Starting Out with C++

ALTERNATE
THIRD ◆ EDITION

Tony Gaddis
Haywood Community College

Judy Walters
North Central College

Godfrey Muganda
North Central College

SCOTT Jones
PUBLISHERS

Scott/Jones Inc.
P.O. Box 696
El Granada, California 94018
Voice: 650-726-2436
Facsimile: 650-726-4693
e-mail: scotjones2@aol.com
Web page: //www.scottjonespub.com

ISBN 1-57676-064-2

Starting Out with C++, Alternate Third Edition

Tony Gaddis, Judy Walters, and Godfrey Muganda

Copyright 2003 Scott/Jones, Inc.

ZYX   543

ISBN: 1-57676-064-2

The publisher wishes to acknowledge the memory and influence of James F. Leisy. Thanks, Jim. We miss you.

Copyediting: Carol Noble
Design and Composition: Stephen Adams
Proofreading: Heather Moehn and Kristin Furino
Cover Design: Stephen Adams
Book Manufacturing: Von Hoffmann Graphics

Scott/Jones Publishing Company
Editorial Group: Richard Jones, Mike Needham, Denise Simon, Leata Holloway, Joe Burns, and Patricia Miyaki
Production Management: Audrey Anderson
Marketing and Sales: Victoria Judy, Page Mead, Hazel Dunlap, Hester Winn, and Donna Cross
Business Operations: Michelle Robelet, Cathy Glenn, Natasha Hoffmeyer, and Bill Overfelt

A Word About Trademarks
All product names identified in this book are trademarks or registered trademarks of their respective companies. We have used the names in an editorial fashion only, and to the benefit of the trademark owner, with no intention of infringing the trademark.

Additional Titles of Interest from Scott/Jones

Computing with Java™: Programs, Objects, Graphics,
    Second Edition and Second Alternate Edition
From Objects to Components with the Java™ Platform
Advanced Java™ Internet Applications, Second Edition
    by Art Gittleman

Developing Web Applications with Active Server Pages
    by Thom Luce

Starting Out with Visual Basic 6.0
Starting Out with Visual Basic.NET
Standard Version of Starting Out with C++, Third Edition
Brief Version of Starting Out with C++, Third Edition
    by Tony Gaddis

C by Discovery, Third Edition
    by L.S. and Dusty Foster

Assembly Language for the IBM PC Family, Third Edition
    by William Jones

The Visual Basic 6 Coursebook, Fourth Edition
QuickStart to JavaScript
QuickStart to DOS for Windows 9X
    by Forest Lin

Advanced Visual Basic.NET, Third Edition
    by Kip Irvine and Jeff Kent

HTML for Web Developers
Server-Side Programming for Web Developers
    by John Avila

The Complete A+ Guide to PC Repair
The Complete Computer Repair Textbook, Third Edition
    by Cheryl Schmidt

Windows 2000 Professional Step-by-Step
Windows XP Professional Step-by-Step
    by Leslie Hardin and Deborah Tice

The Windows 2000 Professional Textbook
Prelude to Programming: Concepts and Design
The Windows XP Textbook
    by Stewart Venit

The Windows 2000 Server Lab Manual
    by Gerard Morris

Preface

Starting Out with C++, Alternate Third Edition can be used in a two-semester C++ programming sequence, or an accelerated one-semester course. Students new to programming, as well those with prior course work in other languages will find this text beneficial. The fundamentals of programming are covered for the novice, while the details, pitfalls, and nuances of the C++ language are explored in-depth for both the beginner and more experienced student. The book is written in clear, easy-to-understand language. At the same time, it covers all the necessary topics of an introductory computer science course. The text is rich in example programs that are concise, practical, and real world oriented. This approach was taken so the student not only learns how to implement the features and constructs of C++, but why and when.

Differences Between This Edition and the Standard Third Edition

The Alternate Third Edition differs from the Standard Third Edition in the following ways:

◆ *Early Objects*

Classes and object-oriented programming techniques are introduced earlier. In this edition, classes are presented in Chapter 7, just after functions and before arrays. The material is structured in a way that minimizes dependency, however. The professor who prefers a different sequence will find that many other possibilities exist. (See the following dependency chart for more information.)

◆ *ANSI Standard Code*

Students using this book are taught to use the newer, standard header files, which do not have a .h extension. All programs in the book use the std namespace as well. Also, function main returns an int value.

◆ *The Standard string Class*

The string class is introduced early and string objects are used throughout the book as the primary method of working with strings. C-strings are covered in their own sections so that students can gain some familiarity with them.

◆ *Data Files*

Data files are introduced early and then used where appropriate in examples throughout the text.

Organization of the Text

Although the chapters can be easily taught in their existing sequence, flexibility is provided. The following dependency diagram suggests possible sequences of instruction.

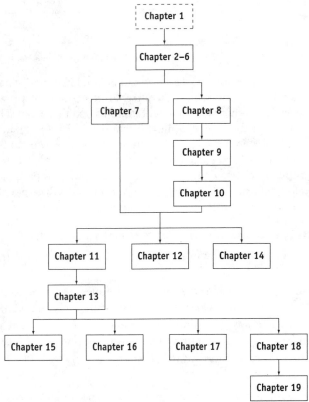

Chapter 1 covers fundamental hardware, software, and programming concepts. The professor may choose to skip this chapter if the class has already mastered those topics. Chapters 2 through 6 cover basic C++ syntax, data types, expressions, selection structures, repetition structures, and functions. Each of these chapters builds on the previous chapter and should be covered in the order presented.

Chapter 7, which discusses the tools for building abstract data types (primarily `structs` and classes) and introduces object-oriented programming, can be covered at any time after Chapter 6, but before Chapters 11, 12, or 14. Chapters 8, 9, and 10 should be covered in order. Note—If Chapter 7 is covered after Chapters 8, 9, or 10, it will only be necessary to postpone the sections on Arrays of Structures and Arrays of Class Objects and the object-oriented case studies in those chapters until Chapter 7 has been covered.

Next, the professor may assign Chapters 11, 12, or 14. Chapter 13 may be assigned only after Chapter 11 has been covered. The remaining chapters can easily be assigned in the order they are presented, but there is flexibility here as well. It is recommended, however, that Chapter 18 precede Chapter 19.

Professors who wish to cover objects early, but to cover arrays before objects, should cover Chapters 1 through 6, then the first half of Chapter 8, before covering Chapter 7. The last part of Chapter 8, which covers arrays of structures and arrays of objects, can then be covered before going on to Chapters 9 through 19.

The following chapter sequence examples illustrate the book's flexibility.

◆ Recommended sequence for early coverage of objects:

Assign the chapters in the order they appear in the book, covering arrays either before or after objects, depending on the professor's preference.

◆ Recommended sequence for late coverage of objects:

Chapter 1 (if necessary)

Chapters 2–6

Chapters 8–10 (skip the material on arrays of structures and objects and the object-oriented case studies for now)

Chapter 7

Return to the object-oriented sections of Chapters 8–10

Chapters 11–19

Brief Overview of Each Chapter:

Chapter 1: Introduction to Computers and Programming   This chapter provides an introduction to the field of computer science and covers the fundamentals of hardware, software, operating systems, programming, problem solving, and software engineering. The components of programs, such as key words, variables, operators, and punctuation are covered. The tools of the trade, such as hierarchy charts and pseudocode are also presented.

Chapter 2: Introduction to C++   This chapter gets the student started in C++ by introducing the basic parts of a C++ program, data types, variable definitions, assignment statements, constants, comments, program output, and simple arithmetic operations. The conventions of programming style are introduced and good programming style is modeled here, as it is throughout the text. An optional section explains the difference between ANSI standard and prestandard C++ programs.

Changes from the Second Alternate Edition: The C++ string class, introduced in this chapter, is now used throughout the text.

Chapter 3: Expressions and Interactivity   In this chapter the student learns to write programs that input and handle numeric, character, and string data. The use of arithmetic operators and the creation of mathematical expressions are covered, with emphasis on operator precedence. Sections are included on conversion and promotion, typecasting, and library functions for working with numbers. Simple output formatting is introduced. For those who wish to cover them, there is also a section on C-strings.

Changes from the Second Alternate Edition: More attention has been given to handling string data. A new section on files has been added to this chapter and sequential text files are now used for I/O at appropriate points throughout the text. Here and throughout the book, output formatting has been simplified.

Chapter 4: Making Decisions   Here the student learns about relational expressions and how to control the flow of a program with the `if`, `if/else`, and `if/else if` statements. Logical operators, the conditional operator, and the `switch` statement are also covered. Applications of these constructs are covered, such as menu-driven programs.

Changes from the Second Alternate Edition: A new section on enumerated data types has been added.

Chapter 5: Looping   This chapter covers C++'s repetitive control mechanisms. The `while` loop, `do-while` loop, and `for` loop are taught, along with a variety of methods to control them. These include using counters, user input, end sentinels, and file eofs. Applications utilizing loops, such as data validation, are covered.

Changes from the Second Alternate Edition: Coverage of data validation has been moved to this chapter and input validation examples have been rewritten to use pretest `while` loops.

Chapter 6: Functions   In this chapter the student learns how and why to modularize programs. Both void and value returning functions are covered. Arguments, parameters, return values, and scope of variables are taught. Overloaded functions are also discussed and demonstrated.

Changes from the Second Alternate Edition: Function prototypes and return values are introduced earlier. More coverage is given to when parameters should be passed by value versus when reference parameters are needed. Here, and throughout the text from this point, functions are preceded by a boxed comment introducing them and visually setting them off.

Chapter 7 Structured Data and Classes   Here the student is introduced to abstract data types and taught how to create them, first using C++ structures and unions, then with classes. In this chapter, the student begins to focus on the object-oriented paradigm. Member variables and functions are discussed. The student learns about private and public access specifications, and reasons to use each. The topics of constructors, overloaded constructors, and destructors are also presented.

Changes from the Second Alternate Edition: Material has been added on nested structures. The introduction to objects has been both simplified and expanded. More coverage has been given in this chapter, and throughout the book from this point, to examples that use classes and objects.

Chapter 8: Arrays   In this chapter the student learns to create and work with single and multi-dimensional arrays, including arrays of structs and arrays of class objects. Programming techniques using parallel arrays are also discussed and demonstrated.

Changes from the Second the Alternate Edition: Additional material has been included on array processing. A section on the `typedef` statement has been added. Additional examples have been provided on using multi-dimensional arrays and arrays of class objects. The student is shown how to use a data file as an input source to populate an array. An optional section has been added on the STL `vector` data type.

Chapter 9: Searching and Sorting Arrays   The student learns the basics of searching for information stored in arrays and of sorting arrays. The chapter covers the Linear Search, Binary Search, Bubble Sort, and Selection Sort algorithms.

Changes from the Second Alternate Edition: An optional section on sorting and searching STL vectors has been added.

Chapter 10: Pointers   This chapter explains how to use pointers. The topics include pointer arithmetic, initialization of pointers, comparison of pointers, pointers and arrays, pointers and functions, dynamic memory allocation, and more.

Changes from the Second Alternate Edition: Changes have been made to comply with the new ANSI standard for handling the allocation of dynamic memory.

Chapter 11: More About Classes   This chapter continues the study of classes. Static members, friends, memberwise assignment, and copy constructors are discussed. The chapter also includes in-depth sections on operator overloading, object conversion, and object composition.

Chapter 12: More about Characters, Strings, and the `string` Class   This chapter covers standard library functions for working with characters and C-strings. A review of the internal storage of C-strings is given. Topics such as passing C-strings to functions, and conversion between numeric and string forms are covered. Additional material about the C++ string class and its member functions and operators is presented.

Changes from the Second Alternate Edition: Now that the book uses string objects as the primary method of working with strings, most of the material on C-strings and C-string functions has been moved from earlier chapters into this chapter.

Chapter 13: Inheritance, Polymorphism, and Virtual Functions   The study of classes continues in this chapter with the subjects of inheritance and polymorphism. The topics covered include base and derived class constructors and destructors, virtual member functions, base class pointers, multiple inheritance, and layers of inheritance.

Changes from the Second Alternate Edition: A new section highlighting the difference between "is-a" and "has-a" relations has been added.

Chapter 14: Files and Advanced I/O   The various modes for opening files are discussed, as well as the many methods for reading and writing file contents. Techniques for working with sequential access, random access, text, and binary files are presented. Advanced output formatting is covered.

Changes from the Second Alternate Edition: The title of this chapter has been revised to reflect its new content. Basic file use (including opening, writing to and reading from, and closing files) has been moved to Chapter 3, leaving this chapter to deal with more advanced file types and techniques. Material on advanced output formatting has been moved from Chapter 3 to this chapter.

Chapter 15: Exceptions, Templates, and the Standard Template Library (STL)   Here the student learns to develop enhanced error trapping techniques using exceptions. Discussion then turns to function and class templates as a method for reusing code. Finally, the student is introduced to the containers, iterators, and algorithms offered by the Standard Template Library (STL).

Chapter 16: Linked Lists   A linked list ADT is developed. The student is taught to code necessary operations such as creating a linked list, appending a node, traversing the list, searching for a node, inserting a node, deleting a node, and destroying a list. A linked list class template is also demonstrated.

Chapter 17: Stacks and Queues   The student learns to create static and dynamic stacks and queues. The operations of stacks and queues are defined, and templates for each ADT are demonstrated.

Chapter 18: Recursion   Recursion is defined and demonstrated. This chapter discusses recursive applications and describes a number of recursive algorithms including a factorial function, a greatest common denominator (GCD) function, printing linked list nodes in reverse, and the QuickSort algorithm.

Changes from the Second Alternate Edition: Coverage of recursion has been expanded with additional examples included. New sections have been added on permutations and on exhaustive and enumeration algorithms.

Chapter 19: Binary Trees   This chapter covers the binary tree ADT and demonstrates many binary tree operations. The student learns to traverse a tree, insert an element, delete an element, replace an element, test for an element, and destroy a tree.

Changes from the Second Alternate Edition: The binary tree class has been rewritten to use references to pointers rather than pointers to pointers.

Appendix A: ASCII Chart   Lists the ASCII and extended ASCII characters and their codes.

Appendix B: Operator Precedence   Lists the C++ operators and their precedence.

Appendix C: Introduction to UML (NEW)   A brief introduction to the Unified Modeling Language (UML).

Appendix D: Type Casts and Run-Time Identification (NEW)

Appendix E: Multi-file Programs   A tutorial on how to create, compile, and link multi-file programs.

Appendix F: Introduction to Microsoft Visual C++ 6.0 (UPDATED)   A tutorial on how to start a Microsoft Visual C++ project, compile a program, save source files, and more. The Visual C++ `getline()` bug is documented and a solution provided.

Appendix G: Introduction to Borland C++ Builder 5.0 (UPDATED)   A tutorial on how to start a Borland C++ Builder project, compile a program, save source files, and more.

Appendix H: The Binary Number System and Bitwise Operations   A guide to the binary number system and the C++ bitwise operators, as well as a tutorial on the internal storage of integers.

Appendix I: Passing Command Line Arguments (NEW)

Appendix J: Header File and Library Function Reference (NEW)

Appendix K: Answers to Checkpoints   Students may test their own progress by comparing their answers to the Checkpoint exercises against this appendix. The answers to all Checkpoint exercises are included.

Appendix L: Answers to Odd-Numbered Review Questions   Another tool that students can use to gauge their progress.

Features of the Text

Concept Statements   Each major section of the text starts with a concept statement. This statement concisely summarizes the meaning of the section.

Example Programs   The text has an abundant number of complete and partial example programs, each designed to highlight the topic currently being studied. In most cases, the programs are practical, real-world examples.

Program Output   After each example program is a sample of its screen output. This immediately shows the student how the program functions.

❓ Checkpoints

Checkpoints are questions placed at intervals throughout each chapter. They are designed as a self-test study aid to help the student check how well he or she has learned a new topic.

Note: Notes appear at appropriate places throughout the text. They are short explanations of interesting or often misunderstood points relevant to the topic at hand.

 WARNING! Warnings are notes that caution the student about certain C++ features, programming techniques, or practices that can lead to malfunctioning programs or lost data.

Case Studies
Case studies that simulate real-world business applications are placed throughout the text. These case studies are designed to highlight the major topics of each chapter they appear in.

Review Questions
Each chapter presents a thorough and diverse set of review questions, including fill-in-the-blank, true-false, multiple-choice, short-answer, and find-the-error.

Programming Challenges
Each chapter offers a pool of programming exercises designed to solidify the student's knowledge of topics at hand. In most cases the assignments present real-world problems to be solved. When applicable, these exercises also include input validation rules.

Group Projects
There are several group programming projects throughout the text, intended to be constructed by a team of students. One student might build the program's user interface, while another student writes the mathematical code, and another designs the file I/O. This process is similar to the way many professional programs are written and encourages team work within the classroom.

Serendipity Booksellers Software Development Project
This is an on-going project requiring the systematic development of a "real world" software package: a point-of-sale program for the fictitious Serendipity Booksellers, a small bookstore located in a shopping mall. The program will act as a cash register, allow the management of an inventory database, and produce a variety of reports.

Supplements
The following supplementary materials are also available for this textbook:

◆ A student disk, containing the source code for each example program in the book

◆ Student CDs containing Borland C++ Builder 5.0 and Microsoft Visual C++ 6.0 compilers.

◆ An instructor's CD, containing answers to the even-numbered review questions, solutions for the programming challenges, (including the Serendipity Booksellers project), a test bank, and a collection of PowerPoint slides with lecture notes

◆ Web resources, described in the next section

Web Resources

The Web site for the Starting Out with C++ series of books is located at the following URL:

http://www.gaddisbooks.com

The Web site offers an ever-growing collection of resources, including:

- ◆ Student downloads
- ◆ A list of any known errors and their corrections
- ◆ A FAQ (frequently asked questions) list
- ◆ A password-protected instructor's site with many downloadable instructional resources

Lab Materials

A lab manual is available for use with this text.

Acknowledgments

There have been many helping hands in the development and publication of this text. I would like to thank the following faculty reviewers for their helpful suggestions and expertise during the production of this manuscript:

Reviewers of the First Edition

David Akins
El Camino College

Don Biggerstaff
Fayetteville Technical Community College

Bill Brown
Pikes Peak Community College

Randall Campbell
Morningside College

Wayne Caruolo
Red Rocks Community College

Dennis Fairclough
Utah Valley State College

James Gifford
University of Wisconsin, Stevens Point

Dennis Heckman
Portland Community College

Patricia Hines
Brookdale Community College

Mike Holland
Northern Virginia Community College

Richard Hull
Lenoir-Rhyne College

Willard Keeling
Blue Ridge Community College

Zhu-qu Lu
University of Maine, Presque Isle

Robert McDonald
East Stroudsburg University

James McGuffee
Austin Community College

Cathi Chambley-Miller
Aiken Technical College

Frank Paiano
Southwestern Community College

Theresa Park
Texas State Technical College

Mark Parker
Shoreline Community College

Dolly Samson
Weber State University

Kirk Stephens
Southwestern Community College

Cherie Stevens
South Florida Community College

Mark Swanson
Red Wing Technical College

Martha Tillman
College of San Mateo

Rober Tureman
Paul D. Camp Community College

Adopters of the Second Edition

Most of us know we can't really tell how good a book is until we teach out of it. The following professors shared their insights and reactions with me after teaching out of *Starting Out with C++*, and helped make it an immeasurably better book:

Ijaz A. Awan
Savannah State University

Randolph Campbell
Morningside College

Ray Larson
Inver Hills Community College

Leon Gleiberman
Touro College

Debbie Mathews
J. Sargeant Reynolds

Stewart Venit
California State Univeristy, Los Angeles

Additionally, the following individuals shared their insight and suggestions on the Alternate Second Edition:

Ahmad Abuhejleh
University of Wisconsin River Falls

Steve Allan
Utah State University

Paul Bladek
Spokane Falls CC

Thomas Cheatham
Middle Tennessee State University

John Cigas
Rockhurst University

John Cross
Indiana University of Pennsylvania

Simon Gray
Ashland University—Ohio

Norman Jacobson
University of California at Irvine

Dr. Eric Jiang
San Diego State University

David Kaeli
Northeastern University

Stephen Leach
Florida State University

Sandeep Mitra
SUNY Brockport

Robert Plantz
Sonoma State University

Dr. Sung Shin
South Dakota State University

Daniel Spiegel
Wright State University

Ray Springston
University of Texas at Arlington

Jane Turk
LaSalle University

Reviewers for the Third Edition

Steve Allan
Utah State University

John Bierbauer
North Central College

Chuck Boehm
Dean Foods, Inc.

Richard Cacace
Pensacola Junior College

James Chegwidden
Tarrant County College

Richard Flint
North Central College

Sheila Foster
California State University Long Beach

David E. Fox
American River College

Cindy Fry
Baylor University

M. Dee Medley
Augusta State University

Cristi Gale
Sterling College

Tino Posillico
SUNY Farmingdale

Ric Heishman
Northern Virginia Community College

Kate Sanders
Rhode Island College

Wayne Horn
Pensacola Junior College

Caroline St. Clair
North Central College

Chris Kardaras
North Central College

Judy Walters
North Central College

Eugene Katzen
Montgomery College—Rockville

Doug White
University of Northern Colorado

Tucjer Maney
George Mason University

Chris Wild
Old Dominion University

Bill Martin
Central Piedmont Community College

Catherine Wyman
DeVry Institute of Technology, Phoenix

The authors wish to thank their families for all the support and encouragement they have provided. We also thank everyone at Scott/Jones, especially our publisher, Richard Jones, for his guiding hand. In addition, we thank Cathy Glenn and Michelle Windell for their hard work. We are deeply grateful to Audrey Anderson, Carol Noble, Stephen Adams, Heather Moehn, and Kristin Furino for making the production of this book a real pleasure. In addition we wish to thank Art Gittleman for contributing his material on the Unified Modeling Language, which appears in Appendix C.

About the Authors

Tony Gaddis is the Coordinator of Advanced Technology at Haywood Community College in North Carolina. He teaches a variety of computer science courses and coordinates IT certification training programs at the Regional High Technology Center. He has also taught C and C++ programming for several corporations and government agencies, including NASA's Kennedy Space Center. Tony is a highly acclaimed instructor who was selected as the North Carolina Community College "Teacher of the Year" in 1994, and received the Teaching Excellence award from the National Institute for Staff and Organizational Development in 1997.

Judy Walters is an Associate Professor of Computer Science at North Central College, where she chairs the Computer Science Department. She has been involved in teaching and curriculum development in industry and in academic settings for more than thirty years. Although she teaches a wide range of computer science courses, undergraduate software development courses are among her favorite courses to teach.

Godfrey Muganda is an Associate Professor of Computer Science at North Central College, where he has taught since 1990. He teaches a wide variety of courses at both the undergraduate and graduate levels including courses in Object-Oriented Programming, Comparative Programming Languages, and Compiler Design. His primary research interests are in the area of Fuzzy Sets and Systems. He won the North Central College faculty award for outstanding scholarship in 1993.

Contents at a Glance

Contents

Introduction to Computers and Programming

Topics

1.1 Why Program?

> **CONCEPT** Computers can do many different jobs because they are programmable.

Every profession has tools that make its job easier to do. Carpenters use hammers, saws, and measuring tapes. Mechanics use wrenches, screwdrivers, and ratchets. Electronics technicians use probes, scopes, and meters. Some tools are unique and can be categorized as belonging to a single profession. For example, surgeons have certain tools that are designed specifically for surgical operations. Those tools probably aren't used by anyone other than surgeons. There are some tools, however, that are used in several professions. Screwdrivers, for instance, are used by mechanics, carpenters, and many others.

The computer is a tool that is used by so many professions, it cannot be easily categorized. It can perform so many different jobs that it is perhaps the most versatile tool ever made. To the accountant, computers balance books, analyze profits and losses, and prepare tax reports. To the factory worker, computers control manufacturing machines and track production. To the mechanic, computers analyze the various systems in an automobile and pinpoint hard-to-find problems.

What makes the computer so useful? Quite simply, the computer can do such a wide variety of tasks because it can be *programmed*. It is a machine specifically designed to follow instructions.

Because of the computer's programmability, it doesn't belong to any single profession. Computers are designed to do whatever job their programs, or *software*, tell them to do.

Computer programmers do a very important job. They create software that transforms computers into the specialized tools of many trades. Without programmers, the users of computers would have no software, and without software, computers would not be able to do anything.

Computer programming is both an art and a science. It is an art because every aspect of a program should be carefully designed. Listed below are a few of the things that must be designed for any real-world computer program:

- The logical flow of the instructions
- The mathematical procedures
- The appearance of the screens
- The way information is presented to the user
- The program's "user-friendliness"
- Manuals and other forms of written documentation

There is also a scientific, or engineering side to programming. Because programs rarely work right the first time they are written, a lot of experimentation, correction, and redesigning is required. This demands patience and persistence of the programmer. Writing software demands discipline as well. Programmers must learn special languages like C++ because computers do not understand English or other human languages. Languages such as C++ have strict rules that must be carefully followed.

Both the artistic and scientific nature of programming makes writing computer software like designing a car: Both cars and programs should be functional, efficient, powerful, easy to use, and pleasing to look at.

1.2   Computer Systems: Hardware and Software

> **CONCEPT**   All computer systems consist of similar hardware devices and software components. This section provides an overview of standard computer hardware and software organization.

Hardware

Hardware refers to the physical components that a computer is made of. A computer, as we generally think of it, is not an individual device, but a system of devices. Like the instruments in a symphony orchestra, each device plays its own part. A typical computer system consists of the following major components:

1. The central processing unit (CPU)
2. Main memory
3. Secondary storage devices
4. Input devices
5. Output devices

The organization of a computer system is depicted in Figure 1-1.

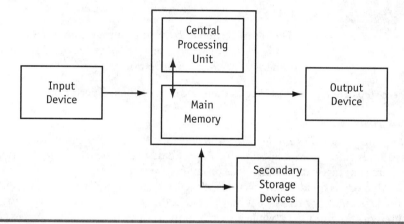

Figure 1-1

The CPU

At the heart of a computer is its *central processing unit*, or *CPU*. The CPU's job is to fetch instructions, follow the instructions, and produce some result or resultant information. Internally, the central processing unit consists of two parts: the *control unit* and the *arithmetic and logic unit (ALU)*. The control unit coordinates all of the computer's operations. It is responsible for determining where to get the next instruction and regulating the other major components of the computer with control signals. The arithmetic and logic unit, as its name suggests, is designed to perform mathematical operations. The organization of the CPU is shown in Figure 1-2.

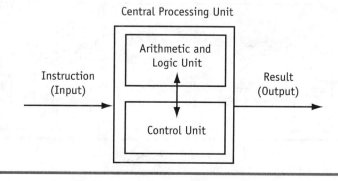

Figure 1-2

A program is a sequence of instructions stored in the computer's memory. When a computer is running a program, the CPU is engaged in a process known formally as the *fetch/decode/execute cycle*. The steps in the fetch/decode/execute cycle are as follows:

Fetch	The CPU's control unit fetches, from main memory, the next instruction in the sequence of program instructions.
Decode	The instruction is encoded in the form of a number. The control unit decodes the instruction and generates an electronic signal.
Execute	The signal is routed to the appropriate component of the computer (such as the ALU, a disk drive, or some other device). The signal causes the component to perform an operation.

These steps are repeated as long as there are instructions to perform.

Main Memory

Commonly known as *random-access memory*, or *RAM*, the computer's main memory is a device that holds information. Specifically, RAM holds the sequences of instructions in the programs that are running and the data those programs are using.

Memory is divided into sections, or cells, that each holds an equal amount of data. Each cell is made of eight "switches" that may be either on or off. A switch that is in the on position usually represents the number 1, while a switch in the off position usually represents the number 0. The computer stores data by setting the switches in a memory cell to a pattern that represents a character of information. Each of these switches is known as a *bit*, which stands for *binary digit*. Each cell, which is a collection of eight bits, is known as a *byte*.

Each byte is assigned a unique number known as an *address*. The addresses are ordered from lowest to highest. A byte is identified by its address in much the same way a post office box is identified by an address. Figure 1-3 shows a group of memory cells with their addresses. In the illustration, sample data is stored in memory. The number 149 is stored in the cell with the address 16, and the number 72 is stored at address 23.

0	1	2	3	4	5	6	7	8	9
10	11	12	13	14	15	16 149	17	18	19
20	21	22	23 72	24	25	26	27	28	29

Figure 1-3

RAM is usually a volatile type of memory, used only for temporary storage. When the computer is turned off, the contents of RAM are erased.

Secondary Storage

Secondary storage is a type of memory that can hold data for long periods of time—even when there is no power to the computer. Frequently used programs are stored in secondary memory and loaded into main memory as needed. Important information, such as word processing documents, payroll data, and inventory figures, is saved to secondary storage as well.

The most common type of secondary storage device is the *disk drive*. A disk drive stores information by magnetically encoding it onto a circular disk. There are several different types of disks, each with advantages and disadvantages. The most common types are hard disks, floppy disks, and zip disks. Hard disks are capable of storing very large amounts of information and can access information quickly. Hard disks are not portable, however. Floppy disks are portable, but hold only a small amount of information and are relatively slow to access. Zip disks, which are also portable, can hold considerably more information than floppy disks and are often used to hold back up copies of hard disk files. Lately CD ROMS, which are now writable as well as readable, are becoming more widely used as a secondary storage medium.

Input Devices

Input is any information the computer collects from the outside world. The device that collects the information and sends it to the computer is called an *input device*. Common input devices are the keyboard, mouse, scanner, and digital camera. Disk drives and CD ROM drives can also be considered input devices because programs and information are retrieved from them and loaded into the computer's memory.

Output Devices

Output is any information the computer sends to the outside world. It might be a sales report, a list of names, or a graphic image. The information is sent to an *output device,* which formats and presents it. Common output devices are monitors and printers. Output sent to a monitor is sometimes called "soft copy," while output sent to a printer is called "hard copy." Disk drives and CD burners can also be considered output devices because the CPU sends information to them so it can be saved.

Software

As previously mentioned, software refers to the programs that run on a computer. There are two general categories of software: *operating systems* and *application software*. An operating system is a set of programs that manages the computer's hardware devices and controls their processes. Operating systems fall into one of the following categories.

Single tasking   A single tasking operating system is capable of running only one program at a time. The computer devotes all its hardware resources and CPU time to each program as it executes. MS-DOS is an example of a single tasking operating system.

> *Multitasking*   A multitasking operating system is capable of running multiple programs at once. Through a technique called *time sharing*, the system divides the allocation of hardware resources and the attention of the CPU among all the executing programs. UNIX and Windows 2000 are multitasking operating systems.

In addition, operating systems fall into one of the following categories, which describe the number of users they can accommodate.

> *Single user*   This type of system allows only one user to operate the computer at a time. MS-DOS and Windows 2000 are single user operating systems.

> *Multiuser*   Multiuser systems allow several users to run programs and operate the computer at once. Most variations of the UNIX operating system are multiuser systems.

Application software refers to programs that make the computer useful to the user. These programs solve specific problems or perform general operations that satisfy the needs of the user. Word processing, spreadsheet, and database packages are all examples of application software.

Checkpoint [1.1–1.2]

1.1   Why is the computer used by so many different people, in so many different professions?

1.2   List the five major hardware components of a computer system.

1.3   Internally, the CPU consists of what two units?

1.4   Describe the steps in the fetch/decode/execute cycle.

1.5   What is a memory address? What is its purpose?

1.6   Explain why computers have both main memory and secondary storage.

1.7   What are the two general categories of software?

1.8   What is the difference between a single tasking system and a multitasking system?

1.9   What is the difference between a single user system and a multiuser system?

1.3 Programs and Programming Languages

> **CONCEPT**   A program is a set of instructions a computer follows in order to perform a task. A programming language is a special language used to write computer programs.

What Is a Program?

Computers are designed to follow instructions. A computer program is a set of instructions that tells the computer how to solve a problem or perform a task. For example, suppose we want the computer to calculate someone's gross pay. Here is a list of things the computer should do:

1. Display a message on the screen asking "How many hours did you work?"
2. Wait for the user to enter the number of hours worked. Once the user enters a number, store it in memory.
3. Display a message on the screen asking "How much do you get paid per hour?"
4. Wait for the user to enter an hourly pay rate. Once the user enters a number, store it in memory.
5. Multiply the number of hours by the amount paid per hour, and store the result in memory.
6. Display a message on the screen that tells the amount of money earned. The message must include the result of the calculation performed in step 5.

Collectively, these instructions are called an *algorithm*. An algorithm is a set of well-defined steps for performing a task or solving a problem. Notice these steps are sequentially ordered. Step 1 should be performed before step 2, and so forth. It is important that these instructions be performed in their proper sequence.

In order for a computer to perform instructions such as the pay-calculating algorithm, the steps must be converted to a form the computer can process. In reality, the CPU only processes instructions written in *machine language*. If you were to look at a machine language program, you would only see a stream of numbers. The CPU interprets these numbers as commands. As you might imagine, the process of encoding an algorithm in machine language is very tedious and difficult. *Computer programming languages,* which use words instead of numbers, were invented to ease this task. Programmers can write their programs in a language such as C++, and then use special software to convert the program into machine language.

Program 1-1 shows how the pay-calculating algorithm might be written in C++.

Program 1-1

```
// This program calculates the user's pay.

#include <iostream>
using namespace std;

int main()
{
    float hours, rate, pay;

    cout << "How many hours did you work? ";
    cin >> hours;
    cout << "How much do you get paid per hour? ";
    cin >> rate;

    pay = hours * rate;

    cout << "You have earned $" << pay << endl;
    return 0;
}
```

Program 1-1

Program Output with Example Input Shown in Bold
```
How many hours did you work? 10
How much do you get paid per hour? 15
You have earned $150
```

The "Program Output with Example Input Shown in Bold" shows what the program will display on the screen when it is running. In the example, the user enters 10 for the number of hours worked and 15 for the hourly pay rate. The program displays the earnings, which are $150.

Programming Languages

In a broad sense, there are two categories of programming languages: low-level and high-level. A *low-level language* is close to the level of the computer, which means it resembles the numeric machine language of the computer more than the natural language of humans. The easiest languages for people to learn are *high-level languages*. They are called "high-level" because they are closer to the level of human-readability than computer-readability. Figure 1-4 illustrates the concept of language levels.

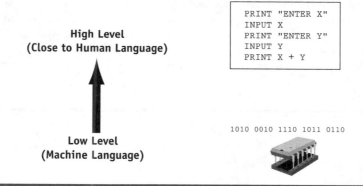

Figure 1-4

Many high-level languages have been created. Table 1-1 lists a few of the well-known ones.

In addition to the high-level features necessary for writing applications such as payroll systems and inventory programs, C++ also has many low-level features. C++ is based on the C language, which was invented for purposes such as writing operating systems and compilers. Since C++ evolved from C, it carries all of C's low-level capabilities with it.

C++ is popular not only because of its mixture of low- and high-level features, but also because of its *portability*. This means that a C++ program can be written on one type of computer and then run on many other types of systems. This usually requires that the program is recompiled on each type of system, but the program itself may need little or no change.

Table 1-1

Language	Description
BASIC	Beginners All-purpose Symbolic Instruction Code. A general programming language originally designed to be simple enough for beginners to learn.
FORTRAN	Formula Translator. A language designed for programming complex mathematical algorithms.
COBOL	Common Business-Oriented Language. A language designed for business applications.
Pascal	A structured, general-purpose language designed primarily for teaching programming.
C	A structured, general-purpose language developed at Bell Laboratories. C offers both high-level and low-level features.
C++	Based on the C language, C++ offers object-oriented features not found in C. Also invented at Bell Laboratories.
Java	An object-oriented language invented at Sun Microsystems. Java may be used to develop programs that run over the Internet, in a Web browser.

 Note: Programs written for specific graphical environments often require significant changes when moved to a different type of system. Examples of such graphical environments are Windows, the X-Window System, and the Macintosh operating system.

Source Code, Object Code, and Executable Code

When a C++ program is written, it must be typed into the computer and saved to a file. A *text editor*, which is similar to a word processing program, is used for this task. The statements written by the programmer are called *source code*, and the file they are saved in is called the *source file*.

After the source code is saved to a file, the process of translating it to machine language can begin. During the first phase of this process, a program called the *preprocessor* reads the source code. The preprocessor searches for special lines that begin with the # symbol. These lines contain commands that cause the preprocessor to modify the source code in some way. During the next phase the *compiler* steps through the preprocessed source code, translating each source code instruction into the appropriate machine language instruction. This process will uncover any *syntax errors* that may be in the program. Syntax errors are illegal uses of key words, operators, punctuation, and other language elements. If the program is free of syntax errors, the compiler stores the translated machine language instructions, which are called *object code*, in an *object file*.

Although an object file contains machine language instructions, it is not a complete program. Here is why: C++ is conveniently equipped with a library of prewritten code for performing common operations or sometimes-difficult tasks. For example, the library contains hardware-specific code for displaying messages on the screen and reading input from the keyboard. It also provides routines for mathematical functions, such as calculating the square root of a number. This collection of code, called the *run-time library*, is extensive. Programs almost always use some part of it. When the compiler generates an object file, however, it does not include machine code for any run-time library routines the programmer might have used. During the last phase of the translation process, another program called the *linker* combines the object file with the necessary library routines. Once the linker has finished with this step, an *executable file* is created. The executable file contains machine language instructions, or *executable code*, and is ready to run on the computer.

Figure 1-5 illustrates the process of translating a source file into an executable file.

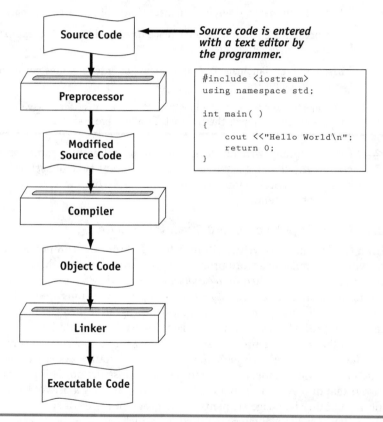

Figure 1-5

The entire process of invoking the preprocessor, compiler, and linker can be initiated with a single action. For example, on a Linux system, the following command causes the C++ program named hello.cpp to be preprocessed, compiled, and linked. The executable code is stored in a file named hello.

```
g++ -o hello hello.cpp
```

Many development systems, particularly those on personal computers, have *integrated development environments (IDEs)*. These environments consist of a text editor, compiler, debugger, and other utilities integrated into a package with a single set of menus. Preprocessing, compiling, linking, and even executing a program is done with a single click of a button, or by selecting a single item from a menu. Figure 1-6 shows a screen from the Microsoft Visual C++ 6.0 IDE.

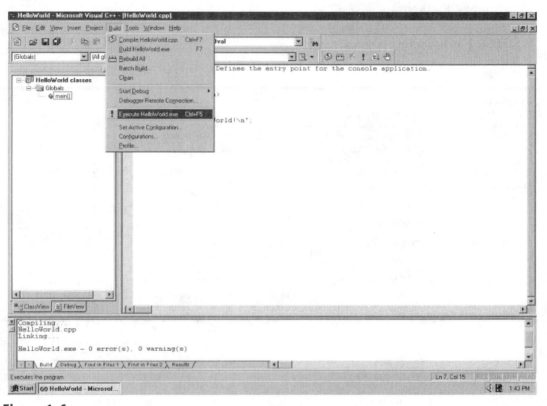

Figure 1-6

Checkpoint [1.3]

1.10 What is an algorithm?

1.11 Why were computer programming languages invented?

1.12 What is the difference between a high-level language and a low-level language?

1.13 What does *portability* mean?

1.14 Explain the operations carried out by the preprocessor, compiler, and linker.

1.15 Explain what is stored in a source file, an object file, and an executable file.

1.16 What is an integrated development environment?

1.4   What Is a Program Made of?

CONCEPT   There are certain elements that are common to all programming languages.

Language Elements

All programming languages have a few things in common. Table 1-2 lists the common elements you will find in almost every language.

Table 1-2

Language Element	Description
Key Words	Words that have a special meaning. Key words may only be used for their intended purpose. Key words are also known as reserved words.
Programmer-Defined Symbols	Words or names defined by the programmer. They are symbolic names that refer to variables or programming routines.
Operators	Operators perform operations on one or more operands. An operand is usually a piece of data, like a number.
Punctuation	Punctuation characters that mark the beginning or ending of a statement, or separate items in a list.
Syntax	Rules that must be followed when constructing a program. Syntax dictates how key words and operators may be used, and where punctuation symbols must appear.

Let's look at some specific parts of Program 1-1 (the pay-calculating program) to see examples of each element listed in the table above. For your convenience, Program 1-1 is listed again, this time with each line numbered.

 Note: The line numbers are NOT part of the program. They are included to help point out specific parts of the program.

Key Words (reserved words)

Four of C++'s key words appear on lines 4 and 6: `using`, `namespace`, `int`, and `main`. The word `float`, which appears on line 8 is also a C++ key word. These words, which are always written in lowercase, each have a special meaning in C++ and can only be used for their intended purposes. As you will see, the programmer is allowed to make up his or her own names for certain things in a program. Key words, however, are reserved and cannot be used for anything other than their designated purposes. Part of learning a programming language is learning what the key words are, what they mean, and how to use them.

 Note: The `#include <iostream>` statement in line 3 is a preprocessor directive.

Program 1-1   (With Line Numbers)

```
 1: // This program calculates the user's pay.
 2:
 3: #include <iostream>
 4: using namespace std;
 5:
 6: int main()
 7: {
 8:     float hours, rate, pay;
 9:
10:     cout << "How many hours did you work? ";
11:     cin >> hours;
12:     cout << "How much do you get paid per hour? ";
13:     cin >> rate;
14:
15:     pay = hours * rate;
16:
17:     cout << "You have earned $" << pay << endl;
18:     return 0;
19: }
```

Programmer-Defined Symbols

The words `hours`, `rate`, and `pay` that appear in the program on lines 8, 11, 13, 15, and 17 are programmer-defined symbols. They are not part of the C++ language but rather are names made up
by the programmer. In this particular program, these are the names of variables. As you will learn
later in this chapter, variables are the names of memory locations that may hold data.

Operators

On line 15 the following statement appears:

```
        pay = hours * rate;
```

The = and * symbols are both operators. They perform operations on pieces of data, known as
operands. The * operator multiplies its two operands, which in this example are the variables
`hours` and `rate`. The = symbol is called the *assignment operator*. It takes the value of the expression on the right and stores it in the variable whose name appears on the left. In this example, the
= operator stores in the `pay` variable the result of the `hours` variable multiplied by the `rate` variable. In other words, the statement says, "Make the `pay` variable equal to `hours` times `rate`" or
"`pay` is assigned the value of `hours` times `rate`."

Punctuation

Notice that all nonblank lines from line 8 through 18 end with a semicolon. A semicolon in C++
is similar to a period in English. It marks the end of a complete sentence (or statement, as it is
called in programming jargon). Semicolons do not appear at the end of every line in a C++ program, however. There are rules that govern where semicolons are required and where they are
not. Part of learning C++ is learning where to place semicolons and other punctuation symbols.

Lines and Statements

Often, the contents of a program are thought of in terms of lines and statements. A "line" is just that—a single line as it appears in the body of a program. Program 1-1 is shown with each of its lines numbered. Most of the lines contain something meaningful; however some of the lines are empty. The blank lines are only there to make the program more readable.

A statement is a complete instruction that causes the computer to perform some action. Here is the statement that appears in line 10 of Program 1-1:

```
cout << "How many hours did you work? ";
```

It causes the computer to display the message "How many hours did you work?" on the screen. Statements can be a combination of key words, operators, and programmer-defined symbols. Statements often occupy only one line in a program, but sometimes they are spread out over more than one line.

Variables

A *variable* is a named storage location in the computer's memory for holding a piece of information. The information stored in variables may change while the program is running (hence the name "variable"). Notice that in Program 1-1 the words hours, rate, and pay appear in several places. All three of these are the names of variables. The hours variable is used to store the number of hours the user worked. The rate variable stores the user's hourly pay rate. The pay variable holds the result of hours multiplied by rate, which is the user's gross pay.

Note: Notice the variables in Program 1-1 have names that reflect their purpose. In fact, it would be easy to guess what the variables were used for just by reading their names. This is discussed further in Chapter 2.

Variables are symbolic names that represent locations in the computer's random-access memory (RAM). When information is stored in a variable, it is actually stored in RAM. Assume a program has a variable named length. Figure 1-7 illustrates the way the variable name represents a memory location.

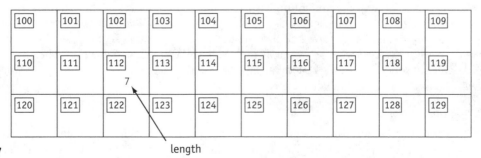

Figure 1-7

In Figure 1-7, the variable `length` is holding the value 7. The number 7 is actually stored in RAM at address 112, but the name `length` symbolically represents this storage location. If it helps, you can think of a variable as a box that holds information. In Figure 1-7, the number 7 is stored in the box named `length`. Only one item may be stored in the box at any given time. If the program stores another value in the box, it will take the place of the number 7.

Variable Definitions

In programming, there are two general types of information: numbers, such as 3, and characters, such as the letter 'A'. Numbers are used to perform mathematical operations and characters are used to print information on the screen or on paper.

Numeric data can be categorized even further. For instance, the following are all whole numbers, or integers:

    5
    7
    -129
    32154

The following are real, or floating-point, numbers:

    3.14159
    6.7
    1.0002

When creating a variable in a C++ program, you must know what type of data the program will be storing in it. Look at line 8 of Program 1-1:

```
float hours, rate, pay;
```

The word `float` in the statement indicates that the variables `hours`, `rate`, and `pay` will be used to hold floating-point numbers. This statement is called a *variable definition*. In C++, all variables must be defined before they can be used because the variable definition is what causes the variables to be created in memory. If you review the listing of Program 1-1, you will see that the variable definitions come before any other statements using those variables.

1.5 Input, Processing, and Output

CONCEPT   The three primary activities of a program are input, processing, and output.

Computer programs typically perform a three-step process of gathering input, performing some process on the information gathered, and then producing output. Input is information a program collects from the outside world. It can be sent to the program from the user, who is entering data at the keyboard or using the mouse. It can also be read from disk files or hardware devices connected to the computer. Program 1-1 allows the user to enter two items of information: the number of hours worked and the hourly pay rate. Lines 11 and 13 use the cin (pronounced "see in") object to perform these input operations:

```
cin >> hours;
cin >> rate;
```

Once information is gathered from the outside world, a program usually processes it in some manner. In Program 1-1, the hours worked and hourly pay rate are multiplied in line 15 to produce the value assigned to the variable pay:

```
pay = hours * rate;
```

Output is information that a program sends to the outside world. It can be words or graphics displayed on a screen, a report sent to the printer, data stored in a file, or information sent to any device connected to the computer. Lines 10, 12, and 17 in Program 1-1 all use the cout (pronounced "see out") object to display messages on the computer's screen.

```
cout << "How many hours did you work? ";
cout << "How much do you get paid per hour? ";
cout << "You have earned $" << pay << endl;
```

You will learn more details about the cin and cout objects in Chapters 2 and 3.

Checkpoint   [1.4–1.5]

1.17 Describe the difference between a key word and a programmer-defined symbol.

1.18 Describe the difference between operators and punctuation symbols.

1.19 Describe the difference between a program line and a statement.

1.20 Why are variables called "variable"?

1.21 What happens to a variable's current contents when a new value is stored there?

1.22 What must take place in a program before a variable is used?

1.23 What are the three primary activities of a program?

1.6 The Programming Process

CONCEPT The programming process consists of several steps, which include design, creation, testing, and debugging activities.

Designing and Creating a Program

Now that you have been introduced to what a program is, it's time to consider the process of creating a program. Quite often, when inexperienced students are given programming assignments, they have trouble getting started because they don't know what to do first. If you find yourself in this dilemma, the steps listed in Figure 1-8 may help. These are the steps recommended for the process of writing a program.

1. Clearly define what the program is to do.
2. Visualize the program running on the computer.
3. Design a hierarchy chart.
4. Check the hierarchy chart for logical errors.
5. Write a pseudocode version of the program.
6. Check the pseudocode for errors.
7. Write the actual program on paper.
8. Desk-check the program for errors.
9. Enter the code and compile it.
10. Correct any errors found during compilation. Repeat steps 9 and 10 as many times as necessary.
11. Run the program with test data for input.
12. Correct any errors found while running the program. Repeat steps 9 through 12 as many times as necessary.
13. Validate the results of the program.

Figure 1-8

The steps listed in Figure 1-8 emphasize the importance of planning. Just as there are good ways and bad ways to paint a house, there are good ways and bad ways to create a program. A good program always begins with planning.

With the pay-calculating program as our example, let's look at each of the steps in more detail.

1. Clearly define what the program is to do.

This step requires that you identify the purpose of the program, the information that is to be input, the processing that is to take place, and the desired output. Here are the requirements for the example program:

Purpose	To calculate the user's gross pay.
Input	Number of hours worked, hourly pay rate.
Process	Multiply number of hours worked by hourly pay rate. The result is the user's gross pay.
Output	Display a message indicating the user's gross pay.

2. Visualize the program running on the computer.

Before you create a program on the computer, you should first create it in your mind. Step 2 is the visualization of the program. Try to imagine what the computer screen looks like while the program is running. If it helps, draw pictures of the screen, with sample input and output, at various points in the program. For instance, here is the screen produced by the pay-calculating program:

```
How many hours did you work? 10
How much do you get paid per hour? 15
You earned $ 150
```

In this step, you must put yourself in the shoes of the user. What messages should the program display? What questions should it ask? By addressing these concerns, you will have already determined most of the program's output.

3. Design a hierarchy chart.

A *hierarchy chart* is a diagram that graphically depicts the structure of a program. It has boxes that represent each step in the program. The boxes are connected in a way that illustrates their relationship to one another. Figure 1-9 shows a hierarchy chart for the pay-calculating program.

A hierarchy chart begins with the overall task, then refines it into smaller subtasks. Each of the subtasks is then refined into even smaller sets of subtasks, until each is small enough to be easily performed. For instance, in the chart in Figure 1-9, the overall task "Calculate Gross Pay" is listed in the top-level box. That task is broken into three subtasks. The first subtask, "Get Payroll Data from User," is broken further into two subtasks. This process of "divide and conquer" is known as *top-down design*.

4. Check the hierarchy chart for logical errors.

Logical errors are mistakes that cause the program to produce erroneous results. Once a hierarchy chart is assembled, it should be checked for these errors. The programmer should trace through the chart, checking the logic of each step. If an error is found, the chart can be corrected before the next step is attempted.

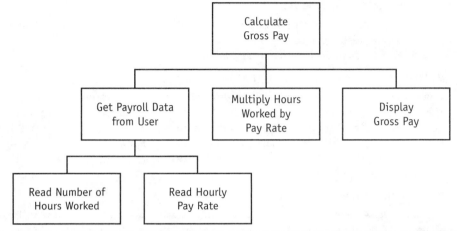

Figure 1-9

5. Write a pseudocode version of the program.

Pseudocode is a cross between human language and a programming language. Although the computer can't understand pseudocode, programmers often find it helpful to write an algorithm in a language that's "almost" a programming language, but still very similar to natural language. For example, this pseudocode describes the pay-calculating program:

```
Get payroll data.
Calculate gross pay.
Display gross pay.
```

Although this pseudocode gives a broad view of the program, it doesn't reveal all the program's details. A more detailed version of the pseudocode follows.

```
Display "How many hours did you work?".
Input hours.
Display "How much do you get paid per hour?".
Input rate.
Store the value of hours times rate in the pay variable.
Display the value in the pay variable.
```

Notice that the pseudocode contains statements that look more like commands than the English statements that describe the algorithm at the beginning of Section 1.3. The pseudocode even names variables and describes mathematical operations.

6. Check the pseudocode for errors.

Once a pseudocode program has been written, it should be checked for logical errors. The programmer should trace through the code, checking each statement for accuracy. If an error is found, the pseudocode can be corrected before the next step is attempted.

7. Write the actual program on paper.

Once the program has been clearly defined, visualized, charted, and roughly modeled in pseudocode, the programmer has enough knowledge to begin writing the program. It's always a good idea before a program is typed on the computer to first write it on paper. During this first step of translating hierarchy charts, pseudocode, and screen diagrams into programming language statements, the programmer sometimes finds more errors or discovers a change that must be made to the algorithm.

8. Desk-check the program for errors.

The term *desk-checking* means the programmer starts reading the program at the beginning and steps through each statement. A sheet of paper is often used in this process to jot down the current contents of all variables and sketch what the screen looks like after each output operation. When a variable's contents change, or information is displayed on the screen, this is noted. By stepping through each statement, a programmer can locate and correct many errors.

9. Enter the code and compile it.

Once the code has been written on paper, desk-checked, and corrected, it is ready to be entered on the computer. The programmer saves the source code to a file and begins the process of translating it to machine language. During this step the compiler will find any syntax errors that may exist in the program.

10. Correct any errors found during compilation.

If the compiler reports any errors, they must be corrected and the code recompiled. This step is repeated until the program is free of compile-time errors.

11. Run the program with test data for input.

Once an executable file is generated, the program is ready to be tested for run-time errors. A run-time error is an error that occurs while the program is running. These are usually logical errors, such as mathematical mistakes.

Testing for run-time errors requires that the program be executed with sample data or sample input. The programmer should select sample data that allows the correct output to be predicted. If the program does not produce the correct output, a logical error is present in the program.

12. Correct any errors found while running the program.

When run-time errors are found in a program, they must be corrected. You must identify the step where the error occurred and determine the cause. If the error is a result of incorrect logic (such as an improperly stated math formula), you must correct the statement or statements involved in the logic. If the error is due to an incomplete understanding of the program requirements, then you must restate the program purpose and modify the hierarchy chart, pseudocode, and source code. The program must then be recompiled and retested. This means steps 9 though 12 must be repeated until the program reliably produces satisfactory results.

13. Validate the results of the program.

When you believe you have corrected all the run-time errors, enter test data to verify that the program solves the original problem.

What Is Software Engineering?

The field of software engineering encompasses the whole process of crafting computer software. It includes designing, writing, testing, debugging, documenting, modifying, and maintaining complex software development projects. Like traditional engineers, software engineers use a number of tools in their craft. Here are a few examples:

- Program specifications
- Charts and diagrams of screen output
- Hierarchy charts
- Pseudocode
- Examples of expected input and desired output
- Special software designed for testing programs

Most commercial software applications are very large. In many instances one or more teams of programmers, not a single individual, develop them. It is important that the program requirements be thoroughly analyzed and divided into subtasks that are handled by individual teams or individuals within a team.

In step 3 of the programming process, you were introduced to the hierarchy chart as a tool for top-down design. The subtasks that are identified in a top-down design can easily become modules, or separate components, of a program. If the program is very large or complex, a team of software engineers can be assigned to work on the individual modules. As the project develops, the modules are coordinated to become a single software application.

1.7 Procedural and Object-Oriented Programming

CONCEPT	Procedural programming and object-oriented programming are two ways of thinking about software development and program design.

C++ is a language that can be used for two methods of writing computer programs: *procedural programming* and *object-oriented programming*. This book is designed to teach you some of both.

In procedural programming, the programmer constructs procedures (or functions, as they are called in C++). The procedures are collections of programming statements that perform a specific task. The procedures each contain their own variables and commonly share variables with other procedures. This is illustrated by Figure 1-10.

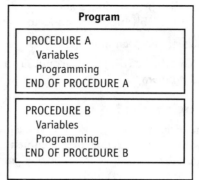

Figure 1-10

Procedural programming is centered on the procedure, or function. Object-oriented programming (OOP), on the other hand, is centered on the object. An object is a programming element that contains data and the procedures that operate on the data. It is a self-contained unit. This is illustrated in Figure 1-11.

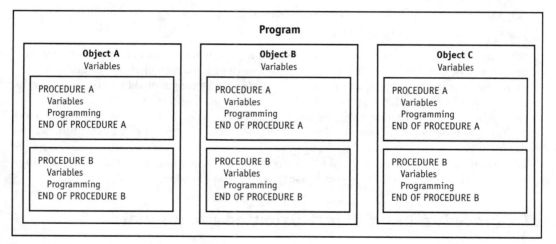

Figure 1-11

The objects contain, within themselves, both information and the ability to manipulate the information. Operations are carried out on the information in an object by sending the object a *message*. When an object receives a message instructing it to perform some operation, it carries out the instruction. As you study this text, you will encounter many other aspects of object-oriented programming.

? Checkpoint [1.6–1.7]

1.24 What four items should you identify when defining what a program is to do?

1.25 What does it mean to "visualize a program running"? What is the value of such an activity?

1.26 What is a hierarchy chart?

1.27 Should a program be written on paper before it is entered into the computer? Why or why not?

1.28 Describe the process of desk-checking.

1.29 Describe what a compiler does with a program's source code.

1.30 What is a run-time error?

1.31 Is a syntax error (such as misspelling a key word) found by the compiler or when the program is running?

1.32 What is the purpose of testing a program with sample data or input?

1.33 Briefly describe the difference between procedural and object-oriented programming.

Review Questions and Exercises

Fill-in-the-Blank

1. Computers can do many different jobs because they can be _____.

2. The job of the _____ is to fetch instructions, carry out the operations commanded by the instructions, and produce some outcome or resultant information.

3. Internally, the CPU consists of the _____ and the _____.

4. A(n) _____ is an example of a secondary storage device.

5. The two general categories of software are _____ and _____.

6. A program is a set of _____.

7. Since computers can't be programmed in natural human language, algorithms must be written in a(n) _____ language.

8. _____ is the only language computers really process.

9. _____ languages are close to the level of humans in terms of readability.

10. _____ languages are close to the level of the computer.

11. A program's ability to run on several different types of computer systems is called _____.

12. Words that have special meaning in a programming language are called _____.

13. Words or names defined by the programmer are called _____.

14. _____ are characters or symbols that perform operations on one or more operands.

15. _____ characters or symbols mark the beginning or ending of programming statements, or separate items in a list.

16. The rules that must be followed when constructing a program are called _____.

17. A(n) _____ is a named storage location.

18. A variable must be _____ before it can be used in a program.

19. The three primary activities of a program are _____, _____, and _____.

20. _____ is information a program gathers from the outside world.

21. _____ is information a program sends to the outside world.

22. A(n) _____ is a diagram that graphically illustrates the structure of a program.

Short Answer

23. Both main memory and secondary storage are types of memory. Describe the difference between the two.

24. What is the difference between operating system software and application software?

25. Indicate all the categories that the following operating systems belong to.

System A	This system allows multiple users to run multiple programs simultaneously.
System B	Only one user can access the system at a time, but multiple programs can be run simultaneously.
System C	Only one user can access the system at a time, and only one program can be run on the system at a time.

26. Why must programs written in a high-level language be translated into machine language before they can be run?

27. Why is it easier to write a program in a high-level language than in machine language?

28. Explain the difference between an object file and an executable file.

29. What is the difference between a syntax error and a logical error?

Predict the Result

Questions 30–32 are programs expressed as English statements. What would each display on the screen if they were actual programs?

30. The variable x starts with the value 0.
    The variable y starts with the value 5.
    Add 1 to x.
    Add 1 to y.
    Add x and y, and store the result in y.
    Display the value in y on the screen.

31. The variable j starts with the value 10.
    The variable k starts with the value 2.
    The variable l starts with the value 4.
    Store the value of j times k in j.
    Store the value of k times l in l.
    Add j and l, and store the result in k.
    Display the value in k on the screen.

32. The variable a starts with the value 1.
    The variable b starts with the value 10.
    The variable c starts with the value 100.
    The variable x starts with the value 0.
    Store the value of c times 3 in x.
    Add the value of b times 6 to the value already in x.
    Add the value of a times 5 to the value already in x.
    Display the value in x on the screen.

Find the Error

33. The following pseudocode algorithm has an error. The program is supposed to ask the user
    for the length and width of a rectangular room, then display the room's area. The program
    must multiply the width by the length in order to determine the area. Find the error.

```
area = width X length.
Display "What is the room's width?".
Input width.
Display "What is the room's length?".
Input length.
Display area.
```

Hierarchy Chart Problems

34. **Available Credit**

    Design a hierarchy chart for a program that calculates a customer's available credit. The
    program should carry out the following steps:

    1. Display the message "Enter the customer's maximum credit."

    2. Wait for the user to enter the customer's maximum credit.

    3. Display the message "Enter the amount of credit used by the customer."

    4. Wait for the user to enter the customer's credit used.

    5. Subtract the used credit from the maximum credit to get the customer's available credit.

    6. Display a message that shows the customer's available credit.

35. **Sales Tax**

Design a hierarchy chart for a program that calculates the total of a retail sale. The program should ask the user for

- The retail price of the item being purchased

- The sales tax rate

Once these items have been entered, the program should calculate and display

- The sales tax for the purchase

- The total of the sale

36. **Account Balance**

Design a hierarchy chart for a program that calculates the current balance in a savings account. The program must ask the user for

- The starting balance

- The total dollar amount of deposits made

- The total dollar amount of withdrawals made

- The monthly interest rate

Once the program calculates the current balance, it should be displayed on the screen.

Serendipity Booksellers Software Development Project—Part 1: *Program Specifications*

Serendipity Booksellers is a small bookstore located in a shopping mall. They have a cashier station equipped with a personal computer. The manager wants you to develop a point-of-sale (POS) software package that will make the computer function as a cash register and keep an inventory file. The inventory file will be a database of all the books in the bookstore. In general, the software is to perform the following tasks:

- Calculate the total of a sale, including sales tax

- When a book is purchased, subtract it from the store's inventory file

- Add, change, delete, and look up books in the inventory file

- Display various reports

At the end of each chapter you will be given assignments that build on the project by implementing newly learned features. At the end of the book, you will have designed and written a fully functional software package that incorporates most of the topics covered in the text.

The Modules

The program will be organized into the following three modules:

- ◆ Cashier module
- ◆ Inventory Database module
- ◆ Report module

When the program runs, a menu will be displayed on the screen, which allows the user to activate any of the modules. A discussion of each module follows.

The Cashier Module

The Cashier module allows the computer to act as a cash register. The user enters information for the books being purchased and the program calculates the sales tax and the total price. In addition, the books being purchased are automatically subtracted from the Inventory Database.

The Inventory Database Module

The Inventory Database will be a file containing a list of all the books in Serendipity's inventory. The following information for each book will be stored in the file:

Field	Description
ISBN	This is the International Standard Book Number. It is a unique number assigned to each book by the publisher.
Title	The title of the book.
Author	The book's author.
Publisher	The company that publishes the book.
Date Added	The date the book was added to the inventory.
Quantity-On-Hand	The number of copies of the book in inventory.
Wholesale Cost	The price paid by Serendipity for each copy of the book.
Retail Price	The price Serendipity is charging for each copy of the book.

The Inventory Database module will allow the user to look up information on any book in the file, add new books to the file, delete books, and change any information in the database.

Case

The Report Module

The Report module will analyze the information in the Inventory Database to produce any of the following reports:

Inventory List.   A list of information on all books in the inventory.

Inventory Wholesale Value.   A list of the wholesale value of all books in the inventory and the total wholesale value of the inventory.

Inventory Retail Value.   A list of the retail value of all books in the inventory and the total retail value of the inventory.

List by Quantity.   A list of all books in the inventory sorted by quantity-on-hand. The books with the greatest quantity-on-hand will be listed first.

List by Cost.   A list of all books in the inventory, sorted by wholesale cost. The books with the greatest wholesale cost will be listed first.

List by Age.   A list of all books in the inventory, sorted by purchase date. The books that have been in the inventory longest will be listed first.

CHAPTER 2

Introduction to C++

Topics

2.1 The Parts of a C++ Program

CONCEPT	C++ programs have parts and components that serve specific purposes.

Every C++ program has an anatomy. Unlike human anatomy, the parts of C++ programs are not always in the same place. Nevertheless, the parts are there and your first step in learning C++ is to learn what they are. We will begin by looking at a simple example:

Program 2-1

```cpp
// A simple C++ program
#include <iostream>
using namespace std;

int main()
{
    cout << "Programming is great fun!";
    return 0;
}
```

The output of the program is shown below. This is what appears on the screen when the program runs.

Program Output

```
Programming is great fun!
```

Let's examine the program line by line. Here's the first line:

```
// A simple C++ program
```

The // marks the beginning of a *comment*. The compiler ignores everything from the double-slash to the end of the line. That means you can type anything you want on that line and the compiler will never complain! Although comments are not required, they are very important to programmers. Real programs are much more complicated than the example in Program 2-1, and comments help explain what's going on.

The next line looks like this:

```
#include <iostream>
```

This line must be included in a C++ program in order to get input from the keyboard or print output to the screen. Since the cout statement (three lines down) will print output to the computer screen, we need to include this line. Because it starts with a #, this line is called a *preprocessor directive*. The preprocessor reads your program before it is compiled and only executes those lines beginning with a # symbol. Think of the preprocessor as a program that "sets up" your source code for the compiler.

Notice that the word inside the brackets, iostream, looks like a filename. There is information in the file iostream that is needed for this program to work properly. Its contents are included in the program at the point the #include statement appears. iostream is called a header file, so it should be included at the head, or top, of the program.

The next line reads

```
using namespace std;
```

Programs usually contain several items with unique names. In this chapter you will learn to create variables. In Chapter 6 you will learn to create functions. In Chapter 7 you will learn to create objects. Variables, functions, and objects are examples of program entities that must have names. C++ uses *namespaces* to organize the names of program entities. The statement `using namespace std;` declares that the program will be accessing entities whose names are part of the namespace called `std`. (Yes, even namespaces have names.) The reason the program needs access to the `std` namespace is because every name created by the `iostream` file is part of that namespace. In order for a program to use the entities in `iostream`, it must have access to the `std` namespace.

The next line reads

```
int main()
```

This marks the beginning of a *function*. A function can be thought of as a group of one or more programming statements that collectively has a name. The name of this function is `main`, and the set of parentheses indicates that it is a function. The word `int` stands for "integer." It indicates that the function sends an integer value to the operating system when it is finished executing.

Although most C++ programs have more than one function, every C++ program must have a function called `main`. It is the starting point of the program. If you're ever reading someone else's program and want to find where it starts, just look for the function called `main`.

 Note: C++ is a case-sensitive language. That means it regards uppercase letters as being entirely different characters than their lowercase counterparts. In C++, the name of the function `main` must be written in all lowercase letters. C++ doesn't see "Main" the same as "main," or "INT" the same as "int." This is true for all the C++ key words.

The next line of our program contains a single, solitary character:

```
{
```

This is called a left-brace, or an opening brace, and it is associated with the beginning of the function `main`. All the statements that make up a function are enclosed in a set of braces. If you look at the third line down from the opening brace you'll see the closing brace. Everything between the two braces is the contents of the function `main`.

 WARNING! Make sure you have a closing brace for every opening brace in your program!

After the opening brace you see the following line:

```
cout << "Programming is great fun!";
```

To put it simply, this line displays a message on the screen. You will read more about `cout` and the `<<` operator later in this chapter. The message "Programming is great fun!" is printed without the quotation marks. In programming terms, the group of characters inside the quotation marks is called a *string constant*.

 Note: This is the only line in the program that causes anything to be printed on the screen. The other lines, like `#include <iostream>` and `int main()`, are necessary for the framework of your program, but they do not cause any screen output. Remember, a program is a set of instructions for the computer. If something is to be displayed on the screen, you must use a programming statement for that purpose.

At the end of the line is a semicolon. Just as a period marks the end of a sentence, a semicolon marks the end of a complete statement in C++. Comments are ignored by the compiler, so the semicolon isn't required at the end of a comment. Preprocessor directives, like #include statements, simply end at the end of the line and never require semicolons.[1] The beginning of a function, like int main(), is not a complete statement, so you don't place a semicolon there either. It might seem that the rules for where to put a semicolon are not clear at all. Rather than worry about it now, just concentrate on learning the parts of a program. You'll soon get a feel for where you should and should not use semicolons.

The next line in the program reads

```
return 0;
```

This sends the integer value 0 back to the operating system upon the program's completion. The value 0 usually indicates that a program executed successfully.

The last line of the program contains the closing brace:

```
}
```

This brace marks the end of the main function. Since main is the only function in this program, it also marks the end of the program.

In the sample program you encountered several sets of special characters. Table 2-1 provides a short summary of how they were used.

Table 2-1 Special Characters

Character	Name	Description
//	Double slash	Marks the beginning of a comment.
#	Pound sign	Marks the beginning of a preprocessor directive.
< >	Opening and closing brackets	Encloses a filename when used with the #include directive.
( )	Opening and closing parentheses	Used in naming a function, as in int main().
{ }	Opening and closing braces	Encloses a group of statements, such as the contents of a function.
" "	Opening and closing quotation marks	Encloses a string of characters, such as a message that is to be printed on the screen.
;	Semicolon	Marks the end of a complete programming statement.

---

[1]Some compilers do not allow you to terminate a preprocessor directive with a semicolon.

Checkpoint [2.1]

2.1 The following C++ program will not compile because the lines have been mixed up.

```
int main()
}
// A crazy mixed up program
#include <iostream>
return 0;
cout << "In 1492 Columbus sailed the ocean blue.";
{
using namespace std;
```

When the lines are properly arranged the program should display the following on the screen:

```
In 1492 Columbus sailed the ocean blue.
```

Rearrange the lines in the correct order. Test the program by entering it on the computer, compiling it, and running it.

2.2 On paper, write a program that will display your name on the screen. Use Program 2-1 as your guide. Place a comment with today's date at the top of the program. Test your program by entering, compiling, and running it.

2.3 Any line that begins with a # symbol is: A) the beginning of a function; B) a preprocessor directive; C) printed on the screen.

2.4 Every complete C++ program must have: A) a function called `main`; B) an `#include` statement; C) a comment.

2.2 The cout Object

CONCEPT Use the cout object to display information on the computer's screen.

One of the primary jobs of a computer is to produce output. When a program is ready to send information to the outside world, it must have a way to transmit that information to an output device. The *monitor* is normally considered the standard output device.

The cout object is referred to as the *standard output object.* Its job is to output information using the standard output device.

cout is classified as a *stream object,* which means it works with streams of data. To print a message on the screen, you send a stream of characters to cout. Let's look at a line from Progam 2-1:

```
cout << "Programming is great fun!";
```

Notice that the << operator is used to send the string "Programming is great fun!" to cout. When the << symbol is used this way, it is called the *stream-insertion operator*. The information immediately to the right of the operator is sent to cout and then displayed on the screen.

Let's look at another way to write the same program.

Program 2-2

```cpp
// A simple C++ program
#include <iostream>
using namespace std;

int main()
{
    cout << "Programming is " << "great fun!";
    return 0;
}
```

Program Output
```
Programming is great fun!
```

As you can see, the stream-insertion operator can be used to send more than one item to cout. The output of this program is identical to Program 2-1. Program 2-3 shows yet another way to accomplish the same thing.

Program 2-3

```cpp
// A simple C++ program
#include <iostream>
using namespace std;

int main()
{
    cout << "Programming is ";
    cout << "great fun!";
    return 0;
}
```

Program Output
```
Programming is great fun!
```

An important concept to understand about Program 2-3 is that, although the output is broken up into two programming statements, this program will still display the message on a single line. Unless you specify otherwise, the information you send to cout is displayed in a continuous stream. Sometimes this can produce less-than-desirable results. Program 2-4 is an example.

Program 2-4

```cpp
// An unruly printing program
#include <iostream>
using namespace std;

int main()
{
    cout << "The following items were top sellers";
    cout << "during the month of June:";
    cout << "Computer games";
    cout << "Coffee";
    cout << "Aspirin";
    return 0;
}
```

Program Output

```
The following items were top sellersduring the month of June:Computer gamesCoff
eeAspirin
```

The layout of the actual output looks nothing like the arrangement of the strings in the source code. First, notice there is no space displayed between the words "sellers" and "during," or between "June:" and "Computer." cout displays messages exactly as they are sent. If spaces are to be displayed, they must appear in the strings.

Second, even though the output is broken up into five lines in the source code, it comes out as one long line that wraps around to a second line since it is too long to fit on one line. This is because cout does not start a new line of output unless it is told to do so. There are two ways to accomplish this. The first is to send cout a *stream manipulator* called endl. Program 2-5 is an example.

Program 2-5

```cpp
// A well-adjusted printing program
#include <iostream>
using namespace std;

int main()
{
    cout << "The following items were top sellers" << endl;
    cout << "during the month of June:" << endl;
    cout << "Computer games" << endl;
    cout << "Coffee" << endl;
    cout << "Aspirin" << endl;
    return 0;
}
```

Program 2-5

Program Output

```
The following items were top sellers
during the month of June:
Computer games
Coffee
Aspirin
```

Every time `cout` encounters an `endl` stream manipulator it advances the output to the beginning of the next line for subsequent printing. The manipulator can be inserted anywhere in the stream of characters sent to `cout`, outside the double quotes. Notice that an `endl` is also used at the end of the last line of output.

Another way to cause subsequent output to begin on a new line is to insert a \n in the string that is being output. Program 2-6 shows an example of this.

Program 2-6

```cpp
// Another well-adjusted printing program
#include <iostream>
using namespace std;

int main()
{
    cout << "The following items were top sellers\n";
    cout << "during the month of June:\n";
    cout << "Computer games\nCoffee";
    cout << "\nAspirin\n";
    return 0;
}
```

Program Output

```
The following items were top sellers
during the month of June:
Computer games
Coffee
Aspirin
```

\n is an example of an *escape sequence*. Escape sequences are written as a backslash character (\) followed by one or more control characters and are used to control the way output is displayed. There are many escape sequences in C++. The newline escape sequence (\n) is just one of them.

When `cout` encounters \n in a string, it doesn't print it on the screen but interprets it as a special command to advance the output cursor to the next line. You have probably noticed inserting the escape sequence requires less typing than inserting `endl`. That's why many programmers prefer it.

WARNING! Do not confuse the backslash (\) with the forward slash (/). An escape sequence will not work if you accidentally start it with a forward slash. Also, do not put a space between the backslash and the control character.

Escape sequences give you the ability to exercise greater control over the way information is output by your program. Table 2-2 lists a few of them.

Table 2-2   Common Escape Sequences

Escape Sequence	Name	Description
\n	Newline	Causes the cursor to go to the next line for subsequent printing.
\t	Horizontal tab	Causes the cursor to skip over to the next tab stop.
\a	Alarm	Causes the computer to beep.
\b	Backspace	Causes the cursor to back up, or move left one position.
\r	Return	Causes the cursor to go to the beginning of the current line, not the next line.
\\	Backslash	Causes a backslash to be printed.
\'	Single quote	Causes a single quotation mark to be printed.
\"	Double quote	Causes a double quotation mark to be printed.

2.3   The #include Directive

CONCEPT   The #include directive causes the contents of another file to be inserted into the program.

Now is a good time to expand our discussion of the #include directive. The following line has appeared near the top of every example program.

```
#include <iostream>
```

The header file iostream must be included in any program that uses the cout object. This is because cout is not part of the "core" of the C++ language. Specifically, it is part of the *input-output stream library*. The header file, iostream, contains information describing iostream objects. Without it, the compiler will not know how to properly compile a program that uses cout.

 Note: cout is not the only object that requires the iostream header file.

Preprocessor directives are not C++ statements. They are signals to the preprocessor, which runs prior to the compiler (hence the name "preprocessor"). The preprocessor's job is to set programs up in a way that makes life easier for the programmer.

For example, any program that uses the cout object must contain the extensive setup information found in iostream. The programmer could type all this information into the program, but it would be too time consuming. An alternative would be to use an editor to "cut and paste" the information into the program, but that would quickly become tiring as well. The solution is to let the preprocessor insert the contents of iostream automatically.

 WARNING! Do not use semicolons at the end of preprocessor directives. Since preprocessor directives are not C++ statements, they do not require them. In fact, in many cases an error will result from a preprocessor directive terminated with a semicolon.

An #include directive must always contain the name of a file. The preprocessor inserts the entire contents of the file into the program at the point it encounters the #include directive. The compiler doesn't actually see the #include directive. Instead it sees the information that was inserted by the preprocessor, just as if the programmer had typed it there.

The information contained in header files is C++ code. Typically it describes complex objects like cout. Later you will learn to create your own header files.

Checkpoint   [2.2–2.3]

2.5   The following C++ program will not compile because the lines have been mixed up.

```
cout << "Success\n";
cout << " Success\n\n";
int main()
cout << "Success";
}
using namespace std;
// It's a mad, mad program
#include <iostream>
cout << "Success\n";
{
return 0;
```

When the lines are properly arranged the program should display the following on the screen:

```
Success
Success Success

Success
```

Rearrange the lines in the correct order. Test the program by entering it on the computer, compiling it, and running it.

2.6 Study the following program and show what it will print on the screen.

```
// The Works of Wolfgang
#include <iostream>
using namespace std;

int main()
{
    cout << "The works of Wolfgang\ninclude the following";
    cout << "\nThe Turkish March" << endl;
    cout << "and Symphony No. 40 ";
    cout << "in G minor." << endl;
    return 0;
}
```

2.7 On paper, write a program that will display your name on the first line, your street address on the second line, your city, state, and ZIP code on the third line, and your telephone number on the fourth line. Place a comment with today's date at the top of the program. Test your program by entering, compiling, and running it.

2.4 Standard and Prestandard C++ (enrichment)

CONCEPT C++ programs written before the language became standardized may appear slightly different from programs written today.

C++ is now a standardized programming language, but it hasn't always been. The language has evolved over the years, and, as a result, there is a "newer style" and an "older style" of writing C++ code. The newer style is the way programs are written with standard C++, while the older style is the way programs were typically written using prestandard C++. Although the differences between the older and newer styles are subtle, it is important that you recognize them. When you go to work as a computer science professional, it is likely that you will see programs written in the older style. It is also possible that your workplace's programming tools only support the older conventions, and you may need to write programs using the older style.

Older Style Header Files

In older style C++, all header files end with the ".h" extension. For example, in a prestandard C++ program the statement that includes the `iostream` header file is written as

```
#include <iostream.h>
```

Absence of `using namespace std;`

Another difference between the newer and older styles is that older style programs typically do not use the `using namespace std;` statement. In fact, some older compilers do not support namespaces at all and will produce an error message if a program has that statement.

An Older Style Program

To illustrate these differences, look at the following program. It is a modification of Program 2-1, written in the older style.

```
// A simple C++ program
#include <iostream.h>

void main(void)
{
   cout << "Programming is great fun!";
}
```

Some standard C++ compilers do not support programs written in the older style, and prestandard compilers normally do not support programs written in the newer style.

2.5 Variables, Constants, and the Assignment Statement

CONCEPT Variables represent storage locations in the computer's memory. Constants are data items whose values do not change while the program is running.

As you discovered in Chapter 1, variables allow you to store and work with data in the computer's memory.[2] They provide an "interface" to RAM. Part of the job of programming is to determine how many variables a program will need and what types of information they will hold. Program 2-7 is an example of a C++ program with a variable.

Program 2-7

```
// This program has a variable.
#include <iostream>
using namespace std;
```

(program continues)

---

[2] The concept of a variable in computer programming is somewhat different from the concept of a variable in mathematics.

Program 2-7 *(continued)*

```
int main()
{
    int number;

    number = 5;
    cout << "The value of number is " << "number" << endl;
    cout << "The value of number is " <<  number  << endl;

    number = 7;
    cout << "Now the value of number is " << number << endl;

    return 0;
}
```

Program Output
```
The value of number is number
The value of number is 5
Now the value of number is 7
```

Let's look more closely at this program. Here is the first line in the function `main`.

```
    int number;
```

This is called a *variable definition*. It tells the compiler the variable's name and the type of data it will hold. This line indicates the variable's name is `number`. The word `int` stands for integer, so `number` will only be used to hold integer numbers. Later in this chapter you will learn all the types of data that C++ allows.

 Note: You must have a definition for every variable you intend to use in a program. In C++, variable definitions can appear at any point in the program. Later in this chapter, and throughout the book, you will learn the best places to define variables.

Notice that variable definitions end with a semicolon. Here is the next line.

```
    number = 5;
```

This is called an *assignment*. The equal sign is an operator that copies the value on its right (5) into the variable named on its left (`number`). After this line executes, `number` will be set to 5.

 Note: This line does not print anything on the computer's screen. It runs silently behind the scenes, storing a value in RAM.

Look at the next two lines. Notice that in the first one, the word `number` has double quotation marks around it and in the second one, it does not.

```
cout << "The value of number is " << "number" << endl;
cout << "The value of number is " <<  number  << endl;
```

Now compare these two lines with the output they produce. In the first `cout` statement, the string constant `"number"` is inserted into the output stream, so the output produced is

```
The value of number is number
```

In the second `cout` statement, because there are no quotation marks around it, it is the variable name `number` that is inserted into the output stream, causing its value to print.

```
The value of number is 5
```

Recall from Chapter 1 that variables are called variables because their values can change. The next line of code

```
number = 7;
```

replaces `number`'s previous value with a 7. Therefore the final `cout` statement

```
cout << "Now the value of number is " << number  << endl;
```

causes the following output to print.

```
Now the value of number is 7
```

Not All Data Are Created Equal

As shown in Program 2-7, placing quotation marks around a variable name made it a string constant. When string constants are sent to `cout`, they are printed exactly as they appear inside the quotation marks. You've probably noticed by now that the `endl` stream manipulator is written with no quotation marks around it. If we were to put the following line in a program

```
cout << "endl";    // Wrong!
```

it would print out the word `endl`, rather than cause subsequent output to begin on a new line.

In fact, placing double quotation marks around anything that is not intended to be a string constant will create an error of some type. For example, in Program 2-7 the number 5 was assigned to the variable `number`. It would have been incorrect to perform the assignment this way:

```
number = "5";
```

In this line, 5 is no longer an integer, but a string constant. Since `number` was declared as an integer variable, you can only store integers in it. The integer 5 and the string constant "5" are not the same thing.

The fact that numbers can be represented as strings frequently confuses students who are new to programming. Just remember that strings are intended for humans to read. They are to be printed on computer screens or paper. Numbers, however, are intended primarily for mathematical operations. You cannot perform math on strings, and you cannot display numbers on the screen without first converting them to strings. (Fortunately, `cout` handles the conversion automatically when you send a number to it.)

Constants

Unlike a variable, a constant is a data item whose value cannot change during the program's execution. Program 2-8 contains both constants and a variable.

Program 2-8

```
// This program has constants and a variable.
#include <iostream>
using namespace std;

int main()
{
    int apples;
    apples = 20;
    cout << "Today we sold " << apples << " bushels ";
    cout << "of apples.\n";
    return 0;
}
```

Program Output
```
Today we sold 20 bushels of apples.
```

Of course, the variable is `apples`. It is declared as an integer. Here is a list of constants found in the program.

Constant	Type of Constant
20	Integer constant
"Today we sold "	String constant
" bushels "	String constant
"of apples.\n"	String constant

What are constants used for? As you can see from this program, they are commonly used to store known values in variables and display messages on the screen or a printout.

 Note: Constants are also called literals.

 # Checkpoint   [2.5]

2.8   Examine the following program.

```cpp
// This program uses variables and constants
#include <iostream>
using namespace std;

int main()
{
    int little;
    int big;
    little = 2;
    big = 2000;
    cout << "The little number is " << little << endl;
    cout << "The big number is " << big << endl;
    return 0;
}
```

List all the variables and constants that appear in the program.

2.9   What will the following program display on the screen?

```cpp
#include <iostream>
using namespace std;

int main()
{
    int number;

    number = 712;
    cout << "The value is " << "number" << endl;
    return 0;
}
```

2.6 Identifiers

CONCEPT	Choose variable names that indicate what the variables are used for.

An *identifier* is a programmer-defined name that represents some element of a program. Variable names are examples of identifiers. You may choose your own variable names in C++, as long as you do not use any of the C++ *key words*. The key words make up the "core" of the language and have specific purposes. Table 2-3 shows a complete list of the C++ key words. Note that they are all lowercase.

Table 2-3   The C++ Key Words

asm	auto	break	bool	case
catch	char	class	const	const_cast
continue	default	delete	do	double
dynamic_cast	else	enum	explicit	extern
false	float	for	friend	goto
if	inline	int	long	mutable
namespace	new	operator	private	protected
public	register	reinterpret_cast	return	short
signed	sizeof	static	static_cast	struct
switch	template	this	throw	true
try	typedef	typeid	typename	union
unsigned	using	virtual	void	volatile
wchar_t	while			

You should always choose names for your variables that give an indication of what the variables are used for. You may be tempted to declare variables with names like this:

```
int x;
```

The rather nondescript name, x, gives no clue as to the variable's purpose. Here is a better example.

```
int itemsOrdered;
```

The name itemsOrdered gives anyone reading the program an idea of the variable's use. This way of coding helps produce self-documenting programs, which means you get an understanding of what the program is doing just by reading its code. Since real-world programs usually have thousands of lines, it is important that they be as self-documenting as possible.

You probably have noticed the mixture of uppercase and lowercase letters in the variable name `itemsOrdered`. Although all of C++'s key words must be written in lowercase, you may use uppercase letters in variable names.

The reason the O in `itemsOrdered` is capitalized is to improve readability. Normally "items ordered" is two words. Unfortunately you cannot have spaces in a variable name, so the two words must be combined into one. When "items" and "ordered" are stuck together you get a variable declaration like this:

```
int itemsordered;
```

Capitalization of the second word and succeeding words makes `itemsOrdered` easier to read. It should be mentioned that this style of coding is not required. You are free to use all lowercase letters, all uppercase letters, or any combination of both. In fact, some programmers use the underscore character to separate words in a variable name, as in the following.

```
int items_ordered;
```

Legal Identifiers

Regardless of which style you adopt, be consistent and make your variable names as sensible as possible. Here are some specific rules that must be followed with all identifiers.

- The first character must be one of the letters a through z, A through Z, or an underscore character (_).
- After the first character you may use the letters a through z or A through Z, the digits 0 through 9, or underscores.
- Uppercase and lowercase characters are distinct. This means `ItemsOrdered` is not the same as `itemsordered`.

Table 2-4 lists variable names and whether each is legal or illegal in C++.

Table 2-4   Some Variable Names

Variable Name	Legal or Illegal
dayOfWeek	Legal.
3dGraph	Illegal. Variable names cannot begin with a digit.
_employee_num	Legal.
June1997	Legal.
Mixture#3	Illegal. Variable names may only use letters, digits, and underscores.

2.7 Integer Data Types

> **CONCEPT** There are many different types of data. Variables are classified according to their data type, which determines the kind of information that may be stored in them. Integer variables can only hold whole numbers.

Computer programs collect pieces of data from the real world and manipulate them in various ways. There are many different types of data. In the realm of numeric information, for example, there are whole numbers and fractional numbers. There are negative numbers and positive numbers. And there are numbers so large, and others so small, that they don't even have a name. Then there is textual information. Names and addresses, for instance, are stored as groups of characters. When you write a program you must determine what types of information it will be likely to encounter.

If you are writing a program to calculate the number of miles to a distant star, you'll need variables that can hold very large numbers. If you are designing software to record microscopic dimensions, you'll need to store very small and precise numbers. Additionally, if you are writing a program that must perform thousands of intensive calculations, you'll want variables that can be processed quickly. The data type of a variable determines all of these factors.

Although C++ offers many data types, in the very broadest sense there are only two: numeric and character. Numeric data types are broken into two additional categories: integer and floating-point. Integers are whole numbers like 12, 157, −34, and 2. Floating-point numbers have a decimal point, like 23.7, 189.0231, and 0.987. Additionally, the integer and floating-point data types are broken into even more classifications. Before we discuss the character data type, let's carefully examine the variations of numeric data.

Your primary considerations for selecting a numeric data type are:

◆ The largest and smallest numbers that may be stored in the variable

◆ How much memory the variable uses

◆ Whether the variable stores signed or unsigned numbers

◆ The number of decimal places of precision the variable has

The size of a variable is the number of bytes of memory it uses. Typically, the larger a variable is, the greater the range it can hold.

Table 2-5 shows the C++ integer data types with their typical sizes and ranges.

 Note: The data type sizes and ranges shown in Table 2-5 are typical on systems using development environments, such as Borland C++ Builder or Microsoft Visual C++. The values used by your system may not be the same.

Table 2-5   Integer Data Types, Sizes, and Ranges

Data Type	Size	Range
short	2 bytes	−32,768 to +32,767
unsigned short	2 bytes	0 to +65,535
int	4 bytes	−2,147,483,648 to +2,147,483,647
unsigned int	4 bytes	0 to 4,294,967,295
long	4 bytes	−2,147,483,648 to +2,147,483,647
unsigned long	4 bytes	0 to 4,294,967,295

Here are some examples of variable definitions:

```
int days;
unsigned speed;
short month;
unsigned short amount;
long deficit;
unsigned long insects;
```

Unsigned data types can only store positive values. They can be used when you know your program will not encounter negative values. For example, variables that hold ages or weights would rarely hold numbers less than 0.

 Note: An `unsigned int` variable can also be declared using only the word `unsigned`. For example, the following variable declarations are equivalent.

```
unsigned int days;
unsigned days;
```

Notice that in Table 2-5, `ints` and `longs` are equivalent, and `unsigned ints` are the same as `unsigned longs`. This is not always true since the size of integers is dependent on the type of machine you are using. Here are the only guarantees:

- Integers are at least as big as short integers.
- Long integers are at least as big as integers.
- Unsigned short integers are the same size as short integers.
- Unsigned integers are the same size as integers.
- Unsigned long integers are the same size as long integers.

Later in this chapter you will learn to use the `sizeof` operator to determine how large all the data types are on your computer.

As mentioned before, variables are defined by giving the data type followed by the name of the variable. In Program 2-9 an integer, an unsigned integer, and a long integer are defined.

Program 2-9

```cpp
// This program has variables of several of the integer types.
#include <iostream>
using namespace std;

int main()
{
    int checking;
    unsigned int miles;
    long days;

    checking = -20;
    miles = 4276;
    days = 186650;
    cout << "We have made a long journey of " << miles;
    cout << " miles.\n";
    cout << "Our checking account balance is " << checking;
    cout << "\nAbout " << days << " days ago Columbus ";
    cout << "stood on this spot.\n";
    return 0;
}
```

Program Output
```
We have made a long journey of 4276 miles.
Our checking account balance is -20
About 186650 days ago Columbus stood on this spot.
```

In most programs you will need more than one variable of any given data type. If a program uses two integers, length and width, they could be defined separately, like this:

```cpp
int length;
int width;
```

It is also possible to combine both variable definitions in a single statement:

```cpp
int length, width;
```

Some instructors, however, prefer that each variable in a variable definition be placed on its own line:

```cpp
int length,
    width;
```

Whether you place multiple variables on the same line or each variable on its own line, when you define several variables of the same type in a single statement, simply separate their names with commas. A semicolon is used at the end of the entire definition. Program 2-10 illustrates this. This program also shows how it is possible to give an initial value to a variable at the time it is defined.

Program 2-10

```
// This program defines three variables in the same statement.
// They are given initial values at the time they are defined.
#include <iostream>
using namespace std;

int main()
{
    int floors =  15,
        rooms  = 300,
        suites =  30;

    cout << "The Grande Hotel has " << floors << " floors\n";
    cout << "with " << rooms << " rooms and " << suites;
    cout << " suites.\n";
    return 0;
}
```

Program Output
```
The Grande Hotel has 15 floors
with 300 rooms and 30 suites.
```

Integer and Long Integer Constants

Look at the following statement from Program 2-10:

```
int floors = 15,
    rooms = 300,
    suites = 30;
```

This statement contains three integer constants. In C++, integer constants are normally stored in memory just as an `int`.

One of the pleasing characteristics of the C++ language is that it allows you to control almost every aspect of your program. If you need to change the way something is stored in memory, the tools are provided to do that. For example, what if you are in a situation where you have an integer constant, but you need it to be stored in memory as a long integer? (Rest assured, this is a situation that does arise.) C++ allows you to force an integer constant to be stored as a long integer by placing the letter L at the end of the number. Here is an example:

```
32L
```

On a computer that uses 2-byte integers and 4-byte long integers, this constant will use 4 bytes. This is called a long integer constant.

 Note: Although C++ allows you to use either an uppercase or lowercase L, the lowercase l looks too much like the number 1, so you should always use the uppercase L.

Hexadecimal and Octal Constants (enrichment)

Programmers are notorious for expressing values in numbering systems other than decimal (or base 10). Hexadecimal (base 16) and octal (base 8) are popular because they make certain programming tasks more convenient than decimal numbers do.

By default, C++ assumes that all integer constants are expressed in decimal. You express hexadecimal numbers by placing 0x in front of them. (This is zero-x, not oh-x.) Here is how the hexadecimal number F4 would be expressed in C++:

```
0xF4
```

Octal numbers must be preceded by a 0 (zero, not oh). For example, the octal 31 would be written

```
031
```

 Note: You will not be writing programs for some time that require this type of manipulation. It is important, however, that you understand this material. Good programmers should develop the skills for reading other people's source code. You may find yourself reading programs that use items like long integer, hexadecimal, or octal constants.

Checkpoint [2.6–2.7]

2.10 Which of the following are illegal variable names, and why?

```
x
99bottles
july97
theSalesFigureForFiscalYear98
r&d
grade_report
```

2.11 Is the variable name Sales the same as sales? Why or why not?

2.12 Refer to the data types listed in Table 2-5 for these questions.

A) If a variable needs to hold numbers in the range 32 to 6,000, what data type would be best?

B) If a variable needs to hold numbers in the range –40,000 to +40,000, what data type would be best?

C) Which of the following constants use more memory, 20 or 20L?

2.13 On any computer, which data type uses more memory, an integer or an unsigned integer?

2.8 The char Data Type

You might be wondering why there isn't a 1-byte integer data type. Actually there is. It is called the char data type, which gets its name from the word "character." A variable defined as a char can hold a single character, but strictly speaking, it is an integer data type.

 Note: On some systems the char data type is larger than 1 byte.

The reason an integer data type is used to store characters is because characters are internally represented by numbers. Each printable character, as well as many nonprintable characters, are assigned a unique number. The most commonly used method for encoding characters is ASCII, which stands for the American Standard Code for Information Interchange. (There are other codes, such as EBCDIC, which is used by many IBM mainframes.)

When a character is stored in memory, it is actually the numeric code that is stored. When the computer is instructed to print the value on the screen, it displays the character that corresponds with the numeric code.

You may want to refer to Appendix A, which shows the ASCII character set. Notice that the number 65 is the code for A, 66 is the code for B, and so on. Program 2-11 demonstrates that when you work with characters, you are actually working with numbers.

Program 2-11

```
// This program demonstrates the close relationship between
// characters and integers.
#include <iostream>
using namespace std;

int main()
{
    char letter;

    letter = 65;
    cout << letter << endl;
    letter = 66;
    cout << letter << endl;
    return 0;
}
```

Program Output
```
A
B
```

Figure 2-1 illustrates that when you think of characters, such as A, B, and C, being stored in memory, it is really the numbers 65, 66, and 67 that are stored.

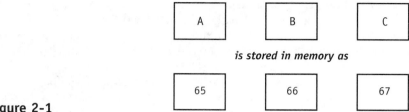

Figure 2-1

Character and String Constants

Although Program 2-11 nicely illustrates the way characters are represented by numbers, it isn't necessary to work with the ASCII codes themselves. Program 2-12 is another version that works the same way.

Program 2-12

```
// This program uses character constants.
#include <iostream>
using namespace std;

int main()
{
    char letter;

    letter = 'A';
    cout << letter << endl;
    letter = 'B';
    cout << letter << endl;
    return 0;
}
```

Program Output
```
A
B
```

Program 2-12 assigns character constants to the variable letter. Anytime a program works with a character, it internally works with the code that represents that character, so this program is still assigning the values 65 and 66 to letter.

Character constants can only hold a single character. To store a series of characters in a constant we need a string constant. In the following example, 'H' is a character constant and "Hello" is a string constant. Notice that a character constant is enclosed in single quotation marks whereas a string constant is enclosed in double quotation marks.

```
cout << 'H' << endl;
cout << "Hello" << endl;
```

Strings allow a series of characters to be stored in consecutive memory locations. The problem with strings is that they can be virtually any length. This means that there must be some way for the program to know how long the string is. In C++ this is done by appending an extra byte to the end of string constants. In this last byte, the number 0 is stored. It is called the *null terminator* or *null character* and marks the end of the string.

Don't confuse the null terminator with the character '0'. If you look at Appendix A you will see that ASCII code 48 corresponds to the character '0', whereas the null terminator is the same as the ASCII code 0. If you want to print the character 0 on the screen, you use ASCII code 48. If you want to mark the end of a string, however, you use ASCII code 0.

Let's look at an example of how a string is stored in memory. Figure 2-2 depicts the way the string "Sebastian" would be stored.

Figure 2-2

| S | e | b | a | s | t | i | a | n | \0 |

First, notice the quotation marks are not stored with the string. They are simply a way of marking the beginning and end of the string in your source code. Second, notice the very last byte of the string. It contains the null terminator, which is represented by the \0 character. The addition of this last byte means that although the string "Sebastian" is 9 characters long, it occupies 10 bytes of memory.

The null terminator is another example of something that sits quietly in the background. It doesn't print on the screen when you display a string, but nevertheless, it is there silently doing its job.

Note: C++ automatically places the null terminator at the end of string constants.

Now let's compare the way a string and a char are stored. Suppose you have the constants 'A' and "A" in a program. Figure 2-3 depicts their internal storage.

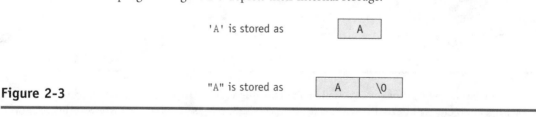

'A' is stored as

| A |

Figure 2-3

"A" is stored as

| A | \0 |

As you can see, 'A' is a 1-byte element and "A" is a 2-byte element. Since characters are really stored as ASCII codes, Figure 2-4 shows what is actually being stored in memory.

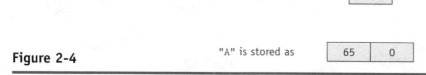

'A' is stored as

| 65 |

Figure 2-4

"A" is stored as

| 65 | 0 |

Since a char variable can only hold a single character, it can be assigned the character 'A', but not the string "A".

```
char letterOne = 'A';        // legal
char letterTwo = "A";        // NOT legal
```

You have learned that some strings look like a single character but really aren't. It is also possible to have a character that looks like a string. A good example is the newline character, \n. Although it is represented by two characters, a slash and an n, it is internally represented as one character. In fact, all escape sequences, internally, are just 1 byte.

Program 2-13 shows the use of \n as a character constant, enclosed in single quotation marks. If you refer to the ASCII chart in Appendix A, you will see that ASCII code 10 is the linefeed character. This is the code C++ uses for the newline character.

Program 2-13

```
// This program uses character constants.
#include <iostream>
using namespace std;

int main()
{
    char letter;

    letter = 'A';
    cout << letter << '\n';
    letter = 'B';
    cout << letter << '\n';
    return 0;
}
```

Program Output

```
A
B
```

Let's review some important points regarding characters and strings:

◆ Printable characters are internally represented by numeric codes. Most computers use ASCII codes for this purpose.

◆ Characters normally occupy a single byte of memory.

◆ Strings are consecutive sequences of characters that occupy consecutive bytes of memory.

◆ String constants have a null terminator at the end. This marks the end of the string.

◆ Character constants are enclosed in single quotation marks.

◆ String constants are enclosed in double quotation marks.

◆ Escape sequences are stored internally as a single character.

2.9   The C++ `string` Class

CONCEPT   Standard C++ provides a special data type for storing and working with strings.

Since a `char` variable can store only one character in its memory location, another data type is needed for a variable able to hold an entire string. While C++ does not have a built-in data type able to do this, Standard C++ provides something called the `string` class that allows the programmer to create a string type variable.

Using the `string` Class

The first step in using the string class is to `#include` the `string` header file. This is accomplished with the following preprocessor directive:

```
#include <string>
```

The next step is to declare a string type variable, called a string object. Declaring a string object is similar to declaring a variable of a primitive type. For example, the following statement declares a string object named `movieTitle`.

```
string movieTitle;
```

You can assign a string value to the `movieTitle` object with the assignment operator:

```
movieTitle = "Wheels of Fury";
```

The contents of `movieTitle` can be displayed on the screen with the `cout` object, as shown in the next statement:

```
cout << "My favorite movie is " << movieTitle << endl;
```

Program 2-14 is a complete program that demonstrates the preceding statements.

Program 2-14

```cpp
// This program demonstrates the string class.
#include <iostream>
#include <string>              // Required for the string class.
using namespace std;

int main()
{
    string movieTitle;

    movieTitle = "Wheels of Fury";
    cout << "My favorite movie is " << movieTitle << endl;
    return 0;
}
```

Program 2-14

Program Output
My favorite movie is Wheels of Fury

As you can see, working with string objects is similar to working with variables of other types. Throughout this text we will continue to discuss string class features and capabilities.

Checkpoint   [2.8–2.9]

2.14   What are the ASCII codes for the following characters? (Refer to Appendix A)

C
F
W

2.15   Which of the following is a character constant?

'B'
"B"

2.16   Assuming the char data type uses 1 byte of memory, how many bytes do the following constants use?

'Q'
"Q"
"Sales"
'\n'

2.17   Write a program that has the following character variables: first, middle, and last. Store your initials in these variables and then display them on the screen.

2.18   What is wrong with the following program?

```cpp
#include <iostream>

int main()
{
    char letter = "Z";

    cout << letter << endl;
    return 0;
}
```

2.19   What header file must you include in order to use string objects?

2.20   Write a program that stores your name, address, and phone number in three separate string objects. Display the contents of the string objects on the screen.

2.10 Floating-Point Data Types

CONCEPT	Floating-point data types are used to declare variables that can hold real numbers.

Whole numbers are not adequate for many jobs. If you are writing a program that works with dollar amounts or precise measurements, you need a data type that allows fractional values. In programming terms, these are called *floating-point* numbers.

Internally, floating-point numbers are stored in a manner similar to *scientific notation*. Take the number 47,281.97. In scientific notation this number is 4.728197×10^4. (10^4 is equal to 10,000, and $4.728197 \times 10,000$ is 47,281.97.) The first part of the number, 4.728197, is called the *mantissa*. The mantissa is multiplied by a power of 10.

Computers typically use *E notation* to represent floating-point values. In E notation, the number 47,281.97 would be 4.728197E4. The part of the number before the E is the mantissa, and the part after the E is the power of 10. When a floating-point number is stored in memory, it is stored as the mantissa and the power of 10.

Table 2-6 shows other numbers represented in scientific and E notation.

Table 2-6   Floating-Point Representations

Decimal Notation	Scientific Notation	E Notation
247.91	2.4791×10^2	2.4791E2
0.00072	7.2×10^{-4}	7.2E−4
2,900,000	2.9×10^6	2.9E6

In C++ there are three data types that can represent floating-point numbers. They are

```
float
double
long double
```

The `float` data type is considered *single precision*. The `double` data type is usually twice as big as `float`, so it is considered *double precision*. As you've probably guessed, the `long double` is intended to be larger than the `double`. Of course, the exact sizes of these data types is dependent on the computer you are using. The only guarantees are

- A `double` is at least as big as a `float`.
- A `long double` is at least as big as a `double`.

Table 2-7 shows the sizes and ranges of floating-point data types usually found on PCs.

Table 2-7   Floating-Point Data Types on PCs

Data Type	Key Word	Description
Single precision	float	4 bytes. Numbers between ±3.4E-38 and ±3.4E38
Double precision	double	8 bytes. Numbers between ±1.7E-308 and ±1.7E308
Long double precision	long double[*]	8 bytes. Numbers between ±1.7E-308 and ±1.7E308

[*]Some compilers use 10 bytes for long doubles. This allows a range of ±3.4E-4932 to 1.1E4832.

You will notice there are no unsigned floating-point data types. On all machines, variables defined as a float, double, or long double can hold positive or negative numbers. Program 2-15 uses floating-point data types.

Program 2-15

```
// This program uses floating-point data types.
#include <iostream>
using namespace std;

int main()
{
    float distance;
    double mass;

    distance = 1.495979E11;
    mass = 1.989E30;
    cout << "The sun is " << distance << " kilometers away.\n";
    cout << "The sun\'s mass is " << mass << " kilograms.\n";
    return 0;
}
```

Program Output
```
The sun is 1.49598e+11 kilometers away.
The sun's mass is 1.989e+30 kilograms.
```

Floating-Point Constants

Floating-point constants may be expressed in a variety of ways. As shown in Program 2-15, E notation is one method. When you are writing numbers that are extremely large or extremely small, this will probably be the easiest way. E notation numbers may be expressed with an upper-case E or a lowercase e. Notice in the source code the constants were written as 1.495979E11 and 1.989E30, but the program printed them as 1.49598e11 and 1.989e+30. The uppercase E and lowercase e are equivalent. (The plus sign in front of the exponent is also optional.) The distance printed with fewer digits of precision than were specified in the program because a float is not large enough to hold a number with as many significant digits as were given.

You can also express floating-point constants in decimal notation. The constant 1.495979E11 could have been written as

```
149597900000.00
```

Obviously the E notation is more convenient for lengthy numbers; but for numbers like 47.39, decimal notation is preferable to 4.739E1.

All of the following floating-point constants are equivalent:

```
1.4959E11
1.4959e11
1.4959E+11
1.4959e+11
149590000000.00
```

Floating-point constants are normally stored in memory as `doubles`. But remember, C++ provides tools for handling just about any situation. Just in case you need to force a constant to be stored as a `float`, you can append the letter F or f to the end of it. For example, the following constants would be stored as `float` numbers:

```
1.2F
45.907f
```

 Note: Because floating-point constants are normally stored in memory as `doubles`, some compilers issue a warning message when you assign a floating-point constant to a `float` variable. For example, assuming `num` is a `float`, the following statement might cause the compiler to generate a warning message:

```
num = 14.725;
```

You can suppress the error message by appending the f suffix to the floating-point constant, as shown:

```
num = 14.725f;
```

If you want to force a value to be stored as a `long double`, append an L or l to it, as in the following examples:

```
1034.56L
89.21
```

The compiler won't confuse these with long integers because they have decimal points. (Remember, the lowercase L looks so much like the number 1 you should always use the uppercase L when suffixing constants.)

2.11 The `bool` Data Type

> **CONCEPT** Boolean variables are set to either `true` or `false`.

Expressions that have a `true` or `false` value are called *Boolean* expressions, named in honor of English mathematician George Boole (1815–1864).

The `bool` data type allows you to create small integer variables that are suitable for holding `true` or `false` values. Program 2-16 demonstrates the declaration and assignment of a `bool` variable.

Program 2-16

```
// A program for demonstrating boolean variables

#include <iostream>
using namespace std;

int main()
{
    bool boolValue;

    boolValue = true;
    cout << boolValue << endl;
    boolValue = false;
    cout << boolValue << endl;
    return 0;
}
```

Program Output
```
1
0
```

As you can see from the program output, the value `true` is represented in memory by the number 1, and `false` is represented by 0.

 Note: Some compilers do not support the `bool` data type. In Chapter 3 you will learn how to create this data type if your compiler does not already include it.

2.12   Determining the Size of a Data Type

CONCEPT   The `sizeof` operator may be used to determine the size of a data type on any system.

Chapter 1 discussed the portability of the C++ language. As you have seen in this chapter, one of the problems of portability is the lack of common sizes of data types on all machines. If you are not sure what the sizes of data types are on your computer, C++ provides a way to find out.

A special operator called `sizeof` will report the number of bytes of memory used by any data type or variable. Program 2-17 illustrates its use. The first line that uses the operator reads

```
cout << "The size of an integer is " << sizeof(int);
```

The name of the data type or variable is placed inside the parentheses that follow the operator. The operator "returns" the number of bytes used by that item. This operator can be invoked anywhere you can use an unsigned integer, including in mathematical operations.

Program 2-17

```
// This program determines the size of integers, long
// integers, and long doubles.
#include <iostream>
using namespace std;

int main()
{
    long double apple;

    cout << "The size of an integer is " << sizeof(int);
    cout << " bytes.\n";
    cout << "The size of a long integer is " << sizeof(long);
    cout << " bytes.\n";
    cout << "An apple can be eaten in " << sizeof(apple);
    cout << " bytes!\n";
    return 0;
}
```

Program Output
```
The size of an integer is 4 bytes.
The size of a long integer is 4 bytes.
An apple can be eaten in 8 bytes!
```

 Checkpoint   [2.10–2.12]

2.21 How would the following number in scientific notation be represented in E notation?

$$6.31 \times 10^{17}$$

2.22   Write a program that declares an integer variable named `age` and a `float` variable named `weight`. Store your age and weight, as constants, in the variables. The program should display these values on the screen in a manner similar to the following:

Program Output
My age is 26 and my weight is 180 pounds

(Feel free to lie to the computer about your age and your weight—it'll never know!)

2.13   More on Variable Assignments and Initialization

CONCEPT   An assignment operation assigns, or copies, a value into a variable. When a value is assigned to a variable as part of the variable's definition, it is called an initialization.

As you have already seen in several examples, a value is stored in a variable with an *assignment statement*. For example, the following statement copies the value 12 into the variable `unitsSold`.

```
unitsSold = 12;
```

The = symbol is called the *assignment operator*. Operators perform operations on data. The data that operators work with are called *operands*. The assignment operator has two operands. In the previous statement, the operands are the variable `unitsSold` and the numeric constant 12.

In an assignment statement, C++ requires the name of the variable receiving the assignment to appear on the left side of the operator. The following statement is incorrect.

```
12 = unitsSold;  //Incorrect!
```

In C++ terminology, the operand on the left side of the = symbol must be an *lvalue*. An lvalue is something that identifies a place in memory whose contents may be changed. Most of the time this will be a variable name. The operand on the right side of the = symbol must be an *rvalue*. An rvalue is any expression that has a value. The assignment statement takes the value of the rvalue and puts it in the memory location of the object identified by the lvalue.

You have also seen that it is possible to assign values to variables when they are defined. This is called *initialization*. When multiple variables are defined in the same statement, it is possible to initialize some of them without having to initialize all of them. Program 2-18 illustrates this.

Program 2-18

```
// This program shows variable initialization.
#include <iostream>
#include <string>
using namespace std;
```

(program continues)

Program 2-18 *(continued)*

```cpp
int main()
{
    string month = "February";        // month is initialized to "February"
    int year,                         // year is not initialized
        days = 29;                    // days is initialized to 29

    year = 2004;                      // Now year is assigned a value.

    cout << "In "   << year << " " << month
         << " has " << days << " days.\n";

    return 0;
}
```

Program Output
In 2004 February has 29 days.

2.14 Scope

CONCEPT	A variable's scope is the part of the program that has access to the variable.

Every variable has a *scope*. The scope of a variable is the part of the program where the variable may be used. The rules that define a variable's scope are complex, and you will only be introduced to the concept here. In other sections of the book we will revisit this topic and expand on it.

The first rule of scope you should learn is that a variable cannot be used in any part of the program before it is defined. Program 2-19 illustrates this.

Program 2-19

```cpp
// This program can't find its variable.
#include <iostream>
using namespace std;

int main()
{
    cout << value;        //Incorrect since value has not been defined yet

    int value = 100;
    return 0;
}
```

The program will not work because it attempts to send the contents of the variable `value` to `cout` before the variable is defined. The compiler reads your program from top to bottom. If it encounters a statement that uses a variable before the variable is defined, an error will result. To correct the program, the variable definition must be put before any statement that uses it.

2.15 Arithmetic Operators

CONCEPT | There are many operators for manipulating numeric values and performing arithmetic operations.

C++ provides many operators for manipulating data. Generally, there are three types of operators: *unary*, *binary*, and *ternary*. These terms reflect the number of operands an operator requires.

Unary operators only require a single operand. For example, consider the following expression:

```
-5
```

Of course, we understand this represents the value negative five. The constant 5 is preceded by the minus sign. The minus sign, when used this way, is called the *negation operator*. Since it only requires one operand, it is a unary operator.

Binary operators work with two operands. The assignment operator is in this category. Ternary operators, as you may have guessed, require three operands. C++ only has one ternary operator, which will be discussed in Chapter 4.

Arithmetic operations are very common in programming. Table 2-8 shows the common arithmetic operators in C++.

Table 2-8   Fundamental Arithmetic Operators

Operator	Meaning	Type	Example
*	Multiplication	Binary	`tax = cost * rate;`
/	Division	Binary	`salePrice = original / 2;`
%	Modulus	Binary	`remainder = value % 3;`
+	Addition	Binary	`total = cost + tax;`
−	Subtraction	Binary	`cost = total - tax;`

Each of these operators work as you probably expect. The addition operator returns the sum of its two operands. In the following assignment statement, the variable `amount` will be assigned the value 12:

```
amount = 4 + 8;
```

The subtraction operator returns the value of its right operand subtracted from its left operand. This statement will assign the value 98 to `temperature`:

```
temperature = 112 - 14;
```

The multiplication operator returns the product of its two operands. In the following statement, `markUp` is assigned the value 3:

```
markUp = 12 * 0.25;
```

The division operator returns the quotient of its left operand divided by its right operand. In the next statement, `points` is assigned the value 5:

```
points = 100 / 20;
```

 WARNING! In C++ when both operands of a division statement are integers, the statement will perform integer division. This means the result of the division will be an integer as well. If there is a remainder, it will be discarded. For example, in the following statement, `parts` is assigned the value 5:

```
parts = 17 / 3;
```

This may seem like an annoyance, but it can actually be useful in some programs. If you want to make sure a statement, like the one shown, performs regular division, express one of the numbers as a floating-point number. Here is an example:

```
parts = 17.0 / 3;
```

In this statement, since 17.0 is interpreted as a floating-point number, the division operation will return a floating-point value. The result of the division is 5.66667.

The modulus operator, which only works with integer operands, returns the remainder of an integer division. The following statement assigns 2 to `leftOver`:

```
leftOver = 17 % 3;
```

In Chapter 3 you will learn how to use these operators in more complex mathematical formulas. For now we will concentrate on their basic usage, as illustrated in Program 2-20.

Program 2-20

```
// This program calculates hourly wages.
// Written by Herbert Dorfmann 12/14/01

#include <iostream>
using namespace std;
```

(program continues)

Program 2-20 *(continued)*

```cpp
int main()
{
    float regHours = 40.0,        // number of regular hours worked
          oTHours = 10,           // number of overtime hours worked
          regPayRate = 18.25,     // hourly pay rate for regular hours
          oTPayRate = 27.78,      // hourly pay rate for overtime hours
          regWages,               // calculated regular wages
          oTWages,                // calculated overtime wages
          totalWages;             // calculated total wages

    regWages = regPayRate * regHours;
    oTWages  = oTPayRate  * oTHours;
    totalWages = regWages + oTWages;

    cout << "Wages for this week are $" << totalWages << endl;
    return 0;
}
```

Program Output
```
Wages for this week are $1007.8
```

Notice that the output displays the wages as $1007.8, with just one decimal point. In Chapter 3 you will learn to format output so you can control how it displays.

Checkpoint [2.13–2.15]

2.23 Is the following assignment statement valid or invalid? If it is invalid, why?

```cpp
72 = amount;
```

2.24 How would you consolidate the following variable definition and assignment statement into a single statement?

```cpp
int apples;
apples = 20;
```

2.25 How would you consolidate the following variable definitions into a single statement?

```cpp
int x = 7;
int y = 16;
int z = 28;
```

2.26 What is wrong with the following program? How would you correct it?

```cpp
#include <iostream>
using namespace std;
```

```
int main()
{
    critter = 62.7;
    float critter;
    cout << critter << endl;
    return 0;
}
```

2.27   Is the following an example of integer division or floating-point division? What value will be stored in `portion`?

```
portion = 70 / 3;
```

2.16   Comments

CONCEPT Comments are notes of explanation that document lines or sections of a program. Comments are part of the program, but the compiler ignores them. They are intended for people who may be reading the source code.

It may surprise you that one of the most important parts of a program has absolutely no impact on the way it runs. In fact, the compiler pretends this part of a program doesn't even exist. Of course, I'm speaking of the comments.

If you are like most programmers, you will be resistant to putting more than just a few comments in your source code. After all, it's painful enough typing the parts of the program that actually do something. It is crucial, however, that you develop the habit of thoroughly annotating your code with descriptive comments. It might take extra time now, but it will almost certainly save time in the future.

Imagine writing a program of medium complexity with about 8,000 to 10,000 lines of C++ code. Once you have written the code and satisfactorily debugged it, you happily put it away and move on to the next project. Ten months later you are asked to make a modification to the program (or worse, track down and fix an elusive bug). You pull out the massive pile of paper that contains your source code and stare at thousands of statements that now make no sense at all. You find variables with names like `z2`, and you can't remember what they are for. If only you had left some notes to yourself explaining all the program's nuances and oddities. Of course it's too late now. All that's left to do is decide what will take less time: figuring out the old program or completely rewriting it!

This scenario might sound extreme, but it's one you don't want to happen to you. Real-world programs are big and complex. Thoroughly documented programs will make your life easier, not to mention the other poor souls who may have to read your code in the future.

Commenting the C++ Way

You have already seen one way to place comments in a C++ program. As illustrated in Program 2-20, you simply place two forward slashes (//) where you want the comment to begin. The compiler ignores everything from that point to the end of the line.

In addition to telling what the program does and describing the purpose of variables, comments can also be used to explain complex procedures in your code and to provide information such as who wrote the program and when it was written or last modified.

Just in case you are one of those who believes "if a little of something is good then a whole lot of it must be better," let me caution you about putting too many comments in your programs. Comments should explain the aspects of your code that are not evident. They do not have to explain every little detail. Program 2-21 is an example of how commenting can be overdone.

Program 2-21

```
// PROGRAM: PAYROLL.CPP
// Written by Herbert Dorfmann 12/14/01
// Also known as "The Dorfmeister"
// This program calculates company payroll.
// The payroll should be done every Friday no later than noon.
// To start the program type PAYROLL and then press the enter key.

#include <iostream>          // Need the iostream file because
using namespace std;         // the program uses cout.
                             //
int main()                   // This is the start of function main.
{                            // This is the opening brace for main.
    float regHours = 40.0,   // regHours is a float variable that
                             // holds the number of regular hours worked.
           oTHours = 10,     // oTHours is a float variable that
                             // holds the number of overtime hours worked.
```

(The remainder of this program is left out.)

Don't feel like you have to comment every line of your program or describe things that are clearly evident. Be sure, however, to thoroughly document the parts that will need explaining 10 months from now!

Commenting the C Way

Recall from Chapter 1 that C++ is a descendent of the C language. Comments in C start with /* (a forward slash followed by an asterisk) and end with */ (an asterisk followed by a forward slash). Everything between these markers is ignored. Program 2-22 illustrates how C style comments may be used in a C++ program.

Program 2-22

```
/* This program calculates hourly wages.
   Written by Herbert Dorfmann 12/14/01
*/

#include <iostream>
using namespace std;

int main()
{
    float regHours = 40.0,     /* number of regular hours worked   */
          oTHours = 10,        /* number of overtime hours worked  */
          regPayRate = 18.25,  /* hourly pay rate for regular hours */
```

(The remainder of this program is left out.)

Unlike a C++ style comment, a C style comment can span several lines. This makes it more convenient to write large, multiline comments because you do not have to mark every line. However, the C style is less convenient for single-line comments because you must type both a beginning and ending comment symbol. Therefore, many programmers prefer to use a combination of both styles, using the C style for multiline comments and the C++ style for single line comments.[3]

When using C style comments:

♦ Be careful not to reverse the beginning symbol with the ending symbol.

♦ Be sure not to forget the ending symbol.

Both of these mistakes can be difficult to track down and will prevent the program from compiling correctly.

2.17 Focus on Software Engineering: *Programming Style*

CONCEPT Programming style refers to the way a programmer uses identifiers, spaces, tabs, blank lines, and punctuation characters to visually arrange a program's source code. These are some, but not all, of the elements of programming style.

In Chapter 1 you learned that syntax rules govern the way a language may be used. The syntax rules of C++ dictate how and where to place key words, semicolons, commas, braces, and other components of the language. The compiler's job is to check for syntax errors and, if there are none, to generate object code.

---

[3]There is anecdotal evidence that some compilers determine whether you are programming in C or C++ by detecting the style of comment being used. If a C++ program contains both C and C++ style comments, such a compiler might mistakenly interpret it as a C program and expect it to follow the syntax of that language.

When the compiler reads a program it processes it as one long stream of characters. The compiler doesn't care that each statement is on a separate line, or that spaces separate operators from operands. Humans, on the other hand, find it difficult to read programs that aren't written in a visually pleasing manner. Consider Program 2-23 for example.

Program 2-23

```
#include <iostream>
using namespace std;int main(){float shares=220.0;float avgPrice=14.67;cout
<<"There were "<<shares<<" shares sold at $"<<avgPrice<<
" per share.\n";return 0;}
```

Program Output
```
There were 220.0 shares sold at $14.67 per share.
```

Although the program is syntactically correct (it doesn't violate any rules of C++), it is very difficult to read. The same program is shown in Program 2-24, written in a more reasonable style.

Program 2-24

```
// This program is visually arranged to make it readable.

#include <iostream>
using namespace std;

int main()
{
    float shares = 220.0;
    float avgPrice = 14.67;

    cout << "There were " << shares << " shares sold at $";
    cout << avgPrice << " per share.\n";
    return 0;
}
```

Program Output
```
There were 220.0 shares sold at $14.67 per share.
```

Programming style refers to the way source code is visually arranged. Ideally, it is a consistent method of putting spaces and indentions in a program so visual cues are created. These cues quickly tell a programmer important information about a program.

For example, notice in Program 2-24 that inside the function `main`'s braces each line is indented. It is a common C++ style to indent all the lines inside a set of braces. You will also notice the blank line between the variable definitions and the `cout` statements. This is intended to visually separate the definitions from the executable statements.

Note: Although you are free to develop your own style, you should adhere to common programming practices. By doing so, you will write programs that visually make sense to other programmers.

Another aspect of programming style is how to handle statements that are too long to fit on one line. Because C++ is a free-flowing language, it is usually possible to spread a statement over several lines. For example, here is a `cout` statement that uses five lines:

```
cout << "The fahrenheit temperature is "
     << fahrenheit
     << " and the centigrade temperature is "
     << centigrade
     << endl;
```

This statement will work just as if it were typed on one line. You have already seen variable definitions treated similarly:

```
int fahrenheit,
    centigrade,
    kelvin;
```

There are many other issues related to programming style. They will be presented throughout the book.

Review Questions and Exercises

Multiple Choice

1. Every complete statement ends with a

   A) `period`
   B) `#` symbol
   C) `semicolon`
   D) `ending brace`

2. Which of the following statements is correct?

   A) `#include (iostream)`
   B) `#include {iostream}`
   C) `#include <iostream>`
   D) `#include [iostream]`
   E) All of the above

3. Every C++ program must have a

   A) `cout` statement
   B) function `main`
   C) `#include` statement
   D) All of the above

4. Preprocessor directives begin with a

   A) #
   B) !
   C) <
   D) *
   E) None of the above

5. The following data

   ```
   72
   'A'
   "Hello World"
   2.8712
   ```

   are all examples of

   A) Variables
   B) Literals or constants
   C) Strings
   D) None of the above

6. A group of statements, such as the contents of a function, are enclosed in

   A) Braces { }
   B) Parenthesis ( )
   C) Brackets < >
   D) Any of the above

7. Which of the following are *not* valid assignment statements? (Circle all that apply.)

   A) `total = 9;`
   B) `72 = amount;`
   C) `profit = 129`
   D) `letter = 'W';`

8. Which of the following are *not* valid `cout` statements? (Circle all that apply.)

   A) `cout << "Hello World";`
   B) `cout << "Have a nice day"\n;`
   C) `cout < value;`
   D) `cout << Programming is great fun;`

9. Assume w = 5, x = 4, y = 8, and z = 2. What value will be stored in `result` in each of the following statements?

   A) `result = x + y;`
   B) `result = z * 2;`
   C) `result = y / x;`
   D) `result = y - z;`
   E) `result = w % 2;`

10. How would each of the following numbers be represented in E notation?

    A) 3.287×10^6
    B) -978.65×10^{12}
    C) 7.65491×10^{-3}
    D) -58710.23×10^{-4}

11. The negation operator is

    A) Unary
    B) Binary
    C) Ternary
    D) None of the above

12. When do preprocessor directives execute?

    A) Before the compiler compiles your program
    B) After the compiler compiles your program
    C) At the same time as the compiler compiles your program
    D) None of the above

True or False

13. T F A variable must be declared before it can be used.

14. T F Variable names may begin with a number.

15. T F Variable names may be up to 31 characters long.

16. T F A left brace in a C++ program should always be followed by a right brace later in the program.

Fill-in-the-Blank and Short Answer

17. How many operands do each of the following types of operators require?

    _____ Unary
    _____ Binary
    _____ Ternary

18. How may the `float` variables `temp`, `weight`, and `age` be declared in one statement?

19. How may the `int` variables `months`, `days`, and `years` be declared in one statement, with `months` initialized to 2 and `years` initialized to 3?

20. Write assignment statements that perform the following operations with the variables `a`, `b`, and `c`.

    A) Adds 2 to `a` and stores the result in `b`.
    B) Multiplies `b` times 4 and stores the result in `a`.
    C) Divides `a` by 3.14 and stores the result in `b`.
    D) Subtracts 8 from `b` and stores the result in `a`.
    E) Stores the value 27 in `a`.
    F) Stores the character `'K'` in `c`.
    G) Stores the ASCII code for `'B'` in `c`.

21. Is the following comment a C style comment, or a C++ style comment?

    ```
    /* This program was written by M. A. Codewriter*/
    ```

22. Is the following comment a C style comment, or a C++ style comment?

    ```
    // This program was written by M. A. Codewriter
    ```

23. Modify the following program so it prints two blank lines between each line of text.

    ```cpp
    #include <iostream>
    using namespace std;

    int main()
    {
        cout << "Two mandolins like creatures in the";
        cout << "dark";
        cout << "Creating the agony of ecstasy.";
        cout << "                    - George Barker";
        return 0;
    }
    ```

24. What will the following programs print on the screen?

    A)
    ```cpp
    #include <iostream>
    using namespace std;

    int main()
    {
        int freeze = 32, boil = 212;
        freeze = 0;
        boil = 100;
        cout << freeze << endl << boil << endl;
        return 0;
    }
    ```

    B)
    ```cpp
    #include <iostream>
    using namespace std;

    int main()
    {
        int x = 0, y = 2;
        x = y * 4;
        cout << x << endl << y << endl;
        return 0;
    }
    ```

    C)
    ```cpp
    #include <iostream>
    using namespace std;
    int main()
    ```

```
        {
            cout << "I am the incredible";
            cout << "computing\nmachine";
            cout << "\nand I will\namaze\n";
            cout << "you.";
            return 0;
        }
```

D)
```
    #include <iostream>
    using namespace std;

    int main()
    {
        cout << "Be careful\n";
        cout << "This might/n be a trick ";
        cout << "question\n";
        return 0;
    }
```

E)
```
    #include <iostream>
    using namespace std;

    int main()
    {
        int a, x = 23;

        a = x % 2;
        cout << x << endl << a << endl;
        return 0;
    }
```

Find the Error

25. There are a number of syntax errors in the following program. Locate as many as you can.

```
        */ What's wrong with this program? /*
        #include iostream
        using namespace std;

        int main();
        }
            int a, b, c\\ Three integers
            a = 3
            b = 4
            c = a + b
            Cout < "The value of c is %d" < C;
            return 0;
        {
```

Programming Challenges

General Requirements

Each program should have a section of comments at the top. The comments should contain your name, the date the program was written, the chapter the assignment appeared in, and the assignment number and name. Here is an example:

```
// Written by Jill Johnson
// March 31, 2003
// Chapter 2
// Assignment 1, Sum of Two Numbers
```

1. Sum of Two Numbers

Write a program that stores the integers 62 and 99 in variables, and stores the sum of these two in a variable named `total`.

2. Sales Prediction

The East Coast sales division of a company generates 62 percent of total sales. Based on that percentage, write a program that will predict how much the East Coast division will generate if the company has $4.6 million in sales this year.

3. Sales Tax

Write a program that will compute the total sales tax on a $52 purchase. Assume the state sales tax is 4 percent and the county sales tax is 2 percent.

4. Cyborg Data Type Sizes

You have been given a job as a programmer on a Cyborg supercomputer. In order to accomplish some calculations, you need to know how many bytes the following data types use: `char`, `int`, `float`, and `double`. You do not have any manuals, so you can't look this information up. Write a C++ program that will determine the amount of memory used by these types and display the information on the screen.

5. Miles per Gallon

A car holds 12 gallons of gasoline and can travel 350 miles before refueling. Write a program that calculates the number of miles per gallon the car gets. Display the result on the screen.

6. Land Calculation

One acre of land is equivalent to 43,560 square feet. Write a program that calculates the number of acres in a tract of land with 389,767 square feet.

7. Circuit Board Price

An electronics company sells circuit boards at a 40 percent profit. Write a program that will calculate the selling price of a circuit board that costs $12.67. Display the result on the screen.

8. Personal Information

Write a program that displays the following information, each on a separate line:

>   Your name
>
>   Your address, with city, state, and zip code
>
>   Your telephone number
>
>   Your college major

Use only a single `cout` statement to display all of this information.

9. Star Pattern

Write a program that displays the following pattern:

```
          *
        * * *
       * * * * *
      * * * * * * *
       * * * * *
        * * *
          *
```

10. Test Average

Write a program that holds five test scores in five variables. Display each test score, as well as the average of the scores.

Serendipity Booksellers Software Development Project—Part 2: *A Problem-Solving Exercise*

Screen Design

For this chapter's assignment, you are to write programs that display the main screens used in the project. The screens have already been designed, so your primary task is to write the C++ code that displays them. For testing purposes you will create a separate program for each screen. (In later chapters you will merge these into one program.) Here is a list of the programs you should have after completing the assignment for this chapter:

```
mainmenu.cpp
cashier.cpp
invmenu.cpp
bookinfo.cpp
reports.cpp
```

Assignments

1. Create the Main Menu Screen.

Create a program called `mainmenu.cpp`. It should display the following screen:

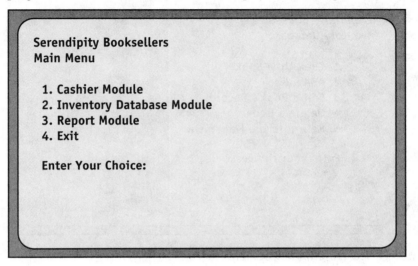

Serendipity Booksellers
Main Menu

  1. Cashier Module
  2. Inventory Database Module
  3. Report Module
  4. Exit

  Enter Your Choice:

2. Create the Cashier Screen.

Create a program called `cashier.cpp`. It should display the following screen:

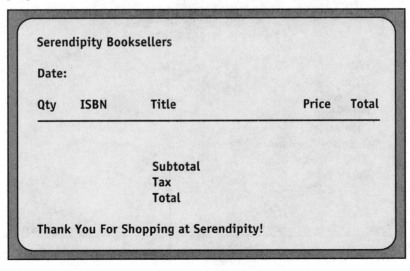

Serendipity Booksellers

Date:

Qty	ISBN	Title	Price	Total

Subtotal
Tax
Total

Thank You For Shopping at Serendipity!

3. Create the Inventory Database Menu Screen.

Create a program called `invmenu.cpp`. It should display the following screen:

```
Serendipity Booksellers
Inventory Database

        1. Look-Up a Book
        2. Add a Book
        3. Edit a Book's Record
        4. Delete a Book
        5. Return to the Main Menu

        Enter your choice:
```

4. Create the Book Information Screen.

Create a program called `bookinfo.cpp`. It should display the following screen:

```
                    Serendipity Booksellers
                      Book Information

        ISBN:
        Title:
        Author:
        Publisher:
        Date Added:
        Quantity-On-Hand:
        Wholesale Cost:
        Retail Price:
```

5. Create the Reports Menu Screen.

Create a program called `reports.cpp`. It should display the following screen:

```
                    Serendipity Booksellers
                           Reports

              1. Inventory Listing
              2. Inventory Wholesale Value
              3. Inventory Retail Value
              4. Listing by Quantity
              5. Listing by Cost
              6. Listing by Age
              7. Return to the Main Menu

              Enter Your Choice:
```

CHAPTER 3

Expressions and Interactivity

Topics

3.1 The `cin` Object

CONCEPT The `cin` object reads information typed at the keyboard.

So far you have written programs with built-in information. Without giving the user an opportunity to enter his or her own data, you have initialized the variables with the necessary starting values. These types of programs are limited to performing their task with only a single set of starting information. If you decide to change the initial value of any variable, the program must be modified and recompiled.

In reality, most programs ask for values that will be assigned to variables. This means the program does not have to be modified if the user wants to run it several times with different sets of information. For example, a program that calculates payroll for a small business might ask the user to enter the name of the employee, the hours worked, and the hourly pay rate. When the paycheck for that employee has been printed, the program could start over again with the name, hours worked, and hourly payrate of the next employee.

Just as cout is C++'s standard output object, cin is the standard input object. It reads input from the console (or keyboard) as shown in Program 3-1.

Program 3-1

```
// This program asks the user to enter the length and width of
// a rectangle. It calculates the rectangle's area and displays
// the value on the screen.

#include <iostream>
using namespace std;

int main()
{
    int length, width, area;

    cout << "This program calculates the area of a ";
    cout << "rectangle.\n";
    cout << "What is the length of the rectangle? ";
    cin >> length;
    cout << "What is the width of the rectangle? ";
    cin >> width;
    area = length * width;
    cout << "The area of the rectangle is " << area << ".\n";
    return 0;
}
```

Program Output with Example Input Shown in Bold
```
This program calculates the area of a rectangle.
What is the length of the rectangle? 10[Enter]
What is the width of the rectangle? 20[Enter]
The area of the rectangle is 200.
```

Instead of calculating the area of one rectangle, this program can be used to get the area of any rectangle. The values that are stored in the length and width variables are entered by the user when the program is running. Look at the following lines:

```
cout << "What is the length of the rectangle? ";
cin >> length;
```

The cout object is used to display the question "What is the length of the rectangle?" This is called a *prompt*. It lets the user know that an input is expected and prompts them as to what must be entered. When a cin statement will be used to get input from the user, it should always be preceded by a prompt.

The next line uses the cin object to get the answer. The >> symbol is the *stream extraction operator*. It gets characters from the stream object on its left and stores them in the variable whose name appears on its right. In the preceding lines, characters are taken from the cin object (which gets them from the keyboard) and are stored in the length variable.

 Note: Notice the >> and << operators appear to point in the direction information is flowing. The >> operator indicates information flows from cin to a variable, and the << operator shows that information flows from a variable (or constant) to cout.

The cin object causes a program to wait until information is typed at the keyboard and the [**Enter**] key is pressed. No other lines in the program will be executed until cin gets its input.

When the user enters characters from the keyboard, they are temporarily placed in an area of memory called the *input buffer*, or *keyboard buffer*. cin automatically converts this information to the data type of the variable it is to be stored in. If the user types 10, it is read as the characters '1' and '0', but cin is smart enough to know this will have to be converted to the int value 10 before it is stored in length. If the user enters a floating-point number like 10.7, however, there is a problem. cin knows such a value cannot be stored in an integer variable, so it stops reading when it gets to the decimal point, leaving the decimal point and the rest of the digits in the input buffer. This can cause a problem when the next value is read in. Program 3-2 illustrates this problem.

Program 3-2

```
// This program illustrates what can happen when a
// floating-point number is entered for an integer variable.

#include <iostream>
using namespace std;

int main()
{
    int intNumber;
    float floatNumber;

    cout << "Input a number.\n";
    cin >> intNumber;
    cout << "Input a second number.\n";
    cin >> floatNumber;
    cout << "You entered: " << intNumber
         << " and " << floatNumber << endl;

    return 0;
}
```

Program Output with Example Input Shown in Bold
```
Input a number.
12.3[Enter]
Input a second number.
You entered: 12 and 0.3
```

When prompted for the first number, the user entered 12.3 from the keyboard. However, because cin was reading a value into intNumber, an integer variable, it stopped reading when it got to the decimal point and a 12 was stored in intNumber. When the second cin statement needed a value to read into floatNumber, it found that it already had a value in the input buffer, the .3 left over from the user's first input. Instead of waiting for the user to enter a second number, the .3 was read in and stored in floatNumber.

Later you will learn how to prevent something like this from happening, but for now this illustrates the need to provide the user with clear prompts. If the user had been specifically prompted to enter an integer for the first number, there would have been less chance of a problem occurring.

 Note: You must include the iostream file in any program that uses cin.

Entering Multiple Values

The cin object may be used to gather multiple values at once. Look at Program 3-3, which is a modified version of Program 3-1.

Program 3-3

```cpp
// This program asks the user to enter the length and width of
// a rectangle. It calculates the rectangle's area and displays
// the value on the screen.

#include <iostream>
using namespace std;

int main()
{
    int length, width, area;

    cout << "This program calculates the area of a ";
    cout << "rectangle.\n";
    cout << "Enter the length and width of the rectangle ";
    cout << "separated by a space.\n";
    cin >> length >> width;
    area = length * width;
    cout << "The area of the rectangle is " << area << endl;
    return 0;
}
```

Program Output with Example Input Shown in Bold
```
This program calculates the area of a rectangle.
Enter the length and width of the rectangle separated by a space.
10 20[Enter]
The area of the rectangle is 200
```

The following line waits for the user to enter two values. The first is assigned to length and the second to width.

```cpp
cin >> length >> width;
```

In the example output, the user entered 10 and 20, so 10 is stored in length and 20 is stored in width.

Notice the user separates the numbers by spaces as they are entered. This is how cin knows where each number begins and ends. It doesn't matter how many spaces are entered between the individual numbers. For example, the user could have entered

    10   20

 Note: The **[Enter]** key is pressed after the last number is entered.

cin will also read multiple values of different data types. This is shown in Program 3-4.

Program 3-4

```
// This program demonstrates how cin can read multiple values
// of different data types.

#include <iostream>
using namespace std;

int main()
{
    int whole;
    float fractional;
    char letter;

    cout << "Enter an integer, a float, and a character: ";
    cin >> whole >> fractional >> letter;

    cout << "Whole: " << whole << endl;
    cout << "Fractional: " << fractional << endl;
    cout << "Letter: " << letter << endl;
    return 0;
}
```

Program Output with Example Input Shown in Bold
```
Enter an integer, a float, and a character: 4 5.7 b[Enter]
Whole: 4
Fractional: 5.7
Letter: b
```

As you can see in the example output, the values are stored in their respective variables. If the user had responded in the following way

    Enter an integer, a float, and a character: 5.7 4 b

the program would have stored 5 in whole, 0.7 in fractional, and 4 in letter. It is important that the values are entered in the correct order.

Checkpoint   [3.1]

3.1   What header file must be included in programs using `cin`?

3.2   What is the `>>` symbol called?

3.3   Where does `cin` read its input from ?

3.4   True or False: `cin` requires the user to press the **[Enter]** key after entering data.

3.5   Assume `value` is an integer variable. If the user enters 3.14 in response to the following programming statement, what will be stored in `value`?

```
cin >> value;
```

A)   3.14
B)   3
C)   0
D)   Nothing. An error message is displayed.

3.6   A program has the following variable definitions.

```
long miles;
int feet;
float inches;
```

Write one `cin` statement that reads a value into each of these variables.

3.7   The following program will run, but the user will have difficulty understanding what to do. How would you improve the program?

```
// This program multiplies two numbers and displays the
// result.
#include <iostream>
using namespace std;

int main()
{
    float first, second, product;

    cin >> first >> second;
    product = first * second;
    cout << product;
    return 0;
}
```

3.8   Complete the following program skeleton so it asks for the user's weight (in pounds) and displays the equivalent weight in kilograms.

```
#include <iostream>
using namespace std;
```

```
int main()
{
        float pounds, kilograms;

        // Write a prompt to tell the user to enter his or her weight
        // in pounds.
        // Write code here that gets the user's weight in pounds.
        // The following line does the conversion.
        // One kilogram weighs 2.21 pounds.
        kilograms = pounds / 2.21;
        // Write code here that displays the user's weight in kilograms.
        return 0;
}
```

3.2 Mathematical Expressions

CONCEPT C++ allows you to construct complex mathematical expressions using multiple operators and grouping symbols.

In Chapter 2 you were introduced to the basic mathematical operators, which are used to build mathematical expressions. An *expression* is a programming statement that has a value. Usually, an expression consists of an operator and its operands. Look at the following statement:

```
sum = 21 + 3;
```

Since 21 + 3 has a value, it is an expression. Its value, 24, is stored in the variable sum. Expressions do not have to be in the form of mathematical operations. In the following statement, 3 is an expression.

```
number = 3;
```

Here are some programming statements where the variable result is being assigned the value of an expression. They are called assignment statements.

```
result = x;
result = 4;
result = 15 / 3;
result = 22 * number;
result = sizeof(int);
result = a + b + c;
```

In each of these statements, a number, variable name, or mathematical expression appears on the right side of the = symbol. A value is obtained from each of these and stored in the variable result. These are all examples of a variable being assigned the value of an expression.

Program 3-5 shows how mathematical expressions can be used with the cout object.

Program 3-5

```
// This program asks the user to enter the numerator
// and denominator of a fraction and it displays the
// decimal value.

#include <iostream>
using namespace std;

int main()

{
    float numerator, denominator;

    cout << "This program shows the decimal value of ";
    cout << "a fraction.\n";
    cout << "Enter the numerator: ";
    cin >> numerator;
    cout << "Enter the denominator: ";
    cin >> denominator;
    cout << "The decimal value is ";
    cout << (numerator / denominator) << endl;
    return 0;
}
```

Program Output with Example Input Shown in Bold
```
This program shows the decimal value of a fraction.
Enter the numerator: 3[Enter]
Enter the denominator: 16[Enter]
The decimal value is 0.1875
```

The cout object will display the value of any legal expression in C++. In the previous program, the value of the expression numerator / denominator is displayed.

 Note: The example input shows the user entering 3 and 16. Since these values are assigned to float variables, they are stored as 3.0 and 16.0.

 Note: When sending an expression that includes an operator to cout, it is always a good idea to put parentheses around the expression. Some advanced operators will yield unexpected results otherwise.

Operator Precedence

It is possible to build mathematical expressions with several operators. The following statement assigns the sum of 17, *x*, 21, and *y* to the variable answer.

```
answer = 17 + x + 21 + y;
```

Some expressions are not that straightforward, however. Consider the following statement:

```
outcome = 12 + 6 / 3;
```

What value will be stored in `outcome`? It could be assigned either 6 or 14, depending on whether the addition operation or the division operation was done first. The answer is 14 because the division operator has higher *precedence* than the addition operator.

Mathematical expressions are evaluated from left to right. However, when there are two operators if one has higher precedence than the other, it is done first. Multiplication and division have higher precedence than addition and subtraction, so the example statement works like this:

A)   6 is divided by 3, yielding a result of 2
B)   12 is added to 2, yielding a result of 14

It could be diagrammed in the following way:

```
12 + 6 / 3
       \ /
12 +   2

14
```

Table 3-1 shows the precedence of the arithmetic operators. The operators at the top of the table have higher precedence than the ones below it

Table 3-1   Precedence of Arithmetic Operators (Highest to Lowest)

(unary negation)   -
*   /   %
+   -

The multiplication, division, and modulus operators have the same precedence. This is also true of the addition and subtraction operators. Table 3-2 shows some expressions with their values.

Table 3-2   Some Expressions

Expression	Value
5 + 2 * 4	13
10 / 2 - 3	2
8 + 12 * 2 - 4	28
4 + 17 % 2 - 1	4
6 - 3 * 2 + 7 - 1	6

Associativity

Associativity is the order in which an operator works with its operands. Associativity is either *left to right* or *right to left*. The associativity of the division operator is left to right, so it divides the operand on its left by the operand on its right. Table 3-3 shows the arithmetic operators and their associativity.

Table 3-3   Associativity of Arithmetic Operators

Operator	Associativity
(unary negation) -	Right to left
* / %	Left to right
+ -	Left to right

Grouping with Parentheses

Parts of a mathematical expression may be grouped with parentheses to force some operations to be performed before others. In the following statement, the sum of a, b, c, and d is divided by 4.

```
average = (a + b + c + d) / 4;
```

Without the parentheses, however, d would be divided by 4 and the result added to a, b, and c. Table 3-4 shows more expressions and their values.

Table 3-4   More Expressions

Expression	Value
(5 + 2) * 4	28
10 / (5 - 3)	5
8 + 12 * (6 - 2)	56
(4 + 17) % 2 - 1	0
(6 - 3) * (2 + 7) / 3	9

Converting Algebraic Expressions to Programming Statements

In algebra it is not always necessary to use an operator for multiplication. C++, however, requires an operator for any mathematical operation. Table 3-5 shows some algebraic expressions that perform multiplication and the equivalent C++ expressions.

Table 3-5 Algebraic and C++ Multiplication Expressions

Algebraic Expression	Operation	C++ Equivalent
6B	6 times B	`6 * B`
(3)(12)	3 times 12	`3 * 12`
4xy	4 times x times y	`4 * x * y`

When converting some algebraic expressions to C++, you may have to insert parentheses that do not appear in the algebraic expression. For example, look at the following expression:

$$X = \frac{A + B}{C}$$

To convert this to a C++ statement, $A + B$ will have to be enclosed in parentheses:

```
x = (a + b) / c;
```

Table 3-6 shows more algebraic expressions and their C++ equivalents.

Table 3-6 Algebraic and C++ Expressions

Algebraic Expression	C++ Expression
$Y = 3\dfrac{X}{2}$	`y = x / 2 * 3;`
$Z = 3BC + 4$	`z = 3 * b * c + 4;`
$A = \dfrac{3X + 2}{4A - 1}$	`a = (3 * x + 2) / (4 * a - 1)`

No Exponents Please!

Unlike many programming languages, C++ does not have an exponent operator. Raising a number to a power requires the use of a *library function*. The C++ library isn't a place where you check out books, but a collection of specialized functions. Think of a library function as a "routine" that performs a specific operation. One of the library functions is called pow, and its purpose is to raise a number to a power. Here is an example of how it's used:

```
area = pow(4, 2);
```

This statement contains a *call* to the pow function. The numbers inside the parentheses are *arguments*. Arguments are information being sent to the function. pow always raises the first argument to the power of the second argument. In this example, 4 is raised to the power of 2. The result is *returned* from the function and used in the statement where the function call appears. In this case, the value 16 is returned from pow and assigned to the variable area. This is illustrated in Figure 3-1.

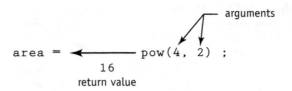

$$\text{area} = \longleftarrow \text{pow}(4, 2) ;$$

16
return value

arguments

Figure 3-1

The statement area = pow(4,2) is equivalent to the following algebraic statement:

$$\text{area} = 4^2$$

Here is another example of a statement using the pow function. It assigns 3 times 6^3 to x:

x = 3 * pow(6, 3);

And the following statement displays the value of 5 raised to the power of 4:

cout << pow(5, 4);

It might be helpful to think of pow as a "black box" that you plug two numbers into, which then sends a third number out. The number that comes out has the value of the first number raised to the power of the second number, as illustrated in Figure 3-2.

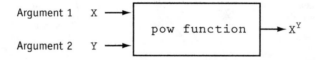

Argument 1   X ⟶   pow function   ⟶ X^Y

Argument 2   Y ⟶

Figure 3-2

There are some rules that must be followed when the pow function is used. First, the program must include the cmath header file. Second, the variable used to store pow's return value should be declared as a double or a float. For example, in the following statement the variable area should be either a double or a float:

area = pow(4, 2);

Note: The pow function is designed to return a double. Remember that a double value will fit in a float variable if the value is small enough. If the arguments of the pow function are large enough to cause pow to produce a value outside the range of a float, a double variable should be used to store the return value.

Program 3-6 solves a simple algebraic problem. It asks the user to enter the radius of a circle and then calculates the area of the circle. The formula is

$$\text{Area} = \pi r^2$$

which is expressed in the program as

area = 3.14159 * pow(radius, 2);

Program 3-6

```
// This program calculates the area of a circle.
// The formula for the area of a circle is pi times
// the radius squared. Pi is 3.14159.

#include <iostream>
#include <cmath>          // Needed for the pow function

int main()
{
    double area, radius;

    cout << "This program calculates the area of a circle.\n";
    cout << "What is the radius of the circle? ";
    cin >> radius;
    area = 3.14159 * pow(radius, 2);
    cout << "The area is " << area << endl;
    return 0;
}
```

Program Output with Example Input Shown in Bold
```
This program calculates the area of a circle.
What is the radius of the circle? 10[Enter]
The area is 314.159
```

 # Checkpoint [3.2]

3.9   In each of the following cases, tell which operator has higher precedence or whether they have the same precedence.

A)   + and *

B)   * and /

C)   / and %

3.10 Complete the following table by writing the value of each expression in the Value column.

Expression	Value
6 + 3 * 5	
12 / 2 - 4	
9 + 14 * 2 - 6	
5 + 19 % 3 - 1	
(6 + 2) * 3	
14 / (11 - 4)	
9 + 12 * (8 - 3)	
(6 + 17) % 2 - 1	
(9 - 3) * (6 + 9) / 3	

3.11 Write C++ expressions for the following algebraic expressions:

$$y = 6x$$

$$a = 2b + 4c$$

$$y = x^2$$

$$g = \frac{x + 2}{z^2}$$

$$y = \frac{x^2}{z^2}$$

3.12 Study the following program and complete the table.

```cpp
#include <iostream>
#include <cmath>

int main()
{
    double value1, value2, value3;
    cout << "Enter a number: ";
    cin >> value1;
    value2 = 2 * pow(value1, 2);
    value3 = 3 + value2 / 2 - 1;
    cout << value3;
    return 0;
}
```

If the User Enters...	The Program Will Display What Number (Stored in `value3`)?
2	
5	
4.3	
6	

3.13 Complete the following program skeleton so it displays the volume of a cylindrical fuel tank. The formula for the volume of a cylinder is

Volume $= \pi r^2 h$

Where
π is 3.14159

r is the radius of the tank
h is the height of the tank

```cpp
#include <iostream>
#include <cmath>

int main()
{
    double volume, radius, height;
    cout << "This program will tell you the volume of\n";
    cout << "a cylinder-shaped fuel tank.\n";
    cout << "How tall is the tank? ";
    cin >> height;
    cout << "What is the radius of the tank? ";
    cin >> radius;

    // You must complete the program.
    return 0;
}
```

3.3 Type Conversion

> **CONCEPT** When an operator's operands are of different data types, C++ will automatically convert them to the same data type. This can affect the results of mathematical expressions.

If a floating-point value is assigned to an `int` variable, what value will the variable receive? If an `int` is multiplied by a `float`, what data type will the result be? What if a `double` is divided by an `unsigned int`? Is there any way of predicting what will happen in these instances? The answer is yes. C++ follows a set of rules when performing mathematical operations on variables of different data types. It's helpful to understand these rules to prevent subtle errors from creeping into your programs.

Just like officers in the military, data types are ranked. One data type outranks another if it can hold a larger number. For example, a `float` outranks an `int`. Table 3-7 lists the data types in order of their rank, from highest to lowest.

Table 3-7 Data Type Ranking

```
long double
double
float
unsigned long
long
unsigned int
int
```

One exception to the ranking in Table 3-7 is when an `int` and a `long` are the same size. In that case, an `unsigned int` outranks `long` because it can hold a higher value.

When C++ is working with an operator, it strives to convert the operands to the same type. This automatic conversion is known as *type coercion*. When a value is converted to a higher data type, it is said to be *promoted*. To *demote* a value means to convert it to a lower data type. Let's look at the specific rules that govern the evaluation of mathematical expressions.

Rule 1: `char`s, `short`s, and `unsigned short`s are automatically promoted to `int`.

You will notice that `char`, `short`, and `unsigned short` do not appear in Table 3-7. That's because anytime they are used in a mathematical expression, they are automatically promoted to an `int`. The only exception to this rule is when an `unsigned short` holds a value larger than can be held by an `int`. This can happen on systems where `short`s are the same size as `int`s. In this case, the `unsigned short` is promoted to `unsigned int`.

Rule 2: When an operator works with two values of different data types, the lower-ranking value is promoted to the type of the higher-ranking value.

In the following expression, assume that `years` is an `int` and `interestRate` is a `float`:

```
years * interestRate
```

Before the multiplication takes place, `years` will be promoted to a `float`.

Rule 3: When the final value of an expression is assigned to a variable, it will be converted to the data type of that variable.

This means that if the variable receiving the value is of a lower data type than the value it is receiving, the value will be demoted to the type of the variable. If the variable's data type does not have enough storage space to hold the value, part of the value will be lost, and the variable could receive an inaccurate result. If the variable receiving the value is an integer and the value being assigned to it is a floating-point number, the value will be *truncated* before being assigned to the variable. This means everything after the decimal point will be "chopped off":

```
int x = 3.75;        // 3.75 will be truncated to integer 3
                     // x will be assigned a 3
```

If the variable receiving the value has a higher data type than the value being assigned to it, there is no problem.

In the following statement, assume that `area` is a `long int`, while `length` and `width` are both `int`:

```
area = length * width;
```

Since `length` and `width` are both `int`s, they will not be converted to any other data type. The result of the multiplication, however, will be converted to `long` so it can be stored in `area`.

 WARNING! Remember, when both operands of a division are integers, the fractional part will be truncated, or thrown away.

Watch out for situations where an expression results in a fractional value being assigned to an integer variable. As discussed, the variable will receive a truncated value. Here is an example:

```
int x, y = 4;
float z = 2.7;
x = y * z;
```

In the expression `y * z`, `y` will be promoted to `float` and 10.8 will result from the multiplication. Since `x` is an integer, however, 10.8 will be truncated and 10 will be stored in `x`.

3.4 Overflow and Underflow

CONCEPT When a variable is assigned a value that is too large or too small in range for that variable's data type, the variable overflows or underflows.

Trouble can arise when a variable is assigned a value that is too large for its type. Here is a statement where a, b, and c are all short integers:

```
a = b * c;
```

If b and c are set to values large enough, the multiplication will produce a number too big to be stored in a. To be prepared for this, a should have been declared as an `int` or `long int`.

When a variable is assigned a number that is too large for its data type, it *overflows*. Likewise, assigning a value that is too small for a variable causes it to *underflow*. Program 3-7 shows what happens when an integer overflows or underflows. (The output shown is from a system with two-byte short integers.)

Program 3-7

```cpp
// This program demonstrates integer overflow and underflow.

#include <iostream>
using namespace std;

int main()
{
    short testVar = 32767;

    cout << testVar << endl;
    testVar = testVar + 1;
    cout << testVar << endl;
    testVar = testVar - 1;
    cout << testVar << endl;
    return 0;
}
```

Program Output
```
32767
-32768
32767
```

Typically, when an integer overflows, its contents wrap around to that data type's lowest possible value. In Program 3-7, testVar wrapped around from 32,767 to −32,768 when 1 was added to it. When 1 was subtracted from testVar, it underflowed, which caused its contents to wrap back around to 32,767. It is common for no warning or error message to be given in such a case, so be careful when working with numbers close to the maximum or minimum range of an integer.

When floating-point variables overflow or underflow, the results depend on which compiler is being used. Your system may produce programs that do any of the following:

♦ Produces an incorrect result and continues running.

♦ Prints an error message and immediately stops when either floating-point overflow or underflow occurs.

♦ Prints an error message and immediately stops when floating-point overflow occurs, but stores a 0 in the variable when it underflows.

♦ Gives you a choice of behaviors when overflow or underflow occurs.

You can find out how your system reacts by compiling and running Program 3-8.

Program 3-8

```cpp
// This program can be used to see how your system handles
// floating-point overflow and underflow.

#include <iostream>
using namespace std;
```

(program continues)

Program 3-8 *(continued)*

```
int main()
{
    float test;

    test = 2.0e38 * 1000;        // Should overflow test
    cout << test << endl;
    test = 2.0e-38 / 2.0e38;     // Should underflow test
    cout << test << endl;
    return 0;
}
```

3.5 The Typecast Operator

CONCEPT The typecast operator allows you to perform manual data type conversion.

The *typecast operator* lets you manually promote or demote a value in the same way automatic conversion takes place. It is a unary operator which appears as the data type name followed by the operand inside a set of parentheses. Here is an example:

```
val = int(number);
```

The typecast operator in the statement above takes a copy of number's value, converts it to an integer, and then stores it in val. If number is a floating-point variable, its value will be truncated before being stored in val. The original value in number is not changed, however.

The typecast operator is useful in situations where you want to prevent integer division from taking place or where C++ will not perform the desired conversion automatically. Program 3-9 shows an example.

Program 3-9

```
// This program uses the typecast operator to avoid an integer
// division.

#include <iostream>
using namespace std;

int main()
{
    int months, books;
    float perMonth;

    cout << "How many books do you plan to read? ";
    cin >> books;
    cout << "How many months will it take you to read them? ";
    cin >> months;
```

(program continues)

Program 3-9   *(continued)*

```
    perMonth = float(books) / months;
    cout << "That is " << perMonth << " books per month.\n";
    return 0;
}
```

Program Output with Example Input Shown in Bold
```
How many books do you plan to read? 30[Enter]
How many months will it take you to read them? 7[Enter]
That is 4.285714 books per month.
```

The statement that uses the typecast operator is

```
    perMonth = float(books) / months;
```

books is an integer variable, but its value is converted to a float before the division takes place. Without the typecast operator, an integer division would have been performed, resulting in an incorrect answer.

 WARNING! In Program 3-9, the following statement would still have resulted in integer division:

```
    perMonth = float(books / months);
```

The result of the expression books / months is 4. When 4 is converted to a float, it is 4.0. To prevent the integer division from taking place, one of the operands should be converted to a float prior to the division operation. This forces C++ to automatically convert the value of the other operand to a float.

Program 3-10 shows another use of the typecast operator.

Program 3-10

```
// This program uses a typecast operator to print a character
// from a number.

#include <iostream>
using namespace std;

int main()
{
    int number = 65;

    cout << number << endl;
    cout << char(number) << endl;
    return 0;
}
```

Program 3-10

Program Output

65
A

cout normally displays variable contents in a format suitable for the variable's native data type. If you want to change this, as in Program 3-10, you can use a typecast operator.

Checkpoint   [3.3–3.5]

3.14 Assume the following variable definitions:

```
int a = 5, b = 12;
float x = 3.4, z = 9.1;
```

What are the values of the following expressions?

A) b / a
B) x * a
C) float(b / a)
D) float(b) / a
E) b / float(a)
F) float(b) / float(a)
G) b / int(x)
H) int(x) * int(z)
I) int(x * z)
J) float(int(x) * int(z))

3.15 Complete the following program skeleton so it asks the user to enter a character. Store the character in the variable letter. Use a typecast operator on the variable in a cout statement to display the character's ASCII code on the screen.

```
#include <iostream>
using namespace std;

int main()
{
    char letter;


    //  Finish this program
    //   as specified above.
    return 0;
}
```

3.16 What will the following program display?

```
#include <iostream>
using namespace std;

int main()
{
    int integer1, integer2;
    float float1;
    integer1 = 19;
    integer2 = 2;
    float1 = integer1 / integer2;
    cout << float1 << endl;
    float1 = float(integer1) / integer2;
    cout << float1 << endl;
    float1 = float(integer1 / integer2);
    cout << float1 << endl;
    return 0;
}
```

3.6   The Power of Constants

CONCEPT	Constants may be given names that symbolically represent them in a program.

In Chapter 2 you learned about numbers and strings being expressed as constants. For example, the following statement contains the numeric constant 0.129:

```
amount2 = amount1 * 0.129;
```

Let's assume this statement appears in a banking program that calculates data pertaining to loans. In such a program, two potential problems arise. First, it is not clear to anyone other than the original programmer what 0.129 is. It appears to be an interest rate, but in some situations there are fees associated with loan payments. How can the purpose of this statement be determined without painstakingly checking the rest of the program?

The second problem occurs if this number is used in other calculations throughout the program and must be changed periodically. Assuming the number is an interest rate, what if the rate changes from 12.9 percent to 13.2 percent? The programmer will have to search through the source code for every occurrence of the number.

Both of these problems can be addressed by using named constants. A *named constant*, also called a *constant variable*, is really a variable whose content is read-only and cannot be changed while the program is running. Here is a definition of a named constant:

```
const float INTERESTRATE = 0.129;
```

It looks just like a regular variable definition except that the word `const` appears before the data type name. The name of the named constant can be any legal C++ identifier name, but some programmers use all uppercase letters, as we have done here, to distinguish them from variables. The key word `const` is a qualifier that tells the compiler to make the variable read-only. Its value will remain constant throughout the program's execution.

An initialization value must be given when a variable with the `const` qualifier is declared, or an error will result when the program is compiled. A compiler error will also result if there are any statements in the program that attempt to change the contents of a named constant.

An advantage of using named constants is that they make programs more self-documenting. The statement

```
amount2 = amount1 * 0.129;
```

can be changed to read

```
amount2 = amount1 * INTERESTRATE;
```

A new programmer can read the second statement and know what is happening. It is evident that `amount1` is being multiplied by the interest rate. Another advantage to this approach is that widespread changes can easily be made to the program. No matter how many places the interest rate is used in the program, if the rate changes the programmer only has to change one line of code—the statement that defines and initializes the named constant. The following line of code, for example, would be used to set a new interest rate of 13.2 percent.

```
const float INTERESTRATE = 0.132;
```

The program is then ready to be recompiled. Every statement that uses `INTERESTRATE` will be updated with the new value.

It is also useful to define named constants for common values that are difficult to remember. For example, Program 3-6 calculated the area of a circle. The number 3.14159 is used for pi in the formula. This value could easily be defined as a named constant, as shown in Program 3-11.

Program 3-11

```
// This program calculates the area of a circle.
// The formula for the area of a circle is pi times
// the radius squared. pi is 3.14159.

#include <iostream>
#include <cmath>            // Needed for the pow function
using namespace std;

int main()
{
    const float PI = 3.14159;
    double area, radius;
```

(program continues)

Program 3-11   (continued)

```
    cout << "This program calculates the area of a circle.\n";
    cout << "What is the radius of the circle? ";
    cin >> radius;
    area = PI * pow(radius, 2);
    cout << "The area is " << area << endl;
    return 0;
}
```

The #define Directive

The older C-style method of creating named constants is with the #define preprocessor directive. Although it is preferable to use the const modifier, there are programs with the #define directive still in use. In addition, the #define directive has other uses, so it is important to understand. Program 3-12 shows how the preprocessor can be used to create a named constant.

Program 3-12

```
// This program calculates the area of a circle.
// The formula for the area of a circle is pi times
// the radius squared. Pi is 3.14159.

#include <iostream>
#include <cmath>        // Needed for the pow function
using namespace std;

#define PI 3.14159

int main()
{
    double area, radius;

    cout << "This program calculates the area of a circle.\n";
    cout << "What is the radius of the circle? ";
    cin >> radius;
    area = PI * pow(radius, 2);
    cout << "The area is " << area << endl;
    return 0;
}
```

Remember, the preprocessor scans your program before it is compiled. It looks for directives, which are lines that begin with the # symbol. Preprocessor directives cause your source code to be modified prior to being compiled. The #define statement in Program 3-12 reads

```
#define PI 3.14159
```

The word PI is a named constant and 3.14159 is its value. Anytime PI is used in the program, it will be replaced by the value 3.14159. The line that reads

```
area = PI * pow(radius, 2);
```

will be modified by the preprocessor to read

```
area = 3.14159 * pow(radius, 2);
```

If there had been a line that read

```
cout << PI << endl;
```

it would have been modified to read

```
cout << 3.14159 << endl;
```

It is important to realize the difference between constant variables declared with the key word `const` and constants created with the #define directive. Constant variables are defined like regular variables. They have a data type and a specific storage location in memory. They are like regular variables in every way except that you cannot change their value while the program is running. Constants created with the #define directive, however, are not variables at all, but textual substitutions. Each occurrence of the named constant in your source code is removed and the value of the constant is written in its place.

Note: It is not required that constants created with the #define directive be named with uppercase letters. Most programmers do this so they can tell the difference between #defined constants and variable names in later sections of the program.

Be careful not to put a semicolon at the end of a #define directive. The semicolon will actually become part of the value of the constant. If the #define directive in Program 3-12 had read like this,

```
#define PI 3.14159;
```

the mathematical statement

```
area = PI * pow(radius, 2);
```

would have been modified to read

```
area = 3.14159; * pow(radius, 2);
```

Because of the semicolon, the preprocessor would have created a syntax error in the statement and the compiler would have given an error message when trying to process this statement.

Note: #define directives are intended for the preprocessor and C++ statements are intended for the compiler. The preprocessor does not look for semicolons to terminate directives.

Creating a Boolean Data Type

In Chapter 2 you learned that Standard C++ has a `bool` data type that has just two values, `true` and `false`. However, if you are using a prestandard C++ compiler, you probably will not be able to use this data type unless you create it yourself. Luckily, C++ provides several ways for programmers to create their own data types. One of the ways to do this is by using #define and named constants, which we have just studied.

To simulate a bool data type using this method, simply include the following preprocessor directive and two named constants in the header section of your program.

```
#define bool int
const int true = 1;
const int false = 0;
```

The #define directive tells the compiler that anytime we define something to be a bool, it is really being stored as an int. The two named constants tell the compiler that anytime we assign true to a variable, we are really storing a 1 and anytime we assign false to a variable, we are really storing a 0.

With these lines in your program, you can now simulate creating and using bool variables. Program 3-13 demonstrates this.

Program 3-13

```
// This program demonstrates creating a bool data type
// for use with a prestandard C++ compiler. It will not
// compile if there is already a built-in bool data type.

#include <iostream.h>    // This is most likely the header file you
                         // are using if you have a prestandard C++ compiler.

#define bool int          // Remember, #define gets no semicolon.
const int true = 1;
const int false = 0;

int main()
{
    bool boolValue;

    boolValue = true;
    cout << boolValue << endl;
    boolValue = false;
    cout << boolValue << endl;

    return 0;
}
```

Program Output
```
1
0
```

Checkpoint [3.6]

3.17 Write statements using the `const` qualifier to create constants for the following values:

Constant Value	Description
2.71828	Euler's number (known in mathematics as e)
5.26E5	Number of seconds in a year
32.2	The gravitational constant (in feet per second^2)
9.8	The gravitational constant (in meters per second^2)
1609	Number of meters in a mile

3.18 Write #define directives for the constants listed in question 3.17.

3.19 Assuming the user enters 6 in response to the question, what will the following program display on the screen?

```
#include <iostream>
using namespace std;

#define GREETING1 "This program calculates the number "
#define GREETING2 "of candy pieces sold."
#define QUESTION "How many jars of candy have you sold? "
#define RESULTS "The number of pieces sold: "
#define YOUR_COMMISSION "Candy pieces you get for commission: "
#define COMMISSION_RATE .20

int main()
{
    const int perJar = 1860;
    int jars, pieces;
    float commission;

    cout << GREETING1;
    cout << GREETING2 << endl;
    cout << QUESTION;
    cin >> jars;
    pieces = jars * perJar;
    cout << RESULTS << pieces << endl;
    commission = pieces * COMMISSION_RATE;
    cout << YOUR_COMMISSION << commission << endl;
    return 0;
}
```

3.20 Complete the following program skeleton so it properly converts a speed entered in miles per hour to feet per second. One mile per hour is 1.467 feet per second.

```
#include <iostream>
using namespace std;

int main()
{
    // Declare a named constant called conversion
    // with the value 1.467.
    float milesPerHour, feetPerSecond;
    cout << "This program converts miles per hour to\n";
    cout << "feet per second.\n";
    cout << "Enter a speed in MPH: ";
    cin >> milesPerHour;
    // Insert a mathematical statement here to
    // calculate feet per second.
    // one mile per hour equals 1.467 feet per second.
    cout << "That is " << feetPerSecond
         << " feet per second.\n";
    return 0;
}
```

3.7   Multiple Assignment and Combined Assignment

CONCEPT   Multiple assignment means to assign the same value to several variables with one statement.

C++ allows you to assign a value to multiple variables at once. If a program has several variables, such as a, b, c, and d, and each variable needs to be assigned a value, such as 12, the following statement may be constructed:

```
a = b = c = d = 12;
```

The value 12 will be copied to each variable listed in the statement.[1]

Program 3-14 uses the following multiple assignment statement to store a value entered by the user into several variables:

```
store1 = store2 = begInv;
```

---

[1]This works because the assignment operations are carried out from right to left. First 12 is assigned to d. Then d's value, now a 12, is assigned to c. Then c's value is assigned to b, and finally b's value is assigned to a.

Program 3-14

```cpp
//    This program tracks the inventory of two widget stores
//    that opened at the same time. Each store started with the
//    same number of widgets in inventory. By subtracting the
//    number of widgets each store has sold from its inventory,
//    the current inventory can be calculated.

#include <iostream>
using namespace std;

int main()
{
    int begInv, sold, store1, store2;

    cout << "One week ago, 2 new widget stores opened\n";
    cout << "at the same time with the same beginning\n";
    cout << "inventory. What was the beginning inventory? ";
    cin >> begInv;
    store1 = store2 = begInv;

    cout << "How many widgets has store 1 sold? ";
    cin >> sold;
    store1 = store1 - sold; // Subtract sold from store1

    cout << "How many widgets has store 2 sold? ";
    cin >> sold;
    store2 = store2 - sold; // Subtract sold from store2

    cout << "\nThe current inventory of each store:\n\n";
    cout << "Store 1: " << store1 << endl;
    cout << "Store 2: " << store2 << endl;

    return 0;
}
```

Program Output with Example Input Shown in Bold
```
One week ago, 2 new widget stores opened
at the same time with the same beginning
inventory. What was the beginning inventory? 100[Enter]
How many widgets has store 1 sold? 25[Enter]
How many widgets has store 2 sold? 15[Enter]

The current inventory of each store:

Store1: 75
Store2: 85
```

Combined Assignment Operators

Notice in Program 3-14 the following statement appears:

```
store1 = store1 - sold; // Subtract sold from store1
```

On the right side of the assignment operator, the value of `sold` is subtracted from the current value of `store1`. The result is then assigned to `store1`, giving it a new value that replaces the value that was previously there. Effectively, this statement subtracts `sold` from `store1`. The variable `store2` is decreased with a similar statement:

```
store2 = store2 - sold; // Subtract sold from store2
```

If you have never seen this type of statement before, it might cause some initial confusion because the same variable name appears on both sides of the assignment operator. Table 3-8 shows other examples of statements written this way.

Table 3-8   (Assume x = 6)

Statement	What It Does	Value of x After the Statement
x = x + 4;	Adds 4 to x	10
x = x - 3;	Subtracts 3 from x	3
x = x * 10;	Multiplies x by 10	60
x = x / 2;	Divides x by 2	3
x = x % 4	Makes x the remainder of x / 4	2

These types of operations are very common in programming. For convenience, C++ offers a special set of operators designed specifically for these jobs. Table 3-9 shows the *combined assignment operators,* also known as *compound operators.*

Table 3-9

Operator	Example Usage	Equivalent To
+=	x += 5;	x = x + 5;
-=	y -= 2;	y = y - 2;
*=	z *= 10;	z = z * 10;
/=	a /= b;	a = a / b;
%=	c %= 3;	c = c % 3;

As you can see, the combined assignment operators do not require the programmer to type the variable name twice. Also, they give a clearer indication of what is happening in the statement. Program 3-15 shows Program 3-14 modified to use combined assignment operators.

Program 3-15

```
//   This program tracks the inventory of two widget stores
//   that opened at the same time. Each store started with the
//   same number of widgets in inventory. By subtracting the
//   number of widgets each store has sold from its inventory,
//   the current inventory can be calculated.

#include <iostream>
using namespace std;

int main()
{
    int begInv, sold, store1, store2;

    cout << "One week ago, 2 new widget stores opened\n";
    cout << "at the same time with the same beginning\n";
    cout << "inventory. What was the beginning inventory? ";
    cin >> begInv;
    store1 = store2 = begInv;

    cout << "How many widgets has store 1 sold? ";
    cin >> sold;
    store1 -= sold; // Subtract sold from store1

    cout << "How many widgets has store 2 sold? ";
    cin >> sold;
    store2 -= sold; // Subtract sold from store2

    cout << "\nThe current inventory of each store:\n\n";
    cout << "Store 1: " << store1 << endl;
    cout << "Store 2: " << store2 << endl;

    return 0;
}
```

Program Output is identical to that of Program 3-14.

More elaborate statements may be expressed with the combined assignment operators. Here is an example:

```
result *= a + 5;
```

In this statement, result is multiplied by the sum of a + 5. When constructing such statements, you must realize the precedence of the combined assignment operators is lower than that of the regular math operators. The statement above is equivalent to

```
result = result * (a + 5);
```

which is different from

```
result = result * a + 5;
```

Table 3-10 shows other examples of such statements and their assignment statement equivalencies.

Table 3-10

Example Usage	Equivalent To
x += b + 5;	x = x + (b + 5);
y -= a * 2;	y = y - (a * 2);
z *= 10 - c;	z = z * (10 - c);
a /= b + c;	a = a / (b + c);
c %= d - 3;	c = c % (d - 3);

⑦ Checkpoint   [3.7]

3.21 Write a multiple assignment statement that assigns 0 to the variables total, subtotal, tax, and shipping.

3.22 Write statements using combined assignment operators to perform the following:

    A)   Add 6 to x.

    B)   Subtract 4 from amount.

    C)   Multiply y by 4.

    D)   Divide total by 27.

    E)   Store in x the remainder of x divided by 7.

    F)   Add y * 5 to x.

    G)   Subtract discount times 4 from total.

    H)   Multiply increase by salesRep times 5.

    I)   Divide profit by shares minus 1000.

3.23 What will the following program display?

```cpp
#include <iostream>
using namespace std;

int main()
{
    int unus, duo, tres;

    unus = duo = tres = 5;
    unus += 4;
    duo *= 2;
    tres -= 4;
    unus /= 3;
    duo += tres;
    cout << unus << endl;
    cout << duo << endl;
    cout << tres << endl;
    return 0;
}
```

3.8 Formatting Output

CONCEPT The cout object provides ways to format data as it is being displayed. This affects the way data appears on the screen.

The same data can be printed or displayed in several different ways. For example, all of the following numbers have the same value, although they look different:

```
720
720.0
720.00000000
        720
7.2e+2
+720.0
```

The way a value is printed is called its *formatting*. The cout object has a standard way of formatting variables of each data type. Sometimes, however, you need more control over the way information is displayed. Consider Program 3-16, for example, which displays three rows of numbers with spaces between each one.

Program 3-16

```cpp
// This program displays three rows of numbers.

#include <iostream>
using namespace std;
```

(program continues)

Program 3-16 *(continued)*

```cpp
int main()
{
    int num1 = 2897, num2 = 5,    num3 = 837,
        num4 = 34,    num5 = 7,    num6 = 1623,
        num7 = 390,   num8 = 3456, num9 = 12;

    // Display the first row of numbers
    cout << num1 << "  " << num2 << "  " << num3 << endl;

    // Display the second row of numbers
    cout << num4 << "  " << num5 << "  " << num6 << endl;

    // Display the third row of numbers
    cout << num7 << "  " << num8 << "  " << num9 << endl;

    return 0;
}
```

Program Output
```
2897   5   837
34   7   1623
390   3456   12
```

Unfortunately, the numbers do not line up in columns. This is because some of the numbers, such as 5 and 7, occupy one position on the screen, while others occupy two or three positions. cout uses just the number of spaces needed to print each number.

To remedy this, cout offers a way of specifying the minimum number of spaces to use for each number. A stream manipulator, setw, can be used to establish print fields of a specified width. Here is an example of how it is used:

```cpp
value = 23;
cout << setw(5) << value;
```

The number inside the parentheses after the word setw specifies the *field width* for the value immediately following it. The field width is the minimum number of character positions, or spaces, on the screen to print the value in. In our example, the number 23 will be displayed in a field of 5 spaces.

To further clarify how this works, look at the following statements:

```cpp
value = 23;
cout << "(" << setw(5) << value << ")";
```

This will produce the following output:

```
(    23)
```

Since the number did not use the entire field, cout filled the extra three positions with blank spaces. Because the number appears on the right side of the field with blank spaces "padding" it in front, it is said to be *right-justified*.

Program 3-17 shows how the numbers in Program 3-16 can be printed in columns that line up perfectly by using setw. In addition, since we used a setw(6), and the largest number has four digits, the numbers will be separated without having to cout a string constant containing blanks, as we did in Program 3-16 to insert extra spaces between them.

Program 3-17

```
// This program uses setw to displays three rows of numbers so they align.

#include <iostream>
#include <iomanip>              // Header file needed to use setw
using namespace std;

int main()
{
    int num1 = 2897, num2 = 5,    num3 = 837,
        num4 = 34,   num5 = 7,    num6 = 1623,
        num7 = 390,  num8 = 3456, num9 = 12;

    // Display the first row of numbers
    cout << setw(6) << num1 << setw(6) << num2 << setw(6) << num3 << endl;

    // Display the second row of numbers
    cout << setw(6) << num4 << setw(6) << num5 << setw(6) << num6 << endl;

    // Display the third row of numbers
    cout << setw(6) << num7 << setw(6) << num8 << setw(6) << num9 << endl;

    return 0;
}
```

Program Output
```
2897     5   837
  34     7  1623
 390  3456    12
```

Because each number uses the same field width, they are displayed in perfect columns.

> **Note:** A new header file, iomanip, is included in Program 3-17. It must be used in any program that uses setw.

Notice how a setw manipulator is used with each value because setw only establishes a field width for the value immediately following it. After that value is printed, cout goes back to its default method of printing.

You might wonder what will happen if the number is too large to fit in the field, as in the following statement:

```
value = 18397;
cout << setw(2) << value;
```

In cases like this, cout will print the entire number. setw only specifies the minimum number of positions in the print field. Any number larger than the minimum will cause cout to override the setw value.

You may specify the field width of any type of data. Program 3-18 shows setw being used with an integer, a floating-point number, and a string.

Program 3-18

```
// This program demonstrates the setw manipulator being
// used with values of various data types.

#include <iostream>
#include <iomanip>
#include <string>
using namespace std;

int main()
{
    int intValue = 3928;
    float floatValue = 91.5;
    string stringObjectValue = "Jill Q. Jones";

    cout << "(" << setw(5) << intValue << ")" << endl;
    cout << "(" << setw(8) << floatValue << ")" << endl;
    cout << "(" << setw(16) << stringObjectValue << ")" << endl;
    return 0;
}
```

Program Output
```
( 3928)
(    91.5)
(   Jill Q. Jones)
```

Program 3-18 can be used to illustrate the following points:

◆ The field width of a floating-point number includes a position for the decimal point.

◆ The field width of a string includes all characters in the string, including spaces.

◆ The values printed in the field are right-justified by default. This means they are aligned with the right side of the print field, and any blanks that must be used to pad it are inserted in front of the value.

Precision

Floating-point values may be rounded to a number of *significant digits,* or *precision,* which is the total number of digits that appear before and after the decimal point. You can control the number of significant digits with which floating-point values are displayed by using the setprecision manipulator. Program 3-19 shows the results of a division operation displayed with different numbers of significant digits.

Program 3-19

```
// This program demonstrates how setprecision rounds a
// floating-point value.

#include <iostream>
#include <iomanip>
using namespace std;

int main()
{
    float quotient, number1 = 132.364, number2 = 26.91;

    quotient = number1 / number2;
    cout << quotient << endl;
    cout << setprecision(5) << quotient << endl;
    cout << setprecision(4) << quotient << endl;
    cout << setprecision(3) << quotient << endl;
    cout << setprecision(2) << quotient << endl;
    cout << setprecision(1) << quotient << endl;
    return 0;
}
```

Program Output
```
4.91877
4.9188
4.919
4.92
4.9
5
```

 Note: With prestandard compilers, your output may be different than that shown in Program 3-19.

The first value is displayed without the setprecision manipulator. (By default, the system in Program 3-19 displays floating-point values with six significant digits.) The subsequent cout statements print the same value, but rounded to five, four, three, two, and one significant digits.

Notice that, unlike `setw`, `setprecision` does not count the decimal point. When we used `setprecision(5)`, for example, the output contained five significant digits, which required six positions to print 4.9188.

If the value of a number is expressed in fewer digits of precision than specified by `setprecision`, the manipulator will have no effect. In the following statements, the value of `dollars` only has four digits of precision, so the number printed by both `cout` statements is 24.51.

```
float dollars = 24.51;
cout << dollars << endl;                  //prints as 24.51
cout << setprecision(5) << dollars << endl;   //prints as 24.51
```

Table 3-11 shows how `setprecision` affects the way various values are displayed. Notice that when fewer digits are to be displayed than the number holds, `setprecision` rounds, rather than truncates, the number.

Table 3-11

Number	Manipulator	Value Displayed
28.92786	setprecision(3)	28.9
21	setprecision(5)	21
109.5	setprecision(4)	109.5
34.78596	setprecision(2)	35

Unlike field width, the precision setting remains in effect until it is changed to some other value. As with all formatting manipulators, you must include the header file `iomanip` to use `setprecision`.

Program 3-20 shows how the `setw` and `setprecision` manipulators may be combined to fully control the way floating-point numbers are displayed.

Program 3-20

```
// This program asks for sales figures for three days.
// The total sales are calculated and displayed in a table.

#include <iostream>
#include <iomanip>
using namespace std;

int main()
{
    float day1, day2, day3, total;
```

(program continues)

Program 3-20 *(continued)*

```cpp
cout << "Enter the sales for day 1: ";
cin >> day1;
cout << "Enter the sales for day 2: ";
cin >> day2;
cout << "Enter the sales for day 3: ";
cin >> day3;
total = day1 + day2 + day3;
cout << "\nSales Figures\n";
cout << "-------------\n";
cout << setprecision(5);
cout << "Day 1: " << setw(8) << day1 << endl;
cout << "Day 2: " << setw(8) << day2 << endl;
cout << "Day 3: " << setw(8) << day3 << endl;
cout << "Total: " << setw(8) << total << endl;
return 0;
}
```

Program Output with Example Input Shown in Bold
```
Enter the sales for day 1: 321.57[Enter]
Enter the sales for day 2: 269.62[Enter]
Enter the sales for day 3: 307.77[Enter]

Sales Figures
- - - - - - - - - - - - -
Day 1:    321.57
Day 2:    269.62
Day 3:    307.77
Total:    898.96
```

If a number is too large to print using the number of digits you have specified with the set-precision manipulator, many systems print it in scientific notation. To prevent this, you can use another stream manipulator, fixed, which indicates that floating-point output should be printed in fixed, or decimal, notation.

```cpp
cout << fixed;
```

When setprecision is used in conjunction with fixed, it behaves differently. It specifies the number of digits to be displayed after the decimal point of a floating-point number, rather than the total number of digits to be displayed. This is usually what we want. For example, look at what happens if we output the following two dollar amounts without using the fixed manipulator, even if we use setw to make both numbers print in the same size field.

```cpp
amount1 = 125.00 * .075;        //amount1 is set to 9.375
amount2 = 125.00 * .06;         //amount2 is set to 7.5

cout << setprecision(4);
cout << setw(5) << amount1 << endl;
cout << setw(5) << amount2 << endl;
```

This produces the following output.

```
9.375
  7.5
```

By using `fixed` and `setprecision` together, we get the desired output. Notice in this case, however, we set the precision to 2, the number of decimal places we wish to see, not to 4.

```
cout << fixed << setprecision(2);
cout << setw(5) << amount1 << endl;
cout << setw(5) << amount2 << endl;
```

This produces the following improved output.

```
9.38
7.50
```

Another useful manipulator is `showpoint`, which indicates that a decimal point should be printed for a floating-point number, even if the value being displayed has no decimal digits. Program 3-21 expands our example to illustrate the use of `fixed`, `showpoint`, and `setprecision`. As with `setprecision`, the `fixed` and `showpoint` manipulators remain in effect until the programmer explicitly changes them.

Program 3-21

```
// This program illustrates the use of the fixed, showpoint,
// and setprecision output stream manipulators.

#include <iostream>
#include <iomanip>                    // Needed to use stream manipulators
using namespace std;
int main()
{
    double amount1 = 125.00 * .075;    //amount1 is set to 9.375
    double amount2 = 125.00 * .06;     //amount2 is set to 7.5
    double amount3 = 125.00 * .20;     //amount3 is set to 25.0

    cout << fixed << showpoint << setprecision(2);
    cout << setw(5) << amount1 << endl;
    cout << setw(5) << amount2 << endl;
    cout << setw(5) << amount3 << endl;

    return 0;
}
```

Program Output
```
 9.38
 7.50
25.00
```

Normally, as you have seen, output is right-justified. This means if the field it prints in is larger than the value being displayed, it is printed on the far right of the field, with leading blanks. There are times when you may wish to force a value to print on the left side of its field, padded by blanks on the right. To do this you can use the `left` manipulator. It remains in effect until you use a `right` manipulator to set it back. These manipulators can be used with any type of value, even a string. Program 3-22 illustrates the `left` and `right` manipulators. It also illustrates that the `fixed`, `showpoint`, and `setprecision` manipulators have no effect on integers, only on floating-point numbers.

Program 3-22

```cpp
// This program illustrates the use of the
// left and right output stream manipulators.

#include <iostream>
#include <iomanip>          // Needed to use stream manipulators
#include <string>
using namespace std;

int main()
{
    string month1 = "January",
           month2 = "February",
           month3 = "March";

    int days1 = 31,
        days2 = 28,
        days3 = 31;

    double high1 = 22.6,
           high2 = 37.4,
           high3 = 53.9;

    cout << fixed << showpoint << setprecision(1);
    cout << "Month       Days    High\n";

    cout << left  << setw(12) << month1
         << right << setw(4)  << days1 << setw(9) << high1 << endl;
    cout << left  << setw(12) << month2
         << right << setw(4)  << days2 << setw(9) << high2 << endl;
    cout << left  << setw(12) << month3
         << right << setw(4)  << days3 << setw(9) << high3 << endl;

    return 0;
}
```

Program 3-22

Program Output

```
Month        Days    High
January        31    22.6
February       28    37.4
March          31    53.9
```

Chapter 14 introduces additional stream manipulators and output formatting methods. However, the six manipulators we have covered in this chapter are normally sufficient to produce the output you desire. Table 3-12 summarizes these six manipulators.

Table 3-12

Stream Manipulator	Description
setw(n)	Sets the display field width to size n.
fixed	Displays floating-point numbers in fixed (i.e., decimal) form.
showpoint	Displays the decimal point for floating-point numbers even if there are no decimal digits.
setprecision(n)	Sets the precision of floating-point numbers.
left	Left-justifies output.
right	Right-justifies output.

✐ Checkpoint   [3.8]

3.24 Write cout statements with stream manipulators that perform the following:

   A) Display the number 34.789 in a field of nine spaces with two decimal places of precision.

   B) Display the number 7.0 in a field of five spaces with three decimal places of precision. The decimal point and any trailing zeroes should be displayed.

   C) Display the number 5.789e+12 in fixed-point notation.

   D) Display the number 67 left-justified in a field of seven spaces.

3.25 The following program skeleton asks for an angle in degrees and converts it to radians. The formatting of the final output is left to you.

```
#include <iostream>
#include <iomanip>
using namespace std;
```

```
int main()
{
    const float pi = 3.14159;
    float degrees, radians;

    cout << "Enter an angle in degrees and I will convert it\n";
    cout << "to radians for you: ";
    cin >> degrees;
    radians = degrees * pi / 180;
    // Display the value in radians left-justified, in fixed-
    // point notation, with four places of precision, in a field
    // five spaces wide, making sure the decimal point is always
    // displayed.
    return 0;
}
```

3.9 Working with Characters and String Objects

CONCEPT Special functions exist for working with characters and string objects.

In Chapter 2 you were introduced to characters and to string objects. A char variable can hold only one character, whereas a variable defined as a string can hold a whole set of characters. The following variable definitions and initializations illustrate this.

```
char letter1 = 'A',
     letter2 = 'B';
string name1 = "Mark Twain",
       name2 = "Samuel Clemens";
```

As with numeric data types, characters and strings can be assigned values.

```
letter2 = letter1;       // Now letter2's value is 'A'
name2 = name1;           // Now name2's value is "Mark Twain"
```

They can also be displayed with the cout statement. The following line of code outputs a character variable, a string constant, and a string object.

```
cout << letter1 << ". " << name1 << endl;
```

The output produced is

```
A. Mark Twain
```

Inputting characters and strings, however, is a little trickier than reading in numeric values.

Inputting a String

Although it is possible to use `cin` with the `>>` operator to input strings, it can cause problems you need to be aware of. When `cin` reads data it passes over and ignores any leading *whitespace* characters (spaces, tabs, or line breaks). However, once it comes to the first nonblank character and starts reading, it stops reading when it gets to the next whitespace character. If we use the following statement

```
cin >> name1;
```

we can input "Mark", or even " Mark", but not "Mark Twain" since `cin` cannot input strings that contain embedded spaces.

To solve this problem, C++ provides a special function called `getline`[2]. This function will read in an entire line, including leading and embedded spaces, and store it in a string object. The `getline` function looks like the following, where `cin` is the input stream we are reading from and `inputLine` is the name of the `string` variable receiving the input string.

```
getline(cin, inputLine);
```

Program 3-23 illustrates using the `getline` function. Remember that to use string objects you must include the `string` header file.

Program 3-23

```
// This program illustrates using the getline function
// to read character data into a string object.
#include <iostream>
#include <string>
using namespace std;

int main()
{
    string name;
    string city;

    cout << "Please enter your name." << endl;
    getline(cin, name);
    cout << "Please enter the city you live in." << endl;
    getline(cin, city);

    cout << "Hello, " << name << endl;
    cout << "You live in " << city << endl;
    return 0;
}
```

[2] Users of the Microsoft Visual C++ 6.0 compiler need to be aware that there is a documented bug in this compiler that prevents the `getline` function from working correctly. More information on this bug, and a way of fixing it, is provided in Appendix F.

Program 3-23

Program Output with Example Input Shown in Bold
```
Please enter your name.
```
John Doe[Enter]
```
Please enter the city you live in.
```
Chicago[Enter]
```
Hello, John Doe
You live in Chicago
```

There is another good reason to use `getline` for reading in characters to be stored in `string` objects. When reading in strings, `getline` not only allows embedded blanks to be read, but it also offers a protection that `cin` does not. If `cin` is used to read in a string and the user embeds a blank in the input, any remaining characters after the blank character are left in the keyboard buffer. The next read will try to use those leftover characters. Program 3-24 illustrates this problem.

Program 3-24

```cpp
// This program illustrates a problem that can occur if
// cin is used to read character data into a string object.
#include <iostream>
#include <string>
using namespace std;

int main()
{
    string name;
    string city;

    cout << "Please enter your name." << endl;
    cin >> name;
    cout << "Please enter the city you live in." << endl;
    cin >> city;

    cout << "Hello, " << name << endl;
    cout << "You live in " << city <<endl;
    return 0;
}
```

Program Output with Example Input Shown in Bold
```
Please enter your name.
```
John Doe[Enter]
```
Please enter the city you live in.
Hello, John
You live in Doe
```

Notice that the user was never given the opportunity to enter the city. In the first input statement, when `cin` came to the space between `John` and `Doe` it stopped reading, storing just `John` as the value of `name`. In the second input statement, `cin` used the leftover characters it found in the keyboard buffer and stored `Doe` as the value of `city`.

Inputting a Character

Quite often a program will ask the user to "Press any key to continue." This can be useful in a program that displays more information than will fit on the screen. The program can keep track of how many lines of text it has displayed and, when the screen is filled, it will wait for the user to press a key before displaying more information. Another instance when it is convenient to read a single character is when a menu of items is displayed for the user to choose from. Often the selections will be denoted by the letters A, B, C, and so forth. The user chooses an item from the menu by typing a character. The simplest way to read a single character is with `cin` and the `>>` operator. Program 3-25 asks the user to enter a character and then displays the character.

Program 3-25

```
#include <iostream>
using namespace std;

int main()
{
    char ch;

    cout << "Type a character and press Enter: ";
    cin >> ch;
    cout << "You entered " << ch << endl;
    return 0;
}
```

Program Output with Example Input Shown in Bold
```
Type a character and press Enter: A[Enter]
You entered A
```

Using `cin.get`

As with string input, there are times when using `cin >>` to read a character does not do what we want. For example, because it passes over all leading whitespace, it is impossible to input just a blank or [**Enter**] with `cin >>`. The program will not continue past the `cin` statement until some character other than the spacebar, the tab key, or the [**Enter**] key has been pressed. (Once such a character is entered, the [**Enter**] key must still be pressed before the program can continue to the next statement.) Thus, programs that ask the user to "Press the enter key to continue." cannot use the `>>` operator to read only the pressing of the [**Enter**] key.

In those situations a member function of `cin`, called `get`, becomes useful. (For more information on member functions, see section 3.13.) The `get` function reads a single character, including any whitespace character. The `get` member function looks like the following, where `ch` is the name of the variable the character is read into.

```
cin.get(ch);
```

Program 3-26 shows the function being used to pause a program.

Program 3-26

```
#include <iostream>
using namespace std;
int main()
{
    char ch;

    cout << "This program has paused. Press Enter to continue.";
    cin.get(ch);
    cout << "Thank you!" << endl;
    return 0;
}
```

Program Output with Example Input Shown in Bold
This program has paused. Press Enter to continue. **[Enter]**
Thank you!

The only difference between the get function and the >> operator is that get reads the first character typed, even if it is a space, tab, or the [**Enter**] key. Program 3-27 is a modification of Program 3-26. It shows the ASCII value of the character entered.

Program 3-27

```
#include <iostream>
using namespace std;

int main()
{
    char ch;

    cout << "Type a character and press Enter: ";
    cin.get(ch);
    cout << "You entered " << ch << endl;
    cout << "Its ASCII code is " << int(ch) << endl;
    return 0;
}
```

Program Output with Example Input Shown in Bold
Type a character and press Enter: **[Enter]**
You entered
Its ASCII code is 10

Mixing `cin >>` and `cin.get`

Mixing `cin >>` with `cin.get` can cause an annoying and hard-to-find problem. For example, look at the following statements:

```
cout << "Enter a number: ";
cin >> number;
cout << "Enter a character: ";
cin.get(ch);
cout << "Thank You!" << endl;
```

These statements allow the user to enter a number but not a character. When the user enters input, the last key pressed is [**Enter**]. Pressing the [**Enter**] key causes a newline (`'\n'`) character to be stored in the keyboard buffer. When `cin >>` reads data, it stops at the newline character, leaving it in the keyboard buffer. But `cin.get` does not skip over leading whitespace; it reads the the next character, whatever it is, from the keyboard buffer. That means the character read by `cin.get` will be the newline character.

Using `cin.ignore`

To solve this problem, the `cin.ignore` member function can be used. This function tells the `cin` object to skip characters in the keyboard buffer. Here is its general form:

```
cin.ignore(n, c);
```

The arguments shown in the parentheses are optional. If they are used, n is an integer and c is a character. They tell `cin` to skip n number of characters, or until the character c is encountered. For example, the following statement causes `cin` to skip the next 20 characters or until a newline is encountered, whichever comes first:

```
cin.ignore(20,'\n');
```

If no arguments are used, `cin` will only skip the very next character. Here's an example:

```
cin.ignore();
```

The statements that mix `cin >>` and `cin.get` can be repaired by inserting a `cin.ignore` statement after the `cin >>` statement:

```
cout << "Enter a number: ";
cin >> number;
cin.ignore();
cout << "Enter a character: ";
cin.get(ch);
cout << "Thank You!" << endl;
```

Using String Operators

The C++ string class provides a number of operators for working with strings. Two of them are studied here. Additional `string` class operators are covered in Chapter 12.

You have already encountered the + operator to add two numeric quantities. Since strings cannot be added, when this operator is applied to two string operands it *concatenates* them, or joins them together. Assume we have the following definitions and initializations in a program.

```
string greeting1 = "Hello ",
       greeting2;
string name1     = "World";
string name2     = "People";
```

The following statements illustrate how string concatenation works.

```
greeting2 = greeting1 + name1; //greeting2 now holds "Hello World"
greeting1 = greeting1 + name2; //greeting1 now holds "Hello People"
```

Notice that the string stored in `greeting1` has a blank as its last character. If the blank were not there, `greeting2` would have been assigned the string `"HelloWorld"`.

The last statement could also have been written using the += combined assignment operator.

```
greeting1 += name2;
```

3.10 Using C-Strings

CONCEPT   C-strings define and manipulate strings as character arrays.

In C, and in C++ prior to the introduction of the `string` class, strings were created by defining them as arrays of characters. Arrays are dealt with in more detail in Chapter 8, but for now just think of them as a set of contiguous memory locations where multiple data values, like a set of characters, can be stored together. Here is a statement that declares word to be an array with enough memory to hold 10 characters and initializes it to `"Hello"`.

```
char word[10] = "Hello";
```

Because this was the way to create a string variable in C, strings defined in this manner are called C-strings. In Chapter 2, you learned how string constants are stored. This, in fact, is how any C-string is stored. Recall from Chapter 2, that because a string can be virtually any length, C appends a special character `'\0'`, whose ASCII code is 0, to the end of the string. This character, called the *null character* or *null terminator*, marks the end of the string. Figure 3-3 shows how the above string would be stored in memory.

Figure 3-3

H	e	l	l	o	\0				

Recall, also, that since one space in the array must be reserved for the null terminator, the `word` array can only hold a string of up to nine characters.

Like string objects, C-strings can have their contents input using `cin >>`, and they can have their contents displayed using `cout <<`. This is illustrated in Program 3-28. Since `name` is defined as an array of size 12, it can store a name of up to 11 characters. Notice that no special header file is needed to use C-strings.

Program 3-28

```
#include <iostream>
using namespace std;

int main()
{
    char name[12];

    cout << "Please enter your first name." << endl;
    cin >> name;
    cout << "Hello, " << name << endl;
    return 0;
}
```

Program Output with Example Input Shown in Bold
```
Please enter your first name.
```
Sebastian[Enter]
```
Hello, Sebastian
```

Notice that in the following two lines from Program 3-28 the brackets and the array size indicator are left out.

```
cin >> name;
cout << "Hello, " << name << endl;
```

When reading a string into an array, or displaying a string stored in an array, you normally use the name of the array only. It would be an error to write the lines as

```
cin >> name[12];                     // Wrong!
cout << "Hello, " << name[12] << endl;  // Wrong!
```

Except for inputting and displaying them with `cin >>` and `cout <<`, almost everything else about using string objects and C-strings is different. This is because the string class has member functions and operators that save the programmer having to worry about many of the details of working with strings. When using C-strings, however, it is the responsibility of the programmer to handle these things.

Assigning a Value to a C-String

The first way in which using a C-string differs from using a string object is that, except for initializing it at the time of its definition, it cannot be assigned a value using the assignment operator. In Program 3-28 we could not, for example, replace the `cin` statement with the line of code

```
name = "Sebastian";        // Wrong!
```

Instead, to assign a value to a C-string, we must use a function called `strcpy` to copy the contents of one string into another. In the following line of code `Cstring` is the name of the variable receiving the value, and `value` is either a string constant or the name of another C-string variable.

```
strcpy(Cstring, value);
```

Program 3-29 shows how the `strcpy` function works.

Program 3-29

```
#include <iostream>
using namespace std;

int main()
{
    char name1[12],
        name2[12];

    strcpy(name1, "Sebastian");
    cout << "name1 now holds the string " << name1 << endl;

    strcpy(name2, name1);
    cout << "name2 now also holds the string " << name2 << endl;

    return 0;
}
```

Program Output
```
name1 now holds the string Sebastian
name2 now also holds the string Sebastian
```

Keeping Track of a How Much a C-String Can Hold

Another crucial way in which using a C-string differs from using a string object involves the memory allocated for it. With a string object, you do not have to worry about there being too little memory to hold a string you wish to place in it. If the storage space allocated to the string object is too small, the string class functions will make sure more memory is allocated to it. With

C-strings this is not the case. A C-string remains whatever size you originally set it to in the definition statement, and it is the job of the programmer to ensure that the number of characters placed in it does not exceed the storage space.

One way to ensure that too many characters are not read into a C-string is by using the `setw` stream manipulator. This manipulator, which we used earlier in this chapter to format output, can also be used to control the number of characters that `cin >>` inputs on its next read, as illustrated here:

```
char word[5];
cin >> setw(5) >> word;
```

Another way to do the same thing is by using the `cin width` member function.

```
char word[5];
cin.width(5);
cin >> word;
```

In both cases the field width specified is 5 and `cin` will read, at most, one character less than this, leaving room for the null character at the end. Program 3-30 illustrates the use of the `setw` manipulator with `cin`, while Program 3-31 uses the `width` member function. Both programs produce the same output.

Program 3-30

```
// This program uses setw with the cin object.
#include <iostream>
#include <iomanip>
using namespace std;

int main()
{
    char word[5];

    cout << "Enter a word: ";
    cin >> setw(5) >> word;
    cout << "You entered " << word << endl;

    return 0;
}
```

Program 3-31

```
// This program uses cin's width member function.

#include <iostream>
#include <iomanip>
using namespace std;
```

(program continues)

Program 3-31   *(continued)*

```
int main()
{
    char word[5];

    cout << "Enter a word: ";
    cin.width(5);
    cin >> word;
    cout << "You entered " << word << endl;

    return 0;
}
```

Program Output for Programs 3-30 and 3-31 with Example Input Shown in Bold
```
Enter a word: Eureka[Enter]
You entered Eure
```

In Program 3-31, `cin` only reads four characters into the word array. Without the field width, `cin` would have written the entire word "Eureka" into the array, overflowing it. Figure 3-4 illustrates the way memory would have been affected by this. The shaded area is the 5 bytes of memory allocated to the C-string array. The word "Eureka" with its null terminator would spill over into the adjacent memory. Anything that was stored there would be destroyed.

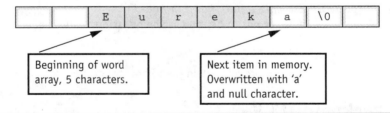

Figure 3-4

There are two important points to remember about the way `cin` handles field widths:

- The field width only pertains to the very next item entered by the user.
- The field width is the maximum number of characters to read. If `cin` comes to a whitespace character before reading the specified number of characters, it will stop reading.

Reading a Line of Input

Still another way in which using C-strings differs from using string objects is that you must use a different set of functions when working with them. To read a line of input, for example, you must use `cin.getline` rather than `getline`. These two names look a lot alike, but they are two different functions and are not interchangeable. Like `getline`, `cin.getline` allows you to read in a string containing spaces. It will continue reading until it has read the maximum specified number of characters, or until the [**Enter**] key is pressed. Here is an example of how it is used:

```
cin.getline(sentence, 20);
```

The `getline` function takes two arguments separated by a comma. The first argument is the name of the array that the string is to be stored in. In the statement above, the name of the array is `sentence`. The second argument is the size of the array. `cin` will read up to one character less than this number, leaving room for the null terminator. This eliminates the need for using the `setw` manipulator or the `width` member function. The statement above will read up to 19 characters. The null terminator will automatically be placed in the array, after the last character. Program 3-32 shows the `getline` member function being used to read a sentence of up to 80 characters.

Program 3-32

```
// This program demonstrates cin's getline member function.
#include <iostream>
using namespace std;

int main()
{
    char sentence[81];

    cout << "Enter a sentence: ";
    cin.getline(sentence, 81);
    cout << "You entered " << sentence << endl;
    return 0;
}
```

Program Output with Example Input Shown in Bold
Enter a sentence: **To be, or not to be, that is the question.[Enter]**
You entered To be, or not to be, that is the question.

Later chapters cover more on C-strings and how they differ from string objects.

Checkpoint [3.9–3.10]

3.26 Will the following string constant fit in the space allocated for `name`? Why or why not?

```
char name[4] = "John";
```

3.27 If a program contains the definition `string name;`
indicate whether each of the following lettered program statements is legal or illegal.

A) `cin >> name;`
B) `cin.getline(name, 20);`
C) `cout << name;`
D) `name = "John";`

3.28 If a program contains the definition `char name[20];`
indicate whether each of the following lettered program statements is legal or illegal.

A) `cin >> name;`
B) `cin.getline(name, 20);`
C) `cout << name;`
D) `name = "John";`

3.11 More Mathematical Library Functions

> **CONCEPT** The C++ run-time library provides several functions for performing complex mathematical operations.

Earlier in this chapter you learned to use the pow function to raise a number to a power. The C++ library has numerous other functions that perform specialized mathematical operations. These functions are useful in scientific and special purpose programs. Table 3-13 shows several of these, each of which requires the cmath header file. These functions take one or more double arguments and return a double value.

Table 3-13

Function	Example	Description
abs	y = abs(x);	Returns the absolute value of the argument. The argument and the return value are integers.
cos	y = cos(x);	Returns the cosine of the argument. The argument should be an angle expressed in radians. The return type and the argument are doubles.
exp	y = exp(x);	Computes the exponential function of the argument, which is x. The return type and the argument are doubles.
fmod	y = fmod(x, z);	Returns, as a double, the remainder of the first argument divided by the second argument. Works like the modulus operator, but the arguments are doubles. (The modulus operator only works with integers.) Take care not to pass zero as the second argument. Doing so would cause division by zero.
log	y = log(x);	Returns the natural logarithm of the argument. The return type and the argument are doubles.
log10	y = log10(x);	Returns the base-10 logarithm of the argument. The return type and the argument are doubles.
sin	y = sin(x);	Returns the sine of the argument. The argument should be an angle expressed in radians. The return type and the argument are doubles.
sqrt	y = sqrt(x);	Returns the square root of the argument. The return type and argument are doubles.
tan	y = tan(x);	Returns the tangent of the argument. The argument should be an angle expressed in radians. The return type and the argument are doubles.

Each of these functions is as simple to use as the `pow` function. The following program segment demonstrates the `sqrt` function, which returns the square root of a number:

```
cout << "Enter a number: ";
cin >> num;
s = sqrt(num);
cout << "The square root of " << num << " is " << s << endl;
```

Here is the output of the program segment, with 25 as the number entered by the user:

```
Enter a number: 25
The square root of 25 is 5
```

Program 3-33 shows the `sqrt` function being used to find the hypotenuse of a right triangle. The program uses the following formula, taken from the Pythagorean theorem:

$$c = \sqrt{a^2 + b^2}$$

In the formula, c is the length of the hypotenuse, and a and b are the lengths of the other sides of the triangle.

Program 3-33

```
// This program asks for the lengths of the two sides of a
// right triangle. The length of the hypotenuse is then
// calculated and displayed.

#include <iostream>
#include <cmath>          // Needed to use the sqrt function
using namespace std;

int main()
{
    float a, b, c;

    cout << "Enter the length of side a: ";
    cin >> a;
    cout << "Enter the length of side b: ";
    cin >> b;
    c = sqrt(pow(a, 2.0) + pow(b, 2.0));

    cout << "The length of the hypotenuse is ";
    cout << c << endl;
    return 0;
}
```

Program 3-33

Program Output with Example Input Shown in Bold
```
Enter the length of side A: 5.0[Enter]
Enter the length of side B: 12.0[Enter]
The length of the hypotenuse is 13
```

The following statement, taken from Program 3-33, calculates the square root of the sum of the squares of the triangle's two sides:

```
c = sqrt(pow(a, 2.0) + pow(b, 2.0));
```

Notice that the following mathematical expression is used as the sqrt function's argument:

```
pow(a, 2.0) + pow(b, 2.0)
```

This expression calls the pow function twice: once to calculate the square of a and again to calculate the square of b. These two squares are then added together, and the sum is sent to the sqrt function.

Random Numbers

Some programming techniques require the use of randomly generated numbers. The C++ library has a function, rand(), for this purpose. (rand() requires the header file cstdlib.) The number returned by the function is an int. Here is an example of its usage:

```
y = rand();
```

After this statement executes, the variable y will contain a random number. In actuality, the numbers produced by rand() are pseudorandom. The function uses an algorithm that produces the same sequence of numbers each time the program is repeated on the same system. For example, suppose the following statements are executed.

```
cout << rand() << endl;
cout << rand() << endl;
cout << rand() << endl;
```

The three numbers displayed will appear to be random, but each time the program runs, the same three values will be generated. In order to randomize the results of rand(), the srand() function must be used. srand() accepts an unsigned int argument, which acts as a seed value for the algorithm. By specifying different seed values, rand() will generate different sequences of random numbers. Program 3-34 demonstrates the two functions.

Program 3-34

```cpp
// This program demonstrates random numbers.

#include <iostream>
#include <cstdlib>
using namespace std;

int main()
{
    unsigned seed;

    cout << "Enter a seed value: ";
    cin >> seed;
    srand(seed);
    cout << rand() << endl;
    cout << rand() << endl;
    cout << rand() << endl;
    return 0;
}
```

Program Output with Example Input Shown in Bold
```
Enter a seed value: 5[Enter]
1731
32036
21622
```

Program Output with Other Example Input Shown in Bold
```
Enter a seed value: 16[Enter]
5540
29663
9920
```

 Note: The stream of random numbers generated on your computer system may be different.

If you wish to limit the range of the random number to an integer between 1 and maxRange, use the following formula.

```cpp
y = 1 + rand() % maxRange;
```

For example, if you wish to generate a random number in the range of 1 through 6 to represent the roll of a dice, you would use

```cpp
dice = 1 + rand() % 6;
```

Note: The `mod` operation gives us the remainder of an integer divide. When the integer returned by `rand()` is divided by 6, the remainder will be a number between 0 and 5. Since we want a number between 1 and 6, we simply add 1 to the result.

Checkpoint [3.11]

3.29 Assume the variables `angle1` and `angle2` hold angles stored in radians. Write a statement that adds the sine of `angle1` to the cosine of `angle2` and stores the result in the variable x.

3.30 To find the cube root (the third root) of a number, raise it to the power of $\frac{1}{3}$. To find the fourth root of a number, raise it to the power of $\frac{1}{4}$. Write a statement that will find the fifth root of the variable x and store the result in the variable y.

3.31 The cosecant of the angle *a* is

$$\frac{1}{\sin a}$$

Write a statement that calculates the cosecant of the angle stored in the variable a and stores it in the variable y.

3.12 Introduction to Files

CONCEPT Program input can be read from a file and program output can be written to a file.

 Note: This section provides an introduction to file input and output using sequential text files. More advanced coverage of files and file operations is found in Chapter 14.

The programs you have written so far require you to re-enter data each time the program runs. This is because the data stored in RAM disappears once the program stops running or the computer is shut down. If a program is to retain data between the times it runs, it must have a way of saving it. Information is saved in a file, which is a collection of data usually stored on a computer's disk. Once the information is saved by writing it into a file, it will remain there after the program stops running. The information can then be retrieved and used at a later time.

There are three steps that must be taken when a file is used by a program:

1. The file must be *opened*.

2. Information is then written to the file, read from the file, or both.

3. When the program is finished using the file, the file must be *closed*.

When a program is actively working with data, the data is located in random-access memory, usually in variables. When data is written into a file, it is copied from variables into the file. This is illustrated in Figure 3-5.

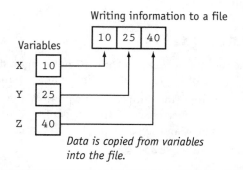

Figure 3-5

When data is read from a file, it is copied from the file into variables. Figure 3-6 illustrates this.

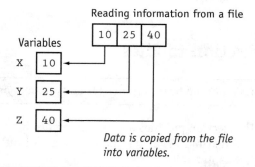

Figure 3-6

Setting Up a Program for File Input/Output

Just as `cin` and `cout` require the `iostream` file to be included in the program, C++ file access requires another header file. The file `fstream` contains all the declarations necessary for file operations. It is included with the following statement:

```
#include <fstream>
```

The next step in setting up a program to perform file I/O is to define one or more *file stream objects*. They are called stream objects because a file can be thought of as a stream of information. File stream objects work very much like `cin` and `cout` objects. A stream of data may be sent to `cout`, which causes values to be displayed on the screen. A stream of data may be read from the keyboard by `cin` and stored in variables. Likewise, streams of information may be sent to a file stream object, which writes the information to a file. Information that is read from a file flows from a file stream object into other variables.

The `fstream` header file contains declarations for the data types `ofstream`, `ifstream`, and `fstream`. Before a C++ program can work with a file, it must define an object of one of these data types. The object will be linked with an actual file on the computer's disk, and the operations that may be performed on the file depend on which of these three data types you pick for the file stream object. Table 3-14 lists and describes file stream data types.

Table 3-14

File Stream Data Type	Description
ofstream	Output file stream. This data type can be used to open *output* files and write information to them. If the file does not yet exist, the `open` operation will automatically create it. If the file already exists, the `open` operation will destroy it and create a new, empty file of the same name in its place. With the `ofstream` data type, information may only be copied from variables to the file, but not vice versa.
ifstream	Input file stream. This data type can be used to open existing *input* files and read information from them into memory. With the `ifstream` data type, information may only be copied from the file into variables, not but vice versa.
fstream	File stream. This data type can be used to open files, write information to them, and read information from them. With the `fstream` data type, information may be copied from variables into a file, or from a file into variables.

 Note: In this section we only discuss the `ofstream` and `ifstream` types. The `fstream` type is covered in Chapter 14.

Here are example statements that define `ofstream` and `ifstream` objects:

```
ofstream outputFile;
ifstream inputFile;
```

These two file stream objects, `outputFile` and `inputFile`, could have been named using any legal C++ identifier names. However, as is good programming practice, they were given descriptive names that clarify their use. The `outputFile` object is of the `ofstream` data type, so information can be written to any file associated with it. The `inputFile` object is of the `ifstream` data type, so information can be read from any file it is associated with.

Opening a File

Before data can be written to or read from a file, the file must be opened. Outside of the C++ program, a file is identified by its name. Inside a C++ program, however, a file is identified by a stream object. The object and the file name are linked when the file is opened.

Files are opened through the `open` member function of a file stream object. Assume `input-File` is an `ifstream` object, defined as

```
ifstream inputFile;
```

The following statement uses `inputFile` to open a file named `customer.dat`:

```
inputFile.open("customer.dat");
```

The argument to the `open` function in this statement is the name of the file. This links the file `customer.dat` with the stream object `inputFile`. Until `inputFile` is associated with another file, any operations performed with it will be carried out on the file `customer.dat`. (Remember, `ifstream` objects can only perform input operations with files. This means information may be read from, but not written to, the `customer.dat` file using the `inputFile` stream object.)

In our example `open` statement, the `customer.dat` file was specified as a simple file name, with no path given. When no path is given, the program will look for the file in a default directory. If the program is being executed from the command line, the default directory is the current directory. If the program is being executed from within an integrated development environment (IDE), the default directory depends on the particular compiler you are using. Further information on default directories can be found in the appendices on Visual C++ and Borland's C++ Builder, and your instructor can provide you with specific information for your particular system.

If the file you want to open is not in the default directory, you will need to specify its location as well as its name. For example, if you were attempting to open a file on the A: drive of a DOS or Windows computer, you would need to specify the file's drive designator and path. Here is an example of a statement that opens a file located on a PC's floppy drive:

```
outputFile.open("a:\\invtry.dat");
```

In this statement, the file `a:\invtry.dat` is opened and linked with `outputFile`.

 Note: Notice the use of two backslashes in the file's path. As mentioned before in this text, two backslashes are needed to represent one backslash in a string.

Closing a File

The opposite of opening a file is closing it. Although a program's files are automatically closed when the program shuts down, it is a good programming practice to write statements that close them. Here are two reasons a program should close files when it is finished using them:

◆ Most operating systems temporarily store information in a *file buffer* before it is written to a file. A file buffer is a small holding section of memory that file-bound information is first written to. When the buffer is filled, all the information stored there is written to the file. This technique improves the system's performance. Closing a file causes any unsaved information that may still be held in a buffer to be saved to its file. This means the information will be in the file if you need to read it later in the same program.

◆ Some operating systems limit the number of files that may be open at one time. When a program keeps open files that are no longer being used, it uses more of the operating system's resources than necessary.

Calling the file stream object's `close` member function closes a file. Here is an example:

```
outputFile.close();
```

Writing Information to a File

You already know how to use the stream insertion operator (<<) with the `cout` object to write information to the screen. It can also be used with file stream objects to write information to a file. Assuming `outputFile` is a file stream object, the following statement demonstrates using the << operator to write a string to a file:

```
outputFile << "I love C++ programming";
```

As you can see, the statement looks like a `cout` statement, except the file stream object name replaces `cout`. Here is a statement that writes both a string and the contents of a variable to a file:

```
outputFile << "Price: " << Price;
```

This statement writes the stream of information to `outputFile` exactly as `cout` would write it to the screen.

Program 3-35 demonstrates opening a file, writing information to the file, and closing the file.

Program 3-35

```cpp
// This program uses the << operator to write information to a file.

#include <iostream>
#include <fstream>                // Needed to use files
using namespace std;

int main()
{
    ofstream outputFile;

    outputFile.open("demofile.txt");

    cout << "Now writing information to the file.\n";

    // Write 3 great names to the file
    outputFile << "Bach\n";
    outputFile << "Beethoven\n";
    outputFile << "Mozart\n";

    // Close the file
    outputFile.close();
    cout << "Done.\n";

    return 0;
}
```

Program 3-35

Program Screen Output
```
Now writing information to the file.
Done.
```

Output to File demofile.txt
```
Bach
Beethoven
Mozart
```

Reading Information from a File

The >> operator not only reads user input from the cin object, but it can also be used to read data from a file. Assuming inFile is a file stream object, the following statement shows the >> operator reading data from the file into the variable name:

```
inFile >> name;
```

In Program 3-35, the file demofile.txt was created and the following list of names was stored there.

```
Bach
Beethoven
Mozart
```

Program 3-36 demonstrates the use of the >> operator to read the names from the file and store them in a variable.

Program 3-36

```
// This program uses the >> operator to read information from a file.

#include <iostream>
#include <fstream>                    // Needed to use files
#include <string>
using namespace std;

int main()
{
    ifstream inFile;
    string name;

    inFile.open("demofile.txt");
    cout << "Reading information from the file.\n\n";
```

(program continues)

Program 3-36 *(continued)*

```
    inFile >> name;              // Read name 1 from the file
    cout << name << endl;        // Display it on the monitor

    inFile >> name;              // Read name 2 from the file
    cout << name << endl;        // Display it on the monitor

    inFile >> name;              // Read name 3 from the file
    cout << name << endl;        // Display it on the monitor

    inFile.close();              // Close the file
    cout << "\nDone.\n";

    return 0;
}
```

Program Screen Output
```
Reading information from the file.

Bach
Beethoven
Mozart

Done.
```

Information is read from files in a sequential manner. When a file is first opened, the file stream object's *read position* is at the first byte of the file. The first read operation extracts data starting at the first byte. As information is read, the file stream object's read position advances through the file.

When the >> operator extracts information from a file, it expects to read pieces of data that are separated by whitespace characters (spaces, tabs, or newlines). In Program 3-36, the following statement reads a string from the file:

```
    inFile >> name;
```

The >> operator extracts a string in this case because name is a string object. Figure 3-7 shows the first 5 bytes in the file:

Figure 3-7

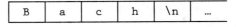

| B | a | c | h | \n | ... |

The >> operator will extract all of the characters up to the newline, so "Bach" is the first string read from the file. After "Bach" is extracted, the file stream object will be positioned so the following read operation would extract the string "Beethoven." This procedure is followed until all three strings have been read from the file.

The file of data read in by Program 3-36 was created by Program 3-35. However, this is not the only way to create a data file. A data file can be created with any text editor (such as Windows Notepad). This is often done when a program has a substantial amount of input. Placing the data in a text file ahead of time and then having the program read the data from the file saves the user having to enter the data when the program is run. Program 3-37, which finds the area of four rectangles, illustrates reading data from a text file named dimensions.txt, which was previously created with a text editor. Here is a sample of the file's contents. Each pair of numbers is the length and width of a different rectangle.

```
10 2
5 7
6 20
8 3
```

Program 3-37

```cpp
// This program uses the >> operator to read information from a file.
// Notice that, as with cin, more than one value can be read in from
// a file with a single statement.

#include <iostream>
#include <fstream>
using namespace std;

int main()
{
    ifstream inFile;
    int length, width;

    inFile.open("dimensions.txt");
    cout << "Reading dimensions of 4 rectangles from the file.\n\n";

    // Process rectangle 1
    inFile >> length >> width;
    cout << "Area of rectangle 1: " << length * width << endl;

    // Process rectangle 2
    inFile >> length >> width;
    cout << "Area of rectangle 2: " << length * width << endl;

    // Process rectangle 3
    inFile >> length >> width;
    cout << "Area of rectangle 3: " << length * width << endl;

    // Process rectangle 4
    inFile >> length >> width;
    cout << "Area of rectangle 4: " << length * width << endl;

    // Close the file
    inFile.close();
    cout << "Done.\n";

    return 0;
}
```

Program 3-37

Program Output
```
Reading dimensions of 4 rectangles from the file.

Area of rectangle 1: 20
Area of rectangle 2: 35
Area of rectangle 3: 120
Area of rectangle 4: 24
Done.
```

 Checkpoint [3.12]

3.32   What header file must be included in a program to use files?

3.33   What is the difference between a file stream object with the data type `ifstream` and one with the data type `ofstream`?

3.34   Which program statement links a file stream object with an actual disk file?

3.35   Assuming `dataFile` is an `ofstream` object associated with a disk file named `payroll.dat`, which of the following statements would write the value of the `salary` variable to the file?

    A)   `cout << salary;`
    B)   `ofstream << salary;`
    C)   `dataFile << salary;`
    D)   `payroll.dat << salary;`

3.13   Focus on Object-Oriented Programming: *Member Functions*

CONCEPT	A member function is a procedure, written in C++ code, that is part of an object. A member function causes the object it is a member of to perform an action.

The concept of object-oriented programming (OOP) was introduced in Chapter 1. Recall that objects are programming elements containing both data and procedures that operate on the data. The packaging together of data and the data's related procedures within an object is known as *encapsulation*.

In C++, the procedures that are part of an object are known as *member functions*. They are called member functions because they are functions that are members of, or belong to, an object. The use of member functions simplifies programming and reduces errors. Anywhere an object is used, it not only contains data, but also the correct algorithms and operations for working with the data. If you are the user of an object (such as `cout` or `cin`) you do not need to write your own code to manipulate the object's data. All that is necessary is that you learn the object's member functions and how to use them.

In this chapter you have used two objects (`cout` and `cin`) and a few of `cin`'s member functions:

- `get`
- `ignore`
- `width`
- `getline`

`cout` also has member functions, which you will learn about in later chapters.

Calling an object's member function causes the object to perform some operation. For example, `cin`'s `getline` member function causes `cin` to read a line of input from the keyboard.

In OOP terminology, calling a member function is also described as *passing a message* to the object. For example, you can think of the following statement as sending a message to the `cin` object, instructing it to read a character from the keyboard and then store the character in the `ch` variable.

```
cin.get(ch);
```

All of `cin`'s and `cout`'s member functions are written in C++ code. In Chapter 7 you will learn to design your own objects, complete with member functions.

Using String Class Member Functions

The `string` class also has member functions. For example, the `length` member function returns the length of the string stored in the object. The value is returned as an unsigned integer.

Assume the following string object definition exists in a program:

```
string town = "Charleston";
```

The following statement in the same program would assign the value 10 to the variable `x`.

```
x = town.length();
```

Program 3-38 further demonstrates the `length` member function.

Program 3-38

```
// This program demonstrates a string object's length member function.

#include <iostream>
#include <string>
using namespace std;
```

(program continues)

Program 3-38 *(continued)*

```cpp
int main()
{
    string town;

    cout << "Where do you live? ";
    cin >> town;
    cout << "Your town's name has " << town.length() ;
    cout << " characters";
    return 0;
}
```

Program Output with Example Input Shown in Bold
```
Where do you live? Jacksonville[Enter]
Your town's name has 12 characters
```

3.14 Focus on Problem Solving and Program Design: A Case Study

General Crates, Inc. builds custom-designed wooden crates. With materials and labor, it costs GCI $0.23 per cubic foot to build a crate. In turn, they charge their customers $0.50 per cubic foot for the crate. You have been asked to write a program that calculates the volume (in cubic feet), cost, customer price, and profit of any crate GCI builds.

Variables

Table 3-15 shows the variables needed.

Table 3-15

Variable	Description
length	A float variable to hold the length of the crate, which is input by the user.
width	A float variable to hold the width of the crate, which is input by the user.
height	A float variable to hold the height of the crate, which is input by the user.
volume	A float variable to hold the volume of the crate. The value stored in this variable is calculated.
cost	A float variable to hold the cost of building the crate. The value stored in this variable is calculated.
charge	A float variable to hold the amount charged to the customer for the crate. The value stored in this variable is calculated.
profit	A float variable to hold the profit GCI makes from the crate. The value stored in this variable is calculated.

Program Design

The program must perform the following general steps:

1. Ask the user to enter the dimensions of the crate (the crate's length, width, and height).
2. Calculate the crate's volume, the cost of building the crate, the customer's charge, and the profit made.
3. Display the data calculated in step 2.

A general hierarchy chart for this program is shown in Figure 3-8.

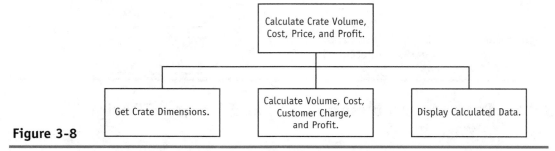

Figure 3-8

The "Get Crate Dimensions" step is shown in greater detail in Figure 3-9.

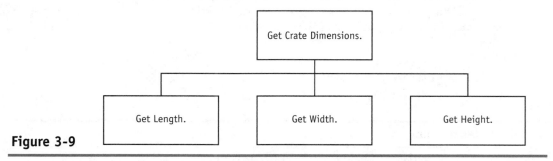

Figure 3-9

The "Calculate Volume, Cost, Customer Charge, and Profit" step is shown in greater detail in Figure 3-10.

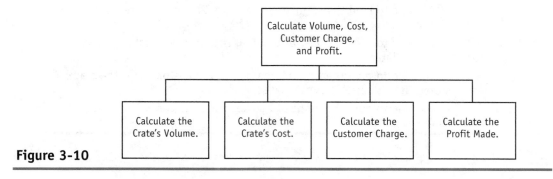

Figure 3-10

The "Display Calculated Data" step is shown in greater detail in Figure 3-11.

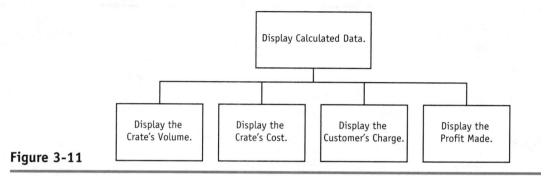

Figure 3-11

Psuedocode for the program is as follows

```
Ask user to input the crate's length.
Ask user to input the crate's width.
Ask user to input the crate's height.
Calculate the crate's volume.
Calculate the cost of building the crate.
Calculate the customer's charge for the crate.
Calculate the profit made from the crate.
Display the crate's volume.
Display the cost of building the crate.
Display the customer's charge for the crate.
Display the profit made from the crate.
```

Calculations

The following formulas will be used to calculate the crate's volume, cost, charge, and profit:

volume = length * width * height
cost = volume * 0.23
charge = volume * 0.5
profit = charge - cost

The Program

The last step is to expand the pseudocode into the final program, which is shown in Program 3-39.

Program 3-39

```
// This program is used by General Crates, Inc. to calculate
// the volume, cost, customer charge, and profit of a crate
// of any size. It calculates this data from user input, which
// consists of the dimensions of the crate.
```

(program continues)

Program 3-39 *(continued)*

```cpp
#include <iostream>
#include <iomanip>
using namespace std;

int main()
{
    float length,  // The crate's length
          width,   // The crate's width
          height,  // The crate's height
          volume,  // The volume of the crate
          cost,    // The cost to build the crate
          charge,  // The customer charge for the crate
          profit;  // The profit made on the crate

    cout << fixed << showpoint << setprecision(2);

    // Prompt the user for the crate's length, width, and height.
    cout << "Enter the dimensions of the crate (in feet):\n";
    cout << "Length: ";
    cin >> length;
    cout << "Width: ";
    cin >> width;
    cout << "Height: ";
    cin >> height;

    // Calculate the crate's volume, the cost to produce it,
    // the charge to the customer, and the profit.
    volume = length * width * height;
    cost = volume * 0.23;
    charge = volume * 0.5;
    profit = charge - cost;

    // Display the calculated data.
    cout << "The volume of the crate is ";
    cout << volume << " cubic feet.\n";
    cout << "Cost to build: $" << cost << endl;
    cout << "Charge to customer: $" << charge << endl;
    cout << "Profit: $" << profit << endl;
    return 0;
}
```

Program Output with Example Input Shown in Bold
```
Enter the dimensions of the crate (in feet):
Length: 10[Enter]
Width: 8[Enter]
Height: 4[Enter]
The volume of the crate is 320.00 cubic feet.
Cost to build: $73.60
Charge to customer: $160.00
Profit: $86.40
```

(program output continues)

Program 3-39   *(continued)*

Program Output with Different Example Input Shown in Bold
```
Enter the dimensions of the crate (in feet):
Length: 12.5[Enter]
Width: 10.5[Enter]
Height: 8[Enter]
The volume of the crate is 1050.00 cubic feet.
Cost to build: $241.50
Charge to customer: $525.00
Profit: $283.50
```

Review Questions and Exercises

Short Answer

1. Assume a string object has been defined as follows:

   ```
   string description;
   ```

   A) Write a `cin` statement that reads in a description.

   B) Write a statement that reads in a description that can contain multiple words separated by blanks.

2. Write a definition statement for a character array large enough to hold any of the following strings:

   ```
   "Billy Bob's Pizza"
   "Downtown Auto Supplies"
   "Betty Smith School of Architecture"
   "ABC Cabinet Company"
   ```

3. Assume the array `name` is declared as follows:

   ```
   char name[25];
   ```

   A) Using a stream manipulator, write a `cin` statement that will read a string into `name`, but will read no more characters than `name` can hold.

   B) Using the `getline` member function, write a `cin` statement that will read a string into `name` but that will read no more characters than `name` can hold.

4. Assume the following variables are defined:

   ```
   int age;
   float pay;
   char section;
   ```

   Write a single `cin` statement that will read input into each of these variables.

5. What header files must be included in the following program?

```
int main()
{
   float amount = 89.7;
   cout << fixed << showpoint << setprecision(1);
   cout << setw(8) << amount << endl;
   return 0;
}
```

6. Write a definition statement for a character array named `city`. It should be large enough to hold a string 30 characters in length.

7. Assume the following statement appears in a program:

```
#define SIZE 12
```

How will the preprocessor rewrite the following lines?

A) `price = SIZE * unitCost;`

B) `cout << setw(SIZE) << 98.7;`

C) `cout << SIZE;`

8. Complete the following table by writing the value of each expression in the Value column.

Expression	Value
28 / 4 - 2	
6 + 12 * 2 - 8	
4 + 8 * 2	
6 + 17 % 3 - 2	
2 + 22 * (9 - 7)	
(8 + 7) * 2	
(16 + 7) % 2 - 1	
12 / (10 - 6)	
(19 - 3) * (2 + 2) / 4	

9. Write C++ expressions for the following algebraic expressions:

A) $a = 12x$

B) $z = 5x + 14y + 6k$

C) $y = x^4$

D) $g = \dfrac{h + 12}{4k}$

E) $c = \dfrac{a^3}{b^2 k^4}$

10. Assume a program has the following variable definitions

```
int units;
float mass;
double weight;
```

and the following statement:

```
weight = mass * units;
```

Which automatic datatype conversion will take place?

A)   `mass` is demoted to an `int`, `units` remains an `int`, and the result of `mass * units` is an `int`.

B)   `units` is promoted to a `float`, `mass` remains a `float`, and the result of `mass * units` is a `float`.

C)   `units` is promoted to a `float`, `mass` remains a `float`, and the result of `mass * units` is a `double`.

11. Assume a program has the following variable definitions

```
int a, b = 2;
float c = 4.2;
```

and the following statement:

```
a = b * c;
```

What value will be stored in `a`?

A)   8.4

B)   8

C)   0

D)   None of the above

12. Assume that `qty` and `salesReps` are both integers. Use a typecast operator to rewrite the following statement so it will no longer perform integer division.

```
unitsEach = qty / salesReps;
```

13. Rewrite the following variable definition so the variable is a named constant with the value 12.

```
int rate;
```

14. Complete the following table by writing statements with combined assignment operators in the right-hand column. The statements should be equivalent to the statements in the left-hand column.

Statements with Assignment Operator	Statements with Combined Assignment Operator

`x = x + 5;`
`total = total + subtotal;`
`dist = dist / rep;`
`ppl = ppl * period;`
`inv = inv - shrinkage;`
`num = num % 2;`	

15. Write a multiple assignment statement that can be used instead of the following group of assignment statements:

```
east = 1;
west = 1;
north = 1;
south = 1;
```

16. Replace the following statements with a single statement that initializes sum to 0 at the time it is defined.

```
int sum;
sum = 0;
```

17. Is the following code legal?

```
const int daysInWeek;
daysInWeek = 7;
```

18. Write a cout statement so the variable divSales is displayed in a field of eight spaces, in fixed point notation, with a precision of two decimal places. The decimal point should always be displayed.

19. Write a cout statement so totalSales is displayed with a decimal point and with its value rounded to two decimal places.

20. Write a cout statement so the variable totalAge is displayed in a field of 12 spaces, in fixed point notation, with a precision of four decimal places.

21. What header file must be included to perform mathematical functions like sqrt?

Fill-in-the-Blank

22. The _____ library function returns the cosine of an angle.

23. The _____ library function returns the sine of an angle.

24. The _____ library function returns the tangent of an angle.

25. The _____ library function returns the exponential function of a number.

26. The _____ library function returns the remainder of a floating-point division.
27. The _____ library function returns the natural logarithm of a number.
28. The _____ library function returns the base-10 logarithm of a number.
29. The _____ library function returns the value of a number raised to a power.
30. The _____ library function returns the square root of a number.
31. The _____ file must be included in a program that uses the mathematical functions.

Find the Errors

32. Each of the following programs has some errors. Locate as many as you can.

    A)
    ```cpp
    using namespace std;

    int main()

    {
    float number1, number2, sum;

    Cout << "Enter a number: ";
    Cin << number1;
    Cout << "Enter another number: ";
    Cin << number2;
    number1 + number2 = sum;
    Cout "The sum of the two numbers is " << sum
    return 0;
    }
    ```

    B)
    ```cpp
    #include <iostream>
    using namespace std;

    int main()
    {
        int number1, number2;
        float quotient;
        cout << "Enter two numbers and I will divide\n";
        cout << "the first by the second for you.\n";
        cin >> number1, number2;
        quotient = number1(float) / number2(float);
        cout << quotient
    }
    ```

    C)
    ```cpp
    #include <iostream>;
    using namespace std;

    int main()
    {
        const int number1, number2, product;
    ```

```cpp
        cout << "Enter two numbers and I will multiply\n";
        cout << "them for you.\n";
        cin >> number1 >> number2;
        product = number1 * number2;
        cout << product
        return 0;
    }
```

D)
```cpp
#include <iostream>;
using namespace std;

main
{
    int number1, number2;

    cout << "Enter two numbers and I will multiply\n"
    cout << "them by 50 for you.\n"
    cin >> number1 >> number2;
    number1 =* 50;
    number2 =* 50;
    return 0;
    cout << number1 << " " << number2;
}
```

E)
```cpp
#include <iostream>;
using namespace std;

main
{
    float number, half;

    cout << "Enter a number and I will divide it\n"
    cout << "in half for you.\n"
    cin >> number1;
    half =/ 2;
}
```

F)
```cpp
#include <iostream>;
using namespace std;

int main()
{
    char name, go;

    cout << "Enter your name: ";
    cin.width(20);
    cin.getline >> name;
```

```
      cout << "Hi " << name << endl;
      cout "Press the ENTER key to end this program.";
      cin >> go;
      return 0;
   }
```

Predict the Output

33. What will each of the following programs display? (Some require a calculator.)

A) *(Assume the user enters 38700. Use a calculator.)*

```cpp
#include <iostream>
using namespace std;

int main()
{
   float salary, monthly;

   cout << "What is your annual salary? ";
   cin >> salary;
   monthly = int(salary) / 12;
   cout << "Your monthly wages are " << monthly << endl;
   return 0;
}
```

B)
```cpp
#include <iostream>
using namespace std;

int main()
{
   long x, y, z;

   x = y = z = 4;
   x += 2;
   y -= 1;
   z *= 3;
   cout << x << " " << y << " " << z << endl;
   return 0;
}
```

C)
```cpp
#include <iostream>
using namespace std;

#define WHO "Columbus"
#define DID "sailed"
#define WHAT "the ocean blue."

int main()
{
   const int when = 1492;
```

```
      cout << "In " << when << " " << WHO << " "
           << DID << " " << WHAT << endl;
      return 0;
   }
```

D) *(Assume the user enters George Washington.)*

```
#include <iostream>
#include <iomanip>
#include <string>
using namespace std;
int main()
{
   string userInput;

   cout << "What is your name? ";
   cin >> userInput;
   cout << "Hello " << userInput << endl;
   return 0;
}
```

E) *(Assume the user enters George Washington.)*

```
#include <iostream>
#include <iomanip>
#include <string>
using namespace std;

int main()
{
   string userInput;

   cout << "What is your name? ";
   getline(cin, userInput);
   cout << "Hello " << userInput << endl;
   return 0;
}
```

F) *(Assume the user enters 36720152. Use a calculator.)*

```
#include <iostream>
#include <iomanip>
using namespace std;

int main()
{
   long seconds;
   float minutes, hours, days, months, years;
```

```
    cout << "Enter the number of seconds that have\n";
    cout << "elapsed since some time in the past and\n";
    cout << "I will tell you how many minutes, hours,\n";
    cout << "days, months, and years have passed: ";
    cin >> seconds;
    minutes = seconds / 60;
    hours = minutes / 60;
    days = hours / 24;
    years = days / 365;
    months = years * 12;
    cout << fixed << showpoint << setprecision(4) << left;
    cout << "Minutes: " << setw(6) << minutes << endl;
    cout << "Hours: " << setw(6) << hours << endl;
    cout << "Days: " << setw(6) << days << endl;
    cout << "Months: " << setw(6) << months << endl;
    cout << "Years: " << setw(6) << years << endl;
    return 0;
}
```

Programming Challenges

General Requirements

Each program should have a section of comments at the top. The comments should contain your name, the date the program was written, the chapter the assignment appeared in, and the assignment number and name. Here is an example:

```
// Written by Jill Johnson
// March 31, 2003
// Chapter 3
// Assignment 1, Miles per Gallon
```

For each program that displays a dollar amount, format the output in fixed-point decimal notation with two places of precision. Be sure the decimal place always displays, even when the number is zero or has no fractional part.

1. Miles per Gallon

Write a program that calculates a car's gas mileage. The program should ask the user to enter the number of gallons of gas the car can hold, and the number of miles it can be driven on a full tank. It should then display the number of miles that may be driven per gallon of gas.

2. Stadium Seating

There are three seating categories at a stadium. For a softball game, Class A seats cost $15, Class B seats cost $12, and Class C seats cost $9. Write a program that asks how many tickets for each class of seats were sold, then displays the amount of income generated from ticket sales. Format your dollar amount in fixed-point notation, with two decimal places of precision, and be sure the decimal point is always displayed.

3. Test Average

Write a program that asks for five test scores. The program should calculate the average test score and display it. The number displayed should be formatted in fixed-point notation, with one decimal point of precision.

4. Average Rainfall

Write a program that calculates the average rainfall for three months. The program should ask the user to enter the name of each month, such as June or July, and the amount of rain (in inches) that fell each month. The program should display a message similar to the following:

```
The average rainfall for June, July, and August is 6.72 inches.
```

5. Box Office

A movie theater only keeps a percentage of the revenue earned from ticket sales. The remainder goes to the distibutor. Write a program that calculates a theater's gross and net box office profit for a night. The program should ask for the name of the movie, and how many adult and child tickets were sold. (The price of an adult ticket is $6.00 and a child's ticket is $3.00.) It should display a report similar to

Movie Name:	"Death Grip"
Adult Tickets Sold:	382
Child Tickets Sold:	127
Gross Box Office Profit:	$ 2673.00
Net Box Office Profit:	$ 534.60
Amount Paid to Distributor:	$ 2138.40

 **Note:** Assume the theater keeps 20 percent of the gross box office profit.

6. How Many Widgets?

The Yukon Widget Company manufactures widgets that weigh 9.2 pounds each. Write a program that calculates how many widgets are stacked on a pallet, based on the total weight of the pallet. The program should ask the user how much the pallet weighs by itself and with the widgets stacked on it. It should then calculate and display the number of widgets stacked on the pallet.

7. Centigrade to Fahrenheit

Write a program that converts centigrade temperatures to Fahrenheit temperatures. The formula is

$$F = \frac{9}{5}C + 32$$

F is the Fahrenheit temperature and C is the centigrade temperature.

8. Currency

Write a program that will convert U.S. dollar amounts to Japanese yen and to euros. The conversion factors to use are 1 dollar = 134.33 yen. 1 dollar = 1.1644 euros. Format your currency amounts in fixed-point notation, with two decimal places of precision, and be sure the decimal point is always displayed.

9. Monthly Sales Tax

A retail company must file a monthly sales tax report listing the sales for the month and the amount of sales tax collected. Write a program that asks for the month, the year, and the total amount collected at the cash register (that is, sales plus sales tax). Assume the state sales tax is 4 percent and the county sales tax is 2 percent.

   If the total amount collected is known and the total sales tax is 6 percent, the amount of product sales may be calculated as

$$S = \frac{T}{1.06}$$

Where S is the product sales and T is the total income (product sales plus sales tax).

The program should display a report similar to

```
Month: October, 2002
--------------------
Total Collected:     $ 26572.89
Sales:               $ 25068.76
County Sales Tax:    $   501.38
State Sales Tax:     $  1002.75
Total Sales Tax:     $  1504.13
```

10. Property Tax

A county collects property taxes on the assessment value of property, which is 60 percent of the property's actual value. If an acre of land is valued at $10,000 its assessment value is $6,000. The property tax is then 64¢ for each $100 of the assessment value. The tax for the acre assessed at $6,000 will be $38.40. Write a program that asks for the actual value of a piece of property and displays the assessment value and property tax.

11. Math Tutor

Write a program that can be used as a math tutor for a young student. The program should display two random numbers to be added, such as

```
  247
+ 129
```

The program should then pause while the student works on the problem. When the student is ready to check the answer, he or she can press a key and the program will display the correct solution

```
  247
+ 129
  376
```

12. Interest Earned

Assuming there are no deposits other than the original investment, the balance in a savings account after one year may be calculated as

$$\text{Amount} = \text{Principal} * \left(1 + \frac{\text{Rate}}{\text{T}}\right)^{\text{T}}$$

Principal is the balance in the savings account, Rate is the interest rate, and T is the number of times the interest is compounded during a year (T is 4 if the interest is compounded quarterly).

Write a program that asks for the principal, the interest rate, and the number of times the interest is compounded. It should display a report similar to

```
Interest Rate:              4.25%
Times Compounded:             12
Principal:            $ 1000.00
Interest:             $   43.33
Amount in Savings:    $ 1043.33
```

13. Monthly Payments

The monthly payment on a loan may be calculated by the following formula:

$$\text{Payment} = \frac{\text{Rate} * (1 + \text{Rate})^{N}}{((1 + \text{Rate})^{N} - 1)} * L$$

Rate is the monthly interest rate, which is the annual interest rate divided by 12. (A 12 percent annual interest would be 1 percent monthly interest.) N is the number of payments and L is the amount of the loan. Write a program that asks for these values and displays a report similar to

```
Loan Amount:          $ 10000.00
Monthly Interest Rate:        1%
Number of Payments:           36
Monthly Payment:      $   332.14
Amount Paid Back:     $ 11957.15
Interest Paid:        $  1957.15
```

14. Pizza Pi

Joe's Pizza Palace needs a program to calculate the number of slices a pizza of any size can be divided into. The program should perform the following steps:

A) Ask the user for the diameter of the pizza in inches.

B) Calculate the number of slices that may be taken from a pizza of that size.

C) Display a message telling the number of slices.

To calculate the number of slices that may be taken from the pizza, you must know the following facts:

◆ Each slice should have an area of 14.125 inches.

◆ To calculate the number of slices, simply divide the area of the pizza by 14.125.

◆ The area of the pizza is calculated with this formula:

Area = πr^2

 Note: π is the Greek letter pi. You can use 3.14159 as its value. The variable r is the radius of the pizza. Divide the diameter by 2 to get the radius.

Make sure the output of the program displays the number of slices in fixed-point notation, rounded to one decimal point of precision. Use a named constant for pi.

15. Angle Calculator

Write a program that asks the user for an angle, entered in radians. The program should then display the sine, cosine, and tangent of the angle. (Use the `sin`, `cos`, and `tan` library functions to determine these values.) The output should be displayed in fixed-point notation, rounded to four decimal places of precision.

Serendipity Booksellers Software Development Project—Part 3: *A Problem-Solving Exercise*

1. The Main Menu

Modify the `mainmenu.cpp` program so it lets the user enter a choice from the menu. The choice will be a number in the range of 1 through 4, so it can be stored in either an `int` or `char` variable.

2. The Cashier Module

You are ready to add some of the point-of-sale functionality to the project. Currently, the `cashier.cpp` program displays a simulated sales slip without any sale information. Modify this program so that prior to displaying the simulated sales slip, it asks for the following information:

◆ The date. Expect the user to enter a date in the form MM/DD/YY. This should be entered as a string and stored in a `string` object.

◆ The quantity of the book being purchased. Store this number in an integer variable.

◆ The ISBN number of the book being purchased. The ISBN number is a string that contains numbers and hyphens. Use a `string` object to store it.

◆ The title of the book. Store the book title in a `string` object.

◆ The unit price of the book. Store this number in a `float` variable.

Case

Here is an example of what the screen might look like:

```
Serendipity Booksellers
Cashier Module

Date: 3/31/03
Quantity of Book: 2
ISBN: 0-333-90123-8
Title: History of Scotland
Price: 19.95
```

Once this information is entered, the program should calculate the merchandise total (multiply quantity by price), and a 6 percent sales tax. The program should then display the simulated sales slip. Here is an example:

```
Serendipity Booksellers

Date: 3/31/03

Qty  ISBN           Title                Price      Total
─────────────────────────────────────────────────────────
2    0-333-90123-8  History of Scotland  $ 19.95   $ 39.90

                    Subtotal                       $ 39.90
                    Tax                            $  2.39
                    Total                          $ 42.29

Thank You For Shopping at Serendipity!
```

The dollar amounts should all be displayed in fields of six spaces with two decimal places of precision. They should always be displayed in fixed-point notation and the decimal point should always appear.

3. The Inventory Database Menu

Modify the `invmenu.cpp` program so it lets the user enter a choice from the menu. The choice will be a number in the range of 1 through 5, so it can be stored in either an `int` or `char` variable.

4. The Reports Menu

Modify the `reports.cpp` program so it lets the user enter a choice from the menu. The choice will be a number in the range of 1 through 7, so it can be stored in either an `int` or `char` variable.

CHAPTER 4

Making Decisions

Topics

4.1   Relational Operators

> **CONCEPT**   Relational operators allow you to compare numeric values and determine if one is greater than, less than, equal to, or not equal to another.

So far, the programs you have written follow this simple scheme:

- ◆ Gather input from the user.
- ◆ Perform one or more calculations.
- ◆ Display the results on the screen.

Computers are good at performing calculations, but they are also quite adept at comparing values to determine if one is greater than, less than, or equal to, the other. These types of operations are valuable for tasks such as examining sales figures, determining profit and loss, checking a number to ensure it is within an acceptable range, and validating the input given by a user.

Numeric data is compared in C++ by using relational operators. Characters can also be compared with these operators, because characters are considered numeric values in C++. Each relational operator determines if a specific relationship exists between two values. For example, the greater-than operator (>) determines if a value is greater than another. The equality operator (==) determines if two values are equal. Table 4-1 lists all of C++'s relational operators

Table 4-1

Relational Operators	Meaning
>	Greater than
<	Less than
>=	Greater than or equal to
<=	Less than or equal to
==	Equal to
!=	Not equal to

 Note: All the relational operators are binary operators with left-to-right associativity. Recall that associativity is the order in which an operator works with its operands.

All of the relational operators are binary. This means they use two operands. Here is an example of an expression using the greater-than operator:

    x > y

This expression is called a *relational expression*. It is used to determine if x is greater than y. The following expression determines if x is less than y:

    x < y

The Value of a Relationship

So, how are relational expressions used in a program? Remember, all expressions have a value. Relational expressions are Boolean expressions, which means their value can only be *true* or *false*. If x is greater than y, the expression x > y will be true, while the expression y == x will be false.

The == operator determines if the operand on its left is equal to the operand on its right. If both operands have the same value, the expression is true. Assuming that a is 4, the following expression is true:

    a == 4

But the following is false:

```
a == 2
```

 WARNING! Notice the equality operator is two = symbols together. Don't confuse this operator with the assignment operator, which is one = symbol. The ==
operator determines if a variable is equal to another value, but the = operator
assigns the value on the operator's right to the variable on its left. There will be
more about this later in the chapter.

A couple of the relational operators actually test for two relationships. The >= operator
determines if the operand on its left is greater than *or* equal to the operand on the right. Assuming
that a is 4, b is 6, and c is 4, both of the following expressions are true:

```
b >= a
a >= c
```

But the following is false:

```
a >= 5
```

The <= operator determines if the operand on its left is less than *or* equal to the operand on its
right. Once again, assuming that a is 4, b is 6, and c is 4, both of the following expressions are true:

```
a <= c
b <= 10
```

But the following is false:

```
b <= a
```

The last relational operator is !=, which is the not-equal operator. It determines if the oper-
and on its left is not equal to the operand on its right, which is the opposite of the == operator. As
before, assuming a is 4, b is 6, and c is 4, both of the following expressions are true:

```
a != b
b != c
```

These expressions are true because a is *not* equal to b and b is *not* equal to c. But the following
expression is false because a *is* equal to c:

```
a != c
```

Table 4-2 shows other relational expressions and their true or false values.

What Is Truth?

The question "what is truth?" is one you would expect to find in a philosophy book, not a C++
programming text. It's a good question for us to consider, though. If a relational expression can

Table 4-2 (Assume x **is 10 and** y **is 7.**)

Expression	Value
x < y	false, because x is not less than y.
x > y	true, because x is greater than y.
x >= y	true, because x is greater than or equal to y.
x <= y	false, because x is not less than or equal to y.
y != x	true, because y is not equal to x.

be either true or false, how are those values represented internally in a program? How does a computer store *true* in memory? How does it store *false*?

As you saw in Program 2-16, those two abstract states are converted to numbers. In C++, relational expressions represent true states with the number 1 and false states with the number 0.

 Note: As you will see later in this chapter, 1 is not the only value regarded as true.

To illustrate this more fully, look at Program 4-1.

Program 4-1

```
// This program displays the values of true and false states.

#include <iostream>
using namespace std;

int main()
{
    int trueValue, falseValue, x = 5, y = 10;

    trueValue = x < y;
    falseValue = y == x;

    cout << "True is " << trueValue << endl;
    cout << "False is " << falseValue << endl;
    return 0;
}
```

Program Output
```
True is 1
False is 0
```

Let's examine the statements containing the relational expressions a little closer:

```
trueValue = x < y;
falseValue = y == x;
```

These statements may seem odd because they are assigning the value of a comparison to a variable. In the first statement, the variable `trueValue` is being assigned the result of x < y. Since x is less than y, the expression is true, and the variable `trueValue` is assigned the value 1. In the second statement the expression y == x is false, so the variable `falseValue` is set to 0.

Notice that in both cases the relational operation was carried out before the assignment operation was performed. Unless parentheses are used to change the order of operations, this is always the case because relational operators have a higher precedence than the assignment operator. Likewise, arithmetic operators have a higher precedence than relational operators. In the statement

```
falseValue = x < y - 8;
```

first y - 8 would be evaluated to yield a 2. Then x's value, 5, would be compared to 2. Since it is false that 5 is less than 2, a zero would be assigned to `falseValue`.

Table 4-3 shows examples of other statements that include relational expressions.

Table 4-3 (Assume x is 10, y is 7, and z, a, and b are all `int`s.)

Statement	Outcome
z = x < y	z is assigned 0 because x is not less than y.
cout << (x > y);	Displays 1 because x is greater than y.
a = x >= y;	a is assigned 1 because x is greater than or equal to y.
cout << (x <= y);	Displays 0 because x is not less than or equal to y.
b = y != x;	b is assigned 1 because y is not equal to x.
cout << (x == y + 3);	Displays 1 because x is equal to y + 3.

Relational operators also have a precedence order among themselves. The four operators that test relative size (>, >=, <, and <=) have the same precedence as each other. The two operators that test for equality or lack of equality (== and !=) have the same precedence as each other. The four relative relational operators have a higher precedence than the two equality relational operators. Table 4-4 shows the precedence of relational operators.

Table 4-4 Precedence of Relational Operators (Highest to Lowest)

>	>=	<	<=
==	!=		

Here is an example of how this is applied. If a = 9, b = 24, and c = 0, the following statement would cause a 1 to print out.

```
cout << (c == a > b);
```

Because of the relative precedence of the operators in this expression, a > b would be evaluated first. Since 9 is not greater than 24, it would evaluate to false, or 0. Then c == 0 would be evaluated. Since c does equal 0, this would evaluate to true, or 1. So a 1 would be inserted into the output stream and printed.

As interesting as relational expressions are, we've only scratched the surface of how to use them. In this chapter's remaining sections you will see how to get the most from relational expressions by using them in statements that take action based on the results of the comparison.

Checkpoint [4.1]

4.1 Assuming x is 5, y is 6, and z is 8, indicate by circling the T or F if each of the following relational expressions is true or false:

A)	x == 5	T	F
B)	7 <= (x + 2)	T	F
C)	z > 4	T	F
D)	(2 + x) != y	T	F
E)	z != 4	T	F
F)	x >= 0	T	F
G)	x <= (y * 2)	T	F

4.2 Indicate if the following statements about relational expressions are correct or incorrect.

A) x <= y is the same as y > x.

B) x != y is the same as y >= x.

C) x >= y is the same as y <= x.

4.3 Answer the following questions with a yes or no.

A) If it is true that x > y and it is also true that x < z, does that mean y < z is true?

B) If it is true that x >= y and it is also true that z == x, does that mean that z == y is true?

C) If it is true that x != y and it is also true that x != z, does that mean that z != y is true?

4.4 What will the following program display?

```
#include <iostream>
using namespace std;
```

```
int main()
{
    int a = 0, b = 2, x = 4, y = 0;

    cout << (a == b) << endl;
    cout << (a != y) << endl;
    cout << (b <= x) << endl;
    cout << (y > a) << endl;
    return 0;
}
```

4.2 The if Statement

CONCEPT The if statement can cause other statements to execute only under certain conditions.

You might think of the statements in a procedural program as individual steps taken as you are walking down a road. To reach the destination, you must start at the beginning and take each step, one after the other, until you reach the destination. The programs you have written so far are like a "path" of execution for the program to follow.

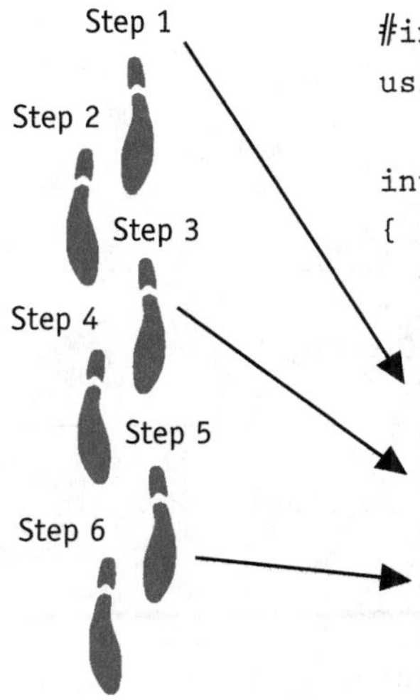

Step 1
Step 2
Step 3
Step 4
Step 5
Step 6

```
// A program to calculate the area of a rectangle

#include <iostream>
using namespace std;

int main()
{
    float length, width, area;

    cout << "Enter the length of the rectangle: ";
    cin >> length;
    cout << "Enter the width of the rectangle: ";
    cin >> width;
    area = length * width;
    cout << "The area is: " << area << endl;
    return 0;
}
```

Figure 4-1

As shown in Figure 4-1, the program's execution flows sequentially from one statement to the next. This type of program is sometimes called an *in-line program*, because the statements are executed in a straight "line," without branching off in another direction.

Wouldn't it be useful, though, if a program could have more than one "path" of execution? What if the program could execute some statements only under certain circumstances? That can be accomplished with the if statement, as illustrated by Program 4-2. The user enters three test scores and the program calculates their average. If the average is greater than 95, the program congratulates the user on obtaining a high score.

Program 4-2

```cpp
// This program averages 3 test scores.

#include <iostream>
#include <iomanip>
using namespace std;

int main()
{
    int score1, score2, score3;
    float average;

    cout << "Enter 3 test scores and I will average them: ";
    cin >> score1 >> score2 >> score3;
    average = (score1 + score2 + score3) / 3.0;
    cout << fixed << showpoint << setprecision(1);
    cout << "Your average is " << average << endl;
    if (average > 95)
        cout << "Congratulations! That's a high score!\n";
    return 0;
}
```

Program Output with Example Input Shown in Bold
Enter 3 test scores and I will average them: **80 90 70[Enter]**
Your average is 80.0

Program Output with Other Example Input Shown in Bold
Enter 3 test scores and I will average them: **100 100 99[Enter]**
Your average is 99.7
Congratulations! That's a high score!

The last two lines of Program 4-2 cause the congratulatory message to be printed:

```cpp
if (average > 95)
    cout << "Congratulations! That's a high score!\n";
```

Here is the general format of the if statement:

```
if (expression)
    statement;
```

The if statement is simple in the way it works: If the expression inside the parentheses is true, the very next statement is executed. Otherwise, it is skipped. The statement is *conditionally executed* because it only executes under the condition that the expression in parentheses is true. In Program 4-2, the cout statement is only executed under the condition that average is greater than 95. If average is not greater than 95, the cout statement is skipped. This is similar to the way we mentally test conditions every day:

> If the car is low in gas, stop at a service station and get gas.
> If it's raining outside, go inside.
> If you're hungry, get something to eat.

The if statement in Program 4-2 is saying the following:

> If the average score is greater than 95, congratulate the user on obtaining a
> high test score average.

Table 4-5 shows other examples of if statements and their outcomes. Assume overTime is a Boolean variable.

Table 4-5

Statements	Outcome
`if (hours > 40)` `    overTime = true;`	Assigns true to overTime only when hours is greater than 40.
`if (value > 32)` `    cout << "Invalid number\n";`	Displays the message "Invalid number" only when value is greater than 32.
`if (overTime == true)` `    payRate *= 2;`	Multiplies payRate by 2 only when overTime is equal to true.

Be Careful with Semicolons

Semicolons do not mark the end of a line, but the end of a complete C++ statement. The if statement isn't complete without the conditionally executed statement that comes after it. So, you must not put a semicolon after the if (expression) portion of an if statement.

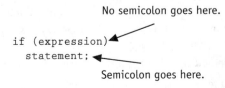

No semicolon goes here.

```
if (expression)
    statement;
```

Semicolon goes here.

If you inadvertently put a semicolon after the `if` part, the compiler will assume you are placing a null statement there. The *null statement* is an empty statement that does nothing. This will prematurely terminate the `if` statement, which disconnects it from the statement that follows it. The statement following the `if` will always execute, as shown in Program 4-3.

Program 4-3

```
//  This program demonstrates how a misplaced semicolon
//  prematurely terminates an if statement.

#include <iostream>
using namespace std;

int main()
{
    int x = 0, y = 10;

    cout << "x is " << x << " and y is " << y << endl;
    if (x > y);                         // Misplaced semicolon
        cout << "x is greater than y\n";  // This statement is always executed.
    return 0;
}
```

Program Output
```
x is 0 and y is 10
x is greater than y
```

 Note: Indentation and spacing are for the human reader of a program, not the computer. Even though the `cout` statement following the `if` statement in Program 4-3 is indented, the semicolon still terminates the `if` statement.

Programming Style and the `if` Statement

Even though `if` statements usually span more than one line, they are technically one long statement. For instance, the following `if` statements are identical except in style:

```
if (a >= 100)
    cout << "The number is out of range.\n";

if (a >= 100) cout << "The number is out of range.\n";
```

The first of these two `if` statements is considered to be better style because it is easier to read. By indenting the conditionally executed statement you are causing it to stand out visually. This is so you can tell at a glance what part of the program the `if` statement executes. This is a standard way of writing `if` statements and is the method you should use. Here are two important style rules you should adopt for writing `if` statements:

◆ The conditionally executed statement should appear on the line after the `if` statement.

◆ The conditionally executed statement should be indented one "level" from the `if` statement.

Note: In most editors, each time you press the tab key, you are indenting one level.

Comparing Floating-Point Numbers

Floating-point numbers should not be tested for equality. Because of round-off errors, a number that should be mathematically equal to another might not be. In Program 4-4, 6 is multiplied by 0.666666, a decimal version of 2/3. Of course, 6 times 2/3 is 4. The program, however, disagrees.

Program 4-4

```cpp
// This program demonstrates how floating-point round-off
// errors can make equality comparisons unreliable.

#include <iostream>
using namespace std;

int main()
{
    float result;

    result = 6.0 * 0.666666;      //Round-off error
    if (result == 4.0)
        cout << "It's true!" << endl;
    else
        cout << "It's false!" << endl;
    return 0;
}
```

Program Output
```
It's false!
```

Typically, the value in `result` will be a number just short of 4, like 3.999996. To prevent errors like this, stick with greater-than and less-than comparisons with floating-point numbers. For example, instead of testing if the result equals 4.0, you could test to see if it is very close to 4.0.

And Now Back to Truth

Now that you've gotten your feet wet with relational expressions and `if` statements, let's look at the subject of truth again. You have seen that a relational expression has the value 1 when it is true and 0 when false. In the world of the `if` statement, however, the concept of truth is expanded. 0 is still false, but all values other than 0 are considered true. This means that any value, even a negative number, represents true as long as it is not 0.

Just as in real life, truth is a complicated thing. Here is a summary of the rules you have seen so far:

- When a relational expression is true it has the value 1.
- When a relational expression is false it has the value 0.

◆ An expression that has the value 0 is considered false by the `if` statement. This includes the `bool` value `false`, which is equivalent to 0.

◆ An expression that has any value other than 0 is considered true by the `if` statement. This includes the `bool` value `true`, which is equivalent to 1.

The fact that the `if` statement considers any nonzero value as true opens many possibilities. Relational expressions are not the only conditions that may be tested. For example, the following is a legal `if` statement in C++:

```
if (value)
    cout << "It is True!";
```

This `if` statement does not test a relational expression, but rather the contents of a variable. If the variable, `value`, contains any number other than 0, the message "It is True!" will be displayed. If `value` is set to 0, however, the `cout` statement will be skipped. Here is another example:

```
if (x + y)
    cout << "It is True!";
```

In this statement the sum of `x` and `y` is tested like any other value in an `if` statement: 0 is false and all other values are true. You may also use the return value of function calls as conditional expressions. Here is an example that uses the `pow` function:

```
if (pow(a, b))
    cout << "It is True!";
```

This `if` statement uses the `pow` function to raise `a` to the power of `b`. If the result is anything other than 0, the `cout` statement is executed. This is a powerful programming technique that you will learn more about in Chapter 6.

Not All Operators Are "Equal"

Earlier you saw a warning not to confuse the equality operator (`==`) with the assignment operator (`=`), as in the following statement:

```
if (x = 2)                          // Caution here!
    cout << "It is True!";
```

This statement does not determine if `x` is equal to 2; it assigns `x` the value 2! Furthermore, the `cout` statement will *always* be executed because the expression `x = 2` evaluates to 2, which is always true.

This occurs because the value of an assignment expression is the value being assigned to the variable on the left side of the `=` operator. Since the value of the expression `x = 2` is 2 and 2 is a nonzero value, it represents a true condition. Program 4-5 is a version of Program 4-2 that attempts to test for a perfect average of 100. The `=` operator, however, was mistakenly used in the `if` statement.

Program 4-5

```cpp
// This program averages 3 test scores. The if statement
// uses the = operator, but the == operator was intended.

#include <iostream>
#include <iomanip>
using namespace std;

int main()
{
    int score1, score2, score3;
    float average;

    cout << "Enter 3 test scores and I will average them: ";
    cin >> score1 >> score2 >> score3;
    average = (score1 + score2 + score3) / 3.0;
    cout << fixed << showpoint << setprecision(1);
    cout << "Your average is " << average << endl;

    if (average = 100)             //Wrong!
        cout << "Congratulations! That's a perfect score!\n";
    return 0;
}
```

Program Output with Example Input Shown in Bold
```
Enter 3 test scores and I will average them: 80 90 70[Enter]
Your average is 80.0
Congratulations! That's a perfect score!
```

Regardless of the average score, this program will print the message congratulating the user on a perfect score.

4.3 Flags

CONCEPT A flag is a variable, usually a Boolean or an integer, that signals when a condition exists.

Flag variables are meant to signal that some condition exists in the program. When the flag contains a 0 (false), it indicates the condition does not yet exist. When the flag contains a nonzero value (true), it means the condition does exist. Many instructors discourage the use of integer flags and encourage their students to use only Boolean flags.[1] Program 4-6 is the test-averaging program modified to use a Boolean flag variable, highScore.

---

[1]If your compiler does not support `bool` variables, see Creating a Boolean Data Type in Section 3.6.

Program 4-6

```cpp
// This program averages 3 test scores.
// It uses the variable HighScore as a flag.

#include <iostream>
#include <iomanip>
using namespace std;

int main()
{
    int score1, score2, score3;
    float average;
    bool highScore = false;

    cout << "Enter 3 test scores and I will average them: ";
    cin >> score1 >> score2 >> score3;
    average = (score1 + score2 + score3) / 3.0;
    if (average > 95)
        highScore = true;                   // Set the flag variable
    cout << fixed << showpoint << setprecision(1);
    cout << "Your average is " << average << endl;
    if (highScore)
        cout << "Congratulations! That's a high score!\n";
    return 0;
}
```

Program Output with Example Input Shown in Bold
Enter 3 test scores and I will average them: **100 100 99[Enter]**
Your average is 99.7
Congratulations! That's a high score!

Notice the flag variable, `highScore`, is initialized to `false`. The first `if` statement changes `high-Score`'s value to `true` if the average is greater than 95. Otherwise, `highScore` keeps its value of `false`. The last `if` statement only prints the message of congratulations if `highScore` is set to `true`. You will find flag variables useful in many circumstances, and we will come back to them in Chapter 5.

 Note: Variables that are created inside a function, like `main`, are not automatically initialized. If you need a variable to start with a particular value, you should initialize it to that value.

4.4 Expanding the `if` Statement

CONCEPT	The `if` statement can conditionally execute more than one statement.

What if you want an `if` statement to conditionally execute a group of statements, not just one line? For instance, what if the test averaging program needed to use several `cout` statements when a high score was reached? The answer is to enclose all of the conditionally executed statements inside a set of braces. Here is the format:

```
if (expression)
{
    statement;
    statement;
    // Place as many statements here as necessary.
}
```

Program 4-7, another modification of the test-averaging program, demonstrates this type of `if` statement.

Program 4-7

```
// This program averages 3 test scores.
// It uses the variable highScore as a flag.

#include <iostream>
#include <iomanip>
using namespace std;

int main()
{
    int score1, score2, score3;
    float average;
    bool highScore = false;

    cout << "Enter 3 test scores and I will average them: ";
    cin >> score1 >> score2 >> score3;
    average = (score1 + score2 + score3) / 3.0;
    if (average > 95)
        highScore = true; // Set the flag variable
```

(program continues)

Program 4-7 *(continued)*

```
    cout << fixed << showpoint << setprecision(1);
    cout << "Your average is " << average << endl;
    if (highScore)
    {
        cout << "Congratulations!\n";
        cout << "That's a high score.\n";
        cout << "You deserve a pat on the back!\n";
    }
    return 0;
}
```

Program Output with Example Input Shown in Bold
Enter 3 test scores and I will average them: **100 100 99[Enter]**
Your average is 99.7
Congratulations!
That's a high score.
You deserve a pat on the back!

Program Output with Different Example Input Shown in Bold
Enter 3 test scores and I will average them: **20 40 30[Enter]**
Your average is 30.0

Program 4-7 prints a more elaborate message when the average score is greater than 95. The if statement was expanded to execute three cout statements when highScore is set to true. Enclosing a group of statements inside a set of braces creates a *block* of code. The if statement will execute all the statements in the block, in the order they appear, only when highScore is set to true. If highScore is false, the block will be skipped.

Notice all the statements inside the braces are indented. As before, this visually separates the statements from lines that are not indented, making it more obvious they are part of the if statement.

 Note: Anytime your program has a block of code, all the statements inside the braces should be indented.

Don't Forget the Braces!

If you intend to conditionally execute a block of statements, rather than just one statement, with an if statement, don't forget the braces. Remember, without a set of braces, the if statement only executes the very next statement. Any following statements are considered to be outside the if statement and will always be executed, even when the if condition is false. Program 4-8 shows the test-averaging program with the braces inadvertently left out of the if statement's block.

Program 4-8

```cpp
// This program averages 3 test scores.
// It uses the variable highScore as a flag.

#include <iostream>
#include <iomanip>
using namespace std;

int main()
{
    int    score1, score2, score3;
    float  average;
    bool   highScore = false;

    cout << "Enter 3 test scores and I will average them: ";
    cin >> score1 >> score2 >> score3;
    average = (score1 + score2 + score3) / 3.0;
    if (average > 95)
        highScore = true;                         // Set the flag variable
    cout << fixed << showpoint << setprecision(1);
    cout << "Your average is " << average << endl;

    // The following statement is missing its braces!
    if (highScore)
        cout << "Congratulations!\n";
        cout << "That's a high score.\n";         // These 2 statements are
        cout << "You deserve a pat on the back!\n"; // outside the if statement.
    return 0;
}
```

Program Output with Example Input Shown in Bold
```
Enter 3 test scores and I will average them: 20 40 30[Enter]
Your average is 30.0
That's a high score.
You deserve a pat on the back!
```

The last two `cout` statements are always executed, even when `highScore` is set to 0. Because all three `cout` statements are no longer inside braces, the `if` statement only controls execution of the first one.

Checkpoint [4.2–4.4]

4.5 True or False: Both of the following `if` statements perform the same operation.

```cpp
if (sales > 10000)
    commissionRate = 0.15;

if (sales > 10000) commissionRate = 0.15;
```

4.6 True or false: Both of the following `if` statements perform the same operation.

```
if (calls == 20)
    rate *= 0.5;

if (calls = 20)
    rate *= 0.5;
```

4.7 Although the following code segments are syntactically correct, each contains an error. Locate the error and indicate what each segment will display.

A)
```
hours = 12;
if (hours > 40);
cout << hours << "hours qualifies for over-time.\n";
```

B)
```
interestRate = .05;
balance = 1000;
if (interestRate = .07)
   cout << "This account is earning the maximum rate.\n";
balance *= interestRate;
cout << "The new balance is " << balance << endl;
```

C)
```
interestRate = .05;
balance = 1000;
if (interestRate > .07)
   cout << "This account earns a $10 bonus.\n";
balance += 10.0;
balance *= interestRate;
cout << "The new balance is " << balance << endl;
```

4.8 Write an `if` statement that assigns 0 to x when y is equal to 20.

4.9 Write an `if` statement that multiplies `payRate` by 1.5 when `hours` is greater than 40.

4.10 Write an `if` statement that assigns .20 to `commission` when `sales` is greater than or equal to 10,000.00.

4.11 Write an `if` statement that sets the variable `fees` to 50 when the flag variable `max` is set.

4.5 The `if/else` Statement

CONCEPT	The `if/else` statement will execute one set of statements if the expression is true, or another set if the expression is false.

The `if/else` statement is an expansion of the `if` statement. Here is its format:

```
if (expression)
    statement or block of statements;
```

```
    else
        statement or block of statements;
```

As with the if statement, an expression is evaluated. If the expression is true, a statement or block of statements is executed. If the expression is false, however, a separate group of statements is executed. Program 4-9 uses the if/else statement along with the modulus operator to determine if a number is odd or even.

Program 4-9

```
// This program uses the modulus operator to determine
// if a number is odd or even. If the number is evenly divisible
// by 2, it is an even number. A remainder indicates it is odd.

#include <iostream>
using namespace std;

int main()
{
    int number;

    cout << "Enter an integer and I will tell you if it\n";
    cout << "is odd or even. ";
    cin >> number;
    if (number % 2 == 0)
        cout << number << " is even.\n";
    else
        cout << number << " is odd.\n";
    return 0;
}
```

Program Output with Example Input Shown in Bold
```
Enter an integer and I will tell you if it
is odd or even. 17[Enter]
17 is odd.
```

The else part at the end of the if statement specifies a statement that is to be executed when the expression is false. When number % 2 does not equal 0, a message is printed indicating the number is odd. Note that the program will only take one of the two paths in the if/else statement. If you think of the statements in a computer program as steps taken down a road, consider the if/else statement as a fork in the road. Instead of being a momentary detour, like an if statement, the if/else statement causes program execution to follow one of two exclusive paths.

Notice the programming style used to construct the if/else statement. The word else is at the same level of indention as if. The statement whose execution is controlled by else is indented one level. This visually depicts the two paths of execution that may be followed.

Like the if part, if you don't use braces the else part controls a single statement. If you wish to control more than one statement with the else part, create a block by writing the lines inside a set of braces. Program 4-10 shows this as a way of handling a classic programming problem: *division by zero*.

Division by zero is mathematically impossible to perform and it normally causes a program to crash. This means the program will prematurely stop running, sometimes with an error message. Program 4-10 shows a way to test the value of a divisor before the division takes place.

Program 4-10

```cpp
// This program asks the user for two numbers, num1 and num2.
// num1 is divided by num2 and the result is displayed.
// Before the division operation, however, num2 is tested
// for the value 0. If it contains 0, the division does not
// take place.

#include <iostream>
using namespace std;

int main()
{
    float num1, num2, quotient;

    cout << "Enter a number: ";
    cin >> num1;
    cout << "Enter another number: ";
    cin >> num2;
    if (num2 == 0)
    {
        cout << "Division by zero is not possible.\n";
        cout << "Please run the program again and enter\n";
        cout << "a number other than zero.\n";
    }
    else
    {
        quotient = num1 / num2;
        cout << "The quotient of " << num1 << " divided by ";
        cout << num2 << " is " << quotient << ".\n";
    }
    return 0;
}
```

Program Output with Example Input Shown in Bold
```
Enter a number: 10[Enter]
Enter another number: 0[Enter]
Division by zero is not possible.
Please run the program again and enter
a number other than zero.
```

The value of num2 is tested before the division is performed. If the user enters 0, the lines controlled by the `if` part execute, displaying a message which indicates the program cannot perform a division by zero. Otherwise, the `else` part takes control, which divides num1 by num2 and displays the result.

⟨? Checkpoint   [4.5]

4.12 True or false: The following `if/else` statements cause the same output to display.

A)
```
if (x > y)
    cout << "x is the greater.\n";
else
    cout << "x is not the greater.\n";
```

B)
```
if (y <= x)
    cout << "x is not the greater.\n";
else
    cout << "x is the greater.\n";
```

4.13 Write an `if/else` statement that assigns 1 to x when y is equal to 100. Otherwise it should assign 0 to x.

4.14 Write an `if/else` statement that assigns 0.10 to commission unless sales is greater than or equal to 50,000.00, in which case it assigns 0.20 to commission.

4.15 Complete the following program skeleton so it computes the correct sales tax. If the customer is an in-state resident, taxRate should be set to .05. If the customer is an out-of-state resident, taxRate should be set to 0.

```
#include <iostream>
using namespace std;

int main()
{
    float taxRate, saleAmount;
    char residence;

    cout << "Enter the amount of the sale: ";
    cin >> saleAmount;
    cout << "Enter I for in-state residence or 0 for out-of-\n";
    cout <<"state: ";
    cin.get(residence);

    // Write code here that assigns 0 to taxRate if residence
    // is set to '0' or .05 to taxRate if residence is set
    // to 'I'

    saleAmount += saleAmount * taxRate;
    cout << "The total is " << saleAmount;
    return 0;
}
```

4.6 The `if/else if` Statement

CONCEPT The `if/else if` statement is a chain of `if` statements. They perform their tests, one after the other, until one of them is found to be true.

We make certain mental decisions by using sets of different but related rules. For example, we might decide the type of coat or jacket to wear by consulting the following rules:

```
if it is very cold, wear a heavy coat,
else, if it is chilly, wear a light jacket,
else, if it is windy, wear a windbreaker,
else, if it is hot, wear no jacket.
```

The purpose of these rules is to determine which type of outer garment to wear. If it is cold, the first rule dictates that a heavy coat must be worn. All the other rules are then ignored. If the first rule doesn't apply, however (if it isn't cold), then the second rule is consulted. If that rule doesn't apply, the third rule is consulted, and so forth.

The way these rules are connected is very important. If they were consulted individually, we might go out of the house wearing the wrong jacket or, possibly, more than one jacket. For instance, if it is windy, the third rule says to wear a windbreaker. What if it is both windy and very cold? Will we wear a windbreaker? A heavy coat? Both? Because of the order that the rules are consulted in, the first rule will determine that a heavy coat is needed. The third rule will not be consulted, and we will go outside wearing the most appropriate garment.

This type of decision making is also very common in programming. In C++ it is accomplished through the `if/else if` statement. Here is its format:

```
if (expression)
   statement or block of statements;
else if (expression)
   statement or block of statements;
//
// Put as many else ifs as needed here.
//
else if (expression)
   statement or block of statements;
```

This construction is like a chain of `if/else` statements. The `else` part of one statement is linked to the `if` part of another. When put together this way, the chain of `if/else`'s becomes one long statement. Program 4-11 shows an example. The user is asked to enter a numeric test score and the program displays the letter grade earned.

Program 4-11

```cpp
// This program uses an if/else if statement to assign a
// letter grade (A, B, C, D, or F) to a numeric test score.

#include <iostream>
using namespace std;

int main()
{
    int testScore;
    char grade;

    cout << "Enter your numeric test score and I will\n";
    cout << "tell you the letter grade you earned: ";
    cin >> testScore;
    if (testScore < 60)
        grade = 'F';
    else if (testScore < 70)
        grade = 'D';
    else if (testScore < 80)
        grade = 'C';
    else if (testScore < 90)
        grade = 'B';
    else if (testScore <= 100)
        grade = 'A';
    cout << "Your grade is " << grade << ".\n";
    return 0;
}
```

Program Output with Example Input Shown in Bold

```
Enter your numeric test score and I will
tell you the letter grade you earned: 88[Enter]
Your grade is B.
```

The if/else if statement has a number of notable characteristics. Let's analyze how it works in Program 4-11. First, the relational expression testScore < 60 is tested.

```cpp
→   if (testScore < 60)
        grade = 'F';
    else if (testScore < 70)
        grade = 'D';
    else if (testScore < 80)
        grade = 'C';
    else if (testScore < 90)
        grade = 'B';
    else if (testScore <= 100)
        grade = 'A';
```

If testScore is less than 60, the letter 'F' is assigned to grade and the rest of the linked if statements are skipped. If testScore is not less than 60, the else part takes over and causes the next if statement to be executed.

```
    if (testScore < 60)
        grade = 'F';
→   else if (testScore < 70)
        grade = 'D';
    else if (testScore < 80)
        grade = 'C';
    else if (testScore < 90)
        grade = 'B';
    else if (testScore <= 100)
        grade = 'A';
```

The first if statement filtered out all of the grades less than 60, so when this if statement executes, testScore will have a value of 60 or greater. If testScore is less than 70, the letter 'D' is assigned to grade and the rest of the if/else if statement is ignored. This chain of events continues until one of the conditional expressions is found true or the end of the statement is encountered. In either case, the program resumes at the statement immediately following the if/else if statement, which is the cout statement that prints the grade. Figure 4-2 shows the paths that may be taken by the if/else if statement.

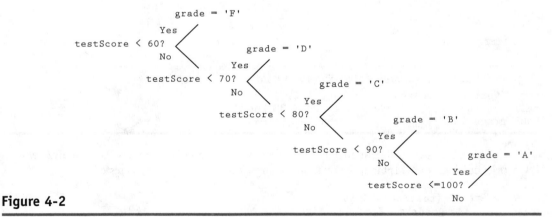

Figure 4-2

Each if statement in the structure depends on all the if statements before it being false. The statements following a particular else if are executed when the conditional expression following the else if is true and all previous conditional expressions are false. To demonstrate how this interconnection works, let's look at Program 4-12, which uses independent if statements instead of an if/else if statement.

Program 4-12

```cpp
// This program uses independent if/else statements to assign a
// letter grade (A, B, C, D, or F) to a numeric test score.
// Do you think it will work?

#include <iostream>
using namespace std;

int main()
{
    int testScore;
    char grade;

    cout << "Enter your test score and I will tell you\n";
    cout << "the letter grade you earned: ";
    cin >> testScore;
    if (testScore < 60)
        grade = 'F';
    if (testScore < 70)
        grade = 'D';
    if (testScore < 80)
        grade = 'C';
    if (testScore < 90)
        grade = 'B';
    if (testScore <= 100)
        grade = 'A';
    cout << "Your grade is " << grade << ".\n";
    return 0;
}
```

Program Output with Example Input Shown in Bold
```
Enter your test score and I will tell you
the letter grade you earned: 40[Enter]
Your grade is A.
```

In Program 4-12, all the `if` statements execute because they are individual statements. In the example output, `testScore` is assigned the value 40, yet the student recieves an A. Here is what happens. Since the student's score is less than 60, the first `if` statement causes `'F'` to be assigned to `grade`. However, since the next `if` statement is not connected to the first through an `else`, it executes as well. Since `testScore` is also less than 70, it causes `'D'` to be assigned to `grade`, replacing the `'F'` that was previously stored there. This continues until all the `if` statements have executed. The last one will cause `'A'` to be assigned to `grade`. (Most students prefer this method since `'A'` is the only grade it gives out!)

4.7   Using a Trailing `else`

CONCEPT   A trailing `else`, placed at the end of an `if`/`else if` statement, provides a default action when none of the `if`s have true expressions.

There is one minor problem with the test score examples shown so far. What if the user enters a test score greater than 100? The `if`/`else if` statement handles all scores through 100, but none greater. If the user were to enter 104, for example, the program would not give a letter grade because there is no code to handle a score greater than 100. Assuming that any grade over 100 is invalid, we can fix the program by placing an `else` at the end of the `if`/`else if` statement.

Program 4-13 is a variation of Program 4-11 which includes a final trailing `else` and which allows more than one statement to be executed when an `if` condition is true. Notice how each block of statments to be conditionally executed is enclosed in braces.

Program 4-13

```cpp
// This program uses an if/else if statement to assign a
// letter grade (A, B, C, D, or F) to a numeric test score.
// A trailing else has been added to catch test scores > 100.

#include <iostream>
using namespace std;

int main()
{
    int testScore;

    cout << "Enter your test score and I will tell you\n";
    cout << "the letter grade you earned: ";
    cin >> testScore;

    if (testScore < 60)
    {
        cout << "Your grade is F.\n";
        cout << "This is a failing grade. Better see your ";
        cout << "instructor.\n";
    }
    else if (testScore < 70)
    {
        cout << "Your grade is D.\n";
        cout << "This is below average. You should get ";
        cout << "tutoring.\n";
    }
```

(program continues)

Program 4-13   *(continued)*

```cpp
    else if (testScore < 80)
    {
        cout << "Your grade is C.\n";
        cout << "This is average.\n";
    }
    else if (testScore < 90)
    {
        cout << "Your grade is B.\n";
        cout << "This is an above average grade.\n";
    }
    else if (testScore <= 100)
    {
        cout << "Your grade is A.\n";
        cout << "This is a superior grade. Good work!\n";
    }
    else                                 //Default action
    {
        cout << testScore << " is an invalid score.\n";
        cout << "Please enter scores no greater than 100.\n";
    }
    return 0;
}
```

Program Output with Example Input Shown in Bold
```
Enter your test score and I will tell you
the letter grade you earned: 104[Enter]
104 is an invalid score.
Please enter scores no greater than 100.
```

The trailing `else` catches any value that "falls through the cracks." It provides a default response when none of the `if`s find a true condition.

4.8   Menus

CONCEPT   You can use the `if`/`else if` statement to create *menu-driven* programs. A menu-driven program allows the user to determine the course of action by selecting it from a list of actions.

A menu is a screen displaying a set of choices the user selects from. For example, a program that keeps a mailing list might give you the following menu:

1. Add a name to the list.
2. Remove a name from the list.
3. Change a name in the list.

4. Print the list.

5. Quit the program.

The user selects one of the operations by entering its number. Entering 4, for example, causes the mailing list to be printed, and entering 5 causes the program to end. The if/else if structure can be used to set up such a menu. After the user enters a number, it compares it to the available selections and executes the statements that perform that operation.

Program 4-14 calculates the charges for membership in a health club. The club has three membership packages to choose from: standard adult membership, child membership, and senior citizen membership. The program presents a menu that allows the user to choose the desired package and then calculates the cost of the membership.

Program 4-14

```
// This program displays a menu and asks the user to make a
// selection. An if/else if statement determines which item
// the user has chosen.

#include <iostream>
#include <iomanip>
using namespace std;

int main()
{
    int choice, months;
    float charges;

    cout << "\t\tHealth Club Membership Menu\n\n";
    cout << "1. Standard Adult Membership\n";
    cout << "2. Child Membership\n";
    cout << "3. Senior Citizen Membership\n";
    cout << "4. Quit the Program\n\n";
    cout << "Enter your choice: ";
    cin >> choice;
    cout << fixed << showpoint << setprecision(2);
    if (choice == 1)
    {
        cout << "For how many months? ";
        cin >> months;
        charges = months * 40.00;
        cout << "The total charges are $" << charges << endl;
    }
    else if (choice == 2)
    {
        cout << "For how many months? ";
        cin >> months;
        charges = months * 20.00;
        cout << "The total charges are $" << charges << endl;
    }
```

(program continues)

Program 4-14 *(continued)*

```cpp
    else if (choice == 3)
    {
        cout << "For how many months? ";
        cin >> months;
        charges = months * 30.00;
        cout << "The total charges are $" << charges << endl;
    }
    else if (choice != 4)
    {
        cout << "The valid choices are 1 through 4. Run the\n";
        cout << "program again and select one of those.\n";
    }
    return 0;
}
```

Program Output with Example Input Shown in Bold
```
    Health Club Membership Menu
1. Standard Adult Membership
2. Child Membership
3. Senior Citizen Membership
4. Quit the Program

Enter your choice: 3[Enter]
For how many months? 6[Enter]
The total charges are $180.00
```

Notice the program also lets the user know when an invalid choice is made. If a number other than 1, 2, 3, or 4 is entered, an error message is printed. This is known as *input validation*.

4.9 Nested `if` Statements

> **CONCEPT** A nested `if` statement is an `if` statement in the conditionally executed code of another `if` statement.

Anytime an `if` statement appears inside another `if` statement, it is considered *nested*. In actuality, the `if`/`else if` structure is a nested `if` statement. Each `if` (after the first one) is nested in the `else` part of the previous `if`.

You may also nest `if`s inside the `if` part, as shown in Program 4-15. Suppose the program is used to determine if a bank customer qualifies for a special interest rate on loans, intended for people who recently graduated from college and are employed.

Program 4-15

```cpp
// This program demonstrates the nested if statement.

#include <iostream>
using namespace std;

int main()
{
    char employed, recentGrad;

    cout << "Answer the following questions\n";
    cout << "with either Y for Yes or ";
    cout << "N for No.\n";
    cout << "Are you employed? ";
    cin >> employed;
    cout << "Have you graduated from college ";
    cout << "in the past two years? ";
    cin >> recentGrad;
    if (employed == 'Y')
    {
        if (recentGrad == 'Y')
        {
            cout << "You qualify for the special ";
            cout << "interest rate.\n";
        }
    }
    return 0;
}
```

Program Output with Example Input Shown in Bold
```
Answer the following questions
with either Y for Yes or N for No.
Are you employed? Y[Enter]
Have you graduated from college in the past two years? Y[Enter]
You qualify for the special interest rate.
```

Program Output with Other Example Input Shown in Bold
```
Answer the following questions
with either Y for Yes or N for No.
Are you employed? Y[Enter]
Have you graduated from college in the past two years? N[Enter]
```

Because the first `if` statement conditionally executes the second one, both the `employed` and `recentGrad` variables must be set to `'Y'` for the message to be printed informing the user he or she qualifies for the special interest rate. This type of nested `if` statement is good for narrowing choices down and categorizing data. The only way the program will execute the second `if` statement is for the conditional expression of the first one to be true.

There is, however, an undesirable feature (otherwise known as a bug) in Program 4-15. If the user enters an `'N'` (or any character other than `'Y'`) for `employed` or `recentGrad`, the program does not print a message letting them know they do not qualify. An `else` statement can be used to remedy this, as illustrated in Program 4-16.

Program 4-16

```cpp
// This program demonstrates the nested if statement.

#include <iostream>
using namespace std;

int main()
{
    char employed, recentGrad;

    cout << "Answer the following questions\n";
    cout << "with either Y for Yes or ";
    cout << "N for No.\n";
    cout << "Are you employed? ";
    cin >> employed;
    cout << "Have you graduated from college ";
    cout << "in the past two years? ";
    cin >> recentGrad;
    if (employed == 'Y')
    {                                           // Nested if
        if (recentGrad == 'Y')                  // Employed and a recent grad
        {
            cout << "You qualify for the special ";
            cout << "interest rate.\n";
        }
        else                                    // Employed but not a recent grad
        {
            cout << "You must have graduated from ";
            cout << "college in the past two\n";
            cout << "years to qualify.\n";
        }
    }
    else                                        // Not employed
    {
        cout << "You must be employed to qualify.\n";
    }
    return 0;
}
```

Program Output with Example Input Shown in Bold
```
Answer the following questions
with either Y for Yes or N for No.
Are you employed? N[Enter]
Have you graduated from college in the past two years? Y[Enter]
You must be employed to qualify.
```
(program output continues)

Program 4-16 *(continued)*

Program Output with Other Example Input Shown in Bold
```
Answer the following questions
with either Y for Yes or N for No.
Are you employed? Y[Enter]
Have you graduated from college in the past two years? N[Enter]
You must have graduated from college in the past two
years to qualify.
```

Program Output with Other Example Input Shown in Bold
```
Answer the following questions
with either Y for Yes or N for No.
Are you employed? Y[Enter]
Have you graduated from college in the past two years? Y[Enter]
You qualify for the special interest rate.
```

 Note: When you are debugging a program with nested `if`/`else` statements, it's important to know which `if` statement each `else` belongs to. The rule for matching `else`s with `if`s is that an `else` goes with the last `if` statement that doesn't have its own `else`. This is easier to see when the `if` statements are properly indented. Each `else` should be lined up with the `if` it belongs to. These visual cues are important because nested `if` statements can be very long and complex.

 ## Checkpoint [4.6–4.9]

4.16 Program 4-13 asks the user for a numeric test score and displays the letter grade for that score. Modify it so an error message is displayed if the user enters a test score less than 0.

4.17 What will the following program display?

```cpp
#include <iostream>
using namespace std;

int main()
{
   int funny = 7, serious = 15;

   funny = serious % 2;
   if (funny != 1)
   {
      funny = 0;
      serious = 0;
   }
   else if (funny == 2)
   {
      funny = 10;
      serious = 10;
   }
```

```
      else
      {
         funny = 1;
         serious = 1;
      }
      cout << funny << serious << endl;
      return 0;
   }
```

4.18 The following program is used in a bookstore to determine how many discount coupons a customer gets. Complete the table that appears after the program.

```
#include <iostream>
using namespace std;

int main()
{
   int numBooks, numCoupons;

   cout << "How many books are being purchased? ";
   cin >> numBooks;
   if (numBooks < 1)
      numCoupons = 0;
   else if (numBooks < 3)
      numCoupons = 1;
   else if (numBooks < 5)
      numCoupons = 2;
   else
      numCoupons = 3;
      cout << "The number of coupons to give is " << numCoupons
           << endl;
   return 0;
}
```

If the Customer Purchases This Many Books...	...This Many Coupons Are Given.
1	
2	
3	
4	
5	
10	

4.19 Write nested if statements that perform the following test: If amount1 is greater than 10 and amount2 is less than 100, display the greater of the two.

4.10   Logical Operators

CONCEPT   Logical operators connect two or more relational expressions into one or reverse the logic of an expression.

In the previous section you saw how a program tests two conditions with two `if` statements. In this section you will see how to use logical operators to combine two or more relational expressions into one. Table 4-6 lists C++'s logical operators.

Table 4-6

Operator	Meaning	Effect
`&&`	AND	Connects two expressions into one. Both expressions must be true for the overall expression to be true.
`||`	OR	Connects two expressions into one. One or both expressions must be true for the overall expression to be true. It is only necessary for one to be true, and it does not matter which.
`!`	NOT	The ! operator reverses the "truth" of an expression. It makes a true expression false, and a false expression true.

The `&&` Operator

The `&&` operator is known as the logical AND operator. It takes two expressions as operands and creates an expression that is true only when both sub-expressions are true. Here is an example of an `if` statement that uses the `&&` operator:

```
if (temperature < 20 && minutes > 12)
    cout << "The temperature is in the danger zone.";
```

Notice that both of the expressions being ANDed together are complete expressions that evaluate to true or false. First `temperature < 20` is evaluated to produce a true or false result. Then `minutes > 12` is evaluated to produce a true or false result. Then, finally, these two results are ANDed together to arrive at a final result for the entire expression. The `cout` statement will only be executed if `temperature` is less than 20 AND `minutes` is greater than 12. If either relational test is false, the entire expression is false and the `cout` statement is not executed.

Table 4-7 shows a truth table for the `&&` operator. The truth table lists all the possible combinations of values that two expressions may have, and the resulting value returned by the `&&` operator connecting the two expressions. As the table shows, both sub-expressions must be true for the `&&` operator to return a true value.

Table 4-7   Logical AND

Expression 1	Expression 2	Expression 1 && Expression 2
false	false	false (0)
false	true	false (0)
true	false	false (0)
true	true	true (1)

 Note: If the sub-expression on the left side of an && operator is false, the expression on the right side will not be checked. Since the entire expression is false if only one of the sub-expressions is false, it would waste CPU time to check the remaining expression.

The && operator can be used to simplify programs that otherwise would use nested if statements. Program 4-17 is a version of Program 4-16, rewritten with a logical operator.

Program 4-17

```cpp
// This program demonstrates the && logical operator.

#include <iostream>
using namespace std;

int main()
{
    char employed, recentGrad;

    cout << "Answer the following questions\n";
    cout << "with either Y for Yes or ";
    cout << "N for No.\n";
    cout << "Are you employed? ";
    cin >> employed;
    cout << "Have you graduated from college ";
    cout << "in the past two years? ";
    cin >> recentGrad;
    if (employed == 'Y' && recentGrad == 'Y')      // Uses the && logical operator
    {
        cout << "You qualify for the special ";
        cout << "interest rate.\n";
    }
    else
    {
        cout << "You must be employed and have \n";
        cout << "graduated from college in the\n";
        cout << "past two years to qualify.\n";
    }
    return 0;
}
```

Program 4-17

Program Output with Example Input Shown in Bold
Answer the following questions
with either Y for Yes or N for No.
Are you employed? **Y[Enter]**
Have you graduated from college in the past two years? **N[Enter]**
You must be employed and have
graduated from college in the
past two years to qualify.

Program Output with Other Example Input Shown in Bold
Answer the following questions
with either Y for Yes or N for No.
Are you employed? **N[Enter]**
Have you graduated from college in the past two years? **Y[Enter]**
You must be employed and have
graduated from college in the
past two years to qualify.

Program Output with Other Example Input Shown in Bold
Answer the following questions
with either Y for Yes or N for No.
Are you employed? **Y[Enter]**
Have you graduated from college in the past two years? **Y[Enter]**
You qualify for the special interest rate.

Note that while this program is similar to Program 4-16, it is not the logical equivalent. In Program 4-17 the message "You qualify for the special interest rate" is displayed when both the expressions `employed == 'Y'` and `recentGrad == 'Y'` are true. If either of these are false, the message "You must be employed and have graduated from college in the past two years to qualify." is printed. Program 4-17 does not display the message "You must be employed to qualify."

The || Operator

The || operator is known as the logical OR operator. It takes two expressions as operands and creates an expression that is true when either of the sub-expressions are true. Here is an example of an if statement that uses the || operator:

```
if (temperature < 20 || temperature > 100)
    cout << "The temperature is in the danger zone.";
```

The cout statement will be executed if temperature is less than 20 OR temperature is greater than 100. If either relational test is true, the entire expression is true and the cout statement is executed.

Note: The two things being ORed should both be logical expressions that evaluate to true or false. It would not be correct to write the if condition as

```
if (temperature < 20 || > 100)
```

 Note: There is no || key on the computer keyboard. Use two | symbols. This symbol is on the backslash key. Press Shift and backslash to print it.

Table 4-8 shows a truth table for the || operator.

Table 4-8   Logical OR

Expression 1	Expression 2	Expression 1 || Expression 2
false	false	false (0)
false	true	true (1)
true	false	true (1)
true	true	true (1)

All it takes for an OR expression to be true is for one of the sub-expressions to be true. It doesn't matter if the other sub-expression is false or true.

 Note: If the sub-expression on the left side of an || operator is true, the expression on the right side will not be checked. Since it's only necessary for one of the sub-expressions to be true, it would waste CPU time to check the remaining expression.

Program 4-18 performs additional tests to qualify a person for a loan. This one determines if the customer earns at least $35,000 per year or has been employed for more than five years.

Program 4-18

```
// This program asks the user for their annual income and
// the number of years they have been employed at their current
// job. The || operator is used in an if statement that
// determines if the income is at least $35,000 or their time
// on the job is more than 5 years.

#include <iostream>
using namespace std;
```

(program continues)

Program 4-18 *(continued)*

```
int main()
{
    float income;
    int years;

    cout << "What is your annual income? ";
    cin >> income;
    cout << "How many years have you worked at "
         << "your current job? ";

    cin >> years;
    if (income >= 35000 || years > 5)             //Uses the || logical operator
        cout << "You qualify.\n";
    else
    {
        cout << "You must earn at least $35,000 or have\n";
        cout << "been employed for more than 5 years.\n";
    }
    return 0;
}
```

Program Output with Example Input Shown in Bold
```
What is your annual income? 40000[Enter]
How many years have you worked at your current job? 2[Enter]
You qualify.
```

Program Output with Other Example Input Shown in Bold
```
What is your annual income? 20000[Enter]
How many years have you worked at your current job? 7[Enter]
You qualify.
```

Program Output with Other Example Input Shown in Bold
```
What is your annual income? 30000[Enter]
How many years have you worked at your current job? 3[Enter]
You must earn at least $35,000 or have
been employed for more than 5 years.
```

The message "You qualify." is displayed when either or both the expressions income >= 35000 or years > 5 are true. If both of these are false, the disqualifying message is printed.

The ! Operator

The ! operator performs a logical NOT operation. It takes an operand and reverses its truth or falsehood. In other words, if the expression is true, the ! operator returns false, and if the expression is false, it returns true. Here is an if statement using the ! operator:

```
if (!(temperature > 100))
    cout << "You are below the maximum temperature.\n";
```

First, the expression (temperature > 100) is tested to be true or false. Then the ! operator is applied to that value. If the expression (temperature > 100) is true, the ! operator returns false. If it is false, the ! operator returns true. In the example, it is equivalent to asking "is the temperature not greater than 100?"

Table 4-9 shows a truth table for the ! operator.

Table 4-9   Logical NOT

Expression	!(Expression)
false	true (1)
true	false (0)

Program 4-19 performs the same task as Program 4-18. The if statement, however, uses the ! operator to determine if the user does *not* make at least $35,000 or has *not* been on the job more than five years.

Program 4-19

```
// This program asks the user for their annual income and
// the number years they have been employed at their current
// job. The ! operator reverses the logic of the expression
// in the if/else statement.

#include <iostream>
using namespace std;

int main()
{
    float income;
    int years;

    cout << "What is your annual income? ";
    cin >> income;
    cout << "How many years have you worked at "
        << "your current job? ";
    cin >> years;
    if (!(income >= 35000 || years > 5))     // Uses the ! operator
    {
        cout << "You must earn at least $35,000 or have\n";
        cout << "been employed for more than 5 years.\n";
    }
    else
        cout << "You qualify.\n";
    return 0;
}
```

Program Output 4-19 is the same as that of Program 4-18.

Boolean Variables and the ! Operator

An interesting feature of a Boolean variable is that its value can be tested just by naming it. Suppose `moreData` is a Boolean variable. Then the test

```
if (moreData == true)
```

can be written simply as

```
if (moreData)
```

and the test

```
if(moreData == false)
```

can be written simply as

```
if(!moreData)
```

This is a common use of the ! operator.

Precedence and Associativity of Logical Operators

Table 4-10 shows the precedence of C++'s logical operators, from highest to lowest.

Table 4-10

Logical Operators in Order of Precedence
!
&&
||

The ! operator has a higher precedence than many of the C++ operators. Therefore, to avoid an error, it is a good idea always to enclose its operand in parentheses, unless you intend to apply it to a variable or a simple expression with no other operators. For example, consider the following expressions:

```
!(x > 2)
!x > 2
```

The first expression applies the ! operator to the expression x > 2. It is asking "is x not greater than 2?" The second expression, however, applies the ! operator to x only. It is asking "is the logical negation of x greater than 2?" Suppose x is set to 5. Since 5 is nonzero, it would be considered true, so the ! operator would reverse it to false, which is 0. The > operator would then determine if 0 is greater than 2. To avoid a catastrophe like this, it is wise to always use parentheses!

The && and || operators rank lower in precedence than relational operators, which means that relational expressions are evaluated before their results are logically ANDed or ORed.

```
a > b && x < y    is the same as    (a > b) && (x < y)
a > b || x < y    is the same as    (a > b) || (x < y)
```

Thus you don't normally need parentheses when mixing relational operators with && and ||, although it does not hurt to use them if you wish.

Parentheses are again recommended, however, anytime && and || operators are both used in the same expression. This is because && has a higher precedence than ||. Without parentheses to indicate which you want done first, && will always be done before ||, which might not be what you intended. Assume recentGrad, employed, and goodCredit are three Boolean variables. Then, the expression

```
recentGrad || employed && goodCredit
```

is the same as

```
recentGrad ||(employed && goodCredit)
```

and not the same as

```
(recentGrad || employed)&& goodCredit
```

4.11 Checking Numeric Ranges with Logical Operators

CONCEPT Logical operators are effective for determining if a number is in or out of a range.

When determining if a number is inside a numeric range, it's best to use the && operator. For example, the following if statement checks the value in x to determine if it is in the range of 20 through 40:

```
if (x >= 20 && x <= 40)
    cout << x << " is in the acceptable range.\n";
```

The expression in the if statement will be true only when x is both greater than or equal to 20 AND less than or equal to 40. x must be within the range of 20 through 40 for this expression to be true.

When determining if a number is outside a range, the || operator is best to use. The following statement determines if x is outside the range of 20 to 40:

```
if (x < 20 || x > 40)
    cout << x << " is outside the acceptable range.\n";
```

It's important not to get the logic of these logical operators confused. For example, the following if statement would never test true:

```
if (x < 20 && x > 40)
    cout << x << " is outside the acceptable range.\n";
```

Obviously, x can never be less than 20 and at the same time greater than 40.

 Note: C++ does not allow you to check numeric ranges with expressions such as 5 < x < 20. Instead, you must use a logical operator to connect two relational expressions, as previously discussed.

 ## Checkpoint [4.10–4.11]

4.20 The following truth table shows various combinations of the values true and false connected by a logical operator. Complete the table by indicating if the result of such a combination is true or false.

Logical Expression	Result (true or false)
true && false	
true && true	
false && true	
false && false	
true || false	
true || true	
false || true	
false || false	
!true	
!false	

4.21 Assume the variables a = 2, b = 4, and c = 6. Indicate by circling the T or F if each of the following conditions is true or false:

```
A)    a == 4 || b > 2     T   F
B)    6 <= c && a > 3     T   F
C)    1 != b && c != 3    T   F
D)    a >= -1 || a <= b   T   F
E)    !(a > 2)            T   F
```

4.22 Assume the variables a = 2, b = 4, and c = 6. Is the following expression true or false?

```
b > a || b > c && c == 5
```

4.23 Rewrite the following using the ! operator.

```
if (activeEmployee == false)
```

4.24 Write an if statement that prints the message "The number is not valid" if the variable speed is outside the range 0 through 200.

4.12 Validating User Input

CONCEPT As long as the user of a program enters bad input, the program will produce bad output. Programs should be written to filter out bad input.

Perhaps the most famous saying of the computer world is "garbage in, garbage out." The integrity of a program's output is only as good as its input, so you should try to make sure garbage does not go into your programs. *Input validation* is the process of inspecting information given to a program by the user and determining if it is valid. A good program should give clear instructions about the kind of input that is acceptable, and not assume the user has followed those instructions. Here are just a few examples of input validations performed by programs:

♦ Numbers are checked to ensure they are within a range of possible values. For example, there are 168 hours in a week. It is not possible for a person to be at work longer than 168 hours in one week.

♦ Values are checked for their "reasonableness." Although it might be possible for a person to be at work for 168 hours per week, it is not probable.

♦ Items selected from a menu or some other set of choices are checked to ensure they are available options.

♦ Variables are checked for values that might cause problems, such as division by zero.

Program 4-20 is a modification of Program 4-11, the test-score program. It rejects any test score less than 0 or greater than 100.

Program 4-20

```cpp
// This program uses an if/else if statement to assign a
// letter grade (A, B, C, D, or F) to a numeric test score.

#include <iostream>
using namespace std;

int main()
{
    int testScore;
    char grade;

    cout << "Enter your test score and I will tell you\n";
    cout << "the letter grade you earned: ";
    cin >> testScore;
    if (testScore < 0 || testScore > 100)
    {
        cout << testScore << " is an invalid score.\n";
        cout << "Run the program again and enter a value\n";
        cout << "in the range of 0 to 100.\n";
    }
```

(program continues)

Program 4-20   *(continued)*

```
    else
    {
        if (testScore < 60)
            grade = 'F';
        else if (testScore < 70)
            grade = 'D';
        else if (testScore < 80)
            grade = 'C';
        else if (testScore < 90)
            grade = 'B';
        else if (testScore <= 100)
            grade = 'A';
        cout << "Your grade is " << grade << endl;
    }
    return 0;
}
```

Program Output with Example Input Shown in Bold
```
Enter your test score and I will tell you
the letter grade you earned: -12[Enter]
-12 is an invalid score.
Run the program again and enter a value
in the range of 0 to 100.
```

Program Output with Other Example Input Shown in Bold
```
Enter your test score and I will tell you
the letter grade you earned: 81[Enter]
Your grade is B
```

In Chapter 5 you will learn about an even better way to validate input data.

4.13   More About Variable Definitions and Scope

CONCEPT   The scope of a variable is limited to the block in which it is defined.

C++ allows you to create variables almost anywhere in a program. It is a common practice to define all of a function's variables at the top of the function. However, especially in longer programs, variables are sometimes defined near the part of the program where they are used. This makes the purpose of the variable more evident. Program 4-21 is a modification of Program 4-18, which determines if the user qualifies for a loan. The definitions of the variables income and years have been moved to later points in the program.

Program 4-21A

```
// This program demonstrates late variable declaration.

#include <iostream>
using namespace std;

int main()
{
    cout << "What is your annual income? ";
    float income;                          // Variable definition
    cin >> income;
    cout << "How many years have you worked at "
        << "your current job? ";
    int years;                             // Variable definition
    cin >> years;
    if (income >= 35000 || years > 5)
        cout << "You qualify.\n";
    else
    {
        cout << "You must earn at least $35,000 or have\n";
        cout << "been employed for more than 5 years.\n";
    }
    return 0;
}
```

Recall from Chapter 2 that the scope of a variable is defined as the part of the program where the variable may be used. Program 4-21B shows the scope of the variable income as a shaded area.

Program 4-21B

```
// This program demonstrates late variable declaration.
#include <iostream>
using namespace std;

int main()
{
    cout << "What is your annual income? ";

    float income;                          // Variable definition
    cin >> income;
    cout << "How many years have you worked at "
        << "your current job? ";
    int years;                             // Variable definition
    cin >> years;
    if (income >= 35000 || years > 5)
        cout << "You qualify.\n";
```

(program continues)

Program 4-21B *(continued)*

```
    else
    {
        cout << "You must earn at least $35,000 or have\n";
        cout << "been employed for more than 5 years.\n";
    }
    return 0;

}
```

Program 4-21C highlights the scope of the variable `years`.

Program 4-21C

```
// This program demonstrates late variable declaration.
#include <iostream>
using namespace std;

int main()
{
    cout << "What is your annual income? ";
    float income;                              // Variable definition
    cin >> income;
    cout << "How many years have you worked at "
        << "your current job? ";

    int years;
    cin >> years;                              // Variable definition
    if (income >= 35000 || years > 5)
        cout << "You qualify.\n";
    else
    {
        cout << "You must earn at least $35,000 or have\n";
        cout << "been employed for more than 5 years.\n";
    }
    return 0;

}
```

The variables `income` and `years` are defined inside function `main`'s braces. Variables defined inside a set of braces are said to have *local scope* or *block scope*. They may only be used in the part of the program between their definition and the block's closing brace.

You may define variables inside any block. For example, look at Program 4-22. This version of the loan program has the variable `years` defined inside the block of the `if` statement. The scope of `years` is shaded.

Program 4-22

```cpp
// This program demonstrates a variable declared in an inner block.
#include <iostream>
using namespace std;

int main()
{
    cout << "What is your annual income? ";
    float income;                                // Variable definition
    cin >> income;
    if (income >= 35000)
    {
        cout << "How many years have you worked at "
             << "your current job? ";

        int years;                               // Variable definition
        cin >> years;
        if (years > 5)
            cout << "You qualify.\n";
        else
        {
            cout << "You must have been employed for\n";
            cout << "more than 5 years to qualify.\n";
        }
    }
    else
    {
        cout << "You must earn at least $35,000 to\n";
        cout << "qualify.\n";
    }
    return 0;
}
```

Notice the scope of `years` is only from the point of its definition to the end of the block in which it is defined. The variable is not visible before its definition or after the closing brace of the block. This is true of any variable defined inside a set of braces.

 Note: When a program is running and it enters the section of code that constitutes a variable's scope, it is said that the variable *comes into scope*. This simply means the variable is now visible and the program may reference it. Likewise, when a variable *leaves scope*, it may no longer be used.

Variables with the Same Name

When a block is nested inside another block, a variable defined in the inner block may have the same name as a variable defined in the outer block. As long as the variable in the inner block is visible, however, the variable in the outer block will be hidden. This is illustrated by Program 4-23.

Program 4-23

```cpp
// This program uses two variables with the same name.

#include <iostream>
using namespace std;

int main()
{
    int number;                              // Variable definition

    cout << "Enter a number greater than 0: ";
    cin >> number;
    if (number > 0)
    {
        int number;                          // Variable definition
        cout << "Now enter another number: ";
        cin >> number;
        cout << "The second number you entered was ";
        cout << number << endl;
    }
    cout << "Your first number was " << number << endl;
    return 0;
}
```

Program Output with Example Input Shown in Bold
```
Enter a number greater than 0: 2[Enter]
Now enter another number: 7[Enter]
The second number you entered was 7
Your first number was 2
```

Program 4-23 has two separate variables named number. The cin and cout statements in the inner block (belonging to the if statement) can only work with the number variable defined in that block. As soon as the program leaves that block, the inner number goes out of scope, revealing the outer number variable.

 WARNING! Although it's perfectly acceptable to define variables inside nested blocks, you should avoid giving them the same names as variables in the outer blocks. It's too easy to confuse one variable with another.

Checkpoint [4.12–4.13]

4.25 The following program skeleton asks the user for two numbers and then multiplies them. The first should be negative and the second should be positive. Write the input validation code for both numbers.

```cpp
#include <iostream>
using namespace std;

int main()
```

```
{
    int first, second, result;
    cout << "Enter a negative integer: ";
    cin >> first;
    cout << "Now enter a positive integer: ";
    cin >> second;
    //
    // Write input validation code
    //
    result = first * second;
    cout << first << " times " << second << " is "
         << result << endl;
    return 0;
}
```

4.26 Find and fix the errors in the following program.

```
#include <iostream>
using namespace std;

int main()
{
    cout << "This program calculates the area of a "
         << "rectangle. Enter the length: ";
    cin >> length;
    cout << "enter the width: ";
    cin >> width;
    int length, width, area;
    area = length * width;
    cout << "The area is " << area << endl;
    return 0;
}
```

4.27 What will the following program display if the user enters 40 for `test1` and 30 for `test2`?

```
#include <iostream>
using namespace std;

int main()
{
    cout << "Enter your first test score: ";
    int test1;
    cin >> test1;
    cout << "Enter your second test score: ";
    int test2;
    cin >> test2;
    int sum = test1 + test2;
    if (sum > 50)
    {
        test1 += 10;
        test2 += 10;
        int sum = test1 + test2;
    }
```

```
cout << "test 1: " << test1 << endl;
cout << "test 2: " << test2 << endl;
cout << "sum    : " << sum << endl;
return 0;
}
```

4.14 Comparing Characters and Strings

CONCEPT | Relational operators can also be used to compare characters and string objects.

Earlier in this chapter you learned to use relational operators to compare numeric values. They can also be used to compare characters and string objects.

Comparing Characters

As you learned in Chapter 3, characters are actually stored in memory as integers. On most systems, this integer is the ASCII value of the character.[2] For example, the letter 'A' is represented by the number 65, the letter 'B' is represented by the number 66, and so on. Table 4-11 shows the ASCII numbers that correspond to some of the commonly used characters.

Table 4-11 ASCII Values of Commonly Used Characters

Character	ASCII value
'0'–'9'	48–57
'A'–'Z'	65–90
'a'–'z'	97–122
blank	32
period	46

Notice that every character, even the blank, has an ASCII code associated with it. Notice also that the ASCII code of a character representing a digit, such as '1' or '2', is not the same as the value of the digit itself. A complete table showing the ASCII values for all characters can be found in Appendix A.

When two characters are compared, it is actually their ASCII values that are being compared. 'A' < 'B' because the ASCII value of 'A' (65) is less than the ASCII value of 'B' (66). Likewise '1' < '2' because the ASCII value of '1' (49) is less than the ASCII value of '2' (50). However, as shown in Table 4-11, lowercase letters have higher numbers than uppercase letters, so 'a' > 'Z'. Program 4-24, which is similar to Program 4-14, shows how characters can be compared with relational operators.

---

[2] A few systems use other character encoding methods (such as EBCDIC), but examples in this text use the ASCII character set.

Program 4-24

```cpp
// This program displays a menu with letters representing selections.
// It compares characters with relational operators.

#include <iostream>
#include <iomanip>
using namespace std;

int main()
{
    char   choice;
    int    months;
    float  charges;

    cout << "   Health Club Membership Menu\n";
    cout << "A. Standard Adult Membership\n";
    cout << "B. Child Membership\n";
    cout << "C. Senior Citizen Membership\n";
    cout << "D. Quit the Program\n\n";
    cout << "Enter your choice: ";
    cin.get(choice);

    cout << fixed << showpoint << setprecision(2);

    if (choice < 'A' || choice > 'D')
    {   cout << "The valid choices are A through D.\n";
        cout << "Run the program again and select one of those.\n";
    }
    else if (choice == 'A')
    {   cout << "For how many months? ";
        cin >> months;
        charges = months * 40.00;
        cout << "The total charges are $" << charges << endl;
    }
    else if (choice == 'B')
    {   cout << "For how many months? ";
        cin >> months;
        charges = months * 20.00;
        cout << "The total charges are $" << charges << endl;
    }
    else if (choice == 'C')
    {   cout << "For how many months? ";
        cin >> months;
        charges = months * 30.00;
        cout << "The total charges are $" << charges << endl;
    }
    return 0;
}
```

Program 4-24

Program Output with Example Input Shown in Bold
```
    Health Club Membership Menu
A. Standard Adult Membership
B. Child Membership
C. Senior Citizen Membership
D. Quit the Program

Enter your choice: C[Enter]
For how many months? 6[Enter]
The total charges are $180.00
```

Comparing String Objects

String objects can also be compared with relational operators. As with individual characters, when two strings are compared, it is actually the ASCII value of the characters making up the strings that are being compared.

For example, assume the following definitions exist in a program:

```
string set1 = "ABC";
string set2 = "XYZ";
```

The object set1 is considered less than the object set2 because the characters "ABC" alphabetically precede (have lower ASCII values than) the characters "XYZ". So, the following if statement will cause the message "set1 is less than set2." to be displayed on the screen.

```
if (set1 < set2)
    cout << "set1 is less than set2.";
```

One by one, each character in the first operand is compared with the character in the corresponding position in the second operand. If all the characters in both strings match, the two strings are equal. Other relationships can be determined if two characters in corresponding positions do not match. The first operand is less than the second operand if the mismatched character in the first operand is less than its counterpart in the second operand. Likewise, the first operand is greater than the second operand if the mismatched character in the first operand is greater than its counterpart in the second operand.

For example, assume a program has the following definitions:

```
string name1 = "Mary";
string name2 = "Mark";
```

The value in name1, "Mary", is greater than the value in name2, "Mark". This is because the first three characters in name1 have the same ASCII values as the first three characters in name2, but the 'y' in the fourth position of "Mary" has a greater ASCII value than the 'k' in the corresponding position of "Mark".

Any of the relational operators can be used to compare two string objects. Here are some of the valid comparisons of `name1` and `name2`.

```
name1 > name2        // true
name1 <= name2       // false
name1 != name2       // true
```

String objects can also, of course, be compared to string constants:

```
name1 < "Mary Jane"  // true
```

Program 4-25 further demonstrates how relational operators can be used to compare string objects.

Program 4-25

```cpp
// This program uses relational operators to compare a string
// entered by the user with valid stereo part numbers.

#include <iostream>
#include <iomanip>
#include <string>
using namespace std;

int main()
{
    const float aPrice = 249.0,
                bPrice = 299.0;
    string partNum;

    cout << "The stereo part numbers are:\n";
    cout << "Boom Box   : part number S147-29A \n";
    cout << "Shelf Model: part number S147-29B \n";
    cout << "Enter the part number of the stereo you\n";
    cout << "wish to purchase: ";
    cin  >> partNum;
    cout << fixed << showpoint << setprecision(2);
    if (partNum == "S147-29A")
        cout << "The price is $" << aPrice << endl;
    else if (partNum == "S147-29B")
        cout << "The price is $" << bPrice << endl;
    else
        cout << partNum << " is not a valid part number.\n";
    return 0;
}
```

Program 4-25

Program Output with Example Input Shown in Bold
```
The stereo part numbers are:
Boom Box   : part number S147-29A
Shelf Model: part number S147-29B
Enter the part number of the stereo you
wish to purchase: S147-29A[Enter]
The price is $249.00
```

> **Note:** C-strings, unlike string objects, cannot be compared with relational operators. To compare C-strings (i.e., strings defined as arrays of characters) you must use the `strcmp` function, which is introduced in Chapter 12.

Checkpoint [4.14]

4.28 Indicate whether each of the following relational expressions is true or false. Refer to the ASCII table in Appendix A if necessary.

```
A) 'a' <  'z'
B) 'a' == 'A'
C) '5' <  '7'
D) 'a' <  'A'
E) '1' ==  1
F) '1' == 49
```

4.29 Indicate whether each of the following relational expressions is true or false. Refer to the ASCII table in Appendix A if necessary.

```
A) "Bill" == "BILL"
B) "Bill" <  "BILL"
C) "Bill" <  "Bob"
D) "189" >  "23"
E) "189" >  "Bill"
F) "Mary" <  "MaryEllen"
G) "MaryEllen" < "Mary Ellen"
```

4.15 The Conditional Operator

> **CONCEPT** You can use the conditional operator to create short expressions that work like `if/else` statements.

The conditional operator is powerful and unique. It provides a shorthand method of expressing a simple `if/else` statement. The operator consists of the question-mark (?) and the colon(:). Its format is

```
expression ? expression : expression;
```

Here is an example of a statement using the conditional operator:

```
x < 0 ? y = 10 : z = 20;
```

This statement is called a *conditional expression* and consists of three sub-expressions separated by the ? and : symbols. The expressions are x < 0, y = 10, and z = 20.

```
  x < 0        ?        y = 10       :        z = 20;
```

Note: Since it takes three operands, the conditional operator is considered a *ternary* operator.

The conditional expression above performs the same operation as the following if/else statement:

```
if (x < 0)
    y = 10;
else
    z = 20;
```

The part of the conditional expression that comes before the question mark is the expression to be tested. It's like the expression in the parentheses of an if statement. If the expression is true, the part of the statement between the ? and the : is executed. Otherwise, the part after the : is executed. Figure 4-3 illustrates the roles played by the three sub-expressions.

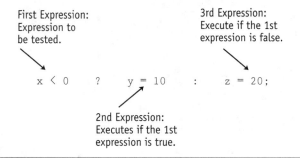

Figure 4-3

If it helps, you can put parentheses around the sub-expressions, as in the following:

```
(x < 0) ? (y = 10) : (z = 20);
```

Using the Value of a Conditional Expression

Remember, in C++ all expressions have a value, and this includes the conditional expression. If the first sub-expression is true, the value of the conditional expression is the value of the second sub-expression. Otherwise it is the value of the third sub-expression. Here is an example of an assignment statement using the value of a conditional expression:

```
a = x > 100 ? 0 : 1;
```

The value assigned to a will be either 0 or 1, depending upon whether x is greater than 100. This statement could be expressed as the following if/else statement:

```
if (x > 100)
    a = 0;
else
    a = 1;
```

Program 4-26 can be used to help a consultant calculate her charges. Her rate is $50.00 per hour, but her minimum charge is for five hours. The conditional operator is used in a statement that ensures the number of hours does not go below five.

Program 4-26

```
// This program calculates a consultant's charges at $50
// per hour, for a minimum of 5 hours. The ?: operator
// adjusts hours to 5 if less than 5 hours were worked.

#include <iostream>
#include <iomanip>
using namespace std;

int main()
{
    const float payRate = 50.0;
    float hours, charges;

    cout << "How many hours were worked? ";
    cin >> hours;
    hours = hours < 5 ? 5 : hours;          // Conditional operator
    charges = payRate * hours;
    cout << fixed << showpoint << setprecision(2);
    cout << "The charges are $" << charges << endl;
    return 0;
}
```

Program Output with Example Input Shown in Bold
```
How many hours were worked? 10[Enter]
The charges are $500.00
```

Program Output with Other Example Input Shown in Bold
```
How many hours were worked? 2[Enter]
The charges are $250.00
```

Here is the statement with the conditional expression:

```
hours = hours < 5 ? 5 : hours;
```

If the value in `hours` is less than 5, then 5 is stored in `hours`. Otherwise `hours` is assigned the value it already has. `hours` will not have a value less than 5 when it is used in the next statement, which calculates the consultant's charges.

As you can see, the conditional operator gives you the ability to pack decision-making power into a concise line of code. With a little imagination it can be applied to many other programming problems. For instance, consider the following statement:

```
cout << "Your grade is: " << (score < 60 ? "Fail." : "Pass.");
```

If you were to use an `if/else` statement, this statement would be written as follows:

```
if (score < 60)
    cout << "Your grade is: Fail.";
else
    cout << "Your grade is: Pass.";
```

 Note: The parentheses are placed around the conditional expression because the `<<` operator has higher precedence than the `?:` operator. Without the parentheses, just the value of the expression `score < 60` would be sent to `cout`.

Checkpoint   [4.15]

4.30 Rewrite the following `if/else` statements as conditional expressions.

A)
```
if (x > y)
    z = 1;
else
    z = 20;
```

B)
```
if (temp > 45)
    population = base * 10;
else
    population = base * 2;
```

C)
```
if (hours > 40)
    wages *= 1.5;
else
    wages *= 1;
```

D)
```
if (result >= 0)
    cout << "The result is positive\n";
        else
            cout << "The result is negative.\n";
```

4.31 Rewrite the following conditional expressions as `if/else` statements.

A)   `j = k > 90 ? 57 : 12;`

B)   `factor = x >= 10 ? y * 22 : y * 35;`

```
C)    total += count == 1 ? sales : count * sales;
D)    cout << ((num % 2) == 0) ? "Even\n" : "Odd\n");
```

4.32 What will the following program display?

```
#include <iostream>
using namespace std;

int main()
{
   const int upper = 8, lower = 2;
   int num1, num2, num3 = 12, num4 = 3;

   num1 = num3 < num4 ? upper : lower;
   num2 = num4 > upper ? num3 : lower;
   cout << num1 << " " <<  num2 << endl;
   return 0;
}
```

4.16 The switch Statement

> **CONCEPT** The switch statement lets the value of a variable or expression determine where the program will branch to.

A branch occurs when one part of a program causes another part to execute. The if/else if statement allows your program to branch into one of several possible paths. It performs a series of tests (usually relational) and branches when one of these tests is true. The switch statement is a similar mechanism. It, however, tests the value of an integer expression and then uses that value to determine which set of statements to branch to. Here is the format of the switch statement:

```
switch (integer expression)
{
   case constant-expression:   // Place one or more statements here.

   case constant-expression:   // Place one or more statements here.

   // Case statements may be repeated as
   // many times as necessary.

   case constant-expression:   // Place one or more statements here.

   default:                    // Place one or more statements here.
}
```

The first line of the statement starts with the word switch, followed by an integer expression inside parentheses. This can be either of the following:

 ◆ A variable of any of the integer data types (including char)

 ◆ An expression whose value is of any of the integer data types

On the next line is the beginning of a block containing several `case` statements. Each `case` statement is formatted in the following manner:

```
case constant expression:    // Place one or more statements here.
```

After the word `case` is a constant expression (which must be of an integer type), followed by a colon. The expression cannot be a variable and it cannot be a Boolean expression such as x < 22 or n == 25. The `case` statement marks the beginning of a section of statements. These statements are branched to if the value of the `switch` expression matches that of the `case` expression.

 WARNING! The expressions of each `case` statement in the block must be unique.

An optional `default` section comes after all the `case` statements. This section is branched to if none of the `case` expressions match the switch expression. Thus it functions like a trailing `else` in an `if/else if` statement.

Program 4-27 shows how a simple `switch` statement works.

Program 4-27

```
// The switch statement in this program tells the user something
// he or she already knows: what they just entered!

#include <iostream>
using namespace std;

int main()
{
    char choice;

    cout << "Enter A, B, or C: ";
    cin >> choice;
    switch (choice)
    {
        case 'A':  cout << "You entered A.\n";
                   break;
        case 'B':  cout << "You entered B.\n";
                   break;
        case 'C':  cout << "You entered C.\n";
                   break;
        default:   cout << "You did not enter A, B, or C!\n";
    }
    return 0;
}
```

Program Output with Example Input Shown in Bold
```
Enter A, B, or C: B[Enter]
You entered B.
```

Program Output with Different Example Input Shown in Bold
```
Enter A, B, or C: F[Enter]
You did not enter A, B, or C!
```

The first case statement is case 'A':, the second is case 'B':, and the third is case 'C':. These statements mark where the program is to branch to if the variable choice contains the values 'A', 'B', or 'C'. (Remember, character variables and constants are considered integers.) The default section is branched to if the user enters anything other than A, B, or C.

Notice the break statements that are in the case 'A', case 'B', and case 'C' sections.

```
switch (choice)
{
    case 'A':cout << "You entered A.\n";
            break;    ◄───────
    case 'B':cout << "You entered B.\n";
            break;    ◄───────
    case 'C':cout << "You entered C.\n";
            break;    ◄───────
    default:cout << "You did not enter A, B, or C!\n";
}
```

The break statement causes the program to exit the switch statement. The next statement executed after encountering a break statement will be whatever statement follows the closing brace that terminates the switch statement. A break statement is needed whenever you want to "break out of" a switch statement because it is not automatically exited after carrying out a set of statements the way an if/else if statement is.

The case statements show the program where to start executing in the block and the break statements show the program where to stop. Without the break statements, the program would execute all of the lines from the matching case statement to the end of the block.

 Note: The default section (or the last case section, if there is no default) does not need a break statement. Some programmers prefer to put one there anyway, for consistency.

Program 4-28 is a modification of Program 4-27 that illustrates what happens if the break statements are omitted.

Program 4-28

```
// The switch statement in this program tells the user something
// he or she already knows: what they just entered!

#include <iostream>
using namespace std;

int main()
{
    char choice;
```

(program continues)

Program 4-28 *(continued)*

```cpp
    cout << "Enter A, B, or C: ";
    cin >> choice;

    // The following switch statement is missing its break statements!
    switch (choice)
    {
        case 'A':  cout << "You entered A.\n";
        case 'B':  cout << "You entered B.\n";
        case 'C':  cout << "You entered C.\n";
        default:   cout << "You did not enter A, B, or C!\n";
    }
    return 0;
}
```

Program Output with Example Input Shown in Bold
```
Enter A, B, or C: A[Enter]
You entered A.
You entered B.
You entered C.
You did not enter A, B, or C!
```

Program Output with Different Example Input Shown in Bold
```
Enter A, B, or C: C[Enter]
You entered C.
You did not enter A, B, or C!
```

Without the break statement, the program "falls through" all of the statements below the one with the matching case expression. Sometimes this is what you want. Program 4-29 lists the features of three TV models a customer may choose from. The model 100 has remote control. The model 200 has remote control and stereo sound. The model 300 has remote control, stereo sound, and picture-in-a-picture capability. The program uses a switch statement with carefully omitted breaks to print the features of the selected model.

Program 4-29

```cpp
// This program is carefully constructed to use the "fall through"
// feature of the switch statement.

#include <iostream>
using namespace std;

int main()
{
    int modelNum;
```

(program continues)

Program 4-29   *(continued)*

```
cout << "Our TVs come in three models:\n";
cout << "The 100, 200, and 300. Which do you want? ";
cin >> modelNum;
cout << "That model has the following features:\n";
switch (modelNum)
{
    case 300: cout << "\tPicture-in-a-picture.\n";
    case 200: cout << "\tStereo sound.\n";
    case 100: cout << "\tRemote control.\n";
              break;
    default:  cout << "You can only choose the 100,";
              cout << "200, or 300.\n";
}
return 0;
}
```

Program Output with Example Input Shown in Bold
```
Our TVs come in three models:
The 100, 200, and 300. Which do you want? 100[Enter]
That model has the following features:
    Remote control.
```

Program Output with Different Example Input Shown in Bold
```
Our TVs come in three models:
The 100, 200, and 300. Which do you want? 200[Enter]
That model has the following features:
    Stereo sound.
    Remote control.
```

Program Output with Different Example Input Shown in Bold
```
Our TVs come in three models:
The 100, 200, and 300. Which do you want? 300[Enter]
That model has the following features:
    Picture-in-a-picture.
    Stereo sound.
    Remote control.
```

Program Output with Different Example Input Shown in Bold
```
Our TVs come in three models:
The 100, 200, and 300. Which do you want? 500[Enter]
You can only choose the 100, 200, or 300.
```

Another example of how useful this "fall through" capability can be is when you want the program to branch to the same set of statements for multiple case expressions. For instance, Program 4-30 asks the user to select a grade of dog food. The available choices are A, B, and C. The switch statement will recognize either upper or lowercase letters.

Program 4-30

```cpp
// The switch statement in this program uses the "fall through"
// feature to catch both uppercase and lowercase letters entered
// by the user.

#include <iostream>
using namespace std;

int main()
{
    char feedGrade;

    cout << "Our dog food is available in three grades:\n";
    cout << "A, B, and C. Which do you want pricing for? ";
    cin >> feedGrade;
    switch(feedGrade)
    {
        case 'a':
        case 'A':   cout << "30 cents per pound.\n";
                    break;
        case 'b':
        case 'B':   cout << "20 cents per pound.\n";
                    break;
        case 'c':
        case 'C':   cout << "15 cents per pound.\n";
                    break;
        default:    cout << "That is an invalid choice.\n";
    }
    return 0;
}
```

Program Output with Example Input Shown in Bold
```
Our dog food is available in three grades:
A, B, and C. Which do you want pricing for? b[Enter]
20 cents per pound.
```

Program Output with Different Example Input Shown in Bold
```
Our dog food is available in three grades:
A, B, and C. Which do you want pricing for? B[Enter]
20 cents per pound.
```

When the user enters 'a' the corresponding case has no statements associated with it, so the program falls through to the next case, which corresponds with 'A'.

```cpp
        case 'a':
        case 'A':   cout << "30 cents per pound.\n";
                    break;
```

The same is technique is used for 'b' and 'c'.

Using `switch` in Menu Systems

The `switch` statement is a natural mechanism for building menu systems. Recall that Program 4-14 gives a menu to select which health club package the user wishes to purchase. The program uses `if/else if` statements to determine which package the user has selected and displays the calculated charges. Program 4-31 is a modification of that program, using a `switch` statement instead of `if/else if`.

Program 4-31

```cpp
// This program displays a menu and asks the user to make a
// selection. A switch statement determines which item
// the user has chosen.

#include <iostream>
#include <iomanip>
using namespace std;

int main()
{
    int choice, months;
    float charges;

    cout << "    Health Club Membership Menu\n\n";
    cout << "1. Standard Adult Membership\n";
    cout << "2. Child Membership\n";
    cout << "3. Senior Citizen Membership\n";
    cout << "4. Quit the Program\n\n";
    cout << "Enter your choice: ";
    cin >> choice;
    cout << "For how many months? ";
    cin >> months;
    cout << fixed << showpoint << setprecision(2);
    switch (choice)
    {
        case 1: charges = months * 40.00;
                cout << "The total charges are $";
                cout << charges << endl;
                break;

        case 2: charges = months * 20.00;
                cout << "The total charges are $";
                cout << charges << endl;
                break;

        case 3: charges = months * 30.00;
                cout << "The total charges are $";
                cout << charges << endl;
                break;
```

(program continues)

Program 4-31 *(continued)*

```
        case 4:  cout << "Thanks for using this program.\n";
                 break;

        default: cout << "The valid choices are 1-4. Run ";
                 cout << "the program again and select one ";
                 cout << "of those.\n";
    }
    return 0;
}
```

Program Output with Example Input Shown in Bold
```
Health Club Membership Menu

1. Standard Adult Membership
2. Child Membership
3. Senior Citizen Membership
4. Quit the Program

Enter your choice: 2[Enter]
For how many months? 6[Enter]
The total charges are $120.00
```

 Checkpoint   [4.16]

4.33 Explain why it would be very difficult to convert the following if/else if statement into a switch statement.

```
if (temp == 100)
    x = 0;
else if (population > 1000)
    x = 1;
else if  (rate < .1)
    x = -1;
```

4.34 What is wrong with the following switch statement?

```
switch (temp)
{
    case temp < 0 :  cout << "Temp is negative.\n";
                     break;
    case temp == 0:  cout << "Temp is zero.\n";
                     break;
    case temp > 0 :  cout << "Temp is positive.\n";
                     break;
}
```

4.35 What will the following program display?

```
#include <iostream>
using namespace std;
```

```
int main()
{
   int funny = 7, serious = 15;

   funny = serious * 2;
   switch (funny)
   {  case 0 :   cout << "That is funny.\n";
               break;
      case 30:   cout << "That is serious.\n";
               break;
      case 32:   cout << "That is seriously funny.\n";
               break;
      default:   cout << funny << endl;
   }
   return 0;
}
```

4.36 Complete the following program skeleton by writing a `switch` statement that displays
   `"one"` if the user has entered 1, `"two"` if the user has entered 2, and `"three"` if the user has
   entered 3. If a number other than 1, 2, or 3 is entered, the program should display an error
   message.

```
#include <iostream>
using namespace std;

int main()
{
   int userNum;

   cout << "Enter one of the numbers 1, 2, or 3: ";
   cin >> userNum;
   //
   // Write the switch statement here.
   //
   return 0;
}
```

4.37 Rewrite the following program. Use a `switch` statement instead of the `if/else if`
   statement.

```
#include <iostream>
using namespace std;

int main()
{
   int selection;

   cout << "Which formula do you want to see?\n\n";
   cout << "1. Area of a circle\n";
   cout << "2. Area of a rectangle\n";
   cout << "3. Area of a cylinder\n"
   cout << "4. None of them!\n";
   cin >> selection;
```

```
   if (selection == 1)
      cout << "Pi times radius squared\n";
   else if (selection == 2)
      cout << "Length times width\n";
   else if (selection == 3)
      cout << "Pi times radius squared times height\n";
   else if (selection == 4)
      cout << "Well okay then, good-bye!\n";
   else
      cout << "Not good with numbers, eh?\n";
   return 0;
}
```

4.17 Enumerated Data Types

CONCEPT An enumerated data type in C++ is a data type whose legal values are a set of named constant integers.

So far we have used data types that are built into the C++ language, such as int and float, and object types, like string, which are provided by C++ classes. However, C++ also allows programmers to create their own data types. An *enumerated data type* is a programmer-defined data type that contains a set of named integer constants. Here is an example of an enumerated type declaration.

```
enum Roster { Tom, Sharon, Bill, Teresa, John };
```

This declaration creates a data type named Roster. It is called an enumerated type because the legal set of values that variables of this data type can have are enumerated, or listed, as part of the declaration. A variable of the Roster data type may only have values that are in the list inside the braces.

It is important to realize that the example enum statement does not actually create any variables—it just defines the data type. It says that when we later create variables of this data type, this is what they will look like—integers whose values are limited to the integers associated with the symbolic names in the enumerated set. The following statement shows how a variable of the Roster data type would be defined.

```
Roster student;
```

The form of this statement is like any other variable definition: first the data type name, then the variable name. Notice that the data type name is Roster, not enum Roster.

Since student is a variable of the Roster data type, we may store any of the values Tom, Sharon, Bill, Teresa, or John in it. An assignment operation would look like this:

```
student = Sharon;
```

The value of the variable could then be tested like this:

```
if (student == Sharon)
```

Notice in the two examples that there are no quotation marks around Sharon. It is a named constant, not a string.

In Chapter 3 you learned that named constants are constant values that are accessed through their symbolic name. So what is the value of Sharon? The symbol Tom is stored as the integer 0. Sharon is stored as the integer 1. Bill is stored as the integer 2, and so forth.

Even though the values in an enumerated data type are actually stored as integers, you cannot always substitute the integer value for the symbolic name. For example, assuming that student is a variable of the Roster data type, the following assignment statement is illegal.

```
student = 2;              // Error!
```

You can, however, test an enumerated variable by using an integer value instead of a symbolic name. For example, the following two if statements are equivalent.

```
if (student == Bill)
if (student == 2)
```

You can also use relational operators to compare two enumerated variables. For example, the following if statement determines if the value stored in student1 is less than the value stored in student2:

```
if (student1 < student2)
```

If student1 equals Bill and student2 equals John, this statement would be true. However, if student1 equals Bill and student2 equals Sharon, the statement would be false.

By default, the symbols in the enumeration list are assigned the integer values 0, 1, 2, and so forth. If this is not appropriate, you can specify the values to be assigned, as in the following example.

```
enum Department { factory = 1, sales = 2, warehouse = 4 };
```

Remember that if you do assign values to the enumerated symbols, they must be integers. The following value assignments would produce an error.

```
enum Department { factory = 1.1, sales = 2.2,
               warehouse = 4.4 };          // Error!
```

While there is no requirement that assigned integer values be placed in ascending order, it is generally considered a good idea to do this.

If you leave out the value assignment for one or more of the symbols, it will be assigned a default value, as illustrated here:

```
enum Colors { red, orange, yellow = 9, green, blue };
```

red will be assigned the value 0, orange will be 1, yellow will be 9, green will be 10, and blue will be 11.

One of the purposes of an enumerated data type is that the symbolic names help to make a program self-documenting. However, since these names are not strings, they are for use inside the program only. Using the `Roster` data type in our example, the following two statements would output a 2, not the name `Sharon`.

```
Roster student1 = Sharon;
cout << student1;
```

Since the symbolic names of an enumerated data type are associated with integer values, they may be used in a switch statement, as shown in Program 4-32. This program also demonstrates that it is possible to use an enumerated data type without actually creating any variables of that type.

Program 4-32

```
// This program demonstrates an enumerated data type.

#include <iostream>
using namespace std;

// Declare the enumerated type
enum Roster { Tom = 1, Sharon, Bill, Teresa, John };
                    // Sharon - John will be assigned default values 2-5.
int main()
{
    int who;

    cout << "This program will give you a student's birthday.\n";
    cout << "Whose birthday do you want to know?\n";
    cout << "1 = Tom\n";
    cout << "2 = Sharon\n";
    cout << "3 = Bill\n";
    cout << "4 = Teresa\n";
    cout << "5 = John\n";
    cin >> who;
    switch (who)
    {
        case Tom   :   cout << "\nTom's birthday is January 3.\n";
                       break;
        case Sharon:   cout << "\nSharon's birthday is April 22.\n";
                       break;
        case Bill  :   cout << "\nBill's birthday is December 19.\n";
                       break;
        case Teresa:   cout << "\nTeresa's birthday is February 2.\n";
                       break;
        case John  :   cout << "\nJohn's birthday is June 17.\n";
                       break;
        default    :   cout << "\nInvalid selection\n";
    }
    return 0;
}
```

Program 4-32

Program Output with Example Input Shown in Bold
```
This program will give you a student's birthday.
Whose birthday do you want to know?
1 = Tom
2 = Sharon
3 = Bill
4 = Teresa
5 = John
2[Enter]
```

Sharon's birthday is April 22.

Checkpoint [4.17]

4.38 Find all the things that are wrong with the following declaration.

```
Enum Pet = { "dog", "cat", "bird", "fish" }
```

4.39 Follow the instructions to complete the following program segment.

```
enum Paint { red, blue, yellow, green, orange, purple };
Paint color = green;

// Write an if/else statement that will print out "primary color"
// if color is red, blue, or yellow, and will print out
// "mixed color" otherwise. The if test should be a relational
// expression.
```

4.18 Focus on Problem Solving and Program Design: A Case Study

Crazy Al's Computer Emporium is a retail seller of home computers. The sales staff at Crazy Al's work strictly on commission. At the end of the month, each salesperson's commission is calculated according to Table 4-12.

Table 4-12

Sales This Month	Commission Rate
Less than $10,000	5%
$10,000–$14,999	10%
$15,000–$17,999	12%
$18,000–$21,999	14%
$22,000 or more	16%

For example, a salesperson with $16,000 in monthly sales will earn a 12% commission ($1,920.00). Another salesperson with $20,000 in monthly sales will earn a 14% commission ($2,800.00).

Since the staff only gets paid once per month, Crazy Al's allows each employee to take up to $1,500 per month in advance. When sales commissions are calculated, the amount of each employee's advanced pay is subtracted from the commission. If any salesperson's commissions are less than the amount of their advance, they must reimburse Crazy Al's for the difference.

Here are two examples: Beverly and John have $21,400 and $12,600 in sales, respectively. Beverly's commission is $2,996 and John's commission is $1,260. Both Beverly and John took $1,500 in advance pay. At the end of the month, Beverly gets a check for $1,496, but John must pay $240 back to Crazy Al's.

You've been asked to write a program that eases the task of calculating the end-of-month commission. Table 4-12 lists the variables needed.

Table 4-13

Variable	Description
sales	A `float` variable to hold a salesperson's total monthly sales.
rate	A `float` variable to hold the salesperson's commission rate.
commission	A `float` variable to hold the commission.
advance	A `float` variable to hold the amount of advanced pay the salesperson has drawn.
pay	A `float` variable to hold the salesperson's amount of pay.

Program Design

The program must perform the following general steps:

1. Ask the user for the salesperson's monthly sales.
2. Ask the user for the amount of advance pay the salesperson has drawn from the company.
3. Determine the commission rate.
4. Calculate the commission.
5. Calculate the salesperson's pay by subtracting the advanced pay from the commission. If the amount is negative, the salesperson must reimburse the company.

Determining the Commission Rate

The commission rate is determined by the monthly sales amount. An `if/else` statement can be used to test the sales amount and assign the correct rate. The following pseudocode expresses the algorithm:

```
If sales is less than $10,000
    rate is 5%.
else if sales is less than $14,999
    rate is 10%.
```

```
else if sales is less than $17,999
    rate is 12%.
else if sales is less than $21,999
    rate is 14%.
else
    rate is 16%.
```

The Program

Before attempting to code the problem, you should first model it entirely in pseudocode:

```
Ask user to enter the salesperson's monthly sales.
Store input in sales.
Ask user to enter the salesperson's amount of advanced pay.
Store input in advance.
If sales is less than $10,000
    rate is 5%.
else if sales is less than $14,999
    rate is 10%.
else if sales is less than $17,999
    rate is 12%.
else if sales is less than $21,999
    rate is 14%.
else
    rate is 16%.
commission = sales * rate.
pay = commission - advance.
Display results.
```

The last step is to expand the pseudocode into the final program, which is shown in Program 4-33.

Program 4-33

```cpp
// This program is used by Crazy Al's Computer Emporium
// to calculate the monthly pay of commissioned salespeople.

#include <iostream>
#include <iomanip>
using namespace std;

int main()
{
    float sales,        // Monthly sales
          rate,         // Rate of commission
          commission,   // Amount of commission
          advance,      // Advanced pay drawn
          pay;          // Amount of pay remaining to be paid
```

(program continues)

Program 4-33 *(continued)*

```cpp
    // Ask user for the salesperson's sales and the
    // amount of advanced pay.
    cout << "Enter the salesperson's monthly sales: ";
    cin >> sales;
    cout << "Enter the amount of advanced pay for this ";
    cout << "salesperson: ";
    cin >> advance;
    // Determine the commission rate.
    if (sales < 10000)
        rate = 0.05;
    else if (sales < 14999)
        rate = 0.1;
    else if (sales < 17999)
        rate = 0.12;
    else if (sales < 21999)
        rate = 0.14;
    else
        rate = 0.16;
    // Calculate the sales commission.
    commission = sales * rate;
    // Calculate the salesperson's pay.
    pay = commission - advance;
    // Display the results.
    cout << fixed << showpoint << setprecision(2);
    cout << "\nPay Results\n";
    cout << "-----------\n";
    cout << "Sales: $" << sales << endl;
    cout << "Commission Rate: " << rate << endl;
    cout << "Commission: $" << commission << endl;
    cout << "Advanced Pay: $" << advance << endl;
    cout << "Remaining Pay: $" << pay << endl;
    return 0;
}
```

Program Output with Example Input Shown in Bold
```
Enter the salesperson's monthly sales: 19600[Enter]
Enter the amount of advanced pay for this salesperson: 1000[Enter]

Pay Results
-----------
Sales: $19600.00
Commission Rate: 0.14
Commission: $2744.00
Advanced Pay: $1000.00
Remaining Pay: $1744.00
```

(program output continues)

Program 4-33   *(continued)*

Program Output with Different Example Input Shown in Bold
```
Enter the salesperson's monthly sales: 9000[Enter]
Enter the amount of advanced pay for this salesperson: 1000[Enter]

Pay Results
-----------
Sales: $9000.00
Commission Rate: 0.05
Commission: $450.00
Advanced Pay: $1000.00
Remaining Pay: $-550.00
```

Review Questions and Exercises

Fill-in-the-Blank

1. An expression using the greater-than, less-than, greater-than-or-equal-to, less-than-or-equal-to, equal, or not-equal operator is called a(n) _____ expression.

2. A relational expression is either _____ or _____.

3. The value of a relational expression is 0 if the expression is _____ or 1 if the expression is _____.

4. The if statement regards an expression with the value 0 as _____.

5. The if statement regards an expression with a nonzero value as _____.

6. For an if statement to conditionally execute a group of statements, the statements must be enclosed in a set of _____.

7. In an if/else statement, the if part executes its statement or block if the expression is _____, and the else part executes its statement or block if the expression is _____.

8. The trailing else in an if/else if statement has a similar purpose as the _____ section of a switch statement.

9. The if/else if statement is actually a form of the _____ if statement.

10. If the sub-expression on the left of the _____ logical operator is false, the right sub-expression is not checked.

11. If the sub-expression on the left of the _____ logical operator is true, the right sub-expression is not checked.

12. The _____ logical operator has higher precedence than the other logical operators.

13. The logical operators have _____ associativity.

14. The _____ logical operator works best when testing a number to determine if it is within a range.

15. The _____ logical operator works best when testing a number to determine if it is outside a range.

16. A variable with _____ scope is only visible when the program is executing in the block containing the variable's definition.

17. C-strings _____ (can/cannot) be compared with relational operators.

18. An expression using the conditional operator is called a(n) _____ expression.

19. The expression that follows the `switch` statement must have a(n) _____ value.

20. The expression following a `case` statement must be a(n) _____ _____.

21. A program will "fall through" a `case` section if it is missing the _____ statement.

22. What value will be stored in the variable `t` after each of the following statements execute?

    A) `t = (12 > 1);`_____

    B) `t = (2 < 0);`_____

    C) `t = (5 == (3 * 2));`_____

    D) `t = (5 == 5);`_____

23. Write an `if` statement that assigns 100 to `x` when `y` is equal to 0.

24. Write an `if/else` statement that assigns 0 to `x` when `y` is equal to 10. Otherwise it should assign 1 to `x`.

25. Using the following chart , write an `if/else if` statement that assigns .10, .15, or .20 to `commission`, depending on the value in `sales`.

Sales	Commission Rate
Up to $10,000	10%
$10,000 to $15,000	15%
Over $15,000	20%

26. Write an `if` statement that sets the variable `hours` to 10 when the flag variable `minimum` is set.

27. Write nested `if` statements that perform the following tests: If `amount1` is greater than 10 and `amount2` is less than 100, display the greater of the two.

28. Write an `if` statement that prints the message "The number is valid" if the variable `grade` is within the range 0 through 100.

29. Write an `if` statement that prints the message "The number is valid" if the variable `temperature` is within the range -50 through 150.

30. Write an `if` statement that prints the message "The number is not valid" if the variable `hours` is outside the range 0 through 80.

31. Write an `if/else` statement that displays the strings in the arrays `title1` and `title2` in alphabetical order.

32. Convert the following `if/else if` statement into a switch statement:

```
if (choice == 1)
{
    cout << fixed << showpoint << setprecision(2);
}
else if (choice == 2 || choice == 3)
{
    cout << fixed << showpoint << setprecision(4);
}

else if (choice == 4)
{
    cout << fixed << showpoint << setprecision(6);
}
else
{
    cout << fixed << showpoint << setprecision(8);
}
```

True or False

33. T   F   The = operator and the == operator perform the same operation.

34. T   F   A variable declared in an inner block may not have the same name as a variable declared in the outer block.

35. T   F   A conditionally executed statement should be indented one level from the `if` statement.

36. T   F   All lines in a block should be indented one level.

37. T   F   It's safe to assume that all uninitialized variables automatically start with 0 as their value.

38. T   F   When an `if` statement is nested in the `if` part of another statement, the only time the inner `if` is executed is when the expression of the outer `if` is true.

39. T   F   When an `if` statement is nested in the `else` part of another statement, as in an `if/else if`, the only time the inner `if` is executed is when the expression of the outer `if` is true.

40. T   F   The scope of a variable is limited to the block in which it is declared.

41. T   F   String objects may be directly compared with the == operator.

42. T   F   x != y is the same as (x > y || x < y).

43. T   F   y < x is the same as x >= y.

44. T   F   x >= y is the same as (x > y && x = y).

45. Assume the variables x = 5, y = 6, and z = 8. Indicate by circling the T or F if each of the following conditions is true or false:

    A) T   F   x == 5 || y > 3

    B) T   F   7 <= x && z > 4

    C) T   F   2 != y && z != 4

    D) T   F   x >= 0 || x <= y

46. Match the conditional expression with the `if/else` statement that performs the same operation.

    A)   q = x < y ? a + b : x * 2;

    B)   q = x < y ? x * 2 : a + b;

    C)   x < y ? q = 0 : q = 1;

```
_____ if (x < y)
          q = 0;
      else
          q = 1;


_____ if (x < y)
          q = a + b;
      else
          q = x * 2;


_____ if (x < y)
          q = x * 2;
      else
          q = a + b;
```

Find the Errors

47. Each of the following programs has errors. Find as many as you can.

    A)
```
// This program averages 3 test scores.
// It uses the variable perfectScore as a flag.
include <iostream>
using namespace std;

int main()
```

```cpp
{
    cout << "Enter your 3 test scores and I will ";
        << "average them:";
    int score1, score2, score3;
    cin >> score1 >> score2 >> score3;
    float average;
    average = (score1 + score2 + score3) / 3.0;
    if (average = 100);
        perfectScore = true;// Set the flag variable
    cout << "Your average is " << average << endl;
    bool perfectScore;
    if (perfectScore);
    {
        cout << "Congratulations!\n";
        cout << "That's a perfect score.\n";
        cout << "You deserve a pat on the back!\n";
    return 0;
}
```

B)
```cpp
// This program divides a user-supplied number by another
// user-supplied number. It checks for division by zero.

#include <iostream>
using namespace std;

int main()
{
    float num1, num2, quotient;

    cout << "Enter a number: ";
    cin >> num1;
    cout << "Enter another number: ";
    cin >> num2;
    if (num2 == 0)
        cout << "Division by zero is not possible.\n";
        cout << "Please run the program again ";
        cout << "and enter a number besides zero.\n";
    else
        quotient = num1 / num2;
        cout << "The quotient of " << num1 <<
        cout << " divided by " << num2 << " is ";
        cout << quotient << endl;
    return 0;
}
```

C)
```cpp
// This program uses an if/else if statement to assign a
// letter grade (A, B, C, D, or F) to a numeric test score.
#include <iostream>
using namespace std;

int main()
```

```
        {
            int testScore;

            cout << "Enter your test score and I will tell you\n";
            cout << "the letter grade you earned: ";
            cin >> testScore;
            if (testScore < 60)
                cout << "Your grade is F.\n";
            else if (testScore < 70)
                cout << "Your grade is D.\n";
            else if (testScore < 80)
                cout << "Your grade is C.\n";
            else if (testScore < 90)
                cout << "Your grade is B.\n";
            else
                cout << "That is not a valid score.\n";
            else if (testScore <= 100)
                cout << "Your grade is A.\n";
            return 0;
        }
```

D)
```
        // This program uses a switch statement to assign a
        // letter grade (A, B, C, D, or F) to a numeric test score.
        #include <iostream>
        using namespace std;

        int main()
        {
            float testScore;

            cout << "Enter your test score and I will tell you\n";
            cout << "the letter grade you earned: ";
            cin >> testScore;
            switch (testScore)
            {
                case (testScore < 60.0):
                        cout << "Your grade is F.\n";
                        break;
                case (testScore < 70.0):
                        cout << "Your grade is D.\n";
                        break;
                case (testScore < 80.0):
                        cout << "Your grade is C.\n";
                        break;
                case (testScore < 90.0):
                        cout << "Your grade is B.\n";
                        break;


                case (testScore <= 100.0):
```

```
                            cout << "Your grade is A.\n";
                            break;
                 default:
                            cout << "That score isn't valid\n"; }
            return 0;
        }
```

48. The following statement should determine if x is not greater than 20. What is wrong with it?

    ```
    if (!x > 20)
    ```

49. The following statement should determine if count is within the range of 0 through 100. What is wrong with it?

    ```
    if (count >= 0 || count <= 100)
    ```

50. The following statement should determine if count is outside the range of 0 through 100. What is wrong with it?

    ```
    if (count < 0 && count > 100)
    ```

51. The following statement should assign 0 to z if a is less than 10; otherwise it should assign 7 to z. What is wrong with it?

    ```
    z = (a < 10) : 0 ? 7;
    ```

Programming Challenges

General Requirements

A) Each program should have a section of comments at the top. The comments should contain your name, the date the program was written, the chapter that the assignment appeared in, and the assignment number and name. Here is an example:

```
// Written by Jill Johnson
// March 31, 2003
// Chapter 4
// Assignment 1, Minimum/Maximum
```

B) For each program that displays a dollar amount, format the output in fixed-point notation with two places of precision. Be sure the decimal place always displays, even when the number is 0 or has no fractional part.

1. Minimum/Maximum

Write a program that asks the user to enter two numbers. The program should use the conditional operator to determine which number is the smaller and which is the larger.

2. Roman Numeral Converter

Write a program that asks the user to enter a number within the range of 1 through 10. Use a switch statement to display the Roman numeral version of that number.

Input Validation: Do not accept a number less than 1 or greater than 10.

3. State Abbreviations

Write a program that asks the user to enter one of the following state abbreviations: NC, SC, GA, FL, or AL. The program should then display the name of the state that corresponds with the abbreviation entered (North Carolina, South Carolina, Georgia, Florida, or Alabama).

Input Validation: Accept abbreviations with both letters in uppercase or both in lowercase. Display an error message if an abbreviation other than what is listed is entered.

4. Math Tutor

This is a modification of problem 11 from Chapter 3. Write a program that can be used as a math tutor for a young student. The program should display two random numbers that are to be added, such as:

```
  247
+ 129
```

The program should then wait for the student to enter the answer. If the answer is correct, a message of congratulations should be printed. If the answer is incorrect, a message should be printed showing the correct answer.

5. Software Sales

A software company sells a package that retails for $99. Quantity discounts are given according to the following table.

Quantity	Discount
10–19	20%
20–49	30%
50–99	40%
100 or more	50%

Write a program that asks for the number of units sold and computes the total cost of the purchase.

Input Validation: Make sure the number of units is greater than 0.

6. Bank Charges

A bank charges $10 per month plus the following check fees for a commercial checking account:

$.10 each for less than 20 checks
$.08 each for 20–39 checks
$.06 each for 40–59 checks
$.04 each for 60 or more checks

The bank also charges an extra $15 if the balance of the account falls below $400 (before any check fees are applied). Write a program that asks for the beginning balance and the number of checks written. Compute and display the bank's service fees for the month.

Input Validation: Do not accept a negative value for the number of checks written. If a negative value is given for the beginning balance, display an urgent message indicating the account is overdrawn.

7. Shipping Charges

The Fast Freight Shipping Company charges the following rates:

Weight of Package (in kilograms)	Rate Per 500 Miles Shipped
2 Kg or less	$1.10
Over 2 Kg but not more than 6 Kg	$2.20
Over 6 Kg but not more than 10 Kg	$3.70
Over 10 Kg but not more than 20 Kg	$4.80

Write a program that asks for the weight of the package and the distance it is to be shipped, and then displays the charges.

Input Validation: Do not accept values of 0 or less for the weight of the package. Do not accept weights of more than 20 Kg (this is the maximum weight the company will ship). Do not accept distances of less than 10 miles or more than 3,000 miles. These are the company's minimum and maximum shipping distances.

8. Fat Gram Calculator

Write a program that asks for the number of calories and fat grams in a food. The program should display the percentage of calories that come from fat. If the calories from fat are less than 30 percent of the total calories of the food, it should also display a message indicating the food is low in fat.

One gram of fat has 9 calories, so

```
Calories from fat = fat grams * 9
```

The percentage of calories from fat can be calculated as

```
Calories from fat ÷ total calories
```

Input Validation: Make sure the number of calories and fat grams are not less than 0. Also, the number of calories from fat cannot be greater than the total number of calories. If that happens, display an error message indicating that either the calories or fat grams were incorrectly entered.

9. Running the Race

Write a program that asks for the names of three runners and the time it took each of them to finish a race. The program should display who came in first, second, and third place.

Input Validation: Only accept positive numbers for the times.

10. Spectral Analysis

If a scientist knows the wavelength of an electromagnetic wave she can determine what type of radiation it is. Write a program that asks for the wavelength of an electromagnetic wave and then displays what that wave is according to the following chart. (For example, a wave with a wavelength of 1E-10 would be an X-ray.)

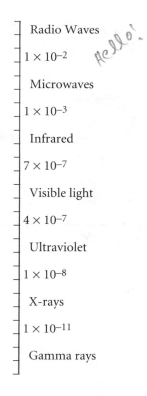

Radio Waves

1×10^{-2}

Microwaves

1×10^{-3}

Infrared

7×10^{-7}

Visible light

4×10^{-7}

Ultraviolet

1×10^{-8}

X-rays

1×10^{-11}

Gamma rays

11. Geometry Calculator

Write a program that displays the following menu:

```
Geometry Calculator

    1.Calculate the Area of a Circle
    2.Calculate the Area of a Rectangle
    3.Calculate the Area of a Triangle
    4.Quit

Enter your choice (1-4):
```

If the user enters 1, the program should ask for the radius of the circle and then display its area. Use the following formula:

$$\text{Area} = \pi r^2$$

Use 3.14159 for π and the radius of the circle for r. If the user enters 2, the program should ask for the length and width of the rectangle, and then display the rectangle's area. Use the following formula:

```
area = length * width
```

If the user enters 3, the program should ask for the length of the triangle's base and its height, and then display its area. Use the following formula:

```
area = base * height * .5
```

If the user enters 4, the program should end.

Input Validation: Display an error message if the user enters a number outside the range of 1 through 4 when selecting an item from the menu. Do not accept negative values for the circle's radius, the rectangle's length or width, or the triangle's base or height.

12. The Speed of Sound

The following table shows the approximate speed of sound in air, water, and steel.

Medium	Speed
Air	1,100 feet per second
Water	4,900 feet per second
Steel	16,400 feet per second

Write a program that displays a menu allowing the user to select air, water, or steel. After the user has made a selection, he or she should be asked to enter the distance a sound wave will travel in the selected medium. The program will then display the amount of time it will take. (Round the answer to four decimal places.)

Input Validation: Check that the user has selected one of the available choices from the menu. Do not accept distances less than 0.

13. Freezing and Boiling Points

The following table lists the freezing and boiling points of several substances. Write a program that asks the user to enter a temperature, and then shows all the substances that will freeze at that temperature and all that will boil at that temperature. For example, if the user enters –20 the program should report that water will freeze and oxygen will boil at that temperature.

Substance	Freezing Point (°F)	Boiling Point (°F)
Ethyl alcohol	–173	172
Mercury	–38	676
Oxygen	–362	–306
Water	32	212

14. Long-Distance Calls

A long-distance carrier charges the following rates for telephone calls:

Starting Time of Call	Rate per Minute
00:00–06:59	0.12
07:00–19:00	0.55
19:01–23:59	0.35

Write a program that asks for the starting time and the number of minutes of the call, and displays the charges. The program should ask for the time to be entered as a floating-point number in the form HH.MM. For example, 07:00 hours will be entered as 07.00, and 16:28 hours will be entered as 16.28.

Input Validation: The program should not accept times that are greater than 23:59. Also, no number whose last two digits are greater than 59 should be accepted. Hint: Assuming num *is a floating-point variable, the following expression will give you its fractional part:*

```
num - int(num)
```

15. Internet Service Provider

An Internet service provider has three different subscription packages for its customers:

Package A:	For $9.95 per month 10 hours of access are provided. Additional hours are $2.00 per hour.
Package B:	For $14.95 per month 20 hours of access are provided. Additional hours are $1.00 per hour.
Package C:	For $19.95 per month unlimited access is provided.

Write a program that calculates a customer's monthly bill. It should ask which package the customer has purchased and how many hours were used. It should then display the total amount due.

Input Validation: Be sure the user only selects package A, B, or C. Also, the number of hours used in a month cannot exceed 744.

16. Internet Service Provider, Part 2

Modify the program in problem 15 so it also displays how much money Package A customers would save if they purchased packages B or C, and how much money package B customers would save if they purchased package C. If there would be no savings, no message should be printed.

17. Internet Service Provider, Part 3

Months with 30 days have 720 hours, and months with 31 days have 744 hours. February, with 28 days, has 672 hours. Enhance the input validation of the Internet Service Provider program by asking the user for the month (by name), and validating that the number of hours entered is not more than the maximum for the entire month. Here is a table of the months, their days, and number of hours in each.

Month	Days	Hours
January	31	744
February	28	672
March	31	744
April	30	720
May	31	744
June	30	720
July	31	744
August	31	744
September	30	720
October	31	744
November	30	720
December	31	744

Serendipity Booksellers Software Development Project—Part 4: *A Problem-Solving Exercise*

1. The Main Menu

A) Modify the `mainmenu.cpp` program so it validates the user's input. If a value outside the range of 1 through 4 is entered, the program should display an error message. Here is an example screen:

```
                        Serendipity Booksellers
                               Main Menu

                1.   Cashier Module
                2.   Inventory Database Module
                3.   Report Module
                4.   Exit

                Enter Your Choice: 5

                Please enter a number in the range 1 - 4.
```

B) Later, in Chapter 6, you will begin merging all the programs you have written into the `main-menu.cpp` file. You will now start making preparations for that. After the user input has been validated, add a `switch` statement that branches to a section of code, depending on which menu choice the user made. For now, the program should simply display a message like "`You selected item 1`" when the user enters a number. Here is an example of the screen:

```
                        Serendipity Booksellers
                               Main Menu

                1.   Cashier Module
                2.   Inventory Database Module
                3.   Report Module
                4.   Exit

                Enter Your Choice: 3

                You selected item 3.
```

2. The Inventory Database Menu

You will make the same modifications to `invmenu.cpp` that you made to `mainmenu.cpp`.

Case

A) Modify the `invmenu.cpp` program so it validates the user's input. If a value outside the range of 1 through 5 is entered, the program should display an error message. Here is an example screen:

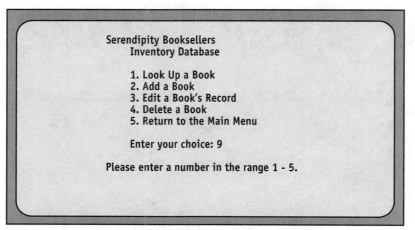

B) After the user input has been validated, add a `switch` statement that branches to a section of code, depending on which menu choice the user made. For now, the program should simply display a message like "`You selected item 1`" when the user enters a number. Here is an example of the screen:

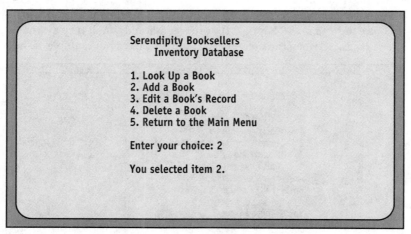

3. The Reports Menu

You will make the same modifications to `reports.cpp` that you made to `mainmenu.cpp` and `invmenu.cpp`.

A) Modify the `reports.cpp` program so it validates the user's input. If a value outside the range of 1 through 7 is entered, the program should display an error message. Here is an example screen:

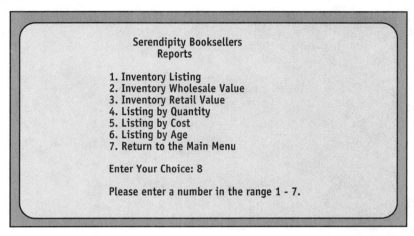

B) After the user input has been validated, add a `switch` statement that branches to a section of code, depending on which menu choice the user made. For now, the program should simply display a message like "`You selected item 1`" when the user enters a number. Here is an example of the screen:

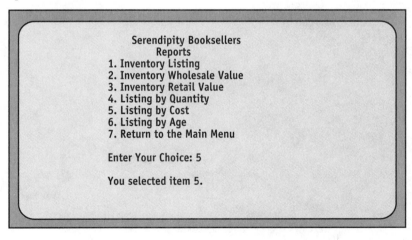

CHAPTER 5

Looping

Topics

5.1   The Increment and Decrement Operators

> **CONCEPT**   ++ and - - are operators that add and subtract 1 from their operands.

To *increment* a value means to increase it by one, and to *decrement* a value means to decrease it by one. Both of the following statements increment the variable num:

```
num = num + 1;
num += 1;
```

And num is decremented in both of the following statements:

```
num = num - 1;
num -= 1;
```

C++ provides a set of simple unary operators designed just for incrementing and decrementing variables. The increment operator is ++ and the decrement operator is --. The following statement uses the ++ operator to increment num:

```
num++;
```

And the following statement decrements num:

```
num--;
```

 Note: The expression num++ is pronounced "num plus plus," and num-- is pronounced "num minus minus."

Our examples so far show the increment and decrement operators used in *postfix mode*, which means the operator is placed after the variable. The operators also work in *prefix mode*, where the operator is placed before the variable name:

```
++num;
--num;
```

In both postfix and prefix mode, these operators add 1 to or subtract 1 from their operand. Program 5-1 shows how they work.

Program 5-1

```cpp
// This program demonstrates the increment and decrement operators.

#include <iostream>
using namespace std;

int main()
{
    int bigVal = 10, smallVal = 1;

    cout << "bigVal is " << bigVal
        << " and smallVal is " << smallVal << endl;
    smallVal++;
    bigVal--;
    cout << "bigVal is " << bigVal
        << " and smallVal is " << smallVal << endl;
    ++smallVal;
    --bigVal;
    cout << "bigVal is " << bigVal
        << " and smallVal is " << smallVal << endl;
    return 0;
}
```

Program Output
```
bigVal is 10 and smallVal is 1
bigVal is 9 and smallVal is 2
bigVal is 8 and smallVal is 3
```

The Difference Between Postfix and Prefix Modes

In the simple statements used in Program 5-1, it doesn't matter if the operator is used in postfix or prefix mode. The difference is important, however, when these operators are used in statements that do more than just incrementing or decrementing. For example, look at the following lines:

```
num = 4;
cout << num++;
```

This `cout` statement is doing two things: (1) displaying the value of `num`, and (2) incrementing `num`. But which happens first? `cout` will display a different value if `num` is incremented first than if `num` is incremented last. The answer depends on the mode of the increment operator.

Postfix mode causes the increment to happen after the value of the variable is used in the expression. In the example, `cout` will display 4, then `num` will be incremented to 5. Prefix mode, however, causes the increment to happen first. In the following statements, `num` will be incremented to 5, then `cout` will display 5:

```
num = 4;
cout << ++num;
```

Program 5-2 illustrates these dynamics further:

Program 5-2

```cpp
// This program demonstrates the prefix and postfix
// modes of the increment and decrement operators.
#include <iostream>
using namespace std;

int main()
{
    int bigVal = 10, smallVal = 1;

    cout << "bigVal starts as " << bigVal;
    cout << " and smallVal starts as " << smallVal << endl;
    cout << "bigVal--: " << bigVal-- << endl;
    cout << "smallVal++: " << smallVal++ << endl;
    cout << "Now bigVal is: " << bigVal << endl;
    cout << "Now smallVal is: " << smallVal << endl;
    cout << "--bigVal: " << --bigVal << endl;
    cout << "++smallVal: " << ++smallVal << endl;
    return 0;
}
```

Program Output
```
bigVal starts as 10 and smallVal starts as 1
bigVal--: 10
smallVal++: 1
Now bigVal is: 9
Now smallVal is: 2
--bigVal: 8
++smallVal: 3
```

Let's analyze the statements in this program. `bigVal` starts with the value 10. The following statement displays the value in `bigVal` and then decrements `bigVal`. The decrement happens last because it is used in postfix mode:

```
cout << "bigVal--: " << bigVal-- << endl;
```

Although this statement displays 10 as the value in `bigVal`, it will be 9 after the statement executes.

`smallVal` starts with the value 1. The following statement displays the number in `smallVal`, then uses the increment operator to add one to it. Because the increment operator is used in postfix mode, it works after the value is displayed:

```
cout<< "smallVal++: " << smallVal++ << endl;
```

This statement displays 1 as the value in `smallVal`, then increments `smallVal`, making it 2.

The last two statements in Program 5-2 use increment and decrement operators in prefix mode. This means they work on their operands before the values are displayed on the screen.

```
cout << "--bigVal: " << --bigVal << endl;
cout<< "++smallVal: " << ++smallVal << endl;
```

In these two statements, `bigVal` is decremented (making it 8) before its value is displayed on the screen. `smallVal` is incremented (making it 3) before its value is displayed.

Using ++ and -- in Mathematical Expressions

The increment and decrement operators can also be used on variables in mathematical expressions. Consider the following program segment:

```
a = 2;
b = 5;
c = a * b++;
cout << a << " " << b << " " << c;
```

In the statement `c = a * b++`, `c` is assigned the value of `a` times `b`, which is 10. The variable `b` is then incremented. The `cout` statement will display

```
2 6 10
```

If the statement were changed to read

```
c = a * ++b;
```

the variable `b` would be incremented before it was multiplied by `a`. In this case `c` would be assigned the value of 2 times 6, so the `cout` statement would display

```
2 6 12
```

You can pack a lot of action into a single statement using the increment and decrement operators, but don't get too tricky with them. You might be tempted to try something like the following, thinking that `c` will be assigned 11:

```
a = 2;
b = 5;
c = ++(a * b);
```

But this assignment statement simply will not work because the operand of the increment and decrement operators must be an lvalue. Recall from Chapter 2 that an lvalue identifies a place in memory whose contents may be changed. The increment and decrement operators usually have variables for their operands, but generally speaking, anything that can go on the left side of an = operator is legal.

Using ++ and -- in Relational Expressions

As you'll see later in this chapter, the ++ and -- operators are sometimes used in relational expressions. Just as in mathematical expressions, the difference between postfix and prefix mode is critical. Consider the following program segment:

```
x = 10;
if (x++ > 10)
    cout << "x is greater than 10.\n";
```

Two operations are happening in this if statement: (1) The value in x is tested to determine if it is greater than 10, and (2) x is incremented. Because the increment operator is used in postfix mode, the comparison happens first. Since 10 is not greater than 10, the cout statement won't execute. If the mode of the increment operator is changed, however, the if statement will compare 11 to 10 and the cout statement will execute:

```
x = 10;
if (++x > 10)
    cout << "x is greater than 10.\n";
```

Checkpoint [5.1]

5.1 What will the following program segments display?

A)
```
x = 2;
y = x++;
cout << x << y;
```
B)
```
x = 2;
y = ++x;
cout << x << y;
```
C)
```
x = 2;
y = 4;
cout << x++ << --y;
```
D)
```
x = 2;
y = 2 * x++;
cout << x << y;
```
E)
```
x = 99;
if (x++ < 100)
    cout "It is true!\n";
else
    cout << "It is false!\n";
```

```
F)    x = 0;
      if (++x)
          cout << "It is true!\n";
      else
          cout << "It is false!\n";
```

5.2 Introduction to Loops: The while Loop

CONCEPT	A loop is part of a program that repeats.

Chapter 4 introduced the concept of control structures, which direct the flow of a program. A *loop* is a control structure that causes a statement or group of statements to repeat. C++ has three looping control structures: the while loop, the do-while loop, and the for loop. The difference between each of these is how they control the repetition.

The while Loop

The while loop has two important parts: (1) an expression that is tested for a true or false value, and (2) a statement or block that is repeated as long as the expression is true. Here is the general format of the while loop:

```
while (expression)
    statement;
```

Notice there is no semicolon after the expression in parentheses. Like the if statement, the while loop is not complete without the statement that follows it.

If you wish the while loop to repeat a block of statements, its format is

```
while (expression)
{
    statement;
    statement;
    // Place as many statements here
    // as necessary.
}
```

The expression inside parentheses is tested and if it has a true value, the next statement or block is executed. (The statement or block that is repeated is known as the *body* of the loop.) This cycle is repeated until the expression in parentheses is false.

The while loop works like an if statement that executes over and over. As long as the expression in the parentheses is true, the conditionally-executed statement or block will repeat. Program 5-3 shows a cin statement inside a loop.

Program 5-3

```cpp
// This program demonstrates a simple while loop.

#include <iostream>
using namespace std;

int main()
{
    int number = 0;

    cout << "This program will let you enter number after\n";
    cout << "number. Enter 99 when you want to quit the ";
    cout << "program.\n";

    while (number != 99)
        cin >> number;
    cout << "Done\n";
    return 0;
}
```

Program Output with Example Input Shown in Bold
```
This program will let you enter number after
number. Enter 99 when you want to quit the program.
 1[Enter]
 2[Enter]
30[Enter]
75[Enter]
99[Enter]
Done
```

This program repeatedly reads values from the keyboard until the user enters 99. The loop controls this action by testing the variable number. As long as number does not equal 99, the loop repeats. The cin statement, inside the loop, puts the user's input into number, where, at the beginning of the next cycle it will be tested again. (Figure 5-1 illustrates the role of the test expression and the body of the loop.) Each repetition is known as an *iteration*.

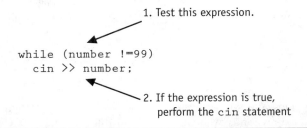

Figure 5-1

Note: Many programmers choose to enclose the body of a loop in braces, even if it only has one statement:

```
while (number != 99)
{
    cin >> number;
}
```

This is a good programming practice since the braces visually offset the body of the loop. The braces are not required for only one statement, however, so the choice of using them in this manner is yours.

while **Is a Pretest Loop**

The while loop is known as a *pretest* loop, which means it tests its expression before each iteration. Notice the variable definition of number in Program 5-3:

```
int number = 0;
```

number is initialized to 0. If number had been initialized to 99, as shown in the following program segment, the loop would never execute the cin statement:

```
int number = 99;
while (number != 99)
    cin >> number;
```

An important characteristic of the while loop is that the loop will never iterate if the test expression is false to start with. If you want to be sure a while loop executes the first time, you must initialize the relevant data in such a way that the test expression starts out as true.

Terminating a Loop

In all but rare cases, loops must contain within themselves a way to terminate. This means that something inside the loop must eventually make the test expression false. The loop in Program 5-3 stops when the user enters 99 at the keyboard, which is subsequently stored in the variable number by the cin object.

If a loop does not have a way of stopping, it is called an *infinite loop*. Infinite loops keep repeating until the program is interrupted. Here is an example:

```
int test = 0;
while (test < 10)
    cout << "Hello\n";
```

This loop will execute forever because it does not contain a statement that changes test. Each time the test expression is evaluated, test will still be equal to 0. Here is another version of the loop. This one will stop after it has executed 10 times:

```
int test = 0;
while (test < 10)
{
    cout << "Hello\n";
    test++;
}
```

This loop increments `test` after each time it prints `"Hello\n"`. When `test` reaches 10, the expression `test < 10` is no longer true, so the loop will stop.

It's also possible to create an infinite loop by accidentally placing a semicolon after the test expression. Here is an example:

```
int test = 0;
while (test < 10);                  // Error: Note the semicolon here.
{
    cout << "Hello\n";
    test++;
}
```

The semicolon after the test expression is assumed to be a null statement and disconnects the `while` statement from the block that comes after it. To the compiler, the loop looks like this:

```
while (test < 10);
```

This `while` loop will forever execute the null statement, which does nothing. The program will appear to have "hung," or "gone into space" because there is nothing to display screen output or show activity.

Another common pitfall with loops is accidentally using the = operator when you intend to use the == operator. The following is an infinite loop because the test expression assigns 1 to `remainder` each time it is evaluated rather than testing if remainder is equal to 1:

```
while (remainder = 1)               // Error: Notice the assignment.
{
    cout << "Enter a number: ";
    cin >> num;
    remainder = num % 2;
}
```

Remember, any nonzero value is evaluated as true.

Programming Style and the `while` Loop

It's possible to create loops that look like this:

```
while (number != 99) cin >> number;
```

as well as this:

```
while (test < 10) { cout << "Hello\n"; test++; }
```

Avoid this style of programming, however. The programming style you should use with the while loop is similar to that of the if statement:

- If there is only one statement repeated by the loop, it should appear on the line after the while statement and be indented one additional level.

- If the loop repeats a block, the block should begin on the line after the while statement and each line inside the braces should be indented.

In general, you'll find a similar style being used with the other types of loops presented in this chapter.

5.3 Counters

CONCEPT	A counter is a variable that is regularly incremented or decremented each time a loop iterates.

Sometimes it's important for a program to control or keep track of the number of iterations a loop performs. For example, Program 5-4 displays a table consisting of the numbers 1 through 10 and their squares, so its loop must iterate 10 times.

Program 5-4

```cpp
// This program displays the numbers 1 through 10 and their squares.

#include <iostream>
using namespace std;

int main()
{
    int num = 1;                            // Initialize counter

    cout << "Number     Number Squared\n";
    cout << "-------------------------\n";
    while (num <= 10)
    {
        cout << num << "\t\t" << (num * num) << endl;
        num++;                              // Increment counter
    }
    return 0;
}
```

Program 5-4

Program Output

```
Number      Number Squared
- - - - - - - - - - - - - - - - - - - - - - - -
1            1
2            4
3            9
4            16
5            25
6            36
7            49
8            64
9            81
10           100
```

In Program 5-4, the variable num, which starts at 1, is incremented each time through the loop. When num reaches 11 the loop stops. num is used as a *counter* variable, which means it is regularly incremented in each iteration of the loop. In essence, num keeps count of the number of iterations the loop has performed. Since num is controlling when to stay in the loop and when to exit from the loop, it is called the *loop control variable*.

 Note: It's important that num be properly initialized. Remember, variables defined inside a function have no guaranteed starting value.

In Program 5-4, num is incremented in the last statement of the loop. Another approach is to combine the increment operation with the relational test, as shown in Program 5-5.

Program 5-5

```cpp
// This program displays the numbers 1 through 10 and their squares.

#include <iostream>
using namespace std;

int main()
{
    int num = 0;

    cout << "Number      Number Squared\n";
    cout << "------------------------\n";
    while (num++ < 10)
        cout << num << "\t\t" << (num * num) << endl;
    return 0;
}
```

Program 5-5

Program Output
```
Number     Number Squared
- - - - - - - - - - - - - - - - - - - - - - -
1             1
2             4
3             9
4             16
5             25
6             36
7             49
8             64
9             81
10            100
```

Notice that num is now initialized to 0, rather than 1, and the relational expression uses the < operator instead of <=. This is because of the way the increment operator works when combined with the relational expression.

The increment operator is used in postfix mode, which means it adds one to num after the relational test. When the loop first executes, num is set to 0, so 0 is compared to 10. The ++ operator then increments num immediately after the comparison. When the cout statement executes, num has the value 1.

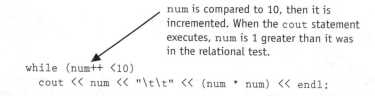

num is compared to 10, then it is incremented. When the cout statement executes, num is 1 greater than it was in the relational test.

```
while (num++ <10)
    cout << num << "\t\t" << (num * num) << endl;
```

Figure 5-2

Inside the loop, num always has a value of 1 greater than the value previously compared to 10. That's why the relational operator is < instead of <=. When num is 9 in the relational test, it will be 10 in the cout statement.

5.4 Letting the User Control a Loop

CONCEPT	We can let the user indicate the number of times a loop should repeat.

Sometimes the user has to decide how many times a loop should iterate. Program 5-6, which is similar to Program 4-2, averages a set of three test scores for any number of students. The program asks the user how many students he or she wishes to enter scores for. This number is stored in numStudents. Each time the while loop is executed, a counter variable is incremented until it exceeds this number, causing the loop to iterate once for each student. This counter is the loop control variable.

Program 5-6

```cpp
// This program averages a set of test scores for multiple
// students. It lets the user decide how many.

#include <iostream>
#include <iomanip>
using namespace std;

int main()
{
    int numStudents, count;

    cout << "This program will give you the average of three\n";
    cout << "test scores per student.\n";
    cout << "How many students do you have test scores for? ";
    cin >> numStudents;
    cout << "Enter the scores for each of the students.\n";
    cout << fixed << showpoint << setprecision(2);

    count = 1;                    // Initialize the loop control variable
    while (count <= numStudents)
    {
        int score1, score2, score3;
        float average;
        cout << "\nStudent " << count << ": ";
        cin >> score1 >> score2 >> score3;
        average = (score1 + score2 + score3) / 3.0;
        cout << "The average is " << average << "\n";
        count++;                  // Increment the loop control variable
    }
    return 0;
}
```

Program Output with Example Input Shown in Bold
```
    This program will give you the average of three
    test scores per student.
    How many students do you have test scores for? 3[Enter]

    Enter the scores for each of the students.

    Student 1: 75 80 82[Enter]
    The average is 79.00

    Student 2: 85 85 90[Enter]
    The average is 86.67

    Student 3: 60 75 88[Enter]
    The average is 74.33
```

In Program 5-6, the student scores were input by the user at run time. The program could easily be modified to have the scores read in from a data file. Program 5-7 does this, reading its data from a file named scores.dat, which holds three scores for each of ten students.

Program 5-7

```cpp
// This program averages a set of test scores for up to ten students.
// The data is read from a file, with the user inputting how may sets
// of scores are to be read.

#include <iostream>
#include <iomanip>
#include <fstream>
using namespace std;

int main()
{
    int numStudents,
        count;                      // Counter to control the loop
    ifstream dataIn;                // Define the input stream variable

    dataIn.open("scores.dat");      // Open the data file

    cout << "This program will give you the average of three\n";
    cout << "test scores per student.\n";
    cout << "How many students do you have test scores for? ";
    cin >> numStudents;
    cout << fixed << showpoint << setprecision(2);
    cout << endl;

    count = 1;                      // Initialize the loop control variable
    while (count <= numStudents)
    {
        int score1, score2, score3;
        float average;
        dataIn >> score1 >> score2 >> score3;       // Read from the file
        average = (score1 + score2 + score3) / 3.0;
        cout << "The average for student " << count
             << " is " << average << "\n";
        count++;                                // Increment the loop control variable
    }
    dataIn.close();                 // Close the data file
    return 0;
}
```

Program Output with Example Input Shown in Bold
```
This program will give you the average of three
test scores per student.
How many students do you have test scores for? 4[Enter]

The average for student 1 is 79.00
The average for student 2 is 86.67
The average for student 3 is 74.33
The average for student 4 is 84.67
```

5.5 Keeping a Running Total

CONCEPT A *running total* is a sum of numbers that accumulates with each iteration of a loop. The variable used to keep the running total is called an *accumulator*.

Some programming tasks require a running total to be kept. Program 5-8, for example, calculates a company's total sales over a period of time by taking daily sales figures as input and keeping a running total of them as they are gathered.

Program 5-8

```cpp
// This program takes daily sales figures over a period of time
// and calculates their total.

#include <iostream>
#include <iomanip>
using namespace std;

int main()
{
    int days,
        count;              // Counter that controls the loop
    float total = 0.0;      // Initialize accumulator

    cout << "For how many days do you have sales figures? ";
    cin >> days;

    count = 1;              // Initialize counter
    while (count <= days)
    {
        float sales;
        cout << "Enter the sales for day " << count << ": ";
        cin >> sales;
        total += sales;     // Accumulate running total
        count++;            // Increment counter
    }
    cout << fixed << showpoint << setprecision(2);
    cout << "The total sales are $" << total << endl;
    return 0;
}
```

Program Output with Example Input Shown in Bold
```
For how many days do you have sales figures? 5[Enter]
Enter the sales for day 1: 489.32[Enter]
Enter the sales for day 2: 421.65[Enter]
Enter the sales for day 3: 497.89[Enter]
Enter the sales for day 4: 532.37[Enter]
Enter the sales for day 5: 506.92[Enter]
The total sales are $2448.15
```

The daily sales figures are stored in `sales` (a variable defined inside the body of the `while` loop). The contents of `sales` is then added to `total`. The variable `total` was initialized to 0, so the first time through the loop it will be set to the same value as `sales`. During each iteration after the first, `total` will be increased by the amount in `sales`. After the loop has finished, `total` will contain the total of all the daily sales figures entered.

5.6 Sentinels

CONCEPT | A *sentinel* is a special value that marks the end of a list of values.

Program 5-8, in the previous section, requires the user to know in advance the number of days he or she wishes to enter sales figures for. Sometimes the user has a list that is very long and doesn't know how many items there are. In other cases, the user might be entering several lists and it is impractical to require that every item in every list be counted.

A technique that can be used in these situations is to ask the user to enter a sentinel at the end of the list. A *sentinel* is a special value that cannot be mistaken as a member of the list and signals that there are no more values to be entered. When the user enters the sentinel, the loop terminates.

In Program 5-3 the number 99 was used as an end sentinel. Program 5-9 provides another example of using an end sentinel. This program calculates the total points earned by a soccer team over a series of games. It allows the user to enter the series of game points, then -1 to signal the end of the list.

Program 5-9

```
// This program calculates the total number of points a
// soccer team has earned over a series of games. The user
// enters a series of point values, then -1 when finished.

#include <iostream>
using namespace std;

int main()
{
    int game = 1,
        points,
        total = 0;

    cout << "Enter the number of points your team has earned\n";
    cout << "so far in the season, then enter -1 when finished.\n\n";
    cout << "Enter the points for game " << game << ": ";
    cin >> points;
```

(program continues)

Program 5-9 *(continued)*

```
    while (points != -1)
    {  total += points;
        cout << "Enter the points for game " << ++game << ": ";
        cin >> points;
    }
    cout << "\nThe total points are " << total << endl;
    return 0;
}
```

Program Output with Example Input Shown in Bold
```
Enter the number of points your team has earned
so far in the season, then enter -1 when finished.

Enter the points for game 1: 7[Enter]
Enter the points for game 2: 9[Enter]
Enter the points for game 3: 4[Enter]
Enter the points for game 4: 6[Enter]
Enter the Points for game 5: 8[Enter]
Enter the points for game 6: -1[Enter]
The total points are 34
```

Notice how the first `cin` statement was placed before the loop. This is so the `while` loop will not try to test the value of `points` until a first value has been read in for it. The value −1 was chosen for the sentinel because it is not possible for a team to score negative points.

Reading Until the End of File

In Program 5-7, data was read in from a file using a loop controlled by a user input value. But what if the user asked to read in more values than there were in the file? This would cause an error. When reading from a file, unless you are absolutely sure how many values are in the file, it is safer to have the program stop trying to read in values when there is no more data in the file. One way to do this is by testing to see if the *end of file* (*eof*) has been reached yet. Most programming languages have a way to determine this; in C++ it is done with the `ifstream` eof member function. The function call

```
    dataIn.eof()
```

tests whether or not the end of file has been reached for the file associated with the `dataIn` file stream object. The function returns a `true` if the end of file has been reached, and returns a `false` otherwise. If we create a loop controlled by the statement

```
    while (!dataIn.eof())
```

the program will continue executing the loop while the `eof` has not yet been reached, which is exactly what we want to do. The `eof` is like an end sentinel. When it is encountered, we leave the loop without trying to read and process any more values. There are several approaches that can be used to read from a file until the `eof` has been reached. The one we will use is shown here in pseudocode:

```
read the first data value from the file
while the eof has not been reached
    process the data value just read
    read the next data value from the file
endwhile
```

Notice that the first read from the data file is done before the `while` loop. This is so that the first `while` test can test if there is any data to read. If the file is empty, the loop body will never be entered and no data values will be processed.

 WARNING! The only problem with this approach to `eof` testing is that there must be at least one whitespace character (a blank or **[Enter]**) in the file after the last data value. Otherwise the `eof` function will return a `true` as soon as it reads the last value, but before it can be processed. We want it to return a `true` only when it attempts to read again and can find no more values to read. So be sure to include a whitespace in the data file after the last value.

Program 5-9 used a sentinel-controlled loop to read in points scored by a soccer team. Program 5-10 modifies this program to read the data from a file and to control the loop by testing for the `eof`.

Program 5-10

```cpp
// This program calculates the total number of points a soccer
// team has earned over a series of games. It reads the data
// from a file until the eof is reached.  The eof acts as an
// end sentinel, signaling that there is no more data to read.

#include <iostream>
#include <fstream>
using namespace std;

int main()
{
    int points,
        total = 0;                // Initialize the accumulator
    ifstream dataIn;              // Define the input stream variable

    dataIn.open("games.dat");     // Open the data file
    dataIn >> points;             // Read the first value from the file

    while (!dataIn.eof())         // Loop while eof has not been reached
    {
        total += points;          // Add the value to the accumulator
        dataIn >> points;         // Read another value from the file
    }
```

(program continues)

Program 5-10 *(continued)*

```
    dataIn.close();              // Close the data file
    cout << "The total points are " << total << endl;
    return 0;
}
```

Program Output for Sample File Containing Data Values 7 9 4 6 8
```
The total points are 34
```

Notice that if the file had been empty, the while loop would never have been entered and total would have remained 0.

Checkpoint [5.2–5.6]

5.2 How many times will "Hello World\n" be printed in the following program segment?

```
int count = 10;
while (count < 1)
{
    cout << "Hello World\n";
    count++;
}
```

5.3 How many times will "I love C++ programming!\n" be printed in the following program segment?

```
int count = 0;
while (count++ < 10)
    cout << "Hello World\n";
    cout << "I love C++ programming!\n";
```

5.4 In the following program segment, which variable is the counter and which is the accumulator?

```
int x = 0, y = 0, z;
cout << "How many numbers do you wish to enter? ";
cin >> z;
while (x++ < z)
{
    int a;
    cout << "Enter a number: ";
    cin >> a;
    y += a;
}
cout << "The sum of those numbers is " << y << endl;
```

5.5 The following program skeleton is a modification of Program 5-4. Instead of starting at 1, however, write this program so it starts at 10 and counts backward down to 1.

```
// This program displays the numbers 10 down to 1 and
// their squares.
#include <iostream>
using namespace std;
```

```
int main()
{
   int num = // Initialize num to the proper value.

   cout << "Number      Number Squared\n";
   cout << "------------------------\n";
   //
   // Insert your while loop here.
   //
   return 0;
}
```

5.6   Modify Program 5-9 so any negative number is a sentinel.

5.7   The `do-while` Loop and `for` Loop

In addition to the `while` loop, C++ also offers the `do-while` and `for` loops. Each loop is appropriate for different programming problems.

The `do-while` loop looks similar to a `while` loop turned upside down. Here is its format when a single statement is to be repeated:

```
do
    statement;
while (expression);
```

Here is the format of the `do-while` loop when repeating a block of statements:

```
do
{
   statement;
   statement;
   // Place as many statements here
   // as necessary.
} while (expression);
```

 Note: The `do-while` loop must be terminated with a semicolon after the closing parenthesis of the test expression.

Besides the way it looks, the difference between the `do-while` loop and the `while` loop is that `do-while` is a *posttest* loop. It tests its expression after each iteration is complete. This means `do-while` always performs at least one iteration, even if the test expression is false from the start. For example, in the following `while` loop the `cout` statement will not execute at all:

```
int x = 1;
while (x < 0)
   cout << x << endl;
```

But the `cout` statement in the following do-while loop will execute once because the do-while loop does not evaluate the expression x < 0 until the end of the iteration.

```
int x = 1;
do
    cout << x << endl;
while (x < 0);
```

You should use do-while when you want make sure the loop executes at least once. Program 5-11, another version of the test-averaging program, uses a do-while loop to repeat as long as the user wishes.

Program 5-11

```
// This program averages 3 test scores. It repeats as
// many times as the user wishes.

#include <iostream>
using namespace std;

int main()
{
    int score1, score2, score3;
    float average;
    char again;

    do
    {
        cout << "Enter 3 scores and I will average them: ";
        cin >> score1 >> score2 >> score3;
        average = (score1 + score2 + score3) / 3.0;
        cout << "The average is " << average << ".\n";
        cout << "Do you want to average another set? (Y/N) ";
        cin >> again;
    } while (again == 'Y' || again == 'y');
    return 0;
}
```

Program Output with Example Input Shown in Bold
```
Enter 3 scores and I will average them: 80 90 70[Enter]
The average is 80.
Do you want to average another set? (Y/N) y[Enter]
Enter 3 scores and I will average them: 60 75 88[Enter]
The average is 74.333336.
Do you want to average another set? (Y/N) n[Enter]
```

The variable again is set by cin inside the body of the loop. Because the test occurs after the body has executed, it doesn't matter that again isn't initialized.

Notice the use of the || operator in the test expression. Any expression that can be evaluated as true or false may be used to control a loop.

Using do-while with Menus

The do-while loop is a good choice for repeating a menu. Recall Program 4-31, which displays a menu of health club packages. Program 5-12 is a modification of that program that uses a do-while loop to repeat the program until the user selects item 4 from the menu.

Program 5-12

```cpp
// This program displays a menu and asks the user to make a
// selection. A switch statement determines which item the
// user has chosen. A do-while loop repeats the program until
// the user selects item 4 from the menu.

#include <iostream>
#include <iomanip>
using namespace std;

int main()
{
    int choice, months;
    float charges;

    cout << fixed << showpoint << setprecision(2);
    do
    {
        cout << "\n\t\tHealth Club Membership Menu\n\n";
        cout << "1.  Standard Adult Membership\n";
        cout << "2.  Child Membership\n";
        cout << "3.  Senior Citizen Membership\n";
        cout << "4.  Quit the Program\n\n";
        cout << "Enter your choice: ";
        cin >> choice;
        if (choice != 4)
        {
            cout << "For how many months? ";
            cin >> months;
        }
```

(program continues)

Program 5-12   *(continued)*

```
        switch (choice)
        {
            case 1:  charges = months * 40.00;
                     cout << "\nThe total charges are $" << charges << endl;
                     break;
            case 2:  charges = months * 20.00;
                     cout << "\nThe total charges are $" << charges << endl;
                     break;
            case 3:  charges = months * 30.00;
                     cout << "\nThe total charges are $" << charges << endl;
                     break;
            case 4:  cout << "Thanks for using this ";
                     cout << "program.\n";
                     break;
            default: cout << "The valid choices are 1-4. ";
                     cout << "Try again.\n";
        }
    } while (choice != 4);
    return 0;
}
```

Program Output with Example Input Shown in Bold

```
                Health Club Membership Menu

1.   Standard Adult Membership
2.   Child Membership
3.   Senior Citizen Membership
4.   Quit the Program

Enter your choice: 1[Enter]
For how many months 12[Enter]

The total charges are $480.00

                Health Club Membership Menu

1.   Standard Adult Membership
2.   Child Membership
3.   Senior Citizen Membership
4.   Quit the Program

Enter your choice: 4[Enter]

Thanks for using this program.
```

The for **Loop**

The third type of loop in C++ is the for loop. It is ideal for situations that require a counter because it has built-in expressions that initialize and update variables. Here is the format of the for loop when used to repeat a single statement:

```
for (initialization; test; update)
    statement;
```

The format of the for loop when used to repeat a block is

```
for (initialization; test; update)
{
    statement;
    statement;
    // Place as many statements here
    // as necessary.
}
```

There are three expressions inside the parentheses, separated by semicolons. (Notice there is no semicolon after the third expression.) The first expression is the *initialization expression*. It is typically used to initialize a counter or other variable that must have a starting value. This is the first action performed by the loop and it is only done once.

The second expression is the *test expression*. Like the test expression in the while and do-while loops, it controls the execution of the loop. As long as this expression is true, the body of the for loop will repeat. The for loop is a pretest loop, so it evaluates the test expression before each iteration.

The third expression is the *update expression*. It executes at the end of each iteration. Typically, it increments a counter or other variable that must be modified in each iteration.

Program 5-13 is another version of Program 5-5, modified to use the for loop instead of the while loop.

Program 5-13

```
// This program displays the numbers 1 through 10 and
// their squares.

#include <iostream>
using namespace std;

int main()
{
    int num;

    cout << "Number      Number Squared\n";
    cout << "---------------------------\n";
```

(program continues)

Program 5-13 *(continued)*

```
    for (num = 1; num <= 10; num++)
        cout << num << "\t\t" << (num * num) << endl;
    return 0;
}
```

Program Output

```
    Number      Number Squared
    - - - - - - - - - - - - - - - - - - - - - - - - -
    1            1
    2            4
    3            9
    4            16
    5            25
    6            36
    7            49
    8            64
    9            81
    10           100
```

Figure 5-3 describes the mechanics of the for loop in Program 5-13.

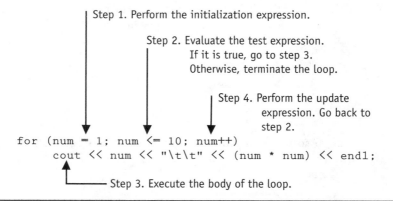

Figure 5-3

 WARNING! Be careful not to place a statement in the body of the for loop that duplicates the update expression. The following loop, for example, increments x twice for each iteration:

```
    for (x = 1; x <= 10; x++)
    {
        cout << x << (x * x) << endl;
        x++;
    }
```

Note: Since the `for` loop performs a pretest, it's possible that it will never iterate. Here is an example:

```
for (x = 11; x < 10; x++)
    cout << x << endl;
```

Since the variable `x` is initialized to a value that makes the test expression false from the beginning, this loop terminates as soon as it begins.

Omitting the `for` Loop's Expressions

The initialization expression may be omitted from inside the `for` loop's parentheses if it has already been performed or if no initialization is needed. Here is an example of the loop in Program 5-11 with the initialization being performed prior to the loop:

```
int num = 1;
for ( ; num <= 10; num++)
    cout << num << "\t\t" << (num * num) << endl;
```

 Note: The semicolon is still required, even though the initialization expression is missing.

You may also omit the update expression if it is being performed elsewhere in the loop or if none is needed. The following `for` loop works just like a `while` loop:

```
int num = 1;
for ( ; num <= 10; )
{
    cout << num << "\t\t" << (num * num) << endl;
    num++;
}
```

You can even go so far as to omit all three expressions from the `for` loop's parentheses. Be warned, however, that if you leave out the test expression, the loop has no built-in way of terminating. Here is an example:

```
for ( ; ; )
    cout << "Hello World\n";
```

Since this loop has no way of stopping, it will display `"Hello World\n"` forever (or until something interrupts the program).

Other Forms of the Update Expression

You are not limited to using increment statements in the update expression. Here is a loop that displays all the even numbers from 2 through 100 by adding 2 to its counter:

```
for (number = 2; number <= 100; number += 2)
    cout << number << endl;
```

And here is a loop that counts backward from 10 down to 0:

```
for (number = 10; number >= 0; number--)
    cout << number << endl;
```

The following loop has no formal body. The combined increment operation and cout statement in the update expression perform all the work of each iteration:

```
for (number = 1; number <= 10; cout << number++);
```

Using Initialization and Update Lists

If your loop needs to perform more than one statement as part of the initialization, separate the statements with commas. Program 5-14 is a version of Program 5-8, modified to let the user input sales figures for one week. It initializes two variables in the for loop's initialization.

Program 5-14

```
// This program takes daily sales figures for one week
// and calculates their total.

#include <iostream>
#include <iomanip>
using namespace std;

int main()
{
    const int days = 7;
    int count;
    float total;

    for (count = 1, total = 0.0; count <= days; count++)
    {
        float sales;
        cout << "Enter the sales for day " << count << ": ";
        cin >> sales;
        total += sales;
    }
    cout << fixed << showpoint << setprecision(2);
    cout << "The total sales are $" << total << endl;
    return 0;
}
```

Program Output with Example Input Shown in Bold
```
Enter the sales for day 1: 489.32[Enter]
Enter the sales for day 2: 421.65[Enter]
Enter the sales for day 3: 497.89[Enter]
Enter the sales for day 4: 532.37[Enter]
Enter the sales for day 5: 506.92[Enter]
Enter the sales for day 6: 489.01[Enter]
Enter the sales for day 7: 476.55[Enter]
The total sales are $3413.71
```

In the `for` loop, `count` is initialized to 1, then `total` is initialized to 0.0. You may place more than one statement in the update expression as well.

```
float sales;
for (count = 1, total = 0.0; count <= days; count++, total += sales)
{
    cout << "Enter the sales for day " << count << ": ";
    cin >> sales;
}
```

In the update expression of this loop, `count` is incremented, then the value in `sales` is added to `total` at the end of each iteration. The two statements are separated by a comma.

Note: In the preceding program segment, the definition of the variable `sales` was moved out of the body of the loop. The scope of a variable defined in the block does not extend outside the braces. In order for the update expression to see `sales`, its definition had to be placed prior to the `for` loop.

Connecting multiple statements with commas works well in the initialization and update expressions, but don't try to connect multiple relational expressions this way in the conditional expression. If you wish to perform more than one conditional test, build an expression with the `&&` or `||` operators, like this:

```
for (count = 1, total = 0; count <= 10 && total < 500; count++)
{
    float amount;
    cout << "Enter the amount of purchase #" << count << ": ";
    cin >> amount;
    total += amount;
}
```

Defining a Variable in the Initialization Expression

Not only may variables be initialized in the initialization expression, but they may be defined there as well. Here is an example:

```
for (int num = 1; num <= 10; num++)
    cout << num << "\t\t" << (num * num) << endl;
```

In this loop, the variable `num` is both defined and initialized in the initialization expression. It makes sense to define variables like counters in this manner when they are only used in a loop. This makes their purpose clearer.

According to the ANSI standard, when a variable is defined in a `for` loop's initialization expression, the scope of the variable is limited to the body of the loop. The variable is not visible to statements outside the loop.

WARNING! Some compilers, such as Visual C++ 6.0, do not follow the ANSI standard on this point. They allow the scope of a variable defined in a `for` loop's initialization expression to extend beyond the body of the loop. These compilers make the variable visible to all statements in the block of code containing the loop, from the definition down. To allow your C++ code to compile and run regardless of which compiler is used, it is wise not to define a variable in a `for` loop initialization expression if the same variable, or another variable with the same name, will be used outside the loop or in a second loop within the same block of code.

Checkpoint [5.7]

5.7 What will the following program segments display?

A)
```cpp
int count = 10;
do
    cout << "Hello World\n";
while (count++ < 1);
```

B)
```cpp
int v = 0;
do
    cout << v++;
while (v < 5);
```

C)
```cpp
int count = 0, funny = 1, serious = 0, limit = 4;
do
{
    funny++;
    serious += 2;
}
while (count++ < limit);
cout << funny << " " << serious << " ";
cout << count << endl;
```

5.8 Write a program segment with a `do-while` loop that asks the user to enter a number. The loop should keep a running total of the numbers entered and stop when the total is greater than 300.

5.9 Name the three expressions in a `for` statement's parentheses.

5.10 What will the following program segments display?

A)
```cpp
for (count = 0; count < 6; count++)
    cout << (count + count);
```

B)
```cpp
for (value = -5; value; value++)
    cout << value;
```

C)
```cpp
for (x = 5; x <= 14; x += 3)
    cout << x << endl;
cout << x << endl;
```

5.11 Write a `for` loop that displays every fifth number, starting at zero, through 100.

5.12 Write a `for` loop that repeats seven times, asking the user to enter a number. The loop should also calculate the sum of the numbers entered.

5.13 Write a `for` loop that calculates the total of the following series of numbers:

$$\frac{1}{30} + \frac{2}{29} + \frac{3}{28} + \frac{4}{27} + \dots \frac{30}{1}$$

5.8 Deciding Which Loop to Use

CONCEPT Although most repetitive algorithms can be written with any of the three types of loops, each works best in different situations.

Each of C++'s three loops are ideal to use in different situations. Here's a short summary of when each loop should be used.

The `while` Loop

The `while` loop is a *pretest* loop. It is ideal in situations where you do not want the loop to iterate if the condition is false from the beginning. It is also ideal if you want to use a sentinel.

```
cout << "This program finds the square of any integer.\n";
cout << "\nEnter an integer, or -99 to quit: ";
cin >> num;
while (num != -99)
{   cout << num << " squared is " << pow(num, 2) << endl;
    cout << "\nEnter an integer, or -99 to quit ";
    cin >> num;
}
```

The `do-while` Loop

The `do-while` loop is a *posttest* loop. It is ideal in situations where you always want the loop to iterate at least once.

```
cout << "This program finds the square of any integer.\n";
do
{   cout << "\nEnter an integer: ";
    cin >> num;
    cout << num << " squared is " << pow(num, 2) << endl;
    cout << "Do you want to square another number? (Y/N) ";
    cin >> doAgain;
} while (doAgain == "Y" || doAgain == "y");
```

The `for` Loop

The `for` loop is a *pretest* loop that first executes an initialization expression. In addition, it automatically executes an update expression at the end of each iteration. It is ideal for situations where a counter variable is needed. The `for` loop is primarily used when the exact number of required iterations is known.

```
cout << "This program finds the squares of the integers "
     << "from 1 to 8.\n\n";
for (num = 1; num <= 8; num++)
{
    cout << num << " squared is " << pow(num, 2) << endl;
}
```

5.9 Nested Loops

CONCEPT A loop that is inside another loop is called a *nested loop*.

In Chapter 4 you saw how one `if` statement could be nested inside another one. It is also possible to nest one loop inside another loop. The first loop is called the *outer loop*. The one nested inside it is called the *inner loop*. This is illustrated by the following two `while` loops. Notice how the inner loop must be completely contained within the outer one.

```
while (some condition)          // Beginning of the outer loop
{    ---
    while (some condition)      // Beginning of the inner loop
    {    ---
        ---
    }                           // End of the inner loop
}                               // End of the outer loop
```

Nested loops are used when, for each iteration of the outer loop, something must be repeated a number of times. Here are some examples from everyday life:

- For *each* batch of cookies to be baked we must put *each* cookie on the cookie sheet.
- For *each* salesman, we must add up *each* of his sales to determine his total commission.
- For *each* teacher we must produce a class list for *each* class he or she teaches.
- For *each* student we must add up *each* the student's test scores to find his or her test average.

Whatever the task, the inner loop will go through all its iterations each time the outer loop is done. This is illustrated by Program 5-15, which handles this last task, finding student test score averages. Any kind of loop can be nested within any other kind of loop. This program uses two for loops.

Program 5-15

```cpp
// This program uses nested loops to average a set of test scores
// for a group of students. It asks the user for the number of
// students and the number of test scores per student.

#include <iostream>
using namespace std;

int main()
{
    int   numStudents,    // Number of students
          numTests,       // Number of tests per student
          total;          // Accumulates total score for each student
    float average;        // Average test score for each student

    cout << "This program averages test scores.\n";
    cout << "How many students are there? ";
    cin  >> numStudents;
    cout << "How many test scores does each student have? ";
    cin  >> numTests;
    cout << endl;

    for (int student = 1; student <= numStudents; student++) // Outer loop
    {
        total = 0;
        for (int test = 1; test <= numTests; test++)          // Inner loop
        {
            int score;
            cout << "Enter score " << test << " for "
                 << "student " << student << ": ";
            cin >> score;
            total += score;
        }                                                     // End of inner loop
        average = total / numTests;
        cout << "The average for student " << student;
        cout << " is " << average << ".\n\n";
    }                                                         // End of outer loop
    return 0;
}
```

Program 5-15

Program Output with Example Input Shown in Bold
```
This program averages test scores.
How many students are there? 2[Enter]
How many test scores does each student have? 3[Enter]

Enter score 1 for student 1: 84[Enter]
Enter score 2 for student 1: 79[Enter]
Enter score 3 for student 1: 97[Enter]
The average for student 1 is 86.

Enter score 1 for student 2: 92[Enter]
Enter score 2 for student 2: 88[Enter]
Enter score 3 for student 2: 94[Enter]
The average for student 2 is 91.
```

Let's trace what happened in Program 5-15, using the sample data shown. In this case, for each of two students, each of three scores were input and summed. First the outer loop was entered and student was set to 1. Then, once the total accumulator was initialized to zero for that student, the inner loop was entered. While the outer loop was still on its first iteration and student was still 1, the inner loop went through all of its iterations, handling tests 1, 2, and 3 for that student. It then exited the inner loop and calculated and output the average for student 1. Only then did the program reach the bottom of the outer loop and go back up to do its second iteration. The second iteration of the outer loop processed student 2. For *each* iteration of the outer loop, the inner loop did *all* its iterations.

It might help to think of each loop as a rotating wheel. The outer loop is a big wheel that is moving slowly. The inner loop is a smaller wheel that is spinning quickly. For every one rotation the big wheel makes, the little wheel makes many rotations. Since, in our example, the outer loop was done twice, and the inner loop was done three times for each iteration of the outer loop, the inner loop was done a total of six times in all. This corresponds to the six scores input by the user. The following points summarize this.

◆ An inner loop goes through all of its iterations for each iteration of an outer loop.

◆ Inner loops complete their iterations faster than outer loops.

◆ To get the total number of iterations of an inner loop, multiply the number of iterations of the outer loop by the number of iterations done by the inner loop each time the outer loop is done.

5.10   Breaking Out of a Loop

CONCEPT The break statement causes a loop to terminate early.

 WARNING! Use the break statement with great caution. Because it bypasses the loop condition to terminate the loop, it violates the rules of structured programming and makes code more difficult to understand, debug, and maintain. For this reason, you should avoid using break, when possible. Because it is part of the C++ language, however, we discuss it briefly in this section.

Sometimes it's necessary to stop a loop before it goes through all its iterations. The break statement, which was used with switch in Chapter 4, can also be placed inside a loop. When it is encountered, the loop stops and the program jumps to the statement immediately following the loop.

The while loop in the following program segment appears to execute 10 times, but the break statement causes it to stop after the fifth iteration.

```cpp
int count = 0;
while (count++ < 10)
{
   cout << count << endl;
   if (count == 5)
      break;
}
```

Program 5-16 uses the break statement to interrupt a for loop. The program asks the user for a number and then displays the value of that number raised to the powers of 0 through 10. The user can stop the loop at any time by entering Q.

Program 5-16

```cpp
// This program raises the user's number to the powers of 0 through 10.

#include <iostream>
#include <cmath>
using namespace std;

int main()
{
   int value;
   char choice;

   cout << "Enter a number: ";
   cin >> value;
   cout << "This program will raise " << value;
   cout << " to the powers of 0 through 10.\n";
```

(program continues)

Program 5-16   *(continued)*

```
for (int count = 0; count <= 10; count++)
{
    cout << value << " raised to the power of ";
    cout << count << " is " << pow(value, count);
    cout << "\nEnter Q to quit or any other key ";
    cout << "to continue. ";
    cin >> choice;
    if (choice == 'Q' || choice == 'q')
        break;
}
return 0;
}
```

Program Output with Example Input Shown in Bold
```
Enter a number: 2[Enter]
This program will raise 2 to the powers of 0 through 10.
2 raised to the power of 0 is 1
Enter Q to quit or any other key to continue. C[Enter]
2 raised to the power of 1 is 2
Enter Q to quit or any other key to continue. C[Enter]
2 raised to the power of 2 is 4
Enter Q to quit or any other key to continue. Q[Enter]
```

Using `break` in a Nested Loop

In a nested loop, the `break` statement only interrupts the loop it is placed in. The following program segment displays five rows of asterisks on the screen. The outer loop controls the number of rows and the inner loop controls the number of asterisks in each row. The inner loop is designed to display 20 asterisks, but the `break` statement stops it after the tenth iteration.

```
for (int row = 0; row < 5; row++)
{
    for (int star = 0; star < 20; star++)
    {
        cout << '*';
        if (int star == 10)
            break;
    }
    cout << endl;
}
```

The output of the program segment above is

```
* * * * * * * * * *
* * * * * * * * * *
* * * * * * * * * *
* * * * * * * * * *
* * * * * * * * * *
```

5.11   The continue Statement

CONCEPT	The continue statement causes a loop to stop its current iteration and begin the next one.

 WARNING! As with the break statement, the continue statement violates the rules of structured programming and makes code more difficult to understand, debug, and maintain. For this reason, you should use continue with great caution. Because it is part of the C++ language, however, we discuss it briefly in this section.

The continue statement causes the current iteration of a loop to end immediately. When continue is encountered, all the statements in the body of the loop that appear after it are ignored, and the loop prepares for the next iteration.

In a while loop, this means the program jumps to the test expression at the top of the loop. As usual, if the expression is still true, the next iteration begins. In a do-while loop, the program jumps to the test expression at the bottom of the loop, which determines if the next iteration will begin. In a for loop, continue causes the update expression to be executed, and then the test expression to be evaluated.

The following program segment demonstrates the use of continue in a while loop:

```
int testVal = 0;
while (testVal++ < 10)
{
   if (testVal == 4)
      continue;
   cout << testVal << " ";
}
```

This loop looks like it displays the integers 1 through 10. When testVal is equal to 4, however, the continue statement causes the loop to skip the cout statement and begin the next iteration. The output of the loop is

```
1 2 3 5 6 7 8 9 10
```

Program 5-17 shows a practical application of the continue statement. The program calculates the charges for DVD rentals where current releases cost $3.50 and all others cost $2.50. If a customer rents several DVDs, every third one is free. The continue statement is used to skip the part of the loop that calculates the charges for every third DVD.

Program 5-17

```cpp
// This program calculates the charges for DVD rentals.
// Every third rental is free.

#include <iostream>
#include <iomanip>
using namespace std;

int main()
{
    int dvdCount = 1, numDVDs;
    float total = 0.0;
    char current;

    cout << "How many DVDs are being rented? ";
    cin >> numDVDs;
    do
    {
        if ((dvdCount % 3) == 0)
        {
            cout << "DVD #" << dvdCount << " is free!\n";
            continue;
        }
        cout << "Is DVD #" << dvdCount;
        cout << " a current release? ";
        cin >> current;
        if (current == 'Y' || current == 'y')
            total += 3.50;
        else
            total += 2.50;
    } while (dvdCount++ < numDVDs);

    cout << fixed << showpoint << setprecision(2);
    cout << "The total is $" << total << endl;
    return 0;
}
```

Program Output with Example Input Shown in Bold
```
How many DVDs are being rented? 6[Enter]
Is DVD #1 a current release? y[Enter]
Is DVD #2 a current release? n[Enter]
DVD #3 is free!
Is DVD #4 a current release? n[Enter]
Is DVD #5 a current release? y[Enter]
DVD #6 is free!
The total is $12.00
```

5.12 Focus on Software Engineering: *Using Loops for Data Validation*

CONCEPT	Loops can be used to create input routines that repeat until acceptable data is entered.

Loops are especially useful for validating input. They can test whether an invalid value has been entered and, if so, require the user to continue entering inputs until a valid one is received.

In Chapter 4 we used `if` statements to validate user inputs, but they do not provide an ideal solution. Examine the following code, which uses an `if` statement to try to ensure that the user enters a number between 1 and 100.

```
cout << "Enter a number in the range 1 - 100: ";
cin >> number;
if (number < 1 || number > 100)
{
    cout << "ERROR: The value must be in the range 1 - 100: ";
    cin >> number;
}
```

Notice that if the user enters a good number initially, the lines of code in the body of the `if` statement are never executed. That is what we want to happen. If the user enters an invalid number, they will be asked to enter a new value. But what if the second number is also invalid? It will never be checked and so will be accepted.

A better approach is to use a `while` loop to validate input data. The following code demonstrates this. Like the previous code, this code is validating that the user enters a number between 1 and 100.

```
cout << "Enter a number in the range 1 - 100: ";
cin >> number;
while (number < 1 || number > 100)
{
    cout << "ERROR: The value must be in the range 1 - 100: ";
    cin >> number;
}
```

Compare this code to the code that used the `if` statement. If the user enters a good value initially, the loop will never be executed. This is what we want. If the user enters an invalid number, however, the loop will be entered and the user will not be able to leave it until a valid input has been entered. Every input will be checked.

Program 5-12, the health club membership billing program, tried to validate the user's menu choice with a `switch` statement. This partially worked since the `switch` statement that caught any invalid input was inside a loop. But the program had a bug. If the user entered an invalid input, the program still asked "`For how many months`" the member was being billed, before reporting that an invalid choice had been made. Program 5-18 modifies Program 5-12 to use a `while` loop to validate the menu choice. Notice that the validation is done as soon as the choice is entered, which is ideal. No further processing is done until a good choice is entered.

Program 5-18

```cpp
// This version of the menu-driven health club membership billing
// program uses a while loop to perform data validation.

#include <iostream>
#include <iomanip>
using namespace std;

int main()
{
    int choice, months;
    float charges;

    cout << fixed << showpoint << setprecision(2);
    do
    {
        cout << "\n\n    Health Club Membership Menu\n\n";
        cout << "1.  Standard Adult Membership\n";
        cout << "2.  Child Membership\n";
        cout << "3.  Senior Citizen Membership\n";
        cout << "4.  Quit the Program\n\n";
        cout << "Enter your choice: ";
        cin  >> choice;

        while (choice < 1 || choice > 4)    // Validate choice
        {   cout << "Choice must be between 1 and 4. \n"
                 << "Please reenter: ";
            cin  >> choice;
        }
        if (choice !=4)
        {   cout << "For how many months? ";
            cin  >> months;
        }
        switch (choice)
        {
            case 1:   charges = months * 40.00;
                      cout << "\nThe total charges are $" << charges << endl;
                      break;
            case 2:   charges = months * 20.00;
                      cout << "\nThe total charges are $" << charges << endl;
                      break;
            case 3:   charges = months * 30.00;
                      cout << "\nThe total charges are $" << charges << endl;
                      break;
            case 4:   cout << "Thanks for using this program.\n";
        }
    } while (choice != 4);
    return 0;
}
```

Program 5-18

Program Output with Example Input Shown in Bold

```
          Health Club Membership Menu

1.  Standard Adult Membership
2.  Child Membership
3.  Senior Citizen Membership
4.  Quit the Program

Enter your choice: 5[Enter]
Choice must be between 1 and 4.
Please reenter: 6[Enter]
Choice must be between 1 and 4.
Please reenter: 1[Enter]
For how many months? 12[Enter]

The total charges are $480.00

          Health Club Membership Menu

1.  Standard Adult Membership
2.  Child Membership
3.  Senior Citizen Membership
4.  Quit the Program

Enter your choice: 4[Enter]
Thanks for using this program.
```

Program 5-19 is another example of using while loops to perform input data validation. This program calculates the number of soccer teams a youth league can create, based on the desired team size and the total number of players.

Program 5-19

```cpp
// This program calculates the number of soccer teams that a
// youth league may create from the number of available players.
// Input validation is performed with while loops.

#include <iostream>
using namespace std;
```

(program continues)

Program 5-19 *(continued)*

```cpp
int main()
{
    int players, teamPlayers, numTeams, leftOver;

    // Get the number of players per team.
    cout << "How many players do you wish per team?\n";
    cout << "(Enter a value in the range 9 - 15): ";
    cin >> teamPlayers;
    while (teamPlayers < 9 || teamPlayers > 15)  // Validate input
    {
        cout << "Team size should be 9 to 15 players.\n";
        cout << "How many players do you wish per team? ";
        cin >> teamPlayers;
    }
    // Get the number of players available.
    cout << "How many players are available? ";
    cin >> players;
    while (players < 0)        // Validate input
    {
        cout << "Please enter a positive number: ";
        cin >> players;
    }
    // Perform calculations.
    numTeams = players / teamPlayers;
    leftOver = players % teamPlayers;
    cout << "There will be " << numTeams << " teams with ";
    cout << leftOver << " players left over.\n";

    return 0;
}
```

Program Output with Example Input Shown in Bold
```
How many players do you wish per team?
(Enter a value in the range 9 - 15): 4[Enter]
Team size should be 9 to 15 players.
How many players do you wish per team? 12[Enter]
How many players are available? -142[Enter]
Please enter a positive number: 142[Enter]
There will be 11 teams with 10 players left over.
```

❓ Checkpoint [5.8–5.12]

5.14 Which loop (while, do-while, or for) would be best to use in the following situations?

A) The user must enter a set of exactly 14 numbers.

B) A menu must be displayed for the user to make a selection.

C) A calculation must be made an unknown number of times. (It is possible the calculation will not be made at all.)

D) A series of numbers must be entered by the user, terminated by a sentinel value.

E) A series of values must be entered. The user specifies exactly how many.

5.15 How many times will the value in *y* be displayed in the following program segment?

```
for (x = 0; x < 20; x++)
{
    for (y = 0; y < 30; y++)
        cout << y << endl;
}
```

5.16 How many times will the value in *y* be displayed in the following program segment?

```
for (x = 0; x < 20; x++)
{
    for (y = 0; y < 30; y++)
    {
        if (y > 10)
            break;
        cout << y << endl;
    }
}
```

5.17 What will the following program segment display?

```
int x = 0, y = 0;
while (x++ < 5)
{
    if (x == 3)
        continue;
    y += x;

    cout << y << endl;
}
```

5.18 Write an input validation loop that asks the user to enter a number in the range of 10 through 25.

5.19 Write an input validation loop that asks the user to enter Y, y, N, or n.

5.20 Write an input validation loop that asks the user to enter "Yes" or "No".

5.13 Focus on Problem Solving and Program Design: *A Case Study*

The Central Mountain Credit Union uses a central data processing system where each branch leases a telephone line to access a minicomputer at the Credit Union's main office. The minicomputer has a tendency to slow down when many users are on the system. Because of this, the loan officer at one of the branch offices has asked you to write a loan amortization program to run locally, on her desktop PC.

Calculations

The credit union uses the following formula to calculate the monthly payment of a loan:

$$\text{Payment} = \frac{\text{Loan} * \text{Rate} / 12 * \text{Term}}{\text{Term} - 1}$$

Where:

Loan = the amount of the loan
Rate = the annual interest rate
Term = $(1 + R/12)^{Y*12}$

Report Requirements

The report produced by the program should show the monthly payment and print four columns for each month in the loan period:

```
Month number
Interest
Principal
Balance
```

The following report may be used as a model. It shows all the required information on a one-year, $5,000 loan at 12.9 percent annual interest.

Month	Interest	Principal	Balance
1	53.75	392.60	4607.40
2	49.53	396.82	4210.58
3	45.26	401.09	3809.49
4	40.95	405.40	3404.09
5	36.59	409.76	2994.33
6	32.19	414.16	2580.17
7	27.74	418.62	2161.55
8	23.24	423.12	1738.44
9	18.69	427.66	1310.77
10	14.09	432.26	878.51
11	9.44	436.91	441.60
12	4.75	441.60	0.00

Variables

Table 5-1 lists the variables needed in the program.

Table 5-1

Variable	Description
loan	A float. Holds the loan amount.
rate	A float. Holds the annual interest rate.
moInterestRate	A float. Holds the monthly interest rate.
years	A float. Holds the number of years of the loan.
balance	A float. Holds the remaining balance to be paid.
term	A float. Used in the monthly payment calculation.
payment	A float. Holds the monthly payment amount.
numPayments	An int. Holds the total number of payments.
month	An int. Loop control variable that holds the current payment number.
moInterest	A float. Holds the monthly interest amount.
principal	A float. Holds the amount of the monthly payment that pays down the loan.

Program Design

Figure 5-4 shows a hierarchy chart for the program.

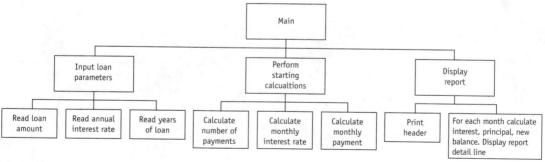

Figure 5-4

The detail of the program can be expanded in pseudocode:

Ask user to input the loan amount.
Ask user to input the annual interest rate.
Ask user to enter the number of years of the loan.
Calculate the number of payments.
Calculate the monthly interest rate
Calculate the monthly payment.
Print the report header.
For each month in the loan period
    Calculate the monthly interest.
    Calculate the principal.
    Calculate the new balance.
    Display the month, payment, interest, principal, and balance.
End For

Program 5-20 lists the final C++ code.

Program 5-20

```cpp
// This program produces a loan amortization chart for the
// Central Mountain Credit Union.

#include <iostream>
#include <iomanip>
#include <cmath>            // Needed for the pow function
using namespace std;

int main()
{
    float loan,            // Loan amount
          rate,            // Annual interest rate
          moInterestRate,  // Monthly interest rate
          years,           // Years of loan
          balance,         // Monthly balance
          term,            // Used to calculate payment
          payment;         // Monthly payment
    int   numPayments;     // Number of payments

    // Ask user for input.
    cout << "Loan amount: $";
    cin >> loan;
    cout << "Annual interest rate (entered as a decimal): ";
    cin >> rate;
    cout << "Years of loan: ";
    cin >> years;
```

(program continues)

Program 5-20 *(continued)*

```cpp
    // Calculate monthly payment.
    numPayments = 12 * years;
    moInterestRate = rate / 12.0;
    term = pow((1 + moInterestRate), numPayments);
    payment = (loan * moInterestRate * term) / (term - 1.0);

    // Display monthly payment.
    cout << fixed << showpoint << setprecision(2);
    cout << "Monthly payment: $" << payment << endl;

    // Display report header.
    cout << endl;
    cout << setw(5)  << "Month";
    cout << setw(10) << "Interest";
    cout << setw(10) << "Principal";
    cout << setw(10) << "Balance" << endl;
    cout << "---------------------------------------\n";

    // Produce a listing for each month.
    balance = loan;

    for (int month = 1; month <= numPayments; month++)
    {
        float moInterest,     // Amt. of monthly pmt that pays interest
              principal;      // Amt. of monthly pmt the brings down the balance

        // Calculate monthly interest
        moInterest = moInterestRate * balance;
        if (month != numPayments)
            principal = payment - moInterest;
        else    // If this is the last month
        {
            principal = balance;
            payment = balance + moInterest;
        }

        // Calculate the new loan balance.
        balance -= principal;

        // Display payment figures
        cout << setw(4)  << month;
        cout << setw(10) << moInterest;
        cout << setw(10) << principal;
        cout << setw(10) << balance << endl;
    }
    return 0;
}
```

Program 5-20

Program Output with Example Input Shown in Bold
Loan amount: $**2500[Enter]**
Annual interest rate: **0.08[Enter]**
Years of loan: **2[Enter]**
Monthly payment: $113.07

Month	Interest	Principal	Balance
1	16.67	96.40	2403.60
2	16.02	97.04	2306.55
3	15.38	97.69	2208.86
4	14.73	98.34	2110.52
5	14.07	99.00	2011.52
6	13.41	99.66	1911.86
7	12.75	100.32	1811.54
8	12.08	100.99	1710.55
9	11.40	101.66	1608.89
10	10.73	102.34	1506.54
11	10.04	103.02	1403.52
12	9.36	103.71	1299.81
13	8.67	104.40	1195.40
14	7.97	105.10	1090.31
15	7.27	105.80	984.51
16	6.56	106.50	878.00
17	5.85	107.21	770.79
18	5.14	107.93	662.86
19	4.42	108.65	554.21
20	3.69	109.37	444.83
21	2.97	110.10	334.73
22	2.23	110.84	223.90
23	1.49	111.58	112.32
24	0.75	112.32	0.00

 Note: You might have noticed in the output that for some months, such as months 2 and 9, the interest amount plus the principal amount does not add up to the monthly payment amount. Also, for some months, the previous balance minus the principal paid does not exactly equal the new balance. These problems are due to *round-off error*, which is caused by a disparity between the precision of a value the computer stores internally and the precision of the value it displays. Do not worry about this for now. You will learn later how to deal with this.

Review Questions and Exercises

Fill-in-the-Blank

1. To _____ a value means to increase it by one, and to _____ a value means to decrease it by one.

2. When the increment or decrement operator is placed before the operand (or to the operand's left), the operator is being used in _____ mode.

3. When the increment or decrement operator is placed after the operand (or to the operand's right), the operator is being used in _____ mode.

4. The statement or block that is repeated is known as the _____ of the loop.

5. Each repetition of a loop is known as a(n) _____.

6. A loop that evaluates its test expression before each repetition is a(n) _____ loop.

7. A loop that evaluates its test expression after each repetition is a(n) _____ loop.

8. A loop that does not have a way of stopping is a(n) _____ loop.

9. A(n)_____ is a variable that "counts" the number of times a loop repeats.

10. A(n) _____ is a sum of numbers that accumulates with each iteration of a loop.

11. A(n) _____ is a variable that is initialized to some starting value, usually zero, and then has numbers added to it in each iteration of a loop.

12. A(n) _____ is a special value that marks the end of a series of values.

13. The _____ loop always iterates at least once.

14. The _____ and _____ loops will not iterate at all if their test expressions are false to start with.

15. The _____ loop is ideal for situations that require a counter.

16. Inside the `for` loop's parentheses, the first expression is the _____ , the second expression is the _____ , and the third expression is the _____.

17. A loop that is inside another is called a(n) _____ loop.

18. The _____ statement causes a loop to terminate immediately.

19. The _____ statement causes a loop to skip the remaining statements in the current iteration.

20. Write a `while` loop that lets the user enter a number. The number should be multiplied by 10 and the result stored in the variable `product`. The loop should iterate as long as `product` contains a value less than 100.

21. Write a `do-while` loop that asks the user to enter two numbers. The numbers should be added and the sum displayed. The user should be asked if he or she wishes to perform the operation again. If so, the loop should repeat; otherwise it should terminate.

22. Write a `for` loop that displays the following set of numbers:

```
0, 10, 20, 30, 40, 50 . . . 1000
```

23. Write a loop that asks the user to enter a number. The loop should iterate 10 times and keep a running total of the numbers entered.

24. Write a nested loop that displays 10 rows of '#' characters. There should be 15 '#' characters in each row.

25. Convert the following `while` loop to a `do-while` loop:

```
int x = 1;
while (x > 0)
{
   cout << "enter a number: ";
   cin >> x;
}
```

26. Convert the following `do-while` loop to a `while` loop:

```
char sure;
do
{
   cout << "Are you sure you want to quit? ";
   cin >> sure;
} while (sure != 'Y' && sure != 'N');
```

27. Convert the following `while` loop to a `for` loop:

```
int count = 0;
while (count++ < 50)
{
   cout << "count is " << count << endl;
}
```

28. Convert the following `for` loop to a `while` loop:

```
for (int x = 50; x > 0; x--)
{
   cout << x << " seconds to go.\n";
}
```

True or False

29. T F The operand of the increment and decrement operators can be any valid mathematical expression.

30. T F The `cout` statement in the following program segment will display 5:

```
int x = 5;
cout << x++;
```

31. T F The `cout` statement in the following program segment will display 5:

```
int x = 5;
cout << ++x;
```

32. T F The `while` loop is a pretest loop.

33. T F The `do-while` loop is a pretest loop.

34. T F The `for` loop is a posttest loop.

35. T   F   It is not necessary to initialize counter variables.

36. T   F   All three of the `for` loop's expressions may be omitted.

37. T   F   One limitation of the `for` loop is that only one variable may be initialized in the initialization expression.

38. T   F   Variables may be defined inside the body of a loop.

39. T   F   A variable may be defined in the initialization expression of the `for` loop.

40. T   F   In a nested loop, the outer loop executes faster than the inner loop.

41. T   F   In a nested loop, the inner loop goes through all of its iterations for every single iteration of the outer loop.

42. T   F   To calculate the total number of iterations of a nested loop, add the number of iterations of all the loops.

43. T   F   The `break` statement causes a loop to stop the current iteration and begin the next one.

44. T   F   The `continue` statement causes a terminated loop to resume.

45. T   F   In a nested loop, the `break` statement only interrupts the loop it is placed in.

Find the Errors

46. Each of the following programs has errors. Find as many as you can.

A)
```cpp
// Find the error in this program.
#include <iostream>
using namespace std;

int main()
{
    int num1 = 0, num2 = 10, result;

    num1++;
    result = ++(num1 + num2);
    cout << num1 << " " << num2 << " " << result;
    return 0;
}
```

B)
```cpp
// This program adds two numbers entered by the user.
#include <iostream>
using namespace std;

int main()
{
    int num1, num2;
    char again;

    while (again == 'y' || again == 'Y')
        cout << "Enter a number: ";
```

```
        cin >> num1;
        cout << "Enter another number: ";
        cin >> num2;
        cout << "Their sum is << (num1 + num2) << endl;
        cout << "Do you want to do this again? ";
        cin >> again;
        return 0;
}
```

C)
```
// This program uses a loop to raise a number to a power.
#include <iostream>
using namespace std;

int main()
{
    int num, bigNum, power, count;

    cout << "Enter an integer: ";
    cin >> num;
    cout << "What power do you want it raised to? ";
    cin >> power;
    bigNum = num;
    while (count++ < power);
        bigNum *= num;
    cout << "The result is << bigNum << endl;
    return 0;
}
```

D)
```
// This program averages a set of numbers.
#include <iostream>
using namespace std;

int main()
{
    int numCount, total;
    float average;

    cout << "How many numbers do you want to average? ";
    cin >> numCount;
    for (int count = 0; count < numCount; count++)
    {
        int num;
        cout << "Enter a number: ";
        cin >> num;
        total += num;
        count++;
    }
    average = total / numCount;
    cout << "The average is << average << endl;
    return 0;
}
```

E)
```cpp
// This program displays the sum of two numbers.
#include <iostream>
using namespace std;

int main()
{
   int choice, num1, num2;

   do
   {
       cout << "Enter a number: ";
       cin >> num1;
       cout << "Enter another number: ";
       cin >> num2;
       cout << "Their sum is " << (num1 + num2) << endl;
       cout << "Do you want to do this again?\n";
       cout << "1 = yes, 0 = no\n";
       cin >> choice;
   } while (choice = 1)
   return 0;
}
```

F)
```cpp
// This program displays the sum of the numbers 1 - 100.
#include <iostream>
using namespace std;

int main()
{
   int count = 1, total;

   while (count <= 100)
       total += count;
   cout << "The sum of the numbers 1 - 100 is ";
   cout << total << endl;
   return 0;
}
```

Programming Challenges

General Requirements

A) Each program should have a section of comments at the top. The comments should contain your name, the date the program was written, the chapter that the assignment appeared in, and the assignment number and name. Here is an example:

```cpp
// Written by Jill Johnson
// March 31, 2003
// Chapter 5
// Assignment 1. Sum of Numbers
```

B) For each program that displays a dollar amount, format the output in fixed point decimal notation with two places of precision. Be sure the decimal place always displays, even when the number is zero or has no fractional part.

1. Sum of Numbers

Write a program that asks the user for a positive integer value. The program should use a loop to get the sum of all the integers from 1 up to the number entered. For example, if the user enters 50, the loop will find the sum of 1, 2, 3, 4, ... 50.

Input Validation: Do not accept a negative starting number.

2. Distance Traveled

The distance a vehicle travels can be calculated as follows:

```
distance = speed * time
```

For example, if a train travels 40 miles per hour for three hours, the distance traveled is 120 miles.

Write a program that asks the user for the speed of a vehicle (in miles per hour) and how many hours it has traveled. It should then use a loop to display the distance the vehicle has traveled for each hour of that time period. Here is an example of the output:

```
What is the speed of the vehicle in mph? 40
How many hours has it traveled? 3
Hour   Distance Traveled
--------------------------------
  1              40
  2              80
  3             120
```

Input Validation: Do not accept a negative number for speed and do not accept any value less than one for time traveled.

3. Pennies for Pay

Write a program that calculates how much a person would earn over a period of time if his or her salary is one penny the first day, two pennies the second day, and continued to double each day. The program should ask the user for the number of days. Display a table showing how much the salary was for each day, and then show the total pay at the end of the period. The output should be displayed in a dollar amount, not the number of pennies.

Input Validation: Do not accept a number less than one for the number of days worked.

4. Math Tutor

This program started in Problem 11 of Chapter 3, and was modified in Problem 4 of Chapter 4. Modify the program again so it displays a menu allowing the user to select an addition, subtraction, multiplication, or division problem. The final selection on the menu should let the user quit the program. After the user has finished the math problem, the program should display the menu again. This process is repeated until the user chooses to quit the program.

Input Validation: If the user selects an item not on the menu, display an error message and display the menu again.

5. Hotel Occupancy

Write a program that calculates the occupancy rate for each floor of a hotel. The program should start by asking the user how many floors the hotel has. A loop should then iterate once for each floor. In each iteration, the loop should ask the user for the number of rooms on the floor and how many of them are occupied. After all the iterations, the program should display how many rooms the hotel has, how many of them are occupied, how many are unoccupied, and the percentage of rooms that are occupied. The percentage may be calculated by dividing the number of rooms occupied by the number of rooms.

 Note: It is traditional that most hotels do not have a thirteenth floor. The loop in this program should skip the entire thirteenth iteration.

Input Validation: Do not accept a value less than one for the number of floors. Do not accept a number less than 10 for the number of rooms on a floor.

6. Average Rainfall

Write a program that uses nested loops to collect data and calculate the average rainfall over a period of years. The program should first ask for the number of years. The outer loop will iterate once for each year. The inner loop will iterate twelve times, once for each month. Each iteration of the inner loop will ask the user for the inches of rainfall for that month.

After all iterations, the program should display the number of months, the total inches of rainfall, and the average rainfall per month for the entire period.

Input Validation: Do not accept a number less than 1 for the number of years. Do not accept negative numbers for the monthly rainfall.

7. Population

Write a program that will predict the size of a population of organisms. The program should ask the user for the starting number of organisms, their average daily population increase (as a percentage), and the number of days they will multiply. A loop should display the size of the population for each day.

Input Validation: Do not accept a number less than two for the starting size of the population. Do not accept a negative number for average daily population increase. Do not accept a number less than one for the number of days they will multiply.

8. Centigrade to Fahrenheit Table

In Programming Challenge 7 of Chapter 3 you were asked to write a program that converts a centigrade temperature to Fahrenheit. Modify that program so it uses a loop to display a table of the centigrade temperatures from 0 to 20 and their Fahrenheit equivalents.

9. The Greatest and Least of These

Write a program with a loop that lets the user enter a series of integers. The user should enter -99 to signal the end of the series. After all the numbers have been entered, the program should display the largest and smallest numbers entered.

10. Payroll Report

Write a program that displays a weekly payroll report. A loop in the program should ask the user for the employee number, gross pay, state tax, federal tax, and FICA withholdings. The loop will terminate when 0 is entered for the employee number. After the data is entered, the program should display totals for gross pay, state tax, federal tax, FICA withholdings, and net pay.

Input Validation: Do not accept negative numbers for any of the items entered. Do not accept values for state, federal, or FICA withholdings that are greater than the gross pay. If the state tax + federal tax + FICA withholdings for any employee are greater than gross pay, print an error message and ask the user to re-enter the data for that employee.

11. Savings Account Balance

Write a program that calculates the balance of a savings account at the end of a period of time. It should ask the user for the annual interest rate, the starting balance, and the number of months that have passed since the account was established. A loop should then iterate once for every month, performing the following:

A) Ask the user for the amount deposited into the account during the month. (Do not accept negative numbers.) This amount should be added to the balance.

B) Ask the user for the amount withdrawn from the account during the month. (Do not accept negative numbers.) This amount should be subtracted from the balance.

C) Calculate the monthly interest. The monthly interest rate is the annual interest rate divided by twelve. Multiply the monthly interest rate by the balance, and add the result to the balance.

After the last iteration, the program should display the ending balance, the total amount of deposits, the total amount of withdrawals, and the total interest earned.

 Note: If a negative balance is calculated at any point, a message should be displayed indicating the account has been closed and the loop should terminate.

12. Bar Chart

Write a program that asks the user to enter today's sales for five stores. The program should then display a bar graph comparing each store's sales. Create each bar in the bar graph by displaying a row of asterisks. Each asterisk should represent $100 of sales.

Here is an example of the program's output. The user input is shown in bold.

```
Enter today's sales for store 1: 1000[Enter]
Enter today's sales for store 2: 1200[Enter]
Enter today's sales for store 3: 1800[Enter]
Enter today's sales for store 4: 800[Enter]
Enter today's sales for store 5: 1900[Enter]

SALES BAR CHART
Store 1: **********
Store 2: ************
Store 3: ******************
Store 4: ********
Store 5: *******************
```

Serendipity Booksellers Software Development Project—Part 5: *A Problem-Solving Exercise*

Revise the input data validation code you wrote for each module in Part 4 of this project to use `while` loops instead of `if` statements. Then add the following additional loops to the program.

1. The Main Menu

Item four on the Main Menu is "Exit," which allows the user to end the program. Add a loop to the `mainmenu.cpp` program that causes it to repeatedly display the menu until the user selects item four.

2. The Inventory Database Menu

Item five on the Inventory Database Menu is "Return to the Main Menu." When the project is complete, this item will cause the program to branch back to the main menu. For now, add a loop to the `invmenu.cpp` program that causes it to repeatedly display the menu until the user selects item five.

3. The Reports Menu

Item seven on the Reports Menu is "Return to the Main Menu." When the project is complete, this item will cause the program to branch back to the main menu. For now, add a loop to the `reports.cpp` program that causes it to repeatedly display the menu until the user selects item seven.

4. The Cashier Module

After the user has entered the information for a sale and the simulated sales slip is displayed, add code that asks the cashier if another transaction is to be processed. If so, the program should repeat.

CHAPTER 6

Functions

Topics

6.1 Focus on Software Engineering: *Modular Programming*

CONCEPT Programs may be broken up into a set of manageable functions, or modules. This is called modular programming.

A function is a collection of statements that performs a specific task. So far you have experienced functions in two ways: (1) you have created a function called `main` in every program you've written, and (2) you have used library functions such as `pow` and `sqrt`. In this chapter you will learn how to create your own functions that can be used like library functions.

One reason to use functions is that they break a program up into small, manageable units. Each unit is a module, programmed as a separate function. Imagine a book that has a thousand pages, but isn't divided into chapters or sections. Trying to find a single topic in the book would be very difficult. Real-world programs can easily have thousands of lines of code, and unless they are modularized, they can be very difficult to modify and maintain.

Another reason to use functions is that they simplify programs. If a specific task is performed in several places in a program, a function can be written once to perform that task, and then be executed anytime it is needed.

6.2 Defining and Calling Functions

> **CONCEPT** A function call is a statement that causes a function to execute. A function definition contains the statements that make up the function.

When creating a function, you must write its *definition*. All function definitions have the following parts:

Return type
: A function can send a value to the part of the program that activated it. The return type is the data type of the value that is sent from the function.

Name
: You should give each function a descriptive name. In general, the same rules that apply to variable names also apply to function names.

Parameter list
: The program can send information into a function. The parameter list is a list of variables that hold the values being passed to the function.

Body
: The body of a function is the set of statements that perform the function's operation. They are enclosed in a set of braces.

Figure 6-1 shows the definition of a simple function with the various parts labeled.

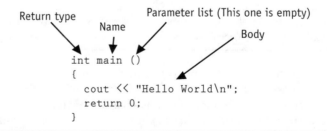

Figure 6-1

 Note: The line in the definition that reads int main () is called the *function header.*

Void Functions

You already know that a function can return a value. The `main` function in all of the programs you have seen in this book is declared to return an `int` value to the operating system. The `return 0;` statement causes the value 0 to be returned when the `main` function finishes executing.

It isn't necessary for all functions to return a value, however. Some functions simply perform one or more statements and then terminate. These are called *void functions*. The `displayMessage` function, shown here, is an example:

```cpp
void displayMessage()
{
    cout << "Hello from the function displayMessage.\n";
}
```

The name of the function is `displayMessage`, since that is what it does. Functions, like variables, should be given names that reflect their purpose.

Notice the function's return type is `void`. This means the function does not return a value to the part of the program that executed it. Also notice the function has no `return` statement. It simply displays a message on the screen and exits.

Calling a Function

A function is executed when it is *called*. Function `main` is called automatically when a program starts, but all other functions must be executed by *function call* statements. When a function is called, the program branches to that function and executes the statements in its body. Let's look at Program 6-1, which contains two functions: `main` and `displayMessage`.

Program 6-1

```cpp
// This program has two functions: main and displayMessage.

#include <iostream>
using namespace std;

//*****************************************
// Definition of function displayMessage  *
// This function displays a greeting.     *
//*****************************************
void displayMessage()
{
    cout << "Hello from the function displayMessage.\n";
}

int main()
{
    cout << "Hello from main.\n";
    displayMessage();
    cout << "Back in function main again.\n";
    return 0;
}
```

Program 6-1

Program Output
```
Hello from main.
Hello from the function displayMessage.
Back in function main again.
```

The function `displayMessage` is called by the following line in `main`:

```
displayMessage();
```

The function call is simply the name of the function followed by a set of parentheses and a semicolon. Let's compare this with the function header:

Function Header ⟶ `void displayMessage()`
Function Call ⟶ `displayMessage();`

The function header is part of the function definition. It declares the function's return type, name, and parameter list. It is not terminated with a semicolon because the definition of the function's body follows it.

The function call is a statement that executes the function, so it is terminated with a semicolon like all other C++ statements. The function call does not list the return type, and, if the program is not passing information into the function, the parentheses are left empty.

 Note: Later in this chapter you will see how information can be passed into a function inside the parentheses.

Even though the program starts executing at `main`, the function `displayMessage` is defined first. This is because the compiler must know the function's return type, the number of parameters, and the type of each parameter before it is called. One way to ensure the compiler will know this information is to place the function definition before all calls to that function. (Later you will see an alternative and preferred method of accomplishing this.)

 Note: You should always document your functions by writing comments that describe what they do. These comments should appear just before the function definition.

Notice how Program 6-1 flows. It starts, of course, in function `main`. When the call to `displayMessage` is encountered, the program branches to that function and performs its statements. Once `displayMessage` has finished executing, the program branches back to function `main` and resumes with the line that follows the function call. This is illustrated in Figure 6-2.

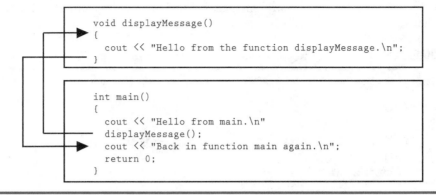

Figure 6-2

Function call statements may be used in control structures like loops, if statements, and switch statements. Program 6-2 places the displayMessage function call inside a loop.

Program 6-2

```cpp
// The function displayMessage is repeatedly called from within a loop.

#include <iostream>
using namespace std;

//*****************************************
// Definition of function displayMessage  *
// This function displays a greeting.      *
//*****************************************

void displayMessage()
{
    cout << "Hello from the function displayMessage.\n";
}

int main()
{
    cout << "Hello from main.\n";
    for (int count = 0; count < 5; count++)
        displayMessage();    // Call displayMessage
    cout << "Back in function main again.\n";
    return 0;
}
```

Program Output
```
Hello from main.
Hello from the function displayMessage.
Hello from the function displayMessage.
Hello from the function displayMessage.
Hello from the function displayMessage.
Hello from the function displayMessage.
Back in function main again.
```

It is possible to have many functions and function calls in a program. Program 6-3 has three functions: main, first, and second.

Program 6-3

```
// This program has three functions: main, first, and second.

#include <iostream>
using namespace std;

//*****************************************
// Definition of function first           *
// This function displays a message.       *
//*****************************************

void first()
{
    cout << "I am now inside the function first.\n";
}

//*****************************************
// Definition of function second          *
// This function displays a message.       *
//*****************************************

void second()
{
    cout << "I am now inside the function second.\n";
}

int main()
{
    cout << "I am starting in function main.\n";
    first();   // Call function first
    second();  // Call function second
    cout << "Back in function main again.\n";
    return 0;
}
```

Program Output
```
I am starting in function main.
I am now inside the function first.
I am now inside the function second.
Back in function main again.
```

In Program 6-3, function main contains a call to first and a call to second:

```
first();
second();
```

Each call statement causes the program to branch to a function and then back to `main` when the function is finished. Figure 6-3 illustrates the paths taken by the program.

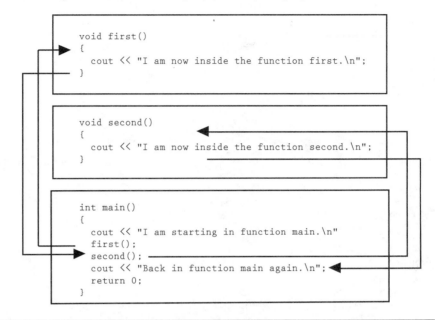

Figure 6-3

Functions may also be called in a hierarchical, or layered fashion. This is demonstrated by Program 6-4, which has three functions: `main`, `deep`, and `deeper`.

Program 6-4

```
// This program has three functions: main, deep, and deeper

#include <iostream>
using namespace std;

//*******************************************
// Definition of function deeper              *
// This function displays a message.          *
//*******************************************

void deeper()
{
    cout << "I am now inside the function deeper.\n";
}
```

(program continues)

Program 6-4   *(continued)*

```
//*******************************************
// Definition of function deep            *
// This function calls function deeper.    *
//*******************************************

void deep()
{
    cout << "I am now inside the function deep.\n";
    deeper();  // Call function deeper
    cout << "Now I am back in deep.\n";
}

int main()
{
    cout << "I am starting in function main.\n";
    deep();    // Call function deep
    cout << "Back in function main again.\n";
    return 0;
}
```

Program Output
```
I am starting in function main.
I am now inside the function deep.
I am now inside the function deeper.
Now I am back in deep.
Back in function main again.
```

In Program 6-4, function main only calls the function deep. In turn, deep calls deeper. The paths taken by the program are shown in Figure 6-4.

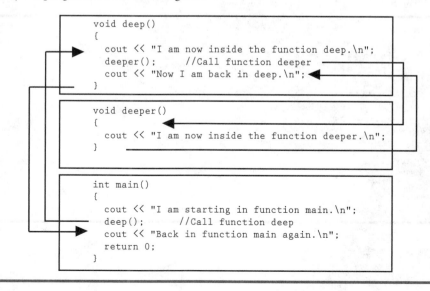

Figure 6-4

Checkpoint   [6.1–6.2]

6.1   Is the following a function header or a function call?

```
calcTotal();
```

6.2   Is the following a function header or a function call?

```
void showResults()
```

6.3   What will the output of the following program be if the user enters 10?

```cpp
#include <iostream>
using namespace std;

void func1()
{
    cout << "Able was I\n";
}

void func2()
{
    cout << "I saw Elba\n";
}

int main()
{
    int input;
    cout << "Enter a number: ";
    cin >> input;
    if (input < 10)
    {
        func1();
        func2();
    }
    else
    {
        func2();
        func1();
    }
    return 0;
}
```

6.4   The following program skeleton determines if a person qualifies for a credit card. To qualify, the person must have worked on his or her current job for at least two years and make at least $17,000 per year. Finish the program by writing the definitions of the functions qualify and noQualify. The function qualify should explain that the applicant qualifies for the card and that the annual interest rate is 12 percent. The function noQualify should explain that the applicant does not qualify for the card and give a general explanation why.

```
#include <iostream>
using namespace std;

// You must write definitions for the two functions qualify
// and noQualify.

int main()
{
    float salary;
    int years;

    cout << "This program will determine if you qualify\n";
    cout << "for our credit card.\n";
    cout << "What is your annual salary? ";
    cin >> salary;
    cout << "How many years have you worked at your ";
    cout << "current job? ";
    cin >> years;
    if (salary >= 17000.0 && years >= 2)
       qualify();
    else
       noQualify();
    return 0;
}
```

6.3   Function Prototypes

> **CONCEPT**   A function prototype eliminates the need to place a function definition before all calls to the function.

Before the compiler encounters a call to a particular function, it must already know certain things about the function. In particular, it must know the number of parameters the function uses, the type of each parameter, and the return type of the function. Parameters allow information to be sent to a function. Certain return types allow information to be returned from a function. You will learn more about parameters and return types in later sections of this chapter. For now, the functions we will use will have no parameters and, except for main, will have a return type of void.

One way of ensuring that the compiler has this required information is to place the function definition before all calls to that function. This was the approach taken in Programs 6-1, 6-2, 6-3, and 6-4. Another method is to declare the function with a *function prototype*. Here is a prototype for the displayMessage function in Program 6-1:

```
void displayMessage();
```

This prototype looks similar to the function header, except there is a semicolon at the end. The statement tells the compiler that the function displayMessage has a void return type (it doesn't return a value) and uses no parameters.

WARNING! You must either place the function definition or the function proto-type ahead of all calls to the function. Otherwise the program will not compile.

Function prototypes are usually placed near the top of a program so the compiler will encounter them before any function calls. Program 6-5 is a modification of Program 6-3. The definitions of the functions first and second have been placed after main, and their function prototypes have been placed above main, directly after the using namespace std statement.

Program 6-5

```cpp
// This program has three functions: main, first, and second.

#include <iostream>
using namespace std;

// Function Prototypes
void first();
void second();

int main()
{
    cout << "I am starting in function main.\n";
    first();    // Call function first
    second();   // Call function second
    cout << "Back in function main again.\n";
    return 0;
}

//*************************************************
// Definition of function first.                 *
// This function displays a message.             *
//*************************************************

void first()
{
    cout << "I am now inside the function first.\n";
}

//*************************************************
// Definition of function second.                *
// This function displays a message.             *
//*************************************************

void second()
{
    cout << "I am now inside the function second.\n";
}
```

Program Output is the same as the output of Program 6-3.

When the compiler is reading Program 6-5, it encounters the calls to the functions `first` and `second` in `main` before it has read the definition of those functions. Because of the function prototypes, however, the compiler already knows the return type and parameter information of `first` and `second`. There should be a prototype for each function in a program except `main`. A prototype is never needed for `main` since it is the starting point of the program.

 Note: Although some programmers make `main` the last function in the program, many prefer it to be first since it is the program's starting point.

6.4   Sending Information into a Function

CONCEPT   When a function is called, the program may send values into the function.

Values that are sent into a function are called *arguments*. You're already familiar with how to use arguments in a function call. In the following statement the function `pow` is being called and two arguments, 2 and 4, are passed to it:

```
result = pow(2, 4);
```

A *parameter* is a special variable that holds a value being passed as an argument into a function. By using parameters, you can design your own functions that accept information this way. Here is the definition of a function that uses a parameter:

```
void displayValue(int num)
{
    cout << "The value is " << num << endl;
}
```

 Note: Parameters are also known as *formal arguments*.

Notice the integer variable definition inside the parentheses (`int num`). The variable `num` is a parameter, or formal argument. This enables the function `displayValue` to accept an integer value as an argument. Program 6-6 is a complete program using this function.

Program 6-6

```
// This program demonstrates a function with a parameter.

#include <iostream>
using namespace std;
```

(program continues)

Program 6-6   *(continued)*

```
// Function Prototype
void displayValue(int);

int main()
{
    cout << "I am passing 5 to displayValue.\n";
    displayValue(5);  // Call displayValue with argument 5
    cout << "Now I am back in main.\n";
    return 0;
}

//*************************************************************
// Definition of function displayValue.                      *
// It uses an integer parameter whose value is displayed.     *
//*************************************************************

void displayValue(int num)
{
    cout << "The value is " << num << endl;
}
```

Program Output
```
I am passing 5 to displayValue.
The value is 5
Now I am back in main.
```

Notice the function prototype for displayValue:

```
    void displayValue(int);
```

It is not necessary to list the name of the parameter variable inside the parentheses. Only its data type is required. This function prototype could optionally have been written as

```
    void displayValue(int num);
```

However, the compiler ignores the name of the parameter variable in the function prototype.

In main, the displayValue function is called with the argument 5 inside the parentheses. The number 5 is passed into num, which is displayValue's parameter. This is illustrated in Figure 6-5.

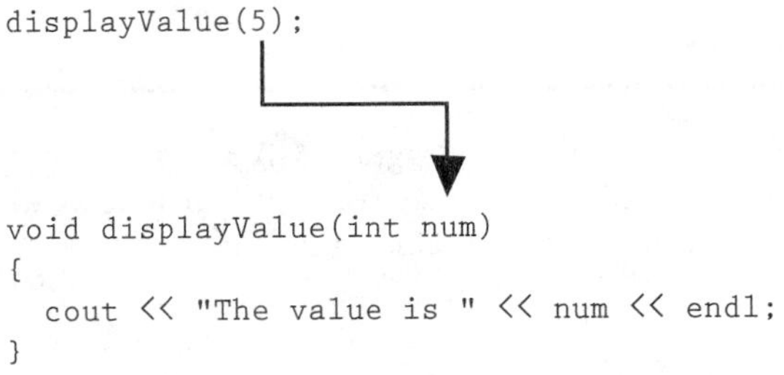

Figure 6-5

Any argument listed inside the parentheses of a function call is copied into the function's parameter variable. In essence, parameter variables are initialized to the value of their corresponding arguments. Program 6-7 shows the function `displayValue` being called several times with a different argument being passed each time.

Program 6-7

```
// This program demonstrates a function with a parameter.

#include <iostream>
using namespace std;

// Function Prototype
void displayValue(int);

int main()
{
    cout << "I am passing several values to displayValue.\n";
    displayValue(5);  // Call displayValue with argument 5
    displayValue(10); // Call displayValue with argument 10
    displayValue(2);  // Call displayValue with argument 2
    displayValue(16); // Call displayValue with argument 16
    cout << "Now I am back in main.\n";
    return 0;
}

//************************************************************
// Definition of function displayValue.                     *
// It uses an integer parameter whose value is displayed.   *
//************************************************************

void displayValue(int num)
{
    cout << "The value is " << num << endl;
}
```

Program Output
```
I am passing several values to displayValue.
The value is 5
The value is 10
The value is 2
The value is 16
Now I am back in main.
```

Each time the function is called in Program 6-7, num takes on a different value. Any expression whose value could normally be assigned to num may be used as an argument. For example, the following function call would pass the value 8 into num:

```
displayValue(3 + 5);
```

If you pass an argument whose type is not the same as the parameter's type, the argument will be promoted or demoted automatically. For instance, since `displayValue`'s parameter is type `int`, the argument in the following function call would be truncated, causing the value 4 to be passed to `num`:

```
displayValue(4.7);
```

Often, it's useful to pass several arguments into a function. Program 6-8 shows the definition of a function with three parameters.

Program 6-8

```
// This program demonstrates a function with three parameters.

#include <iostream>
using namespace std;

// Function Prototype
void showSum(int, int, int);

int main()
{
    int value1, value2, value3;

    cout << "Enter three integers and I will display ";
    cout << "their sum: ";
    cin >> value1 >> value2 >> value3;
    showSum(value1, value2, value3);    // Call showSum with 3 arguments.
    return 0;
}

//*************************************************************
// Definition of function showSum.                           *
// It uses three integer parameters. Their sum is displayed. *
//*************************************************************

void showSum(int num1, int num2, int num3)
{
    cout << (num1 + num2 + num3) << endl;
}
```

Program Output with Example Input Shown in Bold
```
Enter three integers and I will display their sum: 4 8 7[Enter]
19
```

In the function header for `showSum`, the parameter list contains three variable definitions separated by commas:

```
void showSum(int num1, int num2, int num3)
```

WARNING! Each variable must have a data type listed before its name. You can't leave out the data type of any variable in the parameter list. A compiler error would occur if the parameter list were declared as `int num1, num2, num3` instead of `int num1, int num2, int num3`.

In the function call, the variables `value1`, `value2`, and `value3` are passed as arguments:

```
showSum(value1, value2, value3);
```

Notice the syntax difference between the function header and the function call when passing variables as arguments into parameters. In a function call, you do *not* include the variable's data types inside the parentheses. For example, it would be an error to write this function call as

```
showSum(int value1, int value2, int value3); // Wrong!
```

When a function with multiple parameters is called, the arguments are passed to the parameters in order. This is illustrated in Figure 6-6.

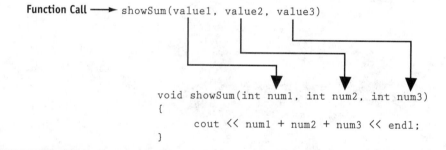

Figure 6-6

The following function call will cause 5 to be passed into the `num1` parameter, 10 to be passed into `num2`, and 15 to be passed into `num3`:

```
showSum(5, 10, 15);
```

However, the following function call will cause 15 to be passed into the `num1` parameter, 5 to be passed into `num2`, and 10 to be passed into `num3`:

```
showSum(15, 5, 10);
```

 Note: Like all variables, parameters have a scope. The scope of a parameter is limited to the body of the function which uses it.

6.5 Passing Information to Parameters by Value

> **CONCEPT** When an argument is passed into a parameter by value, only a copy of the argument's value is passed. Changes to the parameter do not affect the original argument.

As you have seen in this chapter, parameters, or formal arguments, are special-purpose variables that are defined inside the parentheses of a function definition. Their purpose is to hold the information passed to them by the *actual arguments*, which are listed inside the parentheses of a function call. Normally when information is passed to a function it is *passed by value*. This means the parameter receives a copy of the value that is passed to it. If a parameter's value is changed inside a function, it has no effect on the original argument. Program 6-9 demonstrates this concept.

Program 6-9

```cpp
// This program demonstrates that changes to a function parameter
// have no effect on the original argument.

#include <iostream>
using namespace std;

// Function Prototype
void changeThem(int, float);

int main()
{
    int whole = 12;
    float real = 3.5;

    cout << "In main the value of whole is " << whole << endl;
    cout << "and the value of real is " << real << endl;
    changeThem(whole, real); // Call changeThem with 2 arguments
    cout << "Now back in main again, the value of ";
    cout << "whole is " << whole << endl;
    cout << "and the value of real is " << real << endl;
    return 0;
}

//****************************************************************
// Definition of function changeThem.                          *
// It uses i, an int parameter, and f, a float. The values of  *
// i and f are changed and then displayed.                     *
//****************************************************************
```

(program continues)

Program 6-9   *(continued)*

```
void changeThem(int i, float f)
{
    i = 100;
    f = 27.5;
    cout << "In changeThem the value of i is changed to ";
    cout << i << endl;
    cout << "and the value of f is changed to " << f << endl;
}
```

Program Output
```
In main the value of whole is 12
and the value of real is 3.5
In changeThem the value of i is changed to 100
and the value of f is changed to 27.5
Now back in main again, the value of whole is 12
and the value of real is 3.5
```

Even though the parameters i and f are changed in the function changeThem, the arguments whole and real are not modified. The parameters i and f only contain copies of whole and real. The function changeThem does not have access to the original arguments.

Figure 6-7 illustrates that a parameter variable's storage location in memory is separate from that of the original argument.

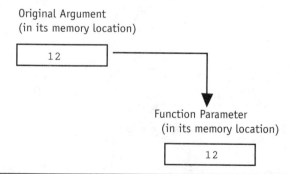

Original Argument
(in its memory location)

12

Function Parameter
(in its memory location)

12

Figure 6-7

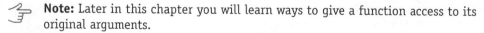 **Note:** Later in this chapter you will learn ways to give a function access to its original arguments.

⍰ Checkpoint   [6.3–6.5]

6.5   Indicate which of the following is the function prototype, the function header, and the function call:

```
void showNum(float num)
void showNum(float);
showNum(45.67);
```

6.6 Write a function named `timesTen`. The function should have an integer parameter named `number`. When `timesTen` is called, it should display the product of `number` times 10. (Note: Just write the function. Do not write a complete program.)

6.7 Write a function prototype for the `timesTen` function you wrote in question 6.6.

6.8 What is the output of the following program?

```
#include <iostream>
using namespace std;

void showDouble(int); // Function prototype

int main()
{
    int num;

    for (num = 0; num < 10; num++)
        showDouble(num);
    return 0;
}

// Definition of function showDouble.
void showDouble(int value)
{
    cout << value << "\t" << (value * 2) << endl;
}
```

6.9 What is the output of the following program?

```
#include <iostream>
using namespace std;

void func1(float, int); // Function prototype

int main()
{
    int x = 0;
    float y = 1.5;

    cout << x << " " << y << endl;
    func1(y, x);
    cout << x << " " << y << endl;
    return 0;
}
```

```
void func1(float a, int b)
{
    cout << a << " " << b << endl;
    a = 0.0;
    b = 10;
    cout << a << " " << b << endl;
}
```

6.10 The following program skeleton asks for the number of hours you've worked and your hourly pay rate. It then calculates and displays your wages. The function showDollars, which you are to write, formats the output of the wages.

```
#include <iostream>
#include <iomanip>
using namespace std;

void showDollars(float); // Function prototype

int main()
{
    float payRate, hoursWorked, wages;

    cout << "How many hours have you worked? "
    cin >> hoursWorked;
    cout << "What is your hourly pay rate? ";
    cin >> payRate;
    wages = hoursWorked * payRate;
    showDollars(wages);
    return 0;
}

// You must write the definition of the function showDollars
// here. It should take one parameter of the type float.
// The function should display the message "Your wages are $"
// followed by the value of the parameter. It should be displayed
// with 2 places of precision after the decimal point, in fixed
// notation, and the decimal point should always display.
```

6.6   The return Statement

CONCEPT   The return statement causes a function to end immediately.

When the last statement in a function has finished executing, the function terminates. The program returns to the module that called it and continues executing from the point immediately following the function call. It's possible, however, to force a function to return to where it was called from before the last statement has been executed. When the return statement is encountered, the function immediately terminates and the program returns. This is demonstrated in Program 6-10.

Program 6-10

```cpp
// This program demonstrates a function with a return statement.

#include <iostream>
using namespace std;

// Function prototype
void halfway();

int main()
{
    cout << "In main, calling halfway...\n";
    halfway();
    cout << "Now back in main.\n";
    return 0;
}

//*************************************************************
// Definition of function halfway                            *
// This function has a return statement that forces it to    *
// terminate before the last statement is executed.          *
//*************************************************************

void halfway()
{
    cout << "In halfway now.\n";
    return;
    cout << "Will you ever see this message?\n";
}
```

Program Output
```
In main, calling halfway...
In halfway now.
Now back in main.
```

The last cout statement in halfway will never be executed because the return statement causes the function to terminate before it is reached. Program 6-11 shows a more practical application of the return statement. The function divide shows the quotient of arg1 divided by arg2. If arg2 is set to zero, the function returns.

Program 6-11

```cpp
// This program uses a function to perform division. If division
// by zero is detected, the function returns.

#include <iostream>
using namespace std;
```

(program continues)

Program 6-11   *(continued)*

```cpp
// Function prototype
void divide(float, float);

int main()
{
    float num1, num2;

    cout << "Enter two numbers and I will divide the first\n";
    cout << "number by the second number: ";
    cin >> num1 >> num2;
    divide(num1, num2);
    return 0;
}

//*******************************************************************
// Definition of function divide                                   *
// Uses two parameters: arg1 and arg2. The function divides arg1*
// by arg2 and shows the result. If arg2 is zero, however, the    *
// function returns.                                               *
//*******************************************************************

void divide(float arg1, float arg2)
{
    if (arg2 == 0.0)
    {
        cout << "Sorry, I cannot divide by zero.\n";
        return;
    }
    cout << "The quotient is " << (arg1 / arg2) << endl;
}
```

Program Output with Example Input Shown in Bold
```
Enter two numbers and I will divide the first
number by the second number: 12 0[Enter]
Sorry, I cannot divide by zero.
```

6.7   Returning a Value from a Function

CONCEPT   A function may send a value back to the part of the program that called the function.

You've seen that information may be passed into a function by way of its parameters. Information may also be returned from a function, back to the part of the program that called it.

Although several arguments may be passed into a function, only one value may be returned from it. Think of a function as having multiple communications channels for receiving data (parameters), but only one channel for sending data (the return value). This is illustrated in Figure 6-8.

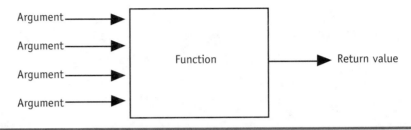

Figure 6-8

 Note: It is possible to return multiple values from a function, but they must be "packaged" in such a way that they are treated as a single value. You will learn to do this in Chapter 7.

The data type of the return value precedes the function name in the header and the prototype. The following prototype declares a function named `square` that returns an integer:

```
int square(int);
```

The function `square` accepts an integer argument. Here is the definition of the function:

```
int square(int number)
{
    return number * number;
}
```

This function only has one line, which is a `return` statement. When a function returns a value, it must have a `return` statement. The expression that follows the `return` key word is evaluated, converted to the data type the function returns, and sent back to the part of the program that called the function. This is demonstrated in Program 6-12.

Program 6-12

```
// This program uses a function that returns a value.

#include <iostream>
using namespace std;
```

(program continues)

Program 6-12 *(continued)*

```
//Function prototype
int square(int);

int main()
{
    int number, result;

    cout << "Enter a number and I will square it: ";
    cin >> number;
    result = square(number);
    cout << number << " squared is " << result << endl;
    return 0;
}

//*********************************************************
// Definition of function square                         *
// This function accepts an int argument and returns     *
// the square of the argument as an int.                 *
//*********************************************************

int square(int number)
{
    return number * number;
}
```

Program Output with Example Input Shown in Bold
```
Enter a number and I will square it: 20[Enter]
20 squared is 400
```

Here is the line that calls the `square` function:

```
result = square(number);
```

An expression is something that has a value. If a function returns a value, a call to that function is an expression. The statement above assigns the value returned from `square` to the variable `result`. So, when 20 is passed as an argument into `square`, 20 times 20, or 400, is returned and assigned to `result`. Figure 6-9 illustrates how information is passed to and returned from the function.

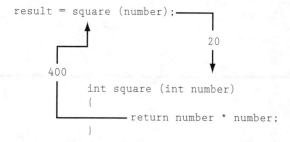

Figure 6-9

Actually, the `result` variable is unnecessary in Program 6-12. The return value of the `square` function could have been displayed by the `cout` object, as shown here:

```
cout << number << " squared is " << square(number) << endl;
```

You have just seen how a value returned by a function can be assigned to a variable or can be printed. It is also possible to use a value returned by a function in a relational test or in an arithmetic expression. For example, the following two statements are both perfectly legal:

```
if (square(number) > 100)      // square function is called and
    cout << "big square\n";    // the returned value is used in
                               // a relational test

sum = 1000 + square(number);   // square function is called and
                               // the returned value is used in
                               // an arithmetic expression
```

Program 6-13 shows a version of the `square` function that returns a `float`. The function is used in a mathematical statement that calculates the area of a circle.

Program 6-13

```
// This program uses the return value of the square function
// in a mathematical statement.

#include <iostream>
#include <iomanip>
using namespace std;

//Function prototypes
float getRadius();
float square(float);

int main()
{
    const float pi = 3.14159;
    float rad;

    cout << fixed << showpoint << setprecision(2);
    cout << "This program calculates the area of ";
    cout << "a circle.\n";
    rad = getRadius();
    cout << "The area is " << pi * square(rad) << endl;
    return 0;
}
```

(program continues)

Program 6-13 *(continued)*

```
//**********************************************************
// Definition of function getRadius                        *
// This function asks the user to enter the radius of      *
// the circle and then returns that number as a float.     *
//**********************************************************

float getRadius()
{
    float radius;

    cout << "Enter the radius of the circle: ";
    cin >> radius;
    return radius;
}


//**********************************************************
// Definition of function square                           *
// This function accepts a float argument and returns      *
// the square of the argument as a float.                  *
//**********************************************************

float square(float number)
{
    return number * number;
}
```

Program Output with Example Input Shown in Bold
```
This program calculates the area of a circle.
Enter the radius of the circle: 10[Enter]
The area is 314.16
```

Program 6-13 also uses a `getRadius` function to get the radius of the circle from the user and return that value back to `main`. This function accepts no arguments and returns a `float`.

The `square` function in Program 6-12 returns an `int`, while the one in Program 6-13 returns a `float`. The return type of a function should be the type of the data you wish to return from the function. For example, if a function is returning a `float` value that is being assigned to a variable, then that variable should also be a `float`. If the `float` value being returned by the `square` function in Program 6-13 were assigned to an `int` variable, the value would be truncated. This is illustrated in the following example:

```
int result;
result = square(2.7);
```

The `square` function returns the value 7.29, but it is truncated to 7 when it is stored in `result`.

 Note: When writing the comments for a function that returns a value, document the purpose of the return value and its data type.

Note: If you give a function a return type other than void, you must have a `return` statement in that function.

6.8   Returning a Boolean Value

CONCEPT   Functions may return `true` or `false` values.

 Note: If your compiler does not support the `bool` data type, see the information in Section 3.6 on Creating a Boolean Data Type.

Frequently there is a need for a function that tests an argument and returns a `true` or `false` value indicating whether or not a condition exists. For example, in a program that needs to know if numbers are even or odd, a function could be written to return `true` if its argument is even, and return `false` if its argument is odd. Program 6-14 demonstrates such a function.

Program 6-14

```
// This program uses a function that returns true or false.

#include <iostream>
using namespace std;

// Function prototype
bool isEven(int);

int main()
{
    int val;

    cout << "Enter an integer and I will tell you ";
    cout << "if it is even or odd: ";
    cin >> val;
    if (isEven(val))
        cout << val << " is even.\n";
    else
        cout << val << " is odd.\n";
    return 0;
}
```

(program continues)

Program 6-14 *(continued)*

```
//****************************************************************
// Definition of function isEven                                 *
// This function accepts an integer argument and tests if it is  *
// even or odd. The function returns true if the argument is even *
// or false if the argument is odd. The return value is a bool.  *
//****************************************************************

bool isEven(int number)
{
   if (number % 2)
       return false; // The number is odd if there's a remainder.
   else
       return true;  // Otherwise, the number is even.
}
```

Program Output with Example Input Shown in Bold
```
Enter an integer and I will tell you if it is even or odd: 5[Enter]
5 is odd.
```

The isEven function is called in the following statement:

```
if (isEven(val))
```

When the if statement executes, isEven is called with val as its argument. If val is even, isEven returns true, otherwise it returns false.

Checkpoint [6.6–6.8]

6.11 How many return values may a function have?

6.12 Write a header for a function named distance. The function should return a float and have two float parameters: rate and time.

6.13 Write a header for a function named days. The function should return an int and have three int parameters: years, months, and weeks.

6.14 Write a header for a function named getKey. The function should return a char and use no parameters.

6.15 Write a header for a function named lightYears. The function should return a long and have one long parameter: miles.

6.9   Using Functions in a Menu-Driven Program

> **CONCEPT** Functions are ideal for use in menu-driven programs. When the user selects an item from a menu, the program can call the appropriate function.

In Chapters 4 and 5 you saw a menu-driven program that calculates the charges for a health club membership. Program 6-15 is an improved *modular* version of that program. A modular program is broken up into functions that perform specific tasks.

Program 6-15

```cpp
// This is a modular menu-driven program that
// computes fees for health club members.

#include <iostream>
#include <iomanip>
#include <string>
using namespace std;

// Function Prototypes
void displayMenu();
int getChoice();
void computeFees(string, double, int);

const double adultRate =  40.00,
             seniorRate = 30.00,
             childRate =  20.00;

int main()
{
    int choice,              // Holds the user's menu choice
        months;              // Number of months being paid for

    cout << fixed << showpoint << setprecision(2);

    do
    {
```

(program continues)

Program 6-15 *(continued)*

```
        displayMenu();
        choice = getChoice(); // Assign choice the choice returned to it
                              // by the getChoice function.
        if (choice != 4)
        {
            cout << "For how many months? ";
            cin >> months;
        }

        switch (choice)
        {
            case 1: computeFees("Adult", adultRate, months);
                    break;
            case 2: computeFees("Child", childRate, months);
                    break;
            case 3: computeFees("Senior", seniorRate, months);
                    break;
            case 4: cout << "Thanks for using this program.\n";
        }
    } while (choice != 4);

    return 0;
}

//**************************************************
// Definition of function displayMenu              *
// Displays the menu choices                       *
//**************************************************

void displayMenu()
{
    cout << "\n\t\tHealth Club Membership Menu\n\n";
    cout << "1.   Standard Adult Membership\n";
    cout << "2.   Child Membership\n";
    cout << "3.   Senior Citizen Membership\n";
    cout << "4.   Quit the Program\n\n";
}

//**************************************************
// Definition of function getChoice                *
// Inputs and validates the user's menu choice     *
//**************************************************

int getChoice()
{
    int choice;
```

(program continues)

Program 6-15 *(continued)*

```
    cin >> choice;
    while (choice < 1 || choice > 4)
    {   cout << "The only valid choices are 1-4.  Please re-enter. ";
        cin >> choice;
    }
    return choice;
}

//****************************************************
// Definition of function computeFees               *
// Uses the monthly rate and number of months       *
// passed to it as parameters to compute and        *
// print the member's total charges.                *
//****************************************************

void computeFees(string memberType, double rate, int months)
{
    cout << endl
        << "Membership Type : " << memberType << "      "
        << "Monthly rate $"    << rate    << endl
        << "Number of months: " << months << endl
        << "Total charges   : $"<< (rate * months)
        << endl << endl;
}
```

Program Output with Example Input Shown in Bold
```
        Health Club Membership Menu

1.  Standard Adult Membership
2.  Child Membership
3.  Senior Citizen Membership
4.  Quit the Program
```

1[Return]
```
For how many months? 3[Return]

Membership Type : Adult     Monthly rate $40
Number of months: 3
Total charges   : $120


        Health Club Membership Menu

1.  Standard Adult Membership
2.  Child Membership
3.  Senior Citizen Membership
4.  Quit the Program
```

4[Return]
```
Thanks for using this program.
```

Notice the versatility of the `computeFees` function, which is called in three different places within the `switch` statement. It is passed three arguments: a `string` holding the membership type, a `double` holding the monthly fee for that membership type, and an `int` holding the number of months being billed. Without these arguments, we would have needed a whole set of functions: one to compute adult membership fees, another to compute child membership fees, and a third to compute senior membership fees. Because we can vary the information passed as arguments to the function, however, we were able to create a single general-purpose function that worked for all three cases.

6.10 Local and Global Variables

> **CONCEPT** A local variable is defined inside a function and is not accessible outside the function. A global variable is defined outside all functions and is accessible to all functions in its scope.

Local Variables

Just as you've defined variables inside function `main`, you may also define them inside other functions. Variables defined inside a function are *local* to that function. They are hidden from the statements in other functions, which normally cannot access them. Program 6-16 shows that because the variables defined in a function are hidden, other functions may have separate, distinct variables with the same name.

Program 6-16

```
// This program shows that variables declared in a function
// are hidden from other functions.

#include <iostream>
using namespace std;

void func();   // Function prototype

int main()
{
    int num = 1;
    cout << "In main, num is " << num << endl;
    func();
    cout << "Back in main, num is still " << num << endl;
    return 0;
}

//****************************************************************
// Definition of function func                                  *
// It has a local variable, num, whose value initial value, 20, *
// is displayed.                                                *
//****************************************************************
```

(program continues)

Program 6-16 *(continued)*

```
void func()
{
    int num = 20;

    cout << "In func, num is " << num << endl;
}
```

Program Output
```
In main, num is 1
In func, num is 20
Back in main, num is still 1
```

Even though there are two variables named num, the program can only "see" one of them at a time. When the program is executing in main, the num variable defined in main is visible. When func is called, however, only variables defined inside it are visible, so the num variable in main is hidden. Figure 6-10 illustrates the closed nature of the two functions. The boxes represent the scope of the variables.

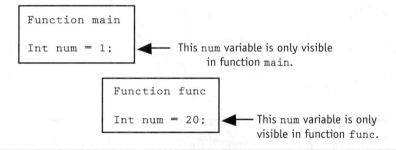

Figure 6-10

Global Variables

Although local variables are safely hidden from other functions, they do not provide a convenient way of sharing information. When large amounts of data must be accessible to all the functions in a program, global variables are an easy alternative.

A global variable is any variable defined outside all the functions in a program. The scope of a global variable is the portion of the program from the variable definition to the end. Program 6-17 shows two functions, main and func, which access the same global variable, num.

Program 6-17

```
// This program shows that a global variable is visible
// to all the functions that appear in a program after
// the variable's declaration.

#include <iostream>
using namespace std;
```

(program continues)

Program 6-17 *(continued)*

```
void func(); // Function prototype
int num = 2; // Global variable

int main()
{
    cout << "In main, num is " << num << endl;
    func();
    cout << "Back in main, num is " << num << endl;
    return 0;
}

//************************************************************
// Definition of function func                             *
// func changes the value of the global variable num.      *
//************************************************************

void func()
{
    cout << "In func, num is " << num << endl;
    num = 50;
    cout << "But, it is now changed to " << num << endl;
}
```

Program Output
```
In main, num is 2
In func, num is 2
But, it is now changed to 50
Back in main, num is 50
```

In Program 6-17, num is defined outside of all the functions. Since its definition appears before the definitions of main and func, both functions have access to it. Program 6-18 is a slight variation of the same program. In it, the definition of num is moved to a point below the definition of function main. The scope of num is shaded.

Program 6-18

```
// This program shows that a global variable is visible
// to all the functions that appear in a program after
// the variable's declaration.

#include <iostream>
using namespace std;
```

(program continues)

Program 6-18 *(continued)*

```cpp
void func(); // Function prototype

int main()
{
    cout << "In main, num is not visible!\n";
    func();
    cout << "Back in main, num still isn't visible!\n";
    return 0;
}

int num = 2; // Global variable

//****************************************************
// Definition of function func                      *
// func changes the value of the global variable num. *
//****************************************************

void func()
{
    cout << "In func, num is " << num << endl;
    num = 50;
    cout << "But, it is now changed to " << num << endl;
}
```

Program Output

```
In main, num is not visible!
In func, num is 2
But, it is now changed to 50
Back in main, num still isn't visible!
```

Global Variables Are Initialized to Zero by Default

Unless you explicitly initialize numeric global variables, they are automatically initialized to zero. Global character variables are initialized to NULL.[1] The variable `globalNum` in Program 6-19 is never set to any value by a statement, but because it is global, it is automatically set to zero.

 Note: Remember that local variables are not automatically initialized like global variables are. The programmer must handle this.

---

[1] The NULL character is stored as ASCII 0.

Program 6-19

```
// This program has an uninitialized global variable.

#include <iostream>
using namespace std;

int globalNum; // Global variable. Automatically set to zero.

int main()
{
    cout << "globalNum is " << globalNum << endl;
    return 0;
}
```

Program Output
```
globalNum is 0
```

Local and Global Variables with the Same Name

If a function has a local variable with the same name as a global variable, only the local variable can be seen by the function. This is demonstrated by Program 6-20 (with apologies to folks living in Maine).

Program 6-20

```
// This program shows that when a local variable has the
// same name as a global variable, the function only sees
// the local variable.

#include <iostream>
using namespace std;

// Function prototypes
void texas();
void arkansas();

int cows = 10;

int main()
{
    cout << "There are " << cows << " cows in main.\n";
    texas();
    arkansas();
    cout << "Back in main, there are " << cows << " cows.\n";
    return 0;
}
```

(program continues)

Program 6-20   *(continued)*

```
//*****************************************
// Definition of function texas          *
// The local variable cows is set to 100. *
//*****************************************

void texas()
{
    int cows = 100;

    cout << "There are " << cows << " cows in texas.\n";
}

//*****************************************
// Definition of function arkansas       *
// The local variable cows is set to 50.  *
//*****************************************

void arkansas()
{
    int cows = 50;

    cout << "There are " << cows << " cows in arkansas.\n";
}
```

Program Output
```
There are 10 cows in main.
There are 100 cows in texas.
There are 50 cows in arkansas.
Back in main, there are 10 cows.
```

When the program is executing in function main, the global variable cows is visible. In the functions texas and arkansas, however, there are local variables with the name cows. The global variable is not visible when the program is executing in those functions.

Program 6-21 is a simple cash register program that uses global and local variables. The function ringUpSale calculates and displays the price, sales tax, and subtotal for each item being purchased. It has a local variable, tax, which has the same name as a global variable. The tax variable in ringUpSale is used to calculate the sales tax on an item, while the global tax variable is used by main to calculate the total sales tax of the purchase.

Program 6-21

```
// This program has local and global variables. In the function
// ringUpSale, there is a local variable named tax. There is
// also a global variable with the same name.
```

(program continues)

Program 6-21   *(continued)*

```cpp
#include <iostream>
#include <iomanip>
using namespace std;

void ringUpSale(); // Function prototype

// Global variables
const float taxRate = 0.06;
float tax, sale, total;

int main()
{
    char again;

    cout << fixed << showpoint << setprecision(2);
    do
    {
        ringUpSale();
        cout << "Is there another item to be purchased? ";
        cin >> again;
    } while (again == 'y' || again == 'Y');
    tax = sale * taxRate;
    total = sale + tax;
    cout << "The tax for this sale is " << tax << endl;
    cout << "The total is " << total << endl;
    return 0;
}

//*************************************************************************
// Definition of function ringUpSale                                      *
// This function asks for the quantity and unit price of an item.         *
// It then calculates and displays the sales tax and subtotal             *
// for those items.                                                       *
//*************************************************************************

void ringUpSale()
{
    int qty;
    float unitPrice, tax, thisSale, subTotal;

    cout << "Quantity: ";
    cin >> qty;
    cout << "Unit price: ";
    cin >> unitPrice;
```

(program continues)

Program 6-21   *(continued)*

```
    thisSale = qty * unitPrice;    // Get the total unit price
    sale += thisSale;              // Update global variable sale
    tax = thisSale * taxRate;      // Get sales tax for these items
    subTotal = thisSale + tax;     // Get subtotal for these items
    cout << "Price for these items: " << thisSale << endl;
    cout << "Tax for these items: " << tax << endl;
    cout << "SubTotal for these items: " << subTotal << endl;
}
```

Program Output with Example Input Shown in Bold
```
Quantity: 2[Enter]
Unit Price: 20.00[Enter]
Price for these items: 40.00
Tax for these items: 2.40
SubTotal for these items: 42.40
Is there another item to be purchased? y[Enter]
Quantity: 3[Enter]
Unit Price: 12.00[Enter]
Price for these items: 36.00
Tax for these items: 2.16
SubTotal for these items: 38.16
Is there another item to be purchased? n[Enter]
The tax for this sale is 4.56
The total is 80.56
```

 WARNING! It's tempting to make all your variables global, especially when you are first learning to program. After all, you can access them from any function without passing their values as parameters. Although this might make your programs easier to create, most likely it will cause problems later. While debugging your program, if you find that the wrong value is being stored in a global variable, you'll have to track down every statement that accesses it to determine where the bad value is coming from. In a program with thousands of lines, this can be a tedious and time-consuming process.

Also, when two or more functions modify the same variable, you must be very careful that what one function does will not upset the correctness of another function. Although global variables make it easy to share information, they should be used carefully and sparingly. Some instructors prefer that you not use them at all.

6.11   Static Local Variables

If a function is called more than once in a program, the values stored in the function's local variables do not persist between function calls. This is because the variables are destroyed when the function terminates and are then re-created when the function starts again. This is shown in Program 6-22.

Program 6-22

```
// This program shows that local variables do not retain
// their values between function calls.

#include <iostream>
using namespace std;

// Function prototype
void showLocal();

int main()
{
    showLocal();
    showLocal();
    return 0;
}

//*************************************************************
// Definition of function showLocal                          *
// The initial value of localNum, which is 5, is displayed.  *
// The value of localNum is then changed to 99 before the    *
// function returns.                                         *
//*************************************************************

void showLocal()
{
    int localNum = 5;   // Local variable

    cout << "localNum is " << localNum << endl;
    localNum = 99;
}
```

Program Output
```
localNum is 5
localNum is 5
```

Even though the last statement in the showLocal function stores 99 in localNum, the variable is destroyed when the function returns. The next time the function is called, localNum is re-created and initialized to 5 again.

Sometimes it's desirable for a program to "remember" what value is stored in a local variable between function calls. This can be accomplished by making the variable `static`. Static local variables are not destroyed when a function returns. They exist for the lifetime of the program, even though their scope is only the function in which they are defined. Program 6-23 demonstrates some characteristics of static local variables.

Program 6-23

```cpp
// This program uses a static local variable.

#include <iostream>
using namespace std;

void showStatic();  // Function prototype

int main()
{
    for (int count = 0; count < 5; count++)
        showStatic();
    return 0;
}

//***************************************************************
// Definition of function showStatic                           *
// statNum is a static local variable. Its value is displayed  *
// and then incremented just before the function returns.      *
//***************************************************************

void showStatic()
{
    static int statNum;

    cout << "statNum is " << statNum << endl;
    statNum++;
}
```

Program Output
```
statNum is 0
statNum is 1
statNum is 2
statNum is 3
statNum is 4
```

In Program 6-23, statNum is incremented in the showStatic function, and it retains its value between each function call. Notice that even though statNum is not explicitly initialized, it starts at zero. Like global variables, all static local variables are initialized to zero by default. (Of course, you can provide your own initialization value, if necessary.)

If you do provide an initialization value for a static local variable, the initialization only occurs once. This is because initialization normally happens when the variable is created, and static local variables are only created once during the running of a program. Program 6-24, which is a slight modification of Program 6-23, illustrates this point.

Program 6-24

```cpp
// This program shows that a static local variable is only initialized once.

#include <iostream>
using namespace std;

void showStatic(); // Function prototype

int main()
{
    for (int count = 0; count < 5; count++)
        showStatic();
    return 0;
}

//*****************************************************************
// Definition of function showStatic                             *
// statNum is a static local variable. Its value is displayed    *
// and then incremented just before the function returns.        *
//*****************************************************************

void showStatic(void)
{
    static int statNum = 5;

    cout << "statNum is " << statNum << endl;
    statNum++;
}
```

Program Output
```
statNum is 5
statNum is 6
statNum is 7
statNum is 8
statNum is 9
```

Even though the definition statement for statNum initializes it to 5, the initialization does not happen each time the function is called. If it did, the variable would not be able to retain its value between function calls.

Checkpoint   [6.10–6.11]

6.16   What is the difference between a static local variable and a global variable?

6.17   What is the output of the following program?

```cpp
#include <iostream>
using namespace std;

void myFunc();  // Function prototype

int main()
{
    int var = 100;

    cout << var << endl;
    myFunc();
    cout << var << endl;
    return 0;
}
// Definition of function myFunc
void myFunc()
{
    int var = 50;

    cout << var << endl;
}
```

6.18   What is the output of the following program?

```cpp
#include <iostream>
using namespace std;

void showVar(); // Function prototype

int main()
{
    for (int count = 0; count < 10; count++)
      showVar();
    return 0;
}

// Definition of function showVar
void showVar()
{
    static int var = 10;

    cout << var << endl;
    var++;
}
```

6.12 Default Arguments

> **CONCEPT** Default arguments are passed to parameters automatically if no argument is provided in the function call.

It's possible to assign *default arguments* to function parameters. A default argument is passed to the parameter when the actual argument is left out of the function call. The default arguments are usually listed in the function prototype. Here is an example:

```
void showArea(float = 20.0, float = 10.0);
```

Default arguments are constant values with an = operator in front of them, appearing after the data types listed in a function prototype. Since parameter names are optional in function prototypes, the example prototype could also be declared as

```
void showArea(float length = 20.0, float width = 10.0);
```

In both example prototypes, the function showArea has two float parameters. The first is assigned the default argument 20.0 and the second is assigned the default argument 10.0. Here is the definition of the function:

```
void showArea(float length, float width)
{
    float area = length * width;
    cout << "The area is " << area << endl;
}
```

The default argument for length is 20.0 and the default argument for width is 10.0. Because both parameters have default arguments, they may optionally be omitted in the function call, as shown:

```
showArea();
```

In this function call, both default arguments will be passed to the parameters. Parameter length will take the value 20.0 and width will take the value 10.0. The output of the function will be

```
The area is 200
```

The default arguments are only used when the actual arguments are omitted from the function call. In the following call, the first argument is specified, but the second is omitted:

```
showArea(12.0);
```

The value 12.0 will be passed to length, while the default value 10.0 will be passed to width. The output of the function will be

```
The area is 120
```

Of course, all the default arguments may be overridden. In the next function call, arguments are supplied for both parameters:

```
showArea(12.0, 5.5);
```

The output of this function call will be

```
The area is 66
```

 Note: If a function does not have a prototype, default arguments may be specified in the function header. The showArea function could be defined as follows:

```
void showArea(float length = 20.0, float width = 10.0)
{
    float area = length * width;
    cout << "The area is " << area << endl;
}
```

 WARNING! A function's default arguments should be assigned in the earliest occurrence of the function name. This will usually be the function prototype.

Program 6-25 uses a function that displays asterisks on the screen. Arguments are passed to the function specifying how many columns and rows of asterisks to display. Default arguments are provided to display 1 row of 10 asterisks.

Program 6-25

```
// This program demonstrates default function arguments.

#include <iostream>
using namespace std;

// Function prototype with default arguments
void displayStars(int = 10, int = 1);

int main()
{
    displayStars();      // Default values 10 and 1 are used for the 2 arguments.
    cout << endl;
    displayStars(5);     // Default value 1 is used for the second argument.
    cout << endl;
    displayStars(7, 3);  // No default values are used.
    return 0;
}
```

(program continues)

Program 6-25 *(continued)*

```
//*********************************************************
// Definition of function displayStars                    *
// The default argument for cols is 10 and for rows is 1. *
// This function displays a square made of asterisks.      *
//*********************************************************

void displayStars(int cols, int rows)
{
    // Nested loop. The outer loop controls the rows
    // and the inner loop controls the columns.
    for (int down = 0; down < rows; down++)
    {
        for (int across = 0; across < cols; across++)
            cout << "*";
        cout << endl;
    }
}
```

Program Output
```
* * * * * * * * * *

* * * * *

* * * * * * *
* * * * * * *
* * * * * * *
```

Although C++'s default arguments are very convenient, they are not totally flexible in their use. When an argument is left out of a function call, all arguments that come after it must be left out as well. In the `displayStars` function in Program 6-25, it is not possible to omit the argument for `cols` without also omitting the argument for `rows`. For example, the following function call would be illegal:

```
displayStars(, 3);       // Illegal function call!
```

It's possible for a function to have some parameters with default arguments and some without. For example, in the following function (which displays an employee's gross pay), only the last parameter has a default argument:

```
// Function prototype
void calcPay(int empNum, float payRate, float hours = 40.0);

// Definition of function calcPay
void calcPay(int empNum, float payRate, float hours)
{
```

```
        float wages;

        wages = payRate * hours;

        cout << "Gross pay for employee number ";
        cout << empNum << " is " << wages << endl;
    }
```

When calling this function, arguments must always be specified for the first two parameters (emp-Num and payRate) since they have no default arguments. Here are examples of valid calls:

```
calcPay(769, 15.75);       // Use default arg for 40 hours
calcPay(142, 12.00, 20);   // Specify number of hours
```

When a function uses a mixture of parameters with and without default arguments, the parameters with default arguments must be declared last. In the calcPay function, hours could not have been declared before either of the other parameters. The following prototypes are illegal:

```
// Illegal prototype
void calcPay(int empNum, float hours = 40.0, float payRate);

// Illegal prototype
void calcPay(float hours = 40.0, int empNum, float payRate);
```

Here is a summary of the important points about default arguments:

- The value of a default argument must be a constant (which can be a literal value or a named constant).
- When an argument is left out of a function call (because it has a default value), all the arguments that come after it must be left out too.
- When a function has a mixture of parameters both with and without default arguments, the parameters with default arguments must be declared last.

6.13 Passing Information to Parameters by Reference

CONCEPT When information is passed to a parameter by reference, the parameter has access to the original argument sent to it, not a copy of it. Any changes to the parameter are also made to the argument.

Earlier you saw that arguments are normally passed to a function by value. This means that parameters receive only a copy of the value sent to them, which they store in the function's local memory. Any changes made to the parameter's value do not affect the value of the original argument.

Sometimes, however, we want a function to be able to change a value in the calling function (i.e., the function that called it). This can be done by making the parameter a *reference variable*. A reference variable is an alias for another variable. Any changes made to the reference variable are actually performed on the variable it is an alias for. When we use a reference variable as a parameter, it becomes an alias for the corresponding variable in the argument list. Any changes made to the parameter are actually made to the variable in the calling function. When information is passed to a parameter in this manner, the argument is said to be passed by reference.

Reference variables are defined like regular variables, except there is an ampersand (&) in front of the name. For example, the following function definition makes the parameter refVar a reference variable:

```
void doubleNum(int &refVar)
{
    refVar *= 2;
}
```

Note: The variable refVar is called "a reference to an int."

This function doubles refVar by multiplying it by 2. Since refVar is a reference variable, this action is actually performed on the variable that was passed to the function as an argument. When prototyping a function with a reference variable, be sure to include the ampersand after the data type. Here is the prototype for the doubleNum function:

```
void doubleNum(int &);
```

Note: Some programmers prefer not to put a space between the data type and the ampersand. The following prototype is equivalent to the one above:

```
void doubleNum(int&);
```

Note: The ampersand must appear in both the prototype and the header of any function that uses a reference variable as a parameter, but not in the call to the function.

Program 6-26 demonstrates how the doubleNum function works.

Program 6-26

```
// This program uses a reference variable as a function parameter.

#include <iostream>
using namespace std;

// Function prototype. The parameter is a reference variable.
void doubleNum(int &);
```

(program continues)

Program 6-26   *(continued)*

```
int main()
{
    int value = 4;

    cout << "In main, value is " << value << endl;
    cout << "Now calling doubleNum..." << endl;
    doubleNum(value);
    cout << "Now back in main, value is " << value << endl;
    return 0;
}

//************************************************************
// Definition of doubleNum                                  *
// The parameter refVar is a reference variable. The value  *
// in refVar is doubled.                                    *
//************************************************************

void doubleNum (int &refVar)
{
    refVar *= 2;
}
```

Program Output
```
In main, value is 4
Now calling doubleNum...
Now back in main, value is 8
```

The parameter `refVar` in Program 6-26 "points" to the `value` variable in function `main`. When a program works with a reference variable, it is actually working with the variable it references, or points to. This is illustrated in Figure 6-11.

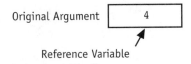

Original Argument

Reference Variable

Figure 6-11

Program 6-27 is a modification of Program 6-26. The function `getNum` has been added. The function asks the user to enter a number, which is stored in `userNum`. The parameter `userNum` is a reference to `main`'s variable `value`.

Program 6-27

```cpp
// This program uses reference variables as function parameters.

#include <iostream>
using namespace std;

// Function prototypes. Both functions use reference variables
// as parameters.
void doubleNum(int &);
void getNum(int &);

int main()
{
    int value;
    getNum(value);
    doubleNum(value);
    cout << "That value doubled is " << value << endl;
    return 0;
}

//****************************************************************
// Definition of getNum                                         *
// The parameter userNum is a reference variable. The user is   *
// asked to enter a number, which is stored in userNum.         *
//****************************************************************

void getNum(int &userNum)
{
    cout << "Enter a number: ";
    cin >> userNum;
}

//****************************************************************
// Definition of doubleNum                                      *
// The parameter refVar is a reference variable. The value      *
// in refVar is doubled.                                        *
//****************************************************************

void doubleNum (int &refVar)
{
    refVar *= 2;
}
```

Program Output with Example Input Shown in Bold
```
Enter a number: 12[Enter]
That value doubled is 24
```

If a function uses more than one reference variable as a parameter, be sure to place the ampersand before each reference variable name. Here is the prototype and definition for a function that uses four reference variable parameters:

```
// Function prototype with four reference variables
// as parameters.
void addThree(int &, int &, int &, int &);

// Definition of addThree.
// All four parameters are reference variables.
void addThree(int &sum, int &num1, int &num2, int &num3)
{
    cout << "Enter three integer values: ";
    cin >> num1 >> num2 >> num3;
    sum = num1 + num2 + num3;
}
```

 WARNING! Don't get carried away with using reference variables as function parameters. Any time you allow a function to alter a variable that's outside the function, you are creating potential debugging problems. Reference variables should only be used as parameters when the situation requires them, as when it is the programmer's intent that a function alter a value passed to it.

When to Pass Arguments by Reference and When to Pass Arguments by Value

New programmers often have a problem determining when an argument should be passed to a function by reference and when it should be passed by value. The problem is further compounded by the fact that if a value must be "sent back" to the calling function there are two ways to do it: by using a reference parameter or by using a return statement. Here are some general guidelines.

- When an argument is a constant, it must be passed by value. Only variables can be passed by reference.

- When a variable passed as an argument should not have its value changed, it should be passed by value. This protects it from being altered.

- When exactly one value needs to be "sent back" from a function to the calling routine, it should generally be returned with a return statement rather than through a reference parameter.

- When two or more variables passed as arguments to a function need to have their values changed by that function, they should be passed by reference.

There are two common instances where reference parameters are used. The first is when new data values being input in a function need to be known by the calling function. The second is when a function must change existing values in the calling function. Program 6-28, which simply inputs and adds two numbers, illustrates the first of these two cases. The getNums function inputs two numbers whose new values must be known to main so that main can pass them to addNums to add them. When main calls getNums, the two arguments are passed by reference. This causes the input values to actually be stored in variables belonging to main. When main calls addNums, however, the two numbers are passed by value, because addNums does not need to place new values in them. It just needs to have a copy of their values to use. Since addNums is passing back just one value to main, it is sent back with a return statement.

Program 6-28

```cpp
// This program illustrates when to pass arguments by reference
// and when to pass them by value. It also illustrates the use of
// reference variables vs. a return statement to send values back
// from a function.

#include <iostream>
using namespace std;

// Function prototypes
void getNums(int&, int&);   // Uses reference parameters so the new values
                            // input in the function will actually be stored
                            // in variables defined in main.

int  addNums(int, int);     // Uses value parameters since addNums just needs
                            // a copy of the argument values and does not need
                            // to change them.
int main()
{
    int num1, num2;

    getNums(num1, num2);
    cout << "The numbers entered are "
         << num1 << " and " << num2 << endl;
    cout << "Their sum is " << addNums(num1, num2) << endl;
    return 0;
}

//**************************************************************
// Definition of getNums                                       *
// The arguments passed into input1 and input2 are passed by   *
// reference so that the values entered in these two           *
// parameters will actually be stored in the memory space of   *
// main's num1 and num2 variables.                             *
//**************************************************************
void getNums(int &input1, int &input2)
{
    cout << "Enter an integer: ";
    cin >> input1;
    cout << "Enter a second integer: ";
    cin >> input2;
}
```

(program continues)

Program 6-28   *(continued)*

```
//**********************************************************
// Definition of addNums                                   *
// The arguments passed into num1 and num2 are passed by    *
// value because addNums does not need to change them.      *
// Since this function is computing and returning just one  *
// value, it is returned with a return statement.           *
//**********************************************************
int addNums (int num1, int num2)
{
    return num1 + num2;
}
```

Program 6-29 illustrates the second instance where it is common to use reference parameters, which is when a function must change existing values in the calling function. This program calls a function to place two integers in ascending order. When the function returns to main, the numbers must have been swapped if they were not already in order.

Program 6-29

```
// This program illustrates another appropriate use of passing
// arguments by reference. It calls function orderNums to put
// two numbers in ascending order if they are not already in order.

#include <iostream>
using namespace std;

// Function prototypes
void getNums (int&, int&);   // Uses reference parameters to input new values
                             // in the function but to actually store them in
                             // variables defined in main.

void orderNums(int&, int&);  // Uses reference parameters to change the
                             // values of existing values stored in main.

int main()
{
    int small, big;

    getNums(small, big);      // Call getNums to input the two numbers.
    orderNums(small, big);    // Call orderNums to put the numbers in order.

    cout << "The two input numbers in order from smallest to biggest are "
         << small << " and " << big << endl;
    return 0;
}
```

(program continues)

Program 6-29   *(continued)*

```
//*********************************************************************
// Definition of getNums                                             *
// The arguments passed into input1 and input2 are passed by         *
// reference so that the values entered in these two                 *
// parameters will actually be stored in the memory space of         *
// main's small and big variables.                                   *
//*********************************************************************
void getNums(int &input1, int &input2)
{
    cout << "Enter an integer: ";
    cin >> input1;
    cout << "Enter a second integer: ";
    cin >> input2;
}


//*********************************************************************
// Definition of orderNums                                           *
// The arguments passed into num1 and num2 are passed by             *
// reference so that if they are out of order main's                 *
// variables small and big can be swapped.  Just swapping            *
// num1 and num2 in orderNum's local memory would not                *
// accomplish the desired result.                                    *
//*********************************************************************
void orderNums (int &num1, int &num2)
{
    int temp;

    if (num1 > num2)   // If the two numbers are out of order, swap them.
    {   temp = num1;
        num1 = num2;
        num2 = temp;
    }
}
```

Checkpoint   [6.12–6.13]

6.19   What kinds of values may be specified as default arguments?

6.20   Write the prototype and header for a function called `compute`. The function should have three parameters: an `int`, a `float`, and a `long` (not necessarily in that order). The `int` parameter should have a default argument of 5, and the `long` parameter should have a default argument of 65536. The `float` parameter should not have a default argument.

6.21   Write the prototype and header for a function called `calculate`. The function should have three parameters: an `int`, a reference to a `float`, and a `long` (not necessarily in that order.) Only the `int` parameter should have a default argument, which is 47.

6.22   What is the output of the following program?

```
#include <iostream>
using namespace std;

void test(int = 2, int = 4, int = 6);

int main()
{
    test();
    test(6);
    test(3, 9);
    test(1, 5, 7);
    return 0;
}

void test (int first, int second, int third)
{
    first += 3;
    second += 6;
    third += 9;
    cout << first << " " << second << " " << third << endl;
}
```

6.23   The following program asks the user to enter two numbers. What is the output of the program if the user enters 12 and 14?

```
#include <iostream>
using namespace std;

void func1(int &, int &);
void func2(int &, int &, int &);
void func3(int, int, int);

int main()
{
    int x = 0, y = 0, z = 0;

    cout << x << " " << y << z << endl;
    func1(x, y);
    cout << x << " " << y << z << endl;
    func2(x, y, z);
    cout << x << " " << y << z << endl;
    func3(x, y, z);
    cout << x << " " << y << z << endl;
    return 0;
}
```

```
void func1(int &a, int &b)
{
    cout << "Enter two numbers: ";
    cin >> a >> b;
}
void func2(int &a, int &b, int &c)
{
    b++;
    c--;
    a = b + c;
}

void func3(int a, int b, int c)
{
    a = b - c;
}
```

6.14   Function Overloading

> **CONCEPT** | Two or more functions may have the same name, as long as their parameter lists are different.

Sometimes you will create two or more functions that perform the same operation, but use a different set of parameters or parameters of different data types. For instance, in Program 6-12 there is a square function that uses an int parameter, and in Program 6-13 there is a square function that uses a float parameter. Both functions do the same thing: return the square of their argument. The only difference is the data type involved in the operation.

If you were to use both these functions in the same program, most programming languages would require you to assign a unique name to each one. For example, the function that squares an int might be named squareInt, and the one that squares a float might be named square-Float. C++, however, allows you to *overload* function names. That means you may assign the same name to multiple functions, as long as their parameter lists are different. The compiler will use the parameter lists to distinguish between them. Program 6-30 uses two square functions.

Program 6-30

```
// This program uses overloaded functions.

#include <iostream>
#include <iomanip>
using namespace std;

// Function prototypes
int square(int);
float square(float);
```

(program continues)

Program 6-30   *(continued)*

```cpp
int main()
{
    int userInt;
    float userFloat;

    cout << fixed << showpoint << setprecision(2);
    cout << "Enter an integer and a floating-point value: ";
    cin >> userInt >> userFloat;
    cout << "Here are their squares: ";
    cout << square(userInt) << " and " << square(userFloat) << endl;
    return 0;
}

//***************************************************************
// Definition of overloaded function square                    *
// This function uses an int parameter, number. It returns the *
// square of number as an int.                                 *
//***************************************************************

int square(int number)
{
    return number * number;
}

//***************************************************************
// Definition of overloaded function square                    *
// This function uses a float parameter, number. It returns the *
// square of number as a float.                                *
//***************************************************************

float square(float number)
{
    return number * number;
}
```

Program Output with Example Input Shown in Bold
```
Enter an integer and a floating-point value: 12 4.2[Enter]
Here are their squares: 144 and 17.64
```

Here are the headers for the `square` functions used in Program 6-30:

```cpp
int square(int number)
```

```cpp
float square(float number)
```

In a C++ function call, not only is the function name used to identify a function, but also the parameter list. In Program 6-30, when an `int` argument is passed to `square`, the version of the function that has an `int` parameter is called. Likewise, when a `float` argument is passed to `square`, the version with a `float` parameter is called. Note that the compiler does not consider the return value when determining which overloaded function to call. The following functions could not be used in the same program because their parameter list isn't different.

```
int square(int)

float square(int)
```

Overloading is also convenient when there are similar functions that use a different number of parameters. For example, consider a program with functions that return the sum of integers. One returns the sum of two integers, another returns the sum of three integers, and yet another returns the sum of four integers. Here are their function headers:

```
int sum(int num1, int num2)

int sum(int num1, int num2, int num3)

int sum(int num1, int num2, int num3, int num4)
```

Because the number of parameters is different in each, they all may be used in the same program. Program 6-31 is an example that uses two functions, each named calcWeeklyPay, to determine an employee's gross weekly pay. One version of the function uses an int and a float parameter, while the other version only uses a float parameter.

Program 6-31

```cpp
// This program demonstrates overloaded functions to calculate
// the gross weekly pay of hourly-wage or salaried employees.

#include <iostream>
#include <iomanip>
using namespace std;

// Function prototypes
void getChoice(char &);
float calcWeeklyPay(int, float);
float calcWeeklyPay(float);

int main()
{
    char selection;
    int worked;
    float rate, yearly;

    cout << fixed << showpoint << setprecision(2);
    cout << "Do you want to calculate the weekly pay of\n";
    cout << "(H) an hourly-wage employee, or \n";
    cout << "(S) a salaried employee? ";
    getChoice(selection);
```

(program continues)

Program 6-31 *(continued)*

```
    switch (selection)
    {
        case 'H' :
        case 'h' :      cout << "How many hours were worked? ";
                        cin >> worked;
                        cout << "What is the hour pay rate? ";
                        cin >> rate;
                        cout << "The gross weekly pay is ";
                        cout << calcWeeklyPay(worked, rate) << endl;
                        break;
        case 'S' :
        case 's' :      cout << "What is the annual salary? ";
                        cin >> yearly;
                        cout << "The gross weekly pay is ";
                        cout << calcWeeklyPay(yearly) << endl;
                        break;
    }
    return 0;
}

//*****************************************************************
// Definition of function getChoice                             *
// The parameter letter is a reference to a char.               *
// This function asks the user for an H or an S and returns     *
// the validated input.                                         *
//*****************************************************************

void getChoice(char &letter)
{
    cin >> letter;

    while (letter != 'H' && letter != 'h' &&
           letter != 'S' && letter != 's')
    {
        cout << "Enter H or S: ";
        cin  >> letter;
    }
}

//*****************************************************************
// Definition of overloaded function calcWeeklyPay              *
// This function calculates the gross weekly pay of             *
// an hourly-wage employee. The parameter hours holds the       *
// number of hours worked. The parameter payRate holds the      *
// hourly pay rate. The function returns the weekly salary.     *
//*****************************************************************
```

(program continues)

Program 6-31 *(continued)*

```
float calcWeeklyPay(int hours, float payRate)
{
    return hours * payRate;
}

//***************************************************************
// Definition of overloaded function calcWeeklyPay             *
// This function calculates the gross weekly pay of            *
// a salaried employee. The parameter holds the employee's     *
// annual salary. The function returns the weekly salary.      *
//***************************************************************

float calcWeeklyPay(float annSalary)
{
    return annSalary / 52.0;
}
```

Program Output with Example Input Shown in Bold
```
Do you want to calculate the weekly pay of
(H) an hourly-wage employee, or
(S) a salaried employee? H[Enter]
How many hours were worked? 40[Enter]
What is the hour pay rate? 18.50[Enter]
The gross weekly pay is 740.00
```

Program Output with Other Example Data Shown in Bold
```
Do you want to calculate the weekly pay of
(H) an hourly-wage employee, or
(S) a salaried employee? S[Enter]
What is the annual salary? 48000.00[Enter]
The gross weekly pay is 923.08
```

6.15 The `exit()` Function

CONCEPT The `exit()` function causes a program to terminate, regardless of which function or control mechanism is executing.

A C++ program stops executing when the end of function `main` is reached, or when a `return` statement in function `main` is encountered. When other functions end, however, the program does not stop. Control of the program goes back to the place immediately following the function call. Sometimes, however, the programmer wishes, under certain conditions, to terminate a program in a function other than `main`. To accomplish this, the `exit` function is used.

When the `exit` function is called, it causes the program to stop, regardless of which function contains the call. Program 6-32 demonstrates this.

Program 6-32

```cpp
// This program shows how the exit function causes a program
// to stop executing.

#include <iostream>
#include <cstdlib>    // For exit
using namespace std;

void function();      // Function prototype

int main()
{
    function();
    return 0;
}

//*************************************************************
// This function simply demonstrates that exit can be used   *
// to terminate a program from a function other than main.   *
//*************************************************************

void function()
{
    cout << "This program terminates with the exit function.\n";
    cout << "Bye!\n";
    exit(0);
    cout << "This message will never be displayed\n";
    cout << "because the program has already terminated.\n";
}
```

Program Output
```
This program terminates with the exit function.
Bye!
```

To use the `exit` function, be sure to include the `cstdlib` header file. Notice the function takes an integer argument. This argument is the exit code you wish the program to pass back to the computer's operating system. This code is sometimes used outside of the program to indicate whether the program ended successfully or as the result of a failure. In Program 6-32, the exit code zero is passed, which commonly indicates a successful exit. If you are unsure which code to use with the `exit` function, there are two named constants, EXIT_FAILURE and EXIT_SUCCESS, defined in `cstdlib` for you to use. The constant EXIT_FAILURE is defined as the termination code that commonly represents an unsuccessful exit under the current operating system. Here is an example of its use:

```cpp
exit(EXIT_FAILURE);
```

The constant EXIT_SUCCESS is defined as the termination code that commonly represents a successful exit under the current operating system. Here is an example:

```
        exit(EXIT_SUCCESS);
```

Since it is considered good programming practice to terminate a program at the end of the main function, many programmers use `exit()` only to handle error conditions. However, Program 6-33 demonstrates the `exit` function used with both the EXIT_SUCCESS and EXIT_FAILURE codes.

Program 6-33

```
// This program demonstrates the exit function.

#include <iostream>
#include <cstdlib>                 // Needed to use exit()
using namespace std;

int main()
{
    char response;

    cout << "This program terminates with the exit function.\n";
    cout << "Enter S to terminate with the EXIT_SUCCESS code\n";
    cout << "or F to terminate with the EXIT_FAILURE code: ";
    cin >> response;

    if (response == 'S')
    {
        cout << "Exiting with EXIT_SUCCESS.\n";
        exit(EXIT_SUCCESS);
    }
    else
    {
        cout << "Exiting with EXIT_FAILURE.\n";
        exit(EXIT_FAILURE);
    }
    return 0;
}
```

Program Output with Example Input Shown in Bold
```
This program terminates with the exit function.
Enter S to terminate with the EXIT_SUCCESS code
or F to terminate with the EXIT_FAILURE code: S[Enter]
Exiting with EXIT_SUCCESS.
```

Program Output with Other Example Input Shown in Bold
```
This program terminates with the exit function.
Enter S to terminate with the EXIT_SUCCESS code
or F to terminate with the EXIT_FAILURE code: F[Enter]
Exiting with EXIT_FAILURE.
```

 WARNING! `exit()` is a nonstructured programming technique. Use with caution.

Checkpoint **[6.14–6.15]**

6.24 Is it required that overloaded functions have different return types, different parameter lists, or both?

6.25 What is the output of the following program?

```cpp
#include <iostream>
using namespace std;

void showVals(float, float);

int main()
{

    float x = 1.2, y = 4.5;

    showVals(x, y);
    return 0;
}

void showVals(float p1, float p2)
{
    cout << p1 << endl;
    return;
    cout << p2 << endl;
}
```

6.26 What is the output of the following program?

```cpp
#include <iostream>
using namespace std;

int manip(int, int);

int main()
{
    int x = 4, y = 7;

    cout << manip(x, y) << endl;
    return 0;
}

int manip(int val1, int val2)
{
    return (val1 + val2) * 2;
}
```

6.27 What is the output of the following program?

```cpp
#include <iostream>
using namespace std;
```

```
        int manip(int);
        int manip(int, int);
        int manip(int, float);

        int main()
        {
           int x = 2, y= 4, z;
           float a = 3.1;

           z = manip(x) + manip(x, y) + manip(y, a);
           cout << z << endl;
           return 0;
        }
        int manip(int val)
        {
           return val + val * 2;
        }
        int manip(int val1, int val2)
        {
           return (val1 + val2) * 2;
        }

        int manip(int val1, float val2)
        {
           return val1 * int(val2);
        }
```

6.28 When completed, the following program skeleton should ask the user for the length and
      width of a yard, and then display the yard's area. You must write the prototype and the def-
      inition of the function `calcArea` to complete the program.

```
// Program to calculate the area of a rectangular yard.
#include <iostream>
using namespace std;

// Place prototype here for calcArea.

int main()
{
   float length, width, area;
   cout << "This program calculates the area of a\n";
   cout << "rectangular yard. It must know the yard's\n";
   cout << "length and width. How long is the yard? ";
   cin >> length;
   cout << "How wide is the yard? ";
   cin >> width;
   area = calcArea(length, width);
   cout << "The area of the yard is " << area;
   return 0;
}
```

```
float calcArea(float len, float wide)
{
    // You must write this function, which is to calculate and return
    // the area of the yard. Simply multiply the length
    // by the width and return the value.
}
```

6.16 Stubs and Drivers

Stubs and drivers are very helpful tools for testing and debugging programs that use functions. They allow you to test the individual functions in a program, in isolation from the parts of the program that call the functions.

A *stub* is a dummy function that is called instead of the actual function it represents. It usually displays a test message acknowledging that it was called, and nothing more. For example, if a stub were used for the computeFees function in Program 6-15 (the modular health club membership program), it might look like this:

```
// Stub for the computeFees function
void computeFees(string memberType, int rate, int months)
{
    cout << "The function computeFees was called with arguments:\n"
         << "Member type: " << memberType << endl
         << "rate: " << rate << endl
         << "months: " << months << endl;
}
```

Here is example output of the program if it were run with these stubs, instead of with the actual computeFees function. Input is shown in bold.

```
    Health Club Membership Menu
1.  Standard Adult Membership
2.  Child Membership
3.  Senior Citizen Membership
4.  Quit the Program
```

1[Enter]
For how many months? **3[Enter]**
The function computeFees was called with arguments:
Member type: Adult
rate: 40
months: 3

```
    Health Club Membership Menu
1.  Standard Adult Membership
2.  Child Membership
3.  Senior Citizen Membership
4.  Quit the Program
```

4[Enter]
Thanks for using this program.

As you can see, by replacing an actual function with a stub, you can concentrate your testing efforts on the parts of the program that call the function. Primarily, the stub allows you to determine if your program is calling a function when you expect it to and confirm that valid values are being passed to the function. If the stub represents a function that returns a value, then the stub should return a test value. This helps you confirm that the return value is being handled properly. When the parts of the program that call a function are debugged to your satisfaction, you can move on to testing and debugging the actual functions themselves. This is where drivers become useful.

A *driver* is a program that tests a function by simply calling it. If the function accepts arguments, the driver passes test data. If the function returns a value, the driver displays the return value on the screen. This allows you to see how the function performs in isolation from the rest of the program it will eventually be part of. Program 6-34 is a driver for testing the computeFees function in the health club membership program.

Program 6-34

```cpp
// This program is a driver for testing the computeFees function.

#include <iostream>
#include <string>
using namespace std;

// Prototype
void computeFees(string, double, int);

int main()
{
    cout << "Calling the computeFees function with arguments "
         << "Adult, 40.00, 3.\n";
    computeFees("Adult", 40.00, 3);

    cout << "Calling the computeFees function with arguments "
         << "Child, 20.00, 2.\n";
    computeFees("Child", 20.00, 2);

    cout << "Calling the computeFees function with arguments "
         << "Senior, 30.00, 4.\n";
    computeFees("Senior", 30.00, 4);

    return 0;
}
```

(program continues)

Program 6-34   *(continued)*

```
//***************************************************
// Definition of function computeFees               *
// Uses the monthly rate and number of months       *
// passed to it as parameters to compute and        *
// print the member's total charges.                *
//***************************************************

void computeFees(string memberType, double rate, int months)
{
    cout << endl
         << "Membership Type : " << memberType << "     "
         << "Monthly rate $"    << rate   << endl
         << "Number of months: " << months << endl
         << "Total charges   : $"<< (rate * months)
         << endl << endl;
}
```

Program Output
```
Calling the computeFees function with arguments Adult, 40.00, 3.

Membership Type : Adult    Monthly rate $40
Number of months: 3
Total charges   : $120

Calling the computeFees function with arguments Child, 20.00, 2.

Membership Type : Child    Monthly rate $20
Number of months: 2
Total charges   : $40

Calling the computeFees function with arguments Senior, 30.00, 4.

Membership Type : Senior   Monthly rate $30
Number of months: 4
Total charges   : $120
```

As shown in Program 6-34, a driver can be used to thoroughly test a function. It can repeatedly call the function with different test values as arguments. When the function performs as desired, it can be placed into the actual program it will be part of.

6.17   Focus on Problem Solving and Program Design: A Case Study

The High Adventure Travel Agency offers four vacation packages for thrill-seeking customers. The rates and options vary for each package. You've been asked to write a program to calculate and itemize the charges for each package.

Devil's Courthouse Adventure Weekend: An action-packed three-day weekend spent camping, rock climbing, and rapelling at Devil's Courthouse, North Carolina. This getaway is for novices and experts alike. Optional climbing instruction is available to beginners at a low price. Camping equipment rental is also available.

Rates:

Base Charge:	$350 per person
Climbing Instruction:	$100 per person
Equipment Rental:	$40/day per person

Scuba Bahama: A week-long cruise to the Bahamas with three days of scuba diving. Those with prior experience may dive right in, while beginners should choose to take optional, but very affordable lessons.

Rates:

Base Charge:	$1,000 per person
Scuba Instruction:	$100 per person

Sky-Dive Colorado: Four thrilling days with expert sky-diving instructors in Colorado Springs, Colorado. For lodging, you may choose either the Wilderness Lodge or the Luxury Inn. (Instruction is included for all members of the party.)

Rates:

Base Charge:	$400 per person
Lodging at Wilderness Lodge:	$65/day per person
Lodging at Luxury Inn:	$120/day per person

Barron Cliff Spelunk: Eight days spent hiking and exploring caves in the Barron Cliff Wilderness Area, Tennessee. Camping equipment rental is available.

Rates:

Base Charge:	$700 per person
Equipment Rental:	$40/day per person

Note: A 10 percent discount on the base charges of any package is given for a party of five or more.

Variables

Table 6-1 lists constant variables that will be declared globally. All these variables will be defined near the top of the program to make modifications easier (in the event the rates change).

Table 6-1

Variable	Description
climbRate = 350.0	A float. Holds base rate of Devil's Courthouse Adventure Weekend package.
scubaRate = 1000.0	A float. Holds base rate of Scuba Bahamas package.
skyDiveRate = 400.0	A float. Holds base rate of Sky-Dive Colorado package.
caveRate = 700.0	A float. Holds base rate of Barron Cliff Spelunk package.
climbInstruct = 100.0	A float. Holds charge for rock climbing instruction.
scubaInstruct = 100.0	A float. Holds charge for scuba instruction.
dailyCampRental = 40.0	A float. Holds daily charge, per person, for camping equipment rental.
dayLodge1 = 65.0	A float. Holds daily cost of lodging option 1 of Sky-Dive Colorado package. (Wilderness Lodge.)
dayLodge2 = 120.0	A float. Holds daily cost of lodging option 2 of Sky-Dive Colorado package. (Luxury Inn.)

Modules

Table 6-2 lists the functions used in the program.

Table 6-2

Function name	Description
main	Calls the menu function and dispatches program control to the appropriate module, based on the user's choice of packages.
menu	Displays a menu listing the vacation packages. Allows the user to enter a selection, which is returned to the main function.
climbing	Asks the user for information necessary to calculate charges for the Devil's Courthouse Adventure Weekend package.
scuba	Asks the user for information necessary to calculate charges for the Scuba Bahamas package.
skyDive	Asks the user for information necessary to calculate charges for the Sky-Dive Colorado package.
spelunk	Asks the user for information necessary to calculate charges for the Barron Cliff Spelunk package.

Program Design

In modular programs, hierarchy charts are used to show the relationship between modules. For example, assume an application has five modules: Module A, Module B, Module C, Module D, and Module E. The relationship between the modules is

Module A calls Module B and Module C.
Module B calls Module D and Module E.

These relationships are shown in the hierarchy chart in Figure 6-12.

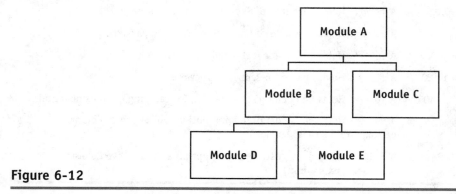

Figure 6-12

Notice that the hierarchy chart does not reveal details about the algorithm or specify when the modules are to be called. Instead, it reveals the relationship between the modules.

Figure 6-13 shows a module hierarchy chart for the High Adventure Travel Agency program.

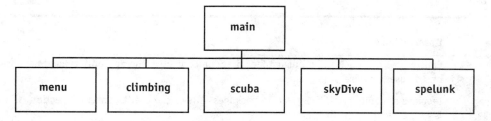

Figure 6-13

The menu that is displayed should list the four vacation packages, plus a fifth option that exits the program. When the user chooses one of the vacation packages, a function is called that asks questions, such as how many people will be going on the trip, and calculates the charges for that particular package. This process repeats until the user chooses to exit the program.

Here is the pseudocode for each of the program's modules.

```
Main Module
    Call Menu Module
    Do-While user does not enter 5
        Switch (User Input)
            Case 1: Call Climbing Module.
            Case 2: Call Scuba Module.
            Case 3: Call SkyDive Module.
            Case 4: Call Spelunk Module.
        End Switch.
    End Do-While.
End of Main Module.

Climbing Module:
    Input number in party needing instruction.
    Input number of advanced climbers in party.
    Input number in party renting equipment.
    Calculate base charges.
    Calculate discount.
    Calculate cost of instruction.
    Calculate cost of equipment rental.
    Calculate total charges.
    Calculate minimum required deposit.
    Display results.
End of Climbing Module.

Scuba Module:
    Input number in party needing instruction.
    Input number of advanced scuba divers in party.
    Calculate base charges.
    Calculate discount.
    Calculate cost of instruction.
    Calculate total charges.
    Calculate minimum required deposit.
    Display results.
End of Scuba Module.

SkyDive Module:
    Input number in party.
    Calculate base charges.
    Calculate discount.
    Input number in party staying at Wilderness Lodge.
    Input number in party staying at Luxury Inn.
    Calculate lodging charges.
    Calculate total charges.
```

> *Calculate minimum required deposit.*
> *Display results.*
> *End of SkyDive Module.*
>
> *Spelunk Module:*
> *Input number in party.*
> *Input number in party renting equipment.*
> *Calculate base charges.*
> *Calculate discount.*
> *Calculate cost of equipment rental.*
> *Calculate total charges.*
> *Calculate minimum required deposit.*
> *Display results.*
> *End of Spelunk Module.*

Program 6-35 lists the C++ code.

Program 6-35

```
// This program will assist the High Adventure Travel Agency
// in calculating the costs of their four major vacation packages.

#include <iostream>
#include <iomanip>
using namespace std;

// Constants for the charges
const float climbRate = 350.0;          // Base rate - Devil's
                                        // Courthouse
const float scubaRate = 1000.0;         // Base rate - Bahamas
const float skyDiveRate = 400.0;        // Base rate - Sky-Dive
const float caveRate = 700.0;           // Base rate - Spelunking
const float climbInstruct = 100.0;      // Climbing instruction
const float scubaInstruct = 100.0;      // Scuba instruction
const float dailyCampRental = 40.0;     // Daily camping equipment rental
const float dayLodge1 = 65.0;           // Lodging option (sky diving)
const float dayLodge2 = 120.0;          // Lodging option (sky diving)

// Function prototypes
void climbing();
void scuba();
void skyDive();
void spelunk();
int menu();
```

(program continues)

Program 6-35   *(continued)*

```cpp
int main()
{
    int selection;

    cout << fixed << showpoint << setprecision(2);
    do
    {
        selection = menu();
        switch(selection)
        {
            case 1 : climbing();
                     break;
            case 2 : scuba();
                     break;
            case 3 : skyDive();
                     break;
            case 4 : spelunk();
                     break;
            case 5 : cout << "Exiting program.\n\n";
        }
    } while (selection != 5);
    return 0;
}
//*********************************************************
// Definition of function menu                           *
// Displays the main menu and asks the user to select    *
// an option. Returns an integer in the range 1 - 5.     *
//*********************************************************

int menu()
{
    int choice;

    cout << "High Adventure Travel Agency\n";
    cout << "----------------------------\n";
    cout << "1) Devil's Courthouse Adventure Weekend\n";
    cout << "2) Scuba Bahama\n";
    cout << "3) Sky-Dive Colorado\n";
    cout << "4) Barron Cliff Spelunk\n";
    cout << "5) Exit Program\n\n";
    cout << "Enter 1, 2, 3, 4, or 5: ";
    cin >> choice;
    while (choice < 1 || choice > 5)  // Validate input
    {
        cout << "Invalid Selection. Enter 1, 2, 3, 4, or 5: ";
        cin >> choice;
    }
    return choice;
}
```

(program continues)

Program 6-35   *(continued)*

```
//****************************************************
// Definition of climbing function                  *
// This function calculates the charges for the     *
// Devil's Courthouse Adventure Weekend package.    *
//****************************************************

void climbing()
{
    int     beginners,      // Those needing instruction
            advanced,       // Those not needing instruction
            needEquip;      // Those renting camping equipment
    float   baseCharges,    // Base charges
            charges,        // Total charges
            instruction,    // Cost of instruction
            equipment,      // Cost of equipment rental
            discount = 0,   // Discount
            deposit;        // Required deposit

    cout << "\nDevil's Courthouse Adventure Weekend\n";
    cout << "-----------------------------------\n";
    cout << "How many will be going who need an instructor? ";
    cin >> beginners;
    cout << "How many advanced climbers will be going? ";
    cin >> advanced;
    cout << "How many will rent camping equipment? ";
    cin >> needEquip;
    // Calculate base charges.
    baseCharges = (beginners + advanced) * climbRate;
    charges = baseCharges;
    // Calculate 10% discount for 5 or more.
    if ((beginners + advanced) > 4)
    {
        discount = (charges * .1);
        charges -= discount;
    }
    // Add cost of instruction.
    instruction = beginners * climbInstruct;
    charges += instruction;
    // Add cost of camping equipment rental
    equipment = needEquip * dailyCampRental * 4;
    charges += equipment;
    // Calculate required deposit.
    deposit = charges / 2.0;
    cout << "Number in party:  " << (beginners + advanced);
    cout << endl;
```

(program continues)

Program 6-35   *(continued)*

```cpp
    cout << "Base charges: $" << baseCharges << endl;
    cout << "Instruction cost: $" << instruction << endl;
    cout << "Equipment Rental: $" << equipment << endl;
    cout << "Discount: $" << discount << endl;
    cout << "Total Charges: $" << charges << endl;
    cout << "Required Deposit: $" << deposit << endl << endl;
}

//*************************************************
// Definition of scuba function                  *
// This function calculates the charges for the   *
// Scuba Bahama package.                          *
//*************************************************

void scuba()
{
    int    beginners,        // Those needing instruction
           advanced;         // Those not needing instruction
    float  baseCharges,      // Base charges
           charges,          // Total charges
           instruction,      // Cost of instruction
           discount = 0,     // Discount
           deposit;          // Required deposit

    cout << "\nScuba Bahama\n";
    cout << "-----------------------------------\n";
    cout << "How many will be going who need an instructor? ";
    cin >> beginners;
    cout << "How many advanced scuba divers will be going? ";
    cin >> advanced;
    // Calculate base charges.
    baseCharges = (beginners + advanced) * scubaRate;
    charges = baseCharges;
    // Calculate 10% discount for 5 or more.
    if ((beginners + advanced) > 4)
    {
        discount = (charges * .1);
        charges -= discount;
    }
    // Add cost of instruction.
    instruction = beginners * scubaInstruct;
    charges += instruction;
    // Calculate required deposit.
    deposit = charges / 2.0;
    cout << "Number in party:  " << (beginners + advanced);
    cout << endl;
```

(program continues)

Program 6-35   *(continued)*

```
    cout << "Base charges: $" << baseCharges << endl;
    cout << "Instruction cost: $" << instruction << endl;
    cout << "Discount: $" << discount << endl;
    cout << "Total Charges: $" << charges << endl;
    cout << "Required Deposit: $" << deposit << endl << endl;
}

//***************************************************
// Definition of skyDive function                  *
// This function calculates the charges for the     *
// Sky-Dive Colorado package.                       *
//***************************************************

void skyDive()
{
    int     party,          // Number in party
            lodge1,         // Number at 1st lodging choice
            lodge2;         // Number at 2nd lodging choice
    float   baseCharges,    // Base charges
            charges,        // Total charges
            discount = 0,   // Discount
            lodging,        // Cost of lodging
            deposit;        // Required deposit

    cout << "\nSky-Dive Colorado\n";
    cout << "------------------------------------\n";
    cout << "How many will be going? ";
    cin >> party;
    // Calculate base charges.
    baseCharges = party * skyDiveRate;
    charges = baseCharges;
    // Calculate 10% discount for 5 or more.
    if (party > 4)
    {
        discount = (charges * .1);
        charges -= discount;
    }
    // Calculate lodging costs.
    cout << "How many will stay at Wilderness Lodge? ";
    cin >> lodge1;
    cout << "How many will stay at Luxury Inn? ";
    cin >> lodge2;
    lodging = (lodge1 * dayLodge1) + (lodge2 * dayLodge2);
```

(program continues)

Program 6-35 *(continued)*

```cpp
    // Calculate required deposit.
    deposit = charges / 2.0;
    cout << "Number in party:  " << party << endl;
    cout << "Base charges: $" << baseCharges << endl;
    cout << "Lodging: $" << lodging << endl;
    cout << "Discount: $" << discount << endl;
    cout << "Total Charges: $" << charges << endl;
    cout << "Required Deposit: $" << deposit << endl << endl;
}

//***************************************************
// Definition of spelunk function                  *
// This function calculates the charges for the     *
// Barron Cliff Spelunk package.                    *
//***************************************************

void spelunk()
{
    int    party,         // Number in party
           needEquip;     // Those renting camping equipment
    float  baseCharges,   // Base charges
           charges,       // Total charges
           equipment,     // Cost of equipment rental
           discount = 0,  // Discount
           deposit;       // Required deposit

    cout << "\nBarron Cliff Spelunk Weekend\n";
    cout << "-----------------------------------\n";
    cout << "How many will be going? ";
    cin >> party;
    cout << "How many will rent camping equipment? ";
    cin >> needEquip;
    // Calculate base charges.
    baseCharges = party * caveRate;
    charges = baseCharges;

    // Calculate 10% discount for 5 or more.
    if (party > 4)
    {
        discount = (charges * .1);
        charges -= discount;
    }
    // Add cost of camping equipment rental
    equipment = needEquip * dailyCampRental * 4;
    charges += equipment;
```

(program continues)

Program 6-35 *(continued)*

```
        // Calculate required deposit.
        deposit = charges / 2.0;
        cout << "Number in party:  " << party << endl;
        cout << "Base charges: $" << baseCharges << endl;
        cout << "Equipment Rental: $" << equipment << endl;
        cout << "Discount: $" << discount << endl;
        cout << "Total Charges: $" << charges << endl;
        cout << "Required Deposit: $" << deposit << endl << endl;
}
```

Program Output with Example Input Shown in Bold
```
High Adventure Travel Agency
----------------------------
1) Devil's Courthouse Adventure Weekend
2) Scuba Bahama
3) Sky-Dive Colorado
4) Barron Cliff Spelunk
5) Exit Program

Enter 1, 2, 3, 4, or 5: 1[Enter]

Devil's Courthouse Adventure Weekend
------------------------------------
How many will be going who need an instructor? 3[Enter]
How many advanced climbers will be going? 2[Enter]
How many will rent camping equipment? 3[Enter]
Number in party:  5
Base charges: $1750.00
Instruction cost: $300.00
Equipment Rental: $480.00
Discount: $175.00
Total Charges: $2355.00
Required Deposit: $1177.50

High Adventure Travel Agency
----------------------------
1) Devil's Courthouse Adventure Weekend
2) Scuba Bahama
3) Sky-Dive Colorado
4) Barron Cliff Spelunk
5) Exit Program

Enter 1, 2, 3, 4, or 5: 2[Enter]
```

(program output continues)

Program 6-35 *(continued)*

```
Scuba Bahama
-------------------------------------
How many will be going who need an instructor? 4[Enter]
How many advanced scuba divers will be going? 0[Enter]
Number in party:  4
Base charges: $4000.00
Instruction cost: $400.00
Discount: $0.00
Total Charges: $4400.00
Required Deposit: $2200.00

High Adventure Travel Agency
----------------------------
1) Devil's Courthouse Adventure Weekend
2) Scuba Bahama
3) Sky-Dive Colorado
4) Barron Cliff Spelunk
5) Exit Program

Enter 1, 2, 3, 4, or 5: 3[Enter]

Sky-Dive Colorado
-------------------------------------
How many will be going? 8[Enter]
How many will stay at Wilderness Lodge? 4[Enter]
How many will stay at Luxury Inn? 4[Enter]
Number in party:  8
Base charges: $3200.00
Lodging: $740.00
Discount: $320.00
Total Charges: $2880.00
Required Deposit: $1440.00

High Adventure Travel Agency
----------------------------
1) Devil's Courthouse Adventure Weekend
2) Scuba Bahama
3) Sky-Dive Colorado
4) Barron Cliff Spelunk
5) Exit Program

Enter 1, 2, 3, 4, or 5: 4[Enter]
```

(program output continues)

Program 6-35   *(continued)*

```
Barron Cliff Spelunk Weekend
-------------------------------------
How many will be going? 6[Enter]
How many will rent camping equipment? 2[Enter]
Number in party:  6
Base charges: $4200.00
Equipment Rental: $320.00
Discount: $420.00
Total Charges: $4100.00
Required Deposit: $2050.00

High Adventure Travel Agency
---------------------------
1) Devil's Courthouse Adventure Weekend
2) Scuba Bahama
3) Sky-Dive Colorado
4) Barron Cliff Spelunk
5) Exit Program

Enter 1, 2, 3, 4, or 5: 5[Enter]
Exiting program.
```

Review Questions and Exercises

Fill-in-the-Blank

1. The _____ is the part of a function definition that shows the function name, return type, and parameter list.

2. If a function doesn't return a value, the word _____ will appear as its return type.

3. If function showValue has the following header: void showValue(int quantity) you would use the statement _____ to call it with the argument 5.

4. Either a function's _____ or its _____ must precede all calls to the function.

5. Values that are sent into a function are called _____.

6. Special variables that hold copies of function arguments are called _____.

7. When only a copy of an argument is passed to a function, it is said to be passed by _____.

8. A(n)_____ eliminates the need to place a function definition before all calls to the function.

9. A(n)_____ variable is declared inside a function and is not accessible outside the function.

10. _____ variables are declared outside all functions and are accessible to any function within their scope.

11. _____ variables provide an easy way to share large amounts of data among all the functions in a program.

12. Unless you explicitly initialize global variables, they are automatically initialized to _____.

13. If a function has a local variable with the same name as a global variable, only the _____ variable can be seen by the function.

14. _____ local variables retain their value between function calls.

15. The _____ statement causes a function to end immediately.

16. _____ arguments are passed to parameters automatically if no argument is provided in the function call.

17. When a function uses a mixture of parameters with and without default arguments, the parameters with default arguments must be defined _____.

18. The value of a default argument must be a(n)_____.

19. When used as parameters, _____ variables allow a function to access the parameter's original argument.

20. Reference variables are defined like regular variables, except there is a _____ in front of the name.

21. Reference variables allow arguments to be passed by _____.

22. The _____ function causes a program to terminate.

23. Two or more functions may have the same name, as long as their _____ are different.

True or False

24. T   F   Functions should be given names that reflect their purpose.

25. T   F   Function headers are terminated with a semicolon.

26. T   F   Function prototypes are terminated with a semicolon.

27. T   F   If other functions are defined before main, the program still starts executing at function main.

28. T   F   When a function terminates, it always branches back to main, regardless of where it was called from.

29. T   F   Arguments are passed to the function parameters in the order they appear in the function call.

30. T   F   Actual arguments passed to a function must agree with the function's formal arguments (i.e., parameters) in number and name.

31. T   F   The scope of a parameter is limited to the function which uses it.

32. T   F   Changes to a function parameter always affect the original argument as well.

33. T   F   In a function prototype, the names of the parameter variables may be left out.

34. T   F   Many functions may have local variables with the same name.

35. T   F   Overuse of global variables can lead to problems as programs become larger and more complex.

36. T   F   Static local variables are not destroyed when a function returns.

37. T   F   All static local variables are initialized to –1 by default.

38. T   F   Initialization of static local variables only happens once, regardless of how many times the function in which they are defined is called.

39. T   F   When a function with default arguments is called and an argument is left out, all arguments that come after it must be left out as well.

40. T   F   It is not possible for a function to have some parameters with default arguments and some without.

41. T   F   The exit function can only be called from main.

42. T   F   A stub is a dummy function that is called instead of the actual function it represents.

Find the Errors

43. Each of the following functions has errors. Locate as many errors as you can.

A)
```
void total(int value1, value2, value3)
{
    return value1 + value2 + value3;
}
```

B)
```
float average(int value1, int value2, int value3)
{
    float average;

    average = value1 + value2 + value3 / 3;
}
```

C)
```
void area(int length = 30, int width)
{
    return length * width;
}
```

D)
```
void getValue(int value&)
{
    cout << "Enter a value: ";
    cin >> value&;
}
```

E) (Overloaded functions)

```
int getValue()
{
    int inputValue;
    cout << "Enter an integer: ";
    cin >> inputValue;
    return inputValue;
}
float getValue()
{
    float inputValue;

    cout << "Enter a floating-point number: ";
    cin >> inputValue;
    return inputValue;
}
```

Programming Challenges

General Requirements

A) Each program should have a section of comments at the top. The comments should contain your name, the date the program was written, the chapter the assignment appeared in, and the assignment number and name. Here is an example:

```
// Written by Jill Johnson
// March 31, 2003
// Chapter 6
// Assignment 1. Markup
```

B) For each program that displays a dollar amount, format the output in fixed-point decimal notation with two places of precision. Be sure the decimal place always displays, even when the number is 0 or has no fractional part.

1. Markup

Write a program that asks for the wholesale cost of an item and its markup percentage. (For example, if an item's wholesale cost is $5 and its retail price is $10, the markup is 100 percent).

The program should have a function that accepts the wholesale cost and markup percentage as arguments, and returns the retail price of the item. The retail price should be displayed.

Input Validation: Do not accept negative values for either the wholesale cost of the item or the percent markup.

2. Lowest Score Drop

This program is to calculate the average of a series of test scores, where the lowest score in the series is dropped. It should use the following functions:

- ◆ getValues should ask for five test scores and store them in variables.
- ◆ findLowest should determine which of the five scores is the lowest and return that value.
- ◆ calcAverage should calculate and display the average of the four highest scores.

Input Validation: Do not accept test scores higher than 100 or lower than 0.

3. Winning Division

This program should calculate which division in a company had the greatest sales for a quarter. It should use the following functions:

- ◆ A function should ask the user for and return the quarterly sales figures for the company's Northeast, Southeast, Northwest, and Southwest divisions.
- ◆ A function should determine which division had the highest sales figures.

A message should be displayed indicating the leading division and its sales figures for the quarter.

Input Validation: Do not accept dollar amounts less than $0.00.

4. Days Out

Write a program that calculates the average number of days a company's employees are absent. The program should have the following functions:

◆ A function that asks the user for the number of employees in the company. This value should be returned as an `int`. (The function accepts no arguments.)

◆ A function that accepts one argument: the number of employees in the company. The function should ask the user to enter the number of days each employee missed during the past year. The total of these days should be returned as an `int`.

◆ A function that takes two arguments: the number of employees in the company and the total number of days absent for all employees during the year. The function should return, as a `float`, the average number of days absent. (This function does not perform screen output and does not ask the user for input.)

Input Validation: Do not accept a number less than 1 or for the number of employees. Do not accept a negative number for the days any employee missed.

5. Order Status

The Middletown Wholesale Copper Wire Company sells spools of copper wiring for $100 each. Write a program that displays the status of an order. The program should have a function that asks for the following information:

◆ The number of spools ordered.

◆ The number of spools in stock.

◆ If there are special shipping and handling charges.

(Shipping and handling is normally $10 per spool.) If there are special charges, it should ask for the special charges per spool.

The information should be passed as arguments to another function that displays:

◆ The number of spools ready to ship from current stock.

◆ The number of spools on backorder (if the number ordered is greater than what is in stock.)

◆ Subtotal of the portion ready to ship (the number of spools ready to ship times $100).

◆ Total shipping and handling charges on the portion ready to ship.

◆ Total of the order ready to ship.

The shipping and handling parameter in the second function should have the default argument 10.00.

Input Validation: Do not accept numbers less than 1 for spools ordered. Do not accept a number less than 0 for spools in stock or shipping and handling charges.

6. Overloaded Hospital

Write a program that computes and displays the charges for a patient's hospital stay. First, the program should ask if the patient was admitted as an in-patient or an out-patient. If the patient was an in-patient, the following information should be entered:

- ◆ The number of days spent in the hospital
- ◆ The daily rate
- ◆ Hospital medication charges
- ◆ Charges for hospital services (lab tests, etc.)

The program should ask for the following information if the patient was an out-patient:

- ◆ Charges for hospital services (lab tests, etc.)
- ◆ Hospital medication charges

The program should use two overloaded functions to calculate the total charges. One of the functions should accept arguments for the in-patient information, while the other function accepts arguments for out-patient information. Both functions should return the total charges.

Input Validation: Do not accept negative numbers for any information.

7. Population

In a population, the birth rate is the percentage increase of the population due to births and the death rate is the percentage decrease of the population due to deaths. Write a program that displays the size of a population for any number of years. The program should ask for the following information:

- ◆ The starting size of a population
- ◆ The annual birth rate
- ◆ The annual death rate
- ◆ The number of years to display

Write a function that calculates the size of the population for a year. The formula is

```
N = P + BP - DP
```

where N is the new population size, P is the previous population size, B is the birth rate, and D is the death rate.

Input Validation: Do not accept numbers less than 2 for the starting size. Do not accept negative numbers for birth rate or death rate. Do not accept numbers less than 1 for the number of years.

Group Project

8. Travel Expenses

This program should be designed and written by a team of students. Here are some suggestions:

♦ One student should design function `main`, which will call the other functions in the program. The remainder of the functions will be designed by other members of the team.

♦ The requirements of the program should be analyzed so each student is given about the same work load.

♦ The parameters and return types of each function should be decided in advance.

♦ Stubs and drivers should be used to test and debug the program.

♦ The program can be implemented either as a multi-file program, or all the functions can be cut and pasted into the main file.

Here is the assignment: Write a program that calculates and displays the total travel expenses of a businessperson on a trip. The program should have functions that ask for and return the following:

♦ The total number of days spent on the trip

♦ The time of departure on the first day of the trip, and the time of arrival back home on the last day of the trip

♦ The amount of any round-trip airfare

♦ The amount of any car rentals

♦ Miles driven, if a private vehicle was used. Calculate the vehicle expense as $0.27 per mile driven

♦ Parking fees (The company allows up to $6 per day. Anything in excess of this must be paid by the employee.)

♦ Taxi fees, if a taxi was used anytime during the trip (The company allows up to $10 per day, for each day a taxi was used. Anything in excess of this must be paid by the employee.)

♦ Conference or seminar registration fees

♦ Hotel expenses (The company allows up to $90 per night for lodging. Anything in excess of this must be paid by the employee.)

♦ The amount of *each* meal eaten. On the first day of the trip, breakfast is allowed as an expense if the time of departure is before 7 a.m. Lunch is allowed if the time of departure is before noon. Dinner is allowed on the first day if the time of departure is before 6 p.m. On the last day of the trip, breakfast is allowed if the time of arrival is after 8 a.m. Lunch is allowed if the time of arrival is after 1 p.m. Dinner is allowed on the last day if the time of arrival is after 7 p.m. The program should only ask for the amounts of allowable meals. (The company allows up to $9 for breakfast, $12 for lunch, and $16 for dinner. Anything in excess of this must be paid by the employee.)

The program should calculate and display the total expenses incurred by the businessperson, the total allowable expenses for the trip, the excess that must be reimbursed by the businessperson, if any, and the amount saved by the businessperson if the expenses were under the total allowed.

Input Validation: Do not accept negative numbers for any dollar amount or for miles driven in a private vehicle. Do not accept numbers less than 1 for the number of days. Only accept valid times for the time of departure and the time of arrival.

Serendipity Booksellers Software Development Project—Part 6: *A Problem-Solving Exercise*

1. Function Name Change

It is now time to make one program from the separate files you have created. Perform the following function name changes:

- Change the name of function `main` in `cashier.cpp` to `cashier`.
- Change the name of function `main` in `invmenu.cpp` to `invMenu`.
- Change the name of function `main` in `bookinfo.cpp` to `bookInfo`.
- Change the name of function `main` in `reports.cpp` to `reports`.

Save each file after you have changed the name of its function `main`.

2. Development Strategy

You must now decide if you are going to develop the project as a multi-file program or simply merge all the functions listed above into the `mainmenu.cpp` file.

Multi-File Program

If you decide on the multi-file program approach, see Appendix E, Multi-file Programs. Additional information on using multiple files with specific compilers is also contained in Appendix F, Introduction to Microsoft Visual C++ 6.0, and Appendix G, Introduction to Borland C++ Builder 5.0. The files that are part of the project are `mainmenu.cpp`, `cashier.cpp`, `invmenu.cpp`, `bookinfo.cpp`, and `reports.cpp`. The file named `mainmenu.cpp` will be the main file.

Single-File Program

If you decide to merge the functions of this project into one file, simply use the cut and paste feature of your editor to perform the following:

- Copy the `cashier` function in `cashier.cpp` and paste it into the `mainmenu.cpp` file.
- Copy the `invMenu` function in `invmenu.cpp` and paste it into the `mainmenu.cpp` file.

◆ Copy the `bookInfo` function in `bookinfo.cpp` and paste it into the `mainmenu.cpp` file.

◆ Copy the `reports` function in `reports.cpp` and paste it into the `mainmenu.cpp` file.

3. Header File Creation

Multi-File Program

If you are developing a multi-file program, create the following header files:

◆ `cashier.h`: This file should contain a function prototype for the `cashier` function. Place an #include directive in `cashier.cpp` that includes `cashier.h`.

◆ `invmenu.h`: This file should contain a function prototype for the `invMenu` function. Place an #include directive in `invmenu.cpp` that includes `invmenu.h`.

◆ `bookinfo.h`: This file should contain a function prototype for the `bookInfo` function. Place an #include directive in `bookinfo.cpp` that includes `bookinfo.h`.

◆ `reports.h`: This file should contain a function prototype for the `reports` function. Place an #include directive in `reports.cpp` that includes `reports.h`.

Single-File Program

If you are developing a single-file program, create a header file named `mainmenu.h`. It should contain function prototypes for the following functions:

```
cashier
invmenu
bookinfo
reports
```

Place an #include "mainmenu.h" statement in the `mainmenu.cpp` file.

4. Switch Modification in `main`

Modify the switch statement in function `main` (of `mainmenu.cpp`) so instead of displaying the number entered by the user, it calls

function `cashier` if the user selects 1,
function `invMenu` if the user selects 2,
function `reports` if the user selects 3.

5. Inventory Database Stub Functions

Add stub functions that will later perform operations selected from the Inventory Database Menu. The functions are

◆ `void lookUpBook()`. This function should simply display the message "You selected Look Up Book."

◆ `void addBook()`. This function should simply display the message "You selected Add Book."

- ◆ void editBook(). This function should simply display the message "You selected Edit Book."

- ◆ void deleteBook(). This function should simply display the message "You selected Delete Book."

Multi-File Program

If you are developing a multi-file program, add the functions above to the invmenu.cpp file. Add function prototypes for each function to invmenu.h.

Single-File Program

If you are developing a single-file program, add the functions above to the mainmenu.cpp file. Add function prototypes for each function to the mainmenu.h file.

6. Switch Modification in invMenu

Modify the switch statement in function invMenu so instead of displaying the number entered by the user, it calls

    function lookUpBook if the user selects 1,
    function addBook if the user selects 2,
    function editBook if the user selects 3,
    function deleteBook if the user selects 4.

7. Report Stub Functions

Add stub functions that will later perform operations selected from the Reports Menu. The functions are

- ◆ void repListing(). This function should simply display the message "You selected Inventory Listing."

- ◆ void repWholesale(). This function should simply display the message "You selected Inventory Wholesale Value."

- ◆ void repRetail(). This function should simply display the message "You selected Inventory Retail Value."

- ◆ void repQty(). This function should simply display the message "You selected Listing By Quantity."

- ◆ void repCost(). This function should simply display the message "You selected Listing By Cost."

- ◆ void repAge(). This function should simply display the message "You selected Listing By Age."

Multi-File Program

If you are developing a multi-file program, add the functions above to the reports.cpp file. Add function prototypes for each function to reports.h.

Single-File Program

If you are developing a single-file program, add the functions above to the `mainmenu.cpp` file. Add function prototypes for each function to the `mainmenu.h` file.

8. Switch Modification in `reports`

Modify the switch statement in function `reports` so instead of displaying the number entered by the user, it calls

function `repListing` if the user selects 1,
function `repWholesale` if the user selects 2,
function `repRetail` if the user selects 3,
function `repQty` if the user selects 4,
function `repCost` if the user selects 5,
function `repAge` if the user selects 6.

CHAPTER 7

Structured Data and Classes

Topics

7.1   Abstract Data Types

CONCEPT An abstract data type (ADT) is a data type that specifies the values the data type can hold and the operations that can be done on them without the need for anyone using the ADT to know how the data type itself is implemented.

The term *abstract data type,* or ADT, is very important in computer science and is especially significant in object-oriented programming. This chapter introduces you to structures and classes, which are C++'s mechanisms for creating abstract data types.

Abstraction

An *abstraction* is a general model of something. It is a definition that includes only the general characteristics of an object. For example, the term "dog" is an abstraction. It defines a general type of animal. The term captures the essence of what all dogs are without specifying the detailed characteristics of any particular type of dog. According to *Webster's New Collegiate Dictionary*, a dog is

> a highly variable carnivorous domesticated mammal (*Canis familiaris*) probably descended from the common wolf.

In real life, however, there is no such thing as a mere "dog." There are specific types of dogs, each with their own set of characteristics. There are poodles, cocker spaniels, great danes, rottwiellers, and many other breeds. There are small dogs and large dogs. There are gentle dogs and ferocious dogs. They come in all shapes, sizes, and dispositions. A real-life dog is not abstract. It is concrete.

Data Types

C++ has a number of *primitive data types* which are defined as a basic part of the language, as shown in Table 7-1.

Table 7-1

bool	int	unsigned long int
char	long int	float
unsigned char	unsigned short int	double
short int	unsigned int	long double

A data type defines what values a variable may hold. Each data type listed in Table 7-1 has its own range of values, such as –32,768 to +32,767 for shorts, and so forth. Data types also define what values a variable may not hold. For example, integer variables may not be used to hold fractional numbers.

In addition to defining a range or domain of values that a variable may hold, data types also define the operations that may be performed on a value. All of the data types listed in Table 7-1 allow the following mathematical and relational operators to be used with them:

```
+, -, *, /, >, <, >=, <=, ==, !=
```

Only the integer data types, however, allow operations with the modulus operator (%). So, a data type defines what values an object may hold and the operations that may be performed on the object.

The primitive data types are abstract in the sense that a data type and an object of that data type are not the same thing. For example, consider the following variable definition:

```
int x = 1, y = 2, z = 3;
```

In this statement the integer variables x, y, and z are defined. They are three separate instances of the data type int. Each variable has its own characteristics (x is set to 1, y is set to 2, and z is set to 3). In this example, the data type int is the abstraction and the variables x, y, and z are concrete occurrences.

Abstract Data Types

An abstract data type (ADT) is a data type created by the programmer. The programmer decides what values are acceptable for the data type, as well as what operations may be performed on the data type. In many cases, the programmer designs his or her own specialized operations.

For example, suppose a program is created to simulate a 12-hour clock. The program could contain three ADTs: hours, minutes, and seconds. The range of values for the hours data type would be the integers 1 through 12. The range of values for the minutes and seconds data types would be 0 through 59. If an hours object is set to 12 and then incremented, it will take on the value 1. Likewise if a minutes object or a seconds object is set to 59 and then incremented, it will take on the value 0.

Abstract data types often combine several values. In the clock program, the hours, minutes, and seconds objects could be combined to form a single clock object. In this chapter you will learn how to combine variables of primitive data types to form your own ADTs.

7.2 Combining Data into Structures

CONCEPT C++ allows you to group several variables together into a single item known as a structure.

So far you've written programs that keep data in individual variables. Sometimes a relationship exists between items of different types. For example, a payroll system might keep the variables shown in Table 7-2. These variables hold information for a single employee.

Table 7-2

Variable Declaration	Information Held
int empNumber;	Employee number
string name;	Employee name
float hours;	Hours worked
float payRate;	Hourly pay rate
float grossPay;	Gross pay

All of the variables listed in Table 7-2 are related because they can hold information about the same employee. Their definition statements, though, do not make it clear that they belong together. To create a relationship between variables, C++ gives you the ability to package them together into a *structure*.

Before a structure can be used, it must be declared. Here is the general format of a structure declaration:

```
struct tag
{
    variable declaration;
    // ... more declarations
    //     may follow...
};
```

The *tag* is the name of the structure. As you will see later, it's used like a data type name. The variable declarations that appear inside the braces declare *members* of the structure. Here is an example of a structure declaration that holds the payroll information listed in Table 7-2:

```
struct PayRoll
{
    int empNumber;
    string name;
    float hours;
    float payRate;
    float grossPay;
};
```

This declaration declares a structure called `PayRoll`. The structure has five members: `empNumber`, `name`, `hours`, `payRate`, and `grossPay`.

 WARNING! Notice that a semicolon is required after the closing brace of the structure declaration.

 Note: In this text we begin the names of structure tags with an uppercase letter. Later you will see the same convention used with unions and classes. This visually differentiates these names from the names of variables.

 Note: The structure declaration shown contains three `float` members, each declared on a separate line. The three could also have been declared on the same line, as

```
struct PayRoll
{
    int empNumber;
    string name;
```

```
        float hours, payRate, grossPay;
};
```

However, many programmers prefer to place each member declaration on a separate line for increased readability.

It's important to note that the structure declaration in our example does not define a variable. It simply tells the compiler what a `PayRoll` structure is made of. In essence, it creates a new data type called `PayRoll`. You can define variables of this type with simple definition statements, just as you would with any other data type. For example, the following statement defines a variable called `deptHead`:

```
        PayRoll deptHead;
```

The data type of `deptHead` is the `PayRoll` structure. The structure tag, `PayRoll`, is listed before the variable name just as the word `int` or `float` would be listed to define variables of those types.

Remember that structure variables are actually made up of other variables known as members. Since `deptHead` is a `PayRoll` structure, it contains the following members:

```
        empNumber, an int
        name, a string object
        hours, a float
        payRate, a float
        grossPay, a float
```

Figure 7-1 illustrates this.

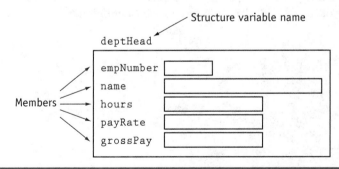

Figure 7-1

Just as it's possible to declare multiple `int` or `float` variables, it's possible to declare multiple structure variables in a program. The following statement declares three `PayRoll` variables: `deptHead`, `foreman`, and `associate`.

```
        PayRoll deptHead, foreman, associate;
```

Figure 7-2 illustrates the existence of these three variables.

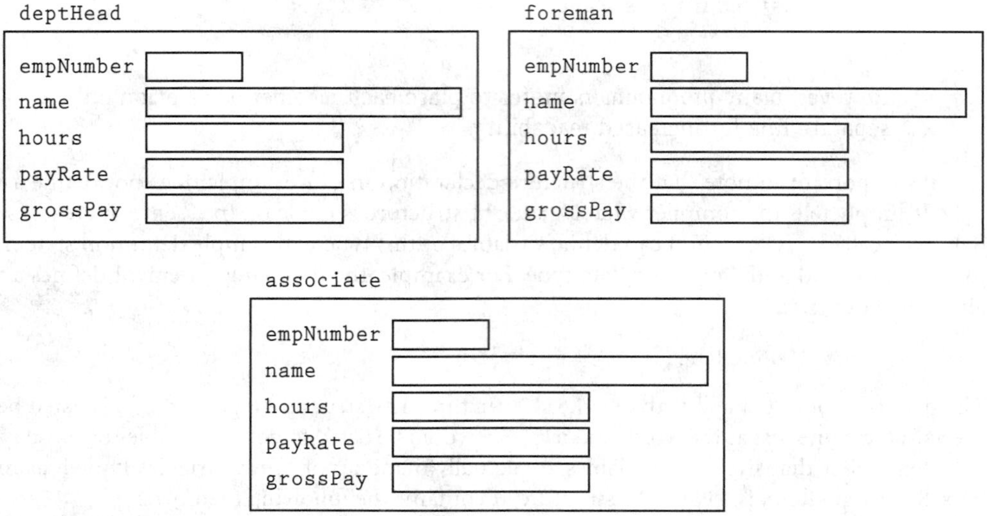

Figure 7-2

Each of the variables defined in this example are separate *instances* of the PayRoll structure and contain their own members. An instance of a structure is a variable that exists in memory. It contains within it all the members described in the structure declaration.

Although the structure variables in the example are separate, each contains members with the same name. (In the next section you'll see how to access these members.) Here are some other examples of structure declarations and variable definitions:

```
struct Time                          struct Date
{                                    {
    int hour;                            int day;
    int minutes;                         int month;
    int seconds;                         int year;
};                                   };
// Definition of the                 // Definition of the structure
// structure variable now.           // variable today.
Time now;                            Date today;
```

In review, there are typically two steps to implementing structures in a program:

◆ Create the structure declaration. This establishes the tag (or name) of the structure and a list of items that are members.

◆ Define variables (or instances) of the structure and use them in the program to hold data.

7.3 Accessing Structure Members

CONCEPT The dot operator allows you to access structure members in a program.

C++ provides the *dot operator* (a period) to access the individual members of a structure. Using our example of `deptHead` as a `PayRoll` structure variable, the following statement demonstrates how to access the `empNumber` member:

```
deptHead.empNumber = 475;
```

In this statement, the number 475 is assigned to the `empNumber` member of `deptHead`. The dot operator connects the name of the member variable with the name of the structure variable it belongs to. The following statements assign values to the `empNumber` members of the `deptHead`, `foreman`, and `associate` structure variables:

```
deptHead.empNumber = 475;
foreman.empNumber = 897;
associate.empNumber = 729;
```

With the dot operator you can use member variables just like regular variables. For example, these statements display the contents of `deptHead`'s members:

```
cout << deptHead.empNumber << endl;
cout << deptHead.name << endl;
cout << deptHead.hours << endl;
cout << deptHead.payRate << endl;
cout << deptHead.grossPay << endl;
```

Program 7-1 is a complete program that uses the `PayRoll` structure.

Program 7-1

```
// This program demonstrates the use of structures.

#include <iostream>
#include <iomanip>
#include <string>
using namespace std;

struct PayRoll
{
    int empNumber;      // Employee number
    string name;        // Employee name
    float hours;        // Hours worked
    float payRate;      // Hourly pay rate
    float grossPay;     // Gross pay
};
```

(program continues)

Program 7-1 *(continued)*

```cpp
int main()
{
    PayRoll employee;    // employee is a PayRoll structure

    //Get inputs
    cout << "Enter the employee's number: ";
    cin >> employee.empNumber;
    cout << "Enter the employee's name: ";
    cin.ignore();         // To skip the remaining '\n' character
    getline(cin, employee.name);
    cout << "How many hours did the employee work? ";
    cin >> employee.hours;
    cout << "What is the employee's hourly payRate? ";
    cin >> employee.payRate;

    // Calculate gross pay
    employee.grossPay = employee.hours * employee.payRate;

    // Display results
    cout << "\nHere is the employee's payroll data:\n";
    cout << "Name: " << employee.name << endl;
    cout << "Number: " << employee.empNumber << endl;
    cout << "Hours worked: " << employee.hours << endl;
    cout << "Hourly pay rate: " << employee.payRate << endl;
    cout << fixed << showpoint << setprecision(2);
    cout << "Gross pay: $" << employee.grossPay << endl;

    return 0;
}
```

Program Output with Example Input Shown in Bold
```
Enter the employee's number: 489[Enter]
Enter the employee's name: Jill Smith[Enter]
How many hours did the employee work? 40[Enter]
What is the employee's hourly payrate? 20[Enter]
Here is the employee's payroll data:
Name: Jill Smith
Number: 489
Hours worked: 40
Hourly pay rate: 20
Gross pay: $800.00
```

 Note: Program 7-1 has the following call to cin's ignore member function:

```cpp
cin.ignore();
```

Recall that the ignore function causes cin to ignore the next character in the input buffer. This is necessary for the getline statement to work properly in Program 7-1.

Note: The contents of a structure variable cannot be displayed by passing the entire variable to `cout`. For example, assuming `employee` is a `PayRoll` structure variable, the following statement will not work:

```
cout << employee << endl;   // Will not work!
```

Instead, each member must be individually passed to `cout`.

As you can see from Program 7-1, structure members can be used with `cin`, `cout`, mathematical statements, and any operation that can be performed with regular variables. The only difference is that the structure variable name and the dot operator must precede the name of the member. Program 7-2 shows a member of a structure variable being passed to the `pow` function.

Program 7-2

```cpp
// This program uses a structure to hold geometric data about a circle.

#include <iostream>
#include <iomanip>
#include <cmath>                 // Needed for the pow function
using namespace std;

struct Circle                    // Declares what a Circle structure looks like
{
    float radius;
    float diameter;
    float area;
};

const double pi = 3.14159;    // Constant is made a double to allow for
                              // greater precision
int main()
{
    Circle c;                 // Defines a variable that is a Circle structure

    // Get the circle diameter
    cout << "Enter the diameter of a circle: ";
    cin >> c.diameter;

    // Perform calulations
    c.radius = c.diameter / 2;
    c.area = pi * pow(c.radius, 2.0);

    // Output results
    cout << fixed << showpoint << setprecision(2);
    cout << "\nThe radius and area of the circle are:\n";
    cout << "Radius: " << setw(6) << c.radius << endl;
    cout << "Area  : " << setw(6) << c.area << endl;

    return 0;
}
```

Program 7-2

Program Output with Example Input Shown in Bold
```
Enter the diameter of a circle: 10[Enter]
The radius and area of the circle are:
Radius:   5.00
Area  :  78.54
```

7.4 Initializing a Structure

CONCEPT The members of a structure variable may be initialized with starting values when the structure variable is defined.

A structure variable may be initialized when it is defined. Assume the following structure declaration exists in a program:

```
struct GeoInfo
{
    string cityName;
    string state;
    long population;
    int distance;
};
```

A variable may then be created with an initialization list, as shown here:

```
GeoInfo location = {"Asheville", "NC", 50000, 28};
```

Some compilers do not allow this method of initializing structure members if the structure contains any string objects. One alternative, in this case, is to assign initial values to the members of the structure after the variable is defined:

```
GeoInfo location;                 // This creates the variable.

location.cityName = "Asheville";  // These statements assign
location.state = "NC";            // initial values to the members.
location.population = 50000;
location.distance = 28;
```

Another alternative is to replace the string objects with C-strings, which were introduced in Section 3.10. The structure would be thus declared as

```
struct GeoInfo
{
    char cityName[30];
    char state[3];
    long population;
    int distance;
};
```

Now the following variable definition and initialization statement will work.

```
GeoInfo location = {"Asheville", "NC", 50000, 28};
```

In either case, whether your compiler allows the initialization of structure variables containing string objects or whether you have replaced the string objects with C-strings, the example statement defines the variable `location` to be a `GeoInfo` structure. The first value in the initialization list is assigned to the first declared structure member, the second value in the list is assigned to the second member, and so on. The `location` variable is thus initialized in the following manner.

The string "Asheville" is assigned to `location.cityName`
The string "NC" is assigned to `location.state`
50000 is assigned to `location.population`
28 is assigned to `location.distance`

You do not have to provide initializers for all the members of a structure variable. For example, the following statement only initializes the `cityName` member of `location`:

```
GeoInfo location = {"Tampa"};
```

The `state`, `population`, and `distance` members are left uninitialized. The following statement only initializes the `cityName` and `state` members, while leaving `population` and `distance` uninitialized:

```
GeoInfo location = {"Atlanta", "GA"};
```

If you leave a structure member uninitialized, you must leave all the members that follow it uninitialized as well. C++ does not provide a way to skip members in a structure. For example, the following statement, which attempts to skip the initialization of the `population` member, is *not* legal:

```
GeoInfo location = {"Knoxville", "TN", , 90};  // Illegal!
```

It's important to note that you cannot initialize a structure member in the declaration of the structure because the structure declaration just creates a new data type. No variables of this type exist yet. For instance the following declaration is illegal:

```
// Illegal structure declaration
struct GeoInfo
{
    char cityName[30] = "Asheville";
    char state[3] = "NC";
    long population = 50000;
    int distance = 28;
};
```

A structure declaration only declares what the structure "looks like." The member variables are created in memory when a structure variable is created with a definition statement. Until this occurs there is no place to store an initial value.

7.5 Nested Structures

> **CONCEPT** It's possible for a structure variable to be a member of another structure variable.

Sometimes it's helpful to nest structures inside other structures. For example, consider the following structure declarations:

```
struct Costs
{
    float wholesale;
    float retail;
};

struct Item
{
    string partNum;
    string description;
    Costs pricing;
};
```

The Costs structure has two float members, wholesale and retail. The Item structure has three members. The first two, partNum and description, are string objects. The third, pricing, is a nested Costs structure. Assume variable widget is defined to be an Item structure:

```
Item widget;
```

Figure 7-3 illustrates its members.

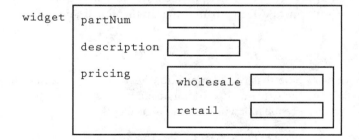

Figure 7-3

They would be accessed as follows:

```
widget.partnum = "123A";
widget.description = "iron widget";
widget.pricing.wholesale = 100.0;
widget.pricing.retail = 150.0;
```

Notice that wholesale and retail are not members of widget; pricing is. To access wholesale and retail, widget's pricing member must first be accessed and then, since it is a Costs structure, its `wholesale` and `retail` members can be accessed. Notice also, as with all structures, it is the member names, not structure tag names, that must be used in accessing members. The following statements would not be legal.

```
cout << widget.retail;          // Wrong!
cout << widget.Costs.wholesale;  // Wrong!
```

When you are deciding whether to use nested structures or not, think about how various members are related. A structure bundles together items that logically belong together. Normally the members of a structure are attributes describing some object. In our example, the object was a widget and its part number, description, and wholesale and retail prices were its attributes. When some of the attributes are related and form a logical subgroup of the object's attributes, it makes sense to bundle them together and use a nested structure. Notice the relatedness of the attributes in the inner structure of Program 7-3, which uses a nested structure.

Program 7-3

```cpp
// This program demonstrates the use of a nested structure.

#include <iostream>
#include <iomanip>
#include <string>
using namespace std;

struct AnnualCostInfo
{
    float food,
          medical,
          license,
          misc;
};

struct PetInfo
{
    string name;
    string type;
    int age;
    AnnualCostInfo cost;
};

int main()
{
    PetInfo pet;        // Define a structure variable
```

(program continues)

Program 7-3   *(continued)*

```
pet.name = "Sassy";
pet.type = "cat";
pet.age = 5;
pet.cost.food = 250.00;
pet.cost.medical = 150.00;
pet.cost.license = 7.00;
pet.cost.misc = 50.00;

cout << fixed << showpoint << setprecision(2);
cout << "Annual costs for my " << pet.age << "-year-old "
     << pet.type << " " << pet.name  << " are $"
     << (pet.cost.food + pet.cost.medical +
          pet.cost.license + pet.cost.misc) << endl;

return 0;
}
```

Sample Output
```
Annual costs for my 5-year-old cat Sassy are $457.00
```

Checkpoint [7.1–7.5]

7.1   Write a structure declaration to hold the following data about a savings account:

Account number (string)
Account balance (float)
Interest rate (float)
Average monthly balance (float)

7.2   Write a definition statement for a variable of the structure you declared in question 7.1. Initialize the members with the following data:

Account number: ACZ42137-B12-7
Account balance: $4512.59
Interest rate: 4%
Average monthly balance: $4217.07

7.3   The following program skeleton, when complete, asks the user to enter the following information about his or her favorite movie:

Name of movie
Name of the movie's motion picture company
Name of the movie's director
Name of the movie's producer
The year the movie was released

Complete the program by declaring the structure that holds this information, defining a structure variable, and writing the individual statements necessary.

```cpp
#include <iostream>
#include <string>
using namespace std;

// Write the structure declaration here to hold the movie information.

int main()
{
    // Define the structure variable here.

    cout << "Enter the following information about your\n";
    cout << "favorite movie.\n";
    cout << "Name: ";
    // Write a statement here that lets the user enter the
    // name of their favorite movie. Store the name in the
    // structure variable.
    cout << "Director: ";
    // Write a statement here that lets the user enter the
    // name of the movie's director. Store the name in the
    // structure variable.
    cout << "Producer: ";
    // Write a statement here that lets the user enter the
    // name of the movie's producer. Store the name in the
    // structure variable.
    cout << "Year of release: ";
    // Write a statement here that lets the user enter the
    // year the movie was released. Store the year in the
    // structure variable.
    cout << "Here is information on your favorite movie:\n";
    // Write statements here that display the information
    // just entered into the structure variable.
    return 0;
}
```

7.4   Write a structure declaration called Measurement, with the following members:

miles, an integer
meters, a long integer

7.5   Write a structure declaration called Destination, with the following members:

city, a string
distance, a Measurement structure (declared in question 7.4)
Also define a variable of this structure type.

7.6   Write statements that store the following information in the variable you defined in question 7.5:

City: Tupelo
Miles 375
Meters: 603,375

7.6   Structures as Function Arguments

Using Individual Structure Members as Function Arguments

Like other variables, the individual members of a structure variable may be used as function arguments. For example, assume the following structure declaration exists in a program:

```
struct Rectangle
{
   float length;
   float width;
   float area;
};
```

Let's say the following function definition exists in the same program:

```
float multiply(float x, float y)
{
    return x * y;
}
```

Assuming that box is a variable of the Rectangle structure type, the following function call will pass box.length into x and box.width into y. The return value will be stored in box.area.

```
box.area = multiply(box.length, box.width);
```

Using an Entire Structure as a Function Argument

Sometimes it's more convenient to pass an entire structure variable into a function instead of individual members. For example, the following function definition uses a Rectangle structure variable as its parameter:

```
void showRect(Rectangle r)
{
    cout << r.length << endl;
    cout << r.width << endl;
    cout << r.area << endl;
}
```

The following function call passes the box variable into r:

```
showRect(box);
```

Inside the function showRect, r's members contain a copy of box's members. This is illustrated in Figure 7-4.

```
showRect(box);


void showRect(Rectangle r)
{
    cout << r.length << endl;
    cout << r.width << endl;
    cout << r.area << endl;
}
```

Figure 7-4

Once the function is called, r.length contains a copy of box.length, r.width contains a copy of box.width, and r.area contains a copy of box.area.

Structures, like all variables, are normally passed to functions by value. If a function needs to have access to the members of the original argument, however, a reference variable may be used as the parameter. Program 7-4 demonstrates this. An entire structure variable is passed to two functions. It is passed by value to the showItem function, which only needs to use a copy of the data members. It is passed by reference to the getItem function, which must access the data members of the original structure variable passed to it.

Program 7-4

```
// This program illustrates passing an entire structure as a
// function argument, both by value and by reference.

#include <iostream>
#include <iomanip>
#include <string>
using namespace std;

struct InvItem
{
    int partNum;          // Part number
    string description;   // Item description
    int onHand;           // Units on hand
    float price;          // Unit price
};
```

(program continues)

Program 7-4 *(continued)*

```
// Function Prototypes
void getItem(InvItem&);     // An entire InvItem structure is being passed
                            // to the getItem function.  It is passed by
                            // reference so that getItem can place new data
                            // into the original structure variable. Note the &.

void showItem(InvItem);     // An entire InvItem structure is being passed
                            // to the showItem function.  It is passed by
                            // value since showItem just needs to use a copy
                            // of the data and does not need to modify the
                            // the original structure variable.

int main()
{
    InvItem part;           // This defines the variable part to be an
                            // InvItem structure.
    getItem (part);
    showItem(part);
    return 0;
}

//****************************************************************
// Definition of function getItem                              *
// This function uses a structure reference variable as its    *
// parameter. It asks the user for information to store in      *
// the structure.                                              *
// ****************************************************************

void getItem(InvItem &piece)    // Note the & indicating this is
{                               // a reference parameter.
    cout << "Enter the part number: ";
    cin >> piece.partNum;
    cout << "Enter the part description: ";
    cin.get();                          // Move past the '\n' left in the
                                        // input buffer by the last input.
    getline(cin, piece.description);
    cout << "Enter the quantity on hand: ";
    cin >> piece.onHand;
    cout << "Enter the unit price: ";
    cin >> piece.price;
}

//****************************************************************
// Definition of function showItem                             *
// This function receives an argument of the InvItem structure *
// type. The contents of the structure are displayed.          *
//****************************************************************
```

(program continues)

Program 7-4 *(continued)*

```
void showItem(InvItem piece)
{
    cout << fixed << showpoint << setprecision(2);
    cout << "\nPart Number: " << piece.partNum << endl;
    cout << "Description: " << piece.description << endl;
    cout << "Units On Hand: " << piece.onHand << endl;
    cout << "Price: $" << piece.price << endl;
}
```

Program Output with Example Input Shown in Bold
```
Enter the part number: 800[Enter]
Enter the part description: Screwdriver[Enter]
Enter the quantity on hand: 135[Enter]
Enter the unit price: 1.25[Enter]

Part Number: 800
Description: Screwdriver
Units On Hand: 135
Price: $1.25
```

Notice in Program 7-4 that the structure declaration of InvItem appears before either the prototype or the definition of the getItem and showItem functions. This is because they each use an InvItem structure variable as a parameter. The compiler must know what InvItem is before it encounters any definitions for variables of that type. Otherwise an error will occur.

Constant Reference Parameters

Sometimes structures can be quite large. Passing large structures by value can decrease a program's performance because a copy of the structure has to be created. When a structure is passed by reference, however, it isn't copied. A reference that points to the original argument is passed instead. So, it's often preferable to pass large objects such as structures by reference.

The disadvantage of passing an object by reference, however, is that the function has access to the original argument, so it can potentially alter the argument's value. This can be prevented by passing the argument as a constant reference. The showItem function from Program 7-4 is modified here to use a constant reference parameter.

```
void showItem(const InvItem &piece)
{
    cout << fixed << showpoint << setprecision(2);
    cout << "\nPart Number: " << piece.partNum << endl;
    cout << "Description: " << pieced.description << endl;
    cout << "Units On Hand: " << piece.onHand << endl;
    cout << "Price: $" << piece.price << endl;
}
```

This function is more efficient than the original version because the amount of time and memory consumed in the function call is reduced. Since the parameter is defined as a constant, the function cannot accidentally corrupt the value of the argument.

7.7 Returning a Structure from a Function

| **CONCEPT** | A function may return a structure. |

Just as functions can be written to return an int, long, float, and other data type, they can also be designed to return a structure. Recall the following structure declaration from Program 7-2:

```
struct Circle
{
    float radius;
    float diameter;
    float area;
};
```

A function, such as the following, could be written to return a variable of the Circle data type:

```
Circle getData()
{
    Circle temp;
    temp.radius = 10.0;
    temp.diameter = 20.0;
    temp.area = 314.159;
    return temp;
}
```

Notice that the function getData has a return data type of Circle. That means the function returns an entire Circle structure when it terminates. The return value can be assigned to any variable that is a Circle structure. The following statement, for example, assigns getData's return value to the Circle structure piePlate:

```
piePlate = getData();
```

After this statement executes, piePlate.radius will be set to 10.0, piePlate.diameter will be set to 20.0, and piePlate.area will be set to 314.159.

When a function returns a structure, it is always necessary for the function to have a local structure variable to hold the member values that are to be returned. In the getData function above, the values for diameter, radius, and area are stored in the local variable temp.

```
temp.radius = 10.0;
temp.diameter = 20.0;
temp.area = 314.159;
```

`temp` is then returned from the function.

```
return temp;
```

Program 7-5 is a modification of Program 7-2. The function `getInfo` gets the circle's diameter from the user and calculates the circle's radius. The diameter and radius are stored in a local structure variable, `round`, which is returned from the function.

Program 7-5

```cpp
// This program uses a function that returns a structure.
// This is a modification of Program 7-2.

#include <iostream>
#include <iomanip>
#include <cmath>        // Needed for the pow function
using namespace std;

// Circle structure declaration
struct Circle
{
    float radius;
    float diameter;
    float area;
};

// Function prototype
Circle getInfo();

// Constant definition for pi
const double pi = 3.14159;

int main()
{
    Circle c;

    c = getInfo();
    c.area = pi * pow(c.radius, 2.0);

    // Output results
    cout << fixed << showpoint << setprecision(2);
    cout << "\nThe radius and area of the circle are:\n";
    cout << "Radius: " << setw(6) << c.radius << endl;
    cout << "Area  : " << setw(6) << c.area << endl;

    return 0;
}
```

(program continues)

Program 7-5   *(continued)*

```
//**********************************************************************
// Definition of function getInfo                                      *
// This function uses a local circle structure variable named          *
// round to hold the input circle diameter and the calculated          *
// circle radius.  The round variable is then returned to the          *
// calling function.                                                   *
//**********************************************************************

Circle getInfo()
{
   Circle round;

   cout << "Enter the diameter of a circle: ";
   cin  >> round.diameter;
   round.radius = round.diameter / 2;
   return round;
}
```

Program Output with Example Input Shown in Bold
```
Enter the diameter of a circle: 10[Enter]

The radius and area of the circle are:
Radius:   5.00
Area  :   78.54
```

> **Note:** In Chapter 6 you learned that C++ only allows you to return a single value from a function. Structures, however, provide a way around this limitation. Even though a structure may have several members, it is technically a single value. By packaging multiple values inside a structure, you can return as many variables as you need from a function.

Checkpoint [7.6–7.7]

Assume the following structure declaration exists for questions 7.7–7.9:

```
struct Rectangle
{
    int length;
    int width;
};
```

7.7   Write a function that accepts a `Rectangle` structure as its argument and displays the structure's contents on the screen.

7.8   Write a function that uses a `Rectangle` structure reference variable as its parameter and stores the user's input in the structure's members.

7.9 Write a function that returns a `Rectangle` structure. The function should store the user's input in the members of the structure before returning it.

7.8 Unions

CONCEPT A *union* is like a structure, except all the members occupy the same memory area.

A union, in almost all regards, is just like a structure. The difference is that all the members of a union use the same memory area, so only one member can be used at a time. A union might be used in an application where the program needs to work with two or more values (of different data types), but only needs to use one of the values at a time. Unions conserve memory by storing all their members in the same memory location.

Unions are declared just like structures, except the key word `union` is used instead of `struct`. Here is an example:

```
union PaySource
{
    short hours;
    float sales;
};
```

A union variable of the data type shown can then be defined as

```
PaySource employee1;
```

The `PaySource` union variable defined here has two members: `hours` (a `short`), and `sales` (a `float`). The entire variable will only take up as much memory as the largest member (in this case, a `float`). The way this variable is stored on a typical PC is illustrated in Figure 7-5.

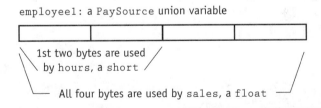

employee1: a PaySource union variable

1st two bytes are used by hours, a short

All four bytes are used by sales, a float

Figure 7-5

As shown in Figure 7-5, the union uses 4 bytes on a typical PC. It can store a `short` or a `float`, depending on which member is used. When a value is stored in the `sales` member, all 4 bytes are needed to hold the data. When a value is stored in the `hours` member, however, only the first 2 bytes are used. Obviously, both members can't hold values at the same time. This union is demonstrated in Program 7-6.

Program 7-6

```
// This program demonstrates a union.

#include <iostream>
#include <iomanip>
using namespace std;

union PaySource                 // Declare a union.
{
    short hours;                // These two variables share
    float sales;               // the same memory space.
};

int main()
{
    PaySource employee1;        // employee1 is a PaySource union.
                                // This employee can have hours or
                                // sales, but not both at once.

    char  hourlyType;           // 'y' if hourly, 'n' if on commission
    float payRate, grossPay;

    cout << fixed << showpoint << setprecision(2);
    cout << "This program calculates either hourly wages or "
         << "sales commission.\n";
    cout << "Is this an hourly employee (y or n)? ";
    cin  >> hourlyType;

    if (hourlyType == 'y')      // This is an hourly employee.
    {
        cout << "What is the hourly pay rate? ";
        cin  >> payRate;
        cout << "How many hours were worked? ";
        cin  >> employee1.hours;
        grossPay = employee1.hours * payRate;
        cout << "Gross pay: $" << grossPay << endl;
    }
    else                        // Employee works on commission.
    {
        cout << "What are the total sales for this employee? ";
        cin  >> employee1.sales;
        grossPay = employee1.sales * 0.10;
        cout << "Gross pay: $" << grossPay << endl;
    }

    return 0;
}
```

Program 7-6

Program Output with Example Input Shown in Bold
```
This program calculates either hourly wages or sales commission.
Is this an hourly employee (y or n)? y[Enter]
What is the hourly pay rate? 20[Enter]
How many hours were worked? 40[Enter]
Gross pay: $800.00
```

Program Output with Other Example Input Shown in Bold
```
This program calculates either hourly wages or sales commission.
Is this an hourly employee (y or n)? n[Enter]
What are the total sales for this employee? 5000[Enter]
Gross pay: $500.00
```

Everything else you already know about structures applies to unions.

Anonymous Unions

The members of an anonymous union have names, but the union itself has no name. Here is the general format of an anonymous union declaration:

```
union
{
    member declaration;
    ...
};
```

An anonymous union declaration actually creates the member variables in memory, so there is no need to separately declare a union variable. Anonymous unions are simple to use because the members may be accessed without the dot operator. Program 7-7, which is a modification of Program 7-6, demonstrates the use of an anonymous union.

Program 7-7

```
// This program demonstrates an anonymous union.

#include <iostream>
#include <iomanip>
using namespace std;

int main()
{
    union                      // Declare an anonymous union.
    {
        short hours;           // These two variables share
        float sales;           // the same memory space.
    };
```

(program continues)

Program 7-7 *(continued)*

```
   char  hourlyType;          // 'y' if hourly, 'n' if on commission
   float payRate, grossPay;

   cout << fixed << showpoint << setprecision(2);
   cout << "This program calculates either hourly wages or "
        << "sales commission.\n";
   cout << "Is this an hourly employee (y or n)? ";
   cin  >> hourlyType;

   if (hourlyType == 'y')    // This is an hourly employee.
   {
      cout << "What is the hourly pay rate? ";
      cin  >> payRate;
      cout << "How many hours were worked? ";
      cin  >> hours;          // Anonymous union member
      grossPay = hours * payRate;
      cout << "Gross pay: $" << grossPay << endl;
   }
   else                       // Employee works on commission.
   {
      cout << "What are the total sales for this employee? ";
      cin  >> sales;          // Anonymous union member
      grossPay = sales * 0.10;
      cout << "Gross pay: $" << grossPay << endl;
   }

   return 0;
}
```

Program Output with Example Input Shown in Bold
```
This program calculates either hourly wages or sales commission.
Is this an hourly employee (y or n)? n[Enter]
What are the total sales for this employee? 12000[Enter]
Gross pay: $1200.00
```

Note: The anonymous union in Program 7-7 is declared inside function `main`. If an anonymous union is declared globally (outside all functions), it must be declared static. This means the word `static` must appear before the word `union`.

 # Checkpoint [7.8]

7.10 Declare a union called `ThreeTypes` with the following members:

`letter`: A character
`whole`: An integer
`real`: A float

7.9 Procedural and Object-Oriented Programming

CONCEPT Procedural programming is a software development approach that is centered on the procedures, or actions, that take place in a program. Object-oriented programming, by contrast, is centered on objects. Objects are entities created from abstract data types that encapsulate together data and the functions that operate on them.

There are two common programming methods in practice today: procedural programming and object-oriented programming (or OOP). Up to this chapter, you have learned to write procedural programs.

In a procedural program, you typically have data stored in a collection of variables and/or structures, coupled with a set of functions that perform operations on the data. The data and the functions are separate entities. For example, in a program that works with the geometry of a rectangle, you might have the variables shown in Table 7-3:

Table 7-3

Variable Declaration	Description
`float width;`	Holds the rectangle's width
`float length;`	Holds the rectangle's length
`float area;`	Holds the area of the rectangle

In addition to the variables listed in Table 7-3, you might also have the functions shown in Table 7-4:

Table 7-4

Function Name	Description
`setData()`	Stores values in `width` and `length`
`calcArea()`	Calculates the rectangle's area
`getWidth()`	Displays the rectangle's width
`getLength()`	Displays the rectangle's length
`getArea()`	Displays the rectangle's area

Usually, variables and data structures are passed to the functions that perform the desired operations. As you can see, procedural programming is centered around functions.

What's Wrong with Procedural Programming?

Even though the most important part of a program is the data and the way the data is organized, the procedural paradigm keeps programmers focused on the functions, or routines, that make up a program. Often this leads to problems such as the following:

1. **Programs with Excessive Global Data**
   The developers of large procedural programs often resort to storing their primary data in global variables and structures. This is so all the functions have convenient access to critical information. This public accessibility, however, opens the door for a programmer to write code that accidentally destroys or corrupts vital data.

2. **Complex and Convoluted Programs**
   Even though a program that is highly modularized (broken into many logical functions) is preferable to one that isn't, there is a limit to the number of functions a person is capable of comprehending. It's common for real-world programs to have hundreds of functions that interact in a myriad of ways. If a new programmer without intimate knowledge of the code is brought into the project, he or she may have difficulty understanding the program.

3. **Programs That Are Difficult to Modify and Extend**
   When a program reaches a certain level of complexity, it becomes difficult to modify and to understand how the modification will impact other parts of the program. Often, there is a delicate dependency between two or more functions. When a programmer alters one function, he or she might unknowingly affect other functions in adverse ways.

What Is Object-Oriented Programming?

Just as procedural programming is centered around functions, object-oriented programming is centered around *objects,* which package together both the data and the functions that operate on the data.

Earlier you learned that variables represent storage locations in the computer's memory. A variable can be an "instance" of an int, a float, or any other built-in data type. You also learned that a program may bundle together, or encapsulate, a group of data items in a structure. A variable defined to be an instance of that structure type represents a storage location in memory where all the data members of the structure are stored. Classes are very similar to structures. However, they normally encapsulate both data members and a set of functions that operate on them. Since they represent more than just memory storage locations, instances of classes are called *objects*, rather than variables.

Figure 7-6 shows a representation of a simple object that contains just one data item and two functions. The object is a Circle object. The data item is its radius. The first function sets the radius, and the second function calculates and returns the area. A data item that is part of an object is called a *member variable*. A function that is part of an object is called a *member function*.

In the object-oriented approach, the member variables and the member functions are both members of the Circle object. They are bound together in a single unit. When an operation is to be performed, such as calculating the area of the circle, a message is passed to the object, telling it

```
Member Variables
float radius;

Member Functions
void setRadius(float r)
{    radius = r; }

void findArea()
{    return 3.14 * pow(radius, 2; }
```

Figure 7-6

to perform the `findArea` function. Since `findArea` is a member of the `Circle` object, it automatically has access to all of the object's member variables. Therefore, there is no need to pass `radius` to the `findArea` function.

 Note: In OOP terminology, an object's member variables are sometimes called its *attributes* and its member functions are sometimes referred to as its *behaviors* or *methods*.

Not only do objects have associated data and functions, they also have the ability to restrict other parts of the program from accessing their member variables and inner workings. This is known as *data hiding*. Data hiding is an important part of object-oriented programming because it allows the creation of objects whose critical data is protected from accidental corruption. It also allows an algorithm's complexity to be hidden from the world outside the object. The only data and functions that are accessible are those necessary to use the object for its intended purpose. These publicly-available members form an interface for using the object. This is illustrated in Figure 7-7.

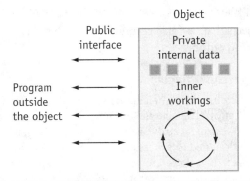

Figure 7-7

An everyday example of object-oriented technology is the automobile. It has a rather simple interface that consists of an ignition switch, steering wheel, gas pedal, brake pedal, and, possibly, a clutch pedal and stick shift for changing gears. If you want to drive an automobile (to become its user), you only have to learn to operate these elements of its interface. To start the motor, you simply turn the key in the ignition switch. What happens internally is irrelevant to the user. If you want to steer the auto to the left, you rotate the steering wheel left. The movements of all the linkages connecting the steering wheel to the front tires occur transparently.

Because automobiles have simple user interfaces, they can be driven by people who have no mechanical knowledge. This is good for the makers of automobiles because it means more people are likely to become customers. It's good for the users of automobiles because it lessens the chance that accidental damage will occur during some simple operation, like starting the motor.

These are also valid concerns in software development. A real-world program is rarely written by only one person. Even the programs you have created so far weren't written entirely by you. If you incorporated C++ library functions, or objects like `cin` and `cout`, you used code written by someone else. In the world of professional software development, programmers commonly work in teams, buy and sell their code, and collaborate on projects. With OOP, programmers can create objects with powerful engines tucked away "under the hood" that have simple interfaces, that safeguard the object's algorithms, and that may be learned quickly.

How Are Objects Used?

Objects are created from programmer-defined abstract data types. Typically, programmers create two types of objects: general purpose and application specific.

General-Purpose Objects

General-purpose objects may be used in a variety of applications. They are commonly designed for purposes such as these:

- ◆ Creating data types that are improvements on C++'s built-in data types

- ◆ Creating data types that are missing from C++. For instance, an object could be designed to process currencies or dates as if they were built-in data types.

- ◆ Creating objects that perform commonly needed tasks, such as input validation and graphical screen output

Application-Specific Objects

Application-specific objects, as their name suggests, are data types created for a specific application. These objects afford the benefits of OOP to the processing of specific types of information. For example, the Westside Hardware Company might have an inventory program that uses objects specifically designed to process their inventory records.

Although objects like these are very useful in their respective applications, they cannot be used for general purposes. For example, the Westside Hardware Company's inventory object could not be used in a program that averages student test scores.

7.10 Introduction to Classes

In C++, the class is the construct primarily used to create objects.

A *class* is very similar to a structure. It is a data type defined by the programmer, consisting of variables and functions. Here is the general format of a class declaration:

```
class class-name
{
    declaration;
    // ... more declarations
    //     may follow...
};
```

We will learn how to implement a class by building one step by step. Our example will be the simple Circle class, depicted in Figure 7-6. The first step is to write the class declaration. This tells the compiler what the class is made of. Here is the declaration for our Circle class.

```
class Circle
{   private:
        float radius;

    public:
        void setRadius(float r)
        {   radius = r;  }

        float findArea()
        {   return 3.14 * pow(radius, 2);  }
};
```

As described earlier, this class contains one member variable, radius, and two member functions, setRadius and findArea.

The class declaration looks very much like Figure 7-6 with the addition of two key words, *private* and *public*. These are called *access specifiers*, since they designate who can access various members of the class. (Notice the access specifiers are followed by a colon.) In our class, the member variable happens to be listed under the private access specifier and the two member functions happen to be listed under the public access specifier. This is not always the case. Both class variables and functions can be designated as either public or private. A public variable is one that can be accessed by functions outside the class and a public function is one that can be called by functions outside the class. Except under special circumstances, however, a private member variable can only be accessed by a function that is a member of the same class and private member function can only be called by another function that is a member of the class.

Note: If a program statement outside a class attempts to access a private member, a compiler error will result. Later you will learn how outside functions may be given special permission to access private class members.

It does not matter whether we list the private or public members first. We could just as easily have first listed the two public members of the `Circle` class and then listed the private member, as shown here:

```
class Circle
{   public:
        void setRadius(float r)
        {   radius = r; }

        float findArea()
        {   return 3.14 * pow(radius, 2);  }

    private:
        float radius;
};
```

Also, even though most programmers consider it more orderly and preferable to separate private and public members as shown in the two examples, it is not actually required that all members of the same access specification be declared together. Here is yet another legal declaration of the `Circle` class.

```
class Circle
{   public:
        void setRadius(float r)
        {   radius = r; }

    private:
        float radius;

    public:
        float findArea()
        {   return 3.14 * pow(radius, 2);  }
};
```

In this text we follow the standard of grouping the private members together first, followed by the public members grouped together.

If we had omitted the words `public` and `private` altogether, everything would have defaulted to being private. This would not have been very useful because, except in special circumstances, no functions outside the class could ever use the class.

Structures can also declare members to be either `private` or `public`, but we normally do not use such access specifiers with structures. This is because, in contrast to classes, the default for structures is for everything to be public, and that is usually what we want when using a structure.

7.11   Introduction to Objects

> **CONCEPT**   Objects are instances of a class. They are created with a definition statement after the class has been declared.

You will recall that a structure declaration only describes what a structure looks like but does not actually create any structure variables. After the structure has been declared, we can write definition statements to define variables of that structure type. Likewise, a class declaration only describes the class, but does not actually create any objects in memory. After the class has been declared, we can write definition statements that define objects. Defining a class object is called the *instantiation* of a class. The following two statements define `Circle` objects.

```
Circle sphere1;
Circle sphere2;
```

Of course these two instances of the `Circle` class could have been defined in the same definition statement, as shown here:

```
Circle sphere1, sphere2;
```

The objects `sphere1` and `sphere2` are two distinct instances of the `Circle` class, with different memory assigned to hold the values of their member variables.

Accessing an Object's Members

The members of a class object are accessed just like the members of a structure: with the dot operator. For example, the following statements call the `setRadius` function of `sphere1` and `sphere2`.

```
sphere1.setRadius(1);     // This sets sphere1's radius to 1
sphere2.setRadius(2.5);   // This sets sphere2's radius to 2.5
```

Now that the radii have been set, we can call the `findArea` member function to return the area of the `Circle` objects:

```
cout << "The area of sphere1 is " << sphere1.findArea() << endl;
cout << "The area of sphere2 is " << sphere2.findArea() << endl;
```

 Note: The class member functions do not need the dot operator to reference member variables of the same class. They are able to access `radius` as if it were a regular variable, without any extra notation.

Program 7-8 is a complete program that demonstrates the `Circle` class.

Program 7-8

```cpp
// This program demonstrates a simple class.

#include <iostream>
#include <cmath>
using namespace std;

// Circle class declaration
class Circle
{   private:
        float radius;

    public:
        void setRadius(float r)
        {   radius = r;  }

        float findArea()
        {   return 3.14 * pow(radius, 2);  }
};

int main()
{
    Circle sphere1,          // Define 2 Circle objects
           sphere2;

    sphere1.setRadius(1);    // This sets sphere1's radius to 1
    sphere2.setRadius(2.5);  // This sets sphere2's radius to 2.5

    cout << "The area of sphere1 is " << sphere1.findArea() << endl;
    cout << "The area of sphere2 is " << sphere2.findArea() << endl;

    return 0;
}
```

Program Output

```
The area of sphere1 is 3.14
The area of sphere2 is 19.625
```

7.12 Defining Member Functions

CONCEPT Class member functions can be defined either inside or outside of the class declaration.

Class member functions are defined similarly to regular functions. Except for a few special cases we will look at later, they have a function header that includes a return type (which may be void), a function name, and a parameter list (which may possibly be empty). The statements that carry out the actions of the function are contained within a pair of braces that follow the function header.

So far, all the class functions we have written have been defined within the class declaration itself. When a class function is defined in this location, it is called an *inline function*. Inline functions provide a convenient way to contain function information within a class declaration, but they can only be used when a function body is very short, usually a single line. When a function body is longer, a prototype for the function appears in the class declaration, instead of the function definition itself. The function definition is placed outside the class declaration, either following it or in a separate file.

Even though the two functions in our `Circle` class are short enough to be written as inline functions, we will rewrite them with regular functions, defined outside the class declaration, to illustrate how this is done. Inside the class declaration the functions would be replaced by the following prototypes:

```
void   setRadius(float);
float findArea();
```

Following the class declaration we would place a *function implementation* section containing the following function definitions:

```
void Circle::setRadius(float r)
{   radius = r;
}

float Circle::findArea()
{   return 3.14 * pow(radius, 2);
}
```

Notice that these look like ordinary functions except that they contain the class name and a double colon (::) before the function name (but after the function type). The :: symbol is called the *scope resolution operator* and is needed to indicate that these are class member functions and to tell the compiler which class they belong to.

 WARNING! Remember, the class name and scope resolution operator extend the name of the function. When the function is defined outside the class declaration, they must be present and must be located after the return type in the function header. The following would both be incorrect.

```
float findArea()        // Wrong! The class name and scope
                        // resolution operator have been omitted.

Circle::float findArea() // Wrong! The class name and scope
                        // resolution operator are misplaced.
```

Program 7-9 revises Program 7-8 to define the class member functions outside of the class declaration.

Program 7-9

```cpp
// This program demonstrates a simple class with member functions
// defined outside the class declaration.

#include <iostream>
#include <cmath>
using namespace std;

// Circle class declaration
class Circle
{   private:
        float radius;

    public:
        void setRadius(float);
        float findArea();
};

// Member function implementation section

//******************************************************************
// setRadius -- Circle class function definition                   *
// This function copies the argument r to                          *
// private member variable radius.                                 *
//******************************************************************

void Circle::setRadius(float r)
{   radius = r;
}


//******************************************************************
// findArea -- Circle class function definition                    *
// This function calculates and returns the Circle object's area.  *
// It does not need any parameters since it already has access     *
// to the member variable radius.                                  *
//******************************************************************

float Circle::findArea()
{   return 3.14 * pow(radius, 2);
}


//******************************************************************
//                            main                                 *
//******************************************************************

int main()
{
    Circle sphere1,          // Define 2 Circle objects
           sphere2;
```

(program continues)

Program 7-9   *(continued)*

```
    sphere1.setRadius(1);     // This sets sphere1's radius to 1
    sphere2.setRadius(2.5);   // This sets sphere2's radius to 2.5

    cout << "The area of sphere1 is " << sphere1.findArea() << endl;
    cout << "The area of sphere2 is " << sphere2.findArea() << endl;

    return 0;
}
```

Program Output is the same as for Program 7-8.

Another Class Demonstration Program

Program 7-10 provides another example using classes and objects. It declares and implements a Rectangle class that has three private member variables and five public member functions. The function definitions are written outside the class declaration.

Program 7-10

```
// This program implements a Rectangle class.

#include <iostream>
using namespace std;

// Rectangle class declaration
class Rectangle
{
    private:
        float length;
        float width;
        float area;
    public:
        void  setData(float, float);
        void  calcArea();
        float getLength();
        float getWidth();
        float getArea();
};

// Member function implementation section

//*****************************************************************
// setData -- Rectangle class function definition                *
// This function copies the argument l to private member length  *
// and w to private member width.                                *
//*****************************************************************
```

(program continues)

Program 7-10 *(continued)*

```cpp
void Rectangle::setData(float 1, float w)
{
    length = 1;
    width = w;
}

//******************************************************************
// calcArea -- Rectangle class function definition                 *
// This function multiplies the private members length and width.  *
// The result is stored in the private member area.                *
//******************************************************************

void Rectangle::calcArea()
{
    area = length * width;
}

//******************************************************************
// getLength -- Rectangle class function definition                *
// This function returns the value in the private member length.   *
//******************************************************************

float Rectangle::getLength()
{
    return length;
}

//******************************************************************
// getWidth -- Rectangle class function definition                 *
// This function returns the value in the private member width.    *
//******************************************************************

float Rectangle::getWidth()
{
    return width;
}

//******************************************************************
// getArea -- Rectangle class function definition                  *
// This function returns the value in the private member area.     *
//******************************************************************

float Rectangle::getArea()
{
    return area;
}
```

(program continues)

Program 7-10 *(continued)*

```
//************************************************************
//                         main                            *
//************************************************************

int main()
{
    Rectangle box;          // This declares a Rectangle object.
    float boxLength, boxWidth;

    // Get box length and width.
    cout << "This program will calculate the area of a rectangle.\n";
    cout << "What is the length? ";
    cin  >> boxLength;
    cout << "What is the width? ";
    cin  >> boxWidth;

    // Call member functions to set the box's dimensions and to
    // calculate its area.
    box.setData(boxLength, boxWidth);
    box.calcArea();

    // Call member functions to get box information to display.
    cout << "\nHere is the rectangle's data:\n";
    cout << "Length: " << box.getLength() << endl;
    cout << "Width : " << box.getWidth()  << endl;
    cout << "Area  : " << box.getArea()   << endl;

    return 0;
}
```

Program Output with Example Input Shown in Bold
```
This program will calculate the area of a rectangle.
What is the length? 10[Enter]
What is the width? 5[Enter]

Here is the rectangle's data:
Length: 10
Width : 5
Area  : 50
```

More on Inline Functions

When designing a class, you will need to decide which member functions to write as inline functions within the class declaration and which ones to define outside the class. Inline functions are implemented completely differently by the compiler than regular functions are. An understanding of this difference may help you decide which to use when.

A lot goes on behind the scenes each time a regular function is called. A number of special items, such as the address to return to when the function has finished executing and the values of the function arguments, must be stored in a section of memory called the *stack*. In addition, local variables are created and a location is reserved to hold the function's return value. All this overhead, which sets the stage for a function call, takes precious CPU time. Although the time needed is miniscule, it can add up if a function is called many times, as in a loop.

Inline functions, on the other hand, are not called in the conventional sense at all. Instead, the compiler replaces all calls to an inline function with the actual code of the function itself. This increases the size of the executable program and is the reason that only functions with very few lines of code should be written as inline functions. However, when member functions are small enough to be written this way, it can improve performance to use them. This is due to the reduced overhead of not having to make actual function calls.[1]

Checkpoint [7.10–7.12]

7.11 True or false: You must declare all private members before the public members.

7.12 Which of the following shows the correct use of the scope resolution operator in a member function definition?

A) `InvItem::void setOnHand(int units)`

B) `void InvItem::setOnHand(int units)`

7.13 An object's private member variables are accessed from outside the object by

A) Public member functions

B) Any function

C) The dot operator

D) The scope resolution operator

7.14 Assuming that `soap` is an instance of the `InvItem` class, which of the following is a valid call to the `setOnHand` member function?

A) `setOnHand(20);`

B) `soap::setOnHand(20);`

C) `soap.setOnHand(20);`

D) `soap:setOnHand(20);`

---

[1]On systems that use paging, however, inline functions can decrease performance because of the additional page faults caused by the increased program size.

7.15 Complete the following code skeleton to define a class called `Date`. The class should contain variables and functions to store and retrieve a date in the form 3/31/03.

```
class Date
{
    private:

    public:

}
```

7.13 Why Have Private Members?

CONCEPT In object-oriented programming, an object should protect its important data by making it private and providing a public interface to access that data.

You might be questioning the rationale behind making the member variables in the `Rectangle` class private. You might also be questioning why member functions were declared for such simple tasks as setting variables and getting their contents. After all, if the member variables were declared as `public`, the member functions wouldn't be needed.

As mentioned early in this chapter, objects usually have some variables and functions that are meant only to be used internally, not outside the object. This protects critical data from being accidentally modified or used in a way that might adversely affect the behavior of the object. When a member variable is declared as `private`, the only way for an application to store values in the variable is through a public member function. Likewise, the only way for an application to retrieve the contents of a private member variable is through a public member function. In essence, the public members become an interface to the object. They are the only members that may be accessed by any application that uses the object.

In the `Rectangle` class, the member variables `length`, `width`, and `area` might be considered critical. Therefore, they are declared as `private` and an interface is constructed with the `public` member functions. The functions allow values to be stored in `length`, `width`, and `area`, and also allow their contents to be retrieved.

7.14 Focus on Software Engineering: *Some Design Considerations*

CONCEPT Usually class declarations are stored in their own header files. Member function definitions are stored in their own `.cpp` files.

In Program 7-9 and 7-10, the class declaration, member function definitions, and application program are all stored in one file. A more conventional way of designing C++ programs is to store class declarations and member function definitions in their own separate files. Typically, program components are stored in the following fashion:

- ◆ Class declarations are stored in their own header files. A header file that contains a class declaration is called a *class specification file*. The name of the class specification file is usually the same as the class, with a .h extension. For example, the Rectangle class would be declared in the file rectangle.h. (If the system doesn't support file names this long, abbreviations will have to be substituted. For example, on DOS systems with an eight-character limit on file names, rectang.h could be used.)

- ◆ The member function definitions for a class are stored in a separate .cpp file, which is called the *class implementaion file*. The file usually has the same name as the class, with the .cpp extension. For example the Rectangle class's member functions would be defined in the file rectangle.cpp. Once again, on systems that limit the length of the file name, an abbreviation must be used.

- ◆ Any program that uses the class should #include its header file. The class's .cpp file (which contains its member function definitions) should be compiled and linked with the main program. This process can be automated with a project or make utility.

Program 7-11 is a revision of Program 7-10. It appears as it would with the class declaration and member function definitions stored in their own files.

 Note: The #ifndef directive shown in Program 7-11 is called an *include guard* and prevents a header file from accidentally being included more than once. In the rectangle.h file, the #ifndef directive checks for the existence of a constant, RECTANGLE_H. If the constant has not been defined, it is immediately defined and the file is included. If the constant has been defined, everything between the #ifndef and #endif directives is skipped.

Program 7-11

Contents of rectang.h
```
#ifndef RECTANGLE_H
#define RECTANGLE_H

// Rectangle class declaration
class Rectangle
{
    private:
        float length;
        float width;
        float area;
```

(program continues)

Program 7-11   *(continued)*

```cpp
   public:
      void  setData(float, float);
      void  calcArea();
      float getLength();
      float getWidth();
      float getArea();
};
#endif
```

Contents of `rectang.cpp`
```cpp
#include "rectang.h"

//******************************************************************
// setData -- Rectangle class function definition                  *
// This function copies the argument 1 to private member length    *
// and w to private member width.                                  *
//******************************************************************

void Rectangle::setData(float 1, float w)
{
    length = 1;
    width = w;
}


//******************************************************************
// calcArea -- Rectangle class function definition                 *
// This function multiplies the private members length and width.  *
// The result is stored in the private member area.                *
//******************************************************************

void Rectangle::calcArea()
{
    area = length * width;
}


//******************************************************************
// getLength -- Rectangle class function definition                *
// This function returns the value in the private member length.   *
//******************************************************************

float Rectangle::getLength()
{
    return length;
}
```

(program continues)

Program 7-11   *(continued)*

```
//*******************************************************************
// getWidth -- Rectangle class function definition               *
// This function returns the value in the private member width.   *
//*******************************************************************

float Rectangle::getWidth()
{
    return width;
}


//*******************************************************************
// getArea -- Rectangle class function definition                *
// This function returns the value in the private member area.    *
//*******************************************************************

float Rectangle::getArea()
{
    return area;
}
```

Contents of the main program, `pr7-11.cpp`

```
// This program implements the Rectangle class, with separate
// files for the class declaration, the implementation of the
// class functions, and the client code that uses the class.

#include <iostream>
#include "rectang.h"        // Contains Rectangle class declaration
using namespace std;
// Remember to link this program with rectang.cpp!

int main()
{
    Rectangle box;          // This declares a Rectangle object.
    float boxLength, boxWidth;

    //Get box length and width.
    cout << "This program will calculate the area of a rectangle.\n";
    cout << "What is the length? ";
    cin  >> boxLength;
    cout << "What is the width? ";
    cin  >> boxWidth;

    // Call member functions to set the box's dimensions and to
    // calculate its area.
    box.setData(boxLength, boxWidth);
    box.calcArea();
```

(program continues)

Program 7-11 *(continued)*

```
// Call member functions to get box information to display.
cout << "\nHere is the rectangle's data:\n";
cout << "Length: " << box.getLength() << endl;
cout << "Width : " << box.getWidth()  << endl;
cout << "Area  : " << box.getArea()   << endl;

return 0;
}
```

Program Output is the same as for Program 7-10.

Table 7-5 summarizes how the different files of Program 7-11 are organized and compiled on a typical DOS or Windows computer.

Table 7-5

rectang.h	Contains the class definition of Rectangle. Included by rectang.cpp and pr7-11.cpp.
rectang.cpp	Contains Rectangle's member function definitions. Compiled to an object file such as rectang.obj.
pr7-11.cpp	Contains function main. Compiled to an object file, such as pr7-11.obj, which is linked with rectang.cpp's object file to form an executable file.
	rectang.cpp is compiled to rectang.obj. pr7-11.cpp is compiled to pr7-11.obj. pr7-11.obj and rectang.obj are linked to make pr7-11.exe.

Performing Input/Output in a Class Object

Another important class design issue is the use of cin and cout in member functions. Notice that none of the Rectangle class's member functions use cin or cout. This is so anyone who writes a program that uses the Rectangle class will not be "locked into" the way the class performs input or output. Unless a class is specifically designed to perform I/O, operations like user input and output are best left to the person designing the application. Classes should provide member functions for retrieving any important data without displaying them on the screen. Likewise, they should provide member functions that store data into private member variables without using cin.

 Note: There are instances where it is appropriate for a class to perform I/O. For example, a class might be designed to display a menu on the screen and get the user's selection. Another example is a class designed to handle a program's file I/O. Classes that hold and manipulate data, however, should not be tied to any particular I/O routines. This will allow them to be more versatile.

7.15   Using Private Member Functions

CONCEPT   A private member function may only be called from a function that is a member of the same class.

Sometimes a class will contain one or more member functions that are necessary for internal processing, but that are not useful to the program outside the class. In some cases a class may contain member functions that initialize member variables or destroy their contents. Those functions should not be accessible by an external part of program because they may be called at the wrong time. In these cases, the member functions should be declared as private. When a member function is declared as private, it may only be called internally.

The Rectangle class can be improved by making the calcArea function private and calling it directly from the setData function. Although calcArea does not do anything destructive, it makes sense that it should execute automatically when the length and width variables are changed. The modified class declaration is shown here. (It is stored on the student diskette in the file rectang2.h.)

```cpp
// Rectangle class declaration
class Rectangle
{
    private:
        float length;
        float width;
        float area;
        void calcArea();

    public:
        void setData(float, float);
        float getLength();
        float getWidth();
        float getArea();
};
```

The modified member function setData is as follows. (It is stored in rectang2.cpp.)

```cpp
//*****************************************************************
// setData -- Rectangle class function definition               *
// This function copies the argument 1 to private member length  *
// and w to private member width and then calls private member   *
// function calcArea to calculate the new area.                  *
//*****************************************************************

void Rectangle::setData(float l, float w)
{
    length = l;
    width = w;
    calcArea();
}
```

Note: None of the other `Rectangle` member functions were modified, so they are not shown again.

Now that `calcArea` is called from `setData`, after the contents of `length` and `width` are modified, the program outside the class doesn't have to explicitly call it. This is shown in Program 7-12.

Program 7-12

```
// This program implements the Rectangle class, with separate
// files for the class declaration, the implementation of the
// class functions, and the client code that uses the class.
#include <iostream>
#include "rectang2.h"  // contains Rectangle class declaration
using namespace std;
// Remember to link this program with rectang2.cpp!

int main()
{
    Rectangle box;          // This declares a Rectangle object.
    float boxLength, boxWidth;

    //Get box length and width.
    cout << "This program will calculate the area of a rectangle.\n";
    cout << "What is the length? ";
    cin  >> boxLength;
    cout << "What is the width? ";
    cin  >> boxWidth;

    // Call member functions to set the box's dimensions.
    box.setData(boxLength, boxWidth);

    // Call member functions to get box information to display.
    cout << "\nHere is the rectangle's data:\n";
    cout << "Length: " << box.getLength() << endl;
    cout << "Width : " << box.getWidth()  << endl;
    cout << "Area  : " << box.getArea()   << endl;

    return 0;
}
```

Program Output is the same as for Program 7-10.

 # Checkpoint   [7.13–7.15]

7.16   Assume the following class components exist in a program:

> `BasePay` class declaration
> `BasePay` member function definitions
> `Overtime` class declaration
> `Overtime` member function definitions

What files would you store each of the components above in?

7.17 What header file should be included in the file containing the `BasePay` member function definitions?

7.18 What is the advantage of using a private member function?

7.19 What is the disadvantage of using a private member function?

7.16 Constructors

> **CONCEPT** A constructor is a member function that is automatically called when a class object is created.

A *constructor* is a special public member function that is automatically called when an object is created in memory, or instantiated. The compiler knows which routines are constructors because they must have the same name as the class. Constructors are used as initialization routines to initialize member variables or perform other setup operations.

To illustrate how constructors work, look at the `Demo` class declaration that follows.

```
class Demo
{
public:
    Demo(){cout << "Welcome to the constructor!\n";} // Constructor
};
```

The class `Demo` only has one member, a function also named `Demo`. This function is the constructor. When a class object is defined, the function `Demo` is automatically called. This is illustrated in Program 7-13.

Program 7-13

```
// This program demonstrates a constructor.
#include <iostream>
using namespace std;

// Demo class declaration
class Demo
{
public:
    Demo() {cout << "Welcome to the constructor!\n";} // Constructor
};

int main()
{
    Demo demoObj; // Define a Demo object

    cout << "This program demonstrates an object "
         << "with a constructor.\n";
    return 0;
}
```

Program 7-13

Program Output
```
Welcome to the constructor!
This program demonstrates an object with a constructor.
```

Notice the constructor's function header looks different than that of a regular member function. There is no return type—not even `void`. This is because constructors are not executed by explicit function calls and cannot return a value.

In Program 7-13, `demoObj`'s constructor executes automatically when the object is defined. Since the object is defined before the `cout` statements in function `main`, the constructor displays its message first.

In Program 7-13, the constructor was defined with an inline function. Program 7-14 illustrates what the constructor's function header looks like when it is defined outside of the class declaration. Since the function name must be the same as the name of the class, the function header will have the form

```
<class name>::<class name>(parameter list)
```

although in Program 7-14 the constructor's parameter list is empty. This program also further illustrates when a constructor executes because, in this case, `demoObj` is defined in the middle of a group of `cout` statements.

Program 7-14

```cpp
// This program demonstrates a constructor.

#include <iostream>
using namespace std;

class Demo
{
public:
    Demo(); // Constructor
};

Demo::Demo()
{
    cout << "Welcome to the constructor!\n";
}

int main()
{
    cout << "This is displayed before the object is created.\n";
    Demo demoObj;   // Define the Demo object.
    cout << "This is displayed after the object is created.\n";
    return 0;
}
```

Program 7-14

Program Output
```
This is displayed before the object is created.
Welcome to the constructor!
This is displayed after the object is created.
```

 Note: When a constructor does not have to accept any arguments, it is called an object's *default constructor*. Like regular functions, constructors may accept arguments, have default arguments, be declared inline, and be overloaded. (You will see examples of these later in this chapter.)

7.17   Constructors That Accept Arguments

CONCEPT	Information can be passed as arguments to an object's constructor.

Often information must be passed to a constructor in order for the object to be properly initialized. For example, consider the Sale class declared here. It is a simple class designed to calculate the total of a retail sale.

```
class Sale
{
private:
   float taxRate;
   float total;
public:
   Sale(float rate) { taxRate = rate; }
   void calcSale(float cost)
      { total = cost + (cost * taxRate); }
   float getTotal(void) { return total; }
};
```

The constructor's purpose is to establish the sales tax rate. The member variable taxRate is used by the calcSale function to compute the total of the sale. The constructor accepts an argument, which is stored in the taxRate member variable. Since the constructor is automatically called when the object is created, the argument is passed to it as part of the object definition. Here is an example:

```
Sale cashier(0.06);
```

This statement declares cashier as an instance of the Sale class. The constructor is called with the value 0.06 passed as its argument. As with all function calls, the argument is copied into the constructor's parameter variable. The contents of the parameter is then assigned by the constructor to the member variable cashier.taxRate. Program 7-15 shows the class in use.

Program 7-15

Contents of sale.h

```
#ifndef SALE_H
#define SALE_H

// Sale class declaration
class Sale
{
private:
    float taxRate;
    float total;
public:
    Sale(float rate) { taxRate = rate; }
    void calcSale(float cost)
        { total = cost + (cost * taxRate) ;}
    float getTotal() { return total; }
};
#endif
```

Contents of main program, pr7-15.cpp

```
#include <iostream>
#include <iomanip>
#include "sale.h"
using namespace std;

int main()
{
    Sale cashier(0.06);   // Create Sale object and pass constructor 6% tax rate
    float amount;

    cout << fixed << showpoint << setprecision(2);
    cout << "Enter the amount of the sale: ";
    cin  >> amount;
    cashier.calcSale(amount);
    cout << "The total of the sale is $";
    cout << cashier.getTotal() << endl;
    return 0;
}
```

Program Output with Example Output Shown in Bold

```
Enter the amount of the sale: 125.00[Enter]
The total of the sale is $132.50
```

Constructors may also have default arguments. Recall from Chapter 6 that default arguments are passed to parameters automatically if no argument is provided in the function call. The default value is listed in the parameter list of the function prototype or definition. Here is the Sale class, with its constructor modified to accept a default argument:

```
class Sale
{
private:
   float taxRate;
   float total;
public:
   Sale(float rate = 0.05) { taxRate = rate; }
   void calcSale(float cost)
      { total = cost + (cost * taxRate) ;}
   float getTotal() { return total; }
};
```

If an object of the Sale class is defined with no argument passed to the constructor, the constructor will be called with the default argument 0.05. This is demonstrated in Program 7-16.

 Note: It was mentioned earlier that when a constructor doesn't have to accept any arguments, it's called a *default constructor*. If a constructor has default arguments for all its parameters, it can be called with no explicit arguments. It then becomes the default constructor.

Program 7-16

Contents of sale2.h
```
#ifndef SALE2_H
#define SALE2_H

// Sale class declaration
class Sale
{
private:
   float taxRate;
   float total;
public:
   Sale(float rate = 0.05) { taxRate = rate; }    //Default constructor
   void calcSale(float cost)
      { total = cost + (cost * taxRate) ;}
   float getTotal() { return total; }
};

#endif
```

Contents of main program, pr7-16.cpp
```
#include <iostream>
#include <iomanip>
#include "sale2.h"
using namespace std;
```

(program continues)

Program 7-16   *(continued)*

```
int main()
{
    Sale cashier1;          // Create Sale object using default tax rate
    Sale cashier2(0.06);    // Create Sale object using 6% tax rate
    float amount;
    cout << fixed << showpoint << setprecision(2);
    cout << "Enter the amount of the sale: ";
    cin >> amount;
    cashier1.calcSale(amount);
    cashier2.calcSale(amount);
    cout << "With a 0.05 sales tax rate, the total\n";
    cout << "of the sale is $";
    cout << cashier1.getTotal() << endl;
    cout << "With a 0.06 sales tax rate, the total\n";
    cout << "of the sale is $";
    cout << cashier2.getTotal() << endl;
    return 0;
}
```

Program Output with Example Input Shown in Bold
```
Enter the amount of the sale: 125.00[Enter]
With a 0.05 sales tax rate, the total
of the sale is $131.25
With a 0.06 sales tax rate, the total
of the sale is $132.50
```

 WARNING! When an object is created with no arguments passed to a constructor, the parentheses must be omitted. Notice in Program 7-16 that the `cashier1` object was created with the statement

```
Sale cashier1;
```

Creating it with the statement

```
Sale cashier1();    // Error!
```

would have caused an error.

 # Checkpoint [7.16–7.17]

7.20 Briefly describe the purpose of a constructor.

7.21 Constructor functions have the same name as the

A) Class

B) Class instance

C) Program

D) None of the above

7.22 A constructor that requires no arguments is called

A) A default constructor

B) An overloaded constructor

C) A null constructor

D) None of the above

7.23 True or false: Constructors are never declared with a return data type.

7.24 Assume the following is a constructor:

```
ClassAct::ClassAct(int x)
{
    item = x;
}
```

Give a declaration for a `ClassAct` object called `sally` that passes the value 25 to the constructor.

7.18 Constructor Overloading

CONCEPT	More than one constructor may be defined for a class.

Recall from Chapter 6 that when two or more functions share the same name, the function name is said to be overloaded. Multiple functions with the same name may exist in a C++ program, as long as their parameter lists are different.

A class's member functions may be overloaded, including the constructor. One constructor might take an integer argument, for example, while another constructor takes a `float`. There could even be a third constructor taking two integers. As long as each constructor takes a different list of parameters, the compiler can tell them apart.

A modified version of the `Sale` class that was presented earlier appears here. This version has three constructors.

Contents of sale3.h
```
#ifndef SALE3_H
#define SALE3_H

// Sale class declaration
class Sale
{
private:
    float taxRate;
    float total;
    void calcSale(float cost)
    { total = cost + (cost * taxRate); }
```

```
       public:
           // Constructor with 2 parameters handles sales with tax.
           Sale(float rate, float cost)
           {  taxRate = rate; calcSale(cost); }

           // Constructor with 1 parameter handles tax-exempt sales.
           Sale(float cost)
           {  taxRate = 0.0; total = cost; }

           // Default constructor
           Sale()
           {  taxRate = 0.0; total = 0.0; }

           float getTotal() { return total; }
       };

    #endif
```

The first constructor handles regular taxed Sale objects. It requires two arguments, the tax rate and the amount of the sale. The second constructor handles tax-exempt Sale objects. Since the tax rate must be zero in this case, only one argument is required, the amount of the sale. The final constructor is the default constructor. Program 7-17 demonstrates how objects are initialized with different Sale class constructors.

Program 7-17

```
#include <iostream>
#include <iomanip>
using namespace std;
#include "sale3.h"

int main()
{
    // Define Sale object with 6% sales tax calculated
    // on a $24.95 sale.
    Sale cashier1(0.06, 24.95);

    // Define a Sale object with a tax-exempt $24.95 sale.
    Sale cashier2(24.95);

    cout << fixed << showpoint << setprecision(2);
    cout << "With a 0.06 sales tax rate, the total\n";
    cout << "of the $24.95 sale is $";
    cout << cashier1.getTotal() << endl;
    cout << "On a tax-exempt purchase, the total\n";
    cout << "of the $24.95 sale is, of course, $";
    cout << cashier2.getTotal() << endl;
    return 0;
}
```

Program 7-17

Program Output
```
With a 0.06 sales tax rate, the total
of the $24.95 sale is $26.45
On a tax-exempt purchase, the total
of the $24.95 sale is, of course, $24.95
```

More on Default Constructors

Notice, in Program 7-17, that we created a default constructor even though it was never called. This is because it is considered good programming practice always to have a default constructor. If we did not have one and inadvertently created an object without passing any arguments to the constructor, its member variables would not be initialized. If the programmer writes no constructors for a class, the compiler automatically creates a default constructor for the class. However, if the programmer writes any constructors at all, even ones which all have parameters, the compiler does not create a default constructor. So it is the responsibility of the programmer to do this.

 Note: A class may have many constructors, but can only have one default constructor.

If multiple functions are to have the same name, the compiler must be able to determine from their parameter lists which one is being called at any given time. It uses the number and type of arguments passed to the function to determine which of the overloaded functions to invoke. Since there can only be one function with the class name that is able to accept no arguments, there can be only one default constructor. Normally, as in Program 7-17, default constructors have no parameters. However, we know from Program 7-16 that it is possible to have a default constructor with parameters if all of its parameters have default values, so that it could be called with no arguments. It would be an error to create one constructor that accepts no arguments and another that has arguments but allows default values for all of them. In this case, if an object were created with no arguments, the compiler would not know which of the two "default" constructors to invoke. For example, the following class declaration illegally declares two default constructors.

```
class Sale
{
private:
   float taxRate;
   float total;
public:
   Sale() { taxRate = 0.05; } // Default constructor with no arguments
   Sale(float r = 0.05)       // Default constructor with a default argument
      { taxRate = r; }
   void calcSale(float cost)
      { total = cost + (cost * taxRate); }
   float getTotal() { return total; }
};
```

As you can see, the first constructor is defined with no parameter list. The second constructor's parameter has a default argument. If an object is defined with no argument list, the compiler will not be able to resolve which constructor to execute.

7.19 Destructors

CONCEPT A destructor is a member function that is automatically called when an object is destroyed.

Destructors are member functions with the same name as the class, preceded by a tilde character (~). For example, the destructor for the `Rectangle` class would be named `~Rectangle`.

Destructors are automatically called when an object is destroyed. In the same way that constructors set things up when an object is created, destructors perform shutdown procedures when the object goes out of existence.

Program 7-18 shows a simple class with a constructor and a destructor. It illustrates when, during the program's execution, each is called.

Program 7-18

```cpp
// This program demonstrates a destructor.

#include <iostream>
using namespace std;

class Demo
{
public:
    Demo();       // Constructor
    ~Demo();      // Destructor
};

Demo::Demo()
{
    cout << "Welcome to the constructor!\n";
}

Demo::~Demo()
{
    cout << "The destructor is now running.\n";
}

int main()
{
    Demo demoObj; // Declare a Demo object;
    cout << "This program demonstrates an object\n";
    cout << "with a constructor and destructor.\n";
    return 0;
}
```

Program 7-18

Program Output

```
Welcome to the constructor!
This program demonstrates an object
with a constructor and destructor.
The destructor is now running.
```

In addition to the fact that destructors are automatically called when an object is destroyed, the following points should be mentioned:

◆ Like constructors, destructors have no return type.

◆ Destructors cannot accept arguments, so they never have a parameter list.

◆ As with default constructors, since destructors can accept no arguments, there can only be one destructor.

Checkpoint [7.18–7.19]

7.25 True or false: Like any C++ function, a constructor may be overloaded, providing each constructor has a unique parameter list.

7.26 True or false: A class may have a constructor with no parameter list, and an overloaded constructor whose parameters all take default arguments.

7.27 Briefly describe the purpose of a destructor.

7.28 A destructor function name always starts with

    A) A number

    B) The tilde character (~)

    C) A data type name

    D) The name of the class

7.29 True or false: Just as a class can have multiple constructors, it can also have multiple destructors.

7.30 What will the following program display on the screen?

```cpp
#include <iostream>
using namespace std;

class Tank
{
private:
    int gallons;
public:
    Tank()
      { gallons = 50; }
    Tank(int gal)
      { gallons = gal; }
    int getGallons()
```

```
          { return gallons; }
};
int main()
{
    Tank storage1, storage2, storage3(20);

    cout << storage1.getGallons() << endl;
    cout << storage2.getGallons() << endl;
    cout << storage3.getGallons() << endl;
    return 0;
}
```

7.31 What will the following program display on the screen?

```
#include <iostream>
using namespace std;

class Package
{
private:
    int value;
public:
    Package()
        { value = 7; cout << value << endl; }
    Package(int v)
        { value = v; cout << value << endl; }
    ~Package()
        { cout << value << endl; }
};
int main()
{
    Package obj1(4);
    Package obj2;
    Package obj3(2);
    return 0;
}
```

7.20 Input Validation Objects

CONCEPT This section shows how classes may be designed to validate user input.

As mentioned earlier in this chapter, one application of OOP is to design general-purpose objects that may be used by a variety of applications. An example of such an object is one that performs input validation. For example, assume a program displays a menu that allows the user to select items A, B, C, or D. The program should validate any character entered by the user and only accept one of these four letters.

In this section, we will design a general-purpose class to handle this type of input validation. Before we discuss the class, let's look at a C++ library function we will need.

The `toupper` Function

Our input validation class will use the `toupper` library function. To use the `toupper` function, you must place the following #include directive in your program:

```
#include <cctype>
```

The `toupper` function accepts a single character as its argument and returns the uppercase equivalent of that character. For example, the following statement will display the character M on the screen:

```
cout << toupper('m');
```

And the following statement assigns the character A to the variable `letter`:

```
letter = toupper('a');
```

If the character passed to `toupper` is already uppercase or is not a letter, that character is returned unchanged.

Among its other uses, the `toupper` function can simplify the task of comparing characters without regard to case. For example, look at the following code segment. It asks the user to enter a letter in the range K through Q, then attempts to validate the character that was entered.

```
cout << "Enter a letter in the range K-Q: ";
cin >> letter;
while (letter < 'K' || letter > 'Q')
{   cout << "That is not a valid letter.\n";
    cout << "Enter a letter from K to Q: ";
    cin >> letter;
}
```

This code will successfully validate the user's input as long as the character entered is uppercase. However, if the user enters a lowercase character in the range k through q, the code will fail. Those characters are higher on the ASCII chart than their uppercase equivalents, so the contents of `letter` will be greater than 'Q' anytime a lowercase letter is entered. We can use the `toupper` function to remedy this problem by comparing the uppercase form of the contents of `letter` to our range of valid characters. The following code shows how.

```
cout << "Enter a letter in the range K-Q: ";
cin >> letter;
while (toupper (letter) < 'K' || toupper(letter) > 'Q')
{   cout << "That is not a valid letter.\n";
    cout << "Enter a letter from K to Q: ";
    cin >> letter;
}
```

Note that the `toupper` function does not actually convert its argument to uppercase but returns the uppercase equivalent of it. After the function `toupper(letter)` has been executed, the content of letter is still the same as it was before the function was called. If we wish to actually convert a variable's contents to uppercase, we must use a statement such as

```
letter = toupper(letter);
```

This statement assigns the return value of toupper(letter) to letter, thus converting the contents of the variable to uppercase. This approach is demonstrated in the following code.

```
cout << "Enter a letter in the range K-Q: ";
cin >> letter;
letter = toupper(letter);
while (letter < 'K' || letter > 'Q')
{   cout << "That is not a valid letter.\n";
    cout << "Enter a letter from K to Q: ";
    cin >> letter;
    letter = toupper(letter);
}
```

The toupper function will be used to implement this type of input validation in the Char-Range class, which is discussed next.

Note: toupper, as well as other character-handling library functions, are discussed further in Chapter 12.

The CharRange **Input Validation Class**

Now we will examine the CharRange class. An object of the CharRange class allows the user to enter a character, then validates that the character is within a specified range of characters. When the user enters a character outside the designated range, the object displays an error message and waits for the user to re-enter the character. The code for the class is shown here.

Contents of chrange.h

```
#ifndef CHRANGE_H
#define CHRANGE_H

class CharRange
{
private:
      char input;      // User input
      char lower;      // Lowest valid character
      char upper;      // Highest valid character
public:
      CharRange(char, char);
      char getChar();
};

#endif
```

Contents of `chrange.cpp`

```cpp
#include <iostream>
#include <cctype>                    // Needed to use toupper
#include "chrange.h"
using namespace std;

//**********************************************
// CharRange constructor                       *
//**********************************************
CharRange::CharRange(char 1, char u)
{
    lower = toupper(1);
    upper = toupper(u);
}


//**********************************************
// CharRange member function getChar           *
// Inputs a character and validates that it    *
// is in the correct range. Then it returns    *
// the valid character.                        *
//**********************************************
char CharRange::getChar()
{
    cin.get(input);              // Get a character
    cin.ignore();                // Ignore the '\n' in the input buffer
    input = toupper(input);      // Uppercase the character

    // Ensure character is in the correct range
    while (input < lower || input > upper)
    {   cout << "That is not a valid character.\n";
        cout << "Enter a value from " << lower;
        cout << " to " << upper << ".\n";
        cin.get(input);
        cin.ignore();
        input = toupper(input);
    }
    return input;
}
```

Let's look at the class's member functions. The constructor establishes the range of valid characters:

```cpp
CharRange::CharRange(char 1, char u)
{
    lower = toupper(1);
    upper = toupper(u);
}
```

The `toupper` function is used to get the uppercase equivalents of the values in the parameters 1 and u. These uppercase values are copied into the private members `lower` and `upper`. The member variables `lower` and `upper` mark the lower and upper ends of the valid range of characters.

Here's an example of how to create an object of the `CharRange` class:

```cpp
CharRange input('A', 'D');
```

This statement creates a `CharRange` object named `input`. The object allows the user to enter a character in the range A through D (valid characters are A, B, C, and D). If the user enters a character outside this range, an error message is displayed and the user is required to re-enter the character.

The actual input validation is performed by the member function `getChar`:

```cpp
char CharRange::getChar()
{
    cin.get(input);            // Get a character
    cin.ignore();              // Ignore the '\n' in the input buffer
    input = toupper(input);    // Uppercase the character

    // Ensure character is in the correct range
    while (input < lower || input > upper)
    {   cout << "That is not a valid character.\n";
        cout << "Enter a value from " << lower;
        cout << " to " << upper << ".\n";
        cin.get(input);
        cin.ignore();
        input = toupper(input);
    }
    return input;
}
```

Note: As mentioned before, you do not always want to use input and output statements in a class's member functions. This, however, is a class that is specifically designed to perform input and output.

Program 7-19 is a simple program that demonstrates the `CharRange` class. (The `CharRange` class will be used again in other programs.)

Program 7-19

```cpp
// This program demonstrates the CharRange class.

#include <iostream>
#include "chrange.h" // Remember to compile and link chrange.cpp
using namespace std;

int main()
{
    // Create an object to check for characters
    // in the range J - N.
    CharRange input('J', 'N');

    cout << "Enter any of the characters J, K, L, M, or N.\n";
    cout << "Entering N will stop this program.\n";
    while (input.getChar() != 'N');
    return 0;
}
```

Program 7-19

Program Output with Example Input Shown in Bold
```
Enter any of the characters J, K, L, M, or N.
Entering N will stop this program.
```
j[Enter]
K[Enter]
q[Enter]
```
That is not a valid character.
Enter a value from J to N.
```
m[Enter]
n[Enter]

7.21   Focus on Problem Solving and Program Design: *An OOP Case Study*

You are a programmer for the Home Software Company. You have been assigned to develop a class that models the basic workings of a bank account. The class should perform the following tasks:

♦ Save the account balance.

♦ Save the number of transactions performed on the account.

♦ Allow deposits to be made to the account.

♦ Allow withrawals to be taken from the account.

♦ Calculate interest for the period.

♦ Report the current account balance at any time.

♦ Report the current number of transactions at any time.

Private Member Variables

Table 7-6 lists the private member variables needed by the object.

Table 7-6

Variable	Description
balance	A float that holds the current account balance
intRate	A float that holds the interest rate for the period
interest	A float that holds the interest earned for the current period
transactions	An integer that holds the current number of transactions

Public Member Functions

Table 7-7 lists the public member functions needed by the object.

Table 7-7

Function	Description
constructor	Takes arguments to be initially stored in the `balance` and `intRate` members. The default value for the balance is zero and the default value for the interest rate is 0.045.
makeDeposit	Takes a `float` argument, which is the amount of the deposit. This argument is added to `balance`.
withdraw	Takes a `float` argument which is the amount of the withdrawal. This value is subtracted from the balance, unless the withdrawal amount is greater than the balance. If this happens, the function reports an error.
calcInterest	Takes no arguments. This function calculates the amount of interest for the current period, stores this value in the `interest` member, and then adds it to the `balance` member.
getBalance	Returns the current balance (stored in the `balance` member).
getInterest	Returns the interest earned for the current period (stored in the `interest` member).
getTransactions	Returns the number of transactions for the current period (stored in the `transactions` member).

The Class Declaration

The following listing shows the class declaration.

Contents of account.h

```
class Account
{
private:
   float balance;
   float intRate;
   float interest;
   int transactions;
public:
   Account(float iRate = 0.045, float bal = 0)
      { balance = bal; intRate = iRate;
        interest = 0; transactions = 0; }
   void makeDeposit(float amount)
      { balance += amount; transactions++; }
   int withdraw(float amount);      // Defined in account.cpp
```

```
        void calcInterest()
          { interest = balance * intRate; balance += interest; }
        float getBalance()
          { return balance; }
        float getInterest()
          { return interest; }
        int getTransactions()
          { return transactions; }
    };
```

The withdraw **Member Function**

The only member function not declared inline in the class declaration is withdraw. The purpose of the function is to subtract the amount of a withdrawal from the balance member. If the amount to be withdrawn is greater than the current balance, however, no withdrawal is made. The function returns 1 if the withdrawal is made or 0 if there is not enough in the account.

Contents of account.cpp

```
    #include "account.h"

    int Account::withdraw(float amount)
    {
        if (balance < amount)
          return 0; // Not enough in the account
        else
        {
          balance -= amount;
          transactions++;
          return 1;
        }
    }
```

The Object's Interface

The balance, intRate, interest, and transactions member variables are private, so they are hidden from the world outside the object. This is because a programmer with direct access to these variables might unknowingly commit any of the following errors:

◆ A deposit or withdrawal might be made without the transactions member being incremented.

◆ A withdrawal might be made for more than is in the account. This will cause the balance member to have a negative value.

◆ The interest rate might be calculated and the balance member adjusted, but the amount of interest might not get recorded in the intRate member.

◆ The wrong interest rate might be used.

Because of the potential for these errors, the object contains public member functions that ensure the proper steps are taken when the account is manipulated.

Implementing the Class

Program 7-20 shows an implementation of the `Account` class. It presents a menu for displaying a savings account's balance, number of transactions, and interest earned. It also allows the user to deposit an amount into the account, make a withdrawal from the account, and calculate the interest earned for the current period. (Note that the `charRange` input validation class, discussed earlier, is also used in the program.)

Program 7-20

```cpp
// This program must be linked with account.cpp and chrange.cpp

#include <iostream>
#include <iomanip>
#include <cctype>
#include "account.h"
#include "chrange.h"
using namespace std;

// Function prototypes
void displayMenu();
void makeDeposit(Account &);
void withdraw(Account &);

int main()
{
    Account savings;            // Account object to model a savings account
    CharRange input('A', 'G');  // CharRange object to do input validation

    cout << fixed << showpoint << setprecision(2);

    for (;;)                    // Infinite loop (terminated by user)
    {
        char choice;

        displayMenu();
        choice = input.getChar();   // getChar() gets and validates choice

        switch(choice)
        {
            case 'A': cout << "The current balance is $";
                      cout << savings.getBalance() << endl;
                      break;
```

(program continues)

Program 7-20   *(continued)*

```
            case 'B': cout << "There have been ";
                      cout << savings.getTransactions()
                           << " transactions.\n";
                      break;
            case 'C': cout << "Interest earned for this period: $";
                      cout << savings.getInterest() << endl;
                      break;
            case 'D': makeDeposit(savings);
                      break;
            case 'E': withdraw(savings);
                      break;
            case 'F': savings.calcInterest();
                      cout << "Interest added.\n";
                      break;
            case 'G': return 0;
         }
   }
   return 0;
}

//*******************************************************************
// Definition of function displayMenu                              *
// This function displays the user's menu on the screen.           *
//*******************************************************************

void displayMenu()
{
cout << "\n\na) Display the account balance\n";
cout << "b) Display the number of transactions\n";
cout << "c) Display interest earned for this period\n";
cout << "d) Make a deposit\n";
cout << "e) Make a withdrawal\n";
cout << "f) Add interest for this period\n";
cout << "g) Exit the program\n\n";
cout << "Enter your choice: ";
}

//*******************************************************************
// Definition of function makeDeposit                              *
// This function accepts a reference to an Account object.         *
// The user is prompted for the dollar amount of the deposit,      *
// and the makeDeposit member of the Account object is             *
// then called.                                                    *
//*******************************************************************
```

(program continues)

Program 7-20 *(continued)*

```
void makeDeposit(Account &account)
{
    float dollars;

    cout << "Enter the amount of the deposit: ";
    cin  >> dollars;
    cin.ignore();
    account.makeDeposit(dollars);
}

//******************************************************************
// Definition of function withdraw                                *
// This function accepts a reference to an Account object.        *
// The user is prompted for the dollar amount of the withdrawal,  *
// and the withdraw member of the Account object is then called.  *
//******************************************************************

void withdraw(Account &account)
{
    float dollars;

    cout << "Enter the amount of the withdrawal: ";
    cin  >> dollars;
    cin.ignore();
    if (!account.withdraw(dollars))
        cout << "ERROR: Withdrawal amount too large.\n\n";
}
```

Program Output with Example Input Shown in Bold
```
a) Display the account balance
b) Display the number of transactions
c) Display interest earned for this period
d) Make a deposit
e) Make a withdrawal
f) Add interest for this period
g) Exit the program

Enter your choice: d[Enter]
Enter the amount of the deposit: 500[Enter]
```

(program output continues)

Program 7-20   *(continued)*

```
a) Display the account balance
b) Display the number of transactions
c) Display interest earned for this period
d) Make a deposit
e) Make a withdrawal
f) Add interest for this period
g) Exit the program

Enter your choice: a[Enter]
The current balance is $500.00

a) Display the account balance
b) Display the number of transactions
c) Display interest earned for this period
d) Make a deposit
e) Make a withdrawal
f) Add interest for this period
g) Exit the program

Enter your choice: e[Enter]
Enter the amount of the withdrawal: 700[Enter]
ERROR: Withdrawal amount too large.

a) Display the account balance
b) Display the number of transactions
c) Display interest earned for this period
d) Make a deposit
e) Make a withdrawal
f) Add interest for this period
g) Exit the program

Enter your choice: e[Enter]
Enter the amount of the withdrawal: 200[Enter]

a) Display the account balance
b) Display the number of transactions
c) Display interest earned for this period
d) Make a deposit
e) Make a withdrawal
f) Add interest for this period
g) Exit the program

Enter your choice: f[Enter]
Interest added.
```

(program output continues)

Program 7-20   *(continued)*

```
a) Display the account balance
b) Display the number of transactions
c) Display interest earned for this period
d) Make a deposit
e) Make a withdrawal
f) Add interest for this period
g) Exit the program

Enter your choice: a[Enter]
The current balance is: $313.50

a) Display the account balance
b) Display the number of transactions
c) Display interest earned for this period
d) Make a deposit
e) Make a withdrawal
f) Add interest for this period
g) Exit the program

Enter your choice: g[Enter]
```

7.22   Focus on Software Engineering: *Object-Oriented Analysis*

The planning phase of any program's development is extremely important. It is during this phase that the programmer carefully examines the program requirements and decides which data structures and algorithms to use. In OOP terminology, this phase of program development is known as the *object-oriented analysis phase.* It is during this time that the programmer determines what classes will be used.

The process of object-oriented analysis can be viewed as the following steps:

1. Identify the objects and classes to be used in the program.

2. Define the attributes for each class.

3. Define the behaviors for each class.

4. Define the relationships between classes.

Let's look at each step more closely.

1. Identify the Objects and Classes.

Remember, a class is a package that consists of data and procedures that perform operations on the data. In order to determine the classes that will appear in a program, the programmer should think of the major data elements and decide what procedures or actions are required for each class. For example, consider a restaurant that uses an object-oriented program to enter customer orders. A customer order is a list of menu items with their respective prices. The restaurant uses this list to charge the customer, so a class could be created to model it. Also, the restaurant's menu has several main entrees, appetizers, side dishes, and beverages to choose from. A class could be designed to represent menu items as well.

Classes can be easily designed to model real-world objects, such as customer orders and a restaurant's menu items. Here are some other types of items that may be candidates for classes in a program:

- ◆ User-interface components, such as windows, menus, and dialog boxes
- ◆ Input/output devices, such as the keyboard, mouse, display, and printer
- ◆ Physical objects, such as vehicles, machines, or manufactured products
- ◆ Recordkeeping items, such as customer histories, and payroll records
- ◆ Any role played by a human (employees, clients, teachers, students, and so forth)

2. Define Each Class's Attributes.

A class's attributes are the data elements used to describe an object instantiated from the class. They are all the important values needed for the object to function properly in the program. Again, let's look at the restaurant example. Here is the beginning of a possible specification for a `menuItem` class:

```
Class name:      MenuItem
Attributes:      description
                 category
                 price
```

The attributes can be described as follows:

`description:` A string object holding the name of the menu item

`category:` An integer holding one of the following codes: 1 = main entree, 2 = appetizer, 3 = side dish, 4 = beverage

`price:` A float holding the individual price of the menu item

Another class mentioned in the restaurant example is the `CustomerOrder` class. Here is the beginning of its specification:

```
Class name:      CustomerOrder
Attributes:      items
                 totalPrice
                 tip
```

The attributes can be described as follows:

`items:` A group of `menuItem` objects

`totalPrice:` A `float` holding the total price of all items ordered

`tip:` A `float` holding the amount of gratuity paid by the customer

3. Define Each Class's Behaviors.

Once the class's attributes have been defined, the programmer must decide what behaviors each class must be capable of performing. For example, a class that holds a student's test scores should be able to average those scores, find the highest and lowest scores, and calculate a letter grade. When each class is finished, they should be complete packages capable of manipulating their data in any necessary way.

Table 7-8 lists some of the `MenuItem` class's behaviors from the restaurant example.

Table 7-8

Behavior	Description
placeOrder	Indicates that the customer has placed an order for a menu item. Stores the description, category, and price in the object.
getDesc	Returns the object's description.
getCategory	Returns the name of the object's category.
getPrice	Returns the object's price.

In C++, a class's behaviors are its *member functions*.

4. Define the Relationships Between Classes.

The last step in our object-oriented analysis phase is to define the relationships that exist between and among the classes in a program. The possible relationships may be formally stated as

- ◆ Access
- ◆ Ownership
- ◆ Inheritance

Informally, these three relationships can be described as

- ◆ Knows
- ◆ Has
- ◆ Is

The first relationship, access, allows an object to modify the attributes of another object. Normally, an object has attributes not accessible to parts of the program outside the object. These are known as private attributes. An access relationship between two objects means that one object will have access to the other object's private attributes. When this relationship exists, it can be said that one object *knows* the other. This type of relationship is discussed in Chapter 11.

The second relationship, ownership, means that one object is an attribute of another object. For example, a personnel system might have an object that represents an employee. That object might have, as an attribute, another object that holds the employee's name. It can be said that the employee object *has* a name object. In OOP terminology, this type of relationship is also called *composition*. This is also discussed in Chapter 11.

The third relationship is inheritance. Sometimes a class is based on another class. This means that one class is a specialized case of the other. For example, consider a program that uses classes representing cars, trucks, and jet planes. Although those three types of classes in the real world are very different, they have some common characteristics: They are all modes of transportation, and they all carry some number of passengers. So each of the three classes could be based on a Vehicle class that has attributes and behaviors common to them all. This is illustrated in Figure 7-8.

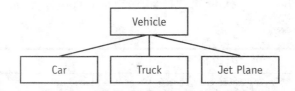

Figure 7-8

In OOP terminology, the Vehicle class is the *base class*. The Car, Truck and Jet Plane classes are *derived* classes. All of the attributes and behaviors of the Vehicle class are inherited by the Car, Truck, and Jet Plane classes. The relationship implies that a car *is a* vehicle, a truck *is a* vehicle and a jet plane *is a* vehicle. Inheritance is discussed in detail in Chapter 13.

In addition to inheriting the attributes and behaviors of the base class, derived classes add their own. For example, the Car class might have attributes and behaviors that set and indicate the number of passengers it can carry, whether it is a sedan or a coupe, and the type of engine it has. The truck class might have attributes and behaviors that set and indicate the maximum amount of weight it can carry, and how many miles it can travel between refuelings. The Jet Plane class might have attributes and behaviors that set and indicate its altitude and heading. These added components of the derived classes make them more specialized than the base class.

Review Questions and Exercises

Fill-in-the-Blank

1. Before a structure variable can be created, the structure must be _____.

2. The _____ is the name of the structure type.

3. The variables declared inside a structure declaration are called _____.

4. A(n) _____ is required after the closing brace of a structure declaration.

5. In the declaration of a structure variable, the _____ is placed before the variable name, just like the data type of a regular variable is placed before its name.

6. The _____ operator allows you to access structure members.

7. The structure Car is declared as follows:

```
struct Car
{
    string carMake;
    string carModel;
    int yearModel;
    float cost;
};
```

Write a definition statement that defines a `Car` structure variable initialized with the following information:

Make: Ford
Model: Mustang
Year: 1997
Cost: $20,000

8. Declare a structure named `TempScale`, with the following members:

`fahrenheit:` a `float`
`centigrade:` a `float`

Next, declare a structure named `Reading`, with the following members:

`windSpeed:` an `int`
`humidity:` a `float`
`temperature:` a `TempScale` structure variable

Next, define a `Reading` structure variable.

9. Write statements that will store the following data in the variable you defined in question 8.

Wind speed: 37 mph
Humidity: 32%
Fahrenheit temperature: 32 degrees
Centigrade temperature: 0 degrees

10. Write a function called `showReading`. It should accept a `Reading` structure variable (see question 8) as its argument. The function should display the contents of the variable on the screen.

11. Write a function called `findReading`. It should use a `Reading` structure reference variable (see question 8) as its parameter. The function should ask the user to enter values for each member of the structure.

12. Write a function called `getReading`, which returns a `Reading` structure (see question 8). The function should ask the user to enter values for each member of a `Reading` structure, and then return the structure.

13. Write the declaration of a union called `Items` with the following members:

`alpha:` a character
`num:` an integer
`bigNum:` a `long` integer
`real:` a `float`

Next, write the definition of an `Items` union variable.

14. Write the declaration of an anonymous union with the same members as the union you declared in question 13.

15. Write a statement that stores the number 452 in the num member of the anonymous union you declared in question 14.

16. The two common programming methods in practice today are _____ and _____.

17. _____ programming is centered around functions or procedures.

18. _____ programming is centered around objects.

19. _____ is an object's ability to contain and manipulate its own data.

20. In C++ the _____ is the construct primarily used to create objects.

21. A class is very similar to a(n) _____.

22. A(n) _____ is a key word inside a class declaration that establishes a member's accessibility.

23. The default access specification of class members is _____.

24. The default access specification of a struct in C++ is _____.

25. Defining a class object is often called the _____ of a class.

26. If you were writing the declaration of a class named Canine, what would you name the file it was stored in? _____

27. If you were writing the external definitions of the Canine class's member functions, what file would you save them in? _____

28. When a member function's body is written inside a class declaration, the function is _____.

29. A(n) _____ is automatically called when an object is created.

30. A(n) _____ is a member function with the same name as the class.

31. _____ are useful for performing initialization or setup routines in a class object.

32. Constructors cannot have a(n) _____ type.

33. A(n) _____ constructor is one that requires no arguments.

34. A(n) _____ is a member function that is automatically called when an object is destroyed.

35. A destructor has the same name as the class, but is preceded by a(n) _____ character.

36. Like constructors, destructors cannot have a(n) _____ type.

37. A constructor whose arguments all have default values is a(n) _____ constructor.

38. A class may have more than one constructor, as long as each has a different _____.

39. A class may only have one default _____ and one _____.

True or False

40. T F A semicolon is required after the closing brace of a structure or union declaration.

41. T F A structure declaration does not define a variable.

42. T F The contents of a structure variable can be displayed by passing the structure variable to the cout object.

43. T   F   Structure variables may not be initialized.
44. T   F   In a structure variable's initialization list, you do not have to provide initializers for all the members.
45. T   F   You may skip members in a structure's initialization list.
46. T   F   A structure variable may not be a member of another structure.
47. T   F   A structure member variable may be passed to a function as an argument.
48. T   F   An entire structure may not be passed to a function as an argument.
49. T   F   A function may return a structure.
50. T   F   When a function returns a structure, it is always necessary for the function to have a local structure variable to hold the member values that are to be returned.
51. T   F   In a `union`, all the members are stored in different memory locations.
52. T   F   All the members of a `union` may be used simultaneously.
53. T   F   An anonymous `union` has no name.
54. T   F   If an anonymous `union` is declared globally (outside all functions), it must be declared `static`.
55. T   F   Private members must be declared before public members.
56. T   F   Class members are private by default.
57. T   F   Members of a `struct` are private by default.
58. T   F   Classes and structures in C++ are very similar.
59. T   F   All private members of a class must be declared together.
60. T   F   All public members of a class must be declared together.
61. T   F   Unless you are designing a class specifically to perform I/O, you should avoid `cin`, `cout`, or other I/O statements in the class's member functions.
62. T   F   A private member function may be called from a statement outside the class, as long as the statement is in the same program as the class declaration.
63. T   F   Constructors do not have to have the same name as the class.
64. T   F   Constructors may not have a return type.
65. T   F   Constructors cannot take arguments.
66. T   F   Destructors cannot take arguments.
67. T   F   Destructors may return a value.
68. T   F   Constructors may have default arguments.
69. T   F   Constructors may be overloaded.
70. T   F   Destructors may be overloaded.
71. T   F   A class may not have a constructor with an empty parameter list, and a constructor whose arguments all have default values.
72. T   F   A class may only have one destructor.

Find the Errors

73. Each of the following declarations, programs, and program segments has errors. Locate as many as you can.

A)
```
struct
{
    int x;
    float y;
};
```

B)
```
struct Values
{
    string name;
    int age;
}
```

C)
```
struct TwoVals
{
    int a, b;
};
int main()
{
    TwoVals.a = 10;
    TwoVals.b = 20;
    return 0;
}
```

D)
```
#include <iostream>
using namespace std;

struct ThreeVals
{
    int a, b, c;
};
int main()
{
    TwoVals vals = {1, 2, 3};
    cout << vals << endl;
    return 0;
}
```

```
E) struct Names
   {
      string first;
      string last;
   };
   int main()
   {
      Names customer = "Smith", "Orley";
      cout << Names.first << endl;
      cout << Names.last << endl;
      return 0;
   }

F) struct FourVals
   {
      int a, b, c, d;
   };
   int main()
   {
      FourVals nums = {1, 2, , 4};
   }

G) struct TwoVals
   {
      int a = 5;
      int b = 10;
   };
   int main()
   {
      TwoVals v;
      cout << v.a << " " << v.b;
      return 0;
   }
```

74. Each of the class declarations or programs below contain errors. Find as many as possible.

```
A) class Circle:
   {
   private
      float centerX;
      float centerY;
      float radius;
   public
      setCenter(float, float);
      setRadius(float);
   }
```

B)
```cpp
#include <iostream>
using namespace std;
Class Moon;
{
Private:
  float earthWeight;
  float moonWeight;
Public:
  moonWeight(float ew);
    { earthWeight = ew; moonWeight = earthWeight / 6; }
  float getMoonWeight();
    { return moonWeight; }
}

int main()
{
  float earth;

  cout >> "What is your weight? ";
  cin << earth;
  Moon lunar(earth);
  cout << "On the moon you would weigh "
      <<lunar.getMoonWeight() << endl;
  return 0;
}
```

C)
```cpp
#include <iostream>
using namespace std;

class DumbBell;
{
  int weight;
public:
  void setWeight(int);
};
void setWeight(int w)
{
  weight = w;
}
int man()
{
  DumbBell bar;

  DumbBell(200);
  cout << "The weight is " << bar.weight << endl;
  return 0;
}
```

```
D) class Change
   {
   public:
      int pennies;
      int nickels;
      int dimes;
      int quarters;
      Change()
          { pennies = nickels = dimes = quarters = 0; }
      Change(int p = 100, int n = 50, d = 50, q = 25);
   };
   void Change::Change(int p, int n, d, q)
   {
      pennies = p;
      nickels = n;
      dimes = d;
      quarters = q;
   }
```

Programming Challenges

General Requirements

A) Each program should have a section of comments at the top. The comments should contain your name, the date the program was written, the chapter the assignment appeared in, and the assignment number and name. Here is an example:

```
// Written by Jill Johnson
// March 31, 2003
// Chapter 7
// Assignment 1, Corporate Sales Data
```

B) For each program that displays a dollar amount, format the output in fixed-point notation with two decimal places of precision. Be sure the decimal place always displays, even when the number is zero or has no fractional part.

1. Corporate Sales Data

Write a program that uses a structure to store the following information on a company division:

> Division name (such as East, West, North, or South)
> First quarter sales
> Second quarter sales
> Third quarter sales
> Fourth quarter sales
> Total annual sales
> Average quarterly sales

The program should create four variables of this structure. Each variable should represent one of the following corporate divisions: East, West, North, and South. The user should be asked for the four quarters' sales figures for each division. Each division's total and average sales should be calculated and stored in the appropriate member of each structure variable. These figures should then be displayed on the screen.

Input Validation: Do not accept negative numbers for any sales figures.

2. Customer Accounts

Write a program that uses a structure to store the following information about a customer account:

> Name
> Address
> City, state, and zip
> Telephone number
> Account balance
> Date of last payment

The program should declare a structure variable. It should let the user enter information into the variable, change the contents of its members, and display all the information stored in the structure. The program should have a menu-driven user interface.

Input Validation: When the information is entered, be sure the user enters data for all the fields. No negative account balances should be entered.

3. Multipurpose Payroll

Write a program that calculates pay for either an hourly wage worker or a salaried worker. Hourly wage workers are paid their hourly pay rate times the number of hours worked. Salaried workers are paid their regular salary plus any bonus they may have earned. The program should declare two structures for the following information:

Hourly Wage
Hours worked
Hourly rate

Salaried
Salary
Bonus

The program should also declare a union with two members. Each member should be a structure variable: one for the hourly wage worker and another for the salaried worker.

The program should ask the user if they are calculating the pay for an hourly wage worker or a salaried worker. Regardless of which the user selects, the appropriate members of the union will be used to store the data that will be used to calculate the pay.

Input Validation: Do not accept negative numbers. Do not accept values greater than 80 for hours worked.

4. Numeric Input Validation Class

Use the CharRange class presented in this chapter as a model for an IntRange class. The IntRange class should allow the user to enter integer values within a specified range. An error message should be displayed when the user enters a value outside the range.

5. Date

Design a class called Date. The class should store a date in three integers: month, day, and year. There should be member functions to print the date in the following forms:

3/31/03
March 31, 2003
31 March 2003

Demonstrate the class by writing a complete program implementing it.

Input Validation: Do not accept values for the day greater than 31 or less than 1. Do not accept values for the month greater than 12 or less than 1.

6. Widget Factory

Design a class for a widget manufacturing plant. Assuming that 10 widgets may be produced each hour, the class object will calculate how many days it will take to produce any number of widgets. (The plant operates two shifts of eight hours each per day.) Write a program that asks the user for the number of widgets that have been ordered and then displays the number of days it will take to produce them.

Input Validation: Do not accept negative values for the number of widgets ordered.

7. Population

In a population, the birth rate and death rate are calculated as follows:

Birth Rate = Number of Births ÷ Population
Death Rate = Number of Deaths ÷ Population

For example, in a population of 100,000 that has 8,000 births and 6,000 deaths per year, the birth rate and death rate are

Birth Rate = 8,000 ÷ 100,000 = 0.08
Death Rate = 6,000 ÷ 100,000 = 0.06

Design a `Population` class that stores a population, number of births, and number of deaths for a period of time. Member functions should return the birth rate and death rate. Implement the class in a program.

Input Validation: Do not accept population figures less than 1, or birth or death numbers less than 0.

8. Mortgage Payment

Design a class that will determine the monthly payment on a home mortgage. The monthly payment with interest compounded monthly can be calculated as follows:

$$\text{Payment} = \frac{\text{Loan} \times \dfrac{\text{Rate}}{12} \times \text{Term}}{\text{Term} - 1}$$

where

$$\text{Term} = \left(1 + \frac{\text{Rate}}{12}\right)^{12 \times \text{Years}}$$

Payment = the monthly payment
Loan = the dollar amount of the loan
Rate = the annual interest rate
Years = the number of years of the loan

The class should have member functions for setting the loan amount, interest rate, and number of years of the loan. It should also have member functions for returning the monthly payment amount and the total amount paid to the bank at the end of the loan period. Implement the class in a complete program.

Input Validation: Do not accept negative numbers for any of the loan values.

9. Inventory Class

Design an `Inventory` class that can hold information and calculate data for items in a retail store's inventory. The class should have the following private member variables:

Variable Name	Description
itemNumber	An int that holds the items item number.
quantity	An int for holding the quantity of the items on-hand.
cost	A float for holding the wholesale per-unit cost of the item
totalCost	A float for holding the total inventory cost of the item (calculated as quantity times cost).

The class should have the following public member functions:

Member Function	Description
default constructor	Sets all the member variables to 0.
constructor #2	Accepts an item's number, cost, and quantity as arguments. The function should copy these values to the appropriate member variables and then call the setTotalCost function.
setItemNumber	Accepts an integer argument that is copied to the itemNumber member variable.
setQuantity	Accepts an integer argument that is copied to the quantity member variable.
setCost	Accepts a floating-point argument that is copied to the cost member variable.
setTotalCost	Calculates the total inventory cost for the item (quantity times cost) and stores the result in totalCost.
getItemNumber	Returns the value in itemNumber.
getQuantity	Returns the value in quantity.
getCost	Returns the value in cost.
getTotalCost	Returns the value in totalCost.

Demonstrate the class in a driver program.

Input Validation: Do not accept negative values for item number, quantity, or cost.

Group Project

10. Patient Fees

This program should be designed and written by a team of students. Here are some suggestions:

- One or more students may work on a single class.
- The requirements of the program should be analyzed so each student is given about the same work load.
- The parameters and return types of each function and class member function should be decided in advance.
- The program will be best implemented as a multi-file program.

Write a program that computes a patient's bill for a hospital stay. The different components of the program are

- The `PatientAccount` class will keep a total of the patient's charges. It will also keep track of the number of days spent in the hospital. The group must decide on the hospital's daily rate.
- The `Surgery` class will have stored within it the charges for at least five types of surgery. It can update the charges variable of the `PatientAccount` class.
- The `Pharmacy` class will have stored within it the price of at least five types of medication. It can update the charges variable of the `PatientAccount` class.
- The `main` program.

The student who designs the main program will design a menu that allows the user to enter a type of surgery and a type of medication, and check the patient out of the hospital. When the patient checks out, the total charges should be displayed.

Serendipity Booksellers Software Development Project—Part 7: *A Problem-Solving Exercise*

For this chapter's assignment, you will begin a class declaration that will hold and manipulate the information on a single book. The class will be named `BookData`, so its declaration should reside in a file named `bookdata.h`, and the member function definitions should reside in a file named `bookdata.cpp`.

1. Create the Class Declaration.

Create a `BookData` class declaration with the following private members:

bookTitle	A string
isbn	A string
author	A string
publisher	A string

dateAdded	A string. The date should be stored in the form MM-DD-YYYY. For example, March 31, 2003 would be stored as 03-31-2003.
qtyOnHand	An integer.
wholesale	A float. This member will hold the wholesale price of a book.
empty	A bool. This member will be set to true when the class object is empty, or false when the object's members hold data. (This member will be used when a book is deleted from inventory.)
retail	A float. This member will hold the retail price of a book.

2. Add the Default Class Constructor

For now, the default constructor should set the qtyOnHand, wholesale, and retail members to zero, and the empty member to true.

3. Add the Following Functions to the BookData Class:

For now, implement these member functions as stubs. You will complete them in later chapters.

setTitle	When this function is complete, it will update the bookTitle member.
setIsbn	When this function is complete, it will update the isbn member.
setAuthor	When this function is complete, it will update the author member.
setPub	When this function is complete, it will update the publisher member.
setDateAdded	When this function is complete, it will update the dateAddded member.
setQty	When this function is complete, it will update the qtyOnHand member.
setWholesale	When this function is complete, it will update the wholesale member.
setRetail	When this function is complete, it will update the retail member.
isEmpty	When this function is complete, it will return the value in the empty member.
removeBook	When this function is complete, it will set the empty member to true.
getTitle	When this function is complete, it will return the value in the bookTitle member.
getIsbn	When this function is complete, it will return the value in the isbn member.
getAuthor	When this function is complete, it will return the value in the author member.
getPub	When this function is complete, it will return the value in the publisher member.
getDateAdded	When this function is complete, it will return the value in the dateAddded member.
getQty	When this function is complete, it will return the value in the qtyOnHand member.
getWholesale	When this function is complete, it will return the value in the wholesale member.
getRetail	When this function is complete, it will return the value in the retail member.

CHAPTER 8

Arrays

Topics

8.1 Arrays Hold Multiple Values

CONCEPT Unlike regular variables, arrays can hold multiple values.

The variables you have worked with so far are designed to hold only one value at a time. Each of the variable definitions in Figure 8-1 cause only enough memory to be reserved to hold one value of the specified data type.

An array is a variable that can store a group of values, all of the same type. The values are stored together in consecutive memory locations. Here is a definition of an array of integers:

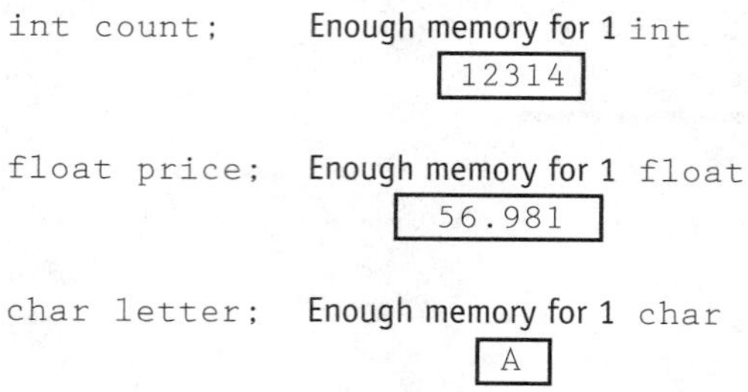

```
int count;    Enough memory for 1 int
              ┌─────────┐
              │  12314  │
              └─────────┘

float price;  Enough memory for 1 float
              ┌─────────┐
              │ 56.981  │
              └─────────┘

char letter;  Enough memory for 1 char
                 ┌───┐
                 │ A │
                 └───┘
```

Figure 8-1

```
int days[6];
```

The name of this array is days. The number inside the brackets is the array's *size declarator*. It indicates the number of *elements,* or values, the array can hold. The days array can store six elements, each one an integer. This is depicted in Figure 8-2.

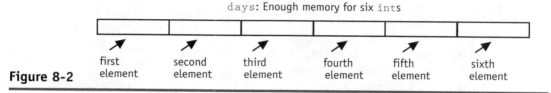

days: Enough memory for six ints

first element   second element   third element   fourth element   fifth element   sixth element

Figure 8-2

An array's size declarator must be a constant integer expression with a value greater than zero. It can be either a literal constant, as in the previous example, or a named constant, as shown here:

```
const int numDays = 6;
int days[numDays];

#define ARRAY_SIZE 6
int days[ARRAY_SIZE];
```

Arrays of any data type can be defined. The following are all valid array definitions:

```
float temperature[100];    // Array of 100 floats
char letter[26];           // Array of 26 characters
long unit[50];             // Array of 50 long integers
double size[1200];         // Array of 1200 doubles
string name[10];           // Array of 10 string objects
```

Memory Requirements of Arrays

The amount of memory used by an array depends on the array's data type and the number of elements. The hours array, defined here, is an array of six shorts.

```
short hours[6];
```

On a typical PC, a `short` uses 2 bytes of memory, so the `hours` array would occupy 12 bytes. This is shown in Figure 8-3.

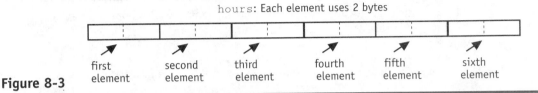

hours: Each element uses 2 bytes

first element   second element   third element   fourth element   fifth element   sixth element

Figure 8-3

The size of an array can be calculated by multiplying the size of an individual element by the number of elements in the array. Table 8-1 shows the sizes of various arrays defined using Borland C++ or Microsoft Visual C++.

Table 8-1

Array declaration	Number of elements	Size of each element	Size of the array
char letter[26];	26	1 byte	26 bytes
short ring[100];	100	2 bytes	200 bytes
int mile[84];	84	4 bytes	336 bytes
float temp[12];	12	4 bytes	48 bytes
double distance[1000];	1000	8 bytes	8,000 bytes

8.2 Accessing Array Elements

CONCEPT | The individual elements of an array are assigned unique subscripts. These subscripts are used to access the elements.

Even though an entire array has only one name, the elements may be accessed and used as individual variables. This is possible because each element is assigned a number known as a *subscript*. A subscript is used as an index to pinpoint a specific element within an array. The first element is assigned the subscript 0, the second element is assigned 1, and so forth. The six elements in the array `hours` would have the subscripts 0 through 5. This is shown in Figure 8-4.

 Note: Subscript numbering in C++ always starts at zero. The subscript of the last element in an array is one less than the total number of elements in the array.

Subscripts

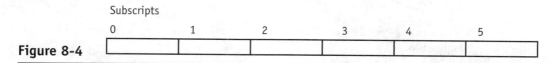

Figure 8-4

This means that in the array shown, the element `hours[6]` does not exist. `hours[5]` is the last element in the array.

Each element in the `hours` array, when accessed by its subscript, can be used as a `short` variable. Here is an example of a statement that stores the number 20 in the first element of the array:

```
hours[0] = 20;
```

Note: The expression `hours[0]` is pronounced "hours sub zero." You would read this assignment statement as "hours sub zero is assigned twenty."

Figure 8-5 shows the contents of the array `hours` after the statement assigns 20 to `hours[0]`.

Subscripts

0	1	2	3	4	5
20	?	?	?	?	?

Figure 8-5

Note: Since values have not been assigned to the other elements of the array, question marks are used to indicate that the contents of those elements are unknown. If an array is declared globally, all of its elements are initialized to zero by default. Local arrays, however, have no default initialization value.

The following statement stores the integer 30 in `hours[3]`, which is the fourth element of the `hours` array:

```
hours[3] = 30;
```

Figure 8-6 shows the contents of the array after this statement executes.

Subscripts

0	1	2	3	4	5
20	?	?	30	?	?

Figure 8-6

Note: It is important to understand the difference between the array size declarator and a subscript. The number inside the brackets in an array definition is the size declarator. It specifies how many elements the array holds. The number inside the brackets in an assignment statement or any statement that works with the contents of an array is a subscript. It specifies which element is being accessed.

Array elements may receive values with assignment statements just like other variables. However, entire arrays may not receive values for all their elements at once. Assume the following two arrays have been defined.

```
int doctorA[5];     // Holds the number of patients seen by Dr. A
                    // on each of 5 days.
int doctorB[5];     // Holds the number of patients seen by Dr. B
                    // on each of 5 days.
```

The following are all legal assignment statements.

```
doctorA[0] = 31;            // doctorA[0] now holds 31.
doctorA[1] = 40;            // doctorA[1] now holds 40.
doctorA[2] = doctorA[0];    // doctorA[2] now also holds 31.
doctorB[0] = doctorA[1];    // doctorB[0] now holds 40.
```

However, the following statements are not legal.

```
doctorA = 152;      // Illegal! An array as a whole may not
doctorB = doctorA;  // be assigned a value. This must be done
                    // one element at a time, using a subscript.
```

8.3 Inputting and Displaying Array Contents

Array elements may also have information read into them using the `cin` object and have their values displayed with the `cout` object, just like regular variables, as long as it is done one element at a time. Program 8-1 shows the array `hours`, introduced in the last section, being used to store and display values entered by the user.

Program 8-1

```
// This program asks the user for the number of hours worked by
// 6 employees. It uses a 6-element short array to store the values.

#include <iostream>
using namespace std;

int main()
{
    short hours[6];
```

(program continues)

Program 8-1   *(continued)*

```
    // Input the hours worked.
    cout << "Enter the hours worked by six employees: ";
    cin >> hours[0];
    cin >> hours[1];
    cin >> hours[2];
    cin >> hours[3];
    cin >> hours[4];
    cin >> hours[5];

    // Display the hours worked.
    cout << "The hours you entered are:";
    cout << " " << hours[0];
    cout << " " << hours[1];
    cout << " " << hours[2];
    cout << " " << hours[3];
    cout << " " << hours[4];
    cout << " " << hours[5] << endl;
    return 0;
}
```

Program Output with Example Input Shown in Bold
```
Enter the hours worked by six employees: 20 12 40 30 30 15[Enter]
The hours you entered are: 20 12 40 30 30 15
```

Figure 8-7 shows the contents of the array hours with the example values entered by the user for Program 8-1.

Subscripts

Figure 8-7

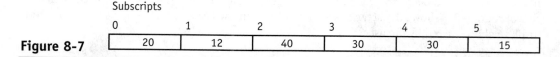

Even though the size declarator of an array definition must be a constant, subscript numbers can be stored in variables. This makes it possible to use a loop to "cycle through" an entire array, performing the same operation on each element. For example, Program 8-1 could be simplified by using two for loops: one for inputting the values into the array and another for displaying the contents of the array. This is shown in Program 8-2.

Program 8-2

```
// This program asks the user for the number of hours worked by
// 6 employees. It uses a 6-element short array to store the values.

#include <iostream>
using namespace std;
```

(program continues)

Program 8-2 *(continued)*

```cpp
int main()
{
    short hours[6];
    int count;

    // Input the hours worked.
    cout << "Enter the hours worked by six employees: ";
    for (count = 0; count < 6; count++)
        cin >> hours[count];

    // Display the hours worked.
    cout << "The hours you entered are:";
    for (count = 0; count < 6; count++)
        cout << " " << hours[count];
    cout << endl;
    return 0;
}
```

Program Output with Example Input Shown in Bold
```
Enter the hours worked by six employees: 20 12 40 30 30 15[Enter]
The hours you entered are: 20 12 40 30 30 15
```

Any integer expression may be used as a subscript. Program 8-3 is a more user-friendly version of Program 8-2. The expression count - 1 is used to calculate the subscript of the desired array element.

Program 8-3

```cpp
// This program asks the user for the number of hours worked by
// 6 employees. It uses a 6-element short array to store the values.

#include <iostream>
using namespace std;

int main()
{
    short hours[6];
    int count;

    // Input the hours worked.
    cout << "Enter the hours worked by six employees.\n";
    for (count = 1; count <= 6; count++)
    {
        cout << "Employee " << count << ": ";
        cin >> hours[count - 1];
    }
```

(program continues)

Program 8-3 *(continued)*

```
    // Display the hours worked.
    cout << "The hours you entered are\n";
    for (count = 1; count <= 6; count++)
    {
        cout << "Employee " << count << ": ";
        cout << hours[count - 1] << endl;
    }
    return 0;
}
```

Program Output with Example Input Shown in Bold
```
Enter the hours worked by six employees.
Employee 1: 20[Enter]
Employee 2: 12[Enter]
Employee 3: 40[Enter]
Employee 4: 30[Enter]
Employee 5: 30[Enter]
Employee 6: 15[Enter]
The hours you entered are
Employee 1: 20
Employee 2: 12
Employee 3: 40
Employee 4: 30
Employee 5: 30
Employee 6: 15
```

Notice in all these examples that the contents of the hours array were input and displayed one element at a time. The following statements would have been incorrect.

```
    cin >> hours;      // Incorrect!
    cout << hours;     // Incorrect!
```

The only time an entire array can be input or displayed as if it were a single value is when it is a C-string or a string object, both of which are really stored as arrays of characters. C-strings are discussed in Section 3.10 and in Chapter 12. String objects are used throughout this text and will be dealt with more in Section 8.5.

No Bounds Checking in C++

One of the reasons for C++'s popularity is the freedom it gives programmers to work with the computer's memory. Many of the safeguards provided by other languages to prevent programs from unsafely accessing memory are absent in C++. For example, C++ does not perform array bounds checking. This means you can write programs with subscripts that go beyond the boundaries of a particular array. Program 8-4 demonstrates this capability.

 WARNING! If you compile and run Program 8-4, an area of memory will be overwritten that the computer might need to continue operating. This could cause the computer to lock up.

Program 8-4

```cpp
// This program unsafely accesses an area of memory by writing
// values beyond an array's boundary.
// WARNING: If you compile and run this program, it could cause
// the computer to crash.

#include <iostream>
using namespace std;

int main ()
{
    short values[3];          // An array of 3 short integers.
    int count;

    cout << "I will store 5 numbers in a 3 element array!\n";
    for (count = 0; count < 5; count++)
        values[count] = 100;
    cout << "If you see this message, it means the computer\n";
    cout << "has not crashed! Here are the numbers:\n";
    for (count = 0; count < 5; count++)
        cout << values[count] << endl;
    return 0;
}
```

The `values` array can hold three short integer elements, with the subscripts 0, 1, and 2. The loop, however, stores the number 100 in elements 0, 1, 2, 3, and 4. The elements with subscripts 3 and 4 do not exist, but C++ allows the program to write beyond the boundary of the array, as if those elements were there. Figure 8-8 depicts the way the array is set up in memory when the program first starts to execute, and what happens when the loop writes data beyond the boundary of the array.

Obviously, the freedom granted by C++ requires a great deal of responsibility. The programmer must make sure that any time values are assigned to array elements, they are written within the array's boundaries.

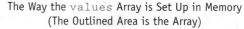

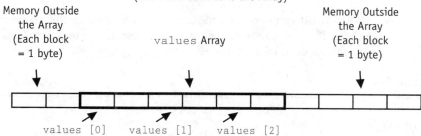

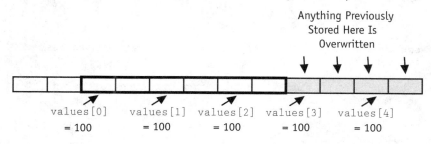

Figure 8-8

? Checkpoint [8.1–8.3]

8.1   Define the following arrays:

A)   empNum, a 100-element array of ints

B)   payRate, a 25-element array of floats

C)   miles, a 14-element array of longs

D)   letter, a 26-element array of chars

E)   lightYears, a 1,000-element array of doubles

8.2   What's wrong with the following array definitions?

```
int readings[-1];
float measurements[4.5];
int size;
char name[size];
```

8.3 What would the valid subscript values be in a four-element array of `doubles`?

8.4 What is the difference between an array's size declarator and a subscript?

8.5 What is "array bounds checking"? Does C++ perform it?

8.6 What is the output of the following program?

```cpp
#include <iostream>
using namespace std;

int main ()
{
    int values[5], count;

    for (count = 0; count < 5; count++)
        values[count] = count + 1;

    for (count = 0; count < 5; count++)
        cout << values[count] << endl;
    return 0;
}
```

8.7 The following program skeleton contains a 20-element array of `ints` called `fish`. When completed, the program should ask how many fish were caught by fishermen 1 through 20, and store this information in the array. Complete the program.

```cpp
#include <iostream>
using namespace std;

int main ()
{
    int fish[20];

    // You must finish this program. It should ask how
    // many fish were caught by fishermen 1 - 20 and
    // store this information in the array fish.
    return 0;
}
```

8.4 Array Initialization

CONCEPT Arrays may be initialized when they are defined.

Writing separate assignment statements for the individual elements of an array can mean a lot of typing, especially for large arrays. For example, consider Program 8-5.

Program 8-5

```cpp
// This program displays the number of days in each month.
// It uses a 12-element int array.

#include <iostream>
using namepsace std;

int main ()
{
    int days[12];

    days[0] = 31;  // January
    days[1] = 28;  // February
    days[2] = 31;  // March
    days[3] = 30;  // April
    days[4] = 31;  // May
    days[5] = 30;  // June
    days[6] = 31;  // July
    days[7] = 31;  // August
    days[8] = 30;  // September
    days[9] = 31;  // October
    days[10] = 30; // November
    days[11] = 31; // December

    for (int count = 0; count < 12; count++)
    {
        cout << "Month " << (count + 1) << " has ";
        cout << days[count] << " days.\n";
    }
    return 0;
}
```

Program Output
```
Month 1 has 31 days.
Month 2 has 28 days.
Month 3 has 31 days.
Month 4 has 30 days.
Month 5 has 31 days.
Month 6 has 30 days.
Month 7 has 31 days.
Month 8 has 31 days.
Month 9 has 30 days.
Month 10 has 31 days.
Month 11 has 30 days.
Month 12 has 31 days.
```

Instead of using a loop to calculate the days of the months (a task not easily done), Program 8-5 uses 12 assignment statements to store the initial values into the array. Fortunately, there is an alternative. Like other variables, C++ allows you to initialize arrays when you define them. The following statement defines the array days and initializes it with the same values established by the set of assignment statements in Program 8-5:

```
int days[12] = {31, 28, 31, 30, 31, 30, 31, 31, 30, 31, 30, 31};
```

The series of values inside the braces and separated with commas is called an *initialization list*. These values are stored in the array elements in the order they appear in the list. (The first value, 31, is stored in days[0], the second value, 28, is stored in days[1], and so forth). Figure 8-9 shows the contents of the array after the initialization.

Subscripts

	0	1	2	3	4	5	6	7	8	9	10	11
Figure 8-9	31	28	31	30	31	30	31	31	30	31	30	31

Program 8-6 is a modification of Program 8-5. It initializes the days array at the time it is created rather than by using separate assignment statements. It also adds an array of string objects to hold the month names.

Program 8-6

```cpp
// This program displays the number of days in each month.
// It uses an array of string objects to hold the month names
// and an int array to hold the number of days in each month.
// Both are initialized with initialization lists at the time
// they are created.

#include <iostream>
#include <iomanip>
#include <string>
using namespace std;

int main()
{
    string month[12] = {"January",   "February", "March",    "April",
                        "May",       "June",     "July",     "August",
                        "September","October",   "November", "December"};

    int days[12] = {31, 28, 31, 30,
                    31, 30, 31, 31,
                    30, 31, 30, 31};
```

(program continues)

Program 8-6 *(continued)*

```
    for (int count = 0; count < 12; count++)
    {
        cout << setw(9) << left << month[count] << " has ";
        cout << days[count] << " days.\n";
    }
    return 0;
}
```

Program Output

```
January   has 31 days.
February  has 28 days.
March     has 31 days.
April     has 30 days.
May       has 31 days.
June      has 30 days.
July      has 31 days.
August    has 31 days.
September has 30 days.
October   has 31 days.
November  has 30 days.
December  has 31 days.
```

 Note: Notice that C++ allows you to spread the initialization list across multiple lines.

So far we have demonstrated how to fill an array with values and then display all the values. Sometimes, however, we want to retrieve one specific value from the array. Program 8-7 is a variation on Program 8-6 that displays how many days are in the month the user selects.

Program 8-7

```
// This program allows the user to select a month and then
// displays how many days are in that month.  It does this
// by "looking up" information it has stored in an array.

#include <iostream>
#include <iomanip>
#include <string>
using namespace std;
```

(program continues)

Program 8-7   *(continued)*

```cpp
int main()
{
    int choice;
    string month[12] = {"January",   "February", "March",     "April",
                        "May",        "June",     "July",      "August",
                        "September","October",   "November",  "December"};

    int days[12] = {31, 28, 31, 30,
                    31, 30, 31, 31,
                    30, 31, 30, 31};

    cout << "This program will tell you how many days are "
         << "in any month.\n\n";

    // Display the months
    for (int count = 1; count <= 12; count++)
        cout << setw(2) << count << "  " << month[count-1] << endl;

    cout << "\nEnter the number of the month you want: ";
    cin >> choice;

    // Use the choice the user entered to get the name of
    // the month and the number of days it has from the array.
    cout << "The month of " << month[choice-1] << " has "
         << days[choice-1]  << " days.\n";
    return 0;
}
```

Program Output with Example Input Shown in Bold
```
This program will tell you how many days are in any month.

 1  January
 2  February
 3  March
 4  April
 5  May
 6  June
 7  July
 8  August
 9  September
10  October
11  November
12  December

Enter the number of the month you want: 4[Enter]
The month of April has 30 days.
```

Partial Array Initialization

An initialization list cannot have more values than the array has elements, but it may have fewer values than there are elements. That is, C++ does not require a value for every element. It's possible to only initialize part of an array, such as

```
int numbers[7] = {1, 2, 4, 8};
```

The definition above only initializes the first four elements of a seven element array, as illustrated in Figure 8-10.

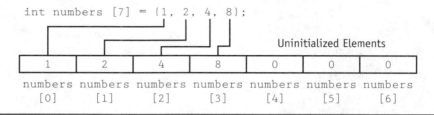

Figure 8-10

It's important to note that if an array is partially initialized, the uninitialized elements will be set to zero for numeric arrays or to the null character for character arrays. This is true even if the array is declared locally. (If a local array is completely uninitialized, its elements will contain "garbage," like all other local variables.) Program 8-8 shows the contents of the array `numbers` after it is partially initialized.

Program 8-8

```
// This program has a partially initialized array.

#include <iostream>
using namespace std;

int main ()
{
    int numbers[7] = {1, 2, 4, 8}; // Initialize the first 4 elements.

    cout << "Here are the contents of the array:\n";
    for (int index = 0; index < 7; index++)
        cout << numbers[index] << endl;
    return 0;
}
```

Program 8-8

___

Program Output
```
Here are the contents of the array:
1
2
4
8
0
0
0
```

___

If you leave an element uninitialized, you must leave all the elements that follow it uninitialized as well. C++ does not provide a way to skip elements in the initialization list. For example, the following is *not* legal:

```
int array[6] = {2, 4, , 8, , 12}; // NOT Legal!
```

Implicit Array Sizing

It's possible to define an array without specifying its size, as long as you provide an initialization list that includes a value for every element. C++ automatically makes the array large enough to hold all the initialization values. For example, the following definitition creates an array with 5 elements:

```
float ratings[] = {1.0, 1.5, 2.0, 2.5, 3.0};
```

Since the size declarator is omitted, C++ counts the number of items in the initialization list and gives the array that many elements.

 Note: You *must* specify an initialization list if you leave out the size declarator. Otherwise, C++ doesn't know how large to make the array.

8.5 Processing Array Contents

> **CONCEPT** Individual array elements are processed like any other type of variable.

Processing array elements is no different than processing other variables. For example, the following statement multiplies `hours[3]` by the variable `rate`:

```
pay = hours[3] * rate;
```

And the following are examples of pre-increment and post-increment operations on array elements:

```
int score[5] = {7, 8, 9, 10, 11};
++score[2];        // Pre-increment operation on the value in score[2]
score[4]++;        // Post-increment operation on the value in score[4]
```

 Note: When using increment and decrement operators, be careful not to confuse the subscript with the array element. The following example illustrates the difference.

```
amount[count]--;  // This decrements the value stored in amount[count].
amount[count--];  // This decrements the variable count, but does
                  // nothing to the value stored in amount[count].
```

Program 8-9 demonstrates the use of array elements in a simple mathematical statement. A loop steps through each element of the array, using the elements to calculate the gross pay of five employees.

Program 8-9

```
// This program stores, in an array, the hours worked by
// a set of employees who all make the same hourly wage.

#include <iostream>
#include <iomanip>
using namespace std;

const int numWorkers = 5;
int main()
{
    int worker;
    int hours[numWorkers];
    float payRate;

    cout << "Enter the hours worked by 5 employees who all\n";
    cout << "earn the same hourly rate.\n";

    for (worker = 0; worker < numWorkers; worker++)
    {
        cout << "Employee #" << (worker+1) << ": ";
        cin  >> hours[worker];
    }
    cout << "\nEnter the hourly pay rate for all the employees: ";
    cin  >> payRate;

    cout << "\nHere is the gross pay for each employee:\n";
    cout << fixed << showpoint << setprecision(2);
```

(program continues)

Program 8-9 *(continued)*

```
    for (worker = 0; worker < numWorkers; worker++)
    {
        float grossPay = hours[worker] * payRate;
        cout << "Employee #" << (worker+1);
        cout << ": $" << setw(6) << grossPay << endl;
    }
    return 0;
}
```

Program Output with Example Input Shown in Bold
```
Enter the hours worked by 5 employees who all
earn the same hourly rate.
Employee #1: 5[Enter]
Employee #2: 10[Enter]
Employee #3: 15[Enter]
Employee #4: 20[Enter]
Employee #5: 40[Enter]

Enter the hourly pay rate for all the employees: 12.75[Enter]

Here is the gross pay for each employee:
Employee #1: $ 63.75
Employee #2: $127.50
Employee #3: $191.25
Employee #4: $255.00
Employee #5: $510.00
```

In Program 8-9, the following statement defines the variable grossPay and initializes it with the value of hours[index] times payRate:

```
    float grossPay = hours[index] * payRate;
```

Array elements may also be used in relational expressions. For example, the following if statement tests cost[20] to determine if it is less than cost[0]:

```
    if (cost[20] < cost[0])
```

And the following statement sets up a while loop to iterate as long as value[place] does not equal 0:

```
    while (value[place] != 0)
```

Summing the Contents of an Array

For many applications we need to sum the contents of an array. Program 8-10 illustrates this. The array holds monthly sales figures for each of 12 regional offices of a particular corporation. The 12 elements are summed to get the total monthly sales for the whole corporation. The data used to fill the array comes from a file.

Program 8-10

```cpp
// This program stores monthly sales figures for each of 12
// regional offices in an array and then sums them to get
// the total monthly sales figure for the entire corporation.
// The sum is used to find the average monthly sales per
// office. The data to fill the array is read in from a file.

#include <iostream>
#include <fstream>        // Needed to use files
#include <iomanip>
using namespace std;

const int numOffices = 12;

int main()
{
    ifstream dataIn;
    int office;
    double sales[numOffices];
    double totalSales = 0;
    double averageSales;

    // Fill the array with data from the file.
    dataIn.open("sales.dat");
    for (office = 0; office < numOffices; office++)
        dataIn >> sales[office];

    dataIn.close();

    // Sum all the array elements.
    for (office = 0; office < numOffices; office++)
        totalSales += sales[office];

    // Calculate average sales.
    averageSales = totalSales / numOffices;

    // Display results.
    cout << fixed << showpoint << setprecision(2);
    cout << "Total Sales: $" << totalSales << endl;
    cout << "Average Sales per office: $"  << averageSales << endl;

    return 0;
}
```

Program 8-10

Program Output
```
Total sales: $899689.00
Average sales per office: $74974.08
```

Comparing the Value of Array Elements to an Average

In Program 8-10, we used an array to demonstrate how to sum the values of all the array elements. However, this program could have been done without even using an array. The 12 values could have just been read into a simple variable and added to a sum as they were read in. This is illustrated by the following code fragment:

```
for (office = 0; office < numOffices; office++)
{   dataIn >> salesAmt;      // SalesAmt is just a double variable.
    totalSales += salesAmt;  // It is not an array.
}
```

Then why use an array at all? There are many reasons. One of the most important is that once the data is in the array it can be used more than once without having to be read in again. Program 8-11 modifies Program 8-10 so that after summing the sales amounts and finding the average, it determines which offices have below-average sales. This requires looking at the data a second time, after the average has been computed. It could not be easily done without an array.

Program 8-11

```
// This program stores monthly sales figures for each of 12
// regional offices in an array as well as sums them to get
// the total monthly sales figure for the entire corporation.
// It then calculates the average sales per office and displays
// the office numbers and sales figures for all offices performing
// below the average.
// The data to fill the array is read in from a file.

#include <iostream>
#include <fstream>        // Needed to use files
#include <iomanip>
using namespace std;

const int numOffices = 12;

int main()
{
    ifstream dataIn;
    int office;
    double sales[numOffices];
    double totalSales = 0;
    double averageSales;
```

(program continues)

Program 8-11   *(continued)*

```cpp
   // Fill the array with data from the file and sum the
   // figures as they are read in.
   dataIn.open("sales.dat");
   for (office = 0; office < numOffices; office++)
   {   dataIn >> sales[office];
       totalSales += sales[office];
   }

   dataIn.close();

   // Calculate average sales.
   averageSales = totalSales / numOffices;

   // Display total and average.
   cout << fixed << showpoint << setprecision(2);
   cout << "Total Sales: $" << totalSales << endl;
   cout << "Average Sales per office: $"  << averageSales << endl;

   // Display figures for offices performing below the average.
   cout << "The following offices have below-average "
        << "sales figures.\n";
   for (office = 0; office < numOffices; office++)
   {   if (sales[office] < averageSales)
       {   cout << "Office "     << setw(2) << office+1
                << " $" << sales[office] << endl;
       }
   }
   return 0;
}
```

Program Output
```
Total sales: $899689.00
Average sales per office: $74974.08
The following offices have below-average sales figures.
Office  1 $62458.00
Office  4 $53460.00
Office  5 $35678.00
Office 10 $43550.00
Office 11 $45679.00
```

Processing Strings

Strings are internally stored as arrays of characters. They are different from other arrays in that the elements can either be treated as a set of individual characters or can be used as a single entity. The following sample code defines a string object and treats it as a single entity, inputting it and displaying it as a single unit.

```
string name;
cout << "Enter your name: ";
cin >> name;
cout << "Hello, " << name << endl;
```

This is, in fact, how strings are normally treated and processed—as single entities. However, C++ provides the ability to index them with a subscript, like any other array, so they can be processed character by character. If "Warren" were entered for the name in the previous code segment, it would be stored in the name string object as shown in Figure 8-11.

'W'	'a'	'r'	'r'	'e'	'n'
name [0]	name [1]	name [2]	name [3]	name [4]	name [5]

Figure 8-11

 Note: Both string objects and C-strings are stored as characters in contiguous bytes of memory, as shown in Figure 8-11. C-strings are terminated by placing a '\0', which represents the null terminator, in the byte of memory following the last character of the string. Since string objects are ADTs, there is no guarantee how they will be implemented. Many versions of C++ do terminate string objects with the null terminator, just like C-strings, but it is never safe to assume they will be terminated this way.

If we wanted to process the string character by character, like a regular array, we could do so. For example the statement

```
cout << name[0];      would print the letter W,
cout << name[1];      would print the letter a, and so forth.
```

Program 8-12 illustrates character by character string processing. It reads in a string and then counts the number of vowels in the string. The string class member function length is used to determine how many characters are in the string.

Program 8-12

```
// This program illustrates how a string can be processed
// as an array of individual characters. It reads in a
// string and then counts the number of vowels in the string.
// It uses the string class member function length() to determine
// how many characters there are in the string.

#include <iostream>
#include <string>
#include <cctype>
using namespace std;
```

(program continues)

Program 8-12 *(continued)*

```cpp
int main()
{
    char ch;
    int vowelCount = 0;
    string sentence;

    cout << "Enter any sentence you wish and I will \n"
         << "tell you how many vowels are in it.\n";
    getline(cin, sentence);

    for (int pos = 0; pos < sentence.length(); pos++)
    {
        // Uppercase a copy of the next character
        // in the string and assign it to ch.
        ch = toupper(sentence[pos]);

        // If the character is a vowel, increment vowelCount.
        switch(ch)
        {   case 'A':
            case 'E':
            case 'I':
            case 'O':
            case 'U': vowelCount++;
        }
    }
    cout << "There are " << vowelCount
         << " vowels in the sentence.\n";

    return 0;
}
```

Program Output with Example Input Shown in Bold.
Enter any sentence you wish and I will
tell you how many vowels are in it.
The quick brown fox jumped over the lazy dog.[Enter]
There are 12 vowels in the sentence.

Additional examples of string processing are introduced in Chapter 12.

8.6 Using Parallel Arrays

CONCEPT By using the same subscript, you can build relationships between data stored in two or more arrays.

Sometimes it is useful to store related data in two or more arrays. It's especially useful when the related data is of different data types. We did this in Program 8-6, where the month array stored the names of the 12 months and the `days` array stored the number of days in a given month. A month name and its number of days were related by having the same subscript. For example, `days[3]` stored the number of days in `month[3]`. When data items stored in two or more arrays are related in this fashion, the arrays are called *parallel arrays*. Program 8-13, which is a variation of the payroll program, uses parallel arrays. An `int` array stores the hours worked by each employee and a `float` array stores each employee's hourly pay rate.

Program 8-13

```
// This program stores, in two arrays, the hours worked by 5
// employees, and their hourly pay rates.

#include <iostream>
#include <iomanip>
using namespace std;

const int numEmps = 5;

int main()
{   int index;
    int hours[numEmps];
    float payRate[numEmps];

    cout << "Enter the hours worked by " << numEmps << " employees ";
    cout << "and their hourly rates.\n";
    for (index = 0; index < numEmps; index++)
    {
        cout << "Hours worked by employee #" << (index + 1) << ": ";
        cin >> hours[index];
        cin >> payRate[index];
    }

    cout << "\nHere is the gross pay for each employee:\n";
    cout << fixed << showpoint << setprecision(2);
    for (index = 0; index < numEmps; index++)
    {
        float grossPay = hours[index] * payRate[index];
        cout << "Employee #" << (index + 1);
        cout << ": $" << grossPay << endl;
    }
    return 0;
}
```

Program 8-13

Program Output with Example Input Shown in Bold
Enter the hours worked by 5 employees and their hourly rates.
Hours worked by employee #1: **10[Enter]**
Hourly pay rate for employee #1: **9.75[Enter]**
Hours worked by employee #2: **15[Enter]**
Hourly pay rate for employee #2: **8.62[Enter]**
Hours worked by employee #3: **20[Enter]**
Hourly pay rate for employee #3: **10.50[Enter]**
Hours worked by employee #4: **40[Enter]**
Hourly pay rate for employee #4: **18.75[Enter]**
Hours worked by employee #5: **40[Enter]**
Hourly pay rate for employee #5: **15.65[Enter]**

Here is the gross pay for each employee:
Employee #1: $97.50
Employee #2: $129.30
Employee #3: $210.00
Employee #4: $750.00
Employee #5: $626.00

Notice in the loops the same subscript is used to access both arrays. That's because the information for one employee is stored in the same relative position in each array. For example, the hours worked by employee #1 are stored in hours[0], and the same employee's pay rate is stored in payRate[0]. The subscript relates the information in both arrays. This concept is illustrated in Figure 8-12.

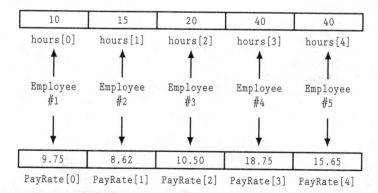

Figure 8-12

Checkpoint [8.4–8.6]

8.8 Define the following arrays:

A) `ages`, a 10-element array of `int`s initialized with the values 5, 7, 9, 14, 15, 17, 18, 19, 21, and 23

B) `temps`, a 7-element array of `float`s initialized with the values 14.7, 16.3, 18.43, 21.09, 17.9, 18.76, and 26.7

C) `alpha`, an 8-element array of `char`s initialized with the values 'J', 'B', 'L', 'A', '*', '$', 'H', and 'M'

8.9 Are each of the following valid or invalid array definitions? (If a definition is invalid, explain why.)

A) `int numbers[10] = {0, 0, 1, 0, 0, 1, 0, 0, 1, 1};`

B) `int matrix[5] = {1, 2, 3, 4, 5, 6, 7};`

C) `float radii[10] = {3.2, 4.7};`

D) `int table[7] = {2, , , 27, , 45, 39};`

E) `char codes[] = {'A', 'X', '1', '2', 's'};`

F) `int blanks[];`

G) `string suit[4] = {"Clubs", "Diamonds", "Hearts", "Spades"};`

8.10 Given the following array definition:

`int values[] = {2, 6, 10, 14};`

what do each of the following display?

A) `cout << values[2];`

B) `cout << ++values[0];`

C) `cout << values[1]++;`

D) `x = 2;`
   `cout << values[++x];`

8.11 Given the following array definition

`int nums[5] = {1, 2, 3};`

what will the following statement display?

`cout << nums[3];`

8.12 What is the output of the following program? (You may need to use a calculator.)

```
#include <iostream>
#include <iomanip>
using namespace std;
```

```
int main ()
{

    float balance[5] = {100.0, 250.0, 325.0, 500.0, 1100.0};
    const float intRate = 0.1;

    cout << fixed << showpoint << setprecision(2);
    for (int count = 0; count < 5; count++)
        cout << (balance[count] * intRate) << endl;
    return 0;
}
```

8.13 What is the output of the following program? (You may need to use a calculator.)

```
#include <iostream>
using namespace std;

int main ()
{
    int count;
    int time[5] = {1, 2, 3, 4, 5},
        speed[5] = {18, 4, 27, 52, 100},
        dist[5];

    for (count = 0; count < 5; count++)
        dist[count] = time[count] * speed[count];
    for (count = 0; count < 5; count++)
    {
        cout << time[count] << " ";
        cout << speed[count] << " ";
        cout << dist[count] << endl;
    }
    return 0;
}
```

8.7 The typedef Statement

CONCEPT	The typedef statement allows an alias to be associated with a simple or structured data type.

The typedef statement allows the programmer to create an alias, or synonym, for an existing data type. This can be a simple data type, like an int, or a structured data type such as an array. The simplest form of the statement is

```
typedef <existing data type> <alias>;
```

For example, the following statements declare examScore to be another name for an int and then define two variables of type examScore.

```
typedef int examScore;
examScore score1, score2;   // score1 and score2 are of type examScore,
                            // which means they are ints.
```

One of the most common uses of the typedef statement is to provide an alias for an array of a specific type. When used with arrays, the [] holding the array size is attached to the alias name, not to the data type name. The following statement creates an alias, named list, for a float array of size 100.

```
typedef float list[100];
```

This means that anything defined to be a list is really an array of 100 floats. The following two statements now do the same thing.

```
float score[100]; // Score is an array of 100 floats.
list score;       // Score is list, which is an array of 100 floats.
```

Sometimes it is desirable to create an alias for an array of a specific data type without specifying its size. The following statement creates an alias, named arrayType for an int array of unspecified size.

```
typedef int arrayType[];
```

In the next section, when you learn how to pass arrays as function arguments, it will become apparent why it is convenient to set up a typedef for an array type.

8.8 Arrays as Function Arguments

CONCEPT   To pass an array as an argument to a function, pass the name of the array.

Quite often you'll want to write functions that process the information in arrays. For example, functions could be written to put values in an array, display an array's contents on the screen, total all of an array's elements, or calculate their average. Usually, such functions accept an array as an argument.

When a single element of an array is passed to a function, it is handled like any other variable. For example, Program 8-14 shows a loop that passes one element of the collection array to the showValue function each time the loop is executed. Since the elements of the collection array are ints, a single int value is passed to the showValue function each time it is called. Notice how this is specified in the showValue function prototype and function header. All showValue knows is that it is receiving an int. It should not know or care that it happens to be coming from an array.

Program 8-14

```
// This program demonstrates that an array element is passed
// to a function like any other variable.
#include <iostream>
using namespace std;

const int arraySize = 8;

void showValue(int);    // Function prototype

int main()
{
    int collection[arraySize] = {5, 10, 15, 20, 25, 30, 35, 40};

    for (int cycle = 0; cycle < arraySize; cycle++)
        showValue(collection[cycle]);
    cout << endl;
    return 0;
}

//**************************************************
// Definition of function showValue                *
// This function accepts an integer argument.       *
// The value of the argument is displayed.          *
//**************************************************

void showValue(int num)
{
    cout << num << " ";
}
```

Program Output
5 10 15 20 25 30 35 40

Since the showValue function simply displays the contents of num and doesn't need to work directly with the array elements themselves, the array elements are passed to it by value. If the function needed to access the original array elements, they would be passed by reference.

If the function were written to accept the entire array as an argument, the parameter would be set up differently. In the following function definition, the parameter nums is followed by an empty set of brackets. This indicates that the argument will be an entire array, not a single value.

```
void showValues (int nums[], int size)
{
    for (int index = 0; index < size; index++)
        cout << nums[index] << " ";
    cout << endl;
}
```

Notice that along with the array containing the values the function will use, the size of the array is also passed to showValues. This is so it will know how many values there are to be processed.

You're probably wondering why there is no size declarator inside the brackets of nums. The reason is because nums is not actually an array—it's a special variable that can accept the address of an array. When an entire array is passed to a function, it is not passed by value. Imagine the CPU time and memory that would be necessary if a copy of a 10,000-element array were created each time it was passed to a function! Instead, only the starting memory address of the array is passed. Program 8-15 shows the function showValues in use.

Program 8-15

```
// This program demonstrates an entire array being passed to a function.

#include <iostream>
using namespace std;

void showValues(int [], int);    // Function prototype

const int arraySize = 8;

int main()
{
    int collection[arraySize] = {5, 10, 15, 20, 25, 30, 35, 40};

    showValues(collection, arraySize);
    return 0;
}

//***************************************************************
// Definition of function showValues                           *
// This function accepts an array of integers and its size     *
// as arguments. The contents of the array are displayed.      *
//***************************************************************

void showValues (int nums[], int size)
{
    for (int index = 0; index < size; index++)
        cout << nums[index] << " ";
    cout << endl;
}
```

Program Output
```
5 10 15 20 25 30 35 40
```

 Note: In the function prototype, empty brackets appear after the data type of the parameter. This indicates that showValues accepts the address of an array, in this case an array of integers.

If a typedef statement is used to create an alias for the array type, the function prototype and header do not need to include a [] to indicate that an array is being passed as a function argument. Program 8-16 modifies Program 8-15 to use a typedef statement.

Program 8-16

```cpp
// This program demonstrates an entire array being passed to a function.
// A typedef statement is used to create an alias for the array type.
#include <iostream>
using namespace std;

// Declare arrayType to be an alias for an array of ints.
typedef int arrayType[];

void showValues(arrayType, int);    // Function prototype

const int arraySize = 8;

int main()
{
    int collection[arraySize] = {5, 10, 15, 20, 25, 30, 35, 40};

    showValues(collection, arraySize);
    return 0;
}

//*****************************************************************
// Definition of function showValues                             *
// This function accepts an array of integers and its size       *
// as arguments. The contents of the array are displayed.        *
//*****************************************************************

void showValues (arrayType nums, int size)
{
    for (int index = 0; index < size; index++)
        cout << nums[index] << " ";
    cout << endl;
}
```

Program Output

5 10 15 20 25 30 35 40

In Programs 8-15 and 8-16, the function showValues is called in the following line:

```cpp
showValues(collection, arraySize);
```

Remember, in C++ the name of an array without brackets and a subscript is actually the address of the array. In this function call, the address of the collection array is being passed to the showValues function.

In the showValues function, the address of collection is copied into the nums parameter variable. The nums variable is then used to reference collection. (Figure 8-13 illustrates the relationship between the array collection and the parameter variable nums.) When the contents of nums[0] is displayed, it is actually the contents of collection[0] that appears on the screen. The nums parameter variable can accept the address of any integer array and can be used to reference that array.

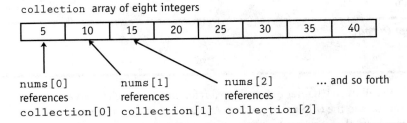

Figure 8-13

> **Note:** Although `nums` is not a reference variable, it works like one.

Program 8-17 uses the `showValues` function to display the contents of two different arrays. Notice that they do not have to be the same size.

Program 8-17

```
// This program demonstrates different arrays being passed to a function.

#include <iostream>
using namespace std;

// Declare arrayType to be an alias for an array of ints.
typedef int arrayType[];

void showValues(arrayType, int);    // Function prototype

int main()
{
    int set1[8] = {5, 10, 15, 20, 25, 30, 35, 40};
    int set2[10] = {2, 4, 6, 8, 10, 12, 14, 16, 18, 20};

    showValues(set1, 8);
    showValues(set2, 10);
    return 0;
}

//****************************************************************
// Definition of function showValues                            *
// This function accepts an array of integers and its size      *
// as arguments. The contents of the array are displayed.       *
//****************************************************************

void showValues (arrayType nums, int size)
{
    for (int index = 0; index < size; index++)
        cout << nums[index] << " ";
    cout << endl;
}
```

Program 8-17

Program Output
```
5 10 15 20 25 30 35 40
2 4 6 8 10 12 14 16 18 20
```

Recall from Chapter 6 that when a reference variable is used as a parameter, it gives the function access to the original argument. Any changes made to the reference variable are actually performed on the argument referenced by the variable. Array parameters work very much like reference variables. They give the function direct access to the original array. Any changes made with the array parameter are actually made on the original array used as the argument. The function `doubleArray` in Program 8-18 uses this capability to double the contents of each element in the array.

Program 8-18

```cpp
// This program uses a function that doubles the contents of
// each element within an array.

#include <iostream>
using namespace std;

typedef int arrayType[];

void doubleArray(arrayType, int);        // Function prototype

const int arraySize = 12;

int main()
{
    int index;
    arrayType set = {1, 2, 3, 4, 5, 6, 7, 8, 9, 10, 11, 12};

    cout << "The arrays values are:\n";
    for (index = 0; index < arraySize; index++)
        cout << set[index] << " ";
    cout << endl;

    doubleArray(set, arraySize);

    cout << "\nAfter calling doubleArray, the values are:\n";
    for (index = 0; index < arraySize; index++)
        cout << set[index] << " ";
    cout << endl;
    return 0;
}
```

(program continues)

Program 8-18 *(continued)*

```
//*****************************************************
// Definition of function doubleArray               *
// This function doubles the value of each element   *
// in the array passed into nums.                    *
//*****************************************************
void doubleArray(arrayType nums, int size)
{
    for (int index = 0; index < size; index++)
        nums[index] *= 2;
}
```

Program Output

```
The array values are:
1 2 3 4 5 6 7 8 9 10 11 12

After calling doubleArray, the values are:
2 4 6 8 10 12 14 16 18 20 22 24
```

Notice in Program 8-18 that the set array was defined to be type arrayType rather than int set[arraySize], though we could have defined it that way. We could do this because the array was initialized with an initialization list at the time of its creation. This means, as you recall, it did not have to have a size declarator.

 WARNING! Like reference variables, array parameters require responsibility. It's important to realize that when an array is passed as an argument, the function has the capability of modifying the original data in the array.

 Checkpoint   [8.7–8.8]

8.14   Given the following array definitions

```
float array1[4] = {1.2, 3.2, 4.2, 5.2};
float array2[4];
```

will the following statement work? If not, why?

```
array2 = array1;
```

8.15   When an array name is passed to a function, what is actually being passed?

8.16   When used as function arguments, are arrays passed by value?

8.17   What is the output of the following program? (You may need to consult the ASCII table in Appendix A.)

```
#include <iostream>
using namespace std;

// Function prototypes
void fillArray(char [], int)
void showArray(char [], int)
```

```
int main ()
{
    char prodCode[8] = {'0', '0', '0', '0', '0', '0', '0', '0'};

    fillArray(prodCode,8);
    showArray(prodCode,8);
    return 0;
}

// Definition of function fillArray
// (Hint: 65 is the ASCII code for 'A'.)
void fillArray(char arr[], int size)
{
    char code = 65;
    for (int k = 0; k < size; code++, k++)
        arr[k] = code;
}

// Definition of function showArray
void showArray(char codes[], int size)
{
    for (int k = 0; k < size; k++)
        cout << codes[k];
}
```

8.18 The following program skeleton, when completed, will ask the user to enter 10 integers which are stored in an array. The function avgArray, which you must write, is to calculate and return the average of the numbers entered.

```
#include <iostream>
using namespace std;

// Write your function prototype here.

int main ()
{
    int userNums[10];

    cout << "Enter 10 numbers: ";
    for (int count = 0; count < 10; count++)
    {
        cout << "#" << (count + 1) << " ";
        cin >> userNums[count];
    }
    cout << "The average of those numbers is ";
    cout << avgArray(userNums, 10) << endl;
    return 0;
}

//
// Write the function avgArray here.
//
```

8.9 Two-Dimensional Arrays

CONCEPT	A two-dimensional array is like several identical arrays put together. It is useful for storing multiple sets of data.

An array is useful for storing and working with a set of information. Sometimes, though, it's necessary to work with multiple sets of information. For example, in a grade-averaging program a teacher might record all of one student's test scores in an array of `floats`. If the teacher has 30 students, that means she'll need 30 arrays of `floats` to record the scores for the entire class. Instead of defining 30 individual arrays, however, it would be better to define a two-dimensional (2D) array.

Two-dimensional arrays can hold multiple sets of values. It's best to think of a two-dimensional array as a table having rows and columns of elements, as shown in Figure 8-14. This figure shows an array of test scores that has three rows and four columns.

	Column 0	Column 1	Column 2	Column 3
Row 0	score[0] [0]	score[0] [1]	score[0] [2]	score[0] [3]
Row 1	score[1] [0]	score[1] [1]	score[1] [2]	score[1] [3]
Row 2	score[2] [0]	score[2] [1]	score[2] [2]	score[2] [3]

Figure 8-14

Notice that the three rows are numbered 0 through 2 and the four columns are numbered 0 through 3. There are a total of 12 elements in the array.

To define a two-dimensional array, two size declarators are required: the first one is for the number of rows and the second one is for the number of columns. Here is an example definition of a two-dimensional array with three rows and four columns:

```
float score[3][4];
```
Rows   Columns

Notice that each number is enclosed in its own set of brackets.

For processing the information in a two-dimensional array, each element has two subscripts: one for its row and another for its column. In the `score` array, the elements in row 0 are referenced as

```
score[0][0]
score[0][1]
score[0][2]
score[0][3]
```

The elements in row 1 are

```
score[1][0]
score[1][1]
score[1][2]
score[1][3]
```

And the elements in row 2 are

```
score[2][0]
score[2][1]
score[2][2]
score[2][3]
```

The subscripted references are used in a program just like the references to elements in a one-dimensional array. For example, the following statement assigns the value 92.25 to the element at row 2, column 1 of the score array:

```
score[2][1] = 92.25;
```

And the following statement displays the element at row 0, column 2:

```
cout << score[0][2];
```

Programs that cycle through each element of a two-dimensional array usually do so with nested loops. Program 8-19 shows an example.

Program 8-19

```
// This program demonstrates a two-dimensional array.

#include <iostream>
#include <iomanip>
using namespace std;

int main()
{
    float sales[3][4];         // 2D array with 3 rows and 4 columns.
    float totalSales = 0;      // Used to accumulate the total sales.
    int div, qtr;              // Loop counters.

    cout << "This program will calculate the total sales of\n";
    cout << "all the company's divisions.\n";
    cout << "Enter the following sales information:\n\n";
```

(program continues)

Program 8-19 *(continued)*

```
    // Nested loops are used to fill the array with
    // quarterly sales figures for each division.
    for (div = 0; div < 3; div++)
    {   for (qtr = 0; qtr < 4; qtr++)
        {
            cout << "Division " << (div + 1);
            cout << ", Quarter " << (qtr + 1) << ": $";
            cin >> sales[div][qtr];
        }
        cout << endl; // Print blank line.
    }

    // Nested loops are used to add all the elements.
    for (div = 0; div < 3; div++)
    {   for (qtr = 0; qtr < 4; qtr++)
            totalSales += sales[div][qtr];
    }

    cout << fixed << showpoint << setprecision(2);
    cout << "The total sales for the company are: $";
    cout << totalSales << endl;
    return 0;
}
```

Program Output with Example Input Shown in Bold
This program will calculate the total sales of
all the company's divisions.
Enter the following sales information:

Division 1, Quarter 1: $**31569.45[Enter]**
Division 1, Quarter 2: $**29654.23[Enter]**
Division 1, Quarter 3: $**32982.54[Enter]**
Division 1, Quarter 4: $**39651.21[Enter]**

Division 2, Quarter 1: $**56321.02[Enter]**
Division 2, Quarter 2: $**54128.63[Enter]**
Division 2, Quarter 3: $**41235.85[Enter]**
Division 2, Quarter 4: $**54652.33[Enter]**

Division 3, Quarter 1: $**29654.35[Enter]**
Division 3, Quarter 2: $**28963.32[Enter]**
Division 3, Quarter 3: $**25353.55[Enter]**
Division 3, Quarter 4: $**32615.88[Enter]**

The total sales for the company are: $456782.34

As with one-dimensional arrays, two-dimensional arrays can be initialized when they are created. When initializing a two-dimensional array, it helps to enclose each row's initialization list in a set of braces. Here is an example:

```
int hours[3][2] = {{8, 5}, {7, 9}, {6, 3}};
```

The same statement could also be written as

```
int hours[3][2] = {{8, 5},
                    {7, 9},
                    {6, 3}};
```

In either case, the values are assigned to hours in the following manner:

```
hours[0][0] is set to 8
hours[0][1] is set to 5
hours[1][0] is set to 7
hours[1][1] is set to 9
hours[2][0] is set to 6
hours[2][1] is set to 3
```

Figure 8-15 illustrates the initialization.

	Column 0	Column 1
Row 0	8	5
Row 1	7	9
Row 2	6	3

Figure 8-15

The extra braces that enclose each row's initialization list are optional. Both of the following statements perform the same initialization:

```
int hours[3][2] = {{8, 5}, {7, 9}, {6, 3}};
int hours[3][2] = {8, 5, 7, 9, 6, 3};
```

Since the extra braces visually separate each row, however, it's a good idea to use them. In addition, the braces give you the ability to leave out initializers within a row without omitting the initializers for the rows that follow it. For instance, look at the following array definition:

```
int table[3][2] = {{1}, {3, 4}, {5}};
```

table[0][0] is initialized to 1, table[1][0] is initialized to 3, table[1][1] is initialized to 4, and table[2][0] is initialized to 5. The uninitialized elements (in this case table[0][1] and table[2][1]) are automatically set to zero.

Passing Two-Dimensional Arrays to Functions

Program 8-20 illustrates how to pass a two-dimensional array to a function. When a two-dimensional array is passed to a function, the parameter type must contain a size declarator for the number of columns. Here is the header for the function showArray, from Program 8-20:

```
void showArray(int array[][4], int numRows)
```

The function can accept any two-dimensional integer array, as long as it has four columns. In Program 8-20, the contents of two separate arrays are displayed by the function.

Program 8-20

```
// This program demonstrates a function that accepts a
// two-dimensional array as an argument.

#include <iostream>
#include <iomanip>
using namespace std;

void showArray(int [][4], int); // Function prototype

int main()
{
    int table1[3][4] = {{1,  2,  3,  4},
                        {5,  6,  7,  8},
                        {9, 10, 11, 12}};

    int table2[4][4] = {{ 10,  20,  30,  40},
                        { 50,  60,  70,  80},
                        { 90, 100, 110, 120},
                        {130, 140, 150, 160}};

    cout << "The contents of table1 are:\n";
    showArray(table1, 3);
    cout << "\nThe contents of table2 are:\n";
    showArray(table2, 4);
    return 0;
}

//*****************************************************************
// Function definition for showArray                             *
// This function accepts two arguments.  The first is a two-     *
// dimensional integer array, which can have any number of rows, *
// but which must have four columns. The second argument specifies*
// the number of rows in the array currently being passed in.    *
// The function displays the contents of the array.              *
//*****************************************************************
void showArray(int array[][4], int numRows)
{
    for (int row = 0; row < numRows; row++)
    {   for (int col = 0; col < 4; col++)
        {
            cout << setw(5) << array[row][col] << " ";
        }
        cout << endl;
    }
}
```

Program 8-20

Program Output
```
The contents of table1 are:
    1    2    3    4
    5    6    7    8
    9   10   11   12

The contents of table2 are:
   10   20   30   40
   50   60   70   80
   90  100  110  120
  130  140  150  160
```

C++ requires the columns to be specified in the function prototype and header because of the way two-dimensional arrays are stored in memory. One row follows another, as shown in Figure 8-16.

Figure 8-16

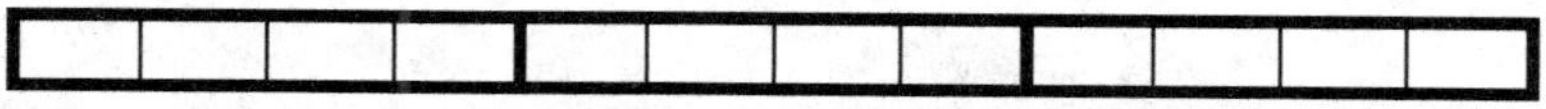

When the compiler generates code for accessing the elements of a two-dimensional array, it needs to know how many bytes separate the rows in memory. The number of columns is a critical factor in this calculation.

The parameter list in the function prototype and the function header can be simplified, however, by using a typedef statement to provide an alias for the array type. Program 8-21 modifies Program 8-20 to use a typedef statement. The alias established by the typedef statement can be used in the definition of the two arrays also, since the number of rows can be determined from their initialization lists.

Program 8-21

```cpp
// This program demonstrates a function that accepts a
// two-dimensional array as an argument.  A typedef statement
// is used to create an alias for the array type.

#include <iostream>
#include <iomanip>
using namespace std;

typedef int intTable[][4];

void showArray(intTable, int); // Function prototype
```

(program continues)

Program 8-21 *(continued)*

```
int main()
{
    intTable table1 =    {{1,   2,   3,   4},
                          {5,   6,   7,   8},
                          {9,  10,  11,  12}};

    intTable table2 =    {{ 10,  20,   30,   40},
                          { 50,  60,   70,   80},
                          { 90, 100,  110,  120},
                          {130, 140,  150,  160}};

    cout << "The contents of table1 are:\n";
    showArray(table1, 3);
    cout << "\nThe contents of table2 are:\n";
    showArray(table2, 4);
    return 0;
}

//********************************************************************
// Function definition for showArray                                *
// This function accepts two arguments.  The first is a two-        *
// dimensional integer array, which can have any number of rows,    *
// but which must have four columns. The second argument specifies  *
// the number of rows in the array currently being passed in.       *
// The function displays the contents of the array.                 *
//********************************************************************
void showArray(intTable array, int numRows)
{
    for (int row = 0; row < numRows; row++)
    {   for (int col = 0; col < 4; col++)
        {
            cout << setw(5) << array[row][col] << " ";
        }
        cout << endl;
    }
}
```

Program Output is the same as for Program 8-20.

Three-Dimensional Arrays and Beyond

C++ allows you to create arrays with virtually any number of dimensions. Here is an example of a three-dimensional (3D) array definition:

```
float seat[3][5][8];
```

This array can be thought of as three sets of five rows, with each row containing eight elements. This array might be used, for example, to store the price of seats in an auditorium that has three sections of seats, with five rows of eight seats in each section.

Figure 8-17 illustrates the concept of a three-dimensional array as "pages" of two-dimensional arrays.

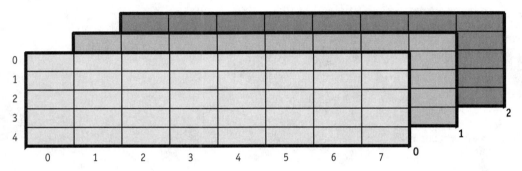

Figure 8-17

Arrays with more than three dimensions are difficult to visualize but can be useful in some programming problems. For example, in a factory warehouse where cases of widgets are stacked on pallets, an array with four dimensions could be used to store a part number for each widget. The four subscripts of each element could represent the pallet number, case number, row number, and column number of each widget. Similarly, an array with five dimensions could be used if there were multiple warehouses.

When writing functions that accept multidimensional arrays as arguments, you must explicitly state all but the first dimension in the parameter list. If the `seat` array, defined here, were passed to a `displaySeats` function, its prototype and function header might look like the following:

```
// Function prototype
void displaySeats(float [][5][8], int);

// Function header
void displaySeats(float array[][5][8], int numGroups);
```

As with one-dimensional and two-dimensional arrays, the parameter lists can be simplified if a `typedef` statement is used to create an alias for the array type. This is demonstrated in Program 8-22, which uses the `seat` array to store theater seat prices. The information to populate the array is read in from a file. The information on number of sections, number of rows in a section, and number of seats in a row is stored in global constants, rather than being passed to the functions.

Program 8-22

```cpp
// This program stores and displays theater seat prices.
// It demonstrates using functions that accept a 3-dimensional
// array as an argument. The data is read in from a file.

#include <iostream>
#include <fstream>
#include <iomanip>
using namespace std;

const int numSections = 3;
const int rowsInSection = 5;
const int seatsInRow = 8;

typedef float seatTable[][rowsInSection][seatsInRow];

// Function prototypes
void fillArray(seatTable);
void showArray(seatTable);

int main()
{
    float seats[3][5][8];    // Holds seat prices.

    fillArray(seats);
    showArray(seats);
    return 0;
}

//****************************************************************
// Function definition for fillArray                            *
// This function accepts a three-dimensional array as an argument *
// and fills the array with data from a file.                   *
//****************************************************************
void fillArray(seatTable array)
{
    ifstream dataIn;
    dataIn.open("seats.dat");
    for (int section = 0; section < numSections; section++)
    {   for (int row = 0; row < rowsInSection; row++)
            for (int seat = 0; seat < seatsInRow; seat++)
                dataIn >> array[section][row][seat];
    }
    dataIn.close();
}
```

(program continues)

Program 8-22 *(continued)*

```
//**********************************************************************
// Function definition for showArray                                   *
// This function accepts a three-dimensional array as an argument      *
// and displays the contents of the array.                             *
//**********************************************************************
void showArray(seatTable array)
{
    cout << fixed << showpoint << setprecision(2);

    for (int section = 0; section < numSections; section++)
    {
        cout << "\n\nSection" << (section+1);
        for (int row = 0; row < rowsInSection; row++)
        {
            cout << "\nRow " << (row+1) << ": ";
            for (int seat = 0; seat < seatsInRow; seat++)
                cout << setw(7) << array[section][row][seat];
        }
    }
    cout << endl;
}
```

Program Output

```
Section1
Row 1:   18.00   18.00   18.00   18.00   18.00   18.00   18.00   18.00
Row 2:   15.00   15.00   15.00   15.00   15.00   15.00   15.00   15.00
Row 3:   15.00   15.00   15.00   15.00   15.00   15.00   15.00   15.00
Row 4:   15.00   15.00   15.00   15.00   15.00   15.00   15.00   15.00
Row 5:   12.00   12.00   12.00   12.00   12.00   12.00   12.00   12.00

Section2
Row 1:   12.00   12.00   12.00   12.00   12.00   12.00   12.00   12.00
Row 2:   12.00   12.00   12.00   12.00   12.00   12.00   12.00   12.00
Row 3:   12.00   12.00   12.00   12.00   12.00   12.00   12.00   12.00
Row 4:   10.00   10.00   10.00   10.00   10.00   10.00   10.00   10.00
Row 5:   10.00   10.00   10.00   10.00   10.00   10.00   10.00   10.00

Section3
Row 1:   10.00   10.00   10.00   10.00   10.00   10.00   10.00   10.00
Row 2:   10.00   10.00   10.00   10.00   10.00   10.00   10.00   10.00
Row 3:    8.00    8.00    8.00    8.00    8.00    8.00    8.00    8.00
Row 4:    8.00    8.00    8.00    8.00    8.00    8.00    8.00    8.00
Row 5:    8.00    8.00    8.00    8.00    8.00    8.00    8.00    8.00
```

Checkpoint [8.9]

8.19 Define a two-dimensional array of `ints` named `grades`. It should have 30 rows and 10 columns.

8.20 How many elements are in the following array?

```
float sales[6][4];
```

8.21 Write a statement that assigns the value 56893.12 to the first column of the first row of the array defined in question 8.20.

8.22 Write a statement that displays the contents of the last column of the last row of the array defined in question 8.20.

8.23 Define a two-dimensional array named `settings` large enough to hold the table of information below. Initialize the array with the values in the table.

12	24	32	21	42
14	67	87	65	90
19	1	24	12	8

8.24 Fill in the table so it shows the contents of the following array:

```
int table[3][4] = {{2, 3}, {7, 9, 2}, {1}};
```


8.25 Write a function called `displayArray7`. The function should accept a two-dimensional array as an argument and display its contents on the screen. The function should work with any of the following arrays:

```
int hours[5][7];
int stamps[8][7];
int autos[12][7];
int cats[50][7];
```

8.26 A DVD rental store keeps DVDs on 50 racks with 10 shelves each. Each shelf holds 25 DVDs. Define a three-dimensional array large enough to represent the store's storage system.

8.10   Vectors (enrichment)

CONCEPT   The Standard Template Library offers a `vector` data type, which in many ways is superior to standard arrays.

The *Standard Template Library* (STL) is a collection of data types and algorithms that you may use in your programs. These data types and algorithms are *programmer-defined*. They are not part of the C++ language but were created in addition to the built-in data types. If you plan to continue your studies in the field of computer science, you should become familiar with the STL. This section introduces one of the STL data types. For more information on the STL, see Chapter 15.

 Note: To use vectors your program header must indicate that you are using `namespace std`, since vectors are contained within that namespace. Many older compilers do not allow namespaces or support the STL.

The data types that are defined in the STL are commonly called *containers*. They are called containers because they store and organize data. There are two types of containers in the STL: *sequence containers* and *associative containers*. A *sequence container* organizes data in a sequential fashion, similar to an array. *Associative containers* organize data with keys, which allow rapid, random access to elements stored in the container.

In this section you will learn to use the `vector` data type, which is a sequence container. A vector is like an array in the following ways:

◆ A vector holds a sequence of values, or elements.

◆ A vector stores its elements in contiguous memory locations.

◆ You can use the array subscript operator `[]` to read the individual elements in the vector.

However, a vector offers several advantages over arrays. Here are just a few:

◆ You do not have to declare the number of elements that the vector will have.

◆ If you add a value to a vector that is already full, the vector will automatically increase its size to accommodate the new value.

◆ Vectors can report the number of elements they contain.

Declaring a Vector

To use vectors in your program, you must first include the `vector` header file with the following statement:

```
#include <vector>
```

The syntax for defining a vector object is somewhat different from the syntax used in defining a regular variable or array. Here is an example:

```
vector<int> numbers;
```

This statement defines `numbers` as a vector of `int`s. Notice that the data type is enclosed in angled brackets, immediately after the word `vector`. Since the vector expands in size as you add values to it, there is no need to declare a size. You can declare a starting size, if you prefer. Here is an example:

```
vector<int> numbers(10);
```

This statement defines `numbers` as a vector of 10 `int`s. This is only a starting size, however. Although the vector has 10 elements, its size will expand if you add more than 10 values to it.

 Note: If you specify a starting size for a vector, the size declarator is enclosed in parentheses, not square brackets.

When you specify a starting size for a vector, you may also specify an initialization value. The initialization value is copied to each element. Here is an example:

```
vector<int> numbers(10, 2);
```

In this statement, `numbers` is defined as a vector of 10 `int`s. Each element in `numbers` is initialized to the value 2.

You may also initialize a vector with the values in another vector. For example, look at the following statement. Assume that `set1` is a vector of `int`s that already has values stored in it.

```
vector<int> set2(set1);
```

After this statement executes, the vector `set2` will be a copy of the vector `set1`.

Table 8-2 summarizes the vector definition procedures we have discussed.

Table 8-2

Declaration Format	Description
`vector<float> amounts;`	Defines `amounts` as an empty vector of `float`s.
`vector<int> scores(15);`	Defines `scores` as a vector of 15 `int`s.
`vector<char> letters(25, 'A');`	Defines `letters` as a vector of 25 characters. Each element is initialized with 'A'.
`vector<double> values2(values1);`	Defines `values2` as a vector of `double`s. All the elements of `values1`, which is also a vector of `double`s, are copied to `value2`.

Storing and Retrieving Values in a Vector

To store a value in an element that already exists in a vector, you may use the array subscript operator []. Program 8-23, which is a modification of Program 8-13, illustrates this.

Program 8-23

```cpp
// This program stores, in two vectors, the hours worked by 5
// employees, and their hourly pay rates.

#include <iostream>
#include <iomanip>
#include <vector>                // Needed to declare vectors
using namespace std;

int main()
{
    vector<int> hours(5);        // Declare a vector of 5 integers
    vector<float> payRate(5);    // Declare a vector of 5 floats
    int index;

    cout << "Enter the hours worked by 5 employees and their "
         << "hourly rates.\n";
    for (index = 0; index < 5; index++)
    {
        cout << "Hours worked by employee #" << (index + 1);
        cout << ": ";
        cin >> hours[index];
        cout << "Hourly pay rate for employee #";
        cout << (index + 1) << ": ";
        cin >> payRate[index];
    }
    cout << "\nHere is the gross pay for each employee:\n";
    cout << fixed << showpoint << setprecision(2);
    for (index = 0; index < 5; index++)
    {
        float grossPay = hours[index] * payRate[index];
        cout << "Employee #" << (index + 1);
        cout << ": $" << grossPay << endl;
    }
    return 0;
}
```

Program 8-23

Program Output with Example Input Shown in Bold
```
Enter the hours worked by 5 employees and their hourly rates.
Hours worked by employee #1: 10[Enter]
Hourly pay rate for employee #1: 9.75[Enter]
Hours worked by employee #2: 15[Enter]
Hourly pay rate for employee #2: 8.62[Enter]
Hours worked by employee #3: 20[Enter]
Hourly pay rate for employee #3: 10.50[Enter]
Hours worked by employee #4: 40[Enter]
Hourly pay rate for employee #4: 18.75[Enter]
Hours worked by employee #5: 40[Enter]
Hourly pay rate for employee #5: 15.65[Enter]

Here is the gross pay for each employee:
Employee #1: $97.50
Employee #2: $129.30
Employee #3: $210.00
Employee #4: $750.00
Employee #5: $626.00
```

Notice that Program 8-23 uses the following statements to define two vectors:

```
vector<int> hours(5);        // Define a vector of 5 ints
vector<float> payRate(5);    // Define a vector of 5 floats
```

Both of the vectors are defined with a starting size: 5. The program uses the following loop to store a value in each element of both vectors:

```
for (index = 0; index < 5; index++)
{
    cout << "Hours worked by employee #" << (index + 1);
    cout << ": ";
    cin >> hours[index];
    cout << "Hourly pay rate for employee #";
    cout << (index + 1) << ": ";
    cin >> payRate[index];
}
```

Because the values entered by the user are being stored in vector elements that already exist, the program uses the array subscript operator [], as shown in the following statements:

```
cin >> hours[index];
cin >> payRate[index];
```

Using the push_back **Member Function**

You cannot, however, use the [] operator to access a vector element that does not exist. To store a value in a vector that does not have a starting size, or that is already full, use the push_back member function. The push_back member function accepts a value as an argument, and stores that value after the last element in the vector. (It pushes the value onto the back of the vector.) Here is an example:

```
numbers.push_back(25);
```

Assuming numbers is a vector of ints, this statement stores 25 as the last element. If numbers is full, the statement creates a new, last element and stores 25 in it. If there are no elements in num-bers, this statement creates an element and stores 25 in it.

Program 8-24 is a modification of Program 8-23. This version, however, allows the user to specify the number of employees. The two vectors, hours and payRate, are defined without start-ing sizes. Since these vectors have no starting elements, the push_back member function is used to store values in the vectors.

Program 8-24

```
// This program stores, in two vectors, the hours worked by a
// specified number of employees, and their hourly pay rates.

#include <iostream>
#include <iomanip>
#include <vector>                    // Needed to declare vectors
using namespace std;

int main()
{
    vector<int> hours;              // hours is an empty vector
    vector<float> payRate;          // payRate is an empty vector
    int numEmployees;               // The number of employees
    int index;

    cout << "How many employees do you have? ";
    cin >> numEmployees;
    cout << "Enter the hours worked by " << numEmployees;
    cout << " employees and their hourly rates.\n";
    for (index = 0; index < numEmployees; index++)
    {
        int tempHours;              // To hold the number of hours entered
        float tempRate;            // To hold the pay rate entered
```

(program continues)

Program 8-24   *(continued)*

```
            cout << "Hours worked by employee #" << (index + 1);
            cout << ": ";
            cin >> tempHours;
            hours.push_back(tempHours);     // Add an element to hours
            cout << "Hourly pay rate for employee #";
            cout << (index + 1) << ": ";
            cin >> tempRate;
            payRate.push_back(tempRate);    // Add an element to payRate
        }
        cout << "\nHere is the gross pay for each employee:\n";
        cout << fixed << showpoint << setprecision(2);
        for (index = 0; index < numEmployees; index++)
        {
            float grossPay = hours[index] * payRate[index];
            cout << "Employee #" << (index + 1);
            cout << ": $" << grossPay << endl;
        }
        return 0;
    }
```

Program Output with Example Input Shown in Bold
```
How many employees do you have? 3[Enter]
Enter the hours worked by 3 employees and their hourly rates.
Hours worked by employee #1: 40[Enter]
Hourly pay rate for employee #1: 12.63[Enter]
Hours worked by employee #2: 25[Enter]
Hourly pay rate for employee #2: 10.35[Enter]
Hours worked by employee #3: 45[Enter]
Hourly pay rate for employee #3: 22.65[Enter]

Here is the gross pay for each employee:
Employee #1: $505.20
Employee #2: $258.75
Employee #3: $1019.25
```

Notice that in Program 8-24 the second loop, which calculates and displays each employee's gross pay, uses the [] operator to access the elements of the hours and payRate vectors:

```
for (index = 0; index < numEmployees; index++)
{
    float grossPay = hours[index] * payRate[index];
    cout << "Employee #" << (index + 1);
    cout << ": $" << grossPay << endl;
}
```

This is possible because the first loop uses the push_back member function to create the elements in the two vectors.

Determining the Size of a Vector

Unlike arrays, vectors can report the number of elements they contain. This is accomplished with the `size` member function. Here is an example of a statement that uses the `size` member function:

```
numValues = set.size();
```

In this statement, assume that `numValues` is an `int` and `set` is a vector. After the statement executes, `numValues` will contain the number of elements in the vector `set`.

The `size` member function is especially useful when you are writing functions that accept vectors as arguments. For example, look at this `showValues` function:

```
void showValues(vector<int> vect)
{
    for (int count = 0; count < vect.size(); count++)
        cout << vect[count] << endl;
}
```

Because the vector can report its size, this function does not need to accept a second argument indicating the number of elements in the vector. Program 8-25 demonstrates this function.

Program 8-25

```
// This program demonstrates the vector size member function.

#include <iostream>
#include <vector>
using namespace std;

// Function prototype
void showValues(vector<int>);

int main()
{
    vector<int> values;

    for (int count = 0; count < 7; count++)
        values.push_back(count * 2);
    showValues(values);

    return 0;
}

//*************************************************
// Definition of function showValues              *
// This function accepts an int vector as its     *
// argument. The value of each of the vector's    *
// elements is displayed.                         *
//*************************************************
```

(program continues)

Program 8-25 *(continued)*

```
void showValues(vector<int> vect)
{
    for (int count = 0; count < vect.size(); count++)
        cout << vect[count] << endl;
}
```

Program Output

```
0
2
4
6
8
10
12
```

Removing Elements from a Vector

Use the `pop_back` member function to remove the last element from a vector. In this example, assume that `collection` is the name of a vector.

```
collection.pop_back();
```

This statement removes the last element from the `collection` vector. Program 8-26 demonstrates the function.

Program 8-26

```
// This program demonstrates the vector size, push_back,
// and pop_back member functions.

#include <iostream>
#include <vector>
using namespace std;

int main()
{
    vector<int> values;

    // Store values in the vector
    values.push_back(1);
    values.push_back(2);
    values.push_back(3);
    cout << "The size of values is " << values.size() << endl;
```

(program continues)

Program 8-26 *(continued)*

```cpp
    // Remove a value from the vector
    cout << "Popping a value from the vector...\n";
    values.pop_back();
    cout << "The size of values is now " << values.size() << endl;

    // Now remove another value from the vector
    cout << "Popping a value from the vector...\n";
    values.pop_back();
    cout << "The size of values is now " << values.size() << endl;

    // Remove the last value from the vector
    cout << "Popping a value from the vector...\n";
    values.pop_back();
    cout << "The size of values is now " << values.size() << endl;

    return 0;
}
```

Program Output
```
The size of values is 3
Popping a value from the vector...
The size of values is now 2
Popping a value from the vector...
The size of values is now 1
Popping a value from the vector...
The size of values is now 0
```

Clearing a Vector

To completely clear the contents of a vector, use the `clear` member function, as shown in this example:

```cpp
    numbers.clear();
```

After the statement executes, the `numbers` vector will be cleared of all its elements. Program 8-27 demonstrates the function.

Program 8-27

```cpp
// This program demonstrates the vector clear member function.

#include <iostream>
#include <vector>
using namespace std;
```

(program continues)

Program 8-27   *(continued)*

```cpp
int main()
{
    vector<int> values(100);

    cout << "The values vector has "
        << values.size() << " elements.\n";

    cout << "I will call the clear member function...\n";
    values.clear();
    cout << "Now the values vector has "
        << values.size() << " elements.\n";

    return 0;
}
```

Program Output
```
The values vector has 100 elements.
I will call the clear member function...
Now the values vector has 0 elements.
```

Detecting an Empty Vector

To determine if a vector is empty, use the `empty` member function. The function returns `true` if the vector is empty, and `false` if the vector has elements stored in it. Assuming `set` is a vector, here is an example of its use:

```cpp
if (set.empty())
    cout << "No values in set.\n";
```

Program 8-28 uses a function named `avgVector`, which demonstrates the `empty` member function.

Program 8-28

```cpp
// This program demonstrates the vector's empty member function.

#include <iostream>
#include <vector>
using namespace std;

// Function prototype
float avgVector(vector<int>);
```

(program continues)

Program 8-28   *(continued)*

```cpp
int main()
{
    vector<int> values;
    int numValues;
    float average;

    cout << "How many values do you wish to average? ";
    cin >> numValues;
    for (int count = 0; count < numValues; count++)
    {
        int tempValue;

        cout << "Enter a value: ";
        cin >> tempValue;
        values.push_back(tempValue);
    }
    average = avgVector(values);
    cout << "Average: " << average << endl;

    return 0;
}

//***********************************************************
// Definition of function avgVector                        *
// This function accepts an int vector as its argument. If *
// the vector contains values, the function returns the    *
// average of those values. Otherwise, an error message is *
// displayed and the function returns 0.0.                 *
//***********************************************************

float avgVector(vector<int> vect)
{
    float total = 0.0;   // accumulator
    float avg;           // average

    if (vect.empty())    // Determine if the vector is empty.
    {
        cout << "No values to average.\n";
        avg = 0.0;
    }
    else
    {
        for (int count = 0; count < vect.size(); count++)
            total += vect[count];
        avg = total / vect.size();
    }
    return avg;
}
```

Program 8-28

Program Output with Example Input Shown in Bold
```
How many values do you wish to average? 5[Enter]
Enter a value: 12[Enter]
Enter a value: 18[Enter]
Enter a value: 3[Enter]
Enter a value: 7[Enter]
Enter a value: 9[Enter]
Average: 9.8
```

Program Output with Different Example Input Shown in Bold
```
How many values do you wish to average? 0[Enter]
No values to average.
Average: 0
```

Summary of Vector Member Functions

Table 8-3 provides a summary of the `vector` member functions we have discussed, as well as some additional ones.

Table 8-3

Member Function	Description
`at(element)`	Returns the value of the element located at *element* in the vector. *Example:* `x = vect.at(5);` assigns the value of the fifth element of `vect` to `x`.
`capacity()`	Returns the maximum number of elements that may be stored in the vector without additional memory being allocated. (This is not the same value as returned by the `size` member function). *Example:* `x = vect.capacity();` assigns the capacity of `vect` to `x`.
`clear()`	Clears a vector of all its elements. *Example:* `vect.clear();` removes all the elements from `vect`.

`empty()`	Returns `true` if the vector is empty. Otherwise, it returns `false`.
	 Example:
	 `if (vect.empty())`
	     `cout << "The vector is empty.";`
	 displays the message if `vect` is empty.

(table continues)

Table 8-3   *(continued)*

Member Function	Description
pop_back()	Removes the last element from the vector. *Example:* vect.pop_back(); removes the last element of vect, thus reducing its size by 1.
push_back(*value*)	Stores a value in the last element of the vector. If the vector is full or empty, a new element is created. *Example:* vect.push_back(7); stores 7 in the last element of vect.
reverse()	Reverses the order of the elements in the vector (the last element becomes the first element, and the first element becomes the last element.) *Example:* vect.reverse(); reverses the order of the element in vect.
resize(*elements*, *value*)	Resizes a vector by *elements* elements. Each of the new elements is initialized with the value in *value*. *Example:* vect.resize(5, 1); increases the size of vect by five elements. The five new elements are initialized to the value 1.
swap(*vector2*)	Swaps the contents of the vector with the contents of *vector2*. *Example:* vect1.swap(vect2); swaps the contents of vect1 and vect2.

Checkpoint [8.10]

8.27   What header file must you #include in order to declare vector objects?

8.28   Write definition statements for the following three vector objects:
frogs (an empty vector of ints), lizards (a vector of 20 floats), and
toads (a vector of 100 chars, with each element initialized to 'Z').

8.29   Assume gators is an empty vector of ints and snakes is a 10-element vector of doubles.
Write a statement that stores the value 27 in gators and a statement that stores the value
12.897 in element 4 of snakes.

8.11   Focus on Problem Solving and Program Design: A Case Study

The National Commerce Bank has hired you as a contract programmer. Your first assignment is to write a function that will be used by the bank's automated teller machines (ATMs) to validate a customer's personal identification number (PIN).

Your function will be incorporated into a larger program that asks the customer to input his or her PIN on the ATM's numeric keypad. (PINs are seven-digit numbers. The program stores each digit in an element of a `short` array.) The program also retrieves a copy of the customer's actual PIN from a database. (The PINs are also stored in the database as seven-element arrays.) If these two numbers match, then the customer's identity is validated. Your function is to compare the two arrays and determine if they contain the same numbers.

Here are the specifications your function must meet.

Parameters   The function is to accept as arguments two short arrays of seven elements each. The first argument will contain the number entered by the customer. The second argument will contain the number retrieved from the bank's database.

Return value   The function should return a Boolean `true` value if the two arrays are identical. Otherwise, it should return `false`.

Here is the pseudocode for the function:

```
For each element in the first array
    Compare the element with the element in the second array
    that is in the corresponding position.
    If the two elements contain different values
        Return false.
    End If.
End For.
Return true.
```

The C++ code is as follows

```cpp
bool testPIN(short custPIN[], short databasePIN[])
{
    for (short index = 0; ndx < 7; index++)
    {
        if (custPIN[index] != databasePIN[index])
            return false;  // We've found two different values.
    }
    return true;       // If we make it to here, the values are the same.
}
```

Since you have only been asked to write a function that performs the comparison between the customer's input and the PIN that was retrieved from the database, you will also need to design a driver. Program 8-29 shows the complete program.

Program 8-29

```
// This program is a driver that tests a function comparing the
// contents of two short arrays.

#include <iostream>
using namespace std;

// Function prototype
bool testPIN(short [], short []);

int main ()
{
    short pin1[7] = {2, 4, 1, 8, 7, 9, 0}; // Base set of values
    short pin2[7] = {2, 4, 6, 8, 7, 9, 0}; // Only 1 element is
                                           // different from pin1.
    short pin3[7] = {1, 2, 3, 4, 5, 6, 7}; // All elements are
                                           // different from pin1.
    if (testPIN(pin1, pin2))
        cout << "ERROR: pin1 and pin2 report to be the same.\n";
    else
        cout << "SUCCESS: pin1 and pin2 are different.\n";

    if (testPIN(pin1, pin3))
        cout << "ERROR: pin1 and pin3 report to be the same.\n";
    else
        cout << "SUCCESS: pin1 and pin3 are different.\n";

    if (testPIN(pin1, pin1))
        cout << "SUCCESS: pin1 and pin1 report to be the same.\n";
    else
        cout << "ERROR: pin1 and pin1 report to be different.\n";
    return 0;
}

//*****************************************************************
// Definition of function testPIN                                *
// The following function accepts two short arrays. The arrays are *
// compared. If they contain the same values, true is returned.   *
// If they contain different values, false is returned.           *
//*****************************************************************
```

(program continues)

Program 8-29   *(continued)*

```
bool testPIN(short custPIN[], short databasePIN[])
{
    for (short index = 0; index < 7; index++)
    {
        if (custPIN[index] != databasePIN[index])
            return false; // We've found two different values.
    }
    return true;           // If we make it to here, the values are the same.
}
```

Program Output
```
SUCCESS: pin1 and pin2 are different.
SUCCESS: pin1 and pin3 are different.
SUCCESS: pin1 and pin1 report to be the same.
```

8.12   Focus on Problem Solving and Program Design: *A Case Study*

In algebra, the intersection of two sets is defined as a new set that contains all the values common to both sets. For instance, consider the following two sets, *A* and *B*:

$A = \{1, 2, 3, 4, 5, 6, 7, 8, 9, 10\}$
$B = \{2, 4, 8, 12, 14, 20, 25, 28, 30, 32\}$

The only values common to both sets are 2, 4, and 8. The intersection of *A* and *B*, which is denoted as $A \cap B$, is

$A \cap B = \{2, 4, 8\}$

This case study illustrates how array contents can be processed to perform an operation such as finding the intersection of two sets. The program will ask the user to enter two sets of values, each stored in an array. Then it will scan the two arrays looking for values common to both. The common values will be stored in a third array, whose contents are displayed on the screen.

Variables

Table 8-4 lists the variables needed.

Table 8-4

Variable	Description
set1	An array of 10 integers to hold the first set
set2	An array of 10 integers to hold the second set
intersection	An array of 10 integers to hold the intersection of set1 and set2
numIntValues	An integer holding the number of intersecting values

Functions

Table 8-5 lists the functions used by the program.

Table 8-5

Function	Description
getArray	set1 and set2 are passed into the function. It prompts the user to enter 10 values for each array.
findIntersection	set1, set2, and intersection are passed into the function. It scans the arrays for values that appear in both. The intersecting values are stored in intersection. This function returns the number of intersecting values found.
displayIntValue	The intersection array and the numIntValues variable are passed into this function. If numIntValues contains a number greater than zero, the function displays that many elements in the intersection array. If there are no intersecting values, the function displays a message indicating so.

The findIntersection Function

The findIntersection function uses two array parameters, first and second. The arrays set1 and set2 are passed into these parameters. The function uses nested loops to find the values that appear in both arrays. Here is the pseudocode.

```
For each element in the first array
    For each element in the second array
        Compare the selected elements in both arrays.
        If they contain the same value
            Store the value in the intersect array.
            Increment the count of intersecting values.
        End If.
    End For.
End For.
Return the count of intersecting values.
```

In the actual code, the outer loop cycles a counter variable (index1) through the values 0 through 9. This variable is used as the subscript for set1. The inner loop also cycles a counter variable (index2) through the values 0 through 9. This variable is used as a subscript for set2. For each iteration of the outer loop, the inner loop goes through all its iterations. An if statement in the inner loop compares first[index1] to second[index2]. Since the inner loop iterates 10 times for each iteration of the outer loop, the function will compare each individual element of the first array to every element of the second array. Here is the C++ code for the function.

```cpp
int findIntersection(int first[], int second[], int intersect[])
{
    int intCount = 0, index3 = 0;

    for (int index1 = 0; index1 < 10; index1++)
    {
        for(int index2 = 0; index2 < 10; index2++)
        {
            if (first[index1] == second[index2])
            {
                intersect[index3] = first[index1];
                index3++;
                intCount++;
            }
        }
    }
    return intCount;
}
```

Program 8-30 shows the entire program's source code.

Program 8-30

```cpp
// This program allows the user to enter two sets of numbers. It finds
// the intersection of the two sets (which is the set of numbers
// contained in both sets). The intersecting values are displayed.

#include <iostream>
using namespace std;

// Function prototypes
void getArrays(int [], int []);
int findIntersection(int [], int [], int []);
void displayIntValues(int [], int);
```

(program continues)

Program 8-30 *(continued)*

```cpp
int main()
{
    int set1[10],          // First set
        set2[10],          // Second set
        intersection[10],  // Set containing intersection values
        numIntValues;      // number of values in intersection

    getArrays(set1, set2);
    numIntValues = findIntersection(set1, set2, intersection);
    displayIntValues(intersection, numIntValues);
    return 0;
}

//*************************************************************
// Definition of function getArrays                         *
// The following function accepts two int arrays as arguments.*
// It prompts the user to enter 10 values for each array.    *
//*************************************************************

void getArrays(int first[], int second[])
{
    int index;

    // Get values for first array.
    cout << "Enter 10 values for the first set:\n";
    for (index = 0; index < 10; index++)
        cin >> first[index];

    // Get values for second array.
    cout << "Enter 10 values for the second set:\n";
    for (index = 0; index < 10; index++)
        cin >> second[index];
}

//*************************************************************
// Definition of function findIntersection                  *
// The following function accepts three arrays as arguments. *
// The first two arrays (first and second) are scanned,      *
// and all values appearing in both are stored in the        *
// third array (intersect). The number of values found       *
// in both arrays is returned.                               *
//*************************************************************
```

(program continues)

Program 8-30 *(continued)*

```
int findIntersection(int first[], int second[], int intersect[])
{
    int intCount = 0, index3 = 0;

    for (int index1 = 0; index1 < 10; index1++)
    {
        for(int index2 = 0; index2 < 10; index2++)
        {
            if (first[index1] == second[index2])
            {
                intersect[index3] = first[index1];
                index3++;
                intCount++;
            }
        }
    }
    return intCount;
}

//**********************************************************
// Definition of function displayIntValues              *
// The following function accepts two arguments: an     *
// array of ints and an int. The second argument is     *
// the number of valid elements contained in the array. *
// These values are displayed, if there are any.        *
//**********************************************************

void displayIntValues(int intersect[], int num)
{
    if (!num)            // Same as saying if (num == 0)
        cout << "There are no intersecting values.\n";
    else
    {
        cout << "Here is a list of the intersecting values:\n";
        for (int index = 0; index < num; index++)
            cout << intersect[index] << " ";
        cout << endl;
    }
}
```

Program Output with Example Input Shown in Bold
```
Enter 10 values for the first set:
1 2 3 4 5 6 7 8 9 10[Enter]
Enter 10 values for the second set:
2 4 8 12 14 20 25 28 30 32[Enter]
Here is a list of the intersecting values:
2 4 8
```

8.13   Arrays of Structures

CONCEPT Elements of arrays can be structures.

Earlier in this chapter you saw that data can be stored in two or more arrays, with a relationship established between the arrays through their subscripts. Because structures can hold several items of varying data types, a single array of structures can be used in place of several arrays of regular variables.

An array of structures is defined like any other array. Assume the following structure declaration exists in a program:

```
struct BookInfo
{
    string title;
    string author;
    string publisher;
    float price;
};
```

The following statement defines an array, `bookList`, which has 20 elements. Each element is a `BookInfo` structure.

```
BookInfo bookList[20];
```

Each element of the array may be accessed through a subscript. For example, `bookList[0]` is the first structure in the array, `bookList[1]` is the second, and so forth. To access a member of any element, simply place the dot operator and member name after the subscript. For example, the following expression refers to the `title` member of `bookList[5]`:

```
bookList[5].title
```

The following loop steps through the array, displaying the information stored in each element:

```
for (int index = 0; index < 20; index++)
{
    cout << bookList[index].title << endl;
    cout << bookList[index].author << endl;
    cout << bookList[index].publisher << endl;
    cout << bookList[index].price << endl << endl;
}
```

 Note: Since the members `title`, `author`, and `publisher` are `string` objects which are stored as character arrays, their individual elements may be accessed as well. The following statement displays the first character of the `title` member of `bookList[10]`:

```
cout << bookList[10].title[0];
```

And the following statement stores the character 't' in the fourth position of the `publisher` member of `bookList[2]`:

```
bookList[2].publisher[3] = 't';
```

Program 8-31 is a modification of Program 8-13 which calculates and displays payroll information for five employees. The original program used two arrays to hold the hours and pay rates of the employees. This modified version, however, uses a single array of structures.

Program 8-31

```
// This program stores, in an array of structures,
// the hours worked by 5 employees, and their hourly
// pay rates. (This is a modification of Program 8-13.)

#include <iostream>
#include <iomanip>
using namespace std;

struct PayInfo
{
    int hours;          // Hours worked
    float payRate;      // Hourly pay rate
};

int main ()
{
    int index;
    PayInfo workers[5];    // Array of 5 structures

    cout << "Enter the hours worked by 5 employees and their ";
    cout << "hourly rates.\n";
    for (index = 0; index < 5; index++)
    {
        cout << "Hours worked by employee #" << (index + 1);
        cout << ": ";
        cin >> workers[index].hours;
        cout << "Hourly pay rate for employee #";
        cout << (index + 1) << ": ";
        cin >> workers[index].payRate;
    }
```

(program continues)

Program 8-31   *(continued)*

```
    cout << "\nHere is the gross pay for each employee:\n";
    cout << fixed << showpoint << setprecision(2);
    for (index = 0; index < 5; index++)
    {
        float gross;
        gross = workers[index].hours * workers[index].payRate;
        cout << "Employee #" << (index + 1);
        cout << ": $" << gross << endl;
    }
    return 0;
}
```

Program Output with Example Input Shown in Bold
```
Enter the hours worked by 5 employees and their hourly rates.
Hours worked by employee #1: 10[Enter]
Hourly pay rate for employee #1: 9.75[Enter]
Hours worked by employee #2: 15[Enter]
Hourly pay rate for employee #2: 8.62[Enter]
Hours worked by employee #3: 20[Enter]
Hourly pay rate for employee #3: 10.50[Enter]
Hours worked by employee #4: 40[Enter]
Hourly pay rate for employee #4: 18.75[Enter]
Hours worked by employee #5: 40[Enter]
Hourly pay rate for employee #5: 15.65[Enter]

Here is the gross pay for each employee:
Employee #1: $97.50
Employee #2: $129.30
Employee #3: $210.00
Employee #4: $750.00
Employee #5: $626.00
```

Initializing a Structure Array

To initialize a structure array, simply provide an initialization list for one or more of the elements. For example, the array in Program 8-31 could have been initialized as follows:

```
    PayInfo workers[5] = {
                            {10, 9.75 },
                            {15, 8.62 },
                            {20, 10.50},
                            {40, 18.75},
                            {40, 15.65}
                         };
```

Like all single-dimensional arrays, you can initialize all or part of the elements in an array of structures, as long as you do not skip elements.

Checkpoint [8.13]

For questions 8.30–8.34, assume the `Product` structure is declared as follows:

```
struct Product
{
    string description;    // Product description
    int partNum;           // Part number
    float cost;            // Product cost
};
```

8.30 Write a definition for an array of 100 `Product` structures. Do not initialize the array.

8.31 Write a loop that will step through the entire array you defined in checkpoint 8.30, setting all the product descriptions to a null string, all part numbers to zero, and all costs to zero.

8.32 Write the statements that will store the following information in the first element of the array you defined in question 8.30:

Description: Claw Hammer
Part Number: 547
Part Cost: $8.29

8.33 Write a loop that will display the contents of the entire array you created in checkpoint 8.30.

8.34 Write the definition for an array of five `Product` structures, initializing the elements with the following information:

Description	Part Number	Cost
Screw driver	621	$ 1.72
Socket set	892	18.97
Claw hammer	547	8.29
Adjustable wrench	229	12.15
Pliers	114	3.17

8.35 Write a structure declaration called `Measurement`, with the following members:

`miles`, an integer
`meters`, a `long` integer

8.36 Write a structure declaration called `Destination`, with the following members:

`city`, a string object
`distance`, a `Measurement` structure (declared in checkpoint 8.35)

8.37 Define an array of 20 `Destination` structures (see checkpoint 8.36). Write statements that store the following information in the fifth array element:

City: Tupelo
Miles: 375
Meters: 603,375

8.14   Arrays of Class Objects

CONCEPT   Elements of arrays can be class objects.

In addition to arrays of built-in data types like `ints`, and arrays of structures, C++ also allows programmers to define arrays of class objects. Program 8-32 creates an array of objects using a slightly modified version of the `Circle` class first used in Program 7-8. Notice that the array is created with the statement.

```
Circle sphere[numCircles];
```

Since the named constant `numCircles` equals 4, this creates an array of four `Circle` objects named `sphere`. The four objects are `sphere[0]`, `sphere[1]`, `sphere[2]`, and `sphere[3]`. Calling a class function for one of these objects is just like calling a class function for any other object, except that a subscript must be included to identify which of the objects in the array is being referenced. For example, the following statement would call the `findArea` function of `sphere[2]`.

```
sphere[2].findArea();
```

In Program 8-32 a variable, named `index`, is used for the array subscript. The following statement, which appears in a loop, calls the `setRadius` function of whichever object is currently being indexed.

```
sphere[index].setRadius(r);
```

Likewise, the following statement is an abbreviated form of a statement which appears in another loop. It calls the `findArea` function of whichever object is currently being indexed.

```
cout << sphere[index].findArea();
```

Program 8-32

```
// This program demonstrates an array of objects.
// The objects are instances of the Circle class.

#include <iostream>
#include <iomanip>
#include <cmath>
using namespace std;
```

(program continues)

Program 8-32 *(continued)*

```
// Circle class declaration
class Circle
{   private:
        float radius;

    public:
        Circle() { radius = 1;}              // Default constructor
        Circle(float r) {radius = r;}        // Overloaded constructor
        void setRadius(float r) {radius = r;}
        float findArea() {return 3.14 * pow(radius, 2);}
};

const int numCircles = 4;

int main()
{
    int index;

    // Define an array that holds 4 Circle objects.
    Circle sphere[numCircles];

    // Use a loop to initialize the radius of each object.
    for (index = 0; index < numCircles; index++)
    {   float r;
        cout << "Enter the radius for sphere " << (index+1) << ": ";
        cin >> r;
        sphere[index].setRadius(r);

    }
    // Use a loop to get and print out the area of each object.
    cout << fixed << showpoint << setprecision(2);
    cout << "\nHere are the areas of the " << numCircles << " spheres.\n";
    for (index = 0; index < numCircles; index++)
    {   cout << "sphere " << (index+1) << setw(8)
             << sphere[index].findArea() << endl;

    }
    return 0;
}
```

Program Output with Example Input Shown in Bold
```
Enter the radius for sphere 1: 0[Enter]
Enter the radius for sphere 2: 2[Enter]
Enter the radius for sphere 3: 2.5[Enter]
Enter the radius for sphere 4: 10[Enter]

Here are the areas of the 4 spheres.
sphere 1    0.00
sphere 2   12.56
sphere 3   19.63
sphere 4  314.00
```

Whenever an array of objects is created with no constructor arguments, the default constructor, if one exists, runs for every object in the array. This occurred in Program 8-32. When the array of Circle objects was first created, the default constructor executed for each object in the array and assigned its radius the value 1. We never saw this because the call to the setRadius member function replaced the 1 with the new value passed to setRadius. It is considered a good idea to always create a default constructor for every class, just as a safeguard, even if you intend to initialize member variables yourself. Program 8-33 eliminates the calls to setRadius in order to illustrate that the default constructor runs for all the objects in the array. Since all the radii have the default value of 1, the program reports that all the Circle objects have the area 3.14.

Program 8-33

```cpp
// This program demonstrates how the default constructor
// runs for every object when an array of objects is created.

#include <iostream>
#include <iomanip>
#include <cmath>
using namespace std;

// Circle class declaration
class Circle
{   private:
        float radius;

    public:
        Circle() { radius = 1;}                 // Default constructor
        Circle(float r) {radius = r;}           // Overloaded constructor
        void setRadius(float r) {radius = r;}
        float findArea() {return 3.14 * pow(radius, 2);}
};

const int numCircles = 4;

int main()
{
    int index;

    // Define an array that holds 4 Circle objects.
    Circle sphere[numCircles];

    // Do not input values for the circle radii. Instead,
    // use the value assigned by the default constructor.
```

(program continues)

Program 8-33 *(continued)*

```
    // Use a loop to get and print out the area of each object.
    cout << fixed << showpoint << setprecision(2);
    cout << "\nHere are the areas of the " << numCircles
         << " spheres.\n";
    for (index = 0; index < numCircles; index++)
    {   cout << "sphere " << (index+1) << setw(8)
             << sphere[index].findArea() << endl;
    }
    return 0;
}
```

Program Output

```
Here are the areas of the 4 spheres.
sphere 1    3.14
sphere 2    3.14
sphere 3    3.14
sphere 4    3.14
```

It is also possible to create an array of objects and have another constructor called for each object. To do this you must use an initialization list. The following array definition and initialization list creates four `Circle` objects and initializes them to the same four values that were input in the Program 8-32 sample run.

```
    Circle sphere[numCircles] = {0.0, 2.0, 2.5, 10.0};
```

This invokes the constructor that accepts one `float` argument and sets the radii as follows:

`sphere[0]` = 0.0, `sphere[1]` = 2.0, `sphere[2]` = 2.5, and `sphere[3]` = 10.0.

If the initialization list had been shorter than the number of objects, any remaining objects would have been initialized by the default constructor. For example, the following statement invokes the constructor that accepts one `float` argument for the first three objects and causes the default constructor to run for the fourth object. The fourth object is assigned a default radius of 1.0.

```
    Circle sphere[numCircles] = {0.0, 2.0, 2.5};
```

This is illustrated in Program 8-34.

Program 8-34

```
// This program demonstrates how an overloaded constructor
// that accepts an argument can be invoked for multiple objects
// when an array of objects is created.
```

(program continues)

Program 8-34 *(continued)*

```
#include <iostream>
#include <iomanip>
#include <cmath>
using namespace std;

// Circle class declaration
class Circle
{   private:
        float radius;

    public:
        Circle() { radius = 1;}                 // Default constructor
        Circle(float r) {radius = r;}           // Overloaded constructor
        void setRadius(float r) {radius = r;}
        float findArea() {return 3.14 * pow(radius, 2);}
};

const int numCircles = 4;

int main()
{
    int index;

    // Define an array that holds 4 Circle objects.  Use an
    // initialization list to call the constructor using one
    // float argument for the first 3 objects. The default
    // constructor will be called for the final object.
    Circle sphere[numCircles] = {0.0, 2.0, 2.5};

    // Use a loop to get and print out the area of each object.
    cout << fixed << showpoint << setprecision(2);
    cout << "\nHere are the areas of the " << numCircles
         << " spheres.\n";
    for (index = 0; index < numCircles; index++)
    {   cout << "sphere " << (index+1) << setw(8)
             << sphere[index].findArea() << endl;
    }
    return 0;
}
```

Program Output

```
Here are the areas of the 4 spheres.
sphere 1    0.00
sphere 2    12.56
sphere 3    19.63
sphere 4    3.14
```

In order to invoke a constructor that accepts more than one argument when an array of objects is created, it is necessary to place a function call in the initialization list for each object to be initialized. In order to demonstrate this we will make some modifications to the Circle class. First, we will add two more member variables, centerX and centerY, which hold the x and y coordinates of the Circle object's center. Second, we will modify the default constructor and the constructor that accepts the radius as an argument so that they both use default values of 0 for centerX and centerY. Third, we will add another overloaded constructor that allows all three member variables to be set. Fourth, we will add member functions to return the center coordinates. Finally, we will eliminate the setRadius member function, which we are no longer using. The class declaration for this enhanced Circle class follows.

```
// Enhanced Circle class declaration
class Circle
{   private:
        float radius;
        int   centerX,
              centerY;
    public:
        // Default constructor
        Circle() { radius = 1.0; centerX = centerY = 0;}

        // Overloaded constructor that accepts one argument
        Circle(float r) {radius = r; centerX = centerY = 0;}

        // Overloaded constructor that accepts three arguments
        Circle(float r, int x, int y)
        {radius = r; centerX = x; centerY = y;}

        float findArea() {return 3.14 * pow(radius, 2);}
        int   getX() {return centerX;}
        int   getY() {return centerY;}
};
```

Program 8-35 uses this enhanced class to illustrate how to invoke overloaded constructors that accept more than one argument when an array of objects is created. Notice that it is not necessary that all objects in the array use the same constructor. In Program 8-35, sphere[0] and sphere[2] use the constructor that accepts three arguments, while sphere[1] uses the constructor that accepts one argument and sphere[3] uses the default constructor. When a constructor with more than one argument is used, a function call appears in the initialization list. Notice that the call uses the name of the class, rather than the name of the array or the object.

Program 8-35

```cpp
// This program demonstrates how an overloaded constructor
// that accepts more than one argument can be invoked when
// an array of objects is created.

#include <iostream>
#include <cmath>
using namespace std;

// Circle class declaration
class Circle
{   private:
        float radius;
        int   centerX,
              centerY;
    public:
        // Default constructor
        Circle() { radius = 1.0; centerX = centerY = 0;}

        // Overloaded constructor that accepts one argument
        Circle(float r) {radius = r; centerX = centerY = 0;}

        // Overloaded constructor that accepts three arguments
        Circle(float r, int x, int y)
        {radius = r; centerX = x; centerY = y;}

        float findArea() {return 3.14 * pow(radius, 2);}
        int   getX() {return centerX;}
        int   getY() {return centerY;}
};

const int numCircles = 4;

int main()
{
    int index;

    // Define an array that holds 4 Circle objects.
    // Invoke the constructor using 3 arguments for object 0.
    // Invoke the constructor using 1 argument  for object 1.
    // Invoke the constructor using 3 arguments for object 2.
    // Invoke the default constructor for object 4.
    Circle sphere[numCircles] = { Circle(0.0, 2, 4),
                                  2.0,
                                  Circle(2.5, -1, -1) };
```

(program continues)

Program 8-35 *(continued)*

```
// Use a loop to get and print out the center
// coordinates and area of each Circle object.
for (index = 0; index < numCircles; index++)
{   cout << "sphere " << (index+1) << " with center at ("
        << sphere[index].getX() << "," << sphere[index].getY()
        << ") has an area of "  << sphere[index].findArea()
        << endl;
}
    return 0;
}
```

Program Output
```
sphere 1 with center at (2,4) has an area of 0
sphere 2 with center at (0,0) has an area of 12.56
sphere 3 with center at (-1,-1) has an area of 19.625
sphere 4 with center at (0,0) has an area of 3.14
```

In summary, there are seven key points to remember.

1. The elements of arrays can be objects.

2. If you do not use an initialization list when an array of objects is created, the default constructor will be invoked for each object in the array.

3. It is not necessary that all objects in the array use the same constructor.

4. If you do use an initialization list when an array of objects is created, the appropriate constructor will be called for each object, depending on the number and type of arguments used.

5. If there are fewer initializer calls in the list than there are objects in the array, the default constructor will be called for all the remaining objects.

6. It is best to always provide a default constructor; but if there is none you must be sure to furnish an initializer for every object in the array.

7. If a constructor requires more than one argument, the initializer must take the form of a constructor function call.

 Checkpoint   [8.14]

8.38 True or false: The default constructor is the only constructor that may be called for objects in an array of objects.

8.39 True or false: The same constructor must be used for all elements in an array of objects.

8.40   What will the following program display on the screen?

```cpp
#include <iostream>
using namespace std;

class Tank
{
private:
    int gallons;
public:
    Tank()
        { gallons = 50; }
    Tank(int gal)
        { gallons = gal; }
    int getGallons()
        { return gallons; }
};
int main ()
{
    Tank storage[3] = { 10, 20 };

    for (int index = 0; index < 3; index++)
        cout << storage[index].getGallons() << endl;
    return 0;
}
```

8.41   Complete the following program so it defines an array of 10 Yard objects. The program should use a loop to ask the user for the length and width of each yard. Then it should loop and display the length and width of each yard. To do this you will need to add two member functions to the Yard class.

```cpp
#include <iostream>
using namespace std;

class Yard
{
private:
    int length, width;
public:
    Yard()
        { length = 0; width = 0; }
    void      setLength(int l)
        { length = l; }
    void      setWidth(int w)
        { width = w; }
};
int main ()
{
    // Finish this program.
}
```

8.15   Focus on Object-Oriented Programming: *Creating an Abstract Array Data Type—Part I*

> **CONCEPT**   The absence of array bounds checking in C++ is a source of potential hazard for many programmers. In this section we discuss a simple integer list class that provides bounds checking.

One of the benefits of object-oriented programming is the ability to create abstract data types that are improvements on built-in data types. As you have seen in this chapter, arrays provide no bounds checking in C++. You can, however, create a class that has array-like characteristics and performs bounds checking. For example, look at this IntList class.

Contents of intlist.h

```
#ifndef INTLIST_H
#define INTLIST_H

class IntList
{
private:
        int list[20];
        bool isValid(int);
public:
        // Constructor
        IntList();
        bool set(int, int);
        bool get(int, int&);
};

#endif
```

Contents of intlist.cpp

```
#include <iostream>
#include "intlist.h"
using namespace std;

//****************************************************************
// Constructor                                                  *
// Initializes each element in the list to zero.                *
//****************************************************************

IntList::IntList()
{
    for (int index = 0; index < 20; index++)
        list[index] = 0;
}
```

```cpp
//****************************************************************
//                    isValid                                   *
// This private member function returns true if the argument    *
// is a valid subscript into the list. Otherwise, it returns    *
// false and displays an error message.                         *
//****************************************************************

bool IntList::isValid(int element)
{
    if (element < 0 || element > 19)
    {
        cout << "ERROR: " << element;
        cout << " is an invalid subscript.\n";
        return false;
    }
    else
        return true;
}


//*****************************************************************
//                         set                                   *
// This public member function is passed an element number and   *
// a value. If the element number is a valid array subscript,    *
// the value is stored in the array at that location and the     *
// function returns true. Otherwise,the function returns false.  *
//*****************************************************************

bool IntList::set(int element, int value)
{
    if (isValid(element))
    {
        list[element] = value;
        return true;
    }
    else
        return false;
}


//  *************************************************************
//                         get                                  *
// This public member function is passed an element number.     *
// If it is a valid array subscript, the value stored in the    *
// array at that location is retrieved and is made available    *
// to the calling function by placing it in a reference         *
// parameter. A true is returned. If the element number passed  *
// in is not a valid subscript, the function returns false.     *
//  *************************************************************
```

```
bool IntList::get(int element, int &value)
{
    if (isValid(element))
    {
        value = list[element];
        return true;
    }
    else
        return false;
}
```

The IntList class allows you to store and retrieve numbers in a 20-element array of integers. Here is a synopsis of the members.

list	A 20-element array of integers used to hold the list.
isValid	This function validates a subscript into the array. It accepts a subscript value as an argument and returns Boolean true if the subscript is in the range 0 to 19. If the value is outside that range, an error message is displayed and Boolean false is returned.
Constructor	The class constructor initializes each element of the list array to zero.
set	The set member function sets a specific element of the list array to a value. The first argument is the element subscript and the second argument is the value to be stored in that element. The function uses isValid to validate the subscript. If an invalid subscript is passed to the function, no value is stored in the array and Boolean false is returned. If the subscript is valid, the function stores the value in the array and returns Boolean true.
get	The get member function retrieves a value from a specific element in the list array. The first argument is the subscript of the element whose value is to be retrieved. The function uses isValid to validate the subscript. If the subscript is valid, the value is copied into the second argument (which is passed to a reference variable), and Boolean true is returned. If the subscript is invalid, no value is retrieved from the array and Boolean false is returned.

Program 8-36 demonstrates the class. A loop uses the set member to fill the array with 9s and prints an asterisk on the screen each time a 9 is successfully stored. Then another loop uses the get member to retrieve the values from the array, and prints them on the screen. Finally, a statement uses the set member to demonstrate the subscript validation by attempting to store a value in element 50.

Program 8-36

```cpp
#include <iostream>
#include "intlist.h"
using namespace std;
//Remember to add intlist.cpp to the project containing this file.

int main()
{
    int x;
    IntList numbers;       // Create an IntList object,
                           // which is an array of 20 ints
    int val;

    // Store 9s in the list and display an asterisk
    // each time a 9 is successfully stored.
    for (x = 0; x < 20; x++)
    {
        if (numbers.set(x, 9))
            cout << "* ";
    }
    cout << endl;

    // Display the 9s
    for (x = 0; x < 20; x++)
    {
        if (numbers.get(x, val))
            cout << val << " ";
    }
    cout << endl;

    // Attempt to store a value outside the list's bounds.
    if (numbers.set(50, 9))
        cout << "Element 50 successfully set.\n";
    return 0;
}
```

Program Output

```
* * * * * * * * * * * * * * * * * * * *
9 9 9 9 9 9 9 9 9 9 9 9 9 9 9 9 9 9 9 9
ERROR: 50 is an invalid subscript.
```

Review Questions and Exercises

Fill-in-the-Blank

1. The _____ indicates the number of elements, or values, an array can hold.

2. The size declarator must be a(n) _____ with a value greater than _____.

3. Each element of an array is accessed and indexed by a number known as a(n) _____.

4. Subscript numbering in C++ always starts at _____.

5. The number inside the brackets of an array declaration is the _____, but the number inside an array's brackets in an assignment statement, or any other statement that works with the contents of the array, is the _____.

6. C++ has no array _____ checking, which means you can inadvertently store information past the end of an array.

7. Starting values for the elements of an array may be specified with a(n) _____ list.

8. If an array is partially initialized, the uninitialized elements will bet set to _____.

9. If the size declarator of an array declaration is omitted, C++ counts the number of items in the _____ to determine how large the array should be.

10. When a character array is initialized with a string constant, the _____ is automatically included at the end.

11. By using the same _____ for multiple arrays, you can build relationships between the data stored in the arrays. These arrays are referred to as parallel arrays.

12. You cannot use the _____ operator to copy data from one array to another in a single statement.

13. Arrays are never passed to functions by _____ since there would be too much overhead in copying all the elements.

14. To pass an array to a function, pass the _____ of the array.

15. A(n) _____ array is like several arrays of the same type put together.

16. It's best to think of a two-dimensional array as having _____ and _____.

17. To define a two-dimensional array, _____ size declarators are required.

18. When initializing a two-dimensional array, it helps to enclose each row's initialization list in _____.

19. When a two-dimensional array is passed to a function, the _____ size must be specified.

Defining and Using Structure Variables

A structure `Car` is declared as follows. Use it for questions 20 to 22.

```
struct Car
{
    string make;
    string model;
    int year;
    float cost;
};
```

20. Define an array of 25 of the `Car` structure variables.

21. Define an array of 35 of the `Car` structure variables. Initialize the first three elements with the following information:

Make	Model	Year	Cost
Ford	Taurus	1997	$ 21,000
Honda	Accord	1992	$ 11,000
Lamborghini	Countach	1997	$200,000

22. Write a loop that will step through the array you defined in question 21, displaying the contents of each element.

True or False

23. T   F   The following expression refers to the fifth element in the array `carInfo`:

    `carInfo.model[5]`

24. T   F   An array of structures may be initialized.

25. T   F   An array's size declarator can either be a literal constant, named constant, or variable.

26. T   F   To calculate the amount of memory used by an array, multiply the number of elements by the number of bytes each element uses.

27. T   T   The individual elements of an array are accessed and indexed by unique numbers.

28. T   F   The first element in an array is accessed by the subscript 1.

29. T   F   The subscript of the last element in an array is one less than the total number of elements in the array.

30. T   F   The contents of an array element cannot be displayed with `cout`.

31. T   F   Subscript numbers may be stored in variables.

32. T   F   You can write programs with subscripts that do not exist for a particular array.

33. T   F   Arrays cannot be initialized when they are defined. A loop or other means must be used.

34. T   F   The values in an initialization list are stored in the array in the order they appear in the list.

35. T   F   C++ allows you to partially initialize an array.

36. T   F   If an array is partially initialized, the uninitialized elements will contain "garbage."

37. T   F   If you leave an element uninitialized, you do not have to leave all the ones that follow it uninitialized.

38. T   F   If you leave out the size declarator of an array declaration, you do not have to include an initialization list.

39. T   F   When initializing an array element with a string, the null terminator is automatically included.

40. T F When an array is passed to a function, the function call must include [] after the array name.

41. T F You cannot use the assignment operator to copy one array's contents to another in a single statement.

42. T F When an array name is used without brackets and a subscript, it is seen as the value of the first element in the array.

43. T F To pass an array to a function, pass the name of the array.

44. T F When defining a parameter variable to hold an array argument, you do not have to include the size declarator.

45. T F When an array is passed to a function, the function has access to the original array.

46. T F A two-dimensional array is like several identical arrays put together.

47. T F It's best to think of two-dimensional arrays as having rows and columns.

48. T F The first size declarator (in the declaration of a two-dimensional array) represents the number of columns. The second size declarator represents the number of rows.

49. T F Two-dimensional arrays may be passed to functions, but the row size must be specified in the declaration of the parameter variable.

50. T F C++ allows you to create arrays with three dimensions and more.

51. T F When an array of objects is defined, the constructor is only called for the first element.

Find the Error

52. Each of the following definitions and program segments has errors. Locate as many as you can.

A) ```
int size;
float values[size];
```

B) ```
int collection[-20];
```

C) ```
int table[10];
for (int x = 0; x < 20; x++)
{
    cout << "Enter the next value: ";
    cin >> table[x];
}
```

D) ```
int hours[3] = 8, 12, 16;
```

E) ```
int score[3] = {90, 80, 88};
cout << score;
```

F) ```
int numbers[8] = {1, 2, , 4, , 5};
```

G) ```
float ratings[];
```

H) ```
values[3] = {6, 8.2, 'A'};
```

I) ```
int array1[4], array2[4] = {3, 6, 9, 12};
array1 = array2;
```
```

```
J)  void showValues(int nums)
    {
        for (int count = 0; count < 8; count++)
            cout << nums[count];
    }
K)  void showValues(int nums[4][])
    {
        for (rows = 0; rows < 4; rows++)
            for (cols = 0; cols < 5; cols++)
                cout << nums[rows][cols];
    }
```

Programming Challenges

General Requirements

A) Each program should have a section of comments at the top. The comments should contain your name, the date the program was written, the chapter the assignment appeared in, and the assignment number and name. Here is an example:

```
// Written by Jill Johnson
// March 31, 2003
// Chapter 7
// Assignment 1. Largest/Smallest Array Values
```

B) For each program that displays a dollar amount, format the output in fixed-point notation with two decimal places of precision. Be sure the decimal place always displays, even when the number is zero or has no fractional part.

1. Largest/Smallest Array Values

Write a program that lets the user enter at least 10 values into an array. The program should then display the largest and smallest values stored in the array.

2. Rainfall Statistics

Write a program that lets the user enter the total rainfall for each of 12 months into an array of floats. The program should calculate and display the total rainfall for the year, the average monthly rainfall, and the months with the highest and lowest amounts.

Input Validation: Do not accept negative numbers for monthly rainfall figures.

3. Lowercase to Uppercase Converter

Write a program that lets the user enter a string into a string object. The program should then convert all the lowercase letters to uppercase. (If a character is already uppercase, or is not a letter, it should be left alone.) Hint: Consult the ASCII chart in Appendix A. Notice that the lowercase letters are represented by the ASCII codes 97 through 122. If you subtract 32 from any lowercase character's ASCII code, it will yield the ASCII code of the uppercase equivalent.

4. Proper Words

Write a function that uses an array parameter to accept a string as its argument. It should convert the first letter of each word in the string to uppercase. If any of the letters are already uppercase, they should be left alone. (See the hint in problem 3 for help on converting lowercase characters to uppercase.) Demonstrate the function in a simple program that asks the user to input a string, passes it to the function, and then displays the string after it has been modified.

5. Quarterly Sales Statistics

Write a program that lets the user enter four quarterly sales figures for six divisions of a company. The figures should be stored in a two-dimensional array. Once the figures are entered, the program should display the following information for each quarter:

- A list of the sales figures by division
- Each division's increase or decrease from the previous quarter. (This will not be displayed for the first quarter.)
- The total sales for the quarter
- The company's increase or decrease from the previous quarter. (This will not be displayed for the first quarter.)
- The average sales for all divisions that quarter
- The division with the highest sales for that quarter

The program should be modular, with functions that calculate these statistics.

Input Validation: Do not accept negative numbers for sales figures.

6. Payroll

Write a program that uses the following arrays:

- `empId`: an array of seven long integers to hold employee identification numbers. The array should be initialized with the following numbers:

5658845	4520125	7895122	8777541
8451277	1302850	7580489	

- `hours`: an array of seven integers to hold the number of hours worked by each employee
- `payRate`: an array of seven `float`s to hold each employee's hourly pay rate
- `wages`: an array of seven `float`s to hold each employee's gross wages

The program should relate the information in each array through the subscripts. For example, the number in element 0 of the `hours` array should be the number of hours worked by the employee whose identification number is stored in element 0 of the `empId` array. That same employee's pay rate should be stored in element 0 of the `payRate` array.

The program should display each employee number and ask the user to enter that employee's hours and pay rate. It should then calculate the gross wages for that employee (hours times pay rate), which should be stored in the `wages` array. After the data has been entered for all the employees, the program should display each employee's identification number and gross wages.

Input Validation: Do not accept negative values for hours or numbers less than $6.00 for pay rate.

7. Weather Statistics

Write a program that uses a structure to store the following weather information for a particular month:

> Total rainfall
> High temperature
> Low temperature
> Average temperature

The program should have an array of 12 structures to hold weather information for an entire year. When the program runs, it should ask the user to enter data for each month. (The average temperature should be calculated). Once the data is entered for all the months, the program should calculate and display the average monthly rainfall, the total rainfall for the year, the highest and lowest temperatures for the year (and the months they occurred in), and the average of all the monthly average temperatures.

Input Validation: Only accept temperatures within the range of −100 to +140 degrees Fahrenheit.

8. Drink Machine Simulator

Write a program that simulates a soft drink machine. The program should use a structure that stores the following information:

> Drink name
> Drink cost
> Number of drinks in machine

The program should create an array of five structures. The elements should be initialized with the following data:

Drink Name	Cost	Number in Machine
Cola	.75	20
Root beer	.75	20
Lemon-lime	.75	20
Grape soda	.80	20
Cream soda	.80	20

Each time the program runs, it should enter a loop that performs the following steps: A list of drinks is displayed on the screen. The user should be allowed to either quit the program or pick a drink. If the user selects a drink, he or she will next enter the amount of money that is to be inserted into the drink machine. The program should display the amount of change that would be returned and subtract one from the number of that drink left in the machine. If the user selects a drink that has sold out, a message should be displayed. The loop then repeats. When the user chooses to quit the program it should display the total amount of money the machine earned.

Input Validation: When the user enters an amount of money, do not accept negative values or values greater than $1.00.

9. Inventory Bins

Write a program that simulates inventory bins in a warehouse. Each bin holds a number of the same type of parts. The program should use a structure that keeps the following information:

Description of the part kept in the bin
Number of parts in the bin

The program should have the following functions:

addParts   A function that accepts as its argument the number of parts being added to a bin. The function increases the bin's part count by this number.

removeParts   A function that accepts as its argument the number of parts being removed from a bin. The function decreases the bin's part count by this number.

The program should have an array of 10 bins, initialized with the following data:

Part Description	Number of Parts in the Bin
Valve	10
Bearing	5
Bushing	15
Coupling	21
Flange	7
Gear	5
Gear housing	5
Vacuum gripper	25
Cable	18
Rod	12

When the program runs, repeat a loop that performs the following steps: The user should see a list of what each bin holds and how many parts are in each bin. The user can choose to either quit the program or select a bin. When a bin is selected, the user can either add parts to it or remove parts from it. The loop then repeats, showing the updated bin information on the screen.

Input Validation: No bin can hold more than 30 parts, so don't let the user add more than a bin can hold. Do not allow the user to remove more items from a bin than it currently holds. Also, don't accept negative values for the number of parts being added or removed.

10. Number Array Class

Design a class that has an array of 10 floating-point numbers. The constructor should set each element to 0.0. There should be a member function to store a number in any element of the array. There should be another member function to return the average of all the numbers in the array. Demonstrate the class in a complete program that lets the user enter numbers into the array and then displays the average.

11. Payroll

Design a `PayRoll` class that has data members for an employee's hourly pay rate, number of hours worked, and total pay for the week. Write a program with an array of seven `PayRoll` objects. The program should ask the user for the number of hours each employee has worked and then display the amount of gross pay each has earned.

Input Validation: Do not accept values less than 0 or greater than 60 for the number of hours worked.

Group Project

12. Theatre Seating

This program should be designed and written by a team of students. Here are some suggestions:

- One student should design function `main`, which will call the other functions in the program. The remainder of the functions will be designed by other members of the team.

- The requirements of the program should be analyzed so each student is given about the same work load.

- The parameters and return types of each function should be decided in advance.

- The program can be implemented either as a multi-file program, or all the functions can be cut and pasted into the main file.

Here is the assignment: Write a program that can be used by a small theater to sell tickets for performances. The theater's auditorium has 15 rows of seats, with 30 seats in each row. The program should display a screen that shows which seats are available and which are taken. For example, the following screen shows a chart depicting each seat in the theater. Seats that are taken are represented by an * symbol, and seats that are available are represented by a # symbol:

```
                      Seats
              123456789012345678901234567890
Row  1        ***####***####*############*****#####
Row  2        ####************####*******####
Row  3        **####*********############****####
Row  4        **########*************####******
Row  5        ********#####*********############
Row  6        ###############*************#####
Row  7        ########*************############
Row  8        ************####****##############
Row  9        ###########*****################****
Row  10       ######************############
Row  11       #***********####################**
Row  12       ################********############*
Row  13       ####***********########**########
Row  14       ################################
Row  15       ################################
```

Here is a list of tasks this program must perform:

◆ When the program begins, it should ask the user to enter the seat prices for each row. The prices can be stored in a separate array.

◆ Once the prices are entered, the program should display a seating chart similar to the one shown. The user may enter the row and seat numbers for tickets being sold. Every time a ticket or group of tickets is purchased, the program should display the total ticket prices and update the seating chart.

◆ The program should keep a total of all ticket sales. The user should be given an option of viewing this amount.

◆ The program should also give the user an option to see a list of how many seats have been sold, how many seats are available in each row, and how many seats are available in the entire auditorium.

Input Validation: When tickets are being sold, do not accept row or seat numbers that do not exist. When someone requests a particular seat, the program should make sure that seat is available before it is sold.

Case

Serendipity Booksellers Software Development Project—Part 8: A Problem-Solving Exercise

For this chapter's exercise you will complete the bookData class member functions, and define an array of bookData objects.

1. Complete the bookData **Member Functions.**

Complete the class's member functions according to the following specifications.

setTitle	The function should accept a string object (assumed to hold the book title) as an argument. The contents of the string object should be copied to the bookTitle member.
setIsbn	The function should accept a string object (assumed to hold the ISBN number) as an argument. The contents of the string object should be copied to the isbn member.
setAuthor	The function should accept a string object (assumed to hold the author's name) as an argument. The contents of the string object should be copied to the author member.
setPub	The function should accept a string object (assumed to hold the name of the book's publisher) as an argument. The contents of the string object should be copied to the publisher member.
setDateAdded	The function should accept a string object (assumed to hold the date) as an argument. The contents of the string object should be copied to the dateAddded member.
setQty	The function should accept an int (assumed to hold the quantity of the book) as an argument. The contents of the argument should be copied to the qtyOnHand member.
setWholesale	The function should accept a float (assumed to hold the wholesale price of the book) as an argument. The contents of the argument should be copied to the wholesale member.
setRetail	The function should accept a float (assumed to hold the retail price of the book) as an argument. The contents of the argument should be copied to the retail member.
isEmpty	This function should return the value in the empty member.

removeBook	This function should set the empty member to true. (This action, in effect, deletes the book from inventory by marking the object as being "empty.")
getTitle	This function should return the value in the bookTitle member.
getIsbn	This function should return the value in the isbn member.
getAuthor	This function should return the value in the author member.
getPub	This function should return the value in the publisher member.
getDateAdded	This function should return the value in the dateAdded member.
getQty	This function should return the value in the qtyOnHand member.
getWholesale	This function should return the value in the wholesale member.
getRetail	This function should return the value in the retail member.

2. Define an array of BookData objects.

In the mainmenu.cpp file, define an array of 20 BookData class objects. You will use this array to test the class member functions and the other program functions. In Chapter 14 you will modify the program to store this information in a file. At that time, the program will be able to keep a much larger inventory.

CHAPTER 9

Searching and Sorting Arrays

Topics

9.1 Focus on Software Engineering: *Introduction to Search Algorithms*

> **CONCEPT** A search algorithm is a method of locating a specific item of information in a larger collection of data. This section discusses two algorithms for searching the contents of an array.

It's very common for programs not only to store and process information stored in arrays, but to search arrays for specific items. This section will show you two methods of searching an array: the linear search and the binary search. Each has its advantages and disadvantages.

The Linear Search

The *linear search* is a very simple algorithm. Sometimes called a *sequential search,* it uses a loop to sequentially step through an array, starting with the first element. It compares each element with the value being searched for, and stops when either the value is found or the end of the array is encountered. If the value being searched for is not in the array, the algorithm will unsuccessfully search to the end of the array.

589

Here is the pseudocode for a function that performs the linear search:

```
Set found to false.
Set position to -1.
Set index to 0.
While index < number of elements and found is false
    If list[index] is equal to search value
        found = true.
        position = index.
    End If
    Add 1 to index.
End While.
Return position.
```

The function searchList, which follows, is an example of C++ code used to perform a linear search on an integer array. The array list, which has a maximum of numElems elements, is searched for an occurrence of the number stored in value. If the number is found, its array subscript is returned. Otherwise, -1 is returned, indicating the value did not appear in the array.

```cpp
int searchList(int list[], int numElems, int value)
{
    int index = 0;          // Used as a subscript to search array
    int position = -1;      // Used to record position of search value
    bool found = false;     // Flag to indicate if the value was found

    while (index < numElems && !found)
    {
        if (list[index] == value)   // If the value is found
        {
            found = true;           // Set the flag
            position = index;       // Record the value's subscript
        }
        index++;                    // Go to the next element
    }
    return position;                // Return the position, or -1
}
```

 Note: The reason –1 is returned when the search value is not found in the array is because –1 is not a valid subscript. Any other nonvalid subscript value could also have been used to signal this.

Program 9-1 is a complete program that uses the searchList function. It searches the five-element array tests to find a score of 100.

Program 9-1

```cpp
// This program demonstrates the searchList function, which
// performs a linear search on an integer array.

#include <iostream>
using namespace std;
```

(program continues)

Program 9-1   *(continued)*

```
// Function prototype
int searchList(int [], int, int);

const int arrSize = 5;

int main()
{
    int tests[arrSize] = {87, 75, 98, 100, 82};
    int results;

    results = searchList(tests, arrSize, 100);
    if (results == -1)
        cout << "You did not earn 100 points on any test.\n";
    else
    {
        cout << "You earned 100 points on test ";
        cout << (results + 1) << ".\n";
    }
    return 0;
}

//*******************************************************************
// The searchList function performs a linear search on an          *
// integer array. The array list, which has a maximum of numElems  *
// elements, is searched for the number stored in value. If the    *
// number is found, its array subscript is returned. Otherwise,    *
// -1 is returned, indicating the value was not in the array.      *
//*******************************************************************

int searchList(int list[], int numElems, int value)
{
    int index = 0;              // Used as a subscript to search array
    int position = -1;          // Used to record position of search value
    bool found = false;         // Flag to indicate if the value was found

    while (index < numElems && !found)
    {
        if (list[index] == value)   // If the value is found
        {
            found = true;           // Set the flag
            position = index;       // Record the value's subscript
        }
        index++;                    // Go to the next element
    }
    return position;                // Return the position, or -1
}
```

Program Output
You earned 100 points on test 4.

Inefficiency of the Linear Search

The advantage of the linear search is its simplicity. It is very easy to understand and implement. Furthermore, it doesn't require the data in the array to be stored in any particular order. Its disadvantage, however, is its inefficiency. If the array being searched contained 20,000 elements, the algorithm would have to look at all 20,000 elements in order to find a value stored in the last element or to determine that a desired element was not in the array.

In an average case, an item is just as likely to be found near the beginning of the array as near the end. Typically, for an array of N items, the linear search will locate an item in N/2 attempts. If an array has 50,000 elements, the linear search will make a comparison with 25,000 of them in a typical case. This is assuming, of course, that the search item is consistently found in the array. (N/2 is the average number of comparisons. The maximum number of comparisons is always N.)

When the linear search fails to locate an item, it must make a comparison with every element in the array. As the number of failed search attempts increases, so does the average number of comparisons. Obviously, the linear search should not be used on large arrays if speed is important.

The Binary Search

The *binary search* is a clever algorithm that is much more efficient than the linear search. Its only requirement is that the values in the array be sorted in order. Instead of testing the array's first element, this algorithm starts with the element in the middle. If that element happens to contain the desired value, then the search is over. Otherwise, the value in the middle element is either greater than or less than the value being searched for. If it is greater than the desired value then the value (if it is in the list) will be found somewhere in the first half of the array. If it is less than the desired value then the value (again, if it is in the list) will be found somewhere in the last half of the array. In either case, half of the array's elements have been eliminated from further searching.

If the desired value wasn't found in the middle element, the procedure is repeated for the half of the array that potentially contains the value. For instance, if the last half of the array is to be searched, the algorithm immediately tests *its* middle element. If the desired value isn't found there, the search is narrowed to the quarter of the array that resides before or after that element. This process continues until the value being searched for is either found or there are no more elements to test.

Here is the pseudocode for a function that performs a binary search on an array whose elements are stored in ascending order.

```
Set first index to 0.
Set last index to the last subscript in the array.
Set found to false.
Set position to - 1.
While found is not true and first is less than or equal to last
    Set middle to the subscript half-way between array[first]
    and array[last].
    If array[middle] equals the desired value
        Set found to true.
        Set position to middle.
    Else If array[middle] is greater than the desired value
        Set last to middle - 1.
```

```
    Else
        Set first to middle + 1.
    End If.
End While.
Return position.
```

This algorithm uses three index variables: `first`, `last`, and `middle`. The `first` and `last` variables mark the boundaries of the portion of the array currently being searched. They are initialized with the subscripts of the array's first and last elements. The subscript of the element halfway between `first` and `last` is calculated and stored in the `middle` variable. If the element in the middle of the array does not contain the search value, the `first` or `last` variables are adjusted so that only the top or bottom half of the array is searched the during the next iteration. This cuts the portion of the array being searched in half each time the loop fails to locate the search value.

The function `binarySearch` in the following example C++ code is used to perform a binary search on an integer array. The first parameter, `array`, which has a maximum of `numElems` elements, is searched for an occurrence of the number stored in `value`. If the number is found, its array subscript is returned. Otherwise, -1 is returned indicating the value did not appear in the array.

```cpp
int binarySearch(int array[], int numElems, int value)
{
    int  first = 0,                    // First array element
         last = numElems - 1,          // Last array element
         middle,                       // Midpoint of search
         position = -1;                // Position of search value
    bool found = false;                // Flag

    while (!found && first <= last)
    {
        middle = (first + last) / 2;   // Calculate midpoint
        if (array[middle] == value)    // If value is found at mid
        {
            found = true;
            position = middle;
        }
        else if (array[middle] > value) // If value is in lower half
            last = middle - 1;
        else
            first = middle + 1;        // If value is in upper half
    }
    return position;
}
```

Program 9-2 is a complete program using the `binarySearch` function. It searches an array of employee ID numbers for a specific value.

Program 9-2

```cpp
// This program demonstrates the binarySearch function, which
// performs a binary search on an integer array. Whose elements
// are in ascending order.

#include <iostream>
using namespace std;

// Function prototype
int binarySearch(int [], int, int);
const int arrSize = 20;

int main()
{
    int tests[arrSize] = {101, 142, 147, 189, 199, 207, 222,
                          234, 289, 296, 310, 319, 388, 394,
                          417, 429, 447, 521, 536, 600};
    int results, empID;

    cout << "Enter the employee ID you wish to search for: ";
    cin >> empID;
    results = binarySearch(tests, arrSize, empID);
    if (results == -1)
        cout << "That number does not exist in the array.\n";
    else
    {
        cout << "That ID is found at element " << results;
        cout << " in the array.\n";
    }
    return 0;
}

//*****************************************************************
// The binarySearch function performs a binary search on an      *
// integer array. array, which has a maximum of numElems         *
// elements, is searched for the number stored in value. If the  *
// number is found, its array subscript is returned. Otherwise,  *
// -1 is returned, indicating the value was not in the array.    *
//*****************************************************************

int binarySearch(int array[], int numElems, int value)
{
    int  first = 0,               // First array element
         last = numElems - 1,     // Last array element
         middle,                  // Midpoint of search
         position = -1;           // Position of search value
    bool found = false;           // Flag
```

(program continues)

Program 9-2   *(continued)*

```
while (!found && first <= last)
{
    middle = (first + last) / 2;        // Calculate midpoint
    if (array[middle] == value)         // If value is found at midpoint
    {
        found = true;
        position = middle;
    }
    else if (array[middle] > value)     // If value is in lower half
        last = middle - 1;
    else
        first = middle + 1;             // If value is in upper half
}
return position;
}
```

Program Output with Example Input Shown in Bold
```
Enter the employee ID you wish to search for: 199[Enter]
That ID is found at element 4 in the array.
```

The Efficiency of the Binary Search

Obviously, the binary search is much more efficient than the linear search. Every time it makes a comparison and fails to find the desired item, it eliminates half of the remaining portion of the array that must be searched. For example, consider an array with 1,000 elements. If the binary search fails to find an item on the first attempt, the number of elements that remains to be searched is 500. If the item is not found on the second attempt, the number of elements that remains to be searched is 250. This process continues until the binary search locates the desired value or determines that it is not in the array. With 1,000 elements in the array, this takes a maximum of 10 comparisons. (Compare this to the linear search, which would make an average of 500 comparisons!)

Powers of 2 are used to calculate the maximum number of comparisons the binary search will make on an array of any size. (A power of 2 is 2 raised to the power of some number.) Simply find the smallest power of 2 that is greater than or equal to the number of elements in the array. For example, a maximum of 16 comparisons will be made on an array of 50,000 elements ($2^{16} = 65,536$), and a maximum of 20 comparisons will be made on an array of 1,000,000 elements ($2^{20} = 1,048,576$).

9.2   Focus on Problem Solving and Program Design: A Case Study

The Demetris Leadership Center (DLC, Inc.) publishes the books, videos, and audio cassettes listed in Table 9-1.

Table 9-1

Product Title	Product Description	Product Number	Unit
Six Steps to Leadership	Book	914	$12.95
"Six Steps to Leadership"	Audio cassette	915	$14.95
The Road to Excellence	Video	916	$18.95
Seven Lessons of Quality	Book	917	$16.95
"Seven Lessons of Quality"	Audio cassette	918	$21.95
Seven Lessons of Quality	Video	919	$31.95
Teams are Made, Not Born	Book	920	$14.95
Leadership for the Future	Book	921	$14.95
"Leadership for the Future"	Audio cassette	922	$16.95

The manager of the Telemarketing Group has asked you to write a program that will help order-entry operators look up product prices. The program should prompt the user to enter a product number and then display the title, description, and price of the product.

Variables

Table 9-2 lists the variables needed.

Table 9-2

Variable	Description
numProds	A constant integer initialized with the number of products the Demetris Leadership Center sells. This value will be used in the declaration of the program's array.
id	Array of integers. Holds each product's number.
title	Array of string objects, initialized with the titles of products.
description	Array of string objects, initialized with the descriptions of each product.
prices	Array of floats. Holds each product's price.

Modules

The program will consist of the functions listed in Table 9-3.

Table 9-3

Function	Description
main	The program's main function. It calls the program's other functions.
getProdNum	Prompts the user to enter a product number. The function validates input and rejects any value outside the range of correct product numbers.
binarySearch	A standard binary search routine. Searches an array for a specified value. If the value is found, its subscript is returned. If the value is not found, –1 is returned.
displayProd	Uses a common subscript into the title, description, and prices arrays to display the title, description, and price of a product.

Function main

Function main contains the variable definitions and calls the other functions. Here is its pseudocode:

```
do
    Call getProdNum.
    Call binarySearch.
    If binarySearch returned -1
        Inform the user that the product number was not found.
    else
        Call displayProd.
    End If.
    Ask the user if the program should repeat.
While the user wants to repeat the program.
```

Here is its actual C++ code:

```
int main()
{
    int id[numProds] = {914, 915, 916, 917, 918, 919, 920,
                        921, 922};

    string title[numProds] = {"Six Steps to Leadership",
                              "Six Steps to Leadership",
                              "The Road to Excellence",
                              "Seven Lessons of Quality",
                              "Seven Lessons of Quality",
                              "Seven Lessons of Quality",
                              "Teams are Made, not Born",
                              "Leadership for the Future",
                              "Leadership for the Future"};
```

```
string description[] = {"Book", "Audio cassette", "Video",
                        "Book", "Audio cassette", "Video",
                        "Book", "Book", "Audio cassette"};

float prices[numProds] = {12.95, 14.95, 18.95, 16.95, 21.95,
                          31.95, 14.95, 14.95, 16.95};
int prodNum, index;
char again;

do
{
    prodNum = getProdNum();
    index = binarySearch(id, numProds, prodNum);
    if (index == -1)
        cout << "That product number was not found.\n";
    else
        displayProd(title, description, prices, index);

    cout << "Would you like to look up another product? (y/n) ";
    cin >> again;
} while (again == 'y' || again == 'Y');
return 0;
}
```

The named constant numProds will be declared globally and initialized to the value 9. Notice that the arrays id, title, description, and prices are initialized with data.

 Note: By using a named constant for the declaration of array sizes, you are making it easier to modify the program in the future.

The getProdNum Function

The getProdNum function prompts the user to enter a product number. It tests the value to ensure it is in the range of 914 to 922 (which are the valid product numbers). If an invalid value is entered, it is rejected and the user is prompted again. When a valid product number is entered, the function returns it. The pseudocode is as follows:

```
Display a prompt to enter a product number.
Read prodNum.
While prodNum is invalid
    Display an error messge.
    Read prodNum.
End While.
Return prodNum.
```

Here is the actual C++ code:

```cpp
int getProdNum()
{
    int prodNum;

    cout << "Enter the item's product number: ";
    cin >> prodNum;

    // Validate input
    while (prodNum < 914 || prodNum > 922)
    {
        cout << "Enter a number in the range 914 - 922: ";
        cin >> prodNum;
    }
    return prodNum;
}
```

The `binarySearch` Function

The `binarySearch` function is identical to the function discussed earlier in this chapter.

The `displayProd` Function

The `displayProd` function has parameter variables named `title`, `desc`, `price`, and `index`. These accept as arguments (respectively) the `title`, `description`, and `price` arrays, and a subscript value. The function displays the data stored in each array at the subscript passed into `index`. Here is the C++ code:

```cpp
void displayProd(string title[], string desc[], float price[], int index)
{
    cout << "Title: " << title[index] << endl;
    cout << "Description: " << desc[index] << endl;
    cout << "Price: $" << price[index] << endl;
}
```

The Entire Program

Program 9-3 shows the entire program's source code.

Program 9-3

```cpp
// This program allows the user to enter a product number
// and then displays the title, description, and price of
// that product.

#include <iostream>
#include <string>
using namespace std;

// Function prototypes
int getProdNum();
int binarySearch(int [], int, int);
void displayProd(string [], string [], float [], int);

// numProds is the number of products produced.
const int numProds = 9;

int main()
{
    int id[numProds] = {914, 915, 916, 917, 918, 919, 920,
                        921, 922};

    string title[numProds] = {"Six Steps to Leadership",
                              "Six Steps to Leadership",
                              "The Road to Excellence",
                              "Seven Lessons of Quality",
                              "Seven Lessons of Quality",
                              "Seven Lessons of Quality",
                              "Teams are Made, not Born",
                              "Leadership for the Future",
                              "Leadership for the Future"};

    string description[] = {"Book", "Audio cassette", "Video",
                            "Book", "Audio cassette", "Video",
                            "Book", "Book", "Audio cassette"};

    float prices[numProds] = {12.95, 14.95, 18.95, 16.95, 21.95,
                              31.95, 14.95, 14.95, 16.95};
    int prodNum, index;
    char again;
```

(program continues)

Program 9-3   *(continued)*

```cpp
   do
   {
       prodNum = getProdNum();
       index = binarySearch(id, numProds, prodNum);
       if (index == -1)
           cout << "That product number was not found.\n";
       else
           displayProd(title, description, prices, index);
       cout << "Would you like to look up another product? (y/n) ";
       cin >> again;
   } while (again == 'y' || again == 'Y');

   return 0;
}

//******************************************************
//                   getProdNum                       *
// The getProdNum function asks the user to enter a    *
// product number. The input is validated, and when    *
// a valid number is entered, it is returned.          *
//******************************************************

int getProdNum()
{
   int prodNum;

   cout << "Enter the item's product number: ";
   cin  >> prodNum;

   // Validate input
   while (prodNum < 914 || prodNum > 922)
   {
       cout << "Enter a number in the range 914 - 922: ";
       cin  >> prodNum;
   }
   return prodNum;
}

//*********************************************************************
//                      binarySearch                                 *
// The binarySearch function performs a binary search on an          *
// integer array. array, which has a maximum of numElems             *
// elements, is searched for the number stored in value. If the      *
// number is found, its array subscript is returned. Otherwise,      *
// -1 is returned, indicating the value was not in the array.        *
//*********************************************************************
```

(program continues)

Program 9-3   *(continued)*

```cpp
int binarySearch(int array[], int numElems, int value)
{
    int  first = 0,                        // First array element
         last = numElems - 1,              // Last array element
         middle,                           // Midpoint of search
         position = -1;                    // Position of search value
    bool found = false;                    // Flag

    while (!found && first <= last)
    {
        middle = (first + last) / 2;       // Calculate midpoint
        if (array[middle] == value)        // If value is found at midpoint
        {
            found = true;
            position = middle;
        }
        else if (array[middle] > value)    // If value is in lower half
            last = middle - 1;
        else
            first = middle + 1;            // If value is in upper half
    }
    return position;
}


//***************************************************************
//                    displayProd                              *
// The displayProd function accepts three arrays and an int.    *
// The array parameters are expected to hold the title,         *
// description, and prices arrays defined in main. The          *
// index parameter holds a subscript. This function displays    *
// the information in each array contained at the subscript.    *
//***************************************************************

void displayProd(string title[], string desc[], float price[], int index)
{
    cout << "Title: " << title[index] << endl;
    cout << "Description: " << desc[index] << endl;
    cout << "Price: $" << price[index] << endl;
}
```

Program 9-3

Program Output with Example Input Shown in Bold

```
Enter the item's product number: 916[Enter]
Title: The Road to Excellence
Description: Video
Price: $18.95
Would you like to look up another product? (y/n) y[Enter]
Enter the item's product number: 920[Enter]
Title: Teams are Made, not Born
Description: Book
Price: $14.95
Would you like to look up another product? (y/n) n[Enter]
```

Checkpoint [9.1–9.2]

9.1 Describe the difference between the linear search and the binary search.

9.2 On average, with an array of 20,000 elements, how many comparisons will the linear search perform? (Assume the items being search for are consistently found in the array.)

9.3 With an array of 20,000 elements, what is the maximum number of comparisons the binary search will perform?

9.4 If a linear search is performed on an array, and it is known that some items are searched for more frequently than others, how can the contents of the array be reordered to improve the average performance of the search?

9.3 Focus on Software Engineering: *Introduction to Sorting Algorithms*

CONCEPT Sorting algorithms are used to arrange data into some order.

Often the information in an array must be sorted in some order. Customer lists, for instance, are commonly sorted in alphabetical order. Student grades might be sorted from highest to lowest. Product codes could be sorted so all the products of the same color are stored together. To sort the information in an array, the programmer must use an appropriate *sorting algorithm*. A sorting algorithm is a technique for scanning through an array and rearranging its contents in some specific order. This section will introduce two simple sorting algorithms: the *bubble sort* and the *selection sort*.

The Bubble Sort

The bubble sort is an easy way to arrange data in *ascending* or *descending order*. If an array is sorted in ascending order, it means the values in the array are stored from lowest to highest. If the values are sorted in descending order, they are stored from highest to lowest. Let's see how the bubble sort is used in arranging the following array's elements in ascending order:

7	2	3	8	9	1
Element 0	Element 1	Element 2	Element 3	Element 4	Element 5

The bubble sort starts by comparing the first two elements in the array. If element 0 is greater than element 1, they are exchanged. After the exchange, the array would appear as

2	7	3	8	9	1
Element 0	Element 1	Element 2	Element 3	Element 4	Element 5

This process is repeated with elements 1 and 2. If element 1 is greater than element 2, they are exchanged. The array would then appear as

2	3	7	8	9	1
Element 0	Element 1	Element 2	Element 3	Element 4	Element 5

Next, elements 2 and 3 are compared. In the array above, these two elements are already in the proper order (element 2 is less than element 3), so no exchange takes place.

As the cycle continues, elements 3 and 4 are compared. Once again, no exchange is necessary because they are already in the proper order. When elements 4 and 5 are compared, however, an exchange must take place because element 4 is greater than element 5. The array now appears as

2	3	7	8	1	9
Element 0	Element 1	Element 2	Element 3	Element 4	Element 5

At this point, the entire array has been scanned, but its contents aren't quite in the right order yet. So the sort starts over again with elements 0 and 1. Since they are in the proper order, no exchange takes place. Elements 1 and 2 are compared next, but once again, no exchange takes place. This continues until elements 3 and 4 are compared. Since element 3 is greater than element 4, they are exchanged. The array now appears as

2	3	7	1	8	9
Element 0	Element 1	Element 2	Element 3	Element 4	Element 5

By now you should see how the sort will eventually cause the elements to appear in the correct order. The sort repeatedly passes through the array until no exchanges are made. Ultimately, the array will appear as

1	2	3	7	8	9
Element 0	Element 1	Element 2	Element 3	Element 4	Element 5

Here is the bubble sort in pseudocode:

```
Do
    Set swap flag to false.
    For count is set to each subscript in array from 0 through the
            next-to-last subscript
        If array[count] is greater than array[count + 1]
            Swap the contents of array[count] and array[count + 1].
            Set swap flag to true.
        End If.
    End For.
While any elements have been swapped.
```

The following C++ code implements the bubble sort as a function. The parameter `array` is an integer array to be sorted. The parameter `elems` contains the number of elements in `array`.

```cpp
void sortArray(int array[], int elems)
{
    int temp;
    bool swap;

    do
    {
        swap = false;
        for (int count = 0; count < (elems - 1); count++)
        {
            if (array[count] > array[count + 1])
            {
                temp = array[count];
                array[count] = array[count + 1];
                array[count + 1] = temp;
                swap = true;
            }
        }
    } while (swap);
}
```

Inside the function is a `for` loop nested inside a `do-while` loop. The `for` loop sequences through the entire array, comparing each element with its neighbor, and swapping them if necessary. Anytime two elements are exchanged, the flag variable `swap` is set to `true`.

The `for` loop must be executed repeatedly until it can sequence through the entire array without making any exchanges. This is why it is nested inside a `do-while` loop. The `do-while` loop sets `swap` to `false`, and then executes the `for` loop. If `swap` is set to `true` after the `for` loop has finished, the `do-while` loop repeats.

Here is the starting line of the `for` loop:

```
for (int count = 0; count < (elems - 1); count++)
```

The variable `count` holds the array subscript values. It starts at zero and is incremented as long as it is less than `elems - 1`. The value of `elems` is the number of elements in the array, and `count` stops just short of reaching this value because the following line compares each element with the one after it:

```
if (array[count] > array[count + 1])
```

When `array[count]` is the next-to-last element, it will be compared to the last element. If the `for` loop were allowed to increment `count` past `elems - 1`, the last element in the array would be compared to a value outside the array.

Let's look at the `if` statement in its entirety:

```
if (array[count] > array[count + 1])
{
    temp = array[count];
    array[count] = array[count + 1];
    array[count + 1] = temp;
    swap = true;
}
```

If `array[count]` is greater than `array[count + 1]`, the two elements must be exchanged. First, the contents of `array[count]` is copied into the variable `temp`. Then the contents of `array[count + 1]` is copied into `array[count]`. The exchange is made complete when `temp` (which holds the previous contents of `array[count]`) is copied to `array[count + 1]`. Last, the `swap` flag variable is set to `true`. This indicates that an exchange has been made.

Program 9-4 demonstrates the bubble sort function in a complete program.

Program 9-4

```
// This program uses the bubble sort algorithm to sort an
// array in ascending order.

#include <iostream>
using namespace std;

// Function prototypes
void sortArray(int [], int);
void showArray(int [], int);

int main()
{
    int values[6] = {7, 2, 3, 8, 9, 1};

    cout << "The unsorted values are:\n";
    showArray(values, 6);
    sortArray(values, 6);
    cout << "The sorted values are:\n";
    showArray(values, 6);
```

(program continues)

Program 9-4 *(continued)*

```
    return 0;
}

//****************************************************************
// Definition of function sortArray                             *
// This function performs an ascending-order bubble sort on     *
// array. The parameter elems holds the number of elements      *
// in the array.                                                *
//****************************************************************

void sortArray(int array[], int elems)
{
    int temp;
    bool swap;

    do
    {
        swap = false;
        for (int count = 0; count < (elems - 1); count++)
        {
            if (array[count] > array[count + 1])
            {
                temp = array[count];
                array[count] = array[count + 1];
                array[count + 1] = temp;
                swap = true;
            }
        }
    } while (swap);
}

//****************************************************************
// Definition of function showArray                             *
// This function displays the contents of array. The parameter  *
// elems holds the number of elements in the array.             *
//****************************************************************

void showArray(int array[], int elems)
{
    for (int count = 0; count < elems; count++)
        cout << array[count] << " ";
    cout << endl;
}
```

Program Output

```
The unsorted values are:
7 2 3 8 9 1
The sorted values are:
1 2 3 7 8 9
```

The Selection Sort

The bubble sort is inefficient for large arrays because items only move by one element at a time. The selection sort, however, usually performs fewer exchanges because it moves items immediately to their final position in the array. Like any sort it can be modified to sort in either ascending or descending order. An ascending sort works like this: The smallest value in the array is located and moved to element 0. Then the next smallest value is located and moved to element 1. This process continues until all of the elements have been placed in their proper order.

Let's see how the selection sort works when arranging the elements of the following array:

5	7	2	8	9	1
Element 0	Element 1	Element 2	Element 3	Element 4	Element 5

The selection sort scans the array, starting at element 0, and locates the element with the smallest value. The contents of this element are then swapped with the contents of element 0. In the example, the 1 stored in element 5 is swapped with the 5 stored in element 0. After the exchange, the array would appear as

1	7	2	8	9	5
Element 0	Element 1	Element 2	Element 3	Element 4	Element 5

The algorithm then repeats the process, but since element 0 already contains the smallest value in the array, it can be left out of the procedure. This time, the algorithm begins the scan at element 1. In the example, the contents of element 2 are exchanged with that of element 1. The array would then appear as

1	2	7	8	9	5
Element 0	Element 1	Element 2	Element 3	Element 4	Element 5

Once again the process is repeated, but this time the scan begins at element 2. The algorithm will find that element 5 contains the next smallest value. This element's contents is exchanged with that of element 2, causing the array to appear as

1	2	5	8	9	7
Element 0	Element 1	Element 2	Element 3	Element 4	Element 5

Next, the scanning begins at element 3. Its contents is exchanged with that of element 5, causing the array to appear as

1	2	5	7	9	8
Element 0	Element 1	Element 2	Element 3	Element 4	Element 5

At this point there are only two elements left to sort. The algorithm finds that the value in element 5 is smaller than that of element 4, so the two are swapped. This puts the array in its final arrangement:

1	2	5	7	8	9
Element 0	Element 1	Element 2	Element 3	Element 4	Element 5

Here is the selection sort algorithm in pseudocode:

```
For startScan is set to each subscript in array from 0 through the
            next-to-last subscript
    Set index variable to startScan.
    Set minIndex variable to startScan.
    Set minValue variable to array[startScan].

    For index is set to each subscript in array from (startScan + 1)
            through the last subscript
        If array[index] is less than minValue
            Set minValue to array[index].
            Set minIndex to index.
        End If.
        Increment index.
    End For.
    Set array[minIndex] to array[startScan].
    Set array[startScan] to minValue.
End For.
```

The following C++ code implements the selection sort in a function. It accepts two arguments: `array` and `elems`. The parameter `array` is an integer array and `elems` is the number of elements in the array. The function uses the selection sort to arrange the values in the array in ascending order.

```cpp
void selectionSort(int array[], int elems)
{
    int startScan, minIndex, minValue;

    for (startScan = 0; startScan < (elems - 1); startScan++)
    {
        minIndex = startScan;
        minValue = array[startScan];
        for(int index = startScan + 1; index < elems; index++)
        {
            if (array[index] < minValue)
            {
                minValue = array[index];
                minIndex = index;
            }
        }
        array[minIndex] = array[startScan];
        array[startScan] = minValue;
    }
}
```

Inside the function are two `for` loops, one nested inside the other. The inner loop sequences through the array, starting at `array[startScan]`, searching for the element with the smallest value. When the element is found, its subscript is stored in the variable `minIndex` and its value is stored in `minValue`. The outer loop then exchanges the contents of this element with array[startScan] and increments startScan. This procedure repeats until the contents of every element have been moved to their proper location.

Program 9-5 demonstrates the selection sort function in a complete program.

Program 9-5

```cpp
// This program uses the selection sort algorithm to sort an
// array in ascending order.

#include <iostream>
using namespace std;

// Function prototypes
void selectionSort(int [], int);
void showArray(int [], int);

int main()
{
    int values[6] = {5, 7, 2, 8, 9, 1};

    cout << "The unsorted values are\n";
    showArray(values, 6);
    selectionSort(values, 6);
    cout << "The sorted values are\n";
    showArray(values, 6);
    return 0;
}

//****************************************************************
// Definition of function selectionSort                        *
// This function performs an ascending-order selection sort on *
// array. The parameter elems holds the number of elements     *
// in the array.                                               *
//****************************************************************

void selectionSort(int array[], int elems)
{
    int startScan, minIndex, minValue;

    for (startScan = 0; startScan < (elems - 1); startScan++)
    {
        minIndex = startScan;
        minValue = array[startScan];
```

(program continues)

Program 9-5 *(continued)*

```
        for(int index = startScan + 1; index < elems; index++)
        {
            if (array[index] < minValue)
            {
                minValue = array[index];
                minIndex = index;
            }
        }
        array[minIndex] = array[startScan];
        array[startScan] = minValue;
    }
}

//****************************************************************
// Definition of function showArray                            *
// This function displays the contents of array. The parameter *
// elems holds the number of elements in the array.            *
//****************************************************************

void showArray(int array[], int elems)
{
    for (int count = 0; count < elems; count++)
        cout << array[count] << " ";
    cout << endl;
}
```

Program Output
```
The unsorted values are
5 7 2 8 9 1
The sorted values are
1 2 5 7 8 9
```

9.4 Focus on Problem Solving and Program Design: A Case Study

Like the previous case study, this is a program developed for the Demetris Leadership Center. Recall that DLC, Inc. publishes books, videos, and audio cassettes. (See Table 9-1 for a complete list of products, with title, description, product number, and price.) Table 9-4 shows the number of units of each product sold during the past six months.

Table 9-4

Product Number	Units Sold
914	842
915	416
916	127
917	514
918	437
919	269
920	97
921	492
922	212

The vice president of sales has asked you to write a sales reporting program that displays the following information:

◆ A list of the products in the order of their sales dollars (not units sold), from highest to lowest

◆ The total number of all units sold

◆ The total sales for the six-month period

Variables

Table 9-5 lists the variables needed.

Table 9-5

Variable	Description
numProds	A constant integer initialized with the number of products DLC, Inc. sells. This value will be used in the definition of the program's arrays.
prodNum	Array of ints. Holds each product's number.
units	Array of ints. Holds each product's number of units sold.
prices	Array of floats. Holds each product's price.
sales	Array of floats. Holds the computed sales amounts (in dollars) of each product.

The four arrays (prodNum, units, prices, and sales) are parallel arrays. That is, the data in any given element of one array corresponds with data in the same element of the other arrays. For example, the product whose number is stored in prodNum[2] will have sold the number of units stored in units[2]. The sales amount for the product will be stored in sales[2].

Modules

The program will consist of the functions listed in Table 9-6.

Table 9-6

Function	Description
main	The program's main function. It calls the program's other functions.
calcSales	Calculates each product's sales.
dualSort	Sorts the sales array so the elements are ordered from highest to lowest. The prodNum array is ordered so the product numbers correspond with the correct sales figures in the sorted sales array.
showOrder	Displays a list of the product numbers and sales amounts from the sorted sales and prodNum arrays.
showTotals	Displays the total number of units sold and the total sales amount for the period.

Function main

Function main is very simple. It contains the variable definitions and calls the other functions. Here is the pseudocode for its executable statements:

```
Call calcSales.
Call dualSort.
Set the desired output formats.
Call showOrder.
Call showTotals.
```

Here is its actual C++ code:

```
int main()
{
    int id[numProds] = {914, 915, 916, 917, 918, 919, 920,
                        921, 922};
    int units[numProds] = {842, 416, 127, 514, 437, 269, 97,
                          492, 212};
    float prices[numProds] = {12.95, 14.95, 18.95, 16.95, 21.95,
                             31.95, 14.95, 14.95, 16.95};
    float sales[numProds];
```

```
        calcSales(units, prices, sales, numProds);
        dualSort(id, sales, numProds);
        cout << fixed << showpoint << setprecision(2);
        showOrder(sales, id, numProds);
        showTotals(sales, units, numProds);
        return 0;
}
```

The named constant `numProds` will be declared globally and initialized to the value 9.

 Note: By using a named constant for the declaration of array sizes, you are making it easier to modify the program in the future.

Notice that the arrays `id`, `units`, and `prices` are initialized with data. (It will be left as an exercise for you to modify this program so the user may enter these values.)

The `calcSales` Function

The `calcSales` function multiplies each product's units sold by its price. The resulting amount is stored in the `sales` array. Here is the function's pseudocode:

> *For index is set to each subscript in the arrays from 0 through the last*
> *subscript.*
> *Set sales[index] to units[index] times prices[index].*
> *End For.*

And here is the function's actual C++ code:

```
    void calcSales(int units[], float prices[], float sales[], int num)
    {
        for (int index = 0; index < num; index++)
            sales[index] = units[index] * prices[index];
    }
```

The `dualSort` Function

The `dualSort` function is a modified version of the selection sort algorithm shown in Program 9-5. The `dualSort` function accepts two arrays as arguments: the `sales` array and the `id` array. The function actually performs the selection sort on the `sales` array. When the function moves an element in the `sales` array, however, it also moves the corresponding element in the `id` array. This is to ensure that the product numbers in the `id` array still have subscripts that match their sales figures in the `sales` array.

The `dualSort` function is also different in another way: It sorts the array in descending order.

Here is the pseudocode for the `dualSort` function:

For startScan variable is set to each subscript in array from 0 through
the next-to-last subscript
    Set index variable to startScan.
    Set maxIndex variable to startScan.
    Set tempId variable to id[startScan].
    Set maxValue variable to sales[startScan].
    For index variable is set to each subscript in array from
                      (startScan + 1) through the last subscript
       If sales[index] is greater than maxValue
          Set maxValue to sales[index].
          Set tempId to tempId[index].
          Set maxIndex to index.
       End If.
    End For.
    Set sales[maxIndex] to sales[startScan].
    Set id[maxIndex] = id[startScan].
    Set sales[startScan] to maxValue.
    Set id[startScan] = tempId.
End For.

Here is the actual C++ code for the dualSort function:

```cpp
void dualSort(int id[], float sales[], int elems)
{
    int startScan, maxIndex, tempId;
    float maxValue;

    for (startScan = 0; startScan < (elems - 1); startScan++)
    {
        maxIndex = startScan;
        maxValue = sales[startScan];
        tempId = id[startScan];
        for(int index = startScan + 1; index < elems; index++)
        {
            if (sales[index] > maxValue)
            {
                maxValue = sales[index];
                tempId = id[index];
                maxIndex = index;
            }
        }
        sales[maxIndex] = sales[startScan];
        id[maxIndex] = id[startScan];
        sales[startScan] = maxValue;
        id[startScan] = tempId;
    }
}
```

Note: Once the `dualSort` function is called, the `id` and `sales` arrays are no longer synchronized with the `units` and `prices` arrays. Since this program doesn't use `units` and `prices` together with `id` and `sales` after this point, it will not be noticed in the final output. It is never good programming practice to sort parallel arrays in such a way that they are out of synchronization. It will be left as an exercise for you to modify the program so all the arrays are synchronized and used in the final output of the program.

The `showOrder` Function

The `showOrder` function displays a heading and the sorted list of product numbers and their sales amounts. It accepts the `id` and `sales` arrays as arguments. Here is its pseudocode:

```
Display heading.
For index variable is set to each subscript of the arrays from 0 through
the last subscript
    Display id[index].
    Display sales[index].
End For.
```

Here is the function's actual C++ code:

```cpp
void showOrder(float sales[], int id[], int num)
{
    cout << "Product Number\tSales\n";

    cout << "------------------------------------\n";
    for (int index = 0; index < num; index++)
    {
        cout << id[index] << "\t\t$";
        cout << setw(8) << sales[index] << endl;
    }
    cout << endl;
}
```

The `showTotals` Function

The `showTotals` function displays the total number of units of all products sold and the total sales for the period. It accepts the `units` and `sales` arrays as arguments. Here is its pseudocode:

```
Set totalUnits variable to 0.
Set totalSales variable to 0.0.
For index variable is set to each subscript in the arrays from 0 through
the last subscript
    Add units[index] to totalUnits[index].
    Add sales[index] to totalSales.
End For.
Display totalUnits with appropriate heading.
Display totalSales with appropriate heading.
```

Here is the function's actual C++ code:

```cpp
void showTotals(float sales[], int units[], int num)
{
    int totalUnits = 0;
    float totalSales = 0.0;
    for (int index = 0; index < num; index++)
    {
        totalUnits += units[index];
        totalSales += sales[index];
    }
    cout << "Total Units Sold:  " << totalUnits << endl;
    cout << "Total Sales:       $" << totalSales << endl;
}
```

The Entire Program

Program 9-6 shows the entire program's source code.

Program 9-6

```cpp
// This program produces a sales report for the Demetris
// Leadership Center.

#include <iostream>
#include <iomanip>
using namespace std;

// Function prototypes
void calcSales(int [], float [], float [], int);
void showOrder(float [], int [], int);
void dualSort(int [], float [], int);
void showTotals(float [], int [], int);

// numProds is the number of products produced.
const int numProds = 9;

int main()
{
    int id[numProds] = {914, 915, 916, 917, 918, 919, 920,
                        921, 922};
    int units[numProds] = {842, 416, 127, 514, 437, 269, 97,
                           492, 212};
    float prices[numProds] = {12.95, 14.95, 18.95, 16.95, 21.95,
                              31.95, 14.95, 14.95, 16.95};
    float sales[numProds];

    calcSales(units, prices, sales, numProds);
    dualSort(id, sales, numProds);
    cout << fixed << showpoint << setprecision(2);
```

(program continues)

Program 9-6 *(continued)*

```
        showOrder(sales, id, numProds);
        showTotals(sales, units, numProds);
        return 0;
}

//**************************************************************
//                      calcSales                             *
// The calcSales function accepts units, prices, and sales    *
// arrays as arguments. The size of these arrays is passed    *
// into the num parameter. This function calculates each      *
// product's sales by multiplying its units sold by each      *
// unit's price. The result is stored in the sales array.     *
//**************************************************************

void calcSales(int units[], float prices[], float sales[], int num)
{
    for (int index = 0; index < num; index++)
        sales[index] = units[index] * prices[index];
}

//****************************************************************
//                      dualSort                                *
// The dualSort function accepts the id and sales arrays as     *
// arguments. The size of these arrays is passed into elems.    *
// This function performs a descending-order selection sort on  *
// the sales array. The elements of the id array are exchanged  *
// identically as those of the sales array.                     *
//****************************************************************

void dualSort(int id[], float sales[], int elems)
{
    int startScan, maxIndex, tempId;
    float maxValue;

    for (startScan = 0; startScan < (elems - 1); startScan++)
    {
        maxIndex = startScan;
        maxValue = sales[startScan];
        tempId = id[startScan];
        for(int index = startScan + 1; index < elems; index++)
        {
            if (sales[index] > maxValue)
            {
                maxValue = sales[index];
                tempId = id[index];
                maxIndex = index;
            }
        }
```

(program continues)

Program 9-6   *(continued)*

```cpp
            sales[maxIndex] = sales[startScan];
            id[maxIndex] = id[startScan];
            sales[startScan] = maxValue;
            id[startScan] = tempId;
        }
    }

//*********************************************************************
//                       showOrder                                    *
// The showOrder function accepts the sales and id arrays             *
// as arguments. The size of these arrays is passed into num.         *
// The function first displays a heading, then the sorted list        *
// of product numbers and sales.                                      *
//*********************************************************************

void showOrder(float sales[], int id[], int num)
{
    cout << "Product Number\tSales\n";
    cout << "-----------------------------------\n";
    for (int index = 0; index < num; index++)
    {
        cout << id[index] << "\t\t$";
        cout << setw(8) << sales[index] << endl;
    }
    cout << endl;
}

//*********************************************************************
//                       showTotals                                   *
// The showTotals function accepts the sales and id arrays as         *
// arguments. The size of these arrays is passed into num.            *
// The function first calculates the total units of all products      *
// sold and the total sales. It then displays these amounts.          *
//*********************************************************************

void showTotals(float sales[], int units[], int num)
{
    int totalUnits = 0;
    float totalSales = 0.0;

    for (int index = 0; index < num; index++)
    {
        totalUnits += units[index];
        totalSales += sales[index];
    }
    cout << "Total Units Sold:  " << totalUnits << endl;
    cout << "Total Sales:      $" << totalSales << endl;
}
```

Program 9-6

Program Output

```
Product Number    Sales
- - - - - - - - - - - - - - - - - - - - - - - - - - - - - -
914               $10903.90
918               $ 9592.15
917               $ 8712.30
919               $ 8594.55
921               $ 7355.40
915               $ 6219.20
922               $ 3593.40
916               $ 2406.65
920               $ 1450.15

Total Units Sold:  3406
Total Sales:       $58827.70
```

9.5   Sorting and Searching Vectors (enrichment)
(Continued from Section 8.10)

CONCEPT	The sorting and searching algorithms you have studied in this chapter may be applied to STL vectors as well as to arrays.

Once you have properly declared an STL vector and populated it with values, you may sort and search the vector with the algorithms presented in this chapter. Simply substitute the vector syntax for the array syntax when necessary. Program 9-7, which illustrates this, is a modification of the case study in Program 9-6.

Program 9-7

```
// This program produces a sales report for the Demetris
// Leadership Center. This version of the program uses
// STL vectors instead of arrays.

#include <iostream>
#include <iomanip>
#include <vector>       // Needed to declare vectors
using namespace std;    // vectors are in the std namespace
```

(program continues)

Program 9-7 *(continued)*

```cpp
// Function prototypes
void initVectors(vector<int> &, vector<int> &, vector<float> &);
void calcSales(vector<int>, vector<float>, vector<float> &);
void showOrder(vector<float>, vector<int>);
void dualSort(vector<int> &, vector<float> &);
void showTotals(vector<float>, vector<int>);

int main()
{
    vector<int> id;
    vector<int> units;
    vector<float> prices;
    vector<float> sales;

    // Required initialization routine
    initVectors(id, units, prices);

    // Calculate and sort the sales totals and display results
    calcSales(units, prices, sales);
    dualSort(id, sales);
    cout << fixed << showpoint << setprecision(2);
    showOrder(sales, id);
    showTotals(sales, units);

    return 0;
}

//*****************************************************************
//                       initVectors                            *
// The initVectors function accepts the id, units, and prices   *
// vectors as reference arguments. This function initializes each *
// vector to a set of starting values.                          *
//*****************************************************************
void initVectors(vector<int> &id, vector<int> &units, vector<float> &prices)
{
    // Initialize the id vector
    for (int value = 914; value <= 922; value++)
        id.push_back(value);
```

(program continues)

Program 9-7   *(continued)*

```
    // Initialize the units vector
    units.push_back(842);
    units.push_back(416);
    units.push_back(127);
    units.push_back(514);
    units.push_back(437);
    units.push_back(269);
    units.push_back(97);
    units.push_back(492);
    units.push_back(212);

    // Initialize the prices vector
    prices.push_back(12.95);
    prices.push_back(14.95);
    prices.push_back(18.95);
    prices.push_back(16.95);
    prices.push_back(21.95);
    prices.push_back(31.95);
    prices.push_back(14.95);
    prices.push_back(14.95);
    prices.push_back(16.95);
}


//*****************************************************************
//                          calcSales                           *
// The calcSales function accepts the units, prices, and sales  *
// vectors as arguments. The sales vector is passed into a      *
// reference parameter. This function calculates each product's *
// sales by multiplying its units sold by each unit's price. The *
// result is stored in the sales vector.                        *
//*****************************************************************

void calcSales(vector<int> units, vector<float> prices, vector<float> &sales)
{
    for (int index = 0; index < units.size(); index++)
        sales.push_back(units[index] * prices[index]);
}
```

(program continues)

Program 9-7   *(continued)*

```
//*******************************************************************
//                         dualSort                                *
// The dualSort function accepts the id and sales vectors as       *
// reference arguments. This function performs a descending-order  *
// selection sort on the sales vector. The elements of the id      *
// vector are exchanged identically as those of the sales vector.  *
//*******************************************************************

void dualSort(vector<int> &id, vector<float> &sales)
{
    int startScan, maxIndex, tempid, elems;
    float maxValue;

    elems = id.size();
    for (startScan = 0; startScan < (elems - 1); startScan++)
    {
        maxIndex = startScan;
        maxValue = sales[startScan];
        tempid = id[startScan];
        for(int index = startScan + 1; index < elems; index++)
        {
            if (sales[index] > maxValue)
            {
                maxValue = sales[index];
                tempid = id[index];
                maxIndex = index;
            }
        }
        sales[maxIndex] = sales[startScan];
        id[maxIndex] = id[startScan];
        sales[startScan] = maxValue;
        id[startScan] = tempid;
    }
}

//*******************************************************************
//                         showOrder                               *
// The showOrder function accepts the sales and id vectors as      *
// arguments. The function first displays a heading, then the      *
// sorted list of product numbers and sales.                       *
//*******************************************************************
```

(program continues)

Program 9-7 *(continued)*

```cpp
void showOrder(vector<float> sales, vector<int> id)
{
    cout << "Product Number\tSales\n";
    cout << "----------------------------------";
    for (int index = 0; index < id.size(); index++)
    {
        cout << id[index] << "\t\t$";
        cout << setw(8) << sales[index] << endl;
    }
    cout << endl;
}


/***************************************************************************
//                          showTotals                                    *
// The showTotals function accepts the sales and id vectors as            *
// arguments. The function first calculates the total units of all        *
// products sold and the total sales. It then displays these amounts.*
//***************************************************************************

void showTotals(vector<float> sales, vector<int> units)
{
    int totalUnits = 0;
    float totalSales = 0.0;

    for (int index = 0; index < units.size(); index++)
    {
        totalUnits += units[index];
        totalSales += sales[index];
    }
    cout << "Total Units Sold:  " << totalUnits << endl;
    cout << "Total Sales:       $" << totalSales << endl;
}
```

Program Output

```
Product Number  Sales
-----------------------------------
914             $10903.90
918             $ 9592.15
917             $ 8712.30
919             $ 8594.55
921             $ 7355.40
915             $ 6219.20
922             $ 3593.40
916             $ 2406.65
920             $ 1450.15

Total Units Sold:  3406
Total Sales:       $58827.70
```

There are some differences between Program 9-7 and Program 9-6. First, the `initVectors` function was added. In Program 9-6, this was not necessary because the `id`, `units`, and `prices` arrays had initialization lists. However, vectors do not accept initialization lists, so this function stores the necessary initial values in the `id`, `units`, and `prices` vectors.

Now look at the function header for `initVectors`:

```
void initVectors(vector<int> &id, vector<int> &units, vector<float> &prices)
```

Notice that the vector parameters are references (as indicated by the `&` that precedes the parameter name). This brings up an important difference between vectors and arrays: By default, vectors are passed by value, whereas arrays are only passed by reference. If you want to change a value in a vector argument, it *must* be passed into a reference parameter. Reference vector parameters are also used in the `calcSales` and `dualSort` functions.

Also, notice that each time a value is added to a vector, the `push_back` member function is called. This is because the `[]` operator cannot be used to store a new element in a vector. It can only be used to store a value in an existing element or to read a value from an existing element.

Next, notice that the `calcSales`, `showOrder`, `dualSort`, and `showTotals` functions do not accept an argument indicating the number of elements in the vectors. This is not necessary because vectors have the `size` member function, which returns the number of elements in the vector. The following code segment, which is taken from the `calcSales` function, shows the `units.size()` member function being used to control the number of loop iterations.

```
for (int index = 0; index < units.size(); index++)
    sales.push_back(units[index] * prices[index]);
```

9.6   Focus on Object-Oriented Programming: *Creating an Abstract Array Data Type—Part II*

In Chapter 8 we demonstrated the `IntList` class, which behaves like 20-element integer array, with the added ability of performing bounds checking. In this section we continue our development of the `IntList` class by adding the following member functions:

`linearSearch` A function that performs a linear search on the array for a specified value. If the value is found in the array, its subscript is returned. If the value is not found in the array, –1 is returned.

`binarySearch` A function that performs a binary search on the array for a specified value. If the value is found in the array, its subscript is returned. If the value is not found in the array, –1 is returned.

`bubbleSort` A function that uses the bubble sort algorithm to sort the array in ascending order.

`selectionSort` A function that uses the selection sort algorithm to sort the array in ascending order.

The member functions are implemented as simple modifications of the algorithms presented in this chapter. The complete code for the class appears here:

Contents of `intlist.h`

```
ifndef INTLIST_H
#define INTLIST_H

class IntList
{
private:
    int  list[20];
    bool isValid(int);
public:
    // Constructor
    IntList();
    bool set(int, int);
    bool get(int, int&);
    int  linearSearch(int);
    int  binarySearch(int);
    void bubbleSort();
    void selectionSort();
};

#endif
```

Contents of `intlist.cpp`

```
#include <iostream>
#include "intlist.h"
using namespace std;

//**********************************************************************
//                         IntList                                     *
// This is the default constructor.                                    *
// It initializes each element in the list to zero.                    *
//**********************************************************************

IntList::IntList()
{
    for (int index = 0; index < 20; index++)
        list[index] = 0;
}

//**********************************************************************
//                          isValid                                    *
// This private member function returns true if the argument           *
// is a valid subscript into the list. Otherwise, it returns           *
// false and displays an error message.                                *
//**********************************************************************
```

```cpp
bool IntList::isValid(int element)
{
    if (element < 0 || element > 19)
    {
        cout << "ERROR: " << element;
        cout << " is an invalid subscript.\n";
        return false;
    }
    else
        return true;
}

//****************************************************************
//                         set                                  *
// This public member function is passed an element number and  *
// a value. If the element number is a valid array subscript,   *
// the value is stored in the array at that location and the    *
// function returns true. Otherwise,the function returns false. *
//****************************************************************

bool IntList::set(int element, int value)
{
    if (isValid(element))
    {
        list[element] = value;
        return true;
    }
    else
        return false;
}

//  ***************************************************************
//                         get                                   *
// This public member function is passed an element number.      *
// If it is a valid array subscript, the value stored in the     *
// array at that location is retrieved and is made available     *
// to the calling function by placing it in a reference          *
// parameter. A true is returned. If the element number passed   *
// in is not a valid subscript, the function returns false.      *
//****************************************************************

bool IntList::get(int element, int &value)
{
    if (isValid(element))
    {
        value = list[element];
        return true;
    }
```

```
        else
            return false;
    }


    // ****************************************************************
    //                       linearSearch                           *
    // This public member function performs a linear search on      *
    // the list, looking for value. If value is found, its array    *
    // subscript is returned. Otherwise, -1 is returned, indicating*
    // the value is not in the array.                               *
    //****************************************************************

    int IntList::linearSearch(int value)
    {
        int index = 0;          // Used as a subscript to search array
        int position = -1;      // Used to record position of search value
        bool found = false;     // Flag to indicate if the value was found

        while (index < 20 && !found)
        {
            if (list[index] == value)// If the value is found
            {
                found = true;           // Set the flag
                position = index;       // Record the value's subscript
            }
            index++;                    // Go to the next element
        }
        return position;                // Return the position, or -1
    }                                   // -1 indicates the value was not found


    // ****************************************************************
    //                       binarySearch                           *
    // This public member function performs a binary search on      *
    // the list, looking for value. If value is found, its array    *
    // subscript is returned. Otherwise, -1 is returned, indicating*
    // the value is not in the array.                               *
    //****************************************************************

    int IntList::binarySearch(int value)
    {
        int    first = 0,
               last = 19,
               middle,
               position = -1;
        bool   found = false;

        // First, sort the list.
        selectionSort();
```

```
    while (!found && first <= last)
    {
        middle = (first + last) / 2;
        if (list[middle] == value)   // If value was found
        {   found = true;
            position = middle;       // Set position to the location
        }                            // where it was found
        else if (list[middle] > value)
            last = middle - 1;
        else
            first = middle + 1;
    }
    return position;                 // If position is still -1 it
}                                    // indicates value was not found


// ***************************************************************
//                      bubbleSort                              *
// This public member function performs an ascending-order      *
// bubble sort on list.                                         *
//****************************************************************

void IntList::bubbleSort()
{
    int temp;
    bool swap;

    do
    {
        swap = false;
        for (int count = 0; count < 19; count++)
        {
            if (list[count] > list[count + 1])
            {
                temp = list[count];
                list[count] = list[count + 1];
                list[count + 1] = temp;
                swap = true;
            }
        }
    } while (swap);
}


// ***************************************************************
//                      selectionSort                          *
// This public member function performs an ascending-order      *
// selection sort on list.                                      *
//****************************************************************
```

```
void IntList::selectionSort()
{
    int startScan, minIndex, minValue;

    for (startScan = 0; startScan < 19; startScan++)
    {
        minIndex = startScan;
        minValue = list[startScan];
        for(int index = startScan + 1; index < 20; index++)
        {
            if (list[index] < minValue)
            {
                minValue = list[index];
                minIndex = index;
            }
        }
        list[minIndex] = list[startScan];
        list[startScan] = minValue;
    }
}
```

Program 9-8 demonstrates the class's selection sort capability by storing 20 random numbers in the array, displaying them, sorting them, and then displaying them again.

Program 9-8

```
// This program demonstrates the IntList's selection sort capability.

#include <iostream>
#include <cstdlib>            // Needed to use the rand() function
#include "intlist.h"
using namespace std;

int main()
{
    IntList numbers;
    int val,
        x;

    // Store random numbers in the list.
    for (x = 0; x < 20; x++)
    {
        if (!numbers.set(x, rand()))
            cout << "Error storing a value.";
    }
    cout << endl;
```

(program continues)

Program 9-8 *(continued)*

```
    // Display the numbers
    for (x = 0; x < 20; x++)
    {
        if (numbers.get(x, val))
            cout << val << endl;
    }
    cout << "Press ENTER to continue...";
    cin.get();

    // Sort the numbers using selectionSort.
    numbers.selectionSort();

    // Display the numbers
    cout << "Here are the sorted values:";
    for (x = 0; x < 20; x++)
    {
        if (numbers.get(x, val))
            cout << val << endl;
    }
    cout << endl;
    return 0;
}
```

Program Output

```
41
18467
6334
26500
19169
15724
11478
29358
26962
24464
5705
28145
23281
16827
9961
491
2995
11942
4827
5436
Press ENTER to continue...
```

(program output continues)

Program 9-8 *(continued)*

```
Here are the sorted values:
41
491
2995
4827
5436
5705
6334
9961
11478
11942
15724
16827
18467
19169
23281
24464
26500
26962
28145
29358
```

Program 9-9 demonstrates the class's binary search algorithm. As in Program 9-8, twenty random numbers are generated and stored in the array. The program displays a list of the numbers and asks the user to pick one. The binarySearch function is then used to find that number's subscript position in the sorted array.

Program 9-9

```cpp
// This program demonstrates the IntList's binary search capability.

#include <iostream>
#include <cstdlib>                    // Needed to use the rand() function
#include "intlist.h"
using namespace std;

int main()
{
    IntList numbers;
    int val,
        searchResult,
        x;
```

(program continues)

Program 9-9   *(continued)*

```cpp
// Store random numbers in the list.
for (x = 0; x < 20; x++)
{
    if (!numbers.set(x, rand()))
        cout << "Error storing a value.\n";
}
cout << endl;

// Display the numbers
for (x = 0; x < 20; x++)
{
    if (numbers.get(x, val))
        cout << val << endl;
}
cout << "Enter one of the numbers shown above: ";
cin >> val;

// Search the list for the entered value
cout << "Searching...\n";
searchResult = numbers.binarySearch(val);
if (searchResult == -1)
    cout << "That value was not found in the array.\n";
else
{
    cout << "After the array was sorted, that value\n";
    cout << "is found at subscript " << searchResult << endl;
}
return 0;
}
```

Program Output

```
41
18467
6334
26500
19169
15724
11478
29358
26962
24464
5705
28145
23281
16827
9961
```

(program output continues)

Program 9-9 *(continued)*

```
491
2995
11942
4827
5436
Enter one of the numbers shown above: 5705
Searching...
After the array was sorted, that value
is found at subscript 5
```

Review Questions and Exercises

Fill-in-the-Blank

1. The _____ search algorithm steps sequentially through an array, comparing each item with the search value.

2. The _____ search algorithm repeatedly divides the portion of an array being searched in half.

3. The _____ search algorithm is adequate for small arrays but not large arrays.

4. The _____ search algorithm requires that the array's contents be sorted.

5. If an array is sorted in _____ order, the values are stored from lowest to highest.

6. If an array is sorted in _____ order, the values are stored from highest to lowest.

True False

7. T F If data are sorted in ascending order, it means they are ordered from lowest value to highest value.

8. T F If data are sorted in descending order, it means they are ordered from lowest value to highest value.

9. T F The *average* number of comparisons performed by the linear search on an array of N elements is N/2 (assuming the search values are consistently found).

10. T F The *maximum* number of comparisons performed by the linear search on an array of N elements is N/2 (assuming the search values are consistently found).

11. Complete the following table by calculating the average and maximum number of comparisons the linear search will perform, and the maximum number of comparisons the binary search will perform.

Array Size →	50 Elements	500 Elements	10,000 Elements	100,000 Elements	10,000,000 Elements
Linear Search (Average Comparisons)					
Linear Search (Maximum Comparisons)					
Binary Search (Maximum Comparisons)					

Programming Challenges

General Requirements

Each program should have a section of comments at the top. The comments should contain your name, the date the program was written, the chapter the assignment appeared in, and the assignment number and name. Here is an example:

```
// Written by Jill Johnson
// March 31, 2003
// Chapter 9
// Assignment 1. Charge Account Validation
```

1. Charge Account Validation

Write a program that lets the user enter a charge account number. The program should determine if the number is valid by checking for it in the following list:

5658845	4520125	7895122	8777541	8451277	1302850
8080152	4562555	5552012	5050552	7825877	1250255
1005231	6545231	3852085	7576651	7881200	4581002

The list of numbers should be initialized in a single dimensional array. A simple linear search should be used to locate the number entered by the user. If the user enters a number that is in the array, the program should display a message saying the number is valid. If the user enters a number that is not in the array, the program should display a message indicating the number is invalid.

2. Charge Account Validation Modification

Modify the program you wrote for problem 1 (Charge Account Validation) so it performs a binary search to locate valid account numbers. Use the selection sort algorithm to sort the array before the binary search is performed.

3. Rainfall Statistics Modification

Modify the Rainfall Statistics program you wrote for problem 2 of Chapter 8. The program should display a list of months, sorted in order of rainfall, from highest to lowest.

4. String Selection Sort

Modify the selectionSort function presented in this chapter so it searches an array of strings instead of an array of ints. Test the function with a driver program. Use Program 9-10 as a skeleton to complete.

Program 9-10

```
#include <iostream>
using namespace std;

int main()
{
    string name[20] = {"Collins, Bill",
                        "Smith, Bart",
                        "Allen, Jim",
                        "Griffin, Jim",
                        "Stamey, Marty",
                        "Rose, Geri",
                        "Taylor, Terri",
                        "Johnson, Jill",
                        "Allison, Jeff",
                        "Looney, Joe",
                        "Wolfe, Bill",
                        "James, Jean",
                        "Weaver, Jim",
                        "Pore, Bob",
                        "Rutherford, Greg",
                        "Javens, Renee",
                        "Harrison, Rose",
                        "Setzer, Cathy",
                        "Pike, Gordon",
                        "Holland, Beth" };

    // Insert your code to complete this program
    return(0);
}
```

5. Binary String Search

Modify the binarySearch function presented in this chapter so it searches an array of strings instead of an array of ints. Test the function with a driver program. Use Program 9-10 as a skeleton to complete. (The array must be sorted before the binary search will work.)

6. Search Benchmarks

Write a program that has an array of at least 20 integers. It should call a function that uses the linear search algorithm to locate one of the values. The function should keep a count of the number of comparisons it makes until it finds the value. The program then should call a function that uses the binary search algorithm to locate the same value. It should also keep count of the number of comparisons it makes. Display these values on the screen.

7. Sorting Benchmarks

Write a program that uses two identical arrays of at least 20 integers. It should call a function that uses the bubble sort algorithm to sort one of the arrays in ascending order. The function should keep a count of the number of exchanges it makes. The program then should call a function that uses the selection sort algorithm to sort the other array. It should also keep count of the number of exchanges it makes. Display these values on the screen.

Serendipity Booksellers Software Development Project—Part 9: *A Problem-Solving Exercise*

For this chapter's assignment you will add searching capabilities to the `addBook`, `lookUpBook`, `editBook`, and `deleteBook` functions.

1. Modify the `addBook` Function

When a new book is added to the inventory, the program will search the `BookData` class array for an empty object. Once an empty object is found in the array, the book's information may be stored in it.

The `addBook` function is currently a stub function. Modify it so it performs the following steps:

◆ First the function should search the `BookData` class array for an empty object. Use the `isEmpty` member to locate an empty object. If no empty object is found, it means the array is full. In that case, the function should display a message indicating that no more books may be added to the inventory, and then terminate.

◆ Once an empty object is found, the function should ask the user to enter the following items:

Book title
ISBN number
Author's name
Publisher's name
The date the book is added to the inventory
The quantity of this book being added
The wholesale cost of the book
The retail price of the book

Each of these items should be added to the object. Note that the wholesale cost and retail price is for a single copy of the book. Also, remember that the date should be entered in the form MM-DD-YYYY, where MM is the month, DD is the day, and YYYY is the year.

2. Modify the `lookUpBook` Function

The `lookUpBook` function is currently a stub function. Modify it so it performs the following tasks:

- It should ask the user for the title of a book. This is a book that is to be looked up in the inventory database.

- The function should search the `BookData` class array for a title that matches the one entered by the user. If no match is found, the function should display a message indicating the book is not in inventory, and terminate. If the book is found, the function should call `bookInfo`, passing the correct information as arguments.

3. Modify the `editBook` Function

The `editBook` function is currently a stub function. Modify it so it performs the following tasks:

- It should ask the user for the title of a book. This is a book whose information is to be edited.

- The function should search the `BookData` class array for a title that matches the one entered by the user. If no match is found, the function should display a message indicating the book is not in inventory, and terminate. If the book is found, the function should call `bookInfo`, passing the correct information as arguments.

- The function should ask the user which of the fields he or she wishes to change. The user is then allowed to enter new values for the selected field. These new values are saved in the arrays, replacing the old values.

4. Modify the `deleteBook` Function

The `deleteBook` function is currently a stub function. Modify it so it performs the following tasks:

- It should ask the user for the title of a book. This is a book that is to be deleted from the inventory database.

- The function should search the `BookData` class array for a title that matches the one entered by the user. If no match is found, the function should display a message indicating the book is not in inventory, and terminate. If the book is found, the function should call `bookInfo`, passing the correct information as arguments.

- The function should ask the user to verify if the book's information is to be deleted from the inventory. If so, call the `removeBook` member funtions to mark the object as empty.

CHAPTER 10

Pointers

Topics

10.1 Getting the Address of a Variable

CONCEPT The address operator (&) returns the memory address of a variable.

Every variable is allocated a section of memory large enough to hold a value of the variable's data type. On a PC, for instance, it's common for 1 byte to be allocated for `chars`, 2 bytes for `shorts`, 4 bytes for `ints`, `longs`, and `floats`, and 8 bytes for `doubles`.

Each byte of memory has a unique *address*. A variable's address is the address of the first byte allocated to that variable. Suppose the following variables are defined in a program:

```
char letter;
short number;
float amount;
```

Figure 10-1 illustrates how they might be arranged in memory and shows their addresses.

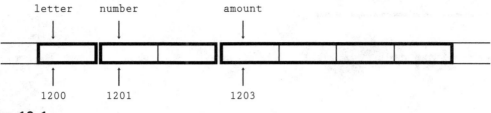

Figure 10-1

In Figure 10-1, the variable `letter` is shown at address 1200, `number` is at address 1201, and `amount` is at address 1203.

 Note: The addresses of the variables shown in Figure 10-1 are arbitrary values used only for illustration purposes.

Getting the address of a variable is accomplished with an operator in C++. When the address operator (&) is placed in front of a variable name, it returns the address of that variable. Here is an expression that returns the address of the variable `amount`:

```
&amount
```

And here is a statement that displays the variable's address on the screen:

```
cout << &amount;
```

Program 10-1 demonstrates the use of the address operator to display the address, size, and contents of a variable.

Program 10-1

```
// This program uses the & operator to determine a variable's
// address and the sizeof operator to determine its size.

#include <iostream>
using namespace std;

int main()
{
    short x = 25;

    cout << "The address of x is " << &x << endl;
    cout << "The size of x is " << sizeof(x) << " bytes\n";
    cout << "The value in x is " << x << endl;
    return 0;
}
```

Program 10-1

Program Output
```
The address of x is 0x8f05
The size of x is 2 bytes
The value in x is 25
```

 Note: The address of the variable x is displayed in hexadecimal. This is the way addresses are normally shown in C++.

10.2 Pointer Variables

 Pointer variables, which are often just called *pointers*, are designed to hold memory addresses. With pointer variables you can indirectly manipulate data stored in other variables.

Although most students agree that the topic of pointers is one of the more difficult subjects in C++, it is also one of the most important. Many operations are best performed with pointers, and some tasks aren't possible without them. They are very useful for things such as the following:

♦ Working directly with memory locations that regular variables don't give you access to

♦ Working with strings and arrays

♦ Creating new variables in memory while the program is running

♦ Creating arbitrarily-sized lists of values in memory

Pointers are special variables that C++ provides for working with memory addresses. Just like int variables are designed to hold and work with integers, pointer variables are designed to hold and work with addresses.

The definition of a pointer variable looks pretty much like any other definition. Here is an example:

```
int *ptr;
```

The asterisk in front of the variable name indicates that ptr is a pointer variable. The int data type indicates that ptr can be used to hold the address of an integer variable. The declaration statement above would read "ptr is a pointer to an int."

 Note: In this definition, the word int does not mean that ptr is an integer variable. It means that ptr can hold the address of an integer variable. Remember, pointers only hold one thing: addresses.

Many programmers prefer to declare pointers with the asterisk next to the type name, rather than the variable name. For example, the declaration shown above could be written as:

```
int* ptr;
```

This style of declaration might visually reinforce the fact that ptr's data type is not int, but pointer-to-int. Both declaration styles are correct.

Program 10-2 demonstrates a very simple usage of a pointer: storing and printing the address of another variable.

Program 10-2

```
// This program stores the address of a variable in a pointer.

#include <iostream>
using namespace std;

int main()
{
    int x = 25;
    int *ptr;

    ptr = &x;    // Store the address of x in ptr
    cout << "The value in x is " << x << endl;
    cout << "The address of x is " << ptr << endl;
    return 0;
}
```

Program Output
```
The value in x is 25
The address of x is 0x7e00
```

In Program 10-2, two variables are defined: x and ptr. The variable x is an int, while ptr is a pointer to an int. The variable x is initialized with 25, while ptr is assigned the address of x with the following statement:

```
ptr = &x;
```

Figure 10-2 illustrates the relationship between ptr and x.

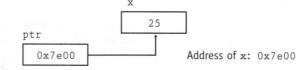

Figure 10-2

As shown in Figure 10-2, the variable x is located at memory address 0x7e00 and contains the number 25, while the pointer ptr contains the address 0x7e00. In essence, ptr "points" to the variable x.

The real benefit of pointers is that they allow you to indirectly access and modify the variable being pointed to. In Program 10-2, for instance, ptr could be used to change the contents of the variable x. This is done with the *indirection operator*, which is an asterisk (*). When the indirection operator is placed in front of a pointer variable name, it *dereferences* the pointer. When you are working with a dereferenced pointer, you are actually working with the value the pointer is pointing to. This is demonstrated in Program 10-3.

Program 10-3

```
// This program demonstrates the use of the indirection
// operator.

#include <iostream>
using namespace std;

int main()
{
    int x = 25;
    int *ptr;

    ptr = &x;    // Store the address of x in ptr
    cout << "Here is the value in x, printed twice:\n";
    cout << x << "   " << *ptr << endl;
    *ptr = 100;
    cout << "Once again, here is the value in x:\n";
    cout << x << "   " << *ptr << endl;
    return 0;
}
```

Program Output
```
Here is the value in x, printed twice:
25   25
Once again, here is the value in x:
100   100
```

Every time the expression *ptr appears in Program 10-3, the program indirectly uses the variable x. The following cout statement displays the value in x twice:

```
cout << x << "   " << *ptr << endl;
```

And the following statement stores 100 in x:

```
*ptr = 100;
```

With the indirection operator, ptr can be used to indirectly access the variable it is pointing to. Program 10-4 demonstrates that pointers can point to different variables.

Program 10-4

```cpp
// This program demonstrates the use of the indirection
// operator.

#include <iostream>
using namespace std;

int main()
{
    int x = 25, y = 50, z = 75;
    int *ptr;

    cout << "Here are the values of x, y, and z:\n";
    cout << x << "   " << y << "   " << z << endl;
    ptr = &x;       // Store the address of x in ptr
    *ptr *= 2;      // Multiply value in x by 2
    ptr = &y;       // Store the address of y in ptr
    *ptr *= 2;      // Multiply value in y by 2
    ptr = &z;       // Store the address of z in ptr
    *ptr *= 2;      // Multiply value in z by 2
    cout << "Once again, here are the values of x, y, and z:\n";
    cout << x << "   " << y << "   " << z << endl;
    return 0;
}
```

Program Output
```
Here are the values of x, y, and z:
25   50   75
Once again, here are the values of x, y, and z:
50   100   150
```

 Note: So far you've seen three different uses of the asterisk in C++:

- As the multiplication operator, in statements such as

    ```
    distance = speed * time;
    ```

- In the definition of a pointer variable, such as

    ```
    int *ptr;
    ```

- As the indirection operator, in statements such as

    ```
    *ptr = 100;
    ```

10.3 The Relationship Between Arrays and Pointers

CONCEPT Array names can be used as pointer constants, and pointers can be used as array names.

You learned earlier that an array name, without brackets and a subscript, actually represents the starting address of the array. This means that an array name is really a pointer. Program 10-5 illustrates this by showing an array name being used with the indirection operator.

Program 10-5

```
// This program shows an array name being dereferenced with the *
// operator.

#include <iostream>
using namespace std;

int main()
{
    short numbers[] = {10, 20, 30, 40, 50};

    cout << "The first element of the array is ";
    cout << *numbers << endl;
    return 0;
}
```

Program Output
```
The first element of the array is 10
```

Since numbers works like a pointer to the starting address of the array in Program 10-5, the first element is retrieved when numbers is dereferenced. So, how could the entire contents of an array be retrieved using the indirection operator? Remember, array elements are stored together in memory, as illustrated in Figure 10-3.

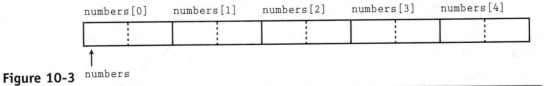

Figure 10-3 numbers

It makes sense that if numbers is the address of numbers[0], values could be added to numbers to get the addresses of the other elements in the array. It's important to know, however, that pointers do not work like regular variables when used in mathematical statements. In C++, when you add a value to a pointer, you are actually adding that value *times the size of the data type being referenced by the pointer*. In other words, if you add one to `numbers`, you are actually adding 1 * `sizeof(short)` to `numbers`. If you add two to `numbers`, the result is `numbers + 2 * sizeof(short)`, and so forth. On a PC, this means the following are true, because `short` integers typically use 2 bytes:

```
*(numbers + 1)  is actually  *(numbers + 1 * 2)
*(numbers + 2)  is actually  *(numbers + 2 * 2)
*(numbers + 3)  is actually  *(numbers + 3 * 2)
```

and so forth.

This automatic conversion means that an element in an array can be retrieved by using its subscript or by adding its subscript to a pointer to the array. If the expression `*numbers`, which is the same as `*(numbers + 0)`, retrieves the first element in the array, then `*(numbers + 1)` retrieves the second element. Likewise, `*(numbers + 2)` retrieves the third element, and so forth. Figure 10-4 shows the equivalence of subscript notation and pointer notation.

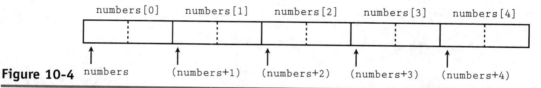

Figure 10-4

 Note: The parentheses are critical when adding values to pointers. The `*` operator has precedence over the `+` operator, so the expression `*numbers + 1` is not equivalent to `*(numbers + 1)`. The expression `*numbers + 1` adds one to the contents of the first element of the array, while `*(numbers + 1)` adds one to the address in `numbers`, then dereferences it.

Program 10-6 shows the entire contents of the array being accessed, using pointer notation.

Program 10-6

```
// This program processes the contents of an array. Pointer
// notation is used.

#include <iostream>
using namespace std;

int main()
{
    int numbers[5];
    int count;
```

(program continues)

Program 10-6 *(continued)*

```cpp
    cout << "Enter five numbers: ";
    for (count = 0; count < 5; count++)
        cin >> *(numbers + count);
    cout << "Here are the numbers you entered:\n";
    for (count = 0; count < 5; count++)
        cout << *(numbers + count)<< " ";
    cout << endl;
    return 0;
}
```

Program Output with Example Input Shown in Bold
```
Enter five numbers: 5 10 15 20 25[Enter]
Here are the numbers you entered:
5 10 15 20 25
```

When working with arrays, remember the following rule:

`array[index]` is equivalent to `*(array + index)`

 WARNING! Remember that C++ performs no bounds checking with arrays. When stepping through an array with a pointer, it's possible to give the pointer an address outside of the array.

To demonstrate just how close the relationship is between array names and pointers, look at Program 10-7. It defines an array of `floats` and a `float` pointer, which is assigned the starting address of the array. Not only is pointer notation then used with the array name, but subscript notation is used with the pointer!

Program 10-7

```cpp
// This program uses subscript notation with a pointer and
// pointer notation with an array name.

#include <iostream>
#include <iomanip>
using namespace std;
```

(program continues)

Program 10-7 *(continued)*

```
int main()
{
    float coins[5] = {0.05, 0.1, 0.25, 0.5, 1.0};
    float *floatPtr;  // Pointer to a float
    int count;        // Array index

    floatPtr = coins; // floatPtr now points to coins array.
    cout << setprecision(2);
    cout << "Here are the values in the coins array:\n";
    for (count = 0; count < 5; count++)
        cout << floatPtr[count] << " ";
    cout << "\nAnd here they are again:\n";
    for (count = 0; count < 5; count++)
        cout << *(coins + count) << " ";
    cout << endl;
    return 0;
}
```

Program Output
```
Here are the values in the coins array:
0.05 0.1 0.25 0.5 1
And here they are again:
0.05 0.1 0.25 0.5 1
```

Notice that the address operator is not needed when an array's address is assigned to a pointer. Since the name of an array is already an address, use of the & operator would be redundant.[1] You can, however, use the address operator to get the address of an individual element in an array. For instance, &numbers[1] gets the address of numbers[1]. This technique is used in Program 10-8.

Program 10-8

```
// This program uses the address of each element in the array.

#include <iostream>
#include <iomanip>
using namespace std;

int main()
{
    float coins[5] = {0.05, 0.1, 0.25, 0.5, 1.0};
    float *floatPtr; // Pointer to a float
    int count;       // Array index
```

(program continues)

---

[1] Some compilers will generate an error message when you use the & operator with the name of an array.

Program 10-8 *(continued)*

```
cout << setprecision(2);
cout << "Here are the values in the coins array:\n";
for (count = 0; count < 5; count++)
{
    floatPtr = &coins[count];
    cout << *floatPtr << " ";
}
cout << endl;
return 0;
}
```

Program Output
```
Here are the values in the coins array:
0.05 0.1 0.25 0.5 1
```

The only difference between array names and pointer variables is that you cannot change the address an array name points to. For example, given the following definitions

```
float readings[20], totals[20];
float *fptr;
```

These statements are legal:

```
fptr = readings;        // Make fptr point to readings
fptr = totals;          // Make fptr point to totals
```

But these are illegal:

```
readings = totals;      // ILLEGAL! Cannot change readings
totals = fptr;          // ILLEGAL! Cannot change totals
```

Array names are *pointer constants*. You can't make them point to anything but the array they represent.

10.4 Pointer Arithmetic

CONCEPT Some mathematical operations may be performed on pointers.

The contents of pointer variables may be changed with mathematical statements that perform addition or subtraction. This is demonstrated in Program 10-9. The first loop increments the pointer variable, stepping it through each element of the array. The second loop decrements the pointer, stepping it through the array backwards.

Program 10-9

```cpp
// This program uses a pointer to display the contents
// of an integer array.

#include <iostream>
using namespace std;

int main()
{
    int set[8] = {5, 10, 15, 20, 25, 30, 35, 40};
    int *nums, index;

    nums = set;
    cout << "The numbers in set are:\n";
    for (index = 0; index < 8; index++)
    {
        cout << *nums << " ";
        nums++;
    }
    cout << "\nThe numbers in set backwards are:\n";
    for (index = 0; index < 8; index++)
    {
        nums--;
        cout << *nums << " ";
    }
    return 0;
}
```

Program Output
```
The numbers in set are:
5 10 15 20 25 30 35 40
The numbers in set backwards are:
40 35 30 25 20 15 10 5
```

 Note: Since `nums` is a pointer, the increment operator adds the size of one integer to `nums`, so it points to the next element in the array. Likewise, the decrement operator subtracts the size of one integer from the pointer.

Not all arithmetic operations may be performed on pointers. For example, you cannot multiply or divide a pointer. The following operations are allowable:

◆ The ++ and -- operators may be used to increment or decrement a pointer variable.

◆ An integer may be added to or subtracted from a pointer variable. This may be performed with the + and - operators, or the += and -= operators.

◆ A pointer may be subtracted from another pointer.

10.5 Initializing Pointers

CONCEPT	Pointers may be initialized with the address of an existing object.

Remember that a pointer is designed to point to an object of a specific data type. When a pointer is initialized with an address, it must be the address of an object the pointer can point to. For instance, the following definition of pint is legal because myValue is an integer:

```
int myValue;
int *pint = &myValue;
```

The following is also legal because ages is an array of integers:

```
int ages[20];
int *pint = ages;
```

But the following definition of pint is illegal because myFloat is not an int:

```
float myFloat;
int *pint = &myFloat;        // Illegal!
```

Pointers may be defined in the same statement as other variables of the same type. The following declaration defines an integer variable, myValue, and then defines a pointer, pint, which is initialized with the address of myValue:

```
int myValue, *pint = &myValue;
```

And the following definition defines an array, readings, and a pointer, marker, which is initialized with the address of the first element in the array:

```
float readings[50], *marker = readings;
```

Of course, a pointer can only be initialized with the address of an object that has already been defined. The following is illegal because pint is being initialized with the address of an object that does not exist yet:

```
int *pint = &myValue;        // Illegal!
int myValue;
```

A programmer can indicate that a pointer variable does not point to a legitimate address by setting the pointer to 0. For example, if ptrToint is a pointer to int, and ptrTofloat is a pointer to float, we can indicate that neither of them points to a legitimate address by assigning 0 to both:

```
int *ptrToint = 0;
float *ptrTofloat = 0;
```

In most computers, the lowest addresses in memory (including address 0) are occupied by special operating system data structures. Because memory occupied by the operating system is off limits to user programs, attempts to use a pointer pointing to address 0 will result in an error. In many cases it is wise to only use a pointer after you have verified that its value is not zero. For example, you might write

```
if (ptrToint != 0)
{
  //use the pointer
  cout << *ptrToint;
}
```

Many header files, including `iostream`, `fstream`, and `cstdlib`, define a constant named NULL whose value is zero. Thus, presuming one of these header files has been included, the code can be written as

```
int *ptrToint = NULL;
float *ptrTofloat = NULL;
```

Likewise, NULL can be used to check a pointer to see if its value is zero:

```
if (ptrToint != NULL)
{
  //use the pointer
  cout << *ptrToint;
}
```

A pointer whose value is the address 0 is often called a *null* pointer.

Checkpoint   [10.1–10.5]

10.1   Write a statement that displays the address of the variable `count`.

10.2   Write the declaration statement for a variable `fltPtr`. The variable should be a pointer to a `float`.

10.3   List three uses of the * symbol in C++.

10.4   What is the output of the following program?

```
#include <iostream>
using namespace std;
int main()
{
   int x = 50, y = 60, z = 70;
   int *ptr;
```

```
cout << x << " " << y << " " << z << endl;
ptr = &x;
*ptr *= 10;
ptr = &y;
*ptr *= 5;
ptr = &z;
*ptr *= 2;
cout << x << " " << y << " " << z << endl;
return 0;
}
```

10.5   Rewrite the following loop so it uses pointer notation (with the indirection operator)
       instead of subscript notation.

```
for (int x = 0; x < 100; x++)
    cout << array[x] << endl;
```

10.6   Assume `ptr` is a pointer to an `int` and holds the address 12000. On a system with 4-byte
       integers, what address will be in `ptr` after the following statement?

```
ptr += 10;
```

10.7   Assume `pint` is a pointer variable. Are each of the following statements valid or invalid?
       If any are invalid, why?

   A) `pint++;`
   B) `--pint;`
   C) `pint /= 2;`
   D) `pint *= 4;`
   E) `pint += x;   // Assume x is an int.`

10.8   Are each of the following declarations valid or invalid? If any are invalid, why?

   A) `int ivar;`
       `int *iptr = &ivar;`
   B) `int ivar, *iptr = &ivar;`
   C) `float fvar;`
       `int *iptr = &fvar;`
   D) `int nums[50], *iptr = nums;`
   E) `int *iptr = &ivar;`
       `int ivar;`

10.6   Comparing Pointers

CONCEPT | If one address comes before another address in memory, the first address is considered "less than" the second. C++'s relational operators may be used to compare pointer values.

Pointers may be compared by using any of C++'s relational operators:

> < == != >= <=

In an array, all the elements are stored in consecutive memory locations, so the address of element 1 is greater than the address of element 0. This is illustrated in Figure 10-5.

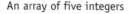
An array of five integers

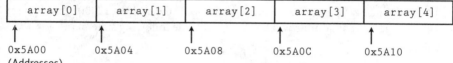

| array[0] | array[1] | array[2] | array[3] | array[4] |

0x5A00   0x5A04   0x5A08   0x5A0C   0x5A10
(Addresses)

Figure 10-5

Since the addresses grow larger for each subsequent element in the array, the following if statements are all true:

```
if (&array[1] > &array[0])
if (array < &array[4])
if (array == &array[0])
if (&array[2] != &array[3])
```

Note: Comparing two pointers is not the same as comparing the values the two pointers point to. For example, the following if statement compares the addresses stored in the pointer variables ptr1 and ptr2:

```
if (ptr1 < ptr2)
```

The following statement, however, compares the values that ptr1 and ptr2 point to:

```
if (*ptr1 < *ptr2)
```

The capability of comparing addresses gives you another way to be sure a pointer does not go beyond the boundaries of an array. Program 10-10 initializes the pointer nums with the starting address of the array set. The pointer nums is then stepped through the array set until the address it contains is equal to the address of the last element of the array. Then the pointer is stepped backwards through the array until it points to the first element.

Program 10-10

```
// This program uses a pointer to display the contents
// of an integer array.

#include <iostream>
using namespace std;

int main()
{
    int set[8] = {5, 10, 15, 20, 25, 30, 35, 40};
    int *nums = set;              // Make nums point to set

    cout << "The numbers in set are:\n";
    cout << *nums << " ";    // Display first element
    while (nums < &set[7])
    {
        nums++;
        cout << *nums << " ";
    }
    cout << "\nThe numbers in set backwards are:\n";
    cout << *nums << " ";    // Display last element
    while (nums > set)
    {
        nums--;
        cout << *nums << " ";
    }
    return 0;
}
```

Program Output
```
The numbers in set are:
5 10 15 20 25 30 35 40
The numbers in set backwards are:
40 35 30 25 20 15 10 5
```

10.7 Pointers as Function Parameters

CONCEPT	A pointer can be used as a function parameter. It gives the function access to the original argument, much like a reference parameter does.

In Chapter 6 you were introduced to the concept of reference variables being used as function parameters. A reference variable acts as an alias to the original variable used as an argument. This gives the function access to the original argument variable, allowing it to change the variable's contents. When a variable is passed into a reference parameter, the argument is said to be passed by reference.

An alternative to passing an argument by reference is to use a pointer variable as the parameter. Admittedly, reference variables are much easier to work with than pointers. Reference variables hide all the "mechanics" of dereferencing and indirection. You should still learn to use pointers as function arguments, however, because some tasks, especially when dealing with C-strings, are best done with pointers.[2] Also, the C++ library has many functions that use pointers as parameters.

Here is the definition of a function that uses a pointer parameter:

```
void doubleValue(int *val)
{
    *val *= 2;
}
```

The purpose of this function is to double the variable pointed to by `val` with the following statement:

```
*val *= 2;
```

When `val` is dereferenced, the `*=` operator works on the variable pointed to by `val`. This statement multiplies the original variable, whose address is stored in `val`, by two. Of course, when the function is called, the address of the variable that is to be doubled must be used as the argument, not the variable itself.

Here is an example of a call to the `doubleValue` function:

```
doubleValue(&number);
```

This statement uses the address operator (`&`) to pass the address of `number` into the `val` parameter. After the function executes, the contents of `number` will have been multiplied by two.

The use of this function is illustrated in Program 10-11.

Program 10-11

```
// This program uses two functions that accept addresses of
// variables as arguments.

#include <iostream>
using namespace std;

// Function prototypes
void getNumber(int *);
void doubleValue(int *);
```

(program continues)

---

[2] It is also important to learn the technique in case you ever have to write a C program. In C, the only way to get the effect of pass by reference is to use a pointer.

Program 10-11 *(continued)*

```cpp
int main()
{
    int number;

    getNumber(&number);      // Pass address of number to getNumber
    doubleValue(&number);    // and doubleValue.
    cout << "That value doubled is " << number << endl;
    return 0;
}

//*********************************************************************
// Definition of getNumber. The parameter, input, is a pointer.    *
// This function asks the user for a number. The value entered     *
// is stored in the variable pointed to by input.                  *
//*********************************************************************

void getNumber(int *input)
{
    cout << "Enter an integer number: ";
    cin >> *input;
}

//*********************************************************************
// Definition of doubleValue. The parameter, val, is a pointer.    *
// This function multiplies the variable pointed to by val by      *
// two.                                                            *
//*********************************************************************
void doubleValue(int *val)
{
    *val *= 2;
}
```

Program Output with Example Input Shown in Bold
```
Enter an integer number: 10[Enter]
That value doubled is 20
```

Program 10-11 has two functions that use pointers as parameters. Notice the function proto-types:

```cpp
void getNumber(int *);
void doubleValue(int *);
```

Each one uses the notation int * to indicate the parameter is a pointer to an int. As with all other types of parameters, it isn't necessary to specify the name of the variable in the prototype. The * is required, though.

The getNumber function asks the user to enter an integer value. The following cin statement stores the value entered by the user in memory:

```
cin >> *input;
```

The indirection operator causes the value entered by the user to be stored, not in input, but in the variable pointed to by input.

 WARNING! It's critical that the indirection operator be used in the previous statement. Without it, cin would store the value entered by the user in input, as if the value were an address. If this happens, input will no longer point to the number variable in function main. Subsequent use of the pointer will result in erroneous, if not disastrous results.

When the getNumber function is called, the address of the number variable in function main is passed as the argument. After the function executes, the value entered by the user is stored in number. Next, the doubleValue function is called, with the address of number passed as the argument. This causes number to be multiplied by two.

It's worth noting that pointer variables can be used to accept array addresses as arguments. Either subscript or pointer notation may then be used to work with the contents of the array. This is demonstrated in Program 10-12.

Program 10-12

```
// This program demonstrates that a pointer may be used as a
// parameter to accept the address of an array. Either subscript
// or pointer notation may be used.

#include <iostream>
#include <iomanip>
using namespace std;

// Function prototypes
void getSales(float *, int);
float totalSales(float *, int);

int main()
{
    float sales[4];

    getSales(sales, 4);
    cout << setprecision(2);
    cout << fixed << showpoint;
    cout << "The total sales for the year are $";
    cout << totalSales(sales, 4) << endl;
    return 0;
}
```

(program continues)

Program 10-12 *(continued)*

```
//****************************************************************
// Definition of getSales. This function uses a pointer to accept *
// the address of an array of floats. The number of elements in   *
// the array is passed as a separate integer parameter. The       *
// function asks the user to enter the sales figures for four     *
// quarters, then stores those figures in the array using         *
// subscript notation.                                            *
//****************************************************************

void getSales(float *array, int size)
{
    for (int count = 0; count < size; count++)
    {
        cout << "Enter the sales figure for quarter ";
        cout << (count + 1) << ": ";
        cin >> array[count];
    }
}

//****************************************************************
// Definition of totalSales. This function uses a pointer to      *
// accept the address of an array of floats whose size is passed  *
// as a separate parameter. The function uses pointer notation    *
// to sum the elements of the array.                              *
//****************************************************************

float totalSales(float *array, int size)
{
    float sum = 0.0;

    for (int count = 0; count < size; count++)
    {
        sum = sum + *array;
        array++;
    }
    return sum;
}
```

Program Output with Example Input Shown in Bold
```
Enter the sales figure for quarter 1: 10263.98[Enter]
Enter the sales figure for quarter 2: 12369.69[Enter]
Enter the sales figure for quarter 3: 11542.13[Enter]
Enter the sales figure for quarter 4: 14792.06[Enter]
The total sales for the year are $48967.86
```

Notice that in the getSales function in Program 10-12, even though the parameter array is defined as a pointer, subscript notation is used in the cin statement:

```
cin >> array[count];
```

In the `totalSales` function, `array` is used with the indirection operator in the following statement:

```
sum += *array;
```

And in the next statement, the address in `array` is incremented to point to the next element:

```
array++;
```

Note: The two previous statements could be combined into the following statement:

```
sum += *array++;
```

The * operator will first dereference `array`, then the ++ operator will increment the address in `array`.

10.8 Focus on Software Engineering: *Dynamic Memory Allocation*

CONCEPT	Variables may be created and destroyed while a program is running.

As long as you know how many variables you will need during the execution of a program, you can declare those variables up front. For example, a program to calculate the area of a rectangle will need three variables: one for the rectangle's length, one for the rectangle's width, and one to hold the area. If you are writing a program to compute the payroll for 30 employees, you'll probably create an array of 30 elements to hold the amount of pay for each person.

But what about those times when you don't know how many variables you need? For instance, suppose you want to write a test-averaging program that will average any number of tests. Obviously the program would be very versatile, but how do you store the individual test scores in memory if you don't know how many variables to declare? Quite simply, you allow the program to create its own variables "on the fly." This is called *dynamic memory allocation* and is only possible through the use of pointers.

To dynamically allocate memory means that a program, while running, asks the computer to set aside a chunk of unused memory large enough to hold a variable of a specific data type. Let's say a program needs to create an integer variable. It will make a request to the computer that it allocate enough bytes to store an `int`. When the computer fills this request, it finds and sets aside a chunk of unused memory large enough for the variable. It then gives the program the starting address of the chunk of memory. The program can only access the newly allocated memory through its address, so a pointer is required to use those bytes.

The way a C++ program requests dynamically allocated memory is through the new opera-tor. Assume a program has a pointer to an int declared as

```
int *iptr;
```

Here is an example of how this pointer may be used with the new operator:

```
iptr = new int;
```

This statement is requesting that the computer allocate enough memory for a new int variable. The operand of the new operator is the data type of the variable being created. This is illustrated in Figure 10-6. Once the statement executes, iptr will contain the address of the newly allocated memory. A value may be stored in this new variable by dereferencing the pointer:

```
*iptr = 25;
```

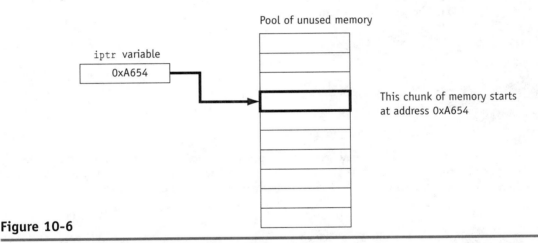

Figure 10-6

Any other operation may be performed on the new variable by simply using the dereferenced pointer. Here are some example statements:

```
cout << *iptr;      // Display the contents of the new variable.
cin >> *iptr;       // Let the user input a value.
total += *iptr;     // Use the new variable in a computation.
```

Although these statements illustrate the use of the new operator, there's little purpose in dynami-cally allocating a single variable. A more practical use of the new operator is to dynamically create an array. Here is an example of how a 100-element array of integers may be allocated:

```
iptr = new int[100];
```

Once the array is created, the pointer may be used with subscript notation to access it. For instance, the following loop could be used to store the value 1 in each element:

```
for (int count = 0; count < 100; count++)
    iptr[count] = 1;
```

But what if there isn't enough free memory to accommodate the request? What if the program asks for a chunk large enough to hold a 100,000-element array of `float`, and that much memory isn't available? Clearly, the program making the request cannot continue to execute normally and in most cases will have no choice but to terminate. When memory cannot be allocated, the `new` operator will by default cause termination of the program with an appropriate error message in a process known as *throwing an exception.* You will learn more about exceptions in Chapter 15.

In older versions of C++, the `new` operator returns the address 0 if it cannot allocate the requested memory. In these versions of C++, a program calling `new` should first check the returned address to make sure it is not 0 before using it. If the returned address is 0, the program should terminate by calling the standard library function `exit`. For example, code to allocate an array of a 100 integers would be written as follows:

```
//for older versions of C++
iptr = new int[100];
if (iptr == NULL)
{
    cout << "Error allocating memory";
    exit(1);
}
//rest of code to use the array
```

When a program is finished using a dynamically allocated chunk of memory, it should release it for future use. The `delete` operator is used to free memory that was allocated with `new`. Here is an example of how `delete` is used to free a single variable, pointed to by `iptr`:

```
delete iptr;
```

If `iptr` points to a dynamically allocated array, the `[]` symbol must be placed between `delete` and `iptr`:

```
delete [] iptr;
```

Memory dynamically allocated in a class constructor should be deleted in the destructor.

 WARNING! Only use pointers with `delete` that were previously used with `new`. If you use a pointer with `delete` that does not reference dynamically allocated memory, unexpected problems could result!

Program 10-13 demonstrates the use of new and delete. It asks for sales figures for any number of days. The figures are stored in a dynamically allocated array, and then totaled and averaged.

Program 10-13

```
// This program totals and averages the sales figures for any
// number of days. The figures are stored in a dynamically
// allocated array.

#include <iostream>
#include <iomanip>
using namespace std;

int main()
{
    float *sales, total = 0, average;
    int numDays;
    int count;

    cout << "How many days of sales figures do you wish ";
    cout << "to process? ";
    cin >> numDays;
    sales = new float[numDays];  // Allocate memory
    if (sales == NULL)           // Test for null pointer
    {
        cout << "Error allocating memory!\n";
        return;
    }

    // Get the sales figures from the user
    cout << "Enter the sales figures below.\n";
    for (count = 0; count < numDays; count++)
    {
        cout << "Day " << (count + 1) << ": ";
        cin >> sales[count];
    }
    // Calculate the total sales
    for (count = 0; count < numDays; count++)
    {
        total += sales[count];
    }
```

(program continues)

Program 10-13   *(continued)*

```
    // Calculate the average sales per day
    average = total / numDays;

    // Display the results
    cout << setprecision(2);
    cout << fixed << showpoint;
    cout << "\n\nTotal Sales: $" << total << endl;
    cout << "Average Sales: $" << average << endl;
    // Free dynamically allocated memory
    delete [] sales;
    return 0;
}
```

Program Output with Example Input Shown in Bold
```
How many days of sales figures do you wish to process? 5[Enter]
Enter the sales figures below.
Day 1: 898.63[Enter]
Day 2: 652.32[Enter]
Day 3: 741.85[Enter]
Day 4: 852.96[Enter]
Day 5: 921.37[Enter]

Total Sales: $4067.13
Average Sales: $813.43
```

10.9   Focus on Software Engineering: *Returning Pointers from Functions*

> **CONCEPT** | Functions can return pointers, but you must be sure the object the pointer references still exists.

Like any other data type, functions may return pointers. For example, the following function locates the null terminator in a string and returns a pointer to it.

```
char *findNull(char *str)
{
    char *ptr = str;

    while (*ptr != '\0')
            ptr++;
    return ptr;
}
```

The char * return type in the function header indicates the function returns a pointer to a char:

```
char *findNull(char *str)
```

When writing functions that return pointers, however, you should take care not to create elusive bugs. For instance, see if you can determine what's wrong with the following function.

```
char *getName()
{
    char name[81];
    cout << "Enter your name: ";
    cin.getline(name, 81);
    return name;
}
```

The problem, of course, is that the function returns a pointer to an object that no longer exists. Because name is declared locally, it is destroyed when the function terminates. Attempting to use the pointer will result in erroneous and unpredictable results.

You should only return a pointer from a function if it is

◆ A pointer to an object that was passed into the function as an argument

◆ A pointer to a dynamically allocated object

For instance, the following function is acceptable:

```
char *getName(char *name)
{
    cout << "Enter your name: ";
    cin.getline(name, 81);
    return name;
}
```

This function accepts a pointer to the memory location where the user's input is to be stored. Since the pointer references a memory location that was valid prior to the function being called, it is safe to return a pointer to the same location. Here is another acceptable function:

```
char *getName()
{
    char *name;

    name = new char[81];
    cout << "Enter your name: ";
    cin.getline(name, 81);
    return name;
}
```

This function uses the new operator to allocate a section of memory. This memory will remain allocated until the delete operator is used or the program ends, so it's safe to return a pointer to it.

Checkpoint [10.6–10.9]

10.9 Assuming `array` is an array of `int`s, will each of the following program segments display "True" or "False"?

A)
```
if (array < &array[1])
    cout << "True";
else
    cout << "False";
```

B)
```
if (&array[4] < &array[1])
    cout << "True";
else
    cout << "False";
```

C)
```
if (array != &array[2])
    cout << "True";
else
    cout << "False";
```

D)
```
if (array != &array[0])
    cout << "True";
else
    cout << "False";
```

10.10 Give an example of the proper way to call the following function:

```
void makeNegative(int *val)
{
    if (*val > 0)
        *val = -(*val);
}
```

10.11 Complete the following program skeleton. When finished, the program should ask the user for a length (in inches), convert that value to centimeters, and display the result. You are to write the function `convert`. (Note: 1 inch = 2.54 cm. Do not modify function `main`.)

```
#include <iostream>
#include <iomanip>
using namespace std;

// Write your function prototype here.

int main()
{
    float measurement;
```

```
        cout << "Enter a length in inches, and I will convert\n";
        cout << "it to centimeters: ";
        cin >> measurement;
        convert(&measurement);
        cout << setprecision(4);
        cout << fixed << showpoint;
        cout << "Value in centimeters: " << measurement << endl;
        return 0;
}
//
// Write the function convert here.
//
```

10.12 Assume ip is a pointer to an int. Write a statement that will dynamically allocate an integer variable and store its address in ip, then write a statement that will free the memory allocated in the statement you just wrote.

10.13 Assume ip is a pointer to an int. Write a statement that will dynamically allocate an array of 500 integers and store its address in ip, then write a statement that will free the memory allocated in the statement you just wrote.

10.14 What is a null pointer?

10.15 Give an example of a function that correctly returns a pointer.

10.16 Give an example of a function that incorrectly returns a pointer.

10.10 Pointers to Structures and Class Objects

CONCEPT You may take the address of structure variables and class objects, and create variables that are pointers to them.

Declaring a variable that is a pointer to a structure is as simple as declaring any other pointer variable: The data type is followed by an asterisk and the name of the pointer variable. Here is an example:

```
circle *cirPtr;
```

This statement declares cirPtr as a pointer to a circle structure. Once again, assuming piePlate is a circle structure, the following statement stores the address of piePlate in the pointer variable cirPtr:

```
cirPtr = &piePlate;
```

Indirectly accessing the members of a structure through a pointer can be clumsy, however, if the indirection operator is used. One might think the following statement will access the radius member of the structure pointed to by cirPtr, but it doesn't:

```
*cirPtr.radius = 10;
```

The dot operator has higher precedence than the indirection operator, so the indirection operator tries to dereference `cirPtr.radius`, not `cirPtr`. To dereference the `cirPtr` pointer, a set of parentheses must be used.

```
(*cirPtr).radius = 10;
```

Because of the awkwardness of this notation, C++ has a special operator for dereferencing structure pointers. It's called the *structure pointer operator*, and it consists of a hyphen (-) followed by the greater-than symbol (>). The previous statement, rewritten with the structure pointer operator, looks like this:

```
cirPtr->radius = 10;
```

The structure pointer operator takes the place of the dot operator in statements using pointers to structures. The operator automatically dereferences the structure pointer on its left. There is no need to enclose the pointer name in parentheses.

 Note: The structure pointer operator is supposed to look like an arrow, thus visually indicating that a "pointer" is being used.

Program 10-14 shows a structure pointer being used to dynamically allocate a structure variable.

Program 10-14

```
// This program uses a structure pointer to dynamically allocate
// a structure variable in memory.

#include <iostream>
#include <string>
#include <iomanip>
#include <cstdlib>
using namespace std;

struct PayRoll
{
    int empNumber;      // Employee number
    string name;        // Employee's name
    float hours;        // Hours worked
    float payRate;      // Hourly pay rate
    float grossPay;     // Gross pay
};
```

(program continues)

Program 10-14 *(continued)*

```cpp
int main()
{
    PayRoll *employee;      // Employee is a pointer to a
                            // PayRoll structure.
    employee = new PayRoll; // Dynamically allocate a struct
        // If new fails to allocate memory, it throws an exception and
        // program will be terminated with an appropriate error message.
    cout << "Enter the employee's number: ";
    cin >> employee->empNumber;
    cout << "Enter the employee's name: ";
    cin.ignore();           // To skip the remaining '\n' character
    getline(cin, employee->name);
    cout << "How many hours did the employee work? ";
    cin >> employee->hours;
    cout << "What is the employee's hourly pay rate? ";
    cin >> employee->payRate;
    employee->grossPay = employee->hours * employee->payRate;
    cout << "Here is the employee's payroll data:\n";
    cout << "Name: " << employee->name << endl;
    cout << "Number: " << employee->empNumber << endl;
    cout << "Hours worked: " << employee->hours << endl;
    cout << "Hourly pay rate: " << employee->payRate << endl;
    cout << setprecision(2);
    cout << fixed << showpoint;
    cout << "Gross pay: $" << employee->grossPay << endl;
    delete employee;        // Free the allocated memory.
    return 0;
}
```

Program Output with Example Input Shown in Bold
```
Enter the employee's number: 489[Enter]
Enter the employee's name: Jill Smith[Enter]
How many hours did the employee work? 40[Enter]
What is the employee's hourly pay rate? 20[Enter]
Here is the employee's payroll data:
Name: Jill Smith
Number: 489
Hours worked: 40
Hourly pay rate: 20
Gross pay: $800.00
```

Pointer variables are commonly used as function parameters. Program 10-15 shows that a pointer to a structure may be used as a function parameter, allowing the function to access the members of the original structure argument.

Program 10-15

```cpp
// This program demonstrates a function that uses a
// pointer to a structure variable as a parameter.

#include <iostream>
#include <string>
#include <iomanip>
using namespace std;

struct Student
{
    string name;        // Student's name
    int idNum;          // Student ID number
    int crdHrs;         // Credit hours enrolled
    float gpa;          // Current GPA
};

void getData(Student *);   // Function prototype

int main()
{
    Student freshman;

    cout << "Enter the following student data:\n";
    getData(&freshman);
    cout << "\nHere is the student data you entered:\n";
        cout << setprecision(4);
    // Now display the data stored in freshman
    cout << "Name: " << freshman.name << endl;
    cout << "ID number: " << freshman.idNum << endl;
    cout << "Credit hours: " << freshman.crdHrs << endl;
        cout << "GPA: " << freshman.gpa << endl;
    return 0;
}

//***************************************************************
// Definition of function getData. Uses a pointer to a        *
// Student structure variable. The user enters student        *
// information, which is stored in the variable.              *
//***************************************************************

void getData(Student *s)
{
    cout << "Student name: ";
    getline(cin, s->name);
    cout << "Student ID number: ";
    cin >> s->idNum;
    cout << "Credit hours enrolled: ";
    cin >> s->crdHrs;
    cout << "Current GPA: ";
    cin >> s->gpa;
}
```

Program 10-15

Program Output with Example Input Shown in Bold
```
Enter the following student data:
Student name: Frank Smith[Enter]
Student ID number: 4876[Enter]
Credit hours enrolled: 12[Enter]
Current GPA: 3.45[Enter]
Here is the student data you entered:
Name: Frank Smith
ID number: 4876
Credit hours: 12
GPA: 3.45
```

Pointers to Class Objects

A pointer to a class object can also be declared. The following statement declares the pointer boxPtr:

```
Rectangle *boxPtr;
```

Assuming box is an object of the Rectangle class, boxPtr can be made to point to it with the following statement:

```
boxPtr = &box;
```

The boxPtr pointer can then be used to call box's member functions by using the -> operator. The following statement calls the setData function, with the arguments 15 and 12:

```
boxPtr->setData(15, 12);
```

Dynamically Allocating Class Objects

In Program 10-14 you saw that a structure may be dynamically allocated in memory. Class objects may be dynamically allocated as well. For example, assume a class named Rectangle exists, and the following class pointer is declared in a program.

```
Rectangle *boxPtr;
```

You may use the pointer above to dynamically allocate an object of the Rectangle class, as shown in the statement below.

```
boxPtr = new Rectangle;
```

When the new operator creates the Rectangle class object in memory, its constructor is executed. You may pass arguments to the dynamically allocated object's constructor in the following fashion.

```
boxPtr = new Rectangle(10, 20);
```

This statement creates a Rectangle class object and passes the arguments 10 and 20 to its constructor. The delete operator destroys dynamically allocated objects, as shown in the next statement:

```
        delete boxPtr;
```

If a dynamically allocated class object has a destructor, the destructor is called when the delete operator destroys the object.

Using Dynamically Allocated Memory in a Class Object

Program 10-16 shows a common use of a class constructor: to dynamically allocate memory. The InvItem class holds simple information about an inventory item. A description of the item is stored in the dynamically allocated array, desc, and the number of units on hand is stored in units. The constructor allocates memory for the desc array, enough for 51 characters. The destructor frees the allocated memory.

Program 10-16

```
#include <iostream>
#include <cstring>
using namespace std;
class InvItem
{
    private:
        char *desc;
        int units;

    public:
        InvItem(void) { desc = new char[51]; }
        ~InvItem() { delete [] desc; }
        void SetInfo(char *dscr, int un) { strcpy(desc, dscr);
                                           units = un;}
        char *getDesc() { return desc; }
        int getUnits() { return units; }
};

int main()
{
    InvItem stock;
    stock.setInfo("Wrench", 20);
    cout << "Item description: " << stock.getDesc() << endl;
    cout << "Units on hand: " << stock.getUnits() << endl;
    return 0;
}
```

Program Output
```
Item description: Wrench
Units on hand: 20
```

10.11   Focus on Software Engineering: *When to Use .,*
When to Use ->, and When to Use *

Sometimes structures and classes contain pointers as members. For example, the following structure declaration has an `int` pointer member:

```
struct GradeInfo
{
    char name[25];    // Student names
    int *testScores;  // Dynamically allocated array
    float average;    // Test average
};
```

It's important to remember that the structure pointer operator (`->`) is used to dereference a pointer to a structure or class object, not a pointer that is a member of a structure or class. If a program dereferences the `testScores` pointer in the structure in the example, the indirection operator must be used. For example, assuming the following variable has been defined:

```
GradeInfo student1;
```

The following statement will display the value pointed to by the `testScores` member:

```
cout << *student1.testScores;
```

It's still possible to declare a pointer to a structure that contains a pointer member. For instance, the following statement declares `stPtr` as a pointer to a `GradeInfo` structure:

```
GradeInfo *stPtr;
```

Assuming `stPtr` points to a valid `GradeInfo` variable, the following statement will display the value pointed to by its `testScores` member:

```
cout << *stPtr->testScores;
```

In this statement, the `*` operator dereferences `stPtr->testScores`, while the `->` operator dereferences `stPtr`. It might help to remember that the expression

```
stPtr->testScores
```

is equivalent to

```
(*stPtr).testScores
```

So, the expression

```
*stPtr->testScores
```

is the same as

```
*(*stPtr).testScores
```

The awkwardness of this expression shows the necessity of the -> operator. Table 10-1 lists some expressions using the *, ->, and . operators, and describes what each references.

Table 10-1

Expression	Description
s->m	s is a pointer to a structure variable or class object, and m is a member. This expression accesses the m member of the structure or class object pointed to by s.
*a.p	a is a structure variable or class object and p, a pointer, is a member of a. This expression accesses the value pointed to by p.
(*s).m	s is a pointer to a structure variable or class object, and m is a member. The * operator dereferences s, causing the expression to access the m member of the object pointed to by s. This expression is the same as s->m.
*s->p	s is a pointer to a structure variable or class object and p, a pointer, is a member of the object pointed to by s. This expression accesses the value pointed to by p. (The -> operator dereferences s and the * operator dereferences p.)
*(*s).p	s is a pointer to a structure variable or class object and p, a pointer, is a member of the object pointed to by s. This expression accesses the value pointed to by p. (*s) dereferences s and the outermost * operator dereferences p. This expression is the same as *s->p.

Checkpoint   [10.10–10.11]

Assume the following structure declaration exists for questions 10.17 through 10.19:

```
struct Rectangle
{
    int length;
    int width;
};
```

10.17   Write the definition of a pointer to a Rectangle structure.

10.18   Assume the pointer you defined in question 10.17 points to a valid Rectangle structure. Write the statement that displays the structure's members through the pointer.

10.19   Assume rptr is a pointer to a Rectangle structure. Which of the expressions, A, B, or C, is equivalent to the expression:

```
rptr->width
```

A)   *rptr.width
B)   (*rptr).width
C)   rptr.(*width)

10.12 Focus on Problem Solving and Program Design: *A Case Study*

CONCEPT This case study demonstrates how an array of pointers can be used to display the contents of a second array in sorted order, without sorting the second array.

The United Cause, a charitable relief agency, solicits donations from businesses. The local United Cause office received the following donations from the employees of CK Graphics, Inc:

$5, $100, $5, $25, $10, $5, $25, $5, $5, $100, $10, $15, $10, $5, $10

The donations were received in the order they appear. The United Cause manager has asked you to write a program that displays the donations in ascending order, as well as in their original order.

You decide to create a class, DonationList, that will hold and process the donation data. The class declaration is

```cpp
class DonationList
{
private:
        int numDonations;
        float *donations;
        float **arrPtr;
        void selectSort();
public:
        DonationList(int num, float gifts[]);
        ~DonationList();
        void show();
        void showSorted();
};
```

Table 10-2 lists and describes the class's member variables

Table 10-2

Member Variable	Description
numDonations	An integer that will hold the number of donations received. This value will be used to dynamically allocate arrays for holding and processing the donation values.
donations	A pointer that will point to a dynamically allocated array of floats containing the donation amounts.
arrPtr	A pointer that will point to an array of pointers. The array of pointers will be dynamically allocated. Each element of the array will point to an element of the donations array.

In this class, the donation values will be stored in their original order in a dynamically allocated array of `float`s. The `donations` member will point to the array. We will refer to this array as the `donations` array. The following statement shows how the `donations` member will be declared.

```
float *donations;
```

The `arrPtr` member will also point to a dynamically allocated array. Its array, however, will be an array of pointers. The elements of the array are pointers to `float`s. The following statement shows how the `arrPtr` member will be declared.

```
float **arrPtr;
```

Since the `arrPtr` member will point to an array of pointers, it is a *pointer-to-a-pointer*. That is why two asterisks appear in the declaration statement. The pointer that `arrPtr` points to is a pointer to a `float`. Figure 10-7 illustrates `arrPtr` as a pointer to an array of pointers-to-`float`s.

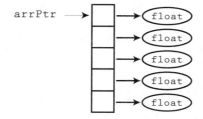

Figure 10-7

We will refer to the array of pointers as the `arrPtr` array. Once the `arrPtr` array is allocated in memory, its elements will be initialized so they point to the elements of the `donations` array, as illustrated in Figure 10-8.

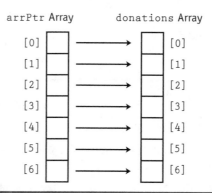

Figure 10-8

The elements of the `arrPtr` array will initially point to the elements of the `donations` array in their natural order (as shown in Figure 10-8). In other words, `arrPtr[0]` will point to `donations[0]`, `arrPtr[1]` will point to `donations[1]`, and so forth. In that arrangement, the following statement would cause the contents of `donations[5]` to be displayed:

```
cout << *(arrPtr[5]) << endl;
```

After the arrPtr array is sorted, however, arrPtr[0] will point to the smallest value in the dona-tions array, arrPtr[1] will point to the next-to-smallest value in the donations array, and so forth. This is illustrated in Figure 10-9.

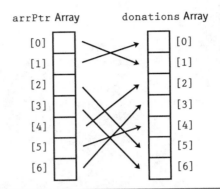

Figure 10-9

This technique gives us access to the elements of the donations array in a sorted order without actually disturbing the contents of the donations array itself.

Table 10-3 lists the class's member functions.

Table 10-3

Member Function	Description
Constructor	The constructor accepts as arguments an integer, which indicates the number of donations received, and an array of floats, which holds the list of donation values. When the constructor is finished, the donations member will point to a dynamically allocated array holding the list of donation values (in their original order), and the arrPtr member will point to a dynamically allocated array of pointers. The elements of the arrPtr array will point, in ascending order, to the elements of the donations array.
Destructor	Deletes the storage that was allocated by the constructor.
selectSort	This function, which performs an ascending-order selection sort on arrPtr, is called by the constructor. Before the sort, arrPtr[0] points to donations[0], arrPtr[1] points to donations[1], and so forth. After the sort, arrPtr will point to the elements of the donations array in ascending order.
show	Displays the contents of the donations array. (This function displays the donations in their original order.)
showSorted	Displays the contents of what each element of the arrPtr array points to. (This function displays the contents of the donations array in sorted order.)

Let's look at each member function in more detail.

The Constructor

The constructor's code is as follows:

```
DonationList::DonationList(int num, float gifts[])
{
    numDonations = num;
    if (num > 0)
    {
        // Allocate an array of floats.
        donations = new float[num];
        // Allocate an array of pointers-to-floats.
        arrPtr = new float*[num];
        // Initialize the arrays.
        for (int count = 0; count < numDonations; count++)
        {
            donations[count] = gifts[count];
            arrPtr[count] = &donations[count];
        }
        // Now sort the array of pointers.
        selectSort();
    }
}
```

The num argument (which is copied to numDonations) holds the number of donations, and the gifts array contains the list of donation values.

If the value in num is greater than 0, the constructor allocates and initializes the elements of the donations and arrPtr arrays. The elements of the gifts array are copied to the elements of the donations array, and the elements of the arrPtr array are set to point to the elements of the donations array.

The selectSort Member Function

The selectSort function is a modified version of the selection sort algorithm. The only difference is that this function sorts an array of pointers. Instead of sorting on the contents of the array's elements, the array is sorted on the contents of what its elements point to. Here is the pseudocode.

For startScan is set to the values 0 up to (but not including) the next-to-last subscript in arrPtr
    Set index variable to startScan.
    Set minIndex variable to startScan.
    Set minElem pointer to arrPtr[startScan].
For index variable is set to the values from (startScan + 1) through the next-to-last subscript in arrPtr

```
        If *(arrPtr[index]) is less than *minElem
            Set minElem to arrPtr[index].
            Set minIndex to index.
        End If.
    End For.
    Set arrPtr[minIndex] to arrPtr[startScan].
    Set arrPtr[startScan] to minElem.
End For.
```

Here is the C++ code for the function:

```cpp
void DonationList::selectSort()
{
    int startScan, minIndex;
    float *minElem;

    for (startScan = 0; startScan < (numDonations - 1); startScan++)
    {
        minIndex = startScan;
        minElem = arrPtr[startScan];
        for(int index = startScan + 1; index < numDonations; index++)
        {
            if (*(arrPtr[index]) < *minElem)
            {
                minElem = arrPtr[index];
                minIndex = index;
            }
        }
        arrPtr[minIndex] = arrPtr[startScan];
        arrPtr[startScan] = minElem;
    }
}
```

The show **Member Function**

The show member function simply displays the contents of the donations array sequentially. Here is its pseudocode:

```
For every element in donations Array
    Display the element's contents
End For.
```

Here is the function's actual C++ code:

```
void DonationList::show()
{
    for (int count = 0; count < numDonations; count++)
        cout << donations[count] << " ";
    cout << endl;
}
```

The showSorted Member Function

The showSorted function displays the values pointed to by the elements of the arrPtr array. Here is its pseudocode:

```
For every element in the arrPtr array
    Dereference the element and display what it points to.
End For.
```

Here is the function's C++ code:

```
void DonationList::showSorted()
{
    for (int count = 0; count < numDonations; count++)
        cout << *(arrPtr[Count]) << " ";
    cout << endl;
}
```

The Entire Class Listing

The class in its entirety is shown here.

Contents of donlist.h
```
#ifndef DONLIST_H
#define DONLIST_H

class DonationList
{
private:
   int numDonations;
   float *donations;
   float **arrPtr;
   void selectSort();
public:
   DonationList(int num, float gifts[]);
   ~DonationList();
   void show();
   void showSorted();
};

#endif
```

Contents of `donlist.cpp`

```cpp
#include <iostream>    //needed for cout
#include "donlist.h"
using namespace std;

//****************************************************************
//                                                               *
// Constructor.                                                  *
// The argument passed to num indicates the number of elements   *
// in array passed to gifts. The gifts array holds the list of   *
// donation values. The constructor allocates the donations      *
// and arrPtr arrays. The gifts array is copied to the           *
// donations array. The elements of the arrPtr array are made    *
// to point to the elements of the donations array,and then      *
// sorted in ascending order by the selectSort function.         *
//****************************************************************

DonationList::DonationList(int num, float gifts[])
{
    numDonations = num;
    if (num > 0)
    {
        // Allocate an array of floats.
        donations = new float[num];
        // Allocate an array of pointers-to-floats.
        arrPtr = new float*[num];
        // Initialize the arrays.
        for (int count = 0; count < numDonations; count++)
        {
            donations[count] = gifts[count];
            arrPtr[count] = &donations[count];
        }
        // Now, sort the array of pointers.
        selectSort();
    }
}

//****************************************************************
// Destructor frees the memory allocated by the constructor*
//****************************************************************

DonationList::~DonationList()
{
    delete [ ] donations;
    delete [ ] arrPtr;
}

//****************************************************************
// The selecSort function performs a selection sort on the    *
// arrPtr array of pointers. The array is sorted on the       *
// values its elements point to.                              *
//****************************************************************
```

```cpp
void DonationList::selectSort()
{
    int startScan, minIndex;
    float *minElem;

    for (startScan = 0; startScan < (numDonations - 1); startScan++)
    {
        minIndex = startScan;
        minElem = arrPtr[startScan];
        for(int index = startScan + 1; index < numDonations; index++)
        {
            if (*(arrPtr[index]) < *minElem)
            {
                minElem = arrPtr[index];
                minIndex = index;
            }
        }
        arrPtr[minIndex] = arrPtr[startScan];
        arrPtr[startScan] = minElem;
    }
}

//*********************************************************
// The show function uses cout to display the donations  *
// array in sequential order.                            *
//*********************************************************

void DonationList::show()
{
    for (int count = 0; count < numDonations; count++)
        cout << donations[count] << " ";
    cout << endl;
}

//*********************************************************
// The showSorted function uses cout to display the values*
// pointed to by the elements of the arrPtr array. Since  *
// arrPtr is sorted, this function displays the elements  *
// of the donations array in ascending order.             *
//*********************************************************

void DonationList::showSorted()
{
    for (int count = 0; count < numDonations; count++)
        cout << *(arrPtr[count]) << " ";
    cout << endl;
}
```

Implementing the Class

Program 10-17 shows how the class is used. The `funds` array is initialized with the 15 donation values.

Program 10-17

```
// This program shows the donations made to the United Cause
// by the employees of CK Graphics, Inc. It displays
// the donations in order from lowest to highest
// and in the original order they were received.'=

#include <iostream>
#include "donlist.h"
using namespace std;

int main()
{
    float funds[] = {5,   100, 5,   25, 10,
                     5,   25,  5,   5,  100,
                     10,  15,  10,  5,  10 };
    DonationList ckGraphics(15, funds);
    cout << "The donations sorted in ascending order are:\n";
    ckGraphics.showSorted();
    cout << "The donations in their original order are:\n";
    ckGraphics.show();
    return 0;
}
```

Program Output
```
The donations sorted in ascending order are:
5 5 5 5 5 5 10 10 10 10 15 25 25 100 100
The donations in their original order are:
5 100 5 25 10 5 25 5 5 100 10 15 10 5 10
```

When the `ckGraphics` object is defined, the value 15 is passed to the constructor's `num` parameter, and the `funds` array is passed to the `gifts` parameter. The `showSorted` member function is called to display the donation values in ascending order (by using the `arrPtr` array to display them), and the `show` member function is called to display the values in their original order.

Review Questions and Exercises

Fill-in-the-Blank

1. Each byte in memory is assigned a unique _____.

2. The _____ operator can be used to determine a variable's address.

3. _____ variables are designed to hold addresses.

4. The _____ operator can be used to work with the variable a pointer points to.

5. Array names can be used as _____ and vice-versa.

6. Creating variables while a program is running is called _____.

7. The _____ operator is used to dynamically allocate memory.

8. If the `new` operator cannot allocate the amount of memory requested, it throws _____.

9. A pointer that contains the address 0 is called a(n) _____ pointer.

10. When a program is finished with a chunk of dynamically allocated memory, it should free it with the _____ operator.

11. You should only use pointers with delete that were previously used with _____.

True or False

12. T   F   Each byte of memory is assigned a unique address.

13. T   F   The * operator is used to get the address of a variable.

14. T   F   Pointer variables are designed to hold addresses.

15. T   F   The & symbol is called the indirection operator.

16. T   F   The & operator dereferences a pointer.

17. T   F   When the indirection operator is used with a pointer variable, you are actually working with the value the pointer is pointing to.

18. T   F   Array names cannot be dereferenced with the indirection operator.

19. T   F   When you add a value to a pointer, you are actually adding that number times the size of the data type referenced by the pointer.

20. T   F   The address operator is not needed when assigning an array's address to a pointer.

21. T   F   You can change the address that an array name points to.

22. T   F   Any mathematical operation, including multiplication and division, may be performed on a pointer.

23. T   F   Pointers may be compared using the relational operators.

24. T   F   When used as function parameters, reference variables are much easier to work with than pointers.

25. T   F   Variables may not be created while a program is running.

26. T   F   The `new` operator dynamically allocates memory.

27. T   F   A pointer that contains a value of 0 is called a null pointer.

28. T   F   The address 0 is generally considered off limits to user programs.

29. T   F   When using a pointer with the `delete` operator, it is not necessary that the pointer was previously used with the new operator.

Find the Error

30. Each of the following declarations and program segments has errors. Locate as many as you can.

A)
```cpp
int ptr*;
```

B)
```cpp
int x, *ptr;
&x = ptr;
```

C)
```cpp
int x, *ptr;
*ptr = &x;
```

D)
```cpp
int x, *ptr;
ptr = &x;
ptr = 100; // Store 100 in x
cout << x << endl;
```

E)
```cpp
int numbers[] = {10, 20, 30, 40, 50};
cout << "The third element in the array is ";
cout << *numbers + 3 << endl;
```

F)
```cpp
int values[20], *iptr;
iptr = values;
iptr *= 2;
```

G)
```cpp
float level;
int fptr = &level;
```

H)
```cpp
int *iptr = &ivalue;
int ivalue;
```

I)
```cpp
void doubleVal(int val)
{
    *val *= 2;
}
```

J)
```cpp
int *pint;
new pint;
```

K)
```cpp
int *pint;
pint = new int;
pint = 100;
```

L)
```cpp
int *pint;
pint = new int[100]; // Allocate memory
    .
    .
  Process the array
    .
    .
delete pint;// Free memory
```

```
M) int *getNum()
   {
        int wholeNum;

        cout << "Enter a number: ";
        cin >> wholeNum;
        return &wholeNum;
   }
```

Programming Challenges

General Requirements

Each program should have a section of comments at the top. The comments should contain your name, the date the program was written, the chapter the assignment appeared in, and the assignment number and name. Here is an example:

```
// Written by Jill Johnson
// March 31, 2003
// Chapter 10
// Assignment 1. Test Averaging
```

1. Test Averaging

Write a program that dynamically allocates a large enough array to hold a user-defined number of test scores. Once all the scores are entered, the array should be passed to a function that sorts them in ascending order. Another function should then be called that calculates the average score. The program should display the sorted list of scores and average, with appropriate headings.

Input Validation: Do not accept negative numbers for test scores.

2. Drop Lowest Score

Modify problem 1 so the lowest test score is dropped. This score should not be included in the calculation of the average.

3. Case Study Modification #1

Modify Program 10-17 (the United Cause case study program) so it can be used with any set of donations. The program should dynamically allocate the `donations` array and ask the user to input its values.

4. Case Study Modification #2

Modify Program 10-17 (the United Cause case study program) so the `arrPtr` array is sorted in descending order instead of ascending order.

5. Mode Function

In statistics, the *mode* of a set of values is the value which occurs most often or with the greatest frequency. Write a function that accepts as arguments the following:

A) An array of integers

B) An integer that indicates the number of elements in the array

The function should determine the mode of the array. That is, it should determine which value in the array occurs most often. The mode is the value the function should return. If the array has no mode (none of the values occur more than once), the function should return -1. (Assume the array will always contain nonnegative values, and that only one element occurs with the highest frequency.)

Demonstrate your pointer prowess by using pointer notation instead of array notation in this function.

6. Median Function

In statistics, when a set of values is sorted in ascending or descending order, its *median* is the middle value. If the set contains an even number of values, the median is the mean, or average, of the two middle values. Write a function that accepts as arguments the following:

A) An array of integers

B) An integer that indicates the number of elements in the array

The function should determine the median of the array. This value should be returned as a float. (Assume the values in the array are already sorted.)

Demonstrate your pointer prowess by using pointer notation instead of array notation in this function.

7. Movie Statistics

Write a program that can be used to gather statistical data about the number of movies college students see in a month. The program should perform the following steps:

A) Ask the user how many students were surveyed. An array of integers with this many elements should then be dynamically allocated.

B) Allow the user to enter the number of movies each student saw into the array.

C) Calculate and display the average, median, and mode of the values entered. (Use the functions you wrote in problems 5 and 6 to calculate the median and mode.)

Input Validation: Do not accept negative numbers for input.

Serendipity Booksellers Software Development Project—Part 10: *A Problem-Solving Exercise*

For this chapter's assignment you will enhance the program's point-of-sale and reporting capabilities.

1. Allow Multiple Transactions

Currently the cashier function only calculates the sale of one title. Modify it so that multiple titles may be purchased. After the information for each book is entered, the function should ask if there are other titles being purchased. If so, it allows the user to enter the information for another book. If not, it calculates the sale subtotal, tax, and total.

2. Enable Automatic Lookup

The `cashier` function currently asks the user to enter the ISBN number, title, and price of the book being purchased. Modify the function so that once the user enters the ISBN number, it automatically looks up the book title and price. It can do so by searching for the ISBN number in the `bookData` array. When an object is found with a matching ISBN number, the title and retail price can be retrieved via the class's member fucntions.

If the function cannot locate the ISBN number in the `isbn` array, it should display a message indicating so. It then should ask the user if he or she wants to re-enter the number and let the user enter that number again.

Once a book's information has been retrieved, the function should check the `qty` member to determine if there are enough copies in stock to fill the order. If so, the function should subtract the number of copies being purchased from the amount in the object. If there aren't enough copies in stock, the function should display a message indicating so, and then return to the main menu.

3. Complete the stub functions called from the `reports` menu

Currently, when the user chooses an option from the `reports` menu, a stub function is called, indicating which option was chosen. Modify the stub functions so they actually display the correct report on the screen.

Here is a list of the reporting functions and what they do:

- The `repListing` function should display a report listing all the books in the inventory. The following information should be included in the report: title, ISBN number, author, publisher, date added to inventory, quantity on hand, wholesale cost, and retail price. The report should display an appropriate title that includes the date. The function should fill the screen with information and then ask the user to press a key to continue to the next screen.

- The `repWholesale` function should display a report that lists the following information on all books in the inventory: title, ISBN number, quantity on hand, and wholesale cost. The report should display an appropriate title that includes the date. The function should fill the screen with information and then ask the user to press a key to continue to the next screen. The last line of the report should give the total wholesale value of the inventory (the sum of each book's wholesale cost multiplied by the quantity on hand.)

- The `repRetail` function should display a report that lists the following information on all books in the inventory: title, ISBN number, quantity on hand, and retail price. The report should display an appropriate title that includes the date. The function should fill the screen with information and then ask the user to press a key to continue to the next screen. The last line of the report should give the total retail value of the inventory (the sum of each book's retail price multiplied by the quantity on hand.)

◆ The `repQty` function should display a report that lists the following information on all books in the inventory: title, ISBN number, and quantity on hand. The list should be sorted by quantity on hand in descending order (the books of the greatest quantity listed first). The report should display an appropriate title that includes the date. The function should fill the screen with information and then ask the user to press a key to continue to the next screen.

◆ The `repCost` function should display a report that lists the following information on all books in the inventory: title, ISBN number, quantity on hand, and wholesale cost. The list should be sorted by wholesale in descending order (the books of the greatest unit cost listed first). The report should display an appropriate title that includes the date. The function should fill the screen with information and then ask the user to press a key to continue to the next screen.

◆ The `repAge` function should display a report that lists the following information on all books in the inventory: title, ISBN number, quantity on hand, and date added to the inventory. The list should be sorted by date added, in descending order (the books that have been in inventory longest will be listed first). The report should display an appropriate title that includes the date. The function should fill the screen with information and then ask the user to press a key to continue to the next screen.

CHAPTER 11

More About Classes

Topics

11.1 Static Members

CONCEPT If a member variable is declared `static`, all objects of that class have access to that variable. If a member function is declared `static`, it may be called before any instances of the class are defined.

Each class object (an instance of a class) has its own copy of the class's member variables. An object's member variables are separate and distinct from the member variables of other objects of the same class. For example, consider the following declaration:

```
class Widget
{
    private:
        float price;
        int quantity;
    public:
        Widget(float p, int q)
            { price = p; quantity = q; }
```

```
          float getPrice()
              { return price; }
          int getQuantity()
              { return quantity; }
};
```

Assume that in a program, two separate instances of the `Widget` class are created by the following declaration:

```
Widget w1(14.50, 100), w2(12.75, 500);
```

This statement creates `w1` and `w2`, two distinct objects. Each has its own `price` and `quantity` member variables. This is illustrated by Figure 11-1.

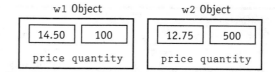

Figure 11-1

When the `getQuantity` member function of either instance is called, it returns the value stored in the calling object's `quantity` variable. Based on the values initially stored in the objects by the example declaration, the following statement will cause 100 500 to be displayed:

```
cout << w1.getQuantity() << " " << w2.getQuantity();
```

Static Member Variables

It's possible to create a member variable that is shared by all the objects of the same class. To create such a member, simply place the key word `static` in front of the variable declaration, as shown in the following class:

```
class StatDemo
{
    private:
        static int x;
        int y;
    public:
        void putx(int a)
            { x = a;}
        void puty(int b)
            { y = b;}
        int getx()
            { return x; }
        int gety()
            { return y; }
};
```

Next, place a separate definition of the variable outside the class, such as:

```
int StatDemo::x;
```

In this example, the member variable x will be shared by all objects of the StatDemo class. When one class object puts a value in x, it will appear in all other StatDemo objects. For example, assume the following statements appear in a program:

```
StatDemo obj1, obj2;
obj1.putx(5);
obj1.puty(10);
obj2.puty(20);
cout << "x: " << obj1.getx() << " " << obj2.getx() << endl;
cout << "y: " << obj1.gety() << " " << obj2.gety() << endl;
```

The cout statements shown will display

```
x: 5 5
y: 10 20
```

The value 5 is stored in the static member variable x by the object obj1. Since obj1 and obj2 share the variable x, the value 5 shows up in both objects. This is illustrated by Figure 11-2.

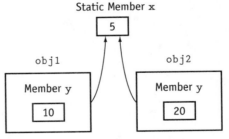

Figure 11-2

Both obj1 and obj2 share the static member x

A more practical use of a static member variable is demonstrated in Program 11-1. The Budget class is used to gather the budget requests for all the divisions of a company. The class uses a static member, corpBudget, to hold the amount of the overall corporate budget. When the member function addBudget is called, its argument is added to the current contents of corpBudget. By the time the program is finished, corpBudget will contain the total of all the values placed there by all the Budget class objects.

Program 11-1

Contents of budget.h

```
#ifndef BUDGET_H
#define BUDGET_H
// Budget class declaration
class Budget
{
    private:
        static float corpBudget;
        float divBudget;
    public:
        Budget() { divBudget = 0; }
        void addBudget(float b)
            { divBudget += b; corpBudget += divBudget; }
        float getDivBudget() { return divBudget; }
        float getCorpBudget() { return corpBudget; }
};
#endif
```

Contents of main program, pr11-1.cpp

```
// This program demonstrates a static class member variable.

#include <iostream>
#include "budget.h"              // For Budget class declaration
using namespace std;

float Budget::corpBudget = 0;    // Definition of static member of Budget class

int main()
{
    Budget divisions[4];
    int count;

    for (count = 0; count < 4; count++)
    {
        float bud;

        cout << "Enter the budget request for Division ";
        cout << (count + 1) << ": ";
        cin >> bud;
        divisions[count].addBudget(bud);
    }
    cout << setprecision(2);
    cout << showpoint << fixed;
    cout << "\nHere are the division budget requests:\n";
    for (count = 0; count < 4; count++)
    {
        cout << "\tDivision " << (count + 1) << "\t$ ";
        cout << divisions[count].getDivBudget() << endl;
    }
```

(program continues)

Program 11-1 *(continued)*

```
        cout << "\tTotal Budget Requests:\t$ ";
        cout << divisions[0].getCorpBudget() << endl;
        return 0;
}
```

Program Output with Example Input Shown in Bold
```
Enter the budget request for Division 1: 100000[Enter]
Enter the budget request for Division 2: 200000[Enter]
Enter the budget request for Division 3: 300000[Enter]
Enter the budget request for Division 4: 400000[Enter]
Here are the division budget requests:
    Division 1    $ 100000.00
    Division 2    $ 200000.00
    Division 3    $ 300000.00
    Division 4    $ 400000.00
    Total Budget Requests:$ 1000000.00
```

Static Member Functions

It is possible to declare a static member function by placing the `static` key word in the function's prototype. Here is the general form:

```
    static <return type><function name>(<parameter type list>);
```

A function that is a static member of a class cannot access any non-static member data in its class. With this limitation in mind, you might wonder what purpose static member functions serve. The following two points are important for understanding their usefulness:

◆ Even though static member variables are declared in a class, they are actually defined outside the class declaration. The lifetime of a class's static member variable is the lifetime of the program. This means that a class's static member variables come into existence before any instances of the class are created.

◆ The static member functions of a class are callable before any instances of the class are created. This means that the static member functions of a class can access the class's static member variables *before* any instances of the class are defined in memory. This gives you the ability to create very specialized setup routines for class objects.

As a rule, member functions such as `getCorpBudget()` that do not access non-static members of their class schould be made static.

Program 11-2, a modification of Program 11-1, demonstrates this. It asks the user to enter the main office's budget request before any division requests are entered. The `Budget` class has been modified to include a static member function named `mainOffice`. This function adds its argument to the static `corpBudget` variable and is called before any instances of the `Budget` class are defined. The `getCorpBdget()` function has also been made static.

Program 11-2

Contents of budget2.h
```
#ifndef BUDGET_H
#define BUDGET_H

// Budget class declaration
class Budget
{
private:
    static float corpBudget;
    float divBudget;
public:
    Budget() { divBudget = 0; }
    void addBudget(float b)
        { divBudget += b; corpBudget += divBudget; }
    float getDivBudget() { return divBudget; }
    static float getCorpBudget() { return corpBudget; }
    static void mainOffice(float);
};
#endif
```

Contents of budget2.cpp
```
#include "budget2.h"

float Budget::corpBudget = 0; // Definition of static member of Budget class

//************************************************************
// Definition of static member function mainOffice.         *
// This function adds the main office's budget request to    *
// the corpBudget variable.                                  *
//************************************************************

void Budget::mainOffice(float moffice)
{
    corpBudget += moffice;
}
```

Contents of main program, pr11-2.cpp
```
// This program demonstrates a static class member function.

#include <iostream>
#include "budget2.h" // For Budget class declaration
using namspace std;
```

(program continues)

Program 11-2 *(continued)*

```
int main()
{
    float amount;
    int count;

    cout << "Enter the main office's budget request: ";
    cin >> amount;
    Budget::mainOffice(amount);
    Budget divisions[4];

    for (count = 0; count < 4; count++)
    {
        float bud;
        cout << "Enter the budget request for Division ";
        cout << (count + 1) << ": ";
        cin >> bud;
        divisions[count].addBudget(bud);
    }
    cout << setprecision(2);
    cout << showpoint << fixed;
    cout << "\nHere are the division budget requests:\n";
    for (count = 0; count < 4; count++)
    {
        cout << "\tDivision " << (count + 1) << "\t$ ";
        cout << divisions[count].getDivBudget() << endl;
    }
    cout << "\tTotal Requests (including main office): $ ";
    cout << Budget::getCorpBudget() << endl;
    return 0;
}
```

Program Output with Example Input Shown in Bold
```
Enter the main office's budget request: 100000[Enter]
Enter the budget request for Division 1: 100000[Enter]
Enter the budget request for Division 2: 200000[Enter]
Enter the budget request for Division 3: 300000[Enter]
Enter the budget request for Division 4: 400000[Enter]

Here are the division budget requests:
    Division 1      $ 100000.00
    Division 2      $ 200000.00
    Division 3      $ 300000.00
    Division 4      $ 400000.00
    Total Requests (including main office): $ 1100000.00
```

Notice the statement that calls the static function `mainOffice`:

```
Budget::mainOffice(amount);
```

Calls to static member functions are normally made by connecting the function name to the class name with the scope resolution operator. If objects of the class have been defined, static member functions can also be called by connecting their names to the object with the dot operator. Thus the last output statement of Program 11-2 could be written as

```
cout << divisions[0].getCorpBudget() << endl;
```

The `this` Pointer

A static member of a class exists independently of any class object and is shared by all objects of the class. A non-static member, on the other hand, exists only inside of an object, or instance, of the class. For this reason, non-static members are often called *instance members*.

An instance member function must be called through an object of its class, and its execution usually depends on values of member variables inside the "calling" object. For example, if we have a class and two objects:

```
class ThisExample
{
private:
        int x;
public:
        ThisExample(int x1) { x = x1; }
        void setX(int x1) { x = x1; }
        int getX() { return x; }
};

ThisExample one(1);
ThisExample two(2);
```

then when we call `one.getX()`, the function `getX` returns 1, the value of x in the object `one`; but when we call `two.getX()`, the same function returns 2, the value of x in the object `two`.

What happens is this. Whenever an instance member function is called, the address of the "calling" object is passed by the compiler to the member function. Thus the address of the object `one` is passed to `getX` when the call `one.getX()` is made, but the address of the object `two` is passed to `getX` when the call `two.getX()` is made. The `getX` function uses this address to find the appropriate x, returning `one.x` in the first call and `two.x` in the latter call.

The pointer to the object through which a non-static member function is called is implicitly passed by the compiler to the member function without the programmer having to do anything. This pointer can be accessed by the programmer by using the keyword `this` inside the member function. This allows a non-static member function to access the object through which it is called by dereferencing the `this` pointer.

As an example of a common use of the `this` pointer, consider the member function

```
void setX(int x1) { x = x1; }
```

of the previously cited class. It is natural to name the formal parameter to setX the same as the class member whose value is to be set; that is, we may want to name it x to indicate that it is a value to be used to set the member variable x. This helps make programs more readable by making the purpose of a formal parameter clear. Unfortunately, calling the formal parameter the same name as a member variable will hide the member variable, making it inaccessible. We can use the this pointer to gain access to members of a class that have been hidden by formal parameters as follows. First, we dereference the this pointer to obtain *this, the object through which the member function is called, and then use the dot operator to access the hidden member. For example, we can write the setX member function as follows:

```
void setX(int x) {(*this).x  = x; }
```

Alternatively, we can use the more user-friendly notation for accessing members of objects and structures through pointers that was covered in the last chapter and write the function as

```
void setX(int x) { this->x = x; }
```

 Note: The this pointer can only be used in an instance member function. In particular, it cannot be used inside of a static member function.

11.2 Friends of Classes

CONCEPT A friend is a function that is not a member of a class, but has access to the private members of the class.

Private members are hidden from all parts of the program outside the class, and accessing them requires a call to a public member function. Sometimes you will want to create an exception to that rule. A *friend* function is a function that is not part of a class, but that has access to the class's private members. In other words, a friend function is treated as if it were a member of the class. A friend function can be a regular stand-alone function, or it can be a member of another class. (In fact, an entire class can be declared a friend of another class.)

In order for a function or class to become a friend of another class, it must be declared as such by the class granting it access. Classes keep a "list" of their friends, and only the external functions or classes whose names appears in the list are granted access. A function is declared a friend by placing the keyword friend in front of a prototype of the function. Here is the general format:

```
friend <return type><function name>(<parameter type list>);
```

In the following declaration of the Budget class, the addBudget function of another class, Aux, has been declared a friend:

```
class Budget
{
private:
    static float corpBudget;
    float divBudget;
public:
    Budget() { divBudget = 0; }
    void addBudget(float b)
        { divBudget += b; corpBudget += divBudget; }
    float getDivBudget() { return divBudget; }
    static float getCorpBudget() { return corpBudget; }
    static void mainOffice(float);
    friend void Aux::addBudget(float);     //A friend
};
```

Let's assume another class, Aux, represents a division's auxiliary office, perhaps in another country. The auxiliary office makes a separate budget request, which must be added to the overall corporate budget. The friend declaration of the Aux::addBudget function tells the compiler that the function is to be granted access to Budget's private members. The function takes a float argument representing an amount to be added to the corporate budget:

```
class Aux
{
private:
    float auxBudget;
public:
    Aux() { auxBudget = 0; }
    void addBudget(float);
    float getDivBudget() { return auxBudget; }
};
```

And here is the definition of the Aux addBudget member function:

```
void Aux::addBudget(float b)
{
    auxBudget += b;
    Budget::corpBudget += auxBudget;
}
```

The parameter b is added to the corporate budget, which is accessed by using the expression Budget::corpBudget. Program 11-3 demonstrates the classes in a complete program.

Program 11-3

Contents of auxil.h
```
#ifndef AUXIL_H
#define AUXIL_H
```

(program continues)

Program 11-3 *(continued)*

```cpp
// Aux class declaration
class Aux
{
private:
    float auxBudget;
public:
    Aux() { auxBudget = 0; }
    void addBudget(float);
    float getDivBudget() { return auxBudget; }
};

#endif
```

Contents of budget3.h
```cpp
#ifndef BUDGET3_H
#define BUDGET3_H
#include "auxil.h"// For Aux class declaration

// Budget class declaration
class Budget
{
private:
    static float corpBudget;
    float divBudget;
public:
    Budget() { divBudget = 0; }
    void addBudget(float b)
        { divBudget += b; corpBudget += divBudget; }
    float getDivBudget() { return divBudget; }
    static float getCorpBudget() { return corpBudget; }
    static void mainOffice(float);
    friend void Aux::addBudget(float);
};

#endif
```

Contents of budget3.cpp
```cpp
#include "budget3.h"

float Budget::corpBudget = 0; // Definition of static member.

//************************************************************
// Definition of static member function mainOffice.         *
// This function adds the main office's budget request to    *
// the corpBudget variable.                                  *
//************************************************************
```

(program continues)

Program 11-3   *(continued)*

```
void Budget::mainOffice(float moffice)
{
    corpBudget += moffice;
}
```

Contents of auxil.cpp
```
#include "auxil.h"
#include "budget3.h"

//**************************************************************
// Definition of member function addBudget.                    *
// This function is declared a friend by the Budget class.      *
// It adds the value of argument b to the static corpBudget     *
// member variable of the Budget class.                         *
//**************************************************************

void Aux::addBudget(float b)
{
    auxBudget += b;
    Budget::corpBudget += auxBudget;
}
```

Contents of main program pr11-3.cpp
```
// This program demonstrates a static class member variable.

#include <iostream>
#include <iomanip>
#include "budget3.h"
using namespace std;

int main()
{
    float amount;
    int count;

    cout << "Enter the main office's budget request: ";
    cin >> amount;
    Budget::mainOffice(amount);
    Budget divisions[4];
    Aux auxOffices[4];
    for (count = 0; count < 4; count++)
    {
        float bud;
```

(program continues)

Program 11-3 *(continued)*

```
        cout << "Enter the budget request for Division ";
        cout << (count + 1) << ": ";
        cin >> bud;
        divisions[count].addBudget(bud);
        cout << "Enter the budget request for Division ";
        cout << (count + 1) << "'s\nauxiliary office: ";
        cin >> bud;
        auxOffices[count].addBudget(bud);
    }
    cout << setprecision(2);
    cout << showpoint << fixed;
    cout << "Here are the division budget requests:\n";
    for (count = 0; count < 4; count++)
    {
        cout << "\tDivision " << (count + 1) << "\t\t\t$ ";
        cout << setw(7);
        cout << divisions[count].getDivBudget() << endl;
        cout << "\tauxiliary Office of Division " << (count+1);
        cout << "\t$   ";
        cout << auxOffices[count].getDivBudget() << endl;
    }
    cout << "\tTotal Requests (including main office): $ ";
    cout << Budget::getCorpBudget() << endl;
    return 0;
}
```

Program Output with Example Input Shown in Bold

```
Enter the main office's budget request: 100000[Enter]
Enter the budget request for Division 1: 100000[Enter]
Enter the budget request for Division 1's
auxiliary office: 50000[Enter]
Enter the budget request for Division 2: 200000[Enter]
Enter the budget request for Division 2's
auxiliary office: 40000[Enter]
Enter the budget request for Division 3: 300000[Enter]
Enter the budget request for Division 3's
auxiliary office: 70000[Enter]
Enter the budget request for Division 4: 400000[Enter]
Enter the budget request for Division 4's
auxiliary office: 65000[Enter]
```

(program output continues)

Program 11-3 *(continued)*

```
Here are the division budget requests:
        Division 1:                        $ 100000.00
        Auxiliary office of Division 1:    $  50000.00
        Division 2:                        $ 200000.00
        Auxiliary office of Division 2:    $  40000.00
        Division 3:                        $ 300000.00
        Auxiliary office of Division 3:    $  70000.00
        Division 4:                        $ 400000.00
        Auxiliary office of Division 4:    $  65000.00
        Total Requests (including main office): $ 1325000.00
```

Note: As mentioned before, it is possible to make an entire class a friend of another class. The Budget class could make the Aux class its friend with the following declaration:

```
friend class Aux;
```

This may not be a good idea, however. Every member function of Aux (including ones that may be added later) would have access to the private members of Budget. The best practice is to declare as friends only those functions that must have access to the private members of the class.

Checkpoint   [11.1–11.2]

11.1 What is the difference between a regular member variable and a static member variable?

11.2 Static member variables are declared inside the class declaration. Where are static member variables defined?

11.3 Does a static member variable come into existence in memory before, at the same time as, or after any instances of its class?

11.4 What limitation does a static member function have?

11.5 What action is possible with a static member function that isn't possible with a regular member function?

11.6 If class X declares function f as a friend, does function f become a member of class X?

11.7 Class Y is a friend of class X, which means the member functions of class Y have access to all the members of class X. Does the friend key word appear in class Y's declaration or in class X's declaration?

11.3 Memberwise Assignment

CONCEPT The = operator may be used to assign one object to another, or to initialize one object with another object's data. By default, each member of one object is copied to its counterpart in the other object.

Like other variables (except arrays), objects may be assigned to each other using the = operator. As an example, consider Program 11-4, which uses a Rectangle class similar to the one discussed in Chapter 7:

Program 11-4

```cpp
#include <iostream>
using namespace std;

class Rectangle
{
private:
    float width;
    float length;
    float area;
    void calcArea() { area = width * length; }
public:
    void setData(float w, float l)
        { width = w; length = l; calcArea(); }
    float getWidth()
        { return width; }
    float getLength()
        { return length; }
    float getArea()
        { return area; }
};

int main()
{
    Rectangle box1, box2;

    box1.setData(10, 20);
    box2.setData(5, 10);
    cout << "Before the assignment:\n";
    cout << "Box 1's width: " << box1.getWidth() << endl;
    cout << "Box 1's length: " << box1.getLength() << endl;
    cout << "Box 1's area: " << box1.getArea() << endl;
    cout << "Box 2's width: " << box2.getWidth() << endl;
    cout << "Box 2's length: " << box2.getLength() << endl;
    cout << "Box 2's area: " << box2.getArea() << endl;
```

(program continues)

Program 11-4   *(continued)*

```
box2 = box1;
cout << endl;
cout << "After the assignment:\n";
cout << "Box 1's width: " << box1.getWidth() << endl;
cout << "Box 1's length: " << box1.getLength() << endl;
cout << "Box 1's area: " << box1.getArea() << endl;
cout << "Box 2's width: " << box2.getWidth() << endl;
cout << "Box 2's length: " << box2.getLength() << endl;
cout << "Box 2's area: " << box2.getArea() << endl;
return 0;
}
```

Program Output
```
Before the assignment:
Box 1's width: 10
Box 1's length: 20
Box 1's area: 200
Box 2's width: 5
Box 2's length: 10
Box 2's area: 50

After the assignment:
Box 1's width: 10
Box 1's length: 20
Box 1's area: 200
Box 2's width: 10
Box 2's length: 20
Box 2's area: 200
```

As you can see, the following statement copies the width, length, and area variables of box1 directly into the width, length, and area variables of box2:

```
box2 = box1
```

Memberwise assignment also occurs when one object is initialized with another object's values. Remember the difference between assignment and initialization: assignment occurs between two objects that already exist, and initialization happens to an object being created. Consider the following program segment:

```
Rectangle box1;
box1.setData(100, 50);
Rectangle box2 = box1;
```

The third statement defines a Rectangle object, box2, and initializes it to the values stored in box1. Because memberwise assignment takes place, the box2 object will contain the exact same values as the box1 object.

11.4 Copy Constructors

> **CONCEPT** A copy constructor is a special constructor that is called whenever a new object is created and initialized with the data of another object of the same class.

Many times it makes sense to create an object and have it start out with its data being the same as that of another, previously created object. For example, if Mary and Joan live in the same house, and an address object for Mary has already been created, it makes sense to initialize Joan's address object to a copy of Mary's. In particular, suppose we have the following class to represent addresses:

```
class Address
{
private:
  string street;
public:
  Address() { street = ""; }
  Address(string st) { setStreet(st); }
  void setStreet(string st) { street = st; }
  string getStreet() { return street; }
};
```

We could then create Mary's address and then initialize Joan's address to a copy of Mary's using the following code:

```
Address mary("123 Main St");
Address joan = mary;
```

Recall that a constructor must execute whenever an object is being created. When an object is created and initialized with another object of the same class, the compiler automatically calls a special constructor, called a *copy constructor,* to perform the initialization using the existing object's data. This copy constructor can be specified by the programmer, as we will shortly show.

The Default Copy Constructor

If the programmer does not specify a copy constructor for the class, then the compiler automatically calls a *default copy constructor.* This default copy constructor simply copies the data of the existing object to the new object using memberwise assignment.

Most of the time, the default copy constructor provides the kind of behavior that we want. For example, if after initializing Joan's address with Mary's, Joan later moves out and gets her own place, we can change Joan's address without affecting Mary's. This is illustrated in Program 11-5.

Program 11-5

```
//This program demonstrates the operation of the default copy constructor

#include <iostream>
using namespace std;

class Address
{
private:
  string street;
public:
  Address() { street = ""; }
  Address(string st) { setStreet(st); }
  void setStreet(string st) { street = st; }
  string getStreet() { return street; }
};

int main()
{
  //Mary and Joan live at same address
  Address mary("123 Main St");
  Address joan = mary;
  cout << "Mary lives at " << mary.getStreet() << endl;
  cout << "Joan lives at " << joan.getStreet() << endl;
  //Now Joan moves out
  joan.setStreet("1600 Pennsylvania Ave");
  cout << "Now Mary lives at " << mary.getStreet() << endl;
  cout << "Now Joan lives at " << joan.getStreet() << endl;

  return 0;
}
```

Program Output
```
Mary lives at 123 Main St
Joan lives at 123 Main St
Now Mary lives at 123 Main St
Now Joan lives at 1600 Pennsylvania Ave
```

Deficiencies of Default Copy Constructors

There are times, however, when the behavior of the default copy constructor is not what we expect. Consider a class

```
class FloatArray
{
private:
  float *aPtr;
  int arraySize;
public:
  FloatArray(int size, float value);
  //~FloatArray(){ if (arraySize > 0) delete [ ] aPtr;}
  void print();
  void setValue(float value);
};
```

that encapsulates an array of floating-point numbers (in practice there may be other members of the class as well). To allow flexibility for different size arrays, the class contains a pointer to the array instead of directly containing the array itself. The constructor of the class allocates an array of a specified size, then sets all the entries of the array to a given value. The class has member functions for printing the array and for setting the entries of the array to a given (possibly different) value. The class's destructor is currently commented out to avoid problems caused by the default copy constructor: We shall shortly point out the specific nature of these problems.

Program 11-6 creates an object of the class, creates and initializes a second object with the data of the first, and then changes the array in the second object. As shown by the output of the program, changing the second object's data changes the data in the first object. In many cases, this is undesirable and leads to bugs.

Program 11-6

Contents of floatarray.h
```
#include <iostream>
using namespace std;

class FloatArray
{
private:
  float *aPtr;
  int arraySize;
public:
  FloatArray(int size, float value);
  //~FloatArray(){ if (arraySize > 0) delete [ ] aPtr; }
  void print();
  void setValue(float value);
};
```

(program continues)

Program 11-6 *(continued)*

Contents of floatarray.cpp

```cpp
//floatarray.cpp
#include <iostream>
#include "floatarray.h"
using namespace std;

//***********************************************
//Constructor allocates an array of the        *
//given size and sets all its entries to the    *
//given value.                                   *
//***********************************************

FloatArray::FloatArray(int size, float value)
{
  arraySize = size;
  aPtr = new float[arraySize];
  setValue(value);
}

//********************************************************
//Sets all the entries of the array to the same value. *
//********************************************************

void FloatArray::setValue(float value)
{
  for(int index = 0; index < arraySize; index++)
    aPtr[index] = value;
}

//***************************************
//Prints all the entries of the array. *
//***************************************

void FloatArray::print()
{
  for(int index = 0; index < arraySize; index++)
    cout << aPtr[index] << "  ";
}
```

(program continues)

Program 11-6 *(continued)*

Contents of Pr11-6.cpp
```
//This program demonstrates the deficiencies of
//the default copy constructor

#include <iostream>
#include <iomanip>
#include "floatarray.h"
using namespace std;

int main()
{
  //Make second a copy of first object.
  FloatArray first(3, 10.5);
  FloatArray second = first;

  cout << setprecision(2) << fixed << showpoint;
  cout << "Value stored in first object is ";
  first.print();
  cout << endl << "Value stored in second object is ";
  second.print();
  cout << endl << "Only the value in second object will be changed."
       << endl;
  //Now change value stored in second object.
  second.setValue(20.5);
  cout << "Value stored in first object is ";
  first.print();
  cout << endl << "Value stored in second object is ";
  second.print();
}
```

Program Output
```
Value stored in first object is 10.50   10.50   10.50
Value stored in second object is 10.50   10.50   10.50
Only the value in second object will be changed.
Value stored in first object is 20.50   20.50   20.50
Value stored in second object is 20.50   20.50   20.50
```

The reason changing the data in one object changes the other object is that the memberwise assignment performed by the default copy constructor copies the value of the pointer in the first object to the pointer in the second object, *leaving both pointers pointing to the same data.* Thus when one of the objects changes its data through its pointer, it affects the other object as well. This is illustrated in Figure 11-3.

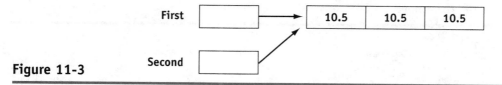

Figure 11-3

The fact that the two pointers point to the same memory location will also cause problems when the destructors for the two objects try to deallocate the same memory (that is why the destructor code in the above class is commented out). In general, classes with pointer members will not behave correctly under the default copy constructor provided by the compiler: They must be provided with a copy constructor written by the programmer.

Programmer-Defined Copy Constructors

A programmer can define a copy constructor for a class. A programmer-defined copy constructor must have a single parameter that is a reference to the *same* class. Thus in the case of the previous example, the prototype for the copy constructor would be

```
FloatArray::FloatArray(FloatArray &obj)
```

This copy constructor avoids the problems of the default copy constructor by allocating separate memory for the pointer of the new object before doing the copy:

```
FloatArray::FloatArray(FloatArray &obj)
{
    arraySize = obj.arraySize;
    aPtr = new float[arraySize];
    for(int index = 0; index < arraySize; index++)
        aPtr[index] = obj.aPtr[index];
}
```

Program 11-7 demonstrates the use of the FloatArray class modified to have a copy constructor. The class declaration is in the floatarray2.h file, with the implementations of its member functions being given in floatarray2.cpp.

Program 11-7

Contents of floatarray2.h
```
#include <iostream>
using namespace std;

class FloatArray
{
private:
    float *aPtr;
    int arraySize;
```

(program continues)

Program 11-7 *(continued)*

```cpp
public:
  FloatArray(FloatArray &);
  FloatArray(int size, float value);
  ~FloatArray() { if (arraySize > 0) delete [] aPtr; }
  void print();
  void setValue(float value);
};
```

Contents of floatarray2.cpp

```cpp
#include <iostream>
#include "floatarray2.h"
using namespace std;

//**********************************
//Copy Constructor.                *
//**********************************

FloatArray::FloatArray(FloatArray &obj)
{
  arraySize = obj.arraySize;
  aPtr = new float[arraySize];
  for(int index = 0; index < arraySize; index++)
    aPtr[index] = obj.aPtr[index];
}

//************************************************
//Constructor allocates an array of the         *
//given size and sets all its entries to the    *
//given value.                                   *
//************************************************

FloatArray::FloatArray(int size, float value)
{
  arraySize = size;
  aPtr = new float[arraySize];
  setValue(value);
}

//***********************************************************
//Sets all the entries of the array to the same value.     *
//***********************************************************
void FloatArray::setValue(float value)
{
  for(int index = 0; index < arraySize; index++)
    aPtr[index] = value;
}
```

(program continues)

Program 11-7   *(continued)*

```
//***************************************
//Prints all the entries of the array. *
//***************************************

void FloatArray::print()
{
  for(int index = 0; index < arraySize; index++)
    cout << aPtr[index] << "   ";
}
```

Contents of Pr11-7.cpp

```
#include <iostream>
#include <iomanip>
#include "floatarray2.h"

using namespace std;

int main()
{
  //Make second a copy of first object.
  FloatArray first(3, 10.5);
  FloatArray second = first;

  cout << setprecision(2) << fixed << showpoint;
  cout << "Value stored in first object is ";
  first.print();
  cout << endl << "Value stored in second object is ";
  second.print();
  cout << endl << "Only the value in second object will be changed."
       << endl;

  //Now change value stored in second object.
  second.setValue(20.5);
  cout << "Value stored in first object is ";
  first.print();
  cout << endl << "Value stored in second object is ";
  second.print();
}
```

Program Output

```
Value stored in first object is 10.50   10.50   10.50
Value stored in second object is 10.50   10.50   10.50
Only the value in second object will be changed.
Value stored in first object is 10.50   10.50   10.50
Value stored in second object is 20.50   20.50   20.50
```

Note: A copy constructor must have a single parameter that is a reference to the same class: Forgetting the & that flags reference parameters will result in compiler errors.

The copy constructor is also automatically called by the compiler to create a copy of an object whenever an object is being passed by *value* in a function call. It is for this reason that the parameter to the copy constructor must be passed by reference; if it was passed by value when the constructor was called, then the constructor would immediately have to be called again to create the copy to be passed by value, leading to an endless chain of calls to the constructor.

The copy constructor is also called to create a copy of an object to be returned from a function.

Using const **Parameters**

Because copy constructors are required to use reference parameters, they have access to their argument's data. Since the purpose of a copy constructor is to make a copy of the argument, there is no reason the constructor should modify the argument's data. With this in mind, it's a good idea to make a copy constructor's parameter constant by specifying the const key word in the parameter list. Here is an example:

```
FloatArray::FloatArray(const FloatArray &obj)
{
    arraySize = obj.arraySize;
    aPtr = new float[arraySize];
    for(int index = 0; index < arraySize; index++)
        aPtr[index] = obj.aPtr[index];
}
```

Checkpoint [11.3–11.4]

11.8 Briefly describe what is meant by memberwise assignment.

11.9 Describe two instances when memberwise assignment occurs.

11.10 Describe a situation in which memberwise assignment should not be used.

11.11 When is a copy constructor called?

11.12 How does the compiler know that a member function is a copy constructor?

11.13 What action is performed by a class's default copy constructor?

11.5   Operator Overloading

CONCEPT   C++ allows you to redefine how standard operators work when used with class objects.

Overloading the = Operator

As we have seen, copy constructors are designed to solve problems that arise when an object containing a pointer is initialized with the data of another object of the same class using memberwise assignment. Similar problems arise in object assignment. For example, with the FloatArray class of the previous section, we may have a program that has defined two objects of that class:

```
FloatArray first(3, 10.5);
FloatArray second(5, 20.5);
```

Now, since C++ allows the assignment operator to be used with class objects, we may execute the statement

```
first = second;
```

if we want to set the first object to exactly the same value as the second. At this point, C++ will once again perform a memberwise copy from the second to the first object, leaving pointers in both objects pointing to the same memory.

Unfortunately, copy constructors only come into play when an object is being initialized at creation time. In particular, copy constructors are not called in an assignment statement. Thus, if the object first has already been created, the statement

```
FloatArray second = first;  //copy constructor called
```

which creates second and initializes it with the value of first, is an *initialization* and causes the copy constructor to be called to perform the initialization. However, the statement

```
second = first;   //copy constructor not called
```

which assumes that both objects have previously been created, is an *assignment*, and therefore no constructor is invoked.

To address the problems that result from memberwise assignment of objects, we need to modify the behavior of the assignment operator so that it does something other than memberwise assignment when it is applied to objects of classes that have pointer members. In effect we are supplying a version of the assignment operator to be used for objects of that class. In so doing, we say that we are *overloading* the assignment operator.

One way to overload the assignment operator for a given class is to define an *operator function* called operator= as a member function of the class. To do this for the FloatArray class, we would write the class declaration as follows:

```
class FloatArray
{
private:
    float *aPtr;
    int arraySize;
public:
    void operator=(const FloatArray &right); //Overloaded operator.
    FloatArray(const FloatArray &);
    FloatArray(int size, float value);
    ~FloatArray() { if (arraySize > 0) delete [ ] aPtr; }
    void print();
    void setValue(float value);
};
```

Let's take a look at the function header, or prototype, before we look at how the operator function itself is implemented. We break the header down into its main parts, as shown in Figure 11-4.

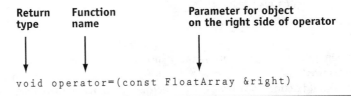

Figure 11-4

The name of the function is operator=. Since the operator function is an instance member of a class, it can only be called through an object of the class. The object of the class through which it is called is considered the left operand of the assignment operator, while the parameter passed to the function is considered the right operand of the assignment operator. To illustrate, let us suppose that two objects, left and right, have been defined in a program:

```
FloatArray left(3,10.5);
FloatArray right(5, 20.5);
```

To assign the value of right to left, we call the member function operator= through the left object, and pass it the right object as parameter:

```
left.operator=(right);
```

While you can call operator functions this way, the compiler will also let you use the more conventional notation

```
left = right;
```

Note: Parameters to operator functions do not have to be passed by reference, nor do they have to be declared `const`. In this example we have used a reference parameter for efficiency reasons: Reference parameters avoid the overhead of copying the object being passed as parameter. The `const` is used to protect the parameter from change.

Let us now consider the implementation of the above operator function. The function starts out by deleting memory allocated to pointers in the object being assigned to, then makes a copy of the other object in pretty much the same way as the copy constructor for the class. Here is the code for the function (although we have used the name `right` for the object that is the right parameter of the assignment, any other name could have been used).

```
void FloatArray::operator=(const FloatArray &right)
{
    if (arraySize > 0) delete [] aPtr;
    arraySize = right.arraySize;
    aPtr = new float[arraySize];
    for (int index = 0; index < arraySize; index++)
      aPtr[index] = right.aPtr[index];
}
```

In general, the assignment operator should be overloaded whenever a non-default copy constructor is used. In particular, classes allocating dynamic memory to a pointer member in any constructor should define both a copy constructor and an overloaded assignment operator. In addition, they should also provide a destructor to deallocate the storage allocated in the constructor.

The class `FloatArray`, with modifications to include both a copy constructor and an overloaded assignment operator, is demonstrated in Program 11-8.

Program 11-8

Contents of `overload.h`
```
#include <iostream>
using namespace std;

class FloatArray
{
private:
  float *aPtr;
  int arraySize;
public:
  void operator=(const FloatArray &right);    // Overloaded operator function
  FloatArray(const FloatArray &);
  FloatArray(int size, float value);
  ~FloatArray() { if (arraySize > 0) delete [ ] aPtr; }
  void print();
  void setValue(float value);
};
```

(program continues)

Program 11-8   *(continued)*

Contents of overload.cpp

```cpp
#include <iostream>
#include "overload.h"
using namespace std;

//**********************************************************
//The overloaded operator function for assignment.    *
//**********************************************************

void FloatArray::operator=(const FloatArray &right)
{
  if (arraySize > 0) delete [] aPtr;
  arraySize = right.arraySize;
  aPtr = new float[arraySize];
  for (int index = 0; index < arraySize; index++)
    aPtr[index] = right.aPtr[index];
}

//**********************************************
//Copy Constructor.                           *
//**********************************************

FloatArray::FloatArray(const FloatArray &obj)
{
  arraySize = obj.arraySize;
  aPtr = new float[arraySize];
  for(int index = 0; index < arraySize; index++)
    aPtr[index] = obj.aPtr[index];
}

//**************************************************
//Constructor.                                    *
//**************************************************

FloatArray::FloatArray(int size1, float value)
{
  arraySize = size1;
  aPtr = new float[arraySize];
  setValue(value);
}

//********************************************************
//Sets the value stored in all entries of the array. *
//********************************************************

void FloatArray::setValue(float value)
{
  for(int index = 0; index < arraySize; index++)
    aPtr[index] = value;
}
```

(program continues)

Program 11-8   *(continued)*

```
//*****************************************
//Print out all entries in the array.    *
//*****************************************

void FloatArray::print()
{
  for(int index = 0; index < arraySize; index++)
     cout << aPtr[index] << "  ";
}
```

Contents of Pr11-8.cpp

```
//This program demonstrates overloading of
//the assignment operator.

#include <iostream>
#include <iomanip>
#include "overload.h"
using namespace std;

int main()
{
   FloatArray first(3, 10.5);
   FloatArray second(5, 20.5);

   cout << setprecision(2) << fixed << showpoint;
   cout << "First object's data is ";
   first.print();
   cout << endl << "Second object's data is ";
   second.print();
   cout << endl << "Now we will assign the second object "
        << "to the first."
   first = second;          //Call overloaded operator.
   cout << "First object's data is ";
   first.print();
   cout << endl << "The second object's data is ";
   second.print();
   return 0;
}
```

Program Output

```
First object's data is 10.50   10.50   10.50
Second object's data is 20.50   20.50   20.50   20.50   20.50
Now we will assign the second object to the first.
First object's data is 20.50   20.50   20.50   20.50   20.50
The second object's data is 20.50   20.50   20.50   20.50   20.50
```

The = Operator's Return Value

There is only one problem with the overloaded = operator shown in Program 11-8: It has a void return type. C++'s built-in assignment operator allows multiple assignment statements such as

```
a = b = c;
```

Multiple assignment statements work because the built-in assignment operator is implemented so that it returns the value of its left operand *after* the assignment has been performed. Thus in this statement, the expression b = c causes c to be assigned to b and then returns the value of b. The return value is then stored in a.

To make an overloaded assignment operator behave similarly, we must redefine the operator function so that it also returns the value of its left operand after the assignment has been performed. In particular, we need to declare the operator function to have a return type of the same type as the class. This is shown in our final modification of the FloatArray class:

```
class FloatArray
{
private:
   float *aPtr;
   int arraySize;
public:
   FloatArray operator=(const FloatArray &right); //Overloaded operator.
   FloatArray(const FloatArray &);
   FloatArray(int size, float value);
   ~FloatArray() { if (arraySize > 0) delete [] aPtr; }
   void print();
   void setValue(float value);
};
```

The only modification we need to make to the assignment operator function is to add a statement at the very end returning the value of its left operand. Since the assignment is equivalent to the statement

```
left.operator=(right);
```

returning the value of the left operand boils down to the operator function returning the value of the object through which it is called. Recall that C++ makes available to each call of a non-static member function, the address of the object through which the call is being made, and that the address of that object is accessed through the pointer this. The value of the object itself can be obtained and returned by dereferencing the this pointer:

```
return *this;
```

The code for the modified assignment operator function is

```
FloatArray FloatArray::operator=(const FloatArray &right)
{
```

```
  if (arraySize > 0)  delete [] aPtr;
  arraySize = right.arraySize;
  aPtr = new float[arraySize];
  for (int index = 0; index < arraySize; index++)
     aPtr[index] = right.aPtr[index];
  return *this;
}
```

Overloading Other Operators

C++ allows the programmer to overload other operators besides assignment. There are many times when it is natural to overload some of C++'s built-in operators to make them work with classes that the programmer has defined. For example, assume that a class named Date exists, and that objects of the Date class hold the day, month, and year in member variables. Suppose the Date class has a member function named add. The add member function adds a number of days to the date and adjusts the member variables if the date goes to another month or year. For example, the following statement adds five days to the date stored in the today object:

```
today.add(5);
```

Although it might be obvious that the statement is adding five days to the date stored in today, the use of an operator might be more intuitive. For example, look at the following statement:

```
today += 5;
```

This statement uses the standard += operator to add 5 to today. This behavior does not happen automatically, however. The += operator must be overloaded for this action to occur. In this section, you will learn to overload many of C++'s operators to perform specialized operations on class objects.

 Note: You have already experienced the behavior of an overloaded operator. The / operator performs two types of division: floating-point and integer. If one of operator's operands is a floating-point type, the result will be a floating-point value. If both of the / operator's operands are integers, however, a different behavior occurs: The result is an integer, and the fractional part is thrown away.

Some General Issues of Operator Overloading

Now that you have had a taste of operator overloading, let's look at some of the general issues involved in this programming technique.

First, you can change an operator's entire meaning, if that's what you wish to do. There is nothing to prevent you from changing the = symbol from an assignment operator to a "display" operator. For instance, the following class does just that:

```
class Weird
{
private:
    int value;
public:
    Weird(int v)
        {value = v; }
    void operator=(const Weird &right)
        { cout << right.value << endl; }
    };
```

Although the `operator=` function overloads the assignment operator, the function doesn't perform an assignment. All the overloaded operator does is display the contents of `right.value`. Consider the following program segment:

```
Weird a(5), b(10);
a = b;
```

Although the statement `a = b` looks like an assignment statement, it actually causes the contents of b's `value` member to be displayed on the screen:

```
10
```

Another operator overloading issue is that you cannot change the number of operands taken by an operator. The = symbol must always be a binary operator. Likewise, ++ and − must always be unary operators.

The last issue is that although you may overload most of the C++ operators, you cannot overload all of them. Table 11-1 shows all of the C++ operators that may be overloaded.

Note: Some of the operators in Table 11-1 are beyond the scope of this book and are not covered.

Table 11-1

+	-	*	/	%	^	&	|	~	!	=	<
>	+=	-=	*=	/=	%=	^=	&=	|=	<<	>>	>>=
<<=	==	!=	<=	>=	&&	||	++	--	->*	,	->
[]	()	new	delete								

The only operators that cannot be overloaded are

```
?:    .    .*    ::    sizeof
```

Overloading Math Operators

Many classes would benefit not only from an overloaded assignment operator, but also from over-loaded math operators. To illustrate this, consider the `FeetInches` class shown in the two files listed here:

Contents of feetinch.h

```
#ifndef FEETINCHES_H
#define FEETINCHES_H

// A class to hold distances or measurements expressed in feet and
inches
class FeetInches
{
private:
   int feet;
   int inches;
   void simplify(); // Defined in feetinch.cpp.
public:
   FeetInches(int f = 0, int i = 0)
      { feet = f; inches = i; simplify(); }
   void setData(int f, int i)
      { feet = f; inches = i; simplify(); }
   int getFeet()
      { return feet; }
   int getInches()
      { return inches; }
};
#endif
```

Contents of feetinch.cpp

```
#include "feetinch.h"
//******************************************************************
// Definition of member function simplify. This function          *
// checks for values in the inches member greater than            *
// 12 and less than 0. If such a value is found, the numbers       *
// in feet and inches are adjusted to conform to a standard feet  *
// and inches expression. For example, 3 feet 14 inches would     *
// be adjusted to 4 feet 2 inches, and 5 feet -2 inches would     *
// be adjusted to 4 feet 10 inches.                               *
//******************************************************************

void FeetInches::simplify()
{
    inches = 12*feet + inches;
    feet = inches /12;
    inches = inches %12;
}
```

The class shown in this example is designed to hold distances or measurements expressed in feet and inches. It consists of five member functions:

- A constructor that allows the `feet` and `inches` members to be set. The default values for these members is 0.

- A `setData` function for storing values in the `feet` and `inches` members.

- A `getFeet` function for returning the value in the `feet` member.

- A `getInches` function for returning the value in the `inches` member.

- A `simplify` function for normalizing the values held in `feet` and `inches`. This function adjusts any set of values where the `inches` member is greater than 12 or less than 0. For example, 3 feet 14 inches would be adjusted to read 4 feet 2 inches, and 5 feet -3 inches would be adjusted to read 4 feet 9 inches.

An enhancement of this class would be the ability to use standard math operators in such a way that one `FeetInches` object could be added to or subtracted from another. For example, assume the `length1` and `length2` objects are declared and initialized as follows:

```
FeetInches length1(3, 5), length2(6, 3);
```

`length1` is holding the value 3 feet 5 inches, and `length2` is holding the value 6 feet 3 inches. Imagine being able to add these two objects in a statement like this:

```
length3 = length1 + length2;
```

Wouldn't it be useful if this statement resulted in `length3` being set to 9 feet 8 inches? That behavior is possible if the + operator is overloaded. Here's the member function that overloads the + operator for the `FeetInches` class:

```
FeetInches FeetInches::operator+(const FeetInches &right)
{
    FeetInches temp;
    temp.inches = inches + right.inches;
    temp.feet = feet + right.feet;
    temp.simplify();
    return temp;
}
```

This function is called anytime the + operator is used with two `FeetInches` objects. Just like the overloaded = operator we defined in the previous section, this function has one parameter: A constant reference object named `right`. This parameter references the object on the right side of the operator. For example, when the following statement is executed, `right` will reference the `length2` object:

```
length3 = length1 + length2;
```

As before, it might be helpful to think of this statement as the following function call:

```
length3 = length1.operator+(length2);
```

The `length2` object is being passed to the function's parameter, `right`. When the function finishes, it will return a `FeetInches` object to `length3`. Now let's see what is happening inside the function. First, notice that a `FeetInches` object called `temp` is declared locally:

```
FeetInches temp;
```

This object is a temporary location for holding the results of the addition. Next, there is a statement that adds `inches` to `right.inches` and stores the result in `temp.inches`:

```
temp.inches = inches + right.inches;
```

`inches` is a member of `length1`, the object making the function call. It is the object on the left side of the operator. `right.inches` references the `inches` member of `length2`. The next statement is very similar. It adds `feet` to `right.feet` and stores the result in `temp.feet`:

```
temp.feet = feet + right.feet;
```

At this point in the function, `temp` contains the sum of the `feet` and `inches` members of both objects in the expression. The next step is to adjust the values so they conform to a normal value expressed in feet and inches. This is accomplished by calling `temp.simplify()`:

```
temp.simplify();
```

The last step is to return the value stored in `temp`:

```
return temp;
```

In the statement `length3 = length1 + length2`, the return statement in the operator function causes the values stored in `temp` to be returned to the `length3` object.

Program 11-9 shows the `FeetInches` class expanded, not only with the + operator overloaded, but the - operator as well. The program also demonstrates the overloaded operators.

Program 11-9

Contents of `feetinc2.h`
```
#ifndef FEETINCHES_H
#define FEETINCHES_H
```

(program continues)

Program 11-9   *(continued)*

```cpp
// A class to hold distances or measurements expressed in feet and inches
class FeetInches
{
    private:
        int feet;
        int inches;
        void simplify();    // Defined in feetinc2.cpp
    public:
        FeetInches(int f = 0, int i = 0)
            { feet = f; inches = i; simplify(); }
        void setData(int f, int i)
            { feet = f; inches = i; simplify(); }
        int getFeet()
            { return feet; }
        int getInches()
            { return inches; }
        FeetInches operator + (const FeetInches &); // Overloaded +
        FeetInches operator - (const FeetInches &); // Overloaded -
};
#endif
```

Contents of feetinc2.cpp
```cpp
#include "feetinc2.h"

//************************************************************
// Definition of member function simplify. This function     *
// checks for values in the inches member greater than       *
// 12 and less than 0. If such a value is found, the numbers  *
// in feet and inches are adjusted to conform to a standard feet *
// and inches expression. For example, 3 feet 14 inches would *
// be adjusted to 4 feet 2 inches, and 5 feet -2 inches would *
// be adjusted to 4 feet 10 inches.                           *
//************************************************************


void FeetInches::simplify()
{
    inches = 12*feet + inches;
    feet = inches / 12;
    inches = inches % 12;
}


//******************************************************
// Overloaded binary + operator.                       *
//******************************************************
```

(program continues)

Program 11-9 *(continued)*

```cpp
FeetInches FeetInches::operator+(const FeetInches &right)
{
    FeetInches temp;

    temp.inches = inches + right.inches;
    temp.feet = feet + right.feet;
    temp.simplify();
    return temp;
}

//*************************************************
// Overloaded binary - operator.                  *
//*************************************************
FeetInches FeetInches::operator-(const FeetInches &right)
{
    FeetInches temp;

    temp.inches = inches - right.inches;
    temp.feet = feet - right.feet;
    temp.simplify();
    return temp;
}
```

Contents of the main program file, pr11-9.cpp

```cpp
// This program demonstrates the FeetInches class's overloaded
// + and - operators.

#include <iostream>
#include "feetinc2.h"
using namespace std;

int main()
{
    FeetInches first, second, third;
    int f, i;
    cout << "Enter a distance in feet and inches: ";
    cin >> f >> i;
    first.setData(f, i);
    cout << "Enter another distance in feet and inches: ";
    cin >> f >> i;
    second.setData(f, i);
    third = first + second;
    cout << "first + second = ";
    cout << third.getFeet() << " feet, ";
    cout << third.getInches() << " inches.\n";
    third = first - second;
    cout << "first - second = ";
    cout << third.getFeet() << " feet, ";
    cout << third.getInches() << " inches.\n";
    return 0;
}
```

Program 11-9

Program Output with Example Input Shown in Bold
```
Enter a distance in feet and inches: 6 5[Enter]
Enter another distance in feet and inches: 3 10[Enter]
first + second = 10 feet, 3 inches.
first - second = 2 feet, 7 inches.
```

Overloading the Prefix ++ Operator

Unary operators, such as ++ and - -, are overloaded in a fashion similar to the way binary operators are implemented. Since unary operators only affect the object making the operator function call, however, there is no need for a parameter. For example, let's say you wish to have a prefix increment operator for the FeetInches class. Assume the FeetInches object distance is set to the values 7 feet and 5 inches. A ++ operator function could be designed to increment the object's inches member. The following statement would cause distance to have the value 7 feet 6 inches:

```
++distance;
```

The following function overloads the prefix ++ operator to work in this fashion:

```
FeetInches FeetInches::operator++()
{
    ++inches;
    simplify();
    return *this;
}
```

This function first increments the object's inches member. The simplify() function is called and then the dereferenced this pointer is returned. This allows the operator to perform properly in statements like this:

```
distance2 = ++distance1;
```

Remember, this statement is equivalent to

```
distance2 = distance1.operator++();
```

Overloading the Postfix ++ Operator

Overloading the postfix ++ operator is only slightly different than overloading the prefix version. Here is the function that overloads the postfix operator with the FeetInches class:

```
FeetInches FeetInches::operator++(int)
{
    FeetInches temp(feet, inches);
    inches++;
    simplify();
    return temp;
}
```

The first difference you will notice is the use of a *dummy parameter*. The word int in the function's parentheses establishes a nameless integer parameter. When C++ sees this parameter in an operator function, it knows the function is designed to be used in postfix mode. The second difference is the use of a temporary local variable, the temp object. temp is initialized with the feet and inches values of the object making the function call. temp, therefore is a copy of the object being incremented, but before the increment takes place. After inches is incremented and the simplify function is called, the content of temp is returned. This causes the postfix operator to behave correctly in a statement like this:

```cpp
distance2 = distance1++;
```

Program 11-10 demonstrates the class implemented with both prefix and postfix ++ operators.

Program 11-10

Contents of feetinc3.h
```cpp
#ifndef FEETINCHES_H
#define FEETINCHES_H

// A class to hold distances or measurements expressed
// in feet and inches
class FeetInches
{
    private:
        int feet;
        int inches;
        void simplify(); // Defined in feetinc3.cpp
    public:
        FeetInches(int f = 0, int i = 0)
            { feet = f; inches = i; simplify(); }
        void setData(int f, int i)
            { feet = f; inches = i; simplify(); }
        int getFeet()
            { return feet; }
        int getInches()
            { return inches; }
        FeetInches operator + (const FeetInches &); // Overloaded +
        FeetInches operator - (const FeetInches &); // Overloaded -
        FeetInches operator++();  // Prefix ++
        FeetInches operator++(int); // Postfix ++
};

#endif
```

(program continues)

Program 11-10 *(continued)*

Contents of feetinc3.cpp

```cpp
#include "feetinc3.h"

//*****************************************************************
// Definition of member function simplify. This function         *
// checks for values in the inches member greater than           *
// 12 and less than 0. If such a value is found, the numbers     *
// in feet and inches are adjusted to conform to a standard feet *
// and inches expression. For example, 3 feet 14 inches would    *
// be adjusted to 4 feet 2 inches, and 5 feet -2 inches would    *
// be adjusted to 4 feet 10 inches.                              *
//*****************************************************************

void FeetInches::simplify()
{
    inches = 12*feet + inches;
    feet = inches / 12;
    inches = inches % 12;
}

//************************************************
// Overloaded binary + operator.                *
//************************************************

FeetInches FeetInches::operator+(const FeetInches &right)
{
    FeetInches temp;

    temp.inches = inches + right.inches;
    temp.feet = feet + right.feet;
    temp.simplify();
    return temp;
}

//************************************************
// Overloaded binary - operator.                *
//************************************************
FeetInches FeetInches::operator-(const FeetInches &right)
{
    FeetInches temp;

    temp.inches = inches - right.inches;
    temp.feet = feet - right.feet;
    temp.simplify();
    return temp;
}
```

(program continues)

Program 11-10   *(continued)*

```
//******************************************************************
// Overloaded prefix ++ operator. Causes the inches member to  *
// be incremented. Returns the incremented object.             *
//******************************************************************
FeetInches FeetInches::operator++()
{
    ++inches;
    simplify();
    return *this;
}


//*******************************************************************
// Overloaded postfix ++ operator. Causes the inches member to  *
// be incremented. Returns the value of the object before the   *
// increment.                                                   *
//*******************************************************************

FeetInches FeetInches::operator++(int)
{
    FeetInches temp(feet, inches);

    inches++;
    simplify();
    return temp;
}
```

Contents of the main program file, pr11-10.cpp

```
// This program demonstrates the FeetInches class's overloaded
// prefix and postfix ++ operators.

#include <iostream>
#include "feetinc3.h"
using namespace std;

int main()
{
    FeetInches first, second(1, 5);
    int count;

    cout << "Demonstrating prefix ++ operator.\n";
    for (count = 0; count < 12; count++)
    {
        first = ++second;
        cout << "First: " << first.getFeet() << " feet, ";
        cout << first.getInches() << " inches. ";
        cout << "Second: " << second.getFeet() << " feet, ";
        cout << second.getInches() << " inches.\n";
    }
```

(program continues)

Program 11-10 *(continued)*

```
    cout << "\nDemonstrating postfix ++ operator.\n";
    for (count = 0; count < 12; count++)
    {
        first = second++;
        cout << "First: " << first.getFeet() << " feet, ";
        cout << first.getInches() << " inches. ";
        cout << "Second: " << second.getFeet() << " feet, ";
        cout << second.getInches() << " inches.\n";
    }
    return 0;
}
```

Program Output
```
Demonstrating prefix ++ operator.
First: 1 feet 6 inches. Second: 1 feet 6 inches.
First: 1 feet 7 inches. Second: 1 feet 7 inches.
First: 1 feet 8 inches. Second: 1 feet 8 inches.
First: 1 feet 9 inches. Second: 1 feet 9 inches.
First: 1 feet 10 inches. Second: 1 feet 10 inches.
First: 1 feet 11 inches. Second: 1 feet 11 inches.
First: 2 feet 0 inches. Second: 2 feet 0 inches.
First: 2 feet 1 inches. Second: 2 feet 1 inches.
First: 2 feet 2 inches. Second: 2 feet 2 inches.
First: 2 feet 3 inches. Second: 2 feet 3 inches.
First: 2 feet 4 inches. Second: 2 feet 4 inches.
First: 2 feet 5 inches. Second: 2 feet 5 inches.

Demonstrating postfix ++ operator.
First: 2 feet 5 inches. Second: 2 feet 6 inches.
First: 2 feet 6 inches. Second: 2 feet 7 inches.
First: 2 feet 7 inches. Second: 2 feet 8 inches.
First: 2 feet 8 inches. Second: 2 feet 9 inches.
First: 2 feet 9 inches. Second: 2 feet 10 inches.
First: 2 feet 10 inches. Second: 2 feet 11 inches.
First: 2 feet 11 inches. Second: 3 feet 0 inches.
First: 3 feet 0 inches. Second: 3 feet 1 inches.
First: 3 feet 1 inches. Second: 3 feet 2 inches.
First: 3 feet 2 inches. Second: 3 feet 3 inches.
First: 3 feet 3 inches. Second: 3 feet 4 inches.
First: 3 feet 4 inches. Second: 3 feet 5 inches.
```

Overloading Relational Operators

In addition to the assignment and math operators, relational operators may also be overloaded. This capability allows objects of classes to be compared in statements that use relational expressions such as

```
if (distance1 < distance2)
{
    ... code ...
}
```

Overloaded relational operators are implemented like other binary operators. The only difference is that a relational operator function should always return a true or false value. Here is the function for overloading the > operator to work with the FeetInches class:

```
bool FeetInches::operator>(const FeetInches &right)
{
    if (feet > right.feet)
        return true;
    else if (feet == right.feet && inches > right.inches)
        return true;
    else return false;
}
```

As you can see, the function compares the feet member (and if necessary, the inches member) with that of the parameter. If the calling object contains a value greater than that of the parameter, the value true is returned. Otherwise, false is returned.

Program 11-11 shows the FeetInches class modified to overload the >, <, and == operators.

Program 11-11

Contents of feetinc4.h
```
#ifndef FEETINCHES_H
#define FEETINCHES_H

// A class to hold distances or measurements expressed
// in feet and inches
class FeetInches
{
    private:
        int feet;
        int inches;
        void simplify(); // Defined in feetinc4.cpp
    public:
        FeetInches(int f = 0, int i = 0)
            { feet = f; inches = i; simplify(); }
        void setData(int f, int i)
            { feet = f; inches = i; simplify(); }
        int getFeet()
            { return feet; }
        int getInches()
            { return inches; }
```

(program continues)

Program 11-11 *(continued)*

```
            FeetInches operator + (const FeetInches &); // Overloaded +
            FeetInches operator - (const FeetInches &); // Overloaded -
            FeetInches operator++();  // Prefix ++
            FeetInches operator++(int); // Postfix ++
            bool operator>(const FeetInches &);
            bool operator<(const FeetInches &);
            bool operator==(const FeetInches &);
};
#endif
```

Contents of feetinc4.cpp
```
#include "feetinc4.h"

//*********************************************************************
// Definition of member function simplify. This function           *
// checks for values in the inches member greater than             *
// 12 and less than 0. If such a value is found, the numbers       *
// in feet and inches are adjusted to conform to a standard feet   *
// and inches expression. For example, 3 feet 14 inches would      *
// be adjusted to 4 feet 2 inches, and 5 feet -2 inches would      *
// be adjusted to 4 feet 10 inches.                                *
//*********************************************************************

void FeetInches::simplify()
{
    inches = 12*feet + inches;
    feet = inches / 12;
    inches = inches % 12;
}


//*************************************************
// Overloaded binary + operator.                 *
//*************************************************

FeetInches FeetInches::operator+(const FeetInches &right)
{
    FeetInches temp;

    temp.inches = inches + right.inches;
    temp.feet = feet + right.feet;
    temp.simplify();
    return temp;
}
```

(program continues)

Program 11-11 *(continued)*

```
//***********************************************
// Overloaded binary - operator.                 *
//***********************************************
FeetInches FeetInches::operator-(const FeetInches &right)
{
    FeetInches temp;

    temp.inches = inches - right.inches;
    temp.feet = feet - right.feet;
    temp.simplify();
    return temp;
}

//*****************************************************************
// Overloaded prefix ++ operator. Causes the inches member to *
// be incremented. Returns the incremented object.              *
//*****************************************************************
FeetInches FeetInches::operator++()
{
    ++inches;
    simplify();
    return *this;
}

//*****************************************************************
// Overloaded postfix ++ operator. Causes the inches member to  *
// be incremented. Returns the value of the object before the   *
// increment.                                                    *
//*****************************************************************

FeetInches FeetInches::operator++(int)
{
    FeetInches temp(feet, inches);

    inches++;
    simplify();
    return temp;
}
//*****************************************************************
// Overloaded > operator. Returns true if the current object is *
// set to a value greater than that of right.                   *
//*****************************************************************
```

(program continues)

Program 11-11 *(continued)*

```cpp
bool FeetInches::operator>(const FeetInches &right)
{
    if (feet > right.feet)
        return true;
    else if (feet == right.feet && inches > right.inches)
        return true;
    else return false;
}

//*******************************************************************
// Overloaded < operator. Returns true if the current object is  *
// set to a value less than that of right.                       *
//*******************************************************************

bool FeetInches::operator<(const FeetInches &right)
{
    if (feet < right.feet)
        return true;
    else if (feet == right.feet && inches < right.inches)
        return true;
    else return false;
}

//*******************************************************************
// Overloaded == operator. Returns true if the current object is *
// set to a value equal to that of right.                        *
//*******************************************************************

bool FeetInches::operator==(const FeetInches &right)
{
    if (feet == right.feet && inches == right.inches)
        return true;
    else return false;
}
```

Contents of the main program file, pr11-11.cpp

```cpp
// This program demonstrates the FeetInches class's overloaded
// relational operators.

#include <iostream>
#include "feetinc4.h"
using namespace std;
```

(program continues)

Program 11-11   *(continued)*

```cpp
int main()
{
    FeetInches first, second, third;
    int f, i;

    cout << "Enter a distance in feet and inches: ";
    cin >> f >> i;
    first.setData(f, i);
    cout << "Enter another distance in feet and inches: ";
    cin >> f >> i;
    second.setData(f, i);
    if (first == second)
        cout << "First is equal to second.\n";
    if (first > second)
        cout << "First is greater than second.\n";
    if (first < second)
        cout << "First is less than second.\n";
    return 0;
}
```

Program Output with Example Input Shown in Bold
```
Enter a distance in feet and inches: 6 5[Enter]
Enter another distance in feet and inches: 3 10[Enter]
First is greater than second.
```

Program Output with Other Example Input Shown in Bold
```
Enter a distance in feet and inches: 5 5[Enter]
Enter another distance in feet and inches: 5 5[Enter]
First is equal to second.
```

Program Output with Other Example Input Shown in Bold
```
Enter a distance in feet and inches: 3 4[Enter]
Enter another distance in feet and inches: 3 7[Enter]
First is less than second.
```

Overloading the << and >> Operators

Overloading the math and relational operators gives you the ability to write those types of expressions with class objects just as naturally as with integers, floats, and other built-in data types. If an object's primary data members are private, however, you still have to make explicit member function calls to send their values to cout. For example, assume distance is a FeetInches object. The following statements display its internal values:

```
cout << distance.getFeet() << " feet, ";
cout << distance.getInches() << " inches";
```

It is also necessary to explicitly call member functions to set a `FeetInches` object's data. For instance, the following statements set the `distance` object to user-specified values:

```
cout << "Enter a value in feet: ";
cin >> f;
distance.setFeet(f);
cout << "Enter a value in inches: ";
cin >> i;
distance.setInches(i);
```

By overloading the stream insertion operator (`<<`), you could send the `distance` object to `cout`, as follows, and have the screen output automatically formatted in the correct way.

```
cout << distance;
```

Likewise, by overloading the stream extraction operator (`>>`), the `distance` object could take values directly from `cin`:

```
cin >> distance;
```

Overloading these operators is done in a slightly different way, however, than overloading other operators. These operators are actually part of the `ostream` and `istream` classes defined in the C++ runtime library. (The `cout` and `cin` objects are instances of `ostream` and `istream`.) You must write operator functions to overload the `ostream` version of `<<` and the `istream` version of `>>`, so they work directly with a class such as `FeetInches`. For example, the following operator function will overload the `<<` operator to format and display the contents of a `FeetInches` object:

```
ostream &operator<<(ostream &strm, FeetInches &obj)
{
    strm << obj.feet << " feet, " << obj.inches << " inches";
    return strm;
}
```

Notice the function has two parameters: an `ostream` reference object and a `FeetInches` reference object. The `ostream` parameter will be a reference to the actual `ostream` object on the left side of the `<<` operator. The second parameter is a reference to a `FeetInches` object. This parameter will reference the object on the right side of the `<<` operator. The function tells C++ how to handle any expression that has the following form:

```
ostream-object << FeetInches-object
```

So, when C++ encounters the following statement, it will call the overloaded `operator<<` function:

```
cout << distance;
```

The function returns an `ostream` object so several of these expressions can be chained together, as in the following statement:

```
cout << distance1 << " " << distance2 << endl;
```

Here is the function that overloads the stream extraction operator to work with the `FeetInches` class:

```
istream &operator>>(istream &strm, FeetInches &obj)
{
    cout << "Feet: ";
    strm >> obj.feet;
    cout << "Inches: "
    strm >> obj.inches;
    return strm;
}
```

The same principles hold true for this operator. It tells C++ how to handle any expression in the following form:

```
istream-object >> FeetInches-object
```

Once again, the function returns an `istream` object so several of these expressions may be chained together.

You have probably realized that neither of these functions are quite ready to work, though. Both functions attempt to directly access the `FeetInches` object's private members. Since the functions aren't themselves members of the `FeetInches` class, they don't have this type of access. The next step is to make the operator functions friends of `FeetInches`. This is shown in the following listing of the `FeetInches` class declaration.

Contents of feetinc5.h

```
#include <iostream> // Needed to overload << and >>
#ifndef FEETINCHES_H
#define FEETINCHES_H
using namespace std;

// A class to hold distances or measurements expressed
// in feet and inches.
class FeetInches
{
private:
    int feet;
    int inches;
    void simplify(); // Defined in feetinc5.cpp
```

```
public:
   FeetInches(int f = 0, int i = 0)
      { feet = f; inches = i; simplify(); }
   void setData(int f, int i)
      { feet = f; inches = i; simplify(); }
   int getFeet()
      { return feet; }
   int getInches()
      { return inches; }
   FeetInches operator + (const FeetInches &); // Overloaded +
   FeetInches operator - (const FeetInches &); // Overloaded -
   FeetInches operator++();  // Prefix ++
   FeetInches operator++(int);   // Postfix ++
   bool operator>(const FeetInches &);
   bool operator<(const FeetInches &);
   bool operator==(const FeetInches &);
   friend ostream &operator<<(ostream &, FeetInches &);
   friend istream &operator>>(istream &, FeetInches &);
};
#endif
```

The last two lines in the class declaration tell C++ to make the overloaded << and >> operator functions friends of the FeetInches class:

```
friend ostream &operator<<(ostream &, FeetInches &);
friend istream &operator>>(istream &, FeetInches &);
```

These statements give the operator functions direct access to the FeetInches class's private members.

Here is a complete listing of feetinc5.cpp, including the overloaded << and >> operator functions:

Contents of feetinc5.cpp

```
#include <iostream>
#include "feetinc5.h"

//*****************************************************************
// Definition of member function simplify. This function          *
// checks for values in the inches member greater than            *
// 12 and less than 0. If such a value is found, the numbers      *
// in feet and inches are adjusted to conform to a standard feet  *
// and inches expression. For example, 3 feet 14 inches would     *
// be adjusted to 4 feet 2 inches, and 5 feet -2 inches would     *
// be adjusted to 4 feet 10 inches.                               *
//*****************************************************************

void FeetInches::simplify()
{
   inches = 12*feet + inches;
   feet = inches / 12;
   inches = inches % 12;
}
```

```
//*************************************************
// Overloaded binary + operator.                  *
//*************************************************

FeetInches FeetInches::operator+(const FeetInches &right)
{
    FeetInches temp;

    temp.inches = inches + right.inches;
    temp.feet = feet + right.feet;
    temp.simplify();
    return temp;
}


//*************************************************
// Overloaded binary - operator.                  *
//*************************************************
FeetInches FeetInches::operator-(const FeetInches &right)
{
    FeetInches temp;

    temp.inches = inches - right.inches;
    temp.feet = feet - right.feet;
    temp.simplify();
    return temp;
}


//************************************************************
// Overloaded prefix ++ operator. Causes the inches member to *
// be incremented. Returns the incremented object.            *
//************************************************************
FeetInches FeetInches::operator++()
{
    ++inches;
    simplify();
    return *this;
}


//************************************************************
// Overloaded postfix ++ operator. Causes the inches member to  *
// be incremented. Returns the value of the object before the   *
// increment.                                                   *
//************************************************************

FeetInches FeetInches::operator++(int)
{
    FeetInches temp(feet, inches);

    inches++;
    simplify();
    return temp;
}
```

```
//****************************************************************
// Overloaded > operator. Returns true if the current object is *
// set to a value greater than that of right.                    *
//****************************************************************

bool FeetInches::operator>(const FeetInches &right)
{
   if (feet > right.feet)
     return true;
   else if (feet == right.feet && inches > right.inches)
     return true;
   else return false;
}

//****************************************************************
// Overloaded < operator. Returns true if the current object is *
// set to a value less than that of right.                       *
//****************************************************************

bool FeetInches::operator<(const FeetInches &right)
{
   if (feet < right.feet)
     return true;
   else if (feet == right.feet && inches < right.inches)
     return true;
   else return false;
}

//****************************************************************
// Overloaded == operator. Returns true if the current object is *
// set to a value equal to that of right.                         *
//****************************************************************

bool FeetInches::operator==(const FeetInches &right)
{
   if (feet == right.feet && inches == right.inches)
     return true;
   else return false;
}
//****************************************************************
// Overloaded << operator. Gives cout the ability to           *
// directly display FeetInches objects.                        *
//****************************************************************

ostream &operator<<(ostream &strm, FeetInches &obj)
{
   strm << obj.feet << " feet, " << obj.inches << " inches";
   return strm;
}
```

```
//**********************************************************
// Overloaded >> operator. Gives cin the ability to      *
// store user input directly into FeetInches objects.    *
//**********************************************************

istream &operator>>(istream &strm, FeetInches &obj)
{
    cout << "Feet: ";
    strm >> obj.feet;
    cout << "Inches: "
    strm >> obj.inches;
    return strm;
}
```

Program 11-12 demonstrates how the overloaded operators work.

Program 11-12

```
// This program demonstrates the << and >> operators,
// overloaded to work with the FeetInches class.

#include <iostream>
#include "feetinc5.h"
using namespace std;

int main()
{
    FeetInches first, second, third;
    cout << "Enter a distance in feet and inches:\n";
    cin >> first;
    cout << "Enter another distance in feet and inches:\n";
    cin >> second;
    cout << "The values you entered are:\n";
    cout << first << " and " << second;
    return 0;
}
```

Program Output with Example Input Shown in Bold
```
Enter a distance in feet and inches:
Feet: 6[Enter]
Inches: 5[Enter]
Enter another distance in feet and inches:
Feet: 3[Enter]
Inches: 10[Enter]
The values you entered are:
6 feet, 5 inches and 3 feet, 10 inches
```

Overloading the [] Operator

In addition to the traditional operators, C++ allows you to change the way the [] symbols work. This gives you the ability to write classes that have array-like behaviors. For example, the string class overloads the [] operator so you can access the individual characters stored in string class objects. Assume the following declaration exists in a program:

```
string name = "William";
```

The first character in the string, W, is stored at name[0], so the following statement will display W on the screen.

```
cout << name[0];
```

Program 11-13 further demonstrates the string class's overloaded [] operator.

Program 11-13

```cpp
// This program demonstrates the string class's
// overloaded [] operator.

#include <iostream>
#include <string>
using namespace std;

int main()
{
    string name = "William";
    int x;  //Loop index.

    cout << "Here are the letters in your name:\n";
    for (x=0; x<name.length(); x++)
        cout << name[x] << endl;
    cout << "Enter a character and press Enter: ";
    cin >> name[2];
    cout << "Now, here are the letters in your name:\n";
    for (x=0; x<name.length(); x++)
        cout << name[x] << endl;
    return 0;
}
```

Program Output with Example Input Shown in Bold
```
Here are the letters in your name:
W
i
l
l
i
a
m
```

(program output continues)

Program 11-13   *(continued)*

```
Enter a character and press Enter: Z[Enter]
Now, here are the letters in your name:
W
i
Z
l
i
a
m
```

You can use the overloaded [] operator to create an array class, like the following one. The class behaves like a regular array but performs the bounds-checking that C++ lacks. It also has several other enhancements over regular integer arrays.

```cpp
class IntArray
{
    private:
        int *aptr;
        int arraySize;
        void subError();            // Handles subscripts out of range.
    public:
        IntArray(int);              // Constructor
        IntArray(const intArray &); // Copy constructor
        ~IntArray();                // Destructor
        int size()
            { return arraySize; }
        int &operator[](int);       // Overloaded [] operator
};
```

Before focusing on the overloaded operator, let's look at the constructors and the destructor. The code for the first constructor is

```cpp
IntArray::IntArray(int s)
{
    arraySize = s;
    aptr = new int [s];
    for (int count = 0; count < size; count++)
        *(aptr + count) = 0;
}
```

When an instance of the class is defined, the number of elements the array is to have is passed into the constructor's parameter, s. This value is copied to the arraySize member, then used to dynamically allocate enough memory for the array. The constructor's final step is to store zeros in all of the array's elements:

```cpp
for (int count = 0; count < size; count++)
    *(aptr + count) = 0;
```

The class also has a copy constructor, which is used when a class object is initialized with another object's data:

```
IntArray::IntArray(const IntArray &obj)
{
   arraySize = obj.arraySize;
   aptr = new int [arraySize];
   for(int count = 0; count < arraySize; count++)
      *(aptr + count) = *(obj.aptr + count);
}
```

A reference to the initializing object is passed into the parameter obj. Once the memory is successfully allocated for the array, the constructor copies all the values in obj's array into the calling object's array.

The destructor simply frees the memory allocated by the class's constructors. First, however, it checks the value in arraySize to be sure the array has at least one element:

```
IntArray::~IntArray()
{
   if (arraySize > 0)
      delete [] aptr;
}
```

The [] operator is overloaded similarly to other operators. Here is the definition of the operator[] function for the IntArray class:

```
int &IntArray::operator[](int sub)
{
   if (sub < 0 || sub >= arraySize)
      subError();
   return aptr[sub];
}
```

The operator[] function can only have a single parameter. The one shown here uses an integer parameter. This parameter holds the value placed inside the brackets in an expression. For example, if table is an IntArray object, the number 12 will be passed into the sub parameter in the following statement:

```
cout << table[12];
```

Inside the function, the value in the sub parameter is tested by the following if statement:

```
if (sub < 0 || sub >= arraySize)
   subError();
```

This statement determines whether sub is within the range of the array's subscripts. If sub is less than zero or greater than or equal to arraySize, it's not a valid subscript, so the subError function is called. If sub is within range, the function uses it as an offset into the array, and returns a reference to the value stored at that location.

One critically important aspect of the function shown is its return type. It's crucial that the function not simply return an integer, but a *reference* to an integer. The reason for this is that expressions such as the following must be possible:

```
table[5] = 27;
```

Remember, the built-in = operator requires the object on its left to be an lvalue. An lvalue must represent a modifiable memory location, such as a variable. The integer return value of a function is not an lvalue. If the operator[] function merely returns an integer, it cannot be used to create expressions placed on the left side of an assignment operator.

A reference to an integer, however, is an lvalue. If the operator[] function returns a reference, it can be used to create expressions like this:

```
table[7] = 52;
```

In this statement, the operator[] function is called with 7 being passed as its argument. Assuming 7 is within range, the function returns a reference to the integer stored at (aptr + 7). In essence, the statement is equivalent to

```
*(aptr + 7) = 52;
```

Because the operator[] function returns actual integers stored in the array, it is not necessary for math or relational operators to be overloaded. Even the stream operators << and >> will work just as they are with the IntArray class.

Here is the complete listing of intarray.h and intarray.cpp:

Contents of intarray.h

```cpp
#ifndef INTARRAY_H
#define INTARRAY_H
#include <cstdlib>

class IntArray
{
    private:
        int *aptr;
        int arraySize;
        void subError();            // Handles subscripts out of range.
    public:
        IntArray(int);              // Constructor
        IntArray(const IntArray &); // Copy constructor
        ~IntArray();                // Destructor
        int size()
            { return arraySize; }
        int &operator[](int);       // Overloaded [] operator
};
#endif
```

Contents of `intarray.cpp`

```cpp
#include <iostream>
#include "intarray.h"
using namespace std;

//*********************************************************
// Constructor for IntArray class. Sets the size of the  *
// array and allocates memory for it.                     *
//*********************************************************

IntArray::IntArray(int s)
{
   arraySize = s;
   aptr = new int [s];
   for (int count = 0; count < arraySize; count++)
     *(aptr + count) = 0;
}

//*********************************************************
// Copy constructor for IntArray class.                  *
//*********************************************************

IntArray::IntArray(const IntArray &obj)
{
   arraySize = obj.arraySize;
   aptr = new int [arraySize];
   for(int count = 0; count < arraySize; count++)
     *(aptr + count) = *(obj.aptr + count);
}

//*********************************************************
// Destructor for IntArray class.                        *
//*********************************************************

IntArray::~IntArray()
{
   if (arraySize > 0)
     delete [] aptr;
}

//*********************************************************
// subError function. Displays an error message and      *
// terminates the program when a subscript is out of range. *
//*********************************************************

void IntArray::subError()
{
   cout << "ERROR: Subscript out of range.\n";
   exit(0);
}
```

```
//***********************************************************
// Overloaded [] operator. The argument is a subscript. *
// This function returns a reference to the element     *
// in the array indexed by the subscript.               *
//***********************************************************

int &IntArray::operator[](int sub)
{
   if (sub < 0 || sub > arraySize)
      subError();
   return aptr[sub];
}
```

Program 11-14 demonstrates how the class works.

Program 11-14

```
#include <iostream>
#include "intarray.h"
using namespace std;

int main()
{
   IntArray table(10);
   int x; //Loop index.

   // Store values in the array.
   for (x = 0; x < 10; x++)
      table[x] = (x * 2);
   // Display the values in the array.
   for (x = 0; x < 10; x++)
      cout << table[x] << " ";
   cout << endl;
   // Use the built-in + operator on array elements.
   for (x = 0; x < 10; x++)
      table[x] = table[x] + 5;
   // Display the values in the array.
   for (x = 0; x < 10; x++)
      cout << table[x] << " ";
   cout << endl;
   // Use the built-in ++ operator on array elements.
   for (x = 0; x < 10; x++)
      table[x]++;
   // Display the values in the array.
   for (x = 0; x < 10; x++)
      cout << table[x] << " ";
   cout << endl;
   return 0;
}
```

Program 11-14

Program Output
```
0 2 4 6 8 10 12 14 16 18
5 7 9 11 13 15 17 19 21 23
6 8 10 12 14 16 18 20 22 24
```

Program 11-15 demonstrates the `IntArray` class's bounds-checking capability.

Program 11-15

```cpp
#include <iostream>
#include "intarray.h"
using namespace std;

int main()
{
    IntArray table(10);
    int x; //Loop index.

    // Store values in the array.
    for (x = 0; x < 10; x++)
        table[x] = x;
    // Display the values in the array.
    for (x = 0; x < 10; x++)
        cout << table[x] << " ";
    cout << endl;
    cout << "Now attempting to store a value in table[11].\n";
    table[11] = 0;
    return 0;
}
```

Program Output
```
0 1 2 3 4 5 6 7 8 9
Now attempting to store a value in table[11].
ERROR: Subscript out of range.
```

Checkpoint [11.5]

11.14 Assume there is a class named `Pet`. Write the prototype for a member function of `Pet` that overloads the = operator.

11.15 Assume that `dog` and `cat` are instances of the `Pet` class, which has overloaded the = operator. Rewrite the following statement so it appears in function call notation instead of operator notation:

```cpp
dog = cat;
```

11.16 What is the disadvantage of an overloaded = operator returning `void`?

11.17 Describe the purpose of the `this` pointer.

11.18 The `this` pointer is automatically passed to what type of functions?

11.19 Assume there is a class named `Animal`, which overloads the = and + operators. In the following statement, assume `cat`, `tiger`, and `wildcat` are all instances of the `Animal` class:

```
wildcat = cat + tiger;
```

Of the three objects, `wildcat`, `cat`, and `tiger`, which is calling the `operator+` function? Which object is passed as an argument into the function?

11.20 What does the use of a dummy parameter in a unary operator function indicate to the compiler?

11.21 Describe the values that should be returned from functions that overload relational operators.

11.22 What is the advantage of overloading the << and >> operators?

11.23 What type of object should an overloaded << operator function return?

11.24 What type of object should an overloaded >> operator function return?

11.25 If an overloaded << or >> operator accesses a private member of a class, what must be done in that class's declaration?

11.26 Assume the class `NumList` has overloaded the [] operator. In the expression below, `list1` is an instance of the `NumList` class:

```
list1[25]
```

Rewrite this expression to explicitly call the function that overloads the [] operator.

11.27 When overloading a binary operator such as + or -, what object is passed into the operator function's parameter?

11.28 Explain why overloaded prefix and postfix ++ and -- operator functions should return a value.

11.29 How does C++ tell the difference between an overloaded prefix and postfix ++ or -- operator function?

11.30 Write member functions of the `FeetInches` class that overload the prefix and postfix -- operators. Demonstrate the functions in a simple program similar to Program 11-12.

11.6 Object Conversion

> **CONCEPT** Special operator functions may be written to convert a class object to any other type.

As you've already seen, operator functions allow classes to work more like built-in data types. Another capability that operator functions can give classes is automatic type conversion.

Data type conversion happens "behind the scenes" with the built-in data types. For instance, suppose a program uses the following variables:

```
int i;
float f;
```

The following statement automatically converts the value in i to a floating-point number and stores it in f:

```
f = i;
```

Likewise, the following statement converts the value in f to an integer (truncating the fractional part) and stores it in i:

```
i = f;
```

The same functionality can also be given to class objects. For example, assuming distance is a FeetInches object and f is a float, the following statement would conveniently convert distance's value into a floating-point number and store it in f, if FeetInches is properly written:

```
f = distance;
```

To be able to use a statement such as this, an operator function must be written to perform the conversion. Here is an operator function for converting a FeetInches object to a float:

```
FeetInches::operator float()
{
    float temp = feet;
    temp += (inches / 12.0);
    return temp;
}
```

This function contains an algorithm that will calculate the decimal equivalent of a feet-and-inches measurement. For example, the value 4 feet 6 inches will be converted to 4.5. This value is stored in the local variable temp.

 Note: No return type is specified in the function header. Since the function is a FeetInches-to-float conversion function, it will always return a float. Also, since the function takes no arguments, there are no parameters.

Program 11-16 demonstrates the `FeetInches` class with both a `float` and an `int` conversion function. (Note that the `int` conversion function simply returns the `feet` member, thus "truncating" the inches value.) The updated class files are also listed.

Program 11-16

Contents of `feetinc6.h`

```
#include <iostream>              // Needed to overload << and >>
#ifndef FEETINCHES_H
#define FEETINCHES_H
using namepspace std;

// A class to hold distances or measurements expressed
// in feet and inches
class FeetInches
{
    private:
        int feet;
        int inches;
        void simplify();          // Defined in feetinc6.cpp
    public:
        FeetInches(int f = 0, int i = 0)
            { feet = f; inches = i; simplify(); }
        void setData(int f, int i)
            { feet = f; inches = i; simplify(); }
        int getFeet()
            { return feet; }
        int getInches()
            { return inches; }
        FeetInches operator + (const FeetInches &);   // Overloaded +
        FeetInches operator - (const FeetInches &);   // Overloaded -
        FeetInches operator++();                      // Prefix ++
        FeetInches operator++(int);                   // Postfix ++
        bool operator>(const FeetInches &);
        bool operator<(const FeetInches &);
        bool operator==(const FeetInches &);
        operator float();
        operator int()            // Truncates the inches value.
            { return feet; }
        friend ostream &operator<<(ostream &, FeetInches &);
        friend istream &operator>>(istream &, FeetInches &);
};
#endif
```

(program continues)

Program 11-16 *(continued)*

Contents of feetinc6.cpp
```cpp
#include <iostream>
#include "feetinc6.h"

//***********************************************************
// Definition of member function simplify. This function    *
// checks for values in the inches member greater than       *
// 12 and less than 0. If such a value is found, the numbers  *
// in feet and inches are adjusted to conform to a standard feet *
// and inches expression. For example, 3 feet 14 inches would  *
// be adjusted to 4 feet 2 inches, and 5 feet -2 inches would  *
// be adjusted to 4 feet 10 inches.                            *
//***********************************************************

void FeetInches::simplify()
{
    inches = 12*feet + inches;
    feet = inches / 12;
    inches = inches % 12;
}


//*************************************************
// Overloaded binary + operator.                 *
//*************************************************

FeetInches FeetInches::operator+(const FeetInches &right)
{
    FeetInches temp;

    temp.inches = inches + right.inches;
    temp.feet = feet + right.feet;
    temp.simplify();
    return temp;
}


//*************************************************
// Overloaded binary - operator.                 *
//*************************************************
FeetInches FeetInches::operator-(const FeetInches &right)
{
    FeetInches temp;

    temp.inches = inches - right.inches;
    temp.feet = feet - right.feet;
    temp.simplify();
    return temp;
}
```

(program continues)

Program 11-16 *(continued)*

```
//******************************************************************
// Overloaded prefix ++ operator. Causes the inches member to  *
// be incremented. Returns the incremented object.             *
//******************************************************************
FeetInches FeetInches::operator++()
{
    ++inches;
    simplify();
    return *this;
}


//******************************************************************
// Overloaded postfix ++ operator. Causes the inches member to  *
// be incremented. Returns the value of the object before the   *
// increment.                                                   *
//******************************************************************

FeetInches FeetInches::operator++(int)
{
    FeetInches temp(feet, inches);

    inches++;
    simplify();
    return temp;
}

//******************************************************************
// Overloaded > operator. Returns true if the current object is *
// set to a value greater than that of right.                   *
//******************************************************************

bool FeetInches::operator>(const FeetInches &right)
{
    if (feet > right.feet)
        return true;
    else if (feet == right.feet && inches > right.inches)
        return true;
    else return false;
}

//******************************************************************
// Overloaded < operator. Returns true if the current object is *
// set to a value less than that of right.                      *
//******************************************************************
```

(program continues)

Program 11-16   *(continued)*

```
bool FeetInches::operator<(const FeetInches &right)
{
    if (feet < right.feet)
        return true;
    else if (feet == right.feet && inches < right.inches)
        return true;
    else return false;
}

//*****************************************************************
// Overloaded == operator. Returns true if the current object is *
// set to a value equal to that of right.                        *
//*****************************************************************

bool FeetInches::operator==(const FeetInches &right)
{
    if (feet == right.feet && inches == right.inches)
        return true;
    else return false;
}

//*****************************************************************
// Conversion function to convert a FeetInches object            *
// to a float.                                                   *
//*****************************************************************

FeetInches::operator float()
{

    float temp = feet;

    temp += (inches / 12.0);
    return temp;
}

//*****************************************************************
// Overloaded << operator. Gives cout the ability to             *
// directly display FeetInches objects.                          *
//*****************************************************************

ostream &operator<<(ostream &strm, FeetInches &obj)
{
    strm << obj.feet << " feet, " << obj.inches << " inches";
    return strm;
}
```

(program continues)

Program 11-16 *(continued)*

```
//**********************************************************
// Overloaded >> operator. Gives cin the ability to      *
// store user input directly into FeetInches objects.    *
//**********************************************************

istream &operator>>(istream &strm, FeetInches &obj)
{
    cout << "Feet: ";
    strm >> obj.feet;
    cout << "Inches: ";
    strm >> obj.inches;
    return strm;
}
```

Main program file, pr11-16.cpp
```
// This program demonstrates the object conversion operators,
// designed to work with the FeetInches class.
#include <iostream>
#include "feetinc6.h"
using namespace std;

int main()
{
    FeetInches distance;
    float f;
    int i;

    cout << "Enter a distance in feet and inches:\n ";
    cin >> distance;
    f = distance;
    i = distance;
    cout << "The value " << distance;
    cout << " is equivalent to " << f << " feet\n";
    cout << "or " << i << " feet, rounded down.\n";
    return 0;
}
```

Program Output with Example Input Shown in Bold
```
Enter a distance in feet and inches:
Feet: 8[Enter]
Inches: 6[Enter]
The value 8 feet, 6 inches is equivalent to 8.5 feet
or 8 feet, rounded down.
```

11.7 Object Composition

Object composition occurs when a class contains an instance of another class.

In Chapter 7 you learned that structures can be nested inside other structures. This leads to the creation of structures with instances of other structures as members. The same technique is possible with classes. Making an instance of one class the member of another class is called *object composition.*

Object composition is useful for creating a "has a" relationship between classes. For example, look at the following Customer class listing. It has several instances of the string and Account classes (discussed in Chapter 7) as members.

Contents of customer.h

```
#include <string>
#include "account.h"

class Customer
{
   public:
      string name;
      string address;
      string city;
      string state;
      string zip;
      Account savings;
      Account checking;
      Customer(string n, string a, string c, string s, string z)
         { name = n; address = a; city = c; state = s; zip = z; }
};
```

The relationship between the different objects that make up this class can be described as follows:

- ◆ The customer has a name
- ◆ The customer has an address
- ◆ The customer has a city
- ◆ The customer has a state
- ◆ The customer has a ZIP code
- ◆ The customer has a savings account
- ◆ The customer has a checking account

Program 11-17 demonstrates this class.

Program 11-17

```cpp
#include <iostream>
#include <iomanip>
#include "customer.h"
using namespace std;

int main()
{
    Customer smith("Smith, John", "127 Pine View Drive",
                   "Brassville", "NC", "28801");

    smith.savings.makeDeposit(1000);
    smith.checking.makeDeposit(500);
    smith.savings.calcInterest();
    smith.checking.calcInterest();
    cout << setprecision(2);
    cout << showpoint << fixed;
    cout << "Customer Name: " << smith.name << endl;
    cout << "Address: " << smith.address << endl;
    cout << "City: " << smith.city << endl;
    cout << "State: " << smith.state << endl;
    cout << "ZIP: " << smith.zip << endl;
    cout << "Savings account balance: ";
    cout << smith.savings.getBalance() << endl;
    cout << "Interest earned from savings: ";
    cout << smith.savings.getInterest() << endl;
    cout << "Checking account balance: ";
    cout << smith.checking.getBalance() << endl;
    cout << "Interest earned from checking: ";
    cout << smith.checking.getInterest() << endl;
    return 0;
}
```

Program Output
```
Customer Name: Smith, John
Address: 127 Pineview Drive
City: Brassville
State: NC
ZIP: 28801
Savings account balance: 1045.00
Interest earned from savings: 45.00
Checking account balance: 522.50
Interest earned from checking: 22.50
```

⁇ Checkpoint

11.31 What are the benefits of having operator functions that perform object conversion?

11.32 Why are no return types listed in the prototypes or headers of operator functions that perform data type conversion?

11.33 Assume there is a class named BlackBox. Write the header for a member function that converts a BlackBox object to an int.

11.34 Assume there are two classes, Big and Small. The Big class has, as a member, an instance of the Small class. Write a sentence that describes the relationship between the two classes.

Review Questions and Exercises

Fill-in-the-Blank

1. If a member variable is declared _____, all objects of that class have access to the same variable.

2. Static member variables are defined _____ the class.

3. A(n) _____ member function cannot access any non-static member variables in its own class.

4. A static member function may be called _____ any instances of its class are defined.

5. A(n) _____ function is not a member of a class, but has access to the private members of the class.

6. A(n) _____ tells the compiler that a specific class will be declared later in the program.

7. _____ is the default behavior when an object is assigned the value of another object of the same class.

8. A(n) _____ is a special constructor, called whenever a new object is initialized with another object's data.

9. _____ is a special built-in pointer that is automatically passed as a hidden argument to all non-static member functions.

10. An operator may be _____ to work with a specific class.

11. When the _____ operator is overloaded, its function must have a dummy parameter.

12. Making an instance of one class a member of another class is called _____.

13. Object composition is useful for creating a(n) _____ relationship between two classes.

14. For each of the following statements or program segments, indicate whether an initialization or an assignment occurs.

```
int x = 47;
y = 12;
if (x == 1)
        cout << "x is equal to 1\n";
```

```
    if (y == 0)
        {
            float z = 12.3;
            cout << z << endl;
        }
    int *ptr = new int[100];
```

15. The class `Stuff` has both a copy constructor and an overloaded = operator. Assume that `blob` and `clump` are both instances of the `Stuff` class. For each of the statements, indicate whether the copy constructor or the overloaded = operator will be called.

```
        Stuff blob = clump;
        clump = blob;
        blob.operator=(clump);
        showValues(blob);    // Blob is passed by value.
```

16. Explain the programming steps necessary to make a class's member variable static.

17. Explain the programming steps necessary to make a class's member function static.

18. Consider the following class declaration:

```
class Thing
{
    private:
        int x;
        int y;
        static int z;
    public:
        Thing()
            { x = y = z; }
        static void putThing(int a)
            { z = a; }
};
    int Thing:: z = 0:
```

Assume a program containing the class declaration defines three `Thing` objects with the following statement:

```
Thing one, two, three;
```

A) How many separate instances of the x member exist?
B) How many separate instances of the y member exist?
C) How many separate instances of the z member exist?
D) What value will be stored in the x and y members of each object?
E) Write a statement that will call the `putThing` member function *before* the `Thing` objects are defined.

19. Describe the difference between making a class a member of another class (object composition) and making a class a friend of another class.

20. What is the purpose of a forward declaration of a class?

21. Explain why memberwise assignment can cause problems with a class that contains a pointer member.

22. Explain why a class's copy constructor is called when an object of that class is passed by value into a function.

23. Explain why the parameter of a copy constructor must be a reference.

24. Assume a class named `Bird` exists. Write the header for a member function that overloads the = operator for that class.

25. Assume a class named `Dollars` exists. Write the headers for member functions that overload the prefix and postfix ++ operators for that class.

26. Assume a class named `Yen` exists. Write the header for a member function that overloads the ‹ operator for that class.

27. Assume a class named `Length` exists. Write the header for a member function that overloads cout's ‹‹ operator for that class.

28. Assume a class named `Collection` exists. Write the header for a member function that overloads the [] operator for that class.

29. Explain why a programmer would want to overload operators rather than use regular member functions to perform similar operations.

True or False

30. T   F   Static member variables cannot be accessed by non-static member functions.

31. T   F   Static member variables are defined outside their class declaration.

32. T   F   A static member function may refer to non-static member variables of the same class, but only after an instance of the class has been defined.

33. T   F   When a function is declared a `friend` by a class, it becomes a member of that class.

34. T   F   A friend function has access to the private members of the class declaring it a `friend`.

35. T   F   An entire class may be declared a `friend` of another class.

36. T   F   In order for a function or class to become a friend of another class, it must be declared as such by the class granting it access.

37. T   F   If a class has a pointer as a member, it's a good idea to also have a copy constructor.

38. T   F   You cannot use the = operator to assign one object's values to another object, unless you overload the operator.

39. T   F   If a class doesn't have a copy constructor, the compiler generates a default copy constructor for it.

40. T   F   If a class has a copy constructor, and an object of that class is passed by value into a function, the function's parameter will *not* call its copy constructor.

41. T   F   The `this` pointer is passed to static member functions.

42. T F All functions that overload unary operators must have a dummy parameter.

43. T F For an object to perform automatic type conversion, an operator function must be written.

44. T F It is possible to have an instance of one class as a member of another class.

Find the Error

45. Each of the following class declarations has errors. Locate as many as you can.

A)
```cpp
class Box
{
    private:
        float width;
        float length;
        float height;
    public:
        Box(float w, 1, h)
            { width = w; length = 1; height = h; }
        Box(Box b) // Copy constructor
            { width = b.width;
              length = b.length;
              height = b.height; }
```

    ... Other member functions follow ...
```cpp
};
```

B)
```cpp
class Circle
{
    private:
        float diameter;
        int centerX;
        int centerY;
    public:
        Circle(float d, int x, int y)
            { diameter = d; centerX = x; centerY = y;   }
        // Overloaded = operator
        void Circle=(Circle &right)
            { diameter = right.diameter;
              centerX = right.centerX;
              centerY = right.centerY; }
```

    ... Other member functions follow ...
```cpp
};
```

C)
```cpp
class Point
{
    private:
        int xCoord;
        int yCoord;
```

```
            public:
                Point (int x, int y)
                    { xCoord = x; yCoord = y; }
                // Overloaded + operator
                void operator+(const &Point Right)
                    { xCoord += right.xCoord;
                      yCoord += right.yCoord;
                      }
```

... Other member functions follow ...

```
        };

D)  class Box
        {
            private:
                float width;
                float length;
                float height;
            public:
                Box(float w, 1, h)
                    { width = w; length = 1; height = h; }
                // Overloaded prefix ++ operator
                void operator++()
                    {   ++width; ++length; }
                // Overloaded postfix ++ operator
                void operator++()
                    {   width++; length++; }
```

... Other member functions follow ...

```
        };

E)  class Yard
        {
            private:
                float length;
            public:
                yard(float 1)
                    { length = 1; }
                // float conversion function
                void operator float()
                    { return length; }
```

... Other member functions follow ...

```
        };
```

Programming Challenges

General Requirements

Each program should have a section of comments at the top. The comments should contain your name, the date the program was written, the chapter the assignment appeared in, and the assignment number and name. Here is an example:

```
// Written by Jill Johnson
// March 31, 2003
// Chapter 11
// Assignment 1, NumDays Class
```

For each program that displays a dollar amount, format the output in fixed-point notation with two decimal places of precision. Be sure the decimal place always displays, even when the number is zero or has no fractional part.

1. NumDays **Class**

Design a class called NumDays. The class's purpose is to store a value that represents a number of work hours and convert it to a number of days. For example, 8 hours would be converted to 1 day, 12 hours would be converted to 1.5 days, and 18 hours would be converted to 2.25 days. The class should have a constructor that accepts a number of hours, as well as member functions for storing and retrieving the hours and days. The class should also have the following overloaded operators:

+   *Addition operator.* When two NumDays objects are added together, the overloaded + operator should return the sum of the two object's hours member.

-   *Subtraction operator.* When one NumDays object is subtracted from another, the overloaded - operator should return the difference of the two object's hours member.

++ *Prefix and postfix increment operators.* These operators should increment the number of hours stored in the object. When incremented, the number of days should be automatically recalculated.

-- *Prefix and postfix decrement operators.* These operators should decrement the number of hours stored in the object. When decremented, the number of days should be automatically recalculated.

2. Time Off

 Note: This assignment assumes you have already completed Programming Challenge 1.

Design a class named TimeOff. The purpose of the class is to track an employee's sick leave, vacation, and unpaid time off. It should have, as members, the following instances of the NumDays class described in Programming Challenge 1:

maxSickDays	A NumDays object that records the maximum number of days of sick leave the employee may take.
sickTaken	A NumDays object that records the number of days of sick leave the employee has already taken.
maxVacation	A NumDays object that records the maximum number of days of paid vacation the employee may take.
vacTaken	A NumDays object that records the number of days of paid vacation the employee has already taken.
maxUnpaid	A NumDays object that records the maximum number of days of unpaid vacation the employee may take.
unpaidTaken	A NumDays object that records the number of days of unpaid leave the employee has taken.

Additionally, the class should have members for holding the employee's name and identification number. It should have an appropriate constructor and member functions for storing and retrieving information in any of the member objects.

Input Validation: Company policy states that an employee may not accumulate more than 240 hours of paid vacation. The class should not allow the maxVacation object to store a value greater than this amount.

3. Personnel Report

Note: This assignment assumes you have already completed Programming Challenges 1 and 2.

Write a program that uses an instance of the TimeOff class you designed in Programming Challenge 2. The program should ask the user to enter the number of months an employee has worked for the company. It should then use the TimeOff object to calculate and display the employee's maximum number of sick leave and vacation days. Employees earn 12 hours of vacation leave and 8 hours of sick leave per month.

4. Date Class Modification

Modify the Date class in Programming Challenge 5 of Chapter 7. The new version should have the following overloaded operators:

++   **Prefix and postfix increment operators.** These operators should increment the object's day member.

--   **Prefix and postfix decrement operators.** These operators should decrement the object's day member.

- *Subtraction operator.* If one `Date` object is subtracted from another, the operator should give the number of days between the two dates. For example, if April 10, 2003 is subtracted from April 18, 2003, the result will be 8.

`<<` `cout`*'s stream insertion operator.* This operator should cause the date to be displayed in the form

```
April 18, 2003
```

`>>` `cin`*'s stream extraction operator.* This operator should prompt the user for a date to be stored in a `Date` object.

The class should detect the following conditions and handle them accordingly:

- ◆ When a date is set to the last day of the month and incremented, it should become the first day of the following month.

- ◆ When a date is set to December 31 and incremented, it should become January 1 of the following year.

- ◆ When a day is set to the first day of the month and decremented, it should become the last day of the previous month.

- ◆ When a date is set to January 1 and decremented, it should become December 31 of the previous year.

Demonstrate the class's capabilities in a simple program.

Input Validation: The overloaded >> operator should not accept invalid dates. For example, the date 13/45/00 should not be accepted.

5. `FeetInches` **Modification**

Modify the `FeetInches` class discussed in this chapter (stored in `feetinc6.h` and `feetinc6.cpp`), so it overloads the following operators:

```
<=
>=
!=
```

Demonstrate the class's capabilities in a simple program.

6. Corporate Sales

A corporation has six divisions, each responsible for sales to different geographic locations. Design a `DivSales` class that keeps sales data for a division, with the following members:

- ◆ An array with four elements for holding four quarters of sales figures for the division

- ◆ A private static variable for holding the total corporate sales for all divisions for the entire year.

◆ A member function that takes four arguments, each assumed to be the sales for a quarter. The value of the arguments should be copied into the array that holds the sales data. The total of the four arguments should be added to the static variable that holds the total yearly corporate sales.

◆ A function that takes an integer argument within the range of 0 to 3. The argument is to be used as a subscript into the division quarterly sales array. The function should return the value of the array element with that subscript.

Write a program that creates an array of six `DivSales` objects. The program should ask the user to enter the sales for four quarters for each division. After the data is entered, the program should display a table showing the division sales for each quarter. The program should then display the total corporate sales for the year.

Input Validation: Only accept positive values for quarterly sales figures.

Serendipity Booksellers Software Development Project—Part 11: *A Problem-Solving Exercise*

1. Add the `titleMatch` Member Function to the `BookData` Class

The standard library `string` class overloads the `==` operator. Since the `BookData` class uses `string` objects to store many of its attributes, you may use the `==` operator when searching for a specific title, ISBN, and so on. Add a member function to the `BookData` class named `titleMatch`. The `titleMatch` function accepts a string as its argument and returns the boolean value `true` if the argument matches the book's title. If the argument and the book title do not match, the function should return `false`.

2. Create the `isbnMatch` Member Function

The `isbnMatch` function accepts a string as its argument and returns the boolean value `true` if the argument matches the book's ISBN. If the argument and the book ISBN do not match, the function should return `false`.

3. Create the `authorMatch` Member Function

The `authorMatch` function accepts a string as its argument and returns the boolean value `true` if the argument matches the author's name. If the argument and the author's name do not match, the function should return `false`.

4. Create the `pubMatch` Member Function

The `pubMatch` function accepts a string as its argument and returns the boolean value `true` if the argument matches the publisher's name. If the argument and the publisher's name do not match, the function should return `false`.

5. Modify `lookUpBook`, `editBook`, and `deleteBook`

Currently the `lookUpBook`, `editBook`, and `deleteBook` functions have their own method of comparing book titles with search strings. Modify them so they use the `titleMatch` function you added to the `BookData` class in step 1.

6. Add Other Classes to the Program

Analyze the program for other ways to implement classes. Here are some suggestions:

- ◆ Consider if the various menus could be managed by class objects. Could a class be constructed to handle the program's user interface?

- ◆ Determine whether input validation could be performed by a class object.

CHAPTER 12

More About Characters, Strings, and the `string` Class

Topics

12.1 Review of the Internal Storage of C-Strings

> **CONCEPT** In C++, a C-string is a sequence of characters stored in consecutive memory locations, terminated by a NULL character.

In this section we will discuss strings, string constants, and C-strings. Although you have previously encountered these terms, make sure you understand what each mean and the differences between them.

String is a generic term that describes any consecutive sequence of characters. A word, a sentence, a person's name, and the title of a song are all strings. In a program, a string may be constant or variable in nature, and may be stored in a variety of ways.

771

String Constants

A *string constant* is the literal representation of a string in a program. In C++, string constants are enclosed in double quotation marks, such as

```
"What is your name?"
```

The term C-*string* describes a string whose characters are stored in consecutive memory locations and are followed by a null character or null terminator. Recall that a null character or null terminator is a byte holding the ASCII code 0. For example, Figure 12-1 illustrates how the string "Bailey" is stored in memory, as a C-string.

Figure 12-1

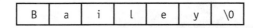

| B | a | i | l | e | y | \0 |

 Note: Remember that \0 ("slash zero") is the escape sequence representing the null terminator. It stands for the ASCII code 0.

The purpose of the null terminator is to mark the end of the C-string. Without it, there would be no way for a function to know the length of a C-string argument. For example, look at Program 12-1.

Program 12-1

```cpp
// This program contains string constants.
#include <iostream>
using namespace std;

int main()
{
    char again;

    do
    {
        cout << "C++ programming is great fun!" << endl;
        cout << "Do you want to see the message again? ";
        cin >> again;
    } while (again == 'Y' || again == 'y');
    return 0;
}
```

Program 12-1 contains two string constants:

```
"C++ programming is great fun!"
"Do you want to see the message again? "
```

Although the strings are not stored in arrays, they are still part of the program's data. The first string occupies 30 bytes of memory (including the null terminator), and the second string occupies 39 bytes. They appear in memory in the forms shown in Figure 12-2.

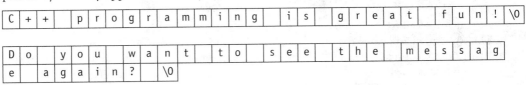

Figure 12-2

It's important to realize that a string constant has its own storage location, just like a variable or an array. When a string constant appears in a statement, it's actually its memory address that C++ uses. Look at the following example:

```
cout << "Do you want to see the message again? ";
```

In this statement, the memory address of the string constant "Do you want to see the message again?" is passed to the `cout` object. `cout` displays the consecutive characters found at this address. It stops displaying the characters when a null terminator is encountered.

Strings Stored in Arrays

Quite often programs need to accept string input, change the contents of a string, or access a string for performing comparisons. One method of storing nonconstant strings is in character arrays, as C-strings. When declaring a character array for holding a C-string, be sure the array is large enough for the null terminator. For example, the following 12-element array can hold a string of no more than 11 characters:

```
char company[12];
```

String input can be performed by the `cin` object. For example, the following statement allows the user to enter a string (with no whitespace characters) into the `company` array:

```
cin >> company;
```

Recall from Chapter 8 that an array name with no brackets and no subscript is converted into the beginning address of the array. In the previous statement, `company` indicates the address in memory where the string is to be stored. Of course, `cin` has no way of knowing that `company` only has 12 elements. If the user enters a string of 30 characters, `cin` will write past the end of the array. This can be prevented by using `cin`'s `getline` member function. Assume the following array has been declared in a program:

```
char line[80];
```

The following statement uses `cin`'s `getline` member function to get a line of input (including whitespace characters) and store it in the `line` array:

```
cin.getline(line, 80);
```

As you will recall from Chapter 3, the first argument tells `getline` where to store the string input. This statement indicates the starting address of the `line` array as the storage location for the string. The second argument (80) indicates the maximum length of the string, including the null terminator. `cin` will read 79 characters, or until the user presses the **[Enter]** key, whichever comes first. `cin` will automatically append the null terminator to the end of the string.

Once a string is stored in an array, it can be processed using standard subscript notation. For example, Program 12-2 displays a string stored in an array. It uses a loop to display each character in the array until the null terminator is encountered.

Program 12-2

```
// This program cycles through a character array, displaying
// each element until a null terminator is encountered.

#include <iostream>
using namespace std;

int main()
{
    char line[80];
    int count = 0;

    cout << "Enter a sentence of no more than 79 characters:\n";
    cin.getline(line, 80);
    cout << "The sentence you entered is:\n";
    while (line[count] != '\0')
    {
        cout << line[count];
        count++;
    }
    return 0;
}
```

Program Output with Example Input Shown in Bold
```
Enter a sentence of no more than 79 characters:
```
C++ is challenging but fun![Enter]
```
The sentence you entered is:
C++ is challenging but fun!
```

12.2 Library Functions for Working with C-Strings

CONCEPT The C++ library has numerous functions for handling C-strings. These functions perform various tests and manipulations.

The C++ library provides many functions for manipulating and testing strings. For instance, the following program segment uses the `strlen` function to determine the length of the string stored in name:

```cpp
char name[50] = "Thomas Edison";
int length;
length = strlen(name);
```

The `strlen` function accepts a pointer to a C-string as its argument. It returns the length of the string, which is the number of characters up to, but not including, the null terminator. As a result, the variable `length` will have the number 13 stored in it. The length of a string isn't to be confused with the size of the array holding it. Remember, the only information being passed to `strlen` is the beginning address of a C-string. It doesn't know where the array ends, so it looks for the null terminator to indicate the end of the string.

 Note: `strlen`, as well as the other functions discussed in this section, require the `cstring` header file to be included.

When using a C-string handling function, you must pass one or more C-strings as arguments. This means passing the address of the C-string, which may be accomplished by using any of the following as arguments:

- The name of the array holding the C-string
- A pointer variable that holds the address of the C-string
- A literal string

Anytime a literal string is used as an argument to a function, the address of the literal string is passed. Here is an example of the `strlen` function being used with such an argument:

```cpp
length = strlen("Thomas Edison");
```

Some functions, such as `strcat`, require two pointers. The `strcat` function *concatenates*, or appends one string to another. Here is an example of its use:

```cpp
char string1[13] = "Hello ";
char string2[7] = "World!";
cout << string1 << endl;
cout << string2 << endl;
strcat(string1, string2);
cout << string1 << endl;
```

These statements will produce the following output:

```
Hello
World!
Hello World!
```

The `strcat` function copies the contents of `string2` to the end of `string1`. In this example, `string1` contains the string "Hello " before the call to `strcat`. After the call, it contains the string "Hello World!". Figure 12-3 shows the contents of both arrays before and after the function call.

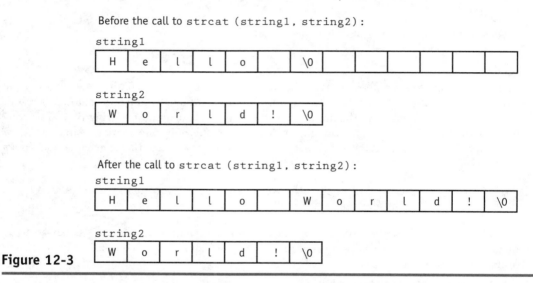

Before the call to `strcat (string1, string2)`:

string1

| H | e | l | l | o | | \0 | | | | | | |

string2

| W | o | r | l | d | ! | \0 |

After the call to `strcat (string1, string2)`:

string1

| H | e | l | l | o | | W | o | r | l | d | ! | \0 |

string2

| W | o | r | l | d | ! | \0 |

Figure 12-3

Notice the last character in `string1` (before the null terminator) is a space. The `strcat` function doesn't insert a space, so it's the programmer's responsibility to make sure one is already there, if needed. It's also the programmer's responsibility to make sure the array holding `string1` is large enough to hold `string1` plus `string2` plus a null terminator. Here is a program segment that uses the `sizeof` operator to test an array's size before `strcat` is called:

```
if (sizeof(string1) >= (strlen(string1) + strlen(string2) + 1))
    strcat(string1, string2);
else
    cout << "String1 is not large enough for both strings.\n";
```

 WARNING! If the array holding the first string isn't large enough to hold both strings, `strcat` will overflow the boundaries of the array.

Recall from Chapter 8 that one array cannot be assigned to another with the = operator. Each individual element must be assigned, usually inside a loop. The strcpy function, which you have already encountered in Chapter 3, can be used to copy one string to another. Here is an example of its use:

```
char name[20];
strcpy(name, "Albert Einstein");
```

The strcpy function's two arguments are C-string addresses. The second C-string is copied to the first C-string, including the null terminator. (The first argument usually references an array.) In this example, the strcpy function will copy the string "Albert Einstein" to the name array.

If anything is already stored in the location referenced by the first argument, it is overwritten, as shown in the following program segment:

```
char string1[10] = "Hello", string2[10] = "World!";
cout << string1 << endl;
cout << string2 << endl;
strcpy(string1, string2);
cout << string1 << endl;
cout << string2 << endl;
```

Here is the output:

```
Hello
World!
World!
World!
```

 WARNING! Being true to C++'s nature, strcpy performs no bounds checking. The array specified by the first argument will be overflowed if it isn't large enough to hold the string specified by the second argument.

Comparing C-Strings

The assignment and relational operators work with the C++ string class because they have been overloaded to work with that class. However, just as the assignment operator cannot be used to assign to C-strings, the relational operators <=, <, >, >=, !=, and == cannot be used to compare C-strings. This is because when used with C-strings, these operators compare the addresses at which the C-strings are stored instead of comparing the actual sequence of characters that comprise the C-strings. Program 12-3 shows the incorrect result of trying to compare C-strings using the equality operator.

Program 12-3

```
// This program illustrates that you cannot compare C-strings
// with relational operators. Although it appears to test the
// strings for equality, that is not what happens.

#include <iostream>
using namespace std;

int main()
{
    char firstString[40], secondString[40];

    cout << "Enter a string: ";
    cin.getline(firstString, 40);
    cout << "Enter another string: ";
    cin.getline(secondString, 40);
    if (firstString == secondString)
        cout << "You entered the same string twice.\n";
    else
        cout << "The strings are not the same.\n";
    return 0;
}
```

Program Output with Example Input Shown in Bold
Enter a string: **Alfonso[Enter]**
Enter another string: **Alfonso[Enter]**
The strings are not the same.

Although two identical strings may be entered, Program 12-3 will always report they are not the same. This is because of the way C++ handles C-strings. When you use the name of an array or a string constant, you are actually working with the *memory address* of the array or constant. In Program 12-3, the following statement is comparing the memory addresses of `firstString` and `secondString`:

```
if (firstString == secondString)
```

Since the addresses of `firstString` and `secondString` are not the same (the two arrays are not located in the same place in memory), the comparison will always be false.

The `strcmp` Function

In C++, C-string comparisons are done with the library function `strcmp`. Here is its format:

```
strcmp(string1, string2);
```

The function compares the contents of string1 with that of string2 and returns one of the following values:

- If the two strings are identical, strcmp returns 0.
- If string1 < string2, strcmp returns a number less than 0 (i.e., a negative number).
- If string1 > string2, strcmp returns a number greater than 0 (i.e., a negative number).

In general, strcmp compares the ASCII codes of each character in the two strings. If it goes all the way through both strings finding no characters different, it returns 0. As soon as it finds two corresponding characters that have different codes, however, it stops the comparison. If the ASCII code for the character in string2 is higher than the code in string1, it returns a negative number. But if the code in string2 is lower than the code in string1, a positive number is returned. Here is the format of an if-else statement using strcmp to determine if two strings are equal:

```
if (strcmp(string1, string2) == 0)
    statement; // The strings are the same
else
    statement; // The strings are not the same
```

Program 12-3, which incorrectly tested two C-strings with a relational operator, can be correctly rewritten with the strcmp function, as shown in Program 12-4.

Program 12-4

```
// This program correctly tests two C-strings for equality
// with the strcmp function.

#include <iostream>
#include <cstring>
using namespace std;

int main()
{
    char firstString[40], secondString[40];

    cout << "Enter a string: ";
    cin.getline(firstString, 40);
    cout << "Enter another string: ";
    cin.getline(secondString, 40);
    if (strcmp(firstString, secondString) == 0)
        cout << "You entered the same string twice.\n";
    else
        cout << "The strings are not the same.\n";
    return 0;
}
```

Program 12-4

Program Output with Example Input Shown in Bold
```
Enter a string: Alfonso[Enter]
Enter another string: Alfonso[Enter]
You entered the same string twice.
```

The function `strcmp` is case sensitive when it compares the two strings. If the user enters "Dog" and "dog" in Program 12-4, it will report they are not the same. Most compilers provide nonstandard versions of `strcmp` that perform case-insensitive comparisons. For instance, Borland C++ has the `stricmp` function. It works identically to `strcmp` except the case of the characters is ignored.

Program 12-5 is a more practical example of how `strcmp` can be used. It asks the user to enter the part number of the stereo they wish to purchase. The part number contains numbers, letters, and a hyphen, so it must be stored as a string. Once the user enters the part number, the program displays the price of the stereo.

Program 12-5

```cpp
// This program uses strcmp to compare the string entered
// by the user with the valid stereo part numbers.

#include <iostream>
#include <cstring>
#include <iomanip>
using namespace std;

int main()
{
    const float aprice = 249.0, bprice = 299.0;
    char partNum[8];

    cout << "The stereo part numbers are:\n";
    cout << "\tBoom Box, part number S147-29A\n";
    cout << "\tShelf Model, part number S147-29B\n";
    cout << "Enter the part number of the stereo you\n";
    cout << "wish to purchase: ";
    cin >> setw(9);    // So they won't enter more than eight characters
    cin >> partNum;
    cout << fixed << showpoint;
    cout << setprecision(2);
    if (strcmp(partNum, "S147-29A") == 0)
        cout << "The price is $" << aprice << endl;
    else if (strcmp(partNum, "S147-29B") == 0)
        cout << "The price is $" << bprice << endl;
    else
        cout << partNum << " is not a valid part number.\n";
    return 0;
}
```

Program 12-5

Program Output with Example Input Shown in Bold
```
The stereo part numbers are:
    Boom Box, part number S147-29A
    Shelf Model, part number S147-29B
Enter the part number of the stereo you
wish to purchase: S147-29B[Enter]
The price is $299.00
```

Using ! with strcmp

Some programmers prefer to use the logical NOT operator with strcmp when testing strings for equality. Since 0 is considered logically false, the ! operator converts that value to true. The expression !strcmp(string1, string2) will return true when both strings are the same, and false when they are different. The two following statements perform the same operation:

```
if (strcmp(firstString, secondString) == 0)
if (!strcmp(firstString, secondString))
```

Sorting Strings

Programs are frequently written to print alphabetically sorted lists of items. For example, consider a department store computer system that keeps customers' names and addresses in a file. The names do not appear in the file alphabetically but in the order the operator entered them. If a list were to be printed in this order, it would be very difficult to locate any specific name. The list would have to be sorted before it was printed.

Because strcmp's return value indicates which of the two strings is higher on the ASCII chart, it can be used in programs that sort strings. Program 12-6 asks the user to enter two names. Then it prints the names alphabetically.

Program 12-6

```
// This program uses the return value of strcmp to alphabetically
// sort two strings entered by the user.

#include <iostream>
#include <cstring>
using namespace std;

int main()
{
    char name1[30], name2[30];
```

(program continues)

Program 12-6   *(continued)*

```
cout << "Enter a name (last name first): ";
cin.getline(name1, 30);
cout << "Enter another name: ";
cin.getline(name2, 30);
cout << "Here are the names sorted alphabetically:\n";
if (strcmp(name1, name2) < 0)
    cout << name1 << endl << name2 << endl;
else if (strcmp(name1, name2) > 0)
    cout << name2 << endl << name1 << endl;
else
    cout << "You entered the same name twice!\n";
return 0;
}
```

Program Output with Example Input Shown in Bold
```
Enter a name (last name first): Smith, Richard[Enter]
Enter another name: Jones, John[Enter]
Here are the names sorted alphabetically:
Jones, John
Smith, Richard
```

Table 12-1 summarizes the string handling functions discussed here, as well as others. (All the functions listed require the `cstring` header file.)

The last function in Table 12-1 is `strstr`, which searches for a string inside of a string. For instance, it could be used to search for the string "seven" inside the larger string "Four score and seven years ago." The function's first argument is the string to be searched, and the second argument is the string to look for. If the function finds the second string inside the first, it returns the address of the occurrence of the second string within the first string. Otherwise it returns the address 0, or the NULL address. Here is an example:

```
char array[] = "Four score and seven years ago";
char *strPtr;
cout << array << endl;
strPtr = strstr(array, "seven");   // search for "seven"
cout << strPtr << endl;
```

 Note: Because C++ does not distinguish between a C-string and a pointer to the first character of the C-string, any of the arguments to these functions may be a pointer to a `char`.

In the preceding program segment `strstr` will locate the string "seven" inside the string "Four score and seven years ago." It will return the address of the first character in "seven", which will be stored in the pointer variable `strPtr`. If run as part of a complete program, the segment will display the following:

Table 12-1 (See your C++ reference manual for more information on these functions.)

Function	Description
strlen	Accepts a C-string as an argument. Returns the length of the C-string (not including the null terminator. *Example Usage:* `len = strlen(name);`
strcat	Accepts two C-strings as arguments. The function appends the contents of the second string to the first C-string. (The first string is altered, the second string is left unchanged.) *Example Usage:* `strcat(string1, string2);`
strcpy	Accepts two C-strings as arguments. The function copies the second C-string to the first C-string. The second C-string is left unchanged. *Example Usage:* `strcpy(string1, string2);`
strncpy	Accepts two C-strings and an integer argument. The third argument, an integer, indicates how many characters to copy from the second C-string to the first C-string. If `string2` has fewer than *n* characters, `string1` is padded with `'\0'` characters. *Example Usage:* `strncpy(string1, string2, n);`
strcmp	Accepts two C-string arguments. If `string1` and `string2` are the same, this function returns 0. If `string2` is alphabetically greater than `string1`, it returns a negative number. If `string2` is alphabetically less than `string1`, it returns a positive number. *Example Usage:* `if (strcmp(string1, string2))`
strstr	Searches for the first occurrence of `string2` in `string1`. If an occurrence of `string2` is found, the function returns a pointer to it. Otherwise, it returns a NULL pointer (address 0). *Example Usage:* `cout << strstr(string1, string2);`

```
Four score and seven years ago
seven years ago
```

The `strstr` function can be useful in any program that must locate information inside one or more strings. Program 12-7, for example, stores a database of product numbers and descriptions in an array of C-strings. It allows the user to look up a product description by entering all or part of its product number.

Program 12-7

```cpp
// This program uses the strstr function to search an array
// of strings for a name.

#include <iostream>
#include <cstring> // For strstr
using namespace std;
```

(program continues)

Program 12-7 *(continued)*

```cpp
int main()
{
    char prods[5][27] = {"TV327   31 inch Television",
                         "CD257   CD Player",
                         "TA677   Answering Machine",
                         "CS109   Car Stereo",
                         "PC955   Personal Computer"};
    char lookUp[27], *strPtr = NULL;
    int index;

    cout << "\tProduct Database\n\n";
    cout << "Enter a product number to search for: ";
    cin.getline(lookUp, 27);
    for (index = 0; index < 5; index++)
    {
        strPtr = strstr(prods[index], lookUp);
        if (strPtr != NULL)
            break;
    }
    if (strPtr == NULL)
        cout << "No matching product was found.\n";
    else
        cout << prods[index] << endl;
    return 0;
}
```

Program Output with Example Input Shown in Bold
```
    Product Database

Enter a product to search for: CD257[Enter]
CD257   CD Player
```

Program Output with Other Example Input Shown in Bold
```
    Product Database

Enter a product to search for: CS[Enter]
CS109   Car Stereo
```

Program Output with Other Example Input Shown in Bold
```
    Product Database

Enter a product to search for: AB[Enter]
No matching product was found.
```

In Program 12-7, the `for` loop cycles through each C-string in the array calling the following statement:

```
strPtr = strstr(prods[index], lookUp);
```

The `strstr` function searches the string referenced by `prods[index]` for the name entered by the user, which is stored in `lookUp`. If `lookUp` is found inside `prods[index]`, the function returns its address. In that case, the following `if` statement causes the `for` loop to terminate:

```
if (strPtr != NULL)
        break;
```

Outside the loop, the following `if-else` statement determines if the string entered by the user was found in the array. If not, it informs the user that no matching product was found. Otherwise, the product number and description are displayed:

```
if (strPtr == NULL)
        cout << "No matching product was found.\n";
else
        cout << prods[index] << endl;
```

Checkpoint   [12.1–12.2]

12.1   Write a short description of each of the following functions:

   A) `strlen`
   B) `strcat`
   C) `strcpy`
   D) `strncpy`
   E) `strcmp`
   F) `strstr`

12.2   What will the following program segment display?

```
char dog[] = "Fido";
cout << strlen(dog) << endl;
```

12.3   What will the following program segment display?

```
char string1[16] = "Have a ";
char string2[9] = "nice day";
strcat(string1, string2);
cout << string1 << endl;
cout << string2 << endl;
```

12.4   Write a statement that will copy the string "Beethoven" to the array `composer`.

12.5 When complete, the following program skeleton will search for the string "Windy" in the array place. If place contains "Windy" the program will display the message "Windy found." Otherwise it will display "Windy not found."

```
#include <iostream>
// include any other necessary header files
int main()
{
    char place[] = "The Windy City";
    // Complete the program. It should search the array place
    // for the string "Windy" and display the message "Windy
    // found" if it finds the string. Otherwise, it should
    // display the message "Windy not found."
}
```

12.6 Indicate whether the following strcmp function calls will return 0, a negative number, or a positive number. Refer to the ASCII table in Appendix A if necessary.

A) strcmp("ABC", "abc");
B) strcmp("Jill", "Jim");
C) strcmp("123", "ABC");
D) strcmp("Sammy", "Sally");

12.7 Complete the if statements in the following program skeleton.

```
#include <iostream>
using namespace std;

int main()
{
    char iceCream[20];
    cout << "What flavor of ice cream do you like best? ";
    cout << "Chocolate, Vanilla, or Pralines and Pecan? ";
    cin.getline(iceCream, 20);
    cout << "Here is the number of fat grams for a half ";
    cout << "cup serving:\n";
    //
    // Finish the following if-else statement
    // so the program will select the ice cream entered
    // by the user.
    //
    if (/* insert your code here */)
        cout << "Chocolate: 9 fat grams.\n";
    else if (/* insert your code here */)
        cout << "Vanilla: 10 fat grams.\n";
    else if (/* insert your code here */)
        cout << "Pralines and Pecan: 14 fat grams.\n";
    else
        cout << "That's not one of our flavors!\n";
    return 0;
}
```

12.3 String/Numeric Conversion Functions

CONCEPT The C++ library provides functions for converting a string representation of a number to a numeric data type and vice versa.

There is a great difference between a number that is stored as a string and one stored as a numeric value. The string "26792" isn't actually a number, but a series of ASCII codes representing the individual digits of the number. It uses six bytes of memory (including the null terminator). Since it isn't an actual number, it's not possible to perform mathematical operations with it, unless it is first converted to a numeric value.

Several functions exist in the C++ library for converting string representations of numbers into numeric values and vice versa. Table 12-2 shows some of these.

Table 12-2 (See your C++ reference manual for more information on these functions.)

Function	Description
atoi	Accepts a C-string as an argument. The function converts the C-string to an integer and returns that value. *Example Usage:* num = atoi("4569");
atol	Accepts a C-string as an argument. The function converts the C-string to a long integer and returns that value. *Example Usage:* lnum = atol("500000");
atof	Accepts a C-string as an argument. The function converts the C-string to a double and returns that value. Use this function to convert a C-string to a float or double. *Example Usage:* fnum = atof("3.14159");
itoa	Converts an integer to a C-string. The first argument, value, is the integer. The result will be stored at the location pointed to by the second argument, string. The third argument, base, is an integer. It specifies the numbering system that the converted integer should be expressed in (8 = octal, 10 = decimal, 16 = hexadecimal, etc.). *Example Usage:* itoa(value, string, base);

The atoi function converts a string to an integer. It accepts a C-string argument and returns the converted integer value. Here is an example of how to use it:

```
int num;
num = atoi("1000");
```

In these statements, atoi converts the string "1000" into the integer 1000. Once the variable num is assigned this value, it can be used in mathematical operations or any task requiring a numeric value.

Note: The `atoi` function as well as the others discussed in this section require that the `cstdlib` header file be included.

The `atol` function works just like `atoi`, except the return value is a `long` integer. Here is an example:

```
long bigNum;
bigNum = atol("500000");
```

As expected, the `atof` function accepts a C-string argument and converts it to a `double`. The numeric `double` value is returned, as shown here:

```
double fnum;
fnum = atof("12.67");
```

 Note: If a string that cannot be converted to a numeric value is passed to any of these functions, the function's behavior is undefined by C++. Many compilers, however, will perform the conversion process until an invalid character is encountered. For example, `atoi("123x5")` might return the integer 123. It is possible that these functions will return 0 if they cannot successfully convert their argument.

The `itoa` function is similar to `atoi`, but it works in reverse. It converts a numeric integer into a string representation of the integer. The `itoa` function accepts three arguments: the integer value to be converted, a pointer to the location in memory where the string is to be stored, and a number that represents the base of the converted value. Here is an example:

```
char numArray[10];
itoa(1200, numArray, 10);
cout << numArray << endl;
```

This program segment converts the integer value 1200 to a string. The string is stored in the array `numArray`. The third argument, 10, means the number should be written in decimal, or base 10 notation. The output of the `cout` statement is

```
1200
```

 WARNING! As always, C++ performs no array bounds checking. Make sure the array whose address is passed to `itoa` is large enough to hold the converted number, including the null terminator.

Now let's look at Program 12-8, which uses a string-to-number conversion function, `atoi`. It allows the user to enter a series of values, or the letters Q or q to quit. The average of the numbers is then calculated and displayed.

Program 12-8

```cpp
// This program demonstrates the strcmp and atoi functions.

#include <iostream>
#include <cstring>                    // For strcmp
#include <cstdlib>                    // For atoi
using namespace std;

int main()
{
    char input[20];
    int total = 0, count = 0;
    float average;

    cout << "This program will average a series of numbers.\n";
    cout << "Enter the first number or Q to quit: ";
    cin.getline(input, 20);

    while ((strcmp(input, "Q") != 0)&&(strcmp(input, "q") != 0))
    {
        total += atoi(input);     // Keep a running total.
        count++;                  // Keep track of how many numbers are entered.
        cout << "Enter the next number or Q to quit: ";
        cin.getline(input, 20);
    }
    if (count != 0)
    {
        average = float(total)/count;
        cout << "Average: " << average << endl;
    }
    return 0;
}
```

Program Output with Example Input Shown in Bold
```
This program will average a series of numbers.
Enter the first number or Q to quit: 74[Enter]
Enter the next number or Q to quit: 98[Enter]
Enter the next number or Q to quit: 23[Enter]
Enter the next number or Q to quit: 54[Enter]
Enter the next number or Q to quit: Q[Enter]
Average: 62.25
```

Recall that strcmp compares two C-strings. If they are identical, it returns 0. Otherwise a nonzero value is returned. The following while statement uses strcmp to determine if the string in input is either "Q" or "q".

```cpp
while ((strcmp(input, "Q") != 0)&&(strcmp(input, "q") != 0))
```

If the user hasn't entered "Q" or "q" the program uses `atoi` to convert the string in `input` to an integer and adds its value to `total` with the following statement:

```
total += atoi(input);  // Keep a running total
```

The user is then asked for the next number. When all the numbers are entered, the user terminates the loop by entering "Q" or "q". If one or more numbers are entered, their average is displayed.

Checkpoint   [12.3]

12.8   Write a short description of each of the following functions.

    A) `atoi`
    B) `atol`
    C) `atof`
    D) `itoa`

12.9   Write a statement that will convert the C-string "10" to an integer and store the result in the variable `num`.

12.10   Write a statement that will convert the C-string "100000" to a `long` and store the result in the variable `num`.

12.11   Write a statement that will convert the C-string "7.2389" to a `float` and store the result in the variable `num`.

12.12   Write a statement that will convert the integer 127 to a C-string, stored in base 10 notation in the array `value`.

12.4   Character Testing

CONCEPT   The C++ library provides several functions for testing characters.

The C++ library provides several functions that allow you to test the value of a character. These functions test a single `char` argument and return either `true` or `false`.[1] For example, the following program segment uses the `isupper` function to determine if the character passed as an argument is an uppercase letter. If it is, the function returns `true`. Otherwise, it returns `false`.

---

[1]These functions actually return an `int` value. The return value is nonzero to indicate `true`, or zero to indicate `false`.

```
char letter = 'a';
if (isupper(letter))
    cout << "Letter is uppercase.\n";
else
    cout << "Letter is lowercase.\n";
```

Since the variable letter, in this example, contains a lowercase character, isupper returns false. The if statement will cause the message "Letter is lowercase" to be displayed.

Table 12-3 lists several character-testing functions. Each of these is implemented in the cctype header file, so be sure to include that file when using the functions.

Table 12-3

Character function	Description
isalpha	Returns true (a nonzero number) if the argument is a letter of the alphabet. Returns false if the argument is not a letter.
isalnum	Returns true (a nonzero number) if the argument is a letter of the alphabet or a digit. Otherwise it returns false.
isdigit	Returns true (a nonzero number) if the argument is a digit from 0 to 9. Otherwise it returns false.
islower	Returns true (a nonzero number) if the argument is a lowercase letter. Otherwise, it returns false.
isprint	Returns true (a nonzero number) if the argument is a printable character (including a space). Returns false otherwise.
ispunct	Returns true (a nonzero number) if the argument is a printable character other than a digit, letter, or space. Returns false otherwise.
isupper	Returns true (a nonzero number) if the argument is an uppercase letter. Otherwise, it returns false.
isspace	Returns true (a nonzero number) if the argument is a whitespace character. Whitespace characters are any of the following: space ' ' vertical tab '\v' newline '\n' tab '\t' Otherwise, it returns false.

Program 12-9 uses several of the functions shown in Table 12-3. It asks the user to input a character and then displays various messages, depending on the return value of each function.

Program 12-9

```cpp
// This program demonstrates some of the character testing
// functions.

#include <iostream>
#include <cctype>
using namespace std;

int main()
{
    char input;

    cout << "Enter any character: ";
    cin.get(input);
    cout << "The character you entered is: " << input << endl;
    cout << "Its ASCII code is: " << int(input) << endl;
    if (isalpha(input))
        cout << "That's an alphabetic character.\n";
    if (isdigit(input))
        cout << "That's a numeric digit.\n";
    if (islower(input))
        cout << "The letter you entered is lowercase.\n";
    if (isupper(input))
        cout << "The letter you entered is uppercase.\n";
    if (isspace(input))
        cout << "That's a whitespace character.\n";
    return 0;
}
```

Program Output with Example Input Shown in Bold
```
Enter any character: A[Enter]
The character you entered is: A
Its ASCII code is: 65
That's an alphabetic character.
The letter you entered is uppercase.
```

Program Output with Other Example Input Shown in Bold
```
Enter any character: 7[Enter]
The character you entered is: 7
Its ASCII code is: 55
That's a numeric digit.
```

Program 12-10 shows a more practical application of the character-testing functions. It tests a seven-character customer number to determine whether it is in the proper format.

Program 12-10

```cpp
// This program tests a customer number to determine whether it is
// in the proper format.

#include <iostream>
#include <cctype>
using namespace std;

// Function prototype
bool testNum(char []);

int main()
{
    char customer[8];
    cout << "Enter a customer number in the form ";
    cout << "LLLNNNN\n";
    cout << "(LLL = letters and NNNN = numbers): ";
    cin.getline(customer, 8);
    if (testNum(customer))
        cout << "That's a valid customer number.\n";
    else
    {
        cout << "That is not the proper format of the ";
        cout << "customer number.\nHere is an example:\n";
        cout << "    ABC1234\n";
    }
    return 0;
}

//*************************************************************
// Definition of function testNum. This function accepts a   *
// character array as its argument and tests its contents    *
// for a valid customer number.                              *
//*************************************************************

bool testNum(char custNum[])
{
    int count;
    // Test the first three characters for alphabetic letters.
    for (count = 0; count < 3; count++)
    {
        if (!isalpha(custNum[count]))
            return false;
    }
    // Test the last four characters for numeric digits.
    for (count = 3; count < 7; count++)
    {
        if (!isdigit(custNum[count]))
            return false;
    }
    return true;
}
```

Program 12-10

Program Output with Example Input Shown in Bold
```
Enter a customer number in the form LLLNNNN
(LLL = letters and NNNN = numbers): RQS4567[Enter]
That's a valid customer number.
```

Program Output with Other Example Input Shown in Bold
```
Enter a customer number in the form LLLNNNN
(LLL = letters and NNNN = numbers): AX467T9[Enter]
That is not the proper format of the customer number.
Here is an example:
   ABC1234
```

In Program 12-10, the customer number is expected to consist of three alphabetic letters followed by four numeric digits. The `testNum` function accepts an array argument and tests the first three characters with the following loop:

```
for (count = 0; count < 3; count++)
{
    if (!isalpha(custNum[count]))
        return false;
}
```

The `isalpha` function returns `true` if its argument is an alphabetic character. The `!` operator is used in the `if` statement to determine whether the tested character is *not* alphabetic. If this is so for any of the first three characters, the function `testNum` returns 0.

Likewise, the next four characters are tested to be numeric digits with the following loop:

```
for (count = 3; count < 7; count++)
{
    if (!isdigit(custNum[count]))
        return false;
}
```

The `isdigit` function returns `true` if its argument is the character representation of any of the digits 0 through 9. Once again, the `!` operator is used to determine if the tested character is *not* a digit. If this is so for any of the last four characters, the function `testNum` returns `false`. If the customer number is in the proper format, the function will cycle through both the loops without returning `false`. In that case, the last line in the function is the `return true` statement, which indicates the customer number is valid.

12.5 Character Case Conversion

CONCEPT The C++ library offers functions for converting a character to upper- or lowercase.

The C++ library provides two functions, `toupper` and `tolower`, for converting the case of a character. The functions are described in Table 12-4. (These functions are prototyped in the header file `cctype`, so be sure to include it.)

Table 12-4

Function	Description
toupper	Returns the uppercase equivalent of its argument.
tolower	Returns the lowercase equivalent of its argument.

Each of the functions in Table 12-4 accepts a single character argument. If the argument is a lowercase letter, the `toupper` function returns its uppercase equivalent. For example, the following statement will display the character A on the screen:

```
cout << toupper('a');
```

If the argument is already an uppercase letter, `toupper` returns it unchanged. The following statement causes the character Z to be displayed:

```
cout << toupper('Z');
```

Any nonletter argument passed to `toupper` is returned as it is. Each of the following statements display `toupper`'s argument without any change:

```
cout << toupper('*');   // Displays *
cout << toupper ('&');  // Displays &
cout << toupper('%');   // Displays %
```

`toupper` and `tolower` don't actually cause the character argument to change, they simply return the upper- or lowercase equivalent of the argument. For example, in the following program segment, the variable `letter` is set to the value 'A'. The `tolower` function returns the character 'a', but `letter` still contains 'A'.

```
char letter = 'A';
cout << tolower(letter) << endl;
cout << letter << endl;
```

These statements will cause the following to be displayed:

```
a
A
```

Program 12-11 demonstrates the `toupper` function in a loop that lets the user enter either Y or N.

Program 12-11

```
// This program calculates the area of a circle. It asks the user
// if he or she wishes to continue. A loop that demonstrates the
// toupper function repeats until the user enters 'y', 'Y',
// 'n', or 'N'.

#include <iostream>
#include <cctype>
#include <iomanip>
using namespace std;

int main()
{
    const float pi = 3.14159;
    float radius;
    char go;

    cout << "This program calculates the area of a circle.\n";
    cout << setprecision(2);
    cout << fixed;
    do
    {
        cout << "Enter the circle's radius: ";
        cin >> radius;
        cout << "The area is " << (pi * radius * radius);
        cout << endl;
        do
        {
            cout << "Calculate another? (Y or N) ";
            cin >> go;
        } while (toupper(go) != 'Y' && toupper(go) != 'N');
    } while (toupper(go) == 'Y');
    return 0;
}
```

Program Output with Example Input Shown in Bold
```
This program calculates the area of a circle.
Enter the circle's radius: 10[Enter]
The area is 314.16
Calculate another? (Y or N) b[Enter]
Calculate another? (Y or N) y[Enter]
Enter the circle's radius: 1[Enter]
The area is 3.14
Calculate another? (Y or N) n[Enter]
```

Checkpoint [12.4–12.5]

12.13 Write a short description of each of the following functions:

    A) `isalpha`
    B) `isalnum`
    C) `isdigit`
    D) `islower`
    E) `isprint`
    F) `ispunct`
    G) `isupper`
    H) `isspace`
    I) `toupper`
    J) `tolower`

12.14 Write a statement that will convert the contents of the `char` variable `big` to lowercase. The converted value should be assigned to the variable `little`.

12.15 Write an `if` statement that will display the word "digit" if the variable `ch` contains a numeric digit. Otherwise, it should display "Not a digit."

12.16 What is the output of the following statement?

```
cout << toupper(tolower('A'));
```

12.17 Write a loop that asks the user "Do you want to repeat the program or quit? (R/Q)". The loop should repeat until the user has entered an R or Q, either uppercase or lowercase.

12.6 Writing Your Own C-String Handling Functions

CONCEPT You can design your own specialized functions for manipulating strings.

By being able to pass arrays as arguments, you can write your own functions for processing C-strings. For example, Program 12-12 uses a function to copy a C-string from one array to another.

Program 12-12

```
// This program uses a function to copy a C-string into an array.

#include <iostream>
using namspace std;

void stringCopy(char [], char []);              // Function prototype
```

(program continues)

Program 12-12 *(continued)*

```cpp
int main()
{
    char first[30], second[30];
    cout << "Enter a string with no more than 29 characters:\n";
    cin.getline(first, 30);
    stringCopy(first, second);
    cout << "The string you entered is:\n" << second << endl;
    return 0;
}

//**************************************************************
// Definition of the stringCopy function.                      *
// This function accepts two character arrays as               *
// arguments. The function assumes the two arrays              *
// contain C-strings. The contents of the first array are      *
// copied to the second array.                                 *
//**************************************************************

void stringCopy(char string1[], char string2[])
{
    int index = 0;
    while (string1[index] != '\0')
    {
        string2[index] = string1[index];
        index++;
    }
    string2[index] = '\0';
}
```

Program Output with Example Input Shown in Bold
```
Enter a string with no more than 29 characters:
```
Thank goodness it's Friday![Enter]
```
The string you entered is:
Thank goodness it's Friday!
```

Notice the function `stringCopy` in Program 12-12 does not accept an argument indicating the size of the arrays. It simply copies the characters from `string1` into `string2` until it encounters a null terminator in `string1`. When the null terminator is found, the loop has reached the end of the C-string. The last statement in the function assigns a null terminator (the `'\0'` character) to the end of `string2`, so it is properly terminated.

 WARNING! Since the `stringCopy` function doesn't know the size of the second array, it's the programmer's responsibility to make sure the second array is large enough to hold the string in the first array.

Program 12-13 uses another C-string handling function: nameSlice. The program asks the user to enter his or her first and last names, separated by a space. The function searches the string for the space and replaces it with a null terminator. In effect, this cuts off the last name of the string.

Program 12-13

```cpp
// This program uses the function nameSlice to cut off the last
// name of a string that contains the user's first and
// last names.

#include <iostream>
using namespace std;

void nameSlice(char []);        // Function prototype

int main()
{
    char name[41];
    cout << "Enter your first and last names, separated ";
    cout << "by a space:\n";
    cin.getline(name, 41);
    nameSlice(name);
    cout << "Your first name is: " << name << endl;
    return 0;
}

//*****************************************************************
// Definition of function nameSlice. This function accepts a     *
// character array as its argument. It scans the array looking   *
// for a space. When it finds one, it replaces it with a null    *
// terminator.                                                   *
//*****************************************************************

void nameSlice(char userName[])
{
    int count = 0;
    while (userName[count] != ' ' && userName[count] != '\0')
        count++;
    if (userName[count] == ' ')
        userName[count] = '\0';
}
```

Program Output with Example Input Shown in Bold

```
Enter your first and last names, separated by a space:
```
Jimmy Jones[Enter]
```
Your first name is: Jimmy
```

The following loop in `nameSlice` starts at the first character in the array and scans the string, searching for either a space or a null terminator:

```
while (userName[count] != ' ' && userName[count] != '\0')
    count++;
```

If the character in `userName[count]` isn't a space or the null terminator, `count` is incremented, and the next character is examined. With the example input "`Jimmy Jones`," the loop finds the space separating "`Jimmy`" and "`Jones`" at `userName[5]`. When the loop stops, `count` is set to 5. This is illustrated in Figure 12-4.

The loop stops when `count` reaches 5 because `userName[5]` contains a space

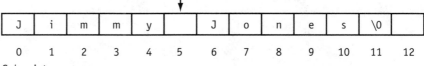

Figure 12-4   Subscripts

 Note: The loop will also stop if it encounters a null terminator. This is so it will not go beyond the boundary of the array if the user didn't enter a space.

Once the loop has finished, `userName[count]` will either contain a space or a null terminator. If it contains a space, the following `if` statement replaces it with a null terminator:

```
if (userName[count] == ' ')
    userName[count] = '\0';
```

This is illustrated in Figure 12-5.

The space is replaced with a null terminator. This now becomes the end of the string.

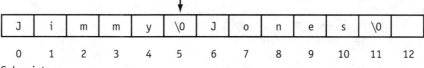

Figure 12-5   Subscripts

The new null terminator now becomes the end of the string.

Using Pointers to Pass C-String Arguments

Pointers are extremely useful for writing functions that process C-strings. If the starting address of a string is passed into a pointer parameter variable, it can be assumed that all the characters, from that address up to the byte that holds the null terminator are part of the string. (It isn't necessary to know the length of the array that holds the string.)

Program 12-14 demonstrates a function, `countChars`, that uses a pointer to count the number of times a specific character appears in a C-string.

Program 12-14

```
// This program demonstrates a function, countChars, that counts
// the number of times a specific character appears in a string.

#include <iostream>
using namespace std;

// Function prototype
int countChars(char *, char);

int main()
{
    char userString[51], letter;
    cout << "Enter a string (up to 50 characters): ";
    cin.getline(userString, 51);
    cout << "Enter a character and I will tell you how many\n";
    cout << "times it appears in the string: ";
    cin >> letter;
    cout << letter << " appears ";
    cout << countChars(userString, letter) << " times.\n";
    return 0;
}

//***************************************************************
// Definition of countChars. The parameter strPtr is a pointer  *
// that points to a string. The parameter ch is a character that *
// the function searches for in the string. The function returns *
// the number of times the character appears in the string.      *
//***************************************************************

int countChars(char *strPtr, char ch)
{
    int times = 0;
    while (*strPtr != '\0')
    {
        if (*strPtr == ch)
            times++;
        strPtr++;
    }
    return times;
}
```

Program Output with Example Input Shown in Bold

```
Enter a string (up to 50 characters): Starting Out With C++[Enter]
Enter a character and I will tell you how many
times it appears in the string: t[Enter]
t appears 4 times.
```

In the function `countChars`, `strPtr` points to the C-string that is to be searched and `ch` contains the character to look for. The `while` loop repeats as long the character `strPtr` points to is not the null terminator:

```
while (*strPtr != '\0')
```

Inside the loop, the following `if` statement compares the character that `strPtr` points to with the character in `ch`:

```
if (*strPtr == ch)
```

If the two are equal, the variable `times` is incremented. (`times` keeps a running total of the number of times the character appears.) The last statement in the loop is

```
strPtr++;
```

This statement increments the address in `strPtr`. This causes `strPtr` to point to the next character in the string. Then the loop starts over. When `strPtr` finally reaches the null terminator, the loop terminates and the function returns the value in `times`.

Checkpoint [12.6]

12.18 What is the output of the following program?

```cpp
#include <iostream>
using namespace std;

// Function prototype
void mess(char []);

int main()
{
    char stuff[] = "Tom Talbert Tried Trains";

    cout << stuff << endl;
    mess(stuff);
    cout << stuff << endl;
    return 0;
}

// Definition of function mess
void mess(char str[])
{
    int step = 0;

    while (str[step] != '\0')
    {
        if (str[step] == 'T')
            str[step] = 'D';
        step++;
    }
}
```

12.7 Focus on Problem Solving and Program Design: A Business Case Study

CONCEPT	This case study demonstrates how C-string manipulation may be used in a program that works primarily with text.

You have been hired as a contract programmer by the Smithfield Natural Gas company. Your first job is to write a program that prints a form letter to customers with an overdue account. The letter should have the form shown in Figure 12-6. When the letter is printed by your program, however, the fields shown in brackets will be replaced by actual values.

```
Dear <Salutation> <Last-Name>:

Our records show that your account has a balance of $<Balance> and
a past-due amount of $<Past-Due>. Your last payment was on <Date>.
Since we haven't heard from you in some time, would you please take
a moment to send us a check for the past-due amount? We value your
business and look forward to serving you in the future.

Sincerely,
The Management

P.S. If you've already sent your payment, ignore this reminder.
```

Figure 12-6

Inside the letter, the fields listed in Table 12-5 are shown in brackets.

Table 12-5

Field	Description
Salutation	Salutation (either Mr. or Ms.)
Last-Name	The customer's last name
Balance	The customer's total account balance
Past-Due	The amount the account is past due
Date	The date the customer last made a payment

Before the letter is printed, your program should ask the user to enter values for the fields listed in Table 12-5. The values should then be inserted into the form letter as it is being printed. The program should perform word-wrap, which means the sentences should be adjusted so no word is split between two lines. Additionally, the letter should have 10-character left and right margins.

You decide to create a class, `FormLetter`, that will process the form letter. The class declaration is as follows.

```
class FormLetter
{
private:
    // Declare arrays to hold portions
    // of the form letter.
    char    part1[6],
            part2[54],
            part3[28],
            part4[26],
            part5[200],
            part6[12],
            part7[17],
            part8[64];
    // Declare arrays to hold the fields.
    char    salutation[4],
            lastName[20],
            balance[20],
            pastDue[20],
            lastPayment[20];
public:
    FormLetter();
    void setFields(char *, char *, char *, char *, char *);
    void printLetter();
    void printLine(char *, int &);
};
```

Table 12-6 lists and describes the class's member variables.

Table 12-6

Variable	Description
part1...part8	Eight global character arrays that hold portions of the form letter
salutation	A character array to hold the salutation
lastName	A character array to hold the customer's last name
lastPayment	A character array to hold the date of the last payment
balance	A character array to hold the text representation of the account balance
pastDue	A character array to hold the text representation of the past-due amount

Table 12-7 lists the class's member functions.

Table 12-7

Member Function	Description
Constructor	The constructor initializes the eight member character arrays (part1 through part8) with strings. The strings are the parts of the form letter that always stay the same.
setFields	Accepts arguments that are to be stored in the form letter fields.
printLetter	Controls the printing of the form letter once the fields have been input by the user. Calls the printLine member function.
printLine	Prints a line of text starting at the current printing position. This function performs word-wrap near the end of a line.

Let's look at each member function in more detail.

The Constructor

The constructor uses the strcpy function to store in the arrays part1 through part8, the parts of the form letter that always stay the same. The constructor's code is as follows:

```
FormLetter::FormLetter()
{
    // Setup part1 through part4.
    strcpy(part1, "Dear ");
    strcpy(part2, "Our records show that your account has a balance of $");
    strcpy(part3, " and a past-due amount of $");
    strcpy(part4, "Your last payment was on ");

    // Setup part5.
    strcpy(part5, "Since we haven't heard from you in some");
    strcat(part5, " time, would you please take a moment to send");
    strcat(part5, " us a check for the past-due amount? We value");
    strcat(part5, " your business and look forward to serving you");
    strcat(part5, " in the future.\n\n");

    // Setup part6 and part7.
    strcpy(part6, "Sincerely,\n");
    strcpy(part7, "The Management\n\n");

    // Setup part8.
    strcpy(part8, "P.S. If you've already sent your payment, ignore");
    strcat(part8, " this reminder.");
}
```

The `setFields` Member Function

The `setFields` member function accepts arguments whose values are stored in the member variables `salutation`, `lastName`, `lastPayment`, `balance`, and `pastDue`. These variables hold the fields that are printed in the form letter. The function's code is as follows:

```
void FormLetter::setFields(char *sal, char *lname,
                           char *bal, char *due, char *lastPay)
{
    strcpy(salutation, sal);
    strcpy(lastName, lname);
    strcpy(balance, bal);
    strcpy(pastDue, due);
    strcpy(lastPayment, lastPay);
}
```

The `printLetter` Member Function

The `printLetter` member function controls the printing of the letter. It has one local variable, `position`, which is an integer. This variable keeps track of the number of characters printed on the current line. This is crucial information for the `printLine` function, which performs word-wrap. Here is the function's pseudocode. (It might help you to refer to the contents of the arrays `part1` through `part8` as you read the code.)

```
// First print the salutation part of the letter.
Set the position variable to zero (for printLine).
Call printLine to print the part1 array.
Print the salutation, followed by a space, followed by the
customer's last name, followed by a colon.
// Next print the body of the letter.
Set the position variable to zero.
Call printLine to print the part2 array.
Print the customer's balance.
Adjust the position variable.
Call printLine to print the part3 array.
Print the past-due amount.
Adjust the position variable.
Call printLine to print the part4 array.
Print the date of the last payment.
Adjust the position variable.
Call printLine to print the part5 array.
// Next print the letter's closing.
Set the position variable to zero (to start a new line.)
Call printLine to print the part6 array.
Set the position variable to zero (to start a new line).
Call printLine to print the part7 array.
// Last, print the PS reminder.
Set the position variable to zero (to start a new line).
Call printLine to print the part8 array.
```

The `printLine` function updates the `position` variable. When `printLetter` prints one of the fields, such as `balance`, it must adjust the position variable. This is so the `printLine` function will accurately detect the end of each line. Notice that every time a new line is to be started, `position` is reset to zero. Here is the C++ code for the function:

```cpp
void FormLetter::printLetter()
{
    int position;

    // Print the salutation part of the letter.
    position = 0;                     // Start a new line.
    printLine(part1, position);
    cout << salutation << " " << lastName << ":" << endl << endl;

    // Print the body of the letter.
    position = 0;                     // Start a new line.
    printLine(part2, position);
    cout << balance;                  // Print account balance.

    // Add length of balance to position.
    position += strlen(balance);
    printLine(part3, position);
    cout << pastDue << ". ";          // Print past-due amount.

    // Add length of pastDue and the period and space at the
    // end of the sentence to position.
    position += strlen(pastDue)+ 2;
    printLine(part4, position);
    cout << lastPayment << ". ";      // Print date of last payment.

    // Now add length of lastPay and the period and space at the
    // end of the sentence to position.
    position += strlen(lastPayment) + 2;
    printLine(part5, position);

    // Print the closing.
    position = 0;                     // Start a new line.
    printLine(part6, position);
    position = 0;                     // Start a new line.
    printLine(part7, position);

    // Print the PS reminder.
    position = 0;                     // Start a new line.
    printLine(part8, position);
}
```

The `printLine` Member Function

The `printLine` member function prints each individual line of the letter. It takes two arguments: the address of the string that is to be printed on the line and the variable used to store the number of characters printed (the `position` variable). The number of characters printed on the line is important because the program must perform word-wrap. This happens when the word being printed at the end of a line will not entirely fit. Instead of printing part of the word on one line and then continuing it on the next line, the program is to start the word on the next line. Here is the function's pseudocode:

```
If the line is at or past the right margin
    Start a new line.
End If.
While not at the end of the string
    If 60 or more characters have been printed AND the next
    character is a space
        Perform word-wrap.
    End If.
    If at the beginning of a new line
        Print the left margin (10 spaces).
        Add 10 to the number of characters printed.
    End If.
    Print the next character.
    Add one to the number of characters printed.
End While.
```

The first `if` statement simply checks to see whether the current printing position is at or beyond the right margin. Since the letter has 10-character margins, any position beyond the seventieth character is in the right margin.

Inside the `while` loop another `if` statement checks to see if 60 or more characters have been printed. This is the part that controls word-wrap. The function begins watching for a space separating words at the sixtieth character. If a break between two words appears anywhere after the sixtieth character, a new line is started. The next `if` statement checks to see whether a new line has begun. If so, it prints the 10 spaces that make the left margin. After all this has taken place, the next character is printed and the character count is incremented.

Here is the C++ code for the function:

```cpp
void FormLetter::printLine(char *line, int &startCount)
{
    int charCount = 0;

    if (startCount >= 70)    // If the line is already at
    {                        // or past the right margin...
        cout << "\n";        // Start a new line.
        startCount = 0;      // Reset startCount.
    }
```

```
// The following while loop cycles through the string
// printing it one character at a time. It watches for
// spaces after the 60th position so word-wrap may be
// performed.
while (line[charCount] != '\0')
{
    if (startCount >= 60 && line[charCount] == ' ')
    {
        cout << "            \n";// Print right margin.
        charCount++;            // Skip over the space.
        startCount = 0;
    }
    if (startCount == 0)
    {
        cout << "            "; // Print left margin.
        startCount = 10;
    }
    cout.put(line[charCount]);// Print the character.
    charCount++;              // Update subscript.
    startCount++;             // Update position counter.
}
}
```

 Note: The `startCount` parameter is a reference to the `position` variable in the `printLetter` function.

Modules

The program will consist of the functions listed in Table 12-8.

Table 12-8

Function	Description
main	The program's `main` function. Calls the `getInfo` and `printLetter` functions.
getInfo	Calls the `getSal` function to get the salutation. Then asks the user to enter the customer's last name, account balance, past-due amount, and date of last payment.
getSal	Prints a menu allowing the user to select either Mr. or Ms. as the salutation.

Function `main`

Function `main` contains its own array declarations for the salutation, last name, date of last payment, account balance, and past due amount. A `do-while` loop calls the `getInfo` and `printLetter` functions. The loop repeats as long as the user wishes to print form letters. Here is the pseudocode:

```
Do
    Call getInfo to get the salutation, last name, balance, past-due amount,
    and date of last payment from the user.
```

Call the FormLetter setFields member function.
Call the FormLetter printLetter member function.
Ask the user if another letter is to be printed.
While the user wants to print another letter.

Here is the function's actual C++ code:

```cpp
int main()
{
    char salutation[4], lastName[16], lastPayment[9],
        balance[9], pastdue[9], again;
    FormLetter letter;

    do
    {
        // Call getInfo to get input from the user.
        getInfo(salutation, lastName, balance, pastdue,
            lastPayment);
        cout << "\n\n";
        // Set the form letter fields.
        letter.setFields(salutation, lastName, balance, pastDue,
                lastPayment);
        // Now print the form letter.
        letter.printLetter();
        cout << "\n\nDo another letter? (Y/N) ";
        cin >> again;
    } while (toupper(again) == 'Y');
    return 0;
}
```

The getInfo Function

This function first calls the getSal function (to get the salutation), then asks the user to enter the customer's last name, account balance, past-due amount, and the date of the last payment. These values are then stored in the arrays whose addresses are passed into the function as arguments. Here is the pseudocode:

Call getSal.
Ask the user to enter the customer's last name.
Convert the first character of the last name to uppercase.
Ask the user to enter the customer's account balance.
Ask the user to enter the account's past-due amount.
Ask the user to enter the date of the last payment.

Notice that after the user enters the customer's last name, the function automatically converts its first character to upper case. This is in case the user entered the name in all lowercase. Here is the function's C++ code:

```
void getInfo(char *sal, char *lname, char *bal, char *due, char *lastPay)
{
    getSal(sal);
    cout << "Last name: ";
    cin >> lname;
    lname[0] = toupper(lname[0]);
    cout << "Account balance: ";
    cin >> bal;
    cout << "Past-due amount: ";
    cin >> due;
    cout << "Date of last payment: ";
    cin >> lastPay;
}
```

The getSal Function

This function displays a menu allowing the user to select a salutation, either Mr. or Ms. The choice is then stored in the array whose address is passed into the function as an argument. Here is the pseudocode:

```
Do
Display menu with choice 1 being Mr. and choice 2 being Ms.
Ask user to select a salutation.
While the user does not select 1 or 2 from the menu.
    If the user selected 1
        The salutation is Mr.
    else
        The salutation is Ms.
End If.
```

Here is the function's C++ code:

```
void getSal(char *sal)
{
    int choice;
    do
    {
        cout << "Salutation:\n";
        cout << "\t1) Mr.\n";
        cout << "\t2) Ms.\n";
        cout << "Select one: ";
        cin >> choice;
    } while (choice != 1 && choice != 2);
    if (choice == 1)
        strcpy(sal, "Mr.");
    else
        strcpy(sal, "Ms.");
}
```

The Entire Program

Program 12-15 shows the entire program's source code.

Program 12-15

Contents of `formletter.h`
```
#ifndef FORMLETTER_H
#define FORMLETTER_H

class FormLetter
{
private:
    // Declare arrays to hold portions
    // of the form letter.
    char    part1[6],
            part2[54],
            part3[28],
            part4[26],
            part5[200],
            part6[12],
            part7[17],
            part8[64];
    // Declare arrays to hold the fields.
    char    salutation[4],
            lastName[20],
            balance[20],
            pastDue[20],
            lastPayment[20];
public:
    FormLetter();
    void setFields(char *, char *, char *, char *, char *);
    void printLetter();
    void printLine(char *, int &);
};

#endif
```

Contents of `formletter.cpp`
```
#include <iostream>
#include <cstring>
#include "formletter.h"
using namespace std;

//**************************************************************
// Constructor.                                                *
// This function initializes the char arrays part1 through     *
// part8 with the strings that make up the form letter.        *
//**************************************************************
```

(program continues)

Program 12-15   *(continued)*

```cpp
FormLetter::FormLetter()
{
    // Set up part1 through part4.
    strcpy(part1, "Dear ");
    strcpy(part2, "Our records show that your account has a balance of $");
    strcpy(part3, " and a past-due amount of $");
    strcpy(part4, "Your last payment was on ");

    // Set up part5.
    strcpy(part5, "Since we haven't heard from you in some");
    strcat(part5, " time, would you please take a moment to send");
    strcat(part5, " us a check for the past-due amount? We value");
    strcat(part5, " your business and look forward to serving you");
    strcat(part5, " in the future.\n\n");

    // Set up part6 and part7.
    strcpy(part6, "Sincerely,\n");
    strcpy(part7, "The Management\n\n");

    // Set up part8.
    strcpy(part8, "P.S. If you've already sent your payment, ignore");
    strcat(part8, " this reminder.");
}
//*************************************************************
// Member function setFields.                                *
// This function stores values in the form letter fields.    *
//*************************************************************

void FormLetter::setFields(char *sal, char *lname, char *bal, char *due,
              char *lastPay)
{
    strcpy(salutation, sal);
    strcpy(lastName, lname);
    strcpy(balance, bal);
    strcpy(pastDue, due);
    strcpy(lastPayment, lastPay);
}


//*********************************************
// Member function printLetter.              *
// This function prints the form letter.     *
//*********************************************

void FormLetter::printLetter()
{
    int position;
```

(program continues)

Program 12-15 *(continued)*

```
// Print the salutation part of the letter
position = 0;                     // Start a new line.
printLine(part1, position);
cout << salutation << " " << lastName << ":" << endl << endl;
// Print the body of the letter.
position = 0;                     // Start a new line.
printLine(part2, position);
cout << balance;                  // Print account balance.

// Add length of balance to position.
position += strlen(balance);
printLine(part3, position);
cout << pastDue << ". ";          // Print past-due amount.

// Add length of pastDue and the period and space at the
// end of the sentence to position.
position += strlen(pastDue)+ 2;
printLine(part4, position);
cout << lastPayment << ". ";      // Print date of last payment.

// Now add length of lastPay and the period and space at the
// end of the sentence to position.
position += strlen(lastPayment) + 2;
printLine(part5, position);

// Print the closing.
position = 0;                     // Start a new line.
printLine(part6, position);
position = 0;                     // Start a new line.
printLine(part7, position);

// Print the PS reminder.
position = 0;                     // Start a new line.
printLine(part8, position);
}

//*********************************************************************
// Member function printLine.                                        *
// This function has two parameters: line and startCount.            *
// The string pointed to by line is printed. startCount is the       *
// starting position of the line in an 80 character field. There     *
// are 10-character left and right margins within the 80             *
// character field. The function performs word-wrap by looking       *
// for space character within the line at or after the 60th          *
// character. A new line is started when a space is found or the      *
// end of the field is reached.                                      *
//*********************************************************************
```

(program continues)

Program 12-15 *(continued)*

```cpp
void FormLetter::printLine(char *line, int &startCount)
{
    int charCount = 0;

    if (startCount >= 70)       // If the line is already at
    {                           // or past the right margin...
        cout << "\n";           // Start a new line.
        startCount = 0;         // Reset startCount.
    }

    // The following while loop cycles through the string
    // printing it one character at a time. It watches for
    // spaces after the 60th position so word-wrap may be
    // performed.

    while (line[charCount] != '\0')
    {
        if (startCount >= 60 && line[charCount] == ' ')
        {
            cout << "            \n";    // Print right margin.
            charCount++;                // Skip over the space
            startCount = 0;
        }
        if (startCount == 0)
        {
            cout << "          ";       // Print left margin.
            startCount = 10;
        }
        cout.put(line[charCount]);      // Print the character.
        charCount++;                    // Update subscript.
        startCount++;                   // Update position counter.
    }
}
```

Contents of main program pr12-15.cpp
```cpp
// This program prints a simple form letter reminding a customer
// of an overdue account balance.

#include <iostream>
#include <cctype>
#include <cstring>
#include "formletter.h"
using namespace std;

// Function prototypes
void getInfo(char *, char *, char *, char *, char *);
void getSal(char *);
```

(program continues)

Program 12-15 *(continued)*

```
int main()
{
    char salutation[4], lastName[16], lastPayment[9],
        balance[9], pastdue[9], again;
    FormLetter letter;

    do
    {
        // Call getInfo to get input from the user.
        getInfo(salutation, lastName, balance, pastdue,
            lastPayment);
        cout << "\n\n";
        // Set the form letter fields.
        letter.setFields(salutation, lastName, balance, pastDue,
                lastPayment);
        // Now print the form letter.
        letter.printLetter();
        cout << "\n\nDo another letter? (Y/N) ";
        cin >> again;
    } while (toupper(again) == 'Y');
    return 0;
}

//****************************************************************
// Definition of function getInfo.                              *
// This function allows the user to enter the following items:  *
// salutation, last name, account balance, past due amount, and *
// date of last payment. The function arguments are pointers to *
// strings where the input will be stored.                      *
//****************************************************************

void getInfo(char *sal, char *lname, char *bal, char *due,
            char *lastPay)
{
    getSal(sal);
    cout << "Last name: ";
    cin >> lname;
    lname[0] = toupper(lname[0]);
    cout << "Account balance: ";
    cin >> bal;
    cout << "Past due amount: ";
    cin >> due;
    cout << "Date of last payment: ";
    cin >> lastPay;
}
```

(program continues)

Program 12-15   *(continued)*

```
//******************************************************************
//                                                                *
// Definition of function getSal.                                 *
// This function gives the user a menu from which to pick a       *
// suitable title for the letter's addressee. The choices are     *
// Mr. and Ms. The choice will be copied to the address pointed   *
// to by sal.                                                     *
//******************************************************************

void getSal(char *sal)
{
    int choice;

    do
    {
        cout << "Salutation:\n";
        cout << "\t1) Mr.\n";
        cout << "\t2) Ms.\n";
        cout << "Select one: ";
        cin >> choice;
    } while (choice != 1 && choice != 2);
    if (choice == 1)
        strcpy(sal, "Mr.");
    else
        strcpy(sal, "Ms.");
}
```

Program Output with Example Input Shown in Bold
```
Salutation:
    1) Mr.
    2) Ms.
Select one: 1[Enter]
Last name: Jones[Enter]
Account balance: 267.98[Enter]
Past-due amount: 57.13[Enter]
Date of last payment: 2/14/02[Enter]

Dear Mr. Jones:

Our records show that your account has a balance of
$267.98 and a past-due amount of $57.13. Your last
payment was on 2/14/02. Since we haven't heard from
you in some time, would you please take a moment to
send us a check for the past-due amount? We value your
business and look forward to serving you in the future.
```

(program output continues)

Program 12-15 *(continued)*

```
Sincerely,
The Management

P.S. If you've already sent your payment, ignore this
letter.

Do another letter? (Y/N) y[Enter]
Salutation:
    1) Mr.
    2) Ms.
Select one: 2[Enter]
Last name: Hildebrand[Enter]
Account balance: 4,598.00[Enter]
Past-due Amount: 1,367.00[Enter]
Date of last payment: 11/23/01[Enter]

Dear Ms. Hildebrand:

Our records show that your account has a balance of
$4,598.00 and a past-due amount of $1,367.00. Your
last payment was on 01/23/02. Since we haven't heard
from you in some time, would you please take a moment
to send us a check for the past-due amount? We value
your business and look forward to serving you in the
future.

Sincerely,
The Management

P.S. If you've already sent your payment, ignore this
letter.

Do another letter? (Y/N) n[Enter]
```

12.8 More About the C++ string Class

From an ease-of-programming point of view, the standard library string class offers several advantages over C-strings. As you have seen throughout this text, the string class has several member functions and overloaded operators. These simplify tasks, such as locating a character or string within a string, that are difficult and tedious to perform with C-strings. In this section we review some basic operations with strings, then discuss more of the string class's member functions.

Any program using the string class must #include the string header file. String objects may then be created using any of several constructors. Program 12-16 provides a simple demonstration.

Program 12-16

```
// This program demonstrates the C++ string class.

#include <iostream>
#include <string>
using namespace std;

int main()
{
    string greeting;
    string name("William Smith");

    greeting = "Hello ";
    cout << greeting << name << endl;
    return 0;
}
```

Program Output
```
Hello William Smith
```

Other examples of the use of string constructors are given in Table 12-9.

Table 12-9

Definition	Description
string address;	Defines an empty string object named address.
string name("William Smith");	Defines a string object named name, initialized with "William Smith."
string person1(person2);	Defines a string object named person1, which is a copy of person2. person2 may be either a string object or character array.
string set1(set2, 5);	Defines a string object named set1, which is initialized to the first five characters in the character array set2.
string lineFull('z', 10);	Defines a string object named lineFull initialized with 10 'z' characters.
string firstName(fullName, 0, 7);	Defines a string object named firstName, initialized with a substring of the string fullName. The substring is seven characters long, beginning at position 0.

Notice in Program 12-16 the use of the = operator to assign a value to the string object. The string class overloads several operators, which are described in Table 12-10.

Table 12-10

Overloaded Operator	Description
>>	Extracts characters from a stream and inserts them into the string. Characters are copied until a whitespace or the end of the string is encountered.
<<	Inserts the string into a stream.
=	Assigns the string on the right to the string object on the left.
+=	Appends a copy of the string on the right to the string object on the left.
+	Returns a string that is the concatenation of the two string operands.
[]	Implements array-subscript notation, as in `name[x]`. A reference to the character in the x position is returned.
Relational Operators	Each of the relational operators are implemented:
	< > <= >= == !=

Program 12-17 demonstrates some of the `string` operators.

Program 12-17

```
// This program demonstrates the C++ string class.

#include <iostream>
#include <string>
using namespace std;

int main()
{
    string str1, str2, str3;
    str1 = "ABC";
    str2 = "DEF";
    str3 = str1 + str2;
    cout << str1 << endl;
    cout << str2 << endl;
    cout << str3 << endl;
    str3 += "GHI";
    cout << str3 << endl;
    return 0;
}
```

Program Output
```
ABC
DEF
ABCDEF
ABCDEFGHI
```

The string class also has several member functions. For example, the size function returns the length of the string. It is demonstrated in the for loop in Program 12-18.

Program 12-18

```cpp
// This program demonstrates the C++ string class.

#include <iostream>
#include <string>
using namespace std;

int main()
{
    string str1, str2, str3;
    str1 = "ABC";
    str2 = "DEF";
    str3 = str1 + str2;
    for (int x = 0; x < str3.size(); x++)
        cout << str3[x];
    cout << endl;
    if (str1 < str2)
        cout << "str1 is less than str2\n";
    else
        cout << "str1 is not less than str2\n";
    return 0;
}
```

Program Output
```
ABCDEF
str1 is less than str2
```

Table 12-11 lists many of the string class member functions and their overloaded variations.

Table 12-11

Member Function Example	Description
theString.append(str);	Appends str to theString. str can be a string object or character array.
theString.append(str, x, n);	n number of characters from str, starting at position x, are appended to theString. If theString is too small, the function will copy as many characters as possible.
theString.append(str, n);	The first n characters of the character array str are appended to theString.
theString.append(n, 'z');	Appends n copies of 'z' to theString.

(table continues)

Table 12-11 *(continued)*

Member Function Example	Description
`theString.assign(str);`	Assigns `str` to `theString`. The parameter `str` can be a string object or a C-string.
`theString.assign(str, x, n);`	n number of characters from `str`, starting at position x, are assigned to `theString`. If `theString` is too small, the function will copy as many characters as possible.
`theString.assign(str, n);`	The first n characters of the character array `str` are assigned to `theString`.
`theString.assign(n, 'z');`	Assigns n copies of `'z'` to `theString`.
`theString.at(x);`	Returns the character at position x in the string.
`theString.begin();`	Returns an iterator pointing to the first character in the string. (For more information on iterators, see Chapter 15.)
`theString.capacity();`	Returns the size of the storage allocated for the string.
`theString.clear();`	Clears the string by deleting all the characters stored in it.
`theString.compare(str);`	Performs a comparison like the `strcmp` function with the same return values. `str` can be a string object or a character array.
`theString.compare(x, n, str);`	Compares `theString` and `str`, starting at position x, and continuing for n characters. The return value is like strcmp. `str` can be a string object or character array.
`theString.copy(str, x, n);`	Copies the character array `str` to `theString`, beginning at position x, for n characters. If `theString` is too small, the function will copy as many characters as possible.
`theString.c_str();`	Returns the C-string value of the `string` object.
`theString.data();`	Returns a character array containing a null terminated string, as stored in `theString`.
`theString.empty();`	Returns true if `theString` is empty.
`theString.end();`	Returns an iterator pointing to the last character of the string in `theString`. (For more information on iterators, see Chapter 15.)
`theString.erase(x, n);`	Erases n characters from `theString`, beginning at position x.

(table continues)

Table 12-11 *(continued)*

Member Function Example	Description
`theString.find(str, x);`	Returns the first position at or beyond position x where the string str is found in theString. The parameter str may be either a string object or a C-string. If str is not found, a position beyond the end of theString is returned.
`theString.find('z', x);`	Returns the first position at or beyond position x where 'z' is found in theString.
`theString.insert(x, str);`	Inserts a copy of str into theString, beginning at position x. str may be either a string object or a character array.
`theString.insert(x, n, 'z');`	Inserts 'z' n times into theString at position x.
`theString.length();`	Returns the length of the string in theString.
`theString.replace(x, n, str);`	Replaces the n characters in theString beginning at position x with the characters in string object str.
`theString.resize(n, 'z');`	Changes the size of the allocation in theString to n. If n is less than the current size of the string, the string is truncated to n characters. If n is greater, the string is expanded and 'z' is appended at the end enough times to fill the new spaces.
`theString.size();`	Returns the length of the string in theString.
`theString.substr(x, n);`	Returns a copy of a substring. The substring is n characters long and begins at position x of theString.
`theString.swap(str);`	Swaps the contents of theString with str.

12.9 Creating Your Own String Class

CONCEPT This section demonstrates some of the programming techniques used to create the C++ string class.

The C++ string class automatically handles many of the tedious tasks involved in using strings, such as dynamic memory allocation and bounds checking. It also overloads operators such as + and =, and offers many member functions that ease the job of working with strings. In this section, we create a string data type with much of the functionality of the C++ class. In the process, we see examples of copy constructors and overloaded operators in full action, as well as examples of programming techniques that are useful in the solution of many problems.

The `MyString` Class

The `MyString` class defined in this section is an abstract data type for handling strings. It has many of the advantages possessed by the C++ `string` class provided by the Standard Template Library:

- Memory is dynamically allocated for any string stored in a `MyString` object. The programmer using this class doesn't need to be concerned with how large to make an array.

- Strings may be assigned to a `MyString` object with the = operator. The programmer using this class does not have to call the `strcpy` function.

- One string may be concatenated to another with the += operator. This eliminates the need for the `strcat` function.

- Strings may be tested for equality with the == operator. The programmer using this class doesn't have to call the `strcmp` function.

The following program listings show the class implementation.

Contents of `mystring.h`

```
#ifndef MYSTRING_H
#define MYSTRING_H

#include <iostream>
#include <cstring>  // For string library functions
#include <cstdlib>  // For exit() function
using namespace std;

// The following declarations are needed
// by some compilers.
class MyString;     // Forward declaration.
ostream &operator<<(ostream &, MyString &);
istream &operator>>(istream &, MyString &);

// MyString class: An abstract data type
// for handling strings.
class MyString
{
private:
   char *str;
   int len;
public:
   MyString() { str = NULL; len = 0; }
   MyString(char *);
   MyString(MyString &); // Copy constructor
      ~MyString() { if (len != 0) delete [] str; }
   int length() { return len; }
   char *getValue() { return str; };
   MyString operator+=(MyString &);
```

```
        MyString operator+=(const char *);
        MyString operator=(MyString &);
        MyString operator=(const char *);
        bool operator==(MyString &);
        bool operator==(const char *);
        bool operator!=(MyString &);
        bool operator!=(const char *);
        bool operator>(MyString &);
        bool operator>(const char *);
        bool operator<(MyString &);
        bool operator<(const char *);
        bool operator>=(MyString &);
        bool operator>=(const char*);
        bool operator<=(MyString &);
        bool operator<=(const char *);
        friend ostream &operator<<(ostream &, MyString &);
        friend istream &operator>>(istream &, MyString &);
    };

    #endif
```

Contents of mystring.cpp

```
    #include "mystring.h"

    //****************************************************
    // Constructor to initialize the str member         *
    // with a string constant.                          *
    //****************************************************

    MyString::MyString(char *sptr)
    {
        len = strlen(sptr);
        str = new char[len + 1];
        strcpy(str, sptr);
    }

    //****************************************************
    // Copy constructor                                 *
    //****************************************************

    MyString::MyString(MyString &right)
    {
        str = new char[right.length() + 1];
        strcpy(str, right.getValue());
        len = right.length();
    }

    //****************************************************
    // Overloaded = operator. Called when operand       *
    // on the right is another MyString object.         *
    // Returns the calling object.                      *
    //****************************************************
```

```
MyString MyString::operator=(MyString &right)
{
   if (len != 0)
      delete [] str;
   str = new char[right.length() + 1];
   strcpy(str, right.getValue());
   len = right.length();
   return *this;
}

//**************************************************
// Overloaded = operator. Called when operand     *
// on the right is a string.                       *
// Returns the calling object.                     *
//**************************************************

MyString MyString::operator=(const char *right)
{
   if (len != 0)
      delete [] str;
   len = strlen(right);
   str = new char[len + 1];
   strcpy(str, right);
   return *this;
}

//***************************************************
// Overloaded += operator. Called when operand      *
// on the right is another MyString object.         *
// Concatenates the str member of right to the      *
// str member of the calling object. Returns the    *
// calling object.                                  *
//***************************************************

MyString MyString::operator+=(MyString &right)
{
   char *temp = str;

   str = new char[strlen(str) + right.length() + 1];
   strcpy(str, temp);
   strcat(str, right.getValue());
   if (len != 0)
      delete [] temp;
   len = strlen(str);
   return *this;
}
```

```
//********************************************************
// Overloaded += operator. Called when operand          *
// on the right is a string. Concatenates the           *
// string right to the str member of                    *
// the calling object.                                  *
// Returns the  the calling object.                     *
//********************************************************

MyString MyString::operator+=(const char *right)
{
    char *temp = str;

    str = new char[strlen(str) + strlen(right) + 1];
    strcpy(str, temp);
    strcat(str, right);
    if (len != 0)
        delete [] temp;
    return *this;
}


//*************************************************************
// Overloaded == operator.                                   *
// Called when the operand on the right is a MyString        *
// object. Returns true if right.str is the same as str.     *
//*************************************************************

bool MyString::operator==(MyString &right)
{
    return !strcmp(str, right.getValue());
}


 //*********************************************************
// Overloaded == operator.                               *
// Called when the operand on the right is a string.     *
// Returns true if right is the same as str.             *
//*********************************************************

bool MyString::operator==(const char *right)
{
    return !strcmp(str, right);
}


//***************************************************************
// Overloaded != operator.                                     *
// Called when the operand on the right is a MyString          *
// object. Returns true if right.str is not equal to str.      *
//***************************************************************
```

```
bool MyString::operator!=(MyString &right)
{
    return strcmp(str, right.getValue());
}

//************************************************************
// Overloaded != operator.                                  *
// Called when the operand on the right is a string.        *
// Returns true if right is not equal to str.               *
//************************************************************

bool MyString::operator!=(const char *right)
{
    return strcmp(str, right);
}

//*************************************************************
// Overloaded != operator.                                   *
// Called when the operand on the right is a string.         *
// Returns true if str is greater than right.getValue.       *
//*************************************************************

bool MyString::operator>(MyString &right)
{
    if (strcmp(str, right.getValue()) > 0)
        return true;
    else
        return false;
}

//************************************************************
// Overloaded > operator.                                   *
// Called when the operand on the right is a string.        *
// Returns true if str is greater than right.               *
//************************************************************

bool MyString::operator>(const char *right)
{
    if (strcmp(str, right) > 0)
        return true;
    else
        return false;
}

 //***********************************************************
// Overloaded < operator.                                    *
// Called when the operand on the right is a MyString        *
// object. Returns true if str is less than right.getValue.  *
//***********************************************************
```

```
bool MyString::operator<(MyString &right)
{
   if (strcmp(str, right.getValue()) < 0)
      return true;
   else
      return false;
}

//********************************************************
// Overloaded < operator.                                *
// Called when the operand on the right is a string.     *
// Returns true if str is less than right.               *
//********************************************************

bool MyString::operator<(const char *right)
{
   if (strcmp(str, right) < 0)
      return true;
   else
      return false;
}

//**********************************************************
// Overloaded >= operator.                                 *
// Called when the operand on the right is a MyString      *
// object. Returns true if str is greater than or          *
// equal to right.getValue                                 *
//**********************************************************

bool MyString::operator>=(MyString &right)
{
   if (strcmp(str, right.getValue()) >= 0)
      return true;
   else
      return false;
}

//************************************************************
// Overloaded >= operator.                                   *
// Called when the operand on the right is a string.         *
// Returns true if str is greater than or equal to right.    *
//************************************************************

bool MyString::operator>=(const char *right)
{
   if (strcmp(str, right) >= 0)
      return true;
   else
      return false;
}
```

```
//******************************************************
// Overloaded <= operator.                             *
// Called when the operand on the right is a MyString   *
// object. Returns true if right.str is less than or equal *
// to str.                                             *
//******************************************************

bool MyString::operator<=(MyString &right)
{
   if (strcmp(str, right.getValue()) <= 0)
      return true;
   else
      return false;
}


//******************************************************
// Overloaded <= operator.                             *
// Called when the operand on the right is a string.    *
// Returns true if str is less than or equal to right.  *
//******************************************************

bool MyString::operator<=(const char *right)
{
   if (strcmp(str, right) <= 0)
      return true;
   else
      return false;
}



//***************************************************
// Overloaded stream insertion operator (<<).      *
//***************************************************

ostream &operator<<(ostream &strm, MyString &obj)
{
   strm << obj.str;
   return strm;
}


//***************************************************
// Overloaded stream extraction operator (>>).     *
//***************************************************

istream &operator>>(istream &strm, MyString &obj)
{
   strm.getline(obj.str, obj.len);
   strm.ignore();
   return strm;
}
```

The Copy Constructor

Since the MyString class has a pointer as a member and dynamically allocates memory to store its string value, a copy constructor is provided. This function will cause the object to properly set up its data when initialized with another MyString object.

The Overloaded = Operators

The MyString class has two overloaded = operators. The first is for assigning one MyString object to another. This operator function is called when the operand on the right of the = sign is a MyString object, as shown in the following code segment:

```
MyString first("Hello"), second;
second = first;
```

The second version of MyString's = operator is for assigning a traditional string to a MyString object. This operator function is called when the operand on the right of = is a string constant or any pointer to a string (such as the name of a char array). This is shown in the following program segment:

```
MyString name;
char who[] = "Jimmy";
name = who;
```

The Overloaded += Operators

The += operator is designed to concatenate the string on its right to the MyString object on its left. Like the = operators, MyString has two versions of +=. The first version is designed to work when the right operand is another MyString object, as shown in this program segment:

```
MyString first("Hello "), second("world");
first += second;
```

The second version of the += operator will be called when the right operand is a literal string or any pointer to a character:

```
MyString first("Hello ");
first += "World";
```

The Overloaded == Operators

The MyString object has overloaded versions of the == operator for performing equality tests. Like the other operators, the first version is designed to work with another MyString object and the second is designed to work with a traditional C++ string.

The == functions return true if the string contained in the right operand matches the str member of the calling object. If the strings of the two operands do not match, the functions return false. These operator functions allow the programmer using this class to construct relational expressions such as these:

```
MyString name1("John"), name2("John");
if (name1 == name2)
    cout << "The names are the same.\n";
else
    cout << "The names are different.\n";

MyString name1("John");
if (name1 == "Jon")
    cout << "The names are the same.\n";
else
    cout << "The names are different.\n";
```

The Overloaded > and < Operators

The `MyString` object has two overloaded versions of the > operator for performing greater-than tests, and the < operator for performing less-than tests. The first version of each is designed to work with another `MyString` object and the second is designed to work with a traditional C++ string. (The functions use the library function `strcmp` to determine if a greater-than or less-than relationship exists.)

The > functions return true if the `str` member of the calling object is greater than the string contained in the right operand. Otherwise, the functions return false. The < functions return true if the `str` member of the calling object is less than the string contained in the right operand. Otherwise, they return false.

These operator functions allow the programmer using this class to construct relational expressions such as those shown in this program segment:

```
MyString name1("John"), name2("Jon");
if (name1 > name2)
    cout << "John is greater than Jon.\n";
else
    cout << "John is not greater than Jon.\n";
MyString name1("John");
if (name1 < "Jon")
    cout << "John is less than Jon.\n";
else
    cout << "John is not less than Jon.\n";
```

The Overloaded >= and <= Operators

The `MyString` object has two overloaded versions of the >= operator for performing greater-than or equal-to tests, and the <= operator for performing less-than or equal-to tests. The first version of each is designed to work with another `MyString` object and the second is designed to work with a traditional C++ string. (The functions use the library function `strcmp` to determine if a greater-than or less-than relationship exists.)

The >= functions return true if the `str` member of the calling object is greater than or equal to the string contained in the right operand. Otherwise, the functions return false. The <= functions return true if the `str` member of the calling object is less than or equal to the string contained in the right operand. Otherwise, they return false.

These operator functions allow the programmer using this class to construct relational expressions such as those shown in this program segment:

```
MyString name1("John"), name2("Jon");
if (name1 >= name2)
    cout << "John is greater than or equal to Jon.\n";
else
    cout << "John is less than Jon.\n";
MyString name1("John");
if (name1 <= "Jon")
    cout << "John is less than or equal to Jon.\n";
else
    cout << "John is greater than Jon.\n";
```

Program 12-19 shows how MyString's += operator performs string concatenation. Additionally, the program's source code demonstrates how MyString allows the programmer to treat strings much like any other built-in data type.

Program 12-19

```
// This program demonstrates the MyString class. Be sure to
// compile this program with mystring.cpp.

#include <iostream>
#include "mystring.h"
using namespace std;

int main()
{
    MyString object1("This"), object2("is");
    MyString object3("a test.");
    MyString object4 = object1;  // Call copy constructor.
    MyString object5("is only a test.");
    char string1[] = "a test.";
    cout << "Object1: " << object1 << endl;
    cout << "Object2: " << object2 << endl;
    cout << "Object3: " << object3 << endl;
    cout << "Object4: " << object4 << endl;
    cout << "Object5: " << object5 << endl;
    cout << "String1: " << string1 << endl;
    object1 += " ";
    object1 += object2;
    object1 += " ";
    object1 += object3;
    object1 += " ";
    object1 += object4;
    object1 += " ";
    object1 += object5;
    cout << "object1: " << object1 << endl;
    return 0;
}
```

Program 12-19

Program Output
```
Object1: This
Object2: is
Object3: a test.
Object4: This
Object5: is only a test.
String1: a test.
object1: This is a test. This is only a test.
```

Program 12-20 shows how `MyString`'s relational operators can be used to compare strings with the same ease that numeric data types are compared.

Program 12-20

```cpp
// This program demonstrates the MyString class. Be sure to
// compile this program with mystring.cpp.

#include <iostream>
#include "mystring.h"
using namespace std;

int main()
{
    MyString name1("Billy"), name2("Sue");
    MyString name3("joe");
    MyString string1("ABC"), string2("DEF");

    cout << "name1: " << name1.getValue() << endl;
    cout << "name2: " << name2.getValue() << endl;
    cout << "name3: " << name3.getValue() << endl;
    cout << "string1: " << string1.getValue() << endl;
    cout << "string2: " << string2.getValue() << endl;
    if (name1 == name2)
        cout << "name1 is equal to name2.\n";
    else
        cout << "name1 is not equal to name2.\n";
    if (name3 == "joe")
        cout << "name3 is equal to joe.\n";
    else
        cout << "name3 is not equal to joe.\n";
    if (string1 > string2)
        cout << "string1 is greater than string2.\n";
```

(program continues)

Program 12-20 *(continued)*

```cpp
   else
      cout << "string1 is not greater than string2.\n";
   if (string1 < string2)
      cout << "string1 is less than string2.\n";
   else
      cout << "string1 is not less than string2.\n";
   if (string1 >= string2)
      cout << "string1 is greater than or equal to "
           << "string2.\n";
   else
      cout << "string1 is not greater than or equal to "
           << "string2.\n";
   if (string1 >= "ABC")
      cout << "string1 is greater than or equal to "
           << "ABC.\n";
   else
      cout << "string1 is not greater than or equal to "
           << "ABC.\n";
   if (string1 <= string2)
      cout << "string1 is less than or equal to "
           << "string2.\n";
   else
      cout << "string1 is not less than or equal to "
           << "string2.\n";
   if (string2 <= "DEF")
      cout << "string2 is less than or equal to "
           << "DEF.\n";
   else
      cout << "string2 is not less than or equal to "
           << "DEF.\n";
   return 0;
}
```

Program Output

```
name1: Billy
name2: Sue
name3: joe
string1: ABC
string2: DEF
name1 is not equal to name2.
name3 is equal to joe.
string1 is not greater than string2.
string1 is less than string2.
string1 is not greater than or equal to string2.
string1 is greater than or equal to ABC.
string1 is less than or equal to string2.
string2 is less than or equal to DEF.
```

12.10   Focus on Problem Solving and Program Design: *A Case Study*

As a programmer for the Home Software Company, you are asked to develop a class named `Currency` that inserts commas and a dollar sign ($) at the appropriate locations in a string containing an unformatted dollar amount. The class's constructor should accept a string object or a pointer to a C-string containing a value such as 1084567.89. The class should provide a member function that returns a string object containing a formatted dollar amount, such as $1,084,567.89.

Table 12-12 lists the class's member variables.

Table 12-12

Member Variable	Description
original	A `string` object holding the original unformatted string.
formatted	A `string` object to hold the formatted string.

Table 12-13 lists the member functions.

Table 12-13

Member Function	Description
Constructor	Accepts a string object as its argument. The object is copied to the `original` member, and the `dollarFormat` member function is called.
Constructor (overloaded)	Accepts a pointer to a C-string as its argument. The string pointed to by the argument is copied to the `original` member, and the `dollarFormat` member function is called.
dollarFormat	Copies the `original` member to the `formatted` member. Commas and a dollar sign are inserted at the appropriate locations in the `formatted` member.
getOriginal	Returns the `original` member.
getFormatted	Returns the `formatted` member.

The contents of the `currency.h` and `currency.cpp` files are shown here.

Contents of `currency.h`
```
#ifndef CURRENCY_H
#define currency_h

#include <string>
using namespace std;
```

```
class Currency
{
private:
   string original;
   string formatted;
public:
   Currency(string);
   Currency(char *);
   void dollarFormat();
   string getOriginal()
      { return original; }
   string getFormatted()
      { return formatted; }
};

#endif
```

Contents of currency.cpp

```
#include "currency.h"

//***********************************************
// Constructor.                                 *
// Copies str to the member original, then      *
// calls the dollarFormat member function.      *
//***********************************************

Currency::Currency(string str)
{
   original = str;
   dollarFormat();
}


//*******************************************
// Constructor.                            *
// Copies string pointed to by strPtr to   *
// the member original, then calls the     *
// dollarFormat member function.           *
//*******************************************

Currency::Currency(char *strPtr)
{
   original.assign(strPtr);
   dollarFormat();
}


//*************************************************
// Member Function dollarFormat.                 *
// This function copies the original string to   *
// the formatted member, then inserts commas     *
// and a dollar sign at the appropriate positions. *
//*************************************************
```

```
void Currency::dollarFormat()
{
    formatted = original;
    // Store position of decimal point in dp.
    int dp = formatted.find('.');
    if (dp > 3)
    {
        for (int x = dp - 3; x > 0; x -= 3)
            formatted.insert(x, ",");
    }
    formatted.insert(0, "$");
}
```

Program 12-21 demonstrates the class.

Program 12-21

```
// This program demonstrates the Currency class.

#include <iostream>
#include <string>
#include "currency.h"
using namespace std;

int main()
{
    string input;

    // Get the dollar amount from the user.
    cout << "Enter a dollar amount in the form nnnnn.nn : ";
    cin >> input;
    //Declare and initialize the Currency object.
    Currency dollars(input);
    // Display the formatted dollar amount.
    cout << "Here is the amount formatted:\n";
    cout << dollars.getFormatted() << endl;
    return 0;
}
```

Program Output with Example Input Shown in Bold
```
Enter a dollar amount in the form nnnnn.nn : 1084567.89[Enter]
Here is the amount formatted:
$1,084,567.89
```

Review Questions and Exercises

Fill-in-the-Blank

1. The _____ function returns true if the character argument is uppercase.

2. The _____ function returns true if the character argument is a letter of the alphabet.

3. The _____ function returns `true` if the character argument is a digit.

4. The _____ function returns `true` if the character argument is a whitespace character.

5. The _____ function returns the uppercase equivalent of its character argument.

6. The _____ function returns the lowercase equivalent of its character argument.

7. The _____ file must be included in a program that uses character testing functions.

8. The _____ function returns the length of a string.

9. To _____ two strings means to append one string to the other.

10. The _____ function concatenates two strings.

11. The _____ function copies one string to another.

12. The _____ function searches for a string inside of another one.

13. The _____ function compares two strings.

14. The _____ function copies, at most, n number of characters from one string to another.

15. The _____ function returns the value of a string converted to an integer.

16. The _____ function returns the value of a string converted to a `long` integer.

17. The _____ function returns the value of a string converted to a `float`.

18. The _____ function converts an integer to a string.

True or False

19. T F Character-testing functions, such as `isupper`, accept strings as arguments and test each character in the string.

20. T F If `toupper`'s argument is already uppercase, it is returned as is, with no changes.

21. T F If `tolower`'s argument is already lowercase, it will be inadvertently converted to uppercase.

22. T F The `strlen` function returns the size of the array containing a string.

23. T F If the starting address of a string is passed into pointer parameter, it can be assumed that all the characters, from that address up to the byte that holds the null terminator, are part of the string.

24. T F String handling functions accept as arguments pointers to strings (array names or pointer variables), or literal strings.

25. T F The `strcat` function checks to make sure the first string is large enough to hold both strings before performing the concatenation.

26. T F The `strcpy` function will overwrite the contents of its first string argument.

27. T F The `strcpy` function performs no bounds checking on the first argument.

28. T F There is no difference between "847" and 847.

Find the Errors

29. Each of the following programs or program segments has errors. Find as many as you can.

    A)
    ```
    char string[] = "Stop";
    if (isupper(string) == "STOP")
        exit(0);
    ```

    B)
    ```
    char numeric[5];
    int x = 123;
    numeric = atoi(x);
    ```

    C)
    ```
    char string1[] = "Billy";
    char string2[] = " Bob Jones";
    strcat(string1, string2);
    ```

    D)
    ```
    char x = 'a', y = 'a';
    if (strcmp(x, y) == 0)
        exit(0);
    ```

Programming Challenges

General Requirements

Each program should have a section of comments at the top. The comments should contain your name, the date the program was written, the chapter the assignment appeared in, and the assignment number and name. Here is an example:

```
// Written by Jill Johnson
// March 31, 2003
// Chapter 12
// Assignment 1, String Length
```

1. String Length

Write a function that returns an integer and accepts a pointer to a C-string as an argument. The function should count the number of characters in the string and return that number. Demonstrate the function in a simple program that asks the user to input a string, passes it to the function, and then displays the function's return value.

2. Backward String

Write a function that accepts a pointer to a C-string as an argument and displays its contents backwards. For instance, if the string argument is "Gravity" the function should display "ytivarG". Demonstrate the function in a program that asks the user to input a string and then passes it to the function.

3. Word Counter

Write a function that accepts a pointer to a C-string as an argument and returns the number of words contained in the string. For instance, if the string argument is "Four score and seven years ago" the function should return the number 6. Demonstrate the function in a program that asks the user to input a string and then passes it to the function. The number of words in the string should be displayed on the screen. *Optional Exercise:* Write an overloaded version of this function that accepts a string class object as its argument.

4. Average Number of Letters

Modify the program you wrote for problem 3 (Word Counter), so it also displays the average number of letters in each word.

5. Sentence Capitalizer

Write a function that accepts a pointer to a C-string as an argument and capitalizes the first character of each sentence in the string. For instance, if the string argument is "hello. my name is Joe. what is your name?" the function should manipulate the string so it contains "Hello. My name is Joe. What is your name?" Demonstrate the function in a program that asks the user to input a string and then passes it to the function. The modified string should be displayed on the screen. *Optional Exercise:* Write an overloaded version of this function that accepts a string class object as its argument.

6. Vowels and Consonants

Write a function that accepts a pointer to a C-string as its argument. The function should count the number of vowels appearing in the string and return that number.

Write another function that accepts a pointer to a C-string as its argument. This function should count the number of consonants appearing in the string and return that number.

Demonstrate the two functions in a program that performs the following steps:

1. The user is asked to enter a string.
2. The program displays the following menu:
   A) Count the number of vowels in the string
   B) Count the number of consonants in the string
   C) Count both the vowels and consonants in the string
   D) Enter another string
   E) Exit the program
3. The program performs the operation selected by the user and repeats until the user selects E, to exit the program.

7. Name Arranger

Write a program that asks for the user's first, middle, and last names. The names should be stored in three different character arrays. The program should then store, in a fourth array, the name arranged in the following manner: the last name followed by a comma and a space, followed by the first name and a space, followed by the middle name. For example, if the user entered "Carol Lynn Smith", it should store "Smith, Carol Lynn" in the fourth array. Display the contents of the fourth array on the screen.

8. Case Manipulator

Write a program with three functions: upper, lower, and reverse. The upper function should accept a pointer to a C-string as an argument. It should step through each character in the string, converting them to uppercase. The lower function, too, should accept a pointer to a C-string as an argument. It should step through each character in the string, converting them to lowercase. Like upper and lower, reverse should also accept a pointer to a string. As it steps through the string, it should test each character to determine whether it is upper- or lowercase. If a character is uppercase, it should be converted to lowercase. Likewise, if a character is lowercase, it should be converted to uppercase.

Test the functions by asking for a string in function main, then passing it to them in the following order: reverse, lower, and upper.

9. Password Verifier

Imagine you are developing a software package that requires users to enter their own passwords. Your software requires that user's passwords meet the following criteria:

- The password should be at least six characters long.
- The password should contain at least one uppercase and at least one lowercase letter.
- The password should have at least one digit.

Write a program that asks for a password and then verifies that it meets the stated criteria. If it doesn't, the program should display a message telling the user why.

10. Phone Number List

Write a program that has an array of at least 10 string objects that hold people's names and phone numbers. You may make up your own strings or use the following:

```
"Becky Warren, 678-1223"
"Joe Looney, 586-0097"
"Geri Palmer, 223-8787"
"Lynn Presnell, 887-1212"
"Holly Gaddis, 223-8878"
"Sam Wiggins, 486-0998"
"Bob Kain, 586-8712"
"Tim Haynes, 586-7676"
"Warren Gaddis, 223-9037"
"Jean James, 678-4939"
"Ron Palmer, 486-2783"
```

The program should ask the user to enter a name or partial name to search for in the array. Any entries in the array that match the string entered should be displayed. For example, if the user enters "Palmer" the program should display the following names from the list:

```
Geri Palmer, 223-8787
Ron Palmer, 486-2783
```

11. Check Writer

Write a program that displays a simulated paycheck. The program should ask the user to enter the date, the payee's name, and the amount of the check. It should then display a simulated check with the dollar amount spelled out, as shown here:

```
                    Date: 11/24/03


  Pay to the Order of: John Phillips          $1920.85

  One thousand nine hundred twenty and 85 cents
```

Be sure to format the numeric value of the check in fixed-point notation with two decimal places of precision. Be sure the decimal place always displays, even when the number is zero or has no fractional part. Use either C-strings or string class objects in this program.

Input Validation: Do not accept negative dollar amounts, or amounts over $10,000.

Serendipity Booksellers Software Development Project—Part 12: *A Problem-Solving Exercise*

For this chapter's assignment you will use library functions to make the program's search capabilities easier.

1. Create the strUpper Function

Write a function called strUpper. This function should accept a string object as its argument. It should convert each character in the string to an uppercase letter.

2. Modify the addBook Function

Modify the addBook function so it calls strUpper to convert each of the following items to all uppercase before they are written to their arrays:

```
    Book Title
    ISBN Number
    Author's Name
    Publisher
```

 Note: These items will be converted to all uppercase so searching will be easier and each book's information will be stored consistently.

3. Modify the lookUpBook Function

The lookUpBook function currently requires the user to enter the full name of the book to search for. Modify it so the user only has to enter part of the book title. Hint: Use the string class's find member function to search the titles in the database.

Note: It is possible to find more than one book that matches a partial title. When this happens, show the book title to the user and ask if it is the one being searched for. If it isn't, continue searching until there are no more book titles in the array.

4. Modify the `editBook` Function

The `editBook` function currently requires the user to enter the full name of the book to search for. Modify it so the user only has to enter part of the book title. Hint: Use the `string` class's `find` member function to search the titles in the database.

 Note: As mentioned before, it is possible to find more than one book that matches a partial title. When this happens, show the book title to the user and ask if it is the one being searched for. If it isn't, continue searching until there are no more book titles in the array.

(Before storing modified book information into the arrays, be sure to use the `strUpper` function to convert the characters in the title, ISBN number, author's name, and publisher's name to all uppercase.)

5. Modify the `deleteBook` Function

The `deleteBook` function currently requires the user to enter the full name of the book to search for. Modify it so the user only has to enter part of the book title. Hint: Use the `string` class's `find` member function to search the titles in the database.

 Note: Once again, it is possible to find more than one book that matches a partial title. When this happens, show the book title to the user and ask if it is the one being searched for. If it isn't, continue searching until there are no more book titles in the array.

CHAPTER 13

Inheritance, Polymorphism, and Virtual Functions

Topics

13.1 What Is Inheritance?

> **CONCEPT** Inheritance allows a new class to be based on an existing class. The new class inherits all the member variables and functions (except the constructors and destructor) of the class it is based on.

An important aspect of object-oriented programming is *inheritance*. Inheritance makes it easy to extend a class or adapt it to a new use. It involves the creation of a new class that is based on, or *derived* from, an existing class. You can think of the *base class* as the parent and the *derived class* as the child. This concept is illustrated in Figure 13-1.

The derived class inherits all of the variables and functions of the base class without any of them being rewritten. Furthermore, new data and functions may be added to the derived class to make it more specialized than the base class.

For example, consider a class that holds test grades. The base class could be designed to hold numeric test scores (like 70, 80, 95, etc.), and alphabetic grades (like A, B, C, etc.). The class could

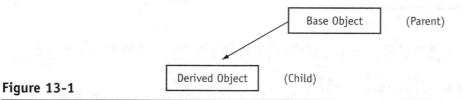

Figure 13-1

have a member function that assigns an alphabetic grade, depending on the numeric score. The declaration of such a class is shown here:

```
class Grade
{
  private:
      char letter;
      float score;
      void calcGrade();
  public:
      void setScore(float s){score = s; calcGrade();}
      float getScore() {return score; }
      char getLetter() { return letter; }
};
```

Here is the definition of the calcGrade function:

```
void Grade::calcGrade()
{
  if (score >= 90)
      letter = 'A';
  else if (score >= 80)
      letter = 'B';
  else if (score >= 70)
      letter = 'C';
  else if (score >= 60)
      letter = 'D';
  else
      letter = 'F';
}
```

The setScore function stores the numeric grade in the member variable score, then assigns a letter grade based on a 10-point scale by calling the calcGrade() function.

Next, we will derive a class from the preceding one. The derived class will have member variables for the number of questions on the test, the number of points each question is worth, and the number of questions missed by the student. Here is the class declaration:

```
class Test : public Grade
{
  private:
      int numQuestions;
      float pointsEach;
      int numMissed;
  public:
      Test(int, int);
};
```

The only new notation in the class is in the first line of the declaration. It reads

```
class Test : public Grade
```

This line indicates the name of the class being declared (Test) and the name of the base class (Grade) as shown here:

```
class Test : public Grade
         ↑               ↑
   Class being      Base class
   declared
```

The word `public` that precedes the name of the base class is the *base class access specification*. It affects how the members of the base class may be accessed by the derived class. (In the next section we discuss class access specification in more detail.)

Here is the definition of the Test class constructor:

```
//************************************************************
// Definition of Test class constructor.                    *
// Parameters: q = Number of questions, m = number of questions *
// missed.                                                   *
//************************************************************
Test::Test(int q, int m)
{
  float numericGrade;
  numQuestions = q;
  numMissed = m;
  pointsEach = 100.0 / numQuestions;
  numericGrade = 100.0 - (numMissed * pointsEach);
  setScore(numericGrade);
}
```

The constructor assigns the parameter q (the number of questions on the test) to numQuestions, and the parameter m (the number of questions missed by the student) to numMissed. The number of points each question is worth is then calculated, as well as the numeric grade. The last statement in the function is a call to setScore. setScore is a member of the Grade class, but since Test is derived from Grade, it is an inherited member of Test. Figure 13-2 illustrates this.

The individual class declarations contain their own members:

Grade Class

Private Members:
    char letter;
    float score;
    void calcGrade();
Public Members:
    void setScore(float);
    float getScore();
    char getLetter();

Test Class

Private Members:
    int numQuestions;
    float pointsEach;
    int numMissed;
Public Members:
    Test (int, int);

When the Test class is derived from the Grade class,
Objects of the Test class apppear to have the following members:

Test Class

Private Members:
    int numQuestions;
    float pointsEach;
    int numMissed;
Public Members:
    Test (int, int);
    void setScore(float);
    float getScore();
    char getLetter();

Figure 13-2

Notice in Figure 13-2 that the private members of the base class (the variables `letter` and `score` and the function `calcGrade`) are not accessible to the derived class. They are still inherited by the derived class, but since they are private members of the base class, only member functions of the base class may access them. They are truly private to the base class.

Since the functions `setScore`, `getScore`, and `getLetter` are public members of the base class, they also become public members of the derived class.

 Note: The base class's access specification affects the way its members are inherited by the derived class. We discuss this in greater detail in the next section.

Program 13-1 shows the `Grade` and `Test` classes in use. The `Grade` class is declared in `grade.h` and its member function `setScore` is defined in `grade.cpp`. The `Test` class is declared in `test.h` and its constructor is defined in `test.cpp`.

Program 13-1

Contents of grade.h

```
#ifndef GRADE_H
#define GRADE_H

// Grade class declaration

class Grade
{
    private:
        char letter;
        float score;
        void calcGrade();
    public:
        void setScore(float s) { score = s; calcGrade();}
        float getScore() {return score; }
        char getLetter() { return letter; }
};
#endif
```

Contents of grade.cpp

```
#include "grade.h"

//****************************************************
// Definition of member function Grade::calcGrade. *
//****************************************************
void Grade::calcGrade()
{
    if (score >= 90)
        letter = 'A';
    else if (score >= 80)
        letter = 'B';
    else if (score >= 70)
        letter = 'C';
    else if (score >= 60)
        letter = 'D';
    else
        letter = 'F';
}
```

Contents of test.h

```
#ifndef TEST_H
#define TEST_H
#include "grade.h"  // Must include Grade class declaration.

// Test class declaration
```

(program continues)

Program 13-1   *(continued)*

```cpp
class Test : public Grade
{
    private:
        int numQuestions;
        float pointsEach;
        int numMissed;
    public:
        Test(int, int);
};
#endif
```

Contents of test.cpp

```cpp
#include "test.h"

//*****************************************************************
// Definition of Test class constructor.                         *
// Parameters: q = Number of questions, m = number of questions  *
// missed.                                                        *
//*****************************************************************
Test::Test(int q, int m)
{
    float numericGrade;
    numQuestions = q;
    numMissed = m;
    pointsEach = 100.0 / numQuestions;
    numericGrade = 100.0 - (numMissed * pointsEach);
    setScore(numericGrade);
}
```

Contents of the main program pr13-1.cpp

```cpp
// This program demonstrates a base class and a derived class.

#include <iostream>
#include <iomanip>
#include "test.h"
using namespace std;

int main()
{
    int questions, missed;

    cout << "How many questions are on the test? ";
    cin >> questions;
    cout << "How many questions did the student miss? ";
    cin >> missed;
```

(program continues)

Program 13-1   *(continued)*

```
    // Declare a Test object.
    Test exam(questions, missed);
    cout << setprecision(4);
    cout << "The score is " << exam.getScore() << endl;
    cout << "The grade is " << exam.getLetter() << endl;
    return 0;
}
```

Program Output with Example Input Shown in Bold

```
How many questions are on the test? 20[Enter]
How many questions did the student miss? 3[Enter]
The score is 85
The grade is B
```

Notice in the following lines from Program 13-1 that the public member functions of the Grade class may be directly called by the exam object:

```
    cout << "The score is " << exam.getScore() << endl;
    cout << "The grade is " << exam.getLetter() << endl;
```

The functions are inherited as public members of the Test class, so they may be accessed as any other public member.

Inheritance does not work in reverse. It is not possible for a base class to call a member function of a derived class. For example, the following classes will not compile in a program because the BadBase constructor attempts to call a function in its derived class:

```
class BadBase
{
  private:
      int x;
  public:
      BadBase() { x = getVal(); }
};

class Derived : public BadBase
{
  private:
      int y;
  public:
      Derived(int z) { y = z; }
      int getVal() { return y; }
};
```

Checkpoint [13.1]

13.1 Here is the first line of a class declaration. Circle the name of the base class.

```
class Truck : public Vehicle
```

13.2 Circle the name of the derived class in the following declaration line.

```
class Truck : public Vehicle
```

13.3 Suppose a program has the following class declarations:

```
// Declaration of Point class.
class Point
{
    private:
        int x;
        int y;
    public:
        void setPoint(int c1, int c2) { x = c1; y = c2; }
        int getX() { return x; }
        int getY() { return y; }
};
// Declaration of Circle class.
class Circle : public Point
{
    private:
        float radius;
        float diameter;
    public:
        void setDiameter(float d)
            {diameter = d; radius = d / 2; }
        void setRadius(float r)
            { radius = r; diameter = r * 2; }
        float getRadius() { return radius; }
        float getDiameter() { return diameter; }
};
```

Answer the following questions concerning the classes:

A) When an object of the Circle class is created, what are its private members?
B) When an object of the Circle class is created, what are its public members?
C) What members of the Point class are not accessible to member functions of the Circle class?

13.2 Protected Members and Class Access

> **CONCEPT** Protected members of a base class are like private members, but they may be accessed by derived classes. The base class access specification determines how private, protected, and public base class members may be accessed by derived classes.

Until now you have used two access specifications within a class: `private` and `public`. C++ provides a third access specification, `protected`. Protected members of a base class are like private members, except they may be accessed by functions in a derived class. To the rest of the program, however, protected members are inaccessible.

Program 13-2 is a modification of Program 13-1. The private members of the `Grade` class have been made protected. A new member function, `adjustScore`, has been added to the `Test` class. This function directly accesses the `score` variable, and makes a call to the `calcGrade` function. If the contents of the `score` variable has a fractional part of .5 or greater, the function rounds `score` up to the next whole number.

Program 13-2

Contents of `grade2.h`
```
#ifndef GRADE2_H
#define GRADE2_H

// Grade class declaration

class Grade
{
    protected:
        char letter;
        float score;
        void calcGrade();
    public:
        void setScore(float s) { score = s; calcGrade(); }
        float getScore() {return score; }
        char getLetter() { return letter; }
};
#endif
```

Contents of `grade2.cpp`
```
#include "grade2.h"

//*********************************************************
// Definition of member function Grade::calcGrade.  *
//*********************************************************
```

(program continues)

Program 13-2 *(continued)*

```
void Grade::calcGrade()
{
    if (score >= 90)
        letter = 'A';
    else if (score >= 80)
        letter = 'B';
    else if (score >= 70)
        letter = 'C';
    else if (score >= 60)
        letter = 'D';
    else
        letter = 'F';
}
```

Contents of test2.h

```
#ifndef TEST2_H
#define TEST2_H
#include "grade2.h"

// Test class declaration

class Test : public Grade
{
    private:
        int numQuestions;
        float pointsEach;
        int numMissed;
    public:
        Test(int, int);
        void adjustScore();
};
#endif
```

Contents of test2.cpp

```
#include "test2.h"

//*********************************************************************
// Definition of Test class constructor.                             *
// Parameters: q = Number of questions, m = number of questions      *
// missed.                                                           *
//*********************************************************************
```

(program continues)

Program 13-2 *(continued)*

```
Test::Test(int q, int m)
{
    float numericGrade;
    numQuestions = q;
    numMissed = m;
    pointsEach = 100.0 / numQuestions;
    numericGrade = 100.0 - (numMissed * pointsEach);
    setScore(numericGrade);
}

//******************************************************************
// Definition of Test::adjustScore. If score is within 0.5 points *
// of the next whole point, it rounds the score up and            *
// recalculates the letter grade.                                 *
//******************************************************************
void Test::adjustScore()
{
    score = int(score + 0.5);
    calcGrade();
}
```

Contents of the main program, pr13-2.cpp

```
// This program demonstrates a base class and a derived class

#include <iostream>
#include <iomanip>
#include "test2.h"
using namespace std;

int main()
{
    int questions, missed;

    cout << "How many questions are on the test? ";
    cin >> questions;
    cout << "How many questions did the student miss? ";
    cin >> missed;
```

(program continues)

Program 13-2 *(continued)*

```
    // Declare a Test object
    Test exam(questions, missed);
    cout << setprecision(4);
    cout << "Unadjusted score: " << exam.getScore() << endl;
    cout << "Unadjusted grade: " << exam.getLetter() << endl;
    exam.adjustScore();
    cout << "Adjusted score is: " << exam.getScore() << endl;
    cout << "Adjusted grade is: " << exam.getLetter() << endl;
    return 0;
}
```

Program Output with Example Input Shown in Bold
```
How many questions are on the test? 200[Enter]
How many questions did the student miss? 21[Enter]
Unadjusted score: 89.5
Unadjusted grade: B
Adjusted score is: 90
Adjusted grade is: A
```

Now look closer at the base class access specification. The first line of the Test class declaration reads

```
class Test : public Grade
```

The declaration gives the public access specification to the base class, Grade. Base class access specification may be public, private, or protected. Be careful not to confuse base class access specification with member access specification. Member access specification determines if a class member is accessible to statements outside the class. Base class access specification determines if functions in the derived class may access members of the base class.

Table 13-1 summarizes how base class specification affects the way base class members appear in the derived class.

As you can see from Table 13-1, base class access specification gives you a great deal of flexibility in determining how base class members will appear in the derived class. Think of a base class's access specification as a filter that base class members must pass through when becoming inherited members of a derived class. This is illustrated in Figure 13-3.

 Note: If the base class access specification is left out of a declaration, the default access specification is private. For example, in the following declaration, Grade is declared as a private base class:

```
class Test : Grade
```

Table 13-1

Base Class Access Specification	How Members of the Base Class Appear in the Derived Class
private	• Private members of the base class are inaccessible to the derived class.
	• Protected members of the base class become private members of the derived class.
	• Public members of the base class become private members of the derived class.
protected	• Private members of the base class are inaccessible to the derived class.
	• Protected members of the base class become protected members of the derived class.
	• Public members of the base class become protected members of the derived class.
public	• Private members of the base class are inaccessible to the derived class.
	• Protected members of the base class become protected members of the derived class.
	• Public members of the base class become public members of the derived class.

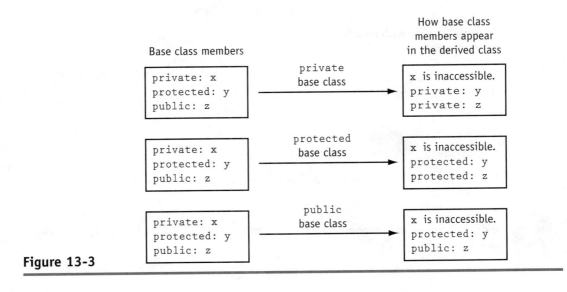

Figure 13-3

Checkpoint [13.2]

13.4 What is the difference between private members and protected members?

13.5 What is the difference between member access specification and base class access specification?

13.6 Suppose a program has the following class declaration:

```cpp
class CheckPoint
{
    private:
      int a;
    protected:
      int b;
      int c;
      void setA(int x) { a = x;}
    public:
      void setB(int y) { b = y;}
      void setC(int z) { c = z;}
};
```

Answer the following questions.

A) Suppose another class, Quiz, is derived from the CheckPoint class. Here is the first line of its declaration:

```cpp
class Quiz : private CheckPoint
```

Indicate whether each member of the CheckPoint class is private, protected, public, or inaccessible:

```
        a
        b
        c
        setA
        setB
        setC
```

B) Suppose the Quiz class, derived from the CheckPoint class, is declared as

```cpp
class Quiz : protected Checkpoint
```

Indicate whether each member of the CheckPoint class is private, protected, public, or inaccessible:

```
        a
        b
        c
```

```
setA
setB
setC
```

C) Suppose the `Quiz` class, derived from the `CheckPoint` class, is declared as

```
class Quiz : public Checkpoint
```

Indicate whether each member of the `CheckPoint` class is `private`, `protected`, `public`, or inaccessible:

```
a
b
c
setA
setB
setC
```

D) Suppose the `Quiz` class, derived from the `CheckPoint` class, is declared as

```
class Quiz : Checkpoint
```

Is the `CheckPoint` class a `private`, `public`, or `protected` base class?

13.3 Constructors and Destructors

CONCEPT The base class's constructor is called before the derived class's constructor. The destructors are called in reverse order, with the derived class's destructor being called first.

When both a base class and a derived class have constructors, the base class's constructor is called first. Destructors are called in reverse order. Program 13-3 shows a simple set of classes, each with a default constructor and a destructor. The `DeriDemo` class is derived from the `BaseDemo` class. Messages are displayed by the constructors and destructors to demonstrate when each is called.

Program 13-3

```
// This program demonstrates the order in which base and
// derived class constructors and destructors are called.
// For the sake of simplicity, all the class declarations
// are in this file.

#include <iostream>
using namespace std;
```

(program continues)

Program 13-3   *(continued)*

```cpp
// BaseDemo class

class BaseDemo
{
    public:
        BaseDemo()   // Constructor
                { cout << "This is the BaseDemo constructor.\n"; }
        ~BaseDemo() // Destructor
                { cout << "This is the BaseDemo destructor.\n"; }
};

class DeriDemo : public BaseDemo
{
    public:
        DeriDemo()   //Constructor
            { cout << "This is the DeriDemo constructor.\n"; }
        ~DeriDemo()  // Destructor
            { cout << "This is the DeriDemo destructor.\n"; }
};

int main()
{
    cout << "We will now create a DeriDemo object.\n";
    DeriDemo object;
    cout << "The program is now going to end.\n";
    return 0;
}
```

Program Output
```
We will now create a DeriDemo object.
This is the BaseDemo constructor.
This is the DeriDemo constructor.
The program is now going to end.
This is the DeriDemo destructor.
This is the BaseDemo destructor.
```

Passing Arguments to Base Class Constructors

In Program 13-3, both the base class and derived class have default constructors, which are called automatically. But what if the base class's constructor takes arguments? What if there is more than one constructor in the base class? The answer to these questions is to let the derived class constructor pass arguments to the base class constructor. For example, consider the following class:

```cpp
class Rect
{ protected:
        float width;
        float length;
        float area;
```

```
public:
    Rect() { width = length = area = 0.0; }
    Rect(float, float);
    float getArea() { return area; }
    float getLen() { return length; }
    float getWidth() { return width; }
};
```

This class is designed to hold information about a rectangle. It specifies two constructors. The first constructor listed is the default constructor, which simply initializes the member variables width, length, and area to 0.0. The second constructor, which takes two float arguments, is defined as

```
Rect::Rect(float w, float l)
{
    width = w;
    length = l;
    area = width * length;
}
```

Now let's look at a class that is derived from Rect:

```
class Cube : public Rect
{
    protected:
        float height;
        float volume;
    public:
        Cube(float, float, float);
        float getHeight() { return height; }
        float getVol() { return volume; }
};
```

The Cube class is designed to hold information about cubes, which not only have a length and width, but a height and volume as well. The constructor takes three arguments and is defined as follows:

```
Cube::Cube(float wide, float length, float high) : Rect(wide, length)
{
    height = high;
    volume = area * high;
}
```

Notice the added notation in the header of the constructor. A colon is placed after the parameter list for the derived class constructor, followed by a function call to the base class constructor. This is illustrated here:

```
Cube::Cube(float wide, float length, float high) : Rect(wide, length)
```

Derived class constructor   Call to base class constructor

The general form of this type of declaration is

```
<class name>::<class name>(parameter list) : <base class name>(argument list)
```

This notation not only causes information to be passed to the base class constructor, but also determines which base class constructor to call if there is more than one.

 Note: In this example, the notation that contains the call to the base class constructor appears in the definition of the derived class constructor. If the derived class constructor is defined in the class declaration (written inline), its definition will contain this notation.

The base class constructor is still executed before the derived class constructor. The `Cube` constructor accepts arguments for the parameters `wide`, `length`, and `high`. The values that are passed to `wide` and `length` are subsequently passed as arguments to the `Rect` constructor. When the `Rect` constructor finishes, the `Cube` constructor is then executed.

Any literal value or variable that is in scope may be used as an argument to the base class constructor. Usually, one or more of the arguments passed to the derived class constructor are, in turn, passed to the base class constructor. The values that may be used as base class constructor arguments are

- Derived class constructor parameters
- Literal values
- Global variables that are accessible to the file containing the derived class constructor definition
- Expressions involving any of the items above

Program 13-4 shows the `Rect` and `Cube` classes in use.

Program 13-4

Contents of `rect.h`
```
#ifndef RECT_H
#define RECT_H

// Rect class declaration
```

(program continues)

Program 13-4 *(continued)*

```
class Rect
{
    protected:
        float width;
        float length;
        float area;
    public:
        Rect() { width = length = area = 0.0; }
        Rect(float, float);
        float getArea() { return area; }
        float getLen() { return length; }
        float getWidth() { return width; }
};
#endif
```

Contents of rect.cpp
```
#include "rect.h"

//*********************************
// Definition of Rect constructor. *
//*********************************
Rect::Rect(float w, float l)
{
    width = w;
    length = l;
    area = width * length;
}
```

Contents of cube.h
```
#ifndef CUBE_H
#define CUBE_H
#include "rect.h"

// Cube class declaration
class Cube : public Rect
{
    protected:
        float height;
        float volume;
    public:
        Cube(float, float, float);
        float getHeight() { return height; }
        float getVol() { return volume; }
};
#endif
```

(program continues)

Program 13-4   *(continued)*

Contents of cube.cpp

```
#include "cube.h"

//**********************************
// Definition of Cube constructor. *
//**********************************
Cube::Cube(float wide, float length, float high) : Rect(wide, length)
{
    height = high;
    volume = area * high;
}
```

Contents of the main program, pr13-4.cpp

```
// This program demonstrates passing arguments to a base
// class constructor.

#include <iostream>
#include "cube.h"
using namespace std;

int main()
{
    float cubeWide, cubeLong, cubeHigh;
    cout << "Enter the dimensions of a Cube:\n";
    cout << "Width: ";
    cin >> cubeWide;
    cout << "Length: ";
    cin >> cubeLong;
    cout << "Height: ";
    cin >> cubeHigh;
    Cube holder(cubeWide, cubeLong, cubeHigh);
    cout << "Here are the Cube's properties:\n";
    cout << "Width: " << holder.getWidth() << endl;
    cout << "Length: " << holder.getLen() << endl;
    cout << "Height: " << holder.getHeight() << endl;
    cout << "Base area: " << holder.getArea() << endl;
    cout << "Volume: " << holder.getVol() << endl;
    return 0;
}
```

Program 13-4

Program Output with Example Input Shown in Bold
```
Enter the dimensions of a Cube:
Width: 10[Enter]
Length: 15[Enter]
Height: 12[Enter]
Here are the Cube's properties:
Width: 10
Length: 15
Height: 12
Base area: 150
Volume: 1800
```

 Note: If the base class has no default constructor then the derived class must have a constructor that calls one of the base class constructors.

Checkpoint   [13.3]

13.7   What will the following program display?

```cpp
#include <iostream>
using namespace std;
class Sky
{
  public:
      Sky() { cout << "Entering the sky.\n"; }
      ~Sky() { cout << "Leaving the sky.\n"; }
};

class Ground : public Sky
{
  public:
      Ground() { cout << "Entering the ground.\n"; }
      ~Ground() { cout << "Leaving the ground.\n"; }
};
int main()
{
  Ground hog;
  return 0;
}
```

13.8 What will the following program display?

```
#include <iostream>
using namespace std;
class Sky
{
  public:
     Sky() { cout << "Entering the sky.\n"; }
     Sky(char *color) { cout << "The sky is " << color << endl; }
     ~Sky() { cout << "Leaving the sky.\n"; }
};

class Ground : public Sky
{
  public:
     Ground() { cout << "Entering the ground.\n"; }
     Ground(char *c1, char *c2) : Sky(c1)
        { cout << "The ground is " << c2 << endl; }
     ~Ground() { cout << "Leaving the ground.\n"; }
};

int main()
{
  Ground hog;
  return 0;
}
```

13.4 Overriding Base Class Functions

CONCEPT A member function of a derived class may have the same name as a member function of a base class.

Inheritance is commonly used to extend a class or give it additional capabilities. Sometimes it may be helpful to equip a derived class with a member function that has the same name and parameters as one in the base class. For example, consider the following class declaration:

```
class MileDist
{
  protected:
     float miles;
  public:
     void setDist(float d) { miles = d; }
     float getDist() { return miles; }
};
```

This class is designed to hold distances, assumed to be measured in miles. The setDist function assigns its argument to the miles variable, and the getDist function returns the value in miles.

Suppose we want to extend the `mileDist` class with the following derived class that can convert between feet and miles:

```
class FtDist : public MileDist
{
  protected:
      float feet;
  public:
      void setDist(float);
      float getDist() { return feet; }
      float getMiles() { return miles; }
};
```

Note: Although the `FtDist` class is not a base class, it still has a protected member section. You will see why in the next section.

Notice that the `FtDist` class also has two member functions, named `setDist` and `getDist`. When a base class and derived class have functions with the same name and parameter list, it is said that the derived class function *overrides* the base class function. This means that objects of the derived class type will call the derived class's version of the function.

There is a distinction between overriding and overloading. An overloaded function is one with the same name as one or more other functions, but with a different parameter list. The compiler uses the arguments passed to the function to tell which version to call. Overloading can take place with regular functions that are not members of a class. Overloading can also take place inside a class when two or more member functions *of the same class* have the same name. These member functions must have different parameter lists for the compiler to tell them apart in function calls.

Overriding, however, is not the same as overloading. Overriding happens when a derived class has a function with the same name and parameter list as a base class function. The parameter lists of the two functions can be the same because the derived class function is always called by objects of the derived class type.

Let's continue our look at the `FtDist` class. Here is the definition of the `FtDist::setDist` function:

```
void FtDist::setDist(float ft)
{
  feet = ft;
  mileDist::setDist(feet / 5280);  // Call base class function
}
```

This function accepts an argument that is stored in the member variable `feet`. (This value is assumed to be a distance measured in feet.) In order to convert the number of feet to miles, the contents of the `feet` variable must be divided by 5,280. The expression `feet / 5280` is passed as an argument to the base class version of the `setDist` function. Notice the use of the scope resolution operator in the function call. A derived class function may call a base class function of the same name using this notation, which takes this form:

<base class name>::<function name>(argument list);

Since the FtDist class also overrides the MileDist::getDist function, it has a third member function named getMiles. getMiles returns the value stored in the miles member variable of the MileDist class. Program 13-5 shows the classes used in a complete program.

Program 13-5

Contents of miledist.h
```
#ifndef MILEDIST_H
#define MILEDIST_H

// MileDist class declaration.

class MileDist
{
    protected:
        float miles;
    public:
        void setDist(float d) { miles = d; }
        float getDist() { return miles; }
};
#endif
```

Contents of ftdist.h
```
#ifndef FTDIST_H
#define FTDIST_H
#include "miledist.h"

// FtDist class declaration.

class FtDist : public MileDist
{
    protected:
        float feet;
    public:
        void setDist(float);
        float getDist() { return feet; }
        float getMiles() { return miles; }
};
#endif
```

(program continues)

Program 13-5 *(continued)*

Contents of `ftdist.cpp`

```
#include "ftdist.h"

void FtDist::setDist(float ft)
{
    feet = ft;
    MileDist::setDist(feet / 5280);  // Call base class function.
}
```

Contents of the main program, `pr13-5.cpp`

```
// This program demonstrates a derived class with
// functions that override base class functions.
// NOTE: ftdist.cpp must be compiled and linked with this
// program.

#include <iostream>
#include <iomanip>
#include "ftdist.h"
using namespace std;

int main()
{
    FtDist feet;
    float ft;
    cout << "Enter a distance in feet and I will convert it\n";
    cout << "to miles: ";
    cin >> ft;
    feet.setDist(ft);
    cout << setprecision(1);
    cout << fixed;
    cout << feet.getDist() << " feet equals ";
    cout << feet.getMiles() << " miles.\n";
    return 0;
}
```

Program Output with Example Input Shown in Bold

```
Enter a distance in feet and I will convert it
to miles: 12600[Enter]
12600 feet equals 2.4 miles.
```

It is important to note that even though a derived class may override a function in the base class, objects of the base class type still call the base class version of the function. This is demonstrated in Program 13-6.

☞ **Note:** The class declarations in Program 13-6 appear in the main program file to simplify the demonstration.

Program 13-6

```cpp
// This program demonstrates that when a derived class function
// overrides a base class function, objects of the base class
// still call the base class version of the function.

#include <iostream>
using namespace std;

class Base
{
   public:
      void showMsg()
         { cout << "This is the Base class.\n"; }
};

class Derived : public Base
{
   public:
      void showMsg()
         { cout << "This is the Derived class.\n"; }
};

int main()
{
   Base b;
   Derived d;

   b.showMsg();
   d.showMsg();
   return 0;
}
```

Program Output
```
This is the Base class.
This is the Derived class.
```

In Program 13-6, a class named Base is declared with a member function named showMsg. A class named Derived is then defined, also with a showMsg function. As their names imply, Derived is derived from Base. Two objects, b and d, are defined in function main. b is a Base class object and d is a Derived class object. When b is used to call the showMsg function, it is the Base class version that is executed. Likewise, when d is used to call showMsg, the Derived class version is used.

13.5 Polymorphism and Virtual Member Functions

> **CONCEPT** A virtual member function in a base class expects to be overridden in a derived class.

The term *polymorphism* means the ability to take many forms. It occurs when member functions in a class hierarchy behave differently, depending on which object performed the call. You have already learned how to override functions in inherited classes. Simple function overriding, however, does not create true polymorphic behavior. For example, consider the following situation:

◆ A base class has member functions named `doCalc()` and `calc()`. The `calc()` function calls the `doCalc()` function.

◆ A derived class overrides the `doCalc()` function, but not the `calc()` function.

In this situation, a problem arises when an object of the derived class calls the inherited function `calc()`. When `calc()` calls `doCalc()`, it is the base class version of `doCalc()` that gets executed, not the overridden version. This is illustrated in Figure 13-4.

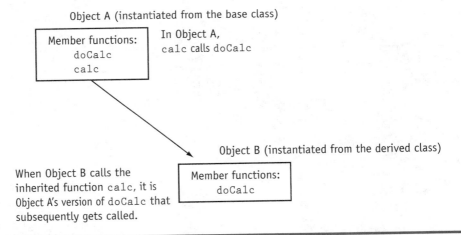

Figure 13-4

As an example, consider a modification of the `MileDist` class:

```
class MileDist
{
  protected:
     float miles;
  public:
     void setDist(float d) { miles = d; }
     float getDist() { return miles; }
     float square() { return getDist() * getDist(); }
};
```

The class has a new member function, square. It returns the square of the getDist function's return value. Now let's see how the function behaves when called from an object of the FtDist class, as shown in Program 13-7.

Program 13-7

Contents of miledis2.h
```
#ifndef MILEDIS2_H
#define MILEDIS2_H

// MileDist class declaration.

class MileDist
{
    protected:
        float miles;
    public:
        void setDist(float d) { miles = d; }
        float getDist() { return miles; }
        float square() { return getDist() * getDist(); }
};
#endif
```

Contents of ftdist2.h
```
#ifndef FTDIST2_H
#define FTDIST2_H

#include "miledis2.h"

// FtDist class declaration.

class FtDist : public MileDist
{
    protected:
        float feet;
    public:
        void setDist(float);
        float getDist() { return feet; }
        float getMiles() { return miles; }
};
#endif
```

Contents of ftdist2.cpp
```
#include "ftdist2.h"

void FtDist::setDist(float ft)
{
    feet = ft;
    MileDist::setDist(feet / 5280);  // Call base class function.
}
```

(program continues)

Program 13-7 *(continued)*

Contents of the main program, pr13-7.cpp

```cpp
// This program demonstrates a base class with an improperly
// overridden function.

#include <iostream>
#include <iomanip>
#include "ftdist2.h"
using namespace std;

int main()
{
    FtDist distObject;
    float ft;
    cout << "Enter a distance in feet and I will convert it\n";
    cout << "to miles: ";
    cin >> ft;
    distObject.setDist(ft);
    cout << setprecision(1);
    cout << fixed;
    cout << distObject.getDist() << " feet equals ";
    cout << distObject.getMiles() << " miles.\n";
    cout << distObject.getDist() << " square feet equals ";
    cout << distObject.square() << " total feet.\n";
    return 0;
}
```

Program Output with Example Input Shown in Bold

```
Enter a distance in feet and I will convert it
      to miles: 12600[Enter]
      12600 feet equals 2.4 miles.
      12600 square feet equals 5.7 total feet.
```

Obviously, since 12,600 square feet does not equal 5.7 total feet, Program 13-7 is not properly calculating the number of square feet. The reason for this is that the square function makes a call to the getDist function. Since the square function belongs to the base class, it is the base class's version of getDist that gets called. The base class's version of getDist returns the number of miles, not the number of feet held by the derived class.

This behavior happens because the C++ compiler performs *static binding* on class member function calls. This means that the compiler binds member function calls with *the version of the function that resides in the same class as the call itself*. In other words, if a call to the getDist function is performed inside the base class, it is the base class's getDist function that will get called, not the one belonging to the derived class.

To remedy this, the getDist function can be made virtual. A *virtual function* is a member function that expects to be overridden in a derived class. The compiler performs *dynamic binding* on virtual functions. This means that function calls are bound at run-time with the member function that resides in the class responsible for the call (which is not necessarily the same class that performed the call). Virtual functions are declared by placing the key word `virtual` in front of the return type in the base class's function declaration, such as

```
virtual float getDist() {return miles; }
```

This declaration tells the compiler to expect `getDist` to be overridden in a derived class. The compiler does not bind calls to the function with the actual function itself. Instead, it allows the program to bind calls, at run time, to the version of the function that belongs to the same class as the object making the call. Program 13-8 is a modification of Program 13-7, where the `getDist` function is declared virtual.

Program 13-8

Contents of `miledis3.h`
```
#ifndef MILEDIS3_H
#define MILEDIS3_H

// MileDist class declaration.

class MileDist
{
    protected:
        float miles;
    public:
        void setDist(float d) { miles = d; }
        virtual float getDist() { return miles; }
        float square() { return getDist() * getDist(); }
};
#endif
```

Contents of `ftdist3.h`
```
#ifndef FTDIST3_H
#define FTDIST3_H
#include "miledis3.h"

// FtDist class declaration.

class FtDist : public MileDist
{
    protected:
        float feet;
```

(program continues)

Program 13-8 *(continued)*

```
   public:
      void setDist(float);
      virtual float getDist() { return feet; }
      float getMiles() { return miles; }
};
#endif
```

Contents of ftdist3.cpp
```
#include "ftdist3.h"

void FtDist::setDist(float ft)
{
   feet = ft;
   MileDist::setDist(feet / 5280);  // Call base class function.
}
```

Contents of the main program, pr13-8.cpp
```
// This program demonstrates a base class with a properly
// overridden function.

#include <iostream>
#include <iomanip>
#include "ftdist3.h"
using namespace std;

int main()
{
   FtDist distObject;
   float ft;
   cout << "Enter a distance in feet and I will convert it\n";
   cout << "to miles: ";
   cin >> ft;
   distObject.setDist(ft);
   cout << setprecision(1);
   cout << fixed;
   cout << distObject.getDist() << " feet equals ";
   cout << distObject.getMiles() << " miles.\n";
   cout << distObject.getDist() << " square feet equals ";
   cout << distObject.square() << " total feet.\n";
   return 0;
}
```

Program Output with Example Input Shown in Bold
```
Enter a distance in feet and I will convert it
to miles: 12600[Enter]
12600 feet equals 2.4 miles.
12600 square feet equals 158760000.0 total feet.
```

13.6 Abstract Base Classes and Pure Virtual Functions

CONCEPT An abstract base class is not instantiated, but other classes are derived from it. A pure virtual function is a virtual member function of a base class that must be overridden. When a class contains a pure virtual function as a member, that class becomes an abstract base class.

Sometimes it is helpful to begin a class hierarchy with an *abstract base class*. An abstract base class is not instantiated itself, but serves as a base class for other classes. The abstract base class represents the generic, or abstract, form of all the classes that are derived from it.

For example, consider a factory that manufactures airplanes. The factory does not make a generic airplane, but makes three specific types of planes: two models of prop-driven planes and one commuter jet model. The computer software that catalogs the planes might use an abstract base class called `Airplane`. That class has members representing the common characteristics of all airplanes. In addition, it has classes for each of the three specific airplane models the factory manufactures. These classes have members representing the unique characteristics of each type of plane. The base class, `Airplane`, is never instantiated, but is used to derive the other classes.

A class becomes an abstract base class when one or more of its member functions is a *pure virtual function*. A pure virtual function is a virtual member function declared in a manner similar to the following:

```cpp
virtual void showInfo() = 0;
```

The = 0 notation indicates that `showInfo` is a pure virtual function. Pure virtual functions have no body, or definition, in the base class. They must be overridden in derived classes. Additionally, the presence of a pure virtual function in a class prevents a program from instantiating the class. The compiler will generate an error if you attempt to define an object of an abstract base class.

For example, look at the abstract base class `Student` declared below. It holds information common to all students, but does not hold all the information needed for students of specific majors.

Contents of `student.h`

```cpp
#ifndef STUDENT_H
#define STUDENT_H
#include <string>
using namespace std;

class Student
{
protected:
    string name;
    string id;
    int yearAdmitted;
    int hoursCompleted;
```

```
public:
    Student()    // Constructor
        {
            name = "";
            id   = "";
            yearAdmitted = hoursCompleted = 0;
        }
    void setName(string n)
        { name = n; }
    void setID(string i)
        { id = i; }
    void setYearAdmitted(int y)
        { yearAdmitted = y; }
    virtual void setHours() = 0;    // Pure virtual function
    virtual void showInfo() = 0;    // Pure virtual function
};
```

```
#endif
```

The `Student` class contains members for storing a student's name, ID number, year admitted, and number of hours completed. It also has member functions for setting values in the `name`, `id`, and `yearAdmitted` members.

Two pure virtual functions are also declared: `setHours` and `showInfo`. These pure virtual functions must be overridden in classes derived from the `Student` class. They were made pure virtual functions because this class is intended to be the base for classes that represent students of specific majors. For example, a `CsStudent` class might hold the data for a computer science student, and a `BiologyStudent` class might hold the data for a biology student. Computer science students must take courses in different disciplines than those taken by biology students. It stands to reason that the `CsStudent` class will calculate the number of hours taken in a different manner than the `BiologyStudent` class, and each will have different types of information to display.

Let's look at an example of the `CsStudent` class.

Contents of csstudent.h

```
#ifndef CSSTUDENT_H
#define CSSTUDENT_H
#include "student.h"

class CsStudent : public Student
{
private:
    int mathHours;     // Hours of math taken
    int csHours;       // Hours of computer science taken
    int genEdHours;    // Hours of general education taken
public:
    void setMathHours(int mh)
        { mathHours = mh; }
    void setCsHours(int csh)
        { csHours = csh; }
```

```
        void setGenEdHours(int geh)
            { genEdHours = geh; }
        void setHours()
            {  hoursCompleted = genEdHours + mathHours + csHours; }
        void showInfo();                    // Defined in csstudent.cpp
    };

    #endif
```

Contents of csstudent.cpp

```
    #include <iostream>
    #include "csstudent.h"
    using namespace std;

    void CsStudent::showInfo()
    {
        cout << "Name: " << name << endl;
        cout << "Student ID: " << id << endl;
        cout << "Year admitted: " << yearAdmitted << endl;
        cout << "Summary of hours completed:\n";
        cout << "\tGeneral Education: " << genEdHours << endl;
        cout << "\tMath: " << mathHours << endl;
        cout << "\tComputer Science: " << csHours << endl << endl;
        cout << "\tTotal Hours Completed: " << hoursCompleted << endl;
    }
```

The CsStudent class, which is derived from the Student class, has member variables and functions for holding and setting the number of hours completed in math, computer science, and general education. In addition it overrides the setHours and showInfo functions.

Program 13-9 demonstrates the Student and CsStudent classes.

Program 13-9

```
// This program demonstrates the CsStudent class, which is
// derived from the abstract base class, Student.

#include <iostream>
#include <string>
#include "csstudent.h"
using namespace std;

int main()
{
    CsStudent student1;
    string strInput;  // Used to read strings.
    int intInput;     // Used to read integers.
```

(program continues)

Program 13-9   *(continued)*

```cpp
      cout << "Enter the following student information:\n";
      // Set the student's name.
      cout << "Name: ";
      getline(cin, strInput);
      student1.setName(strInput);

      // Set the student's ID number.
      cout << "Student ID: ";
      getline(cin, strInput);
      student1.setID(strInput);

      // Set the year admitted.
      cout << "Year admitted: ";
      cin >> intInput;
      student1.setYearAdmitted(intInput);

      // Set the # of general ed hours completed.
      cout << "Number of general ed hours completed: ";
      cin >> intInput;
      student1.setGenEdHours(intInput);

      // Set the # of math hours completed.
      cout << "Number of math hours completed: ";
      cin >> intInput;
      student1.setMathHours(intInput);

      // Set the # of computer science hours completed.
      cout << "Number of computer science hours completed: ";
      cin >> intInput;
      student1.setCsHours(intInput);

      // Total the hours entered.
      student1.setHours();

      // Display the information provided.
      cout << "\nSTUDENT INFORMATION\n";
      student1.showInfo();

      return 0;
};
```

Program 13-9

Program Output with Example Input Shown in Bold
```
Enter the following student information:
Name: Marty Stamey[Enter]
Student ID: 167W98337[Enter]
Year admitted: 2001[Enter]
Number of general ed hours completed: 12[Enter]
Number of math hours completed: 9[Enter]
Number of computer science hours completed: 18[Enter]

STUDENT INFORMATION
Name: Marty Stamey
Student ID: 167W98337
Year admitted: 2001
Summary of hours completed:
        General Education: 12
        Math: 9
        Computer Science: 18

        Total Hours Completed: 39
```

Remember the following points about abstract base classes and pure virtual functions:

◆ When a class contains a pure virtual function, it is an abstract base class.

◆ Pure virtual functions are declared with the = 0 notation.

◆ Abstract base classes cannot be instantiated.

◆ Pure virtual functions have no body, or definition, in the base class.

◆ Pure virtual functions *must* be overridden in derived classes.

13.7   Base Class Pointers

CONCEPT   Pointers to a base class may be assigned the address of a derived class object. The pointer, however, will ignore any overrides the derived class performs.

Pointers to base class objects exhibit behavior that is worth briefly discussing. Here are two important points to remember:

◆ A pointer to a base class object may point to an object that is derived from the base class.

◆ If the derived class overrides any members of the base class, however, the base class pointer will access objects of the base class.

This is shown in Program 13-10.

Program 13-10

```
// This program demonstrates the behavior of a base class pointer
// when it is pointing to an object of a derived class that overrides members
// of the base class.
// The class declarations are placed directly in the file for simplicity.

#include <iostream>
using namespace std;
class Base
{
    public:
        void show()
            { cout << "This is from the Base class.\n"; }
};

class Derived : public Base
{
    public:
        void show()
            { cout << "This is from the Derived class.\n"; }
};

int main()
{
    Base *bptr;
    Derived dobject;

    bptr = &dobject;
    bptr->show();                //Base class pointer, ignores override.
    return 0;
}
```

Program Output
```
This is from the Base class.
```

Since dobject is derived from the Base class, a Base class pointer, such as bptr, may point to it. When bptr is used to call the show function, however, it ignores the fact that dobject has its own version of the function. bptr causes the Base class's show function to execute.

This type of behavior can be altered by the use of virtual functions. If the show function had been declared virtual in the Base class, bptr would have executed the Derived class version.

Checkpoint   [13.4–13.7]

13.9   Explain the difference between overloading a function and overriding a function.

13.10 Explain the difference between static binding and dynamic binding.

13.11 Are virtual functions statically bound or dynamically bound?

13.12 What will the following program display?

```cpp
#include <iostream>
using namespace std;
class First
{
    protected:
        int a;
    public:
        First(int x = 1) { a = x; }
        int getVal() { return a; }
};
class Second : public First
{
    private:
        int b;
    public:
        Second(int y = 5) { b = y; }
        int getVal() { return b; }
};
int main()
{
    First object1;
    Second object2;
    cout << object1.getVal() << endl;
    cout << object2.getVal() << endl;
    return 0;
}
```

13.13 What will the following program display?

```cpp
#include <iostream>
using namespace std;
class First
{
    protected:
        int a;
    public:
        First(int x = 1) { a = x; }
        void twist() { a *= 2; }
        int getVal() { twist(); return a; }
};
class Second : public First
{
    private:
        int b;
    public:
        Second(int y = 5) { b = y; }
        void twist() { b *= 10; }
};
```

```
int main()
{
    First object1;
    Second object2;
    cout << object1.getVal() << endl;
    cout << object2.getVal() << endl;
    return 0;
}
```

13.14 What will the following program display?

```
#include <iostream>
using namespace std;
class First
{
    protected:
        int a;
    public:
        First(int x = 1) { a = x; }
        virtual void twist() { a *= 2; }
        int getVal() { twist(); return a; }
};
class Second : public First
{
    private:
        int b;
    public:
        Second(int y = 5) { b = y; }
        virtual void twist() { b *= 10; }
};
int main()
{
    First object1;
    Second object2;
    cout << object1.getVal() << endl;
    cout << object2.getVal() << endl;
    return 0;
}
```

13.15 What will the following program display?

```
#include <iostream>
using namespace std;
class Base
{
    protected:
        int baseVar;
    public:
        Base(int val = 2) { baseVar = val; }
        int getVar() { return baseVar; }
};
```

```
class Derived : public Base
{
    private:
        int deriVar;
    public:
        Derived(int val = 100) { deriVar = val; }
        int getVar() { return deriVar; }
};

int main()
{
    Base *optr;
    Derived object;

    optr = &object;
    cout << optr->getVar() << endl;
    return 0;
}
```

13.8   Classes Derived from Derived Classes

CONCEPT A base class can also be derived from another class.

Sometimes it is desirable to establish a chain of inheritance in which one class is derived from a second class, which in turn is derived from a third class. Figure 13-5 illustrates this. In some programs, this chaining of classes goes on for many layers.

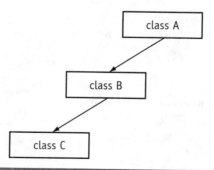

Figure 13-5

In Figure 13-5, class C inherits all of class B's members, including the ones class B inherited from class A. Of course, each class's access specification determines which members are accessible. Let's look at an example of how to create such a chain of inheritance. The InchDist class below is derived from the FtDist class.

```
class InchDist : public FtDist
{
  protected:
     float inches;
  public:
     void setDist(float);
     float getDist() { return inches; }
     float getFeet() { return feet; }
};
```

When FtDist was declared, it had a protected section. Since the InchDist class gives FtDist a public access specification, all of FtDist's protected and public members become protected and public members of InchDist. This includes the protected and public members of MileDist that were inherited by FtDist. Table 13-2 shows all of InchDist's members.

Table 13-2

Member	Access	Description
miles	protected	A member variable, inherited from the FtDist class, which inherited it from the MileDist class
feet	protected	A member variable, inherited from the FtDist class
inches	protected	A member variable
setDist	public	A member function that overrides the setDist functions in the base classes
getDist	public	A member function that overrides the getDist functions in the base classes
getFeet	public	A member function, inherited from the FtDist class
getMiles	public	A member function, inherited from the FtDist class, which inherited it from the MileDist class

The InchDist class also has member functions named setDist and getDist. These functions are designed to work with inches, as shown in the definition of InchDist::setDist:

```
void InchDist::setDist(float in)
{
  inches = in;
  FtDist::setDist(inches / 12);  // Call base class function
}
```

As you can see, a call to the InchDist::setDist function begins a chain of calls to the FtDist::setDist and MileDist functions. This class is demonstrated in Program 13-11. The listings of miledist.h, ftdist.h, and ftdist.cpp have been left out to simplify the illustration.

Program 13-11

Contents of inchdist.h
```cpp
#ifndef INCHDIST_H
#define INCHDIST_H
#include "ftdist3.h" // Needed for FtDist class declaration.

// InchDist class declaration

class InchDist : public FtDist
{
    protected:
        float inches;
    public:
        void setDist(float);
        float getDist() { return inches; }
        float getFeet() { return feet; }
};
#endif
```

Contents of inchdist.cpp
```cpp
#include "inchdist.h"
//*****************************************************
// Definition of setDist member of InchDist class. *
//*****************************************************
void InchDist::setDist(float in)
{
    inches = in;
    FtDist::setDist(inches / 12);   // Call base class function.
}
```

Contents of the main program, pr13-11.cpp
```cpp
// This program demonstrates a derived class derived from another derived class.
// NOTE: inchdist.cpp and ftdist.cpp must be compiled and linked
// with this program.

#include <iostream>
#include <iomanip>
#include "inchdist.h"
using namespace std;

int main()
{
    InchDist inch;
    float in;
    cout << "Enter a distance in inches and I will convert\n";
    cout << "it to feet and miles: ";
    cin >> in;
```

(program continues)

Program 13-11 *(continued)*

```
    inch.setDist(in);
    cout << setprecision(1);
    cout << fixed;
    cout << inch.getDist() << " inches equals ";
    cout << inch.getFeet() << " feet.\n";
    cout << inch.getDist() << " inches equals ";
    cout << inch.getMiles() << " miles.\n";
    return 0;
}
```

Program Output with Example Input Shown in bold
```
Enter a distance in inches and I will convert
it to feet and miles: 115900[Enter]
115900 inches equals 9658.3 feet.
115900 inches equals 1.8 miles.
```

13.9   Multiple Inheritance

CONCEPT   Multiple inheritance is when a derived class has two or more base classes.

In the previous section you saw how a class may be derived from a second class that is itself derived from a third class. The series of classes establishes a chain of inheritance. In such a scheme, you might be tempted to think of the lowest class in the chain as having multiple base classes. A base class, however, should be thought of as the class that another class is directly derived from. Even though there may be several classes in a chain, each class (below the topmost class) only has one base class.

Another way of combining classes is through multiple inheritance. *Multiple inheritance* is when a class has two or more base classes. This is illustrated in Figure 13-6.

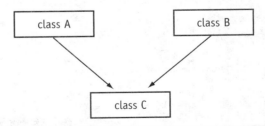

Figure 13-6

In Figure 13-6, class C is directly derived from classes A and B, and inherits the members of both. Neither class A nor B, however, inherits members from the other. Their members are only passed down to class C. Let's look at an example of multiple inheritance. Consider the two classes declared here:

```
class Date
{
  protected:
      int day;
      int month;
      int year;
  public:
      Date(int d, int m, int y) { day = d; month = m; year = y; }
      int getDay() { return day; }
      int getMonth() { return month; }
      int getYear() { return year; }
};

class Time
{
  protected:
      int hour;
      int min;
      int sec;
  public:
      Time(int h, int m, int s) { hour = h; min = m; sec = s; }
      int getHour() { return hour; }
      int getMin() { return min; }
      int getSec() { return sec; }
};
```

These classes are designed to hold integers that represent the date and time. They both can be used as base classes for a third class we will call `DateTime`:

```
class DateTime : public Date, public Time
{
protected:
    string dTString;
public:
    DateTime(int, int, int, int, int, int);
    void getDateTime(string &str) {  str = dTString; }
};
```

The first line in the `DateTime` declaration reads

```
class DateTime : public Date, public Time
```

Notice there are two base classes listed, separated by a *comma*. Each base class has its own access specification. The general format of the first line of a class declaration with multiple base classes is

```
class <derived class name> : <access specification> <base class name>,
<access specification> <base class name>[, ...]
```

The notation in the square brackets indicates that the list of base classes with their access specifications may be repeated. (It is possible to have several base classes.)

Now look at `DateTime`'s constructor:

```
DateTime::DateTime(int dy, int mon, int yr, int hr, int mt, int sc):
        Date(dy, mon, yr), Time(hr, mt, sc)
{
        // Format the date by writing it into a string formatStream.
        strstream formatStream;
        // Store the date in dTString, in the form MM/DD/YY.
        formatStream << getMonth() << '/' << getDay()
                << '/' << getYear();
        // Store the time in dTString, in the form HH:MM:SS.
        formatStream << " " <<getHour() << ':' << getMin()
                << ':' << getSec();
        // Store the entire string in dTString.
        dTString = formatStream.str();
}
```

The function header of the constructor contains notation that is used to pass arguments to the constructors of the base classes:

```
DateTime(int dy, int mon, int yr, int hr, int mt, int sc) :
    Date(dy, mon, yr), Time(hr, mt, sc)
```

After the `DateTime` constructor's parameter list comes a colon, followed by a list of calls to the `Date` and `Time` constructors. The calls are separated by a comma. When using multiple inheritance, the general format of a derived class's constructor's header is

```
<derived class name>(parameter list) : <base class name>(argument list),
<base class name>(argument list)[, ...]
```

The order that the base class constructor calls appear in the list does not matter. They are always called in the order of inheritance. That is, they are always called in the order they are listed in the first line of the class declaration. Since `Date` is listed before `Time` in the `DateTime` class declaration, `Date`'s constructor will always be called first. If the classes use destructors, they are always called in reverse order of inheritance.

The purpose of the constructor is to format date and time information and store it in the string `dTString`. The class has a member function, `getDateTime`, that retrieves and returns the string holding the formatted time. The constructor formats the date and time information by first writing them to a string stream object defined using the statement

```
strstream formatStream;
```

A string stream objects works very similar to a file stream object: The programmer can write and read a string stream object as if she or he were writing or reading a file stream. The use of string stream objects requires inclusion of the `strstream` header file:

```
#include <strstream>
```

Each string stream object contains an internal array of char, which can be accessed using the str() member function:

```
dTString = formatString.str( );
```

Program 13-12 shows the Date, Time, and DateTime classes in use.

Program 13-12

Contents of date.h
```
#ifndef DATE_H
#define DATE_H

class Date
{
    protected:
        int day;
        int month;
        int year;
    public:
        Date(int d, int m, int y) { day = d; month = m; year = y; }
        int getDay() { return day; }
        int getMonth() { return month; }
        int getYear() { return year; }
};
#endif
```

Contents of time.h
```
#ifndef TIME_H
#define TIME_H

class Time
{
    protected:
        int hour;
        int min;
        int sec;
    public:
        Time(int h, int m, int s) { hour = h; min = m; sec = s; }
        int getHour() { return hour; }
        int getMin() { return min; }
        int getSec() { return sec; }
};
#endif
```

(program continues)

Program 13-12   *(continued)*

Contents of datetime.h
```
#ifndef DATETIME_H
#define DATETIME_H

#include <string>
#include "date.h" // For Date class declaration
#include "time.h" // For Time class declaration
using namespace std;

class DateTime : public Date, public Time
{
protected:
    string dTString;
public:
    DateTime(int, int, int, int, int, int);
    void getDateTime(string &str) {  str = dTString; }
};

#endif
```

Contents of datetime.cpp
```
#include "datetime.h"
#include <strstream>

DateTime::DateTime(int dy, int mon, int yr, int hr, int mt, int sc):
        Date(dy, mon, yr), Time(hr, mt, sc)
{
    // Format the date by writing it into a string formatStream.
    strstream formatStream;
    // Store the date in dTString, in the form MM/DD/YY.
    formatStream <<  getMonth() <<  '/' <<  getDay()
                <<  '/' << getYear();
    // Store the time in dTString, in the form HH:MM:SS.
    formatStream <<  " " <<getHour() <<  ':' << getMin()
                <<  ':' << getSec();
    // Store the entire string in dTString.
    dTString = formatStream.str();
}
```

Contents of the main program, pr13-12.cpp
```
// This program demonstrates a class with multiple inheritance.
// NOTE: datetime.cpp must be compiled and linked with this
// file.
```

(program continues)

Program 13-12 *(continued)*

```cpp
#include <iostream>
#include "datetime.h"
using namespace std;

int main()
{
    string formatted;
    DateTime pastDay(4, 2, 60, 5, 32, 27);

    pastDay.getDateTime(formatted);
    cout << formatted << endl;
    return 0;
}
```

Program Output
```
4/2/60 5:32:27
```

 Note: It should be noted that multiple inheritance opens the opportunity for a derived class to have ambiguous members. That is, two base classes may have member variables or functions of the same name. In situations like these, the derived class should always override the member functions. Calls to the member functions of the appropriate base class can be performed within the derived class using the scope resolution operator(::). The derived class can also access the ambiguously-named member variables of the correct base class using the scope resolution operator. If these steps aren't taken, the compiler will generate an error when it can't tell which member is being accessed.

❓ Checkpoint [13.8–13.9]

13.16 Does the following diagram depict multiple inheritance or a chain of inheritance?

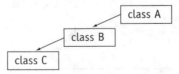

13.17 Does the following diagram depict multiple inheritance or a chain of inheritance?

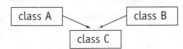

13.18 Examine the following classes. The table lists the variables that are members of the `Third` class (some are inherited). Complete the table by filling in the access specification each member will have in the `Third` class. Write "inaccessible" if a member is inaccessible to the `Third` class.

```
class First
{
  private:
      int a;
  protected:
      float b;
  public:
      long c;
};

class Second : protected First
{
  private:
      int d;
  protected:
      float e;
  public:
      long f;
};

class Third : public Second
{
  private:
      int g;
  protected:
      float h;
  public:
      long i;
};
```

Member Variable	Access Specification in Third class
a	
b	
c	
d	
e	
f	
g	
h	
i	

13.19 Examine the following class declarations:

```
class Van
{
    protected:
        int passengers;
    public:
        Van(int p) { passengers = p; }
};

class FourByFour
{
    protected:
        float cargoWeight;
    public:
        FourByFour(float w) { cargoWeight = w; }
};
```

Write the declaration of a class named SportUtility. The class should be derived from both the Van and FourByFour classes. (This should be a case of multiple inheritance, where both Van and FourByFour are base classes.)

13.10   Composition and Inheritance

CONCEPT Inheritance should model an "is a" relation, rather than a "has a" relation, between the derived and base classes.

Class inheritance in an object-oriented language should be used to model the fact that the type of the derived class is a special case of the type of the base class. Actually, a class can be considered to be the *set* of all objects that can be created from it. Because the derived class is a special case of the base class, the set of objects that correspond to the derived class will be a *subset* of the set of objects that correspond to the base class. Thus, every object of the derived class is also an object of the base class. In other words, each derived class object *is a* base class object.

Class composition occurs whenever a class contains an object of another class as one of its member variables. Composition was covered in Chapter 11, where it was pointed out that composition models a *has a* relation between classes.

Because a derived class inherits all the members of its base class, a derived class effectively contains an object of its base class. Because of this, it is possible to use inheritance where a correct design would call for composition. As an example, consider a program that needs to represent data for a person say the person's name and street address. The street address might consist of two lines:

123 Main Street
Hometown, 12345

Now suppose we had a class for representing a street address:

```
class StreetAddress
{
  private:
    string line1, line2;
  public:
    void setLine1(string);
    void setLine2(string);
    string getLine1();
    string getLine2();
};
```

Because a person's data has a name and a street address, the proper formulation of a class to represent a person's data would use composition in the following way:

```
class PersonData
{
  private:
    string name;
    StreetAddress address;
  public:
    ...
};
```

We have left off the rest of the class declaration for `PersonData` because we don't need it for our purposes.

It is possible to define this class using inheritance instead of composition. For example, we could define a class `PersonData1` as follows:

```
class PersonData1:public StreetAddress
{
  private:
    string name;
  public:
    ...

};
```

While this new definition would compile correctly, it is conceptually the wrong thing to do because it regards a person's data as a special kind of `StreetAddress`, which it is not. This type of conceptual error in design can result in a program that is confusing to understand and difficult to maintain. It is a good design practice to prefer composition to inheritance whenever possible. One reason is that inheritance breaks the encapsulation of the base class by exposing the base class's protected members to the methods of the derived class.

Let us next consider an example where it makes sense to use inheritance rather than composition. Suppose that we have a class `Dog` that represents the set of all dogs. Assuming that each `Dog` object has a member variable `weight` of type `float` and a member function `void bark()`, we might have the following class:

```
class Dog
{
  protected:
    float weight;
  public:
    Dog(float w)
      { weight = w; }
    virtual void bark()
      {
        cout << "I am dog weighing "
             << weight << " pounds." << endl;
      }
};
```

The class also has a constructor to allow Dog objects to be initialized. Note that we have declared the bark() member function as virtual to allow it to be overridden in a derived class.

Suppose that we need to have a class that represents the set of all sheep dogs. Since every sheep dog is also a dog, it makes sense to derive the new SheepDog class from the Dog class. That way, a SheepDog object will inherit every member of the Dog class. In addition to having every characteristic that every dog has, a sheep dog can be expected to have other characteristics peculiar to sheep dogs, so our SheepDog class will have an integer member numberSheep that indicates the maximum number of sheep the dog is trained to herd. In addition, a sheep dog might have a way of barking different from that of a generic dog, perhaps one adapted to the tending of sheep. This is accounted for by overriding the bark() member function of the Dog class.

```
class SheepDog:public Dog
{
  private:
    int numberSheep;
  public:
    SheepDog(float w, int nSheep) : Dog(w)
    {
      numberSheep = nSheep;
    }
    void bark()
    {
      cout << "I am a sheepdog weighing "
           << weight << " pounds \n   and guarding "
           << numberSheep << " sheep." << endl;
    }
};
```

To demonstrate this class, we will set up an array of dogs with some of the dogs in the array being sheep dogs. To get around the fact that an array cannot hold two different types, we will use an array of pointers to Dog. Recall from Section 13.7 that a pointer to a base class (in this case, Dog) can point to any derived class object (in this case, SheepDog). We can therefore create an array of pointers to Dog and have some of those pointers point to Dog objects while others point to SheepDog objects:

```
Dog *kennel[3] = { new Dog(40.5),
                   new SheepDog(45.3, 50),
                   new Dog(24.7)
                 };
```

Finally, we can use a loop to call the `bark()` member function of each `Dog` object in the array.

```
for (int k = 0; k < 3; k++)
   {
      cout << k+1 << ": ";
      kennel[k]->bark();
   }
```

Because of polymorphism, and because the `bark()` function was declared virtual, the same line of code inside the loop will call the original `bark()` function for a regular dog, but will call the specialized `bark()` function for a sheep dog. The complete program is given in Program 13-13.

Program 13-13

```
//This program demonstrates the Is A relationship
//in inheritance.

#include <iostream>
using namespace std;

//Base class

class Dog
{
  protected:
    float weight;
  public:
    Dog(float w)
      { weight = w; }
    virtual void bark()
      {
        cout << "I am dog weighing "
             << weight << " pounds." << endl;
      }
};

//A SheepDog is a special type of Dog.

class SheepDog:public Dog
{
  private:
    int numberSheep;
```

(program continues)

Program 13-13   *(continued)*

```cpp
public:
  SheepDog(float w, int nSheep) : Dog(w)
  {
    numberSheep = nSheep;
  }
  void bark()
  {
    cout << "I am a sheepdog weighing "
         << weight << " pounds \n   and guarding "
         << numberSheep << " sheep." << endl;
  }
};

int main( )
{

  //Create an array of 3 dogs.
  Dog *kennel[3] = { new Dog(40.5),
                     new SheepDog(45.3, 50),
                     new Dog(24.7)
                   };
  //Walk by each kennel and make the dog bark.
  for (int k = 0; k < 3; k++)
  {
    cout << k+1 << ": ";
    kennel[k]->bark();
  }
  return 0;
}
```

Program Output

```
1: I am dog weighing 40.5 pounds.
2: I am a sheepdog weighing 45.3 pounds
   and guarding 50 sheep.
3: I am dog weighing 24.7 pounds.
```

Inheritance is a better choice than composition in this example, since to use composition would be tantamount to saying that a sheep dog *has a* dog, instead of saying that a sheep dog *is a* dog.

There is a third relationship between classes that some authors talk about: the *uses implementation of* relation. Basically, one class uses the implementation of a second class if it calls a member function of an object of the second class.

How can you know when to use inheritance and when to use composition? Suppose that you have an existing class C1 and you need to write a definition for another class C2 which will need the services of an associated C1 object. Should you derive C2 from C1, or should you give C2 a member variable of type C1? In general, you should prefer composition to inheritance. To help determine if inheritance may be appropriate, you might ask the following questions:

- ◆ Is it natural to think of a C2 object as a special type of C1 object? If so, then you should use inheritance.
- ◆ Will objects of class C2 need to be used in places where objects of class C1 are used? For example, will they need to be passed to functions that take reference parameters of type C1, or pointers to C1? If so, then you should make C2 a derived class of C1.

Review Questions and Exercises

Fill-in-the-Blank

1. A derived class inherits the _____ of its base class.

2. The base class named in the following line of code is _____ .

   ```
   class Pet : public Dog
   ```

3. The derived class named in the following line of code is _____ .

   ```
   class Pet : public Dog
   ```

4. In the following line of code, the class access specification for the base class is _____.

   ```
   class Pet : public Dog
   ```

5. In the following line of code, the class access specification for the base class is _____.

   ```
   class Pet : Fish
   ```

6. Protected members of a base class are like _____ members, except they may be accessed by derived classes.

7. Complete the following table by filling in private, protected, public, or inaccessible in the right-hand column:

In a private base class, this base class MEMBER access specification...	...becomes this access specification in the derived class.
private	
protected	
public	

8. Complete the following table by filling in private, protected, public, or inaccessible in the right-hand column:

In a protected base class, this base class MEMBER access specification...	...becomes this access specification in the derived class.
private	
protected	
public	

9. Complete the following table by filling in private, protected, public, or inaccessible in the right-hand column:

In a public base class, this base class MEMBER access specification...	...becomes this access specification in the derived class.
private	
protected	
public	

10. When both a base class and a derived class have constructors, the base class's constructor is called _____ (first/last).

11. When both a base class and a derived class have destructors, the base class's constructor is called _____ (first/last).

12. An overridden base class function may be called by a function in a derived class by using the _____ operator.

13. When a derived class overrides a function of the base class, base class objects will call the version of the function that is defined in the _____ class.

14. A (n)_____ member function in a base class expects to be overridden in a derived class.

15. _____ binding is when the compiler binds member function calls, at compile time, with the version of the function that resides in the same class as the call itself.

16. _____ binding is when a function call is bound at run time with the member function that resides in the class responsible for the call.

17. _____ is when member functions in a class hierarchy behave differently, depending on which object performs the call.

18. When a pointer to a base class is made to point to a derived class, the pointer ignores any _____ the derived class performs, unless the function is _____.

19. A(n) _____ class cannot be instantiated.

20. A (n)_____ member function is meant to be overridden, and has no body, or definition, in the class in which it is declared.

21. A (n)_____ of inheritance is where one class is derived from a second class, which in turn is derived from a third class.

22. _____ is where a derived class has two or more base classes.

23. _____ should be used when all objects of one class are special types of objects of another class.

24. In multiple inheritance, the derived class should always _____ a function that has the same name in more than one base class.

True or False

25. T F The base class's access specification affects the way base class member functions may access base class member variables.

26. T F The base class's access specification affects the way the derived class member functions may access base class member variables and functions.

27. T F Private members of a private base class become inaccessible to the derived class.

28. T F Public members of a private base class become private members of the derived class.

29. T F Protected members of a private base class become public members of the derived class.

30. T F Public members of a protected base class become private members of the derived class.

31. T F Private members of a protected base class become inaccessible to the derived class.

32. T F Protected members of a public base class become public members of the derived class.

33. T F The base class constructor is called after the derived class constructor.

34. T F The base class destructor is called after the derived class destructor.

35. T F It isn't possible for a base class to have more than one constructor.

36. T F Arguments are passed to the base class constructor by the derived class constructor.

37. T F A member function of a derived class may not have the same name as a member function of the base class.

38. T F Pointers to a base class may be assigned the address of a derived class object.

39. T F A base class may not be derived from another class.

Find the Errors

40. Each of the following class declarations and/or member function definitions has errors. Find as many as you can.

A)
```cpp
class Car, public Vehicle
{
    public:
        Car();
        ~Car();
    protected:
        int passengers;
}
```

B)
```cpp
class Truck, public : Vehicle, protected
{
    private:
        float cargoWeight;
    public:
        Truck();
        ~Truck();
};
```

C)
```cpp
class SnowMobile : Vehicle
{
    protected:
        int horsePower;
        float weight;
    public:
        SnowMobile(int h, float w), Vehicle(h)
                { horsePower = h; }
        ~SnowMobile();
};
```

D)
```cpp
class Table : public Furniture
{
    protected:
        int numSeats;
    public:
        Table(int n) : Furniture(numSeats)
                    { numSeats = n; }
        ~Table();
};
```

E)   `class Tank : public Cylinder`
```
    {
        private:
            int fuelType;
            float gallons;
        public:
            Tank();
            ~Tank();
            void setContents(float);
            void setContents(float);
    };
```

F)   `class Three : public Two : public One`
```
    {
        protected:
            int x;
        public:
            Three(int a, int b, int c), Two(b), Three(c)
                    { x = a; }
            ~Three();
    };
```

Programming Challenges

General Requirements

Each program should have a section of comments at the top. The comments should contain your name, the date the program was written, the chapter the assignment appeared in, and the assignment number and name. Here is an example:

```
// Written by Jill Johnson
// March 31, 2003
// Chapter 13
// Assignment 1. Time Format
```

For each program that displays a dollar amount, format the output in fixed-point notation with two decimal places of precision. Be sure the decimal place always displays, even when the number is zero or has no fractional part.

1. Time Format

In Program 13-12, the file `time.h` contains a `Time` class. Design a class called `MilTime` that is derived from the `Time` class. The `MilTime` class should convert time in military (24-hour) format to the standard time format used by the `Time` class. The class should have the following member variables:

`milHours:`	Contains the hour in 24-hour format. For example, 1:00 p.m. would be stored as 1300 hours, and 4:30 p.m. would be stored as 1630 hours.
`milSeconds:`	Contains the seconds in standard format.

The class should have the following member functions:

`MilTime:`	The constructor should accept arguments for the hour and seconds, in military format. The time should then be converted to standard time and stored in the `hours`, `min`, and `sec` variables of the `Time` class.
`setTime:`	Accepts arguments to be stored in the `milHours` and `milSeconds` variables. The time should then be converted to standard time and stored in the `hours`, `min`, and `sec` variables of the `Time` class.
`getHour:`	Returns the hour in military format.
`getStandHr:`	Returns the hour in standard format.

Demonstrate the class in a program that asks the user to enter the time in military format. The program should then display the time in both military and standard format.

Input Validation: The `MilTime` *class should not accept hours greater than 2359 or less than 0. It should not accept seconds greater than 59 or less than 0.*

2. Employee Information

Design a base class named `Employee`. The class should keep the following information in member variables:

- ◆ Employee name
- ◆ Social Security number, in the format XXX-XX-XXXX, where each X is a digit within the range 0 through 9.
- ◆ Employee number, in the format XXX–L, where each X is a digit within the range 0 through 9, and the L is a letter within the range A through M.
- ◆ Hire date

Add a constructor, destructor, and other appropriate member functions to the class. The constructor should dynamically allocate enough memory to hold the employee's name, and the destructor should free the unused memory.

Next, design a class named `EmployeePay`. This class should be derived from the `Employee` class. It should keep the following information in member variables:

Annual pay
Monthly pay
Dependents (the number of dependents the employee claims)

Demonstrate the class in a program that asks the user to enter sample data, and then displays it on the screen.

Input Validation: Only accept valid Social Security numbers (with no alphabetic characters) and valid employee numbers (as described here). Do not accept negative values for annual pay or the number of dependents.

3. Hourly Pay

Design a class called `HourlyPay`, derived from the `EmployeePay` class you designed in assignment 2. The `HourlyPay` class should store the following information in member variables:

> Hourly pay rate
> Overtime pay rate
> Number of hours worked

Demonstrate the class in a program that asks the user to enter sample data and then displays it on the screen.

Input Validation: Do not accept values over 30 or negative values for the hourly pay rate. Do not accept values over 45 or negative values for the overtime pay rate. Do not accept values over 60 for hours worked.

4. Time Clock

Design a class named `TimeClock`. The class should be derived from the `MilTime` class you designed in assignment 1. The class should allow the programmer to pass two times to it: starting time and ending time. The class should have a member function that returns the amount of time elapsed between the two times. For example, if the starting time is 900 hours (9:00 a.m.) and the ending time is 1300 hours (1:00 p.m.), the elapsed time is 4 hours.

Input Validation: The class should not accept hours greater than 2359 or less than 0.

5. Pay Check

Write a program that uses the classes you designed in assignments 3 and 4. The program should ask for sample data for the employee information and the starting and ending work times, and then calculate the employee's pay. Display the information on the screen.

6. Student Information

Design a class called `StudentInfo`. It should have member variables for the following information:

> Student name
> Student ID number (12 characters)
> Major (computer science, business, etc.)

Write appropriate member functions to store and retrieve information in the member variables. The constructor should dynamically allocate enough memory to hold the student's name. The destructor should free the memory.

Design another class called `Grades`. This class should be derived from the `StudentInfo` class. It should have the member variables for the following information:

Test grades (The class should hold 10 test grades.)
Test average

Write appropriate member functions to store and retrieve information in the member variables.

Demonstrate the classes in a program that declares an array of `Grades` objects. The user should enter the test grades for each student, and the program should display each student's average.

Input Validation: Do not accept test scores less than zero or greater than 100 (the teacher doesn't give extra credit!).

7. Products and Services

This assignment is based on Programming Challenge 6 in Chapter 11, which asked you to design a `DivSales` class. Design another class named `SalesType`, which is derived from the `DivSales` class. The `SalesType` class should have the two following member variables:

`products:`   A four-element array for holding the quarterly figures for product sales

`services:`   A four-element array for holding the quarterly figures for sales of services

The sum of each quarter's product and service sales is the total sales of the division for the quarter. (In other words, `products[0]` + `services[0]` = the division's total sales for the first quarter.)

Modify the program you wrote in Chapter 11 so it asks the user to enter the product and service sales for each division. The program should still display each division's total sales for each quarter and the total corporate sales for the year.

Input Validation: Do not accept negative values for any sales figures.

8. Pure Abstract Base Class Project

Define a pure abstract base class called `BasicShape`. The `BasicShape` class should have the following members.

Private Member Variable
`area`, a `double` used to hold the shape's area.

Public Member Functions
`getArea`. This function should return the value in the member variable `area`.
`calcArea`. This function should be a pure virtual function.

Next, define a class named `Circle`. It should be derived from the `BasicShape` class. It should have the following members:

Private Member Variables
`centerX`, a `long` integer used to hold the x coordinate of the circle's center
`centerY`, a `long` integer used to hold the y coordinate of the circle's center
`radius`, a double used to hold the circle's radius

Public Member Functions
Constructor—accepts values for `centerX`, `centerY`, and `radius`. Should call the overridden `calcArea` function described below.
`getCenterX`—returns the value in `centerX`.
`getCenterY`—returns the value in `centerY`.
`calcArea`—calculates the area of the circle using the formula
    `area = 3.14159 * radius * radius`
and stores the result in the inherited member area.

Next, define a class named `Rectangle`. It should be derived from the `BasicShape` class. It should have the following members.

Private Member Variables
`width`, a `long` integer used to hold the width of the rectangle
`length`, a `long` integer used to hold the length of the rectangle

Public Member Functions
Constructor—accepts values for width and length. Should call the overridden `calcArea` function described below.
`getWidth`—returns the value in width.
`getLength`—returns the value in length.
`calcArea`—calculates the area of the rectangle using the formula
    `area = length * width`
and stores the result in the inherited member area.

After you have created these classes, create a driver program that declares a `Circle` object and a `Rectangle` object. Demonstrate that each object properly calculates and reports its area.

Group Project

9. Bank Accounts
This program should be designed and written by a team of students. Here are some suggestions:

- ◆ One or more students may work on a single class.
- ◆ The requirements of the program should be analyzed so each student is given about the same work load.

♦ The parameters and return types of each function and class member function should be decided in advance.

♦ The program will be best implemented as a multi-file program.

Design a generic class to hold the following information about a bank account:

Balance
Number of deposits this month
Number of withdrawals
Annual interest rate
Monthly service charges

The class should have the following member functions:

Constructor:	Accepts arguments for the balance and annual interest rate.
deposit:	A virtual function that accepts an argument for the amount of the deposit. The function should add the argument to the account balance. It should also increment the variable holding the number of deposits.
withdraw:	A virtual function that accepts an argument for the amount of the withdrawal. The function should subtract the argument from the balance. It should also increment the variable holding the number of withdrawals.
calcInt:	A virtual function that updates the balance by calculating the monthly interest earned by the account, and adding this interest to the balance. This is performed by the following formulas:

$$\text{Monthly Interest Rate} = (\text{Annual Interest Rate}/12)$$
$$\text{Monthly Interest} = \text{Balance} * \text{Monthly Interest Rate}$$
$$\text{Balance} = \text{Balance} + \text{Monthly Interest}$$

monthlyProc:	A virtual function that subtracts the monthly service charges from the balance, calls the calcInt function, and sets the variables that hold the number of withdrawals, number of deposits, and monthly service charges to zero.

Next, design a savings account class, derived from the generic account class. The savings account class should have the following additional member:

status (to represent an active or inactive account)

If the balance of a savings account falls below $25, it becomes inactive. (The status member could be a flag variable.) No more withdrawals may be made until the balance is raised above $25, at which time the account becomes active again. The savings account class should have the following member functions:

withdraw: A function that checks to see if the account is inactive before a withdrawal is made. (No withdrawal will be allowed if the account is not active.) A withdrawal is then made by calling the base class version of the function.

deposit: A function that checks to see if the account is inactive before a deposit is made. If the account is inactive and the deposit brings the balance above $25, the account becomes active again. The deposit is then made by calling the base class version of the function.

monthlyProc: Before the base class function is called, this function checks the number of withdrawals. If the number of withdrawals for the month is more than four, a service charge of $1 for each withdrawal above four is added to the base class variable that holds the monthly service charges. (Don't forget to check the account balance after the service charge is taken. If the balance falls below $25, the account becomes inactive.)

Next, design a checking account class, also derived from the generic account class. It should have the following member functions:

withdraw: Before the base class function is called, this function will determine if a withdrawal (a check written) will cause the balance to go below $0. If the blanace goes below $0, a service charge of $15 will be taken from the account. (The withdrawal will not be made.) If there isn't enough in the account to pay the service charge, the balance will become negative and the customer will owe the negative amount to the bank.

monthlyProc: Before the base class function is called, this function adds the monthly fee of $5 plus $0.10 per withdrawal (check written) to the base class variable that holds the monthly service charges.

Write a complete program that demonstrates these classes by asking the user to enter the amounts of deposits and withdrawals for a savings account and checking account. The program should display statistics for the month, including beginning balance, total amount of deposits, total amount of withdrawals, service charges, and the ending balance.

Note: You may need to add more member variables and functions to the classes than those listed here.

Case

Serendipity Booksellers Software Development Project—Part 13: *A Problem-Solving Exercise*

1. Create a Class Hierarchy for the BookData Class

Break the BookData class into two classes: TitleInfo and BookData. TitleInfo will become the base class and BookData will become the derived class. The following variables and functions will become members of TitleInfo:

Member Variables

```
title
isbn
author
publisher
```

Member Functions

```
setTitle
setISBN
setAuthor
setPub
bookMatch
getTitle
getISBN
getAuthor
getPub
```

The following variables and functions will remain members of BookData:

Member Variables

```
dateAdded
qtyOnHand
wholesale
retail
```

Member Functions

```
setDateAdded
setQty
setWholesale
setRetail
isEmpty
removeBook
getDateAdded
getQty
getWholesale
getRetail
```

2. Create the Sale Class

Create a class named Sale, which is derived from the BookData class. Its purpose is to perform the necessary calculations for the sale of one or more books. It should have the following members.

taxRate	A static private member, used to hold the sales tax rate
qtySold	The quantity of a single book title being purchased
tax	The sales tax on a single title times its quantity, calculated as qtySold times retail times taxRate (retail is inherited from BookData.)
subtotal	retail times qtySold plus tax
total	A private static member, used to hold the total of an entire sale

You should determine the member functions needed to initialize, store, and retrieve data with the member variables.

The cashier function should ask the user how many titles the customer is purchasing. It should then dynamically allocate an array of Sale class objects large enough for that many titles. The function will use the array of Sale class objects to compute the necessary information for a customer's sale. The function will then display the simulated sales slip on the screen.

Files and Advanced I/O

Topics

14.1   Files

> **CONCEPT**   A file is a collection of information, usually stored on a computer's disk. Information can be saved to files and later retrieved.

Files are crucial to the operation of many real-world programs. Examples of familiar types of software packages that use files extensively are

- ◆ **Word Processors:** Word processing programs are used to write letters, memos, reports, and other documents. The documents are then saved in files so they can be edited and printed.

- ◆ **Database Management Systems:** DBMSs are used to create and maintain databases. Databases are files that contain large collections of information, such as payroll records, inventories, sales statistics, and customer records.

◆ **Spreadsheets:** Spreadsheet programs are used to work with numerical data. Numbers and mathematical formulas can be inserted into the rows and columns of the spreadsheet. The spreadsheet can then be saved to a file for use later.

◆ **Compilers:** Compilers translate the source code of a program, which is saved in a file, into an executable file. Throughout the previous chapters of this book you have created many C++ source files and compiled them to executable files.

In previous chapters, you learned how to open files, how to read files, and how to store data in files. In this chapter, we briefly review some of what you already know, then cover additional information on the use of files.

File-Naming Conventions

Each operating system has its own rules for naming files. Some systems allow long filenames such as

```
infoFrom1997
corpSalesReport
vehicleRegistrations
```

Other systems only allow shorter file names. MS-DOS, for example, allows filenames of no more than eight characters with an optional three-character extension.

Extensions are commonly used with filenames. The name and extension are separated by a period, called a "dot." While the filename identifies the file's purpose, the extension identifies the type of information contained in the file. For example, the .cpp extension identifies a C++ program. The filename `payroll.cpp` would identify a payroll program written in C++. Table 14-1 lists other example filenames and the type of information they contain.

Table 14-1

File Name and Extension	File Contents
myprog.bas	BASIC program
menu.bat	DOS batch file
install.doc	Microsoft Word file
crunch.exe	Executable file
bob.html	HTML file
model.java	Java program or applet
invent.obj	Object file
prog1.bpr	Borland C++ project file
ansi.sys	System device driver
readme.txt	Text file

Using Files

As you learned in Chapter 3, there are three steps to using a file: The file must be opened, the file is then read or written, and finally, the file should be closed when the program is done with it. In C++, files are used through *file stream objects*. These are objects belonging to the `ifstream`, `ofstream`, and `fstream` classes. Access to these classes is gained by placing the include directive

```
#include <fstream>
```

in your program. Objects of type `ifstream` connect to input files, while objects of type `ofstream` connect to output files. Objects of the `fstream` class can be used for input, output, or both input and output at the same time. For each file that you want to use in your program, you should first determine whether you want to use it for input, output, or both, then define an appropriate file stream object to be used to connect to the file. For example, to read an input file `inFile`, write an output file `outFile`, and use a third file `ioFile` for either input or output, you would define three file stream objects as follows:

```
ifstream inFile;
ofstream outFile;
fstream ioFile;
```

Using Variable File Names

You have already learned how to specify names of files to be opened or created by coding the literal name of the file into your program. For example, to read a file called `demoFile.txt`, you would write

```
inFile.open("demoFile.txt");
```

While this is convenient for student programs, real-world applications cannot require a specific file name: They must read the name of the file the user wants to use. To do this, define an array of characters to hold the name of the file, read the name into the array, and then pass the array to the `open` function:

```
ifstream inFile;
char fileName[81];
cout << "Please enter the name of the file: ";
cin.getline(filename, 81);
inFile.open(fileName);
```

You should be aware that the `open` function of file stream objects expects the name of the file to be a C-string and will not accept C++ `string` objects. If you already have the name of the file in a string object, you need to use the `c_str` or `data` member functions to extract the C-string from the string object:

```
ifstream inFile;
string fileName;
cout << "Please enter the name of the file: ";
getline(cin, fileName);
inFile.open(filename.data());
```

Using a string object for the filename has the drawback of requiring an extra step to extract the C-string, but it has the advantage of avoiding possible buffer overflow problems if the name of the file entered by the user is longer than the array can hold.

How the Program Locates Files

The name of a file being given to a program can be simple, including just the name of the file, as in

```
myfile.dat
```

or it can be a full pathname like

```
C:\csc\programs\myfile.dat
```

which specifies the path through the directories on the system that the computer should follow to locate the file. Generally, the full pathname has to be specified unless the file is located in the current directory. The current directory is the directory the user is in when he or she executes the program from the command line. This will normally be the directory containing the file with the program's executable code.

 Note: The notion of a current directory does not apply if you are executing your program from within your compiler's development environment. In this case, files that are not specified using full pathnames will be searched for in a *default* directory. The default directory is usually the one that contains the program project's source files. For further information, see the appendices for Borland C++ Builder and Microsoft Visual C++.

Using the `fstream` Object

File stream objects require the programmer to specify whether the object will be used for input, output, or both. This is done through the use of *file open modes*. A file open mode is an option, or *flag*, that the programmer can set to determine how the file will be used. The `open` member function of the file stream objects is overloaded to take a file mode as an optional second parameter.

File open modes are predefined values that are members of the `ios` class. The `ios::in` mode is used to set the `fstream` object for input, and `ios::out` is used to set it for output. For example, we can open a file `input.dat` for input, and `output.dat` for output, using the `fstream` object and the appropriate file modes as follows:

```
fstream inFile, outFile;
inFile.open("input.dat", ios::in);
outFile.open("output.dat", ios::out);
```

It is possible to combine several file open mode flags when a file is being opened. The combination of flags is achieved through the *bitwise or* operator `|`. The bitwise or operator, which occupies the same key as the backslash on your keyboard, is discussed further in Appendix H.

Here is an example of combining file mode flags to open a file for both reading and writing:

```
    fstream dataFile;
    myFile.open("myfile.dat", ios::in | ios::out);
```

Reading and Writing Files

File stream objects have a lot of the same member functions as, and behave similarly to, the iostream objects cin and cout. In particular, the insertion operator <<, the extraction operator >>, many member functions such as getline, and even the library function getline for working with string objects work the same way with file stream objects as they do with the iostream objects. In fact, even the I/O manipulators work with the fstream objects. Program 14-1 shows the use of the insertion operator and of the getline function with an fstream object. It opens a file for writing, writes two sentences to it, closes the file, and then opens the file for reading. The contents of the file are then printed on the screen.

Program 14-1

```cpp
//This program demonstrates the use of an fstream object
//and file mode flags.

#include <iostream>
#include <fstream>
using namespace std;

int main()
{
    fstream dataFile;
    string buffer;

    dataFile.open("myfile.dat", ios::out);     //Open for output.
    dataFile << "Now is the time for all good men" << endl
             << "to come to the aid of their country.";
    dataFile.close();
    dataFile.open("myfile.dat", ios::in);      //Open for reading.
    getline(dataFile, buffer);                 //Get first line.
    cout << buffer << endl;                     //Output first line.
    getline(dataFile, buffer);                 //Get second line.
    cout << buffer << endl;                     //Output second line.
    dataFile.close();
}
```

Program Output

```
Now is the time for all good men
to come to the aid of their country.
```

There are other file modes besides ios::in and ios::out. Although we have illustrated file modes for fstream objects, file modes can be used with ifstream and ofstream objects as well. Of course, some file modes do not make sense with certain file stream objects: For example, you should not use the `ios::in` mode with an `ofstream` object. Certain file streams are opened with some of the modes already set by default. Table 14-2 gives details on default modes for `ifstream` and `ofstream` objects.

Table 14-2

File Type	Default Open Mode
ofstream	The file is opened for output only. (Information may be written to the file, but not read from the file.) If the file does not exist, it is created. If the file already exists, its contents are deleted (the file is truncated).
ifstream	The file is opened for input only. (Information may be read from the file, but not written to it.) The file's contents will be read from its beginning. If the file does not exist, the open function fails.

Many times when a program opens a file for output, the assumption is that no file of that name already exists: The intention is to create a new file to hold data generated by the program. This is why the default action in opening a file for output is to delete any existing file of the same name and replace it with a new one. The `ios::app` mode can be used if the data already in the file is to be preserved and new data being generated is to be added, or *appended*, to the end of the file. The `ios::noreplace` flag specifies that an attempt to open a file for output should fail if the file already exists. This protects important files from deletion or modification.

 Note: When used by itself, the `ios::out` causes the file's contents to be deleted if the file already exists. When it is used with the `ios::in` flag, however, the file's existing contents are preserved. If the file does not exist, it is created.

Program 14-2 illustrates the use of the `ios::app` file mode. It opens a file, writes two names to the file, and then closes the file. The program then reopens the file in append mode, adds two more names, closes the file, and terminates.

Program 14-2

```
// This program writes information to a file and closes the file,
// then reopens it and appends more information.

#include <fstream>
using namespace std;

int main()
{
    fstream dataFile;
```

(program continues)

Program 14-2 *(continued)*

```
    dataFile.open("demofile.txt", ios::out);
    dataFile << "Jones\n";
    dataFile << "Smith\n";
    dataFile.close();
    dataFile.open("demofile.txt", ios::out|ios::app);
    dataFile << "Willis\n";
    dataFile << "Davis\n";
    dataFile.close();
    return 0;
}
```

Output to File demofile.txt

```
Jones
Smith
Willis
Davis
```

Table 14-3 gives a list of file mode flags and their meanings.

Table 14-3

File Mode Flag	Meaning
ios::app	Append mode. If the file already exists, its contents are preserved and all output is written to the end of the file. By default, this flag causes the file to be created if it does not exist.
ios::ate	If the file already exists, the program goes directly to the end of it. Output may be written anywhere in the file.
ios::binary	Binary mode. When a file is opened in binary mode, information is written to or read from it in pure binary format. (The default mode is text.)
ios::in	Input mode. Information will be read from the file. If the file does not exist, it will not be created and the open function will fail.
ios::nocreate	If the file does not already exist, this flag will cause the open function to fail. (The file will not be created.)
ios::noreplace	If the file already exists, this flag will cause the open function to fail. (The existing file will not be opened.)
ios::out	Output mode. Information will be written to the file. By default, the file's contents will be deleted if it already exists.
ios::trunc	If the file already exists, its contents will be deleted (truncated). This is the default mode used by ios::out.

Using File Stream Constructors to Open Files

The `ifstream`, `ofstream`, and `fstream` classes all have constructors that can take a name of a file as well as an optional set of file open mode flags and automatically open the file. This eliminates the need for a separate call to the `open` member function. Here are some examples:

```
ifstream infile("names.dat");
fstream iofile("names.dat", ios::in | ios::out);
```

Testing for File Operation Errors

A call to open a file, such as

```
infile.open("names.dat", ios::in);
```

will fail if the `names.dat` file does not exist. It is good programming practice to check whether an attempt to open a file was successful before attempting to use the file. Testing for a successful file open operation is usually accomplished by testing the value of the stream object immediately after the call to open the file (or after the call to the constructor if the file is being opened in the constructor). The value of the stream object will be false (or zero) if the open failed. Thus the expression `!infile` will be true if the open call failed.

```
fstream infile("customer.dat", ios::in)
if (!infile)
  {
    cout << "The customer.dat file could not be opened";
    exit(1);
  }
```

Other file operations, such as attempts to read or write a file can fail for a variety of hardware-related reasons: For example, an attempt to write data will fail if the disk is full, or if the disk drive is malfunctioning. Likewise, an attempt to read a file will fail if there is no more data left to read in the file. File stream objects have a member function, `fail`, which returns `true` if an I/O operation was not successfully completed. For example, a failed attempt to open a file can be detected by using code such as this:

```
infile.open("customer.dat");
if (infile.fail())
  {
    cout << "The customer.dat file could not be opened";
    exit(1);
  }
```

This code will detect a failed attempt to open a file for input and terminate the program.

Testing for the End of a File

Testing for the end of a file is accomplished by calling the `eof` member function, as you learned in Chapter 5. The `eof` function, however, is not the best way to determine whether there is still data left in the file when reading from the file using the extraction operator. Depending on whether the file contains whitespace after the last item, code using `eof` to check for the end of a file will either miss the last data item in the file or read the last data item twice. A better way to determine if there is data left in the file is to attempt a read, and then call the `fail` function to find out if the read was successful. For example, the following code fragment will read and print to the screen all numbers stored in a file:

```
string filename;
cout << "Enter the name of the file:";
getline(cin, filename);
ifstream file(filename.c_str());
if (!file)
  {
    cout << "Cannot open the file " << filename;
    exit(1);
  }
cout << "Contents of the file are:";
cout << endl;
int number;
file >> number;
while (!file.fail())
  {
    cout << number << " ";
    file >> number;
  }
```

There is another way of testing whether a read operation was successful. This method is based on the fact that the extraction operator `>>` returns a value that can be tested to determine the success of the operation. Thus the attempt to read and the subsequent test for success can be done by putting the read operation as the test for loop continuation in a `while` loop as follows:

```
cout << "Contents of the file are:";
cout << endl;
int number;
while (file >> number)
  {
    cout << number << " ";
  }
```

Notice that the initial read outside the loop and the second read at the end of the loop are both eliminated because they are folded into the loop test.

The `eof` function can reliably be used to test for end of data in binary files because there are no whitespace separators in that kind of file. Binary files are covered in a later section.

❓ Checkpoint   [14.1]

14.1   How are files identified outside of a C++ program?

14.2   What are the three steps that must be taken when a file is used by a program?

14.3   What header file is required for a C++ program to perform file operations?

14.4   Describe each of the following file stream types:

```
ofstream
ifstream
fstream
```

14.5   What file operation must be performed before information can be written to or read from a file?

14.6   Assuming `diskInfo` is an `fstream` object, write a statement that opens the file `names.dat` for output.

14.7   Assuming `diskInfo` is an `fstream` object, write a statement that opens the file `customers.dat` for output, where all output will be written to the end of the file.

14.8   Assuming `diskInfo` is an `fstream` object, write a statement that opens the file `payable.dat` for both input and output.

14.9   Write an `if` statement that tests the file stream object `dataBase` to determine whether the file was opened successfully.

14.10 Write a statement that closes the file associated with the file stream object `outFile`.

14.2   Output Formatting

CONCEPT	Output formatting works the same way on all output stream objects.

Output formatting works the same way with file stream objects as with the `cout` object. In particular, the I/O manipulators you learned about in Chapter 3,

```
setw(n)              fixed
showpoint            setprecision(n)
left                 right
```

all work the same way with output file streams as they do with `cout`. Program 14-3 demonstrates the use of `setw(n)` to arrange output being sent to a file into columns.

Program 14-3

```
//This program formats a table of numbers into a file
//using setw(n).
```

(program continues)

Program 14-3 *(continued)*

```cpp
#include <iostream>
#include <fstream>
#include <iomanip>
using namespace std;

int main()
{
    fstream outFile("table.txt", ios::out);
    int nums[3][3] = { 2897, 5, 837,
                       34, 7, 1623,
                       390, 3456, 12 };

    // Write the three rows of numbers
    for (int row = 0; row < 3; row++)
    {
        for (int col = 0; col < 3; col++)
        {
            outFile << setw(4) << nums[row][col] << "   ";
        }
        outFile << endl;
    }
    outFile.close();
    return 0;
}
```

Output to File `table.txt`
```
2897    5   837
  34    7  1623
 390  3456   12
```

Figure 14-1 shows the way the characters appear in the file.

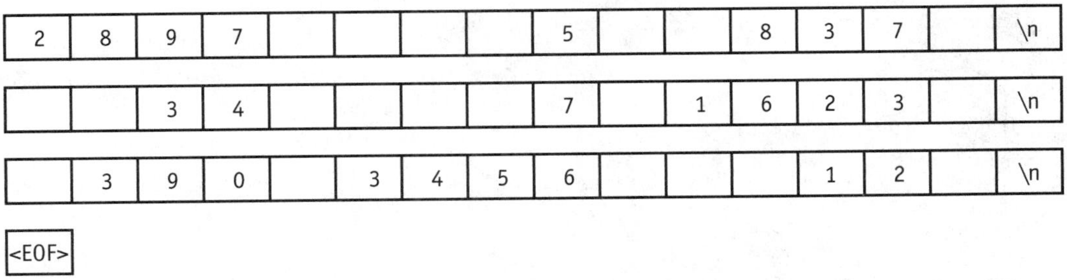

Figure 14-1

Formatting Using strstream Objects

A library class called strstream provides stream objects that write to an array of characters in memory instead of writing to a disk file. This class can be useful in formatting certain types of output. To use the strstream object, you need to include the appropriate header file in your program:

```
#include <strstream>
```

Stream objects of strstream type are defined in the usual way:

```
strstream  outStr;
```

Once a string stream object has been defined, we can write to it using the insertion operator << and the usual formatting manipulators. The C-string in the string stream can then be extracted using the member function str. For example, to print on the screen what has already been written into the string stream object, we can write

```
cout << outStr.str();
```

Program 14-4 demonstrates the use of a string output stream. It simply writes the squares of the first five positive integers to a string object, then extracts the string and prints it on the screen using cout.

Program 14-4

```cpp
//This program demonstrates a string stream output object.

#include <iostream>
#include <strstream>
#include <iomanip>
using namespace std;

int main()
{
    float squares[5] = {1, 4, 9, 16, 25};
    strstream outStr;      //String stream object

    //Format everything in the in-memory string.
    outStr << showpoint << fixed << setprecision(1);
    for (int index = 0; index < 5; index++)
        {
            outStr << setw(10) << squares[index];
        }
    //Print the string on the screen.
    cout << outStr.str();
    return 0;
}
```

Program 14-4

Program Output

```
    1.0       4.0       9.0      16.0      25.0
```

Consider the problem of formatting a set of prices for some products in columns, with the dollar amounts being right-justified in fields of width 10. For example, if we had such a price table of three rows and two columns, it might look like this:

```
$124.45      $5.00
 $67.67     $34.32
 $56.23     $89.00
```

We can format the price into a string object by first writing the dollar sign, followed immediately by the price:

```
strstream outStr;
outStr << showpoint << fixed << setprecision(2);
outStr << '$' << amount;
```

We can then extract the string `outStr.str()` and print it right-justified in a field of 10 spaces. Program 14-5 implements this strategy to format a table of prices. The formatting procedure is embodied in a function that takes as parameters the dollar amount to be formatted and returns the formatted amount as a string object. The main function then writes this string right-justified in a field of 10.

Program 14-5

```cpp
#include <iostream>
#include <iomanip>
#include <strstream>
using namespace std;

string dollarFormat(float amount)
{
  strstream outStr;
  string formattedAmount;
  outStr << showpoint << fixed << setprecision(2);
  outStr << '$' << amount;
  formattedAmount = outStr.str();
  return formattedAmount;
}
```

(program continues)

Program 14-5 *(continued)*

```
int main()
{
  float amount[3][2] = {184.45, 7, 59.13,
                        64.32, 7.29, 1289};

  //Format table of dollar amounts in columns of width 10.
  for (int row = 0; row < 3; row++)
    {
      for (int column = 0; column < 2; column++)
        {
          cout << setw(10) << dollarFormat(amount[row][column]);
        }
      cout << endl;
    }
  return 0;
}
```

Program Output
```
 $184.45      $7.00
  $59.13     $64.32
   $7.29   $1289.00
```

Table 14-4 shows a list of other I/O manipulators that can be used with C++ stream objects and gives a brief description of their meanings.

Table 14-4

Manipulator	Description
dec	Displays subsequent numbers in decimal format.
endl	Writes new line and flushes output stream.
fixed	Uses fixed notation for floating-point numbers.
flush	Flushes output stream.
hex	Inputs or outputs in hexadecimal.
left	Left-justifies output.
oct	Inputs or outputs in octal.
right	Right-justifies output.
scientific	Uses scientific notation for floating-point numbers.
setfill(ch)	Makes ch the fill character.

(table continues)

Table 14-4 *(continued)*

Manipulator	Description
setprecision(n)	Sets floating-point precision to n.
setw(n)	Set width of output field to n.
showpoint	Forces decimal point and trailing zeros to be displayed.
noshowpoint	Prints no trailing zeros and drops decimal point if possible.
showpos	Prints a + with nonnegative numbers.
noshowpos	Prints no + with nonnegative numbers.

You have already encountered some of these manipulators in Chapter 3. The oct, dec, and hex manipulators can be used with both input and output streams; they allow numbers to be read or written using the octal, decimal, or hexadecimal number systems. For example, Program 14-6 will print the numbers 63 in octal, decimal, and hexadecimal, then decimal again.

Program 14-6

```cpp
//This program demonstrates output of numbers using
//the octal, decimal, and hexadecimal number sytems.

#include <iostream>
#include <iomanip>
using namespace std;

int main()
{
    const int x = 63;

    cout << setw(20) << left << "Octal:"  << right <<  oct
         << x <<  endl;
    cout << setw(20) << left << "Decimal:" << right << dec
         << x << endl;
    cout << setw(20) << left << "Hexadecimal:" << right << hex
         << x << endl;
    cout << setw(20) << left << "Decimal:" << right << dec
         << x << endl;
    return 0;
}
```

Program 14-6

Program Output
```
Octal:          77
Decimal:        63
Hexadecimal:    3f
Decimal:        63
```

Recall from Chapter 3 that when a program writes data to an open file, the data does not go directly to the file. Instead, the data is stored in an *output buffer* associated with the file and is later transferred to the file in a process known as *flushing* the buffer. Usually the buffer is only flushed if it is full or when the file is closed. The endl and flush manipulators allow the programmer to flush the buffer at any time, hence forcing transfer of buffered data to the file. For example, the following statement flushes the buffer of an output stream:

```
dataOut << flush;
```

The scientific manipulator causes floating-point numbers to be written out in scientific notation, that is, in the form d.dddEdd. The *fill* character is the character that is written when a printed number does not fill the entire field it is printed in. By default, the fill character is a blank. The programmer can specify a different fill character by using the setfill manipulator. For example,

```
dataOut << setfill('%');
```

will make the percent character (%) the fill character.

Output Formatting with Member Functions

Stream manipulators are not the only way to format data. Field width, precision, and the various format *flags* may also be modified by using member functions of the stream objects. For example, the display field width of an output stream dataOut can be set with the member function

```
dataOut.width(n);
```

This is equivalent to using the stream manipulator

```
dataOut << setw(n);
```

Similarly, there is a member function precision(n) for setting the precision for floating-point numbers; the call

```
dataOut.precision(n);
```

is equivalent to the statement

```
dataOut << setprecision(n);
```

Note that the names of the member functions are different from the names of the corresponding manipulators. There is also a `setf` member function that can be used to do the job done by the manipulator flags: It is passed a flag that is a value defined in the `ios` class. For example, the call

```
dataOut.setf(ios::fixed);
```

is equivalent to the using the manipulator

```
dataOut << fixed.
```

Multiple format flags can be set with a single call to `setf` by combining them using the bitwise or operator. Here is a statement that sets the flags for fixed-point notation, decimal point displaying, and left-justification:

```
dataOut.setf(ios::fixed | ios::showpoint | ios::left);
```

Regardless of the way format flags are set, they can be turned off with the `unsetf` function. It works like `setf`, except the format flags you specify are disabled. The following statement turns off the fixed and left-justification flags:

```
dataOut.unsetf(ios::fixed | ios::left);
```

Table 14-5 shows the member functions that can be used for formatting.

Table 14-5

Member Functions	Description
width()	Sets the display field width.
precision()	Sets the precision of floating-point numbers.
setf()	Sets the specified format flags.
unsetf()	Disables, or turns off, the specified format flags.

Checkpoint [14.2]

14.11 Write `cout` statements with member function calls that perform the following:

A) Set the field width to six spaces.
B) Set the precision to four decimal places.
C) Set the display mode to fixed-point notation.
D) Set the display mode to left-justification and scientific notation.
E) Turn off the scientific notation display mode.

14.12 The following program will not compile because the lines have been mixed up.

```
#include <iomanip>
}
cout << person << endl;
string person = "Wolfgang Smith";
int main()
cout << person << endl;
{
#include <iostream>
cout.setf(ios::left);
cout.width(20);
cout.setf(ios::right);
using namespace std;
return 0;
```

When the lines are properly arranged the program should display the following:

```
        Wolfgang Smith
Wolfgang Smith
```

Rearrange the lines in the correct order. Test the program by entering it on the computer, compiling it, and running it.

14.3 Passing File Stream Objects to Functions

CONCEPT File stream objects may be passed by reference to functions.

When writing actual programs, you'll want to create modularized code for handling file operations. File stream objects may be passed to functions, but they should always be passed by reference. The openFile function shown here uses a fstream reference object parameter:

```
bool openFileIn(fstream &file, char name[51])
{
    bool status;

    file.open(name, ios::in);
    if (file.fail())
        status = false;
    else
        status = true;
    return status;
}
```

The internal state of file stream objects changes with most every operation. They should always be passed to functions by reference to ensure internal consistency. This is demonstrated in Program 14-7.

Program 14-7

```cpp
// This program uses the file stream object's fail() member
// function to detect the end of the data in a file.
// The program also demonstrates how to pass file stream objects
// as parameters.

#include <iostream>
#include <fstream>
#include <string>
using namespace std;

// Function prototypes

bool openFileIn(fstream &, char [51]);
void showContents(fstream &);

int main()
{
    fstream dataFile;

    if (!openFileIn(dataFile,"demofile.txt"))
    {
        cout << "File open error!" << endl;
        exit(1);
    }
    cout << "File opened successfully.\n";
    cout << "Now reading information from the file.\n\n";
    showContents(dataFile);
    dataFile.close();
    cout << "\nDone.\n";
    return 0;
}

//*************************************************************
// Definition of function openFileIn. Accepts a reference     *
// to an fstream object as its argument. The file is opened   *
// for input. The function returns true upon success, false   *
// upon failure.                                              *
//*************************************************************

bool openFileIn(fstream &file, char name[51])
{
    bool status;

    file.open(name, ios::in);
    if (file.fail())
        status = false;
    else
        status = true;
    return status;
}
```

(program continues)

Program 14-7 *(continued)*

```
//***********************************************************
// Definition of function showContents. Accepts an fstream  *
// reference as its argument. Uses a loop to read each name  *
// from the file and displays it on the screen.             *
//***********************************************************

void showContents(fstream &file)

{
    string name;

    file >> name;
    while (!file.fail())
    {
        cout << name << endl;
        file >> name;
    }
}
```

Program Screen Output
```
File opened successfully.
Now reading information from the file.

Jones
Smith
Willis
Davis

Done.
```

14.4   More Detailed Error Testing

CONCEPT	All stream objects have error state bits that indicate the condition of the stream.

All stream objects contain a set of bits that act as flags. These flags indicate the current state of the stream. Table 14-6 lists these bits.

These bits can be tested by the member functions listed in Table 14-7. (You've already learned about the eof() and fail() functions.) One of the functions listed in the table, clear(), can be used to set a status bit.

The function showState, shown here, accepts a file stream reference as its argument. It shows the state of the file by displaying the return values of the eof(), fail(), bad(), and good() member functions:

Table 14-6

Bit	Description
ios::eofbit	Set when the end of an input stream is encountered.
ios::failbit	Set when an attempted operation has failed.
ios::hardfail	Set when an unrecoverable error has occurred.
ios::badbit	Set when an invalid operation has been attempted.
ios::goodbit	Set when all the flags above are not set. Indicates the stream is in good condition.

Table 14-7

Function	Description
eof()	Returns true (nonzero) if the eofbit flag is set, otherwise returns false.
fail()	Returns true (nonzero) if the failbit or hardfail flags are set, otherwise returns false.
bad()	Returns true (nonzero) if the badbit flag is set, otherwise returns false.
good()	Returns true (nonzero) if the goodbit flag is set, otherwise returns false.
clear()	When called with no arguments, clears all the flags listed above. Can also be called with a specific flag as an argument.

```
void showState(fstream &file)
{
    cout << "File Status:\n";
    cout << "   eof bit: " << file.eof() << endl;
    cout << "   fail bit: " << file.fail() << endl;
    cout << "   bad bit: " << file.bad() << endl;
    cout << "   good bit: " << file.good() << endl;
    file.clear();          // Clear any bad bits
}
```

Program 14-8 uses the showState function to display testFile's status after various operations. First, the file is created and the integer value 10 is stored in it. The file is then closed and re-opened for input. The integer is read from the file, and then a second read operation is performed. Since there is only one item in the file, the second read operation will result in an error.

Program 14-8

```cpp
// This program demonstrates the return value of the stream
// object error testing member functions.

#include <iostream>
#include <fstream>
using namespace std;

// Function prototype
void showState(fstream &);

int main()
{
    fstream testFile("stuff.dat", ios::out);
    if (testFile.fail())
    {
        cout << "cannot open the file.\n";
        return 0;
    }
    int num = 10;
    cout << "Writing to the file.\n";
    testFile << num;        // Write the integer to testFile.
    showState(testFile);
    testFile.close();       // Close the file
    testFile.open("stuff.dat", ios::in);                // Open for input.
    if (testFile.fail())
    {
        cout << "cannot open the file.\n";
        return 0;
    }
    cout << "Reading from the file.\n";
    testFile >> num;        // Read the only number in the file
    showState(testFile);
    cout << "Forcing a bad read operation.\n";
    testFile >> num;        // Force an invalid read operation
    showState(testFile);
    testFile.close();       // Close the file.
    return 0;
}
```

(program continues)

Program 14-8 *(continued)*

```cpp
//****************************************************
// Definition of function showState. This function uses        *
// an fstream reference as its parameter. The return values of  *
// the eof(), fail(), bad(), and good() member functions is     *
// displayed. The clear() function is called before the function *
// returns.                                                      *
//****************************************************
void showState(fstream &file)
{
    cout << "file Status:\n";
    cout << "   eof bit: " << file.eof() << endl;
    cout << "   fail bit: " << file.fail() << endl;
    cout << "   bad bit: " << file.bad() << endl;
    cout << "   good bit: " << file.good() << endl;
    file.clear();          // Clear any bad bits.
}
```

Program Output

```
Writing to the file.
File Status:
   eof bit: 0
   fail bit: 0
   bad bit: 0
   good bit: 1
Reading from the file.
File Status:
   eof bit: 0
   fail bit: 0
   bad bit: 0
   good bit: 1
Forcing a bad read operation.
File Status:
   eof bit: 1
   fail bit: 2
   bad bit: 0
   good bit: 0
```

14.5 Member Functions for Reading and Writing Files

> **CONCEPT** File stream objects have member functions for more specialized file reading and writing.

If whitespace characters are part of the information in a file, a problem arises when the file is read by the >> operator. Since the operator considers whitespace characters as delimiters, it does not read them. For example, consider the file murphy.txt, which contains the following information:

Jayne Murphy
47 Jones Circle
Almond, NC 28702

Figure 14-2 shows the way the information is recorded in the file.

J	a	y	n	e		M	u	r	p	h	y	\n	4	7
	J	o	n	e	s		C	i	r	c	l	e	\n	A
l	m	o	n	d	,		N	C			2	8	7	0
2	\n	<EOF>

Figure 14-2

The problem that arises from the use of the >> operator is evident in the output of Program 14-9.

Program 14-9

```
// This program shows the behaviour of the >> operator
// on files that contain spaces as part of the information.

#include <iostream>
#include <fstream>
using namespace std;

int main()
{
    fstream nameFile;
    char input[81];
    nameFile.open("murphy.txt", ios::in);
```

(program continues)

Program 14-9   *(continued)*

```
if (!nameFile)
{
    cout << "File open error!" << endl;
    return 0;
}
nameFile >> input;
while (!nameFile.fail())
{
    cout << input;
    nameFile >> input;
}
nameFile.close();
    return 0;
}
```

Program Screen Output
JayneMurphy47JonesCircleAlmond,NC28702

The `getline` Member Function

The problem with Program 14-9 can be solved by using the file stream object's `getline` member function. The function reads a "line" of information, including whitespace characters. Here is an example of the function call:

```
dataFile.getline(str, 81, '\n');
```

The three arguments in this statement are as follows.

`str`	This is the name of a character array, or a pointer to a section of memory. The information read from the file will be stored here.
`81`	This number is one greater than the maximum number of characters to be read. In this example, a maximum of 80 characters will be read.
`'\n'`	This is a delimiter character of your choice. If this delimiter is encountered, it will cause the function to stop reading before it has read the maximum number of characters. (This argument is optional. If it's left out, `'\n'` is the default.)

The statement is an instruction to read a line of characters from the file. The function will read until it has read 80 characters or encounters a \n, whichever happens first. The line of characters will be stored in the `str` array.

Program 14-10 is a modification of Program 14-9. It uses the `getline` member function to read whole lines of information from the file.

Program 14-10

```cpp
// This program uses the file stream object's getline() member
// function to read a line of information from the file.

#include <iostream>
#include <fstream>
using namespace std;

int main()
{
    fstream nameFile;
    char input[81];

    nameFile.open("murphy.txt", ios::in);
    if (!nameFile)
    {
        cout << "File open error!" << endl;
        return 0;
    }
    nameFile.getline(input,81);              // Use \n as a delimiter.
    while (!nameFile.fail())
    {
        cout << input << endl;
        nameFile.getline(input,81);          // Use \n as a delimiter.
    }
    nameFile.close();
    return 0;
}
```

Program Screen Output

```
Jayne Murphy
47 Jones Circle
Almond, NC 28702
```

Since the third argument of the `getline` function was left out in Program 14-10, its default value is `\n`. Sometimes you might want to specify another delimiter. For example, consider a file that contains multiple names and addresses, and that is internally formatted in the following manner:

> **Contents of** names2.txt
> ```
> Jayne Murphy$47 Jones Circle$Almond, NC 28702\n$Bobbie Smith$
> 217 Halifax Drive$Canton, NC 28716\n$Bill Hammet$PO Box 121$
> Springfield, NC 28357\n$
> ```

Think of this file as consisting of three records. A record is a complete set of information about a single item. Also, the records in the file are made of three fields. The first field is the person's name. The second field is the person's street address or PO box number. The third field contains the person's city, state, and zip code. Notice that each field ends with a $ character, and each record ends with a \n character. Program 14-11 demonstrates how a getline function can be used to detect the $ characters.

Program 14-11

```
// This file demonstrates the getline function with a user-
// specified delimiter.

#include <iostream.h>
#include <fstream.h>
using namespace std;

int main()
{
    fstream dataFile("names2.txt", ios::in);
    char input[81];

    dataFile.getline(input, 81, '$');
    while (!dataFile.fail())
    {
        cout << input << endl;
        dataFile.getline(input, 81, '$');
    }
    dataFile.close();
    return 0;
}
```

Program Output
```
Jayne Murphy
47 Jones Circle
Almond, NC 28702

Bobbie Smith
217 Halifax Drive
Canton, NC 28716

Bill Hammet
PO Box 121
Springfield, NC 28357
```

Notice that the \n characters, which mark the end of each record, are also part of the output. They cause an extra blank line to be printed on the screen, separating the records.

 Note: When using a printable character, such as $, to delimit information in a file, be sure to select a character that will not actually appear in the information itself. Since it's doubtful that anyone's name or address contains a $ character, it's an acceptable delimiter. If the file contained dollar amounts, however, another delimiter would have been chosen.

As demonstrated in Program 14-1, another way to read lines of input is to use a string class object instead of an array of char, and then call the getline library function in place of the get-line member function discussed in this section. An advantage of the member function discussed in this section, however, is that it allows the use of a delimiter other than the end of line.

The get Member Function

Another useful member function is get. It reads a single character from the file. Here is an example of its usage:

```
inFile.get(ch);
```

In this example, ch is a char variable. A character will be read from the file and stored in ch. Program 14-12 shows the function used in a complete program. The user is asked for the name of a file. The file is opened and the get function is used in a loop to read the file's contents, one character at a time.

Program 14-12

```
// This program asks the user for a file name. The file is
// opened and its contents are displayed on the screen.

#include <iostream>
#include <fstream>
using namespace std;

int main()
{
    fstream file;
    char ch, fileName[51];

    cout << "Enter a file name: ";
    cin >> fileName;

    file.open(fileName, ios::in);
    if (!file)
    {
        cout << fileName << " could not be opened.\n";
        return 0;
    }
    file.get(ch);                          // Get a character.
    while (!file.fail())
    {
        cout << ch;
        file.get(ch);                      // Get another character.
    }
    file.close();
    return 0;
}
```

Program 14-12 will display the contents of any file. The get function even reads whitespaces, so all the characters will be shown exactly as they appear in the file.

The put **Member Function**

The put member function writes a single character to the file. Here is an example of its usage:

```
outFile.put(ch);
```

In this statement, the variable ch is assumed to be a char variable. Its contents will be written to the file associated with the file stream object outFile. Program 14-13 demonstrates the put function.

Program 14-13

```cpp
// This program demonstrates the put() member function.

#include <iostream>
#include <fstream>
using namespace std;

int main()
{
    fstream dataFile("sentence.txt", ios::out);
    char ch;

    cout << "Type a sentence and be sure to end it with a ";
    cout << "period.\n";
    cin.get(ch);
    while (ch != '.')
    {
        dataFile.put(ch);
        cin.get(ch);
    }
    dataFile.put(ch);
    dataFile.close();
    return 0;
}
```

Program Screen Output with Example Input Shown in Bold
Type a sentence and be sure to end it with a
period.
I am on my way to becoming a great programmer.[Enter]

Resulting Contents of the File sentence.txt:
I am on my way to becoming a great programmer.

Rewinding a File

Many times it is useful to open a file, process all the data in it, rewind the file back to the beginning, and process it again, perhaps in a slightly different fashion. For example, a user may ask the program to search a database for all records of a certain kind, and when those are found, the user may want to search the database for all records of some other kind.

File stream classes offer a number of different member functions that can be used to move around in a file. One such method is the

```
seekg(offset, place);
```

member function of the input stream classes (the file "seeks" to a certain place in the file; the 'g' is for "get" and denotes that the function works on an input stream, since we "get" data from an input stream). The new location in the file to seek to is given by the two parameters: The new location is at an offset of `offset` bytes from the starting point given by `place`. The offset parameter is a `long` integer, while `place` can be one of three values defined in the `ios` class. The starting place may be the beginning of the file, the current place in the file, or the end of the file. These places are indicated by the constants `ios:beg`, `ios::cur`, and `ios::end`, respectively.

More information on moving around in files will be given in a later section. Here we are interested in moving to the beginning of the file. To move to the beginning of a file, use the call

```
seekg(0L, ios::beg);
```

to move 0 bytes relative to the beginning of the file.

 Note: If you are already at the end of the file, you must clear the end of file flag *before* calling this function. Thus, to move to the beginning of a file stream `dataIn` that you have just read to the end, you need the two statements

```
dataIn.clear();
dataIn.seek(0L, ios::beg);
```

Program 14-14 illustrates how to rewind a file. It creates a file, writes some text to it, and closes the file. The file is then opened for input, read once to the end, rewound, and then read again.

Program 14-14

```
//Program shows how to rewind a file. It writes a text file and
//opens it for reading, then rewinds it to the beginning and reads it
//again.

#include <iostream>
#include <fstream>
using namespace std;
```

(program continues)

Program 14-14 *(continued)*

```cpp
int main()
{
    char ch;
    fstream ioFile("rewind.txt", ios::out);

    if (!ioFile)
      {
        cout << "Error in trying to create file";
        return 0;
      }
    ioFile << "All good dogs " << endl
           << "growl, bark, and eat." << endl;
    ioFile.close();

    //Open the file and read it.
    ioFile.open("rewind.txt", ios::in);
    if (!ioFile)
      {
        cout << "Error in trying to open file";
        return 0;
      }
    ioFile.get(ch);
    while (!ioFile.fail())
      {
        cout.put(ch);
        ioFile.get(ch);
      }

    //Rewind the file.
    ioFile.clear();
    ioFile.seekg(0, ios::beg);

    //Read file again.
    ioFile.get(ch);
    while (!ioFile.fail())
      {
        cout.put(ch);
        ioFile.get(ch);
      }
    return 0;
}
```

Program Output

```
All good dogs
growl, bark, and eat.
All good dogs
growl, bark, and eat.
```

Checkpoint [14.3–14.5]

14.13 Make the required changes to the following program so it writes its output to the file `output.txt` instead of to the screen.

```
#include <iostream>
using namespace std;

int main()
{
    cout << "Today is the first day\n";
    cout << "of the rest of your life.\n";
    return 0;
}
```

14.14 Describe the purpose of the `eof` member function.

14.15 Assume the file `input.txt` contains the following characters:

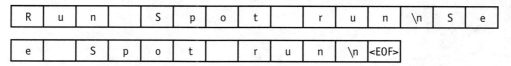

| R | u | n | | S | p | o | t | | r | u | n | \n | S | e |

| e | | S | p | o | t | | r | u | n | \n | <EOF> |

What will the following program display on the screen?

```
#include <iostream>
#include <fstream>
using namespace std;

int main()
{
    fstream inFile("input.txt", ios::in);
    char item[81];
    inFile >> item;
    while (!inFile.fail())
    {
        cout << item << endl;
        inFile >> item;
    }
    return 0;
}
```

14.16 Describe the difference between reading a file with the `>>` operator and with the `getline` member function.

14.17 Describe the difference between the `getline` and `get` member functions.

14.18 Describe the purpose of the `put` member function.

14.19 What will be stored in the file `out.dat` after the following program runs?

```cpp
#include <iostream>
#include <fstream>
#include <iomanip>
using namespace std;

int main()
{
    ofstream outFile("out.dat");
    float nums[5] = {100.279, 1.719, 8.602, 7.777, 5.099};
    outFile << setprecision(2);
    for (int count = 0; count < 5; count++)
    {
        outFile << setw(8) << nums[count];
    }
    outFile.close();
    return 0;
}
```

14.20 The following program skeleton, when complete, will allow the user to store names and telephone numbers in a file. Complete the program.

```cpp
#include <iostream>
#include <fstream>
#include <cctype>  // Needed for toupper
using namespace std;

int main()
{
    //Define a file stream object here and use
    //the file stream to open the file phones.dat.
    char name[81], phone[26];
    cout << "This program allows you to add names and phone\n";
    cout << "numbers to phones.dat.\n";
    do
    {
        char add;
        cout << "Do you wish to add an entry? ";
        cin >> add;
        if (toupper(add) == 'Y')
        {
            // Write code here that asks the user for a name
            // and phone number, then stores it in the file.
        }
    } while (toupper(add) == 'Y');
    // Don't forget to close the file.
    return 0;
}
```

14.6   Working with Multiple Files

CONCEPT It's possible to have more than one file open at once in a program.

Quite often you will need to have multiple files open at once. In many real-world applications, information about a single item is categorized and written to several different files. For example, a payroll system might keep the following files:

emp.dat   A file that contains the following information about each employee: name, job title, address, telephone number, employee number, and the date hired.

pay.dat   A file that contains the following information about each employee: employee number, hourly pay rate, overtime rate, and number of hours worked in the current pay cycle.

withold.dat   A file that contains the following information about each employee: employee number, dependents, and extra withholdings.

When the system is writing paychecks, you can see that it will need to open each of the files listed and read information from them. (Notice that each file contains the employee number. This is how the program can locate a specific employee's information.)

In C++, you open multiple files by declaring multiple file stream objects. For example, if you need to read from three files, you can define three file stream objects, such as:

```
ifstream file1, file2, file3;
```

Sometimes you will need to open one file for input and another file for output. For example, Program 14-15 asks the user for a file name. The file is opened and read. Each character is converted to uppercase and written to a second file called out.txt. This type of program can be considered a *filter*. Filters read the input of one file, change the data in some fashion, and write the data out to a second file. The second file is a modified version of the first file.

Program 14-15

```
// This program demonstrates reading from one file and writing
// to a second file.

#include <iostream>
#include <fstream>
#include <ctype> // Needed for the toupper function.
using namespace std;

int main()
{
```

(program continues)

Program 14-15   *(continued)*

```
    ifstream inFile;
    ofstream outFile("out.txt");
    char fileName[81], ch, ch2;

    cout << "Enter a file name: ";
    cin >> fileName;
    inFile.open(fileName);
    if (!inFile)
    {
        cout << "Cannot open " << fileName << endl;
        return 0;
    }
    inFile.get(ch);                 // Get a character from file 1.
    while (!inFile.fail())          // Test for end of file.
    {
        ch2 = toupper(ch);          // Convert to uppercase.
        outFile.put(ch2);           // Write to file 2.
        inFile.get(ch);             // Get another character from file 1.
    }
    inFile.close();
    outFile.close();
    cout << "File conversion done.\n";
    return 0;
}
```

Program Screen Output with Example Input Shown in Bold

```
Enter a file name: hownow.txt[Enter]
File conversion done.
```

Contents of `hownow.txt`:

```
how now brown cow.
How Now?
```

Resulting Contents of `out.txt`:

```
HOW NOW BROWN COW.
HOW NOW?
```

14.7   Binary Files

> **CONCEPT**   Binary files contain data that is unformatted and not necessarily stored as ASCII text.

All the files you've been working with so far have been text files. That means the data stored in the files has been formatted as ASCII text. Even a number, when stored in a file with the << operator, is converted to text. For example, consider the following program segment:

```
ofstream file("num.dat");
short x = 1297;
file << x;
```

The last statement writes the contents of x to the file. When the number is written, however, it is stored as the characters '1', '2', '9', and '7'. This is illustrated in Figure 14-3.

| '1' | '2' | '9' | '7' | <EOF> |

1297 expressed in ASCII

| 49 | 50 | 57 | 55 | <EOF> |

Figure 14-3

The number 1297 isn't stored in memory (in the variable x) in the fashion depicted in Figure 14-3, however. It is formatted as a binary number, occupying 2 bytes on a typical PC. Figure 14-4 shows how the number is represented in memory, using binary or hexadecimal.

1297 as a short integer, in binary

| 00000101 | 00010001 |

1297 as a short integer, in hexadecimal

| 05 | 11 |

Figure 14-4

The unformatted representation of the number shown in Figure 14-4 is the way the "raw" data is stored in memory. Information can be stored in a file in its pure, binary format. The first step is to open the file in binary mode. This is accomplished by using the ios::binary flag. Here is an example:

```
file.open("stuff.dat", ios::out | ios::binary);
```

Notice the ios::out and ios::binary flags are joined in the statement with the | operator. This causes the file to be opened in both output and binary modes.

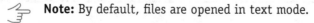 **Note:** By default, files are opened in text mode.

In order to store binary data to a file, the file stream object's write member function is used. This function is particularly useful for writing entire arrays to a file. Following is an example of its usage. (Assume buffer is an array of 10 integers.)

```
file.write((char *)buffer, sizeof(buffer));
```

The two arguments to the function call shown are

(char *)buffer	The first argument is the starting address of the section of memory which is to be written to the file. In this example, buffer is the name of an array. (The write function expects the address to be a pointer-to-char, so the cast operator is used.)
sizeof(buffer)	The second argument is the size, in bytes, of the item being written. Since buffer is an array of 10 integers, sizeof(buffer) returns 40 on a typical PC.

The read function is used to read unformatted data from a file into memory. Following is an example of its usage. Once again, assume buffer is a 10-element array of integers:

```
file.read((char *)buffer, sizeof(buffer));
```

The arguments to the read function serve the same purpose as those to the write function. The only difference is that the read function copies data from the file into memory. Program 14-16 demonstrates both these functions.

Program 14-16

```
// This program uses the write and read functions.

#include <iostream>
#include <fstream>
using namespace std;

int main()
{
    fstream file("nums.dat", ios::out | ios::binary);
    int buffer[10] = {1, 2, 3, 4, 5, 6, 7, 8, 9, 10};
    cout << "Now writing the data to the file.\n";
    file.write((char*)buffer, sizeof(buffer));
    file.close();
    file.open("nums.dat", ios::in);  // Reopen the file.
    cout << "Now reading the data back into memory.\n";
    file.read((char*)buffer, sizeof(buffer));
    for (int count = 0; count < 10; count++)
        cout << buffer[count] << " ";
    file.close();
    return 0;
}
```

Program Screen Output
```
Now writing the data to the file.
Now reading the data back into memory.
1 2 3 4 5 6 7 8 9 10
```

14.8 Creating Records with Structures

CONCEPT Structures may be used to store fixed-length records to a file.

Earlier in this chapter the concept of fields and records was introduced. A field is an individual piece of information pertaining to a single item. A record is made up of fields and is a complete set of information about a single item. For example, a set of fields might be a person's name, age, address, and phone number. Together, all those fields that pertain to one person make up a record.

In C++, structures provide a convenient way to organize information into fields and records. For example, the following structure declaration could be used to create a record containing information about a person.

```
struct Info
{
    char name[51];
    int age;
    char address1[51];
    char address2[51];
    char phone[14];
};
```

Besides providing an organizational structure for information, structures also package information into a single unit. For example, assume the structure variable `person` is declared as

```
Info person;
```

Once the members (or fields) of `person` are filled with information, the entire variable may be written to a file using the `write` function:

```
file.write((char *)&person, sizeof(person));
```

The first argument is the address of the `person` variable. The `(char*)` cast operator is necessary because `write` expects the first argument to be a pointer to a `char`. When you pass the address of anything other than a `char` to the `write` function, you must make it look like a pointer to a `char` with the cast operator. The second argument is the `sizeof` operator. It tells `write` how many bytes to write to the file. Program 14-17 demonstrates this technique.

 Note: Since structures can contain a mixture of data types, you should always use the `ios::binary` mode when opening a file to store them.

Program 14-17 allows you to build a file by filling the members of the `person` variable, then writing the variable to the file. Program 14-18 opens the file and reads each record into the `person` variable, then displays the information on the screen.

Program 14-17

```cpp
// This program demonstrates the use of a structure variable to
// store a record of information to a file.

#include <iostream>
#include <fstream>
#include <cctype>  // for toupper
using namespace std;

// Declare a structure for the record.
struct Info
{
    char name[51];
    int age;
    char address1[51];
    char address2[51];
    char phone[14];
};

int main()
{
    fstream people("people.dat", ios::out | ios::binary);
    Info person;
    char again;
    if (!people)
    {
        cout << "Error opening file. Program aborting.\n";
        return 0;
    }
    do
    {
        cout << "Enter the following information about a "
             << "person:\n";
        cout << "Name: ";
        cin.getline(person.name, 51);
        cout << "Age: ";
        cin >> person.age;
        cin.ignore(); // Skip over remaining newline.
        cout << "Address line 1: ";
        cin.getline(person.address1, 51);
        cout << "Address line 2: ";
        cin.getline(person.address2, 51);
        cout << "Phone: ";
        cin.getline(person.phone, 14);
        people.write((char *)&person, sizeof(person));
        cout << "Do you want to enter another record? ";
```

(program continues)

Program 14-17 *(continued)*

```
        cin >> again;
        cin.ignore();
    } while (toupper(again) == 'Y');
    people.close();
    return 0;
}
```

Program Screen Output with Example Input Shown in Bold

```
Enter the following information about a person:
Name: Charlie Baxter[Enter]
Age: 42[Enter]
Address line 1: 67 Kennedy Bvd.[Enter]
Address line 2: Perth, SC  38754[Enter]
Phone: (803)555-1234[Enter]
Do you want to enter another record? Y[Enter]
Enter the following information about a person:
Name: Merideth Murney[Enter]
Age: 22[Enter]
Address line 1: 487 Lindsay Lane[Enter]
Address line 2: Hazelwood, NC  28737[Enter]
Phone: (704)453-9999[Enter]
Do you want to enter another record? N[Enter]
```

Program 14-18

```cpp
// This program demonstrates the use of a structure variable to
// read a record of information from a file.

#include <iostream>
#include <fstream>
using namespace std;

// Declare a structure for the record.
struct Info
{
    char name[51];
    int age;
    char address1[51];
    char address2[51];
    char phone[14];
};

int main()
{
    fstream people;
    Info person;
    char again;
```

(program continues)

Program 14-18 *(continued)*

```
people.open("people.dat", ios::in | ios::binary);
if (!people)
{
    cout << "Error opening file. Program aborting.\n";
    return 0;
}
cout << "Here are the people in the file:\n\n";
people.read((char *)&person, sizeof(person));
while (!people.eof())
{
    cout << "Name: ";
    cout << person.name << endl;
    cout << "Age: ";
    cout << person.age << endl;
    cout << "Address line 1: ";
    cout << person.address1 << endl;
    cout << "Address line 2: ";
    cout << person.address2 << endl;
    cout << "Phone: ";
    cout << person.phone << endl;
    cout << "\nStrike any key to see the next record.\n";
    cin.get(again);
    people.read((char *)&person, sizeof(person));
}
cout << "That's all the information in the file!\n";
people.close();
return 0;
}
```

Program Screen Output (Using the same file created by Program 14-17 as input)
```
Here are the people in the file:

Name: Charlie Baxter
Age: 42
Address line 1: 67 Kennedy Bvd.
Address line 2: Perth, SC  38754
Phone: (803)555-1234

Strike any key to see the next record.
Name: Merideth Murney
Age: 22
Address line 1: 487 Lindsay Lane
Address line 2: Hazelwood, NC  28737
Phone: (704)453-9999

Strike any key to see the next record.
That's all the information in the file!
```

Note: Structures containing pointers cannot be correctly stored to disk using the techniques of this section. This is because if the structure is read into memory on a subsequent run of the program, it cannot be guaranteed that all program variables will be at the same memory locations. Since `string` class objects contain implicit pointers, they cannot be a part of a structure that has to be stored.

Checkpoint   [14.6–14.8]

14.21 Describe how you set up a C++ program to have multiple files open at the same time.

14.22 How would the number 479 be stored in a text file? (Show the character and ASCII code representation.)

14.23 Describe the differences between the `write` member function and the `<<` operator.

14.24 What are the purposes of the two arguments needed for the `write` member function?

14.25 What are the purposes of the two arguments needed for the `read` member function?

14.26 Describe the relationship between fields and records.

14.27 Assume the following structure declaration, variable, and file stream object definition exist in a program:

```
struct Data
{
    char customer[51];
    int num;
    float balance;
};
Data cust;
fstream file("stuff", ios::out | ios::binary);
```

Write a statement that uses the `write` member function to store the contents of `cust` in the file.

14.9   Random-Access Files

> **CONCEPT**   Random access means nonsequentially accessing information in a file.

All of the programs created so far in this chapter have performed *sequential file access*. When a file is opened, the position where reading and/or writing will occur is at the file's beginning (unless the `ios::app` mode is used, which causes data to be written to the end of the file). If the file is opened for output, bytes are written to it one after the other. If the file is opened for input, data is read beginning at the first byte. As the reading or writing continues, the file stream object's read/write position advances sequentially through the file's contents.

The problem with sequential file access is that in order to read a specific byte from the file, all the bytes that precede it must be read first. For instance, if a program needs information stored at the hundreth byte of a file, it will have to read the first 99 bytes to reach it. If you've ever listened to a cassette tape player, you understand sequential access. To listen to a song at the end of the tape, you have to listen to all the songs that come before it, or fast-forward over them. There is no way to immediately jump to that particular song.

Although sequential file access is useful in many circumstances, it can slow a program down tremendously. If the file is very large, locating information buried deep inside it can take a long time. Alternatively, C++ allows a program to perform *random file access*. In random file access, a program may immediately jump to any byte in the file without first reading the preceding bytes. The difference between sequential and random file access is like the difference between a cassette tape and a compact disc. When listening to a CD, there is no need to listen to or fast-forward over unwanted songs. You simply jump to the track that you want to listen to. This is illustrated in Figure 14-5.

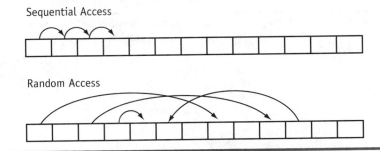

Figure 14-5

The `seekp` and `seekg` Member Functions

File stream objects have two member functions that are used to move the read/write position to any byte in the file. They are `seekp` and `seekg`. The `seekp` function is used with files opened for output and `seekg` is used with files opened for input. (It makes sense if you remember that "p" stands for "put" and "g" stands for "get." `seekp` is used with files that you put information into, and `seekg` is used with files you get information out of.)

Here is an example of `seekp`'s usage:

```
file.seekp(20L, ios::beg);
```

The first argument is a `long` integer representing an offset into the file. This is the number of the byte you wish to move to. In this example, `20L` is used. (Remember, the L suffix forces the compiler to treat the number as a long integer.) This statement moves the file's write position to byte number 20. (All numbering starts at 0, so byte number 20 is actually the twenty-first byte.)

The second argument is called the mode, and it designates where to calculate the offset *from*. The flag `ios::beg` means the offset is calculated from the beginning of the file. Alternatively, the offset can be calculated from the end of the file or the current position in the file. Table 14-8 lists the flags for all three of the random-access modes.

Table 14-8

Mode Flag	Description
ios::beg	The offset is calculated from the beginning of the file.
ios::end	The offset is calculated from the end of the file.
ios::cur	The offset is calculated from the current position.

Table 14-9 shows examples of seekp and seekg using the various mode flags.

Table 14-9

Statement	How It Affects the Read/Write Position
file.seekp(32L, ios::beg);	Sets the write position to the 33rd byte (byte 32) from the beginning of the file.
file.seekp(-10L, ios::end);	Sets the write position to the 11th byte (byte 10) from the end of the file.
file.seekp(120L, ios::cur);	Sets the write position to the 121st byte (byte 120) from the current position.
file.seekg(2L, ios::beg);	Sets the read position to the 3rd byte (byte 2) from the beginning of the file.
file.seekg(-100L, ios::end);	Sets the read position to the 101st byte (byte 100) from the end of the file.
file.seekg(40L, ios::cur);	Sets the read position to the 41st byte (byte 40) from the current position.
file.seekg(0L, ios::end);	Sets the read position to the end of the file.

Notice that some of the examples in Table 14-9 use a negative offset. Negative offsets result in the read or write position being moved backward in the file, while positive offsets result in a forward movement.

Assume the file letters.txt contains the following data:

```
abcdefghijklmnopqrstuvwxyz
```

Program 14-19 uses the seekg function to jump around to different locations in the file, retrieving a character after each stop.

Program 14-19

```
// This program demonstrates the seekg function.

#include <iostream>
#include <fstream>
using namespace std;

int main()
{
    fstream file("letters.txt", ios::in);
    char ch;

    file.seekg(5L, ios::beg);
    file.get(ch);
    cout << "Byte 5 from beginning: " << ch << endl;
    file.seekg(-10L, ios::end);
    file.get(ch);
    cout << "Byte 10 from end: " << ch << endl;
    file.seekg(3L, ios::cur);
    file.get(ch);
    cout << "Byte 3 from current: " << ch << endl;
    file.close();
    return 0;
}
```

Program Screen Output

```
Byte 5 from beginning: f
Byte 10 from end: q
Byte 3 from current: u
```

Program 14-20 shows a more robust example of the seekg function. It opens the people.dat file created by Program 14-17. The file contains two records. Program 14-20 displays record 1 (the second record) first, then displays record 0.

Program 14-20

```
// This program demonstrates the use of a structure variable to
// read a record of information from a file.

#include <iostream>
#include <fstream>
using namespace std;
```

(program continues)

Program 14-20 *(continued)*

```
// Declare a structure for the record.
struct Info
{
    char name[51];
    int age;
    char address1[51];
    char address2[51];
    char phone[14];
};

// Function Prototypes
long byteNum(int);
void showRec(Info);

int main()
{
    fstream people;
    Info person;
    people.open("people.dat", ios::in | ios::binary);
    if (!people)
    {
        cout << "Error opening file. Program aborting.\n";
        return 0;
    }
    cout << "Here is record 1:\n";
    people.seekg(byteNum(1), ios::beg);
    people.read((char *)&person, sizeof(person));
    showRec(person);
    cout << "\nHere is record 0:\n";
    people.seekg(byteNum(0), ios::beg);
    People.read((char *)&person, sizeof(person));
    showRec(person);
    people.close();
    return 0;
}

//**************************************************************
// Definition of function byteNum. Accepts an integer as      *
// its argument. Returns the byte number in the file of the   *
// record whose number is passed as the argument.             *
//**************************************************************

long byteNum(int recNum)
{
    return sizeof(Info) * recNum;
}
```

(program continues)

Program 14-20 *(continued)*

```
//*****************************************************************
// Definition of function showRec. Accepts an Info structure *
// as its argument, and displays the structure's contents.     *
//*****************************************************************
void showRec(Info record)
{
    cout << "Name: ";
    cout << record.name << endl;
    cout << "Age: ";
    cout << record.age << endl;
    cout << "Address line 1: ";
    cout << record.address1 << endl;
    cout << "Address line 2: ";
    cout << record.address2 << endl;
    cout << "Phone: ";
    cout << record.phone << endl;
}
```

Program Screen Output (Using the same file created by Program 14-17 as input)
```
Here is record 1:
Name: Merideth Murney
Age: 22
Address line 1: 487 Lindsay Lane
Address line 2: Hazelwood, NC   28737
Phone: (704)453-9999

Here is record 0:
Name: Charlie Baxter
Age: 42
Address line 1: 67 Kennedy Bvd.
Address line 2: Perth, SC   38754
Phone: (803)555-1234
```

The program has two important functions other than main. The first, byteNum, takes a record number as its argument and returns that record's starting byte. It calculates the record's starting byte by multiplying the record number by the size of the Info structure. This returns the offset of that record from the beginning of the file. The second function, showRec, accepts an Info structure as its argument and displays its contents on the screen.

The tellp and tellg Member Functions

File stream objects have two more member functions that may be used for random file access: tellp and tellg. Their purpose is to return, as a long integer, the current byte number of a file's read and write position. As you can guess, tellp is used to return the write position and tellg is used to return the read position. Assuming pos is a long integer, here is an example of the functions' usage:

```
pos = outFile.tellp();
pos = inFile.tellg();
```

Program 14-21 demonstrates the `tellg` function. It opens the `letters.txt` file, which was also used in Program 14-19. The file contains the following characters:

```
abcdefghijklmnopqrstuvwxyz
```

Program 14-21

```cpp
// This program demonstrates the tellg function.

#include <iostream>
#include <fstream>
#include <cctype>            // For toupper
using namespace std;

int main()
{
    fstream file("letters.txt", ios::in);
    long offset;
    char ch, again;
    do
    {
        cout << "Currently at position " << file.tellg() << endl;
        cout << "Enter an offset from the beginning of the file: ";
        cin >> offset;
        file.seekg(offset, ios::beg);
        file.get(ch);
        cout << "Character read: " << ch << endl;
        cout << "Do it again? ";
        cin >> again;
    } while (toupper(again) == 'Y');
    file.close();
    return 0;
}
```

Program Output with Example Input Shown in Bold

```
Currently at position 0
Enter an offset from the beginning of the file: 5[Enter]
Character read: f
Do it again? y[Enter]
Currently at position 6
Enter an offset from the beginning of the file: 0[Enter]
Character read: a
Do it again? y[Enter]
Currently at position 1
Enter an offset from the beginning of the file: 20[Enter]
Character read: u
Do it again? n[Enter]
```

14.10 Opening a File for Both Input and Output

> **CONCEPT** You may perform input and output on an `fstream` file without closing it and reopening it.

Sometimes you'll need to perform both input and output on a file without closing and reopening it. For example, consider a program that allows you to search for a record in a file and then make changes to it. A read operation is necessary to copy the information from the file to memory. After the desired changes have been made to the information in memory, a write operation is necessary to replace the old data in the file with the new data in memory.

Such operations are possible with `fstream` objects. The `ios::in` and `ios::out` file access flags may be joined with the | operator, as shown in this example declaration:

```
fstream file("data.dat", ios::in | ios::out)
```

The same operation may be accomplished with the `open` member function:

```
file.open("data.dat", ios::in | ios::out);
```

You may also specify the `ios::binary` flag if binary data is to be written to the file. Here is an example:

```
file.open("data.dat", ios::in | ios::out | ios::binary);
```

When an `fstream` file is opened with both the `ios::in` and `ios::out` flags, the file's current contents are preserved and the read/write position is initially placed at the beginning of the file. If the file does not exist, it is created (unless the `ios::nocreate` is also used).

Programs 14-22, 14-23, and 14-24 demonstrate many of the techniques we have discussed. Program 14-22 sets up a file with five blank inventory records. Each record is a structure with members for holding a part description, quantity on hand, and price. Program 14-23 displays the contents of the file on the screen. Program 14-24 opens the file in both input and output modes and allows the user to change the contents of a specific record.

Program 14-22

```
// This program sets up a file of blank inventory records.

#include <iostream>
#include <fstream>
using namespace std;

// Declaration of Invtry structure
struct Invtry
{
    char desc[31];
    int qty;
    float price;
};
```

(program continues)

Program 14-22   *(continued)*

```
int main()
{
    fstream inventory("invtry.dat", ios::out | ios::binary);
    Invtry record = { "", 0, 0.0 };

    // Now write the blank records
    for (int count = 0; count < 5; count++)
    {
        cout << "Now writing record " << count << endl;
        inventory.write((char *)&record, sizeof(record));
    }
    inventory.close();
    return 0;
}
```

Program Screen Output
```
Now writing record 0
Now writing record 1
Now writing record 2
Now writing record 3
Now writing record 4
```

Program 14-23 simply displays the contents of the inventory file on the screen. It can be used to verify that Program 14-22 successfully created the blank records and that Program 14-24 correctly modified the designated record.

Program 14-23

```
// This program displays the contents of the inventory file.

#include <iostream>
#include <fstream>
using namespace std;

// Declaration of Invtry structure
struct Invtry
{
    char desc[31];
    int qty;
    float price;
};
```

(program continues)

Program 14-23 *(continued)*

```cpp
int main()
{
    fstream inventory("invtry.dat", ios::in | ios::binary);
    Invtry record = { "", 0, 0.0 };

    // Now read and display the records
    inventory.read((char *)&record, sizeof(record));
    while (!inventory.eof())
    {
        cout << "Description: ";
        cout << record.desc << endl;
        cout << "Quantity: ";
        cout << record.qty << endl;
        cout << "Price: ";
        cout << record.price << endl << endl;
        inventory.read((char *)&record, sizeof(record));
    }
    inventory.close();
    return 0;
}
```

Here is the screen output of Program 14-23 if it is run immediately after Program 14-22 sets up the file of blank records.

Program Screen Output
```
Description:
Quantity: 0
Price: 0.0

Description:
Quantity: 0
Price: 0.0

Description:
Quantity: 0
Price: 0.0

Description:
Quantity: 0
Price: 0.0

Description:
Quantity: 0
Price: 0.0
```

Program 14-24 allows the user to change the contents of an individual record in the inventory file.

Program 14-24

```cpp
// This program allows the user to edit a specific record in the inventory file.

#include <iostream>
#include <fstream>
using namespace std;

// Declaration of Invtry structure
struct Invtry
{
    char desc[31];
    int qty;
    float price;
};

int main()
{
    fstream inventory("invtry.dat", ios::in | ios::out | ios::binary);
    Invtry record;
    long recNum;
    cout << "Which record do you want to edit?";
    cin >> recNum;
    inventory.seekg(recNum * sizeof(record), ios::beg);
    inventory.read((char *)&record, sizeof(record));
    cout << "Description: ";
    cout << record.desc << endl;
    cout << "Quantity: ";
    cout << record.qty << endl;
    cout << "Price: ";
    cout << record.price << endl;
    cout << "Enter the new data:\n";
    cout << "Description: ";
    cin.ignore();
    cin.getline(record.desc, 31);
    cout << "Quantity: ";
    cin >> record.qty;
    cout << "Price: ";
    cin >> record.price;
    inventory.seekp(recNum * sizeof(record), ios::beg);
    inventory.write((char *)&record, sizeof(record));
    inventory.close();
    return 0;
}
```

Program 14-24

Program Screen Output with Example Input Shown in Bold
Which record do you want to edit? **2[Enter]**
Description:
Quantity: 0
Price: 0.0
Enter the new data:
Description: **Wrench[Enter]**
Quantity: **10[Enter]**
Price: **4.67[Enter]**

Checkpoint [14.9–14.10]

14.28 Describe the difference between the seekg and the seekp functions.

14.29 Describe the difference between the tellg and the tellp functions.

14.30 Describe the meaning of the following file access flags.

```
ios::beg
ios::end
ios::cur
```

14.31 What is the number of the first byte in a file?

14.32 Briefly describe what each of the following statements do.

```
file.seekp(100L, ios::beg);
file.seekp(-10L, ios::end);
file.seekg(-25L, ios::cur);
file.seekg(30L, ios::cur);
```

14.33 Describe the mode that each of the following statements cause a file to be opened in.

```
file.open("info.dat", ios::in | ios::out);
file.open("info.dat", ios::in | ios::app);
file.open("info.dat", ios::in | ios::out | ios::ate);
file.open("info.dat", ios::in | ios::out | ios::binary);
```

14.11 Focus on Problem Solving and Program Design: A Business Case Study

This chapter's case study is a modification of the one presented in Chapter 6. Recall that chapter's program, written for the High Adventure Travel Agency, which calculates and itemizes the charges for each of four vacation packages. For this chapter's assignment you have been asked to enhance the program so it keeps a list of the vacation packages sold in a disk file. First, you will design structures and a class to hold and process the information about each package. Then you will complete the program with the addition of file I/O capabilities.

Creating the Data Structures

The original program, in Chapter 6, uses functions to process each vacation package. The functions keep their data in local variables. The new version of the program does not hold the vacation package information in local variables, but in a series of structures. As shown in the following declarations, there is a structure for each of the four vacation packages.

```
struct Package1              // Climbing Package
{
    int      num;            // Number in party
    int      beginners;      // Those needing instruction
    int      advanced;       // Those not needing instruction
    int      needEquip;      // Those renting camping equipment
    float    baseCharges;    // Base charges
    float    charges;        // Total charges
    float    instruction;    // Cost of instruction
    float    equipment;      // Cost of equipment rental
    float    discount;       // Discount
    float    deposit;        // Required deposit
};

struct Package2              // Scuba Package
{
    int      num;            // Number in party
    int      beginners;      // Those needing instruction
    int      advanced;       // Those not needing instruction
    float    baseCharges;    // Base charges
    float    charges;        // Total charges
    float    instruction;    // Cost of instruction
    float    discount;       // Discount
    float    deposit;        // Required deposit
};

struct Package3              // Sky Diving Package
{
    int      num;            // Number in party
    int      party;          // Number in party
    int      lodge1;         // Number at 1st lodging choice
    int      lodge2;         // Number at 2nd lodging choice
    float    baseCharges;    // Base charges
    float    charges;        // Total charges
    float    discount;       // Discount
    float    lodging;        // Cost of lodging
    float    deposit;        // Required deposit
};
```

```
struct Package4              // Spelunking Package
{
    int      num;            // Number in party
    int      needEquip;      // Those renting camping equipment
    float    baseCharges;    // Base charges
    float    charges;        // Total charges
    float    equipment;      // Cost of equipment rental
    float    discount;       // Discount
    float    deposit;        // Required deposit
};
```

When the modifications to the program are complete, a record will be stored in a file each time a vacation package is sold. Since each record will record the information on a single package, the structures can be combined into a union. Here is the declaration:

```
union Pack
{
    Package1 climb;
    Package2 scuba;
    Package3 sky;
    Package4 spel;
};
```

Figure 14-6 illustrates that the union can hold in memory the information for any one of the structures at any given time.

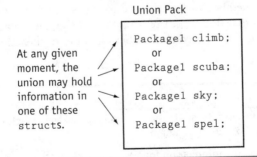

Figure 14-6

The `Package1`, `Package2`, `Package3`, and `Package4` structures along with the `Pack` union are declared in the file `packages.h`.

The next step is to create the `Reservation` class:

```
class Reservation
{
private:
    int packNum;
    Pack packs;
    void displayPack1();
```

```
        void displayPack2();
        void displayPack3();
        void displayPack4();
    public:
        void climbing();
        void scuba();
        void skyDive();
        void spelunk();
        void displayInfo();
};
```

The class declaration is stored on the student disk in the file reservation.h. Table 14-10 describes the class's member variables.

Table 14-10

Member Variable	Description
packNum	An integer, stored as a private member. This variable holds the values 1 through 4. The value stored in the variable indicates which vacation package the union packs holds. 1=Climbing, 2=Scuba, 3=Sky Diving, and 4=Spelunking.
packs	An instance of the pack union, stored as a private member, which holds the information for any of the four vacation packages.

In addition to the member variables, the class has several member functions. Table 14-11 describes them. (Notice that the climbing, scuba, skyDive, and spelunk functions written in Chapter 6 have been modified to become member functions of the Reservation class.)

Table 14-11

Member Function	Description
displayPack1	Displays the information for a Climbing package, which is stored in the climb member of the pack union.
displayPack2	Displays the information for a Scuba package, which is stored in the scuba member of the pack union.
displayPack3	Displays the information for a Sky-Diving package, which is stored in the sky member of the pack union.
dispayPack4	Displays the information for a Spelunking package, which is stored in the spel member of the pack union.
climbing	Prompts the user for information about the Climbing package, and calculates the charges for the trip. The information, along with the calculated charges, is stored in the climb member of the pack union.

(table continues)

Table 14-11   *(continued)*

Member Function	Description
scuba	Prompts the user for information about the Scuba package and calculates the charges for the trip. The information, along with the calculated charges, is stored in the scuba member of the pack union.
skyDive	Prompts the user for information about the Sky-Diving package and calculates the charges for the trip. The information, along with the calculated charges, is stored in the sky member of the pack union.
spelunk	Prompts the user for information about the Spelunking package and calculates the charges for the trip. The information, along with the calculated charges, is stored in the spel member of the pack union.
displayInfo	This function evaluates the packNum member variable to determine which vacation package information is stored in the pack union. The following action is taken, based on the value of packNum: If packNum holds 1, the displayPack1() member function is called. If packNum holds 2, the displayPack2() member function is called. If packNum holds 3, the displayPack3() member function is called. If packNum holds 4, the displayPack4() member function is called.

The code for the member functions is shown at the end of the case study.

You are now ready to add file I/O capabilities. When complete, the program will be able to save the cost information of booked vacation packages to a reservation file. It will also display a list of all the information stored in the file. The menu that is displayed lists the four vacation packages, plus a fifth option, which causes the information stored in the reservation file to be displayed. A sixth option exits the program.

New Program Modules

Three new modules, or program functions, will be added: openFile, saveInfo, and showRes. Table 14-12 describes the purpose of each module.

Table 14-12

Module Name	Description
openFile	Opens the requested file.
saveInfo	Saves the cost information of a vacation package reservation to the file currently open.
showRes	Displays all of the package reservation information in the file currently open.

The `openFile` Module

The `openFile` module is called prior to the menu being displayed. It first asks the user to enter the name of a file. That file is then opened for input and output, in binary mode. Here is the pseudocode:

```
openFile Module
    Ask user for file name.
    Open file in binary mode for input and output.
    If file failed to open
        Display error message.
        Exit program.
    End If.
End Module.
```

The C++ code is shown here:

```cpp
void openFile(fstream &resFile)
{
    char fileName[256];

    cout << "File name: ";
    cin.getline(fileName, 256);
    resFile.open(fileName, ios::out | ios::in | ios::binary);
    if (!resFile)
    {
        cout << "Error opening " << fileName << endl;
        exit(0);
    }
}
```

The `saveInfo` Module

The `saveInfo` module is called after the costs for a specific vacation package have been calculated. The user is asked if he or she wants to save the information. If so, the data structure holding the data is written to the reservation file currently open. Here is the pseudocode:

```
saveInfo Module
    Do
        Ask user "Do you want to save this information?".
    While user provides invalid input.
    If "yes"
        Write record to the file.
        If write operation failed
            Display error message.
        End If.
    End If.
End Module.
```

The C++ code is shown here:

```
void saveInfo(const Reservation &group, fstream &resFile)
{
    char yOrN;

    do
      {
        cout << "Do you want to save this information? (Y/N) ";
        cin >> yOrN;
        yOrN = toupper(yOrN);
        if (yOrN != 'Y' && yOrN != 'N')
            cout << "Please enter Y or N\n";
    } while (yOrN != 'Y' && yOrN != 'N');
    if (yOrN == 'Y')
      {
        cout << "Saving reservation data.\n";
        resFile.write((char *)&group, sizeof(group));
        if (!resFile)
            cout << "Could not write to resFile!\n";
      }
}
```

The showRes Module

When the user selects option 5 from the menu, the showRes module is called. This function moves the file's read position to the beginning of the file. It then begins a loop that reads each record from the file and displays its information. The loop repeats until the end of the file is encountered. Here is the pseudocode:

```
showRes Module
    Seek beginning of file.
    While not at the end of file
        Read a record from the file.
        Display the record.
        Ask user to press a key to continue.
    End While.
End Module.
```

The C++ code is shown here:

```
void showRes(fstream &resFile)
{

    Reservation temp;
    char skip[2];

    resFile.seekg(0L, ios::beg); // Go to beginning of resFile.
    while (!resFile.eof())
      {
```

```
            resFile.read((char *)&temp, sizeof(temp));
            if (!resFile.eof())
            {
                temp.displayInfo();
                cout << "Type a character and press Enter "
                    << "to continue:";
                cin >> skip;
            }
        }
        if (resFile.fail())
            resFile.clear();
    }
```

The function declares a local object, temp, which is a Reservation class object. It's used to hold each record as they are read from the file. After each record's information is displayed, the message "Type a character and press Enter" is displayed. When the user performs this action, the function repeats the loop, reading the next record.

The last if statement tests the condition of the file's fail bit. If file.fail returns true, the fail bit is cleared so processing may resume. (The fail bit may be set after the last record has been read, as a result of the read member trying to read past the end of the file.)

Program 14-25 shows the entire program.

Program 14-25

Contents of packages.h
```
#ifndef PACKAGES_H
#define PACKAGES_H

// Data Structures

struct Package1                 // Climbing Package
{
    int     num;                // Number in party
    int     beginners;          // Those needing instruction
    int     advanced;           // Those not needing instruction
    int     needEquip;          // Those renting camping equipment
    float   baseCharges;        // Base charges
    float   charges;            // Total charges
    float   instruction;        // Cost of instruction
    float   equipment;          // Cost of equipment rental
    float   discount;           // Discount
    float   deposit;            // Required deposit
};
```

(program continues)

Program 14-25 *(continued)*

```
struct Package2                // Scuba Package
{
    int      num;              // Number in party
    int      beginners;        // Those needing instruction
    int      advanced;         // Those not needing instruction
    float    baseCharges;      // Base charges
    float    charges;          // Total charges
    float    instruction;      // Cost of instruction
    float    discount;         // Discount
    float    deposit;          // Required deposit
};

struct Package3                // Sky Diving Package
{
    int      num;              // Number in party
    int      party;            // Number in party
    int      lodge1;           // Number at 1st lodging choice
    int      lodge2;           // Number at 2nd lodging choice
    float    baseCharges;      // Base charges
    float    charges;          // Total charges
    float    discount;         // Discount
    float    lodging;          // Cost of lodging
    float    deposit;          // Required deposit
};

struct Package4                // Spelunking Package
{
    int      num;              // Number in party
    int      needEquip;        // Those renting camping equipment
    float    baseCharges;      // Base charges
    float    charges;          // Total charges
    float    equipment;        // Cost of equipment rental
    float    discount;         // Discount
    float    deposit;          // Required deposit
};

union Pack
{
    Package1 climb;
    Package2 scuba;
    Package3 sky;
    Package4 spel;
};

#endif
```

(program continues)

Program 14-25   *(continued)*

Contents of reservation.h

```
#ifndef RESERVATION_H
#define RESERVATION_H

#include "packages.h"

class Reservation
{
private:
    int packNum;
    Pack packs;
    void displayPack1(void);
    void displayPack2(void);
    void displayPack3(void);
    void displayPack4(void);
public:
    void climbing(void);
    void scuba(void);
    void skyDive(void);
    void spelunk(void);
    void displayInfo(void);
};

#endif
```

Contents of reservation.cpp

```
#include <iostream>
#include "reservation.h"
using namespace std;

// Constants for the charges.
const float climbRate = 350.0;      // Base rate - Devil's
                                    // Courthouse
const float scubaRate = 1000.0;     // Base rate - Bahamas
const float skyDiveRate = 400.0;    // Base rate - Sky diving
const float caveRate = 700.0;       // Base rate - Spelunking
const float climbInstruct = 100.0;  // Climbing instruction
const float scubaInstruct = 100.0;  // Scuba instruction
const float dailyCampRental = 40.0;// Daily camping equip. rental
const float dayLodge1 = 65.0;       // Lodging option (sky diving)
const float dayLodge2 = 120.0;      // Lodging option (sky diving)
```

(program continues)

Program 14-25 *(continued)*

```cpp
//****************************************************
// Definition of climbing member function.          *
// This function calculates the charges for the      *
// Devil's Courthouse Adventure Weekend package.     *
//****************************************************

void Reservation::climbing()
{
    packNum = 1;
    cout << "\nDevil's Courthouse Adventure Weekend\n";
    cout << "-------------------------------------\n";
    cout << "How many will be going who need an instructor? ";
    cin >> packs.climb.beginners;
    cout << "How many advanced climbers will be going? ";
    cin >> packs.climb.advanced;
    packs.climb.num = packs.climb.beginners +
                packs.climb.advanced;
    cout << "How many will rent camping equipment? ";
    cin >> packs.climb.needEquip;
    // Calculate base charges.
    packs.climb.baseCharges = packs.climb.num *
                    climbRate;
    packs.climb.charges = packs.climb.baseCharges;
    // Calculate 10% discount for 5 or more.
    if (packs.climb.num > 4)
    {
        packs.climb.discount = packs.climb.charges
                    * .1;
        packs.climb.charges -= packs.climb.discount;
    }
    else
      packs.climb.discount = 0;
    // Add cost of instruction.
    packs.climb.instruction = packs.climb.beginners
                        * climbInstruct;
    packs.climb.charges += packs.climb.instruction;
    // Add cost of camping equipment rental
    packs.climb.equipment = packs.climb.needEquip *
                dailyCampRental * 4;
    packs.climb.charges += packs.climb.equipment;
    // Calculate required deposit.
    packs.climb.deposit = packs.climb.charges / 2.0;
}
```

(program continues)

Program 14-25 *(continued)*

```cpp
//****************************************************
// Definition of scuba member function.             *
// This function calculates the charges for the     *
// Scuba Bahama package.                             *
//****************************************************

void Reservation::scuba()
{
     packNum = 2;
     cout << "\nScuba Bahama\n";
     cout << "------------------------------------\n";
     cout << "How many will be going who need an instructor? ";
     cin >> packs.scuba.beginners;
     cout << "How many advanced scuba divers will be going? ";
     cin >> packs.scuba.advanced;
     packs.scuba.num = packs.scuba.beginners +
               packs.scuba.advanced;
     // Calculate base charges.
     packs.scuba.baseCharges = packs.scuba.num *
               scubaRate;
     packs.scuba.charges = packs.scuba.baseCharges;
     // Calculate 10% discount for 5 or more.
     if (packs.scuba.num > 4)
     {
          packs.scuba.discount = packs.scuba.charges
               * .1;
          packs.scuba.charges -= packs.scuba.discount;
     }
     else
       packs.scuba.discount = 0;
     // Add cost of instruction.
     packs.scuba.instruction = packs.scuba.beginners
               * scubaInstruct;
     packs.scuba.charges += packs.scuba.instruction;
     // Calculate required deposit.
     packs.scuba.deposit = packs.scuba.charges / 2.0;
}

//****************************************************
// Definition of skyDive member function.           *
// This function calculates the charges for the     *
// Sky Dive Colorado package.                        *
//****************************************************

void Reservation::skyDive()
{
     packNum = 3;
     cout << "\nSky Dive Colorado\n";
```

(program continues)

Program 14-25   *(continued)*

```cpp
    cout << "-----------------------------------\n";
    cout << "How many will be going? ";
    cin >> packs.sky.num;

    // Calculate base charges.
    packs.sky.baseCharges = packs.sky.num *
                 skyDiveRate;
    packs.sky.charges = packs.sky.baseCharges;
    // Calculate 10% discount for 5 or more.
    if (packs.sky.num > 4)
    {
         packs.sky.discount = packs.sky.charges * .1;
         packs.sky.charges -= packs.sky.discount;
    }
    else
       packs.sky.discount = 0;
    // Calculate lodging costs.
    cout << "How many will stay at Wilderness Lodge? ";
    cin >> packs.sky.lodge1;
    cout << "How many will stay at Luxury Inn? ";
    cin >> packs.sky.lodge2;
    packs.sky.lodging = (packs.sky.lodge1 *
      dayLodge1) + (packs.sky.lodge2 * dayLodge2);
    // Calculate required deposit.
    packs.sky.deposit = packs.sky.charges / 2.0;
}
//****************************************************
// Definition of spelunk member function.          *
// This function calculates the charges for the     *
// Barron Cliff Spelunk package.                    *
//****************************************************

void Reservation::spelunk()
{
    packNum = 4;
    cout << "\nBarron Cliff Spelunk Weekend\n";
    cout << "-----------------------------------\n";
    cout << "How many will be going? ";
    cin >> packs.spel.num;
    cout << "How many will rent camping equipment? ";
    cin >> packs.spel.needEquip;
    // Calculate base charges.
    packs.spel.baseCharges = packs.spel.num *
                caveRate;
    packs.spel.charges = packs.spel.baseCharges;
```

(program continues)

Program 14-25 *(continued)*

```cpp
    // Calculate 10% discount for 5 or more.
    if (packs.spel.num > 4)
    {
         packs.spel.discount = packs.spel.charges * .1;
         packs.spel.charges -= packs.spel.discount;
    }
    else
      packs.spel.discount = 0;
    // Add cost of camping equipment rental
    packs.spel.equipment = packs.spel.needEquip *
            dailyCampRental * 4;
    packs.spel.charges += packs.spel.equipment;
    // Calculate required deposit.
    packs.spel.deposit = packs.spel.charges / 2.0;
}

//****************************************************
// Definition of member function displayPack1.      *
// This function displays the information stored     *
// for vacation package 1.                           *
//****************************************************

void Reservation::displayPack1()
{
    cout << "Package: Devil's Courthouse Adventure Weekend\n";
    cout << "Number in party:  "
         << packs.climb.num << endl;
    cout << "Base Charges: $"
         << packs.climb.baseCharges << endl;
    cout << "Instruction cost: $"
         << packs.climb.instruction << endl;
    cout << "Equipment Rental: $"
         << packs.climb.equipment << endl;
    cout << "Discount: $"
         << packs.climb.discount << endl;
    cout << "Total Charges: $"
         << packs.climb.charges << endl;
    cout << "Required Deposit: $"
         << packs.climb.deposit << endl << endl;
}
```

(program continues)

Program 14-25 *(continued)*

```
//********************************************
// Definition of member function displayPack2.    *
// This function displays the information stored   *
// for vacation package 2.                         *
//********************************************

void Reservation::displayPack2()
{
    cout << "Package: Scuba Bahama\n";
    cout << "Number in party:   "
         << packs.scuba.num << endl;
    cout << "Base Charges: $"
         << packs.scuba.baseCharges << endl;
    cout << "Instruction cost: $"
         << packs.scuba.instruction << endl;
    cout << "Discount: $"
         << packs.scuba.discount << endl;
    cout << "Total Charges: $"
         << packs.scuba.charges << endl;
    cout << "Required Deposit: $"
         << packs.scuba.deposit << endl << endl;
}

//********************************************
// Definition of member function displayPack3.    *
// This function displays the information stored   *
// for vacation package 3.                         *
//********************************************

void Reservation::displayPack3()
{
    cout << "Package: Sky Dive Colorado\n";
    cout << "Number in party:   "
         << packs.sky.num << endl;
    cout << "Base Charges: $"
         << packs.sky.baseCharges << endl;
    cout << "Lodging: $"
         << packs.sky.lodging << endl;
    cout << "Discount: $"
         << packs.sky.discount << endl;
    cout << "Total Charges: $"
         << packs.sky.charges << endl;
    cout << "Required Deposit: $"
         << packs.sky.deposit << endl << endl;
}
```

(program continues)

Program 14-25 *(continued)*

```cpp
//****************************************************
// Definition of member function displayPack4.    *
// This function displays the information stored  *
// for vacation package 4.                        *
//****************************************************

void Reservation::displayPack4()
{
    cout << "Package: Barron Cliff Spelunk\n";
    cout << "Number in party:   "
         << packs.spel.num << endl;
    cout << "Base Charges: $"
         << packs.spel.baseCharges << endl;
    cout << "Equipment Rental: $"
         << packs.spel.equipment << endl;
    cout << "Discount: $"
         << packs.spel.discount << endl;
    cout << "Total Charges: $"
         << packs.spel.charges << endl;
    cout << "Required Deposit: $"
         << packs.spel.deposit << endl << endl;
}

//**********************************************************
// Definition of member function displayInfo.            *
// This function looks in the packNum member to           *
// determine which member function to call to display the *
// vacation package information.                          *
//**********************************************************

void Reservation::displayInfo()
{
    switch (packNum)
    {
        case 1:displayPack1();
                break;
        case 2:displayPack2();
                break;
        case 3:displayPack3();
                break;
        case 4:displayPack4();
                break;
        default: cout << "ERROR: Invalid package number.\n";
    }
}
```

(program continues)

Program 14-25 *(continued)*

Contents of the main program, pr14-25.cpp
```cpp
// This program will assist the High Adventure Travel Agency
// in booking reservations for any of their 4 major
// vacation packages.

#include <iostream>
#include <fstream>
#include <iomanip>
#include <cstdlib>
#include <cctype>
#include "packages.h"
#include "reservation.h"
using namespace std;

// Function prototypes
void openFile(fstream &);
void saveInfo(const Reservation &, fstream &);
int menu();
void showRes(fstream &);

int main()
{
    int selection;
    Reservation group;
    fstream resFile;

    cout << setprecision(2);
    cout << fixed << showpoint;
    openFile(resFile);
    do
    {
     selection = menu();
     switch(selection)
     {
        case 1 :  group.climbing();
                  break;
        case 2 :  group.scuba();
                  break;
        case 3 :  group.skyDive();
                  break;
        case 4 :  group.spelunk();
                  break;
        case 5 :  showRes(resFile);
                  break;
        case 6 :  cout << "Exiting program.\n\n";
     }
```

(program continues)

Program 14-25 *(continued)*

```
        if (selection < 5)
            {
            group.displayInfo();
            saveInfo(group, resFile);
            }
    } while (selection != 6);
    resFile.close();
    return 0;
}

//****************************************************
// Definition of function openFile.               *
// Accepts an fstream object as an argument. The   *
// resFile is opened for both input and output, in *
// binary mode.                                    *
//****************************************************

void openFile(fstream &resFile)
{
    char fileName[256];

    cout << "File name: ";
    cin.getline(fileName, 256);
    resFile.open(fileName, ios::out | ios::in | ios::binary);
    if (!resFile)
    {
        cout << "Error opening " << fileName << endl;
        exit(0);
    }
}


//********************************************************************
// Definition of function saveInfo.                               *
// Accepts a Reservation object and an fstream object.            *
// The user is asked if the information in the structure          *
// is to be saved. If so, it is saved at the end of the resFile.  *
//********************************************************************

void saveInfo(const Reservation &group, fstream &resFile)
{
    char yOrN;

    do
      {
        cout << "Do you want to save this information? (Y/N) ";
        cin >> yOrN;
        yOrN = toupper(yOrN);
        if (yOrN != 'Y' && yOrN != 'N')
            cout << "Please enter Y or N\n";
    } while (yOrN != 'Y' && yOrN != 'N');
```

(program continues)

Program 14-25 *(continued)*

```cpp
   if (yOrN == 'Y')
   {
      cout << "Saving reservation data.\n";
      resFile.write((char *)&group, sizeof(group));
      if (!resFile)
         cout << "Could not write to resFile!\n";
   }
}


//*********************************************************
// Definition of function menu.                          *
// Displays the main menu and asks the user to select    *
// an option. Returns an integer in the range 1 - 5.     *
//*********************************************************

int menu()
{
    int choice;

    do
    {
    cout << "High Adventure Travel Agency\n";
    cout << "----------------------------\n";
    cout << "1) Devil's Courthouse Adventure Weekend\n";
    cout << "2) Scuba Bahama\n";
    cout << "3) Sky Dive Colorado\n";
    cout << "4) Barron Cliff Spelunk\n";
    cout << "5) Show Booked Reservations\n";
    cout << "6) Exit Program\n\n";
    cout << "Enter 1, 2, 3, 4, 5, or 6: ";
    cin >> choice;
    if (choice < 1 || choice > 6)
         cout << "Invalid Selection\n";
    } while (choice < 1 || choice > 6);
    return choice;
}

//*********************************************************
// Definition of function showRes.                       *
// Accepts an fstream object as an argument. Seeks the   *
// beginning of the resFile and then reads and displays  *
// each record.                                          *
//*********************************************************

void showRes(fstream &resFile)
{

    Reservation temp;
    char skip[2];
```

(program continues)

Program 14-25 *(continued)*

```
    resFile.seekg(0L, ios::beg);          // Go to beginning of resFile.
    while (!resFile.eof())
    {
        resFile.read((char *)&temp, sizeof(temp));
        if (!resFile.eof())
        {
            temp.displayInfo();
            cout << "Type a character and press Enter "
                 << "to continue:";
            cin >> skip;
        }
    }
    if (resFile.fail())
        resFile.clear();
}
```

Program Output with Example Input Shown in Bold

```
File name: resfile[Enter]
High Adventure Travel Agency
----------------------------
1) Devil's Courthouse Adventure Weekend
2) Scuba Bahama
3) Sky Dive Colorado
4) Barron Cliff Spelunk
5) Show Booked Reservations
6) Exit Program

Enter 1, 2, 3, 4, 5, or 6: 1[Enter]
Devil's Courthouse Adventure Weekend
------------------------------------
How many will be going who need an instructor? 3[Enter]
How many advanced climbers will be going? 2[Enter]
How many will rent camping equipment? 3[Enter]
Package: Devil's Courthouse Adventure Weekend
Number in party:  5
Base Charges: $1750.00
Instruction cost: $300.00
Equipment Rental: $480.00
Discount: $175.00
Total Charges: $2355.00
Required Deposit: $1177.50
```

(program output continues)

Program 14-25 *(continued)*

```
Do you want to save this information? (Y/N) y[Enter]
Saving reservation data.
High Adventure Travel Agency
----------------------------
1) Devil's Courthouse Adventure Weekend
2) Scuba Bahama
3) Sky Dive Colorado
4) Barron Cliff Spelunk
5) Show Booked Reservations
6) Exit Program

Enter 1, 2, 3, 4, 5, or 6: 3[Enter]
Sky Dive Colorado
------------------------------------
How many will be going? 8[Enter]
How may will stay at Wilderness Lodge? 4[Enter]
How many will stay at Luxury Inn? 4[Enter]
Package: Sky Dive Colorado
Number in party:  8
Base Charges: $3200.00
Lodging: $740.00
Discount: $320.00
Total Charges: $2880.00
Required Deposit: $1440.00

Do you want to save this information? (Y/N) y[Enter]
Saving reservation data.

High Adventure Travel Agency
----------------------------
1) Devil's Courthouse Adventure Weekend
2) Scuba Bahama
3) Sky Dive Colorado
4) Barron Cliff Spelunk
5) Show Booked Reservations
6) Exit Program

Enter 1, 2, 3, 4, 5, or 6: 5[Enter]
Package: Devil's Courthouse Adventure Weekend
Number in party:  5
Base Charges: $1750.00
Instruction cost: $300.00
Equipment Rental: $480.00
Discount: $175.00
Total Charges: $2355.00
Required Deposit: $1177.50

Type a character and press Enter to continue: g[Enter]
```

(program output continues)

Program 14-25 *(continued)*

```
Package: Sky Dive Colorado
Number in party:  8
Base Charges: $3200.00
Lodging: $740.00
Discount: $320.00
Total Charges: $2880.00
Required Deposit: $1440.00

Type a character and press Enter to continue: g[Enter]

High Adventure Travel Agency
- - - - - - - - - - - - - - - - - - - - - - - - - -
1) Devil's Courthouse Adventure Weekend
2) Scuba Bahama
3) Sky Dive Colorado
4) Barron Cliff Spelunk
5) Show Booked Reservations
6) Exit Program

Enter 1, 2, 3, 4, 5, or 6: 6[Enter]

Exiting program.
```

Review Questions and Exercises

Fill-in-the-Blank and Short Answer

1. All files are assigned a(n)_____ that is used for identification purposes by the operating system and the user.

2. Before a file can be used, it must first be _____.

3. When a program is finished using a file, it should _____ it.

4. The _____ header file is required for file I/O operations.

5. The three file stream data types are _____, _____, and _____.

6. The _____ file stream data type is for output files.

7. The _____ file stream data type is for input files.

8. The _____ file stream data type is for output files, input files, or files that perform both input and output.

9. Write a statement that defines a file stream object named people. The object will be used for file output.

10. Write a statement that defines a file stream object named pets. The object will be used for file input.

11. Write a statement that defines a file stream object named `places`. The object will be used for both output and input.

12. Write two statements that use the `people` file stream object to open a file named `people.dat`. (Show how to open the file with a member function and at definition.) The file should be opened for output.

13. Write two statements that use the `pets` file stream object to open a file named `pets.dat`. (Show how to open the file with a member function and at definition.) The file should be opened for input.

14. Write two statements that use the `places` file stream object to open a file named `places.dat`. (Show how to open the file with a member function and at definition.) The file should be opened for both input and output.

15. If a file fails to open, the file stream object will be set to _____.

16. Write a program segment that defines a file stream object named `employees`. The file should be opened for both input and output (in binary mode). If the file fails to open, the program segment should display an error message.

17. The same formatting techniques used with _____ may also be used when writing information to a file.

18. The _____ member function reports when the end of the file has been encountered.

19. The _____ member function reads a line of text from a file.

20. The _____ member function reads a single character from a file.

21. The _____ member function writes a single character to a file.

22. _____ files contain data that is unformatted and not necessarily stored as ASCII text.

23. _____ files contain information formatted as _____.

24. A(n) _____ is a complete set of information about a single item and is made up of _____.

25. In C++, _____ provide a convenient way to organize information into fields and records.

26. The _____ member function writes "raw" binary data to a file.

27. The _____ member function reads "raw" binary data from a file.

28. The _____ operator is necessary if you pass anything other than a pointer to `char` as the first argument of the two functions mentioned in questions 26 and 27.

29. In _____ file access, the contents of the file are read in the order they appear in the file, from the file's start to its end.

30. In _____ file access, the contents of a file may be read in any order.

31. The _____ member function moves a file's read position to a specified byte in the file.

32. The _____ member function moves a file's write position to a specified byte in the file.

33. The _____ member function returns a file's current read position.

34. The _____ member function returns a file's current write position.

35. The _____ mode flag causes an offset to be calculated from the beginning of a file.

36. The _____ mode flag causes an offset to be calculated from the end of a file.

37. The _____ mode flag causes an offset to be calculated from the current position in the file.

38. A negative offset causes the file's read or write position to be moved _____ in the file from the position specified by the mode.

True or False

39. T F   Different operating systems have different rules for naming files.

40. T F   It isn't required that a file be opened before information is written to it, but it's a good programming practice.

41. T F   When data is written to a file, it is copied from random-access memory (RAM) to the file.

42. T F   When data is read from a file, it is copied from the file into random-access memory (RAM).

43. T F   The `iostream` file is the only header file necessary for file operations.

44. T F   `fstream` objects are only capable of performing file output operations.

45. T F   `ofstream` objects, by default, delete the contents of a file if it already exists when opened.

46. T F   `ifstream` objects, by default, create a file if it doesn't exist when opened.

47. T F   Several file access flags may be joined by using the | operator.

48. T F   A file may be opened in the definition of the file stream object.

49. T F   If a file is opened in the definition of the file stream object, no mode flags may be specified.

50. T F   A file stream object may be tested for a zero value to determine if the file was successfully opened.

51. T F   The >> operator may be used to write information to a file.

52. T F   The same output formatting techniques used with `cout` may also be used with file stream objects.

53. T F   The << operator may be used to read information from a file.

54. T F   The >> operator expects information to be delimited by whitespace characters.

55. T F   The `eof` member function returns `true` when the end of the file has not been reached.

56. T F   The `getline` member function can be used to read text that contains whitespaces.

57. T F It is not possible to have more than one file open at once in a program.

58. T F Binary files contain unformatted data, not necessarily stored as text.

59. T F Binary is the default mode in which files are opened.

60. T F The `tellp` member function tells a file stream object which byte to move its write position to.

61. T F It is possible to open a file for both input and output.

Find the Error

62. Each of the following programs or program segments has errors. Find as many as you can.

A)
```
fstream file(ios::in | ios::out);
file.open("info.dat");
if (!file)
{
    cout << "Could not open file.\n";
}
```

B)
```
ofstream file;
file.open("info.dat", ios::in);
if (file)
{
    cout << "Could not open file.\n";
}
```

C)
```
fstream file("info.dat");
if (!file)
{
    cout << "Could not open file.\n";
}
```

D)
```
fstream dataFile("info.dat", ios:in | ios:binary);
int x = 5;
dataFile << x;
```

E)
```
fstream dataFile("info.dat", ios:in);
int x;
while (dataFile.eof())
{
    dataFile >> x;
    cout << x << endl;
}
```

F)
```
fstream dataFile("info.dat", ios:in);
char line[81];
dataFile.getline(line);
```

G)
```
fstream dataFile("info.dat", ios:in);
char stuff[81];
dataFile.get(stuff);
```

H)
```
fstream dataFile("info.dat", ios:in);
char stuff[81] = "abcdefghijklmnopqrstuvwxyz";
dataFile.put(stuff);
```

I)
```
fstream dataFile("info.dat", ios:out);
struct Date
{
    int month;
    int day;
    int year;
};
Date dt = { 4, 2, 98 };
dataFile.write(&dt, sizeof(int));
```

J)
```
fstream inFile("info.dat", ios:in);
int x;
inFile.seekp(5);
inFile >> x;
```

Programming Challenges

General Requirements

A) Each program should have a section of comments at the top. The comments should contain your name, the date the program was written, the chapter the assignment appeared in, and the assignment number and name. Here is an example:

```
// Written by Jill Johnson
// March 31, 2003
// Chapter 14
// Assignment 1. Head Program
```

B) For each program that displays a dollar amount, format the output in fixed point notation with two decimal places of precision. Be sure the decimal place always displays, even when the number is zero or has no fractional part.

1. Head Program

Write a program that asks the user for the name of a file. The program should display the first 10 lines of the file on the screen (the "head" of the file). If the file has fewer than 10 lines, the entire file should be displayed, with a message indicating the entire file has been displayed.

 Note: Using an editor, you should create a simple text file that can be used to test this program.

2. File Display Program

Write a program that asks the user for the name of a file. The program should display the contents of the file on the screen. If the file's contents won't fit on a single screen, the program should display 24 lines of output at a time, and then pause. Each time the program pauses, it should wait for the user to strike a key before the next 24 lines are displayed.

 Note: Using an editor, you should create a simple text file that can be used to test this program.

3. Tail Program

Write a program that asks the user for the name of a file. The program should display the last 10 lines of the file on the screen (the "tail" of the file). If the file has less than 10 lines, the entire file should be displayed, with a message indicating the entire file has been displayed.

 Note: Using an editor, you should create a simple text file that can be used to test this program.

4. Line Numbers

(This assignment could be done as a modification of the program in problem 2.) Write a program that asks the user for the name of a file. The program should display the contents of the file on the screen. Each line of screen output should be preceded with a line number, followed by a colon. The line numbering should start at 1. Here is an example:

```
1:George Rolland
2:127 Academy Street
3:Brasstown, NC  28706
```

If the file's contents won't fit on a single screen, the program should display 24 lines of output at a time, then pause. Each time the program pauses, it should wait for the user to strike a key before the next 24 lines are displayed.

 Note: Using an editor, you should create a simple text file that can be used to test this program.

5. String Search

Write a program that asks the user for a file name and a string to search for. The program should search the file for every occurrence of a specified string. When the string is found, the line that contains it should be displayed. After all the occurrences have been located, the program should report the number of times the string appeared in the file.

 Note: Using an editor, you should create a simple text file that can be used to test this program.

6. Sentence Filter

Write a program that asks the user for two file names. The first file will be opened for input and the second file will be opened for output. (It will be assumed that the first file contains sentences that end with a period.) The program will read the contents of the first file, change all the letters to lowercase except the first letter of each sentence, which should be made uppercase. The revised contents should be stored in the second file.

 Note: Using an editor, you should create a simple text file that can be used to test this program.

7. File Encryption Filter

File encryption is the science of writing the contents of a file in a secret code. Your encryption program should work like a filter, reading the contents of one file, modifying the information into a code, and then writing the coded contents out to a second file. The second file will be a version of the first file, but written in a secret code.

Although there are complex encryption techniques, you should come up with a simple one of your own. For example, you could read the first file one character at a time, and add 10 to the ASCII code of each character before it is written to the second file.

8. File Decryption Filter

Write a program that decrypts the file produced by the program in assignment 7. The decryption program should read the contents of the coded file, restore the information to its original state, and write it to another file.

9. Corporate Sales Data Output

Write a program that uses a structure to store the following information on a company division:

Division name (such as East, West, North, or South)
Quarter (1, 2, 3, or 4)
Quarterly sales

The user should be asked for the four quarters' sales figures for the East, West, North, and South divisions. The information for each quarter for each division should be written to a file.

Input Validation: Do not accept negative numbers for any sales figures.

10. Corporate Sales Data Input

Write a program that reads the information in the file created by the program in assignment 9. The program should calculate and display the following figures:

- Total corporate sales for each quarter
- Total yearly sales for each division
- Total yearly corporate sales
- Average quarterly sales for the divisions
- The highest and lowest quarters for the corporation

11. Inventory Program

Write a program that uses a structure to store the following inventory information in a file:

    Item description
    Quantity on hand
    Wholesale cost
    Retail cost
    Date added to inventory

The program should have a menu that allows the user to perform the following tasks:

- Add new records to the file.
- Display any record in the file.
- Change any record in the file.

    Input Validation: The program should not accept quantities, or wholesale or retail costs less than 0. The program should not accept dates that the programmer determines are unreasonable.

12. Inventory Screen Report

Write a program that reads the information in the file created by the program in assignment 11. The program should calculate and display the following information:

- The total wholesale value of the inventory
- The total retail value of the inventory
- The total quantity of all items in the inventory

Group Project

14. Customer Accounts

This program should be designed and written by a team of students. Here are some suggestions:

- One student should design function `main`, which will call other program functions or class member functions. The remainder of the functions will be designed by other members of the team.

- The requirements of the program should be analyzed so each student is given about the same workload.

Write a program that uses a structure to store the following information about a customer account:

- Name
- Address
- City, state, and ZIP
- Telephone number
- Account balance
- Date of last payment

The structure should be used to store customer account records in a file. The program should have a menu that lets the user perform the following operations:

- Enter new records into the file.
- Search for a particular customer's record and display it.
- Search for a particular customer's record and delete it.
- Search for a particular customer's record and change it.
- Display the contents of the entire file.

Input Validation: When the information for a new account is entered, be sure the user enters data for all the fields. No negative account balances should be entered.

Serendipity Booksellers Software Development Project—Part 14: *A Problem-Solving Exercise*

For this chapter's assignment you are going to modify the program so it works with an inventory file instead of an array of class objects. You will still keep the `BookData` class declaration you created in Chapter 7. However, it will now be used to define the records in the file.

1. Set Up the Program to Work with the Inventory File

Include the appropriate header file and decide where you want to declare the file stream object for the inventory file. One approach is to declare a global file stream object. That way, it will be available to all functions needing file access. Another approach is to declare the object only in the functions that need to open the file, then pass references to it to functions that need to work with the file.

2. Modify the `addBook` Function

Change the `addBook` function so it works with the file instead of the array of `BookData` objects. When a new book is added to the inventory, the program will step through the file, reading each record into a single `BookData` object. The program will then call the `isEmpty` member function of the class. When it finds an empty structure, it will ask the user for the book's information. The function will then call the structure's member functions to set its variable members to the new data. Once the structure is filled with the new data, it will be written to the file, over the old record.

3. Modify the `lookUpBook` Function

The `lookUpBook` function should be changed to search the file, instead of the `BookData` class object array, for a book whose title matches the user's input. When a book is found, its information should be passed to the `bookInfo` function.

4. Modify the `editBook` Function

The `editBook` function should be changed to search and modify information in the file instead of in the `BookData` class object array. When it finds a book whose information the user wishes to modify, it should pass the new data to the class's appropriate member functions. Once the data has been modified, the record should be written to the file over the old information.

5. Modify the `deleteBook` Function and the `removeBook` Member Function

The `deleteBook` function should be changed to work with the file instead of with the `BookData` structure array. When a book is to be removed from inventory, this function should search for it in the file, and then call the class's `removeBook` member function to delete it. The `removeBook` member function should be modified so it writes the deleted record to the file.

Exceptions, Templates, and the Standard Template Library (STL)

Topics

15.1 Exceptions

> **CONCEPT** Exceptions are used to signal errors or unexpected events that occur while a program is running.

Error testing is usually a straightforward process involving `if` statements or other control mechanisms. For example, the following code segment will trap a division-by-zero error before it occurs:

```
if (denominator == 0)
    cout << "ERROR: Cannot divide by zero.\n";
else
    quotient = numerator / denominator;
```

But what if similar code is part of a function that returns the quotient as in the following example:

```
// An unreliable division function
float divide(int numerator, int denominator)
{
    if (denominator == 0)
    {
        cout << "ERROR: Cannot divide by zero.\n";
        return 0;
    }
    else
        return float(numerator) / denominator;
}
```

Functions commonly signal error conditions by returning a predetermined value. Apparently, the function in the example returns 0 when division by zero has been attempted. This is unreliable, however, because 0 is a valid result of a division operation. Even though the function displays an error message, the part of the program that calls the function will not know when an error has occurred. Problems like these require sophisticated error-handling techniques.

Throwing an Exception

One way of handling complex error conditions is with *exceptions*. An exception is a value or an object that signals an error. When the error occurs, an exception is "thrown." For example, the following code shows the divide function, modified to throw an exception when division by zero has been attempted.

```
float divide(int numerator, int denominator)
{
    if (denominator == 0)
        throw "ERROR: Cannot divide by zero.\n";
    else
        return float(numerator) / denominator;
}
```

The following statement causes the exception to be thrown.

```
throw "ERROR: Cannot divide by zero.\n";
```

The throw keyword is followed by an argument, which can be any value. As you will see, the value of the argument is used to determine the nature of the error. The function above simply throws a string containing an error message.

The line containing a throw statement is known as the *throw point*. When a throw statement is executed, control is passed to another part of the program known as an *exception handler*. When an exception is thrown by a function, the function aborts.

Handling an Exception

To handle an exception, a program must have a *try/catch* construct. The general format of the try/catch construct is

```
try
{
    // code here calls functions or object member
    // functions that might throw an exception.
}
catch(exception parameter)
{
    // code here handles the exception
}
// Repeat as many catch blocks as needed.
```

The first part of the construct is the *try block*. This starts with the key word `try` and is followed by a block of code executing any statements that might directly or indirectly cause an exception to be thrown. The try block is immediately followed by one or more *catch blocks,* which are the exception handlers. A catch block starts with the key word `catch`, followed by a set of parentheses containing the declaration of an exception parameter. For example, here is a try/catch construct that can be used with the `divide` function:

```
try
{
    quotient = divide(num1, num2);
    cout << "The quotient is " << quotient << endl;
}
catch (char *exceptionString)
{
    cout << exceptionString;
}
```

Since the `divide` function throws an exception whose value is a string, there must be an exception handler that catches a string. The catch block shown catches the error message in the `exceptionString` parameter, then displays it with `cout`.

Now let's look at an entire program to see how `throw`, `try`, and `catch` work together. In the first sample run of Program 15-1, valid data is given. This shows how the program should run with no errors. In the second sample running, a denominator of 0 is given. This shows the result of the exception being thrown.

Program 15-1

```cpp
#include <iostream>
using namespace std;

// Function prototype
float divide(int, int);

int main()
{
    int num1, num2;
    float quotient;
    cout << "Enter two numbers: ";
    cin >> num1 >> num2;

    try
    {
        quotient = divide(num1, num2);
        cout << "The quotient is " << quotient << endl;
    }
    catch (char *exceptionString)
    {
        cout << exceptionString;
    }

    cout << "End of the program.\n";
    return 0;
}

float divide(int numerator, int denominator)
{
    if (denominator == 0)
        throw "ERROR: Cannot divide by zero.\n";
    else
        return float(numerator) / denominator;
}
```

Program Output with Example Input Shown in Bold
```
Enter two numbers: 12 2[Enter]
The quotient is 6
End of the program.
```

Program Output with Example Input Shown in Bold
```
Enter two numbers: 12 0[Enter]
ERROR: Cannot divide by zero.
End of the program.
```

As you can see from the second output screen, the exception caused the program to jump out of the `divide` function and into the catch block. After the catch block has finished, the program resumes with the first statement after the try/catch construct.

Handling the Exception Thrown by `new`

The `new` operator throws a system-defined exception of type `bad_alloc` if it is unable to allocate the requested storage. For example, the following fragment of code attempts to allocate an array of two integers using the `new` operator inside of the try block. If the allocation fails, the resulting `bad_alloc` exception is caught in the attached catch block and the program is terminated with an appropriate error message. If the allocation succeeds, the code goes on to print the numbers 10 and 20.

```
int *p;
try
  {
    p = new int[2];
    p[0] = 10;
    p[1] = 20;
  }
catch(bad_alloc exceptParam)
  {
    cout << "Memory cannot be allocated";
    exit(1);
  }
cout << p[0] << " " << p[1];
```

Notice that, unlike the previous example in which the parameter to the catch block is used inside the block, this example never uses `exceptParam`. C++ allows parameters that are never used to be omitted (the type of the exception must still be specified). Thus, this catch block could be written as follows:

```
catch(bad_alloc)
  {
    cout << "Memory cannot be allocated";
    exit(1);
  }
```

What If an Exception Is Not Caught?

There are two possible ways for a thrown exception to go uncaught. The first possibility is for the try/catch construct to contain no catch blocks with an exception parameter of the right data type. The second possibility is for the exception to be thrown from outside a try block. In either case, the exception will cause the entire program to abort execution.

Object-Oriented Exception Handling with Classes

Now that you have an idea of how the exception mechanism in C++ works, we will examine an object-oriented approach to exception handling. Let's begin by looking at the IntRange class:

Contents of IntRange.h

```
#ifndef INTRANGE_H
#define INTRANGE_H

class IntRange
{
private:
  int input; // For user input
  int lower; // Lower limit of range
  int upper; // Upper limit of range
public:
  // Exception class
  class OutOfRange
    { };   // Empty class declaration
  // Member functions
  IntRange(int low, int high)// Constructor
    { lower = low; upper = high; }
  int getInput()
    { cin >> input;
      if (input < lower || input > upper)
        throw OutOfRange();
      return input;
      }
};

#endif
```

IntRange is a simple class whose member function, getInput, lets the user enter an integer value. The value is compared against the member variables lower and upper (which are initialized by the class constructor). If the value entered is less than lower or greater than upper, an exception is thrown indicating the value is out of range. Otherwise, the value is returned from the function.

Instead of throwing a character string or other primitive value, this function throws an *exception class*. Notice the empty class declaration that appears in the public section:

```
class OutOfRange
    { };   // Empty class declaration
```

The class OutOfRange has no members, and no instances of the class are ever created. The only important part of this class is its name, which will be used by the exception handling code. Look at the if statement in the getinput function:

```
if (input < lower || input > upper)
    throw OutOfRange();
```

The throw statement's argument, OutOfRange(), causes an instance of the OutOfRange class to be created and thrown as an exception. All that remains is for a catch block to handle the exception. Here is an example:

```cpp
catch (IntRange::OutOfRange)
{
    cout << "That value is out of range.\n";
}
```

All that must appear inside the catch block's parentheses is the name of the exception class. The exception class is empty, so there is no need to declare an actual parameter. All the catch block needs to know is the type of the exception.

Since the OutOfRange class is declared in the IntRange class, its name must be fully qualified with the scope resolution operator. Program 15-2 shows the class at work in a driver program.

Program 15-2

```cpp
#include <iostream>
#include "IntRange.h"
using namespace std;

int main()
{
    IntRange range(5, 10);
    int userValue;

    cout << "Enter a value in the range 5 - 10: ";
    try
    {
        userValue = range.getInput();
        cout << "You entered " << userValue << endl;
    }
    catch (IntRange::OutOfRange)
    {
        cout << "That value is out of range.\n";
    }
    cout << "End of the program.\n";
    return 0;
}
```

Program Output with Example Input Shown in Bold
```
Enter a value in the range 5 - 10: 12[Enter]
That value is out of range.
End of the program.
```

Multiple Exceptions

The programs we have studied so far test only for a single type of error and throw only a single type of exception. In many cases a program will need to test for several different types of errors and signal which one has occurred. C++ allows you to throw and catch multiple exceptions. The only requirement is that each different exception be of a different type. You then code a separate catch block for each type of exception that may be thrown in the try block.

For example, suppose we wish to expand the `IntRange` class so it throws one type of exception if the user enters a value that is too low, and another type if the user enters a value that is too high. First, we declare two different exception classes, such as

```
// Exception classes
class TooLow
    { };
class TooHigh
    { };
```

An instance of the `TooLow` class will be thrown when the user enters a low value, and an instance of the `TooHigh` class will be thrown when a high value is entered.

Next we modify the `getInput` member function to perform the two error tests and throw the appropriate exception:

```
if (input < lower)
    throw TooLow();
else if (input > upper)
    throw TooHigh();
```

The entire modified class, which is named `IntRange2`, is shown here:

Contents of `IntRange2.h`
```
#ifndef INTRANGE2_H
#define INTRANGE2_H

class IntRange2
{
  private:
      int input; // For user input
      int lower; // Lower limit of range
      int upper; // Upper limit of range
  public:
      // Exception classes
      class TooLow
          { };
      class TooHigh
          { };
      // Member functions
      IntRange2(int low, int high)// Constructor
          { lower = low; upper = high; }
      int getInput()
          { cin >> input;
            if (input < lower)
                throw TooLow();
```

```
                          else if (input > upper)
                              throw TooHigh();
                          return input;
                     }
          };

          #endif
     Program 15-3 is a simple driver that demonstrates this class.
```

Program 15-3

```cpp
// This program demonstrates the IntRange2 class.

#include <iostream>
#include "IntRange2.h"
using namespace std;

int main()
{
    IntRange2 range(5, 10);
    int userValue;

    cout << "Enter a value in the range 5 - 10: ";
    try
    {
        userValue = range.getInput();
        cout << "You entered " << userValue << endl;
    }
    catch (IntRange2::TooLow)
    {
        cout << "That value is too low.\n";
    }
    catch (IntRange2::TooHigh)
    {
        cout << "That value is too high.\n";
    }

    cout << "End of the program.\n";
    return 0;
}
```

Program Output with Example Input Shown in Bold
```
Enter a value in the range 5 - 10: 3[Enter]
That value is too low.
End of the program.
```

Extracting Information from the Exception Class

Sometimes we might want an exception to pass information back to the exception handler. For example, suppose we would like the `IntRange` class not only to signal when an invalid value has been entered, but to pass the value back. This can be accomplished by giving the exception class members in which information can be stored.

`IntRange3`, our next modification of the `IntRange` class, goes back to using a single exception class: `OutOfRange`. This version of `OutOfRange`, however, has a member variable and a constructor that initializes it:

```
// Exception class
class OutOfRange
{   public:
        int value;
        OutOfRange(int i)
        {   value = i;  }
};
```

When we throw this exception, we want to pass the value entered by the user to `OutOfRange`'s constructor. This is done with the following statement:

```
throw OutOfRange(input);
```

This `throw` statement creates an instance of the `OutOfRange` class and passes a copy of the `input` variable to the constructor. The constructor then stores this number in `OutOfRange`'s member variable, `value`. The class instance carries this member variable to the catch block that intercepts the exception.

Back in the catch block, the value is extracted:

```
catch (IntRange3::OutOfRange ex)
{
    cout << "That value " << ex.value
        << " is out of range.\n";
}
```

Notice that catch block declares a parameter object named `ex`. This is necessary, since the exception has a member variable that we want to examine. The entire `IntRange3` class is as follows, and Program 15-4 is a driver that demonstrates it.

Contents of `IntRange3.h`
```
#ifndef INTRANGE3_H
#define INTRANGE3_H

class IntRange3
{
private:
  int input; // For user input
```

```
                int lower; // Lower limit of range
                int upper; // Upper limit of range
            public:
                // Exception class
                class OutOfRange
                {   public:
                        int value;
                        OutOfRange(int i)
                        {   value = i; }
                };

                // Member functions
                IntRange3(int low, int high)// Constructor
                    { lower = low; upper = high; }
                int getInput()
                    { cin >> input;
                        if (input < lower || input > upper)
                            throw OutOfRange(input);
                        return input;
                    }
            };

        #endif
```

Program 15-4

```
// This program demonstrates the IntRange3 class.

#include <iostream>
#include "IntRange3.h"
using namespace std;

int main()
{
    IntRange3 range(5, 10);
    int userValue;
    cout << "Enter a value in the range 5 - 10: ";
    try
    {
        userValue = range.getInput();
        cout << "You entered " << userValue << endl;
    }
    catch (IntRange3::OutOfRange ex)
    {
        cout << "That value " << ex.value
             << " is out of range.\n";
    }

    cout << "End of the program.\n";
    return 0;
}
```

Program 15-4

Program Output with Example Input Shown in Bold
```
Enter a value in the range 5 - 10: 12[Enter]
That value 12 is out of range.
End of the program.
```

Unwinding the Stack

Once an exception has been thrown, the program cannot jump back to the throw point. The function that executes a throw statement will immediately terminate. If that function was called by another function, the calling function will terminate as well. This process, known as *unwinding the stack,* continues for the entire chain of nested function calls, from the throw point all the way back to the try block.

If an exception is thrown by the member function of a class object, then the class destructor is called. If statements in the try block, or branching from the try block created any other objects, their destructors will be called as well.

Rethrowing an Exception

It is possible for try blocks to be nested. For example, look at this code segment:

```
try
{
    doSomething();
}
catch(exception1)
{
    // code to handle exception 1
}
catch(exception2)
{
    // code to handle exception 2
}
```

In this try block the function doSomething is called. There are two catch blocks, one that handles exception1, and another that handles exception2. If the doSomething function also has a try block, then it is nested inside the one shown.

With nested try blocks, it is sometimes necessary for an inner exception handler to pass an exception to an outer exception handler. Sometimes, both an inner and an outer catch block must perform operations when a particular exception is thrown. These situations require that the inner catch block *rethrow* the exception so the outer catch block has a chance to catch it.

A catch block can rethrow an exception with the throw; statement. For example, suppose the doSomething function (called in the try block above) calls the doSomethingElse function, which potentially can throw exception1 or exception3. Suppose doSomethingElse does not want to handle exception1. Instead, it wants to rethrow it to the outer block. The following code segment illustrates how this is done.

```
try
{
    doSomethingElse();
}
catch(exception1)
{
    throw; // Rethrow the exception
}
catch(exception3)
{
    // Code to handle exception 3
}
```

When the first catch block catches exception1, the throw; statement simply throws the exception again. The catch block in the outer try/catch construct will then handle the exception.

Checkpoint [15.1]

15.1 What is the difference between a try block and a catch block?

15.2 What happens if an exception is thrown, but not caught?

15.3 If multiple exceptions can be thrown, how does the catch block know which exception to catch?

15.4 After the catch block has handled the exception, where does program execution resume?

15.5 How can an exception pass information to the exception handler?

15.2 Function Templates

CONCEPT A function template is a "generic" function that can work with any data type. The programmer writes the specifications of the function, but substitutes parameters for data types. When the compiler encounters a call to the function, it generates code to handle the specific data type(s) used in the call.

Introduction

Overloaded functions make programming convenient because only one function name must be remembered for a set of functions that perform similar operations. Each of the functions, however, must still be written individually, even if they perform the same operation. For example, Program 6-34 uses the following overloaded square functions.

```
int square(int number)
{
    return number * number;
}

float square(float number)
{
    return number * number;
}
```

The only differences between these two functions are the data types of their return values and their parameters. In situations like this, it is more convenient to write a *function template* than an overloaded function. Function templates allow you to write a single function definition that works with many different data types, instead of having to write a separate function for each data type used.

A function template is not an actual function, but a "mold" the compiler uses to generate one or more functions. When writing a function template, you do not have to specify actual types for the parameters, return value, or local variables. Instead, you use a *type parameter* to specify a generic data type. When the compiler encounters a call to the function, it examines the data types of its arguments and generates the function code that will work with those data types.

Here is a function template for the `square` function:

```
template <class T>
T square(T number)
{
    return number * number;
}
```

The beginning of a function template is marked by a *template prefix*, which begins with the key word `template`. Next is a set of angled brackets that contains one or more generic data types used in the template. A generic data type starts with the key word `class`, followed by a parameter name that stands for the data type. The example just given only uses one, which is named T. (If there were more, they would be separated by commas.) After this, the function definition is written as usual, except the type parameters are substituted for the actual data type names. In the example the function header reads

```
T square(T number)
```

T is the type parameter, or generic data type. The header defines `square` as a function that returns a value of type T and uses a parameter, `number`, which is also of type T.

As mentioned before, the compiler examines each call to `square` and fills in the appropriate data type for T. For example, the following call uses an `int` argument:

```
int y, x = 4;
y = square(x);
```

This code will cause the compiler to generate the function:

```
int square(int number)
{
    return number * number;
}
```

while the statements

```
float y, f = 6.2
y = square(f);
```

will result in the generation of the function

```
float square(float number)
{
    return number * number;
}
```

Program 15-5 demonstrates how this function template is used.

Program 15-5

```
// This program uses a function template.

#include <iostream>
#include <iomanip>
using namespace std;

// Template definition for square function.
template <class T>
T square(T number)
{
    return number * number;
}

int main()
{
    int userInt;
    float userFloat;

    cout << setprecision(5);
    cout << "Enter an integer and a floating-point value: ";
    cin >> userInt >> userFloat;
    cout << "Here are their squares: ";
    cout << square(userInt) << " and " << square(userFloat) << endl;
    return 0;
}
```

Program Output With Example Input Shown in Bold
```
Enter an integer and floating-point value: 12 4.2[Enter]
Here are their squares: 144 and 17.64
```

☞ **Note:** All type parameters defined in a function template must appear at least once in the function parameter list.

Since the compiler encountered two calls to square in Program 15-5, each with different parameter types, it generated the code for two instances of the function: one with an int parameter and int return type, the other with a float parameter and float return type. This is illustrated in Figure 15-1.

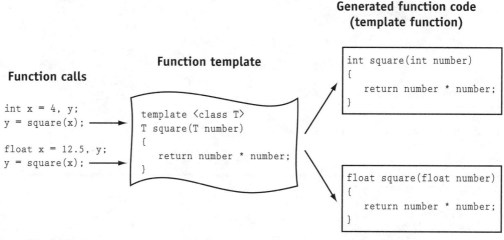

Figure 15-1

Notice in Program 15-5 that the template appears before all calls to square. As with regular functions, the compiler must already know the template's contents when it encounters a call to the template function. Templates, therefore, should be placed near the top of the program or in a header file.

☞ **Note:** A function template is merely the specification of a function and by itself does not cause memory to be used. An actual instance of the function is created in memory when the compiler encounters a call to the template function.

Program 15-6 shows another example of a function template. The function, swap, uses two references to type T as parameters. The function swaps the contents of the variables referenced by the parameters.

Program 15-6

```
// This program demonstrates the use of the swap function template.

#include <iostream>
using namespace std;
```

(program continues)

Program 15-6   *(continued)*

```cpp
template <class T>
void swap(T &var1, T &var2)
{
    T temp;

    temp = var1;
    var1 = var2;
    var2 = temp;
}

int main()
{
    char firstChar, secondChar;
    int firstInt, secondInt;
    float firstFloat, secondFloat;

    // Get and swap two chars
    cout << "Enter two characters: ";
    cin >> firstChar >> secondChar;
    swap(firstChar, secondChar);
    cout << firstChar << " " << secondChar << endl;

    // Get and swap two ints
    cout << "Enter two integers: ";
    cin >> firstInt >> secondInt;
    swap(firstInt, secondInt);
    cout << firstInt << " " << secondInt << endl;

    // Get and swap two floats
    cout << "Enter two floating-point numbers: ";
    cin >> firstFloat >> secondFloat;
    swap(firstFloat, secondFloat);
    cout << firstFloat << " " << secondFloat << endl;
    return 0;
}
```

Program Output With Example Input Shown in Bold
```
Enter two characters: A B[Enter]
B A
Enter two integers: 5 10[Enter]
10 5
Enter two floating-point numbers: 1.2 9.6[Enter]
9.6 1.2
```

Using Operators in Function Templates

The square template shown in this section uses the * operator with the number parameter. This works well as long as number is of a primitive data type such as int, or float. If a user-defined class object is passed to the square function, however, the class must contain code for an overloaded * operator. If not, the compiler will generate a function with an error.

Always remember that a class object passed to a function template must support all the operations the function will perform on the object. For instance, if the function performs a comparison on the object (with >, <, ==, or another relational operator), those operators must be overloaded by the class.

Function Templates with Multiple Types

More than one generic type may be used in a function template. Each type must have its own parameter, as shown in the following modified version of the swap template.

```
template <class T1, class T2>
void swap(T1 &var1, T2 &var2)
{
    T1 temp;

    temp = var1;
    var1 = (T1)var2;
    var2 = (T2)temp;
}
```

This template uses two type parameters: T1 and T2. Since the function parameters, var1 and var2, are specified with different types, the function generated from this template can accept two arguments of different types. The template is demonstrated in Program 15-7.

Program 15-7

```
// This program demonstrates the use of the swap function template
// with two type parameters.

#include <iostream>
using namespace std;

template <class T1, class T2>
void swap(T1 &var1, T2 &var2)
{
    T1 temp;

    temp = var1;
    var1 = (T1)var2;
    var2 = (T2)temp;
}
```

(program continues)

Program 15-7 *(continued)*

```
int main()
{
    char character;
    int intNum;
    float floatNum;

    // Get and swap a char and an int
    cout << "Enter a character and an int: ";
    cin >> character >> intNum;
    swap(character, intNum);
    cout << character << " " << intNum << endl;

    // Get and swap a float and an int
    cout << "Enter a float and an int: ";
    cin >> floatNum >> intNum;
    swap(floatNum, intNum);
    cout << floatNum << " " << intNum << endl;
    return 0;
}
```

Program Output with Example Input Shown in Bold
```
Enter a character and an int: A 78[Enter]
N 65
Enter a float and an int: 12.9 7[Enter]
7 12
```

 Note: Each type parameter declared in the template prefix must be used somewhere in the template definition.

Overloading with Function Templates

Function templates may be overloaded. As with regular functions, function templates are overloaded by having different parameter lists. For example, there are two overloaded versions of the sum function in Program 15-8. The first version accepts two arguments, and the second version accepts three.

Program 15-8

```
// This program demonstrates an overloaded function template.

#include <iostream>
using namespace std;
```

(program continues)

Program 15-8 *(continued)*

```
template <class T>
T sum(T val1, T val2)
{
    return val1 + val2;
}
template <class T>
T sum(T val1, T val2, T val3)
{
    return val1 + val2 + val3;
}

int main()
{
    float num1, num2, num3;

    cout << "Enter two values: ";
    cin >> num1 >> num2;
    cout << "Their sum is " << sum(num1, num2) << endl;
    cout << "Enter three values: ";
    cin >> num1 >> num2 >> num3;
    cout << "Their sum is " << sum(num1, num2, num3) << endl;
    return 0;
}
```

Program Output with Example Input Shown in bold
```
Enter two values: 12.5 6.9[Enter]
Their sum is 19.4
Enter three values: 45.76 98.32 10.51[Enter]
Their sum is 154.59
```

There are other ways to perform overloading with function templates as well. For example, a program might contain a regular (non-template) version of a function as well as a template version. As long as each has a different parameter list, they can coexist as overloaded functions.

15.3 Focus on Software Engineering: *Where to Start When Defining Templates*

Quite often, it is easier to convert an existing function into a template than to write a template from scratch. With this in mind, you should start designing a function template by writing it first as a regular function. For example, the swap template in Program 15-6 would have been started as something like the following:

```
void swap(int &var1, int &var2)
{
    int temp;

    temp = var1;
    var1 = var2;
    var2 = temp;
}
```

Once this function is properly tested and debugged, converting it to a template is a simple process. First, the `template <class T>` header is added, then all the references to `int` that must be changed are replaced with the data type parameter `T`.

Checkpoint [15.2–15.3]

15.6   When does the compiler actually generate code for a function template?

15.7   The following function accepts an `int` argument and returns half of its value as a float:

```
float half(int number)
{
    return number / 2.0;
}
```

Write a template that will implement this function to accept an argument of any type.

15.8   What must you be sure of when passing a class object to a function template that uses an operator, such as * or >?

15.9   What is the best method for writing a function template?

15.4 Class Templates

CONCEPT Templates may also be used to create generic classes and abstract data types. Class templates allow you to create one general version of a class without having to duplicate code to handle multiple data types.

Recall the `IntArray` class from Chapter 11. If you overload the `[]` operator, this class allows you to implement `int` arrays that perform bounds checking. But suppose you would like to have a version of this class for other data types? Of course, you could design specialized classes such as `LongArray`, `FloatArray`, `DoubleArray`, and so forth. A better solution, however, is to design a single class template that works with any primitive data type. In this section, we will convert the `IntArray` class into a generalized template named `SimpleVector`.

Declaring a class template is very similar to declaring a function template. First, a template prefix, such as `template<class T>` is placed before the class declaration. As with function templates, `T` (or whatever identifier you choose to use) is a data type parameter. Then, throughout the class declaration the data type parameter is used wherever you wish to support any data type. The following is the `SimpleVector` class template declaration.

```
template <class T>
class SimpleVector
{
private:
  T *aptr;
  int arraySize;
  void subError();              // Handles subscripts out of range.
public:
  SimpleVector()                // Default constructor
    { aptr = 0; arraySize = 0;}
  SimpleVector(int);            // Constructor
  SimpleVector(const SimpleVector &); // Copy constructor
  ~SimpleVector();              // Destructor
  int size()
      { return arraySize; }
  T &operator[](int);           // Overloaded [] operator
};
```

If you compare this template with the original `IntArray` class, you will see that the only difference is the addition of the template prefix and the use of the type parameter.

 Note: The `arraySize` variable remains an `int`. This is because it holds the size of the array, which will be an integer value, regardless of the data type of the array. This is also why the `size` member function returns an `int`.

The entire class template is shown as follows:

Contents of `SimpleVector.h`
```
#ifndef SIMPLEVECTOR_H
#define SIMPLEVECTOR_H
#include <iostream>
#include <cstdlib>
using namespace std;

template <class T>
class SimpleVector
{
private:
  T *aptr;
  int arraySize;
  void subError();                      // Handles subscripts out of range.
```

```
public:
  SimpleVector()                        // Default constructor
    { aptr = 0; arraySize = 0;}
  SimpleVector(int);                    // Constructor
  SimpleVector(const SimpleVector &);   // Copy constructor
  ~SimpleVector();                      // Destructor
  int size()
    { return arraySize; }
  T &operator[](int);                   // Overloaded [] operator
};
//****************************************************************
// Constructor for SimpleVector class. Sets the size of the *
// array and allocates memory for it.                        *
//****************************************************************
template <class T>
SimpleVector<T>::SimpleVector(int s)
{
  arraySize = s;
  aptr = new T [s];
  for (int count = 0; count < arraySize; count++)
      *(aptr + count) = 0;
}

//*********************************************
// Copy Constructor for SimpleVector class. *
//*********************************************
template <class T>
SimpleVector<T>::SimpleVector(const SimpleVector &obj)
{
  arraySize = obj.arraySize;
  aptr = new T [arraySize];
  for(int count = 0; count < arraySize; count++)
      *(aptr + count) = *(obj.aptr + count);
}

//***************************************
// Destructor for SimpleVector class. *
//***************************************
template <class T>
SimpleVector<T>::~SimpleVector()
{
  if (arraySize > 0)
      delete [] aptr;
}

//*****************************************************************
// subError function. Displays an error message and             *
// terminates the program when a subscript is out of range.     *
//*****************************************************************
```

```
template <class T>
void SimpleVector<T>::subError()
{
  cout << "ERROR: Subscript out of range.\n";
  exit(0);
}

//***********************************************************
// Overloaded [] operator. The argument is a subscript.   *
// This function returns a reference to the element        *
// in the array indexed by the subscript.                  *
//***********************************************************
template <class T>
T &SimpleVector<T>::operator[](int sub)
{
  if (sub < 0 || sub > arraySize)
      subError();
  return aptr[sub];
}

#endif
```

Defining Objects of the Class Template

Class template objects are defined like objects of ordinary classes, with one small difference: The data type you wish to pass to the type parameter must be specified. Placing the data type name inside angled brackets immediately following the class name does this. For example, the following declarations create two SimpleVector objects: intTable and floatTable.

```
SimpleVector<int> intTable(10);
SimpleVector<float> floatTable(10);
```

In the first definition (of intTable), the data type int will be used in the template everywhere the type parameter T appears. This will cause intTable to store an array of ints. Likewise, the definition of floatTable passes the data type float into the parameter T, causing it to store an array of floats. This is demonstrated in Program 15-9.

Program 15-9

```
// This program demonstrates the SimpleVector template.

#include <iostream>
#include "SimpleVector.h"
using namespace std;
```

(program continues)

Program 15-9 *(continued)*

```cpp
int main()
{
    SimpleVector<int> intTable(10);
    SimpleVector<float> floatTable(10);
    int x;

    // Store values in the arrays.
    for (x = 0; x < 10; x++)
    {
        intTable[x] = (x * 2);
        floatTable[x] = (x * 2.14);
    }

    // Display the values in the arrays.
    cout << "These values are in intTable:\n";
    for (x = 0; x < 10; x++)
        cout << intTable[x] << " ";
    cout << endl;
    cout << "These values are in floatTable:\n";
    for (x = 0; x < 10; x++)
        cout << floatTable[x] << " ";
    cout << endl;

    // Use the built-in + operator on array elements.
    for (x = 0; x < 10; x++)
    {
        intTable[x] = intTable[x] + 5;
        floatTable[x] = floatTable[x] + 1.5;
    }

    // Display the values in the array.
    cout << "These values are in intTable:\n";
    for (x = 0; x < 10; x++)
        cout << intTable[x] << " ";
    cout << endl;
    cout << "These values are in floatTable:\n";
    for (x = 0; x < 10; x++)
        cout << floatTable[x] << " ";
    cout << endl;

    // Use the built-in ++ operator on array elements.
    for (x = 0; x < 10; x++)
    {
        intTable[x]++;
        floatTable[x]++;
    }
```

(program continues)

Program 15-9 *(continued)*

```
    // Display the values in the array.
    cout << "These values are in intTable:\n";
    for (x = 0; x < 10; x++)
        cout << intTable[x] << " ";
    cout << endl;
    cout << "These values are in floatTable:\n";
    for (x = 0; x < 10; x++)
        cout << floatTable[x] << " ";
    cout << endl;
    return 0;
}
```

Program Output
```
These values are in intTable:
0 2 4 6 8 10 12 14 16 18
These values are in floatTable:
0 2.14 4.28 6.42 8.56 10.7 12.84 14.98 17.12 19.26
These values are in intTable:
5 7 9 11 13 15 17 19 21 23
These values are in floatTable:
1.5 3.64 5.78 7.92 10.06 12.2 14.34 16.48 18.62 20.76
These values are in intTable:
6 8 10 12 14 16 18 20 22 24
These values are in floatTable:
2.5 4.64 6.78 8.92 11.06 13.2 15.34 17.48 19.62 21.76
```

Class Templates and Inheritance

Inheritance can easily be applied to class templates. For example, in the following template, `SearchableVector` is derived from the `SimpleVector` class.

Contents of SearchVect.h

```
#ifndef SEARCHABLEVECTOR_H
#define SEARCHABLEVECTOR_H

#include "SimpleVector.h"

template <class T>
class SearchableVector : public SimpleVector<T>
{
public:
    SearchableVector(int s) : SimpleVector<T>(s) // Constructor
        { }
    SearchableVector(SearchableVector &);        // Copy constructor
    SearchableVector(SimpleVector<T> &obj): SimpleVector<T>(obj)
        { }
    int findItem(T);
};
```

```cpp
template <class T>
SearchableVector<T>::SearchableVector(SearchableVector &obj) :
SimpleVector<T>(obj)
{
    for(int count = 0; count < this->size(); count++)
        this->operator[](count) = obj[count];
}

template <class T>
int SearchableVector<T>::findItem(T item)
{
    for (int count = 0; count <= this->size(); count++)
    {
        if (this->operator[](count) == item)
            return count;
    }
    return -1;
}

#endif
```

This class template defines a searchable version of the `SimpleVector` class. The member function `findItem` accepts an argument, and performs a simple linear search to determine whether the argument's value is stored in the array. If the value is found in the array, its subscript is returned. Otherwise, −1 is returned.

Notice that each time the name `SimpleVector` is used in the class template, the type parameter `T` is used with it. For example, here is the first line of the class declaration, which names `SimpleVector` as the base class:

```cpp
class SearchableVector : public SimpleVector<T>
```

And here is the header for the first constructor:

```cpp
SearchableVector(int s) : SimpleVector<T>(s)
```

Because `SimpleVector` is a class template, the type parameter must be passed to it.

Program 15-10 demonstrates the class by storing values in two `SearchableVector` objects and then searching for a specific value in each.

Program 15-10

```cpp
// This program demonstrates the SearchableVector template.

#include <iostream>
#include "SearchVect.h"
using namespace std;
```

(program continues)

Program 15-10 *(continued)*

```
int main()
{
    SearchableVector<int> intTable(10);
    SearchableVector<float> floatTable(10);
    int x, result;

    // Store values in the arrays.
    for (x = 0; x < 10; x++)
    {
        intTable[x] = (x * 2);
        floatTable[x] = (x * 2.14);
    }

    // Display the values in the arrays.
    cout << "These values are in intTable:\n";
    for (x = 0; x < 10; x++)
        cout << intTable[x] << " ";
    cout << endl;
    cout << "These values are in floatTable:\n";
    for (x = 0; x < 10; x++)
        cout << floatTable[x] << " ";
    cout << endl;

    // Now search for values in the arrays.
    cout << "Searching for 6 in intTable.\n";
    result = intTable.findItem(6);
    if (result == -1)
        cout << "6 was not found in intTable.\n";
    else
        cout << "6 was found at subscript " << result << endl;

    cout << "Searching for 12.84 in floatTable.\n";
    result = floatTable.findItem(12.84);
    if (result == -1)
        cout << "12.84 was not found in floatTable.\n";
    else
        cout << "12.84 was found at subscript " << result << endl;
    return 0;
}
```

Program Output
```
These values are in intTable:
0 2 4 6 8 10 12 14 16 18
These values are in floatTable:
0 2.14 4.28 6.42 8.56 10.7 12.84 14.98 17.12 19.26
Searching for 6 in intTable.
6 was found at subscript 3
Searching for 12.84 in floatTable.
12.84 was found at subscript 6
```

The SearchableVector class demonstrates that a class template may be derived from another class template. In addition, class templates may be derived from ordinary classes, and ordinary classes may be derived from class templates.

Specialized Templates

Suppose you have a template that works for all data types but one. For example, the SimpleVector and SearchableVector classes work well with numeric, and even character data. But they will not work with C-strings. Situations like this require the use of *specialized templates*. A specialized template is one that is designed to work with a specific data type. In the declaration, the actual data type is used instead of a type parameter. For example, the declaration of a specialized version of the SimpleVector class might start like this:

```
class SimpleVector<char *>
```

The compiler would know that this version of the SimpleVector class is intended for the char * data type. Anytime an object is declared of the type SimpleVector<char*>, the compiler will use this template to generate the code.

Checkpoint [15.4]

15.10 Suppose your program uses a class template named List, which is defined as

```
template<class T>
class List
{
    // Members are declared here...
};
```

Give an example of how you would use int as the data type in the declaration of a List object. (Assume the class has a default constructor.)

15.11 As the following Rectangle class declaration is written, the width, length, and area members are floats. Rewrite the class as a template that will accept any data type for these members.

```
class Rectangle
{
    private:
      float width;
      float length;
      float area;
    public:
      void setData(float w, float 1)
            { width = w; length = 1;}
```

```
        void calcArea()
                { area = width * length; }
        float getWidth()
                { return width; }
        float getLength()
                { return length; }
        float getArea()
                { return area; }
};
```

15.5   Introduction to the Standard Template Library

CONCEPT   The Standard Template Library contains many templates for useful algorithms and data structures.

In addition to its run-time library, which you have used throughout this book, C++ also provides a library of templates. The *Standard Template Library* (or *STL*) contains numerous generic templates for implementing abstract data types and algorithms. In this section you will be introduced to the general types of ADTs and algorithms that may be found in the STL.

 Note: The STL is a relatively new addition to the C++ language. Older compilers may not support it.

Abstract Data Types

The most important data structures in the STL are *containers* and *iterators*. A container is a class that stores data and organizes it in some fashion. An iterator is like a pointer. It is used to access the individual data elements in a container.

There are two types of container classes in the STL: *sequence* and *associative*. A sequence container organizes data in a sequential fashion similar to an array. The three sequence containers currently provided are listed in Table 15-1.

Table 15-1

Container Name	Description
vector	An expandable array. Values may be added to or removed from the end or middle of a vector.
deque	Like a vector, but allows values to be added to or removed from the front or back.
list	A doubly-linked list of data elements. Values may be inserted to or removed from any position. (You will learn more about linked lists in Chapter 16.)

Performance Differences Between Vectors, Deques, and Lists

There is a difference in performance between vectors, deques, and lists. When choosing one of these templates to use in your program, remember the following points:

- ◆ A vector is capable of quickly adding values to its end. Insertions at other points are not as efficient.

- ◆ A deque is capable of quickly adding values to its front and its end. deques are not efficient at inserting values at other positions, however.

- ◆ A list is capable of quickly inserting values anywhere in its sequence. Lists do not, however, provide random access.

An associative container uses keys to rapidly access elements. (If you've ever used a relational database, you are probably familiar with the concept of keys.) The four associative containers currently supported are shown in Table 15-2.

Table 15-2

Container Name	Description
set	Stores a set of keys. No duplicate values are allowed.
multiset	Stores a set of keys. Duplicates are allowed.
map	Maps a set of keys to data elements. Only one key per data element is allowed. Duplicates are not allowed.
multimap	Maps a set of keys to data elements. Many keys per data element are allowed. Duplicates are allowed.

Iterators are generalizations of pointers and are used to access information stored in containers. The types of iterators are shown in Table 15-3.

Table 15-3

Iterator Type	Description
Forward	Can only move forward in a container (uses the ++ operator).
Bidirectional	Can move forward or backward in a container (uses the ++ and -- operators).
Random-access	Can move forward and backward, and can jump to a specific data element in a container.
Input	Can be used with cin to read information from an input device or a file.
Output	Can be used with cout to write information to an output device or a file.

Iterators are associated with containers. The type of container you have determines the type of iterator you use. For example, `vectors` and `deques` require random-access iterators, while `lists`, `sets`, `multisets`, `maps`, and `multimaps` require bidirectional iterators.

Algorithms

The algorithms provided by the STL are implemented as function templates and perform various operations on elements of containers. There are many algorithms in the STL; Table 15-4 lists a few of them. (The table gives only general descriptions.)

Table 15-4

Algorithm	Description
`binary_search`	Performs a binary search for an object and returns `true` if the object is found, `false` if not.
	Example: `binary_search(iter1, iter2, value);`
	In this statement, `iter1` and `iter2` define a range of elements within the container. (`iter1` points to the first element in the range and `iter2` points to just after the last element in the range.) The statement performs a binary search on the range of elements, searching for `value`. The `binary_search` function returns `true` if the element was found and `false` if the element was not found.
`count`	Returns the number of times a value appears in a range.
	Example: `number = count(iter1, iter2, value);`
	In this statement, `iter1` and `iter2` define a range of elements within the container. (`iter1` points to the first element in the range and `iter2` points to just after the last element in the range.) The statement returns the number of times `value` appears in the range of elements.
`for_each`	Executes a function for each element in a container.
	Example: `for_each(iter1, iter2, func);`
	In this statement, `iter1` and `iter2` define a range of elements within the container. (`iter1` points to the first element in the range and `iter2` points to just after the last element in the range.) The third argument, `func`, is the name of a function. The statement calls the function `func` for each element in the range, passing the element as an argument.

(table continues)

Table 15-4   *(continued)*

Algorithm	Description
find	Finds the first object in a container that matches a value and returns an iterator to it.
	Example: `iter3 = find(iter1, iter2, value);`
	In this statement, `iter1` and `iter2` define a range of elements within the container. (`iter1` points to the first element in the range and `iter2` points to just after the last element in the range.) The statement searches the range of elements for `value`. If `value` is found, the function returns an iterator to the element containing it, otherwise, it returns the iterator `iter2`.
max_element	Returns an iterator to the largest object in a range.
	Example: `iter3 = max_element(iter1, iter2);`
	In this statement, `iter1` and `iter2` define a range of elements within the container. (`iter1` points to the first element in the range and `iter2` points to just after the last element in the range.) The statement returns an iterator to the element containing the largest value in the range.
min_element	Returns an iterator to the smallest object in a range.
	Example: `iter3 = min_element(iter1, iter2);`
	In this statement, `iter1` and `iter2` define a range of elements within the container. (`iter1` points to the first element in the range and `iter2` points to just after the last element in the range.) The statement returns an iterator to the element containing the smallest value in the range.
random_shuffle	Randomly shuffles the elements of a container.
	Example: `random_shuffle(iter1, iter2);`
	In this statement, `iter1` and `iter2` define a range of elements within the container. (`iter1` points to the first element in the range and `iter2` points to just after the last element in the range.) The statement randomly reorders the elements in the range.

(table continues)

Table 15-4   *(continued)*

Algorithm	Description
sort	Sorts a range of elements. ***Example:*** `sort(iter1, iter2);` In this statement, `iter1` and `iter2` define a range of elements within the container. (`iter1` points to the first element in the range and `iter2` points to just after the last element in the range.) The statement sorts the elements in the range in ascending order.

Example Programs Using the STL

Now that you have been introduced to the types of data structures and algorithms offered by the STL, let's look at some simple programs that use them.

Containers

Program 15-11 provides a limited demonstration of the `vector` class template. The member functions of `vector` used in this program are listed in Table 15-5.

Table 15-5

Member Function	Description
size()	Returns the number of elements in the vector.
push_back()	Accepts as an argument a value to be inserted into the vector. The argument is inserted after the last element. (Pushed onto the back of the vector.)
pop_back()	Removes the last element from the vector.
operator[]	Allows array-like access of existing vector elements. (The vector must already contain elements for this operator to work. It cannot be used to insert new values into the vector.)

The `vector` class template has many more member functions, but these are enough to demonstrate the class.

Program 15-11

```
// This program provides a simple demonstration of the
// vector STL template.
```

(program continues)

Program 15-11   *(continued)*

```cpp
#include <iostream>
#include <vector>          // Needed to use vectors
using namespace std;

int main()
{
   int x;
   vector<int> vect;       // Declare a vector object

   // Use the size member function to get
   // the number of elements in the vector.
   cout << "vect starts with " << vect.size()
      << " elements.\n";
   // Use push_back to push values into the vector.
   for (x = 0; x < 10; x++)
      vect.push_back(x);
   cout << "Now Vect has " << vect.size()
      << " elements. Here they are:\n";
   // Use the [] operator.
   for (x = 0; x < vect.size(); x++)
      cout << vect[x] << " ";
   cout << endl;
   // Use the pop_back member function.
   cout << "Popping the values out of vect...\n";
   for (x = 0; x < 10; x++)
      vect.pop_back();
   cout << "Now vect has " << vect.size() << " elements.\n";
   return 0;
}
```

Program Output
```
Vect starts with 0 elements.
Now vect has 10 elements. Here they are:
0 1 2 3 4 5 6 7 8 9
Popping the values out of vect...
Now vect has 0 elements.
```

Notice in Program 15-11 the inclusion of the vector header file, which is required for the vector container. The vector container is one of the simplest types of containers in the STL. In the following chapters, you will see examples using other types of containers.

Iterators

In Program 15-11, the vector's elements were accessed by the container's member functions. Iterators may also be used to access and manipulate container elements. Program 15-12 demonstrates the use of an iterator with a vector object.

Program 15-12

```cpp
// This program provides a simple demonstration of an
// iterator.

#include <iostream>
#include <vector>
using namespace std;

int main()
{
    int x;
    vector<int> vect;            // Declare a vector object
    vector<int>::iterator iter;  // Declare an iterator

    // Use push_back to push values into the vector.
    for (x = 0; x < 10; x++)
        vect.push_back(x);
    // Step the iterator through the vector,
    // and use it to display the vector's contents.
    cout << "Here are the values in vect: ";
    for (iter = vect.begin(); iter < vect.end(); iter++)
    {
        cout << *iter << " ";
    }
    cout << "\nand here they are backwards: ";
    for (iter = vect.end() - 1; iter >= vect.begin(); iter--)
    {
        cout << *iter << " ";
    }
    return 0;
}
```

Program Output
```
Here are the values in vect: 0 1 2 3 4 5 6 7 8 9
and here they are backwards: 9 8 7 6 5 4 3 2 1 0
```

The declaration of an iterator is closely related to the declaration of the container it is to be used with. For example, Program 15-12 declares a vector of ints as

```cpp
vector<int> vect;
```

The iterator that will work with the vector is declared as

```cpp
vector<int>::iterator iter;
```

This declaration creates an iterator specifically for a vector of ints. The compiler automatically chooses the right type (in this case, a random-access iterator).

The first `for` loop in Program 15-12 causes the iterator to step through each element in the `vector`:

```
for (iter = vect.begin(); iter < vect.end(); iter++)
```

The loop's initialization expression uses the container's `begin()` member function, which returns an iterator pointing to the beginning of the `vector`. The statement

```
iter = vect.begin();
```

causes `iter` to point to the first element in the `vector`. The loop continuation expression uses the `end()` member function, which returns an iterator pointing to the location just past the end of the container:

```
iter < vect.end();
```

As long as `iter` points to an element prior to the end of the `vector`, this statement will be true.

The loop's update expression uses the `++` operator to increment the iterator. This causes the iterator to point to the next element in the vector.

The body of the loop uses a `cout` statement to display the element that the iterator points to

```
cout << *iter << " ";
```

Like a pointer, iterators may be dereferenced with the `*` operator. This statement causes the value pointed to by `iter` to be displayed.

Back to the `vector` Template

Table 15-6 lists several more member functions of the `vector` class template. Some of these accept iterators as arguments and/or return an iterator.

Table 15-6

Member Function	Description
`at(position)`	Returns the value of the element located at *position* in the vector. **Example:** `x = vect.at(5);` This statement assigns the value of the fifth element of `vect` to `x`.
`back()`	Returns a reference to the last element in the vector. **Example:** `cout << vect.back() << endl;`
`begin()`	Returns an iterator pointing to the vector's first element. **Example:** `iter = vect.begin();`

(table continues)

Table 15-6 *(continued)*

Member Function	Description
capacity()	Returns the maximum number of elements that may be stored in the vector without additional memory being allocated. (This is not the same value as returned by the size member function). *Example:* `x = vect.capacity();` This statement assigns the capacity of vect to x.
clear()	Clears a vector of all its elements. *Example:* `vect.clear();` This statement removes all the elements from vect.

empty()	Returns true if the vector is empty. Otherwise, it returns false.
	Example:
	`if (vect.empty())`
	    `cout << "The vector is empty.";`

end()	Returns an iterator pointing to just after the last element of the vector. *Example:* `iter = vect.end();`
erase()	Causes the vector element pointed to by the iterator iter to be removed. *Example:* `vect.erase(iter);`
erase(iter1, iter2)	Removes all vector elements in the range specified by the iterators iter1 and iter2. *Example:* `vect.erase(iter1, iter2);`
front()	Returns a reference to the vector's first element. *Example:* `cout << vector.front() << endl;`
insert(iter, value)	Inserts an element into the vector. *Example:* `vect.insert(iter, x);` This statement inserts the value x just before the element pointed to by the iterator iter.

(table continues)

Table 15-6 *(continued)*

Member Function	Description
insert(iter, n, value)	Inserts *n* copies of *value* into the vector, starting at the position pointed to by the iterator *iter*. **Example:** `vect.insert(iter, 7, x);` This statement inserts 7 copies of the value x just before the element pointed to by the iterator iter.
pop_back()	Removes the last element from the vector. **Example:** `vect.pop_back();` This statement removes the last element of vect, thus reducing its size by one.
push_back(value)	Stores *value* as the new last element of the vector. If the vector is already filled to capacity, it is automatically resized. **Example:** `vect.push_back(7);` This statement stores 7 as the new last element of vect.
reverse()	Reverses the order of the elements in the vector (the last element becomes the first element, and the first element becomes the last element.) **Example:** `vect.reverse();.`
resize(n, value)	Resizes a vector by adding *n* new entries, each of which is initialized to *value*. **Example:** `vect.resize(5, 1);` This statement increases the size of vect by 5 elements. The 5 new elements are initialized to the value 1.
size()	Returns the number of elements in the vector. **Example:** `cout << vector.size() << endl;`
swap(vector2)	Swaps the contents of the vector with the contents of *vector2*. **Example:** `vect1.swap(vect2);` The statement above swaps the contents of vect1 and vect2.

Algorithms

There are a multitude of algorithms in the STL, implemented as function templates. Program 15-13 demonstrates `random_shuffle`, `sort`, and `binary_search`.

Program 15-13

```
// This program provides a simple demonstration of the
// STL algorithms.

#include <iostream>
#include <vector>          // Include the vector header
#include <algorithm>       // Required for STL algorithms
using namespace std;

int main()
{
    int x;
    vector<int> vect;      // Declare a vector object

    // Use push_back to push values into the vector.
    for (x = 0; x < 10; x++)
        vect.push_back(x);
    // Display the vector's elements
    cout << "Vect has " << vect.size() << " elements. Here they are:\n";
    for (x = 0; x < vect.size(); x++)
    cout << vect[x] << " ";
    cout << endl;

    // Randomly shuffle the vector's contents.
    random_shuffle(vect.begin(), vect.end());
    // Display the vector's elements
    cout << "The elements have been shuffled:\n";
    for (x = 0; x < vect.size(); x++)
        cout << vect[x] << " ";
    cout << endl;

    // Now sort them.
    sort(vect.begin(), vect.end());
    // Display the vector's elements again
    cout << "The elements have been sorted:\n";
    for (x = 0; x < vect.size(); x++)
        cout << vect[x] << " ";
    cout << endl;

    // Now search for an element.
    if (binary_search(vect.begin(), vect.end(), 7))
        cout << "The value 7 was found in the vector.\n";
    else
        cout << "The value 7 was not found in the vector.\n";
    return 0;
}
```

Program 15-13

Program Output

```
Vect has 10 elements. Here they are:
0 1 2 3 4 5 6 7 8 9
The elements have been shuffled:
4 3 0 2 6 7 8 9 5 1
The elements have been sorted:
0 1 2 3 4 5 6 7 8 9
The value 7 was found in the vector.
```

 Note: The STL algorithms require the `algorithm` header file.

The `random_shuffle` function rearranges the elements of a container. In Program 15-13, it is called in the following manner:

```
random_shuffle(vect.begin(), vect.end());
```

The function takes two arguments, which together represent a range of elements within a container. The first argument is an iterator to the first element in the range. In this case, `vect.begin()` is used. The second argument is an iterator to just after the last element in the range. Here we have used `vect.end()`. These arguments tell `random_shuffle` to rearrange all the elements from the beginning to the end of the `vect` container.

The `sort` algorithm also takes iterators to a range of elements. Here is the function call that appears in Program 15-13:

```
sort(vect.begin(), vect.end());
```

All the elements within the range are sorted in ascending order.

The `binary_search` algorithm searches a range of elements for a value. If the value is found, the function returns `true`. Otherwise, it returns `false`. For example, the following function call searches all the elements in `vect` for the value 7.

```
binary_search(vect.begin(), vect.end(), 7)
```

Program 15-14 demonstrates the `count` algorithm.

Program 15-14

```
// This program demonstrates the STL count algorithm.

#include <iostream>
#include <vector>           // Needed to declare the vector
#include <algorithm>        // Needed for the for_each algorithm
using namespace std;
```

(program continues)

Program 15-14 *(continued)*

```
int main()
{
    vector<int> values;
    vector<int>::iterator iter;

    // Store some values in the vector.
    values.push_back(1);
    values.push_back(2);
    values.push_back(2);
    values.push_back(3);
    values.push_back(3);
    values.push_back(3);

    // Display the values in the vector.
    cout << "The values in the vector are:\n";
    for (iter = values.begin(); iter < values.end(); iter++)
        cout << *iter << endl;
    cout << endl;

    // Display the count of each number.
    cout << "The number of 1s in the vector is ";
    cout << count(values.begin(), values.end(), 1) << endl;
    cout << "The number of 2s in the vector is ";
    cout << count(values.begin(), values.end(), 2) << endl;
    cout << "The number of 3s in the vector is ";
    cout << count(values.begin(), values.end(), 3) << endl;
    return 0;
}
```

Program Output

```
The values in the vector are:
1
2
2
3
3
3

The number of 1s in the vector is 1
The number of 2s in the vector is 2
The number of 3s in the vector is 3
```

Program 15-15 demonstrates the max_element and min_element algorithms.

Program 15-15

```cpp
// This program demonstrates the STL max_element and min_element
// algorithms.

#include <iostream>
#include <vector>          // Needed to declare the vector
#include <algorithm>       // Needed for the algorithms
using namespace std;

int main()
{
    vector<int> numbers;
    vector<int>::iterator iter;

    // Store some numbers in the vector.
    for (int x = 0; x < 10; x++)
        numbers.push_back(x);

    // Display the numbers in the vector.
    cout << "The numbers in the vector are:\n";
    for (iter = numbers.begin(); iter != numbers.end(); iter++)
        cout << *iter << endl;
    cout << endl;

    // Find the largest value in the vector.
    iter = max_element(numbers.begin(), numbers.end());
    cout << "The largest value in the vector is " << *iter << endl;

    // Find the smallest value in the vector.
    iter = min_element(numbers.begin(), numbers.end());
    cout << "The smallest value in the vector is " << *iter << endl;
    return 0;

}
```

Program Output
```
The numbers in the vector are:
0
1
2
3
4
5
6
7
8
9

The largest value in the vector is 9
The smallest value in the vector is 0
```

Program 15-16 demonstrates the find algorithm.

Program 15-16

```
// This program demonstrates the STL find algorithm.

#include <iostream>
#include <vector>              // Needed to declare the vector
#include <algorithm>          // Needed for the find algorithm
using namespace std;

int main()
{
    vector<int> numbers;
    vector<int>::iterator iter;

    // Store some numbers in the vector.
    for (int x = 0; x < 10; x++)
        numbers.push_back(x);

    // Display the numbers in the vector.
    cout << "The numbers in the vector are:\n";
    for (iter = numbers.begin(); iter != numbers.end(); iter++)
        cout << *iter << endl;
    cout << endl;

    // Find 7 in the vector.
    iter = find(numbers.begin(), numbers.end(), 7);
    cout << *iter << endl;
    return 0;
}
```

Program Output
```
The numbers in the vector are:
0
1
2
3
4
5
6
7
8
9

7
```

Program 15-17 demonstrates the for_each algorithm.

Program 15-17

```cpp
// This program demonstrates the for_each find algorithm.

#include <iostream>
#include <vector>          // Needed to declare the vector
#include <algorithm>       // Needed for the for_each algorithm
using namespace std;

// Function prototype
void doubleValue(int &);

int main()
{
    vector<int> numbers;
    vector<int>::iterator iter;

    // Store some numbers in the vector.
    for (int x = 0; x < 10; x++)
        numbers.push_back(x);

    // Display the numbers in the vector.
    cout << "The numbers in the vector are:\n";
    for (iter = numbers.begin(); iter != numbers.end(); iter++)
        cout << *iter << endl;
    cout << endl;

    // Double the values in the vector.
    for_each(numbers.begin(), numbers.end(), doubleValue);

    // Display the numbers in the vector again
    cout << "Now the numbers in the vector are:\n";
    for (iter = numbers.begin(); iter != numbers.end(); iter++)
        cout << *iter << endl;
    cout << endl;
    return 0;
}

//***********************************************************
// Function doubleValue. This function accepts an int        *
// reference as its argument. The value of the argument      *
// is doubled.                                               *
//***********************************************************

void doubleValue(int &val)
{
    val *= 2;
}
```

Program 15-17

Program Output
```
The numbers in the vector are:
0
1
2
3
4
5
6
7
8
9

Now the numbers in the vector are:
0
2
4
6
8
10
12
14
16
18
```

In Program 15-17, the following statement calls `for_each`:

```
for_each(numbers.begin(), numbers.end(), doubleValue);
```

The first and second arguments specify a range of elements. In this case, the range is the entire vector. The third argument is the name of a function. The `for_each` algorithm calls the function once for each element in the range, passing the element as an argument to the function.

The programs in this section give you a brief introduction to using the STL by demonstrating simple operations on a `vector`. In the remaining chapters you will be given specific examples of how to use other STL containers, iterators, and algorithms.

Review Questions and Exercises

Fill-in-the-Blank

1. The line containing a throw statement is known as the _____.

2. The _____ block contains code that directly or indirectly might cause an exception to be thrown.

3. The _____ block handles an exception.

4. When writing function or class templates, you use a(n) _____ to specify a generic data type.

5. The beginning of a template is marked by a(n) _____.

6. When declaring objects of class templates, the _____ you wish to pass into the type parameter must be specified.

7. A(n) _____ template works with a specific data type.

8. A(n) _____ container organizes data in a sequential fashion similar to an array.

9. A(n) _____ container uses keys to rapidly access elements.

10. _____ are pointer-like objects used to access information stored in a container.

True or False

11. T   F   There can be only one catch block in a program.

12. T   F   When an exception is thrown but not caught, the program ignores the error.

13. T   F   Information may be passed with an exception by storing it in members of an exception class.

14. T   F   Once an exception has been thrown, it is not possible for the program to jump back to the throw point.

15. T   F   All type parameters defined in a function template must appear at least once in the function parameter list.

16. T   F   The compiler creates an instance of a function template in memory as soon as it encounters the template.

17. T   F   A class object passed to a function template must overload any operators used on the class object by the template.

18. T   F   Only one generic type may be used with a template.

19. T   F   In the function template definition, it is not necessary to use each type parameter declared in the template prefix.

20. T   F   It is possible to overload function templates.

21. T   F   It is possible to overload a function template and an ordinary (non-template) function.

22. T   F   A class template may not be derived from another class template.

23. T   F   A class template may not be used as a base class.

24. T   F   Specialized templates work with a specific data type.

25. T   F   When declaring an iterator from the STL, the compiler automatically creates the right kind, depending upon the container it is to be used with.

26. T   F   STL algorithms are implemented as function templates.

Find the Error

27. Each of the following declarations or code segments have errors. Locate as many as possible.

A)
```cpp
catch
{
    quotient = divide(num1, num2);
    cout << "The quotient is " << quotient << endl;
}
try (char *exceptionString)
{
    cout << exceptionString;
}
```

B)
```cpp
try
{
    quotient = divide(num1, num2);
}
cout << "The quotient is " << quotient << endl;
catch (char *exceptionString)
{
    cout << exceptionString;
}
```

C)
```cpp
template <class T>
T square(T number)
{
    return T * T;
}
```

D)
```cpp
template <class T>
int square(int number)
{
    return number * number;
}
```

E)
```cpp
template <class T1, class T2>
T1 sum(T1 x, T1 y)
{
    return x + y;
}
```

F) Assume the following declaration appears in a program that uses the `SimpleVector` class template presented in this chapter.

```cpp
int <SimpleVector> array(25);
```

G) Assume the following statement appears in a program that has declared `valueSet` as an object of the `SimpleVector` class presented in this chapter. Assume that `valueSet` is a vector of `int`s, and has 20 elements.

```
cout << valueSet<int>[2] << endl;
```

Programming Challenges

Each program should have a section of comments at the top. The comments should contain your name, the date the program was written, the chapter the assignment appeared in, and the assignment number and name. Here is an example:

```
// Written by Jill Johnson
// March 31, 2003
// Chapter 15
// Assignment 1.  Date Exceptions
```

1. Date Exceptions

Modify the `Date` class you wrote for Programming Challenge 5 of Chapter 7. The class should implement the following exception classes:

`InvalidDay`   Throw when an invalid day (< 1 or > 31) is passed to the class.

`InvalidMonth`   Throw when an invalid month (< 1 or > 12) is passed to the class.

Demonstrate the class in a driver program.

2. Time Format Exceptions

Modify the `MilTime` class you created for Programming Challenge 1 of Chapter 13. The class should implement the following exceptions:

`BadHour`   Throw when an invalid hour (< 0 or > 2359) is passed to the class.

`BadSeconds` Throw when an invalid number of seconds (< 0 or > 59) is passed to the class.

Demonstrate the class in a driver program.

3. Min/Max Templates

Write templates for the two functions `min` and `max`. `min` should accept two arguments and return the value of the argument that is the lesser of the two. `max` should accept two arguments and return the value of the argument that is the greater of the two. Design a simple driver program that demonstrates the templates with various data types.

4. Absolute Value Template

Write a function template that accepts an argument and returns its absolute value. The absolute value of a number is its value with no sign. For example, the absolute value of –5 is 5, and the absolute value of 2 is 2. Test the template in a simple driver program.

5. Total Template

Write a template for a function called `total`. The function should keep a running total of values entered by the user, then return the total. The argument sent into the function should be the number of values the function is to read. Test the template in a simple driver program that sends values of various types as arguments and displays the results.

6. `SimpleVector` Modification

Modify the `SimpleVector` class template, presented in this chapter, to include the member functions `push_back` and `pop_back`. These functions should emulate the STL vector class member functions of the same name. (See Table 15-5.) The `push_back` functon should accept an argument and insert its value at the end of the array. The `pop_back` function should accept no argument and remove the last element from the array. Test the class with a driver program.

7. `SearchableVector` Modification

Modify the `SearchableVector` class template, presented in this chapter, so it performs a binary search instead of a linear search. Test the template in a driver program.

8. `SortableVector` Class Template

Write a class template named `SortableVector`. The class should be derived from the `Simple-Vector` class presented in this chapter. It should have a member function that sorts the array elements in ascending order. (Use the sorting algorithm of your choice.) Test the template in a driver program.

9. Inheritance Modification

Assuming you have completed Programming Challenges 7 and 8, modify the inheritance hierarchy of the `SearchableVector` class template so it is derived from the `SortableVector` class instead of the `SimpleVector` class. Implement a member function named `sortAndSearch`, both a sort and a binary search.

10. Specialized Templates

In this chapter, the section *Specialized Templates* describes how to design templates that are specialized for one particular data type. The section introduces a method for specializing a version of the `SimpleVector` class template so it will work with strings. Complete the specialization for both the `SimpleVector` and `SearchableVector` templates. Demonstrate them with a simple driver program.

11. Rainfall Vector

Modify Programming Challenge 2 in Chapter 8 (Rainfall Statistics) to use an STL vector instead of an array. Refer to the information in Tables 15-5 and 15-6 if you wish to use any of the member functions.

12. Test Averaging Vector

Modify Programming Challenge 2 in Chapter 10 (Test Averaging) to use an STL vector instead of a dynamically-allocated array. Refer to the information in Tables 15-5 and 15-6 if you wish to use any of the member functions.

13. STL Binary Search

Modify programming Challenge 1 in Chapter 9 so it uses a vector instead of an array. Also, modify the program so it uses the STL `binary_search` algorithm to locate valid account numbers.

Serendipity Booksellers Software Development Project—Part 15: *A Problem-Solving Exercise*

For this chapter's exercise, you are to implement exception handlers to intercept critical errors (such as memory allocation failures, file open failures, etc.).

First, locate each point in the program where the inventory file is opened. If the program fails to open the file, an exception should be thrown. The exception handler should display an urgent error message indicating the nature of the problem, and terminate the program.

The second modification will be in the `cashier` function. In Chapter 13 you modified that function to ask how many titles the customer is purchasing and to dynamically allocate an array of `sale` objects large enough to hold that many titles. In the event that the new operator fails to allocate the required memory, the `cashier` function should throw an exception. Once again, the exception handler should display an urgent error message and terminate the program.

Linked Lists

Topics

16.1   Introduction to the Linked List ADT

> **CONCEPT**   Dynamically allocated data structures may be linked together in memory to form a chain.

A linked list is a series of connected *nodes,* where each node is a data structure. The nodes of a linked list are usually dynamically allocated, used, and then deleted, allowing the linked list to grow or shrink in size as the program runs. If new information needs to be added to a linked list, the program simply allocates another node and inserts it into to the series. If a particular piece of information needs to be removed from the linked list, the program deletes the node containing that information.

Advantages of Linked Lists over Arrays and Vectors

Although linked lists are more complex to code and manage than arrays, they have some distinct advantages. First, a linked list can easily grow or shrink in size. In fact, the programmer doesn't need to know how many nodes will be in the list. They are simply created in memory as they are needed.

One might argue that linked lists are not superior to vectors (found in the Standard Template Library), because they too can expand or shrink. The advantage that linked lists have over vectors, however, is the speed at which a node may be inserted into or deleted from the list. To insert a value into the middle of a vector requires all the elements after the insertion point to be moved one position toward the vector's end, thus making room for the new value. Likewise, removing a value from a vector requires all the elements after the removal point to be moved one position toward the vector's beginning. When a node is inserted into, or deleted from a linked list, none of the other nodes have to be moved.

The Composition of a Linked List

Each node in a linked list contains one or more members that hold data. (Perhaps the nodes hold inventory records, or customer names, addresses, and telephone numbers.) In addition to the data, each node contains a pointer, which can point to another node. The makeup of a node is illustrated in Figure 16-1.

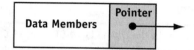

Figure 16-1

A linked list is called "linked" because each node in the series has a pointer that points to the next node in the list. This creates a chain where the first node points to the second node, the second node points to the third node, and so on. This is illustrated in Figure 16-2.

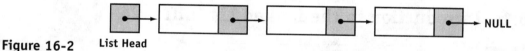

Figure 16-2   List Head

The list depicted in Figure 16-2 has three nodes, plus a pointer known as the list *head*. The head simply points to the first node in the list. Each node, in turn, points to the next node in the list. (Node 1 points to node 2, which points to node 3.) Since node 3 is the last one, it points to the NULL address (address 0). This is usually how the end of a linked list is signified—by letting the last node point to NULL.

 Note: Figure 16-2 depicts the nodes in the linked list as being very close to each other, neatly arranged in a row. In reality, the nodes may be scattered around various parts of memory.

Declarations

So how is a linked list declared in C++? First you must declare a data structure that will be used for the nodes. For example, the following struct could be used to create a list where each node holds a float:

```
struct ListNode
{
    float value;
    ListNode *next;
};
```

The first member of this `ListNode` structure is a `float` named `value`. It will be used to hold the node's data. The second member is a pointer named `next`. The pointer can hold the address of any object that is a `ListNode` structure. This allows each `ListNode` structure to point to the next `ListNode` structure in the list.

Since the `ListNode` structure shown contains a pointer to an object of the same type as that being declared, it is a *self-referential data structure*. This structure makes it possible to create nodes that point to other nodes of the same type.

The next step is to declare a pointer to serve as the list head, as shown here:

```
ListNode *head;
```

Before you use the `head` pointer in any linked list operations, you must be sure it is initialized to NULL, since that marks the end of the list. Once you have declared a node data structure and have created a NULL head pointer, you have an empty linked list. The next step is to implement operations with the list.

Checking for NULL pointers

When working with linked lists, we will frequently have occasion for testing a pointer such as

```
ListNode *p;
```

to see if its value is NULL. For example, we may have an if statement such as

```
if (p != NULL)
{
    //do something
}
```

Because any nonzero value is considered to be equivalent to true by an if statement, we can substitute any value for the test condition `p != NULL` in the preceding if statement, as long as the substituted value is nonzero when `p` is not NULL (that is, the value must be nonzero when `p` is nonzero) and the substituted value is zero when `p` is NULL (that is the value must be zero when `p` is zero). Because the value `p` itself fits this criterion, we can write

```
if (p)
{
    //do something
}
```

in place of the preceding if statement. Similarly, a while statement such as

```
while (p != NULL)
{
    //do something
}
```

can be replaced by the equivalent code

```
while (p)
    {
        //do something
    }
```

Similar reasoning shows that the expression !p is true precisely when p is false, or equivalently, when p is zero. Thus the expression !p in a test condition of an if statement or while loop is equivalent to the expression p == NULL. Thus instead of writing

```
if (p == NULL)
    {
        //do something
    }
```

you can write

```
if (!p)
    {
        //do something
    }
```

Many programmers use both forms of testing the value of a pointer against NULL.

Checkpoint   [16.1]

16.1   Describe the two parts of a node.

16.2   What is a list head?

16.3   What signifies the end of a linked list?

16.4   What is a self-referential data structure?

16.2   Linked List Operations

CONCEPT The basic linked list operations are appending a node, traversing the list, inserting a node, deleting a node, and destroying the list.

In this section we will develop an abstract data type that performs basic linked list operations using the ListNode structure and head pointer defined in the previous section. We will use the following class declaration, which is stored in FloatList.h.

```
class FloatList
{
```

```
private:
    // Declare a structure for the list
    struct ListNode
    {
        float value;
        ListNode *next;
    };
    ListNode *head;              // List head pointer
public:
    FloatList()                  // Constructor
        { head = NULL; }
    ~FloatList();                // Destructor
    void appendNode(float);
    void insertNode(float);
    void deleteNode(float);
    void displayList();
};
```

Notice that the constructor initializes the head pointer to NULL. This establishes an empty linked list. The class has member functions for appending, inserting, and deleting nodes, as well as a displayList function that displays all the values stored in the list. The destructor destroys the list by deleting all its nodes. These functions are defined in FloatList.cpp. First we will examine the functions individually. At the end of the section the entire contents of FloatList.cpp will be shown.

Appending a Node to the List

To append a node to a linked list means to add the node to the end of the list. The appendNode member function accepts a float argument, num. The function will allocate a new ListNode structure, store the value in num in the node's value member, and append the node to the end of the list. Here is a pseudocode representation of the general algorithm:

```
Create a new node.
Store data in the new node.
If there are no nodes in the list
    Make the new node the first node.
Else
    Traverse the list to find the last node.
    Add the new node to the end of the list.
End If.
```

Here is the actual C++ code for the function:

```
void FloatList::appendNode(float num)
{
    ListNode *newNode, *nodePtr;
```

```
// Allocate a new node and store num in it
newNode = new ListNode;
newNode->value = num;
newNode->next = NULL;

// If there are no nodes in the list
// make newNode the first node
if (!head)
    head = newNode;
else
    // otherwise, determine where to
    // insert the new node.
{
    // Initialize nodePtr to head of list
    nodePtr = head;
    // Find the last node in the list
    while (nodePtr->next)
        nodePtr = nodePtr->next;
    // Insert the new Node as the last node
    nodePtr->next = newNode;
}
}
```

Let's examine the statements in detail. First, our function will declare the following local variables:

```
ListNode *newNode, *nodePtr;
```

The newNode pointer will be used to allocate and point to the new node. The nodePtr pointer will be used to travel down the linked list, in search of the last node.

The following statements create a new node and store num and NULL in its value and next members respectively:

```
newNode = new ListNode;
newNode->value = num;
newNode->next = NULL;
```

The last statement shown is important. Since this node will become the last node in the list, its next pointer must point to NULL.

Next, we test the head pointer to determine whether there are any nodes already in the list. If head points to NULL, we will make the new node the first in the list. Making head point to the new node does this. Here is the code:

```
if (!head)
    head = newNode;
```

If head does not point to NULL, however, there are nodes in the list. The else part of the if statement must contain code to find the end of the list and insert the new node. The code is shown here:

```
else
{
    // Initialize nodePtr to head of list
```

```
        nodePtr = head;

        // Find the last node in the list
        while (nodePtr->next)
            nodePtr = nodePtr->next;

        // Insert newNode as the last node
        nodePtr->next = newNode;
    }
```

The code uses `nodePtr` to travel down the linked list. It does this by first assigning to `nodePtr` the address stored in `head`, thus making it point to the same node that `head` points to:

```
        nodePtr = head;
```

A `while` loop is then used to *traverse* (or travel through) the list searching for the last node. The last node will be the one whose `next` member points to NULL:

```
        while (nodePtr->next)
          nodePtr = nodePtr->next;
```

When `nodePtr` points to the last node in the list, we make that node's `next` member point to the new node with the following statement:

```
        nodePtr->next = newNode;
```

This inserts the new node at the end of the list. (Remember, `newNode->next` has already been set to NULL.)

Program 16-1 demonstrates the function.

Program 16-1

```
// This program demonstrates a simple append
// operation on a linked list.

#include <iostream>
#include "FloatList.h"
using namespace std;

int main()
{
    FloatList list;

    list.appendNode(2.5);
    list.appendNode(7.9);
    list.appendNode(12.6);
    return 0;
}
```

(This program displays no output.)

Let's step through Program 16-1, observing how the `appendNode` function builds a linked list to store the three argument values used.

The `head` pointer, a member variable of the `FloatList` class, is automatically initialized to NULL by the constructor when the list is created. This indicates that the list is initially empty.

The first call to `appendNode` passes 2.5 as the argument. In the following statements, a new node is allocated in memory, 2.5 is copied into its `value` member, and NULL is assigned to the node's `next` pointer:

```
newNode = new ListNode;
newNode->value = num;
newNode->next = NULL;
```

Figure 16-3 illustrates the state of the `head` and `newNode` pointers.

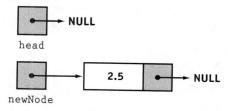

Figure 16-3

The next statement to execute is the following `if` statement:

```
if (!head)
    head = newNode;
```

Since `head` points to NULL, the condition `!head` is true. The statement `head = newNode;` is executed, making the new node the first node in the list. This is illustrated in Figure 16-4.

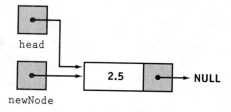

Figure 16-4

There are no more statements to execute, so control returns to function `main`. In the second call to `appendNode`, 7.9 is passed as the argument. Once again, the first three statements in the function create a new node, store the argument in the node's `value` member, and assign its `next` pointer to NULL. Figure 16-5 illustrates the current state of the list and the new node.

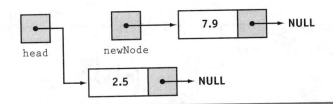

Figure 16-5

Since head no longer points to NULL, the else part of the if statement executes:

```
else
    // Otherwise, insert the new node at end
{
    // Initialize nodePtr to head of list
    nodePtr = head;

    // Find the last node in the list
    while (nodePtr->next)
        nodePtr = nodePtr->next;
    // Insert the new node as the last node
    nodePtr->next = newNode;
}
```

The first statement in the else block assigns the value in head to nodePtr. This causes nodePtr to point to the same node that head points to. This illustrated in Figure 16-6.

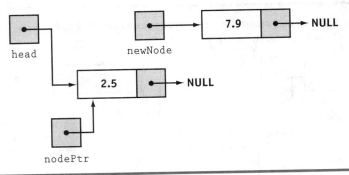

Figure 16-6

Look at the next member of the node that nodePtr points to. Its value is NULL, which means that nodePtr->next also points to NULL. Therefore, nodePtr is already at the end of the list, and the while loop immediately terminates. The last statement

```
nodePtr->next = newNode;
```

causes nodePtr->next to point to the new node. This inserts the new node at the end of the list, as shown in Figure 16-7.

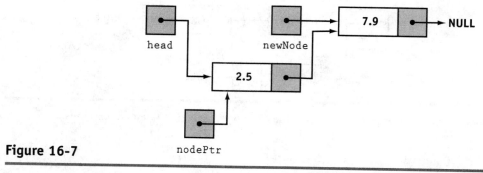

Figure 16-7

The third time appendNode is called, 12.6 is passed as the argument. Once again, the first three statements create a node with the argument stored in the value member. This is shown in Figure 16-8.

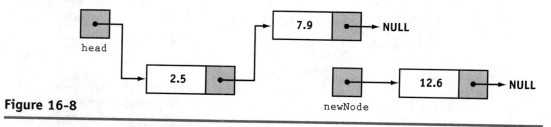

Figure 16-8

Next, the else part of the if statement executes. As before, nodePtr is made to point to the same node as head; as shown in Figure 16-9.

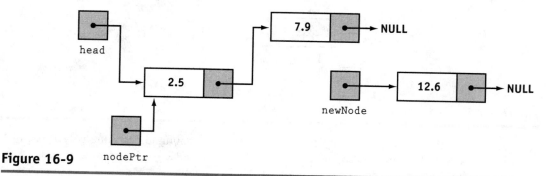

Figure 16-9

Since nodePtr->next is not NULL, the while loop will execute. After its first iteraton, nodePtr will point to the second node in the list. This is shown in Figure 16-10.

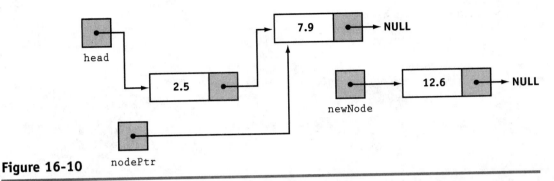

Figure 16-10

The `while` loop's conditional test will fail after the first iteration because `nodePtr->next` now points to NULL. The last statement,

```
nodePtr->next = newNode;
```

causes `nodePtr->next` to point to the new node. This inserts `newNode` at the end of the list, as shown in Figure 16-11.

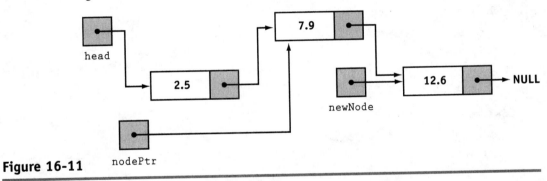

Figure 16-11

Figure 16-11 depicts the final state of the linked list.

Traversing a Linked List

The `appendNode` function demonstrated in the previous section contains a `while` loop that traverses, or travels through, the linked list. In this section we will demonstrate the `displayList` member function that traverses the list, displaying the `value` member of each node. The following pseudocode represents the algorithm.

```
Assign List head to node pointer.
While node pointer is not NULL
    Display the value member of the node pointed to by node pointer.
    Make node pointer point to the next node in the list
End While.
```

The function is shown here:

```
void FloatList::displayList(void)
{
    ListNode *nodePtr;
    nodePtr = head;
    while (nodePtr)
    {
        cout << nodePtr->value << endl;
        nodePtr = nodePtr->next;
    }
}
```

Program 16-2, a modification of Program 16-1, demonstrates the function.

Program 16-2

```
// This program calls the displayList member function.
// The function traverses the linked list, displaying
// the value stored in each node.

#include <iostream>
#include "FloatList.h"
using namespace std;

int main()
{
    FloatList List;

    list.appendNode(2.5);
    list.appendNode(7.9);
    list.appendNode(12.6);
    list.displayList();
    return 0;
}
```

Program Output
```
2.5
7.9
12.6
```

Usually, when an operation is to be performed on some or all the nodes in a linked list, a traversal algorithm is used. You will see variations of this traversal algorithm throughout this chapter.

Inserting a Node

Appending a node is a straightforward procedure. Inserting a node in the middle of a list, however, is more involved. For example, suppose the values in a list are sorted and you wish all new values to be inserted in their proper position. This will preserve the order of the list. Using the ListNode structure again, the following pseudocode shows an algorithm for finding a new node's proper position in the list and inserting there. The algorithm assumes the nodes in the list are already in order.

```
Create a new node.
Store data in the new node.
If there are no nodes in the list
    Make the new node the first node.
Else
    Find the first node whose value is greater than or equal the new
    value, or the end of the list (whichever is first).
    Insert the new node before the found node, or at the end of the list
    if no such node was found.
End If.
```

Notice that the new algorithm finds the first node whose value is greater than or equal to the new value. The new node is then inserted before the found node. This will require the use of two node pointers during the traversal: one to point to the node being inspected and another to point to the previous node. The code for the traversal algorithm is as follows. (As before, num holds the value being inserted into the list.)

```
// Initialize nodePtr to head of list
nodePtr = head;

// Skip all nodes whose value member is less
// than num.
while (nodePtr != NULL && nodePtr->value < num)
{
    previousNode = nodePtr;
    nodePtr = nodePtr->next;
}
```

This code segment uses the ListNode pointers nodePtr and previousNode. As nodePtr moves down the list, the previousNode pointer points to the node before the one pointed to by nodePtr. The entire insertNode function is shown here:

```
void FloatList::insertNode(float num)
{
    ListNode *newNode, *nodePtr, *previousNode;

    // Allocate a new node and store num in it
    newNode = new ListNode;
    newNode->value = num;
    newNode->next = NULL;

    // If there are no nodes in the list or new node
    // is smaller than the first node then make
    // the new node the first node
```

```
            if (!head || num <= head->value)
            {
                newNode->next = head;
                head = newNode;
            }
            else
                // Otherwise, insert the new node at
                // correct place in the list
            {
                // Initialize nodePtr to head of list
                nodePtr = head;

                // Skip all nodes whose value member is less
                // than num.
                while (nodePtr != NULL && nodePtr->value < num)
                {
                    previousNode = nodePtr;
                    nodePtr = nodePtr->next;
                }
                // Insert the node after the one pointed to
                // by previousNode and before the one pointed to
                // by nodePtr.
                previousNode->next = newNode;
                newNode->next = nodePtr;
            }
        }
    }
```

Program 16-3 is a modification of Program 16-2. It uses the insertNode member function to insert a value in its ordered position in the list.

Program 16-3

```
// This program illustrates the FloatList
// appendNode, insertNode, and displayList
// member functions.

#include <iostream>
#include "floatlist.h"
using namespace std;

int main()
{
    FloatList list;

    // Build the list
    list.appendNode(2.5);
    list.appendNode(7.9);
    list.appendNode(12.6);
```

(program continues)

Program 16-3 *(continued)*

```
// Insert a node in the middle
// of the list.
list.insertNode(10.5);

// Display the list
list.displayList();
return 0;
}
```

Program Output
```
2.5
7.9
10.5
12.6
```

Like Program 16-2, Program 16-3 calls the appendNode function three times to build the list with the values 2.5, 7.9, and 12.6. The insertNode function is then called, with the argument 10.5. In insertNode, a new node is created and the function argument is copied to its value member. Since the list already has nodes stored in it, the else part of the if statement will execute. It begins by assigning to nodePtr the address stored in head, thus making nodePtr point to the beginning of the list. Figure 16-12 illustrates the state of the list at this point.

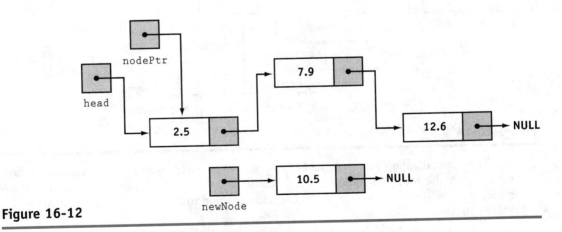

Figure 16-12

Since nodePtr is not NULL and nodePtr->value is less than num, the while loop will iterate. During the iteration, previousNode will be made to point to the node that nodePtr is pointing to. nodePtr will then be advanced to point to the next node. This is shown in Figure 16-13.

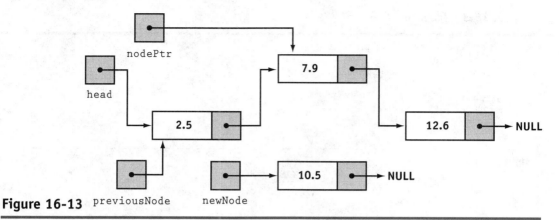

Figure 16-13 previousNode   newNode

Once again, the loop performs its test. Since nodePtr is not NULL and nodePtr->value is less than num, the loop will iterate a second time. During the second iteration, both previous-Node and nodePtr are advanced by one node in the list. This is shown in Figure 16-14.

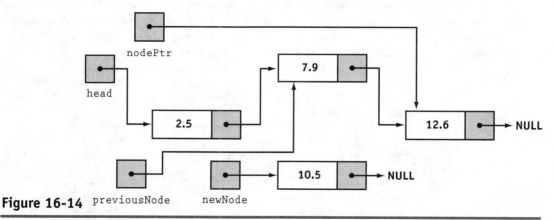

Figure 16-14 previousNode   newNode

This time, the loop's test will fail because nodePtr->value is not less than num. The statements after the loop will execute, which cause previousNode->next to point to the new node, and newNode->next to point to the node pointed to by nodePtr. This is illustrated in Figure 16-15.

This leaves the list in its final state. If you follow the links, from the head pointer to the NULL, you will see that the nodes are stored in the order of their value members.

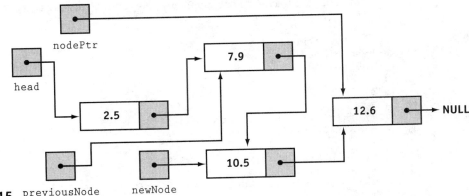

Figure 16-15 previousNode   newNode

Checkpoint   [16.2]

16.5   What is the difference between appending a node to a list and inserting a node into a list?

16.6   Which is easier to code: appending or inserting?

16.7   Why does the insertNode function shown in this section use a previousNode pointer?

Deleting a Node

Deleting a node from a linked list requires two steps:

1. Remove the node from the list without breaking the links created by the next pointers.

2. Delete the node from memory.

The deleteNode member function searches for a node containing a particular value and deletes it from the list. It uses an algorithm similar to the insertNode function. Two node pointers, nodePtr and previousNode, are used to traverse the list. The previousNode pointer always points to the node whose position is just before the one pointed to by nodePtr. When nodePtr points to the node that is to be deleted, previousNode->next is made to point to nodePtr->next. This removes the node pointed to by nodePtr from the list. The final step performed by this function is to free the memory used by the node with the delete operator. The entire function is shown here:

```
void FloatList::deleteNode(float num)
{
    ListNode *nodePtr, *previousNode;

    // If the list is empty, do nothing.
    if (!head)
        return;
```

```
          // Determine if the first node is the one to delete.
          if (head->value == num)
          {
            nodePtr = head;
            head = head->next;
            delete nodePtr;
          }
          else
          {
            // Initialize nodePtr to head of list
            nodePtr = head;

            // Skip all nodes whose value member is
            // not equal to num.
            while (nodePtr != NULL && nodePtr->value != num)
            {
                previousNode = nodePtr;
                nodePtr = nodePtr->next;
            }
            // Link the previous node to the node after
            // nodePtr, then delete nodePtr.
            if (nodePtr)
            {
                previousNode->next = nodePtr->next;
                delete nodePtr;
            }
          }
        }
    }
```

Program 16-4 demonstrates the function by first building a list of three nodes, then deleting them one by one.

Program 16-4

```
// This program demonstrates the deleteNode member function

#include <iostream>
#include "FloatList.h"
using namespace std;

int main()
{
    FloatList list;
```

(program continues)

Program 16-4   *(continued)*

```cpp
    // Build the list
    list.appendNode(2.5);
    list.appendNode(7.9);
    list.appendNode(12.6);
    cout << "Here are the initial values:\n";
    list.displayList();
    cout << endl;

    cout << "Now deleting the node in the middle.\n";
    cout << "Here are the nodes left.\n";
    list.deleteNode(7.9);
    list.displayList();
    cout << endl;

    cout << "Now deleting the last node.\n";
    cout << "Here are the nodes left.\n";
    list.deleteNode(12.6);
    list.displayList();
    cout << endl;

    cout << "Now deleting the only remaining node.\n";
    cout << "Here are the nodes left.\n";
    list.deleteNode(2.5);
    list.displayList();
    return 0;
}
```

Program Output

```
Here are the initial values:
2.5
7.9
12.6

Now deleting the node in the middle.
Here are the nodes left.
2.5
12.6

Now deleting the last node.
Here are the nodes left.
2.5

Now deleting the only remaining node.
Here are the nodes left.
```

To illustrate how `deleteNode` works, we will step through the first call which deletes the node containing 7.9 as its value. This node is in the middle of the list.

Look at the `else` part of the second `if` statement. This is where the function will perform its action since the list is not empty, and the first node does not contain the value 7.9. Just like `insertNode`, this function uses `nodePtr` and `previousNode` to traverse the list. The `while` loop terminates when the value 7.9 is located. At this point, the list and the other pointers will be in the state depicted in Figure 16-16.

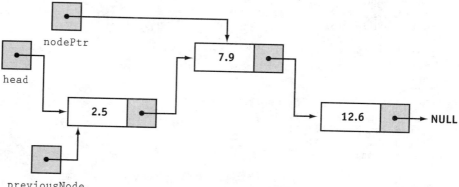

Figure 16-16 `previousNode`

Next, the following statement executes.

```
previousNode->next = nodePtr->next;
```

This statement causes the links in the list to bypass the node that `nodePtr` points to. Although the node still exists in memory, this removes it from the list, as illustrated in Figure 16-17.

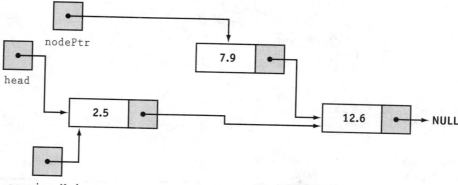

Figure 16-17 `previousNode`

The last statement uses the `delete` operator to free the memory used by the deleted node.

Destroying the List

It's important for the class's destructor to release all the memory used by the list. It does so by stepping through the list, deleting one node at a time. The code is shown here:

```cpp
FloatList::~FloatList()
{
  ListNode *nodePtr, *nextNode;

  nodePtr = head;
  while (nodePtr != NULL)
  {
    nextNode = nodePtr->next;
    delete nodePtr;
    nodePtr = nextNode;
  }
}
```

Notice the use of nextNode instead of previousNode. The nextNode pointer is used to hold the position of the next node in the list, so it will be available after the node pointed to by nodePtr is deleted.

For your reference, the entire FloatList class is shown here:

Contents of FloatList.h

```cpp
#ifndef FLOATLIST_H
#define FLOATLIST_H

class FloatList
{
private:
  // Declare a structure for the list
  struct ListNode
  {
    float value;
    ListNode *next;
  };

  ListNode *head;              // List head pointer
public:
  FloatList()                  // Constructor
    { head = NULL; }
  ~FloatList();                // Destructor
  void appendNode(float);
  void insertNode(float);
  void deleteNode(float);
  void displayList();
};

#endif
```

Contents of FloatList.cpp

```
#include <iostream>  // For cout and NULL
#include "floatlist.h"
using namespace std;

//**********************************************************
// appendNode appends a node containing the             *
// value passed into num, to the end of the list.       *
//**********************************************************

void FloatList::appendNode(float num)
{
   ListNode *newNode, *nodePtr;

   // Allocate a new node and store num in it
   newNode = new ListNode;
   newNode->value = num;
   newNode->next = NULL;

   // If there are no nodes in the list
   // make the new node the first node
   if (!head)
      head = newNode;
   else
      // otherwise, determine where to
      // insert the new node.
   {
      // Initialize nodePtr to head of list
      nodePtr = head;
      // Find the last node in the list
      while (nodePtr->next)
          nodePtr = nodePtr->next;
      // Insert the new Node as the last node
      nodePtr->next = newNode;
   }
}


//**********************************************************
// displayList shows the value                          *
// stored in each node of the linked list               *
// pointed to by head.                                  *
//**********************************************************

void FloatList::displayList()
{
   ListNode *nodePtr;
```

```
    nodePtr = head;
    while (nodePtr)
    {
        cout << nodePtr->value << endl;
        nodePtr = nodePtr->next;
    }
}

//********************************************************
// The insertNode function inserts a node with          *
// num copied to its value member.                       *
//********************************************************

void FloatList::insertNode(float num)
{
    ListNode *newNode, *nodePtr, *previousNode;

    // Allocate a new node and store num in it
    newNode = new ListNode;
    newNode->value = num;
    newNode->next = NULL;

    // If there are no nodes in the list or new node
    // is smaller than the first node then make
    // the new node the first node
    if (!head || num <= head->value)
    {
        newNode->next = head;
        head = newNode;
    }
    else
        // Otherwise, insert the new node at
        // correct place in the list
    {
        // Initialize nodePtr to head of list
        nodePtr = head;

        // Skip all nodes whose value member is less
        // than num.
        while (nodePtr != NULL && nodePtr->value < num)
        {
            previousNode = nodePtr;
            nodePtr = nodePtr->next;
        }
        // Insert the node after the one pointed to
        // by previousNode and before the one pointed to
        // by nodePtr.
        previousNode->next = newNode;
        newNode->next = nodePtr;
    }
}
```

```cpp
//**********************************************************
// The deleteNode function searches for a node          *
// with num as its value. The node, if found, is        *
// deleted from the list and from memory.               *
//**********************************************************

void FloatList::deleteNode(float num)
{
   ListNode *nodePtr, *previousNode;

   // If the list is empty, do nothing.
   if (!head)
      return;
   // Determine if the first node is the one to delete.
   if (head->value == num)
   {
     nodePtr = head;
     head = head->next;
     delete nodePtr;
   }
   else
   {
     // Initialize nodePtr to head of list
     nodePtr = head;

     // Skip all nodes whose value member is
     // not equal to num.
     while (nodePtr != NULL && nodePtr->value != num)
     {
        previousNode = nodePtr;
        nodePtr = nodePtr->next;
     }
     // Link the previous node to the node after
     // nodePtr, then delete nodePtr.
     if (nodePtr)
     {
        previousNode->next = nodePtr->next;
        delete nodePtr;
     }
   }
}

//**********************************************************
// Destructor                                           *
// This function deletes every node in the list.        *
//**********************************************************

FloatList::~FloatList()
{
   ListNode *nodePtr, *nextNode;
```

```
   nodePtr = head;
   while (nodePtr != NULL)
   {
      nextNode = nodePtr->next;
      delete nodePtr;
      nodePtr = nextNode;
   }
}
```

Checkpoint [16.2]

16.8 What are the two steps involved in deleting a node from a linked list?

16.9 When deleting a node, why can't you just use the `delete` operator to remove it from memory? Why must you take the steps you listed in response to question 16.8?

16.10 In a program that uses several linked lists, what might eventually happen if the class destructor does not destroy its linked list?

16.3 A Linked List Template

CONCEPT   A template can be easily created to store linked lists of any type.

The limitation of the `FloatList` class is that it can only hold float values. The class can easily be converted to a template that will accept any data type, as shown here:

Contents of `LinkedList.h`

```
#ifndef LINKEDLIST_H
#define LINKEDLIST_H

template <class T>
class LinkedList
{
private:
  // Declare a structure for the list
  struct ListNode
  {
    T value;
    ListNode *next;
  };

   ListNode *head;        // List head pointer
public:
   LinkedList()           // Constructor
     { head = NULL; }
   ~LinkedList();         // Destructor
```

```
      void appendNode(T);
      void insertNode(T);
      void deleteNode(T);
      void displayList();
};

//*******************************************************
// appendNode appends a node containing the         *
// value passed into num, to the end of the list.   *
//*******************************************************

template <class T>
void LinkedList<T>::appendNode(T num)
{
   ListNode *newNode, *nodePtr;

   // Allocate a new node and store num in it
   newNode = new ListNode;
   newNode->value = num;
   newNode->next = NULL;

   // If there are no nodes in the list
   // make the new node the first node.
   if (!head)
      head = newNode;
   else   // Otherwise, insert the new node at the end
   {
      // Initialize nodePtr to head of list
      nodePtr = head;
      // Find the last node in the list
      while (nodePtr->next)
         nodePtr = nodePtr->next;

      // Insert the new node as the last node
      nodePtr->next = newNode;
   }
}

//*******************************************************
// displayList shows the value                      *
// stored in each node of the linked list           *
// pointed to by head.                              *
//*******************************************************

template <class T>
void LinkedList<T>::displayList()
{
   ListNode *nodePtr;

   nodePtr = head;
```

```
   while (nodePtr)
   {
      cout << nodePtr->value << endl;
      nodePtr = nodePtr->next;
   }
}

//*********************************************************
// The insertNode function inserts a node with           *
// num copied to its value member.                        *
//*********************************************************

template <class T>
void LinkedList<T>::insertNode(T num)
{
   ListNode *newNode, *nodePtr, *previousNode;

   // Allocate a new node and store num in it
   newNode = new ListNode;
   newNode->value = num;
   newNode->next = NULL;

   // If there are no nodes in the list or the new node
   // is smaller than the first node then make newNode
   // the first node.
   if (!head || num <= head->value)
   {
      newNode->next = head;
      head = newNode;
   }
   else // Otherwise, insert newNode at correct
        // place in the list
   {
      // Initialize nodePtr to head of list
      nodePtr = head;
      // Skip all nodes whose value member is less
      // than num.
      while (nodePtr != NULL && nodePtr->value < num)
      {
         previousNode = nodePtr;
         nodePtr = nodePtr->next;
      }
      // Insert the node after the one pointed to
      // by previousNode and before the one pointed to
      // by nodePtr.
      previousNode->next = newNode;
      newNode->next = nodePtr;
   }
}
```

```
//*********************************************************
// The deleteNode function searches for a node       *
// with num as its value. The node, if found, is      *
// deleted from the list and from memory.             *
//*********************************************************

template <class T>
void LinkedList<T>::deleteNode(T num)
{
   ListNode *nodePtr, *previousNode;

   // If the list is empty, do nothing.
   if (!head)
      return;
   // Determine if the first node is the one.
   if (head->value == num)
   {
      nodePtr = head;
      head = head->next;
      delete nodePtr;
   }
   else
   {
      // Initialize nodePtr to head of list
      nodePtr = head;
      // Skip all nodes whose value member is
      // not equal to num.
      while (nodePtr != NULL && nodePtr->value != num)
      {
         previousNode = nodePtr;
         nodePtr = nodePtr->next;
      }
      // Link the previous node to the node after
      // nodePtr, then delete nodePtr.
      if (nodePtr)
      {
         previousNode->next = nodePtr->next;
         delete nodePtr;
      }
   }
}


//*********************************************************
// Destructor                                          *
// This function deletes every node in the list.       *
//*********************************************************
```

```
template <class T>
LinkedList<T>::~LinkedList()
{
    ListNode *nodePtr, *nextNode;

    nodePtr = head;
    while (nodePtr != NULL)
    {
        nextNode = nodePtr->next;
        delete nodePtr;
        nodePtr = nextNode;
    }
}

#endif
```

Of course, there are still limitatons, since the template uses the == operator to search for values. Any type passed to the template must support the == operator.

Program 16-5 shows the template being used to create a list of integers.

Program 16-5

```
// This program demonstrates the deleteNode member fucntion.

#include <iostream>
#include "LinkedList.h"
using namespace std;

int main()
{
    LinkedList<int> list;
    // Build the list
    list.appendNode(2);
    list.appendNode(4);
    list.appendNode(6);
    cout << "Here are the initial values:\n";
    list.displayList();
    cout << endl;

    cout << "Now inserting the value 5.\n";
    list.insertNode(5);
    cout << "Here are the nodes now.\n";
    list.displayList();
    cout << endl;

    cout << "Now deleting the last node.\n";
    list.deleteNode(6);
    cout << "Here are the nodes left.\n";
    list.displayList();
    return 0;
}
```

Program 16-5

Program Output
```
Here are the initial values:
2
4
6
Now inserting the value 5.
Here are the nodes now.
2
4
5
6
Now deleting the last node.
Here are the nodes left.
2
4
5
```

16.4 Variations of the Linked List

CONCEPT There are many ways to link dynamically allocated data structures together. Two variations of the linked list are the doubly linked list and the circular linked list.

The linked list examples that we have discussed are considered *singly linked lists*: Each node is linked to a single other node. A variation of this is the *doubly linked list*. In this type of list, each node not only points to the next node, but also to the previous one. This is illustrated in Figure 16-18.

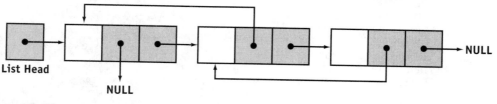

List Head NULL NULL

Figure 16-18

In Figure 16-18, the last node and the first node in the list have pointers to the NULL address. When the program traverses the list it knows when it has reached either end.

Another variation is the *circular linked list*. The last node in this type of list points to the first, as shown in Figure 16-19.

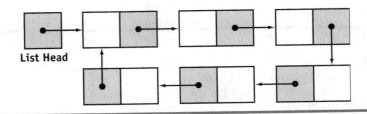

Figure 16-19

16.5 The STL `list` Container

> **CONCEPT** The Standard Template Library provides a linked list container.

The `list` container, found in the Standard Template Library, is a template version of a doubly linked list. STL `list`s can insert elements or add elements within the list more quickly than vectors can, because lists do not have to shift the other elements. Lists are also efficient at adding elements at their back because they have a built-in pointer to the last element in the list (no traversal required).

Table 16-1 describes some of the `list` member functions.

Table 16-1

Member Function	Examples and Description
back	`cout << list.back() << endl;` The `back` member function returns a reference to the last element in the list.

erase	`list.erase(iter);`
	`list.erase(firstIter, lastIter)`
	The first example causes the `list` element pointed to by the iterator `iter` to be removed. The second example causes all of the `list` elements from `firstIter` to `lastIter` to be removed.

empty	`if (list.empty())` The `empty` member function returns `true` if the `list` is empty. If the `list` has elements, it returns `false`.
end	`iter = list.end();` `end` returns a bidirectional iterator to the end of the list.
front	`cout << list.front() << endl;` `front` returns a reference to the first element of the `list`.

(table continues)

Table 16-1 *(continued)*

Member Function	Examples and Description
insert	`list.insert(iter, x)` The insert member function inserts an element into the list. The example inserts an element with the value x, just before the element pointed to by iter.
merge	`list1.merge(list2);` merge inserts all the items in list2 into list1. list1 is expanded to accommodate the new elements plus any elements already stored in list1. The merge function expects both lists to be sorted. When list2 is merged into list1, the elements are inserted into their correct position, so the resulting list is also sorted.
pop_back	`list.pop_back();` pop_back removes the last element of the list.
pop_front	`list.pop_front();` pop_front removes the first element of the list.
push_back	`list.push_back(x);` push_back inserts an element with value x at the end of the list.
push_front	`list.push_front(x);` push_front inserts an element with value x at the beginning of the list.
reverse	`list.reverse();` reverse reverses the order in which the elements appear in the list.
size()	Returns the number of elements in the list.
swap	`list1.swap(list2)` The swap member function swaps the elements stored in two lists. For example, assuming list1 and list2 are lists, the statement shown will exchange the values in the two lists.
unique	`list.unique();` unique eliminates duplicate values by removing any element that has the same value as the element before it.

Program 16-6 demonstrates some simple operations with the STL lists.

Program 16-6

```
// This program demonstrates the STL list container.

#include <iostream>
#include <list>      // Include the list header
using namespace std;
```

(program continues)

Program 16-6   *(continued)*

```
int main()
{
    list<int> myList;
    list<int>::iterator iter;

    // Add values to the list
    for (int x = 0; x < 100; x += 10)
        myList.push_back(x);

    // Display the values
    for (iter = myList.begin(); iter != myList.end(); iter++)
        cout << *iter << " ";
    cout << endl;

    // Now reverse the order of the elements
    myList.reverse();

    // Display the values again
    for (iter = myList.begin(); iter != myList.end(); iter++)
        cout << *iter << " ";
    cout << endl;
    return 0;
}
```

Program Output
```
0 10 20 30 40 50 60 70 80 90
90 80 70 60 50 40 30 20 10 0
```

Review Questions and Exercises

Fill-in-the-Blank

1. The _____ points to the first node in a linked list.

2. A data structure that points to an object of the same type as itself is known as a(n) _____ data structure.

3. After creating a linked list's head pointer, you should make sure it points to _____ before using it in any operations.

4. _____ a node means adding it to the end of a list.

5. _____ a node means adding it to a list, but not necessarily to the end.

6. _____ a list means traveling through the list.

7. In a(n) _____ list, the last node has a pointer to the first node.

8. In a(n) _____ list, each node has a pointer to the one before it and the one after it.

True or False

9. T   F   The programmer must know in advance how many nodes will be needed in a linked list.

10. T   F   It is not necessary for each node in a linked list to have a self-referential pointer.

11. T   F   In physical memory, the nodes in a linked list may be scattered around.

12. T   F   When the head pointer points to NULL, it signifies an empty list.

13. T   F   Insertion of elements in the middle of the container is more efficient for STL vectors than for linked lists.

14. T   F   Deleting a node in a linked list is a simple matter of using the `delete` operator to free the node's memory.

15. T   F   A class that builds a linked list should destroy the list in the class destructor.

Find the Error

16. Each of the following member functions has errors in the way it performs a linked list operation. Find as many mistakes as you can.

    A)
    ```
    void FloatList::appendNode(float num)
    {
        ListNode *newNode, *nodePtr;
        // Allocate a new node and store num in it
        newNode = new listNode;
        newNode->value = num;

        // If there are no nodes in the list
        // make newNode the first node
        if (!head)
            head = newNode;
        else // Otherwise, insert the new node at end
        {
            // Find the last node in the list
            while (nodePtr->next)
                nodePtr = nodePtr->next;
            // Insert the new node as the last node
            nodePtr->next = newNode;
        }
    }
    ```

    B)
    ```
    void FloatList::deleteNode(float num)
    {
        ListNode *nodePtr, *previousNode;
        // If the list is empty, do nothing.
        if (!head)
            return;
    ```

```
        // Determine if the first node is the one to delete.
        if (head->value == num)
           delete head;
        else
        {
           // Initialize nodePtr to head of list
           nodePtr = head;

           // Skip all nodes whose value member is
           // not equal to num.
           while (nodePtr->value != num)
           {
              previousNode = nodePtr;
              nodePtr = nodePtr->next;
           }
           // Link the previous node to the node after
           // nodePtr, then delete nodePtr.
           previousNode->next = nodePtr->next;
           delete nodePtr;
        }
     }
C) FloatList::~FloatList()
   {
      ListNode *nodePtr, *nextNode;

      nodePtr = head;
      while (nodePtr != NULL)
      {
         nextNode = nodePtr->next;
         nodePtr->next = NULL;
         nodePtr = nextNode;
      }
   }
```

Programming Challenges

General Requirements

Each program should have a section of comments at the top. The comments should contain your name, the date the program was written, the chapter the assignment appeared in, and the assignment number and name. Here is an example:

```
// Written by Jill Johnson
// March 31, 2003
// Chapter 16
// Assignment 1. Your Own Linked List
```

1. Your Own Linked List

Design your own linked list class to hold a series of integers. The class should have member functions for appending, inserting, and deleting nodes. Don't forget to add a destructor that destroys the list. Demonstrate the class with a driver program.

2. Rainfall Statistics Modification

Modify Programming Challenge 2 in Chapter 8 (Rainfall Statistics) to let the user decide how many months of data will be entered. Use a linked list instead of an array to hold the monthly data.

3. Payroll Modification

Modify Programming Challenge 6 in Chapter 8 (Payroll) to use three linked lists instead of three arrays to hold the employee IDs, hours worked, and wages. When the program starts, it should ask the user to enter the employee IDs. There should be no limit on the number of IDs the user can enter.

4. List Search

Modify the `LinkedList` template shown in this chapter to include a member function named `search`. The function should search the list for a specified value. If the value is found, it should return a number indicating its position in the list. (The first node is node 1, the second node is node 2, and so forth.) If the value is not found, the function should return 0. Demonstrate the function in a driver program.

5. Linked List Copy Constructor

Since classes that create linked lists dynamically allocate memory, they should have copy constructors. Write a copy constructor for the `LinkedList` template shown in this chapter. Use a simple driver program to demonstrate it.

6. Float Merge

Modify the `FloatList` class shown in this chapter to include a member function named `mergeArray`. The `mergeArray` function should take an array of floats as its first argument, and an integer as its second argument. (The second argument will specify the size of the array being passed into the first argument.)

The function should merge the values in the array into the linked list. The value in each element of the array should be inserted (not appended) into the linked list. When the values are inserted, they should be in numerical order. Demonstrate the function with a driver program. When you are satisfied with the function, incorporate it into the `LinkedList` template.

7. Reverse Order

Modify the `LinkedList` template to include a member function named `reverse`. The function should reverse the order of the nodes in the linked list. Hint: This can be done by creating a second linked list. Copy the nodes from the original list, starting at the last node. When this is done, destroy the first list and replace it with the second list.

8. Rainfall Statistics Modification #2

Modify the program you wrote for Programming Challenge 2 so it saves the information in the linked list to a file. Write a second program that reads the information from the file into a linked list and displays it on the screen.

Serendipity Booksellers Software Development Project—Part 16: *A Problem-Solving Exercise*

The system's reporting module produces the following reports:

Inventory Listing
Inventory Wholesale Value
Inventory Retail Value
Listing by Quantity
Listing by Cost
Listing by Age

The functions that produce these reports must read the records from the inventory file (which you implemented in Chapter 14). Modify the system so it reads the records from a linked list instead of the inventory file. Implement the linked list in the following manner:

1. Modify the `LinkedList` template presented in this chapter. The template must be able to store `BookData` class objects.

2. Modify the reporting module so it reads the entire contents of the inventory file into a linked list when the user enters the Reports menu. When the user selects one of the reports from the Reports menu, the system will read the information stored in the linked list instead of the inventory file. This will increase performance when the user is requesting more than one report.

3. When the user exits the Reports menu, the system destroys the linked list.

CHAPTER 17

Stacks and Queues

Topics

17.1   Introduction to the Stack ADT

> **CONCEPT** A stack is a data structure that stores and retrieves items in a last-in-first-out manner.

Definition

Like an array or a linked list, a stack is a data structure that holds a sequence of elements. Unlike arrays and lists, however, stacks are *last-in-first-out (LIFO)* structures. This means that when a program retrieves elements from a stack, the last element inserted into the stack is the first one retrieved (and likewise, the first element inserted is the last one retrieved).

When visualizing the way a stack works, think of a stack of plates at the beginning of a cafeteria line. When a cafeteria worker replenishes the supply of plates, the first one he or she puts on the stack is the last one taken off. This is illustrated in Figure 17-1.

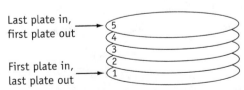

Figure 17-1

The LIFO characteristic of a stack of plates in a cafeteria is also the primary characteristic of a stack data structure. The last data element placed on the stack is the first data retrieved from the stack.

Applications of Stacks

Stacks are useful data structures for algorithms that work first with the last saved element of a series. For example, computer systems use stacks while executing programs. When a function is called, they save the program's return address on a stack. They also create local variables on a stack. When the function terminates, the local variables are removed from the stack and the return address is retrieved. Also, some calculators use a stack for performing mathematical operations.

Static and Dynamic Stacks

There are two types of stack data structure: static and dynamic. Static stacks have a fixed size and are implemented as arrays. Dynamic stacks grow in size as needed and are implemented as linked lists. In this section you will see examples of both static and dynamic stacks.

Stack Operations

A stack has two primary operations: *push* and *pop*. The push operation causes a value to be stored, or pushed onto the stack. For example, suppose we have an empty integer stack that is capable of holding a maximum of three values. With that stack we execute the following push operations.

```
push(5);
push(10);
push(15);
```

Figure 17-2 illustrates the state of the stack after each of these push operations.

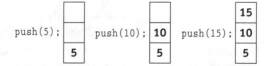

Figure 17-2

The pop operation retrieves (and hence, removes) a value from the stack. Suppose we execute three consecutive pop operations on the stack shown in Figure 17-2. Figure 17-3 depicts the results.

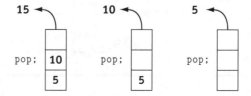

Figure 17-3

As you can see from Figure 17-3, the last pop operation leaves the stack empty.

For a static stack (one with a fixed size), we will need a boolean *isFull* operation. The isFull operation returns `true` if the stack is full, and `false` otherwise. This operation is necessary to prevent a stack overflow in the event a push operation is attempted when all the stack's elements have values stored in them.

For both static and dynamic stacks we will need a boolean *isEmpty* operation. The isEmpty operation returns `true` when the stack is empty, and `false` otherwise. This prevents an error from ocurring when a pop operation is attempted on an empty stack.

A Static Stack Class

Now we examine a class, `IntStack`, that stores a static stack of integers and performs the stack operations listed above. The class has the member variables described in Table 17-1.

Table 17-1

Member Variable	Description
stackArray	A pointer to `int`. When the constructor is executed, it uses `stackArray` to dynamically allocate an array for storage.
stackSize	An integer that holds the size of the stack. This is the maximum number of elements the stack can hold, not the number of elements currently in the stack.
top	An integer that is used to mark the top of the stack.

The class's member functions are listed in Table 17-2.

Table 17-2

Member Functions	Description
Constructor	The class constructor accepts an integer argument, which specifies the size of the stack. An integer array of this size is dynamically allocated and assigned to `stackArray`. Also, the variable `top` is initialized to –1 to indicate that the stack is currently empty.
push	The `push` function accepts an integer argument, which is pushed onto the top of the stack.
pop	The `pop` function uses an integer reference parameter. The value at the top of the stack is removed and copied into the reference parameter.
isFull	Returns `true` if the stack is full and `false` otherwise. The stack is full when `top` is equal to `stackSize` –1.
isEmpty	Returns `true` if the stack is empty, and `false` otherwise. The stack is empty when `top` is set to –1.

 Note: Even though the constructor dynamically allocates the stack array, it is still considered a static stack since the size of the stack does not change once it is allocated.

The code for the class is shown here:

Contents of IntStack.h

```
#ifndef INTSTACK_H
#define INTSTACK_H

class IntStack
{
private:
   int *stackArray;
   int stackSize;
   int top;

public:
   IntStack(int);
   ~IntStack()
      {
          delete [] stackArray;
      }
   void push(int);
   void pop(int &);
   bool isFull();
   bool isEmpty();
};

#endif
```

Contents of IntStack.cpp

```
#include <iostream>
#include "intstack.h"

//********************
// Constructor       *
//********************

IntStack::IntStack(int size)
{
   stackArray = new int[size];
   stackSize = size;
   top = -1;
}


//*****************************************************
// Member function push pushes the argument onto   *
// the stack.                                       *
//*****************************************************
```

```
void IntStack::push(int num)
{
  if (isFull())
  {
     cout << "The stack is full.\n";
     exit(1);
  }
  else
  {
     top++;
     stackArray[top] = num;
  }
}

//**********************************************************
// Member function pop pops the value at the top          *
// of the stack off, and copies it into the variable      *
// passed as an argument.                                 *
//**********************************************************

void IntStack::pop(int &num)
{
  if (isEmpty())
  {
     cout << "The stack is empty.\n";
     exit(1);
  }
  else
  {
     num = stackArray[top];
     top--;
  }
}

//**********************************************************
// Member function isFull returns true if the stack       *
// is full, or false otherwise.                           *
//**********************************************************

bool IntStack::isFull()
{
  bool status;

  if (top == stackSize - 1)
     status = true;
  else
     status = false;

  return status;
}
```

```
//********************************************************
// Member function isEmpty returns true if the stack  *
// is empty, or false otherwise.                       *
//********************************************************

bool IntStack::isEmpty()
{
  bool status;

  if (top == -1)
      status = true;
  else
      status = false;

  return status;
}
```

The constructor dynamically allocates the stack array and initializes the stackSize and top member variables. Remember that items are stored to and retrieved from the top of the stack. In this class, the top of the stack is actually the end of the array. The variable top is used to mark the top of the stack by holding the subscript of the last element. When top holds –1, it indicates that the stack is empty. (See the isEmpty function, which returns true if top is –1, or false otherwise.) The stack is full when top is at the maximum subscript, which is stackSize - 1. This is the value that isFull tests for. It returns true if the stack is full, or false otherwise.

Program 17-1 is a simple driver that demonstrates the IntStack class.

Program 17-1

```
// This program demonstrates the IntStack class.

#include <iostream>
#include "IntStack.h"
using namespace std;

int main()
{
    IntStack stack(5);
    int catchVar;

    cout << "Pushing 5\n";
    stack.push(5);
    cout << "Pushing 10\n";
    stack.push(10);
    cout << "Pushing 15\n";
    stack.push(15);
```

(program continues)

Program 17-1 *(continued)*

```
cout << "Pushing 20\n";
stack.push(20);
cout << "Pushing 25\n";
stack.push(25);

cout << "Popping...\n";
stack.pop(catchVar);
cout << catchVar << endl;
stack.pop(catchVar);
cout << catchVar << endl;
stack.pop(catchVar);
cout << catchVar << endl;
stack.pop(catchVar);
cout << catchVar << endl;
stack.pop(catchVar);
cout << catchVar << endl;
return 0;
}
```

Program Output

```
Pushing 5
Pushing 10
Pushing 15
Pushing 20
Pushing 25
Popping...
25
20
15
10
5
```

In Program 17-1, the constructor is called with the argument 5. This sets up the member variables, as shown in Figure 17-4. Since top is set to –1, the stack is empty.

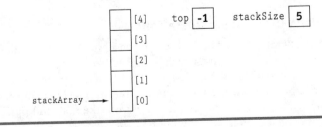

Figure 17-4

Figure 17-5 shows the state of the member variables after the push function is called the first time (with 5 as its argument). The top of the stack is now at element 0.

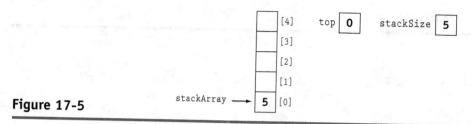

Figure 17-5

Figure 17-6 shows the state of the member variables after all five calls to the push function. Now the top of the stack is at element 4, and the stack is full.

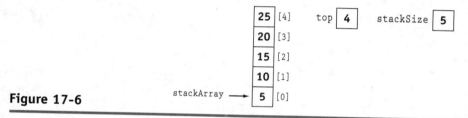

Figure 17-6

Notice that the pop function uses a reference parameter, num. The value that is popped off the stack is copied into num so it can be used later in the program. Figure 17-7 depicts the state of the class members and the num parameter, just after the first value is popped off the stack.

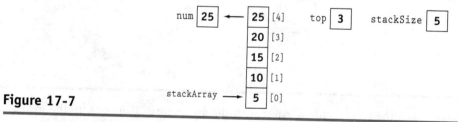

Figure 17-7

The program continues to call the pop fuction until all the values have been removed from the stack.

Implementing Other Stack Operations

More complex operations may be built on the basic stack class previously shown. In this section, we will discuss a class, MathStack, which is derived from IntStack. The MathStack class has two member functions: add() and sub(). The add() function pops the first two values off the stack, adds them together, and pushes the sum onto the stack. The sub() function pops the first two values off the stack, subtracts the second value from the first, and pushes the difference onto the stack. The class declaration is as follows:

Contents of `MathStack.h`

```
#ifndef MATHSTACK_H
#define MATHSTACK_H
#include "IntStack.h"

class MathStack : public IntStack
{
  public:
      MathStack(int s) : IntStack(s) {}
      void add();
      void sub();
};

#endif
```

The defnitions of the member functions are shown here:

Contents of `MathStack.cpp`

```
#include "MathStack.h"

//**********************************************
// Member function add. add pops                *
// the first two values off the stack and       *
// adds them. The sum is pushed onto the stack.  *
//**********************************************

void MathStack::add()
{
  int num, sum;

  pop(num);
  sum = num;
  pop(num);
  sum += num;
  push(sum);
}

//**********************************************
// Member functon sub. sub pops the             *
// first two values off the stack. The          *
// second value is subtracted from the          *
// first value. The difference is pushed        *
// onto the stack.                              *
//**********************************************

void MathStack::sub()
{
  int num, diff;
```

```
              pop(num);
              diff = num;
              pop(num);
              diff -= num;
              push(diff);
        }
```

The class is demonstrated in Program 17-2, a simple driver.

Program 17-2

```
// This program demonstrates the MathStack class.

#include <iostream>
#include "MathStack.h"
using namespace std;

int main()
{
    MathStack stack(5);
    int catchVar;

    cout << "Pushing 3\n";
    stack.push(3);
    cout << "Pushing 6\n";
    stack.push(6);
    stack.add();
    cout << "The sum is ";
    stack.pop(catchVar);
    cout << catchVar << endl;

    cout << "Pushing 7\n";
    stack.push(7);
    cout << "Pushing 10\n";
    stack.push(10);
    stack.sub();
    cout << "The difference is ";
    stack.pop(catchVar);
    cout << catchVar << endl;
    return 0;
}
```

Program Output
```
Pushing 3
Pushing 6
The sum is 9
Pushing 7
Pushing 10
The difference is 3
```

It will be left as a Programming Challenge for you to implement the `mult()`, `div()`, and `mod()` functions that will complete the `MathStack` class.

Stack Templates

The stack classes shown in this chapter work only with integers. A stack template can be easily designed to work with any data type. This, too, will be left as a Programming Challenge for you to complete.

17.2 Dynamic Stacks

CONCEPT A stack may be implemented as a linked list, and expand or shrink with each push or pop operation.

A dynamic stack is built on a linked list instead of on an array. A stack based on a linked list offers two advantages over a stack based on an array. First, there is no need to specify the starting size of the stack. A dynamic stack simply starts as an empty linked list, then expands by one node each time a value is pushed. Second, a dynamic stack will never be full, as long as the system has enough free memory.

In this section we will look at a dynamic stack class, `DynIntStack`. This class is a dynamic version of the `IntStack` class previously discussed. The class declaration is shown here:

Contents of `DynIntStack.h`

```
#ifndef DYNINTSTACK_H
#define DYNINTSTACK_H

class DynIntStack
{
private:
    struct StackNode
    {
        int value;
        StackNode *next;
    };

    StackNode *top;

public:
    DynIntStack()
        { top = NULL; }
    void push(int);
    void pop(int &);
    bool isEmpty();
};

#endif
```

The `StackNode` structure is the data type of each node in the linked list. It has a `value` member and a `next` pointer. Notice that instead of a `head` pointer, a `top` pointer is declared. This member will always point to the first node in the list, which will represent the top of the stack. It is initialized to NULL by the constructor, to signify that the stack is empty.

The definitons of the other member functions are shown here:

Contents of `DynIntStack.cpp`

```cpp
#include <iostream>
#include "DynIntStack.h"
using namespace std;

//*****************************************************
// Member function push pushes the argument onto     *
// the stack.                                         *
//*****************************************************

void DynIntStack::push(int num)
{
    StackNode *newNode;

    // Allocate a new node and store num in it.
    newNode = new StackNode;
    newNode->value = num;
    // add the new node at new top of the stack
    newNode->next = top;
    top = newNode;
}

//*****************************************************
// Member function pop removes the value at the top  *
// of the stack and copies it into the variable      *
// passed as an argument.                             *
//*****************************************************

void DynIntStack::pop(int &num)
{
    StackNode *temp;

    if (isEmpty())
    {
        cout << "The stack is empty.\n";
        exit(1);
    }
    else    // pop value off top of stack
    {
        num = top->value;
        temp = top;
        top = top->next;
        delete temp;
    }
}
```

```
//*********************************************************
// Member function isEmpty returns true if the stack     *
// is empty, or false otherwise.                         *
//*********************************************************

bool DynIntStack::isEmpty()
{
    bool status;
    if (!top)
        status = true;
    else
        status = false;
    return status;
}
```

Let's look at the push operation. First, a new node is allocated in memory and the function argument is copied into its value member:

```
newNode = new StackNode;
newNode->value = num;
```

The new node is then added at the top of the stack with the following code:

```
newNode->next = top;
top = newNode;
```

Note that this code works correctly even if the stack was empty previous to the call to push. This is because in that case, top is NULL, and the code newNode->next = top will correctly set newNode->next to NULL.

Now let's look at the pop function. Just as the push function must insert nodes at the head of the list, pop must delete nodes at the head of the list. First, the function calls isEmpty to determine whether there are any nodes in the stack. If not, an error message is displayed and the program is terminated.

```
if (isEmpty())
{
    cout << "The stack is empty.\n";
    exit(1);
}
```

If isEmpty returns false, then the following statements are executed.

```
else    // pop value off top of stack
{
    num = top->value;
    temp = top;
    top = top->next;
    delete temp;
}
```

First, a copy of the `value` member of the node at the top of the stack is saved in the `num` reference parameter. A temporary pointer `temp` is then set to point to the node that is to be deleted, that is, the node currently at the top of the stack. The `top` pointer is then set to point to the node after the one that is currently at the top: The same code will set `top` to NULL if there are no nodes after the one that is currently at the top of the stack. It is then safe to delete the top node through the temporary pointer.

The `isEmpty` function is simple. If `top` is NULL, then the list (the stack) is empty. Program 17-3 is a driver that demostrates the `DynIntStack` class.

Program 17-3

```
// This program demonstrates the dynamic stack
// class DynIntClass.

#include <iostream>
#include "DynIntStack.h"
using namespace std;

int main()
{
    DynIntStack stack;
    int catchVar;

    cout << "Pushing 5\n";
    stack.push(5);
    cout << "Pushing 10\n";
    stack.push(10);
    cout << "Pushing 15\n";
    stack.push(15);
    cout << "Popping...\n";
    stack.pop(catchVar);
    cout << catchVar << endl;
    stack.pop(catchVar);
    cout << catchVar << endl;
    stack.pop(catchVar);
    cout << catchVar << endl;

    cout << "\nAttempting to pop again... ";
    stack.pop(catchVar);
    return 0;
}
```

Program 17-3

Program Output
```
Pushing 5
Pushing 10
Pushing 15
Popping...
15
10
5

Attempting to pop again... The stack is empty.
```

17.3 The STL stack Container

CONCEPT	The Standard Template Library offers a stack template, which may be implemented as a vector, a linked list, or a deque.

So far, the STL containers you have learned about are vectors and lists. The STL stack container may be implemented as a vector or a list. (It may also be implemented as a deque, which you will learn about later in this chapter.) One class is said to *adapt* another class if it provides a new interface for it. The purpose of the new interface is to make it more convenient to use the class for specialized tasks. Because the stack container is used to adapt the list, vector, and deque containers, it is often referred to as a *container adapter*.

Here are examples of how to declare a stack of ints, implemented as a vector, a list, and a deque.

```
stack< int, vector<int> > iStack;    // Vector stack
stack< int, list<int> > iStack;      // List stack
stack< int > iStack;                 // Deque stack (the default)
```

 Note: Be sure to put spaces between the angled brackets that appear next to each other. This will prevent the compiler from mistaking >> for the stream extraction operator, >>.

Table 17-3 lists and describes some of the stack template's member functions.

Table 17-3

Member Function	Examples and Description
empty	`if (myStack.empty())` The `empty` member function returns `true` if the stack is empty. If the stack has elements, it returns `false`.
pop	`myStack.pop();` The `pop` function removes the element at the top of the stack
push	`myStack.push(x);` The `push` function pushes an element with the value `x` onto the stack.
size	`cout << myStack.size() << endl;` The size function returns the number of elements currently in the stack.
top	`x = myStack.top();` The `top` function returns a reference to the element at the top of the stack.

 Note: The `pop` function in the stack template does not retrieve the value from the top of the stack, it only removes it. To retrieve the value, you must call the `top` function first.

Program 17-4 is a driver that demonstrates an STL stack implemented as a vector.

Program 17-4

```
// This program demonstrates the STL stack
// container adapter.

#include <iostream>
#include <vector>
#include <stack>
using namespace std;

int main()
{
    int x;

    stack< int, vector<int> > iStack;

    for (x = 2; x < 8; x += 2)
    {
        cout << "Pushing " << x << endl;
        iStack.push(x);
    }
```

(program continues)

Program 17-4   *(continued)*

```
    cout << "The size of the stack is ";
    cout << iStack.size() << endl;

    for (x = 2; x < 8; x += 2)
    {
        cout << "Popping " << iStack.top() << endl;
        iStack.pop();
    }
    return 0;
}
```

Program Output
```
Pushing 2
Pushing 4
Pushing 6
The size of the stack is 3
Popping 6
Popping 4
Popping 2
```

Checkpoint   [17.1–17.3]

17.1   Describe what LIFO means.

17.2   What is the difference between static and dynamic stacks? What advantages do dynamic stacks have over static stacks?

17.3   What are the two primary stack operations? Describe them both.

17.4   What STL types does the STL stack container adapt?

17.4   Introduction to the Queue ADT

CONCEPT   A queue is a data structure that stores and retrieves items in a first-in-first-out manner.

Definition

Like a stack, a *queue* (pronounced "cue") is a data structure that holds a sequence of elements. A queue, however, provides access to its elements in *first-in, first-out (FIFO)* order. The elements in a queue are processed like customers standing in a grocery checkout line: The first customer in line is the first one served.

Application of Queues

Queue data structures are commonly used in computer operating systems. They are especially important in multiuser/multitasking environments where several users or tasks may be requesting the same resource simultaneously. Printing, for example, is controlled by a queue because only one document may be printed at a time. A queue is used to hold print jobs submitted by users of the system, while the printer services those jobs one at a time.

Communications software also uses queues to hold information received over networks and dial-up connections. Sometimes information is transmitted to a system faster than it can be processed, so it is placed in a queue when it is received.

Static and Dynamic Queues

Queues, like stacks, can be implemented as arrays or linked lists. Dynamic queues offer the same advantages over static queues that dynamic stacks offer over static stacks. In fact, the primary difference between queues and stacks is the way data elements are accessed in each structure.

Queue Operations

Just like checkout lines in a grocery store, think of queues as having a front and a rear. This is illustrated in Figure 17-8. When an element is added to a queue, it is added to the rear. When an element is removed from a queue, it is removed from the front. The two primary queue operations are enqueuing and dequeuing. To *enqueue* means to insert an element at the rear of a queue, and to *dequeue* means to remove an element from the front of a queue. There are several algorithms for implementing these operations. We will begin by looking at the simplest.

Figure 17-8

Suppose we have an empty static integer queue that is capable of holding a maximum of three values. With that queue we execute the following enqueue operations:

```
enqueue(3);
enqueue(6);
enqueue(9);
```

Figure 17-9 illustrates the state of the queue after each of these enqueue operations.

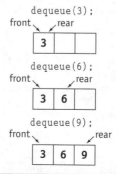

Figure 17-9

Notice that the front index (which is a variable holding a subscript or perhaps a pointer) always references the same physical element. The rear index moves in the array as items are enqueued. Now let's see how dequeue operations are performed. Figure 17-10 illustrates the state of the queue after each of three consecutive dequeue operations.

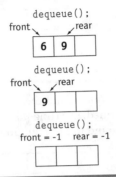

Figure 17-10

In the dequeuing operation, the element at the front of the queue is removed. This is done by moving all the elements after it forward by one position. After the first dequeue operation, the value 3 is removed from the queue and the value 6 is at the front. After the second dequeue operation, the value 6 is removed and the value 9 is at the front. Notice that when only one value is stored in the queue, that value is at both the front and the rear.

When the last dequeue operation is performed in Figure 17-10, the queue is empty. An empty queue can be signified by setting both front and rear indices to −1.

The problem with this algorithm is its inefficiency. Each time an item is dequeued, the remaining items in the queue are copied forward to their neighboring element. The more items there are in the queue, the longer each successive dequeue operation will take.

Here is one way to overcome the problem: Make both the front and rear indices move in the array. As before, when an item is enqueued, the rear index is moved to make room for it. But in this design, when an item is dequeued, the front index moves by one element toward the rear of the queue. This logically removes the front item from the queue and eleminates the need to copy the remaining items to their neighboring elements.

With this approach, as items are added and removed, the queue gradually "crawls" toward the end of the array. This is illustrated in Figure 17-11. The shaded squares represent the queue elements (between the front and rear).

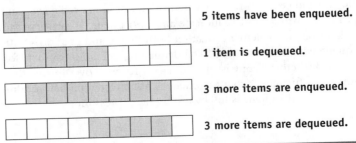

Figure 17-11

The problem with this approach is that the rear index cannot move beyond the last element in the array. The solution is to think of the array as circular instead of linear. When an item moves past the end of a circular array, it simply wraps around to the beginning. For example, consider the queue depicted in Figure 17-12.

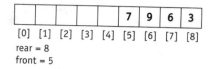

Figure 17-12

rear = 8
front = 5

The value 3 is at the rear of the queue, and the value 7 is at the front of the queue. Now, suppose an enqueue operation is performed, inserting the value 4 into the queue. Figure 17-13 shows how the rear of the queue wraps around to the beginning of the array.

4				7	9	6	3
[0]	[1]	[2]	[3]	[4]	[5]	[6]	[7]	[8]

Figure 17-13

rear = 0
front = 5

So, what is the code for wrapping the rear marker around to the opposite end of the array? One straightforward approach is to use an `if` statement such as

```
if (rear == queueSize - 1)
    rear = 0;
else
    rear++;
```

Another approach is with modular arithmetic:

```
rear = (rear + 1) % queueSize;
```

This statement uses the % operator to adjust the value in `rear` to the proper position. Although this approach appears more elegant, the choice of which code to use is yours.

Detecting Full and Empty Queues with Circular Arrays

In our implementation of a queue using a circular array, we have adopted the convention that the front and rear indices both reference items that are *still in the queue*, and that the front and rear indices will both be set to −1 to indicate an *empty* queue. To preserve this convention, the operation for dequeueing an element must set both `front` and `rear` to −1 after removing an element from a queue with only one item. The dequeuing operation can test for a queue with only one item by testing whether `front` is equal to `rear`. To avoid overflowing the queue, the operation for enqueuing must first check that the queue is not already full before adding another element. We can check to see if the queue is full by testing the expression

```
(rear + 1) % queueSize == front
```

to see if it is true.

There is another way for detecting full and empty queues: A counter variable can be used to keep a count of the number of items currently stored in the queue. With this convention, the counter is incremented with each enqueue operation and decremented with each dequeue operation. The queue is empty when the counter is zero, and is full when the counter equals the size allocated for the queue.

Because it might be helpful to keep a count of items in the queue anyway, we will use the second method in our implementation. Accordingly, we introduce the variables

```
int *queueArray;
int queueSize;
int front;
int rear;
int numItems;
```

with `numItems` being the counter variable, and `queueArray` the pointer to a dynamically allocated array of size `queueSize`. We adopt the following two conventions:

- ◆ `rear` points to the place in the queue holding the item that was last added to the queue.
- ◆ `front` points to the place in the queue that used to hold the item that was last removed from the queue.

Because of the convention on where the rear index is pointing to, the enqueue operation must first (circularly) move `rear` one place to the right before adding a new item `num`:

```
rear = (rear + 1) % queueSize;
queueArray[rear] = num;
numItems ++;
```

Similarly, because whatever is at `front` has already been removed, the dequeue operation must first move `front` before retrieving a queue item.

A Static Queue Class

The declaration of the `IntQueue` class is as follows:

Contents of `IntQueue.h`
```
#ifndef INTQUEUE_H
#define INTQUEUE_H

class IntQueue
{
  private:
      int *queueArray;
      int queueSize;
      int front;
      int rear;
      int numItems;
```

```
    public:
        IntQueue(int);
        ~IntQueue();
        void enqueue(int);
        void dequeue(int &);
        bool isEmpty();
        bool isFull();
        void clear();
};

#endif
```

Notice that in addition to the operations discussed in this section, the class also declares a member function named clear. This function clears the queue by resetting the front and rear indices, and setting the numItems member to 0. The member function definitions are listed here:

Contents of IntQueue.cpp

```
#include <iostream>
#include "IntQueue.h"
using namespace std;

//*************************
// Constructor            *
//*************************

IntQueue::IntQueue(int s)
{
  queueArray = new int[s];
  queueSize = s;
  front = -1;
  rear = -1;
  numItems = 0;
}

//*************************
// Destructor             *
//*************************

IntQueue::~IntQueue()
{
  delete [] queueArray;
}

//**********************************************
// Function enqueue inserts the value in num   *
// at the rear of the queue.                   *
//**********************************************
```

```cpp
void IntQueue::enqueue(int num)
{
  if (isFull())
      {
         cout << "The queue is full.\n";
         exit(1);
      }
  else
    {
       // Calculate the new rear position
       rear = (rear + 1) % queueSize;
       // Insert new item
       queueArray[rear] = num;
       // Update item count
       numItems++;
    }
}

//**************************************************
// Function dequeue removes the value at the       *
// front of the queue, and copies it into num.     *
//**************************************************

void IntQueue::dequeue(int &num)
{
  if (isEmpty())
    {
       cout << "The queue is empty.\n";
       exit(1);
    }
  else
    {
       // Move front
       front = (front + 1) % queueSize;
       // Retrieve the front item
       num = queueArray[front];
       // Update item count
       numItems--;
    }
}

//**************************************************
// Function isEmpty returns true if the queue     *
// is empty, and false otherwise.                 *
//**************************************************

bool IntQueue::isEmpty()
{
  bool status;
```

```cpp
   if (numItems)
       status = false;
   else
       status = true;

   return status;
}

//*********************************************
// Function isFull returns true if the queue *
// is full, and false otherwise.              *
//*********************************************

bool IntQueue::isFull()
{
  bool status;

  if (numItems < queueSize)
      status = false;
  else
      status = true;

  return status;
}

//*********************************************
// Function clear resets the front and rear  *
// indices, and sets numItems to 0.           *
//*********************************************

void IntQueue::clear()
{
  front = -1;
  rear = -1;
  numItems = 0;
}
```

Program 17-5 is a driver that demonstrates the IntQueue class.

Program 17-5

```cpp
// This program demonstrates the IntQeue class

#include <iostream>
#include "IntQueue.h"
using namespace std;
```

(program continues)

Program 17-5 *(continued)*

```cpp
int main()
{
    IntQueue iQueue(5);

    cout << "Enqueuing 5 items...\n";
    // Enqueue 5 items.
    for (int x = 0; x < 5; x++)
        iQueue.enqueue(x);

    // deqeue and retrieve all items in the queue
    cout << "The values in the queue were:\n";
    while (!iQueue.isEmpty())
    {
        int value;
        iQueue.dequeue(value);
        cout << value << endl;
    }
    return 0;
}
```

Program Output
```
Enqueuing 5 items...
The values in the queue were:
0
1
2
3
4
```

17.5 Dynamic Queues

CONCEPT A queue may be implemented as a linked list, and expand or shrink with each enqueue or dequeue operation.

Dynamic queues, which are built around linked lists, are much more intuitive to understand than static queues. A dynamic queue starts as an empty linked list. With the first enqueue operation, a node is added, which is pointed to by the front and rear pointers. As each new item is added to the queue, a new node is added to the rear of the list, and the rear pointer is updated to point to the new node. As each item is dequeued, the node pointed to by the front pointer is deleted, and front is made to point to the next node in the list. Figure 17-14 shows the structure of a dynamic queue.

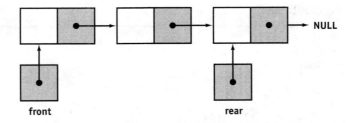

Figure 17-14

A dynamic integer queue class is listed here:

Contents of DynIntQueue.h

```
#ifndef DYNINTQUEUE_H
#define DYNINTQUEUE_H

class DynIntQueue
{
  private:
     struct QueueNode
     {
        int value;
        QueueNode *next;
     };

     QueueNode *front;
     QueueNode *rear;
     int numItems;
  public:
     DynIntQueue();
     ~DynIntQueue();
     void enqueue(int);
     void dequeue(int &);
     bool isEmpty();
     bool isFull();
     void clear();
};

#endif
```

Contents of DynIntQueue.cpp

```
#include <iostream>
#include "DynIntQueue.h"
using namespace std;

//************************
// Constructor           *
//************************
```

```
DynIntQueue::DynIntQueue()
{
   front = NULL;
   rear = NULL;
   numItems = 0;
}

//************************
// Destructor            *
//************************

DynIntQueue::~DynIntQueue()
{
   clear();
}

//************************************************
// Function enqueue inserts the value in num *
// at the rear of the queue.                  *
//************************************************

void DynIntQueue::enqueue(int num)
{
    QueueNode *newNode;

    newNode = new QueueNode;
    newNode->value = num;
    newNode->next = NULL;
    if (isEmpty())
    {
       front = newNode;
       rear = newNode;
    }
    else
    {
       rear->next = newNode;
       rear = newNode;
    }
    numItems++;
}

//************************************************
// Function dequeue removes the value at the   *
// front of the queue, and copies it into num. *
//************************************************

void DynIntQueue::dequeue(int &num)
{
   QueueNode *temp;
```

```
        if (isEmpty())
        {
            cout << "The queue is empty.\n";
            exit(1);
        }
        else
        {
            num = front->value;
            temp = front;
            front = front->next;
            delete temp;
            numItems--;
        }
    }

    //***********************************************
    // Function isEmpty returns true if the queue  *
    // is empty, and false otherwise.              *
    //***********************************************

    bool DynIntQueue::isEmpty()
    {
        bool status;

        if (numItems > 0)
            status = false;
        else
            status = true;
        return status;
    }

    //***********************************************
    // Function clear dequeues all the elements    *
    // in the queue.                               *
    //***********************************************

    void DynIntQueue::clear()
    {
        int value;   // Dummy variable for dequeue

        while(!isEmpty())
            dequeue(value);
    }
```

Program 17-6 is a driver that demonstrates the DynIntQueue class.

Program 17-6

```cpp
// This program demonstrates the DynIntQeue class

#include <iostream>
#include "DynIntQueue.h"
using namespace std;

int main()
{
    DynIntQueue iQueue;

    cout << "Enqueuing 5 items...\n";
    // Enqueue 5 items.
    for (int x = 0; x < 5; x++)
        iQueue.enqueue(x);

    // Dequeue and retrieve all items in the queue
    cout << "The values in the queue were:\n";
    while (!iQueue.isEmpty())
    {
        int value;
        iQueue.dequeue(value);
        cout << value << endl;
    }
    return 0;
}
```

Program Ouput
```
Enqueuing 5 items...
The values in the queue were:
0
1
2
3
4
```

17.6 The STL `deque` and `queue` **Containers**

CONCEPT	The Standard Template Library provides two containers, `deque` and `queue`, for implementing queue-like data structures.

In this section we will examine two ADTs offered by the Standard Template Library: `deque` and `queue`. A deque (pronounced "deck" or "deek") is a double-ended queue. It similar to a vector, but allows efficient access to values at both the front and the rear. The queue ADT is like the stack ADT: It is actually a container adapter.

The deque Container

Think of the deque container as a vector that provides quick access to the element at its front as well as at the back. (Like vector, deque also provides access to its elements with the [] operator.)

Programs that use the deque ADT must include the deque header. Since we are concentrating on its queue-like characteristics, we will focus our attention on the push_back, pop_front, and front member functions. Table 17-4 describes them.

Table 17-4

Member Function	Examples and Description
push_back	iDeque.push_back(7); Accepts as an argument a value to be inserted into the deque. The argument is inserted after the last element. (Pushed onto the back of the deque.)
pop_front	iDeque.pop_front(); Removes the first element of the deque and discards it.
front	cout << iDeque.front() << endl; front returns a reference to the first element of the deque.

Program 17-7 demonstrates the deque container.

Program 17-7

```cpp
// This program demonstrates the STL deque
// container.

#include <iostream>
#include <deque>
using namespace std;
int main()
{
    int x;
    deque<int> iDeque;

    cout << "I will now enqueue items...\n";
    for (x = 2; x < 8; x += 2)
    {
    cout << "Pushing " << x << endl;
        iDeque.push_back(x);
    }
    cout << "I will now dequeue items...\n";
    for (x = 2; x < 8; x += 2)
    {
        cout << "Popping "<< iDeque.front() << endl;
        iDeque.pop_front();
    }
    return 0;
}
```

(program continues)

Program 17-7 *(continued)*

```
    for (x = 2; x < 8; x += 2)
    {
        cout << "Popping "<< iDeque.front() << endl;
        iDeque.pop_front();
    }
    return 0;
}
```

Program Output
```
I will now enqueue items...
Pushing 2
Pushing 4
Pushing 6
I will now dequeue items...
Popping 2
Popping 4
Popping 6
```

The queue **Container Adapter**

The queue container adapter can be built upon vectors, lists, or deques. By default, it uses a deque as its base.

The insertion and removal operations supported by queue are the same as those supported by the stack ADT: push, pop, and top. There are differences in their behavior, however. The queue version of push always inserts an element at the rear of the queue. The queue version of pop always removes an element from the structure's front. The top function returns the value of the element at the front of the queue.

Program 17-8 demonstrates a queue. Since the declaration of the queue does not specify which type of container is being adapted, the queue will be built on a deque.

Program 17-8

```
// This program demonstrates the STL queue
// container adapter.

#include <iostream>
#include <queue>
using namespace std;

int main()
{
    int x;
    queue<int> iQueue;
```

(program continues)

Program 17-8   *(continued)*

```
    cout << "I will now enqueue items...\n";
    for (x = 2; x < 8; x += 2)
    {
        cout << "Pushing "<< x << endl;
        iQueue.push(x);
    }
    cout << "I will now dequeue items...\n";
    for (x = 2; x < 8; x += 2)
    {
        cout << "Popping "<< iQueue.front() << endl;
        iQueue.pop();
    }
    return 0;
}
```

Program Output

```
I will now enqueue items...
Pushing 2
Pushing 4
Pushing 6
I will now dequeue items...
Popping 2
Popping 4
Popping 6
```

Review Questions and Exercises

Fill-in-the-Blank

1. The _____ element saved onto a stack is the first one retrieved.

2. The two primary stack operations are _____ and _____.

3. _____ stacks and queues are implemented as arrays.

4. _____ stacks and queues are implemented as linked lists.

5. The STL stack container is an adapter for the _____, _____, and _____ STL containers.

6. The _____ element saved in a queue is the first one retrieved.

7. The two primary queue operations are _____ and _____.

8. The two ADTs in the Standard Template Library that exhibit queue-like behavior are _____ and _____.

9. The queue ADT, by default, adapts the _____ container.

True or False

10. T   F   A static stack or queue is built around an array.

11. T   F   The size of a dynamic stack or queue must be known in advance.

12. T F   The `push` operation inserts an element at the end of a stack.

13. T F   The `pop` operation retrieves an element from the top of a stack.

14. T F   The STL stack container's `pop` operation does not retrieve the top element of the stack, it just removes it.

Short Answer

15. Suppose the following operations were performed on an empty stack:

```
push(0);
push(9);
push(12);
push(1);
```

Insert numbers in the following diagram to show what will be stored in the static stack after the operations have executed.

```
┌─────────┐
│         │  top of stack
├─────────┤
│         │
├─────────┤
│         │
├─────────┤
│         │  bottom of stack
└─────────┘
```

16. Suppose the following operations were performed on an empty stack:

```
push(8);
push(7);
pop();
push(19);
push(21);
pop();
```

Insert numbers in the following diagram to show what will be stored in the static stack after the operations have executed.

```
┌─────────┐
│         │  top of stack
├─────────┤
│         │
├─────────┤
│         │
├─────────┤
│         │  bottom of stack
└─────────┘
```

17. Suppose the following operations are performed on an empty queue:

```
enqueue(5);
enqueue(7);
enqueue(9);
enqueue(12);
```

Insert numbers in the following diagram to show what will be stored in the static queue after the operations have executed.

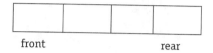

front   rear

18. Suppose the following operations are performed on an empty queue:

```
enqueue(5);
enqueue(7);
dequeue();
enqueue(9);
enqueue(12);
dequeue();
enqueue(10);
```

Insert numbers in the following diagram to show what will be stored in the static queue after the operations have executed.

front   rear

19. What problem is overcome by using a circular array for a static queue?

20. Write two different code segments that may be used to wrap an index back around to the beginning of an array when it moves past the end of the array. Use an if statement in one segment and modular arithmetic in the other.

Programming Challenges

General Requirements

Each program should have a section of comments at the top. The comments should contain your name, the date the program was written, the chapter the assignment appeared in, and the assignment number and name. Here is an example:

```
// Written by Jill Johnson
// March 31, 2003
// Chapter 17
// Assignment 1. Static Stack Template
```

1. Static Stack Template

In this chapter you studied `IntStack`, a class that implements a static stack of integers. Write a template that will create a static stack of any data type. Demonstrate the class with a driver program.

2. Dynamic Stack Template

In this chapter you studied `DynIntStack`, a class that implements a dynamic stack of integers. Write a template that will create a dynamic stack of any data type. Demonstrate the class with a driver program.

3. Static Queue Template

In this chapter you studied `IntQueue`, a class that implements a static queue of integers. Write a template that will create a static queue of any data type. Demonstrate the class with a driver program.

4. Dynamic Queue Template

In this chapter you studied `DynIntQueue`, a class that implements a dynamic queue of integers. Write a template that will create a dynamic queue of any data type. Demonstrate the class with a driver program.

5. Error Testing

The `DynIntStack` and `DynIntQueue` classes shown in this chapter are abstract data types using a dynamic stack and dynamic queue, respectively. The classes do not currently test for memory allocaton errors. Modify the classes so they determine if new nodes cannot be created, and handle the error condition in an appropriate way. (You will need to catch the predefined exception `bad_alloc`.)

 Note: If you have already done Programming Challenges 2 and 4, modify the templates you created.

6. Dynamic String Queue

Design a class that stores strings on a dynamic queue. The strings should not be fixed in length. Demonstrate the class with a driver program.

7. Dynamic MathStack

The `MathStack` class shown in this chapter only has two member functions: `add` and `sub`. Write the following additonal member functions:

Function	Description
mult	Pops the top two values off the stack, multiplies them and pushes their product onto the stack.
div	Pops the top two values off the stack, divides the second value by the first, and pushes the quotient onto the stack.
addAll	Pops all values off the stack, adds them and pushes their sum onto the stack.
multAll	Pops all values off the stack, multiplies them and pushes their product onto the stack.

Demonstrate the class with a driver program.

8. Dynamic MathStack Template

Currently the MathStack class is derived from the IntStack class. Modify it so it is a template, derived from the template you created in Programming Challenge 2.

9. File Reverser

Write a program that opens a text file and reads its contents into a stack of characters. The program should then pop the characters from the stack and save them in a second text file. The order of the characters saved in the second file should be the reverse of their order in the first file.

10. File Filter

Write a program that opens a text file and reads its contents into a queue of characters. The program should then dequeue each character, convert it to uppercase, and store it in a second file.

11. File Compare

Write a program that opens two text files and reads their contents into two separate queues. The program should then determine whether the files are identical by comparing the characters in the queues. When two unidentical characters are encountered, the program should display a message indicating the files are not the same. If both queues contain the same set of characters, a message should be displayed indicating the files are identical.

12. Inventory Bin Stack

Design an inventory class that stores the following members.

> serialNum: An integer that holds a part's serial number
> manufactDate: A member that holds the date the part was manufactured
> lotNum: An integer that holds the part's lot number

The class should have appropriate member funtions for storing data into, and retrieving data from, these members.

Next, design a stack class that can hold objects of the class. If you wish, you may use the template you designed in Programming Challenge 1 or 2.

Last, design a program that uses the stack class. The program should have a loop that asks the user whether he or she wishes to add a part to iventory or take a part from inventory. The loop should repeat until the user is finished.

If the user wishes to add a part to inventory, the program should ask for the serial number, date of manufacture, and lot number. The information should be stored in an inventory object and pushed onto the stack.

If the user wishes to take a part from inventory, the program should pop the top-most part from the stack and display the contents of its member variables.

When the user finishes, the program should display the contents of the member values of all the objects that remain on the stack

13. Inventory Bin Queue

Modify the program you wrote for Programming Challenge 12 so it uses a queue instead of a stack. Compare the order in which the parts are removed from the bin for each program.

14. Exception Project

This assignment assumes you have completed Programming Challenge 2 of Chapter 13 (Employee Information). For this assignment, you are to modify the `Employee` and `EmployeePay` classes so they throw exceptions when error conditions occur.

Here are the specific instructions:

- If the `Employee` class receives an invalid Social Security Number, it should throw an exception named `InvalidSSN`.
- If the `Employee` class receives an invalid employee number, it should throw an exception named `InvalidEmpNumber`.
- If the `EmployeePay` class receives a negative number for the annual pay, it should throw an exception named `InvalidAnnualPay`.
- If the `EmployeePay` class receives a negative number for the monthly pay, it should throw an exception named `InvalidMonthlyPay`.
- If the `EmployeePay` class receives a negative number for the number of dependents, it should throw an exception named `InvalidDependents`.

Demonstrate each of these exceptions in a driver program.

Serendipity Booksellers Software Development Project—Part 17: *A Problem-Solving Exercise*

For this chapter's assignment, you will implement a queue data structure for processing items purchased at the cash register.

Previously you modified the `cashier` function to ask how many titles the customer is purchasing, and dynamically allocate an array of `Sale` objects large enough to hold that many titles. Modify the function so it stores the `Sale` objects in a queue instead of in a dynamic array. As the function dequeues the objects, it should perform the necessary calculations to compute the customer's sale and display the simulated sales slip.

Recursion

Topics

18.1 Introduction to Recursion

CONCEPT A recursive function is one that calls itself.

You have seen instances of functions calling other functions. Function A can call function B, which can then call Function C. It's also possible for a function to call itself. A function that calls itself is a *recursive function*. Look at this `message` function:

```
void message()
{
    cout << "This is a recursive function.\n";
    message();
}
```

This function displays the string "This is a recursive function.\n", and then calls itself. Each time it calls itself, the cycle is repeated. Can you see a problem with the function? There's no way to stop the recursive calls. This function is like an infinite loop because there is no code to stop it from repeating.

 Note: The example function will eventually cause the program to crash. Do you remember learning in Chapter 17 that the system stores temporary information on a stack each time a function is called? Eventually, these recursive function calls will use up all available stack memory and cause it to overflow.

Like a loop, a recursive function must have some algorithm to control the number of times it repeats. The following is a modification of the message function. It passes an integer argument, which holds the number of times the function is to call itself.

```
void message(int times)
{
    if (times > 0)
    {
        cout << "This is a recursive function.\n";
        message(times - 1);
    }
    return;
}
```

This function contains an if statement that controls the repetition. As long as the times argument is greater than zero, it will display the message and call itself again. Each time it calls itself, it passes times - 1 as the argument. For example, let's say a program calls the function with the following statement:

```
message(5);
```

The argument, 5, will cause the function to call itself five times. The first time the function is called, the if statement will display the message and call itself with 4 as the argument. Figure 18-1 illustrates this.

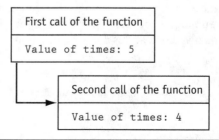

Figure 18-1

The diagram in Figure 18-1 illustrates two separate calls of the message function. Each time the function is called, a new instance of the times parameter is created in memory. The first time the function is called, the times parameter is set to 5. When the function calls itself, a new instance of `times` is created, and the value 4 is passed into it. This cycle repeats until zero is passed to the function. This is illustrated in Figure 18-2.

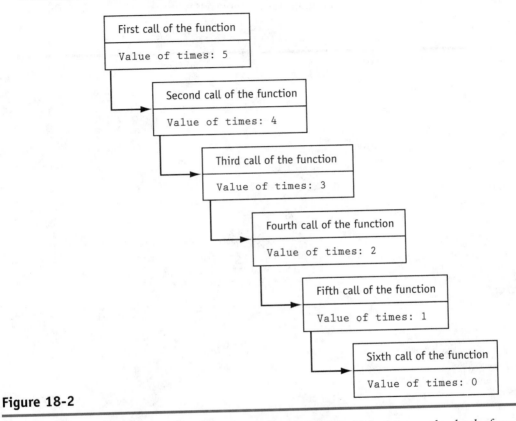

Figure 18-2

As you can see from Figure 18-2, the function will call itself six times, so the *depth of recursion* is six. When the function reaches its sixth call, the `times` parameter will be set to 0. At that point, the if statement will stop the recursive calls by executing a `return` statement. Control of the program will return from the sixth instance of the function to the point in the fifth instance directly after the recursive function call:

```
if (times > 0)
{
    cout << "This is a recursive function.\n";
    message(times - 1);
}
return;
```

Control returns here.

Since there are no more statements to be executed after the function call, the fifth instance of the function returns control of the program back to the fourth instance. This repeats until all instances of the function return. Program 18-1 demonstrates the recursive `message` function.

Program 18-1

```cpp
// This program demonstrates a simple recursive function.

#include <iostream>
using namespace std;

// Function prototype
void message(int);

int main()
{
    message(5);
    return 0;
}

//*************************************************************
// Definition of function message. If the value in times is  *
// greater than 0, the message is displayed and the          *
// function is recursively called with the argument          *
// times - 1.                                                 *
//*************************************************************

void message(int times)
{
    if (times > 0)
    {
        cout << "This is a recursive function.\n";
        message(times - 1);
    }
    return;
}
```

Program Output
```
This is a recursive function.
This is a recursive function.
This is a recursive function.
This is a recursive function.
This is a recursive function.
```

To further illustrate the inner workings of this recursive function, let's look at another version of the program. In Program 18-2, a message is displayed each time the function is entered, and another message is displayed just before the function returns.

Program 18-2

```
// This program demonstrates a simple recursive function.

#include <iostream>
using namespace std;

// Function prototype
void message(int);

int main()
{
    message(5);
    return 0;
}

//****************************************************************
// Definition of function message. If the value in times is    *
// greater than 0, the message is displayed and the            *
// function is recursively called with the argument            *
// times - 1.                                                  *
//****************************************************************

void message (int times)
{
    cout << "message called with " << times << " in times.\n";
    if (times > 0)
    {
        cout << "This is a recursive function.\n";
        message(times - 1);
    }
    cout << "message returning with " << times;
    cout << " in times.\n";
}
```

Program Output
```
message called with 5 in times.
This is a recursive function.
message called with 4 in times.
This is a recursive function.
message called with 3 in times.
This is a recursive function.
message called with 2 in times.
This is a recursive function.
message called with 1 in times.
This is a recursive function.
message called with 0 in times.
```

(program output continues)

Program 18-2 *(continued)*

```
message returning with 0 in times.
message returning with 1 in times.
message returning with 2 in times.
message returning with 3 in times.
message returning with 4 in times.
message returning with 5 in times.
```

The true role of recursive functions in programming is to break a complex problem down into a solvable problem. The solvable problem is known as the *base case*. A recursive function is designed to terminate when it reaches its base case.

Let's look at a simple example of recursion that performs a useful task. The function numChars counts the number of times a specific character appears in a string.

```
int numChars(char search, char str[], int subscript)
{
    if (str[subscript] == '\0')
        return 0;
    else
    {
        if (str[subscript] == search)
            return 1 + numChars(search, str, subscript+1);
        else
            return numChars(search, str, subscript+1);
    }
}
```

The function's parameters are

- search: The character to be searched for and counted
- str: An array containing the string to be searched
- subscript: The starting subscript for the search

The first if statement determines whether the end of the string has been reached:

```
if (str[subscript] == '\0')
```

If the end of the string has been reached, the function returns 0, indicating there are no more characters to count. Otherwise, the following if statement is executed:

```
if (str[subscript] == search)
    return 1 + numChars(search, str, subscript+1);
else
    return numChars(search, str, subscript+1);
```

If `str[subscript]` contains the search character, the function performs a recursive call. The return statement returns 1 + the number of times the search character appears in the string, starting at `subscript + 1`. If `str[subscript]` does not contain the search character, a recursive call is made to search the remainder of the string. Program 18-3 demonstrates the program.

Program 18-3

```cpp
// This program demonstrates a recursive function for
// counting the number of times a character appears
// in a string.

#include <iostream>
using namespace std;

int numChars(char, char [], int);

int main()
{
    char array[] = "abcddddef";

    cout << "The letter d appears "
         << numChars('d', array, 0) << " times.\n";
    return 0;
}

//**************************************************
// Function numChars. This recursive function       *
// counts the number of times the character         *
// search appears in the string str. The search     *
// begins at the subscript stored in subscript.      *
//**************************************************

int numChars(char search, char str[], int subscript)
{
    if (str[subscript] == '\0')
        return 0;
    else
    {
        if (str[subscript] == search)
            return 1 + numChars(search, str, subscript+1);
        else
            return numChars(search, str, subscript+1);
    }
}
```

Program Output
```
The letter d appears 4 times.
```

Direct and Indirect Recursion

The examples show recursive functions that directly call themselves. This is known as *direct recursion*. There is also the possibility of creating *indirect recursion* in a program. This occurs when function A calls function B, which in turn calls function A. There can even be several functions involved in the recursion. For example, function A could call function B, which could call function C, which calls function A.

⍰ Checkpoint [18.1]

18.1   What happens if a recursive function never returns?

18.2   What is a recursive function's base case?

18.3   What will the following program display?

```cpp
#include <iostream>
using namespace std;

// Function prototype
void showMe(int arg);

int main()
{
    int num = 0;

    showMe(num);
    return 0;
}

void showMe(int arg)
{
    if (arg < 10)
        showMe(++arg);
    else
        cout << arg << endl;
}
```

18.4   What is the difference between direct and indirect recursion?

18.2   The Recursive Factorial Function

CONCEPT   The recursive factorial function accepts an argument and calculates its factorial. Its base case is when the argument is 0.

Let's use an example from mathematics to examine an application of recursion. In mathematics, the notation $n!$ represents the factorial of the number n. The factorial of a number is defined as

$$n! = 1 \times 2 \times 3 \times \ldots \times n; \qquad \text{if } n > 0$$
$$ = 1; \qquad \text{if } n = 0$$

The rule states that when n is greater than 0, its factorial is the product of all the positive integers from 1 up to n. For instance, 6! can be calculated as $1 \times 2 \times 3 \times 4 \times 5 \times 6$. The rule also states that the factorial of 0 is 1.

Another way of defining the factorial of a number, using recursion, is

$$\text{factorial}(n) = n \times \text{factorial}(n-1) \qquad \text{if } n > 0$$
$$\phantom{\text{factorial}(n)} = 1; \qquad \text{if } n = 0$$

The following C++ function implements this recursive definition:

```cpp
int factorial(int num)
{
    if (num > 0)

        return num * factorial(num - 1);
    else
        return 1;
}
```

Consider a program that displays the value of 4! with the following statement:

```cpp
cout << factorial(4) << endl;
```

The first time the function is called, `num` is set to 4. The `if` statement will execute the following line:

```cpp
return num * factorial(num - 1);
```

Although this is a `return` statement, it does not immediately return. Before the return value can be determined, the value of `factorial(num - 1)` must be determined. The function is called recursively until the fifth call, in which the `num` parameter will be set to zero. The diagram in Figure 18-3 illustrates the value of `num` and the return value during each call of the function.

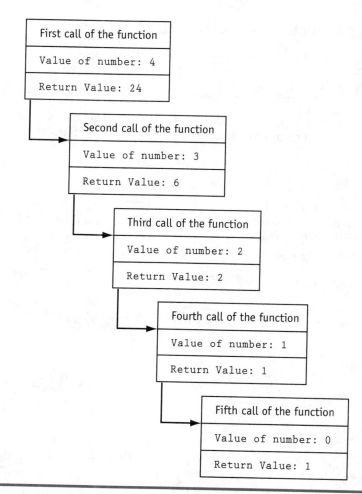

Figure 18-3

Program 18-4 demonstrates the `factorial` function.

Program 18-4

```
// This program demonstrates a recursive function to
// calculate the factorial of a number.

#include <iostream>
using namespace std;

// Function prototype
int factorial(int);
```

(program continues)

Program 18-4   *(continued)*

```cpp
int main()
{
    int number;

    cout << "Enter an integer value and I will display\n";
    cout << "its factorial: ";
    cin >> number;
    cout << "The factorial of " << number << " is ";
    cout << factorial(number) << endl;
    return 0;
}

//****************************************************************
// Definition of factorial. A recursive function to calculate  *
// the factorial of the parameter, num.                        *
//****************************************************************

int factorial(int num)
{
    if (num > 0)
        return num * factorial(num - 1);
    else
        return 1;
}
```

Program Output with Example Input
```
Enter an integer value and I will display
its factorial: 4
The factorial of 4 is 24
```

18.3   The Recursive gcd Function

CONCEPT The gcd function uses recursion to find the greatest common divisor (gcd) of two numbers.

Our next example of recursion is the calculation of the greatest common divisor, or gcd, of two numbers. Using Euclid's algorithm, the gcd of two positive integers, x and y, is

$$\gcd(x, y) = y; \quad \text{if } y \text{ divides } x \text{ evenly}$$
$$= \gcd(y, \text{ remainder of } x/y); \quad \text{otherwise}$$

This definition states that the gcd of x and y is y if x/y has no remainder. Otherwise, the answer is the gcd of y and the remainder of x/y. Program 18-5 shows the recursive C++ implementation:

Program 18-5

```cpp
// This program demonstrates a recursive function to calculate
// the greatest common divisor (gcd) of two numbers.

#include <iostream>
using namespace std;

// Function prototype
int gcd(int, int);

int main()
{
    int num1, num2;

    cout << "Enter two integers: ";
    cin >> num1 >> num2;
    cout << "The greatest common divisor of " << num1;
    cout << " and " << num2 << " is ";
    cout << gcd(num1, num2) << endl;
    return 0;
}

//*************************************************************
// Definition of gcd. This function uses recursion to        *
// calculate the greatest common divisor of two integers,    *
// passed into the parameters x and y.                       *
//*************************************************************

int gcd(int x, int y)
{
    if (x % y == 0)
        return y;
    else
        return gcd(y, x % y);
}
```

Program Output with Example Input Shown in Bold
```
Enter two integers: 49 28
The greatest common divisor of 49 and 28 is 7
```

18.4   Solving Recursively Defined Problems

CONCEPT	Some problems naturally lend themselves to recursive solutions.

Some problems naturally lend themselves to recursive solutions. One well-known example is the calculation of *Fibonacci numbers*. The Fibonacci numbers, named after the Italian mathematician Leonardo Fibonacci (born circa 1170), form the following sequence:

0, 1, 1, 2, 3, 5, 8, 13, 21, 34, 55, 89, 144, 233, ...

Notice that after the second number, each number in the sequence is the sum of the two previous numbers. The Fibonacci series can be defined as:

$$F_0 = 0,$$
$$F_1 = 1,$$
$$F_N = F_{N-1} + F_{N-2} \quad \text{for all } N \geq 2.$$

A recursive C++ function to calculate the nth number in the Fibonacci series is shown here:

```cpp
int fib(int n)
{
    if (n <= 0)
        return 0;
    else if (n == 1)
        return 1;
    else
        return fib(n - 1) + fib(n - 2);
}
```

The function is demonstrated in Program 18-6, which displays the first 10 numbers in the Fibonacci series.

Program 18-6

```cpp
// This program demonstrates a recursive function
// that calculates Fibonacci numbers.

#include <iostream>
using namespace std;

// Function prototype
int fib(int);

int main()
{
    cout << "The first 10 Fibonacci numbers are:\n";
    for (int x = 0; x < 10; x++)
        cout << fib(x) << " ";
    cout << endl;
    return 0;
}
```

(program continues)

Program 18-6 *(continued)*

```
//*******************************************
// Function fib. Accepts an int argument   *
// in n. This function returns the nth      *
// Fibonacci number.                        *
//*******************************************

int fib(int n)
{
    if (n <= 0)
        return 0;
    else if (n == 1)
        return 1;
    else
        return fib(n - 1) + fib(n - 2);
}
```

Program Output
```
The first 10 Fibonacci numbers are:
0 1 1 2 3 5 8 13 21 34
```

Another such example is Ackermann's function. A Programming Challenge at the end of this chapter asks you to write a recursive function that calculates Ackermann's function.

18.5 Recursive Linked List Operations

> **CONCEPT** Recursion can be used to traverse the nodes in a linked list. This section presents a function that prints the values of a list's nodes in reverse order.

Recall that in Chapter 16 we discussed a class named FloatList that holds a linked list of float values. In this section we will modify the class by adding recursive member functions. The functions will use recursion to traverse the linked list and perform the following operations:

- **Count the number of nodes in the list.** To count the number of nodes in the list by recursion, we introduce two new member functions: numNodes, and countNodes. countNodes is a private member function that uses recursion, and numNodes is the public interface that calls it.

- **Display the value of the list nodes in reverse order.** To display the nodes in the list in reverse order, we introduce two new member functions: displayBackwards and showReverse. showReverse is a private member function that uses recursion, and displayBackwards is the public interface that calls it.

The class declaration, which is saved in FloatList2.h, is shown here.

```
class FloatList
{
private:
  // Declare a structure for the list
  struct ListNode
  {
      float value;
      ListNode *next;
  };

  ListNode *head;   // List head pointer
  int countNodes(ListNode *);
  void showReverse(ListNode *);
public:
  FloatList()    // Constructor
      { head = NULL; }
  ~FloatList();      // Destructor
  void appendNode(float);
  void insertNode(float);
  void deleteNode(float);
  void displayList();
  int numNodes()
      { return countNodes(head); }
  void displayBackwards()
      { showReverse(head); }
};
```

Counting the Nodes in the List

The numNodes function is declared inline. It simply calls the countNodes function and passes the head pointer as an argument. (Because the head pointer, which is private, must be passed to countNodes, the numNodes function is needed as an interface.)

The function definition for countNodes is shown here.

```
int FloatList::countNodes(ListNode *nodePtr)
{
    if (nodePtr != NULL)
        return 1 + countNodes(nodePtr->next);
    else
        return 0;
}
```

The function's recursive logic can be expressed as:

```
If the current node has a value
    Return 1 + the number of the remaining nodes
Else
    Return 0
End If.
```

Program 18-7 demonstrates the function.

Program 18-7

```
#include <iostream>
#include "FloatList2.h"
using namespace std;

int main()
{
    FloatList list;

    for (int x = 0; x < 10; x++)
        list.insertNode(x);
    cout << "The number of nodes is "
        << list.numNodes() << endl;
    return 0;
}
```

Program Output
```
The number of nodes is 10
```

Displaying List Nodes in Reverse Order

The technique for displaying the list nodes in reverse order is designed like the node counting procedure: A public member function, which serves as an interface, passes the head pointer to a private member function. The public displayBackwards function, declared inline, is the interface. It calls the showReverse function and passes the head pointer as an argument. The function definition for showReverse is shown here.

```
void FloatList::showReverse(ListNode *nodePtr)
{
    if (nodePtr != NULL)
    {
        showReverse(nodePtr->next);
        cout << nodePtr->value << " ";
    }
}
```

The base case for the function is nodePtr being equal to NULL. When this is true, the function has reached the last node in the list, so it returns. It is not until this happens that any instances of the cout statement execute. The instance of the function whose nodePtr variable points to the last node in the list will be the first to execute the cout statement. It will then return, and the previous instance of the function will execute its cout statement. This repeats until all the instances of the function have returned.

The modified class declaration is stored in `FloatList2.h`, and its member function implementation is in `FloatList2.cpp`. The remainder of the class implementation is unchanged from Chapter 16, so it is not shown here. Program 18-8 demonstrates the function.

Program 18-8

```cpp
// This program demonstrates the FloatList class's
// recursive function for displaying the list's nodes
// in reverse.

#include <iostream>
#include "FloatList2.h"
using namespace std;

int main()
{
    FloatList list;

    for (float x = 1.5; x < 15; x += 1.1)
        list.appendNode(x);
    cout << "Here are the values in the list:\n";
    list.displayList();
    cout << "Here are the values in reverse order:\n";
    list.displayBackwards();
    return 0;
}
```

Program Output
```
Here are the values in the list:
1.5
2.6
3.7
4.8
5.9
7
8.1
9.2
10.3
11.4
12.5
13.6
14.7
Here are the values in reverse order:
14.7 13.6 12.5 11.4 10.3 9.2 8.1 7 5.9 4.8 3.7 2.6 1.5
```

18.6 A Recursive Binary Search Function

CONCEPT	The binary search algorithm can be defined as a recursive function.

In Chapter 9 you learned about the binary search algorithm and saw an iterative example written in C++. The binary search algorithm can also be implemented recursively. For example, the procedure can be expressed as

If array[middle] equals the search value, then the value is found.

Else, if array[middle] is less than the search value, perform a binary search on the upper half of the array.

Else, if array[middle] is greater than the search value, perform a binary search on the lower half of the array.

The recursive binary search algorithm is an example of breaking a problem down into smaller pieces until it is solved. A recursive binary search function is shown here:

```cpp
int binarySearch(int array[], int first, int last, int value)
{
    int middle;// Mid point of search

    if (first > last)
        return -1;
    middle = (first + last) / 2;
    if (array[middle] == value)
        return middle;
    if (array[middle] < value)
        return binarySearch(array, middle+1,last,value);
    else
        return binarySearch(array, first,middle-1,value);
}
```

The first parameter, array, is the array to be searched. The next parameter, first, holds the subscript of the first element in the search range (the portion of the array to be searched). The next parameter, last, holds the subscript of the last element in the search range. The last parameter, value, holds the value to be searched for. Like the iterative version, this function returns the subscript of the value if it is found, or −1 if the value is not found. Program 18-9 demonstrates the function.

Program 18-9

```cpp
// This program demonstrates the recursive binarySearch function, which
// performs a binary search on an integer array.

#include <iostream>
using namespace std;

// Function prototype
int binarySearch(int [], int, int, int);

const int arrSize = 20;

int main()
{
    int tests[arrSize] = {101, 142, 147, 189, 199, 207, 222,
                          234, 289, 296, 310, 319, 388, 394,
                          417, 429, 447, 521, 536, 600};
    int results, empID;

    cout << "Enter the Employee ID you wish to search for: ";
    cin >> empID;
    results = binarySearch(tests, 0, arrSize - 1, empID);
    if (results == -1)
        cout << "That number does not exist in the array.\n";
    else
    {
        cout << "That ID is found at element " << results;
        cout << " in the array\n";
    }

    return 0;
}

//*****************************************************************
// The binarySearch function performs a recursive binary search  *
// on a range of elements of an integer array passed into the    *
// parameter array.The parameter first holds the subscript of    *
// the range's starting element, and last holds the subscript    *
// of the ranges's last element. The parameter value holds the   *
// the search value. If the search value is found, its array     *
// subscript is returned. Otherwise, -1 is returned indicating   *
// the value was not in the array.                               *
//*****************************************************************
```

(program continues)

Program 18-9   *(continued)*

```
int binarySearch(int array[], int first, int last, int value)
{
    int middle;            // Mid point of search

    if (first > last)
        return -1;
    middle = (first + last)/2;
    if (array[middle]==value)
        return middle;
    if (array[middle]<value)
        return binarySearch(array, middle+1,last,value);
    else
        return binarySearch(array, first,middle-1,value);
}
```

Program Output with Example Input Shown in Bold
```
Enter the Employee ID you wish to search for: 521 [Enter]
That ID is found at element 17 in the array
```

18.7   Focus on Problem Solving and Program Design: *The QuickSort Algorithm*

CONCEPT	The QuickSort algorithm uses recursion to efficiently sort a list.

The QuickSort algorithm is a popular, general purpose sorting routine developed in 1960 by C. A. R. Hoare. It can be used to sort lists stored in arrays or linear linked lists. It sorts a list by dividing it into two sublists. Between the sublists is a selected value known as the *pivot*. This is illustrated in Figure 18-4.

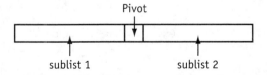

Figure 18-4

Notice in Figure 18-4 that sublist 1 is positioned to the left of (before) the pivot, and sublist 2 is positioned to the right of (after) the pivot. Once a pivot value has been selected, the algorithm exchanges the other values in the list until all the elements in sublist 1 are less than the pivot, and all the elements in sublist 2 are greater than the pivot.

Once this is done, the algorithm repeats the procedure on sublist 1, and then on sublist 2. The recursion stops when there is only one element in a sublist. At that point the original list is completely sorted.

The algorithm is coded primarily in two functions: `quickSort` and `partition`. `quickSort` is a recursive function. Its pseudocode is shown here:

```
quickSort:
If Starting Index < Ending Index
        Partition the List around a Pivot.
        quickSort Sublist 1.
        quickSort Sublist 2.
End If.
```

Here is the C++ code for the `quickSort` functon:

```
void quickSort(int set[], int start, int end)
{
   int pivotPoint;

   if (start < end)
   {
      // Get the pivot point.
      pivotPoint = partition(set, start, end);
      // Sort the first sub list.
      quickSort(set, start, pivotPoint - 1);
      // Sort the second sub list.
      quickSort(set, pivotPoint + 1, end);
   }
}
```

This version of `quickSort` works with an array of integers. Its first argument is the array holding the list that is to be sorted. The second and third arguments are the starting and ending subscripts of the list.

The subscript of the pivot element is returned by the `partition` function. `partition` not only determines which element will be the pivot, but also controls the rearranging of the other values in the list. Our version of this function selects the element in the middle of the list as the pivot, then scans the remainder of the list searching for values less than the pivot.

The code for the `partition` function is

```
int partition(int set[], int start, int end)
{
   int pivotValue, pivotIndex, mid;

   mid = (start + end) / 2;
   exchange(set[start], set[mid]);
   pivotIndex = start;
   pivotValue = set[start];
   for (int scan = start + 1; scan <= end; scan++)
```

```
        {
            if (set[scan] < pivotValue)
            {
                pivotIndex++;
                exchange(set[pivotIndex], set[scan]);
            }
        }
        exchange(set[start], set[pivotIndex]);
        return pivotIndex;
    }
```

 Note: The `partition` function does not initially sort the values into their final order. Its job is only to move the values that are less than the pivot to the pivot's left, and move the values that are greater than the pivot to the pivot's right. As long as that condition is met, the values may appear in any order. The ultimate sorting order of the entire list is achieved cumulatively, through the recursive calls to `quickSort`.

There are many different ways of partitioning the list. As previously stated, the method shown in the preceding function selects the middle value as the pivot. That value is then moved to the beginning of the list (by exchanging it with the value stored there). This simplifies the next step, which is to scan the list.

A `for` loop scans the remainder of the list; when an element is found whose value is less than the pivot, that value is moved to a location left of the pivot point.

A third function, `exchange`, is used to exchange the values found in any two elements of the list. The function is

```
    void exchange(int &value1, int &value2)
    {
      int temp = value1;
      value1 = value2;
      value2 = temp;
    }
```

Program 18-10 demonstrates the QuickSort algorithm shown here.

Program 18-10

```
// This program demonstrates the QuickSort algorithm

#include <iostream>
using namespace std;

// Function prototypes
void quickSort(int [], int, int);
int partition(int [], int, int);
void exchange(int &, int &);
```

(program continues)

Program 18-10 *(continued)*

```cpp
int main()
{
    int array[10] = {7, 3, 9, 2, 0, 1, 8, 4, 6, 5};
    int x;      // Counter

    for (x = 0; x < 10; x++)
        cout << array[x] << " ";
    cout << endl;
    quickSort(array, 0, 9);
    for (x = 0; x < 10; x++)
        cout << array[x] << " ";
    cout << endl;
    return 0;
}

//************************************************
// quickSort uses the QuickSort algorithm to     *
// sort set, from set[start] through set[end].    *
//************************************************

void quickSort(int set[], int start, int end)
{
    int pivotPoint;

    if (start < end)
    {
        // Get the pivot point.
        pivotPoint = partition(set, start, end);
        // Sort the first sublist.
        quickSort(set, start, pivotPoint - 1);
        // Sort the second sublist.
        quickSort(set, pivotPoint + 1, end);
    }
}

//*********************************************************
// partition selects the value in the middle of the       *
// array set as the pivot. The list is rearranged so       *
// all the values less than the pivot are on its left      *
// and all the values greater than pivot are on its right. *
//*********************************************************

int partition(int set[], int start, int end)
{
    int pivotValue, pivotIndex, mid;
```

(program continues)

Program 18-10 *(continued)*

```
    mid = (start + end) / 2;
    exchange(set[start], set[mid]);
    pivotIndex = start;
    pivotValue = set[start];
    for (int scan = start + 1; scan <= end; scan++)
    {
        if (set[scan] < pivotValue)
        {
            pivotIndex++;
            exchange(set[pivotIndex], set[scan]);
        }
    }
    exchange(set[start], set[pivotIndex]);
    return pivotIndex;
}

//**************************************************
// exchange simply exchanges the contents of      *
// value1 and value2.                             *
//**************************************************

void exchange(int &value1, int &value2)
{
    int temp = value1;
    value1 = value2;
    value2 = temp;
}
```

Program Output
```
7 3 9 2 0 1 8 4 6 5
0 1 2 3 4 5 6 7 8 9
```

18.8   Focus on Problem Solving and Program Design: *Permutations*

> **CONCEPT** | A permutation of a set is an arrangement of the elements of the set in some order. Recursive techniques are useful when working with permutations.

A *permutation* of a set is an arrangement of the elements of the set in some order. For example, the set of two numbers 1, 2 has two permutations because it can be ordered in two different ways: 1 2 and 2 1. The set of 3 numbers 1, 2, and 3 has six permutations as shown in the following table:

1 2 3	2 1 3	3 1 2
1 3 2	2 3 1	3 2 1

Since a permutation is basically a list of elements, it can be represented any way lists are represented, such as with an array, a linked list, or some STL container like a list or a vector.

Permutations have many applications. For example, a teacher giving a makeup examination to a student who missed a multiple choice test may wish to reorder the questions on the test by randomly *permuting* the test questions. Likewise, in many card games, play begins by shuffling the deck to obtain a random permutation of the deck of cards.

How can we create a random permutation of a set? Consider an example of the set of four integers: 1, 2, 3, and 4. We can start by recursively creating a random permutation of the one size smaller set: 1, 2, and 3. Say that we get

3   1   2

as the random permutation of the smaller set. We would then need to insert 4 at a random place within this smaller permutation. There are four choices for such an insertion location: We could insert the 4 just before any of the three elements already there, or we could insert the 4 after the last element.

Let us now consider the implementation of this recursive strategy. To represent a permutation, we need to use a data structure that maintains order among its elements and allows easy insertion of new elements at arbitrary points. The vector container provided in the Standard Template Library fits all these criteria, so we will represent a permutation as a vector of int.

We will use the recursive function

```
void createRandomPerm(perm, numElements)
```

to create a random permutation of a set of numElements elements, which it will place in the perm vector. The parameter perm will be a vector of int that is passed by reference. The elements of the set are represented by the numbers 1 through numElements. The function assumes that the number of elements being permuted is at least one.

The base case for the recursion is when the number of elements in the set to be permuted is one, and the set itself consists of the single element 1. This case is handled by setting the argument perm to the vector containing the single element with the statements

```
perm.clear();
perm.push_back(1);
```

The non-base case is handled by recursively creating a random permutation of the set one size smaller (i.e., the set whose elements are the numbers 1 through numElements - 1), then inserting the final number, which will equal numElements, at a random position within it.

```
createRandomPerm(perm, numElements-1);
insertPosition = rand() % numElements;
perm.insert(perm.begin() + insertPosition, numElements);
```

In Chapter 3 you learned that the random number generator in the standard library has to be provided with a seed in order to produce different sequences of random numbers on different program runs, and that such a seed is provided by passing an unsigned integer to the library function `srand()`. A convenient way to have the computer create such a seed is to call the library function `time()` with argument 0. The value returned by this function will be a seed that depends on the time that the program executes, and so is likely to be different each time the program runs. All of this can be done in a single function called `randomize()`. The Borland compiler provides such a function. In Visual C++, this function call must be replaced with the following line of code:

```
srand((unsigned int)time(0));
```

and the following two libraries must be included in your program.

```
#include <cstdlib>
#include <time.h>
```

Program 18-11 demonstrates the use of our `createRandomPerm` function to create a random permutation of the four integers 1, 2, 3, 4.

Program 18-11

```
//This program demonstrates the creation of a random permutation.

#include <iostream>
#include <vector>
using namespace std;

typedef vector<int> Permutation;

//function prototype

void createRandomPerm(Permutation&, int);

int main()
{
    Permutation perm;              // Define vector to hold permutation elements

    randomize();                   // Set up random number generator
    createRandomPerm(perm, 4);     // Create random permutation of size 4

    cout << "A random permutation of a set of  size 4 is" << endl;
    for (int index = 0; index < perm.size(); index++)
        cout << perm[index] << "   ";
    return 0;
}
```

(program continues)

Program 18-11 *(continued)*

```
//*************************************************************
//This function creates a random permutation of size numElements *
//and stores it in the Permutation variable perm.              *
//*************************************************************
void createRandomPerm(Permutation &perm, int numElements)
{
    if (numElements == 1)          // Handle the base case
    {                              // There is only one permutation of 1 element
        perm.clear();
        perm.push_back(1);
    }
    else                           // Recursively call createRandomPerm to create
    {                              // a random permutation of size numElements-1
        createRandomPerm(perm, numElements-1);
        int insertPosition = rand() % numElements;
        perm.insert(perm.begin() + insertPosition, numElements);
    }
}
```

Program Output
```
A random permutation of a set of size 4 is
4  2  1  3
```

18.9 Focus on Problem Solving and Program Design: *Generating Permutations*

> **CONCEPT** | Recursion can be used to generate all permutations of a set.

Recursion is a natural technique to use when solving problems that can be broken down into smaller problems of the same type. For example, in the previous section, we saw how the problem of generating a random permutation of a set can be solved by eliminating one of the elements, generating a random permutation of the remaining elements, then inserting the previously left out element at a random position.

A similar problem that can also be solved by recursion is that of generating all the permutations of a given set. Assume again that the elements of the set to be permuted are the positive integers from 1 through some maximum value that we will call numElements.

As seen in Section 18.8, such a permutation, being a list of numbers, can be represented by a vector of integers:

```
typedef vector<int> Permutation;
```

We can similarly represent a list of permutations as a vector of permutations:

```
typedef vector<Permutation> PermutationList;
```

To create a list of permutations, we will write a recursive function

```
void createPermList(permList, numElements)
```

which when called will create a list of all permutations of the set of size numElements. The permutations will be stored in the permList argument, which is a reference parameter of type PermutationList. Note that numElements is the number of elements being arranged, not the number of permutations. For example, if numElements is 4, there will be 24 different permutations of the numbers 1, 2, 3, 4. The function assumes that the size of the set is at least one.

The base case is when the size of the set is one. In this case the sole element of the set is 1, and the list of permutations consists of only one permutation. We can build this list of permutations by first creating an empty permutation perm, inserting 1 into it, then inserting perm into an initially empty list of permutations permList.

```
permutation perm;   //empty permutation
perm.push_back(1);  //permutation of one element
permList.clear();
permList.push_back(perm); //list has a single permutation
```

To handle the non-base case, we first form the set one size smaller by leaving out the largest value of the original set (this largest value is numElements). We can then recursively create a list of permutations for the smaller set by calling

```
CreatePermList(permList, numElements - 1);
```

Once we have all the permutations of the smaller set, we can generate all permutations of the original set by inserting the left out element, numElements, at all possible positions in each permutation of the smaller set.

For example, if numElements is 4, we would first recursively create a list of all permutations of the set 1, 2, 3. To create the list of permutations of the set 1, 2, 3, 4 we must insert 4 at every possible position in each permutation of the set 1, 2, 3. For example, if we take the permutation 2 1 3 and insert 4 at each possible position, we get the four permutations

$$4\ 2\ 1\ 3 \qquad 2\ 4\ 1\ 3 \qquad 2\ 4\ 3\ 1 \qquad 2\ 3\ 1\ 4$$

As you can see, a single permutation of size 3 must give rise to four different permutations of size 4. This can be done by creating three extra *copies* of the original permutation of size 3, and then inserting 4 at a different position in each of the three copies. To get the fourth permutation of size 4, we just insert 4 at the very end of the *original* permutation of size 3. More generally, using the variable numElements in place of 4, and assuming that permList already holds a list of all permutations of size one smaller, we can create all the permutations of size numElements that arise from a given "smaller" permutation using the following fragment of code:

```
    //permList[index] is a given "smaller" permutation

    //pos represents a position in the "smaller" permutation
    for (int pos = 0; pos < permSize-1; pos++)
    {
      Permutation permCopy;
      permCopy = permList[index]; //make a copy of the smaller permutation
      //insert permSize at this position
      permCopy.insert(permCopy.begin() + pos, permSize);
      //add the modified copy to the list of permutations
      permList.push_back(permCopy);
    }
    //for the very last position, no need to use a copy
    //so just insert permSize at the end.
    permList[index].push_back(permSize)
```

Code for the complete `createPermList` function is given in Program 18-12. The `main` function illustrates the use of the function to create a list of all permutations of a set of 3 elements.

Program 18-12

```
//This program demonstrates the use of the function for
//creating a list of all permutations of a set of some given size.

#include <iostream>
#include <vector>
using namespace std;

typedef vector<int> Permutation;
typedef vector<Permutation> PermutationList;

//Function prototype
void createPermList(PermutationList&, int);

int main()
{
    PermutationList permList;

    cout << "Here is a list of all permutations of the set 1,2,3" << endl;
    //Create a list of all permutations of the set 1,2,3
    createPermList(permList, 3);
    //Output the list of permutations
    for (int permIndex = 0; permIndex < permList.size( ); permIndex++)
    {
        Permutation  perm = permList[permIndex];
```

(program continues)

Program 18-12   *(continued)*

```cpp
      //output an individual permutation
      //elemIndex indexes a set element within the permutation
      for (int elemIndex = 0; elemIndex < perm.size( ); elemIndex++)
        {
          cout << perm[elemIndex] << "  ";
        }
      cout << endl;
    }
}

//**************************************************************
//Create a list of all permutations of a set of size          *
//numElements whose elements are 1, 2, through numElements     *
//and returns them in the parameter permList                   *
//**************************************************************

void createPermList(PermutationList& permList, int numElements)
{
  if (numElements ==1)
    {
      Permutation perm;            //empty permutation
      perm.push_back(1);           //permutation of one element
      permList.clear();            //make sure list of permutations is empty
      permList.push_back(perm);    //list has one permutation
      return;
    }
  // Create a list of permutations of the set whose
  // elements are 1 through numElements-1
  createPermList(permList, numElements-1);
  int numberOfPerms = permList.size( );
  for (int permIndex = 0; permIndex < numberOfPerms; permIndex++)
  {
    //permList[permIndex] is a permutation of the smaller set
    //pos represents a position at which to insert numElements
    for (int pos = 0; pos < numElements-1; pos++)
    {
      Permutation permCopy;
      //Make a copy of current permutation of the smaller set
      permCopy = permList[permIndex];
      //Extend the copy by inserting numElements at this position
      permCopy.insert(permCopy.begin()+ pos, numElements);
      //Add the modified copy to the end of the permutation list
      permList.push_back(permCopy);
    }
    //Modify the original permutation in the list by adding numElements
    permList[permIndex].push_back(numElements);
  }
}
```

Program 18-12

Program Output
```
Here is a list of all permutations of the set 1,2,3
1   2   3
2   1   3
3   1   2
1   3   2
3   2   1
2   3   1
```

18.10 Focus on Problem Solving and Program Design: *Exhaustive and Enumeration Algorithms*

CONCEPT An enumeration algorithm is one that generates all possible combinations of items of a certain type; an exhaustive algorithm is one that searches through such a set of combinations to find the best one.

Many problems can only be solved by examining all possible combinations of items of a certain type and then choosing the best one. For example, consider the problem of making change for $1.00 using the U.S. system of coins. A few of the solutions to this problem are:

> one dollar coin
> two fifty-cent coin
> four quarters
> one fifty-cent coin and two quarters
> three quarters, two dimes, and one nickel

Although there are many ways to make change for $1.00, some ways are better than others: Most people would prefer a single dollar piece over a 100 pennies. The best solution is the one that gives the fewest coins.

A strategy for this problem that almost immediately suggests itself is to give as many of the largest coin as possible, then as many of the second largest coin as possible, and so on, until you have made change for the complete account. It turns out that for the U.S. system of coins, this procedure, which is called the *greedy strategy,* always finds the best solution. Unfortunately, the procedure does not work for other systems of coins. For example, if there are only three coin sizes,

> 1, 20, 25

and one has to make change for 44 cents, the greedy strategy will give one quarter and 19 pennies, for a total of 20 coins. The best solution uses six coins: two twenty-cent pieces and four pennies.

In general, one would have to try all possible ways of making change to determine the best one. An algorithm that searches through all possible combinations to solve a problem is called an *exhaustive* algorithm; an algorithm that generates all possible combinations is an *enumeration* algorithm.

Recursive techniques are often useful in exhaustive and enumeration algorithms. In this section, we look at a recursive algorithm that counts the number of different ways to make change for a given amount. With some modification, the algorithm can be adapted to keep track of the different combinations, and either enumerate the list of all such combinations, or report which combination is best. Although the algorithm works for any system that includes a one-cent piece among its coins, we will assume the American system with the six coin values: 1, 5, 10, 25, 50, and 100.

The main idea is this. Suppose we want to calculate the number of ways to make change for 24 cents using coins in the set 1, 5, 10, 25, 50, 100. Since there is no way to make change for 24 cents that uses coins in the set 25, 50, 100, the largest usable coin is a dime and we can just calculate the number of ways to make change for 24 cents using coins in the set 1, 5, 10. Moreover, we cannot use more than two 10-cent pieces in making change for 24 cents, so we only need to count the number of ways to make change that use zero, one, or two 10-cent pieces and add them all together to get our answer. Table 18-1 lists these possibilities, shows how each possibility can be broken down into a smaller problem of the same type, and shows the call to the recursive `mkChange` function that would be invoked to solve the subproblem. The parameters for the `mkChange` function will be explained shortly.

Table 18-1

number of ways to make change for 24 cents using no dimes	=	number of ways to make change for 24 cents using coins in the set 1, 5	`mkChange(24,1);`
number of ways to make change for 24 cents using one dime	=	number of ways to make change for 14 cents using coins in the set 1, 5	`mkChange(14,1);`
number of ways to make change for 24 cents using two dimes	=	number of ways to make change for 4 cents using coins in the set 1, 5	`mkChange(4,1);`

We are now ready to present the implementation of the algorithm. The set of possible coin values is given by an array

```
const int coinValues[] = {1, 5, 10, 25, 50, 100};
```

and the algorithm itself is embodied in the recursive function

```
int mkChange(amount, largestIndex)
```

where the first parameter is the amount to make change for, the second is the index of the largest coin in the `coinValues` array to be used in making that amount, and the integer returned is the number of combinations possible to make the specified amount of change using the specified maximum coin value. Thus the call to make change for 24 cents using coin values 1, 5 is

```
mkChange(24,1);
```

In this case, the second parameter, 1, is the index of the largest coin to be used, that is, it is the index of the nickel in the `coinValues` array. Likewise, the call to make change for 14 cents using the same coin values is

```
mkChange(14,1);
```

Program 18-13 implements this algorithm for the U.S. system of coins. It would work for any other coin system by simply changing the coin set size and the values in the `coinValues` array. The algorithm assumes that the `coinValues` array lists its values in increasing order.

Program 18-13

```cpp
// This program demonstrates a recursive function that finds and counts all
// possible combinations of coin values to make a specified amount of change.

#include <iostream>
using namespace std;

const int coinSetSize = 6;
const int coinValues[ ] = {1, 5, 10, 25, 50, 100};

//************************************************************************
// This function returns the number of ways to make change for an      *
// amount if we can only use coinValues in the array positions         *
// 0 through largestIndex                                              *
//************************************************************************

int mkChange(int amount, int largestIndex)
{
    int waysToMakeChange = 0;

    while(coinValues[largestIndex] > amount) // Don't use coin values bigger
        largestIndex--;                      // than amount.

    if (largestIndex == 0)                   // There is only one way to make
        return 1;                            // the specified amount.
```

(program continues)

Program 18-13 *(continued)*

```
    // qty is how many of the largest coin to use
    for (int qty = 0; qty <= amount/coinValues[largestIndex]; qty++)
    {
        int amountLeft;                           // amount of change left to be given
                                                  // after using the specified quantity
                                                  // of the largest coin

        amountLeft = amount - qty * coinValues[largestIndex];

        if (amountLeft == 0)
            waysToMakeChange = waysToMakeChange + 1;
        else
            waysToMakeChange = waysToMakeChange + mkChange(amountLeft, largestIndex-
1);
    }
    return waysToMakeChange;
}


int main( )
{
    int amount;

    //display possible coin values
    cout << "Here are the valid coin values, in cents: ";
    for (int index = 0; index < coinSetSize; index ++)
        cout << coinValues[index] << "  ";
    cout << endl;

    //get input from user
    cout << "Enter (as an integer) the amount of cents to make change for: ";
    cin >> amount;
    cout << "Number of possible combinations is "
         << mkChange(amount, coinSetSize-1)  // coinSetSize-1 is the index of the
         << endl;                            // largest coin value to be considered
    return 0;
}
```

Program Output with Example Input Shown in Bold
```
Here are the valid coin values, in cents: 1 5 10 25 50 100
Enter (as an integer) the amount of cents to make change for: 11[Enter]
Number of possible combinations: 4
```

18.11   Focus on Software Engineering:
Recursion Versus Iteration

> **CONCEPT**   Recursive algorithms can also be coded with iterative control structures. There are advantages and disadvantages to each approach.

Any algorithm that can be coded with recursion can also be coded with an iterative control structure, such as a `while` loop. Both approaches achieve repetition, but which is best to use?

There are several reasons not to use recursion. Recursive algorithms are certainly less efficient than iterative algorithms. Each time a function is called, the system incurs overhead that is not necessary with a loop. Also, in many cases an iterative solution may be more evident than a recursive one. In fact, the majority of repetitive programming tasks are best done with loops.

Some problems, however, are more easily solved with recursion than with iteration. For example, the mathematical definition of the gcd formula is well-suited for a recursive approach. The QuickSort algorithm is also an example of a function that is easier to code with recursion than iteration.

The speed and amount of memory available to modern computers diminishes the performance impact of recursion so much that inefficiency is no longer a strong argument against it. Today the choice of recursion or iteration is primarily a design decision. If a problem is more easily solved with a loop, that should be the approach you take. If recursion results in a better design, that is the choice you should make.

Review Questions and Exercises

Fill-in-the-Blank

1. The _____ of recursion is the number of times a function calls itself.
2. A recursive function's solvable problem is known as its _____. This causes the recursion to stop.
3. _____ recursion is when a function explicitly calls itself.
4. _____ recursion is when function A calls function B, which in turn calls function A.

Predict the Output

5. What is the output of the following programs?

```
A)    #include <iostream>
      using namespace std;
```

```
    int function(int);
    int main()
    {
        int x = 10;

        cout << function(x) << endl;
        return 0;
    }

    int function(int num)
    {
        if (num <= 0)
            return 0;
        else
            return function(num - 1) + num;
    }
```

B)
```
    #include <iostream>
    using namespace std;

    void function(int);

    int main()
    {
        int x = 10;

        function(x);
        return 0;
    }

    void function(int num)
    {
        if (num > 0)
        {
            for (int x = 0; x < num; x++)
                cout << '*';
            cout << endl;
            function(num - 1);
        }
    }
```

C)
```
    #include <iostream>
    using namespace std;

    void function(char [], int, int);
```

```
int main()
{
    char names[] = "Adam and Eve";
    function(names, 0, 13);
    return 0;
}
void function(char array[], int pos, int size)
{
    if (pos < size - 1)
    {
        function(array, pos + 1, size);
        cout << array[pos];
    }
}
```

Short Answer

6. What is the base case of each of the recursive functions listed in question 5?

7. What type of recursive function do you think would be more difficult to debug; one that uses direct recursion, or one that uses indirect recursion? Why?

8. Which repetition approach is less efficient; a loop or a recursive function? Why?

9. When should you choose a recursive algorithm over an iterative algorithm?

10. Explain what is likely to happen when a recursive function that has no way of stopping executes.

Programming Challenges

Each program should have a section of comments at the top. The comments should contain your name, the date the program was written, the chapter the assignment appeared in, and the assignment number and name. Here is an example:

```
// Written by Jill Johnson
// March 31, 2003
// Chapter 18
// Assignment 1.  Iterative Factorial
```

1. Iterative Factorial

Write an iterative version (using a loop instead of recursion) of the factorial function shown in this chapter. Test it with a driver program.

2. Recursive Conversion

Convert the following function to one that uses recursion.

```
void sign(int n)
{
  while (n-- > 0)
     cout << "No Parking\n";
}
```

Demonstrate the function with a driver program.

3. QuickSort Template

Create a template version of the `quickSort` algorithm that will work with any data type. Demonstrate the template with a driver function.

4. Recursive Array Sum

Write a function that accepts an array of integers and a number indicating the number of elements as arguments. The function should recursively calculate the sum of all the numbers in the array. Demonstrate the function in a driver program.

5. Recursive Multiplication

Write a recursive function that accepts two arguments into the parameters x and y. The function should return the value of x times y. Remember, multiplication can be performed as repeated addition:

$$7 * 4 = 4 + 4 + 4 + 4 + 4 + 4 + 4$$

6. `isMember` Function

Write a recursive boolean function named `isMember`. The function should accept three parameters: an array of integers, an integer denoting the number of elements in the array, and an integer value. The function should return `true` if the value is found in the array, or `false` if the value is not found in the array. Demonstrate the function in a driver program.

7. String Reverser

Write a recursive function that accepts a string as its argument and prints the string in reverse order. Demonstrate the function in a driver program.

8. Ackermann's Function

Ackermann's function is a recursive mathematical algorithm that can be used to test how well a computer performs recursion. Write a function A(m, n) that solves Ackermann's function. Use the following logic in your function:

```
If m = 0 then    return n + 1
If n = 0 then    return A(m-1, 1)
Otherwise,       return A(m-1, A(m, n-1))
```

Test your function in a driver program that displays the following values:

A(0, 0)   A(0, 1)   A(1, 1)   A(1, 2)   A(1, 3)   A(2, 2)   A(3, 2)

Serendipity Booksellers Software Development Project—Part 18:
A Problem-Solving Exercise

Previously you completed functions for displaying a series of inventory reports:

```
repListing
repWholesale
repRetail
repQty
repCost
repAge
```

Modify your program so it uses the `quickSort` algorithm to sort the information stored in the linked list of `BookData` structures before the reports are printed. The book information should be sorted by ISBN number.

CHAPTER 19

Binary Trees

Topics

19.1 Definition and Applications of Binary Trees

CONCEPT A binary tree is a nonlinear linked list where each node may point to two other nodes. Binary trees expedite the process of searching large sets of information.

A standard linked list is a linear data structure in which one node is linked to the next. A *binary tree* is a nonlinear linked list. It is nonlinear because each node can point to two other nodes. Figure 19-1 illustrates the organization of a binary tree.

The data structure is called a tree because it resembles an upside-down tree. It is anchored at the top by a *tree pointer,* which is like the head pointer in a standard linked list. The first node in the list is called the *root node.* The root node has pointers to two other nodes, which are called *children,* or *child nodes.* Each of the children have their own set of two pointers, and can have their own children. Notice that not all nodes have two children. Some point to only one node, and some point to no other nodes. A node that has no children is called a *leaf node.* All pointers that do not point to a node are set to NULL.

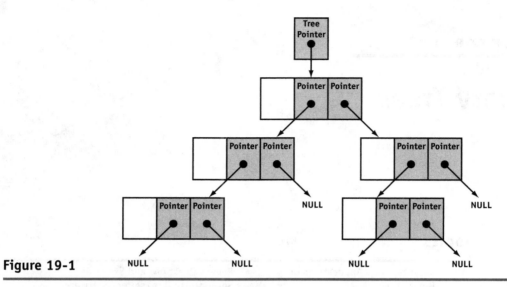

Figure 19-1

Binary trees can be divided into *subtrees*. A subtree is an entire branch of the tree, from one particular node down. For example, Figure 19-2 shows the left subtree from the root node of the tree shown in Figure 19-1.

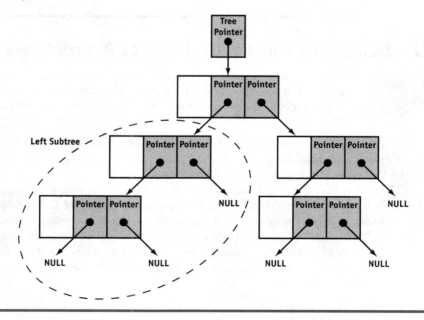

Figure 19-2

Applications of Binary Trees

Searching any linear data structure, such as an array or a standard linked list, is slow when the structure holds a large amount of information. This is because of the sequential nature of linear data structures. Binary trees are excellent data structures for searching large amounts of information. They are commonly used in database applications to organize key values that index database records. When used to facilitate searches, a binary tree is called a *binary search tree*. Binary search trees are the primary focus of this chapter.

Information is stored in binary search trees in a way that makes a binary search simple. For example, look at Figure 19-3.

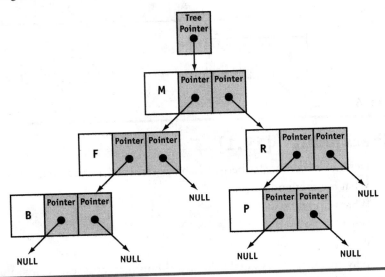

Figure 19-3

The figure depicts a binary search tree where each node stores a letter of the alphabet. Notice that the root node holds the letter M. The left child of the root node holds the letter F, and the right child holds R. Values are stored in a binary search tree so that a node's left child holds data whose value is less than the node's data, and the node's right child holds data whose value is greater than the node's data. This is true for all nodes in the tree that have children.

It is also true that *all* the nodes to the left of a node hold values less than the node's value. Likewise, all the nodes to the right of a node hold values that are greater than the node's data. When an application is searching a binary tree, it starts at the root node. If the root node does not hold the search value, the application branches either to the left or right child, depending on whether the search value is less than or greater than the value at the root node. This process continues until the value is found. Figure 19-4 illustrates the search pattern for finding the letter P in the binary tree shown.

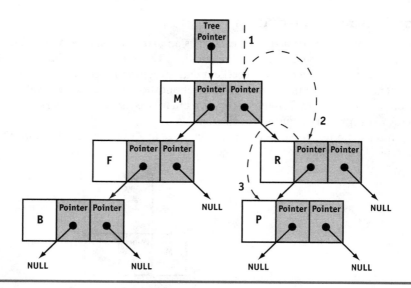

Figure 19-4

☞ Checkpoint [19.1]

19.1   Describe the difference between a binary tree and a standard linked list.

19.2   What is a root node?

19.3   What is a child node?

19.4   What is a leaf node?

19.5   What is a subtree?

19.6   Why are binary trees suitable for algorithms that must search large amounts of information?

19.2   Binary Search Tree Operations

> **CONCEPT**   There are many operations that may be performed on a binary search tree; including creating a binary search tree, inserting, finding, and deleting nodes.

In this section you will learn some basic operations that may be performed on a binary search tree. We will study a simple class that implements a binary tree for storing integer values.

Creating a Binary Tree

We will demonstrate the fundamental binary tree operations using a simple ADT: the Int-BinaryTree class. The basis of our binary tree node is the following struct declaration:

```
struct TreeNode
{
    int value;
    TreeNode *left;
    TreeNode *right;
};
```

Each node has a `value` member, for storing its integer data, as well as `left` and `right` pointers. The `struct` is implemented in the class declaration shown here:

Contents of `IntBinaryTree.h`
```
#ifndef INTBINARYTREE_H
#define INTBINARYTREE_H

class IntBinaryTree
{
private:
  struct TreeNode
  {
      int value;
      TreeNode *left;
      TreeNode *right;
  };

  TreeNode *root;
  void destroySubTree(TreeNode *);
  void deleteNode(int, TreeNode *&);
  void makeDeletion(TreeNode *&);
  void displayInOrder(TreeNode *);
  void displayPreOrder(TreeNode *);
  void displayPostOrder(TreeNode *);
public:
  IntBinaryTree()    // Constructor
      { root = NULL; }
  ~IntBinaryTree() // Destructor
      { destroySubTree(root); }
  void insertNode(int);
  bool searchNode(int);
  void remove(int);
  void showNodesInOrder(void)
        { displayInOrder(root); }
  void showNodesPreOrder()
        { displayPreOrder(root); }
  void showNodesPostOrder()
        { displayPostOrder(root); }
};

#endif
```

The `root` pointer will be used as the tree pointer. Similar to the `head` pointer in a linked list, `root` will point to the first node in the tree, or to NULL if the tree is empty. It is initialized in the constructor, which is declared inline. The destructor calls `destroySubTree`, a private member function that recursively deletes all the nodes in the tree.

Inserting a Node

The code to insert a new value in the tree is fairly straightforward. First, a new node is allocated and its `value` member is initialized with the new value. The `left` and `right` child pointers are set to NULL, because all nodes must be inserted as leaf nodes.

Next, we determine whether the tree is empty. If so, we simply make `root` point to it and there is nothing else to be done. But if there are nodes in the tree, we must find the new node's proper insertion point. If the new value is less than the `root` node's value, we know it will be inserted somewhere in the left subtree. Otherwise, the value will be inserted into the right subtree. We simply traverse the subtree, comparing each node along the way with the new node's value, deciding whether we should continue to the left or the right. When we reach a child pointer that is set to NULL, we have found our insertion point.

 Note: We assume that our binary tree will store no duplicate values.

The `insertNode` member function, which is in the `IntBinaryTree.cpp` file, is listed here:

```
void IntBinaryTree::insertNode(int num)
{
   TreeNode *newNode,    // Pointer to a new node
            *nodePtr;    // Pointer to traverse the tree

   // Create a new node
   newNode = new TreeNode;
   newNode->value = num;
   newNode->left = newNode->right = NULL;

   if (!root)            // Is the tree empty?
      root = newNode;
   else
   {
      nodePtr = root;
      while (nodePtr != NULL)
      {
         if (num < nodePtr->value)
         {
            if (nodePtr->left)
               nodePtr = nodePtr->left;
            else
            {
               nodePtr->left = newNode;
               break;
            }
         }
```

```
                else if (num > nodePtr->value)
                {
                    if (nodePtr->right)
                        nodePtr = nodePtr->right;
                    else
                    {
                        nodePtr->right = newNode;
                        break;
                    }
                }
                else
                {
                    cout << "Duplicate value found in tree.\n";
                    break;
                }
            }
        }
    }
```

Program 19-1 demonstrates the function.

Program 19-1

```
// This program builds a binary tree with 5 nodes.

#include <iostream>
#include "IntBinaryTree.h"
using namespace std;

int main()
{
    IntBinaryTree tree;

    cout << "Inserting nodes.";
    tree.insertNode(5);
    tree.insertNode(8);
    tree.insertNode(3);
    tree.insertNode(12);
    tree.insertNode(9);
    cout << "Done.\n";
    return 0;
}
```

Figure 19-5 shows the structure of the binary tree built by Program 19-1.

 Note: The shape of the tree is determined by the order in which the values are inserted. The root node in Figure 19-5 holds the value 5 because that was the first value inserted. By stepping through the function, you can see how the other nodes came to appear in their depicted positions.

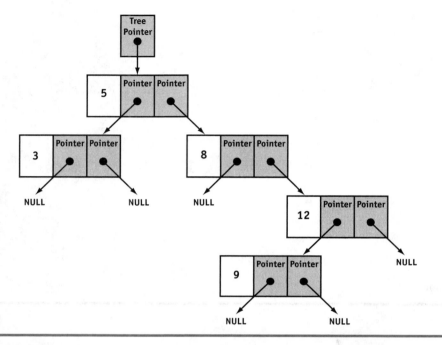

Figure 19-5

Traversing the Tree

There are three common methods for traversing a binary tree and processing the value of each node: *inorder, preorder,* and *postorder.* Each of these methods is best implemented as a recursive function. The algorithms are described as follows.

◆ *Inorder traversal*
   1. The node's left subtree is traversed.
   2. The node's data is processed.
   3. The node's right subtree is traversed.

◆ *Preorder traversal*
   1. The node's data is processed.
   2. The node's left subtree is traversed.
   3. The node's right subtree is traversed.

◆ *Postorder traversal*
   1. The node's left subtree is traversed.
   2. The node's right subtree is traversed.
   3. The node's data is processed.

The `IntBinaryTree` class can display all the values in the tree using all three of these algorithms. The algorithms are initiated by the following inline public member functions:

```
void showNodesInOrder()
    {   displayInOrder(root);  }
void showNodesPreOrder()
    {   displayPreOrder(root);  }
void showNodesPostOrder()
    {   displayPostOrder(root);  }
```

Each of the public member functions calls a recursive private member function and passes the root pointer as an argument. The recursive functions are very simple and straightforward:

```
//**********************************************************
// The displayInOrder member function displays the values  *
// in the subtree pointed to by nodePtr, via inorder traversal.  *
//**********************************************************

void IntBinaryTree::displayInOrder(TreeNode *nodePtr)
{
  if (nodePtr)
  {
     displayInOrder(nodePtr->left);
     cout << nodePtr->value << endl;
     displayInOrder(nodePtr->right);
  }
}


//**********************************************************
// The displayPreOrder member function displays the values  *
// in the subtree pointed to by nodePtr, via preorder traversal.  *
//**********************************************************

void IntBinaryTree::displayPreOrder(TreeNode *nodePtr)
{
  if (nodePtr)
  {
     cout << nodePtr->value << endl;
     displayPreOrder(nodePtr->left);
     displayPreOrder(nodePtr->right);
  }
}


//**********************************************************
// The displayPostOrder member function displays the values  *
// in the subtree pointed to by nodePtr, via postorder traversal.*
//**********************************************************

void IntBinaryTree::displayPostOrder(TreeNode *nodePtr)
{
  if (nodePtr)
  {
     displayPostOrder(nodePtr->left);
     displayPostOrder(nodePtr->right);
     cout << nodePtr->value << endl;
  }
}
```

Program 19-2, which is a modification of Program 19-1, demonstrates each of the traversal methods.

Program 19-2

```
// This program builds a binary tree with 5 nodes.
// The nodes are displayed with inorder, preorder,
// and postorder algorithms.

#include <iostream>
#include "IntBinaryTree.h"
using namespace std;

int main()
{
    IntBinaryTree tree;

    cout << "Inserting nodes.\n";
    tree.insertNode(5);
    tree.insertNode(8);
    tree.insertNode(3);
    tree.insertNode(12);
    tree.insertNode(9);
    cout << "Inorder traversal:\n";
    tree.showNodesInOrder();
    cout << "\nPreorder traversal:\n";
    tree.showNodesPreOrder();
    cout << "\nPostorder traversal:\n";
    tree.showNodesPostOrder();
    return 0;
}
```

Program Output
```
Inserting nodes.
Inorder traversal:
3
5
8
9
12
Preorder traversal:
5
3
8
12
9

Postorder traversal:
3
9
12
8
5
```

Searching the Tree

The `IntBinaryTree` class has a public member function, `searchNode`, which returns `true` if a value is found in the tree, or `false` otherwise. The function simply starts at the `root` node and traverses the tree until it finds the search value, or runs out of nodes. The code is shown here:

```cpp
bool IntBinaryTree::searchNode(int num)
{
   TreeNode *nodePtr = root;

   while (nodePtr)
   {
      if (nodePtr->value == num)
         return true;
      else if (num < nodePtr->value)
         nodePtr = nodePtr->left;
      else
         nodePtr = nodePtr->right;
   }
   return false;
}
```

Program 19-3 demonstrates this function.

Program 19-3

```cpp
// This program builds a binary tree with 5 nodes.
// The SearchNode function determines if the
// value 3 is in the tree.

#include <iostream>
#include "IntBinaryTree.h"
using namespace std;

int main()
{
   IntBinaryTree tree;

   cout << "Inserting nodes.\n";
   tree.insertNode(5);
   tree.insertNode(8);
   tree.insertNode(3);
   tree.insertNode(12);
   tree.insertNode(9);
```

(program continues)

Program 19-3 *(continued)*

```
    if (tree.searchNode(3))
        cout << "3 is found in the tree.\n";
    else
        cout << "3 was not found in the tree.\n";
    return 0;
}
```

Program Output
```
Inserting nodes.
3 is found in the tree.
```

Deleting a Node

Deleting a leaf node is not difficult. We simply find its parent and set the child pointer that links to it to NULL, then free the node's memory. But what if we want to delete a node that has child nodes? We must delete the node while at the same time preserving the subtrees that the node links to.

There are two possible situations to face when deleting a nonleaf node: the node has one child, or the node has two children. Figure 19-6 illustrates a tree in which we are about to delete a node with one subtree.

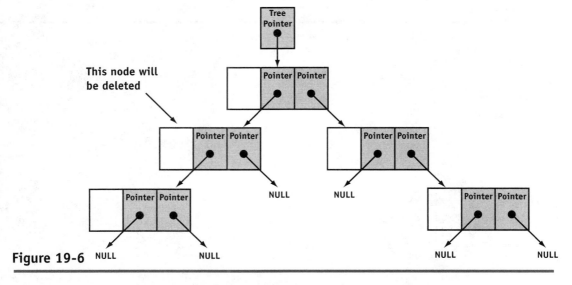

Figure 19-6

Figure 19-7 shows how we will link the node's subtree with its parent.

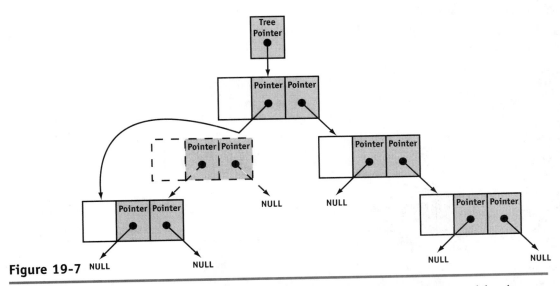

Figure 19-7

The problem is not as easily solved, however, when the node we are about to delete has two subtrees. For example, look at Figure 19-8.

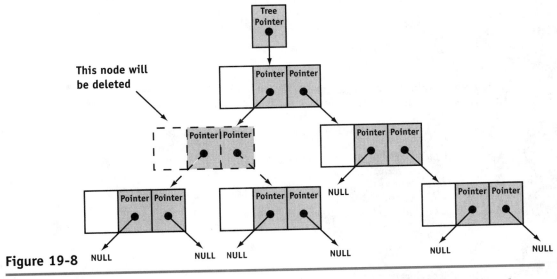

Figure 19-8

Obviously, we cannot attach both of the node's subtrees to its parent, so there must be an alternative soluton. One way of addressing this problem is to attach the node's right subtree to the parent, then find a position in the right subtree to attach the left subtree. The result is shown in Figure 19-9.

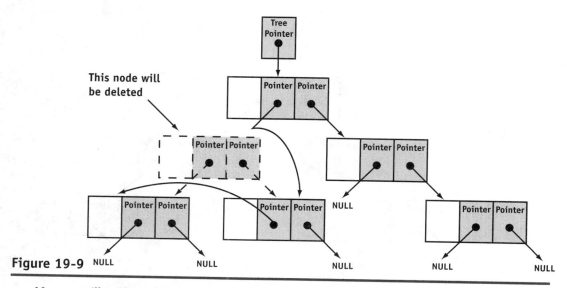

Figure 19-9

Now we will see how this action is implemented in code. To delete a node from the IntBinary-Tree, call the public member remove. The argument passed to the function is the value of the node you wish to delete. The remove member function is

```
void IntBinaryTree::remove(int num)
{
    deleteNode(num, root);
}
```

The remove member function calls the deleteNode member function. It passes the value of the node to delete and the root pointer. The deleteNode member function is

```
void IntBinaryTree::deleteNode(int num, TreeNode *&nodePtr)
{
    if (nodePtr == NULL) return;
    if (num < nodePtr->value)
        deleteNode(num, nodePtr->left);
    else if (num > nodePtr->value)
        deleteNode(num, nodePtr->right);
    else
        makeDeletion(nodePtr);
}
```

Notice the declaration of the nodePtr parameter variable:

```
TreeNode *&nodePtr
```

nodePtr is not simply a pointer to a TreeNode structure, but a *reference* to a pointer to a TreeNode structure. This means that any action performed on nodePtr is actually performed on the argument that was passed into nodePtr. The reason for this is explained momentarily.

The `deleteNode` function uses an if statement. The first part of the statement is

```
if (num < nodePtr->value)
    deleteNode(num, nodePtr->left);
```

This statement compares the parameter `num` with the `value` member of the node that `nodePtr` points to. If `num` is less, then the value being searched for will appear somewhere in `nodePtr`'s left subtree (if it appears in the tree at all). In this case, the `deleteNode` function is recursively called with `num` as the first argument and `nodePtr->left` as the second argument.

If `num` is not less than `nodePtr->value`, the following `else if` statement is executed.

```
else if (num > nodePtr->value)
    deleteNode(num, nodePtr->right);
```

If `num` is greater than `nodePtr->value`, then the value being searched for will appear somewhere in `nodePtr`'s right subtree (if it appears in the tree at all). In that case, the `deleteNode` function is recursively called with `num` as the first argument and `nodePtr->right` as the second argument.

If `num` is equal to `nodePtr->value`, then neither of the `if` statements will find a true condition. In this case, `nodePtr` points to the node that is to be deleted, and the trailing `else` will execute.

```
else
    makeDeletion(nodePtr);
```

The trailing `else` statement calls the `makeDeletion` function and passes `nodePtr` as its argument. The `makeDeletion` function actually deletes the node from the tree and must reattach the deleted node's subtrees, as shown in Figure 19-9. Therefore, it must have access to the actual pointer, in the binary tree, to the node that is being deleted (not just a copy of the pointer). This is why the `nodePtr` parameter in the `deleteNode` function is a reference. It must pass to `makeDeletion` the actual pointer, in the binary tree, to the node that is to be deleted. The `makeDeletion` function's code is as follows:

```
void IntBinaryTree::makeDeletion(TreeNode *&nodePtr)
{
    TreeNode *tempNodePtr;   // Temporary pointer, used in reattaching
                             // the left subtree.

    if (nodePtr->right == NULL)
    {
        tempNodePtr = nodePtr;
        nodePtr = nodePtr->left;      // Reattach the left child
        delete tempNodePtr;
    }
    else if (nodePtr->left == NULL)
    {
        tempNodePtr = nodePtr;
        nodePtr = nodePtr->right;     // Reattach the right child
        delete tempNodePtr;
    }
```

```
        // If the node has two children.
        else
        {
            // Move one node to  the right.
            tempNodePtr = nodePtr->right;
            // Go to the end left node.
            while (tempNodePtr->left)
                tempNodePtr = tempNodePtr->left;
            // Reattach the left subtree.
            tempNodePtr->left = nodePtr->left;
            tempNodePtr = nodePtr;
            // Reattach the right subtree.
            nodePtr = nodePtr->right;
            delete tempNodePtr;
        }
    }
```

Program 19-4 demonstrates these functions.

Program 19-4

```
// This program builds a binary tree with 5 nodes.
// The deleteNode function is used to remove two
// of them.

#include <iostream>
#include "IntBinaryTree.h"
using namespace std;

int main()
{
    IntBinaryTree tree;
    cout << "Inserting nodes.\n";
    tree.insertNode(5);
    tree.insertNode(8);

    tree.insertNode(3);
    tree.insertNode(12);
    tree.insertNode(9);

    cout << "Here are the values in the tree:\n";
    tree.showNodesInOrder();
```

(program continues)

Program 19-4 *(continued)*

```
   cout << "Deleting 8...\n";
   tree.remove(8);
   cout << "Deleting 12...\n";
   tree.remove(12);

   cout << "Now, here are the nodes:\n";
   tree.showNodesInOrder();
   return 0;
}
```

Program Output
```
Inserting nodes.
Here are the values in the tree:
3
5
8
9
12
Deleting 8...
Deleting 12...
Now, here are the nodes:
3
5
9
```

For your reference, the entire contents of IntBinaryTree file are shown here:

Contents of IntBinaryTree.cpp
```
#include <iostream>
#include "IntBinaryTree.h"
using namespace std;

//*********************************************************
// insertNode creates a new node to hold num as its value, *
// and inserts it into the tree.                           *
//*********************************************************

void IntBinaryTree::insertNode(int num)
{
   TreeNode *newNode,      // Pointer to a new node
            *nodePtr;      // Pointer to traverse the tree

   // Create a new node
   newNode = new TreeNode;
   newNode->value = num;
   newNode->left = newNode->right = NULL;
```

```
    if (!root)// Is the tree empty?
        root = newNode;
    else
    {
        nodePtr = root;
        while (nodePtr != NULL)
        {
            if (num < nodePtr->value)
            {
                if (nodePtr->left)
                    nodePtr = nodePtr->left;
                else
                {
                    nodePtr->left = newNode;
                    break;
                }
            }
            else if (num > nodePtr->value)
            {
                if (nodePtr->right)
                    nodePtr = nodePtr->right;
                else
                {
                    nodePtr->right = newNode;
                    break;
                }
            }
            else
            {
                cout << "Duplicate value found in tree.\n";
                break;
            }
        }
    }
}

//*****************************************************
// destroySubTree is called by the destructor. It    *
// deletes all nodes in the tree.                     *
//*****************************************************

void IntBinaryTree::destroySubTree(TreeNode *nodePtr)
{
    if (!nodePtr) return;
    destroySubTree(nodePtr->left);
    destroySubTree(nodePtr->right);
    delete nodePtr;
}
```

```cpp
//*******************************************************
// searchNode determines if a value is present in   *
// the tree. If so, the function returns true.       *
// Otherwise, it returns false.                      *
//*******************************************************

bool IntBinaryTree::searchNode(int num)
{
  TreeNode *nodePtr = root;

  while (nodePtr)
  {
     if (nodePtr->value == num)
         return true;
     else if (num < nodePtr->value)
         nodePtr = nodePtr->left;
     else
         nodePtr = nodePtr->right;
  }
  return false;
}

//**********************************************
// remove calls deleteNode to delete the      *
// node whose value member is the same as num. *
//**********************************************

void IntBinaryTree::remove(int num)
{
   deleteNode(num, root);
}


//********************************************
// deleteNode deletes the node whose value   *
// member is the same as num.                *
//********************************************

void IntBinaryTree::deleteNode(int num, TreeNode *&nodePtr)
{
   if (nodePtr == NULL) return;
   if (num < nodePtr->value)
      deleteNode(num, nodePtr->left);
   else if (num > nodePtr->value)
      deleteNode(num, nodePtr->right);
   else
      makeDeletion(nodePtr);
}
```

```
//*************************************************************
// makeDeletion takes a reference to a pointer to the node    *
// that is to be deleted. The node is removed and the         *
// branches of the tree below the node are reattached.        *
//*************************************************************

void IntBinaryTree::makeDeletion(TreeNode *&nodePtr)
{
    TreeNode *tempNodePtr;  // Temporary pointer, used in reattaching the
                            // left subtree.

  if (nodePtr->right == NULL)
  {
      tempNodePtr = nodePtr;
      nodePtr = nodePtr->left;    // Reattach the left child
      delete tempNodePtr;
  }
  else if (nodePtr->left == NULL)
  {
      tempNodePtr = nodePtr;
      nodePtr = nodePtr->right;  // Reattach the right child
      delete tempNodePtr;
  }
  // If the node has two children.
  else
  {
      // Move one node the right.
      tempNodePtr = nodePtr->right;
      // Go to the end left node.
      while (tempNodePtr->left)
          tempNodePtr = tempNodePtr->left;
      // Reattach the left subtree.
      tempNodePtr->left = nodePtr->left;
      tempNodePtr = nodePtr;
      // Reattach the right subtree.
      nodePtr = nodePtr->right;
      delete tempNodePtr;
  }
}


//*************************************************************
// The displayInOrder member function displays the values    *
// in the subtree pointed to by nodePtr, via inorder traversal. *
//*************************************************************
```

```
void IntBinaryTree::displayInOrder(TreeNode *nodePtr)
{
  if (nodePtr)
  {
     displayInOrder(nodePtr->left);
     cout << nodePtr->value << endl;
     displayInOrder(nodePtr->right);
  }
}

//***************************************************************
// The displayPreOrder member function displays the values      *
// in the subtree pointed to by nodePtr, via preorder traversal. *
//***************************************************************

void IntBinaryTree::displayPreOrder(TreeNode *nodePtr)
{
  if (nodePtr)
  {
     cout << nodePtr->value << endl;
     displayPreOrder(nodePtr->left);
     displayPreOrder(nodePtr->right);
  }
}

//***************************************************************
// The displayPostOrder member function displays the values      *
// in the subtree pointed to by nodePtr, via postorder traversal.*
//***************************************************************

void IntBinaryTree::displayPostOrder(TreeNode *nodePtr)
{
  if (nodePtr)
  {
     displayPostOrder(nodePtr->left);
     displayPostOrder(nodePtr->right);
     cout << nodePtr->value << endl;
  }
}
```

Checkpoint [19.2]

19.7 Describe the sequence of events in an inorder traversal.

19.8 Describe the sequence of events in a preorder traversal.

19.9 Describe the sequence of events in a postorder traversal.

19.10 Describe the steps taken in deleting a leaf node.

19.11 Describe the steps taken in deleting a node with one child.

19.12 Describe the steps taken in deleting a node with two children.

19.3 Template Considerations for Binary Search Trees

> **CONCEPT** Binary search trees may be implemented as templates, but any data types used with them must support the ⟨, ⟩, and == operators.

The actual implementation of a binary tree template has been left as a Programming Challenge. When designing your template, remember that any data types stored in the binary tree must support the ⟨, ⟩, and == operators. If you use the tree to store class objects, these operators must be overridden.

Review Questions and Exercises

Fill-in-the-Blank

1. The first node in a binary tree is called the _____.
2. A binary tree node's left and right pointers point to the node's _____.
3. A node with no children is called a(n) _____.
4. A (n)_____ is an entire branch of the tree, from one particular node down.
5. The three common types of traversal with a binary tree are _____, _____, and _____.

True or False

6. T F Each node in a binary tree must have at least two children.
7. T F When a node is inserted into a binary search tree, it must be inserted as a leaf node.
8. T F Values stored in the current node's left subtree are less than the value stored in the current node.
9. T F The shape of a binary search tree is determined by the order in which values are inserted.
10. T F In inorder traversal, the node's data is processed first, then the left and right nodes are visited.

Short Answer

11. Write a pseudocode algorithm for inserting a node in a tree.
12. Write a pseudocode algorithm for the inorder traversal.
13. Write a pseudocode algorithm for the preorder traversal.
14. Write a pseudocode algorithm for the postorder traversal.
15. Write a pseudocode algorithm for searching a tree for a specified value.

16. Suppose the following values are inserted into a binary search tree, in the order given:

    12, 7, 9, 10, 22, 24, 30, 18, 3, 14, 20

    Draw a diagram of the resulting binary tree.

17. How would the values in the tree you sketched for queston 16 be displayed in an inorder traversal?

18. How would the values in the tree you sketched for queston 16 be displayed in a preorder traversal?

19. How would the values in the tree you sketched for queston 16 be displayed in a postorder traversal?

Programming Challenges

General Requirements

Each program should have a section of comments at the top. The comments should contain your name, the date the program was written, the chapter the assignment appeared in, and the assignment number and name. Here is an example:

```
// Written by Jill Johnson
// March 31, 2003
// Chapter 19
// Assignment 2. Node Counter
```

1. Binary Tree Template

In this chapter you studied `IntBinaryTree`, a class that implements a binary tree of integers. Write a template that will create a binary tree that can hold values of any data type. Demonstrate the class with a driver program.

2. Node Counter

Write a member function, for either the template you designed in Programming Challenge 1, or the `IntBinaryTree` class, that counts and returns the number of nodes in the tree. Demonstrate the function in a driver program.

3. Leaf Counter

Write a member function, for either the template you designed in Programming Challenge 1, or the `IntBinaryTree` class, that counts and returns the number of leaf nodes in the tree. Demonstrate the function in a driver program.

4. Tree Height

Write a member function, for either the template you designed in Programming Challenge 1, or the `IntBinaryTree` class, that returns the height of the tree. The height of the tree is the number of levels it contains. For example, the tree shown in Figure 19-10 has three levels.

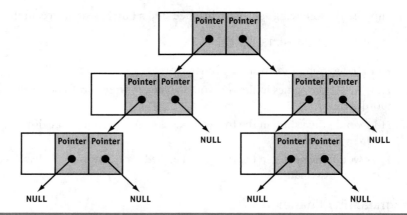

Figure 19-10

Demonstrate the function in a driver program.

5. Tree Width

Write a member function, for either the template you designed in Programming Challenge 1, or the IntBinaryTree class, that returns the width of the tree. The width of the tree is the largest number of nodes in the same level. Demonstrate the function in a driver program.

6. Tree Assignment Operator and Copy Constructor

Design an overloaded assignment operator and a copy constructor for either the template you designed in Programming Challenge 1, or the IntBinaryTree class. Demostrate them in a driver program.

7. Queue Converter

Write a program that stores a series of numbers in a binary tree. Then have the program insert the values into a queue in ascending order. Dequeue the values and display them on the screen to confirm that they were stored in the proper order.

8. Employee Tree

Design an EmployeeInfo class that holds the following employee information:

Employee ID Number: an integer
Employee Name: a string

Next, use the template you designed in Programming Challenge 1 to implement a binary tree whose nodes hold an instance of the EmployeeInfo class. The nodes should be sorted on the Employee ID number.

Test the binary tree by inserting nodes with the following information.

Employee ID Number	Name
1021	John Williams
1057	Bill Witherspoon
2487	Jennifer Twain
3769	Sophia Lancaster
1017	Debbie Reece
1275	George McMullen
1899	Ashley Smith
4218	Josh Plemmons

Your program should allow the user to enter an ID number, then search the tree for the number. If the number is found, it should display the employee's name. If the node is not found, it should display a message indicating so.

Serendipity Booksellers Software Development Project—Part 19: *A Problem-Solving Exercise*

Currently, the inventory data is stored by the Reports module in a linked list of BookData objects. For this chapter's assignment, you are to modify the program so it stores the objects in a binary tree.

The BookData objects should be keyed on the ISBN number. This means your algorithm will use the book's ISBN number to find its insertion point in the tree. You will need to modify the BookData class so it has overloaded ==, <, and > operators, or equivalent member functions for allowing comparisons with the ISBN number.

Appendix A
The ASCII Character Set

Nonprintable ASCII Characters			
Dec	Hex	Oct	Name of Character
0	0	0	NULL
1	1	1	SOTT
2	2	2	STX
3	3	3	ETY
4	4	4	EOT
5	5	5	ENQ
6	6	6	ACK
7	7	7	BELL
8	8	10	BKSPC
9	9	11	HZTAB
10	a	12	NEWLN
11	b	13	VTAB
12	c	14	FF
13	d	15	CR
14	e	16	SO
15	f	17	SI
16	10	20	DLE
17	11	21	DC1
18	12	22	DC2
19	13	23	DC3
20	14	24	DC4
21	15	25	NAK
22	16	26	SYN
23	17	27	ETB
24	18	30	CAN
25	19	31	EM
26	1a	32	SUB
27	1b	33	ESC
28	1c	34	FS
29	1d	35	GS
30	1e	36	RS
31	1f	37	US
127	7f	177	DEL

Printable ASCII Characters			
Dec	Hex	Oct	Character
32	20	40	(Space)
33	21	41	!
34	22	42	"
35	23	43	#
36	24	44	$
37	25	45	%
38	26	46	&
39	27	47	'
40	28	50	(
41	29	51	)
42	2a	52	*
43	2b	53	+
44	2c	54	,
45	2d	55	-
46	2e	56	.
47	2f	57	/
48	30	60	0
49	31	61	1
50	32	62	2
51	33	63	3
52	34	64	4
53	35	65	5
54	36	66	6
55	37	67	7
56	38	70	8
57	39	71	9
58	3a	72	:
59	3b	73	;
60	3c	74	<
61	3d	75	=
62	3e	76	>
63	3f	77	?
64	40	100	@
65	41	101	A
66	42	102	B
67	43	103	C

	Printable ASCII Characters		
Dec	**Hex**	**Oct**	**Character**
68	44	104	D
69	45	105	E
70	46	106	F
71	47	107	G
72	48	110	H
73	49	111	I
74	4a	112	J
75	4b	113	K
76	4c	114	L
77	4d	115	M
78	4e	116	N
79	4f	117	O
80	50	120	P
81	51	121	Q
82	52	122	R
83	53	123	S
84	54	124	T
85	55	125	U
86	56	126	V
87	57	127	W
88	58	130	X
89	59	131	Y
90	5a	132	Z
91	5b	133	[
92	5c	134	\
93	5d	135	]
94	5e	136	^
95	5f	137	_
96	60	140	`
97	61	141	a
98	62	142	b
99	63	143	c
100	64	144	d
101	65	145	e
102	66	146	f
103	67	147	g
104	68	150	h
105	69	151	i
106	6a	152	j
107	6b	153	k
108	6c	154	l
109	6d	155	m
110	6e	156	n
111	6f	157	o
112	70	160	p
113	71	161	q

	Printable ASCII Characters		
Dec	**Hex**	**Oct**	**Character**
114	72	162	r
115	73	163	s
116	74	164	t
117	75	165	u
118	76	166	v
119	77	167	w
120	78	170	x
121	79	171	y
122	7a	172	z
123	7b	173	{
124	7c	174		
125	7d	175	}
126	7e	176	~

	Extended ASCII Characters		
Dec	**Hex**	**Oct**	**Character**
128	80	200	Ç
129	81	201	ü
130	82	202	é
131	83	203	â
132	84	204	ä
133	85	205	à
134	86	206	å
135	87	207	ç
136	88	210	ê
137	89	211	ë
138	8a	212	è
139	8b	213	ï
140	8c	214	î
141	8d	215	ì
142	8e	216	Ä
143	8f	217	Å
144	90	220	É
145	91	221	æ
146	92	222	Æ
147	93	223	ô
148	94	224	ö
149	95	225	ò
150	96	226	û
151	97	227	ù
152	98	230	ÿ
153	99	231	Ö
154	9a	232	Ü
155	9b	233	¢

Extended ASCII Characters			
Dec	Hex	Oct	Character
156	9c	234	£
157	9d	235	ù
158	9e	236	û
159	9f	237	ƒ
160	a0	240	á
161	a1	241	í
162	a2	242	ó
163	a3	243	ú
164	a4	244	ñ
165	a5	245	Ñ
166	a6	246	ª
167	a7	247	º
168	a8	250	¿
169	a9	251	©
170	aa	252	Ñ
171	ab	253	´
172	ac	254	¨
173	ad	255	¡
174	ae	256	
175	af	257	»
176	b0	260	∞
177	b1	261	±
178	b2	262	≤
179	b3	263	≥
180	b4	264	¥
181	b5	265	µ
182	b6	266	∂
183	b7	267	Σ
184	b8	270	Π
185	b9	271	π
186	ba	272	∫
187	bb	273	ª
188	bc	274	º
189	bd	275	Ω
190	be	276	æ
191	bf	277	ø
192	c0	300	¿
193	c1	301	¡
194	c2	302	¬
195	c3	303	√
196	c4	304	ƒ
197	c5	305	≈
198	c6	306	Δ
199	c7	307	
200	c8	310	»
201	c9	311	…
202	ca	312	
203	cb	313	À
204	cc	314	Ã
205	cd	315	Õ

Extended ASCII Characters			
Dec	Hex	Oct	Character
206	ce	316	Œ
207	cf	317	œ
208	d0	320	–
209	d1	321	—
210	d2	322	"
211	d3	323	"
212	d4	324	'
213	d5	325	'
214	d6	326	÷
215	d7	327	◊
216	d8	330	ÿ
217	d9	331	Ÿ
218	da	332	/
219	db	333	¤
220	dc	334	‹
221	dd	335	›
222	de	336	fi
223	df	337	fl
224	e0	340	‡
225	e1	341	·
226	e2	342	'
227	e3	343	"
228	e4	344	‰
229	e5	345	Â
230	e6	346	Ê
231	e7	347	Á
232	e8	350	Ë
233	e9	351	È
234	ea	352	Í
235	eb	353	Î
236	ec	354	Ï
237	ed	355	Ì
238	ee	356	Ó
239	ef	357	Ô
240	f0	360	
241	f1	361	Ò
242	f2	362	Ú
243	f3	363	Û
244	f4	364	Ù
245	f5	365	ı
246	f6	366	^
247	f7	367	~
248	f8	370	¯
249	f9	371	˘
250	fa	372	˙
251	fb	373	•
252	fc	374	¸
253	fd	375	˝
254	fe	376	˛
255	ff	377	ˇ

Appendix B
Operator Precedence and Associativity

The operators are shown in order of precedence, from highest to lowest.

Operator	Associativity
: :	unary: left to right
( ) [ ] -> .	left to right
++ - + - ! ~ (type) * & sizeof	right to left
* / %	left to right
+ -	left to right
<< >>	left to right
< <= > >=	left to right
== !=	left to right
&	left to right
^	left to right
|	left to right
&&	left to right
||	left to right
? :	right to left
= += -= *= /= %= &= ^= |= <<= >>=	right to left
,	left to right

Appendix C
Introduction to UML
Contributed by Art Gittleman

The Unified Modeling Language (UML) has become the standard for object-oriented modeling. The UML *class diagram* of Figure C-1 represents the BankAccount class, showing the common structure of all BankAccount objects. The top section in the figure gives the class name; the middle section lists the variables used to represent the state of a BankAccount; and the bottom section lists each BankAccount's operations used to provide its services.

```
BankAccount

balance

getBalance()
deposit()
withdraw()
```

Figure C-1   **The** BankAccount **Class Diagram**

The class describes the attributes (data) and behavior (operations) each object instance possesses; it is like a pattern or template for specifying the state and behavior of each of its instances.

We create one or more BankAccount objects to instantiate the BankAccount class. In the UML notation, *object diagrams*, as pictured in Figure C-2, represent objects. The objects myAccount and yourAccount are *instances* of the BankAccount class.

```
┌─────────────────────────────┐      ┌─────────────────────────────┐
│ myAccount:BankAccount       │      │ yourAccount:BankAccount     │
├─────────────────────────────┤      ├─────────────────────────────┤
│ balance = 24.50             │      │ balance = 142.11            │
├─────────────────────────────┤      ├─────────────────────────────┤
│ getBalance()                │      │ getBalance()                │
│ deposit()                   │      │ deposit()                   │
│ withdraw()                  │      │ withdraw()                  │
└─────────────────────────────┘      └─────────────────────────────┘
```

Figure C-2   **Two** BankAccount **Objects**

Object diagrams also have three parts. In the top part of the figure, we name the object and indicate the class that defines it, underlining both as in

myAccount:BankAccount

The middle section shows the balance with a specific value, for example

balance = 24.50

The BankAccount class specifies each account must have a balance. In the object itself, the balance has a specific value. This is analogous to the concept of a chair that specifies a seat and legs, contrasted with an actual chair object that has a hard seat and curved legs.

The third part of the object diagram in Figure C-2 lists the services the object provides. Each BankAccount object can deposit, withdraw, or get its balance.

Use Cases and Scenarios

We identify the types of objects we need by considering the typical uses of the system, called *use cases*, and various *scenarios*, which show, in a step-by-step manner, the interaction between the user and the use cases. When designing with objects, we may start by identifying the use cases. For example, if we were modeling a customer order at a fast food restaurant, one use case would be a customer placing an order. To better understand each use of the system, we describe typical scenarios. For each use case, we develop a primary scenario showing the normal interactions and several secondary scenarios that list the interactions that take place in more unusual or error situations.

Associations and Relationships Between Classes

We also use UML to show the associations between classes. An association represents a relationship between instances of the associated classes. For example, a customer places an order with a waiter, while a waiter asks the cook to make a burger. The diagram in Figure C-3 is a simplification of these associations.

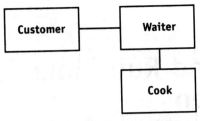

Figure C-3   **Association Between Classes**

UML diagrams show inheritance by using unfilled arrows to denote the relationship. For example, Figure C-4 shows an inheritance relationship between the BankAccount class and its SavingsAccount and CheckingAccount subclasses. The subclasses inherit from their parent superclass.

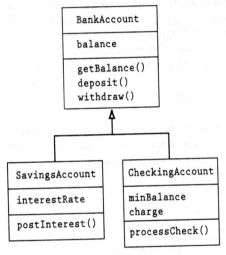

Figure C-4   **Inheritance**

UML provides many more diagram types and tools for modeling object-oriented systems. See http://www.rational.com/uml for more information.

Appendix D
C++ Casts and Run-Time Type Identification

Introduction

There are many times when a programmer needs to use type casts to tell the compiler to convert the type of an expression to another type, or to treat an expression of a known type as if it were of a different type. An example of the former is when you have computed the sum of n integer values in an integer variable sum, and would like to compute the average and store it in a variable average of type float. In this case, you must tell the compiler to first convert the integer sum to float before performing the division by using a type cast:

```
float average;
average = (float) sum / n;
```

An example of the latter occurs frequently in reading from an I/O device (perhaps a modem, a network connection, or a disk) from which data arrives as a stream of bytes. In this case, to store the data in a data item of some type, say a structure

```
struct PersonData
{
    char name[20];
    int age;
};
PersonData pData;
```

the address of pData must be treated as the address of a location where a sequence of bytes will be stored. In other words, a pointer to pData must be treated as a pointer to a byte. Since C++ treats bytes as if they were characters, this just means that a pointer to the type PersonData must be regarded as if it were a pointer to char. Again, this is accomplished through the use of a type cast:

```
char *pChar = (char *)&pData;
```

It is clear that these two examples of casting are different, not only in their purpose, but also in the way that they are implemented by the compiler. In converting an int to a float, the

1198

compiler must change the internal bit representation of an integer into the bit representation of a `float`, whereas in the second example, no transformation of the bit representation is performed. The designers of the C++ standard decided to introduce different casting notations to represent the two different kinds of casts mentioned, as well as two other kinds of casts also used in the language. The designers introduced four different ways of casting:

1. `static_cast`
2. `reinterpret_cast`
3. `const_cast`
4. `dynamic_cast`

Using the new style casts clarifies the programmer's intent to the compiler and enables the compiler to catch casting errors.

In this appendix, we will discuss the four ANSI C++ style type casts and briefly touch on the related topic of using the `typeid` operator.

Static_cast

A `static_cast` is used to convert an expression to a value of a specified type. For example, to convert an expression `expr1` to a value of type `Type1` and assign it to a variable `var1`, you would write

```
Type1 var1 = static_cast< Type1 >(expr1);
```

in place of the traditional C-style cast

```
Type1 var1 = (Type1) expr1;
```

For example, to perform the conversion of `int` to `float` mentioned in the first example of the introductory section, you would write

```
float average = static_cast< float >(sum) / n;
```

A `static_cast` is used to convert an expression of one type to a second type when the compiler has information on how to perform the indicated conversion. For example, `static_cast` can be used to perform all kinds of conversions between `char`, `int`, `long`, `float`, and `double` because the knowledge for performing those types of conversions is already built into the compiler. A `static_cast` can also be used if information on how to perform the conversion has been provided by the programmer through type conversion operators. For example, consider the class

```
class FeetInches
{
  private:
    int feet;
    int inches;
```

```
    public:
    FeetInches(int f, int i)
    {
      feet = f;
      inches = i;
    }
    //type conversion operator
    operator float()
    {
      return feet + inches/12.0;
    }
};
```

This class provides information to the compiler on how to convert a `FeetInches` object to a `float`. As a result, the following `main` function will compile correctly and print 3.5 and 3 when it executes.

```
#include <iostream>
#include "FeetInchesEx.h"
using namespace std;

int main()
{
  FeetInches ftObject(3, 6);
  //use static_cast to convert to float
  float ft = static_cast< float >(ftObject);
  cout << ft;
  //use static_cast to convert to int
  cout << endl << static_cast< int >(ftObject);
  return 0;
}
```

Here we have assumed that the class declaration is stored in the indicated header file. The static cast to `float` succeeds because of the presence of the type conversion operator, while the cast to `int` succeeds because the compiler already knows how to convert `float` to `int`.

An example of an improper use of `static_cast` might be instructive. Assuming the same declaration of `FeetInches` as earlier, the following `main` function will be rejected by the compiler:

```
int main()
{
  FeetInches ftObject(3, 6);
  //illegal use of static_cast
  char *pInt = static_cast< int * >(&ftObject);
  cout << *pInt;
  return 0;
}
```

The program fails to compile because the compiler has been given no information on how to convert a pointer to a `FeetInches` object to a pointer to `int`.

Finally, a `static_cast` can be used to cast a pointer to a base class to a pointer to a derived class. We will see an example of this in the last section of this appendix.

Reinterpret_cast

A `reinterpret_cast` is used to force the compiler to treat a value as if it were of a different type when the compiler knows of no way to perform the type conversion. A `reinterpret_cast` is mostly used with pointers, when a pointer to one type needs to be treated as if it were a pointer to a different type. In other words, `reinterpret_cast` is useful with the second kind of casting discussed in the introductory section. No change in the bit representation takes place: The value being cast is just used as is.

The notation for `reinterpret_cast` is similar to that for `static_cast`. To force expression `expr1` to be regarded as a value of type `Type1`, we would write

```
Type1 var1 = reinterpret_cast< Type1 >(expr1);
```

instead of the old C-style cast. For example, if for some reason we needed to treat a `FeetInches` object as a pair of integers, we could set a pointer to `int` to point to the object, and then access the integer components of the object by dereferencing the pointer. The `reinterpret_cast` would be used to force the change of type in the pointer. The following `main` program would print 3 on one line and 6 on the next.

```cpp
int main()
{
  FeetInches ftObject(3, 6);
  //point to beginning of object
  int *p = reinterpret_cast< int * >(&ftObject);
  cout << *p << endl;
  //advance the pointer by size of one int
  p++;
  cout << *p;
  return 0;
}
```

The compiler will reject the use of `reinterpret_cast` where there is adequate information on how to perform the type conversion. In particular, the following statement generates a compiler error:

```cpp
cout << reinterpret_cast< int >(ftObject);
```

Well-designed programs that do not work directly with hardware should have little need for this type of casting. Indeed, a need to use `reinterpret_cast` may well be an indication of a design error.

Const_cast

This type of casting is only used with *pointers to constants*. A pointer to a constant may not be used to change the memory location it points to. For example, we may define a pair of integer variables and a pointer to a constant int as follows:

```
int  k = 4;
int m = 20;
const int *pToC;
```

We may then make the pointer pToC point to different integer variables, as in

```
pToC = &k;
cout << *pToC; //prints 4
pToC = &m;
cout << *pToC; //prints 20
```

but we cannot use pToC to change whatever variable pToC points to. For example, the code

```
*pToC = 23;
```

is illegal. Moreover, you cannot assign the value of a pointer to a constant to another pointer that is not itself a pointer to a constant, since the constant might then be changed through the second pointer:

```
int *p1; //not a pointer to constant
p1 = pToC;  //error!!
```

For the same reason, a pointer to a constant can only be passed to a function if the corresponding formal parameter is a pointer to a constant. Thus, with the function definition

```
void print(int *p)
{
    cout << *p;
}
```

the call

```
print(pToC);
```

would be illegal. Such a call, however, would be all right if the function was modified to take a parameter that is a pointer to a constant. Thus, in the presence of

```
void constPrint(const int *p)
{
    cout << *p;
}
```

the call

```
constPrint(pToC);
```

would be okay.

We have purposely kept these examples simple. In real programs, the pointer to a constant might be returned by a member function of a class, and might point to a member of the class that needs to be protected from modification (the pointer to a constant might be returned to avoid copying the value of a large member). This pointer might need to be passed to a function such as `print` above which perhaps through poor planning was not written to take a pointer to a constant. In this case, the compiler can be persuaded to accept the call by "casting away" the "constness" of the pointer using a `const_cast`:

```
print( const_cast< int * >(pToC) );
```

Naturally, `const_cast` can also be used to allow assignment of a pointer to a constant to a regular pointer:

```
int *p = const_cast< int * >(pToC);
```

As in the case of `reinterpret_cast`, we note that the use of `const_cast` should not be necessary in most well-designed programs. We can now summarize the purpose of `const_cast`: *it is used treat a pointer to a constant as though it were a regular pointer.*

Dynamic_cast

Polymorphic code is code that is capable of being invoked with objects belonging to different classes within the same inheritance hierarchy. Because objects of different classes have different storage requirements, polymorphic code does not use the objects directly. Instead, it accesses them through references or pointers. In this appendix, we will deal mainly with the access of polymorphic objects through pointers: access through references is similar.

Polymorphic code processes objects of different classes by treating them as belonging to the same base class. At times, however, it is necessary to determine at run time the specific derived class of the object, so that its methods can be invoked. Objects designed to be processed by polymorphic code carry type information within them to make this type of run-time type identification possible. In C++, such objects must belong to a polymorphic class. A polymorphic class is a class with at least one virtual member function, or one that is derived from such a class.

In C++, a `dynamic_cast` is used to take a pointer (or reference) to an object of a polymorphic class, determine whether the object is of a specified *target class*, and if so, return that pointer cast as a pointer to the target class. If the object cannot be regarded as belonging to the target class, `dynamic_cast` returns the special pointer value 0.

A typical use of `dynamic_cast` is as follows. Let `pExpr` be a pointer to an object of some derived class of a polymorphic class `PolyClass`, and let `DerivedClass` be one of several classes derived from `PolyClass`. We can determine whether the object pointed to by `pExpr` is a `DerivedClass` object by writing

```
DerivedClass *dP = dynamic_cast<DerivedClass *>(pExpr);
if (dP)
 {
   // the object *dP belongs to DerivedClass
   ...
 }
else
 {
   // *dp does not belong to DerivedClass
   ...
 }
```

Here DerivedClass is what we have called the specified target class.

As an example, consider a farm that keeps cows for milk as well as a number of dogs to guard the homestead. All the animals eat (have an eat member function), the cows give milk (have a giveMilk member function), and the dogs keep watch (have a guardhouse member function). We can describe all of these by using the following hierarchy of classes:

```
#include <iostream>
using namespace std;

class DomesticAnimal
{
   public:
     virtual void eat()
       {
         cout << "Animal eating: Munch munch." << endl;
       }
};

class Cow:public DomesticAnimal
{
  public:
    void giveMilk()
      {
        cout << "Cow giving milk." << endl;
      }
};

class Dog:public DomesticAnimal
{
  public:
    void guardHouse()
      {
        cout << "Dog guarding house." << endl;
      }
};
```

Note that the eat member function has been declared as a virtual member function in order to make all the classes polymorphic.

Many applications work with collections, usually arrays of objects belonging to the same inheritance hierarchy. For example, our farm may have two cows and two dogs, which can be stored in an array as follows:

```
DomesticAnimal *a[4] = {new Dog, new Cow,
                        new Dog, new Cow
                       };
```

We have to use an array of pointers since an array of DomesticAnimal would not be able to hold Dog or Cow objects, either of which would normally require more storage than a DomesticAnimal. Now suppose that we wanted to go through the entire array of animals and milk all the cows. We couldn't just go through the array with a loop such as

```
for (int k = 0; k < 4; k++)
  a[k]->giveMilk();
```

for then we would cause run-time errors whenever a[k] points to a Dog. A dynamic_cast will take a pointer such as a[k], look at the actual type of the object being pointed to, and return the address of the object if the object matches the target type of the dynamic_cast. If the object does not match the target type of the cast, then 0 is returned in place of the address. As mentioned, the general format for casting an expression expr1 to a target type TargetType is

```
dynamic_cast< TargetType >(expr1);
```

where TargetType must be a pointer or reference type. In our case, to determine if a domestic animal pointed to by a[k] is a cow we would write

```
Cow *pC = dynamic_cast< Cow * >(a[k]);
```

and then test pC to see if it was 0. If it is 0, we know the animal is not a cow and that it is useless to attempt to milk it; otherwise, we can milk the animal by invoking

```
a[k]->giveMilk();
```

Here is a main function that puts all of this together.

```
int main()
{
    DomesticAnimal *a[4] = {new Dog, new Cow,
                            new Dog, new Cow,
                           };
    for (int k = 0; k < 4; k++)
    {
      Cow *pC = dynamic_cast<Cow *>(a[k]);
      if (pC)
        {
          //pC not 0, so we found a cow
          pC->giveMilk();
        }
```

```
        else
        {
          cout << "This animal is not a cow." << endl;
        }
      }
    return 0;
}
```

When executed, the output will be

```
This animal is not a cow.
Cow giving milk.
This animal is not a cow.
Cow giving milk.
```

The `dynamic_cast` is so called because the type of the object of a polymorphic class cannot always be determined statically, that is, at compile time without running the program. For example, in the statement

```
a[k]->giveMilk();
```

it is impossible to determine at compile time whether `a[k]` points to a `Dog` or a `Cow` since it can point to objects of either type. In contrast, `static_cast` uses information available at compile time.

Run-Time Type Identification

As we have seen, `dynamic_cast` can be used to identify the class type of a polymorphic object within an inheritance hierarchy at run time. More generally, the `typeid` operator can be used to identify the type of any expression at run time. The `typeid` operator can be applied to both data and type expressions:

```
typeid(data_expression)
```

or

```
typeid(type_expression)
```

For example, if we have the definitions

```
int i;
Cow c;
Cow *pC;
```

then we could apply the `typeid` operator to the data items i+12, c, and pC, giving

```
typeid(i+12)
typeid(c)
typeid(pC)
```

which would respectively be equal to the results of applying `typeid` to the corresponding type expressions

```
typeid(int)
typeid(Cow)
typeid(Cow *)
```

In the program in the last section, evaluating the expression

```
typeid(a[k]) == typeid(DomesticAnimal)
```

would always yield the value true. To find out if the animal pointed to by `a[k]` is a cow, we would test the expression

```
typeid(*a[k]) == typeid(Cow)
```

to see if it was true. If it was true, we could then use a `static_cast` to cast `a[k]` to the appropriate type in order to milk the cow:

```
static_cast<Cow *>(a[k])->giveMilk();
```

The cast is necessary since without it, the statement

```
a[k]->giveMilk();
```

will not compile. This is because the type of `a[k]` is a pointer to a `DomesticAnimal`, and domestic animals do not have a `giveMilk()` member function.

Appendix E
Multi-File Programs

Programming students normally begin by writing programs that are contained in a single file. Once the size of a program grows large enough, however, it becomes necessary to break it up into multiple files. This results in smaller files that compile more quickly and are easier to manage. In addition, dividing the program into several files facilitates the parceling out of different parts of the program to different programmers when the program is being developed by a team.

Generally, a multi-file program consists of two types of files: those that contain function definitions, and those that contain function prototypes and templates. Here is a common strategy for creating such a program:

♦ Group all specialized functions that perform similar tasks into the same file. For example, a file might be created for functions that perform mathematical operations. Another file might contain functions for user input and output.

♦ Group function `main` and all functions that play a primary role into one file.

♦ For each file that contains function definitions, create a separate header file to hold the prototypes for each function and any necessary templates.

As an example, consider a multi-file banking program that processes loans, savings accounts, and checking accounts. Figure E-1 illustrates the different files that might be used. Notice the file-naming conventions used and how the files are related.

♦ Each file that contains function definitions has a filename with a `.cpp` extension.

♦ Each `.cpp` file has a corresponding header file with the same name, but with the a `.h` file extension. The header file contains function prototypes and templates for all functions that are part of the corresponding `.cpp` file.

♦ Each `.cpp` file has an #include directive for its own header file. If the `.cpp` file contains calls to functions in another `.cpp` file, it will also have an #include directive for the header file for that function.

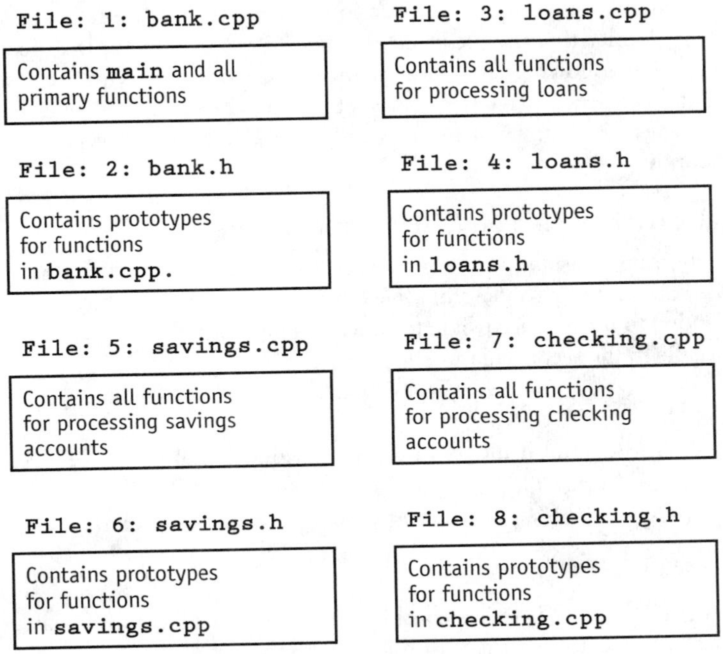

File: 1: `bank.cpp`

> Contains **main** and all
> primary functions

File: 3: `loans.cpp`

> Contains all functions
> for processing loans

File: 2: `bank.h`

> Contains prototypes
> for functions
> in **bank.cpp**.

File: 4: `loans.h`

> Contains prototypes
> for functions
> in **loans.h**

File: 5: `savings.cpp`

> Contains all functions
> for processing savings
> accounts

File: 7: `checking.cpp`

> Contains all functions
> for processing checking
> accounts

File: 6: `savings.h`

> Contains prototypes
> for functions
> in **savings.cpp**

File: 8: `checking.h`

> Contains prototypes
> for functions
> in **checking.cpp**

Figure E-1

Compiling and Linking a Multi-File Program

In a program with multiple source code files, all of the `.cpp` files are compiled into separate *object* files. The object files are then linked into a single executable file. Integrated development environments, such as those provided by Borland's C++ Builder and Microsoft Visual C++, facilitate this process by allowing you to organize a collection of source code files into a *project* and then use menu items to add files to the project. The individual source files can be compiled, and an executable program can be created, by invoking a command called MAKE or BUILD on the project menu.

 Note: See Appendix F for instructions on creating multi-file projects in Microsoft Visual C++ 6.0, and Appendix G for instructions on creating multi-file projects in Borland C++ Builder 5.

If you are using a command line compiler, such as gcc, you can compile all source files and create an executable by passing the names of the source files to the compiler as command line arguments.

```
g++ -o bankprog bank.cpp loans.cpp checking.cpp savings.cpp
```

This command will compile the four source code files and link them into an executable called `bankprog`. Notice that the file listed after the `-o` is the name of the file where the executable will be placed. The following `.cpp` files are the source code files, with the first one listed being the file that contains the `main` function. Notice that the `.h` header files do not need to be listed because the contents of each one will automatically be added to the program when it is #included by the corresponding `.cpp` file.

Global Variables in a Multi-File Program

Normally, global variables can only be accessed in the file in which they are defined. For this reason, they are said to have *file scope*. However, the scope of a global variable defined in one file can be extended to make it accessible to functions in another file by placing an `extern` declaration of the variable in the second file, as shown here.

```
extern int accountNum;
```

The `extern` declaration does not define another variable; it just permits access to a variable defined in some other file.

Only true variables, not constant variables, should be declared to be `extern`.

```
const int maxCustomers = 35;        // Don't declare this as extern.
```

This is because some compilers compile certain types of constant variables right into the code and do not allocate space for them in memory, thereby making it impossible to access the constant variable from another file. So how can functions in one file be allowed to use the value of a variable defined in another file while ensuring that they do not alter its value? The solution is to use the `const` key word in conjunction with the `extern` declaration. Thus the variable is defined in the original file, as shown here:

```
string nameOfBank = "First Federal Savings Bank";
```

In the other file that will be allowed to access that variable, the `const` key word is placed on the `extern` declaration, as shown here:

```
extern const string nameOfBank;
```

If you want to protect a global variable from any use outside the file in which it is defined, you can declare the variable to be `static`. This limits its scope to the file in which it is defined and hides its name from other files:

```
static float balance;
```

Figure E-2 shows some global variable declarations in the example banking program. The variables `customer` and `accountNum` are defined in `bank.cpp`. Since they are not declared to be `static` variables, their scope is extended to `loans.cpp`, `savings.cpp`, and `checking.cpp`, the three files that contain an `extern` declaration of these variables. Even though the variables are defined in `bank.cpp`, they may be accessed by any function in the three other files.

bank.cpp

```
#include "bank.h"
#include "loans.h"
#include "savings.h"
#include "checking.h"
...
      (other #include
      directives)

char customer[35];
int accountNum;

int main()
{
...
}
function1()
{
...
}
function2()
{
...
}
```

loans.cpp

```
#include "loans.h"
...
      (other #include
      directives)

extern char customer[];
extern int accountNum;
static float loanAmount;
static int months;
static float interest;
static float payment;

 function3()
 {
...
 }
 function4()
 {
...
 }
```

checking.cpp

```
#include "checking.h"
...
      (other #include
      directives)

extern char customer[];
extern int accountNum;
static float balance;
static float checkAmnt;
static float deposit;

function5()
{
...
}
function6()
{
...
}
```

savings.cpp

```
#include "savings.h"
...
      (other #include
      directives)

extern char customer[];
extern int accountNum;
static float balance;
static int interest;
static float deposit;
static float withdrawl;

function7()
{
...
}
function8()
{
...
}
```

Figure E-2

Figure E-2 includes examples of static global variables. These variables may not be accessed outside the file they are defined in. The variable `interest`, for example, is defined as a static global in both `loans.cpp` and `savings.cpp`. This means each of these two files has its own variable named `interest`, which is not accessible outside the file it is defined in. The same is true of the variables `balance` and `deposit`, defined in `savings.cpp` and `checking.cpp`.

In our example, the variable `customer` is defined to be an array of characters. It could have been defined to be a `string` object, but it was made a C-string instead to illustrate how an `extern` declaration handles arrays. Notice that in `bank.cpp`, the array is defined with a size declarator

```
char customer[35];
```

but in the `extern` declarations found in the other files, it is referenced as

```
extern char customer[];
```

In a one-dimensional array, the size of the array is normally omitted from the `extern` declaration. In a multidimensional array, the size of the first dimension is usually omitted. For example, the two-dimensional array defined in one file as

```
int myArray[20][30];
```

would be made accessible to other files by placing the following declaration in them.

```
extern  int myArray[][30];
```

Object-Oriented Multi-File Programs

When creating object-oriented programs that define classes and create objects of those classes, it is common to store class declarations and member function definitions in separate files. Typically, program components are stored in the following fashion.

- ◆ **The class declaration**—The class declaration is stored in its own header file, which is called the *class specification file*. The name of the specification file is usually the same as the class, with a `.h` extension.

- ◆ **Member function definitions**—The member function definitions for the class are stored in a separate `.cpp` file, which is called the *class implementation file*. This file, which must #include the class specification file, usually has the same name as the class, with a `.cpp` extension.

- ◆ **Client functions that use the class**—Any files containing functions that create and use class objects should also #include the class specification file. They must then be linked with the compiled class implementation file.

These components are illustrated in the following example, which creates and uses an `Address` class. Notice how a single program is broken up into separate files. The `.cpp` files making up the program can be separately compiled and then linked to create the executable program.

```
//**************************************************************************
// contents of address.h
// This is the specification file that contains the class declaration.
//**************************************************************************

#include <string>
using namespace std;

class Address
{private:
    string name;
    string street;
    string city;

 public:
    Address(string name, string street, string city);
    Address( );
    void print();
};

//**************************************************************************
// contents of address.cpp
// This is the implementation file that contains the function definitions
// for the class member functions.
//**************************************************************************

#include "address.h"
#include <iostream>

Address::Address(string name_in, string street_in, string city_in)
{
    name = name_in;
    street = street_in;
    city = city_in;
}

Address::Address()
{
    name = street = city = "";
}

void Address::print()
{
    cout << name   << endl
         << street << endl
         << city   << endl;
}
```

```
//****************************************************************************
// contents of userfile.cpp
// This file contains the client code that uses the Address class.
//****************************************************************************

#include "address.h"

int main( )
{
    //Create an address and print it.
    Address addr("John Doe", "123 Main Street", "Hometown, USA");
    addr.print();

    // Other code could go here.
    return 0;
}
```

For additional information on creating multi-file programs using Microsoft Visual C++ 6.0 and Borland Builder 5, see Appendices F and G.

Appendix F
Introduction to
Microsoft Visual C++ 6.0

This appendix serves as a quick reference for performing the following operations using the Microsoft Visual C++ integrated development environment (IDE):

- ◆ Starting a new project and entering code
- ◆ Saving a project to disk
- ◆ Compiling and executing a project
- ◆ Opening an existing project
- ◆ Creating multi-file projects

Starting a New Project

The first step in creating a program with Visual C++ is to start a *project*. A project is a group of one or more files that make up a software application. (Even if your program consists of no more than a single source code file, it still must belong to a project.)

To start a project:

1. Launch Microsoft Visual C++. The IDE window opens, as shown in Figure F-1.

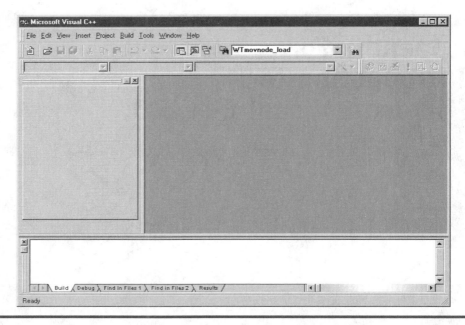

Figure F-1

2. Click **File** on the menu bar. On the File menu, click **New**. You see the dialog box shown in Figure F-2.

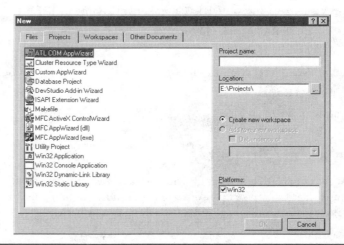

Figure F-2

3. All of the programs in this book are console programs, so click **WIN32 Console Application** in the list of project types.

4. Enter the name of the project (such as lab6, or program5) in the Project name text box. (Do not enter an extension.)

5. The Location text box should list the name of a folder. The folder will have the same name as your project. This is where Visual C++ will store all the files associated with this project. The dialog box should now appear similar to Figure F-3.

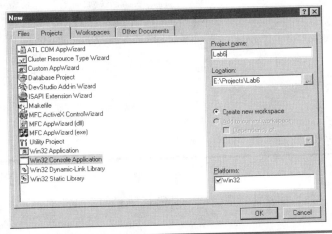

Figure F-3

6. Click the **OK** button. You now see the dialog shown in Figure F-4.

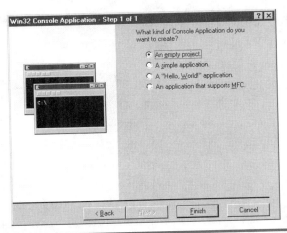

Figure F-4

7. Make sure **"An empty project"** is selected and click the **Finish** button. You see the dialog box shown in Figure F-5.

Figure F-5

8. Click the **OK** button. You return to the IDE, as shown in Figure F-6.

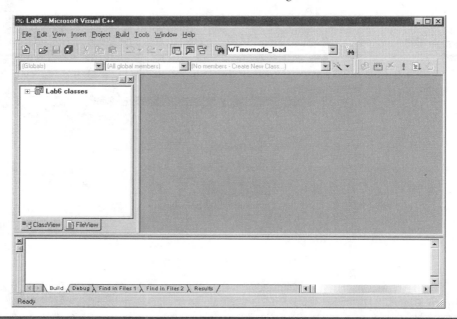

Figure F-6

9. Now you must insert a new C++ source file into the project. Click **Project** on the menu bar. On the Project menu, click **Add to project**, then click **New...** You see the dialog box shown in Figure F-7.

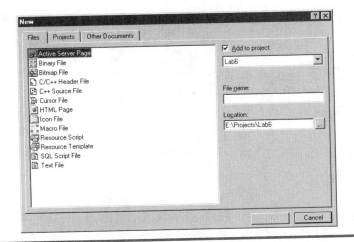

Figure F-7

10. In the list of file types, click **C++ Source File**.

11. In the File name text box, enter the name of the source file. (This can be the same as the project name, if you wish.) Be sure to type the .cpp extension. Your screen should look similar to Figure F-8.

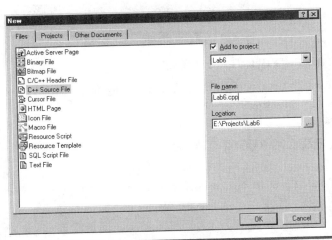

Figure F-8

12. Click the **OK** button. You will return to the IDE. The right pane is now a text editor. This is where you type your C++ source code, as shown in Figure F-9.

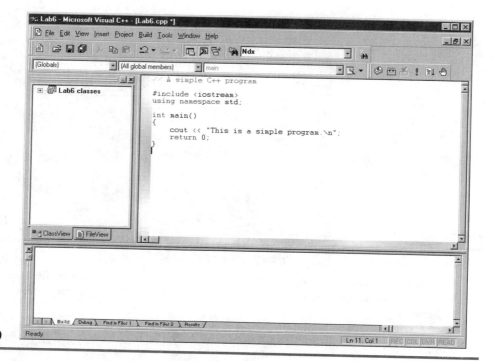

Figure F-9

Saving Your Project to Disk

It is important to periodically save your work. To do so, click **File** on the menu bar, then click **Save Workspace** on the File menu.

Opening an Existing Project

To open an existing project, click **File** on the menu bar, then click on **Open Workspace....** Use the resulting dialog box to browse to the location of your project. When you have located your project, double-click it.

Compiling and Executing

Once you have entered a program's source code, you may compile and execute it by any of the following methods:

- By clicking the ! button
- By pressing **Ctrl+F5**
- By clicking **Build** on the menu bar, then clicking **Execute.**

The window at the bottom of the screen shows status messages as the program is compiled. Error messages are also displayed there. If you see an error message, double-click it and the editor will move the text cursor to the line of code where the error was encountered.

For example, look at the program in Figure F-10. The first `cout` statement is missing a semi-colon. When the error message is double-clicked, the text cursor moves to the line with the error. (Actually, in this case the cursor appears on the line after the statement with the missing semicolon. The compiler did not detect that the semicolon was missing until it encountered the beginning of the next line. Finding errors is not always straightforward.)

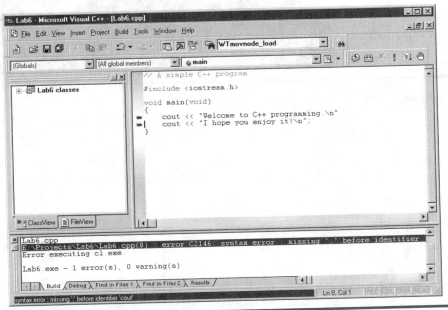

Figure F-10

If the program compiles successfully, an MS-DOS window appears and the program runs. This is illustrated in Figure F-11.

Creating a Multi-File Project

Many of your programs consist of more than one file. For example, consider the following program:

```
// Filename: RectData.cpp
// This program uses multiple files
#include <iostream>
#include "rectang.h"  // contains Rectangle class declaration
using namespace std;
```

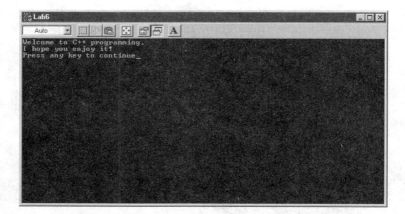

Figure F-11

```
// Don't forget to link this program with rectang.cpp!
int main()
{
    Rectangle box;
    float wide, long;

    cout << "This program will calculate the area of a\n";
    cout << "rectangle. What is the width? ";
    cin >> wide;
    cout << "What is the length? ";
    cin >> long;
    box.setData(Wide, Long);
    box.calcArea();
    cout << "Here rectangle's data:\n";
    cout << "Width: " << box.getWidth() << endl;
    cout << "Length: " << box.getLength() << endl;
    cout << "Area: " << box.getArea() << endl;
    return 0;
}
```

This program relies on two other files: `rectang.h` and `rectang.cpp`. Before this program can be compiled, `rectang.h` and `rectang.cpp` must be added to the project. The following steps show you how to set the project up with all three of the existing files as members.

1. Start a new project by following steps 1 through 8 under the section *Starting a New Project*, at the beginning of this appendix. Name the project `RectData`.

2. Insert the main C++ source file into the project. Click **Project** on the menu bar. On the Project menu, click **Add to project**, then click **Files….** You see the **Insert Files into Project** dialog box. Use the dialog box to find the file `RectData.cpp` on the student disk. When you locate the file, click it and then click the **OK** button. The file `RectData.cpp` is now a member of the project.

3. Now insert the `rectang.cpp` source file into the project. Click **Project** on the menu bar. On the Project menu, click **Add to project**, then click **Files…**. Again, you see the **Insert Files into Project** dialog box. Use the dialog box to find the file `rectang.cpp` on the student disk. When you locate the file, click it and then click the **OK** button. The file `rectang.cpp` is now a member of the project.

4. Now insert the `rectang.h` header file into the project. Click **Project** on the menu bar. On the Project menu, click **Add to project**, then click **Files…**. As before, you see the **Insert Files into Project** dialog box. Use the dialog box to find the file `rectang.h` on the student disk. When you locate the file, click it and then click the **OK** button. The file `rectang.h` is now a member of the project.

5. At this point, `RectData.cpp`, `rectang.cpp`, and `rectang.h` are members of the project. The left pane of the IDE, which is called the *workspace window*, is shown in Figure F-12. This window allows you to navigate among all the files in the project.

Figure F-12

The two tabs at the bottom of the workspace window allow you to switch between Class View and File View. Click on the **File View** tab. You should see a display similar to Figure F-13.

Figure F-13

6. Click the small + sign that appears next to `RectData` files. The display expands, as shown in Figure F-14, to show folders labeled Source Files, Header Files, and Resource Files. These folders organize the names of the files that are members of the project.

Figure F-14

7. Notice that the Source Files and Header Files folders have small + signs next to them. This indicates the folders hold filenames. Click on the small + sign next to the Source Files and Header Files folders. The filenames `RectData.cpp`, `rectang.cpp`, and `rectang.h` are listed, as shown in Figure F-15.

Figure F-15

8. Double-click on the name `RectData.cpp`. The file is displayed in the editor. (You may display any of the files in the editor by double-clicking its name.)
9. You may compile and execute the project by following the steps listed under the section *Compiling and Executing.*

Creating a New Multi-File Project

If you are creating a new multi-file project (not from existing files), follow steps 1 through 12 under the section *Starting a New Project.* Type the code for the main source file into the editor. When you are ready to create another source file (such as a header file for a class declaration, or a .cpp file to contain class member function definitions), follow these steps.

1. Click **Project** on the menu bar, click **Add to project**, then click **New**.
2. In the New dialog box, click **C++ Source File** if you are creating a new .cpp file, or **C/C++ Header File** if you are creating a new header file.
3. In the File name text box, enter the name of the file. Be sure to include the proper extension.
4. Click the **OK** button. You will return to the text editor. Enter the code for the new file.
5. Repeat the steps above for each new file you wish to add to the project.

Removing a File from a Project

To remove a file from a project, simply select the file's name in the project browser window and press the **Delete** key. This operation removes the file from the project, but does not delete it from the disk.

Project Directories

When you create a project, Visual C++ allows you to specify a directory as a location for saving your project files. Within the directory that you specify, Visual C++ will create a folder with the same name as your project, and will save your files there. This folder, which we call the *project directory*, will hold the source files for your project, along with other files that Visual C++ creates to help it keep track of your project files. For example, if you specify the location `cscprogs` and the name of your project is `project1`, then the project directory created by Visual C++ will be

```
cscprogs\project1
```

Within this project directory, Visual C++ will create yet another folder, named `Debug`, and will store your executable code in there. The executable code has the same name as the project, but has a `.exe` extension.

When you execute your program from within the development environment, the program will look for input files in the project directory unless a full pathname is given. Similarly, output files created by the program will be stored in the project directory unless a full pathname is specified. To avoid having to specify full pathnames of files, you should store input files in the project directory before you run your program.

For example, to have your program open a file named `myfile.dat`, you simply write

```
fstream inFile("myfile.dat", ios::in);
```

if the file is stored in the project directory. If the file is in a directory `A:\mydata` on the floppy drive A:, however, you must write

```
fstream inFile("A:\\mydata\\myfile.dat", ios::in);
```

Doubling up on the backspace character \ is only necessary if the file name is being hard-coded into your program. If the file name is being entered in at the keyboard at the program's request, just type in

```
A:\mydata\myfile.dat
```

in response to the program prompt.

Once the project executable has been created, it is possible to exit the Visual C++ environment, change directory to the `Debug` folder, and execute the program from the MSDOS command line. When you execute the program this way, the program expects files whose full pathnames are not given to be in the *current directory*. The current directory is the directory from which you give the command to run the program at the DOS command line: It is usually the directory containing the executable code. If you plan to execute program this way, you should store your input files in the same directory as the program executable.

Correcting the `getline` bug

The `getline` function in Microsoft Visual C++ 6.0 does not work correctly. The source code responsible for the error is in the ⟨string⟩ include file, and can be corrected after you have installed Visual C++ on your system. You only need to apply the correction once each time you install or reinstall Visual C++.

To apply the fix, carefully follow these steps:

1. Start up Visual C++, select **File** from the menu, then **New…**, and then from the resulting New dialog box, select the **Files** tab.

2. Select **C++ Source Files** and then click **OK**. You should now be in an edit window editing an empty file.

3. At the top of the edit window, type the include directive

   ```
   #include <string>
   ```

   and then using the mouse, right click on the word `string` in that directive. A pop up menu appears: select the option *Open Document* ⟨*string*⟩.

4. You now need to find the line of code that has to be fixed. This is best done using the Find command in the Edit menu. Select **Edit** on the main menu, then **Find**. In the resulting dialog box, carefully type in the phrase

   ```
   _Tr::eq((
   ```

   in the Find What text box and then click **OK**.

5. You should see the block of code

   ```
   else if (_Tr::eq((_E)_C, _D))
           {_Chg = true;
           _I.rdbuf()->snextc();
           break; }
   ```

   Modify it to

   ```
   else if (_Tr::eq((_E)_C, _D))
           {_Chg = true;
               //_I.rdbuf()->snextc();
               //(comment the bad code out)
           _I.rdbuf()->sbumpc();
           break; }
   ```

then save and close the ⟨string⟩ header file. Close the other file that you were editing that contains the #include ⟨string⟩ directive.

The `getline` function should now work correctly.

Appendix G
Introduction to Borland C++ Builder 5.0

This appendix serves as a quick reference for performing the following operations using the Borland C++ Builder integrated development environment (IDE):

◆ Starting a new project and entering code

◆ Saving a project to disk

◆ Compiling and executing a project

◆ Opening an existing project

◆ Creating multi-file projects

Starting a New Project

The first step in creating a program with Borland C++ Builder is to start a *project*. A project is a group of one or more files that make up a software application. (Even if your program consists of no more than a single source code file, it still must belong to a project.)

To start a project:

1. Launch Borland C++ Builder. The IDE windows open on the desktop, similar to what is shown in Figure G-1.

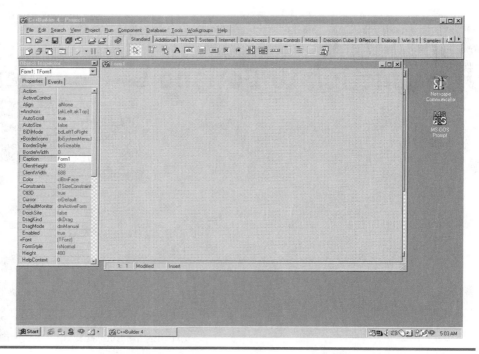

Figure G-1

2. When C++ Builder starts, it automatically begins an empty project. This project is usually named Project1. This project is not set up properly for the programs in this book, however, so you will begin a new project. Click **File** on the menu bar. On the File menu, click **New**. You see the dialog box shown in Figure G-2. (Make sure the **New** tab is selected.)

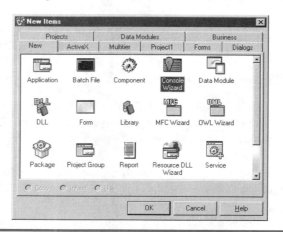

Figure G-2

3. All of the programs in this book are console programs, so click **Console Wizard,** then click the **OK** button. The dialog box shown in Figure G-3 is displayed.

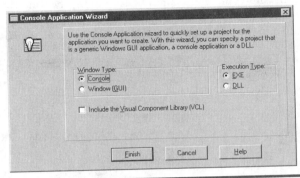

Figure G-3

4. Make sure **Console** is selected under Window Type, and **EXE** is selected under Execution Type. Click the **Finish** button. A dialog box appears asking "Save changes to Project1?" (The name you see may be different from Project1.) Since the default project is empty, click the **No** button. Your screen now looks similar to Figure G-4.

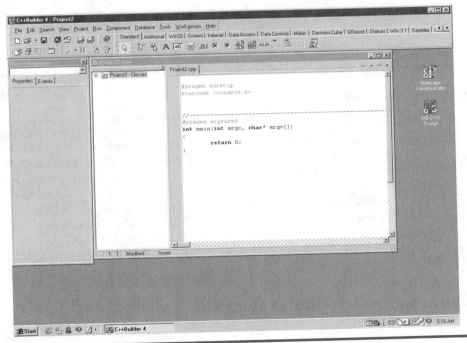

Figure G-4

5. The right-most pane in the window shown in Figure G-4 is the text editor. C++ Builder automatically creates a program skeleton for you. The skeleton contains some preprocessor directives and an empty function main. You can modify the code skeleton, or erase it and write your own program form scratch. For example, Figure G-5 shows a simple program that has been written in the editor after the default program skeleton has been erased.

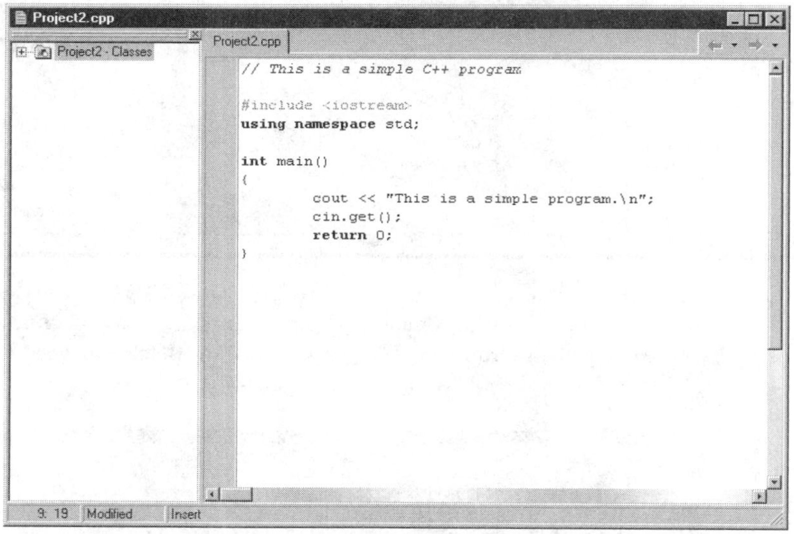

Figure G-5

Saving Your Project to Disk

It is important to periodically save your work. To save your project for the first time, click **File** on the menu bar, and then click **Save Project As...** on the File menu. A **Save As** dialog box appears for the C++ source file. The source file's default name is Unit1.cpp. Click the **OK** button if you want to keep this name. If you wish to save the source file under a different name, enter the new name and click the **OK** button. Next, a Save As dialog box appears for the project file. A default name, such as Project2.bpr, will appear as the project file's name. Click the **OK** button if you want to keep this name. If you wish to save the project file under a different name, enter the new name and click the **OK** button.

After you have saved the project the first time, you may save it subsequent times by clicking **File** on the menu bar, then clicking **Save All**.

Opening an Existing Project

To open an existing project, click **File** on the menu bar, then click on **Open Project....** Use the resulting dialog box to browse to the location of your project. When you have located your project, double-click it.

Compiling and Executing

Once you have entered a program's source code, you may compile and execute it by any of the following methods:

- By clicking the button
- By pressing **F9**
- By clicking **Run** on the menu bar, and then clicking **Run**

A window at the bottom of the editor pane appears if errors are found in your program. Double-click an error message in the window, and the editor will highlight the line of code where the error was encountered.

For example, look at the program in Figure G-6. The cout statement is missing a semicolon. When you double-click the error message, the text cursor moves to the line with the error. (Actually, in this case the cursor appears on the line after the statement with the missing semicolon. The compiler did not detect that the semicolon was missing until it encountered the beginning of the next line. Finding errors is not always straightforward.)

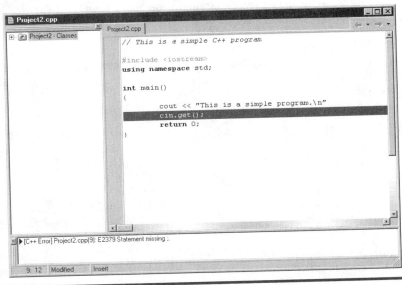

Figure G-6

If the program compiles successfully, an MS-DOS window appears and the program runs. This is illustrated in Figure G-7.

> **Note:** The program shown in Figure G-6 has a cin.get() statement as the last statement in the program. The statement causes the program to pause until the user presses the Enter key. The statement is in the program because the

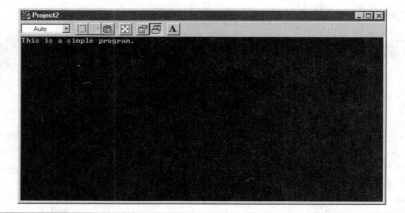

Figure G-7

MS-DOS window automatically closes as soon as the program is finished. If the program did not have the `cin.get()` statement, it would quickly flash the message "This is a simple program" on the screen, and the MS-DOS window would suddenly close.

Sometimes a single `cin.get()` statement will not pause the screen. (This is because a previous `cin` statement has left a newline character in the keyboard buffer.) A better way of pausing the screen is to include the `conio.h` header file, and use the `getch()` function at the end of the program. This is demonstrated in the next example.

Creating a Multi-File Project

Many of your programs consist of more than one file. For example, consider the following program:

```cpp
// This program demonstrates a simple class
#include <condefs.h>          // For Borland Console Applications
#include <conio.h>            // For the getch() function
#include <iostream>
#include "rectang.h"          // Contains Rectangle class declaration
using namespace std;

// Don't forget to link this program with rectang.cpp!

int main()
{
    Rectangle box;
    float wide, long;

    cout << "This program will calculate the area of a\n";
    cout << "rectangle. What is the width? ";
    cin >> wide;
```

```
cout << "What is the length? ";
cin >> long;
box.setData(wide, long);
box.calcArea();
cout << "Here rectangle's data:\n";
cout << "Width: " << box.getWidth() << endl;
cout << "Length: " << box.getLength() << endl;
cout << "Area: " << box.getArea() << endl;
getch();
return 0;
}
```

Note: Include the Borland header file `condefs.h` when creating multi-file console programs.

This program relies on two other files: `rectang.h` and `rectang.cpp`. Before this program can be compiled, `rectang.cpp` must be added to the project. The following steps show you how to set up the project.

1. Start a new project by following steps 1 through 5 under the section *Starting a New Project*, at the beginning of this appendix.

2. Enter the `main` C++ source code into the text editor. Your editor window will look similar to Figure G-8.

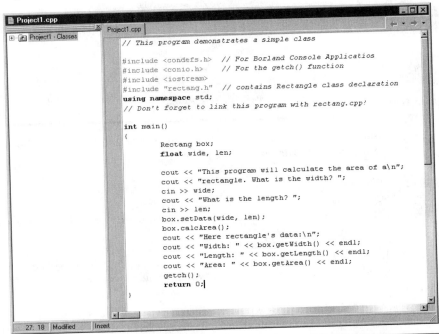

Figure G-8

3. Now insert the `rectang.cpp` source file into the project. Click **Project** on the menu bar. On the Project menu, click **Add To Project…**. The **Add to Project** dialog box. Use the dialog box to find the file `rectang.cpp` in the Chapter 13 folder. on the student disk. When you locate the file, click it and then click the **OK** button. The file `rectang.cpp` is now a member of the project. Your editor window now looks similar to Figure G-9.

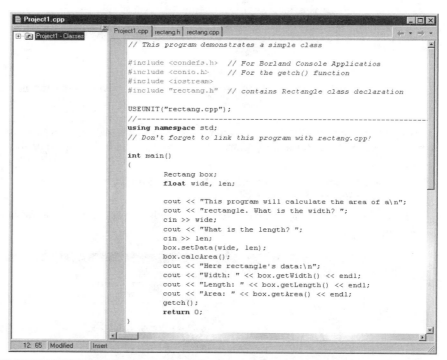

Figure G-9

 Note: Notice that C++ Builder has automatically inserted the following statement into the main source file:

```
USEUNIT("rectang.cpp");
```

The Borland IDE needs this statement to properly compile and link the `rectang.cpp` file with the main file.

4. At this point, the main source file and `rectang.cpp` are members of the project. At the top of the editor window are tabs for the two files. Click on either tab to bring the file's contents into view.

The left pane of the editor window, which is called the *Class Explorer*, is used to bring class declarations into the editor window. In Figure G-9, a folder titled Project1–Classes appears. (Your screen will look similar, but the project name may be different.) Click the small + sign to expand the view. The window looks similar to Figure G-10.

Figure G-10

5. Click the small + sign next to **Rectang**. The view expands further to show entries for all the members of the Rectangle class. Your window should be similar to Figure G-11.

Figure G-11

6. By double-clicking any of the Rectangle class's member names in the Class Explorer window, you bring the source file containing the member's declaration into the editor. For example, by double-clicking the area member, the rectang.h file is brought into the editor, as shown in Figure G-12.

```
#ifndef RECTANG_H
#define RECTANG_H

// Rectang class declaration.
class Rectang
{
        private:
                float width;
                float length;
                float area;
        public:
                void setData(float, float);
                void calcArea();
                float getWidth();
                float getLength();
                float getArea();
};

#endif
```

Figure G-12

7. You may compile and execute the project by following the steps listed under the section *Compiling and Executing*.

Removing a File from a Project

To remove a file from a project, click **Project** on the menu bar, then click **Remove from Project....** The Remove from Project dialog box appears, as shown in Figure G-13.

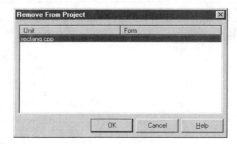

Figure G-13

Select the name of the file you wish to remove from the project and click the **OK** button. The file will be removed from the project. (It will not be erased from the disk, however.)

Project Directories

When you save your project, C++ Builder will normally save your project files in a subdirectory of the folder in which C++ Builder itself is installed. On a typical Windows installation, this will be the folder

```
Program Files\Borland\Cbuilder5\Projects.
```

Your project files include the source code, the object and executable files that result from compiling and making your program, and other files that the C++ Builder environment uses to keep track of your project. We will refer to the folder storing your project files as the *Project Directory*.

When you execute your program from within the development environment, the program will look for input files in the project directory unless a full pathname is given. Similarly, output files created by the program will be stored in the project directory unless a full pathname is specified. To avoid having to specify full pathnames of files, you should store input files in the project directory before you run your program.

For example, to have your program open a file named `myfile.dat`, you simply write

```
fstream inFile("myfile.dat", ios::in);
```

if the file is stored in the project directory, whereas if the file is in a directory `A:\mydata` on the floppy drive A:, you must write

```
fstream inFile("A:\\mydata\\myfile.dat", ios::in);
```

Doubling up on the backspace character \ is only necessary if the file name is being hard-coded into your program as shown above. If the file name is being entered in at the keyboard at the program's request, just type in

```
A:\mydata\myfile.dat
```

in response to the program prompt.

Appendix H
The Binary Number System and Bitwise Operations

One of the many powers that C++ gives the programmer is the ability to work with the individual bits of an integer field. The purpose of this appendix is to give an overview of how integer types are stored in binary and explain the bitwise operators that the C++ offers. Finally, we will look at bit fields, which allow us to treat the individual bits of a variable as separate entities.

Integer Forms

The integer types that C++ offers are as follows:

```
char
int
short
long
unsigned char
unsigned (same as unsigned int)
unsigned short
unsigned long
```

When you assign constant values to integers in C++, you may use decimal, octal, or hexadecimal. Placing a zero in the first digit creates an octal constant. For example, 0377 would be interpreted as an octal number. Hexadecimal constants are created by placing 0x or 0X (zero-x, not O-x) in front of the number. The number 0X4B would be interpreted as a hex number.

Binary Representation

Regardless of how you express constants, integer values are all stored the same way internally—in binary format. Let's take a quick review of binary number representation.

Let's assume we have a one-byte field. The diagram below shows our field broken into its individual bits.

Bit	Bit	Bit	Bit	Bit	Bit	Bit	Bit
7	6	5	4	3	2	1	0

High Order ------------------------> Low Order

The leftmost bits are called the *high order* bits and the rightmost bits are called the *low order* bits. Bit number 7 is the highest order bit, so it is called the *most significant* bit.

Each of these bits has a value assigned to it. The diagram below shows the values of each bit:

	Bit	Bit	Bit	Bit	Bit	Bit	Bit	Bit
	7	6	5	4	3	2	1	0
Values ->	128	64	32	16	8	4	2	1

These values are actually powers of two. The value of bit 0 is 2^0, which is 1. The value of bit 1 is 2^1, which is 2. Bit 2 has the value 2^2, which is 4. It progresses to the last bit.

When a number is stored in this field, the bits may be set to either 1 or 0. Here is an example.

	Bit	Bit	Bit	Bit	Bit	Bit	Bit	Bit
	7	6	5	4	3	2	1	0
	0	1	1	0	0	1	1	0
Values ->	128	64	32	16	8	4	2	1

Here, bits 1, 2, 5, and 6 are set to 1. To calculate the overall value of this bit pattern, we add up all of the bit values of the bits that are set to 1.

Bit 1's value	2
Bit 2's value	4
Bit 5's value	32
Bit 6's value	64
Overall Value	102

The bit pattern 01100110 has the decimal value 102.

Negative Integer Values

One way that a computer can store a negative integer is to use the leftmost bit as a sign bit. When this bit is set to 1, it would indicate a negative number, and when it is set to 0 the number would be positive. The problem with this, however, is that we would have two bit patterns for the number 0. One pattern would be for positive 0, the other would be for negative 0. Because of this, most systems use two's complement representation for negative integers.

To calculate the two's compliment of a number, first you must get the one's compliment. This means changing each 1 to a 0, and each 0 to a 1. Next, add 1 to the resulting number. What you have is the two's compliment. Here is how the computer stores the value –2.

2 is stored as	00000010
Get the one's compliment	11111101
Add 1	1
And the result is	11111110

As you can see, the highest order bit is still set to 1, indicating not only that this is a negative number, but it is stored in two's compliment representation.

Bitwise Operators

C++ provides operators that let you perform logical operations on the individual bits of integer values, and shift the bits right or left.

The Bitwise Negation Operator

The bitwise negation operator is the ~ symbol. It is a unary operator that performs a negation, or one's compliment on each bit in the field. The expression

```
~val
```

returns the one's compliment of `val`. It does not change contents of `val`. It could be used in the following manner:

```
negval = ~val;
```

This will store the one's compliment of `val` in `negval`.

The Bitwise AND Operator

The bitwise AND operator is the & symbol. This operator performs a logical AND operation on each bit of two operands. This means that it compares the two operands bit by bit. For each position, if both bits are 1, the result will be 1. If either or both bits are 0, the results will be 0. Here is an example:

```
andval = val & 0377;
```

The result of the AND operation will be stored in `andval`. There is a combined assignment version of this operator. Here is an example:

```
val &= 0377;
```

This is the same as

```
val = val & 0377;
```

The Bitwise OR Operator

The bitwise OR operator is the | symbol. This operator performs a logical OR operation on each bit of two operands. This means that it compares the two operands bit by bit. For each position, if either of the two bits is 1, the result will be 1. Otherwise, the results will be 0. Here is an example:

```
orval = val | 0377;
```

The result of the OR operation will be stored in `orval`. There is a combined assignment version of this operator. Here is an example:

```
val |= 0377;
```

This is the same as

```
val = val | 0377;
```

The Bitwise EXCLUSIVE OR Operator

The bitwise EXCLUSIVE OR operator is the ^ symbol. This operator performs a logical XOR operation on each bit of two operands. This means that it compares the two operands bit by bit. For each position, if one of the two bits is 1, but not both, the result will be 1. Otherwise, the results will be 0. Here is an example:

```
xorval = val ^ 0377;
```

The result of the XOR operation will be stored in `xorval`. There is a combined assignment version of this operator. Here is an example:

```
val ^= 0377;
```

This is the same as

```
val = val ^ 0377;
```

Using Bitwise Operators with Masks

Suppose we have the following variable declarations:

```
char value = 110, cloak = 2;
```

The binary pattern for each of these two variables will be as follows:

| value --> | 0 | 1 | 1 | 0 | 1 | 1 | 1 | 0 | = 110 |
| cloak --> | 0 | 0 | 0 | 0 | 0 | 0 | 1 | 0 | = 2 |

The operation

```
value &= cloak;
```

will perform a logical bitwise AND on the two variables `value` and `cloak`. The result will be stored in `value`. Remember a bitwise AND will produce a 1 only when both bits are set to 1. Here is a diagram showing the result of the AND operation.

value -->	0	1	1	0	1	1	1	0

AND

cloak -->	0	0	0	0	0	0	1	0

equals

result -->	0	0	0	0	0	0	1	0

The 0's in the `cloak` variable "hide" the values that are in the corresponding positions of the `value` variable. This is called *masking*. When you mask a variable, the only bits that will "show through" are the ones that correspond with the 1's in the mask. All others will be turned off.

Turning Bits On

Sometimes you may want to turn on selected bits in a variable and leave all of the rest alone. This operation can be performed with the bitwise OR operator. Let's see what happens when we OR the `value` and `cloak` variables we used before, but using a different value for cloak.

```
char value = 110, cloak = 16;
value |= mask;
```

This diagram illustrates the result of the OR operation:

value -->	0	1	1	0	1	1	1	0

OR

cloak -->	0	0	0	1	0	0	0	0

equals

result -->	0	1	1	1	1	1	1	0

This caused bit 4 to be turned on and all the rest to be left alone.

Turning Bits Off

Suppose that instead of turning specific bits on, you wish to turn them off. Assume we have the following declaration:

```
char status = 127, cloak = 8;
```

Bit 3 of `cloak` is set to 1, and all the rest are set to 0. If we wish to set bit 3 of status to 0 we must AND it with the negation of `cloak`. In other words, we must get the one's compliment of `cloak`, then AND it with `status`. The statement would look like this:

```
status &= ~cloak;
```

Here is what `cloak`'s bit pattern looks like:

cloak --> | 0 | 0 | 0 | 0 | 1 | 0 | 0 | 0 |
| --- | --- | --- | --- | --- | --- | --- | --- |

And here is the one's compliment of `cloak`:

~cloak --> | 1 | 1 | 1 | 1 | 0 | 1 | 1 | 1 |
| --- | --- | --- | --- | --- | --- | --- | --- |

Here is what we get when we AND status and the one's compliment of `cloak`:

status --> | 0 | 1 | 1 | 1 | 1 | 1 | 1 | 1 |
| --- | --- | --- | --- | --- | --- | --- | --- |

AND

~cloak --> | 1 | 1 | 1 | 1 | 0 | 1 | 1 | 1 |
| --- | --- | --- | --- | --- | --- | --- | --- |

equals

result --> | 0 | 1 | 1 | 1 | 0 | 1 | 1 | 1 |
| --- | --- | --- | --- | --- | --- | --- | --- |

Bit 3 of status is turned off, and all other bits were left unchanged.

Toggling Bits

To toggle a bit is to flip it off when it is on, and on when it is off. This can be done with the EXCLUSIVE OR operator. We will use the following variables to illustrate.

```
char status = 127, cloak = 8;
```

Our objective is to toggle bit 3 of `status`, so we will use the XOR operator.

```
status ^= cloak;
```

Here is the diagram of the operation:

status --> | 0 | 1 | 1 | 1 | 1 | 1 | 1 | 1 |
| --- | --- | --- | --- | --- | --- | --- | --- |

XOR

cloak -->

0	0	0	0	1	0	0	0

equals

result -->

0	1	1	1	0	1	1	1

Bit 3 of `status` will be set to 0. If we repeat this operation with the new value of `status`, this is what will happen:

status -->

0	1	1	1	0	1	1	1

XOR

cloak -->

0	0	0	0	1	0	0	0

equals

result -->

0	1	1	1	1	1	1	1

Bit 3 of `status` will be toggled again, restoring it to its previous state.

Testing the Value of a Bit

To test the value of an individual bit, you must use the AND operator. For example, if we want to test the variable `bitvar` to see if bit 2 is on, we must use a mask that has bit 2 turned on. Here is an example of the test:

```
if ((bitvar & 4) == 4)
    cout << "Bit 2 is on.\n";
```

Remember that ANDing a value with a mask will produce a value that hides all of the bits but the ones turned on in the mask. If bit 2 of `bitvar` is on, the expression `bitvar & 4` will return the value 4.

The parentheses around `bitvar & 4` are necessary because the `==` operator has higher precedence than the `&` operator.

The Bitwise Left Shift Operator

The bitwise left shift operator is two less-than signs (`<<`). It takes two operands. The operand on the left is the one to be shifted, and the operand on the right is the number of places to shift. When the bit values are shifted left, the vacated positions to the right are filled with 0 and the bits that shift out of the field are lost. Suppose we have the following variables:

```
char sand = 2, shiftsand;
```

The following statement will store in `shiftsand` the value of `sand` shifted left two places.

```
shiftsand = sand << 2;
```

Let's see what is happening behind the scenes with the value in `sands`

Before shift	0	0	0	0	0	0	1	0
After shift	0	0	0	0	1	0	0	0

Realize, however that `sand` itself is not being shifted. The variable `shiftsand` is being set to the value of `sand` shifted left two places. If we wanted to shift `sand` itself, we could use the combined assignment version of the left shift operator.

```
sand <<= 2;
```

Shifting a number left by n places is the same as multiplying it by 2^n. So the example above is the same as

```
sand *= 4;
```

The bitwise shift will almost always work faster, however.

The Bitwise Right Shift Operator

The bitwise right shift operator is two greater-than signs ($>>$). Like the left shift operator, it takes two operands. The operand on the left is the one to be shifted, and the operand on the right is the number of places to shift. When the bit values are shifted right, and the variable is signed, what the vacated positions to the left are filled with depends on the machine. They could be filled with 0 or with the value of the sign bit. If the variable is unsigned, the places will be filled with 0. The bits that shift out of the field are lost.

Suppose we have the following variables:

```
char sand = 8, shiftsand;
```

The following statement will store in `shiftsand` the value of `sand` shifted right two places.

```
shiftsand = sand >> 2;
```

Let's see what is happening behind the scenes with the value in `sand`.

Before shift	0	0	0	0	1	0	0	0
After shift	0	0	0	0	0	0	1	0

As before, sand itself is not being shifted. The variable shiftsand is being set to the value of sand shifted right two places. If we wanted to shift sand itself, we could use the combined assignment version of the right shift operator.

```
sand >>= 2;
```

Shifting a number right by n places is the same as dividing it by 2^n (as long as the number is not negative). So, the example is the same as

```
sand /= 4;
```

The bitwise shift will almost always work faster, however.

Bit Fields

C++ allows you to create data structures that use bits as individual variables. Bit fields must be declared as part of a structure. Here is an example.

```
struct {
    unsigned field1 : 1;
    unsigned field2 : 1;
    unsigned field3 : 1;
    unsigned field4 : 1;
    } fourbits;
```

The variable fourbits contains four bit fields: field1, field2, field3, and field4. Following the colon after each name is a number that tells how many bits each field should be made up of. In this example, each field is 1 bit in size. This structure is stored in memory in a regular unsigned int. Since we are only using four bits, the remaining ones will go unused.

Values may be assigned to the fields just as if it were a regular structure. In this example, we assign the value 1 to the field1 member:

```
fourbits.field1 = 1;
```

Since these fields are only 1 bit in size, we can only put a 1 or a 0 in them. We can expand the capacity of bit fields by making them larger, as in the following example:

```
struct {
    unsigned field1 : 1;
    unsigned field2 : 2;
    unsigned field3 : 3;
    unsigned field4 : 4;
    } mybits;
```

Here, mybits.field1 is only 1 bit in size, but others are larger. mybits.field2 occupies 2 bits, mybits.field3 occupies 3 bits, and mybits.field4 occupies 4 bits. Here is a table that shows the maximum values of each field:

Field Name	Number of Bits	Maximum Value
mybits.field1	1	1
mybits.field2	2	3
mybits.field3	3	7
mybits.field4	4	15

This data structure uses a total of 10 bits. If you create a bit field structure that uses more bits than will fit in an int, the next int sized area will be used. Suppose we declare the following bit field structure on a system that has 16 bit integers.

```
struct {
    unsigned tiny    : 1;
    unsigned small   : 4;
    unsigned big     : 6;
    unsigned bigger  : 8;
    unsigned biggest : 9;
} flags;
```

The problem that occurs here is that flags.bigger will straddle the boundary between the first and second integer area. The compiler won't allow this to happen. flags.tiny, flags.small, and flags.big will occupy the first integer area, and flags.bigger will reside in the second integer area. There will be five unused bits in the first. Likewise, since flags.bigger and flags.biggest cannot fit within one integer area, flags.biggest will reside in a third area. There will be eight unused bits in the second area, and seven unused bits in the third.

You can force a field to be aligned with the next integer area by putting an unnamed bit field with a length of 0 before it. Here is an example:

```
struct {
    unsigned first  : 1;
                    : 0;
    unsigned second : 1;
                    : 0;
    unsigned third  : 2;
} scattered;
```

The unnamed fields with the 0 width force scattered.second and scattered.third to be aligned with the next int area.

You can create unnamed fields with lengths other than 0. This way you can force gaps to exist at certain places. Here is an example.

```
struct {
    unsigned first  : 1;
                    : 2;
    unsigned second : 1;
                    : 3;
    unsigned third  : 2;
} gaps;
```

This will cause a 2-bit gap to come between `gaps.first` and `gaps.second`, and a 3-bit gap to come between `gaps.second` and `gaps.third`.

Bit fields are not very portable when the physical order of the fields and the exact location of the boundaries are used. Some machines order the bit fields from left to right, but others order them from right to left.

Appendix I
Passing Command Line Arguments

If you are working in a command line environment, such Unix, Linux, or the MS-DOS prompt, it might be helpful to write programs that take arguments from the command line. For example, suppose we have a program called sum, which takes two numbers as command line arguments and displays their sum. We could enter the following command at the operating system prompt:

```
sum 12 16
```

The arguments, which are separated by a space, are 12 and 16. Since a C++ program starts its execution with function main, command line arguments are passed to main. Function main can be optionally written with two special parameters. These parameters are traditionally named argc and argv. The argc parameter is an int, and the argv parameter is an array of char pointers. Here is an example function header for main, using these two parameters:

```
void main(int argc, char *argv[])
```

The argc parameter contains the number of items that were typed on the command line, including the name of the program. For example, if the sum program is executed with the command sum 12 16, the argc parameter will contain 3.

As previously mentioned, the argv parameter is an array of char pointers. In the function header, the brackets are empty because argv is an external array of unknown size. The number that is stored in argc, however, will be the number of elements in the argv array. Each pointer in the argv array points to a C-string holding a command line argument. Once again, assume the sum program is executed with the command sum 12 16. The elements of the argv array will reference the items on the command line in the following manner:

```
argv[0] = "sum"
argv[1] = "12"
argv[2] = "16"
```

Before we look at the code for the sum program, let's look at Program I-1. It is a simple program that displays its command line arguments. (The program is named argdemo.)

Program I-1   (argdemo.cpp)

```cpp
// This program demonstrates how to read
// command line arguments.

#include <iostream>

int main(int argc, char *argv[])
{
    cout << "You entered " << (argc - 1)
    cout << " command line arguments.\n";
    if (argc > 1)
    {
        cout << "Here they are:\n";
        for (int count = 1; count < argc; count++)
            cout << argv[count] << endl;
    }
    return 0;
}
```

Example Session on a Unix System

```
$ argdemo Hello World [Enter]
You entered 2 command line arguments.
Here they are:
Hello
World
$
```

Now let's look at the code for the sum program.

Program I-2   (sum.cpp)

```cpp
// This program takes two command line arguments,
// assumed to be numbers, and displays their sum.

#include <iostream>
#include <cstdlib>// Needed for atof

int main(int argc, char *argv[])
{
    double total = 0;

    if (argc > 1)
    {
        for (int count = 1; count < argc; count++)
            total += atof(argv[count]);
        cout << total << endl;
    }
    return 0;
}
```

Example Session on a Unix System

```
$ sum 12 16 [Enter]
28
$ sum 1 2 3 4 5 [Enter]
15
$
```

Appendix J
Header File and Library Function Reference

This appendix provides a reference for the C++ library functions discussed in the book. The following table gives an alphabetical list of functions. Tables of functions that are organized by their header files follow it.

Alphabetical Listing of Selected Library Functions

Function	Details
abs(m)	**Header File:** cstdlib **Description:** Accepts an integer argument. Returns the absolute value of the argument as an integer. **Example:** a = abs(m);
atof(str)	**Header File:** cstdlib **Description:** Accepts a C-string as an argument. The function converts the string to a double and returns that value. **Example:** num = atof("3.14159");
atoi(str)	**Header File:** cstdlib **Description:** Accepts a C-string as an argument. The function converts the string to an int and returns that value. **Example:** num = atoi("4569");
atol(str)	**Header File:** cstdlib **Description:** Accepts a C-string as an argument. The function converts the string to a long and returns that value. **Example:** num = atol("5000000");

(table continues)

Alphabetical Listing of Selected Library Functions *(continued)*

Function	Details
`cos(m)`	***Header File:*** `cmath` ***Description:*** Accepts a `double` argument. Returns the cosine of the argument. The argument should be an angle expressed in radians. The return type is `double`. ***Example:*** `a = cos(m);`
`exit(status)`	***Header File:*** `cstdlib` ***Description:*** Accepts an `int` argument. Terminates the program and passes the value of the argument to the operating system. ***Example:*** `exit(0);`
`exp(m)`	***Header File:*** `cmath` ***Description:*** Accepts a `double` argument. Computes the exponential function of the argument, which is e^x. The return type is `double`. ***Example:*** `a = exp(m);`
`fmod(m, n)`	***Header File:*** `cmath` ***Description:*** Accepts two `double` arguments. Returns, as a `double`, the remainder of the first argument divided by the second argument. Works like the modulus operator, but the arguments are doubles. (The modulus operator only works with integers.) Take care not to pass zero as the second argument. Doing so would cause division by zero. ***Example:*** `a = fmod(m, n);`

`isalnum(ch)`	***Header File:*** `cctype`
	Description:
	Accepts a `char` argument. Returns `true` if the argument is a letter of the alphabet or a digit. Otherwise, it returns `false`.
	Example:
	`if (isalnum(ch))`
	`    cout << ch << " is alphanumeric.\n";`

`isdigit(ch)`	***Header File:*** `cctype`
	Description:
	Accepts a `char` argument. Returns `true` if the argument is a digit from 0 to 9. Otherwise, it returns `false`.
	Example:
	`if (isdigit(ch))`
	`    cout << ch << " is a digit.\n";`

(table continues)

Alphabetical Listing of Selected Library Functions *(continued)*

Function	Details

islower(ch)	**Header File:** cctype
	Description:
	Accepts a char argument. Returns true if the argument is a lowercase letter. Otherwise, it returns false.
	Example:
	`if (islower(ch))`
	`    cout << ch << " is lowercase.\n";`

isprint(ch)	**Header File:** cctype
	Description:
	Accepts a char argument. Returns true if the argument is a printable character (including a space). Returns false otherwise.
	Example:
	`if (isprint(ch))`
	`    cout << ch << " is printable.\n";`

ispunct(ch)	**Header File:** cctype
	Description:
	Accepts a char argument. Returns true if the argument is a printable character other than a digit, letter, or space. Returns false otherwise.
	Example:
	`if (ispunct(ch))`
	`    cout << ch << " is punctuation.\n";`

isspace(ch)	**Header File:** cctype
	Description:
	Accepts a char argument. Returns true if the argument is a whitespace character. Whitespace characters are any of the following:
	• space.................' '
	• newline..............'\n'
	• tab...................'\t'
	• vertical tab.........'\v'
	Otherwise, it returns false.
	Example:
	`if (isspace(ch))`
	`    cout << ch << " is whitespace.\n";`

isupper(ch)	**Header File:** cctype
	Description:
	Accepts a char argument. Returns true if the argument is an uppercase letter. Otherwise, it returns false.
	Example:
	`if (isupper(ch))`
	`    cout << ch << " is uppercase.\n";`

(table continues)

Alphabetical Listing of Selected Library Functions *(continued)*

Function	Details
`log(m)`	***Header File:*** `cmath` ***Description:*** Accepts a `double` argument. Returns, as a `double`, the natural logarithm of the argument. ***Example:*** `a = log(m);`
`log10(m)`	***Header File:*** `cmath` ***Description:*** Accepts a `double` argument. Returns, as a `double`, the base-10 logarithm of the argument. ***Example:*** `a = log10(m);`
`pow(m, n)`	***Header File:*** `cmath` ***Description:*** Accepts two `double` arguments. Returns the value of its first argument raised to the power of the second argument. ***Example:*** `a = pow(m, n);`
`rand()`	***Header File:*** `cstdlib` ***Description:*** Generates a pseudorandom number. ***Example:*** `x = rand();`
`sin(m)`	***Header File:*** `cmath` ***Description:*** Accepts a `double` argument. Returns, as a `double`, the sine of the argument. The argument should be an angle expressed in radians. ***Example:*** `a = sin(m);`
`sqrt(m)`	***Header File:*** `cmath` ***Description:*** Accepts a `double` argument. Returns, as a `double`, the square root of the argument. ***Example:*** `a = sqrt(m);`

(table continues)

Alphabetical Listing of Selected Library Functions *(continued)*

Function	Details
`srand(m)`	**Header File:** `cstdlib` **Description:** Accepts an `unsigned int` argument. The argument is used as a seed value to randomize the results of the `rand()` function. **Example:** `srand(m);`
`strcat(str1, str2)`	**Header File:** `cstring` **Description:** Accepts two C-strings as arguments. The function appends the contents of the second string to the first string. (The first string is altered; the second string is left unchanged.) **Example:** `strcat(string1, string2);`

`strcmp(str1, str2)`	**Header File:** `cstring`
	Description:
	Accepts pointers to two string arguments. If `str1` and `str2` are the same, this function returns 0. If `str2` is alphabetically greater than `str1`, it returns a positive number. If `str2` is alphabetically less than `str1`, it returns a negative number.
	Example:
	`if (strcmp(str1, str2) == 0)`
	`    cout << "The strings are equal.\n";`

`strcpy(str1, str2)`	**Header File:** `cstring` **Description:** Accepts two C-strings as arguments. The function copies the second string to the first string. The second string is left unchanged. **Example:** `strcpy(string1, string2);`
`strlen(str)`	**Header File:** `cstring` **Description:** Accepts a C-string as an argument. Returns the length of the string (not including the null terminator) **Example:** `len = strlen(name);`

(table continues)

Alphabetical Listing of Selected Library Functions *(continued)*

Function	Details
strncpy(str1, str2, n)	***Header File:*** cstring ***Description:*** Accepts two C-strings and an integer argument. The third argument, an integer, indicates how many characters to copy from the second string to the first string. If str2 has fewer than n characters, str1 is padded with '\0' characters. ***Example:*** strncpy(string1, string2, n);
strstr(str1, str2)	***Header File:*** cstring ***Description:*** Searches for the first occurrence of str2 in str1. If an occurrence of str2 is found, the function returns a pointer to it. Otherwise, it returns a null pointer (address 0). ***Example:*** cout << strstr(string1, string2);
tan(m)	***Header File:*** cmath ***Description:*** Accepts a double argument. Returns, as a double, the tangent of the argument. The argument should be an angle expressed in radians. ***Example:*** a = tan(m);
tolower(ch)	***Header File:*** cctype ***Description:*** Accepts a char argument. Returns the lowercase equivalent of its argument. ***Example:*** ch = tolower(ch);
toupper(ch)	***Header File:*** cctype.h ***Description:*** Accepts a char argument. Returns the uppercase equivalent of its argument. ***Example:*** ch = toupper(ch);

Selected `cstdlib` functions

Function	Details
`atof(str)`	**Header File:** `cstdlib` **Description:** Accepts a C-string as an argument. The function converts the string to a `double` and returns that value. **Example:** `num = atof("3.14159");`
`atoi(str)`	**Header File:** `cstdlib` **Description:** Accepts a C-string as an argument. The function converts the string to an `int` and returns that value. **Example:** `num = atoi("4569");`
`atol(str)`	**Header File:** `cstdlib` **Description:** Accepts a C-string as an argument. The function converts the string to a `long` and returns that value. **Example:** `num = atol("5000000");`
`exit(status)`	**Header File:** `cstdlib` **Description:** Accepts an `int` argument. Terminates the program and passes the value of the argument to the operating system. **Example:** `exit(0);`
`rand()`	**Header File:** `cstdlib` **Description:** Generates a pseudorandom number. **Example:** `x = rand();`
`srand(m)`	**Header File:** `cstdlib` **Description:** Accepts an `unsigned int` argument. The argument is used as a seed value to randomize the results of the `rand()` function. **Example:** `srand(m);`

Selected cmath **Functions**

Function	Details
abs(m)	**Header File:** cmath **Description:** Accepts an integer argument. Returns the absolute value of the argument as an integer. **Example:** a = abs(m);
cos(m)	**Header File:** cmath **Description:** Accepts a double argument. Returns the cosine of the argument. The argument should be an angle expressed in radians. The return type is double. **Example:** a = cos(m);
exp(m)	**Header File:** cmath **Description:** Accepts a double argument. Computes the exponential function of the argument, which is e^x. The return type is double. **Example:** a = exp(m);
fmod(m, n)	**Header File:** cmath **Description:** Accepts two double arguments. Returns, as a double, the remainder of the first argument divided by the second argument. Works like the modulus operator, but the arguments are doubles. (The modulus operator only works with integers.) Take care not to pass zero as the second argument. Doing so would cause division by zero. **Example:** a = fmod(m, n);
log(m)	**Header File:** cmath **Description:** Accepts a double argument. Returns, as a double, the natural logarithm of the argument. **Example:** a = log(m);

(table continues)

Selected cmath **Functions** *(continued)*

Function	Details
log10(m)	**Header File:** cmath **Description:** Accepts a double argument. Returns, as a double, the base-10 logarithm of the argument. **Example:** a = log10(m);
pow(m, n)	**Header File:** cmath **Description:** Accepts two double arguments. Returns the value of its first argument raised to the power of the second argument. **Example:** a = pow(m, n);
sin(m)	**Header File:** cmath **Description:** Accepts a double argument. Returns, as a double, the sine of the argument. The argument should be an angle expressed in radians. **Example:** a = sin(m);
sqrt(m)	**Header File:** cmath **Description:** Accepts a double argument. Returns, as a double, the square root of the argument. **Example:** a = sqrt(m);
tan(m)	**Header File:** cmath **Description:** Accepts a double argument. Returns, as a double, the tangent of the argument. The argument should be an angle expressed in radians. **Example:** a = tan(m);

Selected `cstring` **Functions**

Function	Details
`strcat(str1, str2)`	***Header File:*** `cstring` ***Description:*** Accepts two C-strings as arguments. The function appends the contents of the second string to the first string. (The first string is altered; the second string is left unchanged.) ***Example:*** `strcat(string1, string2);`

`strcmp(str1, str2)`	***Header File:*** `cstring`
	 Description:
	 Accepts pointers to two string arguments. If `str1` and `str2` are the same, this function returns 0. If `str2` is alphabetically greater than `str1`, it returns a positive number. If `str2` is alphabetically less than `str1`, it returns a negative number.
	 Example:
	 `if (strcmp(string1, string2) == 0)`
	 `    cout << "The strings are equal.\n";`

`strcpy(str1, str2)`	***Header File:*** `cstring` ***Description:*** Accepts two C-strings as arguments. The function copies the second string to the first string. The second string is left unchanged. ***Example:*** `strcpy(string1, string2);`
`strlen(str)`	***Header File:*** `cstring` ***Description:*** Accepts a C-string as an argument. Returns the length of the string (not including the null terminator) ***Example:*** `len = strlen(name);`
`strncpy(str1, str2, n)`	***Header File:*** `cstring` ***Description:*** Accepts two C-strings and an integer argument. The third argument, an integer, indicates how many characters to copy from the second string to the first string. If `str2` has fewer than n characters, `str1` is padded with '\0' characters. ***Example:*** `strncpy(string1, string2, n);`

(table continues)

Selected `cstring` Functions *(continued)*

Function	Details
`strstr(str1, str2)`	***Header File:*** `cstring` ***Description:*** Searches for the first occurrence of `str2` in `str1`. If an occurrence of `str2` is found, the function returns a pointer to it. Otherwise, it returns a NULL pointer (address 0). ***Example:*** `cout << strstr(string1, string2);`

Selected `cctype` Functions and Macros

Function	Details

`isalnum(ch)`	***Header File:*** `cctype`
	Description:
	Accepts a char argument. Returns `true` if the argument is a letter of the alphabet or a digit. Otherwise, it returns `false`.
	Example:
	`if (isalnum(ch))`
	`    cout << ch << " is alphanumeric.\n";`

`isdigit(ch)`	***Header File:*** `cctype`
	Description:
	Accepts a char argument. Returns `true` if the argument is a digit from 0 to 9. Otherwise, it returns `false`.
	Example:
	`if (isdigit(ch))`
	`    cout << ch << " is a digit.\n";`

`islower(ch)`	***Header File:*** `cctype`
	Description:
	Accepts a char argument. Returns `true` if the argument is a lowercase letter. Otherwise, it returns `false`.
	Example:
	`if (islower(ch))`
	`    cout << ch << " is lowercase.\n";`

`isprint(ch)`	***Header File:*** `cctype`
	Description:
	Accepts a char argument. Returns `true` if the argument is a printable character (including a space). Returns `false` otherwise.
	Example:
	`if (isprint(ch))`
	`    cout << ch << " is printable.\n";`

(table continues)

Selected cctype **Functions and Macros** *(continued)*

Function	Details

ispunct(ch)	**Header File:** cctype
	Description:
	Accepts a char argument. Returns true if the argument is a printable character other than a digit, letter, or space. Returns false otherwise.
	Example:
	`if (ispunct(ch))`
	`    cout << ch << " is punctuation.\n";`

isspace(ch)	**Header File:** cctype
	Description:
	Accepts a char argument. Returns true if the argument is a whitespace character. Whitespace characters are any of the following:
	• space................ ' '
	• newline............. '\n'
	• tab................. '\t'
	• vertical tab........ '\v'
	Otherwise, it returns false.
	Example:
	`if (isspace(ch))`
	`    cout << ch << " is whitespace.\n";`

isupper(ch)	**Header File:** cctype
	Description:
	Accepts a char argument. Returns true if the argument is an uppercase letter. Otherwise, it returns false.
	Example:
	`if (isupper(ch))`
	`    cout << ch << " is uppercase.\n";`

tolower(ch)	**Header File:** cctype **Description:** Accepts a char argument. Returns the lowercase equivalent of its argument. **Example:** `ch = tolower(ch);`
toupper(ch)	**Header File:** cctype **Description:** Accepts a char argument. Returns the uppercase equivalent of its argument. **Example:** `ch = toupper(ch);`

Appendix K
Answers to Checkpoints

Chapter 1

1.1 Because the computer can be programmed to do so many different tasks

1.2 The central processing unit (CPU), main memory, secondary storage devices, input devices, and output devices

1.3 Arithmetic and logic unit (ALU) and control unit

1.4 Fetch: The CPU's control unit fetches the program's next instruction from main memory.
Decode: The control unit decodes the instruction, which is encoded in the form of a number. An electrical signal is generated.
Execute: The signal is routed to the appropriate component of the computer, which causes a device to perform an operation.

1.5 A unique number assigned to each section of memory

1.6 Program instructions and data are stored in main memory while the program is operating. Main memory is volatile and loses its contents when power is removed from the computer. Secondary storage holds data for long periods of time—even when there is no power to the computer.

1.7 Operating systems and application software

1.8 A single tasking operating system is capable of running only one program at a time. All the computer's resources are devoted to the program that is running. A multitasking operating system is capable of running multiple programs at once. A multitasking system divides the allocation of the hardware resources among the running programs using a technique known as time sharing.

1.9 A single user system allows only one user to operate the computer at a time. A multiuser system allows several users to operate the computer at once.

1.10 A set of well-defined steps for performing a task or solving a problem

1.11 To ease the task of programming. Programs may be written in a programming language, then converted to machine language.

1.12 A low-level language is close to the level of the computer and resembles the system's numeric machine language. A high-level language is closer to the level of human readability and resembles natural languages.

1.13 That a program may be written on one type of computer and run on another type

1.14 The preprocessor reads the source file searching for commands that begin with the # symbol. These are commands that cause the preprocessor to modify the source file in some way. The compiler translates each source code instruction into the appropriate machine language instruction, and creates an object file. The linker combines the object file with necessary library routines.

1.15 Source file: Contains program statements written by the programmer.

Object file: Machine language instructions, generated by the compiler translated from the source file.

Executable file: Code ready to run on the computer. Includes the machine language from an object file, and the necessary code from library routines.

1.16 A programming environment that includes a text editor, compiler, debugger, and other utilities, integrated into one package

1.17 A key word has a special purpose and is defined as part of a programming language. A programmer-definedsymbol is a word or name defined by the programmer.

1.18 Operators perform operations on one or more operands. Punctuation symbols mark the beginning or ending of a statement, or separates items in a list.

1.19 A line is a single line as it appears in the body of a program. A statement is a complete instruction that causes the computer to perform an action.

1.20 Because their contents may be changed

1.21 The original value is overwritten.

1.22 The variable must be defined in a declaration.

1.23 Input, processing, and output

1.24 The program's purpose, information to be input, the processing to take place, and the desired output.

1.25 To imagine what the computer screen looks like while the program is running. This helps define input and output.

1.26 A chart that depicts each logical step of the program in a hierarchical fashion

1.27 Yes. In this stage, errors and necessary changes are sometimes found.

1.28 The programmer steps through each statement in the program from beginning to end. The contents of variables are recorded, and screen output is sketched.

1.29 It translates each source code statement into the appropriate machine language statement.

1.30 A logical error that occurs while the program is running

1.31 By the compiler

1.32 To determine if a logical error is present in the program

1.33 Procedural programs are made of procedures or functions. Object-oriented programs are centered on objects, which contain both data and the procedures that operate on the data.

Chapter 2

2.1
```
// A crazy mixed up program
#include <iostream>
using namespace std;
```

```cpp
int main()
{
    cout << "In 1492 Columbus sailed the ocean blue.";
    return 0;
}
```

2.2
```cpp
// Today's Date: March 31, 2003
#include <iostream>
using namespace std;

int main()
{
    cout << "Teresa Jones";
    return 0;
}
```

2.3   B

2.4   A

2.5
```cpp
// It's a mad, mad program
#include <iostream>
using namespace std;

int main()
{
    cout << "Success\n";
    cout << "Success";
    cout << " Success\n\n";
    cout << "Sucess\n";
    return 0;
}
```

2.6   The works of Wolfgang
include the following:
The Turkish March
and Symphony No. 40 in G minor.

2.7
```cpp
// Today's Date: March 31, 2003
#include <iostream>
using namespace std;

int main()
{
    cout << "Teresa Jones\n";
    cout << "127 West 423rd Street\n";
    cout << "San Antonio, TX  78204\n";
    cout << "555-475-1212\n";
    return 0;
}
```

2.8   Variables: little and big
Constants: 2, 2000, "The little number is ", "The big number is"

2.9   The value is number

2.10   `99bottles`: Variable names cannot begin with a number.

`r&d`: Variable names may only use alphabetic letters, digits, or underscores.

2.11   No. Variable names are case sensitive.

2.12   A)   `short` or `unsigned short`

B)   `int`

C)   They both use the same amount of memory.

2.13   They both use the same amount of memory.

2.14   67, 70, 87

2.15   'B'

2.16   'Q' uses 1 byte

"Q" uses 2 bytes

"Sales" uses 6 bytes

'\n' uses 1 byte

2.17
```cpp
#include <iostream>
using namespace std;

int main()
{
    char first, middle, last;
    first = 'T';
    middle = 'E';
    last = 'G';
    cout << first << " " << middle << " " << last << endl;
    return 0;
}
```

2.18   The string constant "Z" is being stored in the character variable `letter`.

2.19   `string`

2.20
```cpp
// Substitute your name, address, and phone
// number for those shown in this program.
#include <iostream>
#include <string>
using namespace std;

int main()
{
    string name, address, phone;
    name = "George Davis";
    address = "179 Ravenwood Lane";
    phone = "555-6767";
    cout << name << endl;
    cout << address << endl;
    cout << phone << endl;
    return 0;
}
```

2.21   6.31E17

2.22
```cpp
#include <iostream>
using namespace std;

int main()
{
    int age;
    float weight;

    age = 26;
    weight = 180;
    cout << "My age is " << age << "and my weight is " << weight;
    cout << endl;
    return 0;
}
```

2.23   Invalid. The value on the left of the = operator must be an `lvalue`.

2.24   `int apples = 20;`

2.25
```cpp
int x = 7,
    y = 16,
    z = 28;
```

2.26   The variable `critter` is assigned a value before it is declared. Correct the program by moving the statement `critter = 62.7;` to the point after the variable declaration. Here is the corrected program:

```cpp
#include <iostream>
using namespace std;

int main()
{
    float critter;
    critter = 62.7;
    cout << critter << endl;
    return 0;
}
```

2.27   Integer division. The value 23 will be stored in `portion`.

Chapter 3

3.1   `iostream`

3.2   The stream extraction operator

3.3   The console (or keyboard)

3.4   True

3.5   B

3.6   `cin >> miles >> feet >> inches;`

3.7   Include one or more `cout` statements explaining what values the user should enter.

3.8
```
#include <iostream>
using namespace std;

int main()
{
    float pounds, kilograms;

    cout << "Enter your weight in pounds: ";
    cin >> pounds;
    // The following line does the conversion.
    // One kilogram weighs 2.21 pounds.
    kilograms = pounds / 2.21;
    cout << "Your weight in kilograms is ";
    cout << kilograms << endl;
    return 0;
}
```

3.9   A) *

     B) same

     C) same

3.10   *Value*

21

2

31

5

24

2

69

0

30

3.11
```
y = 6 * x;

a = 2 * b + 4 * c;

y = x * x;   or   y = pow(x, 2);

g = (x + 2) / (z * z);   or   g = (x + 2) / pow(z, 2);

y = (x * x) / (z * z);   or   y = pow(x, 2) / pow (z, 2);
```

3.12   *If the user enters...*   *The program displays...*

       2   6

       5   27

     4.3   20.49

       6   38

3.13
```
#include <iostream>
#include <cmath>
using namespace std;

int main()
{
    double volume, radius, height;
    cout << "This program will tell you the volume of\n";
```

```
    cout << "a cylinder-shaped fuel tank.\n";
    cout << "How tall is the tank? ";
    cin >> height;
    cout << "What is the radius of the tank? ";
    cin >> radius;
    volume = 3.14159 * pow(radius, 2.0) * height;
    cout << "The volume of the tank is " << volume << endl;
    return 0;
}
```

3.14   A)   2

        B)   17.0

        C)   2.0

        D)   2.4

        E)   2.4

        F)   2.4

        G)   4

        H)   27

        I)   30

        J)   27.0

3.15
```cpp
#include <iostream>
using namespace std;

int main()
{
    char letter;

    cout << "Enter a character: ";
    cin >> letter;
    cout << "The ASCII code for " << letter;
    cout << " is " << int(letter) << endl;
    return 0;
}
```

3.16   9
       9.5
       9

3.17
```cpp
const float e = 2.71828;
const float yearSecs = 5.26e5;
const float gf = 32.2;
const float gm = 9.8;
const int metersPerMile = 1609;
```

3.18
```cpp
#define E 2.71828
#define YEARSECS 5.26e5
#define GF 32.2
#define GM 9.8
#define METERSPERMILE 1609
```

3.19   This program calculates the number of candy pieces sold.
       How many jars of candy have you sold?
       6[Enter]
       The number of pieces sold: 11160
       Candy pieces you get for commission: 2232

3.20   ```cpp
       #include <iostream>
       using namespace std;

       int main()
       {
               const float conversion = 1.467;
               float milesPerHour, feetPerSecond;

               cout << "This program converts miles-per-hour to\n";
               cout << "feet-per-second.\n";
               cout << "Enter a speed in MPH: ";
               cin >> milesPerHour;
               feetPerSecond = MilesPerhour * conversion;
               cout << "That is " << feetPerSecond
                   << " feet-per-second.\n";
               return 0;
       }
       ```

3.21   total = subtotal = tax = shipping = 0;

3.22   A) x += 6;

       B) amount -= 4;

       C) y *= 4;

       D) total /= 27;

       E) x %= 7;

       F) x += (y * 5);

       G) total -= (discount * 4);

       H) increase *= (salesRep * 5);

       I) profit /= (shares - 1000);

3.23   3
       11
       1

3.24

       A) cout << fixed
                << setprecision(2);
          cout << setw(9) << 34.789;
       B) cout << fixed << showpoint
                << setprecision(3);
          cout << setw(5) << 7.0;
       C) cout << fixed << 5.789e12;
       D) cout << left << setw(7) <<67;

3.25   ```cpp
       #include <iostream>
       #include <iomanip>
       using namespace std;
       ```

```
int main()
{
    const float pi = 3.14159;
    float degrees, radians;
    cout << "Enter an angle in degrees and I will convert it\n";
    cout << "to radians for you: ";
    cin >> degrees;
    radians = degrees * pi / 180;
    cout << degrees << " degrees is equal to ";
    cout << fixed << showpoint << setprecision(4);
    cout << left << setw(5) << radians << "radians.\n ";
    return 0;
}
```

3.26   No. Space is needed for a fifth character, to hold the null terminator.

3.27   A)   Legal (Though no embedded blanks can be input)

      B)   Illegal (This works for C-strings only)

      C)   Legal

      D)   Legal

3.28   A)   Legal (Though no embedded blanks can be input)

      B)   Legal

      C)   Legal

      D)   Illegal (Arrays cannot be assigned to)

3.29   `x = sin(angle1) + cos(angle2);`

3.30   `y = pow(x, 0.2);   // 0.2 is equal to 1/5`

3.31   `y = 1 / sin(a);`

3.32   `fstream`

3.33   `ifstream` objects can only be used to read from file into memory. `ofstream` objects can only be used to write from memory to a file.

3.34   The `open` statement

3.35   C

Chapter 4

4.1   T, T, T, T, T, T, T

4.2   A)   Incorrect

      B)   Incorrect

      C)   Correct

4.3   A)   Yes

      B)   No

      C)   No

4.4   0
0
1
0

4.5   True

4.6   False

4.7   A) The `if` statement is terminated with a semicolon.

          B) The = operator is used instead of the == operator.

          C) Only the first statement after the `if` statement is conditionally executed. The first three statements after the `if` statement should be enclosed in a set of braces.

4.8
```
if (y == 20)
    x = 0;
```

4.9
```
if (hours > 40)
    payRate *= 1.5;
```

4.10
```
if (sales >= 10000.00)
    commission = .20;
```

4.11
```
if (max)
    fees = 50;
```

4.12   False

4.13
```
if (y == 100)
    x = 1;
else
    x = 0;
```

4.14
```
if (sales >= 50000.00)
    commission = 0.20;
else
    commission = 0.10;
```

4.15
```cpp
#include <iostream>
using namespace std;

int main()
{
    float taxRate, saleAmount;
    char residence;

    cout << "Enter the amount of the sale: ";
    cin >> saleAmount;
    cout << "Enter I for in-state residence or O for out-of-\n";
    cout "state: ";
    cin.get(residence);
    if (residence == 'O')
        taxRate = 0;
    else
        taxRate = 0.05;
    saleAmount += saleAmount * taxRate;
    cout << "The total is " << saleAmount;
    return 0;
}
```

4.16
```cpp
// This program uses an if/else if statement to assign a
// letter grade (A, B, C, D, or F) to a numeric test score.
// A trailing else has been added to catch test scores > 100.

#include <iostream>
using namespace std;

int main()
{
    int testScore;

    cout << "Enter your test score and I will tell you\n";
    cout << "the letter grade you earned: ";
    cin >> testScore;
    if (testScore < 0)
    {
        cout << testScore << " is an invalid score.\n";
        cout << "Please enter scores greater than 0.\n";
    }
    else if (testScore < 60)
    {
        cout << "Your grade is F.\n";
        cout << "This is a failing grade. Better see your ";
        cout << "instructor.\n";
    }
    else if (testScore < 70)
    {
        cout << "Your grade is D.\n";
        cout << "This is below average. You should get ";
        cout << "tutoring.\n";
    }
    else if (testScore < 80)
    {
        cout << "Your grade is C.\n";
        cout << "This is average.\n";
    }
    else if (testScore < 90)
    {
        cout << "Your grade is B.\n";
        cout << "This is an above average grade.\n";
    }
    else if (testScore <= 100)
    {
        cout << "Your grade is A.\n";
        cout << "This is a superior grade. Good work!\n";
    }
```

```
        else
        {
            cout << testScore << " is an invalid score.\n";
            cout << "Please enter scores no greater than 100.\n";
        }
        return 0;
    }
```

4.17 11

4.18
If the customer purchases this many books...	this many coupons are given.
1	1
2	1
3	2
4	2
5	3
10	3

4.19
```
if (amount1 > 10)
    if (amount2 < 100)
        if (amount1 > amount2)
            cout << amount1;
        else
            cout << amount2;
```

4.20

Logical Expression	Result (True or False)
TRUE && FALSE	False
TRUE && TRUE	True
FALSE && TRUE	False
FALSE && FALSE	False
TRUE || FALSE	True
TRUE || TRUE	True
FALSE || TRUE	True
FALSE || FALSE	False
!TRUE	False
!FALSE	True

4.21 T, F, T, T, T

4.22 True (&& is done before ||)

4.23 if (!activeEmployee)

4.24
```
if (speed < 0 || speed > 200)
    cout << "The number is not valid.";
```

4.25
```cpp
#include <iostream>
using namespace std;

int main()
{
    int first, second, result;

    cout << "Enter a negative integer: ";
    cin >> first;
    cout << "Now enter a positive integer: ";
    cin >> second;
    if (first >= 0 || second < 0)
    {
        cout << "The first number should be negative\n";
        cout << "and the second number should be\n";
        cout << "positive. Run the program again and\n";
        cout << "enter the correct values.\n";
    }
    else
    {
        result = first * second;
        cout << first << " times " << second << " is "
            << result << endl;
    }
    return 0;
}
```

4.26   The variables length, width, and area should be declared before they are used.

4.27
```
Enter your first test score: 40
Enter your second test score: 30
Test 1: 50
Test 2: 40
Sum   : 70
```

4.28   A) True
      B) False
      C) True
      D) False
      E) False
      F) True

4.29   A) False
      B) False
      C) True
      D) False
      E) False
      F) True
      G) False

4.30   A) `z = x > y ? 1 : 20;`
      B) `population = temp > 45 ? base * 10 : base * 2;`
      C) `wages *= hours > 40 ? 1.5 : 1;`
      D) `cout << (result >= 0 ? "The result is positive\n" :`
                             `"The result is negative.\n");`

4.31   A)
```
if (k > 90)
    j = 57;
else
    j = 12;
```
      B)
```
if (x >= 10)
    factor = y * 22;
else
    factor = y * 35;
```
      C)
```
if (count == 1)
    total += sales;
else
    total += count * sales;
```
      D)
```
if (num % 2)
    cout << "Even\n";
else
    cout << "Odd\n";
```

4.32   2 2

4.33   Because the `if`/`else` statement tests several different conditions, consisting of different variables.

4.34   The case statements must be followed by an integer constant, not a relational expression.

4.35   `That is serious.`

4.36
```
switch (userNum)
{
    case 1 : cout << "One";
            break;
    case 2 : cout << "Two";
            break;
    case 3 : cout << "Three";
            break;
    default: cout << "Enter 1, 2, or 3 please.\n";
}
```

4.37
```
switch (selection)
{
    case 1  : cout << "Pi times radius squared\n";
            break;
    case 2  : cout << "lengthtimes width\n";
            break;
```

```
        case 3  : cout << "Pi times radius squared times height\n";
                  break;
        case 4  : cout << "Well okay then, good bye!\n";
                  break;
        default : cout << "Not good with numbers, eh?\n";
    }
```

4.38   1. enum must be lowercase.

2. There should be no = sign.

3. The symbolic names in the enumeration list should not be in quotes.

4. It should end with a semicolon.

4.39
```
if (color z = yellow)
    cout "primary color \n";
else
    cout "mixed color \n";
```

Chapter 5

5.1   A) 32
       B) 33
       C) 23
       D) 34
       E) It is true!
       F) It is true!

5.2   None

5.3   Once

5.4   x is the counter, y is the accumulator.

5.5
```
#include <iostream>
using namespace std;

int main()
{
    int num = 10;

    cout << "number          number Squared\n";
    cout << "-------------------------------------------\n";
    while (num > 0)
    {
        cout << num << "\t\t" << (num * num) << endl;
        num--;
    }
    return 0;
}
```

5.6
```
// This program calculates the total number of points a
// soccer team has earned over a series of games. The user
// enters a series of point values, then a negative number
// when finished.

#include <iostream>
using namespace std;

int main()
{
    int count = 0, points = 0, total = 0;

    cout << "Enter the number of points your team has earned\n";
    cout << "so far in the season, then enter a negative number\n";
    cout << "when finished.\n";
    while (points >= 0)
    {
        count++;
        cout << "Enter the points for game " << count << ": ";
        cin >> points;
        if (points >= 0)
            total += points;
    }
    cout << "The total points are " << total << endl;
    return 0;
}
```

5.7   A) Hello World
      B) 01234
      C) 6 10 5

5.8
```
int number, total = 0;
do
{
    cout << "Enter a number: ";
    cin >> number;
    total += number;
} while (total <= 300);
```

5.9   The initialization, the test, and the update

5.10 A) 0246810
      B) -5-4-3-2-1
      C) 5
          8
          11
          14
          17

5.11
```
for (count = 0; count <= 100; count += 5)
            cout << count << endl;
```

5.12
```
int count, number, total = 0;
for (count = 0; count < 7; count++)
{
        cout << "Enter a number: ";
        cin >> number;
        total += number;
}
cout << "The total is " << total << endl;
```

5.13
```
float x, y, quotient, total = 0;
for (x = 1, y = 30; x <= 30; x++, y--)
{
        quotient = x / y;
        total += quotient;
}
cout << "The total is " << total << endl;
```

5.14   A) for
       B) do-while
       C) while
       D) while
       E) for

5.15   600 times (20 times 30)

5.16   220 times (20 times 11)

5.17   1
       3
       7
       12

5.18
```
do
{
    cout << "Enter a number in the range 10 - 25: ";
    cin >> number;
    if (number < 10 || number > 25)
        cout << "That value is out of range. Try again.\n";
} while (number < 10 || number > 25);
```

5.19
```
char letter;
do
{
    cout << "Enter y, y, N, or n: ";
    cin >> letter;
    if (letter != 'y' && letter != 'y' &&
        letter != 'N' && letter != 'n')
            cout << "That is not a valid choice. Try again.\n";
} while (letter != 'y' && letter != 'y' &&
            letter != 'N' && letter != 'n');
```

5.20
```
char response[4];
do
{
    cout << "Enter Yes or No: ";
    cin >> response;
    if (strcmp("Yes", response)!=0 && strcmp("No", response)!=0)
        cout << "That is not a valid choice. Try again.\n";
}while (strcmp("Yes", response)!=0 && strcmp("No", response)!=0);
```

Chapter 6

6.1   Function call

6.2   Function header

6.3   I saw Elba
       Able was I

6.4
```
void qualify()
{
    cout << "Congratulations, you qualify for\n";
    cout << "the loan. The annual interest rate\n";
    cout << "is 12%\n";
}

void noQualify()
{
    cout << "You do not qualify. In order to\n";
    cout << "qualify you must have worked on\n";
    cout << "your current job for at least two\n";
    cout << "years and you must earn at least\n";
    cout << "$17,000 per year.\n";
}
```

6.5   Header
       Prototype
       Function call

6.6
```
void timesTen(int number)
{
    cout << (number * 10);
}
```

6.7
```
void timesTen(int);
```

6.8
```
0        0
1        2
2        4
3        6
4        8
5        10
6        12
7        14
8        16
9        18
```

6.9
```
0 1.5
1.5 0
0 10
0 1.5
```

6.10
```
void showDollars(float amount)
{
    cout << fixed << showpoint << setprecision(2);
    cout << "Your wages are $" << amount << endl;
```

6.11   One

6.12   `float distance(float rate, float time)`

6.13   `int days(int years, int weeks, int months)`

6.14   `char getKey()`

6.15   `long lightYears(long miles)`

6.16   A static local variable's scope is limited to the function in which it is declared. A global variable's scope is the portion of the program beginning at its declaration to the end.

6.17
```
100
50
100
```

6.18
```
10
11
12
13
14
15
16
17
18
19
```

6.19   Constants

6.20   *Prototype:*
```
void compute(float, int = 5, long = 65536);
```

Header:
```
void compute(float x, int y, long z)
```

6.21   *Prototype:*
```
void calculate(long, &float, int = 47);
```

Header:
```
void calculate(long x, float &y, int z)
```

6.22
```
5 10 15
9 10 15
6 15 15
4 11 16
```

6.23   0 00
Enter two numbers: 12 14
12 140
14 15-1
14 15-1

6.24   Different parameter lists

6.25   1.2

6.26   22

6.27   30

6.28   *Function Prototype:*

```cpp
float calcArea(float, float);
```

Definition of the function:

```cpp
float calcArea(float len, float wide)
{
        return len * wide;
}
```

Chapter 7

7.1
```cpp
struct Account
{
    string acctNum;
    float acctBal;
    float intRate;
    float avgBal;
};
```

7.2
```cpp
Account savings = {"ACZ42137-B12-7",
                    4512.59,
                    0.04,
                    4217.07 };
```

7.3
```cpp
#include <iostream>
using namespace std;

struct Movie
{
    string name;
    string director;
    string producer;
    string year;
};

int main()
{
    Movie favorite;

    cout << "Enter the following information about your\n";
    cout << "favorite movie.\n";
```

```cpp
        cout << "Name: ";
        getline(cin, favorite.name);
        cout << "Director: ";
        getline(cin, favorite.director);
        cout << "Producer: ";
        getline(cin, favorite.producer);
        cout << "Year of release: ";
        getline(cin, favorite.year);
        cout << "Here is information on your favorite movie:\n";
        cout << "Name: " << favorite.name << endl;
        cout << "Director: " << favorite.director << endl;
        cout << "Producer: " << favorite.producer << endl;
        cout << "Year of release: " << favorite.year << endl;
        return 0;
    }
```

7.4
```cpp
    struct Measurement
    {
        int miles;
        long meters;
    }
```

7.5
```cpp
    struct Destination
    {
        string city;
        Measurement distance;
    };
    Destination place;
```

7.6
```cpp
    place.city = "Tupelo";
    place.distance.miles = 375;
    place.distance.meters = 603375;
```

7.7
```cpp
    void showRect(Rectangle r)
    {
        cout << r.length << endl;
        cout << r.width << endl;
    }
```

7.8
```cpp
    void getRect(Rectangle &r)
    {
        cout << "Width: ";
        cin >> r.width;
        cout << "Length: ";
        cin >> r.length;
    }
```

7.9
```cpp
    Rectangle getRect()
    {
        Rectangle r;
        cout << "Width: ";
        cin >> r.width;
        cout << "Length: ";
        cin >> r.length;
        return r;
    }
```

7.10
```
union ThreeTypes
{
    char letter;
    int whole;
    float real;
};
```

7.11   False

7.12   B

7.13   A

7.14   C

7.15
```
class Date
{
private:
    int month;
    int day;
    int year;
public:
    void setDate(int m, int d, int y)
        { month = m; day = d; year = y; }
    int getMonth()
        { return month; }
    int getDay()
        { return day; }
    int getYear()
        { return year; }
}
```

7.16   The `BasePay` class declaration would reside in `basepay.h`

The `BasePay` member function definitions would reside in `basepay.cpp`

The `Overtime` class declaration would reside in `overtime.h`

The `Overtime` member function declarations would reside in `Overtime.cpp`

7.17   The file `basepay.cpp`, which contains the `BasePay` member function definitions, should `#include "basepay.h."`

7.18   Some functions may have adverse effects if they are called at the wrong time. For example, a function might initialize member variables, or destroy a member variable's contents. To prevent a member function from being called at the wrong time, it can be made private. Then, it can only be called from another member function, which can determine if it appropriate to call the private function.

7.19   It adds the additional overhead of coding a public member function to act as an interface to the private member function.

7.20   A constructor is automatically called when the class object is created. It is useful for initializing member variables or performing setup operations.

7.21   A

7.22   A

7.23   True

7.24   `ClassAct sally(25);`

7.25   True

7.26   False

7.27   A destructor is automatically called before a class object is destroyed. It is useful for performing housekeeping operations, such as freeing memory that was allocated by the class object's member functions.

7.28   B

7.29   False

7.30   50
       50
       20

7.31   4
       7
       2
       2
       7
       4

Chapter 8

8.1   A) `int empNum[100];`
      B) `float payRate[25];`
      C) `long miles[14];`
      D) `char letter[26];`
      E) `double lightYears[1000];`

8.2   `int readings[-1];  // Size declarator cannot be negative`

      `float measurements[4.5];  // Size declarator must be an integer`

      `int size;`
      `char name[size]; // Size declarator must be a constant`

8.3   0 through 3

8.4   The size declarator is used in the array declaration statement. It specifies the number of elements in the array. A subscript is used to access an individual element in an array.

8.5   Array bounds checking is a safeguard provided by some languages. It prevents a program from using a subscript that is beyond the boundaries of an array. C++ does not perform array bounds checking.

8.6   1
      2
      3
      4
      5

8.7
```cpp
#include <iostream>
using namespace std;

int main()
{
    int fish[20], count;

    cout << "Enter the number of fish caught\n";
    cout << "by each fisherman.\n";
    for (count = 0; count < 20; count++)
    {
        cout << "fisherman " << (count+1) << ": ";
        cin >> fish[count];
    }
    return 0;
}
```

8.8
A) `int ages[10] = {5, 7, 9, 14, 15, 17, 18, 19, 21, 23};`
B) `float temps[7] = {14.7, 16.3, 18.43, 21.09, 17.9, 18.76, 26.7};`
C) `char alpha[8] = {'J', 'B', 'L', 'A', '*', '$', 'H', 'M'};`

8.9
`int numbers[10] = {0, 0, 1, 0, 0, 1, 0, 0, 1, 1};`
The definition is valid.

`int matrix[5] = {1, 2, 3, 4, 5, 6, 7};`
The definition is invalid because there are too many values in the initialization list.

`float radii[10] = {3.2, 4.7};`
The definition is valid. Elements 2-9 wll be initialized to 0.0.

`int table[7] = {2, , , 27, , 45, 39};`
The definition is invalid. Values cannot be skipped in the initialization list.

`char codes[] = {'A', 'X', '1', '2', 's'};`
The definition is valid. The codes array will be allocated space for five characters.

`int blanks[];`
The definition is invalid. An initialization list must be provided when an array is implicitly sized.

`string suit[4] = {"Clubs", "Diamonds", "Hearts", "Spades"};`
The definition above is valid.

8.10
A) 10
B) 3
C) 6
D) 14

8.11   0

8.12   10.00
        25.00
        32.50
        50.00
        110.00

8.13   1 18 18
        2 4 8
        3 27 81
        4 52 208
        5 100 500

8.14   No. An entire array cannot be copied in a single statement with the = operator. The array must be copied element by element.

8.15   The address of the array

8.16   The address of the array is passed by value, but not the array elements.

8.17   ABCDEFGH

8.18   *(The entire program is shown here.)*

```
#include <iostream>
using namespace std;

// Function prototype here
float avgArray(int [], int);

int main()
{
    int userNums[10];

    cout << "Enter 10 numbers: ";
    for (int count = 0; count < 10; count++)
    {
        cout << "#" << (count + 1) << " ";
        cin >> userNums[count];
    }
    cout << "The average of those numbers is ";
    cout << avgArray(userNums, 10) << endl;
    return 0;
}

// Function avgArray
float avgArray(int array[], size)
{
    float total = 0.0, average;
    for (int count = 0; count < size; count++)
        total += array[count];
    average = total / size;
    return average;
}
```

8.19   `int grades[30][10];`

8.20   24

8.21   `sales[0][0] = 56893.12;`

8.22   `cout << sales[5][3];`

8.23   `int settings[3][5] = {{12, 24, 32, 21, 42},`
                                   `{14, 67, 87, 65, 90},`
                                   `{19,  1, 24, 12,  8}};`

8.24

2	3	0	0
7	9	2	0
1	0	0	0

8.25
```
void displayArray7(int array[][7], int numRows)
{
    for (int row = 0; row < numRows; row ++)
    {
        for (int col = 0; col < 7; col ++)
        {   cout << array[row][col] <<" ";
        }
        cout << endl;
    }
}
```

8.26   `int vidNum[50][10][25];`

8.27   `vector`

8.28   `vector <int> frogs;`
        `vector <float> lizards(20);`
        `vector <char> toads(100, 'Z');`

8.29   `vector <int> gators;`
        `gators.push_back(27);`
        `snakes[4] = 12.897`

8.30   `Product items[100];`

8.31
```
for (int x = 0; x < 100; x++)
{
    items[x].description " ";
    items[x].partNum = 0;
    items[x].cost = 0.0;
}
```

8.32   `items[0].description = "Claw Hammer";`
        `items[0].partNum = 547;`
        `items[0].cost = 8.29;`

8.33
```
for (int x = 0; x < 100; x++)
{
    cout << items[x].description << endl;
    cout << items[x].partNum << endl;
    cout << items[x].cost  << endl << endl;
}
```

8.34   Product items[5] = { {"Screw Driver", 621, 1.72},
                            {"Socket Set", 892, 18.97},
                            {"Claw Hammer", 547, 8.29},
                            {"Adjustable Wrench", 229, 12.15},
                            {"Pliers", 114, 3.17}};

8.35   struct Measurement
       {
           int miles;
           long meters;
       };

8.36   struct Destination
       {
           string city;
           Measurement distance;
       };

8.37   Destination places [20];
       places[4].city = "Tupelo";
       places[4].distance.miles = 375;
       places[4].distance.meters = 603375;

8.38   **False**

8.39   **Fasle**

8.40   10
       20
       50

8.41   #include <iostream>
       using namespace std;

       class Yard
       {
       private:
           int length, width;
       public:
           Yard()
               { length = 0; width = 0; }
           void setLength(int len)
               { length = len; }
           void setWidth(int wide)
               { width = wide; }
           int getLength() {return length;}
           int getWidth() {return width;}
       };

       int main()
       {
           Yard lawns[10];
           cout << "Enter the length and width of "
               << "each yard.\n";

```
for (int count = 0; count < 10; count++)
{
    int input;
    cout << "Yard " << (count + 1) << ":\n";
    cout << "length: ";
    cin >> input;
    lawns[count].setLength(input);
    cout << "width: ";
    cin >> input;
    lawns[count].setWidth(input);
}
return 0;
}
```

Chapter 9

9.1   The linear search algorithm simply uses a loop to step through each element of an array, comparing each element's value with the value being searched for. The binary search algorithm, which requires the values in the array to be sorted in order, starts searching at the element in the middle of the array. If the middle element's value is greater than the value being searched for, the algorithm next tests the element in the middle of the first half of the array. If the middle element's value is less than the value being searched for, the algorithm next tests the element in the middle of the last half of the array. Each time the array tests an array element and does not find the value being searched for, it eliminates half of the remaining portion of the array. This method continues until the value is found, or there are no more elements to test. The binary search is more efficient than the linear search.

9.2   10,000

9.3   15

9.4   The items frequently searched for can be stored near the beginning of the array.

Chapter 10

10.1   `cout << &count;`

10.2   `float *fltPtr;`

10.3   Multiplication operator, pointer declaration, indirection operator

10.4   50   60   70
            500   300   140

10.5
```
for (int x = 0; x < 100; x++)
      cout << *(array + x) << endl;
```

10.6   12040

10.7   A)   Valid
        B)   Valid
        C)   Invalid. Only addition and subtraction are valid arithmetic operations with pointers.
        D)   Invalid. Only addition and subtraction are valid arithmetic operations with pointers.
        E)   Valid

10.8   A) Valid
        B) Valid
        C) Invalid. `fvar` is a float and `iptr` is a pointer to an `int`.
        D) Valid
        E) Invalid. `ivar` must be declared before `iptr`.

10.9   A) True
        B) False
        C) True
        D) False

10.10   `makeNegative (&num);`

10.11
```
void convert(float *val)
{
    *val *= 2.54;
}
```

10.12
```
ip = new int;
delete ip;
```

10.13
```
ip = new int[500];
delete [] ip;
```

10.14   A pointer that contains the address 0

10.15
```
char *getname(char *name)
{
    cout << "Enter your name: ";
    cin.getline(name, 81);
    return name;
}
```

10.16
```
char *getname()
{
    char name[81];
    cout << "Enter your name: ";
    cin.getline(name, 81);
    return name;
}
```

10.17   `Rectangle *rptr;`

10.18   `cout << rptr->length << endl << rptr->width << endl;`

10.19   B

Chapter 11

11.1   Each class object (an instance of a class) has its own copy of the class's regular member variables. If a class's member variable is static, however, only one instance of the variable exists in memory. All objects of that class have access to that one variable.

11.2   Outside the class declaration

11.3   Before

11.4   Static member functions can only access member variables that are also static.

11.5   You can call a static member function before any instances of the class have been created.

11.6   No, but it has access to all of class X's members, just as if it were a member.

11.7   Class X

11.8   Each member of one object is copied to its counterpart in another object of the same class.

11.9   When one object is copied to another with the = operator, and when one object is initialized with another object's data

11.10   When an object contains a pointer to dynamically allocated memory

11.11   When an object is initialized with another object's data, and when an object is passed by value as the argument to a function

11.12   It has a reference parameter of the same class type as the constructor's class.

11.13   It performs memberwise assignment.

11.14   `void operator=(const Pet &);`

11.12   It has a reference parameter of the same class type as the constructor's class.

11.15   `dog.operator=(cat);`

11.16   It cannot be used in multiple assignment statements or other expressions.

11.17   It's a built-in pointer, available to a class's non-static member functions, that always points to the instance of the class making the function call.

11.18   Non-static member functions

11.19   `cat` is calling the operator+ function. `tiger` is passed as an argument.

11.20   The operator is used in postfix mode.

11.21   They should always return true or false values.

11.22   The object may be directly used with `cout` and `cin`.

11.23   An `ostream` object should be returned by reference.

11.24   An `istream` object should be returned by reference.

11.25   The operator function must be declared as a `friend`.

11.26   `list1.operator[](25);`

11.27   The object whose name appears on the right of the operator in the expression

11.28   So statements using the overloaded operators may be used in other expressions

11.29   The postfix version has a dummy parameter.

11.30   *(Overloaded operator functions)*

```
// Overloaded prefix -- operator
FeetInches FeetInches::operator--()
{
    --inches;
    simplify();
    return *this;
}
```

```cpp
// Overloaded postfix -- operator
FeetInches FeetInches::operator--(int)
{
    FeetInches temp(feet, inches);
    inches--;
    simplify();
    return temp;
}
```

(Demonstration program)

```cpp
// This program demonstrates the prefix and postfix -
// operators, overloaded to work with the FeetInches class.

#include <iostream>
#include "feetinc5.h"
using namespace std;

int main()
{
    FeetInches distance;

    cout << "Enter a distance in feet and inches: ";
    cin >> distance;
    cout << "Demonstrating the prefix - operator: \n";
    cout << "Here is the value: " << --distance << endl;
    cout << "Demonstrating the postfix - operator: \n";
    cout << "Here is the value: " << distance-- << endl;
    cout << "Here is the final value: " << distance << endl;
    return 0;
}
```

11.31   Objects are automatically converted to other types. This ensures that an object's data is properly converted.

11.32   They always return a value of the data type they are converting to.

11.33   `BlackBox::operator int()`

11.34   The `Big` class "has a" `Small` class as its member.

Chapter 12

12.1

strlen	Accepts a C-string as an argument. Returns the length of the string (not including the null terminator).
strcat	Accepts two C-strings as arguments. The function appends the contents of the second string to the first string. (The first string is altered, the second string is left unchanged.)

strcpy	Accepts two C-strings as arguments. The function copies the second string to the first string. The second string is left unchanged.
strncpy	Accepts two C-strings and an integer argument. The third argument, an integer, indicates how many characters to copy from the second string to the first string. If the string2 has fewer than n characters, string1 is padded with '\0' characters.
strcmp	Accepts two C-string arguments. If string1 and string2 are the same, this function returns 0. If string2 is alphabetically greater than string1, it returns a positive number. If string2 is alphabetically less than string1, it returns a negative number.
strstr	Searches for the first occurrence of string2 in string1. If an occurrence of string2 is found, the function returns a pointer to it. Otherwise, it returns a NULL pointer (address 0).

12.2   4

12.3   Have a nice day
        nice day

12.4   strcpy(composer, "Beethoven");

12.5
```cpp
#include <iostream>
#include <cstring>
using namespace std;

int main()
{
    char place[] = "The Windy City";
    if (strstr(place, "Windy"))
        cout << "Windy found.\n";
    else
        cout << "Windy not found.\n";
    return 0;
}
```

12.6   A) negative
        B) negative
        C) negative
        D) positive

12.7
```cpp
if (strcmp(iceCream, "Chocolate") == 0)
        cout << "Chocolate: 9 fat grams.\n";
else if (strcmp(iceCream, "Vanilla") == 0)
        cout << "Vanilla: 10 fat grams.\n";
else if (strcmp(iceCream, "Pralines & Pecan") == 0)
        cout << "Pralines & Pecan: 14 fat grams.\n";
else
        cout << "That's not one of our flavors!\n";
```

12.8

atoi	Accepts a C-string as an argument. The function converts the string to an integer and returns that value.
atol	Accepts a C-string as an argument. The function converts the string to a long integer and returns that value.
atof	Accepts a C-string as an argument. The function converts the string to a float and returns that value.
itoa	Converts an integer to a C-string. The first argument is the integer. The result will be stored at the location pointed to by the second argument. The third argument is an integer. It specifies the numbering system that the converted integer should be expressed in. (8 = octal, 10 = decimal, 16 = hexadecimal, etc.)

12.9   `num = atoi("10");`

12.10   `num = atol("10000");`

12.11   `num = atof("7.2389");`

12.12   `itoa(127, strValue, 10);`

12.13

isalpha	Returns `true` (a nonzero number) if the argument is a letter of the alphabet. Returns `false` if the argument is not a letter.
isalnum	Returns `true` (a nonzero number) if the argument is a letter of the alphabet or a digit. Otherwise it returns `false`.
isdigit	Returns `true` (a nonzero number) if the argument is a digit 0–9. Otherwise it returns `false`.
islower	Returns `true` (a nonzero number) if the argument is a lowercase letter. Otherwise, it returns `false`.
isprint	Returns `true` (a nonzero number) if the argument is a printable character (including a space). Returns `false` otherwise.
ispunct	Returns `true` (a nonzero number) if the argument is a printable character other than a digit, letter, or space. Returns `false` otherwise.
isupper	Returns `true` (a nonzero number) if the argument is an uppercase letter. Otherwise, it returns `false`.

isspace	Returns `true` (a nonzero number) if the argument is a whitespace character. Whitespace characters are any of the following: space................ `' '` newline............. `'\n'` tab................. `'\t'` vertical tab........ `'\v'` Otherwise, it returns `false`.
toupper	Returns the uppercase equivalent of its argument.
tolower	Returns the lowercase equivalent of its argument.

12.14   `little = tolower(big);`

12.15
```
if (isdigit(ch))
        cout << "digit";
else
        cout << "Not a digit.";
```

12.16   A

12.17
```
char choice;
do
{
    cout << "Do you want to repeat the program or quit? (R/Q) ";
    cin >> choice;
} while (toupper(choice) != 'R' && toupper(choice) != 'Q');
```

12.18
```
Tom Talbert Tried Trains
Dom Dalbert Dried Drains
```

Chapter 13

13.1   The base class is `Vehicle`.

13.2   The derived class is `Truck`.

13.3   A) The variables `radius` and `diameter`

      B) `setPoint` function (inherited)
            `getX` function (inherited)
            `getY` function (inherited)
            `setDiameter` function
            `setRadius` function
            `getRadius`
            `getDiameter`

      C) The variables `x` and `y`

13.4   Protected members may be accessed by derived classes. Private members are inaccessible to derived classes.

13.5 Member access specification determines whether a class member is accessible to statements outside the class. Base class access specification determines whether functions in a derived class may access members of the base class.

13.6 A) a is inaccessible; the rest are private.
B) a is inaccessible; the rest are protected.
C) a is inaccessible; b, c, and setA are protected; setB and setC are public.
D) Private

13.7 Entering the sky
Entering the ground
Leaving the ground
Leaving the sky

13.8 Entering the sky
Entering the ground
Leaving the ground
Leaving the sky

13.9 An overloaded function is one with the same name as one or more other functions, but with a different parameter list. The compiler determines which function to call based on the arguments used. Overriding occurs when a derived class has a function with the same name as a base class function. The two functions must have the same parameter list. Objects that are of the derived class always call the derived class's version of the function, while objects that are of the base class always call the base class's version.

13.10 Static binding means the compiler binds member function calls with the version of the function that resides in the same class as the call itself. Dynamic binding means that function calls are bound at runtime with member functions that reside in the class responsible for the call.

13.11 Dynamically

13.12 1
5

13.13 2
2

13.14 2
1

13.15 2

13.16 Chain of inheritance

13.17 Multiple inheritance

13.18 A) Inaccessible
B) Protected
C) Protected
D) Inaccessible
E) Protected
F) Public
G) Private
H) Protected
I) Public

13.19
```
class SportUtility : public van, public FourByFour
{
};
```

Chapter 14

14.1   By filenames

14.2   Open, information saved to or read from the file, and close

14.3   `fstream`

14.4   `ofstream`   Output file stream. This data type can be used to create files and write information to them. With the `ofstream` data type, information may only be copied from variables to the file, but not vice versa.

        `ifstream`   Input file stream. This data type can be used to create files and read information from them into memory. With the `ifstream` data type, information may only be copied from the file into variables, but not vice versa.

        `fstream`   File stream. This data type can be used to create files, write information to them, and read information from them. With the `fstream` data type, information may be copied from variables into a file or from a file into variables.

14.5   The file must be opened.

14.6   `diskInfo.open("names.dat", ios::out);`

14.7   `diskInfo.open("customers.dat", ios::out | ios::app);`

14.8   `diskInfo.open("payable.dat", ios::in | ios::out | ios::app);`

14.9
```
if (dataBase)
     cout << "The file was successfully opened.\n";
else
     cout << "The file was not opened.\n";
```

14.10 `outFile.close();`

14.11
```
A)  cout.width(6);
B)  cout.precision(4);
C)  cout.setf(ios::fixed);
D)  cout.setf(ios::left | ios::scientific);
E)  cout.unsetf(ios::scientific);
```

14.12
```
#include <iostream>
#include <iomanip>
using namespace std;

int main()
{
    char person[15] = "Wolfgang Smith";
    cout.setf(ios::right);
    cout.width(20);
    cout << person << endl;
    cout.setf(ios::left);
    cout << person << endl;
    return 0;
}
```

14.13
```
#include<iostream>
#include <fstream>
using namespace std;

int main()
{
    fstream outFile;
    outFile.open("output.txt", ios::out);
    outFile << "Today is the first day\n";
    outFile << "of the rest of your life.\n";
    return 0;
}
```

14.14   It reports when the end of a file has been encountered.

14.15
```
Run
Spot
run
See
Spot
run
```

14.16   The >> operator considers whitespace characters as delimiters and does not read them. The get-line() member function does read whitespace characters.

14.17   The getline function reads a line of text; the get function reads a single character.

14.18   Writes a single character to a file.

14.19   1e+002   1.7   8.6   7.8   5.1

14.20
```
#include <iostream>
#include <fstream>
#include <cctype>            // Needed for toupper
using namespace std;

int main()
{
    fstream namesFile;
    namesFile.open("phones.dat", ios::app);
    char name[81], phone[26];

    cout << "This program allows you to add names and phone\n";
    cout << "numbers to phones.dat.\n";
    do
    {
        char add;
        cout << "Do you wish to add an entry? ";
        cin >> add;
        if (toupper(add) == 'Y')
        {
            // Write code here that asks the user for a name
            // and phone number, then stores it in the file.
```

```
                    cout << "name: ";
                    cin.getlin(name, 81);
                    cout << "phone number: ";
                    cin.getline(phone, 26);
                    namesFile << name << endl;
                    namesFile << phone << endl;
                }
            } while (toupper(add) == 'Y');
            namesFile.close();
            return 0;
        }
```

14.21 You define multiple file stream objects, one for each file you wish to work with.

14.22 Character representation: "479"
ASCII codes: 52 55 57

14.23 The << operator writes text to a file. The write member function writes binary data to a file.

14.24 The first argument is the starting address of the section of memory, which is to be written to the file. The second argument is the size, in bytes, of the item being written.

14.25 The first argument is the starting address of the section of memory where information read from the file is to be stored. The second argument is the size, in bytes, of the item being read.

14.26 A filed is an individual piece of information pertaining to a single item. A record is made up of fields and is a complete set of information about a single item.

14.27 `file.write((char *)&cust, sizeof(cust));`

14.28 `seekg` moves the file's read position (for input) and `seekp` moves the file's write position (for output).

14.29 `tellg` reports the file's read position and `tellp` reports the files write position.

14.30 `ios::beg` The offset is calculated from the beginning of the file
`ios::end` The offset is calculated from the end of the file
`ios::curr` The offset is calculated from the current position

14.31 0

14.32 `file.seekp(100L, ios::beg);`
Moves the write position to the one hundred first byte (byte 100) from the beginning of the file.

`file.seekp(-10L, ios::end);`
Moves the write position to the eleventh byte (byte 10) from the end of the file.

`file.seekp(-25L, ios::cur);`
Moves the write position backward to the twenty sixth byte from the current position.

`file.seekp(30L, ios::cur);`
Moves the write position to the thirtieth byte (byte 31) from the current position.

14.33   `file.open("info.dat", ios::in | ios::out);`
Input and output

       `file.open("info.dat", ios::in | ios::app);`
Input and output. Output will be appended to the end of the file.

       `file.open("info.dat", ios::in | ios::out | ios::ate);`
Input and output. If the file already exists, the program goes immediately to the end of the file.

       `file.open("info.dat", ios::in | ios::out | ios::binary);`
Input and output, binary mode

Chapter 15

15.1   The try block contains one or more statements that may directly or indirectly throw an exception. The catch block contains code that handles, or responds to an exception.

15.2   The entire program will abort execution.

15.3   Each exception must be of a different type. The catch block whose parameter matches the data type of the exception handles the exception.

15.4   With the first statement after the try/catch construct

15.5   By giving the exception class a member variable, and storing the desired information in the variable. The throw statement creates an instance of the exception class, which must be caught by a catch statement. The catch block can then examine the contents of the member variable.

15.6   When it encounters a call to the function

15.7
```
template <class T>
float half(T number)
{
        return number / 2.0;
}
```

15.8   That the operator has been overloaded by the class object

15.9   First write a regular, nontemplated version of the function. Then, after testing the function, convert it to a template.

15.10   `List<int> myList;`

15.11
```
template <class T>
class Rectangle
{
    private:
        T width;
        T length;
        T area;
```

```
    public:
        void setData(T W, T L)
{ width = W; length = L;}
        void calcArea()
            { area = width * length; }
        T getWidth()
            { return width; }
        T getLength()
            { return length; }
        T getArea()
            { return area; }
};
```

Chapter 16

16.1   A data member contains the data stored in the node. A pointer points to another node in the list.

16.2   A pointer to the first node in the tree

16.3   The last node in the list will point to the NULL address.

16.4   A data structure that contains a pointer to an object of the same data structure type

16.5   Appending a node is adding a new node to the end of the list. Inserting a node is adding a new node in a position between two other nodes.

16.6   Appending

16.7   Since the new node is being inserted between two other nodes, previousNode points to the node that will appear before the new node.

16.8   A)   Remove the node from the list without breaking the links created by the next pointers.
       B)   Delete the node from memory.

16.9   Because there is probably a node pointing to the node being deleted. Additionally, the node being deleted probably points to another node. These links in the list must be preserved.

16.10 The unused memory is never freed, so it could eventually be used up.

Chapter 17

17.1   Last-in-first-out. The last item stored in a LIFO data structure is the first item extracted.

17.2   A static stack has a fixed size, and is implemented as an array. A dynamic stack grows in size as needed, and is implemented as a linked list. Advantages of a dynamic stack: There is no need to specify the starting size of the stack. The stack automatically grows each time an item is pushed, and shrinks each time an item is popped. Also, a dynamic stack is never full (as long as the system has free memory).

17.3   Push: An item is pushed onto, or stored in, the stack.

       Pop: An item is retrieved (and hence, removed) from the stack.

17.4   Vector, linked list, or deque

Chapter 18

18.1   The function calls itself with no way of stopping. It creates an infinite recursion.

18.2   The solvable problem that the recursive algorithm is designed to solve. When the recursive algorithm reaches the base case, it terminates.

18.3   10

18.4   In direct recursion, a recursive function calls itself. In indirect recursion, function A calls function B, which in turn calls function A.

Chapter 19

19.1   A standard linked list is a linear data structure in which one node is linked to the next. A binary tree is nonlinear, because each node can point to two other nodes.

19.2   The first node in the tree

19.3   A node pointed to by another node in the tree

19.4   A node that points to no other nodes

19.5   An entire branch of the binary tree, from one particular node down

19.6   Information can be stored in a binary tree in a way that makes a binary search simple.

19.7   1. The node's left subtree is traversed.
       2. The node's data is processed.
       3. The node's right subtree is traversed.

19.8   1. The node's data is processed.
       2. The node's left subtree is traversed.
       3. The node's right subtree is traversed.

19.9   1. The node's left subtree is traversed.
       2. The node's right subtree is traversed.
       3. The node's data is processed.

19.10 The node to be deleted is node D.
       1. Find node D's parent and set the child pointer that links the parent to node D, to NULL.
       2. Free node D's memory.

19.11 The node to be deleted is node D.
       1. Find node D's parent.
       2. Link the parent node's child pointer (that points to node D) to node D's child.
       3. Free node D's memory.

19.12 1. Attach the node's right subtree to the parent, and then find a position in the right subtree to attach the left subtree.
       2. Free the node's memory.

Appendix L
Solutions to Odd-Numbered
Review Questions

Chapter 1

1. Programmed
3. Arithmetic logic unit and control unit
5. Operating systems and application software
7. Programming language
9. High-level
11. Portability
13. Programmer-defined symbols
15. Punctuation
17. Variable
19. Input, processing, output
21. Output
23. Main memory, or RAM, is volatile, which means its contents are erased when power is removed from the computer. Secondary memory, such as a disk, does not lose its contents when power is removed from the computer.
25. System A: Multiuser, multitasking
    System B: Single user, multitasking
    System C: Single user, single tasking
27. Because high-level languages are more like natural language
29. A syntax error is the misuse of a key word, operator, punctuation, or other part of the programming language. A logical error is a mistake that causes the program to produce the wrong results.
31. 28
33. The error is that the program performs its math operation before the user has entered values for the variables width and length.

35. Hierarchy chart:

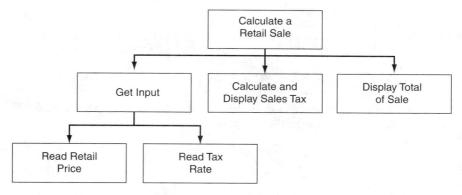

Chapter 2

1. C
3. B
5. B
7. B, C
9. A) 12   B) 4   C) 2   D) 6   E) 1
11. A
13. True
15. True
17. 1, 2, 3
19. `int months = 2, days, years = 3;`
21. C style
23.
```
#include <iostream>
using namespace std;

int main()
{
    cout << "Two mandolins like creatures in the\n\n\n";
    cout << "dark\n\n\n";
    cout << "Creating the agony of ecstasy.\n\n\n";
    cout << "                   - George Barker\n\n\n";
    return 0;
}
```

25. The C-style comments symbols are backward.
    `iostream` should be enclosed in angle brackets.
    There shouldn't be a semicolon after `int main()`.

The opening and closing braces of function main are reversed.
There should be a semicolon after `int a, b, c.`
The comment `\\ Three integers` should read `// Three integers.`
There should be a semicolon at the end of the following lines:

```
a = 3
b = 4
c = a + b
```

`cout` begins with a capital letter.
The stream insertion operator (that appears twice in the cout statement) should read `<<` instead of `<`.
The `cout` statement uses the variable `C` instead of `c`.

Chapter 3

1. A) `cin >> description;`
   B) `getline (cin, description);`
3. A) `cin >> setw(25) >> name;`
   B) `cin.getline(name, 25);`
5. `iostream` and `iomanip`
7. A) `price = 12 * unitCost;`
   B) `cout << setw(12) << 98.7;`
   C) `cout << 12;`
9. `a = 12 * x;`
   `z = 5 * x + 14 * y + 6 * k;`
   `y = pow(x, 4);`
   `g = (h + 12) / (4 * k);`
   `c = pow(a, 3) / (pow(b, 2) * pow(k, 4));`
11. B
13. `const int rate = 12;`
15. `east = west = north = south = 1;`
17. No
19. `cout << fixed << showpoint << setprecision(2);`
    `cout << totalSales;`
21. `cmath`
23. `sin`
25. `exp`
27. `log`
29. `pow`
31. `cmath`
33. A) `Your monthly wages are 3225.000000`
    B) `6 3 12`
    C) `In 1492 Columbus sailed the ocean blue.`

```
D)  Hello George
E)  Hello George Washington
F)  Minutes: 612002.0000
    Hours: 10200.0332
    Days: 425.0014
    Months: 13.9726
    Years: 1.1644
```

Chapter 4

1. Relational

3. False, true

5. True

7. True, false

9. `if/else`

11. `||`

13. left to right

15. `||`

17. Cannot

19. Integer

21. `break`

23.
```
if (y == 0)
    x = 100;
```

25.
```
if (sales < 10000)
        commission = .10;
else if (sales <= 15000)
        commission = .15;
else
        commission = .20;
```

27.
```
if (amount1 > 10)
        if (amount2 < 100)
            cout << (amount1 > amount2 ? amount1 : amount2);
```

29.
```
if (temperature >= -50 && temperature <= 150)
    cout << "The number is valid.";
```

31.
```
if (strcmp(title1, title2) < 0)
        cout << title1 << " " << title2 << endl;
else
        cout << title2 << " " << title1 << endl;
```

33. False

35. True

37. False

39. False
41. True
43. False
45. T, F, T, T
47. A) The first `cout` statement is terminated by a semicolon too early.
    The definition of `score1`, `score2`, and `score3` should end with a semicolon.
    The statement
    ```
    if (average = 100)
    ```
    should read
    ```
    if (average == 100)
    ```
    `perfectScore` is used before it is declared.
    The following `if` statement should not be terminated with a semicolon:
    ```
    if (perfectScore);
    ```
    The conditionally executed block in the `if` statement shown above should end with a closing brace.
    B) The conditionally executed blocks in the `if/else` construct should be enclosed in braces.
    The statement
    ```
    cout << "The quotient of " << num1 <<
    ```
    should read
    ```
    cout << "quotient of " << num1;
    ```
    C) The trailing `else` statement should come at the end of the `if/else` construct.
    D) A switch case construct cannot be used to test relational expressions. An `if/else` statement should be used instead.
49. It should use `&&` instead of `||`.
51. The `:` and `?` are transposed. The statement should read:
    ```
    z = (a < 10) ? 0 : 7;
    ```

Chapter 5

1. Increment, decrement
3. Postfix
5. Iteration
7. Posttest loop
9. Counter
11. Accumulator
13. `do-while`
15. `for`
17. Nested
19. `continue`

21.
```
do
{
    float num1, num2;
    char again;
    cout << "Enter two numbers: ";
    cin >> num1 >> num2;
    cout << "Their sum is " << (num1 + num2) << endl;
    cout << "Do you wish to do this again? (Y/N) ";
    cin >> again;
} while (again == 'Y' || again == 'y');
```

23.
```
float total, num;
for (int count = 0; count < 10; count++)
{
    cout << "Enter a number: ";
    cin >> num;
    total += num;
}
```

25.
```
int x;
do
{
    cout << "Enter a number: ";
    cin >> x;
} while (x > 0);
```

27.
```
for (int count = 0; count < 50; count++)
            cout << "count is " << count << endl;
```

29. False

31. False

33. False

35. False

37. False

39. True

41. True

43. False

45. True

Chapter 6

1. Header

3. `showValue(5);`

5. Arguments

7. Value

9. Local

11. Global

13. Local

15. Return

17. Last

19. Reference

21. Reference

23. Parameter lists

25. False

27. True

29. True

31. True

33. True

35. True

37. False

39. True

41. False

43. A)   The data type of `value2` and `value3` must be declared.
    The function is declared void but returns a value.

    B)   The assignment statement should read:

    ```
    average = (value1 + value2 + value3) / 3.0;
    ```
    The function is declared as a `float` but returns no value.

    C)   `width` should have a default argument value.
    The function is declared `void` but returns a value.

    D)   The parameter should be declared as:

    ```
    int &value
    ```
    The `cin` statement should read:

    ```
    cin >> value;
    ```

    E)   The functions must have different parameter lists.

Chapter 7

1. Declared

3. Members

5. Tag

7. `Car hotRod = {"Ford", "Mustang", 1997, 20000};`

9. ```
   today.windSpeed = 37;
   today.humidity = .32;
   today.temperature.fahrenheit = 32;
   today.temperature.centigrade = 0;
   ```
   ```

11.
```
void findReading(Reading &r)
{
    cout << "Enter the wind speed: ";
    cin >> r.windSpeed;
    cout << "Enter the humidity: ";
    cin >> r.humidity;
    cout << "Enter the fahrenheit temperature: ";
    cin >> r.temperature.fahrenheit;
    cout << "Enter the centigrade temperature: ";
    cin >> r.temperature.centigrade;
}
```

13.
```
union Items
{
    char alpha;
    int num;
    long bigNum;
    float real;
};
Items x;
```

15. `num = 452;`

17. Procedural

19. Encapsulation

21. Structure

23. Private

25. Instantiation

27. `canine.cpp`

29. Constructor

31. Constructors

33. Default

35. ~

37. Default

39. Constructor, destructor

41. True

43. False

45. False

47. True

49. True

51. False

53. True

55. False

57. False

59. False
61. True
63. False
65. False
67. False
69. True
71. True
73. A)   The structure declaration has no tag.
    B)   The semicolon is missing after the closing brace.
    C)   No structure variable has been declared. TwoVals is the structure tag.
    D)   In the declaration of vals, TwoVals is used as the type instead of ThreeVals.
         An entire struct cannot be sent to cout.
    E)   The initialization list of the customer variable must be enclosed in braces.
    F)   An initializer cannot be skipped before the end of the initialization list.
    G)   Structure members cannot be initialized in the structure definition.

Chapter 8

1. Size declarator
3. Subscript
5. Size declarator, subscript
7. Initialization
9. Initialization list
11. Subscript
13. An address
15. Multidimensional
17. Two
19. Column
21.
```
Car forSale[35] = {{"Ford", "Taurus", 1997, 21000.0},
                   {"Honda", "Accord", 1992, 11000.0},
                   {"Lamborghini", "Countach", 200000.0}};
```
23. False
25. False
27. True
29. True
31. True
33. False
35. True
37. False

39. True
41. True
43. True
45. True
47. True
49. False
51. False

Chapter 9

1. Linear
3. Linear
5. Ascending
7. True
9. True
11.

Array Size →	50 Elements	500 Elements	10,000 Elements	100,000 Elements	10,000,000 Elements
Linear Search (Average Comparisons)	25	250	5,000	50,000	5,000,000
Linear Search (Maximum Comparisons)	50	500	10,000	100,000	10,000,000
Binary Search (Maximum Comparisons)	6	9	14	17	24

Chapter 10

1. Address
3. Pointer
5. Pointers
7. new
9. Null
11. new
13. False

15. False
17. True
19. True
21. False
23. True
25. True
27. True
29. False

Chapter 11

1. Static
3. Static
5. Friend
7. Memberwise assignment
9. `this`
11. Postfix increment (or decrement)
13. Has a
15. Copy constructor
    Overloaded = operator
    Overloaded = operator
    Copy constructor
17. Place the static key word in the function's prototype. Calls to the function are performed by connecting the function name to the *class* name with the scope resolution operator.
19. In object composition, one object is nested inside another object, which creates a "has a" relationship. When a class is a friend of another class, there is no nesting. If object A is a friend of object B, object A has access to all of object B's private members.
21. If a pointer member is used to reference dynamically allocated memory, a memberwise assignment operation will only copy the contents of the pointer, not the section of memory referenced by the pointer. This means that two objects will exist with pointers to the same address in memory. If either object manipulates this area of memory, the changes will show up for both objects. Also, if either object frees the memory, it will no longer contain valid information for either object.
23. If an object were passed to the copy constructor by value, the copy constructor would create a copy of the argument and store it in the parameter object. When the parameter object is created, its copy constructor will be called, thus causing another parameter object to be created. This process will continue indefinitely.
25. `Dollars Dollars::operator++() // Prefix`
    `Dollars Dollars::operator++(int)  // Postfix`
27. `ostream &operator<<(ostream &strm, Length &obj)`
29. The overloaded operators offer a more intuitive way of manipulating objects, similar to the way primitive data types are manipulated.

31. True
33. False
35. True
37. True
39. True
41. False
43. True
45. A) The types of the parameters l and h of the first constructor are not declared, and the parameter of the copy constructor needs to be passed by reference.
    B) The overloaded = operator function header should read
       ```
       void operator=(const Circle &right)
       ```
    C) The overloaded + operator function header should read
       ```
       Point operator+(const Point &right)
       ```
       The body of the operator function should return an object that is the result of performing the addition. It is also best if the operator does not change the object through which it is called.
    D) The types of the parameters l and h of the first constructor are not declared. Both overloaded operators need to declare a return type Point. In addition, the overloaded postfix operator should declare a dummy integer parameter:
       ```
       Point operator++(int)
       ```
       The bodies of both overloaded operator functions should return an appropriate value.
    E) The float conversion operator function header should read
       ```
       operator float()
       ```
       and the first letter of the identifier of the constructor Yard should be uppercase.

Chapter 12

1. isupper
3. isdigit
5. toupper
7. cctype
9. Concatenate
11. strcpy
13. strcmp
15. atoi
17. atof
19. False
21. False
23. True
25. False
27. True
29. A) C-strings cannot be compared with the == operator.
    B) atoi converts a string to an integer, not an integer to a string.
    C) The compiler will not allocate enough space in string1 to accommodate both strings.
    D) strcmp compares C-strings, not characters.

Chapter 13

1. Public and protected members
3. `Pet`
5. Private
7. Inaccessible, private, private
9. Inaccessible, protected, public
11. Last
13. Base
15. Static
17. Polymorphism
19. Abstract
21. Chain
23. Inheritance
25. False
27. True
29. False
31. True
33. False
35. False
37. False
39. False

Chapter 14

1. Filename
3. Close
5. `ifstream, ofstream, fstream`
7. `ifstream`
9. `ofstream people("people.dat");`
11. `fstream places("places.dat");`
13. `pets.open("pets.dat");`
    `fstream pets("pets.dat");`
15. `NULL` or 0
17. `cout`
19. `getline`
21. `put`
23. Text, ASCII text
25. Structures
27. `read`
29. Sequential

31. `seekg`
33. `tellg`
35. `ios::beg`
37. `ios::cur`
39. True
41. True
43. False
45. True
47. True
49. False
51. False
53. False
55. False
57. False
59. False
61. True

Chapter 15

1. Throw point
3. Catch
5. Template prefix
7. Specialized
9. Associative
11. False
13. True
15. True
17. True
19. False
21. True
23. False
25. True
27. A) The try block must appear before the catch block.
    B) The cout statement should not appear between the try and catch blocks.
    C) The return statement should read `return number * number;`
    D) The type parameter, T, is not used.
    E) The type parameter, T2, is not used.
    F) The declaration should read `SimpleVector<int> array(25);`
    G) The statement should read `cout << valueSet[2] << endl;`

Chapter 16

1. Head pointer
3. NULL
5. Inserting
7. Circular
9. False
11. True
13. False
15. True

Chapter 17

1. Last
3. Static
5. Vector, list, and deque
7. Enqueuing and dequeuing
9. deque
11. False
13. True
15.

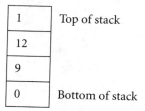

17.

5	7	9	12

front   rear

19. It allows the queue elements to wrap around the end of the array. This, in turn, makes the queue more efficient by eliminating the need to copy the queue elements forward each time an item is enqueued.

Chapter 18

1. Depth
3. Direct

5. A) `55`

   B) ```
      ****
      ****
      ****
      ****
      ******
      *****
      ****
      ***
      **
      *
      ```

   C) `evE dna madA`

7. Indirect recursion. There are more function calls to keep up with.

9. When the problem is more easily solved with recursion, and a better program design is possible.

# Chapter 19

1. Root node

3. Leaf node

5. Inorder, preorder, and postorder

7. True

9. True

11. *Create a new node.*
    *Store a value in the new node.*
    *Set the new node's children pointers to NULL.*
    *If the tree is empty*
        *Make root point to the new node.*
    *Else*
        *Starting at the root node, compare the new node's value with*
        *the existing nodes' values. When the new node's value is less*
        *than the existing node's value, go the node's left child for the*
        *next comparison. Otherwise, go to the right.*
        *Repeat this process until a NULL child pointer is found.*
        *That is the insertion point.*
    *End If.*

13. *(Recursive Function)*

    *Display Pre Order(Node Pointer)*
        *If Node Pointer is not Null*
            *Display the node's Value.*
            *Display Pre Order (Node Pointer -> Left).*
            *Display Pre Order (Node Pointer -> Right).*
        *End If*
    *End Display Pre Order*
      ```

15. *Node Pointer = Root.*
    While Node Pointer is not Null
        If Node Pointer -> Value equals the Search Value
            Return True. // Item found
        Else If the Search Value is less than Node Pointer -> Value
            Node Pointer = Node Pointer -> Left.
        Else
            Node Pointer = Node Pointer -> Right.
        End If.
    End While.
    Return False. // Item not found

17. 3 7 9 10 12 14 18 20 22 24 30

19. 3 10 9 7 14 20 18 30 24 22 12

Index